D1000600

THE STRATEGY OF WORLD ORDER

Volume III

THE UNITED NATIONS

Edited by

RICHARD A. FALK

SAUL H. MENDLOVITZ

Foreword by Oscar Schachter

WORLD LAW FUND

1966 *New York*

Library of Congress Catalog Card No. 66-14524

Manufactured in the United States of America
First edition, 1966

Foreword

IT IS HARDLY surprising that the United Nations has been given a prominent place in a work which lays emphasis on the transformation of the present international system. Many have seen in its Charter the beginnings of a transition: on the one side, the acceptance of State sovereignty and the traditional forms of international cooperation; on the other, the introduction of elements of international authority—expressly as in the case of the Security Council and more subtly as in the General Assembly and the international Secretariat. The experience of the Organization has reflected both the old and the new conceptions and also the clash between them. Dag Hammarskjöld alluded to this in the midst of the bitter controversy over the Congo action; he contrasted the "static" conception of the Organization as "conference machinery" for the solution of conflicts of interest through expanded diplomatic facilities with the idea of the Organization as a "dynamic instrument of government" through which international executive action would be undertaken on behalf of all the Members in pursuance of the agreed purposes.[1] The adjectives reveal Hammarskjöld's own preference—as did his conduct in office—but he was far from certain that Members were prepared to take that path in the immediate future. Still, the vision of an ultimate international constitutional order remained significant for him, even though its exact shape could not be foreseen. It would have to be attained, he believed, through organic growth responsive to felt needs, rather than by imposing ideal patterns. "We, like our ancestors, can only press against this receding wall which hides the future."[2] The United Nations itself was for him an experimental operation with no claim to "*a priori* validity"; someday a wholly new start might have to be made; even so, one could best conquer the essential new ground for the future through pursuing the present effort to the limits of one's ability, energy and dedication.[3]

These ideas seem to be implicit in most of the commentary in this volume. There is clearly a feeling that the Organization should be plastic and

1. See Chapter 11, "Two Views of the United Nations Assayed."
2. Dag Hammarskjöld, "Development of a Constitutional Framework for International Cooperation" (University of Chicago, 1960). Reprinted in Dag Hammarskjöld Servant of Peace, edited by Wilder Foote (1962) p. 251, 252.
3. *ibid*, p. 255.

adaptable, endeavouring to cope with felt needs without much regard to future constitutional lines. One finds reluctance to speculate about long-range objectives and an assumption that present solutions would be impeded by undue concern with distant goals. "Le mieux est l'ennemi du bien." Perhaps this attitude would change if there were—as Professors Falk and Mendlovitz envisage—a "social science of international relations" with models and verifiable data that could be applied to actual issues. But that seems a long distance away and in the practical world of the United Nations it does not appear destined to play a role in the near future.

If long-range speculation is rare, other forms of intellectual activity are not. The principal activity of the United Nations is the gathering and analysis of data—the vast array of political, economic, technological and psychological data that bear upon the troubles and tensions of the contemporary world. These facts are subjected in the Organization to a process of scrutiny and appraisal which has an international and as a rule an expert character. The heterogeneity and basic divergence of outlook and experience tend to produce a wider and sharper examination than could be achieved by more homogeneous groups. Moreover, the United Nations needs no reminders that it should be "value-oriented" and "problem-solving." It is, after all, an institution for the attainment of express purposes and it is inevitably the target of the demands and claims of a large portion of dissatisfied mankind. Though only a fraction of these can be dealt with, that fraction still involves an immense range of questions which press for solution. Not that solutions are always forthcoming, but the effort goes on, vitalized by the continuous pressures for action and by the diverse points of view. In most cases it focuses on a quest for points of common interest needed to override ideological or political divisions and thus serve as the foundation for common action.

This aspect of United Nations activity also has special implications for the development of law. It will be observed that when controversial issues are submitted to a United Nations forum the Member governments (whatever their motives) are impelled to justify their positions on grounds that will be generally accepted by other States with different ideologies and political attitudes. That is why expressions of principle and law in United Nations decisions cannot be dismissed merely as homages of hypocrisy; they are realistically the necessary result of a multipartisan process of deliberation. It is also apparent that such decisions will have normative effects for future cases. That is so even though governments may assert—as they frequently do—that particular resolutions are limited to the facts of the case and are not intended to establish precedents. For once a decision is premised on principle or law there is a high probability that it will be looked to for future guidance and that considerations of equity and equal treatment will tend to favour its application to similar situations. Thus we now have in the United Nations an embryonic "common law" procedure by which new rules emerge on a case-by-case basis and, on the basis of State acceptance, form part of the body of international norms.

One should not of course assume that this process—desirable as it may be—will in itself be a major source of strength for international order. Indeed, as the essays in this volume amply demonstrate, there are no certain paths to an effective war-prevention system. Throughout the history of the United Nations, replete with one crisis after another, there has been a continuing flow of proposed panaceas each summed up in a then-favoured phrase. "Quiet diplomacy," "executive action," "peace-keeping" are the recent successors to earlier favourites such as the "town-meeting of the world," arbitration, conciliation and others. Each such concept represented an approach or technique that was useful; each was a response to a particular circumstance; but none has served or could serve to meet all the varying problems. The range of problems and conditions faced by the United Nations is far too wide and complex to be solved through any single formula or for that matter in any single political ideology.

The editors have wisely recognized this in the breadth and catholicity of their selections. There is no taint of parochialism in this volume, even if national representation is not as wide as might have been desirable. The reader will have no difficulty in learning of the numerous illusions, frustration and dissension which are part of United Nations history; he will also acquire an understanding of the enormous complexity of maintaining peace in a world continuously at the brink of destruction and, most important, he will become aware of the effort, ingenuity and perseverance that have been exhibited in the United Nations and which offer some encouragement for the eventual attainment of a warless world.

OSCAR SCHACHTER
The United Nations

Prefatory Note

THE FOUR VOLUMES that comprise *The Strategy of World Order* are an attempt to study the subject of world order from the interrelated perspectives of international law, international organization, disarmament, and economic development. Although the four volumes are part of a single enterprise, each is an autonomous unit that is meant to be able to exist on its own. In each the focus is upon world order and the sub-focus is upon war prevention. In each *World Peace through World Law* by Grenville Clark and Louis B. Sohn serves as a model of the kind of world order that is needed if the prospect of major warfare is to be eliminated from international life. The strategy of study is to clarify the nature of order in the existing international political system, to postulate the Clark-Sohn model as an alternative international system, and on this basis to analyze the techniques for transforming the one into the other and thereby achieve a transition to a warless world. For a fuller statement of the intellectual rationale of *The Strategy of World Order*, see the essay by Mendlovitz, **I-4**.

R.A.F.
S.H.M.

NOTE: *Where references are made in the text to other volumes of* The Strategy of World Order, *the volume is designated by roman numeral, the chapter by arabic numeral, and (where applicable) the section heading by letter. Thus,* **I-4B** *refers to Volume I, Chapter 4, Section B. Reference to materials contained in the same volume are designated by chapter number. Thus, "see Chapter 4."*

THE STRATEGY OF WORLD ORDER has been made possible through the generosity of the D. S. and R. H. Gottesman Foundation and the Miriam and Ira D. Wallach Foundation.

Acknowledgments

The sheer mass of an enterprise of this sort makes its principal organizers very dependent upon the aid and comfort of many others, a dependence that far exceeds the gesture of acknowledgment. We mention here only those who made contributions beyond the normal line of duty.

First of all, we wish to thank the Rutgers Law School Secretarial Pool, especially Mary Connolly, Eleanore Yurkutat and Florence Wotherspoon for their patient and expert labors.

In The Netherlands the editors were especially lucky to have the benefit of the prodigious and proficient secretarial service of Miss Nora W. Allen who made a habit of twenty-hour working days.

We thank Willard Heckel, Dean of the Rutgers Law School, for making available the funds for research assistance, and Blair Crawford, Barbara Kulzer, and Miriam Nusbaum, for giving us much needed assistance with the research and related matters. Thanks are also due to the Harvard Law School and especially the staff of the International Legal Studies Center for providing Mendlovitz with office and library facilities, and to Klaus Knorr, Director of the Center of International Studies at Princeton, for providing similar facilities in the final stages of the study, thus speeding the collaborative process considerably.

We are most indebted to Professor Ellen Frey-Wouters for many kindnesses, including especially the delicate handling of permissions with several of the more refractory of the foreign publishers.

William Cowan deserves especial mention because he did such an excellent job as technical editor with such short notice. Susan Newman's proofreading under similar circumstances is also greatly appreciated.

We are, of course, very grateful to the staff of the World Law Fund for handling the whole undertaking, and to Miss Florence Goldstein for her superb managerial services in master-minding the entire complex process of translating an assemblage of materials into a series of books.

And in the spirit of dedication, Saul Mendlovitz seeks also to mention Roberta Mendlovitz and their family—Jessica, Michael, Jamie, John, and Martha.

Contents

*WPTWL is the abbreviation used to designate *World Peace through World Law* by Grenville Clark and Louis B. Sohn.

Introduction

As historical time tends to be measured, experiments with the formal organization of international society are of recent vintage. The League of Nations was founded after World War I, the United Nations after World War II. Despite the failure of the League to avert World War II, there was no disposition to abandon the attempt to create international institutions as the political basis for an enduring peace. Today, despite the many weaknesses of the United Nations, there are few responsible people who favor its abolition. On the contrary, a consensus of the nations and their publics appears to favor strengthening the international organization, and there is apparent a slow but discernible trend toward the growth of organizations in international affairs.

The objective of this volume is to examine the contribution of the United Nations to world order. It thus carries forward the inquiry which was initiated in Volumes I and II, which concentrated upon the definition of the problem of world order in terms of war prevention, and which explored the relevance of international law to the regulation of violence in world politics. In Volume III these earlier themes are further developed, both in the context of the United Nations as it presently operates, and in the context of a United Nations revised along the lines proposed by Clark and Sohn in *World Peace through World Law* (Harvard University Press, 1964). As elsewhere in these volumes, this comparison between alternative systems of world order is bridged by the study of transition devices that might act to strengthen the existing system and to build confidence in the realistic prospects for the adoption of a new, less war-prone system of world order.

In evaluating law as a method of achieving and maintaining world peace, it becomes clear that intricate relationships exist between the character of international law and the development of a global community. In addition, questions were raised in Volume II about the capacity of authority structures to control the use of violence and the degree to which a global community needs the support of a consensus among its members on matters of value and interest. What, for example, is the minimum consensus needed for effective action? One way to begin answering this question is to clarify and appraise various alternative approaches to world order. We have attempted to do this in the earlier chapters, emphasizing throughout the choice between gradual and radical approaches to world order. At each stage we tried to ask what evidence exists to support the assumption that a radical change cannot be brought about by peaceful processes. This question is central, because the Clark-Sohn plan entails a drastic change in international society; this drastic change encounters all of the skepticism present whenever a nongradualist prescription is offered as a solution for a problem in human affairs.

To emphasize the nature of a system change in world order, we have used the admittedly somewhat vague notion of a warless world as a way to dramatize the contrast between the Clark-Sohn image of the world and the existing war-prone world. Our ideal model is warless only in the sense that nation-states will no longer be entitled to maintain the capacity to wage war. In estimating the possible attainment of this ideal, we have laid stress upon the idea and techniques of transition; we have emphasized the problem of moving from where we are to where we would like to be. In this connection it is necessary to take account of the existence of diverse views of the world, as well as the consequences of diversity for any program to improve the quality of world order. It is also important to examine writers who suggest that most of the order in world affairs results from nations interacting with one another, rather than from the acts or the mere existence of international organizations. These writers doubt whether central institutions with a strength comparable to the institutions that have emerged in domestic society will be acceptable to national governments in the foreseeable future. In order to take this skepticism seriously, the chapters in Volume III will consider the possibilities for improving international order by the evolutionary growth of international organizational activity. It will also consider the possibility of substituting the Clark-Sohn scheme, or one of equivalent magnitude, for the existing system of international relations.

In studying the future of international organization, we confine ourselves to the possibilities and problems that relate to revising and strengthening the United Nations in order to achieve and maintain peace. This focus upon the United

Nations is properly understood as the expression of an editorial judgment that formal organization on the global level has become increasingly important for the prevention of international violence.

At the same time it is evident that regional organizations play an increasingly important role in world affairs, although it is impossible to consider this role in any detail in these readings. Most recently, the Organization of American States has embarked upon a full-scale regional peace-keeping operation in the Dominican Republic. This regional undertaking aims to achieve domestic order in a situation of civil strife that prompted military intervention by the United States in April of 1965. See Ronald J. Yalem, *Regionalism and World Order* (Public Affairs Press, Washington, D.C., 1965).

It is clear that the effective limits of the United Nations are set by the political and social processes at work in the world community, especially as these processes are influenced by the policies and behavior of the principal states. Nevertheless, the impact of formal organizations can both transcend and transform these underlying forces. That is, the United Nations can come to have status as an independent actor, in additon to its primary role as an agency for the fulfillment of the goals of national actors; this aspect of independence allows the organs of the United Nations to carry out certain initiatives, in some instances going far beyond the preferences of many members and even beyond the express limits of its own Charter. These initiatives arouse hostility among those that oppose them and account for some of the lines of criticism of the United Nations; they also explain, in part, the refusal of several major states to pay their assessed share of the cost of major peace-keeping operations. It is difficult to measure this independent impact and to assess its relationship to the risks of war implicit in the international system. Those who propose drastic reforms in the United Nations in order to reduce further the risks of war deem its present basis of organization inadequate. A concern with the development of a warless world leads us to examine ways to strengthen the war prevention capabilities of the United Nations.

One way to examine these issues is to compare the present structure and practices of the United Nations with those envisaged by Clark and Sohn. In carrying out this comparison it is important to organize appraisals around the criterion of war prevention. Above all, we want to consider whether the Clark-Sohn plan involves too little or too much alteration of the existing United Nations; that is whether, given this central objective of reducing the risk of major war to the lowest attainable level, does it propose about the right degree of revision. From this perspective, the degree to which the political unacceptability of their scheme, or an attribute of it, makes its adoption less likely is a factor to be weighed. Thus, given the Soviet opposition to the use of the International Court of Justice (ICJ) to settle international disputes, it might be advantageous to reduce the role of the Court to the lowest level consistent with other aspects of systemic stability, such as the need for impartial procedures to resolve a conflict before violence erupts. The techniques of ordering the world must be evaluated partly in light of the willingness of states to use them.

When examining the Clark-Sohn proposal, it is important to keep in mind that each revision is offered as an integral part of an organic set of proposals, and that many of the specific revisions are closely related to a detailed plan for a peace-keeping force and for general and complete disarmament. It is important, at the same time, to appreciate that many of these proposals may be considered apart from their total scheme, and it is sensible to ask whether any particular proposal itself is necessary and feasible within the present political context—either to facilitate transition, or as a constituent element in a stable peace system. Finally, assuming that there is agreement that the proposals made by Clark and Sohn are instructive, at least in the sense of being an alternative to what now exists, then it follows that these proposals provide us with an explicit standard that is also useful for the evaluation of present practices and procedures of the United Nations. To summarize, then, the Clark-Sohn plan offers a useful model *first*, as an ideal situated in the future, *second*, as a basis upon which to appraise the actual, and *third*, as an aid in structuring thought about how to make the transition from the actual to the ideal. In essence, we are given a framework within which to assess the various aspects of the problem of transforming one international system into another.

The League of Nations and the United Nations: Continuities and Discontinuities

1

It is useful to begin investigation of the United Nations by looking back briefly at its predecessor, the League of Nations. The League was created in 1919 to avoid recurrence of major warfare. The intention of its creators was to substitute a collective security system for a balance of power system. Collective security envisages that the aggregated power of the world community shall be used to frustrate any and every attempt at aggression; it was conceived as a way to avoid the risks and instabilities of the balance of power approach to international peace and security. However, the League in practice, as distinct from the League in theory, proved unable to transform politics in international society. When the peace was broken by Japanese aggression in Manchuria, Italian aggression in Ethopia, and German aggression in Europe, it became evident that the members of the League were unwilling to pool their strength to frustrate aggression. There existed neither the disposition to make the material sacrifices needed to make a collective security system work, nor the ethical commitment to support a central ordering role in world affairs for the League. The principal powers were more intent upon keeping alliance possibilities open than in defeating a country which had taken aggressive steps against their nonvital interests. In the 1930's, for example, France and the United Kingdom looked upon Italy as a potential ally in a struggle against Germany for the control of Europe.

In addition, critics of the League pointed out that its cumbersome procedure, its excessive deference to sovereign status, and its structure contributed to the failure of this first major experiment with international organization. The United Nations was organized in such a way as to mitigate, if not altogether avoid, these perceived defects in the functioning of the League. Once again an international organization—the United Nations—was predicated upon the expectation that only a reliable system of collective security, organized on a global basis, would be capable of keeping the peace. But once again the Great Powers seem to have placed more reliance upon alliances than upon genuine collective security. It is reasonable to characterize international society as still dominated by the balance of power patterns of belief and action. See Claude in **II-3** and Hoffmann in Chapter 11, for developments of this theme.

In the United Nations system the grant of a veto to the five permanent members of the Security Council made it clear that the original intention was to confine the peace-keeping role of the Organization to disputes between secondary powers. The very structure of the United Nations, then, makes explicit the modest limits of current efforts by international organizations to control war and violent conflict among states. Even allowing for some development beyond these original limits, it seems clear that the organized international community is not able to act against threats or breaches of the peace by the Great Powers. Nevertheless, the contributions of the United Nations to the maintenance of peace have been surprisingly significant. For a fuller account of these matters, see Inis P. Claude, *Swords Into Plowshares* (3rd rev. ed., Random House, 1964).

As later portions of this volume will develop, the United Nations has undertaken to act on the basis of collective security principles on several occasions. See especially Chapter 9. Perhaps the most notable occasions were Suez in 1956 and the Congo in 1960. The response by the United Nations to North Korean aggression in 1950 was a more ambiguous instance of collective security; the Organization was able to act only because of the accident of a Soviet boycott at the time the authorization was granted and because the entire operation was more of an American security undertaking than an action taken by the international community. There is no simple way to characterize the international political system, but it does seem reasonable to conclude that it exhibits more of the attributes of a collective security system than it did during the League period. There is visible a growth of support for the principles of collective security that includes a willingness to make material and diplomatic sacrifices, such as U.S. opposition to French and British action in Suez. This growth appears to be taking place despite the countertrends that are manifest in the financing crisis (Chapter 10) and the apparent swing toward greater use of regional action to deal with political violence.

Clark and Sohn argue that a collective security system, even supposing it to be currently in operation, is not a sufficiently reliable basis for world peace in the nuclear age. In its stead, they propose a scheme for limited world government organized around the central task of war prevention. Clark and Sohn regard total disarmament as essential, in view of the destructive consequences of modern warfare. It is not enough to be able to detect an aggressor; it is necessary to abolish the war system that is an outgrowth of permitting nations to use their own discretion where the needs of national security are concerned. According to Clark and Sohn, international society must be established in such a way that states no longer rely upon national military establishments for the conduct of their foreign policy, or for the satisfaction of their security interests. To achieve this objective, a set of structural revisions in the present United Nations are proposed. These include a police force, a world development authority, and an international conciliation system. In this chapter the emphasis is placed upon the continuities and discontinuities between the League of Nations, the United Nations, and the Clark-Sohn scheme as systems of world order. A way to bring this comparison into focus is to consider the allocation of function and authority between nation-states and the international organization in each of the three peace systems.

In many respects the League of Nations is the first truly "general international organization"—"general," in the sense that it performed a variety of functions, including the broad one of upholding peace and security. The League represented the establishment of an international organization that was potentially universal; membership was open to all states, rather than limited exclusively to Western states. The League was also expected to deal with a wide range of matters of international concern, to hold meetings on an annual and continuing basis, and to possess an articulated structure of organs that were supposed to operate according to stated rules. It was also equipped with a permanent staff to carry on its bureaucratic activities. The combination of these elements clearly distinguishes the League from the experiences with international organization during the nineteenth and early part of the twentieth centuries. A particular pattern of activity developed in this earlier period. Meetings of the Concert of Europe during the nineteenth century were held to allow the Great Powers to discuss their problems; a series of multilateral conferences was convened to deal with specific issues on an ad hoc basis. The development of international private and public organizations formalized the results of these meetings, but each organization was created to deal with a narrow subject such as postal or customs regulation, or the joint administration of an international waterway. The Hague Peace Conferences of 1899 and 1907, although devoted to war-peace issues, did not produce much machinery to deal with the problems which the states had convened to discuss.

The two authors presented in this chapter disagree about the extent of continuity between the League and the United Nations. The first selection, by Clyde Eagleton, "Covenant of the League of Nations and the Charter of the United Nations: Points of Difference," *Department of State Bulletin* (August 19, 1945) pp. 263–269, was prepared just a few months after the United Nations came into existence. The article recites the differences between the United Nations and the League of Nations. Eagleton carefully scrutinizes the constitutional documents of both organizations—the League Covenant and the United Nations Charter—and then lists fifty differences between them. He finds that these differences give the United Nations more scope and greater flexibility in dealing with matters of international concern. He concludes that the United Nations thus constitutes "an improvement over the League of Nations."

Leland Goodrich, on the other hand, writing in 1947 after some disillusioning experiences, stresses the practice of the League. It is Goodrich's contention that the League of Nations represented a far more radical departure from the established pattern of international relations at the time of its adoption than did the United Nations Charter in 1945. In his article, "From League of Nations to United Nations," *International Conciliation,* vol. I, no. 1 (Carnegie Endowment for International Peace, New York, 1947) pp. 3–21, Goodrich acknowledges that there are formal differences between the Charter and the Covenant, but he minimizes their significance by demonstrating that the Charter provisions codify practices that evolved during the life of the League. Thus, he argues, the patterns of practice of the two organizations are far more similar than a comparison of their constitutional texts, in the manner of Eagleton, would indicate.

Before reading these two selections, it would be useful to read through the United Nations Charter. In addition, the questions below will help one to evaluate any proposals for a general international organization with war prevention pretensions:

1. What obligations did states undertake by joining each organization?

2. How do the obligations of membership enlarge the duties imposed by international law on all states?

3. What is the authority of the League of Nations and the United Nations to deal with dangers to the peace and with

international uses of force?

4. What procedures are used by the principal organs of each organization to exercise their authority?

5. What kinds of authoritative results—discussion, recommendation, decision, legislation—is each organization permitted to reach?

6. What enforcement methods are relied upon to attain compliance with the will of each organization?

Covenant of the League of Nations and Charter of the United Nations: Points of Difference

BY CLYDE EAGLETON

THE COMMUNITY OF NATIONS is now engaged in changing over from the Covenant of the League of Nations to the Charter of the United Nations. It is natural, therefore, to compare the two and to inquire as to the differences between them.

Comparison is one of the usual methods of scientific study. It leads in this case to a clearer understanding of both systems and is an excellent means of becoming acquainted with the new United Nations.

Although there is a resemblance between the two systems in structure and general appearance, fundamental differences show, when added up, that the United Nations is quite different in concept and character. Thus, in the League of Nations the Council and the Assembly had a coordinate jurisdiction over most matters; in the United Nations a clear division of function is stated. The Security Council is given primary responsibility for the maintenance of international peace and security; and within the Security Council, a large degree of control is entrusted to the five great powers, which would have, in any case, the actual responsibility for maintaining peace. The United Nations will also exercise control over non-members for purposes of peace and security, thus making the Organization universal in this respect. In order that the United Nations may be really effective in the maintenance of peace, the decisions of the Security Council are binding upon members, who undertake to furnish armed forces or other assistance when the Security Council decides that they are needed.

The other functions of the United Nations are in general put under the supervision of the General Assembly. A much wider provision of institutions and agencies is made through which the cooperative endeavor of nations may be carried on. An Economic and Social Council and a Trusteeship Council will direct work in their respective fields; and a number of "specialized agencies" are contemplated which are to be organized independently of the United Nations but brought into relation with it. The United Nations has many additional functions to perform, particularly in relation to "human rights and fundamental freedoms".

The United Nations is, in general, a more flexible system than that of the League of Nations. The over-all rule of unanimity is abandoned; no tests of aggression are stated, and the Council is left a wide discretion in determining what constitutes an act of aggression; the specialized agencies have room for more functional operation; there are more bodies of the United Nations which can ask the Court for an advisory opinion or which can call to the attention of the Security Council matters dangerous to peace. This flexibility leaves to each member state freedom of decision and complete protection over matters of domestic jurisdiction; at the same time, it affords the widest possible opportunity and encouragement for cooperation in those fields in which sovereign states wish to cooperate.

A more detailed, though not exhaustive, list of points of difference between the League of Nations and the United Nations is given below. The relative merits of the two systems will always be, with regard to each point, a matter of subjective judgment for the reader, but there would be general agreement, it seems safe to say, that in most of these specific comparisons the new system represents an improvement over the League of Nations.

Constitutional Characteristics

1. One of the grounds upon which the Covenant of the League of Nations was criticized in the United States was that it was part of the treaties of peace at the end of the last World War. The Charter of the United Nations is an independent instrument which has nothing to do with war issues but which deals exclusively with the international Organization. Indeed, article 107 dissociates the United Nations entirely from responsibility for action in relation to the enemy states.[2]

2. The Charter contains a statement of purposes and principles for the guidance of the Organization and its members which was not found in the Covenant of the League (arts. 1 and 2).

3. Although article 17 of the Covenant of the League enabled the Council to intervene in disputes to which non-members were parties, the Charter of the United Nations is more definitely applicable to non-members: So far as the maintenance of peace and security is concerned, a non-member may be subjected to the same principles and procedures as a member, although of course without the rights of a member (e. g. art. 2, par. 6; art. 32; art. 35, par. 2).

4. An effort was made, in the League system (art. 24), to centralize all international activities under one organization. In the United Nations system, a purposed decentralization leaves many international activities under independently organized specialized agencies. These agencies, it is intended, should be brought into relation with the United Nations, which should coordinate their activities (art. 57).

5. The most characteristic feature of the United Nations system is the concentration of authority, for purposes of international peace and security, in the hands of the five great powers. Under the Charter, only these five states are given the right of veto; under the Covenant, every member of the Council had that right. The security function in the League was shared by and might be transferred to the Assembly; the Security Council of the United Nations is given the exclusive right to make decisions in this field. Also, the five powers are authorized to act together, in the period until the Security Council has forces at its disposal, for the maintenance of peace and security in the world.

6. Amendment of the Covenant of the League required a unanimous vote of the Assembly (thus giving any member of the League a veto) and ratification by two thirds of the members, including all members of the Council. Amendment of the Charter of the United Nations requires a two-thirds vote in the General Assembly and ratification by two thirds of all members, including the permanent members of the Security Council (thus giving an individual veto only to the five states having permanent seats). The Charter has an additional article authorizing a general conference for review of the Charter to be held at a time and place fixed by a two-thirds vote of the Assembly and any seven members of the Security Council. If such a conference has not been held within ten years, it is automatically placed upon the agenda at the General Assembly and will be held if a majority of the Assembly and any seven members of the Security Council so vote (arts. 108 and 109).

7. Article 104 of the Charter assures to the United Nations such legal capacity as may be necessary for the exercise of its functions and the fulfilment of its purposes. The lack of such a provision in the Covenant led to numerous debates concerning the juridical status of the League of Nations.

Structure and General Procedure

8. In both systems, membership is open to any state regarded as able and willing to meet the obligations of membership, and in both, new members are admitted by two-thirds vote of the Assembly, though the Security Council, under the Charter, must recommend a state for admission (art. 4). Both systems allow also for the expulsion of members: Under the Covenant, by the Council; and under the Charter, by the General Assembly upon recommendation of the Security Council. The Covenant provided for withdrawal by a member on two years' notice and on condition that its international obligations had been met (art. 1 [par. 3]); no mention whatever of withdrawal is found in

[2] For text of the Charter of the United Nations, see BULLETIN of June 24, 1945, p. 1119, and also Department of State publication 2353, Conference Series 74. For text of the Covenant of the League of Nations see III *Treaties, Conventions, International Acts, Protocols and Agreements Between the United States of America and Other Powers* (Redmond, 1923) 3154.

the Charter.[3] The Charter contains an additional provision, however, not found in the Covenant, according to which a member may be suspended from the exercise of the rights and privileges of membership by the General Assembly on recommendation by the Security Council (arts. 5 and 6).

9. Although the principal organs of the League of Nations and the United Nations appear to be similar, the United Nations Charter provides a much clearer division of functions between Council and Assembly than did the Covenant of the League of Nations. Under the Charter primary responsibility for security matters is placed upon the Security Council. On the other hand, the General Assembly has exclusive control over all other matters. In the League system the two bodies in general had competence over the same fields. The United Nations has also an Economic and Social Council and a Trusteeship Council, and various specialized agencies are contemplated.

10. While the provision for meeting the expenses of the Organization is much the same in both, the Charter provides a sanction against the non-payment of dues for which there was no correlative provision in the Covenant (art. 19).

11. A general rule for voting was put into article 5 of the Covenant; provisions for voting are stated separately for each organ of the United Nations. It is an important gain, however, that the unanimity rule, which was of general application in the League system, is abandoned in the Charter of the United Nations. In the Security Council, only the five states having permanent seats thereon have an individual veto, and no veto is possible in the General Assembly (art. 27). Under the League Covenant, each member had a veto in any organ of the League, with very few specified exceptions.

The Security Council

12. With regard to the composition of the Council, permanent and non-permanent members are provided in each system. The Covenant authorized the Council, with the approval of the majority of the Assembly, to name other permanent members of the Council (art. 4 [par. 2]); the Charter makes no provision, except amendment, for changing the status of the permanent members. No qualifications are set in either case for permanent members, but the Charter provides that certain stated criteria must be taken into account in the choice of non-permanent members of the Security Council (art. 23).

13. The Covenant of the League called for at least one meeting of the Council a year (art. 4, [par. 3]), although in practice the Council met three or four times a year. The Charter of the United Nations requires the Security Council to be organized so that it will be able to function continuously, and it obligates each member of the Council to have a representative at all times at the seat of the Organization (art. 28).

14. In both the Council of the League and the Security Council of the United Nations, each state has only one vote. In the Council of the League, however, action upon any substantive matter required a unanimous vote of all its members; in the Security Council, on non-procedural matters a decision may be taken by a vote of seven of the eleven members, provided this includes all members having permanent seats. Thus, in the Council of the League any member had a veto, whereas in the Security Council only five states have such a right.

With regard to the vote of the parties to a dispute, the Covenant of the League specifically excepted such votes under article 15, though it did not do so under article 11. The Charter requires a disputant to abstain from voting in any case of pacific settlement of disputes to which it is a party (art. 27).

The Security Functions

15. When the Security Council, having decided that a threat to or breach of the peace, or act of aggression, has occurred, determines upon enforcement measures to be taken, then members of the United Nations are obligated to carry out the decisions of the Security Council in accordance with the Charter (art. 25 and ch. VII). Under the Covenant of the League of Nations, and under the interpretative resolutions of 1921–22, each member could decide for itself whether an aggression had been committed which obligated it to take action under article 16 of the Covenant, and that member was obligated only after it had itself made that decision.

[3] It was, however, explained in the Report to the President that "withdrawal is permissible but it will have to be justified" (*Report to the President on the Results of the San Francisco Conference by the Chairman of the United States Delegation, the Secretary of State.* Department of State publication 2349, p. 49).

16. No tests or definitions of aggression are provided in the Charter of the United Nations. The Security Council has much more freedom of action than had the Council of the League in determining what constitutes a threat to or breach of the peace, or act of aggression, which authorizes action against an aggressor (art. 39). Under article 16 of the League Covenant, action could be taken only in case of "resort to war in disregard of its covenants under Articles 12, 13 or 15"; under the Charter, no restriction is set upon the power of the Security Council to determine that any dispute or situation is a threat to the peace, breach of the peace, or act of aggression.

17. In neither instrument is war declared to be illegal. The Charter, however, makes a large advance over the Covenant by omitting the word "war" and forbidding *the use of force* by a state in a manner inconsistent with the purposes of the Organization (art. 2, par. 4, and ch. VII).

18. Under the Covenant, members guaranteed to respect and preserve against external aggression the territorial integrity and existing political independence of all members of the League (art. 10). Under the Charter, members undertake to refrain from the threat or use of force against the territorial integrity or political independence of any state in a manner inconsistent with the purposes of the United Nations (art. 2, par. 4).

19. The Charter of the United Nations obligates members to supply armed forces or facilities or other assistance, while under the Covenant the Council could only recommend that members should contribute certain amounts. The obligation in the Charter is, however, to be implemented by subsequent agreements specifying the contribution to be made by each member; and if and when the agreements for supply of forces by members have been made under article 43 of the Charter, the United Nations will have behind its decisions a military strength, derived from the obligation upon its members, which was never available to the League of Nations. During the interim until these agreements are made, provision is made in chapter XVII for the maintenance of security and peace by the five powers.

20. Chapter VII of the Charter more definitely contemplates and more specifically provides for military enforcement measures than did the Covenant of the League. The League system included a Permanent Advisory Commission to advise the Council on reduction of armaments and on military matters in general. The Charter establishes a Military Staff Committee with specific functions concerning all military requirements for the maintenance of international peace and security, including the employment and command of forces used for this purpose (arts. 45–47).

21. The League of Nations had some difficulty in securing its participation in non-military measures, since it was held that members were not obligated by a decision of the Council in this respect. By article 41 of the Charter, as well as by article 25, it is clear that members of the United Nations are obligated to apply such measures upon call of the Security Council.

22. The Covenant spoke in more detail concerning reduction of armaments than does the Charter. The Security Council is, however, instructed to formulate plans for a system for the regulation of armaments with the assistance of the Military Staff Committee (art. 26). The Covenant spoke only of "reduction of armaments"; the Charter refers to "regulation of armaments".

Settlement of Disputes

23. Article 33 of the Charter emphasizes, as the first step, the obligation of parties to a dispute to seek a settlement by means of their own choice. This obligation was not stated as such in the Covenant, though it was doubtless assumed as a preliminary step.

24. Article 37 of the Charter requires all disputes which have not been settled by means of the parties' own choice to be submitted to the Security Council. Under articles 12, 13, and 15 of the Covenant, legal disputes were required to be submitted to arbitration or judicial settlement, and other disputes, to the Council.

25. Under the Charter of the United Nations, no provision is made for enforcement of terms of settlement, except the limited provision regarding a decision of the Court found in article 94, paragraph 2. By article 15 [paragraph 6] of the Covenant, members of the League undertook not to go to war against any party to a dispute which complied with a unanimous recommendation of the Council.

26. The League of Nations and the Permanent Court of International Justice were separate institutions, though with some connections. The International Court of Justice is designated as the chief judicial organ of the United Nations; its Statute is an integral part of the Charter of the United Nations; and all members of the latter are *ipso facto* parties to the Statute of the Court. In neither system, however, does the Court have compulsory jurisdiction, except so far as is conferred upon it by the Optional Clause, or by treaties of arbitration or other treaties. (Ch. XIV.)

27. The Covenant provided that the Council or Assembly could ask an advisory opinion of the Court (art. 14). The Charter does the same but provides additionally that other organs of the United Nations or specialized agencies, when so authorized by the General Assembly, may also request advisory opinions (art. 96).

The General Assembly and Its Functions

28. As has been suggested above, the functions of the General Assembly are more clearly differentiated from those of the Security Council under the Charter than under the Covenant. In comparison with the Security Council, it has a more exclusive field of activity, since the Council can deal only with peace and security; on the other hand, the Assembly, although with much more limited authority, can deal with these and with practically all other international matters.

29. A dispute, under the League system, might be referred to and handled by the Assembly. Under the Charter, the Assembly may discuss and make recommendations concerning a dispute, but it can make recommendations only if the matter is not being dealt with by the Security Council (art. 12).

30. A more detailed structure for handling international cooperative activities, especially economic, social, and humanitarian advancement, is provided than was found in the League Covenant. The Assembly was the only organ provided by the Covenant for these purposes; under the Charter, there is to be an Economic and Social Council, with such commissions as it may need; a Trusteeship Council; and various agencies specializing in particular fields.

31. The Charter states more fully the specific functions and objectives aimed at, such as human rights, higher standards of living, full employment, cultural and educational cooperation, or the development of international law.

32. Although the Assembly under the Covenant had more control over the Council than the General Assembly does under the Charter (e.g. as to its composition), the latter has, in the new system, a more exclusive supervision over other agencies, such as the new Economic and Social Council or the new Trusteeship Council. Under the Covenant, Council and Assembly both had authority over such organs. The General Assembly is more of an over-all directing agency under the Charter than was the Assembly under the Covenant.

33. Voting upon substantive matters in the General Assembly is by a two-thirds majority (art. 18); voting in the Assembly of the League of Nations required unanimity. In both cases, procedural matters are determined by a majority.

Secretariat

34. The Secretary-General is chosen in the same manner under both systems. His functions under the Charter, however, are broader. He acts as Secretary-General for all the chief organs of the United Nations; he is required to make an annual report to the General Assembly (art. 98); and he is given the important additional authority to bring to the attention of the Security Council any matter which may, in his opinion, threaten peace and security (art. 99).

35. The staff of the secretariat is in both cases chosen by the Secretary-General, but where the Covenant required approval by the Council (art. 6) the Charter submits his choice to regulations established by the General Assembly (art. 101).

36. The Charter contains qualifications for the staff which, with the exception of the provision concerning equal opportunity for both sexes, were not stated in the Covenant. Article 100 of the Charter obligates both members and staff to respect the international position and responsibility of staff members; and article 101 states as the paramount consideration in employment efficiency, competence, and integrity, though due regard is to be given to the geographical basis of selection.

International Law and Treaties

37. The principle that international law should furnish the rule of conduct in the achievement of peace and security was vaguely referred to in the Preamble to the Covenant of the League. More precise legal effect is given to this idea in the Charter by stating in the first article of the text that disputes should be settled in conformity with the principles of justice and international law.

38. The Charter states as one of the functions f the General Assembly the development of inter-ational law (art. 13). The Covenant of the eague contained no such statement, although the eague actually did perform this function in ractice.

39. The provision with regard to "domestic uestions" is stated in broader terms under the harter. Under the Covenant of the League, the ouncil could make no recommendation upon a ispute which the Council found to be a matter hich, by international law, was solely within the omestic jurisdiction of a state (art. 15, [par. 8]), nd the application of this clause was limited to isputes. The Charter provision is put among the rinciples and therefore applies to all parts of the harter; it does not include, as did the Covenant, e right of the Security Council to decide whether matter is a domestic question or the requirement at the decision be made according to interna-onal law.

40. With regard to treaties, both instruments equire that every treaty and every international ngagement entered into by members shall be egistered and published; but, where the Covenant tipulates that no such treaty shall be binding un-ess registered, the Charter (art. 102) says that a reaty not registered cannot be invoked before any rgan of the United Nations. Both instruments rovide, in effect, that obligations thereunder con-racted prevail over obligations assumed by embers under any other agreement.

41. The Covenant of the League contained an neffective article with regard to revision of reaties; the Charter of the United Nations makes o specific mention of this problem but encourages n various ways the adjustment of situations which night lead to friction (arts. 1, 10, 14; chs. IX nd X).

Trusteeship

42. Article 22 of the Covenant of the League vas to apply "To those colonies and territories which as a consequence of the late war have ceased o be under the sovereignty of the States which formerly governed them . . . ". Article 77 of the Charter of the United Nations applies the rusteeship provisions "to such territories in the following categories as may be placed thereunder by means of trusteeship agreements"; the cate-gories mentioned are (1) territories now under mandate, (2) territories detached from the enemy as a result of the second World War, and (3) other territories voluntarily placed thereunder.

43. The provisions of the Covenant applied only to peoples placed under mandate; chapter XI of the Charter establishes standards for dependent peoples whether or not under trusteeship.

44. The Covenant provided a Mandates Com-mission, which was a group of experts not repre-senting their own states; the Charter elevates the Trusteeship Council to the rank of a principal organ composed of the official representatives of designated states (ch. III).

45. Under the League of Nations, no military use could be made of a mandated territory. The Charter of the United Nations allows for military contributions in such areas, whether for interna-tional peace and security or for local defense. It also distinguishes strategic areas, under the Se-curity Council, from non-strategic areas, under the General Assembly and the Trusteeship Council (arts. 82, 83, 84, 85).

46. The mandates of the League of Nations were in a rigid classification known as *A*, *B*, and *C* mandates. The trusteeship system of the United Nations is more flexible in that a separate agreement is to be made with regard to each trust area (art. 81).

47. The trusteeship provisions of the Charter state more fully and more definitely than did the Covenant such objectives as development toward self-government or independence and respect for human rights and fundamental freedoms (art. 76).

Regional Arrangements

48. The Covenant of the League contained a vague and negative statement in article 21: "Noth-ing in this Covenant shall be deemed to affect the validity of international engagements, such as treaties of arbitration or regional understandings like the Monroe doctrine, for securing the main-tenance of peace." The Charter of the United Nations permits and encourages, though it does not create, "regional arrangements and agencies" for the maintenance of regional peace, provided they are consistent with the purposes and prin-ciples of the United Nations.

49. The League had no provision for settle-ment of disputes by regional means. Under arti-cle 52 of the Charter, both members and the Secu-rity Council are to encourage the pacific settlement of local disputes by regional agencies before they are referred to the Security Council.

50. The League made no provision for "sanctions", or enforcement measures, on a regional basis. The Charter permits the Security Council to make use of regional arrangements or agencies for enforcement action, but carefully insures that such action shall be under its authority, and that no regional enforcement action shall be taken without the authorization of the Security Council—though the individual and collective right of self-defense is maintained under article 51.

FROM LEAGUE OF NATIONS TO UNITED NATIONS

by LELAND M. GOODRICH

I.

On April 18, 1946, the League Assembly adjourned after taking the necessary steps to terminate the existence of the League of Nations and transfer its properties and assets to the United Nations. On August 1, this transfer took place at a simple ceremony in Geneva. Thus, an important and, at one time, promising experiment in international cooperation came formally to an end. Outside of Geneva, no important notice was taken of this fact. Within the counsels of the United Nations, there was an apparent readiness to write the old League off as a failure, and to regard the new organization as something unique, representing a fresh approach to the world problems of peace and security. Quite clearly there was a hesitancy in many quarters to call attention to the essential continuity of the old League and the new United Nations for fear of arousing latent hostilities or creating doubts which might seriously jeopardize the birth and early success of the new organization.

This silence regarding the League could well be understood at a time when the establishment of a general world organization to take the place of the discredited League was in doubt, when it was uncertain whether the United States Senate would agree to American participation, and when the future course of the Soviet Union was in the balance. Though careful consideration had been given within the Department of State to League experience in the formulation of American proposals, it was quite understandable that officers of the Department, in the addresses which they delivered and reports which they made on the Dumbarton Oaks Proposals, should have for the most part omitted all references to the League except where it seemed possible to point to the great improvements that had been incorporated in the new Proposals. Nor was it surprising, in view of the past relation of the United States to the League and the known antipathy of the Soviet Union to that organization, that Secretary of State Stettinius in his address to the United Nations Conference in San Francisco on April 26, 1945, failed once to refer to the League of Nations, or the part of an American President in the establishment of it.[1] In fact, from the addresses and debates at the San Francisco Conference, the personnel assembled for the Conference Secretariat, and the organization and procedure of the Conference, it would have been quite possible for an outside observer to draw the conclusion that this was a pioneer effort in world organization.[2] Since the United Nations came into being as a functioning organization there has been a similar disinclination on the part of those participating in its work to call attention to its true relation to the League of Nations.

While the circumstances which make it necessary for those officially connected with the United Nations to be so circumspect in their references to the League of Nations can be appreciated, the student of international organization is free, in fact is duty bound, to take a more independent and objective view of the relations of the two organizations. If his studies lead him to the conclusion that the United Nations is in large measure the result of a continuous evolutionary development extending well into the past, instead of being the product of new ideas conceived under pressure of the recent war, that should not be the occasion for despair, as we know from the past that those social institutions which have been most successful in achieving their purposes are those which are the product of gradual evolutionary development, those which in general conform to established habits of thought but which nevertheless have the inner capacity for adaptation to new conditions and new needs.

While progress largely depends upon the discovery and application of new ideas and techniques, it has always been considered the test of practical statesmanship to be able to build on the past, adapting what has been proven to be useful in past experience to the needs and requirements of the changing world. Thus the framers of the American Constitution, while they created much that was new, did not hesitate to draw heavily upon the institutions and principles which were a part of their common background of experience in America and in England. At the time of the establishment of the League of Nations, the view was commonly held, certainly with more justification than today in relation to the United Nations, that something really unique was being created. However, we have come to recognize that even the League system was primarily a systematization of pre-war ideas and practices, with some innovations added in the light of war experience. Sir Alfred Zimmern has expressed this fact very well in these words:

> . . . The League of Nations was never intended to be, nor is it, a revolutionary organization. On the contrary, it accepts the world

[1] United Nations Conference on International Organization, Document 15, P/3, April 27, 1945.

[2] For an authoritative description of the Conference, see Grayson Kirk and Lawrence H. Chamberlain, "The Organization of the San Francisco Conference," in *Political Science Quarterly*, LX (1945), p. 321.

> of states as it finds it and merely seeks to provide a more satisfactory means for carrying on some of the business which these states transact between one another. It is not even revolutionary in the more limited sense of revolutionizing the methods for carrying on interstate business. It does not supersede the older methods. It merely supplements them.[3]

We have come to recognize the various strands of experience—the European Concert of Powers, the practice of arbitration in the settlement of disputes, international administrative cooperation, to mention only a few—which entered into the fabric of the League. Should we be surprised to find that what was true of the League of Nations is even more true of the United Nations?

Those who have thus far attempted a comparison of the United Nations with the League of Nations have, generally speaking, been concerned with pointing out the differences.[4] Furthermore, comparison has been made of the textual provisions of the Covenant and the provisions of the Charter, not taking into account actual practice under the Covenant. Such a basis of comparison naturally leads to an exaggerated idea of the extent of the gap which separates the two systems. If in similar fashion the Constitution of the United States as it existed on paper at the time it became effective in 1789 were compared with the Constitution as it is applied today, the conclusion undoubtedly would be that a revolution had occurred in the intervening period. Obviously, any useful comparison of the League and the United Nations must be based on the League system as it developed under the Covenant. If that is done, it becomes clear that the gap separating the League of Nations and the United Nations is not large, that many provisions of the United Nations system have been taken directly from the Covenant, though usually with changes of names and rearrangements of words, that other provisions are little more than codifications, so to speak, of League practice as it developed under the Covenant, and that still other provisions represent the logical development of ideas which were in process of evolution when the League was actively functioning. Of course there are many exceptions, some of them important. But the point upon which attention needs to be focused for the serious student of international affairs is that the United Nations does not represent a break with the past, but rather the continued application of old ideas and methods with some changes deemed necessary in the light of past experience. If people would only recognize this simple truth, they might be more intelligent in their evaluation of past efforts and more tolerant in their appraisal of present efforts.

[3] Alfred Zimmern, *The League of Nations and the Rule of Law*, London, 1936, p. 4.

[4] See, for example, Clyde Eagleton, "Covenant of the League of Nations and Charter of the United Nations: Points of Difference," in Department of State, *Bulletin*, XIII, p. 263.

II.

Space does not permit a detailed analysis with a view to establishing the exact extent to which the United Nations is a continuation of the League system. All that is attempted here is to consider the more important features of the United Nations system, particularly those with respect to which claims to uniqueness have been made, with a view to determining to what extent in general this continuity can be said to exist.

Relation to the Peace Settlement

One point that has been made in favor of the United Nations as a special claim to uniqueness is that its Charter is an independent instrument, unconnected with the treaties which are in process of being made for settling the political and economic issues of World War II.[5] In contrast, it is argued that the League, by virtue of the fact that its Covenant was made at the Paris Peace Conference, and incorporated in each of the peace treaties, was from the beginning so involved in the issues of the peace settlement that it was never able to overcome the initial handicap of being a League to enforce the peace treaties. It is true, of course, that under the Covenant and under other provisions of the peace treaties, the League had placed upon it certain responsibilities in connection with the carrying out of the peace settlement.[6] This connection was not, in the early years of the League, regarded as an unmixed evil. One distinguished observer, while recognizing that a principal function of the League was "to execute the peace treaties," concluded on the basis of the first years of experience that this connection on balance served a useful world purpose.[7] It might be suggested that the criticism that later came to be made of the League on the ground of its relation to the peace treaties was primarily an attack upon the treaties themselves and would have been directed against any international organization which proved incapable of revising them. Without further arguing this point, however, the question can be raised as to how different will be the relation of the United Nations to the peace settlement following World War II?

While the Charter is a separate instrument and was made at a conference called specially for the purpose, the United Nations will inevitably become intimately and directly associated with the peace treaties once they are made. For one thing the original Members of the United Nations were those states that were at war with one or more of the Axis powers at the time of the San Francisco Conference. Furthermore, the interpre-

[5] See, for example, Clyde Eagleton, "Covenant of the League of Nations and Charter of the United Nations: Points of Difference," in Department of State, *Bulletin*, XIII, p. 264.

[6] See, for example, the provision of the Treaty of Versailles relating to the administration of the Saar Basin and the protection of Danzig. *Treaty of Peace with Germany*, Part III, section IV, Annex, chapter II, and section XI.

[7] W. E. Rappard, *International Relations Viewed from Geneva*, New Haven, 1925, p. 14–16.

tation to date of the provisions of Article 4 of the Charter makes it clear that the conduct of a non-member state during the war is an important factor in determining whether that state shall be admitted to membership. While Article 107 dissociates the United Nations as a peace organization from action taken in relation to enemy states, once the peace treaties have been made they will become part of the existing economic and political order on the basis of which the United Nations will seek to maintain peace and security. It is difficult to see how an international organization for maintaining peace and security, such as the United Nations is, can do so on any other basis. Furthermore, in connection with the making of the peace treaties, we already see the United Nations being called upon to exercise important functions of administration or guarantee similar to those which the League was asked to perform. Thus the United Nations guarantee of the special regime for Trieste parallels very closely the League guarantee of Danzig in its basic conception, and the proposed role of the United Nations in connection with "territories detached from enemy states in connection with the Second World War"[8] is almost identical to that of the League in relation to "colonies and territories which as a consequence of the late war [World War I] have ceased to be under the sovereignty of the States which formerly governed them."[9]

In this same connection we should consider the respective powers and responsibilities of the two organizations in regard to the revision of the two peace settlements. One serious criticism made of the League of Nations was its ineffectiveness as an instrumentality for the revision of those provisions of the peace treaties which had come to be recognized as unfair and unjust. Under the Covenant of the League the Assembly was empowered to advise the revision of treaties which had become "inapplicable" and the consideration of international conditions whose continuation might affect the peace of the world.[10] This provision remained a dead letter from the beginning, due to the Assembly's lack of power of decision and means of enforcement.[11] How much more effective is the United Nations likely to be in this respect? According to Article 14 of the Charter the General Assembly may recommend measures for the peaceful adjustment of any situation, regardless of origin, which is likely to impair friendly relations among nations. While there is no specific mention made of the revision of treaties, the General Assembly is clearly authorized under this Article to discuss any situation having its origin in unsatisfactory treaty provisions and to make recommendations thereon.[12] There is, however,

[8] *Charter of the United Nations*, Article 77.

[9] *Covenant of the League of Nations*, Article 12, paragraph 1.

[10] *Ibid.*, Article 19.

[11] Frederick S. Dunn, *Peaceful Change*, New York, 1937, p. 106–11.

[12] See discussion in Leland M. Goodrich and Edvard Hambro, *Charter of the United Nations: Commentary and Documents*, Boston, 1946, p. 104–06.

no obligation on the part of Members to accept any recommendation that may be made. Thus the power conferred under this Article does not go substantially beyond that of the Assembly under Article 19 of the Covenant and there is the same chance, if not likelihood, that the United Nations will be ineffective as an instrument for treaty revision. Furthermore, while the Security Council is given broad powers to take necessary action to maintain peace and security, the powers which the Council has to bind Members are limited to those falling within the general category of enforcement action and do not extend to the power to impose upon parties to a dispute or states interested in a particular situation any particular terms of settlement or adjustment. That was made clear in the discussions at San Francisco.[13]

Basic Character of Two Organizations

The statement has been made that the United Nations is "potentially and actually much stronger" than the League of Nations.[14] That statement might lend itself to some misunderstanding, particularly in view of the fact that it is only one of many statements that have been made suggesting that the United Nations inherently is a more powerful organization and therefore more likely to achieve its purpose by virtue of the specific provisions of its Charter than was the League of Nations.

We can start, I think, with the fundamental proposition that the United Nations, as was the League of Nations, is primarily a cooperative enterprise and falls generally within the category of leagues and confederations instead of within that of federal unions. Except in one situation, neither the United Nations nor its principal political organs have the authority to take decisions binding on Members without their express consent. Without this power, it is impossible to regard the organs of the United Nations as constituting a government in the sense of the federal government of the United States. The essential character of the United Nations is specifically affirmed in the first of the principles laid down in Article 2 of the Charter where it is stated that "the organization is based on the principle of the sovereign equality of all its members." This principle was not expressly stated in the Covenant of the League of Nations, but was, nevertheless, implicit in its provisions.

Since both the United Nations and the League of Nations are based primarily upon the principle of voluntary cooperation, the point that needs special consideration is whether, more or less as an exception to the general principle, the Charter contains provisions which give to the organs of the United Nations greater authority than was vested in the corre-

[13] See Goodrich and Hambro, *op. cit.*, p. 152–53, 155–59.

[14] Louis Dolivet, *The United Nations: A Handbook on the New World Organization*, New York, 1946, p. 16.

sponding organs of the League. In this connection a great deal of emphasis has been placed upon the provisions of the Charter regulating voting in the General Assembly and the Security Council. It is, of course, true that under Article 18 of the Charter decisions of the General Assembly can be taken by a two-thirds majority of the members present and voting, instead of by unanimous vote of those present, as was the requirement for the League Assembly. It must be borne in mind, however, that on questions of policy the General Assembly can only recommend, and that consequently any decision taken is a decision to make a recommendation. Also, it is quite unfair to compare these provisions without taking into account the practice of the League Assembly under the Covenant. In several important respects the rule of the Covenant was interpreted so as to bring actual League practice fairly close to the provisions of the Charter.[15] For one thing, it was provided in the rules of the Assembly that a state which abstained from voting was not to be counted as present, with the result that abstention was a means by which certain of the consequences of the unanimity rule could be avoided. More important, however, was the rule which was established in the first session of the League Assembly, that a resolution expressing a wish, technically known as a "voeu," might be adopted by a majority vote. This had the effect of making possible a whole range of Assembly decisions by majority vote which did not differ in any important respect from decisions which may be taken by the General Assembly by majority or two-thirds votes.[16] Furthermore, it should be noted that the League Assembly early came to the conclusion that the decision to recommend an amendment to the Covenant under Article 26 might be taken by a majority vote,[17] with the result that the power of the Assembly to initiate amendments actually could be exercised more easily than under the Charter of the United Nations. Thus it would seem erroneous to view the provisions of the Charter with respect to the power of the General Assembly to make decisions as representing any fundamentally different approach from or any great advance over the comparable provisions of the Covenant of the League of Nations as interpreted in practice.

When we turn our attention to the Security Council we find admittedly that an important change has been made. Under the League Covenant the Council was governed by the unanimity rule except in procedural matters, and this proved a serious handicap, particularly when the Council was acting under Article 11 of the Covenant. It was possible for a member of the Council, accused of threatening or disturbing the peace, to prevent any effective action under this Article by the interposition

[15] See Margaret E. Burton, *The Assembly of the League of Nations*, Chicago, 1941, p. 175–205.

[16] See C. A. Riches, *Majority Rule in International Organization*, Baltimore, 1940, p. 24.

[17] League of Nations, *Records of the Second Assembly*, Plenary Meetings, p. 733–35. See also, Burton, *op. cit.*, p. 187.

of its veto, as happened in the case of Japanese aggression in Manchuria in 1931 and the threat of Italian aggression in Ethiopia in 1935. Under the Charter it is possible for a decision to be taken binding Members of the United Nations without their express consent. Furthermore, this decision may require specific acts upon the part of the Members of the United Nations and is not to be regarded as a simple recommendation as was the case with decisions taken by the League Council under Articles 10 and 16.

Nevertheless, there are important points to be kept in mind before we conclude that a revolutionary step has been taken. In the first place, a decision by the Security Council can only have the effect of a recommendation when the Security Council is engaged in the performance of its functions under Chapter VI, *i.e.* when it is seeking to achieve the pacific settlement or adjustment of a dispute or situation. Furthermore, while the decision of the Security Council with respect to enforcement action under Chapter VII is binding upon Members of the United Nations, including those not represented on the Security Council, such decisions cannot be taken without the concurrence of all the permanent members of the Security Council. Consequently, in a situation comparable to that of Japanese aggression against China in Manchuria in 1931 and the threat of Italian aggression against Ethiopia in 1935, where the League Council admittedly failed on account of the unanimity principle, the Security Council would be prevented from taking any decision. Under the Charter the Security Council has power, which the League Council did not have, to take action against the small powers, but the experience of the past would seem to show that it is not the smaller powers, acting alone, who are most likely to disturb the peace. When dealing with threats by smaller powers acting alone the League Council was reasonably effective; it failed only when small powers had the backing of great powers. In spite of important changes in the technical provisions of the Charter, one is forced to the conclusion that so far as the actual possession of power is concerned, the United Nations has not advanced much beyond the League of Nations and that in comparable situations much the same result is to be anticipated. In the last analysis under either system success or failure is dependent upon the ability of the more powerful members to cooperate effectively for common ends.

Finally, the provisions of the Charter with regard to amendments and withdrawal follow in all essential respects the provisions of the Covenant and the practices developed thereunder. Under both Charter and Covenant no amendment recommended by the Assembly can become effective until ratified by the great powers. The Covenant was a little more restrictive than the Charter in one respect, requiring ratification by all members of the League whose representatives composed the Council, plus a majority of all other members, thereby giving any Council member a "veto." On the other hand, the Charter, while limiting the "veto" to permanent members, requires approval by two-thirds of the Members of the United Nations. In practice, the charter provisions are not likely to have substantially different results.

Likewise, with respect to withdrawal, the League and the United Nations systems do not differ in any important respect. The Covenant of the League expressly permitted withdrawal under certain conditions which were not, however, enforced in practice.[18] The Charter says nothing about withdrawal but it is understood on the basis of a declaration adopted at San Francisco that the right of withdrawal can be exercised.[19] No doubt influenced by the League practice and conforming to it, it was decided that no legal conditions should be attached to the exercise of this right and that no attempt should be made to force a state to remain a Member, although it was made clear that a moral obligation to continue as a Member exists and that the right of withdrawal should only be exercised for very good reasons.

Basic Obligations of Members

Enumerated in Article 2 of the Charter are certain basic obligations of Members of the United Nations. These include the obligation to settle disputes by peaceful means in such a manner that international peace and security are not endangered, the obligation to refrain from the threat or the use of force against the territorial integrity or political independence of any state, and the obligation to give assistance to the United Nations in any action taken under the terms of the Charter. Similar commitments phrased in somewhat different language and with somewhat different meanings were to be found in various Articles of the Covenant.[20] From the point of view of form the Charter does represent a somewhat different approach in that these basic commitments are grouped together as Principles binding upon all Members. The phraseology of the Charter in certain respects undoubtedly represents improvement. For instance, the provision of Article 2, paragraph 4, by which Members are to refrain "from the threat or use of force against the territorial integrity or political independence of any state" represents an advance over the corresponding provisions of the Covenant which made it possible for members to take refuge in the technicality that an undeclared war in the material sense was no war and that therefore such use of armed force did not constitute a "resort to war." On the other hand, in one important respect, the basic

[18] Article 1, paragraph 2.

[19] For text, see UNCIO, *Verbatim Minutes of the Ninth Plenary Session*, June 25, 1945, Document 1210, P/20, p. 5–6; for text and comment, see Goodrich and Hambro, *op. cit.*, p. 86–89.

[20] Articles 10; 12, paragraph 1; 13, paragraphs 1 and 4; 15, paragraphs 1 and 6; 16, paragraphs 1 and 3; and 17.

obligations of the Members of the United Nations may prove to be less satisfactory since, in the matter of enforcement action, the obligation of the Members of the United Nations is to accept and carry out decisions of the Security Council and to give assistance to the United Nations in any action taken under the Charter, while under Article 16 of the Covenant, the obligation of members extended to the taking of specific measures against any state resorting to war in violation of its obligations under the Covenant. While this obligation was weakened by resolutions adopted by the Assembly in 1921, it nevertheless proved capable of providing the legal basis for important action against Italy in 1935.

III.

The element of continuity in the progression from League of Nations to United Nations is perhaps most obvious when we examine the structure of the two organizations. The General Assembly is the League Assembly, from the point of view of the basic principles of its composition, powers and procedures. We have already seen from an examination of voting procedures that the practical difference between the League provisions and their actual application and the Charter provisions has been greatly exaggerated. The powers of the General Assembly, as compared with those of the League Assembly, have been somewhat restricted, it is true. The General Assembly's powers of discussion under Article 10 of the Charter and succeeding articles are fully as broad and comprehensive as the League Assembly's powers under Article 3, paragraph 3 of the Covenant. Only in respect to the making of recommendations has the power of the General Assembly been limited, and this, it can be argued, is in line with the practice which developed under the Covenant according to which the Council, and not the Assembly, ordinarily dealt with disputes and situations which endangered peace and good understanding.[21] The significant difference is that under the Charter a party to a dispute cannot by its act alone transfer the dispute from the Council to the Assembly, as was possible under Article 15, paragraph 9, of the Covenant.

The Security Council, from the point of view of composition, is the old League Council. One important change, however, has been introduced into the Charter. The League Council had general responsibilities and functions, whereas the Security Council is a highly specialized organ. Instead of having one council with broad powers as did the League, the United Nations has three, among which the various functions and powers of the League Council are divided. To a certain extent this new set-up was anticipated in League practice. At the time when the League's prestige as a peace and security organization was low, the Assembly created a special committee known as the Bruce Committee to inquire

[21] See Burton, *op. cit.*, p. 284–374.

and report on the possibilities of giving the economic and social work of the League greater autonomy. This Committee recommended the establishment of a new organ to be known as the Central Committee for Economic and Social Questions to which would be entrusted the direction and supervision of the work of the League committees in this field.[22] This proposed Committee, while it never was set up, was in effect the forerunner of the present Economic and Social Council.

So far as the Trusteeship Council is concerned, there is a somewhat similar background of development. While the Council was responsible under the Covenant for the supervision of the administration of mandates, in actual practice the Council came to rely very heavily on the Mandates Commission which, under the Charter, has come to be elevated to the rank of a principal organ, responsible not to the Council but to the General Assembly. This very responsibility of the Trusteeship Council to the General Assembly was to some extent anticipated in the practice of the League. Over the protest of some members, the League Assembly early asserted and exercised the right to discuss and express its opinion on mandates questions. While the Council was technically responsible for the enforcement of the provisions of the Covenant, there can be little doubt but what the Assembly exercised a real influence both on Council action and upon the mandatory powers.[23]

The Secretariat of the United Nations is clearly a continuation of the League Secretariat, not only in name, but also largely in substance. While the Charter provisions would permit its organization on somewhat different lines, with separate staffs for the principal organs of the United Nations, it seems clear that the conception of a unified Secretariat has prevailed.[24] "The role of the Secretary-General as the administrator of the United Nations derives from that of his counterpart in the League of Nations," [25] but has clearly assumed greater importance and scope under the provisions of the Charter. Due to political circumstances and the personality of the first holder of the office, the Secretary-General of the League never came to exercise a strong guiding hand in the direction of the League's work. The Charter of the United Nations, however, both expressly and by implication, gives the Secretary-General greater power and seems to expect more constructive leadership from him. More particularly, the role which the Secretary-General will be called upon to play in connection with the coordination of the work of the specialized agencies will require the exercise of initiative and strong leadership.[26]

[22] *League of Nations, Monthly Summary*, August 1939, Special Supplement.

[23] See Quincy Wright, *Mandates under the League of Nations*, Chicago, 1930, p. 133–35.

[24] See Report of the Preparatory Commission of the United Nations, PC/20, 23 December 1945, p. 84–94; Walter H. C. Laves and Donald Stone, "The United Nations Secretariat," *Foreign Policy Reports*, October 15, 1946.

[25] Laves and Stone, *op. cit.*, p. 183.

[26] *Ibid.*, p. 186 et seq.

With respect to the Court, it is clearly recognized that, while it was decided to set up a new Court under a new name, it will be essentially the same as the Permanent Court of International Justice.[27] The fact that this Court is regarded as one of the principal organs of the United Nations does not in substance distinguish it from the Permanent Court. For purposes of expediency it seemed advisable to maintain the fiction that the Permanent Court of International Justice was independent of the League system, but a careful examination of the actual organization and work of the Court will leave no doubt that the Court functioned as fully within the framework of the League as will the International Court of Justice within the framework of the United Nations.

IV.

Like the League of Nations, the United Nations is a "general international organization" in the sense that its functions and actions cover the whole range of matters of international concern. Both the Preamble and the statement of Purposes contained in Article I of the Charter make this clear. In fact this generality of purpose and function is more explicitly stated in the Charter than it was in the Covenant, though in the practice of the League it came to be fully recognized. The Charter of the United Nations, in its general arrangement and substantive provisions, divides the major activities of the Organization into three categories: (1) the maintenance of international peace and security, by the pacific settlement of disputes and the taking of enforcement measures; (2) the promotion of international economic and social cooperation; and (3) the protection of the interests of the peoples of non-self-governing territories.

The Pacific Settlement of Disputes

The Charter system for the pacific settlement of disputes,[28] while differing from that of the League in many details of substance and phraseology, follows it in accepting two basic principles: (1) that parties to a dispute are in the first instance to seek a peaceful settlement by means of their own choice; and (2) that the political organs of the international organization are to intervene only when the dispute has become a threat to the peace, and then only in a mediatory or conciliatory capacity.

The obligation which Members of the United Nations accept under Article 2, paragraph 3 is to "settle their international disputes by peaceful means in such a manner that international peace and security, and justice, are not endangered." Under Article 34, paragraph 1, the parties to any

[27] UNCIO, Report of the Rapporteur of Committee IV/1, Document 913, IV/1/74 (1). See also Manley O. Hudson, "The Twenty-Fourth Year of the World Court," in *American Journal of International Law*, LX (1946), p. 1–52.

[28] For detailed analysis, see Leland M. Goodrich, "Pacific Settlement of Disputes," in *American Political Science Review*, XXXIX (1945), p. 956–970.

dispute "the continuance of which is likely to endanger the maintenance of international peace and security, shall, first of all seek a solution" by peaceful means of their own choice. Furthermore, by the terms of Article 36 of the Statute of the Court, Members may by declaration accept under certain conditions the compulsory jurisdiction of the Court. Declarations made by Members of the United Nations accepting the compulsory jurisdiction of the Permanent Court of International Justice and still in force are declared to be acceptances under this Article.

The legal obligations which Members of the United Nations have thus assumed are substantially the same as the obligations of League members under the Covenant and supplementary agreements. The Covenant itself did not place upon members of the League the obligation to settle all their disputes by peaceful means. However, forty-six states accepted the compulsory jurisdiction of the Permanent Court by making declarations under Article 36 of the Statute.[29] By Article 2 of the General Pact for the Renunciation of War of 1928 (Kellogg-Briand Pact), the signatories agreed that "the settlement or solution of all disputes or conflicts of whatever nature or of whatever origin they may be . . . shall never be sought except by pacific means."

The powers of the United Nations organs for the pacific settlement of disputes are substantially the same as those of the principal organs of the League. Under the Charter, as under the Covenant, the functions of political organs in this connection are limited to discussion, inquiry, mediation and conciliation. It is clear from the words of the Charter and from the discussions at San Francisco, that the Security Council has no power of final decision in connection with its functions of pacific settlement.[30] The Charter does, however, seek to differentiate between the functions and powers of the General Assembly and the Security Council in a way that the Covenant did not do. More specifically it makes the Security Council primarily responsible for the maintenance of peace and security, does not permit a party to a dispute to have the matter transferred at its request to the General Assembly, and limits the power of the General Assembly in principle to that of discussion. This constitutes an important departure from the textual provisions of the League Covenant which gave the Council and Assembly the same general competence and expressly allowed a party, acting under Article 15, paragraph 9, to have a dispute transferred at its request to the Assembly. It is significant, however, that out of some 66 disputes that came before the League, only three were actually brought before the Assembly under this provision. It would thus appear, and this is the conclusion of a careful student of the Assem-

[29] See Manley O. Hudson, "The Twenty-Fourth Year of the World Court," *op. cit.*, p. 33.

[30] See UNCIO, Report of the Rapporteur of Committee III/2, Document 1027 III/2/31(1), p. 4.

bly,[31] that actual practice under the Covenant resulted in a differentiation of function. This the Charter seeks to make obligatory.

In certain other respects the Charter system departs from the League pattern, but the importance of these differences can be greatly exaggerated. The elimination of the requirement of unanimity in voting theoretically increases the power of the Security Council, as compared with the League Council, in dealing with disputes and situations, but considering that the Security Council can only recommend, and that in League practice, agreement of the great powers was likely to result in the necessary agreement among all members of the Council, the practical importance of this difference is not likely to be great. Furthermore, under the Charter provision is made for the consideration by the Security Council and General Assembly of situations as well as disputes, but this does not mean any increase in the powers of the United Nations organs, particularly the Security Council, as compared with those of the corresponding organs of the League. In fact, it can be argued that the provisions of the Charter suffer somewhat in flexibility and capacity for growth, as compared with the corresponding provisions of the Covenant, because of the greater detail and consequent rigidity of certain of its terms. A comparison of experience under the Charter to date in the peaceful settlement or adjustment of disputes and situations with that of the League gives little basis for a confident conclusion that the Charter system is inherently better than, or for that matter, significantly different from, that which operated under the terms of the Covenant.[32]

Enforcement Action

It is in respect to enforcement action that the provisions of the Charter seem to offer the most marked contrast to the provisions of the Covenant,[33] but here again when we compare the Charter provisions with the way in which the Covenant provisions were actually applied the differences do not appear so great. The League system, as originally conceived, was based on the principle that once a member had resorted to war in violation of its obligations under the Covenant, other members were immediately obligated to apply economic and financial sanctions of wide scope against the offending state. The Council was empowered to recommend

[31] See Margaret E. Burton, *The Assembly of the League of Nations*, p. 284 et seq.

[32] On the operation of the League system, see William E. Rappard, *The Quest for Peace*, Cambridge, 1940, p. 134–207; Burton, *op. cit.*, p. 284–374; and T. P. Conwell-Evans, *The League Council in Action*, London, 1929. On the work of the Security Council to date, see Clyde Eagleton, "The Jurisdiction of the Security Council over Disputes," in *American Journal of International Law*, XI (July, 1946), p. 513–33; and United Nations, *Report of the Security Council to the General Assembly*, A/93, October 3, 1946.

[33] For analysis of the United Nations system for the enforcement of peace and security, see Grayson Kirk, "The Enforcement of Security," in *Yale Law Journal*, LV (August 1946), p. 1081–1196.

military measures which members of the League were technically not required to carry out. As a matter of fact, in the one case where the provisions of Article 16 were given anything like a real test, the application of sanctions against Italy in 1936, acting under the influence of the resolutions adopted by the Assembly in 1921,[34] the members of the League established a mechanism for the coordination of their individual acts, and proceeded to apply selected economic and financial measures. No recommendation was made by the Council for the application of military measures.[35]

The Charter makes the Security Council responsible for deciding what enforcement measures are to be used to maintain the peace. Obligations arise for Members of the United Nations only when such decisions have been taken. This is a further development of the principle recognized in the 1921 Assembly resolutions and in the application of sanctions against Italy, that a central coordinating agency is needed to insure the taking of necessary measures with the maximum of effectiveness and the minimum of inconvenience and danger to the participating members. However, the provisions of the Charter go much further than did the Covenant in providing for obligatory military measures and advance commitments to place specific forces at the disposal of the Security Council. Even though certain members of the League, notably France, were insistent upon the need of specific military commitments, little was done in League practice to meet this need. The Geneva Protocol of 1924 was one notable attempt to meet this demand, by methods which in certain respects anticipated the Charter, but it never came into force. The framers of the Charter, no doubt recognizing this as a defect in the League system, sought to remedy the deficiency by providing in some detail for military agreements between members of the United Nations and the Security Council, and for a military staff committee to assist the Security Council in drawing up advanced plans and in applying military measures.

It can, however, be queried whether the Charter system will be more effective than the League system, in view of the requirement of unanimity of the permanent members of the Security Council. If we imagine its application in situations such as the Italian-Ethiopian and Sino-Japanese affairs, it is difficult to see how the United Nations would achieve any better results than did the League. Like the League, but for somewhat different technical reasons, the United Nations, in so far as its enforcement activities are concerned, is an organization for the enforcement of peace among the smaller states. If the permanent members of the Security Council are in agreement, it will be possible to take effective action under

[34] League of Nations, *Records of the Second Assembly*, Plenary Meetings, p. 803.

[35] For summary of this experience, see *International Sanctions* (A Report by a Group of Members of the Royal Institute of International Affairs), London, 1938, p. 204–213.

the Charter. It is not likely that such agreement will be reached to take measures against one of these great powers or against a protégé of such a great power. Consequently the sphere of effective enforcement action by the United Nations is restricted in advance, even more perhaps than was that of the League. Within the area of possible operation, the actual effectiveness of the United Nations system will depend upon political conditions which, if they had existed, would have also assured the success of the League of Nations.[36]

Administration of Non-Self-Governing Territories

Here we encounter new names and phraseology in the United Nations Charter, but the substance is very much the substance of the League mandates system. There are, of course, important differences. For one thing, Chapter XI, "Declaration Regarding Non-Self-Governing Territories," is definitely an addition. The idea, however, is not new, as it has been accepted by various colonial administrations in recent years, and has found expression both in official statements and in authoritative writings on the subject.[37] However, it is new to have embodied in an international instrument a definite statement of principles binding upon all states engaged in the administration of non-self-governing territories and to place upon such states the additional obligation to make reports to an international authority.

So far as the trusteeship system, strictly speaking, is concerned, it follows in general the lines of the mandates system.[38] The three categories of A, B, and C mandates do not appear, but due to the freedom allowed in the drafting of trusteeship agreements, there can be the same, if not greater, variety of provisions. Like the League mandates system, the institution of the trusteeship system is not made obligatory for any particular territories; it is simply declared applicable to certain territories to the extent that they are placed under it by agreement. Following the practice under the mandates system, the trusteeship agreements, according to the Charter, are to be made by the states "directly concerned." They must in addition have the approval of the General Assembly or the Security Council, depending upon whether or not they apply to strategic areas, but neither organ has any authority to draft and put into effect a trusteeship agreement for any territory without the specific approval at least of the state in actual possession of it.

The machinery for supervision and the lines of responsibility have been changed in that for trusteeship areas other than strategic areas the ad-

[36] See Kirk, *op. cit.*, p. 1082.

[37] See, for example, Baron Lugard, *The Dual Mandate in British Tropical Africa*, 2nd ed., London, 1923.

[38] For detailed analysis of the United Nations trusteeship system, see Ralph J. Bunche, "Trusteeship and Non-Self-Governing Territories in the Charter of the United Nations," in *Organizing the United Nations*, Department of State Publication 2573.

ministrative authorities are responsible to the General Assembly and its agent, the Trusteeship Council. As has been pointed out above, however, this change as compared with the League mandates system, was to some extent anticipated in League practice by the right which the Assembly asserted and exercised to discuss and make recommendations with respect to the administration of mandated territories. There is, however, in the Charter one important power vested in the United Nations organs, though in somewhat qualified form, which the Council and Mandates Commission of the League did not have and the lack of which was regarded as a serious weakness of the League system. I refer to the provision for periodical visits to the trusteeship territories which should make it possible for the Organization to get information on the spot and thereby check upon and supplement the reports of the administrative authorities.

International Economic and Social Cooperation

Perhaps the most important advance of the Charter over the Covenant of the League is to be found in its provisions defining the objectives, policies, machinery and procedure of international economic and social cooperation. In this respect, the Charter offers a wide contrast to the Covenant, which had only three articles dealing specifically with the subject. In fact, the Preamble of the Covenant, containing the statement of purposes of the League, made no specific mention of cooperation in economic and social matters, though the very general phrase "in order to promote international order and cooperation" was relied upon to justify numerous activities for which no express authority was to be found.

It is, nevertheless, true that the League in practice was a quite different matter.[39] It has been generally observed that the most permanently worthwhile activities of the League of Nations were in the field of international economic and social cooperation. There was in the course of the League's existence a tremendous proliferation of organization and an impressive record of substantial achievement in making available necessary information, in promoting administrative and legislative action by member states, and in dealing directly with international economic and social evils by administrative action. We have seen how in 1939 the recognition of the scope and importance of this work led to the proposal that a Central Committee for Economic and Social Questions should be set up to coordinate League activities in this field.

Apart from the provision for a separate economic and social council there is one important organizational difference between the League and United Nations systems, a difference which may prove to be of great

[39] See, for example, Denys P. Myers, *Handbook of the League of Nations*, Boston, 1935, for evidence of the relative importance on a quantitative basis, at least, of the League's economic and social activities during the first fifteen years of the League's existence.

importance, depending upon how the provisions of the Charter are applied in practice. Whereas the League technical organizations dealing with health, economic and financial cooperation were developed within the framework of the League and operated under the general direction and control of the principal League organs, the approach of the United Nations has been a different one. This time we have proceeded on the assumption that special needs as they arise should be met by the creation of appropriate autonomous organizations and that subsequently, these organizations should be brought into relationship with each other and with the United Nations by agreements negotiated by the organs empowered to act in such matters. The result is that instead of having a number of technical organizations functioning within the general international organization and subject to the general direction and supervision of its principal organs, as under the League system, we now have a number of specialized inter-governmental agencies, each operating within a defined area and more or less independently of the others.

Such a system clearly has possibilities as to the range and type of action that may be taken which were denied to the League system operating more completely under the influence of political considerations. On the other hand, there are obviously certain advantages in having some effective coordination of the operation of these various agencies as there will be many points at which their interests and activities will overlap.[40] Under the Charter the proposal is to take care of these common concerns by the special agreements referred to above. It is too early to be certain as to what the practical consequences of this approach will prove to be.

V.

To the student of international organization, it should be a cause neither of surprise nor of concern to find that the United Nations is for all practical purposes a continuation of the League of Nations. Rather it would be disturbing if the architects of world organization had completely or largely thrown aside the designs and materials of the past. One cannot build soundly on the basis of pure theory. Man being what he is, and the dominant forces and attitudes of international relations being what they are, it is idle to expect, and foolhardy to construct the perfect system of world government in our day. Profiting from the lessons of past experience, we can at most hope to make some progress toward the attainment of a goal which may for a long time remain beyond our reach. The United Nations is not world government and it was not intended to be such. Rather it represents a much more conservative and cautious approach

[40] See Herman Finer, *The United Nations Economic and Social Council*, Boston, 1945, 121 p.; also *Report of the Preparatory Commission of the United Nations*, PC/20, December 23, 1945, p. 40–48.

to the problem of world order. As such, it inevitably falls into the stream of institutional development represented by the League of Nations and its predecessors. Different names may be used for similar things, and different combinations of words may be devised to express similar ideas. There may be changes of emphasis, and in fact important substantive changes, deemed desirable in the light of past experience or thought necessary in order to meet changed conditions. But there is no real break in the stream of organizational development.

The student of international organization must recognize the United Nations for what it quite properly is, a revised League, no doubt improved in some respects, possibly weaker in others, but nonetheless a League, a voluntary association of nations, carrying on largely in the League tradition and by the League methods. Important changes have occurred in the world distribution of power, in the world's economic and political structure, in the world's ideological atmosphere. These changes create new problems and modify the chances of success or failure in meeting them, but the mechanics remain much the same. Anyone desiring to understand the machinery, how it operates, the conditions of its success, must look to the experience of the past, and particularly to the rich and varied experience of that first attempt at a general international organization, the League of Nations.

NOTES AND QUESTIONS

1. It would be helpful to get some sense of the extent to which international organizations have grown during the past one-hundred years. Can this long period be viewed as preparation for the further growth recommended by the Clark-Sohn plan? If one acquires an historical perspective, then the Clark-Sohn scheme may seem to be a culmination of an historical process of growth, rather than a radical discontinuity. It is, of course, difficult to say what kind of "preparation" is relevant or crucial. Once a change, however drastic, has taken place, we can find an abundance of antecedents to account for it; however, before it happens, it often appears inconceivable. Domestic revolutions often possess this dual character. Perhaps the Clark-Sohn model only appears radical because we are looking forward to it. We need to know much more about the relations between the temporal perspective of the observer and the transformation phenomena, if we are to grasp whatever reality may exist in the widely-held position that social and political change must take place gradually rather than suddenly. What makes us view a change in social and political circumstance as sudden? Could we have looked ahead to the dissolution of the colonial system in 1935? What brought it about? Do we now look back on it as a radical change? If we do, then radical change has happened; if we do not, then the idea of "radical" is conditioned by whether we are looking backward or forward.
2. Summarize the main structural changes introduced by the United Nations. Are these changes more apparent than real? Do they, as Goodrich suggests, merely formalize what had taken place under League practice? Can you think of ways that United Nations practice has gone beyond League practice?

3. The most definitive study of the League is Francis Walters' *A History of the League of Nations* (Oxford University Press, London, 1952). The great tests of the peace-keeping capacity of the League were the Japanese conquest of Manchuria in 1931 and the Italian aggression against Ethiopia in 1935. The failure to curtail the Spanish Civil War was a final indication of the inability of the League to curb the tendencies inclining international society in the direction of world war. See Sadako Ogata, *Defiance in Manchuria* (University of California Press, 1964); Westel W. Willoughby, *The Sino-Japanese Controversy and the League of Nations* (Johns Hopkins University Press, 1935); George Martelli, *Italy against the World* (Chatto & Windus, London, 1937). For a critical analysis of the League experiment, see Roland N. Stromberg, *Collective Security and American Foreign Policy* (Praeger, New York, 1962). See, also, Inis P. Claude, *Swords into Plowshares* (3rd rev. ed., Random House, New York, 1964) Ch. I and II; D. W. Bowett, *Law of International Institutions* (Praeger, New York, 1963); and Hoffmann in Chapter 11.

The Relevance of Law to the Operations of the United Nations

2

Volume II examined the relevance of international law to the conduct of world politics, including its relevance to the control of international violence. In the present chapter we shall concentrate upon the role of the United Nations as a source of law and upon the degree to which the operations of the Organization are law-conditioned, in the sense of relying upon the procedures and rhetoric of law. It is generally assumed that the political organs of the United Nations are responsive to whatever the majority happens to favor. This has led some commentators to characterize the activities of these organs as "political" in the sense of being the opposite of "legal." Such a way of thinking holds that there are two boxes, one for law and the other for politics, and that it is up to the analyst to show that a particular issue or institution belongs in one rather than the other. In contrast, this chapter argues that, at least with respect to the organs of the United Nations, legal and political factors are intertwined, and that various organs with relation to various issues exhibit both kinds of institutional behavior to varying degrees.

It has become increasingly evident that the consensus of the organized international community has a law-creating impact when expressed through formal acts. In Chapter 5, consideration will be given to the legal effect of resolutions of the General Assembly. Here, too, that subject will be touched upon in the opening three selections which are devoted to the legislative capacity of the political organs of the United Nations. In passing, it should be noted that Clark and Sohn confer upon the General Assembly a limited legislative competence for the discharge of its functions connected directly with war prevention, but rule out any exercise of legislative competence in connection with all other subject matter. One of our chief concerns will be the extent to which it is possible to make this distinction in practice. Might not the objectives of war prevention require the potential regulation of subject matter as seemingly remote from recourse to violence as immigration and trade policy? For is not the risk of war created whenever actors in a social system feel strongly enough about an issue to contemplate the use of violence for its rectification? See Nieburg in **I-2**.

The first selection—Rosalyn Higgins', "Law, Politics and the United Nations," *The Development of International Law through the Political Organs of the United Nations* (Oxford University Press, London, 1963) pp. 1–10—sets forth with great clarity a method used to connect the activities of the organs of the United Nations with the traditional sources of international law in international society. Mrs. Higgins' discussion of the sources of international law as they are set forth in Article 38 of the Statute of the ICJ deserves particular attention because it is a major theme of the first three readings in this chapter.

ROSALYN HIGGINS

LAW, POLITICS, AND THE UNITED NATIONS

To choose highly political organs as the frame of reference for a study on the development of law seems curious and perhaps eccentric; in any event, it is a decision which calls for further explanation. While at one time it may have been correct to describe international law as the collection of legal norms applicable to inter-state relations, now, with the growing tendency to acknowledge that the sovereign state is not the only recipient of rights and duties under international law, it is more correct to observe that international law is the body of legal norms which apply to relations across state boundaries. Basically, this legal system derives from two sources—contractual law and general international law. Contractual law comprises bilateral treaties, giving rise to a special régime, and multilateral treaties, giving rise to a general régime. The United Nations Charter is, of course, a multilateral treaty of this latter type. General international law refers to customary rules which are evidenced by the practice of states; it also includes general principles which are widely accepted. All these sources of public international law are expressly recognized in the Statute of the International Court of Justice, and an additional source—judicial decisions and the writings of distinguished jurists—is also mentioned.[1]

Of all these sources, international custom is the most flexible, the most fluid, and as such, is exceedingly responsive to the changing needs of the international community. Treaty-making and judicial decisions are far more self-conscious methods of legal regulation and pronouncement. International custom is modified and developed by the practice of states. It does not stem from weighty pronouncements of an international tribunal or long-negotiated agreements recorded in a formal treaty. Customary international law is therefore perhaps the most 'political' form of international law, reflecting the consensus of the great majority of states. The emergence of a customary rule of law occurs where there has grown up a clear and continuous habit of performing certain actions in the conviction

1. Art. 38(1) of the Statute of the ICJ states that in deciding disputes it will apply:
(*a*) international conventions, whether general or particular, establishing rules expressly recognized by the contesting states;
(*b*) international custom, as evidence of a general practice accepted as law;
(*c*) the general principles of law as recognized by civilized nations;
(*d*) judicial decisions and the teachings of the most highly qualified publicists of the various nations, as subsidiary means for the determination of rules of law.

that they are obligatory under international law. It matters not that the action performed accords with the convenience of the state—it would be a curious form of puritanism which insisted that convenience and legality could never run side by side; what is relevant is the belief in the nature of the obligation as binding. It is essential at this point to distinguish international custom from international usage, for while the latter may reflect the growth of a habit, the habit is not performed from conviction of legal obligation.

The legal organs of the United Nations—that is to say, the International Court of Justice and the International Law Commission, are concerned only to a limited degree with the application and development of customary international law. The Court uses it as one source of law among several to guide it in its judicial decisions, and the prime task of the Commission is to codify and develop law through the preparation of draft treaties and codes. The political organs of the United Nations, however, are vitally concerned with the development of customary international law. Although they are political bodies, they are none the less bound by legal rules—rules which are both specific, reflecting formal consent to the terms of the Charter, and general, being the rules of general international law. The application of these rules of general international law may well lead to the growth of new practices and to developments in the customary rules.

The United Nations is a very appropriate body to look to for indications of developments in international law, for international custom is to be deduced from the practice of states, which includes their international dealings as manifested by their diplomatic actions and public pronouncements. With the development of international organizations, the votes and views of states have come to have legal significance as evidence of customary law. Moreover, the practice of states comprises their collective acts as well as the total of their individual acts; and the number of occasions on which states see fit to act collectively has been greatly increased by the activities of international organizations.[2] Collective acts of states, repeated by and acquiesced in by sufficient numbers with sufficient frequency, eventually attain the status of law. The existence of the United Nations—and especially its accelerated trend towards universality of membership since 1955—now provides a very clear, very concentrated, focal point for state practice. Here, then, is the reason for looking to United Nations practice in a search for the direction of the development of international law.

Within the United Nations, the practice of the political organs—that is to say the General Assembly, the Security Council, the Secretariat, the Trusteeship Council, and the Economic and Social Council—is perhaps the most significant so far as the development of law is concerned. It is true that the International Law Commission was established by the Assembly to

2. On this point, see Jenks, 'Development of Law by the UN', 37 *TGS* (1952), 23.

'encourage the progressive development of International Law and its codification',[3] but its work, while useful, has been limited. The distinction between its tasks of developing and codifying has been difficult to sustain, and until recently the Commission has been occupied with the unrewarding and hazardous method of codifying and developing law by international treaty. The topics agreed upon or codified in international conventions are limited and, almost by definition, are matters upon which general consensus has already been readily available. The capacity of the International Court to develop the law has been hampered by the absence of any *a priori* system of compulsory jurisdiction, which has restricted the occasions and questions on which it has been called to pronounce. Yet international law, if it is to be fully effective, *must* concern itself with the controversial and the political. The lack of compulsory jurisdiction does not, it is true, affect the ability of the Court to develop the law through advisory opinions; however, the General Assembly and the Security Council, which may themselves ask for an Advisory Opinion from the International Court,[4] have shown little inclination to do so.[5] A similar by-passing of the Sixth (Legal) Committee of the Assembly may be observed. The work of that Committee has become more and more restricted and political problems with important legal implications are debated in the First or Ad Hoc Committees. As early as the sixth session the United Kingdom delegation raised the problem of the handling of legal questions, and a special committee was set up to study the matter. Its recommendation that the Legal Committee should be consulted in certain defined cases was so watered down in the Assembly that consultation of that Committee became optional in most cases.[6]

These observations are not to denigrate the law-developing activities of the legal organs of the United Nations; rather are they to suggest that for a study of the most dynamic and significant method it seems well to look to the role being played by the political organs of that body. The following parts of this study will therefore examine the development of international law by the practice of the General Assembly, Security Council, and Secretariat, and, to a lesser degree, of the Trusteeship Council and Economic and Social Council.

How, in practice, do political bodies such as these contribute to the development of international law? These organs are called upon, in the

3. Art. 13(1) of the Charter. The ILC was set up under GA res. 174(II).
4. Under Art. 96(1).
5. The Assembly has requested an Advisory Opinion on very few occasions (see UN *Repertory* (1955), v. 38 & Suppl. (1958), ii. 317; also the recent request under GA res. 1731 (XVI). The SC has requested no opinions and it recommended recourse to the Court in only one case (Corfu). For observations on the reluctance to use the International Court see Fitzmaurice, 'The UN & the Rule of Law', 38 *TGS* (1953), 135; Stone 'The Int. Court & World Crisis', *Int. Conc.* (1962); and Liang, 'Int. Law Questions', *Ann. R. UN Aff., 1949*, p. 272.
6. See Cheng, *YBWA 1954*, p. 171.

course of their ordinary work, to interpret their own constitution. This constitution not only is an international treaty, but also contains many accepted concepts of international law. Interpretative decisions inevitably must reflect upon the meaning of international law. Moreover, even the decisions taken on the internal workings of the United Nations, on its constitutional powers under the Charter, ultimately reflect on general international law, and not only on the Charter itself; for such practice 'may come in time to evidence a special new branch of the customary law on the interpretation of treaties'.[7] The political organs of the United Nations not only interpret their own constitutional powers[8] and the specific provisions of the Charter, but are often called upon to consider situations which concern general international law, such as reparation for damages and injury (involving concepts of international responsibility) or questions of diplomatic immunity. New institutional arrangements generate law and legal procedures, often purely out of administrative necessity: much that has happened in the Congo may be described in this way. Usage and precedent in political organs develop into legal rules—that is to say into norms which are accepted as legally binding by the vast majority of the states and organs of the United Nations.[9] Furthermore, such organs have from time to time promulgated declarations of purportedly existing rules of law: such pronouncements are not only evidence of a customary law—they may also affect the direction of development of that law.

It is necessary at this point to ask ourselves if political organs do in fact have the authority to prescribe rules of law, or may they only recommend solutions? That they have authority for internal prescription is not in doubt; and we have already mentioned that this may well give rise to a more far-reaching legal effect than is at first appreciated. Similarly, it may be observed that political organs sometimes make declarations of consciously legal content—the Declaration on the Nuremberg principles and the resolutions on sovereignty over natural resources may both be cited as examples.[10]

7. Hammarskjöld, 'Int. Law & the UN', *Philippine Law J.* (1955), 542.

8. For confirmation that each organ is competent to interpret the Charter within the scope of its activities, see rep. of Rapporteur of Cttee IV/2 of San Francisco Conf., UNCIO *Docs*, xiii. 646. Fitzmaurice has made the interesting point that this rule is in fact a protection of sovereignty as it protects states from the attempts of others to determine such matters unilaterally (92 *HR* (1957), ii. at 5).

9. Thus, looked at from the point of view of treaty law, the Charter may in part be interpreted by the 'subsequent practice' of the parties. The ICJ has indicated its approval (*International Status of South-West Africa, ICJ Rep. 1950*, p. 128; *Competence of the GA regarding admission to the UN*, ibid. pp. 4, 9). Cf. Judge Sir Percy Spender, *ICJ Rep. 1962*, pp. 182 ff.

10. GA res. 95(I) & A/AC.97/13; also the study on the Status of Permanent Sovereignty over Natural Wealth and Resources prepared by the Secretariat: A/AC.97/Rev. 1, i & ii. See also the statement by the Netherlands Govt: 'A certain amount of law creating power cannot be denied to the General Assembly, because in those cases which might give rise to doubt whether a rule belongs already to international law or is still *jus constituendum*, a formal declaration of the General Assembly might well make the rule concerned one of recognized positive international law' (A/1338 Add. 1, p. 2).

However, the Assembly certainly has no right to legislate in the commonly understood sense of the term. Resolutions of the Assembly are not *per se* binding:[11] though those rules of general international law which they may embody are binding on member states, with or without the help of the resolution. But the body of resolutions as a whole, taken as indications of a general customary law, undoubtedly provide a rich source of evidence. Those resolutions of the Assembly which deliberately—rather than incidentally—provide declarations on international law are invariably based on other quasi-judicial forms of support.[12] Thus the Nuremberg principles were adopted on the recommendation of the International Law Commission, and pronouncements on the status of prisoners of war have been based on the work of commissions set up specifically to study these aspects of the problem.

In the case of the Security Council—and to a lesser extent, the Assembly —the reference to specific legal authority is muted, in the sense that decisions are often demanded with some urgency. The prescription of law, rather than its application, thus becomes involved. This is especially true of decisions made concerning peace and security, where the feeling may well be that, quite apart from traditional law on the subject concerned, it is essential to pacify the situation. Although, in such a situation, the Security Council is likely to state that it is basing itself on the law as it conceives it to be, the line between applying law and legislating it becomes thin: certainly a question of developing law becomes involved.[13]

It is worth adding that all these examples of the development of international law by the United Nations occur quite apart from the question of whether the Charter may now be considered a part of general international law.[14]

While there seems to be every reason for examining the law-developing role of political organs, it must be admitted that this entails a quantitative problem of some magnitude. That is to say it is often far from easy to see, when analysing the practice of states, the point at which a repeated practice

11. Sloan, 'The Binding Force of a "Recommendation" of the General Assembly of the UN', 25 *BYIL* (1948), 1 & Rosenne, 'Recognition of States by the UN', ibid. 26 (1949), 437.

12. The author is indebted to Dr Schachter for drawing her attention to this point.

13. Dr Schachter has commented that this method of 'law development' does not normally occur in economic fields, as the requisite degree of urgent necessity is not present. In these areas the law-making process takes a different form—e.g. a treaty—or the topic may for some reason warrant a *sui generis* approach, as in the case of disarmament (Lecture at Yale Law School, 16 May 1961).

14. For an interesting analysis of the relationship of the Charter to international law, see Robinson, 'Metamorphosis of the UN', 94 *HR* (1958), ii. 565 & Kelsen, 'General Int. Law and the Law of the UN', in *The UN; Ten Years' Legal Progress* (1956). On the inroads made into formerly sovereign areas by international law, Scheuner, 'Sovereignty and the UN', ibid. Also Van Kleffens, 'Sovereignty in Int. Law', 82 *HR* (1953), i. 83; St Korowicz, 'Modern Doctrines of Sovereignty', 5 *Ned. Tijd. Int. Recht* (1958); & Weinschel, 'The Doctrine of Equality of States and its Recent Modifications', 45 *AJIL* (1951), 417.

has hardened into a rule of law. How many resolutions incorporating the same legal doctrine must be passed before that doctrine is deemed an international custom? How many states must vote in favour of those resolutions? —a simple majority?—a two-thirds majority? Must all the major Powers be in favour of the implied legal prescription? The problem revealed by these questions is in reality the familiar one of where to draw the line between usage and customary international law; and it admits of no easy answer.

The question is perhaps even more complex when it concerns the political organs of the United Nations, for the manifestations of state practice are very diverse, incorporating voting and debating and diplomatic correspondence. Moreover, the fact that voting patterns to some extent conform to political pressures rather than to legal beliefs must be recognized.[15] It is also true that developments in international law have been accelerated by the emergence of new Afro-Asian states, whose common expectations do not always conform to traditional law;[16] and by the new needs of states, which cause rules once thought firmly established—such as freedom of the high seas and the limits of territorial waters—to be put in doubt.[17] It may well be that such factors render the 'waiting-period' during which a new custom must be proved considerably shorter than in the past.[18] The only possible answer to the problem of at what stage a usage becomes law must be *at that point at which states regard themselves as legally bound by the practice*—a point which can only be ascertained by the close examination of states' attitudes and public statements. No precise percentage of the members of the Society of Nations can be said to constitute the prescribed 'quorum' to consider a new development binding: it can only be said that there must be a considerable majority of nations. Nor does there seem any good reason why the Permanent Members have to number among these nations—though exclusion of *all* the Big Powers may in present circumstances render the new custom ineffective. Members of the United Nations have shown themselves to be not unaware of the difficulties inherent in this type of law-making.

As regards custom, that is, the repetition of legal facts sanctioned by the practice of States, it is difficult to determine at what stage this repetition acquires the force of law. . . . International custom results . . . from the need for a social rule and,

15. Riggs, *Politics in the UN* (1958) & Hovet, *Bloc Politics in the UN* (1960) are very instructive on this point.

16. For analysis of Asian attitudes to international law, Syatauw, *Some Newly Established Asian States and the Dev. of Int. Law* (1961).

17. See Eagleton, 'Legal Matters', *Ann. R. UN Aff., 1955–6*, p. 140 & Robinson in 94 *HR* (1958), ii. 565.

18. Lauterpacht has suggested that 'any tendency to exact a prolonged period for the crystallization of custom must be proportionate to the degree and intensity of the change that it purports, or is asserted, to effect'.

therefore, mere negation of a generally established custom does not exempt a State from its responsibility with regard to such a rule.[19]

There may well exist a period during which a resolution or resolutions of the Assembly may command considerable moral force without yet constituting new law. Obviously the larger the majority in favour of the resolution, the more impressive is its moral force.[20] It is possible to state the case even more strongly:

> Whatever may be the content of the recommendation, and whatever may be the nature and circumstances of the majority by which it has been reached, it is nevertheless, a legal act by the principal organ of the United Nations which members of the United Nations are under a duty to treat with a degree of respect appropriate to a resolution of the General Assembly.[21]

This respect, Lauterpacht adds, includes the consideration of the resolution in good faith and the offering of detailed reasons for any decision to reject it.[22] The pages which follow attempt to take all these considerations into account in assessing the trend of development of customary law.

The choice of the political organs of the United Nations for a study on international law is thus explained by a belief that they are concerned in a multitude of ways with general international law, and are likely to provide evidence of state practice, an accepted source of law. To justify the choice, however, it is necessary to answer the objection that in reality political bodies are not in the least concerned with international law, that they will merely pay lip-service to it when it suits them, while in fact doing exactly as they please with political expediency as their sole guide.

This all too common attitude—frequently assumed by its holders to be a mark of worldly cynicism and political sophistication—reflects a fundamental misconception about the relationship between law and politics, and about the nature of international law. It assumes both that the application of legal rules is only meaningful within a judicial framework and that international law can only be effective if subject to a system of sanctions. The first assumption is well answered in the observation that:

> Perhaps the purest analytical conception of 'law' is that in which an impartial judge objectively applies a pre-established rule to decide a controversy. And perhaps the purest analytical concept of 'politics' is that in which the stronger influence or

19. Per the Canadian representative (A/1338, p. 4).

20. And indeed, where unanimous resolutions are concerned—such as the Assembly Declaration on the Granting of Independence to Colonial Countries (GA res. 1514 (XV)) a question of estoppel and *mala fides* may well arise.

21. Lauterpacht, *South-West Africa Voting Procedure* case, *ICJ Rep. 1955*, p. 120.

22. It is perhaps too commonly assumed that no resolutions of the Assembly are binding: a certain legal obligation, albeit amorphous and ill defined, attaches to all of them, and resolutions dealing with certain internal appointments and budgetary matters are binding in the full legal sense.

interest regulates the social distribution of values. In the real world, however, judges cannot avoid exercising at least some political discretion in the decision of cases. And in any stable political system, the political process is also subject to normative constraints.[23]

The second assumption fails to appreciate that the particular 'sanction system' built into international law is simply the sanction of reciprocity. It is not, by and large, sanctions in the sense of physical compulsion or physical punishment. There is some attempt in the Charter to regulate major illegal coercion by enforcement measures; yet none of the other norms of international law upon which the Charter rests, and within which the United Nations must operate, is subject to a centralized sanctioning process. Yet international law as it applies to a multitude of questions—recognition, state responsibility, diplomatic immunities, law of the sea, and so forth—is widely heeded because its breach would incur a reciprocal response. It is often *in the interests* of the state concerned that reference be made to a legal process. Nor should it be thought that rules of international law which deal with matters other than the regulation of force are unimportant. They are the very foundation of stability and order in international intercourse. Indeed, 'we must put over the idea that Mr Jessup has written about, that international law is involved in a diplomatic dialectical usage in the everyday conduct of international affairs'.[24]

It is equally in the interest of an international organization such as the United Nations not to ignore the legal process. Its conciliatory functions will be considerably hampered if it does. Oscar Schachter has clearly shown the advantages in diplomacy in having a legal authority—a *locus standi*—available to a third-party mediator in a dispute.[25] If the Secretary-General departs too radically in his actions from the expectations of international law he will lose the confidence of the member states.

All this is not to deny that international law is sometimes ignored; what *is* denied, however, is that international law is more honoured in its breach than in its observance. As a descriptive statement of fact this is manifestly untrue. The popularity of this view stems only from an ignorance of the range and scope of international law and of the hard political factors working in favour of respect for it. All systems of law tend to break down in crisis situations; revolutionary justice following the collapse of the Vichy régime in France is but one example in constitutional law.[26] The crisis situations

23. Kaplan & Katzenbach, *Political Foundations of Int. Law* (1961), p. 1.
24. Oliver, 'Relation of Int. Law to Int. Relations', *Proc. ASIL* (1954), 108. Oliver's views on Kennan's attitude towards international law, as shown in *American Diplomacy, 1900–50* (1951), are pertinent in this context (Lipsky, *Law and Politics in the World Community* (1953), at p. 196).
25. Schachter, 'Dag Hammarskjöld on Law and Politics', 56 *AJIL* (1962), 6.
26. Kaplan & Katzenbach, p. 6.

with which international law is faced are perhaps more frequent and more dramatic; breaches of international law are perhaps more common and certainly are subject to more publicity. None the less, there is a hard core of adherence to international law which continues day in and day out.

The Parts which follow in this book assume, for all the reasons stated here, that there is an essential relationship between law and politics. They reject equally the view of certain political scientists who believe that law is a mere façade for unfettered political power[27] and the view of those international lawyers who deplore the introduction of political realities into legal decisions.[28] To set law up against politics, or politics against law, is an abortive exercise—better by far 'to find within the limits of power the elements of common interest on the basis of which joint action and agreed standards could be established'.[29] The ensuing study accepts this as the proper function of the international lawyer, identifying itself in this respect with the opinions of those who view law essentially as a branch of social engineering.[30] The proper and vital integration of law and politics was dynamically realized and adroitly practised in the office of the late Secretary-General, Dag Hammarskjöld. He viewed the body of law 'not merely as a technical set of rules and procedures, but as the authoritative expression of principles that determine the goals and direction of collective action'.[31]

The belief that law and politics are not necessarily inimical leads to certain consequences of importance so far as this particular study is concerned. In the first place, it means that it has not been considered beyond the ambit of the lawyer to comment on the political and diplomatic pressures causing certain legal decisions to be taken; on the contrary, the necessity of interdisciplinary co-operation between lawyers and political scientists is predicated. Secondly, it is argued here that political considerations must be taken in account when interpreting ambiguous or imprecise legal rules. To insist that every international problem admits of an 'impartial' legal answer is essentially a dishonest position. All rules of international law are open to interpretation, and as many of the rules are fluid and unclearly stated, the interpretive element is very great. It is not possible always to choose between alternative interpretations purely on grounds of 'legal correctness'. It is necessary on some occasions to examine the political preferences involved in each alternative, and to decide accordingly. Unless such considerations are taken into account, the growth of international law

27. See e.g. Werner Levi, *Fundamentals of World Organization* (1950); Bloomfield, *Evolution or Revolution* (1957), at p. 125.

28. See e.g. Zslawski, 35 *TGS* (1949), 4.

29. Schachter, 56 *AJIL* (1962), 7.

30. See e.g. McDougal, *Studies in World Public Order* (1960) & *Law and Minimum World Public Order* (1961); Kaplan & Katzenbach; and the comments of Falk thereon, 10 *Am. J. Comp. Law* (1961), 296 & 'Reality of Int. Law', 14 *Wld Pol.* (1962), 355.

31. Schachter, at 2.

will be stunted and its content unsatisfactory.[32] In each Part of this study it has therefore seemed desirable to include a brief analysis of policy considerations which are relevant to the topic under discussion. Reference to these may provide a guideline in choosing between two possible interpretations, both of which have some legal merit.

Many of the traditional techniques for legal analysis are ill suited for revealing this dynamic interplay between law and politics. The often arbitrary sections into which legal topics are subdivided reveal no clear relationship to each other and fail to highlight new trends or show the reasons for them. For this reason international law questions are here examined within a framework that is sometimes unfamiliar to traditional analysis. This framework does not conform to classical textbook headings or to articles of the United Nations Charter; instead, the *actual claims* made before United Nations organs, and the *responses thereto* have been thought to reveal more closely law in the making.

The political organs of the United Nations have been vitally concerned in the course of their work with the application of certain groups of rules. As a result the law on statehood, domestic jurisdiction, recognition, the use of force, and treaties is developing and evolving. Seventeen years' work by the United Nations has provided us with an important new source of customary international law.

32. See Kerno, 46 *Proc. ASIL* (1952), at 13, 15. It may also be noted that the inherent difficulty of 'impartial interpretation' is not peculiar to international law: there is no certain legal answer to any problem of complexity in national law either. Law in fact is never a geometry.

NOTES AND QUESTIONS

1. What is the relation between the doctrine of sovereignty and the formation of customary international law? To what extent do the formal acts of the political organs of the United Nations contribute to the formation of customary international law? Is the consent of states the basis of international obligations? Or can international obligations be deduced through the use of reason or by determining what is natural or by widely held ethical standards?
2. According to Mrs. Higgins, what is the basis of international customary law? Why does she call it the most "political" of all the forms of international law? What does "political" mean in this usage? What is the role of the concept of consensus?
3. How does Mrs. Higgins differentiate the legal organs from the political organs of the United Nations? Contrast their relative contributions to the development of international law.
4. What is the relationship between the authority of the political organs and their role as law-creating agents? Does Mrs. Higgins suggest that recommendations of the General Assembly can act as binding interpretations of legal obligations? Note the difference between these recommendations as *evidence* of and as a *source* of international law. When do the preferences of a majority of states have the capacity to

generate a binding international legal norm? Does the answer depend upon the *extent* of the majority, or upon the *intensity* of their feeling, or upon the *subject matter* at issue? Recall that the Clark-Sohn plan restricts legislative competence to matters of war prevention. Who decides what makes a subject of international concern a matter of war prevention?

The next selection was the first of a series of lectures delivered several years ago by A. J. P. Tammes at the Hague Academy of International Law, under the title "The Introduction of a New Legislative Technique." The series of lectures is called "Decisions of International Organs as a Source of International Law," *Recueil des Cours,* vol. 94, no. II (A. Sijthoff, Leyden, 1958) pp. 265–284. Tammes shares the same concern as Mrs. Higgins for the need to reconcile the law-creating activities of the organs of the United Nations with the traditional sources of international law as set forth in Article 38 of the Statute of the ICJ. What Tammes adds, in particular, is a sense of historical perspective, thereby showing the extent to which ordering activities in international society rested upon quasi-legislative techniques before the advent of the United Nations. One way to consider this subject is to identify the extent of legislative competence operative in the present international system and to consider the extent to which this competence must be augmented, if at all, in a totally disarmed world.

DECISIONS OF INTERNATIONAL ORGANS AS A SOURCE OF INTERNATIONAL LAW

A. J. P. TAMMES

THE INTRODUCTION OF A NEW LEGISLATIVE TECHNIQUE

The life of international organs is marked by certain nodal points called resolutions, that is to say formal decisions. Most activities of international organs are moulded according to a pattern consisting of the preparation and the implementation of resolutions. Many formal decisions themselves are milestones along the road towards and from major resolutions. It might be observed that the same could be said of other organs, such as those belonging to the State: the passing of laws, ordinances or motions or the making of decrees is likewise the formal manifestation of their activity. Yet although this in itself is true, it is only one of the many aspects of the intensive and all-embracing life of the organization known as the State. In public international organizations, on the other hand, because of their diplomatic origin, the making of a decision in a collegiate organ is often a major event, a laborious step on the road of international co-operation.

Little wonder, then, that the process of decision-making is a matter of such interest to everyone who takes an active part in, or who studies the functioning of an international organization. Studies are made, indeed, of the voting procedure, majority and unanimity rule, equality and inequality of representation and voting rights in the organs of various international organizations. In addition, as intergovernmental organizations have become

The author acknowledges his indebtedness to Dr. J. F. Engers, New York, and to Dr. M. N. G. Dukes, Rotterdam, for their valuable advice and information during the preparation of the final text of this study.

an increasingly widespread and important phenomenon of international relations, so more comparative studies have been undertaken, aiming at generalized observations and conclusions regarding the decision-making process in such organizations taken as a whole [1] This widening of the scope of research is only natural, international organizations being too closely connected not to influence each other's practice and to inspire a general theory. In the light of this development, however, it is remarkable that international decisions as such have only rarely become the subject of a comparative and generalizing study as to their function and their effect [2].

This lack is the more felt because decisions of international organs comprise a source of public international law [3]. All categories of sources of public international law, conventions, custom, general principles and so on, have been thoroughly studied as to their characteristics. To a similar study of international decisions it cannot be objected that those decisions are only of importance within the limited range of the organization from which they derive. For this is equally the case with regard to the limited participation in bilateral or multilateral treaties; yet such treaties are published in bulky collections, and are regularly studied and compared as a source of international law. Further, certain decisions make their influence felt far beyond the constitutional orbit of a particular organization.

1. For instance: C. A. Riches, *Majority Rule in International Organization*, 1940; Wellington Koo, Jr., *Voting Procedures in International Political Organizations*, 1947; A. J. P. Tammes, *Hoofdstukken van Internationale Organisatie* (Chapters of International Organization), 1951, Chapter I.

2. Apart from the remarks of a comparative nature made in the present author's *Hoofdstukken* reference can be made to the more recent study of M. Virally, *La valeur juridique des recommandations des organisations internationales*, Annuaire français de droit international, II (1956), pp. 66 ff.

3. Among authors recognizing decisions of international organs as a separate source of international law, reference can be made to: P. Fauchille, *Traité de droit international public*, Vol. I, first part, 1922, p. 48; J. P. A. François, *Handboek van het Volkenrecht*, Vol. I, 1949, p. 709; M. Sibert, *Traité de droit international public*, Vol. I, 1951, pp. 35 ff.; H. Kelsen, *Principles of International Law*, 1952, pp. 365 ff.; A. Verdross, *Völkerrecht*, 1955, p. 129; G. Piotrowski, *Les Résolutions de l'Assemblée générale des Nations Unies et la portée du droit conventionnel*; Revue de droit international (Sottile), (1955), pp. 111 ff., pp. 211 ff.; P. Reuter, *Organisations internationales et évolution du droit*, in *L'Évolution du droit public, Études en l'honneur d'Achille Mestre*, 1956, p. 452.

And, finally, there are between a number of organizations actual formal ties, whereby certain decisions of one organization become legally relevant to the decisions of another.

When we turn, then, to the study of decisions of international organs as a source of public international law, several points should be made clear from the outset. In the first place, there is no need to enter here into the well known controversy concerning the adequacy of the term "source of law", which, admittedly, can refer to the sociological cause or psychological motive behind the law as well as to the formal act intended to create law, or evidence of a consensus of opinion as to what the law may be. In the present study the term "source" is taken in the second sense, as referring to the way in which rules become part of a legal system, and more particularly, with regard to our subject, to the formal act intended to create law. We are further occupied with the fact *that* a number of decisions of international organs create law (as opposed to others not so intended), and only subsidiarily with the question as to *what* they have contributed to the mass of public international law. In this connection it also must be made clear from the start that the term "public international law" is meant to include all the internal law of public international organizations. Even if some would be inclined to consider the law of certain organizations as "pre-federal" it still seems permissible to consider it as international as well, so long as an "international" tribunal, like the International Court of Justice [1], if granted jurisdiction, would declare itself competent to apply this particular kind of law.

Article 38 of the Statute of the I.C.J. Silent on Decisions

Any study of decisions of international organs as a source of public international law carries with it the basic assumption that such decisions can be adequately distinguished from other categories of sources. If, however, we glance at the enumeration of the sources of international law in Article 38, paragraph 1, of the Statute of the International Court of Justice, it will be

1. "The Court, whose function is to decide in accordance with international law . . ." Article 38, paragraph 1, first sentence, of the Statute.

seen that decisions of international organs are not among the categories that are listed separately. Though the enumeration in Article 38 has been criticized, it may be safely stated that it represents the most authoritative enumeration of the sources of international law and that it has been especially referred to in numerous provisions prescribing the law to be applied by particular international tribunals [1]. As late as 1953, in its Draft Convention on Arbitral Procedure, the International Law Commission of the United Nations proposed that "in the absence of any agreement between the parties concerning the law to be applied, the tribunal shall be guided by Article 38, paragraph 1, of the Statute of the International Court of Justice" [2]. By adding that "the tribunal may not bring in a finding of *non liquet* on the ground of the silence or obscurity of international law or of the *compromis*", the Commission stresses the implication that Article 38, paragraph 1, enumerates all the sources of international law.

How significant is it, then, that decisions of international organs are not explicitly referred to in that paragraph, nor in the almost identical provision on the Statute of the Permanent Court of International Justice of 1920? In its practice the Court does not seem to have found any difficulty in applying and interpreting resolutions, of international organs. For giving its numerous advisory opinions the Court has always had to base its competence upon a request laid down in a resolution of the Assembly or the Council of the League of Nations [3], or, since 1945, of the General Assembly or the Security Council of the United Nations [4], or of another international organ, itself authorized, by resolution of the General Assembly, to request advisory opinions [5]. Often the Court has had to proceed to a careful examination of the text of the request; in one case it

1. *Systematic Survey of Treaties for the Pacific Settlement of International Disputes, 1928-1948*, United Nations, pp. 116 ff., referring to the corresponding provision of the Statute of the Permanent Court of International Justice.
2. Art. 12, Report of the I.L.C., Fifth Session, U.N. Doc, A/2456, p. 10.
3. Art. 65 of the Statute of the Permanent Court of International Justice.
4. Art. 96, par. 1, of the Statute of the International Court of Justice.
5. *Ibidem*, par. 2.

found the request related to an actual dispute which the Court had no jurisdiction to decide [1]. But, apart from such determination of the basis and scope of the terms of reference, the Court more than once had to apply and interpret legislative resolutions of international organs. Thus, in the Advisory Opinions of July 13th, 1954, and of October 23rd, 1956, the Court, in order to determine the nature and competence of the Administrative Tribunals of the United Nations and of the International Labour Organization, respectively, proceeded to an elaborate examination of their Statutes, the one laid down in a resolution of the General Assembly, the other originally adopted in a resolution of the League of Nations Assembly.

One is drawn to the conclusion that the Court, in applying resolutions of international organs, is basically applying the international conventions such as the Charter of the United Nations, from which the decision-making power of such organs is derived. The Court, therefore, has no need of an explicit reference, in Article 38, paragraph 1, to decisions of international organs as a source of international law distinct from conventions. As a very experienced member of the Court pointed out in the Committee of Jurists, entrusted, in 1945, with reviewing the old Statute: while Article 38 is not well drafted the Court had operated very well under it and time should not be spent in redrafting it [2].

But for the purpose of clear legal distinctions decisions can most conveniently be considered as a separate source of international law. This would be well illustrated in practice, if the Court had to apply and interpret, not a resolution of a principal organ established by the convention constituting an organization, but a resolution of a subsidiary organ itself established by resolution of a principal organ. In such a case the connection with the basic instrument would appear rather tenuous. Therefore, just as in national law it would be confusing to maintain that a court, dealing with an act of parliament, is applying the

1. *Eastern Carelian Question;* Adv. Op. of July 23rd, 1923, A/B No. 4.

2. Mr. Basdevant (France) in the meeting of April 13th, 1945; United Nations Conference on International Organization (UNCIO), Vol. XIV, p. 170.

Constitution, for the same reason in international law it would be unpractical not to recognize that applying a resolution is applying something different from a convention. The most obvious difference is that there are no parties to a decision.

International Legislation as Conceived in 1920

The distinction will appear as a matter of course now that the practice of international organizations has produced an immense mass of decisions. The General Assembly of the United Nations, for instance, which is only one of hundreds of international bodies, though a large and productive one, had a jubilee when, on November 5th, 1956, it adopted Resolution 1000 (ES-1) establishing a United Nations Command for an Emergency International Force in the Near East. But has the concept of international decisions always been a matter of course? Was it so understood at the time, say, of the drafting of the Statute of the World Court in 1920? It is of more than historical interest to survey here briefly the ideological and practical development of the concept up to that decisive moment in international co-operation, when the League of Nations was founded. Such a survey will also throw light on certain elements of our problem which will then be better recognized when we meet them again among the complicated facts of present-day international organization.

The eminent jurists who drafted the Statute were not interested, as far as the substantive law forming the basis of the future Court's judgments was concerned, in the phenomenon of decisions of international organs. That such deciding organs did exist, they must well have realized, the more so because the Advisory Committee was itself established by a resolution of the Council of the League of Nations. But what they were interested in was the question of to what extent, by permitting the legal conscience of civilized nations, principles of justice and even equity to be applied, the Court would be given, in view of *lacunae* existing in international law, an increasing latitude of appreciation as to what the law should be and, therefore, a degree of law-making power. Conventions, on the other hand, were the source of public international law *par excellence* and it fitted well into that train of thought that the Committee proposed an order of priority, headed by conventions [1]. The legal signifiance of decisions of international organs never was a subject of discussion in the Advisory Committee nor, when the draft-Statute was reviewed, in the subcommittee of the Third Committee of the First League of Nations Assembly.

But the Advisory Committee did touch indirectly on the matter, when dealing with the possibility that a wide appreciation left to the Court would in effect give it law-making powers. Among various shades of opinion there were two clearly opposite approaches. One was strongly favoured by Mr. Albert de Lapradelle, Professor in the University of Paris. He preferred a short wording, for instance "the Court shall judge in accordance with law, justice and equity", rather than any attempt to define law and indicate its sources.

> "This was interesting but useless. It was useless, for instance, to mention that the Court must take treaties into account. On the other hand it would be useful to specify that the Court must not act as a legislator. It was necessary to give parties an assurance that the Court would concern itself only with the application of law, to administer justice, and would not succomb to the temptation to deal with diplomacy . . . However it would be too strict and even unjust to force the Court to consider only law. There would be no danger in allowing the Court to consider whether any particular legal solution were just and equitable and if necessary to modify, if the situation arose, the legal solution according to the exigencies of justice and equity. Confidence must be put in the judges, and they must be allowed to consider these different elements for themselves." [2].

The champion of the opposite point of view was the former United States Secretary of State Elihu Root, supported by Lord Phillimore, a member of the Judicial Committee of the Privy Council. Mr. Root warned that it was "inconceivable that a Government would agree to allow itself to be arraigned

1. Following the example of the unratified Hague Convention XII, of 1907, proposing an International Prize Court, and of other projects referred to in *Documents presented to the Advisory Committee of Jurists relating to existing plans*, 1920, p. 103. The order of *précédence* of the sources of international law was deleted by the subcommittee of the Third Committee of the First Assembly of the League of Nations.

2. *Procès-Verbaux of the Proceedings of the Committee*, June 16th-July 24th, 1920, pp. 295 f.

before a Court which bases its sentences on its subjective conceptions of justice. The Court must not have the power to legislate. "[1]. Making the same point, Lord Phillimore especially referred to the so-called project of the Five Neutral Powers where it proposed that the Court, "should no rules applicable to the case exist, shall enter judgment according to its own opinion of what the rule of international law on the subject should be" [2]. This part of the project, according to Lord Phillimore,

> "in fact, gave the Court a legislative power, but legislation in matters of international law could only be carried out by the universal agreement of all States. Apart from this legislation, what remains? In the first place Conventional law, and in the second place, international law actually in force [2]." ...

But a complaint could be justified, though it might not fall within the bounds of actual law, and consequently could not be recognized according to law.

> "If cases of this nature arise in international affairs, two solutions are possible: either the Assembly may be asked to fill the gap by means of legislation, or the question may be submitted to the Council for decision [3]. . . .The Council is the body which must give satisfaction in cases which cannot be dealt with according to the law". [4].

As appears from the context the word *legislation* is used in five more or less different meanings. In all cases it means law-making, but there are degrees in law-making. There is, in the first place, the adjustment of the applicable law if, in a concrete dispute, it would lead to apparent injustice. This mode of law-making, advocated by M. de Lapradelle, was rejected as "legislation", and in the final text of Article 38, as it still stands, it only appears as a power to decide *ex aequo et bono* where this is agreed to by the parties. (In view of the fact that this power has played a relatively small part in international practice and that "judicial legislation" [5] is outside the scope of the present study, we will

1. *Ibidem*, p. 309.
2. *Ibidem*, p. 295.
3. *Ibidem*, p. 320.
4. *Ibidem*, p. 316.
5. As discussed by H. Lauterpacht in *The Function of Law in the International Community*, 1933, Chapter XV, where attention is also paid to the extension of judicial legislation by conferment of the power to lay down regulations and to propose recommendations. And see the same author's essay "*Some Observations on the Prohibition of "Non Liquet" and the Completeness of the Law*," in *Symbolae Verzijl*, 1958, pp. 196 ff.

deal only incidentally with decisions of international tribunals and of other bodies which may be called upon to settle disputes [1] as a source of international law.) But apart from this disagreement the Committee was unanimous as to the obvious fact that all other forms of international legislation must be left to more appropriate bodies. There is "diplomacy", explicitly denied to the Court by M. de Lapradelle, a non-institutionalized means of settlement of international disputes. Then there is the finding of a solution by the Council of the League of Nations. Entirely distinct from these means for the creation of new law in an actual and concrete case, there is the making of rules for abstract future situations. This can be done either in the form of negotiated treaties as referred to by Lord Phillimore in his first intervention (and by Mr. Manley Hudson in the title of his well known collection *International Legislation*), or by an established international body such as the Assembly of the League of Nations, referred to by Lord Phillimore in a later intervention.

Readjustment and Peaceful Settlement of Disputes

The references, in the Advisory Committee, to international legislation reflect very well the state of thinking and practice up to that time. When studying international institutions throughout the nineteenth century we are struck by a distinction between two groups of related phenomena. Basic to the first group is the idea of maintaining the established order as laid

1. Although, in those latter cases, it will not always be easy to determine whether the essence of the decision is on the judicial or rather on the legislative side. Reference is made to those provisions of the Articles of Agreement of the International Monetary Fund (Article XVIII) and of the International Bank for Reconstruction and Development (Article IX), of the International Wheat Agreement (Article XIX), of the International Sugar Agreement (Article 40) and of the International Tin Agreement (as drafted by the United Nations Tin Conference, held in Geneva 1953; Article XVII) according to which disputes concerning the interpretation or application of the Agreements shall be submitted to the Executive Directors, the Board of Governors (Bank and Fund), or to the Council for decision. Decision is taken according to the regular procedure adopted for those organizations, that is to say by a system of weighted voting. However, as far as the method of decision-making is concerned, in the commodity agreements the judicial element has been reinforced by directing the Council in certain cases to seek the opinion of an advisory panel (See S. D. Metzger, *Settlement of International Disputes by Non-Judicial Methods*, 48 American J. Int. Law (1954), pp. 408 ff.)

down, legally, in the treaty-system of Vienna and, politically, in the concept of the Balance of Power. The framework of that order must be kept intact, but certain readjustments, from time to time, are inevitable. For that purpose either traditional diplomacy can be used when pressure between equals should be exerted, or, in the form of collective mediation and intervention, a more organized action can be taken when the "Powers of the first order" [1] wish to enforce such changes as the separation of Greece from Turkey or of Belgium from the Netherlands. In the latter case unanimous decisions are taken (in the absence of the Powers directly involved) by a conference of ambassadors, instructed to this effect by the "Pentarchy [2]". But the final legislative work is completed in the conventional diplomatic form of treaties with participation of all the parties, including those whose rights have been disposed of. The directive and pre-legislative function of the conferences of ambassadors provides a precedent for the League of Nations Council or the Security Council. When, however, between two equals, France and Prussia, conflicting claims regarding Luxemburg threaten to upset the balance of power, resort is had to more traditional methods of diplomacy by conference [3].

It is noteworthy that the diplomatic approach co-exists satisfactorily with a pacifist movement which has arbitration as the main item on its program of action. Against arbitration as a panacea for all problems of war and peace only rare voices are heard, denouncing it as the sanction of the forcibly established order and as the continuation of injustice. Towards the end of

1. Despatch of Viscount Castlereagh to the Earl of Liverpool, Vienna, September 24, 1814. Appendix I to C. K. Webster, *The Congress of Vienna, 1814-15*, (1919), p. 149.

2. The Conference on Belgian Affairs in London held 70 sittings from November, 1830 to October, 1832. The protocol of the first sitting states: "The Powers who signed the Treaties of Paris and Vienna have agreed, through the instrumentality of *(par l'organe de)* their Ambassadors and Ministers accredited to the Court of London on the following resolutions *(les déterminations suivantes)*. Martens, *Nouveau Recueil*, X, 78.

The Conference relative to the Affairs of Greece, July, 1827-May, 1832, was held in London between the representatives of Great Britain, Russia and France; Austria and Prussia not participating.

3. Conference respecting Luxemburg, London, May, 1867.

the century arbitration, even in the diplomatic world, is an accepted and even fashionable institution, overshadowing by far questions of the creation of new law and interest in methods of developing law as an instrument of social progress. Forasmuch as there is any public interest in this field, it is in codification, the crystallization of rules of customs and practice and, as far as it goes a very valuable contribution to the reliability and calculability of international law.

The Climate of the Union

In the meantime a silent evolution has taken place, belonging to a world other than that of diplomacy and arbitration. It is silent because it is not accompanied by sonorous motions of parliaments and conferences. It is an evolution because it is recognized only after it has proceeded a long way. And the world to which it belongs is that of men not primarily interested in international relations as such, but concentrating on specialized matters which might be better promoted by international action. The matters themselves—such as labour, intellectual property, health, agriculture and communications of all kinds—often have little in common, so that the development in each field follows its own course. Nevertheless, when at the end of the century the balance is struck [1], it appears that often similar solutions are found for similar organizational problems.

Typical of all those specialized activities, and essentially different from diplomatic situations, is that in these cases the treaty is the starting point and the legislative basis of a progressive work, whereas in diplomacy the treaty merely sets the seal on a process of change accomplished through negotiation and pressure. It follows that in the former cases, after the constitutional framework has been set up, methods of law-making must be adapted to the needs of a continuous task, whether it be the collection and distribution of technical and scientific information

1. Among a number of studies published in various countries the work of Paul S. Reinsch, *Public International Unions* (Boston and London, 1911), was the most influential. It is extensively used by Walter Schücking in his *Staatenverband der Haager Konferenzen* (1912) and by L. S. Woolf in his two reports, prepared for the Fabian Society; *International Government* (London, 1916).

for common use, the making of studies, the control of the observance and implementation of conventions and regulations, or the administration of a common undertaking. Or the task may be the creation of law itself, either by a process of unification of national laws, or by regulations binding upon the participating States and Administrations, or even by a system under which the basic convention is revised, developed and adjusted to new requirements. It is in this dynamic climate that, besides the international treaty, the international decision wins its place as a practical means of international legislation.

There is one other aspect, which in contrast to diplomatic situations, is often characteristic of the activities referred to. That is the concept of union, applied and limited to a technical or economic matter, as in the current conception of a European common market. From the point of view of navigation an international river will be considered as a perfect unity throughout its course, or, for the purposes of the international organization, a number of national telecommunication networks will be regarded as an integrated system, or "the countries between which the present treaty is concluded will form a single postal territory for the reciprocal exchange of correspondence" [1], or the union is aimed at the creation of an area of uniform national law in a particular field. It is clear that such an approach is essentially different from, and necessarily leads to international techniques unknown to all methods of peaceful settlement of disputes implying plurality instead of unity.

Links of Continuity

We have no opportunity, in this rapid survey, to take many illustrations from nineteenth century international organizations. Attention can only be drawn to a group of early unions, whose significance has somewhat been obscured by the establishment, in 1865, of the International Telegraph Union, which eventually developed to the present International Telecommunication Union, and, in 1874, of the General Postal Union, soon to be-

1. Treaty of October 9th, 1874, concerning the formation of a General Postal Union, Article 1.

come the Universal Postal Union, now the most venerable member of the family of specialized agencies. Most of their characteristics, however, did already belong to similar Germanic Unions of the eighteen-fifties, and it was those unions which served as examples to build on. In 1850 a Postal Union was concluded between Austria and Prussia [1] and a Telegraph Union between the same States, together with Bavaria and Saxony [2], and in the following years both organizations, through various revisions and bilateral treaties, expanded to several more States including, in the case of the Telegraph Union, the Netherlands [3]. From the point of view of the history of international law those forgotten [4] unions are important for the following reasons.

History shows various examples of confederations which are, in their structure and functioning, very similar to modern international organizations. There is the constituent treaty between sovereign States, there is the differentiation of organs, there is the taking of decisions after a prescribed process of initiation, preparation, discussion and voting. It has rightly been observed [5] that, though this similarity is striking as to the outward form, politically there is the difference that the confederates, already having much in common, in concluding the union brought in more and bigger interests than is typical of the later international organizations. When, indeed, in the second half of the century that word came into use as an adequate term for an improved form of international relations [6], the last confederations were going to disappear because the relations they served were no longer fully international.

The historical significance of the unions of the eighteen-fifties

1. Treaty of August 6th, 1850. L. Neumann, *Recueil des traités et conventions conclus par l'Autriche*, Vol. V, pp. 161 ff.

2. Treaty of July 25th, 1850, Neumann, *Ibid.*, pp. 196 ff.

3. E. G. Lagemans, *Recueil des traités et conventions conclus par le Royaume des Pays-Bas*, Vol. IV, p. 90.

4. See, however, G. A. Codding Jr., *The International Telecommunication Union*, 1952, pp. 14 ff., extensively dealing with the Austro-German Telegraph Union.

5. H. Rehm, *Allgemeine Staatslehre*, 1899, pp. 97 ff.

6. Already used by C. Frantz, *Der Federalismus*, 1879, pp. 371 ff.

is that, by making their influence felt outside the Germanic States and on the conventions of 1865 and 1874, they form the link between international organization as experienced in the confederations on the one hand, and international organization properly so-called on the other hand. There is no doubt that the practice of the Germanic Confederation was responsible for the fact that as early as 1851 in the revised postal convention a differentiated system of international legislation is to be found, allowing for modifications of the convention and of the regulations through decisions of a postal conference. Three categories of decisions are distinguished: in the first place, and nearest to the diplomatic form, decisions concerning enumerated kinds of important matters, unanimously to be taken and to be ratified by all Member States; further, decisions concerning "less important cases", to be taken by a majority of three-fourths and requiring no ratification; and lastly, decisions regarding the regulations, to be taken by an absolute majority and requiring no ratification [1]. The latter category presents the first example in the history of international organization (apart from the confederations) of legislation by majority vote finally and formally binding upon the Member States. (Thus Article XVII of Annex 16 B of the Final Act of the Congress of Vienna and the corresponding Article 94 of the Treaty of Mayence of 1831-32 [2] prescribed the additional consent of the riparian States for such majority decisions, taken in the Central Commission for the Navigation of the Rhine [3], in order to make them binding.)

Though each organization, as has been observed earlier, showed a development of its own, according to its special functions and needs, a process of mutual stimulation can be traced as a connecting thread running through the organizational evolution until the First World War. When the General Postal Union was set up in 1874, a draft submitted by the first Post-

1. Treaty of December 5th, 1851, Article LXXV, Neumann, *Ibid.* pp. 496 ff. And see Agreement between the Administrations of the Austro-German Telegraph Union, August 31st, 1861, Article 4, Lagemans, *Ibid.*, Vol. V, p. 116.

2. Article 94, Lagemans, *Ibid.*, Vol. II, pp. 259 ff.

3. The first permanent international organ.

master-General of the German Empire, Heinrich von Stephan, was used as a basis of discussion; in this draft von Stephan had turned to profitable use his personal experiences with the Austro-German Postal Union [1]. In the Convention of 1874 several features, among them the Bureau, were taken from the successive Telegraph Conventions up to 1865. In 1882, during a congress of the Association Littéraire et Artistique Internationale held in Rome, the idea of a union for the protection of literary and artistic works was inspired by the examples of the Universal Postal Union and others [2]. The convention for that purpose, signed in 1886, was very similar to that for the protection of industrial property, signed a few years earlier. The first official initiative for international labour legislation proposed in the Swiss Federal Council in 1887 by Decurtins, referred to the international conventions already concluded on posts, telegraphs, railways and copyrights [3]. When in an official Italian memorandum Lubin's plan for an international institute of agriculture was favourably considered and the first step was taken for the establishment of the Institute in 1905, reference was made to the form, though not the substance, of the first international conference on the regulation of factory and mine labour, held in Berlin in 1890 after the Swiss initiative already referred to, and following a German invitation [4].

When the League of Nations was under discussion, the ground was well prepared for adopting two achievements of a century of international relations. In the specialized sphere the making of decisions, rather than agreements, had become the regular practice of permanent organs dealing with an expanding variety of economical, technical, scientific, humanitarian, cultural and legal matters. In the diplomatic sphere the Hague conferences of 1899 and 1907, the succession of inter-American conferences

1. *Documents du Congres Postal International, réuni à Berne du 15 Septembre au 9 Octobre, 1874*, pp. 3 f.

2. F. Ruffini in 12 Recueil des Cours (1926, II), p. 455.

3. J. W. Follows, *Antecedents of the International Labour Organization*, 1951, p. 121.

4. A. Hobson, *The International Institute of Agricuture,*, Thesis, Geneva, 1931, p. 35.

from 1899 onwards, and, during the First World War, the inter-Allied co-operation which Lord Hankey from personal experience described as "diplomacy by conference" [1], had made the statesmen of the world accustomed to the idea of international bodies regularly convening and dealing with political matters. To a certain extent and for a few years only the idea had been put into practice after the Congress of Vienna and again, on a lower level, in the form of the London conferences of ambassadors between 1827 and 1833, dealing with two limited problems. In 1918, however, permanent bodies were for the first time entrusted with duties concerning world affairs of a general political nature.

Still Limited Scope of Legislation by Decision

The fact that, henceforth, no field of international activity was to be excluded from being dealt with by way of decisions, did not however mean that legislative decisions were thereby introduced in the political sphere. As was clearly stated in the official British commentary on the Covenant: "At the present stage of national feeling, sovereign States will not consent to be bound by legislation voted by a majority, even an overwhelming majority, of their fellows". [2]. And this standpoint was confirmed by the fact that the provision, drafted by President Wilson, whereby the expedience of territorial readjustments was to be decided by three-fourths majority, was finally dropped [3].

Though this particularly refers to the Assembly, no more was it the intention to entrust the Council with legislative power in the sense of power to impose upon a Member State more than it had already undertaken by the Covenant itself, that is, in the first place, to respect the territorial integrity and existing political independence of all Members. In its early practice the Council excluded from the required unanimity of its decisions

1. Lecture delivered at the British Institute of International Affairs in 1920 and Chapter I of *Diplomacy by Conference*, 1946.

2. C. A. Kluyver, *Documents on the League of Nations*, p. 102.

3. Article III of Wilson's First, Second and Third Draft; D. H. Miller, *The Drafting of the Covenant*, 1928, Vol. II, pp. 12, 70, 98; Vol. I, p. 71. Otherwise, the provision required an additional agreement of the peoples concerned.

the votes of the parties to a dispute, even where such exclusion was not explicitly prescribed by the Covenant [1]. Nevertheless, even acting in a broad capacity in the settlement of disputes under the Covenant, the Council never went further than confirming already existing legal obligations. It never considered the possibility [2], theoretically contained in the Covenant, of binding a party against its will to a proposal of territorial readjustment, by unanimous report (not counting the votes of the parties: Article 15, paragraph 6) [3]. It never acted (in the words of Lord Phillimore in the Advisory Committee of Jurists) [1] as "the body which must give satisfaction in cases which cannot be dealt with according to the law".

The limitations, which we have just discussed, on the powers of the League, apply similarly to other international organizations. It may be questioned whether such limitations were always clearly understood. While it took some time before the organizational evolution of the nineteenth century was recognized, conversely there was a tendency to over-estimate the development once it was discovered. A survey of all cases in which some form of majority vote already was accepted, and of all types of decisions by which sovereign States were bound without their consent (or with a token consent), certainly did not give a true picture of the progress already achieved or further to be expected. For the evaluation of that progress it is necessary to take into consideration the purposes for which, and the political conditions under which, the decisions were taken.

In the first place, it is relevant to consider the stage of law-making at which a decision is made. For obvious reasons decisions can be more easily taken, and with less qualified majorities, when the decision is sufficiently remote from the final, definite satges of the law-making process. It therefore was relatively early in the organizational evolution that majority vote was accep-

1. That was in the happy days when the Greco-Bulgar dispute, coming before the Council under Articles 10 and 11, could be decided by "dictatorial request".

2. As considered by D. Schindler, *Die Verbindlichkeit der Beschlüsse des Völkerbundes*, 1927, p. 14.

3. *Supra*, p. 12.

ted for decisions in committees, even of such highly political conferences as the Congress of Berlin of 1878 [1]. (From the point of view of our subject a committee established by an international conference can be regarded as its organ, irrespective of the fact that the conference itself is not, strictly speaking, an organ in the sense that the conferences and assemblies of international organizations are their organs.) It is further relevant to consider the function which a particular type of decision fulfils in the constitutional machinery of an organization. There is a whole gamut of categories of decisions, varying from those which are primarily of an internal character and effect, such as those determining the meeting-place of organs, to those regarding appointment or designation, admission or expulsion of Members, and, finally, those which imply for Members direct, though limited and calculable, obligations, *inter alia* of a financial nature. Though all decisions required for the regular functioning of an organization indirectly concern the national interests of each Member, it is clear that typical "internal" matters, such as the functioning of the "Bureau", could be most easily decided by a simple majority vote [2].

Secondly, we have the cases in which the Great Powers of the day imposed their will on defeated enemies, or on otherwise weak States or new-born States, in such a way that the latter formally agreed in advance to be bound by future decisions of the Powers. If, then, the Powers acted through some agency, established by them for that purpose, there was an organ competent to create law for States without the requirement of their consent. (In this connection neither the London Conferences on Greek and on Belgian Affairs [3], nor the Constantinople Conference of Ambassadors and other organs, which after 1896 were created by the Great Powers to deal with Cretan affairs, are clear examples, because their decisions were directly imposed by pressure and force, while in the other cases there was a treaty-

1. E. Satow, *International Congresses*, Peace Handbooks, No. 151 (Vol. XXIII), p. 3. S. Maiwald, *Der Berliner Kongress 1878 und das Völkerrecht*, 1948, p. 75.
2. See further *infra*, pp. 50 ff.
3. *Supra* p. 14.

based competence allowing legal interpretation [1].) For two examples, we may cite, first, the Conference of Ambassadors of the Four Allied Powers, which met regularly between 1815 and 1818 and was entrusted with the execution of the Second Peace Treaty of Paris, and secondly, the Conference of Ambassadors of the Great Powers, meeting in London between December, 1912 and August, 1913 to deal with Balkan Affairs, after the belligerents in the First Balkan War had accepted the mediation of the Powers. Under the Treaty of London of May 17-30th, 1930 the task of settling the frontiers of Albania and any other questions regarding Albania was reserved to them, and it was one of their decisions in fulfilment of this task that was submitted to the Permanent Court of International Justice for an advisory opinion on the question of the Monastery of Saint-Naoum [2].

But the most important case in point is that of the Conference of Ambassadors, constituted in 1920 by the Supreme Council of the Principal Allied and Associated Powers to complete the Peace Treaties and to supervise their execution. The activities of this body, which was terminated only in 1931, are most ably described by Dr. Gerhard P. Pink [3]. It is to be noted that, particularly during the first years of its existence, it was most actively engaged in laying down a long series of binding decisions, some of which dealt with new constitutions (Dantzig, Memel) and with new boundaries. A number of decisions of this organ, as well as of its parent body, the Supreme Council, again played a part in proceedings before the International Court of Justice [4].

At the same time, the Council of the League of Nations, though resulting from a more static conception, was invested by the Austrian, Hungarian and Bulgarian Peace Treaties with certain legislative powers, to be exerted by majority vote, in regard to

1. However, according to some treaties of which Turkey also was a party for instance: Article 15 of the Peace Treaty of December 4th, 1897 between Turkey and Greece: De Martens, XXVIII *N.R.G.*, 2ème Série, p. 636) a few disputes between Turkey and Greece were referred to the decision of the Powers.

2. Series B, No. 9 (1921).

3. *The Conference of Ambassadors (Paris, 1920-1931)*; XII Geneva Studies, (1942), Nos. 4-5.

4. *Question of St. Naoum; Question of Jaworzina*, Series B, No. 8 (1923).

modification of the provisions relating to minorities [1], and the Treaty of Lausanne contained the provision (which became known from another advisory opinion of the Court) that in the event of no agreement being reached between Turkey and Great Britain, the determination of the frontier between Turkey and Iraq was to be referred to the Council. It was on this occasion that the Court confirmed the principle [2] that the votes of the parties must not be counted in ascertaining whether there was unanimity [3].

It may be concluded that, though the taking of formal decisions had become a natural manifestation of the functioning of international organs, including political bodies, decisions involving new legal obligations for States remained the exception. Apart from the special and transient situations following from peace treaties and as such not fully representative from the point of view of the development of international organization, legislation remained confined to relatively rare examples of a facilitated modification of technical regulations [4], navigation tolls [5] and prescriptions of a similar nature [6]. To a large extent, this applies also to the period until the Second World War.

1. St. Germain, Article 69, paragraph 1; Trianon, Article 60, paragraph 1; Neuilly, Article 57, paragraph 1.

2. *Supra*, p. 21.

3. Article 3, paragraph 2, of the Treaty of Lausanne; Series B, No. 12 (1925). Comp. Annex XI, paragraph 3, of the Treaty of Peace with Italy, 1947, whereby the Powers concerned agreed to accept the recommendation of the General Assembly of the U.N. on the disposal of the former Italian colonies. The recommendation referred to was adopted 21 November, 1949 as Res. 289 (IV).

4. *Infra*, p. 85, n. 2.

5. Navigation tolls as established by Article 16 of the Treaty of Paris of March 30th, 1856, could be modified by majority vote of the European Commission of the Danube (Article 16 of its *Règlement*)

6. Such as Article 7, par. (c), of the International Sugar Convention of March 5, 1902, authorizing a Permanent Commission by majority vote to pronounce whether bounties exist in the Non-Signatory States, and to estimate the amount thereof for the purpose of determining the compensatory duties which all signatory States must then put into effect.

NOTES AND QUESTIONS

1. What does Tammes mean by a new legislative technique? Is it comparable to what Mrs. Higgins depicts as the role of the United Nations political organs in the creation of customary international law?
2. How does Tammes interpret the failure of Article 38 to specify decisions of international organizations as a source of international law? Does the failure prevent the International Court of Justice from treating resolutions of international organs as relevant to the performance of its adjudicative role?
3. Does the experience of functional international unions contribute to our understanding of the law-creating role of United Nations organs? Note that Tammes stresses the contrast between the making of decisions within an organizational setting and the making of agreements within a diplomatic or interstate setting. International agreements—such as treaties and conventions—depend for legal obligation upon the expressions of consent of the states concerned. Traditionally, the binding force of customary international law was explained by the idea of tacit or implied consent; that is, general practice and a sense of legal obligation plus the absence of protest. Does sovereignty imply the authority of a state to limit its international obligations to those to which it has given consent? If international organizations can bind dissenting states, then the organized international community comes to acquire a governmental character. On what foundation of law does this governmental character rest?

The next selection—Report of Committee on Study of Legal Problems of the United Nations, "Should the Laws of War Apply to United Nations Enforcement Action?," *Proceedings of The American Society of International Law* (1952) pp. 216–220—examines the relationship between international law and the United Nations from quite another perspective. It raises questions concerning the extent to which the Organization as an actor is itself subservient to international law. This revives the theme of **II-1**, especially the articles of McDougal and Hoffmann which held that the organizing concepts of international law arose at a time when the only significant actors in international law were states.

REPORT OF COMMITTEE ON STUDY OF LEGAL PROBLEMS OF THE UNITED NATIONS*

SHOULD THE LAWS OF WAR APPLY TO UNITED NATIONS ENFORCEMENT ACTION?

The Committee on Legal Problems of the United Nations undertook this year study of a problem which turned out to be more than the Committee, widely scattered and consulting by mail, was able to handle. We therefore present a brief report which presents the problem for your consideration, and urge further study of it.

The problem under consideration can be summarily presented by the question: Should the laws of war be applied to United Nations enforcement action? This single question ramifies in a surprising number of directions, many of which are for the future and can hardly be answered at the present time.

I

It must be admitted that, under present circumstances, there may be war and, therefore, a need for laws of war. One of the members of this Committee asserts that war is still possible under general international law; and that under the Charter of the United Nations war remains possible illegally in breach of the Charter, and legally under Articles 106, 107, and 51, and in the case of enforcement action. He asserts further that it has been, since Grotius, and is today positive international law that the "laws of war" apply to any large-scale international fighting, whether legal or illegal. The laws of war, however, are in a chaotic condition, and the first and most urgent proposal *de lege ferenda* is a study of the revision of the laws of war.[1]

Other questions were raised as to the nature of the enforcement action which can be taken by the United Nations. The Security Council, while theoretically able to take a decision, would in most cases be blocked by a veto and could do no more than, as in the case of Korea, recommend that Members contribute to such action against an aggressor. The same situation would exist in regard to action under the Uniting for Peace Resolution, since the General Assembly here also can only recommend. In this situation, is the action to be regarded as enforcement action under the authority of the United Nations, or simply as separate national action by Members,

[1] See Josef L. Kunz, "The Chaotic Status of the Laws of War and the Urgent Necessity for Their Revision," *American Journal of International Law*, Vol. 45 (1951), pp. 37–61.

even though jointly conducted? Even decisions of the Security Council, it is suggested, are subject to the proviso that they must be "in accordance with the present Charter," and apparently each Member may decide for itself whether there is such accordance.

Over such questions, the members of the Committee disagreed in such various ways that few conclusions could be reached. Certain points, however, are submitted for your consideration.

In the first place, the use of the term "war" is itself debatable. War has never been satisfactorily defined, and its changed character today makes its meaning even more uncertain.[2] Whether in reference to an insurance or other contract or in reference to the action which ought to be restrained by collective security, the word "war" is not sufficiently definable to be of much value; what the world wants today is restriction of illegal use of force. The Charter of the United Nations does not employ the word "war" (except for an oratorical reference in the Preamble).

The assertion that United Nations enforcement action is war arouses strong opposition. Whatever the definition of war may be, this much of it would be generally accepted, that war is conflict between states, between units of equal legal status; whereas the United Nations, acting on behalf of the organized community of nations against an offender, has a superior legal and moral position as compared with the other party to the conflict. A war is fought by a state for its own national interest; United Nations enforcement action is on behalf of order and peace among nations. It is the duty of all Members of the United Nations to help it in its action against an aggressor; while there may be exceptions under the Charter making war possible, there is in the theory of the Charter no room for neutrality. War as between states of equal legal status has in the past been regarded as honorable; the use of force against the United Nations is now to be regarded as an offense against all Members.

The United Nations action in Korea is being conducted, at least in part, according to the law of war. The United Nations has announced that it will follow the 1949 Geneva Conventions regarding prisoners of war, civilians, etc.; it has not announced that the whole of the law of war is to be followed. Since no other rules have been stated, it was natural that the United Nations should accept existing rules insofar as they seem relevant and proper; this was especially true as regards humanitarian principles. It is not true, however, that the United Nations considers itself to be a combatant in the sense of the old laws of war, and bound to apply all of them. It is maintained by some that acceptance of the Charter by Member States meant acceptance by them of the superior legal position of the United Nations as regards the use of force and that, consequently, the United Nations may apply such rules as it wishes. It might, for ex-

[2] See F. Grob, The Relativity of War and Peace (New Haven: Yale University Press, 1949).

ample, forbid use of atomic bombs by a state while reserving the right to use them itself. Presumably, its rules would be of high humanitarian character and it would respect them carefully.

Even if it could be said that the laws of war must be applied since no other rules have been prepared, it can also be said that there remain today few distinguishable rules of the law of war. So many changes have appeared in the character of war itself, and in the attitudes and obligations of states respecting the use of force, that agreement as to the validity of most of the rules of the old law of war would be impossible to obtain. This leads us into the question of new rules, to which we now turn.

II

At this point, a number of difficult questions appear, and we raise them for your future thinking, and for possible further research.

In the first place, assuming a new approach to a new problem, on what theory shall we proceed? Is United Nations enforcement action to be regarded as old-time war, or as police action analogous to the theory of policing within a state, or as something quite new, *sui generis?* We have already revealed the debate as to whether it should be regarded as war; even if—debated—one must in present circumstances accept it as war, is it necessary to accept it as war in planning for the future?

If one wishes to proceed on a police theory, one is forced to ask what is the theory and differentiation of police activity within a state? Just what is meant by the word "police"? Assuming an answer to this—and apparently some research would be required to find an answer—it would be necessary to take into account the structure, functions and authority of the United Nations as now constituted, and then ask how it compares in ability to do such police work. The assumption here would be an independent United Nations force, rather than the national contingents contemplated in the Charter. What would be the ability of the United Nations to act in accordance with a theory of police as regards:

1. The decision in accordance with which the police may or must act?

2. The extent to which discretion is to be left to the policeman? How far may he decide on the merits of the case? In what situations shall the United Nations police be free to act, and in which must it await orders from the Security Council or the General Assembly or other organ?

3. Recruiting, organizing and maintaining police forces? Bases? Production of equipment? Supplies? Transportation?

4. The purposes, or objectives, of police action: To prevent the use of force? Before or after it has begun? To settle the dispute or to enforce a settlement decided upon by a higher authority? What authority would this be in the United Nations?

5. What weapons would be available to the international police, and what would be forbidden—and how—to the aggressor?

6. What obligations to assist in police action would rest upon Member States? Would they be entitled to assume that responsibility rests entirely upon the international police?

7. What protection or guarantees would be provided against the international police force seizing control of the entire world?

Such questions would need to be answered before it would be possible to decide whether to build rules for United Nations enforcement action upon a police theory. When they have been answered, it would then be necessary to ask what changes, if any, in the Charter of the United Nations would be needed in order to enable the United Nations to act in accordance with a theory of police. Only then would it be possible to draw up rules for the conduct of the United Nations police in an enforcement action.[3] Such an investigation is desirable, but far beyond the capacity of your Committee as now constituted.

The above line of questioning leads also into the status of individuals. Should rules for the conduct of enforcement apply to states, to individuals, or to both? Can war be controlled by action against states alone, or must individuals who conspire to aggression be regarded as criminals? Is there now developing an international law which would, on the one hand, protect the individual (human rights) and, on the other hand, hold him responsible to an international authority for certain acts (genocide, Nuremberg principles, acts against the peace and security of nations, etc.)? This would confront the individual with a choice between loyalty to his own state and loyalty to the United Nations. How far, in this conflict, can the proposals for rights and duties of individuals under international law reasonably be pushed? Furthermore, the division of rights and duties of individuals between states and the United Nations means a constitutional division of legal powers: Does this imply that the United Nations must become a federal system? And finally, would the provision of rules for conduct of United Nations enforcement action which are applicable to individuals mean the establishment or beginning of an international criminal law, with all its problems of implementation and enforcement?

III

Some of the above discussion may seem far-fetched, yet it is all related to current developments in international law. It is obviously difficult, and I am sure that you can see why your Committee feels unable to provide all the answers, and why it will content itself with this very general conclusion:

[3] It is to be observed that the above questions, or some of them, could be asked as regards presents enforcement action under the Charter.

The Committee agrees that the use of force by the United Nations to restrain aggression is of a different nature from war-making by a state. The purposes for which the laws of war were instituted are not entirely the same as the purposes of regulating the use of force by the United Nations. This we may say without deciding whether United Nations enforcement action is war, police enforcement of criminal law, or *sui generis*. In the present circumstances, then, the proper answer would seem to be, for the time being, that the United Nations should not feel bound by all the laws of war, but should select such of the laws of war as may seem to fit its purposes (*e.g.,* prisoners of war, belligerent occupation), adding such others as may be needed, and rejecting those which seem incompatible with its purposes. We think it beyond doubt that the United Nations, representing practically all the nations of the earth, has the right to make such decisions.

WILLIAM J. BIVENS — JOSEF L. KUNZ
LELAND M. GOODRICH — LOUIS B. SOHN
HANS KELSEN — CLYDE EAGLETON, *Chairman*

NOTES AND QUESTIONS

1. What authoritative decision-maker is available to appraise a violation by the United Nations of international law?
2. On what basis should the United Nations be entitled to violate the rules of war in relation to a state that is alleged to be acting in violation of the Charter? See the last paragraph of the Schelling article in Chapter 9C. Is it desirable to liberate the United Nations from the laws of war? Why? On what basis can one predicate a legal duty of the Organization to comply?
3. For a full discussion of the issues in the Report of the Committee on Study of Legal Problems of the United Nations, see Derek Bowett, *United Nations Forces* (Praeger, New York, 1964) pp. 484–516.

To illustrate the way in which law emerges from the activities of the political organs of the United Nations it seems helpful to consider the *South West Africa Cases* brought against the Republic of South Africa in 1960 by Liberia and Ethiopia. The litigation is relevant because an issue in controversy is whether or not the activities of the political organs of the United Nations shall be accorded a law-creating effect. Because the controversy is before the ICJ it allows an analysis of the relation between law and politics from the perspective and with the techniques of the principal judicial arm of the United Nations. A short background statement is needed to put the issue in its proper setting.

After World War I the victorious Allied and Associated Powers agreed to place German colonies under mandate. The objective was to avoid their annexation by the victors and, at the same time, to acknowledge their inability to exist as independent states. The Mandate System was written into the Covenant of the League of Nations in Article 22. The basic character of the mandate concept is expressed by the first two paragraphs of Article 22:

1. To those colonies and territories which as a consequence of the late war have ceased to be under the sovereignty of the States which formerly governed them and which are inhabited by peoples not yet able to stand by themselves under the strenuous conditions of the modern world, *there should be applied the principle that the well-being and development of such peoples form a sacred trust of civilization* and that securities for the performance of this trust should be embodied in this Covenant.

2. The best method of giving practical effect to this principle is that the tutelage of such peoples should be entrusted to advanced nations who by reason of their resources, their experience or their geographical position can best undertake this responsibility, and who are willing to accept it, and *that this tutelage should be exercised by them as Mandatories of the League*. (Emphasis added.)

The Union of South Africa, now the Republic, was made the Mandatory of the Territory of South-West Africa. In the Mandate instrument of 1920, Article 2(2) carries forth this idea of a sacred trust administered by the Mandatory on behalf of the League:

The Mandatory shall promote to the utmost the material and moral well-being and social progress of the territory subject to the present Mandate.

South Africa, as Mandatory, was given in Article 2(1) considerable governmental discretion:

The Mandatory shall have full power of administration and legislation over the territory subject to the present Mandate as an integral portion of the Union of South Africa, and may apply the laws of the Union of South Africa to the territory, subject to such local modifications as circumstances may require.

Under this authority South Africa has extended its racial policies of *apartheid* to the mandated territory. Since the formation of the United Nations these racial policies have been the subject of debate and censure. South Africa, in response, has refused to cooperate, claiming that its obligations as Mandatory came to an end with the dissolution of the League. The General

Assembly by Resolution 338 (IV) in 1949 requested the ICJ to render an Advisory Opinion on certain questions related, *inter alia,* to the survival of the Mandate. The Court rejected South Africa's contention about the lapse of the Mandate: "The Mandate was created in the interests of the inhabitants of the territory, and of humanity in general, as an international institution with an international object—a sacred trust of civilization." "International Status of South-West Africa," *Advisory Opinion: I. C. J. Reports* (1950) p. 128. The Court added that the obligations under the Mandate "represent the very essence of the sacred trust of civilization. The raison d'être and original object remain. Since their fulfillment did not depend upon the existence of the League of Nations, they could not be brought to an end merely because this supervisory organ ceased to exist." [Id. at 133.] In Resolution 449A(V) the General Assembly voted to accept the Advisory Opinion of 1950. However, South Africa continued to refuse to comply with its obligation under the Mandate to submit to international supervision.

The course of the dispute is very complicated, but finally Ethiopia and Liberia in 1960 instituted a suit in the ICJ alleging that South Africa was violating the terms of the Mandate in several respects, including especially its obligation in Article 2(2) to promote the well-being of the inhabitants. Under Article 7 of the Mandate any Member of the League was entitled to submit a dispute connected with the Mandate, in the event that it could not be settled by negotiation, to the Permanent Court of International Justice for decision. Ethiopia and Liberia, as Members of the League, took advantage of this compromissory clause to bring the case on the theory that every state had a legal interest in securing compliance by a Mandatory with its obligation to administer the Mandate on behalf of the organized international community. In 1962 the Court, by a narrow margin (8–7), upheld its jurisdiction to decide the case on its merits. As yet, the South-West Africa Cases have not been decided, although lengthy pleadings and oral proceedings have been held.

The extract that follows is taken from the oral presentation by Ernest A. Gross, Agent for Ethiopia and Liberia, on the central issue of whether the practice of apartheid violates Article 2(2) of the Mandate, requiring the Mandatory to promote the moral well-being of the inhabitants. The legal problem is to convince the Court that the numerous condemnations of apartheid by the organs of the United Nations provide an authoritative basis for the interpretation of Article 2(2). In essence, Liberia and Ethiopia argued that these organs had evolved standards on the issue of moral well-being and that, given the idea of a sacred trust laid upon the organized international community, there was established a minimum obligation in Article 2(2) with respect to race relations. This minimum standard was described in the written pleadings, *Reply*, p. 274, as a norm of nondiscrimination or non-separation and defined as follows: "stated negatively, the terms refer to the absence of governmental policies or action which allot status, rights, duties, privileges or burdens on the basis of membership in a group, class or race rather than on the basis of individual merit, capacity or potential; stated affirmatively, the terms refer to governmental policies and actions the objective of which is to protect equality of opportunity and equal protection of the laws to individual persons as such."

South Africa argues that no such norm exists, and even if it does exist, it is not binding upon it, given the discretion vested in the Mandatory by Article 2(1). Furthermore, the Republic contends that its only obligation in Article 2 is to pursue in good faith the welfare of the inhabitants, and that even the complaining states do not question the sincerity of its belief in apartheid as the best mode of governmental administration. To overcome this argument and to make the action of the organs of the United Nations *legally relevant* to an interpretation of Article 2 of the Mandate, Mr. Gross is arguing in the proceedings reprinted below that the practice of apartheid violates international law, as defined by Article 38 of the Statute, and that the Mandatory, however great its discretion might be, must administer the Mandate in accordance with international law, especially as its rules bear on moral well-being. Underlying the presentation of the argument is a long sequence of Resolutions by the General Assembly and actions by the Security Council asserting the practice of apartheid to be in violation of Charter obligations; a virtual unanimity of states joining in the condemnation of South Africa in terms that have also, on occasion, declared the practice of apartheid to be in violation of international law. But how can it be proved to the satisfaction of the ICJ that an international legal norm came into being over South Africa's vigorous protest? Does the will of the international community expressed through its competent organs have a law-creating effect? We cannot know the definitive answer to these questions until the Court hands down its decision, a decision likely to have a vital bearing upon the material considered in this chapter.

What follows are excerpts from the uncorrected version of Mr. Gross's Oral Argument of May 19, 1965.

The Honorable ERNEST A. GROSS

Extracts from an Address

Agent for the Government of Ethopia and Liberia Delivered before the International Court of Justice, May 19, 1965. (*Taken from the Verbatim Record of the Public Sitting of the ICJ in the South West Africa Cases*)

As the Applicants contend with respect to the international legal norm, such norm would, if it exists and if it is applicable as the Applicants contend, render irrelevant, as a matter of law, any issue with regard to the limits of the Respondents discretion pursuant to the first paragraph of Article 2. Even as a sovereign State, Respondent must govern in accordance with international law. Its obligation as a mandatory to promote well-being and social progress, in accordance with the obligations of the sacred trust, do, of course, require that the international law, the international legal norms pertaining to the Respondent's obligations as a sovereign State and as mandatory, apply *a fortiori* to the Mandate itself. The jurisdiction of the Court to determine the obligations pursuant to international law, to the international legal norm for which the Applicants contend, would be founded on, and cognizable under, the compromissory clause of the Mandate.

The Applicants contend that the international standard of nondiscrimination and non-separation qualifies as law, qualifies as a legal norm, in accordance with, and pursuant to, the several sub-sections of Article 38, paragraph 1, of the Statute. Such demonstration depends upon acceptance by the Court of the Applicants' contention that formal acts of international institutions in certain circumstances, which the Applicants contend apply here, may and do possess a law-creating effect within the meaning of Article 38, paragraph 1, of the Statute.

* * *

In the first place, the diversity and multitude of states comprising the contemporary international order have brought in their wake new concepts and needs regarding the normative process itself. Collective judgments are, at once, more difficult to come by and more important to respect. Special significance is to be attributed, in the face of cultural, ideological and economic diversity of the members of the international community, to the fact that so high a degree of consensus, approaching unanimity, has been achieved regarding the incompatibility of apartheid with contemporary international norms of official behaviour.

Secondly, technological development and the spread of information in the arts of war and of transportation have made international society more interdependent. There is increasing awareness that events in one State cannot be isolated from concerns of international society in the maintenance of a system of minimal order. There is ever increasing awareness that what is going on in the Territory of South West Africa has had great impact upon the welfare of nations and of peoples even in remote areas of the world, and, above all, that the demand increases that something be done in deference to minimum expectations concerning the content of human diginity.

* * *

Thirdly, the connection between world peace and the protection of human rights in the international sphere has become increasingly manifest. International co-operation in the human rights field has proceeded from this premise with a sense of increasing urgency. It is a trend especially evident in connection with the effort by the organs of the United Nations to deal with Respondent's policies of separation and discrimination. The organized international community insistently proclaims the need to correct perceived abuses of human rights, most particularly where such abuses are implemented as part of authorized government policy.

* * *

Fourthly, within the area of human rights the most significant developments have focussed upon the evolution of standards pertaining to matters of racial equality, nondiscrimination and non-separation. This subject matter, as the Court will be aware, and as the record makes clear, has dominated the human rights activities of international institutions, and abuse in this area has been identified with a consensus approximating unanimity as an affront to human dignity, as a serious impediment to individual well-being, and as a grave threat to international peace and security. It is not too much to say that one of the foundation stones of international peace is the establishment and implementation of international standards pertaining to racial discrimination, and this marks a vast advance, as the Court will be aware, from the Covenant of the League to the Charter of the United Nations.

Sixthly, [*sic*] international society lacks legislative organs, and for this reason it has had to rely on other than legislative procedures to change and evolve international standards and norms, and the Applicants will consider shortly the implications of this requirement. The need has grown acute, in the light of expansion of international society and the increasing role of international institutions. For this reason scholars have increasingly urged that suitable and, in appropriate cases, *quasi* legislative effect be given to official acts of international institutions. Only thus can an important gap in the international legal order be filled.

The absence of a legislative capacity as such in the international order has an important bearing, of course, upon the outlook of international judicial organs. As Judge Sir Gerald Fitzmaurice has written—and I refer to his article "Hersch Lauterpacht, The Scholar as Judge," vol. 37, *British Yearbook of International Law, 1961,* I quote from pages 14 to 15—

> Domestic courts can, if they wish, plead with some plausibility as a ground for not going beyond what is barely necessary for a decision that a national legislature exists which can, by legislative action, remedy any gaps or obscurities in the law. In the international field there is at present nothing comparable to a legislature, and the operation of the so-called law-making treaty is both uncertain and leaves many loose ends. The international community is therefore peculiarly dependent on its international tribunals for the development and clarification of the law, and for lending to it an authority more substantial and less precarious than can be drawn from the often uncertain and divergent practices of States, or even from the opinion of individual publicists, whatever their repute.

Seventhly, consideration closely connected with the need in international society for at least *quasi* legislative capacity in appropriate situations, in cases, is appreciation of the ordering role played by the organs and specialized agencies in the great system of the United Nations itself, of which this Court forms the judicial arm. The same is true of regional institutions in world affairs. The world order attributes increasing importance to the normative functions of international institutions and acknowledges that actors other than States may evolve authoritative international standards as well as international legal norms. Fundamental to such a modernization process is the degree to which a single, recalcitrant State, or a small minority of States, may be permitted to veto or block the emergence of authoritative standards, or legal norms, in international society, and thus paralyse the growth and development of international law itself.

Underlying this question is the extent to which the reality of unanimous sovereign consent is an essential ingredient in the formation of an international legal norm or international standards binding upon all States. The Applicants contend that the Court should confirm the role of international consensus as a source of international law within the meaning of Article 38 of the Statute of the Court and within clear, practical limitations. "Consensus" is used by the Applicants to refer to an overwhelming majority, a convergence of international opinion, a predominance of view; it means considerably more than a simple majority, but something less than unanimity. These words and phrases introduce no ambiguity in the context of this case. There is a virtual unanimity with regard to the practice and policy of apartheid, and the shadings and nuances of language or terminology are irrelevant here.

If the resources of law are not available only force is left to implement the preponderant will of the international community, most manifest in this case. The use of force, if accepted in the context of a threat to or breach of international peace or act of aggression, is accepted without positing the necessity of the consent of all States. The notion of literal universality should not constitute an impediment to the legal order, to pacific settlement, particularly in the face of governmental policies which have been denounced by the international community to be sources of international tension and even threats to the peace.

The need for judicial settlement by the application of the consensus of civilized States becomes even more compelling in such a situation, and if the use of force itself does not rest upon unanimity the maintenance of peace should rest on no narrower basis.

A substantial increase in the normative function of the organized international community is found in the relaxation of the requirement of unanimous consent in the decision-making procedures of the United Nations in contrast to the procedures obtaining during the lifetime of the League of Nations. Such normative capacities of the General Assembly are relevant to the Applicants' submission that the principle of non-discrimination is an international legal norm: the relevance is established in at least two respects.

First, there has been authoritative definition of the scope, character and applicability to Respondent's policies of the international legal norm found in Article 55(c) and Article 56 of the Charter, read in the light of the overall affirmation of the Charter of the connection between human rights and obligation of Members.

Secondly, conclusive evidence is to be found in the many judgments of Member States that the standards evolved by the organs in the United Nations do in fact constitute an international legal norm. Further evidence of the law-creating competence of the United Nations is dramatically evidenced by Article 2, paragraph 6 of the Charter which I quote:

> The Organization shall ensure that States which are not Members of the United Nations act in accordance with these principles so far as may be necessary for the maintenance of international peace and security.

This provision in itself makes clear the extent to which the international legal order has found it necessary to abandon the strict requirements of universal sovereign consent.

Article 38 (1) (a) of the Statute has in a sense been disposed of and covered in connection with the discussion of the development of standards. This material, which was covered in the oral proceedings yesterday, would, in the Applicants' submission, be relevant here as well since it falls within the rubric paragraph (a) of Article 38(1) in the context of the development of a legal norm as well as the development of an international standard.

The Applicants have sought to demonstrate that international practice in conjunction with the human rights and non-discrimination provisions and purposes of the United Nations Charter, and of the Constitution of the I. L. O., have evolved authoritative standards of non-discrimination and non-separation; and, as I have said, the same evidence, the same materials, the same sources, support the Applicants' contention that these standard-creating procedures have eventuated in an international legal norm of the same content and scope.

The essence of the position is that the articles in question, Articles 55 (c) and 56, impose legal duties susceptible of definition by a consensus of the membership of the Organization when such consensus, as in this case, approaches unanimity and, indeed, in many resolutions, actual unanimity but for the sole dissenting vote and voice of the Respondent itself.

Specifically in this context, the formal acts of the constituent organs of the United Nations have produced an authoritative construction of Articles 55 (c) and 56 of the Charter, *inter alia,* such that the practice of apartheid is legally impermissible. Thus, the norm of non-discrimination and non-separation emanates from the Charter itself and is binding upon Respondent as a treaty norm within the meaning of Article 38 (1) (a).

With regard to Article 38 (1) (b)—international custom, as evidence of a general practice accepted as law—the Applicants respectfully submit the following.

Sub-section (b) of Article 38, paragraph 1, says nothing about unanimous consent as a prerequisite to the coming into being of a customary norm. It does not posit that practice must be universally accepted, nor that all States in their sovereign capacity must accept this practice as law. The language of paragraph 1 (b) is more in accord with the view that custom of a preponderant majority of States may in appropriate situations generate norms.

In common parlance, a custom may develop and exist despite objection during its period of emergence. So long as international society was highly decentralized it was necessary to rest law-creating procedures on State practice. With the growth of an organized international community, with constituent organs, it is increasingly reasonable to regard the collective acts of the competent international institutions as evidence of general practice accepted as law.

The resolutions of the General Assembly identifying apartheid as contrary to the Charter and to international law are, accordingly, relevant to an appraisal by the Court of the Applicants' contention that Respondent's policies violate an international legal norm of non-discrimination and non-separation.

As was noted in an authoritative work on the Charter of the United Nations, by that title—*Charter of the United Nations*—in the revised edition, at page 457: this is the well-known work by Goodrich and Hambro:

> All the various organs of the United Nations will simultaneously be engaged in thus interpreting different provisions of the Charter and will build up the practice which will gradually assume the character of customary law.

Where, as here, there is virtually unanimous agreement among the various organs as to the impermissible and illegal character of Respondent's policy, the views just quoted from the work of these learned authorities assume even more persuasive force.

* * *

Traditional doctrine concerning the formation of customary international law, both as it has been formulated by this Court and by international jurists, has encountered a difficulty, already mentioned, arising from the concept that sovereign States are bound only by rules to which they give their consent, either expressly or tacitly, the argument being that custom rests on tacit consent or at least on acquiescense or the absence of protest. Thus, the International Law Commission has stated, [and] I quote from the *Yearbook of the International Law Commission,* vol. I, 1950, at page 275, as follows:

> The emergence of a principle of rule of custom in international law is generally thought to require presence of the following elements: concordant practice by a number of States with reference to a situation falling within the domain of international relations; continuation or repetition of the practice over some period of time; conception by the States engaged that the practice is not forbidden by prevailing international law; and general acquiescence in the practice by States other than those engaged.

Such a formulation clearly is meshed with the emergence of customary international law as a consequence of State practice, rather than as a result of the form standard and norm-setting processes of the organized international community, through its competent organs. As such, the statement just quoted overlooks the centralization of the normative process in international society resulting from the existence and the expanding role and the ever-increasing importance of a decisive nature of the international institutions themselves. It is principally in the light of such an expanding role, and its peculiar relevance to the norm contended for by the Applicants that makes it appropriate to judge in these proceedings, that a broad interpretation of Article 38, paragraph 1, of the Statute, especially sub-section (b) applies to and governs the establishment of an international legal norm of the character described and which has particular reference to the territory under mandate.

* * *

In the *Asylum* case, *I. C. J. Reports 1950,* at page 266, as the Court will be aware, of course, the subject matter in dispute involved the existence of a norm in the field of human rights; there an unreviewable discretion on the part of a State to grant asylum in its Embassy to a political fugitive. The Court held, I quote from page 276, that:

> The Party which relies on a custom of this kind must prove that this custom is established in such a manner that it has become binding on the other Party. The Colombian Government must prove that the rule invoked by it is in accordance with the constant and uniform usage practised by the States in question, and that this usage is the expression of a right appertaining to the State granting asylum and a duty incumbent on the territorial State.

Notwithstanding the phrase just quoted, "constant and uniform usage," the Court rejected the claim of customary norm on the ground, and I quote here again, this time from page 231 of the Opinion, that—

> The facts brought to the knowledge of the Court disclose so much uncertainty and contradiction, so much fluctuation and discrepancy in the exercise of diplomatic asylum and in the official views expressed on various occasions, there has been so much inconsistency in the rapid succession of conventions on asylum, ratified by some States and rejected by others, and the practice has been so much influenced by considerations of political expediency in the various cases, that it is not possible to

discern in all this any constant and uniform usage, accepted as law, with regard to the alleged rule of unilateral and definitive qualification of the offense.

It would be difficult to find a case in which the situation from a factual and legal point of view is more in contrast than the pattern described in the passage just quoted from the *Asylum* case. The *Asylum* case involved an adjustment of directly competing interests of States. On the other hand, indeed to the contrary, the norm of non-discrimination and non-separation involves the promotion of common interests and collective interests of States, and of the organized international community taken as a whole. These are, moreover, common interests which rest upon a widely shared and deeply felt and often eloquently expressed humanitarian conviction. In this respect apartheid corresponds to genocide, and the nature of the law-creating process in response to both has been remarkably similar: one in which the collective will of the international community has been shocked into virtual unanimity, and in which the moral basis of law is most visible. It is precisely because there is an offender that there has been a drive to create a norm. If the offender is allowed to avoid the legal condemnation of his action by stating a protest, then international law is rendered impotent in the face of a grave challenge to the values underlying the international social order.

In the *Fisheries* case the Court affirmed, as I have said, that "the ten-mile rule would appear inapplicable as against Norway inasmuch as she has always opposed any attempt to apply it to the Norwegian coast." But the Court emphasized many other factors as well, including Norway's long historical claims, its peculiar economic dependence on fisheries, the general toleration of other States, and the acquiescence by Great Britain, the other party, itself over a long period of time. Here again the alleged customary norm was a matter of adjusting directly competing or conflicting interests of States differently situated, littoral States versus maritime States; it did not involve the enforcement of a world community standard against a sole dissenter who is moreover discharging responsibilities on behalf of that very community. The proof of custom appropriate to the evolution of a customary norm of international law of this character is a consensus manifest from the formal acts of the competent organs of the international community. Such a law-creating procedure is a functional requirement of the contemporary order, even given the rudimentary nature of the collective processes now existing. Such a procedure parallels the evolution of custom by State practice, which is ascertained by the inter-action of States. Here it is generated through expressions manifesting a collective judgment, a collective will. The Court in the past has been faced essentially with claims alleging the existence of norms arising out of State inter-action. It is in this respect that the Applicants may perhaps appropriately refer to this case as rare in the annals of this Court or its predecessor, inasmuch as the background of precedents, two of which I have cited, is less relevant than might at first appear from the generality of the language traditionally used by this

Court and its predecessor in cases involving the conflicting or competing interests of States and the inter-action of States.

The late Judge Sir Hersch Lauterpacht suggested that concepts of sovereign consent and universality, if taken literally, would impoverish the dynamic possibilities for the growth of international law, as well as undercut much of the law in being. The learned author asked and responded to a revealing rhetorical question—I quote from his work *The Development of International Law by the International Court of Justice,* 1958, pages 191–192, as follows:

> If universal acceptance alone is the hall-mark of the existence of a rule of international law, how many rules of international law can there be said to be in effective existence? Any such acceptance of the standard of universality as the test of the existence of a rule of international law may be open to the objection that it puts into question the existence of most rules and principles of international law. For this would appear to be the result of a judicial method which declines to treat a widely adopted practice as constituting accepted international law and which elevates the attitude of a small number of States to the authority of a practice entitled to equal—or greater—respect.

Respondent's insistence that its protest should be permitted to obstruct the formation of a legal norm, even in a context in which the world community has an interest as manifest as in the Mandate, would seem to paralyze the dynamic aspects of international supervision by allowing the Mandatory's objection to freeze the content of Article 2, paragraph 2, the core and essence of the sacred trust itself. Such a discretion vested in a mandatory may be exercised with appropriate appreciation of the relevance of the will of the organized international community on the issue whether or not the norm contended for by the Applicants actually exists. Such an appreciation, if taken together with Judge Lauterpacht's advocacy of "predominance" rather than "universality" as the measure of general practice and acceptance by nations, makes out an overwhelming case for the Court to acknowledge the existence of the norm of non-discrimination and non-separation as a matter of customary international law, and once so acknowledged, makes its application to the Mandate a *per se* matter, in the Applicants' submission.

Article 38(1)(c): ". . . the general principles of law recognized by civilized nations."

* * *

In the jurisprudence of the Court "The general principles of law" have been generally used to fill in gaps in international law by relying upon private law analogies, based upon legal rules and institutions commonly found in municipal legal systems. As such, Article 38 (1) (c) provides a way to enrich international law on the basis of what may be called comparative law research. There is no tradition, as with customary international law, of premising the existence of a general principle of law upon evidence of universality, or the absence of any protest, or upon a sense of obligation with respect to the duty. As such, it is the source of law least closely tied to the ideas of legal obligation associated with the approach of legal positivism In this regard Article 38 (1)(c) has frequently been identified as the manner by which the perspectives of natural law can be most easily accommodated in a developing international system. But in addition, in relation to Article 38 (1)(c), it would seem most appropriate for the Court to confirm the role of consensus as manifest in the formal acts and proceedings of the competent organs of the international community as a source or basis of international legal norms.

In this respect there would be two ways in which Article 38 (1) (c) might establish, or at least strengthen, the Applicants' contention that a legal norm of non-discrimination and non-separation has come into being in international society. The first would be to regard the presence of laws and regulations against racial discrimination and segregation in the municipal systems of virtually every State as establishing, by comparative law analysis, an essential precondition for the assertion of the norm of non-discrimination and non-separation as a "general principle of law," within the meaning of Article 38 (1) (c).

The second approach might be to regard the international consensus, as, for example, evidenced in the Reply at pages 274–291, as a general principle of law recognized by civilized nations everywhere in the world. Such an approach would view the interpretation of the sub-divisions of Article 38 in light of the needs of the developing international legal order, giving to Article 38 a dynamic content, and thereby giving full scope to the fact that the Statute of the Court is an integral part of the Charter of the United Nations and is itself capable of, and entitled to, the same flexible principles of interpretation as have been applied to the remaining provisions of the Charter itself. This of course applies with even greater force to the Mandate Instrument and international regime. The Statute of the Court, as an integral portion of the Charter, underscores the point that this Court itself is formally constituted as an institutional component of the organized international community, thereby making it highly appropriate to give effect to the law-creating processes active in other segments of this same international community, of which the Court is the high judicial tribunal.

All legal systems, of course, have evolved from some social consensus on matters of basic social rights and duties. International law has developed and established much of its content by crystallizations of the *jus gentium* or consensus *gentium*, if we may use that phrase, in the period of its growth over the centuries which preceded the formulation of Article 38 of the Statute.

* * *

Mr. Rosenne has come to the following conclusion concerning the character of Article 38 (1) (c):

> These instances show that the 'general principles of law recognized by civilized nations' are not so much generalizations reached by application of comparative law . . . as particularizations of a common underlying sense of what is just in the

circumstances. Having an independent existence, their validity as legal norms does not derive from the consent of the parties as such, provided they are norms which the Court considers civilized States ought to recognize. (*The International Court of Justice*, p. 423.)

This, of course, is a conception of Article 38(1)(c) which demonstrates the relevance of general principles of law to (a) the acceptance of the consensus of the organized international community as a source of international legal norms, and (b) a construction on a *per se* basis of the meaning and intent of Article 2(2) of the Mandate in question here.

International crimes, such as piracy, evidence processes by which the international community has *acted as a whole* to uphold its *common* interests, making use of norms and standards in those cases to confer an extraordinary power of jurisdiction upon member States and nation States. In the absence of international institutions, the manner of dealing with common danger historically has been the expansion of the normal competence of States, making each, in this sense, an agent of the whole, and to count upon decentralized actions, uncoordinated actions, discontinuous actions of self-help to realize the common interest of the world, for example, in the suppression of crimes such as piracy.

* * *

Similarly, the international crime of genocide has come to be accepted as part of the law of nations. Without an extended discussion of this point, the prohibition of genocide rests principally upon generality of practice, reinforced by a moral consensus and by a common set of interests in the suppression of that offence. The Court's Advisory Opinion in the case of *Reservations to the Convention on the Prevention of Punishment of Genocide* states:

The origins of the Convention show that it was the intention of the United Nations to condemn and punish genocide as 'a crime under international law' involving a denial of the right of existence of entire human groups, a denial which shocks the conscience of mankind and results in great losses to humanity, and which is contrary to moral law and to the spirit and aims of the United Nations (Resolution 96 (1) of the General Assembly 11 December 1946). The first consequence arising from this conception is that the principles underlying the Convention are principles which are recognized by civilized nations as binding on States, even without any conventional obligation. A second consequence is the universal character both of the condemnation of genocide and of the cooperation required 'in order to liberate mankind from such an odious scourge' (Preamble to the Convention). (*I. C. J. Reports 1951*, p. 23.)

The foregoing passage is relevant to the issues now before the Court. The Court relied there, in the *Genocide Convention* case, upon a General Assembly resolution to construe the character of an international legal norm presented for consideration and, furthermore, the Court found it legally relevant to discuss the impact of genocide upon the conscience of mankind, the moral law, and the underlying spirit, purposes and aims of the United Nations itself. Furthermore, it is apparent from the quoted language that the Court regarded genocide as violative of international law even without the convention then before it. The law-creating process operative in the context of genocide seems clearly, in the opinion of the Court, to have been the manifest will of the organized international community.

It is, of course, true that when the Genocide Convention came before the Court no State was defending the practice of genocide. Respondent, of course, today stoutly defends the practice of apartheid.

The result of taking universality as a literal precondition of law formation is to make the organized international community incapable *in law* of taking action against an existing practice or policy, notwithstanding the self-evident fact that it is universally condemned.

General principles of law, for reasons set forth in the discussion just now presented to the Court, seem to the Applicants to provide a juridically sound basis where a decision that the international standard of non-discrimination and non-separation does qualify with the status of a legal norm. But, even if the Court should reject the international legal norm, as such, as a general principle of international law recognized by civilized nations within the meaning of Article 38 paragraph 1(c), this source of law, nevertheless, would provide in any event the basis for an interpretation of Article 2, paragraph 2, which would establish the practice of apartheid as a *per se* violation in the light of the international standards for which the Applicants contend and which are confirmed and demonstrated by precisely the same considerations upon which the Applicants vest their case for the establishment of an international legal norm, as well.

* * *

The juristic background for the Applicants' theory of the case has been developed fully and explicitly in the writings of Dr. Jenks, to whom I have already referred, and in our view most clearly and persuasively in an essay by Dr. Jenks entitled "The Will of the World Community as the Basis of Obligation in International Law" in his work entitled *Law, Freedom and Welfare* (1963). Dr. Jenks' concept of the will of the international community is equivalent to and analogous to the Applicants' reliance upon consensus as a basis of international legal obligation. In this regard it may be appropriate to call to the attention of the Court the recent decision by the United States Supreme Court in the well-known case *Banco Nacional de Cuba v. Sabbatino*, 376 United States 398 decided in 1964.

In conclusion of this discussion of Article 38, paragraph 1, rubrics or sub-sections, I should like to read from the work of Dr. Jenks' *Law, Welfare and Freedom*, published in 1963, at page 93. In the context in which Dr. Jenks was demonstrating the possibilities, as the Applicants perceived the context, for accommodating law-creating by the organized international community within the three main sub-sections of Article 38 (1) of the Statute, Dr. Jenks writes as follows, at the cited page:

> The will of the community constitutes the basis of obligation but the law of the community comes into being by all the processes of legal development and growth known to mature legal systems. It is the will of the community that principles and

rules evolved in accordance with these processes of growth shall be regarded as binding. Treaty, custom, the general principles of law recognized by civilized nations, judicial precedent and the opinions of the most highly qualified publicists, all fall naturally into place as methods by which, in accordance with the will of the community, the law is developed to meet the changing and growing needs of an evolving society.

NOTES AND QUESTIONS

1. If you were a judge on the Court, how would you react to this line of argument? If you were responding on behalf of South Africa, what points would you emphasize?
2. Is the legal relevance of the will of the international community altered by the character of the arena? Does it matter that this is a judicial arena? How?
3. If the political organs of the United Nations are denied legislative competence by the Court, how will it be possible to generate new legal norms in contemporary international society? If legislative competence is confirmed, how will it be constrained in the interests of a dissenting state or states? Are there intermediate doctrinal lines available between a position of denial and one of affirmation with regard to the legislative competence of the General Assembly?

Judge Sir Percy Spender, current President of the ICJ, advanced a conservative view of the subject of Charter interpretation in a separate opinion in the Advisory Opinion, "Certain Expenses of the United Nations," *Reports of Judgments, Advisory Opinions and Orders* (International Court of Justice, 1962) pp. 195–197. See the Opinion of the Court, reprinted below in Chapter 10A. The argument as to the incompatibility between apartheid and the Charter rests in large upon the role of the practice of the Organization in providing the basis for an authoritative interpretation of human rights provisions, especially Articles 55(c) and 56. In the very brief excerpt taken from Sir Percy's Opinion, the learned Judge argues against giving any weight to subsequent practice in the interpretation of Charter obligations:

(Excerpts from)

SEPARATE OPINION OF JUDGE SIR PERCY SPENDER IN THE CASE OF THE CERTAIN EXPENSES OF THE UNITED NATIONS

Apart from a practice which is of a peaceful, uniform and undisputed character accepted in fact by all current Members, a consideration of which is not germane to the present examination, I accordingly entertain considerable doubt whether practice of an organ of the United Nations has any probative value either as providing evidence of the intentions of the original Member States or otherwise a criterion of interpretation. As presently advised I think it has none.

If however it has probative value, what is the measure of its value before this Court?

An organ of the United Nations, whether it be the General Assembly, the Security Council, the Economic and Social Council, the Secretariat or its subsidiary organs, has in practice to interpret its authority in order that it may effectively function. So, throughout the world, have countless governmental and administrative organs and officials to interpret theirs. The General Assembly may thus in practice, by majority vote, interpret Charter provisions as giving it authority to pursue a certain course of action. It may continue to give the same interpretation to these Charter provisions in similar or different situations as they arise. In so doing action taken by it may be extended to cover circumstances and situations which had never been contemplated by those who framed the Charter. But this would not, for reasons which have already been given, necessarily involve any departure from the terms of the Charter.

On the other hand, the General Assembly may in practice construe its authority beyond that conferred upon it, either expressly or impliedly, by the Charter. It may, for example, interpret its powers to permit it to enter a field prohibited to it under the Charter or in disregard of the procedure prescribed in the Charter. Action taken by the General Assembly (or other organs) may accordingly on occasions be beyond power.

The Charter establishes an Organization. The Organization must function through its constituted organs. The functions and authorities of those organs are set out in the Charter. However the Charter is otherwise described the essential fact is that it is a multilateral treaty. It cannot be altered at the will of the majority of the Member States, no matter how often that will is expressed or asserted against a protesting minority and no matter how large be the majority of Member States which assert its will in this manner or how small the minority.

It is no answer to say that the protesting minority has the choice of remaining in or withdrawing from the Organization and that if it chooses to remain or because it pays its contributions according to apportionment under Article 17 (2) the Members in the minority "acquiesce" in the practice or must be deemed to have done so. They are bound to pay these contributions and the minority has a right to remain in the Organization and at the same time to assert what it claims to be any infringement of its rights under the Charter or any illegal use of power by any organ of the United Nations.

In practice, if the General Assembly (or any organ) exceeds its authority there is little that the protesting minority may do except to protest and reserve its rights whatever they may be. If, however, the authority purported to be exercised against the objection of any Member State is beyond power it remains so.

So, if the General Assembly were to "intervene in matters which are essentially within the domestic jurisdiction of any State" within the meaning of Article 2 (7) of the Charter, whatever be the meaning to be given to these words, that intervention would be the entering into a field prohibited to it under the Charter and be beyond the authority of the General Assembly. This would continue to be so, no matter how frequently and consistently the General Assembly had construed its authority to permit it to make intervention in matters essentially within the domestic jurisdiction of any States. The majority has no power to extend, alter or disregard the Charter.

Each organ of the United Nations, of course, has an inherent right to interpret the Charter in relation to its authority and functions. But the rule that they may do so is not in any case applicable without qualification. Their interpretation of their respective authorities under the Charter may conceivably conflict one with the other. They may agree. They may, after following a certain interpretation for many years, change it. In any case, their right to interpret the Charter gives them no power to alter it.

The question of constitutionality of action taken by the General Assembly or the Security Council will rarely call for consideration except within the United Nations itself, where a majority rule prevails. In practice this may enable action to be taken which is beyond power. When, however, the Court is called upon to pronounce upon a question whether certain authority exercised by an organ of the Organization is within the power of that organ, only legal considerations may be invoked and *de facto* extension of the Charter must by disregarded.

* * *

Once a request for an Advisory Opinion is made to this Court and it decides to respond to that request, the question on which the Opinion has been sought passes, as is claimed by the Republic of France in its written statement in this case, on to the legal plane and takes on a new character, in the determination of which legal considerations and legal considerations only may be invoked.

In the present case, it is sufficient to say that I am unable to regard any usage or practice followed by any organ of the United Nations which has been determined by a majority therein against the will of a minority as having any legal relevance or probative value.

(Signed) Percy C. SPENDER.

The same issues are developed by Oscar Schachter, Director of the General Legal Division of the United Nations Secretariat since 1953, in the course of a series of lectures delivered at the Hague Academy in 1963. In these lectures, "The Relation of Law, Politics and Action in the United Nations," *Recueil des Cours*, vol. II (A. W. Sijthoff, Leyden, 1963) pp. 171–200, Schachter develops an approach that is, in addition, relevant and useful to the whole subject of law and the United Nations, both with respect to law in the activities of the Organization, and with respect to the activities of the Organization as an independent source of law.

OSCAR SCHACHTER

THE RELATION OF LAW, POLITICS AND ACTION IN THE UNITED NATIONS

LAW AND THE PROCESS OF DECISION IN THE POLITICAL ORGANS OF THE UNITED NATIONS

The first question to which I shall address myself is whether the normative structure of the United Nations—in particular, as expressed in the purposes and principles of the Charter—constitutes a significant element in the decisions of its political organs and in the achievement of its main objectives. The issue is sometimes put more sharply: of what use are legal principles in the conditions of crisis, deep-seated mistrust, the bipolar concentration of power and the demands for radical change that characterize the intensely political atmosphere of the United Nations?

The inadequacies of the legal process in the United Nations have received much emphasis. International lawyers have frequently drawn attention to the absence of mandatory judicial or other impartial third party procedures governed by legal rules. They have taken it for granted that in the political bodies—the General Assembly and the Security Council—Governments act and decide for reasons of power or expediency, even though the issues may be formulated in terms of legal norms.[2] The references to law common in the debates are regarded as merely rhetorical, fig leaves to cover the play of power and interest, and at times as a deception, destructive of law observance.[3]

Some international lawyers have also laid stress on the generality, even the vacuity, of the stated principles and standards of the Charter. They cite as evidence the multitude of conflicting

2. C. Eagleton, "The United Nations: A Legal Order?" in Law and Politics in the World Community, (ed. G. A. Lipsky, 1953) pp. 129 ff; Ch. de Visscher, Theory and Reality in Public International Law (Corbett trans. 1957) pp. 113-114, 146-147; J. Robinson, "Metamorphosis of the United Nations" in 94 Recueil des Cours (1958) pp. 560-581.

3. Bin Cheng "International Law in the United Nations" in 8 Yearbook of World Affairs (London University 1954) pp. 170 et seq; Dean Acheson in 1963 Proc. Am. Soc. Int. Law; J. Stone, Aggression and World Order (1958) pp. 104 ff.

interpretations, especially those regarding the crucial rule against the use of force and the frequently invoked principles of self-determination and human rights. The fact that those and other principles may be paired off with their apparent "opposites"—each pointing to different conclusions in specific cases—has been regarded as proof that decisions are necessarily taken on the basis of political interests and preferences rather than legal criteria.[4]

There have been also the arguments of the "Realpolitiker"—who emphasize the inevitable weakness of law and international authority in the face of power and the widespread assault on the status quo.[5] For them, law in the United Nations must necessarily be restricted to the minor and somewhat technical rules imposed by requirements of international intercourse and sanctioned mainly by considerations of reciprocity. In regard to the major issues, some would conclude that it is preferable to do away with the pretense of legality so as to avoid illusion and confusion. It would be better, as they see it, to make it clear that the highsounding norms of the Charter cannot be taken seriously until we have achieved the kind of integrated world community which has a common ethos and consequently is prepared to accept as binding the decisions of impartial international organs.

All of these positions contain elements of truth and understandably appeal to the sceptical temper of the contemporary international lawyer and political scientist. Yet they ignore significant aspects of the United Nations; in particular it seems to me they underestimate the extent to which its constitutional and procedural norms influence political proceedings and contribute to the development and observance of international law.

Normative Conceptions in Political Organs

It may be useful to begin with some observations on the role and procedure of the main political bodies of the United Nations. These organs understandably have evoked diverse images: they

4. Kelsen, Law of the United Nations, (1950) Preface on Interpretation pp. xiii et seq.; J. Stone "What Price Effectiveness" in 1956 Proc. Am. Soc. Int. Law, pp. 198 et seq.
5. Corbett, Law and Society in the Relation of States (1951) pp. 11, 75 ff.; Schwarzenberger, Power Politics (2d ed. 1951) at pp. 203, 206, 713; Morgenthau, In Defense of the National Interest (1951) pp. 101, 102, 144.

seem to behave at times like parliaments, on occassion like courts, most frequently as arenas for propaganda or diplomatic negotiation. Each one of these images has its obvious functional counterpart and each accordingly has a partial validity. But the various functions are not sharply differentiated and the representatives are not required to play their parts in the manner of a character actor who adopts a new guise as he moves from role to role. They are expected at all times to act as representatives of Governments and to further the interests of those Governments, whatever may be the specific issue at stake.

Yet as we look more closely at their functions and the kinds of decisions they take it becomes apparent that the "furthering of interests" may involve more than calculations of power and expediency. For we must remember that the activities in the political organs take place in the framework of a fairly well defined system, characterized by expressly stated common values, by a process of interaction and by collective decisions which are related, at least verbally, to the accepted values and goals. The individual participants naturally act within the terms of the system. They employ the common vocabulary of the Charter principles and purposes to justify their positions and conduct. They conform to the rules of procedure in seeking their objectives and they rely on agreements and established practice in adopting their strategies and tactics. The outcomes sought are those which are believed to fall within the patterns of decision laid down by the Charter and related constitutional practice. In short, within this system the pursuit of their particular interests by Governments is inevitably influenced by the norms of that system and the attitudes as to legitimacy and propriety that arise from it.

This may seem fairly obvious when stated in these terms but it is often overlooked by those who lay stress on the "conflict" between law and politics, and the opposition between "obligation" and self-interest. This difference in approach seems to me to be of significance in understanding United Nations decisions (as well as political decisions in a wider context) and I should like to make quite clear what I mean. For one thing, I do *not* mean to suggest that there are no conflicts or choices between obligation and self-interest. Obviously in many particular situations government officials have to face a choice between following a course of action which they believe is called for by the "law" and one that does not conform to legal prescription but appears required for other reasons. At the same time it is quite evident that conceptions of what is "legal", "right" and "appropriate" do play a role in shaping the proceedings and their outcome in regard to various questions. To see this we must generally look at a whole series of decisions rather than merely a single case since it is the uniformities and patterns that most clearly exhibit the attitudes as to what is or is not permissible and legitimate. The single case is rarely decisive; it is like trying to establish a point of social etiquette by examining one or two controversial situations instead of seeking the rule in the repetitive patterns of relevant acts and communications. I am not, of course, suggesting that mere repetition establishes the normative rules; an essential element is that the patterns of decisions made over a period of time exhibit the psychological element of "opinio juris", whether such opinion is based on the Charter, international convention, customary law or general principles accepted as law.

If we consider the broad stream of decisions (together with related communications and conduct) that have come from the United Nations political bodies, we can readily identify a number of subjects in regard to which conceptions of legality can be seen to have played a significant part. These questions include, for example:

(1) questions of the competence of the political organs to discuss and deal with various matters of state conduct;[6]

(2) questions of the participation or exclusion of certain territorial communities in the international decision process;[7]

6. As for example the questions of competence raised in regard to Apartheid in South Africa or the Question of Algeria. See vol. I U.N. Repertory of Practice (1955) and Supp. No. 1 (1958). Studies in Art. 2 para. 7. Also Vallat "The Competence of the United Nations General Assembly" in 97 Recueil des Cours (1959) 207-292.

7. As for example, questions raised in regard to admission of Mongolia, Ceylon, et al and in regard to participation of Eastern Germany, and other "divided" countries. See R. Higgins, The Development of International Law Through the Political Organs of the United Nations (1963), pp. 11-57; Rosenne, "Recognition of States by the U.N.", 26 Brit. Y. Bk. Int. Law (1949), pp. 427 ff; C. H. Alexandrowicz, "The Quasi-Judicial Function in Recognition of States and Governments", 46 Am. J. Int. L. (1952) pp. 631-640.

(3) questions relating to the material resources (e.g., military, financial and personnel) that may be utilized under international direction to achieve objectives determined by the Organization;[8]

(4) questions relating to the authority of the international organ to obtain information regarding events in national States and to discuss and evaluate such data in terms of international objectives and principles;[9]

(5) questions of whether agreed general norms—such as those relating to the use of force or human rights—apply to the conduct of states in particular situations and circumstances;[10]

(6) questions of projecting—either by recommendation or agreement—new norms of state conduct of a more specific character than those stated in the Charter and general international law.[11]

These six categories do not of course exhaust the list but they are important examples of subjects which have been dealt with by the political organs and which—as their terms show—necessarily involve considerations of a normative and legal character.

In pointing out that attitudes as to legitimacy and propriety inevitably play a role in the political decision process I do not intend to imply that the Governments are not also concerned with, and influenced by, other considerations involving their own advantage and national sympathies. We must accept the fact that Governments in political organs as elsewhere take into account a variety of considerations and are subjected to a multitude of influences bearing on the positions they adopt. It is as unrealistic to believe that considerations of law are necessarily given priority as to assert that they are invariably mere rationalizations without influence on the decisions. However, to

8. For example, issues raised in regard to UNEF and the Congo. See Adv. Op. of Int. Court of Justice of July 20, 1962 on "Certain Expenses of the United Nations", I.C.J. Reports, 1962, pp. 151 et seq. For further discussion, chapters III and IV of these lectures.

9. See U.N. Repertory of Practice (1955), Vol. IV on Article 73 (re non-self-governing territories). See also discussions relating to inquiry on "forced labor", Repertory ibid., Vol. III, study on Articles 55 and 62.

10. As for example questions in regard to Suez, Hungary, Apartheid and Treatment of Indians in South Africa. See Vallat op. cit. n. 6 and R. Higgins op. cit. n. 7, pp. 167-221.

11. See Gen. Assem. resolutions 1721 (XVI) on outer space, 1653 (XVI) on nuclear weapons and 1803 (XVII) on permanent sovereignty over natural resources. Also reports of Sixth Committee 17th sess. on "Principles of Int. Law concerning friendly relations and cooperation among States" G.A.O.R., 17th sess., agenda item No. 75, Doc. A/5356.

attempt to assess the relative importance of various factors in the whole decision process (or for that matter in any important segment or series of cases) is a task of vast complexity and one that I shall not attempt.

It seems to me we must take for granted the multiplicity of factors and influences and the uncertainties as to their relative priority in actual decision making. But this should not preclude us from undertaking the more limited, and probably more useful, task of trying to understand clearly the process of "authoritative decision" in political organs and the ways in which legal prescriptions influence that process.

From the General to the Specific

It has often been observed that the acceptance of standards of legitimacy and propriety (especially among States with different social systems and in different stages of political and economic development) is limited largely to highly general norms. Clearly, there is a remarkable identity in the formulation of the major legal prescriptions accepted by all States; all tend to employ the terms of the United Nations Charter in proclaiming their own aims and obligations in matters of international concern.

But this identity and consensus do not appear to go beyound the highly abstract level of Charter principles on most matters of importance. On a more specific level, sharp cleavages exist both in regard to rules of a lower order of generality and in respect of judgments and attitudes concerning particular cases. One can readily think of examples in the first category which have been the subject of much controversial discussion in U.N. bodies: the criteria of aggression, principles governing use of outer space, the declaration on permanent sovereignty over natural resources (particularly in regard to acquired rights and responsibility in cases of nationalization), and the norms for international trade and economic cooperation. In the second category, the specific cases, one has only to recall some of the major U.N. controversies: notably, those relating to Cuba, Goa, Hungary, Suez, Katanga, to appreciate the gulf between agreement on principles and disagreement on the interpretation and application of these principles in concrete situations. In addition to these differences, it is also apparent that there is often a wide discrepancy between the proclaimed norms and actual conduct, although opinions would of course differ as to which governments have departed from the norms to a greater extent than others and the degree of justification for such deviations.

While these observations may seem pessimistic as to the role of law, they do not tell the whole story and for that we must look rather more closely at the way in which legal principles are used in concrete cases.

When a government proposes an item for consideration by a U.N. organ, it necessarily asserts or implies a position relative to one or more legal propositions. At the very least, it is claiming that the U.N. organ has the competence (the "jurisdiction") to deal with that item. This in itself is often a complex legal assertion, since it may—and indeed normally does—presuppose first that the issue raised falls within the terms of a Charter provision and second that the organ has the authority to take some kind of decision or action to meet the problem. Even on this relatively simple level, one can readily see that the mere proposal of an agenda item implies the submission of normative issues; the "law", so to speak, is being invoked.

That contention may of course involve no more than a fairly well settled and non-controversial point. On the other hand, it may concern a basic norm and a highly unsettled and controversial issue. Illustration of this can easily be found in the hotly disputed debates on "competence" characteristic of the whole series of colonial cases (beginning with the Indonesian dispute in 1947) and of the running controversies regarding human rights, especially those concerned with South Africa.[12] Moreover, in many, if not most, of the "peace and security" cases, the issue of competence has similarly focussed on controversies as to the specific meaning and application of the Charter prescriptions, especially those relating to the use of force, self-defense and domestic jurisdiction.[13] In all of these classes of situations which involve the conduct of a State on matters which it considers "vital" and within its authority, the simple submission of an agenda item almost necessarily entails a controversial assertion regarding the specific import of a Charter obligation. In fact,

12. References to the legal contentions may be found in the U.N. Repertory of Practice (1955) and Supplements in studies of Articles 2 (7), 10, 11, 14, 55 interalia.

13. See U.N. Repertory of Practice (1955) and Supplements, Studies of Articles 2 (4), 39 and 51. See also Higgins, op. cit. n. 7.

one must add that rarely, if ever, is a single obligation involved; generally one finds that a whole set of related principles have been relied upon by different groups of States in support of their conduct and positions. (Perhaps I should parenthetically observe that it is an unwarranted simplification to conceive of these controversies arising in regard to "competence" as necessarily involving sharp choices between an international interest and a national interest. To be sure, in many cases this may be a useful perspective but we must bear in mind that the legal prescriptions invoked against international competence may themselves express international aims which are entitled to consideration and appropriate application in deciding the specific issue).

A significant point is that when these issues relating to competence come before a collective body of diverse points of view, such as the General Assembly and the Security Council, the issues can no longer remain on the highly abstract level of the Charter principles. To the casual observer they may often still appear to be on that level since so much of the debate consists of repetition of Charter phrases and simple assertion that policies and conduct either conform to or deviate from the general principles.

However, if one examines the proceedings more closely, it becomes apparent that the repetitious references to Charter norms are also accompanied by references to and descriptions of specific practices which are explained and justified in terms of the basic values considered to be expressed in the Charter principles. In short, the necessities of the collective procedures have imposed a more concrete level of discourse and justification.

Thus, Governments asserting U.N. competence to take up violations of human rights in regard to specific areas such as South Africa or practices such as forced labour have usually had to support the jurisdictional basis for their claims by specifying the actions considered to constitute deviations from the Charter conception of human rights and fundamental freedoms. The Governments which are opposed to U.N. consideration or which have doubts will respond similarly by citing specific events and practices in their country or elsewhere. The discussion thus moves from the mere reiteration of broad principles to a more concrete level of facts and evaluations of facts thought to be relevant to the general norms.[14] As a result of this confrontation on the more factual level, the organ may undertake further inquiries through its own multilateral procedures or through its international officials. This has been done in most of the major controversies regarding human rights and self-determination and has often been the procedure followed in peace and security cases.[15] As a consequence of these organizational inquiries, the factual accounts—since they are no longer unilateral and have now been subjected to public scrutiny—acquire a more authoritative character. (There are, of course, variations in practice; an inquiry might have been so dominated by an idée fixe that its results would not receive wide acceptance). But whether or not there are investigations by the organ or its subsidiary, the whole process of consideration in the organ generates a wealth of assertions and observations which are evidence of the attitudes and convictions of the Governments regarding the more specific meaning of the Charter norms and of other general formulations of international law. The importance of this in regard to the development and strengthening of international law, has, in my view, been largely overlooked by international lawyers and I should like to place considerable emphasis on it. There are several aspects which merit attention.

The Significance of Multipartisan Proceedings

The first aspect has to do not merely with the fact but with the significance of what I have referred to as a "more concrete level of discourse and justification." Surely, some may say, this only shows that States agree on the "law" in general terms but differ on the facts or the modalities of application. But the process of "specification" involves a good deal more than this. It is, for one thing, a creative process which establishes a relation between the conceptual framework and the "operational" activity, between the basic principles and the specific practices. This can

14. In regard to South Africa, see for example debates at General Assembly 9th sess. (1954) 511th mtg. and Ad Hoc Pol. Comm. Mtgs 42-47 (1954); 10th sess., Mtgs. 3-12 (1955)

15. For example, commissions of inquiry have reported on Greek Frontier Incidents, on withdrawal of troops in Korea, on the dispute between India and Pakistan, on the Racial Situation in South Africa, on Forced Labor, Repatriation of Prisoners of War, etc., etc.

be seen in almost all of the major areas of controversy—including those which are seemingly the most chaotic and "political".

One such example may be found in the consideration by the General Assembly of non-self-governing territories, a subject which has been singled out by many (especially in Western Europe) as revealing an excess of political emotionalism and a lack of concern with legal concepts. Yet the massive record of U.N. activity in this field reveals a considerable collective effort to relate such Charter concepts as self-government, political advancement, "just treatment" and others to a multitude of diverse institutional practices that have been empirically described. The proceedings indicate the extent and depth of this effort; almost every aspect of political and social life has been dealt with: educational opportunities, rights of women, penal conditions, representation in local government, access to lands, relative wage levels, collective bargaining, freedom of travel and so on.[16]

The important point is not simply that many facts have emerged but that institutions and practices have been linked to the objectives and legal concepts of the Charter in ways that facilitated further inquiry, criticism and conclusions. This is not to say that the elucidation of facts always brought about agreement between holders of diverse views; opinions would still differ as to whether a particular educational arrangement was a step toward self-government. However, it has been possible—as seen in the many recommendations on which there has been agreement—to establish a consensus on whether a given practice or arrangement served to develop or impede the evolution toward responsible self-government and the Charter goals. Whether or not such agreement was formalized in a resolution, the general consensus which can often be ascertained from the record is evidence of what the international community considers to be the concrete meaning of the Charter criteria in a specific context:

This can also be illustrated by reference to another subject which is somewhat more familiar to the international lawyer and which was dealt with in the General Assembly under the rubric of "permanent sovereignty over natural resources".

16. See for example, Gen. Assem. Off. Rec., 15th sess., Fourth Committee, Mtgs. 1005-1024; 16th sess., 4th Cttee. Mtgs. 1181-1188; 17th sess., 4th Cttee. Mtgs. 1409-1424.

Here the U.N. effort assumed a legislative form—it looked to the elaboration of "principles" which would apply to the relations of States and foreign business enterprise in the light of certain fundamental ideas and attitudes about the rights of "peoples" to self-determination in respect of their wealth and resources.[17] This approach was broadened in successive discussions to include the ideas (also linked to the Charter) regarding the interdependence of States in economic cooperation and their obligations under customary international law and international agreements.[18] After a decade of debate and surveys, the General Assembly adopted a declaration of principles—a declaration which achieved near-unanimity of support by its deference to diverse (and perhaps not entirely consistent) objectives aided by a measure of vagueness and equivocation.[19]

But it would be misleading to consider the declaration as the only outcome of the proceedings; it is in fact more like the upper part of the iceberg, by far the larger part remaining beneath the surface. This larger part, in my view, must be found in the whole record of the case, for those proceedings contain material bearing upon the contemporary attitudes of States toward their rights and obligations in regard to their resources. What is interesting is that these attitudes were justified by the participants—not so much in terms of "classic" rules of State responsibility or of ideological conceptions (although these too were employed) as on the basis of empirical data bearing on the relation between foreign enterprise and objectives of economic development and political independence. Thus data were introduced on the flow of private capital and technological know-how as factors in promoting higher standards of living; and on the other side, statistics were cited on the exclusion of indigenous inhabitants from arable land in certain areas and on the insufficiency of employment opportunities for them in foreign owned firms.[20]

17. Gen. Assem. res. 523 (VI) and 626 (VII)
18. Gen. Assem. res. 1314 (XIII)
19. Gen. Assem. res. 1803 (XVII)
20. See records of U.N. Commission on Permanent Sovereignty over Natural Resources, Third Session (1961), Docs. A/AC. 97/SR. 19-33. Also Gen. Assem. 17th sess., Second Committee Mtgs. 835, 850-860 (1962). See O. J. Lissitzyn, "International Law in a Divided World", International Conciliation, No. 542, (March 1963) pp. 40-49. J. N. Hyde, "Permanent Sovereignty over Natural Wealth and Resources", 50 Am. J. Int. Law (Oct. 1956) p. 854.

A voluminous report of the Secretariat similarly introduced facual material and information on legislation, treaties and administrative practice—all of which bore in some degree on the issues of State responsibility.[21] If it did nothing else, this material served to draw attention to the variety of problems and of institutional practices that are germane to the two main objectives of self-determination and economic well-being.

In the United Nations debates as well as outside them, such discussions of specific practices and empirical data are often characterized as political in a somewhat invidious sense. One reason for this is that the discussions appear to consist largely of self-serving material introduced to support a particular pre-determined point of view. But while this may be true, it does not follow that the proceedings are "merely" political in their consequences. There is an enormous difference between the consideration of these matters in a collective body and the making of unilateral statements in an unorganized context. In the U.N. organs, as we have seen, the expression of self-serving statements is subject to a process of scrutiny and appraisal. The fact that few, if any, of the participants are impartial or non-partisan does not eliminate their role as a "judging" element. Even if they have commitments and political interests they will be expected to, and they will in fact, pass judgement on the issues presented.

Moreover, the plurality of interests and political philosophies represented in a universal collective organ has a tendency to reduce the distinctive "ideological" content of the debate. This is not as paradoxical as it may seem; when appeals and arguments have to be addressed to groups who do not share the same ideologies, the discussion is more likely to be cast in terms of a shared vocabulary and widely accepted formulations of law and policy. Consequently the common normative element is given emphasis and more specific rules are proposed in language that reflects the broadly accepted concepts of the Charter and international law. This is illustrated in the discussion of "permanent sovereignty over resources" by the fact that the proposals which dealt with nationalization and private enterprise were not couched in the ideological language of socialism or capitalism.

21. U.N. Secretariat, Survey of the Permanent Sovereignty over Natural Wealth and Resources (U.N. Pub. Sales No. 62. V. 6).

They tended instead to use neutral phrases of a descriptive character or Charter phrases in expressing basic purposes and attitudes (as for example, sovereign and equal rights, respect for international law, and promotion of cooperation for economic development).

The important conclusion that can be drawn is that even though the United Nations organs are mainly arenas for the expression of political interests, their "multipartisan" character within a constitutional system results in a process of examination and evaluation of State behavior in terms of its conformity with the principles of the Charter and international law (as these norms are interpreted contemporaneously by diverse groups of States). Collective judgements are in fact being made as to what is legal and permissible and new, more specific legal norms are being elaborated to meet felt necessities. Whatever may be its shortcomings, the process of examination and evaluation constitutes a centralized institutional means on the international level for performing functions that in the national sphere are normally the province of judicial and legislative institutions. No one will maintain that these activities are adequate for the needs or that the procedures cannot be improved. But it can be suggested that international lawyers might look more sympathetically at the political organs of the United Nations and seek ways to clarify and strengthen the role of these bodies in furthering the growth of international law and its acceptance throughout the world.

II

LAW AND THE PROCESS OF DECISION IN THE POLITICAL ORGANS OF THE UNITED NATIONS (CONTINUED)

In the previous lecture, I endeavoured to show some ways in which the process of decision in the political organs is influenced by, and in turn influences, the normative conceptions of the international community. In the present lecture I shall continue with this theme and consider several problems which arise as a consequence of this interaction of law and politics and which bear especially on the complexities of interpretation and implementation of the Charter.

The Difference between Interpretation and Recommendation

It is perhaps useful at the outset to emphasize the distinction between the interpretation of the Charter and resolutions that are purely recommendatory. Typically, the U.N. political organs, in accordance with the Charter, submit "recommendations" to Governments, but an examination of such recommendations reveals that many of them are accompanied by assertions of legal rights and obligations under the Charter. Such assertions of law are advanced in the process of reaching recommendations; they may be stated in the resolutions or they may be implied from the consensus expressed in the debates. It is evident that these assertions are not themselves recommendatory; they are expressed by States or adopted by the organs as authoritative precepts derived from the Charter or accepted rules of international law. Frequently they set forth limitations on the competence or authority of the organs or procedures which they must follow; in some cases they are legal determinations of a substantive character which specify obligations of Members.[1]

The question of primary interest to the international lawyer has generally been the extent to which the interpretations reached by, or within, the political organs are to be regarded as legally authoritative when the organ has not been accorded the competence to make binding decisions. In considering this, one might start with the principle that an "authentic" interpretation of a treaty by the parties is legally binding on them to the same degree as the treaty itself.[2] I believe it is generally accepted that this conclusion would hold for an interpretation of the Charter adopted by all the Members (or even "by the overwhelming majority" except for some abstentions) in the General Assembly; the interpretation would be characterized by international lawyers as having the same legal force and effect as the Charter itself.[3] Moreover, there would seem to be no substantial reason why this conclusion would not be applied in cases where a virtually unanimous consensus in a matter of Charter interpretation is made known through statements and actions expressed separately by Governments either within or outside the United Nations, even though no vote is taken.[4]

1. *The Repertory of Practice of United Nations Organs* (U.N. Secretariat publication No. 1955 V. 2) contains for each article of the Charter the decisions and relevant statements on the meaning of that article. Examples of resolutions that assert substantive obligations based on the Charter may be found, inter alia, in regard to apartheid, colonialism, use of nuclear weapons, outer space, and sovereignty over natural resources. They will also be found in connection with specific disputes and situations involving peace and security. See R. Higgins, The Development of International Law Through the Political Organs of the United Nations (1963); Castaneda, "The Underdeveloped Nations and the Development of International Law", 15 Int. Org. (Winter 1961) 38, 44-48.
2. Oppenheim (Lauterpacht 7th ed.) International law, vol. 1, p. 857. Kelsen, The Law of the United Nations (1950) pp. xiii et seq.
3. See, Lachs "The Law in and of the United Nations" in 1 Indian Journal of International Law (April 1961) p. 429, 439. See Castaneda, op. cit. n. 1.
4. In the oft-quoted statement on the interpretation of the Charter made at the San Francisco Conference, it is said that if an interpretation "is not generally acceptable it will be without binding force", thus in effect recognizing that an interpretation receiving general approval will be authoritative and binding. See Report of the Rapporteur of Committee IV/2, UNCIO Doc. 933, IV/2/42, Vol. 13 p. 710.
It is generally agreed that authentic interpretation does not require a particular procedure. See Oppenheim n. 9 supra, Lachs n. 10 supra, Ehrlich, "L'interprétation des traités", 24 Recueil des Cours (1928) p. 36.

However, when the proceedings do not reveal a general consensus, and particularly when there is a substantial difference in points of view, the foregoing analysis does not apply. The usual distinction then drawn is that between an interpretation of a treaty which is considered to be binding because it has been accepted by all of the parties and an interpretation which is rejected by some and therefore would be regarded as effective only if the treaty should be amended accordingly.[5] This point is often bolstered by emphasizing that the political organs have not been granted authority to adopt binding decisions except in the limited cases covered by Chapter VII and certain organizational matters such as admission of members and financial assessments.[6]

I do not wish to take issue with this conclusion, but I would observe that it does not entirely settle the question of the authority of such interpretation. There are two qualifications to be considered. In the first place we must take account of generally accepted practice regarding the competence of the organs to decide definitively certain issues. For example, the right of the United Nations General Assembly to determine which territories fall within the scope of Article 73 has received such continuing support that it may now be regarded as fairly well settled.[7] My point here is that when the practice of states in the United Nations has served by general agreement to vest in the organs the competence to deal definitively with certain questions, then the decisions of the organs in regard to those questions acquire an authoritative juridical status even though these decisions had not been taken by unanimous decison or "general approval".[8]

5. See San Francisco statement on interpretation referred to supra n. 4 which states that an interpretation that has not been generally accepted would require a Charter amendment in order to be made binding.
6. I.C.J. Advisory Opinion of July 20, 1962 on "Certain Expenses of the United Nations." I.C.J. Reports 1962 p. 151 and Written Statements, I.C.J. Doc. 62/21.
7. U.N. Repertory of Practice (1955). Vol. IV, Study on Article 73, especially paras. 226 et seq. See also M.K. Nawaz, "Colonies, Self-Government and the United Nations", Indian Year Book of International Affairs (1962) pp. 3-47.
8. I.C.J. "Competence of the General Assembly for the Admission of a State to the United Nations," I.C.J. Reports 1950 pp. 8-9. For what appears

In this way evolutionary growth in regard to fields of competence has an important positive effect on the law-making potentialities of the organs.[9]

The second qualification relates to the significance of conflicting interpretative positions which have not been resolved by a competent organ or in a clearly evidenced general consensus. It seems plain to me that such positions when taken by governments are not and should not be regarded as irrelevant to the meaning of the Charter norms. Official positions of States announced in the General Assembly or Security Council regarding their understanding of the obligations of the Charter cannot be considered in legal effect as no more than judgments of private persons. They constitute evidence of contemporaneous construction by the parties that is entitled to weight in determining the meaning and effect of a treaty provision. This is in line with accepted doctrine, expressed by the International Court of Justice in several cases recognizing that the views of the parties as to the meaning of an international instrument even if not binding are relevant evidence of the correct legal interpretation of the instrument.[10]

Criteria for Choosing between Conflicting Interpretations

If the interpretative statements of Governments have evidentiary value but are in disagreement, what criteria are available and appropriate for evaluating them and choosing between them? Such choices are of course often made: they are made by Governments in the political organs when faced with conflicting interpretation; they may on occasion be made by judicial tribunals; and they are of course frequently made by legal scholars who scrutinize and appraise positions from a relatively

to be a contrary view, see Separate Opinion of Sir Percy Spender, relating to "Certain Expenses of the United Nations" Opinion. I.C.J. Reports 1962 pp. 186-197.

9. Cf. De Visscher, Theory and Reality in Public International Law (Eng. trans. 1957) p. 253.

10. I.C.J. Advisory Opinions on South West Africa, I.C.J. Reports 1950 p. 128; and on Competence of the General Assembly for the Admission of a State, ibid p. 8; and I.C.J. Judgments in Iranian Oil Company Case, I.C.J. Reports 1952 pp. 106-107.

"disinterested" point of view. Each of these "decision-makers" will see the problem from a different perspective arising from the difference in their roles but all will be concerned with the criteria that may properly be employed in reaching an "interpretative" decision and justifying it to others. The last point warrants emphasis; for it must be borne in mind that even if a government decides (or thinks it does) for reasons of immediate advantage, it will still be required to justify that decision in terms of criteria and principles acceptable to others in the political organs and in the international community generally.

It is of course impossible to consider criteria and principles of interpretation without examining more closely than we have yet done the various types of norms contained in the Charter and the diverse questions of meaning and specification which they present. As a preliminary observation I would note that the application of all general propositions—whether legal or not—to diverse facts and events has necessarily a substantial degree of uncertainty or ambiguity; such general propositions have what logicians aptly describe as "an open texture". That of course does not imply that they are without any clear meaning; normally there will be some central cases in respect of which everyone may be expected to agree that the proposition applies. But there will also be, inevitably, an outer area of uncertainty—that is, there will be cases in regard to which there exist reasons for both asserting and denying that the general rule applies.[11]

While this is true of many norms of the Charter, it is essential in considering the criteria of interpretation to bear in mind the great differences that exist in these norms in regard to their degree of generality and the nature of the choices they require. To show this, it seems convenient to employ four categories which serve roughly to bring out these differences: they are "rules", "principles", "standards" and "doctrine" (or "general theory").[12] These are not, of course, hard and fast categories or

11. H.L.A. Hart, The Concept of Law (Oxford 1961) p. 119. Cf. Cardozo, The Paradoxes of Legal Science (N.Y. 1928) pp. 4-7.

12. The first three categories are those employed by Hardy Dillard in his various discussions of the normative hierarchy. See Dillard in 91 Recueil des Cours (1957) pp. 477 et seq.

refined from a logician's standpoint; they are simply terms which are commonly used and which suggest distinctions which are germane to the task of interpretation.

The Specific "Rules"

The first category—the "rules"—refers to the norms which have relatively precise and explicit terms and which are generally intended to be applied without discrimination as to individual characteristics. In the Charter most of such specific rules concern procedure and organizational activities. Typical examples are those relating to composition of the organs: "the General Assembly shall consist of all Members . . . ", "the Economic and Social Council of eighteen Members elected by the General Assembly", or on voting "Each Member shall have one vote." In these rules the terms used have generally accepted definitions in the context of U.N. procedures and other Charter definitions. Much as it may be desired, an increase in membership of the Economic and Social Council is not considered admissible under the existing Charter provisions; the text is regarded as explicit and conclusive on this point.[13]

What is important to bear in mind is that in saying a rule is regarded as "explicit", we mean that in point of fact its meaning is taken for granted at a particular time. It is, so to speak, a given datum, not subject to question at that time. But this does not mean that its "explicit" meaning may not be challenged, or indeed changed in another context. In the history of the United Nations many apparently precise rules have been interpreted anew in new situations.[14] Even a rule as explicit as that providing for a two-year term for non-permanent Members of the Security Council has on occasion been modified in practice; and the express requirement of a "concurring" vote of a Perma-

13. U.N. General Assembly Official Records XIII Session Supp. No. 3, ch. I, Sec. VI. See also General Assembly resolutions 1300 (XIII) and 1404 (XIV) which recognize the necessity of an amendment to increase the size of the Economic and Social Council.

14. Kelsen op. cit. n. 2 at p. 244-5. Also cf. Robinson "Metamorphosis of the United Nations" 94 Recueil des Cours pp. 547-559 (1958).

nent Member has been interpreted to apply only if the Member actually casts an affirmative or negative vote and not if it abstains. But even in citing these examples, one should observe that in both situations, there was general support for the interpretation.

Other cases can be cited where majorities considered themselves clearly restricted by specific rules and required to reject proposals otherwise desired. My main point in this connection is not that specific "rules" do not require interpretation but rather that they contain key terms and expressions, the meaning of which is taken for granted in almost all cases which arise. (This is perhaps another way of saying their terms are definite and specific but it also suggests that such "precision" is always open to question.) We would be closing our eyes to a significant difference in practical interpretation if we ignored this large category of "specific" rules and treated the problem which they present as essentially no different from that raised by the more general norms.

The General Principles

The category of "principles" includes, of course, the broadly stated precepts of Article 2 of the Charter—such as the obligation to settle disputes by peaceful means, the prohibiton against the use of force, the duty to refrain from assisting a State against which the U.N. is taking preventive or enforcement action. Article 2 is not the only source of authoritative principles; they are found throughout the Charter, although not expressly designated as such. There are also general principles of law accepted as binding; such are the obligation to carry out agreements and the duty to make reparation for breach of obligations. All of these principles are invoked and appealed to as "law" in the same way as "rules", except that they are generally treated as higher in the normative hierachy. However, the significant difference for the decision-maker arises from the much greater "generality" of the principles. Their key terms are often highly abstract—hence, applicable to an indeterminate series of events, which may be viewed as extending outward from a "core meaning". Consider the various connotations which concepts like "force" and "political independence" can have in ordinary political usage. There are undoubtedly some core cases which everyone would say fall within those terms but in a large number of other situations there can be arguments for and against inclusion.[15] Does "force" embrace economic boycott or financial support of subversive movements? Is "political independence" interfered with by "force" when an unpopular de jure government facing an insurection receives foreign military support?

Moreover, because principles are general and fundamental, they tend to clash with each other in specific cases—thus every principle in the Charter can be paired off with a contrary or opposing principle in the context of a particular situation. (This, by the way, would not be true of the category of "rules"—there are no contraries in the Charter of specific precepts such as "each member shall have one vote".) Even the salient rule against force is "balanced by" the right of self-defence and collective enforcement measures and the most fervent supporters of the principle of self-determination have recognized the opposing claims of the obligation of peaceful settlement and the principle of "territorial integrity". This characteristic opposition of principles is not, as some have suggested, the result of political confusion or defective drafting; on the contrary, it is a desirable and necessary way of expressing the diverse and competing aims and interests of mankind. An attempt to eliminate such inconsistencies can only result in an artificial emphasis on some abstractions and a suppression of valid and basic human values.[16]

From the standpoint of the "law-applying function", it is

15. See Repertory of U.N. Practice (1955) and Supp. No. 1 (1958) on Article 2 (4); Report of the Secretary-General of the U.N. on "The Question of Defining Aggression" General Assembly Official Records VII Session, Annexes to Agenda Item 54 pp. 17-81 (1952). McDougal and Feliciano, Law and Minimum World Public Order (Yale 1961) pp. 121-206. J. Stone, Aggression and World Order (London, 1958).
16. O. Schachter, "Dag Hammarskjöld and the Relation of Law to Politics" 56 Am. J. Int. Law (1962) pp. 1, 3-5. For a wider conception of "polarity" in a philosophic context, see M. R. Cohen, Reason and Nature (N.Y. 1931) p. 165.

apparent that the opposition and indeterminancy of the principles of the Charter call for a frame of reference that is quite different from that required in deciding the issues presented by specific rules. The importance of "dictionary" and "ordinary" meaning is greatly reduced, often indeed they have little significance; emphasis necessarily shifts to an assessment of a complex factual situation and a consideration of the consequences of a decision in the light of more basic values that are regarded as implicit in the Charter.

The Category of "Standards" and the Facts of the Case

I have referred to a third category of norms as "standards". In this context, it refers to highly general prescriptions which involve evaluating the individual features of events. By contrast rules (and to some degree principles) assume a relatively uniform application, irrespective of individual characteristics. "Standards" in this sense are common in both public and private domestic law; notable examples are: "due care", "reasonable rates", "unfair competition", "good moral character". They are used to judge conduct of a kind which docs not seem susceptible of treatment under more specific criteria and requires that each case be judged largely on its own facts.[17] The Charter of the U.N. contains a number of these concepts: "good faith", "peace-loving", "with due regard to equitable geographical distribution." The organs may also be obliged to apply "standards" which are not expressly stated in the Charter but are necessarily implied by a principle or rule.

A good example of this is presented by the principle or right of self-determination. Neither the Charter nor "logic" provides specific criteria to determine what group or what territorial unit is entitled to exercise that "right" (recall the issues over Katanga, Cyprus, West Irian, Togo).[18] The organs must therefore—if they are to apply the principle of self-determination in specific cases—determine which territorial entity or group of persons is

17. See Dillard op. cit. n. 12.
18. U.N. Repertory of Practice (1955) and Supp. No. 1 (1958), Articles 1 (2) and 55. See also Eagleton, "Self-Determination in the United Nations" 47 Am. J. Int. Law (1953) 88.

the "appropriate" or "reasonable" unit in that case. The fact that a standard of this kind is used rather than a definition or rule shows that it has not been found possible to stipulate in advance which elements are decisive—in other words, that the judgments of what unit is appropriate for the purpose of self-determination depend so much on the individual and contingent facts of the case that it cannot be expected that a general formula will provide an adequate basis for decision.[19] It is evident that the problem of applying standards of this type to particular circumstances cannot be resolved by appeal to textual meaning or on the basis of legal formulae; it necessarily requires consideration of the basic aims of the Charter and of the "felt necessities of time and place". Obviously this has significance for determining which organ can best apply standards and what frame of reference is appropriate.

The Significance of "Doctrine" and "General Theory" of the Charter

We have not quite exhausted the classes of norms relevant to the interpretation concerning Charter principles. For over and above rules, principles and standards, there is a still more generalized category that may aptly be described as "doctrine" or "general theory" which comes into play particularly in cases of conflict between competing principles and in giving concrete meaning to broad concepts of the Charter. The influence of "general theory", in this sense, has been apparent in some of the great constitutional debates in the U.N.—for example that which took place in 1950 on the Uniting for Peace resolution or that in 1960 and 1961 on the legitimacy of the Congo operation. In the first case, the opposing positions were based in part on broad theoretical conceptions of the Charter which were at odds with each other: one could roughly be described as a collective security position, emphasizing the primacy of the responsibility to take "collective measures", the other treating as essential the unanimity rule of the Security Council and

19. Cf. General Assembly Official Records 12th Session, 3d Committee Meetings 820-825 (1957); 13th Sess., 3d Comm. Meetings 886-893 (1958).

perhaps described as a type of balance of power conception.[20] Both of these theoretical constructions were justified by their respective advocates in terms of the essentials of Charter doctrine and therefore implicitly presented as governing the choice between competing interpretations.

In the second of the examples mentioned, that relating to the Congo operation, the different doctrinal conceptions of the Charter that seemed pertinent in the context of that debate were emphasized in Mr. Hammarskjöld's last Annual Report.[21] He referred to one as a "static" conception in which the Organization was essentially "conference machinery" for the solution of conflicts of interest and ideology through expanded diplomatic facilities. In the opposing doctrine the Organization was also a "dynamic instrument of Government" through which international executive action would be undertaken on behalf of all Members in implementation of the purposes and principles of the Charter. Mr. Hammarskjöld went on to suggest these two different conceptions would lead to different emphasis and different interpretation of the major precepts of the Charter.

It may perhaps be questioned whether these and other theoretical concepts are appropriately classified as "legal" norms since they are not formulated as such in the Charter. But are not constitutions generally considered to have certain underlying and implicit premises, which are literally extra-constitutional, but which provide a "higher-law" rationale to justify choices between competing principles?[22] (The concepts of popular sovereignty or of inalienable natural rights are obvious exam-

20. General Assembly Official Records, 5th Sess., 279, 280th meetings (Sept. 1950). See also Ruth B. Russell, "The Management of Power and Political Organization" in *International Organization*, vol. XV, No. 4, Autumn 1961, p. 630.

21. "Introduction to the Annual Report of the Secretary-General on the work of the Organization, 16 June 1960-15 June 1961", Gen. Assem. Off. Rec., 16th Sess., Supplement 1 A (1961).

22. There are several references in opinions of the United States Supreme Court to the underlying premises or "inherent limitations" of constitutional provisions. Chief Justice Hughes stated "Behind the words of the constitutional provisions are postulates which limit and control". Principality of Monaco v. Miss. 292 U.S. 313, 322 (1934). See also Marshall, C.J. in Fletcher v. Peck 10 U.S. 87 (1810).

ples). Concepts of this character play so significant a role that it would be myopic to exclude them from the categories of Charter norms.

The Complexity of the Interpretative Task

No doubt these four categories of legal norms can be refined by further logical and syntactical analysis and replaced by more precise classification. Yet our analysis is sufficient to show that the organs face widely diverse tasks when they are called on to apply the "law of the Charter" to a complicated political situation. Certainly the words of the Charter must be the starting point, but as we have seen, in relatively few cases can the words provide a substantial part of the answer. In most cases the dictionary and the texts themselves can do little to resolve the issues which are presented as a result of generality, indeterminancy, conflicts and inconsistencies of the Charter norms. It is apparent from the various types of norms that the range of relevant considerations will vary considerably from problem to problem, but it is also clear that in a great many cases the organs have to evaluate complex situations in terms of a diversity of factors, including some which clearly involve judgements of "reasonableness", importance, intent, expectations and "necessity". Perhaps most important as we have seen is the requirement that the process of interpretation must include in many cases an assessment of the consequences of a decision on the major purposes of the Charter.[23] For this reason, a constitutional instrument like the Charter should not be subject to the restrictive interpretation appropriate to "bargaining treaties of the traditional type" where the contracting parties acted in terms of precise interests on a basis of reciprocity. As Charles de Visscher has put it, "always of capital importance in the interpretation" of a treaty such as the Charter "is the master idea or fundamental conception" that led to its conclusion, and he cites by way of example of such fundamental conceptions "the

23. ICJ Advisory Opinion on Reparation for Injuries, ICJ Reports, 1949, p. 174; Advisory Opinion on the International Status of South West Africa (July 11, 1950), ICJ Reports, 1950, p. 128.

protection of the independence and international character of the Organization's functions" and "the primary demands of peaceful coexistence and more precisely the efficacy of coercive action against aggression".[24]

It will perhaps be suggested that these general ideas as well as other considerations which I have suggested as guides to interpretation are political principles, rather than legal concepts and therefore involve subjective preferences and should not be employed to impose obligations on States without their consent. I am quite prepared to admit that many of the principles I have mentioned can be appropriately described as "political" in the sense that they express basic policies and social values. That is not a sufficient reason, however, to deny their legal relevance for they are at the same time criteria which are expressed in the Charter or which involve accepted legal techniques for applying standards in particular cases. The fact that opinions may differ as to the specific content of a general norm or on the assessment of the relevant facts does not means that all interpretations are on the same juridical footing. In many cases it will be possible to choose between conflicting positions by employing criteria which as I have indicated can be justified in terms of the Charter or other generally accepted principles.[25] This has been demonstrated in several decisions of the International Court of Justice and indeed in many individual statements in the political bodies.

In suggesting that interpretation can and should be justified in terms of principle (rather than expediency or self-interest) I am not asserting that there is no act of choice or that there is necessarily only one correct interpretation. On the contrary it seems to me that the element of human choice and preference cannot be eliminated—at least not in most controversial issues. But my main submission is that the act of choice must be validated and justified in terms of the "shared values" which have

24. De Visscher, Theory and Reality in Public International Law (Eng. transl., 1957), p. 253.
25. See Lauterpacht, "Restrictive Interpretation and the Principle of Effectiveness in the Interpretation of Treaties", 26 B.Y.I.L., (1949), 48 at p. 82 and footnote; see also McDougal and Gardner, "The Veto and the Charter". 60 Yale L.J. 258-92 (1951).

been expressed in the Charter or manifested through other consensual procedures[26]. This is so, even though the dominant motivation of a government was its own advantage; the essential point is that this motive cannot be the *justification* to others of an interpretation which is claimed to have legal effect. In this sense, it is "principle" rather than "politics" that must be decisive.

The Relation of Legal Obligation to the Behavior of States

It is not enough to observe that the specific norms which are asserted in the political organs may be legally authoritative on the basis of their acceptance and validity as interpretation of the Charter or other generally accepted principles of law. For unless they do actually influence actual behavior they remain no more than verbal admonitions and their presumed obligatory character merely nominal. To be sure, the fact that "law-applying" and "law-declaring" functions are extensively employed indicates some degree of efficacy; it can be assumed that States would not focus on legal prescriptions—whether in general terms or in specific cases—unless they had an expectation that normative decisions had an ascertainable impact on conduct outside of the organ itself.

While this assumption seems reasonably safe as a generality, the degree to which conduct is influenced and the specific mechanisms that operate are much more difficult to describe. In the three lectures which follow I shall attempt to do this in some measure by analyzing certain activities of the United Nations directed towards the maintenance of peace and the tasks of economic development. It is important to remember in this connection that the U.N. political organs are more than arenas for debate and for the assertion of recommendations or conclusions of law. They are also centers of authority for a complex

26. In other words, the purposes and values employed in the task of interpretation cannot be merely the preferences of the interpreter; they must be justified by evidence of their acceptance by the Members, whether in the form of legal texts or other expressions—in words and acts—of their views. Cf. McDougal "The Ethics of Applying Systems of Authority" in The Ethic of Power, edited by Lasswell and Cleveland (N.Y. 1962) pp. 221-240.

institutional system through which activities are undertaken that have an influence in many ways on the policies and conduct of Government. We shall examine some of these activities closely, and it will be apparent that the conclusions of a legal character expressed by the political organs have often been considered as essential elements in the action taken in the name of the Organization.

Apart from these institutional activities the effect of U.N. decisions is commonly thought to depend on "public opinion", a somewhat amorphous sanction, the impact of which is usually conjectural and uncertain. More solid and predictable than "opinion" (and in some respects its cause) are the interests and values which motivate Governments and which are reflected in the norms and procedures accepted by States in the Charter and in practice. For in the relatively decentralized international legal structure (epitomized by the concept of "sovereign States") the observance of international norms by national States is largely a function of their perceived self-interest, and it must be borne in mind that such perceived self-interest extends not only to immediate gains and losses but also includes a recognition of reciprocity and long-term perspectives of order and stability. Rarely will responsible national decision-makers lose sight of the fact that a failure on their part to observe the rules can be used "against" them and generally weaken the basis for their own reliance on commonly accepted restraints.

Of course these factors do not mean that the norms expressed in the U.N. are always carried out; there are inevitably intense pressures of an immediate character which in a given case may override the recognition of long-range interests in mutual restraint and stability. But it can be said with confidence that, generally speaking, the collective processes in a United Nations organ do focus attention on the desirability and indeed the necessity of mutual restraint and reciprocal observance of the rules. It is not only that they express or "declare" a norm; they also place emphasis on the common interest served by that norm since that is the most compelling reason for its adoption by States of diverse views and interests. Thus by translating the broad principles and purposes of the Charter into more specific norms, and by linking these norms to the interest of all or most States, the collective procedures in the United Nations inevitably generate pressures for the observance of such norms in the self-interest of the States concerned. Nor should we be so abstract about this significant point. When I speak about the common interest today, I have in mind above all the threat of nuclear disaster and the demands for effective recognition of the dignity of all human beings. These are at present the "hard facts" which find their expression both in the Charter and the more specific norms which emanate from the deliberations in the United Nations. It is the perception of these common interests by national decison-makers that constitutes the principal bond between law and political behavior in the contemporary world.

NOTES AND QUESTIONS

1. Compare the views of Spender and Schachter on Charter interpretation. What considerations guide your choice of the "correct" position? How do these two positions bear upon the resolution of the litigation in the *South-West Africa Cases*?
2. According to Schachter, how does law arise from the activities of the political organs of the United Nations? Compare Tammes and Higgins. Note the list compiled by Schachter in Lecture I of decisions in which "conceptions of legality seem to have played a significant part."
3. In conceiving of the operation of law in the Clark-Sohn world, would it be necessary to modify Schachter's approach in any significant respect? Do Clark and Sohn imply that legislative action by the competent international organs is an independent source of law within the meaning of Article 38 in the area of war prevention?
4. What kind of transition steps might be taken through the use of legal techniques within the United Nations? Would greater law-conditioning in the political organs improve the image of the Organization as a responsible forum for international action? Does this relate to the willingness of states to transfer sovereignty and give up national control over the instruments of international violence?
5. What kind of transition steps might be taken through the expanding use of the organs of the United Nations as a *source* of international law? Might such use develop a capacity for the Organization to satisfy the needs of peaceful change? Does a social system need legislative substitutes for violence? See Nieburg, **I-2**. Does the transition to war prevention and total disarmament presuppose the emergence of a legislative process? Have Clark and Sohn taken adequate account of this general need for legislative action? But might not the actuality of legislative competence make powerful and privileged states less willing than ever to renounce sovereign prerogatives? What sorts of checks can you posit as feasible and desirable upon the will of the majority? Have Clark and Sohn made the checks too rigid (e.g., on legislation, on revenue-raising) or too vague (e.g., no boundaries on the idea of war prevention, no veto)?

Membership in the United Nations 3

Political disagreements will often express themselves in disputes about the character of formal organizational structure. Each side will try to shape the organization to promote its political interests. This has certainly been the experience of the United Nations. Its capacity as a peace-keeping agency is restricted by the reluctance of the Great Powers to create a capability for decisive action that might operate against their political interests. In fact, one useful focus for studying the United Nations is to examine the extent to which antagonistic political interests have been offset by a common interest in the prevention of nuclear war. How much political violence to realize cold war ends is compatible with the satisfaction of this common interest? It is a matter of comparative risk-taking. When is the risk of escalation too high? Communist governments disagree with one another. Peking seems to favor the acceptance of higher risks to promote their revolutionary goals abroad than does Moscow. We will look at these matters directly in Chapter 9, which concerns peace-keeping.

At this point it is useful to associate the analysis of organizational issues with the subject matter of war prevention. Membership is hardly worth studying for its own sake, but rather because it illuminates the effective limits of the United Nations as it is presently constituted.

A. Problems of Membership

Some insight into the United Nations arises by studying its membership practices and procedures—who the Organization admits, who it excludes, by what procedures, for what reasons. Such lines of inquiry lead to an appraisal of proposed changes in these procedures and practices that would strengthen the United Nations as an Organization constituted to prevent war. It may be useful to compare foreign policy perspectives with world order considerations on membership problems. Such a comparison recalls the "level of analysis problem" as outlined by J. David Singer, **I-3B**.

In 1945, the United Nations Charter was signed by the representatives of 51 states. At the time of this writing, 117 states are Members of the Organization. Most of these new members are states in Africa and Asia that have emerged as independent political units in the course of decolonization. The process of decolonization is likely to produce another 6 to 10 new states in the near future. As has been noted in the previous materials, these new states are eager to participate in international relations and to influence the decision-making processes of international organizations. Their emergence is an important element in the dynamics of world order. From the viewpoint of understanding an evolving world order capable of eliminating international violence, it is useful to recall that at the time the Charter was adopted, there were 24 states who were denied the privileges of membership. Only those states that had declared war against Germany or Japan, or had at least broken diplomatic relations with the Axis Powers, were invited to participate in the initial meetings that set up the United Nations Organization. While the primary reason for not inviting these other states to join in the formation of the Organization undoubtedly arose from the feeling that these states had not made a contribution to the victorious alliance formed during World War II, other considerations involving national interests, ideological commitments, and differing attitudes toward world order were also present.

The creation of procedures for the admission of new members makes these additional considerations become explicit. In fact, Article 4 of the Charter sets forth criteria for admission that have no direct relation to World War II sympathies.

Article 4(1) reads as follows:

Membership in the United Nations is open to all other peace-loving states which accept the obligations contained in the present Charter and, in the judgment of the Organization, are able and willing to carry out these obligations.

The procedure used to apply Article 4(1) is set forth in Article 4(2):

The admission of any such state to membership in the United Nations will be effected by a decision of the General Assembly upon the recommendation of the Security Council.

As a consequence the five permanent members of the Security Council must recommend admission with unanimity and, as well, there must be a two-thirds majority in favor of admission in the General Assembly. As with other aspects of the Charter this voting procedure is best understood as a compromise between those that would want to confer competence on the United Nations to act whenever a strong consensus exists and those who regard action by the United Nations as requiring the consent of every sovereign state presently a member.

In addition to these procedures the drafters did seek to confine admission to the substantive standards set forth in Article 4(1), the most important of which is the requirement that the applicant state be "peace-loving." Such a requirement reflects the view that the Organization joins together those states committed by their foreign policy and ideology to an anti-war position. If a state were not peace-loving in this sense, then it would not contribute to the work of the United Nations as it would not share the basic premise of the Organization. There are three implications of this approach that seem worth noting. First, the founders of the United Nations did not consider universality of membership an important enough requirement to justify admitting non-peace-loving states. Second, as Article 2(6) suggests, the Organization, as agent of the world community, assumed responsibility and authority to control even the activities of nonmembers to the extent necessary for the maintenance of international peace and security. And third, the discussions at San Francisco took it for granted that most states would want to become Members of the Organization and that this desire would influence nonmembers to abide by the Principles of the Charter. It is, of course, clear that the procedures for applying the substantive standards do not assure that a state whose behavior warrants admission will be admitted, or that one whose behavior warrants exclusion will be excluded. Political forces have influenced, if not altogether controlled, voting on membership questions in the United Nations.

An Advisory Opinion of the International Court of Justice has dealt with the conditions of membership in the United Nations and is reproduced below under the title, "Conditions of Admission of a State to Membership in the United Nations" as it appears in *Cases on United Nations Law,* edited by Louis B. Sohn (Foundation Press, New York, 1956) pp. 9–20. The Court in its judgment takes seriously the objective of universal membership and considers whether the positive value of attaining universal membership should lead to the relaxation of the requirements in Article 4 that only peace-loving states be deemed eligible for admission.

In 1955 the so-called package deal resulted in the admission of 16 states. This deal broke a cold war deadlock on admission questions and was an important step in the direction of universality. In effect, since 1955, applicants for admission have been admitted almost without question and certainly without paying much attention to their ideological orientation. Except for Indonesia which withdrew in 1965, the states which remain outside are the divided states of Germany, Korea and Vietnam. (Note that China is a member; the controversy is centered on whether to shift accreditation from the representatives of Nationalist China to those of Peking China.)

This universalizing of membership practice has transformed the Organization in a fundamental way. At the outset, the Organization was dominated by the outlook of the victorious coalition of World War II. Increasingly, in recent years the United Nations has been dominated by the concerns and attitudes of the African and Asian states, including their posture of nonalignment with regard to the cold war. This contrasts with the early years of the Organization when cold war issues were more salient and when the United Nations took positions that almost always accorded with United States foreign policy.

In the first selection we wish to emphasize several issues:

(1) To what extent should membership in the United Nations be open only to peace-loving states?

(2) To what extent is universal membership a positive achievement?

(3) Do the Clark-Sohn proposals on membership vary from your responses to questions (1) and (2)? What requirements would a state have to meet to qualify for membership in their altered United Nations?

(4) What kind of argument on membership issues is it appropriate to make with regard to each of the principal organs of the United Nations? What kinds of evidence are appropriate to show that a state is or is not peace-loving in the General Assembly?——in the Security Council?——in the ICJ?

(5) How does law function in each of the three principal organs of the United Nations? What is the relation between law and politics in each of these organs?

(6) The answers to (5) might be changed considerably by the adoption of the Clark-Sohn scheme. How do they conceive of legal and political questions *within* each organ and in the relations *among* the three organs? See WPTWL, Articles 4–6, pp. 12–17.

CONDITIONS OF ADMISSION OF A STATE TO MEMBERSHIP IN THE UNITED NATIONS

Advisory Opinion of the International Court of Justice, 28 May 1948.
ICJ Reports, 1948, pp. 57–115.

On November 17th, 1947, the General Assembly of the United Nations adopted the following Resolution:

The General Assembly,

"Considering Article 4 of the Charter of the United Nations,

"Considering the exchange of views which has taken place in the Security Council at its Two hundred and fourth, Two hundred and fifth and Two hundred and sixth Meetings, relating to the admission of certain States to membership in the United Nations,

"Considering Article 96 of the Charter,

"Requests the International Court of Justice to give an advisory opinion on the following question:

" 'Is a Member of the United Nations which is called upon, in virtue of Article 4 of the Charter, to pronounce itself by its vote, either in the Security Council or in the General Assembly, on the admission of a State to membership in the United Nations, juridically entitled to make its consent to the admission dependent on conditions not expressly provided by paragraph 1 of the said Article? In particular, can such a Member, while it recognizes the conditions set forth in that provision to be fulfilled by the State concerned, subject its affirmative vote to the additional condition that other States be admitted to membership in the United Nations together with that State?' . . ."

* * * *

. . . the Court holds that it is competent, on the basis of Article 96 of the Charter and Article 65 of the Statute, and considers that there are no reasons why it should decline to answer the question put to it.

In framing this answer, it is necessary first to recall the "conditions" required, under paragraph 1 of Article 4, of an applicant for admission. This provision reads as follows:

"Membership in the United Nations is open to all other peace-loving States which accept the obligations contained in the present Charter and, in the judgment of the Organization, are able and willing to carry out these obligations."

The requisite conditions are five in number: to be admitted to membership in the United Nations, an applicant must (1) be a State; (2) be peace-loving; (3) accept the obligations of the Charter; (4) be able to carry out these obligations; and (5) be willing to do so.

All these conditions are subject to the judgment of the Organization. The judgment of the Organization means the judgment of the two organs mentioned in paragraph 2 of Article 4, and, in the last analysis, that of its Members. The question put is concerned with the individual attitude of each Member called upon to pronounce itself on the question of admission.

Having been asked to determine the character, exhaustive or otherwise, of the conditions stated in Article 4, the Court must in the first place consider the text of that Article. The English and French texts of paragraph 1 of Article 4 have the same meaning, and it is impossible to find any conflict between them. The text of this paragraph, by the enumeration which it contains and the choice of its terms, clearly demonstrates the intention of its authors to establish a legal rule which, while it fixes the conditions of admission, determines also the reasons for which admission may be refused; for the text does not differentiate between these two cases and any attempt to restrict it to one of them would be purely arbitrary.

The terms "Membership in the United Nations is open to all other peace-loving States which . . ." and *"Peuvent devenir Membres des Nations unies tous autres États pacifiques"*, indicate that States which fulfil the conditions stated have the qualifications requisite for admission. The natural meaning of the words used leads to the conclusion that these conditions constitute an exhaustive enumeration and are not merely stated by way of guidance or example. The provision would lose its significance and weight, if other conditions, unconnected with those laid down, could be demanded. The conditions stated in paragraph 1 of Article 4 must therefore be regarded not merely as the necessary conditions, but also as the conditions which suffice.

Nor can it be argued that the conditions enumerated represent only an indispensable minimum, in the sense that political considerations could be superimposed upon them, and prevent the admission of an applicant which fulfils them. Such an interpretation would be inconsistent with the terms of paragraph 2 of Article 4, which provide for the admission of *"tout État* remplissant ces conditions"—"any *such* State". It would lead to conferring upon Members an indefinite and practically unlimited power of discretion in the imposition of new conditions. Such a power would be inconsistent with the very character of paragraph 1 of Article 4 which, by reason of the close connexion which it establishes between membership and the observance of the principles and obligations of the Charter, clearly constitutes a legal regulation of the question of the admission of new States. To warrant an interpretation other than that which ensues from the natural meaning of the words, a decisive reason would be required which has not been established.

Moreover, the spirit as well as the terms of the paragraph preclude the idea that considerations extraneous to these principles and obligations can prevent the admission of a State which complies with them. If the authors of the Charter had meant to leave Members free to import into the application of this provision considerations extraneous to the conditions laid down therein, they would undoubtedly have adopted a different wording.

The Court considers that the text is sufficiently clear; consequently, it does not feel that it should deviate from the consistent practice of the Permanent Court of International Justice, according to which there is no occasion to resort to preparatory work if the text of a convention is sufficiently clear in itself.

The Court furthermore observes that Rule 60 of the Provisional Rules of Procedure of the Security Council is based on this interpretation. The first paragraph of this Rule reads as follows:

"The Security Council shall decide whether in its judgment the applicant is a peace-loving State and is able and willing to carry out the obligations contained in the Charter, and accordingly whether to recommend the applicant State for membership."

It does not, however, follow from the exhaustive character of paragraph 1 of Article 4 that an appreciation is precluded of such circumstances of fact as would enable the existence of the requisite conditions to be verified.

Article 4 does not forbid the taking into account of any factor which it is possible reasonably and in good faith to connect with the conditions laid down in that Article. The taking into account of such factors is implied in the very wide and very elastic nature of the prescribed conditions; no relevant political factor—that is to say, none connected with the conditions of admission—is excluded.

It has been sought to deduce either from the second paragraph of Article 4, or from the political character of the organ recommending or deciding upon admission, arguments in favour of an interpretation of paragraph 1 of Article 4, to the effect that the fulfilment of the conditions provided for in that Article is necessary before the admission of a State can be recommended or decided upon, but that it does not preclude the Members of the Organization from advancing considerations of political expediency, extraneous to the conditions of Article 4.

But paragraph 2 is concerned only with the procedure for admission, while the preceding paragraph lays down the substantive law. This procedural character is clearly indicated by the words "will be effected", which, by linking admission to the decision, point clearly to the fact that the paragraph is solely concerned with the manner in which admission is effected, and not with the subject of the judgment of the Organization, nor with the nature of the appreciation involved in that judgment, these two questions being dealt with in the preceding paragraph. Moreover, this paragraph, in referring to the "recommendation" of the Security Council and the "decision" of the General Assembly, is designed only to determine the respective functions of these two organs which consist in pronouncing upon the question whether or not the applicant State shall be admitted to membership after having established whether or not the prescribed conditions are fulfilled.

The political character of an organ cannot release it from the observance of the treaty provisions established by the Charter when they constitute limitations on its powers or criteria for its judgment. To ascertain whether an organ has freedom of choice for its decisions, reference must be made to the terms of its constitution. In this case, the limits of this freedom are fixed by Article 4 and allow for a wide liberty of appreciation. There is therefore no conflict between the functions of the political organs, on the one hand, and the exhaustive character of the prescribed conditions, on the other.

It has been sought to base on the political responsibilities assumed by the Security Council, in virtue of Article 24 of the Charter, an argument justifying the necessity for according to the Security Council as well as to the General Assembly complete freedom of appreciation in connexion with the admission of new Members. But Article 24, owing to the very general nature of its terms, cannot, in the absence of any provision, affect the special rules for admission which emerge from Article 4.

The foregoing considerations establish the exhaustive character of the conditions prescribed in Article 4.

The second part of the question concerns a demand on the part of a Member making its consent to the admission of an applicant dependent on the admission of other applicants.

Judged on the basis of the rule which the Court adopts in its interpretation of Article 4, such a demand clearly constitutes a new condition, since it is entirely unconnected with those prescribed in Article 4. It is also in an entirely different category from those conditions, since it makes admission dependent, not on the conditions required of applicants, qualifications which are supposed to be fulfilled, but on an extraneous consideration concerning States other than the applicant State.

The provisions of Article 4 necessarily imply that every application for admission should be examined and voted on separately and on its own merits; otherwise it would be impossible to determine whether a particular applicant fulfils the necessary conditions. To subject an affirmative vote for the admission of an applicant State to the condition that other States be admitted with that State would prevent Members from exercising their judgment in each case with complete liberty, within the scope of the prescribed conditions. Such a demand is incompatible with the letter and spirit of Article 4 of the Charter.

For these reasons,

THE COURT,

by nine votes to six,

is of opinion that a Member of the United Nations which is called upon, in virtue of Article 4 of the Charter, to pronounce itself by its vote, either in the Security Council or in the General Assembly, on the admission of a State to membership in the United Nations, is not juridically entitled to make its consent to the admission dependent on conditions not expressly provided by paragraph 1 of the said Article;

and that, in particular, a Member of the Organization cannot, while it recognizes the conditions set forth in that provision to be fulfilled by the State concerned, subject its affirmative vote to the additional condition that other States be admitted to membership in the United Nations together with that State. . . .

Judges Alvarez and Azevedo, whilst concurring in the opinion of the Court, have availed themselves of the right conferred on them by Article 57 of the Statute and appended to the opinion a statement of their individual opinion.

Judges Basdevant, Winiarski, McNair, Read, Zoričić and Krylov, declaring that they are unable to concur in the opinion of the Court, have availed themselves of the right conferred on them by Article 57 of the Statute and appended to the opinion a statement of their dissenting opinion. . . .

Individual Opinion by M. ALVAREZ.—I. I do not agree with the method adopted by the Court in giving the opinion for which it has been asked by the General Assembly of the United Nations.

The Court has inferred from the enumeration of the conditions prescribed in Article 4, paragraph 1, of the Charter for the admission of a State to membership in the United Nations, that nothing else can be adduced to justify a negative vote. This question cannot be answered merely by a clarification of the texts, nor by a study of the preparatory work; another method must be adopted and, in particular, recourse must be had to the great principles of the new international law.

More changes have taken place in international life since the last great social cataclysm than would normally occur in a century. Moreover, this life is evolving at a vertiginous speed: inter-State relations are becoming more and more various and complex. The fundamental principles of international law are passing through a serious crisis, and this necessitates its reconstruction. A new international law is developing, which embodies not only this reconstruction, but also some entirely new elements.

For a long time past I have insisted on the rôle which the Court must play in the renewal and development of international law. A recent event supports my opinion. The General Assembly of the United Nations in its Resolution No. 171 of November 14th, 1947, declares that it is of paramount importance, in the first place, that the interpretation of the Charter should be based on recognized principles of international law and, in the second place, that the Court should be utilized, to the greatest practicable extent, in the progressive development of this law, both in regard to legal issues between States and in regard to constitutional interpretation or to questions of a general nature submitted to it for its opinion.

I hold that in this connexion the Court has a free hand to allow scope to the new spirit which is evolving in contact with the new conditions of international life: there must be a renewal of international law corresponding to the renewal of this life.

With regard to the interpretation of legal texts, it is to be observed that, while in some cases preparatory work plays an important part, as a rule this is not the case. The reason lies in the fact that delegates, in discussing a subject, express the most varied views on certain matters and often without a sufficient knowledge of them; sometimes also they change their views without expressly saying so. The preparatory work on the constitution of the United Nations Organization is of but little value. Moreover, the fact should be stressed that an institution, once established, acquires a life of its own, independent of the elements which have given birth to it, and it must develop, not in accordance with the views of those who created it, but in accordance with the requirements of international life.

II. As the question put to the Court concerns the admission of new States to the United Nations Organization, the character of the international community and the place in it occupied by the Organization must be borne in mind.

As a result of the increasingly closer relations between States, which has led to their ever greater interdependence, the old *community* of nations has been transformed into a veritable international *society,* though it has neither an executive power, nor a legislative power, nor yet a judicial power, which are the characteristics of a national society, but not of international society. This society comprises all States throughout the world, without there being any need for consent on their part or on that of other States; it has aims and interests of its own; States no longer have an absolute sovereignty but are interdependent; they have not only rights, but also *duties* towards each other and towards this society; finally, the latter is organized and governed to an ever increasing extent, by a law of a character quite different from that of customary law.

The foregoing indicates the place occupied by the United Nations Organization in the universal international society. The creation of the League of Nations constituted a great effort to organize this society, particularly from the standpoint of the maintenance of peace. The present United Nations Organization, which is destined to replace it and has the same aims, is therefore merely an institution within the universal international society.

The aims of this Organization are not confined to certain States or to a great number of States, but are of a world-wide nature. They are concerned with the maintenance of peace and the development of cooperation among all States of the world; it will suffice to read the Preamble and Chapter I of the Charter to appreciate this.

But to become a Member of this Organization, a State must apply for admission, must fulfil certain conditions and must be admitted by the Organization. States which are not yet Members of the Organization have not the rights and duties which it has laid down, but they have these conferred or imposed upon them as members of the universal society of nations. Moreover, such States may enter into relations of every kind with those which belong to the United Nations Organization, and these relations are governed by international law.

III. Before giving the opinion asked of it by the General Assembly of the United Nations, the Court has had to make up its mind as to the legal or political character of the question put.

The traditional distinction between what is legal and what is political, and between law and politics, has to-day been profoundly modified. Formerly, everything dependent on precepts of law was regarded as legal and anything left to the free will of States was regarded as political.

Relations between States have become multiple and complex. As a result, they present a variety of aspects: legal, political, economic, social, etc.; there are, therefore, no more strictly legal issues. Moreover, many questions regarded as essentially legal, such as the interpretation of a treaty, may, in certain cases, assume a political character, especially in the case of a peace treaty. Again, many questions have both a legal and a political character, notably those relating to international organization.

A new conception of law in general, and particularly of international law, has also emerged. The traditionally *juridical* and *individualistic* conception of law is being progressively superseded by the following conception: in the first place, international law is not strictly juridical; it is also political, economic, social and psychological; hence, all the fundamental elements of traditional individualistic law are profoundly modified, a fact which necessitates their reconstruction. In the next place, strictly individualistic international law is being more and more superseded by what may be termed the *law of social interdependence*. The latter is the outcome, not of theory, but of the realities of international life and of the juridical conscience of the nations. The Court is the most authoritative organ for the expression of this juridical conscience, which also finds expression in certain treaties, in the most recent national legislative measures and in certain resolutions of associations devoted to the study of international law.

This *law of social interdependence* has certain characteristics of which the following are the most essential: (*a*) it is concerned not only with the delimitation of the rights of States, but also with harmonizing them; (*b*) in every question it takes into account all its various aspects; (*c*) it takes the general interest fully into account; (*d*) it emphasizes the notion of the *duties* of States, not only towards each other but also towards the international society; (*e*) it condemns the abuse of right; (*f*) it adjusts itself to the necessities of international life and evolves together with it; accordingly, it is in harmony with policy; (*g*) to the rights conferred by strictly juridical law it adds that which States possess to belong to the international organization which is being set up.

Far therefore from being in opposition to each other, law and policy are to-day closely linked together. The latter is not always the selfish and arbitrary policy of States; there is also a collective or individual policy inspired by the general interest. This policy now exercises a profound influence on international law; it either confirms it or endows it with new life, or even opposes it if it appears out of date. It is also one of the elements governing the relations between States when no legal precepts exist.

It is however always necessary to differentiate between juridical and political elements, particularly from the standpoint of the Court's jurisdiction.

The United Nations Charter makes the Court one of its organs (Art. 7), and Article 92 lays down that it is its principal judicial organ. The Statute of the present Court, like that of the old, indicates that its task is to hear and determine legal questions, and not political questions. The advisory opinions for which it may be asked must also relate to legal questions (Articles 36, No. 3, and 96 of the Charter; Article 65 of the Statute of the Court).

When a question is referred to the Court, the latter therefore must decide whether its dominant element is legal, and whether it should accordingly deal with it, or whether the political element is dominant and, in that case, it must declare that it has no jurisdiction.

In the questions which it is called upon to consider, the Court must, however, take into account all aspects of the matter, including the political aspect when it is closely bound up with the legal aspect. It would be a manifest mistake to seek to limit the Court to consideration of questions solely from their legal aspect, to the exclusion of other aspects; it would be inconsistent with the realities of international life.

It follows from the foregoing that the constitutional Charter cannot be interpreted according to a strictly legal criterion; another and broader criterion must be employed and room left, if need be, for political considerations.

The Court has decided that the question on which its advisory opinion has been asked is a legal one because it concerns the interpretation of the Charter of the United Nations, which is a treaty.

In reality, this question is both legal and political, but the legal element predominates, not so much because it is a matter of interpreting the Charter but because it is concerned with the problem whether States have a *right* to membership in the United Nations Organization if they fulfil the conditions required by the Statute of the Organization. The question is at the same time a political one, because it is the States comprising the Security Council and those belonging to the General Assembly which determine whether these conditions are, or are not, fulfilled by the applicant.

IV. As regards the essential conditions to be fulfilled by every State desiring to be admitted to membership in the United Nations Organization, these are prescribed in Article 4, paragraph 1, of the

Charter. These conditions are exhaustive because they are the only ones enumerated. If it had been intended to require others, this would have been expressly stated.

Moreover, having regard to the nature of the universal international society, the purposes of the United Nations Organization and its mission of universality, it must be held that all States fulfilling the conditions required by Article 4 of the Charter have a *right* to membership in that Organization. The exercise of this right cannot be blocked by the imposition of other conditions not expressly provided for by the Charter, by international law or by a convention, or on grounds of a political nature.

Nevertheless, it has to be judged in each case whether the conditions of admission required by the Charter are fulfilled. The units which may form this judgment are the States composing the Security Council and the members of the General Assembly. They must be guided solely by considerations of justice and good faith, i. e., they must confine themselves to considering whether the applicant fulfils the conditions required by Article 4, paragraph 1. In actual fact, however, these States are mainly guided by considerations of their own policy and, consequently, if not directly, at all events indirectly, they sometimes require of an applicant conditions other than those provided for in Article 4, since they vote against its admission if such other conditions are not fulfilled. That is an abuse of right which the Court must condemn; but at the present time no sanction attaches to it save the reprobation of public opinion.

Nevertheless, cases may arise in which the admission of a State is liable to disturb the international situation, or at all events the international organization, for instance, if such admission would give a very great influence to certain groups of States, or produce profound divergencies between them. Consequently, even if the conditions of admission are fulfilled by an applicant, admission may be refused. In such cases, the question is no longer a legal one; it becomes a political one and must be regarded as such. In a concrete case of this kind, the Court must declare that it has no jurisdiction.

A claim by a Member of the United Nations Organization, which recognizes the conditions of Article 4 of the Charter to be fulfilled by an applicant State, to subject its affirmative vote to the condition that other States be admitted to membership together with this applicant, would be an act contrary to the letter and spirit of the Charter. Nevertheless, such a claim may be justified in exceptional circumstances, for instance, in the case of applications for admission by two or more States simultaneously brought into existence as the result of the disappearance of the State or colony of which they formed part. It is natural in that case that their admission should be considered simultaneously.

NOTES AND QUESTIONS

1. Clark and Sohn propose that we eliminate "peace-lovingness" as a qualification for membership in the United Nations. Such a proposal is an aspect of their overall plan for limited world government. In a political system based upon centralized government the idea of voluntary membership seems inappropriate. In fact, in a national system the obligation to remain a member is, perhaps, the most basic obligation. Consider the frequent civil wars that have been fought between central governments and sub-systems seeking to opt out of the national system. Note that Clark and Sohn do not allow a state to be expelled from or to withdraw from membership, although the act of joining remains a voluntary one. That is, there is the possibility of nonmembership in the Clark-Sohn plan, but only for those states who never join. Once a state has been accepted as a member, then it is required to remain one, although if it persists in violating the Charter it may, according to Clark and Sohn, be suspended from the privileges of membership.
2. In January of 1965 Indonesia withdrew from the United Nations. This is the first time that a state has withdrawn from the United Nations since its inception. What kind of response would the United Nations have been able to make if we suppose that the present Charter had disallowed withdrawal? Note that the prestige and role of the League was greatly reduced by the withdrawal of Japan and Germany in 1933, by the withdrawal of Italy in 1937, and by the subsequent withdrawal of 14 other states. But is an international organization in a position to enforce an obligation to remain a member? How would such an enforcement action be carried out in the altered environment of the Clark-Sohn world? One could suggest that the obligation to remain a member is purely a formal one—that the United Nations would merely refuse to take note of a state's decision to withdraw. But what about the enforcement of the obligations of membership upon a state that considers itself a nonmember? What about the enforcement of financial obligations? Can one develop a security community on a global scale without being able to make the participation of the constituent political units mandatory? Can one even afford to allow states to have the discretion to refrain from joining at the outset?
3. Supposing, however, that we look now at the one test of admission under the Clark-Sohn plan: statehood. Traditional definitions of a state have emphasized four elements: a *government* administering *a fixed population* within *territorial boundaries* and *capable of discharging its international obligations*. In a given case arguments against admission could be posed by reference to alleged failures to satisfy this definition of a state. If and when the United Nations attains universality, the problem of qualifications for membership becomes academic. However, so long as withdrawal and readmission remain possible, it is important to understand the procedures and standards used to assess an application for membership even if the United Nations should eventually have universal membership. It is also likely that federations of existing states and dissolutions of existing federations will create a series of complex membership problems. Must each new political entity seek membership in the Organization?
4. At the moment issues of representation are more conspicuous than are issues of membership in the United Nations. This is a consequence of the attention that has been given to Chinese representation in recent United Nations history. Which governmental elite is entitled to represent China in the United Nations—National-

ist or Peking China? The problem is generally important because there are likely to be many internal struggles for power in the years ahead, accompanied by competing claims as to which faction is entitled to represent the state concerned in international organizations. We mention the issue of representation here to indicate its connection to the problems of membership. In Section B representation will be studied on its own.

5. In Article 3(2) Clark and Sohn propose that "In case the legal status of the applicant as an independent state is thus questioned, the General Assembly shall refer the question to the International Court of Justice for final decision." They observe in a comment that the assurance that any nation "having the legal status of an independent state would be absolutely entitled to membership, should also be a strong influence toward universality." Can a court decide this kind of an issue? Can a court decide whether a state is "independent" and whether it is willing to meet its obligations under the Charter? Can a court adequately decide who should represent China in the United Nations? See Fuller, Chapter 8.
6. To what extent is the nation-state the permanent unit entitled to be the exclusive participant in world organization? Suppose regional groupings based on geography, race, ideology, or common interest emerge as powerful political actors of an autonomous sort in various parts of the world? Should not these regional actors be allowed to become members of the global organization? Suppose, for instance, that African security and trade becomes dominated by the autonomous activities of the Organization of African Unity. Should there not be a place for the OAU in the UN? Is there any historical basis for supposing states to be the permanently significant units of interaction in world politics? In the medieval world feudal principalities were the principal units of political interaction.

   In the opposite vein, is there any reason to suppose that a state will be capable of representing the interests of individuals? Should there not be provision for taking the individual into more direct account in an evolving international system? Such a question suggests the importance of creating a human community of global dimensions based upon universal sentiments sufficient to reinforce the universal structure of an augmented United Nations. If we wish to depress conflict among nations, one way to go about it would be to emphasize human concerns and to moderate emphasis on national concerns. Thus conflict patterns in intergroup relations may be shifted to new patterns with less stress on inter-nation conflict. This might be quite beneficial as the military capability has been monopolized by national governments. If the most intense rivalries were no longer between nations, then it might be much more feasible to persuade nations that their security does not depend upon their relative degree of military strength.

B. Problems of Representation: The Affiliation of Communist China with the United Nations

The most vexing problem of membership is a problem of representation. Since 1949 upwards of 700,000,000 Chinese have been ruled by a government in Peking that has been denied access to the United Nations. This denial of access makes more difficult the settlement of the international disputes that center upon the destiny of the divided states of Germany, Vietnam, and Korea—political entities which also remain outside the United Nations. Throughout the last 15 years demands have been made in the official organs of the United Nations that representatives of the Chinese People's Republic be seated as the representatives of the state of China in place of those from the Nationalist government, which remains in control of the island of Formosa.

Prior to the Sixteenth Session, matters pertaining to this question had been debated within the context of whether or not the matter should even be placed on the agenda for the General Assembly. The Assembly had answered this question in the negative each year. In the Sixteenth Session, however, two items referring to the matter were placed on the agenda. After a debate in which 56 members participated, the Assembly voted that the question of Chinese representation was an "important matter" under Article 18 (requiring, therefore, an affirmative vote of two-thirds and not just a simple majority of the members present and voting). It then voted 48–37–19 that the delegation from Taiwan should continue to represent China in the United Nations. See: UN General Assembly, "Question of Representation of China in the UN," *Provisional Verbatim Record of the 1069th Plenary Meeting of the General Assembly, A/PV. 1069* (December 1, 1961) pp. 2–17; and the 1070th Meeting, *A/PV. 1070* (December 4, 1961) pp. 21–24.

The next selection consists of two speeches, one by the late Ambassador Adlai Stevenson of the United States and the other by Dr. G. P. Malaskera, head of the Ceylonese delegation. These speeches were given during the debate in 1961 in the Assembly and suggest the major points in contention on the issue of Chinese representation.

It might be possible to regard the Chinese People's Republic as a new state seeking admission rather than as a government alleging exclusive rights of representation. In fact, one popular solution of the issue of Chinese exclusion is the so-called "Two Chinas" proposal. This proposal is emphatically rejected by both Chinese governments as each is very insistent upon being the sole rightful representative of the entire state of China. Both from the viewpoint of legal analysis and from that of universality, it is important to decide whether the issue of Chinese affiliation is properly to be decided as one of representation or one of membership. It is uncertain when and whether the issue of Chinese affiliation will be settled. It is far from evident that Peking China now seeks, or seeks very eagerly, to participate in the United Nations. The issue of Chinese affiliation has become a very provocative one in the United States. Why is this? Why should it matter so much to the United States that one more large Communist state is in the United Nations? Does the United States Government—its officials—seriously feel that Mao's China is less qualified for membership than is the Soviet Union, Haiti, the Republic of South Africa or Portugal?——by what criteria?

In addition to the intrinsic importance of commenting upon the issue of Chinese affiliation within the United Nations, the speeches of the two ambassadors also contribute to the inquiry into the content and scope of appropriate argument for the different organs within the United Nations. More concretely, it is important to be able to distinguish between those kinds of arguments considered appropriate and persuasive before the ICJ, as compared with those appropriate and persuasive before the General Assembly. Are there any genuine differences between the two? If so, what are they? Are there any formal limitations upon the kinds of arguments that can be properly made before the General Assembly? Which organ of the United Nations is the most appropriate to decide questions of admission and representation? Should the questions be dealt with separately by each organ? Should there be different standards applied to each question? To what extent should the provisions concerning expulsion or suspension from membership be treated as functionally equivalent to those dealing with admission and representation? Do the standards found in Articles 5 and 6 of the present Charter clarify a reasonable basis for a vote against admission or representation? If the issue is one of representation is it appropriate to ask whether the government is peace-loving?

SIXTEENTH SESSION GENERAL ASSEMBLY DEBATE ON AGENDA ITEMS 90 AND 91 DECEMBER 1, 1961 QUESTION OF THE REPRESENTATION OF CHINA IN THE UNITED NATIONS RESTORATION OF THE LAWFUL RIGHTS OF THE PEOPLE'S REPUBLIC OF CHINA IN THE UNITED NATIONS

Mr. STEVENSON (United States of America): The question confronting the Assembly of the representation of China in the United Nations is of world-wide and historical importance.

We live in an age when the ever-expanding family of nations is striving anew to realize the vision of the United Nations Charter: a world community, freed from the overhanging menace of war, acting together in equal dignity and mutual tolerance to create a better life for humanity. This very Assembly, in its majestic diversity, is both the physical symbol and the practical embodiment - however imperfect - of that transcendent vision.

In striving toward that vision, what we decide regarding the representation of China will have momentous consequences. For more is at stake than the status of certain delegations. More is at stake than the registering or reflecting of existing facts of power. Indeed, the underlying question is how the great people of China, who by a tragedy of history have been forcibly cut off from their own traditions and even led into war against the community of nations, can be enabled to achieve their own destinies and live with themselves and with the rest of the world in peace and tolerance.

This question, as we all know, has a long history. For twelve years past, ever since the Communist armies conquered the Chinese mainland and the Republic of China relocated its Government in Taipei, the community of nations has been confronted with a whole set of profoundly vexing problems. Most of them have arisen from aggressive military actions by the Chinese Communists - against Korea, against the Government of the Republic of China on its island refuge, against Tibet, and against South and Southeast Asia.

The problem before us, in its simplest terms, is this. The authorities who have carried out those aggressive actions, who have for twelve years been in continuous and violent defiance of the principles of the United Nations and of the resolutions of the General Assembly and deaf to the restraining pleas of law-abiding Members - these same warlike authorities claim the right to occupy the seat of China here, and demand that we eject from the United Nations the representatives of the Republic of China.

The gravity of this problem is heightened in its world-wide political and moral significance by the fact that the place of the Republic of China in the United Nations, since its founding in 1945, has been filled by its representatives with distinction - filled by representatives of a law-abiding Government which, under most difficult circumstances, has done its duty well and faithfully in the United Nations, and against which there is no ground for serious complaint, let alone expulsion.

The United States believes, as we have believed from the beginning, that the United Nations would make a tragic and perhaps irreparable mistake if it yielded to the claim of an aggressive and unregenerate "People's Republic of China" to replace the Republic of China in the United Nations. I realize that we have sometimes been charged with "unrealism", and even with "ignoring the existence of 600 million people" - to quote familiar phrases.

This seems to us a strange charge indeed. My country's soldiers fought with other soldiers of the United Nations in Korea for nearly three years against a huge invading army from the mainland of China. My country's negotiators have done their best, for nearly ten years, at Panmunjon, at Geneva, at Warsaw, to negotiate with the emissaries of Peking. Almost no country, I dare say, is more aware of the existence of these people than mine.

I think that it could be said with more justice that it would be dangerously unrealistic if this Assembly were to bow to the demands of Peking to expel and replace the Republic of China in the United Nations; it would be ignoring the warlike character and the aggressive behaviour of the rulers who dominate 600 million people and who talk of the inevitability of war as an article of faith and refuse to renounce the use of force.

To consider this subject in its proper light, we must see it against the background of the era in which we live. It is an era of sweeping revolutionary changes. We cannot clearly see the end. With dramatic swiftness the classic age of the empire is drawing to a close. More than one third of the Member States of the United Nations have won their independence since the United Nations itself was founded. Today, together with all other free and aspiring nations, they are working to perfect their independence by developing their economies and training their peoples. Already they play a vital part in the community of nations and in the work of this Organization.

Thus, for the first time on this grand scale, we have seen an imperial system end, not in violent convulsions and the succession of still another empire, but in the largely peaceful rise of new independent states - equal members of a world-wide community.

So diverse is that community in traditions and attitudes, so small and closely knit together is our modern world, so much do we have need of one another - and so frightful are the consequences of war - that all of us whose representatives gather in this General Assembly must more than ever be determined, as the Charter says, "To practice tolerance and live together in peace with one another as good neighbours." For there can be no independence any more except in a community - and there can be no community without tolerance.

Such is one of the great revolutionary changes of our time: a spectacular revolution of emancipation and hope. But this century has also bred more sinister revolutions born out of reaction to old injustices and out of the chaos of world war. These movements have brought into being a plague of warrior States - the scourge of our age. These regimes have been characterized not by democracy but by dictatorship; they have been concerned not with people but with power; not with the consent of the people but with control of the people; not with tolerance and conciliation but with hatred, falsehood and permanent struggle. They have varied in their names and in their ideologies but this has been their essential character.

Nowhere have these qualities been carried to a greater extreme, or on a grander scale, than on the mainland of China under Communist rule. The regime has attempted through intimidation, through hunger, through ceaseless agitation - and through a so-called commune system which even allied Communist States view with distaste - to reduce a brilliant and spirited civilization to a culture of military uniformity and iron discipline. Day and night, by poster, by loudspeaker and by public harangue, the people are reminded of their duty to hate the foreign enemy.

Into the international sphere these leaders have carried the same qualities of arrogance, of regimentation and of aggression. Many persons hoped, after their invasion of Korea ended, that they would thereupon give up the idea of foreign conquest. Instead they sponsored and supplied the communizing of North Vietnam; they resumed their warlike threats against Taiwan; they launched a campaign of armed conquest to end the autonomy of Tibet; and all along their southern borders they have pressed forward into new territory. To this day, in a fashion recalling the earlier authoritarian emperors of China, they pursue all these policies, and in addition seek to use the millions of Chinese residing abroad as agents of their political designs.

In fact, these modern Chinese imperialists have gone further than their imperial ancestors ever dreamed of going. There are at this time in Communist China, in training centres for guerrilla warfare, young men from Asia, from Africa and from Latin America being trained in sabotage and guerrilla tactics for eventual use in their own countries. Thus the strategy of what Mao Tse-tung calls "Protracted Revolutionary War in the Rural Areas," has become one of the principal world exports - and no longer an "Invisible Export" - of Communist China.

We have exact information about some of these activities. For example, we have the testimony of six young men from the Republic of Cameroun who travelled clandestinely from their country to the mainland of China last year. They arrived in China on 9 June; they left on 30 August. During that period they had a ten-week course from French-speaking instructors in a military academy outside Peking. The curriculum of this educational institution, taken from the syllabus that these men brought home, included such items as these - they make interesting reading: The correct use of explosives and grenades; Planning a sabotage operation; How to use explosives against houses, rails, bridges, tanks, guns, trucks, tractors, etc; Manufacture of explosives from easily obtained materials; Manufacture and use of mines and grenades; Use of semi-automatic rifles and carbines; Theory and practice of guerrilla warfare, ambushes, attacks on communications. And then there were political lectures with such titles as "The People's War", "The Party", "The United Front" and, of course, "The Imperialists Are Only Paper Tigers".

This, incidentally, was the fourth in a series of courses to train Camerounians to fight for the overthrow, not of European colonial rulers - for their rule had already ended - but of their own sovereign African Government.

Such an affinity for aggressive violence, and for subversive interference in other countries, is against all the rules of the civilized world; but it accords with the outlook and objective of the rulers in Peking. It was the supreme leader of Chinese Communism, Mao Tse-tung, who summed up his world outlook in these words: "Everything can be made to grow out of the barrel of a gun." And again, to quote him: "The central duty and the highest form of revolution is armed seizure of political power and the settling of problems by means of war. This Marxist-Leninist principle is universally correct, whether in China or in foreign countries; it is always true."

President Tito of Yogoslavia knows to what extremes this dogma of violence has been carried. In a speech to his people in 1958, he quoted the "Chinese Leaders" as saying with apparent complacency "that in any possible war. . . there would still be 300 million left; that is to say, 300 million would get killed and 300 million would be left behind. . . ."

In an age when reasonable men throughout the world fear and detest the thought of nuclear war, from the Chinese Communist thinkers there comes the singular boast that, after such a war, "on the debris of a dead imperialism the victorious people would create with extreme rapidity a civilization thousands of times higher than the capitalist system and a truly beautiful future for themselves."

In fact, only three months ago it was the same Chinese Communist leaders who officially acclaimed the resumption of atmospheric nuclear tests by the Soviet Union as, "A powerful inspiration to all peoples striving for world peace." What a queer idea of world peace.

With such a record and with such a philosophy of violence and of fanaticism, no wonder this regime, after twelve years still has no diplomatic relations with almost two-thirds of the Governments of the world. One cannot help wondering what the representatives of such a predatory regime would contribute in our United Nations Councils to the solutions of the many dangerous questions which confront us.

I believe these facts are enough to show how markedly Communist China has deviated from the pattern of progress and peace embodied in our Charter and toward which the community of nations is striving. In its present mood it is a massive and brutal threat to man's very survival. Its gigantic power, its reckless ambition and its unconcern for human values, make it the major world problem.

Now - what is to be done about this problem? And what in particular can the United Nations do?

The problem is, in reality, age-old. How can those who prize tolerance and humility, those whose faith commands them to "love those that hate you", how can they make a just reply to the arrogant, the rapacious and the bitterly intolerant? To answer with equal intolerance would be to betray our humane values. But to answer with meek submission or with a convenient pretense that wrong is not really wrong--this would betray the institutions on which the future of a peaceful world depend.

There are some who acknowledge the illegal and aggressive conduct of the Chinese Communists, but who believe that the United Nations can somehow accommodate this unbridled power, and bring it in some measure under the control - or at least the influence - of the community of nations. They maintain that this can be accomplished by bringing Communist China unconditionally into participation in the United Nations. By this step - so we are told - the interplay of ideas and interests in the United Nations would sooner or later cause these latter-day empire builders to abandon their warlike ways and accommodate themselves to the rule of law and the comity of nations.

This is a serious view and I intend to discuss it seriously. Certainly we must never abandon hope of winning over even the most stubborn antagonist.

But reason born of sober experience obliges us to restrain our wishful thoughts. There are four principal reasons which I think are of overriding importance, and I most earnestly urge the Assembly to consider them with great care, for the whole future of the United Nations may be at stake.

My first point is that the step advocated, once taken, is irreversible. We cannot try it and then give it up if it fails to work. Given the extraordinary and forbidding difficulty of expulsion under the Charter, we must assume that, once in our midst, the Peking representatives would stay - for better or for worse.

Secondly, there are ample grounds to suspect that a power given to such bitter words and ruthless actions as those of the Peking regime, far from being reformed by its experience in the United Nations, would be encouraged by its success in gaining admission to exert, all the more forcefully, by threats and manoevres, a most disruptive and demoralizing influence on the Organization at this critical moment in its history.

Thirdly, its admission, in circumstances in which it continues to violate and to defy the principles of the Charter, could seriously shake public confidence in the United Nations - I can assure you it would do so among the people of the United States - and this alone would significantly weaken the Organization.

Elementary prudence requires the General Assembly to reflect that there is no sign or record of any intension to pursue a course of action consistent with the Charter. Indeed, the signs all point the other way. The Peking authorities have shown nothing but contempt for the United Nations. They go out of their way to deprecate it and to insult its Members. They refuse to abandon the use of force in the Taiwan Straits. They continue to encroach on the territorial integrity of other States. They apparently do not even get along very well with the Soviet Union.

Fourth, and with particular emphasis, let me recall to the attention of my fellow representatives the explicit conditions which the Chinese Communists themselves demand to be fulfilled before they will deign to accept a seat in the United Nations. I quote here their Prime Minister, Chou En-Lai:

> "The United Nations must expel the Chiang Kai-shek clique and restore China's legitimate rights, otherwise it would be impossible for China to have anything to do with the United Nations."

Now in this short sentence are two impossible demands. The first is that we should expel from the United Nations the Republic of China. The second, "to restore China's legitimate rights," in this context and in the light of Peking's persistent demands, can have only one meaning: that the United Nations should acquiesce in Communist China's design to conquer Taiwan and the 11 million people who live there, and thereby contribute to the overthrow and the abolition of the independent Government of the Republic of China.

The effrontery of these demands is shocking. The Republic of China, which we are asked to expel and whose conquest and overthrow we are asked to approve, is one of the founding Members of the United Nations. Its rights in this Organization extend in an unbroken life from 1945, when the Charter was framed and went into effect, to the present.

The Republic of China is a Charter Member of this Organization. The seat of the Republic of China is not empty; it is occupied and should continue to be occupied by the able representatives of the Government of the Republic of China.

The fact that control over the Chinese mainland was wrested from the Government of the Republic of China by force of arms, and its area of actual control was thus greatly reduced, does not in the last justify expulsion, or alter the legitimate rights of that Government.

The de jure authority of the Government of the Republic of China extends throughout the territory of China. Its effective jurisdiction extends over an area of over 14,000 square miles, an area greater than the territory of Albania, Belgium, Cyprus, El Salvador, Haiti, Israel, Lebanon or Luxembourg - all of them Member States of the United Nations. It extends over 11 million people, that is, over more people than exist in the territory of sixty-five United Nations Members. Its effective control, in other words, extends over more people than does the legal jurisdiction of two-thirds of the Governments represented here. The economic and social standard of living of the people under its jurisdiction is one of the highest in all Asia, and is incomparably higher than the standard prevailing on the mainland. The progressive agrarian policy of the Government of the Republic of China and its progress in political, economic and cultural affairs contrast starkly with the policies of the rulers in Peking under whom the unhappy lot of the mainland people has been but little but oppression, communes, famine and cruelty.

All those who have served with the representatives of the Republic of China in the United Nations know their integrity and know their loyalty to the Charter, which we all respect, their high standards of conduct, their unfailing dignity and courtesy, their contributions, and their consistent devotion to the principles and the success of our Organization.

The notion of expelling the Republic of China is thus absurd and unthinkable. But what are we to say of the other condition sought by Peking - that the United Nations stand aside and let them conquer Taiwan and the 11,000,000 people who live there? In effect, Peking is asking the United Nations to set its seal of approval in advance upon what would be as massive a resort to arms as the world has witnessed since the end of World War II. Of course, the United Nations will never stultify itself in such a way.

The issue we face is, among other things, this question - whether it is right for the United Nations to drive the Republic of China from this Organization in order to make room for a regime whose aggressive appetite seems to be insatiable. It is whether we intend to abandon the Charter requirement that all United Nations Members be peace-loving and to give our implicit blessing to an aggressive and bloody war against those Chinese who are still free in Taiwan. What an invitation to aggression the Soviet proposal would be - and what a grievous blow to the good name of the United Nations.

In these circumstances the United States earnestly believes that it is impossible to speak seriously today of "bringing Communist China into the United Nations." No basis exists on which such a step could be taken. We believe that we must first do just the opposite: we must instead find a way to bring the United Nations - its law and its spirit - back into the whole territory of China.

The root of the problem lies, as it has lain from the beginning, in the hostile, callous, and seemingly intractable minds of the rulers of the mainland. Let those members who advocate Peking's admission seek to exert upon its rulers whatever benign influence they can, in the hope of persuading them to accept the standards of the community of nations. Let those rulers respond to these appeals; let them give up trying to impose their demands on this Organization; let them cease their aggression, direct and indirect, and their threats of aggression; let them show respect for the rights of others; let them recognize and accept the independence and diversity of culture and institutions among their neighbors.

Therefore, let the Assembly declare the transcendent importance of this question of the representation of China. Let us reaffirm the position which the General Assembly took ten years ago, that such a question as this "should be considered in the light of the purposes of the Charter."

The issue on which peace and the future of Asia so greatly depend is not simply whether representatives from Peking should take a place in the General Assembly. More profoundly still, it is whether the United Nations, with its universal purposes of peace and tolerance, shall be permitted to take its rightful place in the minds of the people of all of China.

Today the rulers in Peking still repeat the iron maxim of Mao Tsetung: "All political power grows out of the barrel of a gun." If that maxim had been followed, the United Nations would never have been created, and this world would long since have been blanketed with lethal radioactive ashes. It is an obsolete maxim, and the sooner it is abandoned, the sooner the people of all of China are allowed to resume their traditionally peaceful policies, the better for the world.

The United States will vote against the Soviet draft resolution and give its full support to the continued participation of the representatives of the Government of the Republic of China in the United Nations.

No issue remaining before the United Nations this year has such fateful consequences for the future of this Organization. The vital significance which would be attached to any alteration of the current situation needs no explanation. The United States has therefore joined today with the delegations of Australia, Colombia, Italy and Japan in presenting a resolution under which the Assembly would determine that any proposal to change the representation of China would be considered an important question in accordance with the Charter. Indeed, it would be hard to consider such a proposal in any other light, and we trust it will be solidly endorsed by the Assembly.

Mr. Malalasekera (Ceylon): The views of my Government, my people and my delegation on the issue before us are already well known. We hold, as we have always held, that a people must be represented in the United Nations by those who are their effective Government. I stress the word "effective," because we thereby want to say that representation which affects the daily lives of the people through the economic, social and political efforts of the United Nations can be carried out only by the day-to-day partnership and hourly collaboration of a people and its Government. This is obviously what the then Secretary-General had in mind when he wrote his letter of 8 March 1950 to the President of the Security Council, contained in document S/1466. Here is part of what he said:

> "This Article"--meaning Article 4 of the Charter--"requires that an applicant for membership must be able and willing to carry out the obligations of membership. The obligations of membership can be carried out only by Governments which in fact possess the power to do so. Where a revolutionary Government presents itself as representing a State, in rivalry to an existing Government, the question at issue should be which of these two Governments in fact is in a position to employ the resources and and direct the people of the State in fulfilment of the obligations of membership. In essence, this means an inquiry as to whether the new Government exercises effective authority within the territory of the State and is habitually obeyed by the bulk of the population.
>
> "If so, it would seem to be appropriate for the United Nations organs, through their collective action, to accord it the right to represent the State in the Organization, even though individual Members of the Organization refuse, and may continue to refuse, to accord it recognition as the lawful Government for reasons which are valid under their national policies."

These things are well known. Equally well known are the arguments for and against which are adduced in this controversy. Indeed we all know them by heart after twelve years of airing them on a procedural level.

But now for the first time we are discussing this issue on a substantive level. There is the danger that in the next ten days to two weeks we shall expend much time and energy rehashing the old arguments. I shall try my best to avoid this and to deal with the new aspects, whatever new factors can be extracted.

Among these new factors, there is a new American administration and, of course, there is its distinguished

Ambassador, Governor Adlai Stevenson for whom, personally, I have great respect and, may I be allowed to add, even affection. I followed him with great attention when in a somewhat formidable manner he presented his case against a positive solution of the China issue.

Mr. Stevenson's statement, I must confess to my regret, I found a little puzzling, because there are apparently not only two Chinas but two streams of thinking in the United States delegation. There seem to be those who supply the brilliant premises and also, alas, others who insist on arriving at the same old conclusions, the wrong conclusions. Take, for instance, these brilliant words, sweeping and majestic in their scope. Speaking of the ever-expanding family of nations, the United States statement said:

> "This very Assembly, in its majestic diversity, is both a physical symbol and a practical embodiment--however imperfect--of that transcendent vision." (A/PV. 1069, pp. 2-3.)

Further on the United States statement resumes this theme of "majestic diversity" and says:

> "So diverse is that community in traditions and attitudes, so small and closely knit together is our modern world, so much do we have need of one another--and so frightful are the consequences of war--that all of us whose representatives gather in this General Assembly must more than ever be determined, as the Charter says, 'To practice tolerance and live together in peace with one another as good neighbours'." (A/PV. 1069, p. 6).

These are noble words and excellent arguments. They are especially good arguments for the universal representation of all people in the United Nations and they are based on an eloquent interpretation of the Charter which the United States statement quotes with such approval.

Now let us imagine to ourselves that some day in an age of Utopia and reason the same delegation is instructed by its Government by some strange and unforeseen development, perhaps by an affiliation against another mighty Communist State, to plead for the seating of mainland China. Could it find words better fitted to speak in favour of the admission of the People's Republic of China? I do not think so.

But then the United States statement embarks on a long journey to nowhere when it sets forth in its discussion of regimes. Where in the Charter, I ask, is the United Nations described as an Organization of regimes? The United Nations Charter in its first three words, "We the peoples," establishes at once the hegemony of peoples. There is no mention here of regimes but only of peoples.

The United Nations programmes also are for peoples. The great revolution of our time, which the United States statement so eloquently described, is the revolution of the common people. The United Nations programme for under-developed areas, the United Nations social programme, the United Nations programme for children, the various agencies for health and food and culture--all these are for people, not for regimes.

Therefore the paramount question we must consider is the question not of regimes but of people. In China there are 650 million people, one-quarter of the human race. These 650 million people are not represented in the United Nations. It is true that somebody in Taiwan claims to represent them. The United States statement claims that that somebody does in fact represent them. We cannot and do not agree with this claim. Let us make it clear that we have no personal quarrel with the representatives from Taiwan. We have no desire at all to refer to them except in terms of great courtesy and correctness. Neither do we approve, therefore, of some of the unfortunate phraseology used in reference to them in the Soviet draft resolution.

But we are forced by the realities of the situation to ask a question: Has the regime in Taiwan, which makes that claim, implemented any of the programmes that I have mentioned earlier, for the benefit of these 650 million people who live on the mainland of China? The answer is an emphatic no. How then can we morally justify a world Organization which denies to so many millions of people the ordinary benefits of existence?

I am not speaking here of any abstraction alien to the United States Government, a Government which speaks so much of "people-to-people programmes." The United States Government is very intelligently aware of the difference between regimes and peoples.

In this connection the statement I refer to has struck off a clever bit of counterpoint. It says, in so many words, Let us not bring the Chinese People's Republic into the United Nations, but rather let us bring the United Nations to the Chinese people. Good. But how does the United States propose to do this? By sending them a United Nations flag? Or shall we send them 650 million copies of the Charter, or perhaps 650 million copies of the United States statement?

I submit, there is only one way to bring the United Nations to the Chinese people or to any other people, and that is by admitting them to membership of this world Organization. Then we shall have a United Nations literature in China. We shall have--as we have in the Soviet Union--a Chinese Association for the United Nations. We shall Have United Nations agencies for China.

Let me cite an illustration. Throughout the life of the

League of Nations the United States Government kept the American people out of the League. Then came World War II. The most intelligent and enlightened Americans--Mr. Stevenson among them--rightly pointed out the danger to the American people of being isolated from a world community. It was even said at the time that this isolationism may have actually contributed to the coming of the Second World War. The problem was how to win over the American people to this great co-operative enterprise after years of isolationism. Well, eventually the United Nations was brought into the United States and that is where we are now. But before this happened it was found necessary for the United States first to become a Member of the United Nations, and through being a Member of the United Nations the American people made this brilliant and historic transition from isolationism to internationalism, one of the most brilliant and constructive evolutions effected by any people anywhere.

Now, the United States, having abandoned American isolationism, preaches the doctrine of enforced isolationism for the Chinese people. If the isolationism of a big Power like America probably contributed to World War II, could it not be deduced, by the same thinking, that a similar isolation of a big Power like China might well become a contributing factor to World War III?

Beyond this, there is really not much more to say. All else--this discussion of how good or how bad certain regimes are; this talk about "dictatorship"; this talk about the system of "communes" in China--seems to my delegation a heap of irrelevancies. Dictatorships indeed! If the United Nations, in 1945 and thereafter, had kept out all the peoples who lived under one dictatorship or another, who but a handful of nations would be here today? The United States has friendly relations with many Governments controlled by dictatorial power, and some of the allies of the United States that started out with parliamentary experiments have later turned to dictatorship, some of them, strangely enough, on the excuse that dictatorial regimes could make better use of American economic aid. Is the "good" Chinese regime in Taiwan a model of democracy? There have been four Presidents in the United States during the reign of Chiang Kai-shek. It is worth recalling that Chiang Kai-shek has been in power much longer than Mao Tse-tung.

No, we shall get nowhere at all if we get lost in the bewildering jungle of passing judgment on political regimes as a qualification for Membership in the United Nations. It would not be difficult at all for my delegation or any other to produce a list of dictators enjoying the friendship and even the aid of the United States. And let me add that in saying this I make no criticism of any Government before this Assembly.

Then of course, there is the very much worn-out and dog-eared catalogue of China's aggressions. The United States statement mentioned Korea, Tibet, South East Asia. Let us take Korea because that is cited as a flagrant case.

The Korean War broke out in 1950. The Chinese People's Republic was set up in 1949. The United States statement cites Chinese intervention in the Korean War as a reason for not admitting the Chinese People's Republic to this Organization. Did the United States express great enthusiasm in support of the Chinese demand for a seat in the United Nations before the Korean War broke out? I have no such recollection. The truth is that United States opposition was not due to China's intervention in Korea, but rather to China's socialist system--and that remains true even today. All the other reasons are so much new cellophane wrapping on the same old package.

Speaking of the Korean War, perhaps that war need never have broken out at all if the Chinese People's Republic had been in the United Nations at that time. Some of the older Members here may recall how at Lake Success the United States, aware of China's fears, sought through various United Nations agencies to allay those fears with unofficial assurances that the United Nations armies in Korea would not cross the Yalu River. But China was not at the United Nations to accept those assurances. On the other hand, non-recognition tended to keep China's fears and suspicions alive. Perhaps the United States Government could have saved its people all those terrible casualties if the true representatives of China had been around the Security Council table and in the Assembly hall, where rising tensions leading to the war might have been anticipated, discussed, reduced and blunted, as they frequently are here. It might be pertinent to ask, would the United States be more afraid or less afraid if the Soviet Union were not in the United Nations? There are scores of speeches by United States officials to the American people explaining why it is better that the Soviet Union is in the United Nations. The American people are told, for instance, that it is better to have the Soviet Union in the Organization here where the United States can keep an eye on it--or, as it is sometimes said, "Better a war of words than a war of bullets"; or as it is also said, at the United Nations the Soviet system could be "exposed"; or, in the United Nations this "bad" Soviet Union can be made amenable to benevolent influences; or, at the United Nations, informal consultations could be had such as solved the Berlin crisis in 1949. Mr. Stevenson himself has sometimes used these arguments to explain why it is better for an allegedly warlike nation to be in the United Nations, rather than out of it. Why can we not apply the same arguments to the Chinese People's Republic? The United States statement speaks of the warlike aims of the Peking Government. This argument is based on two things; on China's pronouncements with regard to war and peace in the cold war and on certain directives issued in the training guerilla units.

On this point, I must note that Mr. Kennedy, the President of the United States, recently announced a new training programme for guerillas. I am certain that the manual of arms which is issued to them is not a memo on passive resistance. Mr. Mao Tse-tung allegedly spoke of using nuclear bombs. Can we say in this connection that we have an outright commitment from the nuclear Members of the United Nations that they will never use nuclear bombs? And it is they that have them, while Peking does not have any nuclear bombs. Surely we have more reason to fear Governments who have the bombs and will not say that they will never use them than we have of Governments who say they will use bombs but who, in fact, have no bombs to use.

Reading the United States statement, one gets an impression of a Hollywood script, long out of fashion, in which everybody is good except the villain. At this very moment I see before me here the faces of a number of delegations whose governmental policies and actions in certain parts of the world have been described by other delegations as "warlike". I need not call the roll of the territories, particularly in Africa, where full-scale wars are not being conducted by Western nations, some of them democracies, not against regimes but against people. I refer to Algeria, Angola, Oman, South Africa, Bizerta. Who attacked in the Suez? Does the United States delegation therefore want us to expel all of these warlike Governments? Then there are other Governments which, not I but Mr. Stevenson, would call warlike. Would we expel them? These Governments, in turn, call the Government of the United States warlike. Should they, then, ask for the expulsion of the United States?

Who is going to be the judge? Who is to judge? We do pass judgments on each other on various issues--sometimes much too freely--but we do so because we know that as long as we do it in the United Nations, as Members of the Organization, there is a chance that warlike policies, words and actions can be turned to the ways of peace.

This is not only a house of peace; it is the school of peace where all nations come to learn the lessons of peace. None, therefore, should be kept out of it. The United States statement has expressed fear of making what it calls an "irreversible" decision. As I understand it, the thinking of this Administration on the question of China was not as positive on the issue as the United States statement would seem to convey, according to United States Press reports themselves. The Administration, it was once reported, was inclined to reverse its policy on China and then it was reported that, under great pressure, the reversal was reversed. At what stage in this pondering were the arguments advanced in the United States statement correct?

Let me turn back to the major issue, which is whether a Government can be so judged as to affect either its membership or its desire for membership in the United Nations. It so happens that while Mr. Stevenson was talking in this hall on the China issue, two floors below in the Fourth Committee, at exactly the same time, the American delegate strongly denounced the apartheid policies in the Union of South Africa. The American delegate had some harsh words to say about the policies of the Union Government. Some delegates called the policies genocidal; I think that this is the highest form of destruction and the lowest form of war. But when certain delegates suggested that these policies disqualified the Union of South Africa from continued membership in the Organization, did the United States representative support that stand? He did not even support less drastic sanctions. Yet in the case of the Peking regime, the United States would apply the highest sanction of all--excommunication from this world community. I use the word excommunication in its harshest historic meaning, which amounts to a death sentence.

Let us assume that the United States, as Mr. Stevenson says, abhors the regime but is concerned with the plight of the Chinese people. Then why keep the Chinese People's Republic out of the specialized agencies, most of whose programmes are humanitarian? Much is said about the lack of food in China, a sad plight in which the Food and Agricultural Organization could have been of assistance. The same could be said of the World Health Organization. But the United States fought every attempt to give the People's Republic of China membership even in those agencies.

What the United States is waging is not a war against a regime; it is a war against the Chinese people. This is a blockage, an embargo. It is a Western-imposed iron curtain.

The United States statement cites the failure of Peking to conclude negotiations at Panmunjom, at Geneva, and at Warsaw which, it says proved futile although, Mr. Stevenson says, "My country's negotiators have done their best." This is a strange admission for a country that has a fabulous reputation for doing its best--a best which invariably ends in success. Is it possible that perhaps these negotiations might have made a little more progress and even ended successfully if both negotiating States had been Members in the United Nations?

Let me turn for a moment to the four reasons given in the United States statement for not making a decision now. The first reason is that the decision would be "irreversible." I fail to understand this argument, I must confess. I hope, in the name of the universality which we all desire, that all membership in the United Nations is irreversible and that, unlike the League of Nations, the United Nations will never cease to exist as a result of reversible membership.

The second argument is that the Peking delegation here might be "a most disruptive and demoralizing influence." In answer to this argument, we might consider the record of the United Nations. It seems to me that the question of China's representation here has been more disruptive and demoralizing than anything any new State could do. It is a strange theory and, to me, utterly contradictory to the philosophy of a world organization that representation, rather than non-representation, could undermine the United Nations. The United Nations, we would have thought, was by common acceptance the world's answer and antidote to the disruptive forces which begot two world wars.

We could go further and state that this cold war between the United Nations and the Chinese People's Republic, which the United States statement seeks to promulgate, is today one of the most dangerous challenges to the peace of the world--so disruptive, so demoralizing that tomorrow it could be one thousand times as great as the threat of Berlin.

Let us look at things a little more closely. There are other disruptive elements in the United Nations. We have representatives here who refuse to take their seats when their interests are under discussion. We have many States which refuse, at least temporarily, to accept Assembly decisions. Who is disrupting the United Nations in the Congo? Shall those who are responsible be expelled? We heard the United States representative tell the General Assembly that his Government could not accept the resolution on the moratorium on test explosions, that it could not accept the resolution on the denuclearization of Africa, that it could not accept the resolution leading to a ban on the use of terror weapons in wartime. Is that attitude constructive, or disruptive? There have been charges of disruption in the selection of the Acting Secretary-General, in the assessments on the Congo. The United States statement bristles with moral judgments and self-righteousness.

How are we to judge? Who is to pass judgment? Obviously, no Government in the world is without sin. Judgment, it seems to me, should be reserved to the world community, and then only with the greatest caution. Unilateral judgments, apart from being unobjective, are too frequently regarded as acts of hostility.

The third reason given in the United States statement is that the seating of the Peiping delegation would seriously shake public confidence in the United Nations. If public confidence in the United Nations were shaken every time some Government offended it in one way or another, the United Nations would have been dead long ago. Fortunately, the moral strength of world public opinion is a hardier plant than the Governments which represent it. It is part of the glorious chapter of modern times and a supreme expression of true faith in the future that world public opinion has stood by the United Nations through thick and thin and in its darkest moments. World opinion, if it is to be defined, means the public opinion of all the peoples of the world, and not of a world divided.

Why do some people wish to perpetuate an indefinitely protracted situation of bitterness, of harsh words, pitting the great people of the United States--175 million of them--against 650 million people of China, an ancient people of glorious achievements, a people who have seen and lived through many regimes and who do not need the United Nations to give them a lesson in the ways of peace? Experiments in peace were made in China centuries ago, culminating in the doctrines of Lao Tse and Confucius. These are hopeful traditions in the great history of China. These traditions will emerge here in this great laboratory of peace with a new vigour and a rediscovery.

The United States statement wishes the General Assembly of the United Nations to pass a judgment on Peiping's claim to Taiwan. Well, for ten or twelve years we have heard about Taiwan and Korea and other places as reasons for avoiding a positive decision. But let us ask: Have we succeeded in settling these problems with the Chinese People's Republic outside the United Nations?

To complete its lurid picture of an "unregenerate" Government in Peiping--that was the word used--and of a Government which cannot get along with anybody, the United States statement says: "They"--meaning the Chinese People's Republic--"apparently do not even get along very well with the USSR." I should have thought that, given the United States attitude to the USSR, it would welcome that Government into the United Nations if only for that very reason. At any rate, if the USSR is worried about it, if Moscow is afraid of Peiping's future might, the USSR is taking another course--it is the Soviet Union which is leading the campaign to bring Peiping into the United Nations.

I have mentioned the wall of hatred which, it seems to me, its present policy on China is building between the American and the Chinese peoples. It is my delegation's sincere conviction that such a policy cannot add to the security of America. This is the nuclear and missile age. The people who were the first to invest gunpowder will not lose too much time in becoming a nuclear Power--even without outside aid. When that day comes, the United States will be confronted by two mighty nuclear Powers, and that two-front war which was America's nightmare in the Second World War will re-emerge as the double nuclear front of the future.

The General Assembly is now trying desperately to hold the dissemination and spread of these nuclear weapons. If the Chinese People's Republic is seated here now, at this session, there is a good chance that we might head off such a development in one of the world's largest areas. China is building its economy and its social system with national plans which will require decades and which will tax all the national resources which it can muster. Thus engaged, it cannot afford now to divert billions in order to match the existing nuclear Powers. But if China is pushed to the wall or isolated from the forces of peace in the United Nations, it will find itself forced to build for itself a mighty fortress against those who make themselves its enemies. Does anyone doubt that mighty China will meet that challenge? When that day comes, China will be the only nuclear Power outside the United Nations. That, we submit, would be positively dangerous. If the United States Government really believes all it says about the warlike attitude of China, then it seems to me that it should do everything in its power to scotch this cold war and hatred as quickly as possible. Six hundred and fifty million people isolated from the world community of nations and compelled to build themselves into a mighty fortress, soon with nuclear and missile weapons, goaded by harsh words, taunts and insults, can never add to the security of the world. The greatest single reason for seating Peiping now is that it may spare the world another big nuclear Power. And this would be a contribution to world peace worth working for.

But if we miss this opportunity--and next year may be too late in the current high-speed armaments race--the United Nations and world peace itself will be not only disrupted but wrecked and will open the way for one quarter of the world fully armed outside the United Nations. Against this mighty war machine, that puny procedural paper resolution, in which five Powers have joined, will become the comedy of history and the tragedy of mankind. My delegation would like to say, with all respect but with the utmost seriousness, that this procedural obstructionism is unworthy of a delegation representing the wonderful American people, and that we most sincerely hope it will be brought to a halt.

We have talked of what the United Nations can do for China. But this Organization is not a one-way street. There is much that China can do for the United Nations. The Chinese people have much to offer in science, in culture and in industry. Its great strides in these fields have been a loss to the specialized agencies. Economically, China is a mighty laboratory in the way in which a nation can pull itself up by its own bootstraps from under-development. Politically, it is a giant in the rising tide of nationalism which has given birth to many new States and will produce many more as our decolonization programme accelerates. Both in terms of production and consumption, China's mighty population will always be an important factor in world trade.

The important resolutions adopted in the Second Committee of the Assembly, on the promotion of world trade, on industrialization, on the opening of new markets for one-commodity nations and the building of a world planned economy, on the building of the regional autonomy through ECAFE --all these resolutions must remain only partially implemented when the present and potential economic forces of China are left out.

One of these resolutions speaks of making available the benefit of central planning to under-developed countries. Regardless of ideologies, the great experiments and achievements of China in this respect cannot be ignored. They are too valuable a lesson to many new smaller nations desperately hunting for blue-prints in planned economies.

Many nations are now receiving such aid from the Chinese People's Republic bilaterally. China is highly developed medically, socially and scientifically. It is a country whose people and whose leaders are consumed with an unceasing ambition to build a nation from the remnants of colonialist fragmentization into a nationalist unity, seeking a social order based on justice and self-sufficiency.

I could go on indefinitely listing the great benefits which China can make in the fields of technical assistance, engineering, land reform, flood control, the building of dams, irrigation, literacy and education.

When the West says "no" to all these, let us recall the great contribution which China made to the early history of Western Civilization. The caravans moving from the Italian cities to China for its textiles, its art, its culture, is one of the most dramatic chapters in the history of modern civilization.

The nations of the world are being asked to ignore, to bypass, to snub that daring vision and imagination of the Italian and Arab traders who built a golden bridge across oceans, mountains, and deserts to bring China to Europe. In other words, we are being asked to throw progress back by 1,000 years.

Is this the time to move backward in the world which Mr. Stevenson so eloquently described as revolutionary? The United States is the country of the revolution of 1776, and China is the country of the revolution of 1948. In the historic perspective it is the same revolution in different forms. All modern revolutions--the French, the Russian and those of other countries--are a part of that great tidal wave of humanity increasing in vast numbers, marching across the globe and filling every inch of it with hundreds of different cultures.

In this vast and complicated panorama of change, these revolutions have sometimes developed into different and sometimes opposing patterns. The League of Nations was born to resolve the clashes of nations. The United Nations is challenged to resolve the clashes of revolutions. They can be resolved only if they are all represented in this World Organization, and they must be resolved not only in the settling of disputes but even more so in those positive and creative elements which arise from co-operative efforts. Peace in our time can be made not so much by stopping the aggressor as by the organization of a community of peoples in which no nation will find aggression desirable, necessary or even possible.

Therefore, we say that it is essential to bring the United Nations to China and China to the United Nations so that not only their joint economic co-operation but also their joint co-operation can become the epic of peace in our time.

For these reasons the issue under discussion here is not a procedural issue except as a simple matter of credentials. It is an issue which strikes at the deepest roots of the question of war and peace in Asia and in the whole world. We have made a correct decision in abandoning petty procedural tactics in dealing with this great problem and we are now for the first time dealing with it in a substantive manner. Let us have the courage to take the next bold step and dispose of this issue once and for all. Representatives who have an effective and a de facto relationship with the 650 million people of China seated in this House could make one of the greatest contributions to the universality of this Organization by admitting China. Such action could make this Assembly emerge from its present session with splendour. It could make the biggest contribution to peace which the United Nations can make today. Let us, here and now, resolve to make that contribution with vision and unflinching courage.

NOTES AND QUESTIONS

1. In an article entitled "The Question of China in the United Nations," *International and Comparative Law Quarterly* (October, 1963) p. 1232, Franz B. Schick summarizes many of the pertinent legal and political arguments that have been made concerning the problem. He first argues that, from the viewpoint of international law, the question has been posed incorrectly as one of admission; it is his contention that China, as one of the founding members of the Organization, is already a member and that the only legal question concerns the identification of the rightful representative of China. In this connection he states that effective control over a territory by a government establishes its legitimacy, regardless of the means by which it acquires power. Furthermore, neither the change of name nor the fact that it does not control Taiwan defeats the claim of the Communist government at Peking to represent China. Schick's analysis leads him to conclude that the government on Taiwan is the political entity for which that admission procedure would be appropriate, since it, rather than Peking, is in fact the "new" state. Schick's analysis is, of course, hotly contested by Formosa and her supporters.

   The consequence of phrasing the question as one of representation rather than admission seems to imply that the proper criterion of "peace loving" found in Article 4 is not relevant to the assessment of Peking's claims to representation. The Charter is silent on representation problems and the various organs of the United Nations accept the practices of their credential committees in defining their own procedures and standards for representation. Having argued to this effect, Schick then states the following:

   > Only cursory attention need be given to United Nations debates which have frequently presented other criteria either in favour of or against the exclusion of the Chiang Kai-shek régime or the seating of the People's Republic of China in the United Nations. As a whole, these arguments have referred to ideological-political points. Illustrations are the Korean War, Tibet, the border conflict with India, alleged acts of genocide by the Communist Government against "millions of Chinese on the mainland," the rejection by Communist China of the concept of peaceful coexistence by favouring a thermonuclear war, or the weight of world public opinion allegedly supporting the representation of the one or the other of the two Chinese régimes. The debates have also raised some more serious organizational questions such as the need for a ban on nuclear testing, and an agreement to reserve the use of outer space for peaceful purposes as well as the problem of disarmament. It has been stated that all such problems may defy an effective solution without the cooperation of the People's Republic of China in the United Nations. Finally, the Chinese question has also been linked with the principle of universality towards which the United Nations must strive if it is to achieve more effectively the purposes and principles enumerated in Chapter I of the Charter. The political importance of these issues can hardly be doubted. However, they have no direct bearing on the legal aspects of the question under consideration.

   Assuming that the question is one of representation and not admission, is there any legal argument for considering those matters that Schick describes as political? Would it make any difference whether the question was being decided by the General Assembly or by the ICJ? See Kaplan and Katzenbach, Chapter 8.

2. The Chinese question whether phrased as admission or representation, has been frequently tied to the problem of diplomatic recognition. It has been frequently argued that if the Chinese Communist government were to be seated in the United Nations, this would constitute formal recognition by all Member States of the Chinese People's Republic. In 1950, a legal memorandum from the Secretary-

General's Office disputed this contention and stated that as a juridical matter the collective decision of members could not be seen as implying individual diplomatic recognition: "Legal Aspects of Problems of Representation in the United Nations," S/1466; SCOR, V, Supp. for January to May, 1950, pp. 18–23. This memorandum has been commented on frequently since then. Whether the position is legally sound or not, it nevertheless remains true that within the domestic politics of the United States, membership of the Communist government of China in the United Nations would certainly be considered as the equivalent of recognition by the vast majority of the American public.

In traditional international law a state has unlimited discretion to decide whether or not to accord a foreign government or state diplomatic recognition. The United States, sensitive to its own revolutionary origins, was strongly in favor of a factual approach to recognition during the early part of its history. It was Thomas Jefferson who put this policy on paper and into practice. In the Jeffersonian view, the United States was prepared to recognize a foreign government whenever it was in firm control of the government machinery and, as a second requirement, whenever it seemed to rule with the consent of the population. Only in the twentieth century did new, more normative approaches to recognition crop up in American foreign policy. Woodrow Wilson, concerned with the instability of Latin American politics, sought to use nonrecognition as a way to bolster constitutional procedures in the Western Hemisphere. According to Wilson's approach, no government would be recognized that seized power by violence, at least not until it had held free elections. When the Soviet government came to power, the United States withheld recognition, both because it disapproved of communism as a political system, and because the American government was angry about the unwillingness of the Soviet government to discharge its financial obligations to compensate aliens for confiscated property and to pay the public debts incurred by earlier Russian régimes. In 1933, fifteen years after it came into existence, the Soviet Union was recognized by the United States. Many years have elapsed since Mao gained control over the Chinese mainland. What considerations prompt us to withhold recognition? Note that our two main European allies, Great Britain and France, have recognized China without adverse consequences. See generally, Sir Hersch Lauterpacht, *Recognition in International Law* (Cambridge University Press, 1948); and Quincy Wright, "Chinese Recognition Problem," *American Journal of International Law*, vol. 49 (July, 1955) p. 320.

3. Schick suggests that the question of representation might be referred to the ICJ for an Advisory Opinion. Schick predicts that the Peking government would undoubtedly be viewed as legally entitled to represent China in the Organization. It is sometimes argued that such a legal opinion might permit governments who face domestic opposition to the participation of the Peking government in the United Nations to reconcile themselves more gracefully to this eventuality.
4. There is considerable controversy about whether, from the perspective of world order, it would be a net gain or a net loss to take Peking China into the United Nations *at this time*. Some contend that the Organization is too weak at present to withstand the possible strain of Chinese participation, whereas others suggest that the earliest possible entry is desirable as otherwise progress in the areas of peace-keeping and disarmament will be retarded. Few students of world order contend that it would be desirable to exclude China permanently from the Organization. Disagreement centers upon whether the Organization must develop greater

cohesiveness than it presently possesses and upon whether China's revolutionary animus must first disappear, at least with respect to the use of violence as a means to attain her political goals.

5. So long as China remains outside the Organization the claims of the United Nations to be the sole authoritative agent of the organized world community remain precarious. A second center of authority can at any time be established, undermining the hitherto unchallenged legitimacy of the claims asserted on behalf of the United Nations. This fear has become less fanciful in light of Indonesia's withdrawal from the United Nations and the alienation of several of the more radical African states from the policies of the Organization, as well as by Pakistan's threat in 1965 to leave the United Nations unless it grows more satisfied with the role of the Organization with respect to the resolution of the dispute with India about the future status of Kashmir.

4

The Security Council

The previous chapter considered the varied problems connected with membership in the United Nations. It seems logical now to go on to the Organization itself, and to begin by getting some sense of its constitutional structure through an examination of the character and operation of the Security Council and the General Assembly. Consistent with the emphasis throughout the book, an appraisal of these organs will proceed from the perspective of war prevention. Are these organs presently equipped both with the formal authority and the means of implementation to safeguard international society from a major war? What deficiencies in structure and action do they exhibit in this respect? How can they be strengthened within the existing system of international society, so as to foster transition to a new system, and to uphold peace and security in the Clark-Sohn world?

The formal organization of the United Nations consists of six major organs and some twenty-five specialized agencies. See diagram of the UN structure, p. 839. With the exception of the ICJ, each major organ and many of the agencies also have a relatively complicated network of committees consisting of standing committees, subcommittees and ad hoc and special committees. A complete study of the structure and function of these organs, agencies, and committees would require an investigation of at least the following topics: membership composition; general principles underlying the authority of each structural unit to deal with specific substantive areas; rules of procedures, especially voting; permissible techniques for the discharge of functions, including sanctioning processes; and finally, the relationships that exist among the various units with regard to each of these topics. Such an investigation is well beyond the scope of this book.

At the same time, to assess realistically the present capacity of an international organization to deal with problems of peace and security, and to determine what changes are necessary if a global international organization is to become the major vehicle for achieving stable world order, it is important to obtain some understanding of the way in which international political processes operate within these structures and to evaluate what influence, if any, these structures may be said to have upon the international political system. For a pioneering effort to do just this in the principal context of the International Labor Organization, see Ernest B. Haas, *Beyond the Nation-State* (Stanford University Press, 1964).

The Security Council and the General Assembly are the logical places to begin a study of the structure of the United Nations. The Charter confers upon these two organs the major responsibility and authority for upholding international peace and security. The direct link of these two organs with the peace-keeping problems of the day does not imply that the Security Council and the General Assembly are either the most important or the most fundamental elements in a global international organization charged with maintaining a peaceful world. A compulsory system of dispute settlement before the ICJ or, even seemingly more remote from immediate peace-keeping efforts, a much more ambitious program by the Economic and Social Council allowing it to eliminate the sources of many international disputes and conflicts might turn out to be among the most crucial elements in the construction and operation of a stable peace system. For it has often been argued that without effective procedures for pacific settlement and without a more solid basis for significant world-wide cooperation on social and economic problems, it is impossible to diminish appreciably either the incidence or scale of existing patterns of international violence, or to reduce the risk of a major war. Nevertheless, during the past twenty years the Security Council, the General Assembly (and, as we shall see later, the Office of the Secretary-General) have been directly involved in a variety of efforts to regulate international violence; whether or not important changes are made in the structure and operation of the United Nations, these organs are likely to remain so engaged in the foreseeable future.

One final word of introduction: the term "political organ" is frequently used to describe the Security Council and General Assembly. We inquire here whether it is really appropriate to designate them as such.

The interrelatedness of legal and political behavior has been stressed throughout these materials. See especially, **II-1**, and Chapter 2. The activities of an organ of any social system consist necessarily of both a series of decisions and a sequence of acts by authoritative officials. These decisions and acts are both subject to normative and institutional restraints in terms of community expectations. This has the effect of making law and politics organic in the sense of being aspects of or ways of talking about a single phenomenon. Morton A. Kaplan and

Nicholas deB. Katzenbach accept, and then only reluctantly, a separation between law and politics that is based upon the degree of formal structuring in the decision-making procedures and in the extent to which coercion is made available as an instrument for achieving the institutional ends. What is clearly rejected is any notion that a certain subject matter or a certain arena (say, the General Assembly or the ICJ) is either intrinsically political or intrinsically legal.

The relation between what is legal and what is political has been frequently debated and raises many complicated issues. In addition to the cross-references referred to above, see Lincoln P. Bloomfield, *Law, Politics, and International Disputes* (Carnegie Endowment for International Peace, New York, 1960); and Charles de Visscher, *Theory and Reality in Public International Law* (Princeton University Press, 1957). For our purposes here it suffices to say that the use of the term "political organ" to describe the Security Council and the General Assembly accepts the conventional distinction found in the literature about the United Nations. In such writing, these organs are each seen as a forum within which political considerations are manifest and policy for the international community is discussed and formulated. Such political organs are contrasted with legal organs, especially the ICJ, that are expected to decide cases according to international law and to exclude any considerations deriving from international politics. The validity and usefulness of this distinction is a subject for reflection in relation to the materials that follow. But, let us be clear: law emanates from political organs and politics is rife in legal organs. The conventional usage is retained, but it does cause some confusion about the way in which legal and political factors coexist in any social process that is regarded as authoritative—vested with authority—by a substantial portion of the community.

The Security Council is the organ that is given primary responsibility by the Charter for the maintenance of international peace and security. Its membership consists of eleven states, five of which are permanent; the permanent members are France, the Republic of China, the Union of Soviet Socialist Republics, the United Kingdom, and the United States. The other six members are states elected from the membership of the General Assembly. According to the Charter, they are to be "elected for a term of two years" and "in the first instance" on the basis of their contributions "to the maintenance of international peace and security and to other purposes of the Organization" and, in addition, to achieve for the Council an "equitable geographical distribution." This composition of Security Council membership represented a compromise intended to accommodate the various attitudes present in the existing system of international relations at the time the Organization was conceived. In view of what has happened since 1945, what changes can and should be made in this system of Security Council representation?

In the following article—"The United Nations Security Council," *International Organization*, vol. XII, no. 3 (1958) pp. 273–287—Leland M. Goodrich assesses how well the original conception of the structure and function of the Security Council has responded to the realities and needs of international life during its period of operation. From the viewpoint of an evolving world order it is appropriate to emphasize that the *formal authority* of the Security Council, its combination of substantive competence with its authority to make legal decisions obligatory for the entire membership of the United Nations (and, perhaps, for nonmembers, as well, see Article 2(6)), on matters "relating to the threats to the peace, breach of the peace, or acts of aggression" represents a high mark of supranational authority. While reading Goodrich it is important to bear in mind the distinction between the *formal authority* conferred in the Charter and the *socially effective control* manifest in the history of its operations.

The extensive authority of the Security Council is subject to several important qualifying observations. First, the permanent members of the Security Council are given the right of veto. Second, the competence of the Security Council is not so remarkable when one appreciates that in some respects the Council of the League of Nations possessed a comparable degree of authority. Third, there exists at present several unresolved legal and political problems relating to the competence and authority of the organ to act. Despite these remarks, the Security Council has unprecedented authority in at least one central respect: insofar as its five permanent members agree and are joined by any two nonpermanent members on a matter coming under Articles 39, 40 and 41 of the Charter, the Security Council is empowered to make decisions that are binding upon *all* Member States, although some of the states affected by the decision have not had an opportunity to vote and, in some instances, might have voted against the particular measure. From the viewpoint of traditional international law and international organization, this represents a dramatic change; it does not make the existence of an international obligation depend upon the consent of the state or states that are bound. See J. L. Brierly, *The Basis of*

Obligation in International Law (Clarendon Press, Oxford, 1958) Ch. I; C. W. Jenks, "The Will of the International Community as the Basis of International Obligation," *Law, Freedom and Welfare* (Oceana, Dobbs Ferry, N. Y., 1964); Richard A. Falk, "The Adequacy of Contemporary Theories of International Law—Gaps in Legal Thinking," *Virginia Law Review*, vol. 50 (1964) p. 231.

It is, of course, difficult to evaluate what differences, if any, might have developed in the contemporary system of international relations had this formal authority not been granted to the Security Council; on the basis of the record, however, it seems reasonable to argue that the presence of this formal authority has not produced any significant change in international life. To begin with, the formal authority of the Security Council has been severely limited in its application as a result of ideological and political conflict among the major powers. It is true that the General Assembly and the Secretary-General have, in consequence, assumed a greater role in matters of international peace and security than had been anticipated at the outset, but their activities have not been able to establish a formal authority comparable to that given to the Security Council in the Charter, nor have they effectuated a significant change in the international system.

Not only has the cold war restricted the role of the Security Council, but, as well, the large number of new states emerging from a colonial status after World War II have been particularly sensitive about the prerogatives of national sovereignty, including the idea of legal equality on the international level that is summarized in the principle: one-state-one-vote, and have thus not favored a dominant role for the Council within the Organization. It is also relevant that this group of recently independent states have used their influence to emphasize the role of the United Nations in the area of economic and social development instead of in the area of international peace and security. For these and other reasons, many who have appraised the structure of the United Nations, including Clark and Sohn, conclude that the Security Council is not the appropriate organ within which to vest the primary responsibility for preventing and regulating international violence.

The article written by Goodrich in 1958, when such views were quite widely held, reviews the events that have led others to recommend curtailing the role of the Security Council and gives the reasons that have led him to question, in part, their conclusion—"From League of Nations to United Nations," *International Organization*, vol. I, no. 1 (World Peace Foundation,

Boston, 1947) pp. 3–21. It is his view that the Security Council should retain an important role in matters of international peace and security; we shall want to evaluate this position. Goodrich also makes a number of specific suggestions for revision of the Council that might be regarded as transition techniques for achieving a less war-prone world.

THE UN SECURITY COUNCIL

Leland M. Goodrich

It has been the unfortunate fate of the United Nations to have been most conspicuously unsuccessful in performing that task which was to be its major responsibility and for which it was supposed to be best equipped. Naturally this has also been the fate of the Security Council upon which the Members of the Organization, by the terms of Article 24, conferred "primary responsibility for the maintenance of international peace and security". Against this background of failure and consequent dissatisfaction, many have been asking whether the Security Council is fated to become like the human appendix, an atrophied organ with no useful function to perform or whether the present condition is not one that can and should be remedied or that perhaps will be changed in any case by an improvement in the state of international relations. To form a judgment on these possibilities it is necessary to recall the original conception of the Security Council, to review its record, and to analyze the causes of its decline and the likelihood of their elimination or counterbalancing by other forces.

I.

The peace and security provisions of the Charter appear to have been based in part on conclusions that were drawn by their authors with respect to the causes of the failure of the League system. First of all, it was rightly believed that a major cause of the failure of the League system was its lack of universality, and particularly the absence of the United States. Consequently, the first concern of the Charter-makers was to have as members all the major powers in the Organization, and above all the Soviet Union and the United States. Secondly, it was believed that a weakness of the League system was its provision that sanctions should be applied against every aggressor, irrespective of whether or not it was a major power, and whether or not all the major powers joined in applying them. Consequently the authors of the Charter stressed the need of agreement among the permanent members of the Security Council as a condition of enforcement action, thus returning to the principle underlying the European Concert in the nineteenth century. Thirdly, it was believed that an important reason for the failure of the League system was the absence of any effective provision for the use of military force and the unwillingness of states under a voluntary system to take such extreme measures for defeating aggression. Therefore, the authors of the Charter were concerned with placing effective military force at the disposal of the Organization and making certain that it would be used when necessary. Finally, it was apparently believed, by some at least, that the League system

The author is indebted to Mr. Yasushi Akachi, a former Fulbright Scholar and at present member of the Department of Security Council and Political Affairs of the United Nations Secretariat, for assistance in the preparation of this article.

was weakened by the failure of the Covenant clearly to delimit the respective responsibilities of Council and Assembly. Therefore the Charter-makers sought to define the limits of the responsibilities of the UN counterparts of these two organs.

As written at San Francisco, after a lengthy process of elaboration in which the United States government played a leading role, the Charter set the maintenance of international peace and security as the first purpose of the Organization. It prescribed two principal approaches to the achievement of this purpose: collective measures for preventing or removing threats to the peace and suppressing acts of aggression or breaches of the peace, and adjustment or settlement of international disputes or situations by peaceful means. The regulation of armaments was made a subsidiary approach with emphasis upon agreements to make armed forces and facilities available to the Security Council and upon achieving "the least diversion for armaments of the world's human and economic resources"[1] consistent with the assured maintenance of international peace and security.

The primary responsibility for doing these things was placed on the Security Council, an organ so constructed and with voting procedures so defined that no decision other than a procedural one could be taken except with the concurrence of the five permanent members.[2] This gave assurance that no action could be taken against a permanent member or without its consent. The powers given to the Security Council were such as to give assurance that once the permanent members were in agreement and had the support of two other members—which would in all likelihood not be difficult to achieve—effective action could be taken to maintain peace and security. The requirement of unanimity, moreover, was regarded as assurance that the coercive power vested in the Council would not be abused. Thus, in effect, the maintenance of international peace and security was to be made the responsibility of a "concert of the permanent members".

It was assumed that the members of this concert would each have an interest in the maintenance of peace and security, following a war which had imperilled them all. Furthermore, the members of the Council were required to act in accordance with the Purposes and Principles of the Organization, as set forth in Chapter I, in discharging their responsibilities. But it was also recognized that the concert might not always materialize in fact.

> The underlying theory, however, was that if one of the major powers were to prove recalcitrant, or were to refuse to abide by the rules of international behaviour that were being inscribed in the Charter, a situation would be created in which the recalcitrant nation might have to be coerced; and it was apparent that no major nation could be coerced except by the combined forces of the other major nations. This would be the equivalent of a world war, and a decision to embark upon such a war would necessarily have to be made by each of the other major nations for itself and not by any international organization.[3]

There was no disagreement among the major powers at San Francisco or in previous discussions on the principle that unanimity of the major powers should be required. There was disagreement as

[1] Article 26 of the Charter.

[2] The one qualification was that a permanent member must abstain from voting when a decision was being taken under Chapter VI or Article 52, para. 3.

[3] Leo Pasvolsky, "The United Nations in Action," *Edmund J. James Lectures on Government*, Fifth Series, Urbana, University of Illinois Press, 1951, p. 80-81.

to how far the principle should be applied in disputes involving one or more of the major powers. The view of the United Kingdom was that no one, even a permanent member of the Council, should be allowed to vote in its own case. The Soviet view was that the unity of the major powers was the important consideration and no provision should be included in the Charter which would tend to encourage disagreement. At Yalta, however, Stalin accepted President Roosevelt's proposal that a member of the Council, party to a dispute, even though a permanent member, should not be allowed to veto a decision which the Council might take in the performance of its function of peaceful settlement or adjustment. The agreement reached at Yalta did not fully hold at San Francisco, however, when it became evident that it was not interpreted in like manner by all the parties to it. Extensive further discussions among the four sponsoring governments were necessary before final agreement was reached on the scope of the unanimity requirement.[4] By the San Francisco agreement, accepted by France, it was made clear that the requirement of unanimity of the permanent members did not apply to Council decisions to consider and discuss matters brought to its attention, or to decisions inviting parties to disputes to be heard. On the other hand, the "chain of events" theory as elaborated in the Statement was interpreted as preventing the Security Council from deciding to conduct an investigation or take any subsequent non-procedural decisions save with the concurrence of the permanent members, the one exception to the rule being that above indicated. Furthermore, the Statement asserted that the question whether or not a particular matter was procedural was itself non-procedural. While the Statement contained no commitment not to use the right of veto excessively or unreasonably, it did contain the statement that it was

> not to be assumed . . . that the permanent members, any more than the non-permanent members, would use their "veto" power wilfully to obstruct the operation of the Council,

and representatives of the permanent members reaffirmed their sense of responsibility in Conference discussions.

With respect to the division of powers between the Security Council and the General Assembly, there was even less disagreement among the permanent members up to the time of the San Francisco Conference. The Tentative Proposals of July 18, 1944,[5] which the United States submitted to the other participants in the Dumbarton Oaks Conversations gave the executive council (Security Council) the "primary responsibility for the peaceful settlement of international disputes, for the prevention of threats to the peace and breaches of the peace, and for such other activities as may be necessary for the maintenance of international peace and security". They empowered the General Assembly "to take action in matters of concern to the international organization which are not allocated to other organs by the basic instrument", and specifically

> a. to make on its own initiative or on request of a member state, reports on and recommendations for the peaceful

[4] See Dwight E. Lee, "The Genesis of the Veto," *International Organization*, February 1947 (Vol. 1, No. 1), p. 33–42. For text of Statement by the Delegations of the Four Sponsoring Governments on Voting Procedure in the Security Council, see United Nations Conference on International Organization, *Documents*, XI, p. 710–714, and Goodrich and Hambro, *Charter of the United Nations: Commentary and Documents*, rev. ed., Boston, World Peace Foundation, 1949, p. 216–218.

[5] *Post-War Foreign Policy Preparation*, Department of State Publication 3580, p. 595–606.

adjustment of any situation or controversy, the continuance of which it deems likely to impair the general welfare;

b. to assist the executive council, upon its request, in enlisting the cooperation of all states toward giving effect to action under consideration in or decided upon by the council with respect to:
   1) the settlement of a dispute the continuance of which is likely to endanger security or to lead to a breach of the peace;
   2) the maintenance or restoration of peace; and
   3) any other matters within the jurisdiction of the Council.

This proposed delimitation of the respective responsibilities of the two organs was substantially accepted at Dumbarton Oaks and incorporated into the Dumbarton Oaks Proposals.[6] This not only represented Department of State thinking, but it was in line with Soviet reluctance to permit extensive participation by the lesser powers in the activities of the Organization in the maintenance of international peace and security.

At San Francisco, a variety of pressures —the insistence of the lesser powers on a larger measure of participation, growing skepticism regarding the likelihood of cooperation among the major powers, and the insistence of Republican leaders and Congressional members of the United States delegation[7]—led to the broadening of the powers of the General Assembly, particularly by the inclusion of Articles 10 and 14, and the consequent blurring of the line dividing Security Council and General Assembly responsibilities and powers. Thus the Charter foundation was laid for the subsequent development of the role of the General Assembly in the field of action originally reserved to the Security Council.[8] The primary role of the Security Council was further jeopardized by the inclusion of Article 51 recognizing explicitly "the inherent right of individual or collective self-defense" in case of an armed attack upon a Member, until such time as the Security Council has taken measures necessary to the maintenance of international peace and security.

II.

The most striking trend in the practice of the UN since its establishment has been the increasing inability of the Security Council to serve the purposes for which it was intended and the growing preference of Members to make use of the General Assembly. This trend has been accompanied by the gradual breakdown of the lines of functional separation between the Security Council and the General Assembly, drawn up at Dumbarton Oaks and preserved, though with important modifications, at San Francisco, and by the gradual assumption by the General Assembly of an active role in the maintenance of international peace and security.

A quantitative measurement of the trend, though obviously inadequate, provides us with an indication of the changing role of the Security Council within the UN machinery. The declining frequency of the meetings of the Security Council in a world beset with conflicts, together with the increasing number of political questions considered by the General Assembly in comparison with the number considered by the Council,

[6] Department of State *Bulletin*, October 8, 1944 (Vol. 11, No. 276), p. 368 and following.

[7] See John Foster Dulles, *War or Peace*, New York, Macmillan, 1950, p. 36–41.

[8] See Goodrich and Hambro, *op. cit.*, p. 150–163 and 178–181 and H. Field Haviland, Jr., *The Political Role of the General Assembly*, New York, Carnegie Endowment for International Peace, 1951, p. 5–28.

underscores the diminishing role of the Council. The figures are extremely illuminating:[9]

Period	*Meetings of the SC*	*Substantive Political Questions Considered by the*	
		SC	*GA*
Jan. 17, 1946–July 15, 1946	50	5	2
July 16, 1946–July 15, 1947	108	8	4
1947–1948	180	8	5
1948–1949	92	8	11
1949–1950	46	6	10
1950–1951	72	7	19
1951–1952	43	6	12
1952–1953	26	1	14
1953–1954	59	4	11
1954–1955	22	3	15
1955–1956	32	1	11
1956–1957	52	6	13

Since the peak reached in the period from July 1947 to July 1948, there has been a general decline in the number of meetings. Even in the period comprising the crises which simultaneously arose in the Middle East and Hungary in the fall of 1956, the frequency of Council meetings registered merely a moderate reversal of the trend. The provision of Rule I of the Provisional Rules of Procedure of the Security Council that "the interval between meetings shall not exceed fourteen days" was fairly well observed during the first three years, when there were only three instances in which the interval between meetings exceeded fourteen days. The situation began to deteriorate in 1949, and has not been remedied since.

Although the decline in the number of meetings of the Security Council and the number of new questions submitted to it would appear to be indicative of a decline in the importance attached to the work of the organ, one would not be justified in drawing conclusions regarding the effectiveness of the Council from these figures alone. Before passing final judgment upon the degree to which the Council has been effective in performing its Charter responsibilities, it is necessary to examine in some detail the Council's actual record of performance in the principal fields of its activity. These can be roughly defined as four in number: 1) the taking of collective measures to keep or restore international peace and security in case of threat or actual violation; 2) the peaceful settlement or adjustment of disputes and situations; 3) the regulation of armaments; and 4) the performance of certain organizational functions, including the recommendation of new members and the recommendation of a Secretary-General.

In the performance of the first function, the Council has achieved a considerable measure of success in dealing with those situations where its permanent

[9] Substantive political questions are those designated "Political and Security Questions" in the Annual Reports of the Secretary-General on the Work of the Organization and which do not relate to constitutional, organizational or procedural matters, including the admission of new Members or the representation of Members. For detailed information, see the Secretary-General's reports and the Reports of the Security Council to the General Assembly.

members, for whatever reasons, have had a sufficient interest in the maintenance of restoration of international peace and security to agree on a common course of action. Thus in dealing with the situation in Indonesia created by Dutch "police" action to re-establish the authority of the Netherlands in Indonesia, the Security Council was able eventually to get the parties to agree to the cessation of hostilities leading to an acceptable political settlement. It must be recognized, however, that Security Council action alone might not have been effective without strong supporting action of an economic nature by the United States and certain Asian states. The major powers were unwilling, however, to use military force to achieve their purpose.

In dealing with the Palestine question during the initial period of crisis, the Security Council achieved considerable success. Although it was not willing to undertake the enforcement of the partition plan recommended by the General Assembly in its resolution of November 29, 1947, it did exercise steady and increasing pressure on the parties to the hostilities which broke out after the Israeli declaration of independence of May 14, 1948, to cease fighting and agree to permanent armistice arrangements. Largely as a result of this pressure, the armistice agreements were concluded, and a system of international supervision under the general oversight of the Council was established. Until the Israeli attack of late October 1956, this system was effective in preventing a resumption of general hostilities, notwithstanding the failure of the UN to achieve a peaceful settlement of outstanding issues, occasional incidents of violence, and the deterioration of relations between the Soviet Union and the western powers.

The Security Council also achieved a considerable measure of success in dealing with hostilities involving India and Pakistan over Kashmir. The parties acceded to the proposal made by the Council's commission that a ceasefire be concluded under a system of international observation established with the consent of the parties, and a condition of nonfighting has since been maintained, even though efforts to settle the dispute have failed.

Only under exceptional conditions, has the Council been at all effective in dealing with threats to or breaches of the peace where the vital interests of permanent members have been directly in conflict. When, following the Communist *coup* in Czechoslovakia in February 1948, the complaint of Soviet intervention in that country was brought before the Council, any action, even the appointment of a committee to study the situation, was prevented by Soviet vetoes. It is difficult to see how any effective action could have been taken in any case, even if the right of veto had not existed, unless the western powers were willing to risk the unleashing of a general war.

In September 1948, the Council was asked to consider the situation resulting from the Soviet blockade of Berlin. The Soviet Union, by its veto, prevented any action from being taken. Again it is difficult to see what the Council could have done, even without the veto, without risking a general war, other than provide, as it did, the occasion for representatives of the interested parties to meet and negotiate.

When north Korean forces attacked the Republic of Korea on June 25, 1950, the Security Council was presented with a unique opportunity to take action in a situation involving the conflicting vital interests of permament members, since the Soviet representative was absent in protest against the seating of the Chinese representative appointed by the Nationalist government. This condition of affairs proved to be temporary, and when the Soviet representative returned to the Council at the beginning of August, the possibility of making further use of the Council to guide and determine UN action ceased.

It was this situation which led to the adoption by the Assembly of the "Uniting for Peace" resolution of November 3, 1950,[10] by which the Assembly asserted for itself, under a liberal interpretation of Charter provisions, the right to consider any threat to the peace, breach of the peace, or act of aggression, if the Council, because of lack of unanimity of its permanent members, had failed to discharge its primary responsibility, and to make appropriate recommendations, "including in the case of a breach of the peace or act of aggression the use of armed force when necessary". While the General Assembly was to exercise this "residual responsibility" only after the Council had failed to take action and had removed the item from its agenda, the fact that this could be done by a procedural vote made it impossible for a permanent member by its veto to prevent Assembly consideration. Thus, the relationship between Council and Assembly which had been spelled out in the Department of State proposal of July 18, 1944, and in the Dumbarton Oaks Proposals and maintained in principle in the Charter was explicitly redefined to permit a majority of seven in the Council, in the face of opposition by as many as four of the permanent members, to transfer the consideration of an alleged threat to or breach of the peace to the General Assembly. Thus the way was prepared for making the Council's "primary responsibility" largely nominal, unless the permanent members were in full accord, and for making the Assembly's "residual responsibility"—based on extremely liberal Charter interpretation—major in fact, at least for as long as the cold war continued.

The Hungarian and Middle East crises in October 1956 again demonstrated that the Council was incapable of acting in a situation involving the conflicting vital interests of the major powers, though in the latter case it was not the cold war that was mainly responsible. In both cases, action was taken by the General Assembly, in the first case with no visible effect on the actual course of events and in the second case effectively. This experience tended to show that even when the General Assembly acts, the chances of successful action are small unless the United States and the Soviet Union are on the same side.

In discharging its second function, the peaceful settlement or adjustment of international disputes and situations, the Security Council has had very limited effectiveness. The disputes and situations that have been brought to its attention have, almost without exception, fallen into one or the other of two main categories: 1) disputes and situations resulting from the cold war—the ideological-power conflict between the communist powers and the western powers; and 2) disputes and situations resulting from the conflict of interests between the more advanced western powers, including particularly the colonial powers, and the states, mainly of Asia and Africa, which had recently emerged from colonial domination or have strong attachments to the cause of Asian-African nationalism.

In dealing with disputes and situations

[10] General Assembly Resolution 377 (V).

in the first category, the Council has only exceptionally had some measure of success. Pressure brought to bear through the Council appears to have influenced the Soviet Union to withdraw its military forces from Iran in 1946 after that country had complained of their illegal presence. Following a Council recommendation, the dispute between the United Kingdom and Albania over damage to United Kingdom ships in the Corfu Channel was submitted to the International Court of Justice for decision. However, Albania did not accept the award of damages. The Council was not able to agree on the appointment of a governor of the Free Territory of Trieste. It was unable by its own action to bring about a settlement of the dispute leading to the Berlin blockade. It was unable to take decision on various complaints submitted to it at the time of the Korean conflict. For the most part, the parties initiating UN consideration of cold war questions have considered the General Assembly better suited to their purposes.

In handling disputes and situations in the second category, the Council has not been much more effective. Only in the Indonesian case did it play a major part in bringing about an agreed settlement. The fact that the Soviet Union has generally aligned itself with the Asian and African states in their differences with the West and that some of the other permanent members have taken a rigid stand in opposition has largely eliminated the possibility of agreement among the permanent members of the Council on any course of action. Even the major western powers themselves have often been in disagreement, largely due to the unwillingness of the United States to go as far as the United Kingdom and France in opposing Asian and African claims. Generally speaking, the Asian and African Members have preferred to bring the questions involving claims against the West before the General Assembly where their voting strength is proportionately greater. When the western powers find it in their interest to bring a question before the Security Council, as in the case of the Anglo-Iranian oil dispute or the Suez Canal dispute, any effective Council action is likely to be prevented by a Soviet opposition or by disagreement among the western powers themselves.

The disputes between the Arab states and Israel and between India and Pakistan over Kashmir do not completely fit into either of the above categories. Here, too, the Council has failed as an organ of peaceful settlement. And one of the decisive factors in these cases, as in the ones previously considered, has been the failure of the permanent members to agree, as the result of their conflicting interests in the cold war. Without this agreement, not only may the Council be prevented from taking a decision, but even if it is able to take a decision as the result of one or more abstentions by a permanent member, the authority of the Council is greatly weakened.

In the performance of its third function, the achievement of agreement on the regulation of armaments, the Council has a record of complete failure. In the first place, it has been unable to conclude any agreement with Members by which they would undertake to place military forces and facilities at the disposal of the Council. This has been due to the inability of the permanent members, the members of the Military Staff Committee, to agree on the principles to be applied in the conclusion of these agreements.[11] As a result, the Council has not had available to it the military forces essential to the full discharge of its responsibility for the maintenance of peace. Without these forces it can only recommend military measures, as it did in the Korean case. Secondly, all efforts that the Security Council has made to prepare proposals for the regulation of national armaments, whether atomic or conventional, have ended in complete deadlock due to the inability of the major powers to agree. Nor has the Assembly, which has taken the leading initiative in disarmament discussions, been more successful.

In discharging its functions relating to membership and the internal organization of the UN, the Security Council has had a mixed record. Because of vetoes cast by the Soviet Union, a deadlock developed over the admission of new members with the result that from 1950 to 1955 not a single new member was admitted. Indicative of the seriousness of the situation was the fact that in 1953 21 applications for membership were listed by the UN as not having been favorably acted upon by the Council. Down to December 14, 1955, the UN admitted only nine new members. The log-jam was broken in December 1955 when, under the terms of a "package deal", sixteen new members were admitted and since that time, six other new members have been taken in. At the present time, only the Republic of Korea, the Mongolian People's Republic, the Democratic People's Republic of Korea, the Democratic People's Republic of Vietnam and Vietminh stand outside because of refusal of the Council to act favorably on their applications, and of these only two are outside solely because of the use of the veto in the Council.[12] It would be highly subjective to attempt any evaluation of how well the Security Council has performed its membership function. Probably the UN is nearer universality of membership at the present time as the result of the deadlock in the Security Council and the resulting necessity of a "package deal" than it would have been if the Assembly alone had controlled admissions. On the other hand, many qualified states were kept out for years, when the Assembly stood ready to admit them, solely because the use of the veto prevented favorable Council action.

In performing its recommending function in connection with the appointment of a Secretary-General, the Council has probably contributed to strengthening the role of that official in the work of the Organization. The requirement of agreement of the major powers increases the likelihood that the Secretary-General will have their confidence, which in turn is helpful, if not essential, to the full and most effective use of his powers. While the Council, due to the Soviet veto, did prevent the reappointment of Trygve Lie in 1950, the use of the General Assembly to break the deadlock did not produce very satisfactory results. In 1953, the Council recommended, and the Assembly appointed, Dag Hammerskjöld as Lie's successor. Experience since then has demonstrated the advantage of having a Secretary-General who commands the confidence of the major powers.

III.

Clearly the Security Council has failed to discharge its Charter responsibilities in the manner and with the degree of ef-

[11] See Goodrich and Simons, *The United Nations and the Maintenance of International Peace and Security*, Washington, Brookings Institution, 1955, p. 397–405.

[12] The Federal Republic of Germany undoubtedly would have applied and been admitted before now if it had not been for the knowledge that its application would be vetoed by the Soviet Union.

fectiveness which the authors of the Charter envisaged. Furthermore, there can be little doubt that the Council has declined greatly in prestige and has seemed to most Members of the UN less useful than in the beginning. This decline has been accompanied by a corresponding increase in the prestige and use of the General Assembly. What have been the reasons for the Council's decline?

The one reason upon which most people would seem to agree is the "veto". It is common to cite the number of vetoes cast and to draw the conclusion that the excessive use of the veto has been the cause of the Council's failure. Eighty-nine vetoes were cast in the Security Council up to May 2, 1958. The number of vetoes cast, however, does not tell the whole story regarding the influence of the veto on the work of the Council. It is necessary, first of all, to consider the nature of the proposals that have been vetoed. Of the total number, 48 vetoes were cast on proposals to admit new members, and in some instances the same country was "vetoed" four times.[13] Thirty-nine were used to defeat proposals made in connection with the discharge by the Council of its responsibility for the maintenance of international peace and security. Two vetoes have been cast in connection with the appointment of the Secretary-General.

If we consider only the vetoes that fall into this second category, we find a number of cases where the majority of the Council's members appear to have maneuvered to force the minority permanent member to repeat its veto on substantially the same issue for the record. For example, during the consideration of the Greek complaint against its northern neighbors in August 1947, the Soviet Union cast two vetoes consecutively, first on the Australian draft resolution and then on the United States draft resolution. The second veto must have been anticipated since the United States resolution was stronger than the Australian and therefore more objectionable to the Soviet Union.

The veto of a proposal has not necessarily prevented its substance from being put into effect. In the Syrian and Lebanese case, for example, the United States draft resolution expressing the confidence of the Security Council that the United Kingdom and French troops would be withdrawn "as soon as practicable" was not adopted due to the negative vote of the Soviet Union, which wanted a stronger resolution urging the immediate withdrawal of foreign forces. Nevertheless, the representatives of France and the United Kingdom declared that their governments were willing to give effect to the majority opinion, and the withdrawal of forces was carried out to the satisfaction of all concerned.

On the other hand, in those situations where the cooperation of the vetoing power is necessary to the carrying out of the proposal, the veto simply registers a factual situation. Even if the right of veto did not exist and the proposal were adopted by the required majority, there would be little likelihood that the dissenting major power would back down, if a vital interest was at stake, except under compulsion that might risk general war. Thus, if the Security Council had been able to take a decision in the Czechoslovak and Hungarian cases notwithstanding Soviet opposition, there is little reason to believe that the results would have been different since the majority members were not prepared to take those

[13] Italy's application was vetoed 6 times.

measures of coercion which alone had any chance of influencing Soviet action.

Concentration of attention upon the voting procedure of the Council as an explanation of Council weakness seems somewhat misplaced, since the real cause lies deeper than a mere organizational or procedural defect. The veto, when used, reflects the schism in the relations among the permanent members of the Council. It is a symptom, rather than the cause, of a disunited world.

The primary cause of the decline of the Security Council and especially of its role in relation to the General Assembly must be sought in the breakdown since 1945 of the wartime alliance of the Soviet Union, the United Kingdom, and the United States—the alliance whose continuation was the assumption upon which the idea of the Security Council as the guarantor of peace was constructed. The rivalry among the major powers induced them in many cases to use the Security Council as a tool for propaganda purposes to advance their divergent political objectives rather than to harmonize the action of nations in the attainment of common purposes, as intended by the authors of the Charter. Furthermore, these same powers discovered that for purposes of appealing to world opinion, and gaining support for their respective policies and programs in the cold war the General Assembly provided a more effective forum than the Security Council.

The work of the Security Council has been hampered by the conflicts among former Allied powers over the peace settlements. The authors of the Charter had remembered the onus attached to the Covenant of the League because of its close association with the settlements after the First World War. Accordingly, they provided a separate machinery for the making of the peace treaties with the Axis powers after the Second World War. Contrary to their hopes, however, the Allied unity broke down soon after the disappearance of the common enemies, and from the outset the Security Council had to carry burdens beyond its capacity, to deal with questions arising from the differences among the major powers concerning the peace settlements, such as the questions of Greece, Iran, and Czechoslovakia, the status of the Free Territory of Trieste, and the Berlin and the Korean questions. Deadlocks over the terms of the major peace settlements, moreover, were bound to make agreement on other issues more difficult to achieve.

Another cause contributing to the diminishing role of the Security Council has been the post-war emergence of numerous new nations in Asia and Africa, their crucial role in the world's balance of power, and their general preference for the Assembly rather than the Council for bringing their influence to bear in connection with the issues of colonialism, human rights, and disarmament. The anxiety of the major powers to win resounding political victories by the support of these newly independent states has helped the Assembly to gain further importance.

In addition, the advance in the use of mass media of communications and the increasing role of public opinion in the governmental process have tended to revolutionize traditional views on the relative merits of public discussion and participation in foreign policy making on the one hand, and quiet diplomacy and private negotiations on the other. The result has been that the attention of the strategists of national policy has turned to the manipulation and exploitation of the General Assembly as a world forum.

Doubtless the Assembly provides a more spectacular arena to wage the "war of ideas" than a small body like the Council.

IV.

It would seem likely that any amelioration of the relations among the major powers would bring about an improvement in the effectiveness of the Security Council; it would also reduce the desire of the major powers to turn to the General Assembly for political propaganda reasons. Amelioration of the major power relations does not, however, appear to be a sufficient condition to bring about the complete revival of the Security Council as the predominant organ for the maintenance of international peace and security as envisaged by the authors of the Charter, because the newly independent, non-western nations would be most reluctant to relinquish their power of effectively influencing political developments in the world through the General Assembly rather than through the Security Council, unless the composition of the Security Council is revised to meet their objections to its west-slanted membership. With the world situation as it is, it seems probable that the major questions of political adjustment, of the cold war as well as of the liquidation of colonialism, will remain the primary concern of the General Assembly rather than of the Council. The Security Council is more likely to confine itself to dealing with specific disputes or situations related to the maintenance of peace and security, which require swiftness of action and continuity of study and surveillance by the international organization, and about which the permanent members are able to achieve some measure of agreement.

The inclination of the western states to clarify and bring to the fore the residual responsibility of the Assembly in matters related to peace and security, as exemplified by their support for the "Uniting for Peace" resolution, appears to have been checked as a result of their realization of the new situation brought about by the increase in the voting power of the Asian and African states, often unsympathetic to the West. In fact, the Asian and African states have come to possess a potential veto over Assembly decisions. In consequence, the passage of west-sponsored resolutions through the Assembly can no longer be taken for granted. It was noteworthy that when the Syrian-Turkish question (1957) was brought before the Assembly, the representatives of Australia, France, the Netherlands, the United Kingdom, and the United States raised the constitutional issue that the proper place to deal with a threat to the peace under the Charter was the Security Council, not the Assembly.[14] This was in marked contrast to the Soviet silence regarding the competence of the Assembly in connection with the question. The seeming reversal of the positions of the western and communist states on the respective roles of the Security Council and the General Assembly on questions of peace and security is indicative of the fluidity of Members' preferences for one organ over another, stemming from the changing political configuration of these organs, caused partly by the addition to the Asian and African group of recently admitted states and partly by the trend of some members of this group of nations towards neutralism.

[14] Documents A/PV.706 (October 18, 1957); A/-BUR/SR.116 (October 21, 1957); and A/PV.708 (October 22, 1957).

Setting aside broad political considerations which would ultimately determine the relative roles for peacemaking of the Security Council and the General Assembly, several advantages which the Council possesses over the Assembly, from an organizational point of view, are worth noting. The Security Council is an executive committee of a small size in a state of constant alertness. Its members, even non-permanent members chosen for two year periods, can accumulate considerable knowledge and skill with respect to disputes and situations brought to its attention. It is able to act at a moment's notice, continue its supervisory functions without intermission, and serve as an effective negotiating body. In comparison, the size and lack of continuity of the General Assembly, together with the publicity attendant on its consideration of questions and the deficiency of experience of some of the delegates to the Assembly, suggest that it is primarily a forum of the nations for the discussion of questions of a general character, rather than an organ suited to perform intricate diplomatic functions of negotiation and conciliation. The establishment of subsidiary organs like the Interim Committee, the United Nations Commission on Korea, and the Advisory Committee on the United Nations Emergency Force, may overcome some of the organizational deficiencies of the Assembly. But an effective use of the Security Council would have several advantages not possessed by the subsidiary organs of the Assembly. It would also avoid an unnecessary duplication of functions.

Proposals have been made for the strengthening of the Security Council to enable it to perform more effectively the functions assigned to it by the Charter.[15] These may be divided into two categories: those calling for revision of the powers and voting procedures of the Council, and those involving some change of the Council's composition.

The frustration resulting from the frequent use of the veto has led to the following suggestions[16]: 1) abolish the veto completely and accord equality in voting to all members of the Security Council; 2) substitute for the requirement of the absolute unanimity of all permanent members that of a qualified unanimity by which the favorable votes of three or four of the permanent members would be necessary for a decision; 3) restrict the use of the veto to clearly defined areas and eliminate it from the pacific settlement of disputes and the admission of new members; 4) alter the fundamental nature of the Security Council by substituting powers of recommendation for its present enforcement powers; and 5) strengthen further the role of the General Assembly by giving it enforcement powers. Suggestions 1) and 2) seem unacceptable at the present to any of the permanent members. Suggestion 3) has been espoused by the United States since the Vandenberg Resolution of June 1948. This was confirmed by President Eisenhower in his letter to Premier Bulganin dated January 12, 1958.[17] Formal adoption of suggestion 4) would mean a retrogression of international organization, although it is not more than an acknowledgment of the existing state of affairs in the Security Council arising from the failure to implement provisions of Article 43. It is also unlikely that the major

[15] See Francis O. Wilcox and Carl M. Marcy, *Proposals for Changes in the United Nations*, Washington, Brookings Institution, 1955, Chapts. X and XI.

[16] U. S. Senate Committee on Foreign Relations, Subcommittee on the United Nations Charter, *The Problem of the Veto in the United Nations Security Council*, Staff Study No. 1, Washington, 1954.

[17] Department of State *Bulletin*, January 27, 1958 (Vol. 38, No. 970), p. 125.

powers would agree to the expansion of the powers of the Assembly, unless they have a share in the voting commensurate with the responsibility which they have to assume. A prerequisite to such agreement would be solution of the complicated question of weighted voting in the General Assembly. In short, suggestion 3) appears to be the only proposal which has some hope of acceptance by the powers constituting the permanent members, although there is no indication that the Soviet Union has changed its view on the "chain of events" theory by which it justified extension of the veto to the peaceful settlement of disputes.[18] Thus, even the adoption of suggestion 3) would have to await substantial relaxation of tensions between the western powers and the communist bloc, and this relaxation would make it largely unnecessary.

The question of change of composition of the Security Council has two facets, namely, the increase in the number of the non-permanent members of the Council, and additions to or elimination of the permanent members. The former question has already arisen in the Assembly and is probably easier to solve than the latter. Though an informal "gentleman's agreement" was reached among the major powers in London in 1946 on the allocation of non-permanent seats, the increase in the number of Member States, in particular from Asia and Africa, has brought about intensified pressures for a reconsideration of the original allocation. It has also given rise to contests for non-permanent seats, as evidenced in the Yugoslav-Philippine rivalry of 1955 and the Japanese-Czechoslovakian competition of 1957. In its eleventh and twelfth sessions the General Assembly had before it a proposal by Latin American states and Spain to increase the number of non-permanent members of the Security Council, but decided to postpone consideration until the following session.[19] The Latin American proposal for an increase of two non-permanent seats in the Council was favored by the western powers, but was opposed by many Asian and African nations who felt that the allocation of merely one of the two proposed seats to their region and the other to Europe was not proportionate to their increased number.

The question of the expansion of membership of the Council must be carefully weighed in the light of the aspirations of various regions of the world to be justly represented on the Council and the requirement to preserve the advantages inherent in a small, compact Council. The rise of India as a spokesman of the neutral nations and the recovery of west Germany, Italy, and Japan as influential powers, though west Germany is not yet a Member of the UN, may give rise to the question of their permanent—or semi-permanent—membership in the Council. There is no doubt that the question of the representation of China also has a crucial importance for the revitalization of the Council as an organ reflective of the reality of the power in the world.[20]

Of more importance than formal changes for the immediate future of the Security Council would be the improvement of the Council proceedings by the use of informal techniques not requiring revision of voting procedure or composi-

[18] See Premier Bulganin's letter to President Eisenhower, February 1, 1958, *ibid.*, March 10, 1958, p. 378.

[19] General Assembly *Official Records* (eleventh session), Annexes, Agenda items 56, 57, and 58; A/SPC/SR.74 and 75 (December 1957); A/PV.728 (December 12, 1957).

[20] See Herbert W. Briggs, "Chinese Representation in the United Nations," *International Organization*, May 1952 (Vol. 6, No. 2), p. 192–209; and an address given by the Secretary-General at a recent meeting of members of the British Houses of Parliament held under the auspices of the British group of the Inter-parliamentary Union, *United Nations Review*, May 1958 (Vol. 4, No. 11), p. 9.

tion. Among such techniques, mention might be made of the following: an effective use of private, as against public, meetings of the Council, depending on the nature of the problem, as illustrated by the three private Council meetings held in connection with the question of the nationalization of the Suez Canal in October 1956; the vitalization of the provisions of Article 28 (2), which have remained dormant, regarding periodic meetings of the Council attended by foreign ministers or heads or other members of government;[21] the appointment of a rapporteur or conciliator for a situation or dispute brought to the Council, who would make efforts at conciliation before the Council enters into the consideration of the substance of the question, along the lines of the Assembly resolution 268 B (III); and other measures of private diplomacy within the framework of the Security Council, making use of the good offices of the Secretary-General, as exemplified by his repeated trips to the Middle East since the spring of 1956 at the request of the Security Council.

The Security Council may indeed have an increasingly important role to play in the task of keeping the peace, provided that a discriminating choice is made by its members of the various instruments and techniques of diplomacy at its disposal. As part of the "evolution of emphasis and practice"[22] of the over-all United Nations machinery, it may yet become an active and vigorous guardian of the peace, though it is not likely to achieve the stature envisioned by the architects of the Charter.

[21] Proposals dealing with the periodic meetings of the Security Council have been made by the Secretary-General in the past. Cf. General Assembly *Official Records* (sixth session) Supplement No. 15 (A/1902), "Development of a Twenty-Year Programme for Achieving Peace Through the United Nations"; General Assembly *Official Records* (tenth session), Supplement No. 1 (A/2911), "Annual Report of the Secretary-General on the Work of the Organization, 1 July 1954—15 June 1955".

[22] General Assembly *Official Records* (twelfth session), Supplement No. 1A (A/3594/Add.I), "Introduction to the Annual Report of the Secretary-General on the Work of the Organization, 16 June 1956—15 June 1957".

NOTES AND QUESTIONS

1. As Goodrich has noted, the Security Council has four major functions: (1) the taking of collective measures to keep or restore international peace and security; (2) the peaceful settlement or adjustment of disputes and situations; (3) the regulation of armaments; and (4) the performance of certain organizational functions including the recommendation of new members and the recommendation of a Secretary-General. The first three of these are significantly related to war prevention. On the basis of his analysis Goodrich concludes that the Council has had success, and then only of a limited nature, in the performance of the first of these four functions; Goodrich explains the successes and failures of the Security Council by reference to the presence or absence of common interests by the big powers. Under what conditions are common interests present and perceived as the basis for international cooperation in the United Nations? For an analysis of the cold war in these terms, see Louis Henkin, "A Rule of Law Community," *The Promise of World Tensions*, edited by Harlan Cleveland (Macmillan, New York, 1961). For a comprehensive analysis of international order that emphasizes the relevance of common interests, see Wolfgang Friedmann, *The Changing Structure of International Law* (Columbia University Press, 1964). See also, Charles Burton Marshall, "Notes on Conferencemanship," *New Republic* (February 16, 1963), for the distinction between common interests and joint interests.

Throughout the remainder of this volume we shall be concerned with the functions of the Security Council that are spelled out in Chapters V, VI and VII of the United Nations Charter. Some familiarity with the actual wording of the Charter and the structure of these chapters would probably be useful. It would also be helpful to read *World Peace through World Law*, pp. 75–129, but not the Clark-Sohn revisions and comments as yet.

The excerpt from D. W. Bowett's descriptive book, *The Law of International Institutions* (Praeger, New York, 1963) pp. 30–37, reproduced below offers a trenchant summary of these provisions, as well as a brief account of some of the more significant circumstances in which they have been invoked. The Charter attempts to deal with problems of international peace and security through a relatively complicated system of classification and gradation of the various situations that might disturb the peace. It then correlates the gravity of the situation with the comprehensiveness and coerciveness of the procedures available to the Organization in response. An evaluation of these procedures, especially as they are concerned with the way in which political problems are related to the norms and processes of the United Nations system, will be deferred until after there has been an opportunity to study the materials on the General Assembly (Chapter 5A) and the range of problems connected with the peace-keeping operation of the United Nations (Chapter 9B).

(Excerpt from)

D. W. BOWETT

The Security Council

3. Functions and Powers

These are stated in Articles 24–26 of the Charter. In conferring on the Council "primary responsibility for the maintenance of international peace and security", the members of the Organisation agree that it "acts on their behalf". The Council thus acts as the agent of all the members and not independently of their wishes; it is, moreover, bound by the Purposes and Principles of the Organisation, so that it cannot, in principle, act arbitrarily and unfettered by any restraints. At the same time, when it does act "intra vires", the members of the Organisation are bound by its actions and, under Article 25, they "agree to accept and carry out the decisions of the Security Council in accordance with the present Charter". This agreement would not extend to a mere "recommendation" as opposed to a "decision".

Although Article 24 (2) refers to "the specific powers granted . . . in Chapters VI, VII, VIII and XII", practice has now confirmed the view that this enumeration is not exhaustive. There exist such other "implied" powers as may be required in the execution of its overall responsibility.[14]

The Council's primary function, the maintenance of international peace and security, is to be exercised by two means; the first is the pacific settlement of such international disputes as are likely to endanger international peace and security, and the second (which presupposes the failure or inapplicability of the first) is the taking of enforcement action.

(A) *Pacific settlement of disputes*

Chapter VI sets out the various means by which the Council may assist in the settlement of disputes and, as Article 33 makes clear, the methods of Chapter VI are supplementary to those methods tradition-

[14] See *Repertory*, Vol. II, p. 19–25: a good example is the responsibility the Security Council was to assume under the Statute of the Free Territory of Trieste, including a power to appoint a Governor.

ally established in international law and which the parties must "first of all" utilise, as appropriate. Moreover it is with disputes "likely to endanger international peace and security" that the Council is concerned, and not with all disputes.

The following have a *right* to submit disputes to the Council: the Assembly (Arts. 11 and 12), the Secretary-General (Art. 99), member States (Art. 35 (1)), and non-member States (Art. 35 (2)). It will be noted that the non-member States are bound, in so doing, to accept in advance and for the purposes of the dispute "the obligations of pacific settlement provided in the present Charter". There is also a *duty* imposed on parties to a dispute likely to endanger international peace and security to submit the dispute to the Council if they cannot settle it by the traditional means enumerated in Article 33; this is provided for in Article 37, but would, presumably, only apply to member States and not non-members.

The dispute, once submitted, is not automatically incorporated on the Council's agenda. The Council itself decides, by a majority of seven (*i.e.*, a procedural decision), whether or not to place the matter on the agenda and even this decision is without prejudice to the question of competence. It may well be that the Council, after considering the matter, decides that the dispute is not an "international" one – in other words it is precluded from exercising any jurisdiction by virtue of the domestic jurisdiction clause of Article 2 (7). Similarly, it is for the Council itself to decide whether and when a dispute shall be removed from its agenda, and again by a procedural vote.[15]

Once seised of a "dispute" the Council is *bound* under Article 32 to invite the parties to participate in the discussion (but without the right to vote); the Council *may* invite member States under Article 31 to participate in the discussion of "any question", whether or not a "dispute", when the Council considers the interests of that State are specially affected. Naturally the Council is not limited by the statements of the parties. It may undertake its own investigations[16] of the matter by setting up an investigation under Article 34, using a subsidiary organ for that purpose. If the purpose of the investigation is as defined in that Article, it is not permissible for the Council to utilise its general power under Article 29 to establish subsidiary organs. Under

[15] For details of the controversy which arose over this question in the Iranian dispute of 1946, see *Repertoire*, 1946–51, p. 92–93.

[16] See Kerley, "The powers of investigation of the UN Security Council", (1961) 55 A.J.I.L. 892.

Article 29 the vote is procedural; under Article 34 it is non-procedural and the Council's decision to investigate a dispute should, as agreed at San Francisco, be made only with the concurrence of the five permanent members.[17] There is no legal obligation spelt out in the Charter to the effect that a State must comply with the decision of the Council in the sense of permitting a commission of investigation to have access to its territory. Yet, without such access, the value of a commission is much decreased and it can be, and has been, argued that such an obligation exists by virtue of the general terms of Article 25.

In dealing with a dispute the Council has a number of alternative ways of proceeding open to it. It may, under Article 33 (2), simply call upon the parties to utilise the traditional means of settlement, leaving the choice of any particular means to the parties. Or it may, under Article 36 (1), recommend a particular means of settlement, but taking into consideration that "legal disputes should as a general rule be referred by the parties to the International Court of Justice . . ." (Art. 36 (3)). The Council may even go further and, under Article 37 (2), recommend the actual terms of a settlement in addition to the means or procedures for settlement; this is tantamount to assuming a quasi-judicial function where the dispute affects the legal rights of the parties. This way of proceeding is available only where the dispute is considered by the Council to endanger international peace and security; otherwise the Council could only so act, under Article 38, with the consent of all the parties. A final alternative is for the Council to set up a machinery for settlement within the United Nations – such as the Committee of Good Offices in Indonesia in 1947 or the Mediator between India and Pakistan over Kashmir – or to refer the dispute to an existing organ, as was done by the Council in referring the Palestine question to the General Assembly.

Whatever the course adopted under Chapter VI, it must be adopted by a non-procedural decision. The justification for this lay in the so-called "chain of events" theory. This was that, it being granted that any permanent member could veto enforcement action, it was necessary to grant the same veto in matters of pacific settlement lest the permanent member should otherwise become committed to a course of action against its wishes which might ultimately lead to taking enforcement action. This reasoning does not really bear close examination. As we shall see, any permament member can, whatever course

[17] See, as an example of controversy on this point, the discussion in the Czechoslovakian question in 1948: *Repertory*, Vol. II, p. 231–233.

has been adopted under Chapter VI, cast its veto to prevent the determination of a "threat to the peace, breach of the peace or act of aggression" under Article 39 without which none of the enforcement measures under Chapter VII can be applied.

One final point must be noted in connection with Chapter VI, and that is that the powers of the Security Council are to make "recommendations". These are not binding on the States to whom they are addressed, for Article 25 relates only to "decisions". Hence the recommendation by the Council to the parties in the Corfu Channel dispute, that they submit their dispute to the International Court of Justice, was not regarded by the majority of the Court as creating a legal obligation to submit to the Court's jurisdiction.

(B) *Enforcement action*

The striking difference between the Covenant of the League of Nations and the Charter of the United Nations lies in the degree of centralisation accorded to the Council – the executive organ of limited membership. Under the League each member State reserved the right to determine for itself whether a particular State had resorted to war in breach of the Covenant, and also whether or not to comply with the recommendation of the Council with regard to the "sanctions" to be taken. In the United Nations the Security Council has the power, under Article 39, to determine, on behalf of the Organisation as a whole, whether or not there has been a "threat to the peace, breach of the peace or act of aggression", and its decisions with regard to any enforcement action to be taken are, theoretically at least, binding on the member States by virtue of Article 25.

The Security Council has two forms of enforcement action available to it; those described in Article 41, *i.e.*, not involving the use of armed force, and those described in Article 42, *i.e.*, involving action by air, sea or land forces. Before deciding upon either it is necessary for the Council to "determine the existence of any threat to the peace, breach of the peace, or act of aggression" under Article 39. This determination, as with all other decisions under Chapter VII, can only be made by a non-procedural vote. The unanimity of the permanent members is, therefore, essential and it is unlikely that any enforcement action can be taken under Chapter VII against any of the permanent members or any other State securing their support; the veto ensures that result. It is for this reason, above all others, that the measures envisaged in Chapter VII are virtually useless in an age in which the threats to the peace, breaches of the peace or acts of aggression occur in situations in which there is a conflict of interests between, notably, the U.S.A. and the U.S.S.R. and, consequently, no unanimity amongst the permanent members. Hence, after the Indonesian affair in 1947 (in which there was unanimity) and until the Congo crisis of July 1960, there had been no occasion on which the Security Council effectively used its powers under Chapter VII, except that of Korea in 1950, and this only due to the fortuitous absence of the U.S.S.R.[18] The successive crises of Berlin, Palestine, Indo-China, Hungary and Suez, to pick random examples, have all involved the East-West conflict of interests and, therefore, the Council has never used its enforcement powers. The East-West conflict destroyed the principle of unanimity upon which the whole structure of Chapter VII (and indeed UNO itself) depends for its ability to work as intended under the Charter. The Congo crisis of 1960 appeared, at the outset, to be a unique example of a situation which called for UN action but which did not involve the East-West conflict. Hence the three major resolutions of July 14, 22 and August 9 came from the Security Council, enabling the Secretary-General to provide military assistance to the government of the Congo. Admittedly the action taken was not "enforcement action" under Articles 41 or 42, but rather the "provisional measures" envisaged in Article 40,[19] but it nevertheless marked an unprecedented and initially successful use by the Security Council of its powers under Chapter VII. However, in due course the conflict between East and West re-emerged even here, and with the loss of unanimity effective control passed to the Assembly, convened in emergency session under the Resolution on Uniting for Peace procedure by the Security Council on September 17, 1960, against the votes of the U.S.S.R. and Poland. It is for the very reason that lack of unanimity has almost invariably frustrated the Council that the following discussion of the enforcement procedures under Chapter VII is of a somewhat cursory character.

The determination of a "threat to the peace, breach of the peace or act of aggression" under Article 39 must precede the use of the Council's powers under Articles 41 and 42, whether or not that Article is

[18] See *ante*, p. 29.

[19] See Schachter, "Legal Aspects of the UN Action in the Congo", (1961) 55 A.J.I.L. 1. The I.C.J., in its advisory opinion of July 20, 1962, on *Certain Expenses of the UN*, took the view that ONUC was not "enforcement action" against any State, and that the S.C. could "police a situation" (p. 167) without agreements existing under Art. 43, and without characterising its actions as "enforcement action".

specifically invoked or cited. The practice of the Council has been to avoid specific reference to that Article[20] (a practice, incidentally, not limited to Article 39); even in determining that the armed attack upon the Republic of Korea constituted a "breach of the peace", no specific reference to Article 39 was made by the Council in its resolution of June 25, 1950.[21] Two difficulties in the making of this determination call for comment. The first is that the "peace" referred to must mean "international" peace. It would be contrary to the intention of the Charter to assume that the Council could forcibly intervene in any civil strife which did not threaten international peace, and both in the Korean question and in the earlier Indonesian question the argument was advanced that action by the Council was barred on the ground that it intervened in the purely domestic jurisdiction of the State concerned. However, that argument was in both cases implicitly rejected. In the Congo affair, although the Council probably acted under Article 40, and although there was there a specific request from the government for UN intervention, it may also be recalled that the principle of non-intervention guided the Secretary-General in instructing the UN Force not to intervene in the internal struggle for political power but to confine its activities to the maintenance of law and order, the protection of human life and the elimination of the foreign elements (originally Belgian troops and later mercenaries) which tended to create a threat to *international* peace.[22] The second difficulty arises from the lack of any definition of the terms used, *i.e.*, "threat to the peace, breach of the peace or act of aggression". This lack was intentional. At San Francisco an area of discretion was intentionally left to the Council and although, subsequently, the United Nations has established a Committee on Defining Aggression, it has so far not succeeded, any more than the League did, in agreeing upon a definition. Whether a definition is desirable, and if so what type, is a debatable matter and it should not be assumed that the Council has thus far been handicapped by the absence of a definition. In practice the problem may be one of acquiring accurate factual knowledge of events, rather

[20] See *Repertory*, Vol. II, p. 334 *et seq.*

[21] S/1501; similarly in the resolution of June 27, 1950 (S/1511). It may be noted that neither resolution, the latter of which recommended Members to furnish assistance to the Republic of Korea, cited Articles 41 or 42. One construction of these resolutions is that they were in exercise of the power of "recommendation" under Art. 39.

[22] Schachter, *loc. cit.*, p. 15–20, and see especially the S.G.'s statement to the Security Council (UN Doc. S/P.V. 887).

than one of legal definition, and in Korea the Council relied heavily on the report of UNCOK (UN Commission on Korea) then in Korea, just as in considering the situation in Lebanon in 1958 it relied on the reports from UNOGIL (UN Observer Group in Lebanon). The presence of such groups "on the spot" is a tremendous advantage and, as has already been suggested, the Council has the power under Article 34 to send a committee or group where none already exists.

The practice of the Council rather suggests that the power under Article 40 to call upon the parties to comply with "provisional measures" does not depend upon a prior determination under Article 39. In the Palestine question Article 40 was specifically invoked, in ordering a cease-fire and calling for a withdrawal behind provisional truce-lines; similar measures were ordered by the Council in Kashmir. In the Congo, whilst there was abundant evidence, both in the terms of the request for assistance by the government of the Congo and in statements by representatives in the Security Council, that a "threat to international peace" existed, no specific determination under Article 39 was made. The resolutions of the Council were, however, probably based upon Article 40. The question whether a resolution "calling upon" States or other bodies to comply with the provisional measures is mandatory cannot be answered in the abstract. It was, however, clear that the three resolutions of July 14, 22 and August 9 were considered as mandatory, for the Secretary-General's conclusion[23] that Articles 25 and 49 applied was confirmed by the Security Council in the resolution of August 9. Both those articles refer to the *decisions* of the Security Council which are, of course, binding on all members. The "provisional measures" ordered under Article 40 do not prejudice the rights of the parties; they are simply a means of preventing an aggravation of the situation and the Council may take account of a failure to comply with such provisional measures.

The crux of the scheme envisaged in Chapter VII lay in the provision to the Security Council of the armed forces necessary to enforce its decisions against recalcitrant States, and this was to be effected by agreements between the member States and the Council, for which provision is made in Article 43. No such agreements have ever been concluded, so that the Council lacks the "teeth" with which to bite, and the Military Staff Committee for which provision is made in Articles 46 and 47 (although established since 1946) has no real function since its purpose was to make plans for the application of armed force

[23] Statement to the S.C. on August 8; Doc. S/P.V. 884, p. 9–10.

and to advise and assist the Council in the use of forces placed at its disposal. The absence of agreements under Article 43 would not, however, prevent member States from agreeing *ad hoc*, and in relation to a particular situation, to place forces at the disposal of the Council; in fact this is precisely how the United Nations Command was composed in Korea in 1950 and how the UN Force in the Congo was subsequently constituted. However, dependence on "voluntary contributions" cannot be said to be the surest guarantee of effectiveness.

The failure of the Security Council to fulfil its primary purpose of maintaining international peace and security has led to two major developments which will be considered later. The first is the assumption by the General Assembly of a role which was certainly never intended for it, namely that of determining a breach of the peace or an act of aggression and recommending action by members, including the use of armed forces.[24] The second is the development of powerful regional security systems of alliances outside the UN, such as NATO or the Warsaw Treaty Organisation, a development symptomatic of the breach of unity between the permanent members and the lack of confidence in the efficacy of the general collective security system based on the Security Council.[25]

II. The General Assembly

1. Composition

The General Assembly is the plenary organ of the United Nations, consisting of all the member States, each with one vote but entitled to five representatives. It would be this organ, therefore, which would reflect the extent to which the Organisation had become truly universal and thus a "world forum", an effective sounding-board for world opinion. For many years the Organisation fell far short of universality, for admission to membership was dependant on the fulfilment of certain conditions, and was to be achieved via a certain process, as Article 4 makes clear:

> "1. Membership in the United Nations is open to all other peace-loving states which accept the obligations contained in the present Charter and, in the judgment of the Organisation, are able and willing to carry out these obligations.

[24] See *post*, p. 45.
[25] See *post*, p. 152.

2. The admission of any such state to membership in the United Nations will be effected by a decision of the General Assembly upon the recommendation of the Security Council."

Thus Statehood is not alone sufficient; the applicant for membership has to satisfy the Organisation that it is "peace-loving", that it "accepts" the Charter obligations and, moreover, is "able and willing" to carry them out. The criteria are all capable of subjective appreciation by the existing member States in voting on an application for admission.

NOTES AND QUESTIONS

1. From the viewpoint of structure, the most significant revisions proposed by Clark and Sohn would involve relocating the primary responsibility for maintaining international peace and security in the General Assembly. The Security Council would henceforth be considered an agent of the General Assembly, although it would be given very important functions connected with the supervision of disarmament and peace-keeping activities. Since the Clark-Sohn revision of the Security Council is closely related to the extraordinary grant of legislative and executive power they propose to give to the General Assembly and to changes in the voting procedures of the Assembly, we defer evaluation of their proposal until after an opportunity has been had to study the General Assembly. A number of recent events concerning the relationship between the General Assembly and Security Council are relevant, however, to an understanding of their respective roles in matters of international peace and security.

During the period between 1958 and 1963 the role of the Security Council vis-a-vis the General Assembly and the Secretary-General has remained relatively fixed in the manner described by Goodrich. In the latter part of 1963 and during 1964 there was, however, a sudden flurry of activity within the Security Council. The following account by Marion McVitty from the *Independent Observer* (New York, June, 1964), tells how these developments relate to the allocation of authority and functions between the Security Council and General Assembly in the area of peace-keeping; it also points out the fundamental constitutional and political problems that have arisen in connection with the supranational quality of the United Nations:

> In 1963 the Security Council dealt with the future of Southern Rhodesia and the status of the Portuguese territories in Africa. And since March 1964 the Security Council has been extremely busy. It has dealt with the Cyprus emergency, Kashmir, the Cambodian complaint about interference and Apartheid.
>
> As a result of these activities some observers have argued that the Security Council is having a renaissance. In addition to these items being placed on the agenda, there have been efforts to negotiate drafts that could generally be agreed upon before resolutions are introduced into the Council. This has avoided the exercise of the veto by any major power. It seems fair to say that in the case of Cyprus this method produced extraordinarily positive results in view of the extremely complex and controversial nature of the emergency. In the case of the Cambodian complaint the method properly avoided having either Cambodia or the United Nations become involved in a political situation that they were unable

to deal with successfully. On the other hand, avoidance of the veto has thus far simply avoided the issues in the case of Kashmir, Southern Rhodesia, and the Portuguese territories; limited positive action with regard to South Africa has hardly had any more effective outcome.

If the pendulum swings back towards greater recourse to the Security Council, it is important to understand what forces have been operating in this direction. One such force is undoubtedly the controversy over the authority of the General Assembly in connection with its power to make the assessments needed to pay for peace-keeping operations. So long as the USSR and France maintain the position that the peace-keeping operations of the Organization cannot be authoritatively initiated by the General Assembly, or more narrowly, that the General Assembly does not have authoritative power to assess member states for peace-keeping operations, it is highly unlikely that the General Assembly will be able to assume responsibility for international peace and security. At the same time, the United Nations financial crisis is but a symptom of the political disaffection that has been experienced by certain major powers more severely than others but by all of them to some extent. While the USSR and France have fought openly against any form of authoritative power by the General Assembly, the United States and the United Kingdom have gone along with the binding nature of General Assembly assessments for emergency operations only so long as they remain ad hoc. These two Western powers, however, have shown an increasing uneasiness about the Uniting for Peace Resolution now that an Afro-Asian majority could determine the outcome by invoking that detour around the special control over events that major nations can exert in the Security Council. Furthermore, the Secretary-General is quite naturally concerned to avoid adding liabilities and is almost certain to avoid any new peace-keeping effort that does not emanate from the Security Council and include assessments to pay for the proposed United Nations action.

There is still another reason for a return of the Security Council. The vast majority of the small and new members are determined to implement the declaration granting independence to colonial peoples and countries. While zealous in prescribing remedies and demanding action in the Assembly, their experiences force them to realize that Assembly recommendations, no matter how reasonable or how passionately desired, can be ignored with impunity by the parties to whom they are addressed. Thus the Afro-Asians and other sympathetic states have evidently decided that the Security Council with is capacity to prescribe penalties may exert the kind of pressure that could produce results.

The question remains open as to which United Nations body can deal most effectively with international problems of serious concern. The General Assembly has the weight of numbers in expressing world opinion. The Security Council has the authority to make legally binding decisions and to apply sanctions. In addition, it is highly unlikely that the Organization would be able to make any major or significant decisions that would affect the international political system without at least the tacit consent of both the Soviet Union and the United States.

2. The financial crisis to which McVitty refers shall be dealt with more extensively in Chapter 10. Here it is sufficient to note that the crisis is an aspect of the question of whether or not the General Assembly or Security Council should have the major responsibility for dealing with matters of international peace and security. Those who wish to give the General Assembly the major responsibility are in large measure attempting, of course, to avoid the necessity to achieve unanimity among the five permanent members of the Security Council in peace-keeping actions. There are many observers who are strong supporters of greater supranational authority for the United Nations who feel, however, that it is unrealistic to expect any significant change in the capacity of the Organization to deal with international peace and security until the Soviet Union and the United States, at a minimum, achieve a greater consensus on how to deal with war-peace issues. As some

of these observers see it, an important step that might enhance the capacity of the United Nations to maintain international security is to make the Security Council a forum for the conduct of serious international diplomacy and negotiation. The Commission to Study the Organization of Peace, which consists of a group of prominent American scholars and public figures, has twice during the past seven years urged a diplomatic role upon the Security Council—"Development of the Process of Political Accomodation," Thirteenth Report of the Commission to Study the Organization of Peace, *Developing the United Nations: A Response to the Challenge of a Revolutionary Era* (New York, 1961) pp. 22–35. In its 1960 report the Commission wrote:

> We emphasize at the outset that no conceivable transformation of the United Nations will involve making international political adjustment a function performed exclusively by the world organization; whatever structural and procedural changes may be instituted in the United Nations, the importance of improving the methods and manners of diplomacy and of adapting it to the rapid changes in the character of international relations will remain undiminished. Even in the most mature national legislature, diplomacy—in the popular rather than the technical meaning of the term—plays an important part in adjusting the viewpoints of legislators and in preparing the way for acceptance of legislation by the considerable fraction of the citizens whose support or acquiescence is essential to the effectiveness of the legislation. Without such diplomatic preparation, legislation may require so much enforcement as to be ineffective. In short, the process of political accommodation is to some degree decentralized, even in a national state.

3. The term "parliamentary diplomacy" was first used by Dean Rusk and is most frequently thought to refer to the General Assembly where full-scale debate by all members on the total range of UN matters is possible in contrast with the more restricted membership and concerns of the Security Council. However, the characteristics of "parliamentary diplomacy" as they have been elucidated by Rusk and others seem also to apply to the behavior of statesmen in the Security Council. Perhaps the most quoted statement on this subject is the following paragraph from an article by Rusk entitled "Parliamentary Diplomacy—Debate v. Negotiation," *World Affairs Interpreter*, vol. 26, no. 2 (Summer, 1955) pp. 121–122:

> What might be called parliamentary diplomacy is a type of multilateral negotiation which involves at least four factors: First, a continuing organization with interest and responsibilities which are broader than the specific items that happen to appear upon the agenda at any particular time—in other words, more than a traditional international conference called to cover specific agenda. Second, regular public debate exposed to the media of mass communication and in touch, therefore, with public opinions around the globe. Third, rules of procedure which govern the process of debate and which are themselves subject to tactical manipulation to advance or oppose a point of view. And lastly, formal conclusions, ordinarily expressed in resolution, which are reached by majority votes of some description, on a simple or two-thirds majority or based upon a financial contribution or economic stake—some with and some without a veto. Typically, we are talking about the United Nations and its related organizations, although not exclusively so, because the same type of organization is growing up in other parts of the international scene.

An important exposition of the character of parliamentary diplomacy is to be found in a series of lectures by Judge Philip C. Jessup, "Parliamentary Diplomacy: An Examination of the Legal Quality of the Rules of Procedure of Organs of the U.N.," *Récueil des Cours*, vol. 89-I (A. W. Sijthoff, Leyden, 1956) pp. 185–319. See also, Hardy Dillard, "Some Aspects of Law and Diplomacy," *Recueil des Cours,* vol. 91-I (1957) p. 449–550; and Percy E. Corbett, *Law in Diplomacy* (Princeton University Press, 1959).

Goodrich notes that the reforms most often discussed for strengthening the Security Council are concerned with revisions of its authority, voting procedures, and the composition of its membership. Discussion of proposals for reform is here restricted to the Clark-Sohn proposals for voting in the Security Council and, especially, to their proposed elimination of the veto.

Clark and Sohn feel that the retention of the veto by a single state interferes with the efficient operation of the Organization under conditions of international strain; at the same time, given the important functions conferred upon this body, Clark and Sohn feel that binding decisions by the Council, renamed the Executive Council, on important matters should be reached only if supported by a special majority. This special majority is based ultimately on population and results in giving relatively more influence to the most heavily populated states. In addition, in order to accommodate the much larger numbers of states that would be in the United Nations, as contrasted with the original 51 Members, they would expand the Council to 17 members. Although the gist of their proposals on voting is to be found in their revision of Article 27, this appears to be an approriate time to examine their proposals for the composition and functions of the Executive Council. In reading these materials, consider to what extent their revision of the present Security Council seems sensible and feasible, given the present political context, even if the rest of their scheme should not be adopted. Which groups of nations would be adversely affected by the revision? Why and under what conditions would it be rational for them to accept it?

Read WPTWL, pp. 66–88.

NOTES AND QUESTIONS

1. Evaluate the Clark-Sohn proposals for eliminating the veto. Is there any hope of changing the veto provision as it stands in the present UN Charter? Note the suggestions outlined by Goodrich's article in this chapter.
2. The veto poses a perplexing problem for those who feel that additional supranational authority is necessary for the effective control of international violence. As Goodrich points out, however, the veto has probably not been as obstructive as is commonly believed. Furthermore, if the veto is expressive of an underlying political cleavage that can only begin to close when intense ideological and political tensions diminish, or when an agreement can be reached between the superpowers to

change the methods by which international conflict is waged, then its retention may serve to disclose the effective limits of action by the Security Council in the current world.

The Commission's report underscores this point by seeking a way to make the Security Council an important forum for negotiation and discussion, that is, for overcoming the cleavage, rather than to propose the elimination of the veto, so as to make it a less hampered authoritative decision-making body. Some observers have gone even further in their reluctance to oppose the veto and have suggested that there are some positive functions for the veto. For example, Roger Fisher offers an analysis of the role of the veto in a proposed agreement on arms control inspection in his article entitled "Should We Veto the Troika?" *The New Republic*, vol. 145 (August 21, 1961) pp. 278–280, and p. 283. His comments apply almost equally well in the context of the Security Council.

> In the light of the physical power which a major nation has to use its army or its police to veto proposed international action against it, the continued existence of an international organization may depend upon there being some legal way of exercising that power. To provide a right of veto at some stage is to recognize the limited power which any international organization has, for example, over the United States and over the Soviet Union. If the Soviet Union had not had the legal right of veto within the Security Council during the last 15 years, it is unlikely that the United Nations would exist today. It is at least probable the Russians would have wrecked a veto-less UN dominated by the West.
>
> The existence of a legal right to exercise a political veto may protect an international administrative machine in another way. If there is no permissible veto, the international civil servants or neutrals who are making decisions must take that into account. They will have to ponder the political resistance to their decisions and whether a particular decision might be "unacceptable" to a major power. One can conceive of a neutral in a veto-less test-ban organization being approached by the Soviet representative with the suggestion that he has been voting too often with the Western members and that the Soviet Union may have to break up the organization unless he will go along with the Soviet Union on a particular vote. Or such an approach might be made by a US representative who thinks that a neutral has been too pro-Soviet. In such a situation, a conscientious neutral may conclude that it is better to preserve the international organization than to conduct an inspection. ("Both sides have such quantities of nuclear weapons that even one test, if it did occur, is not terribly important; far better to vote in a way which will preserve the chances of continued international cooperation and eventual disarmament.") Requiring the administrative staff to take into account the factor of political unacceptability runs the risk of corrupting its integrity.
>
> On the other hand, the existence of a legal right of veto at the political level tends to free the international civil servant from having to modify his judgment to make it politically acceptable. He can give his honest, scientific or impartial views, without having to assume the risk of wrecking the institution by his own action, since if the decision is unacceptable to a major power, that country may veto it. ("If you don't like my decision you can veto it, but I must do my duty as I see it.")
>
> Moreover, the veto, like the group decision, is deeply rooted in Anglo-American law. For centuries we have insisted that representatives of the people be given a veto power over the enforcement of the criminal laws. Many famous trials, such as that of Peter Zenger in 1735 for printing a libel against the Governor of New York, demonstrate that one of the purposes behind trial by jury is to give people a veto over the enforcement against one of them of laws which the people do not want to see enforced. Not only does the jury as a unit have a veto in every major criminal case; the requirement that the jury's verdict be unanimous gives each of the 12 jurors veto power over a verdict either way. And on the other side the

prosecutor is usually given unreviewable discretion to veto the prosecution of any case. There are, of course, differences between the restraints which people impose on a government and those which governments impose upon international organizations. But if within a community like the US we are so distrustful of authority that we insist upon a system of checks and balances, we should understand that comparable checks and balances may be necessary in a community where there is far less mutual trust.

As a matter of fact, the draft nuclear test ban treaty submitted this spring by the United States and the United Kingdom included a significant number of provisions involving a veto. For example, the major powers are given a right of veto over the appointment of both the Administrator and the Deputy Administrator. The initial location of fixed air inspection routes is subject to veto by the country being inspected, as are the locations of the fixed components of the inspection system. More significantly, perhaps, under the Anglo-American draft treaty "the total amount of each annual budget shall require the concurring votes of the original Parties." The US Government has thus adopted a flexible attitude towards the veto. Not only did we include various veto provisions within our draft treaty but undoubtedly we would have given consideration to additional provisions. We thus recognized the veto as something to be dealt with in practical terms depending upon particular circumstances.

The Soviet position has been represented as being that a veto must apply to everything. With respect to nuclear testing *Life* magazine reported: "The Soviets say now they will accept only the 'troika' system whereby any of three members could veto any inspection." This is incorrect. The Soviet Union has publicly recognized that the veto is not something to be applied across the board. With respect to nuclear testing its troika proposal involves a veto on matters to be decided by the vote of the Administrative Council. In a section of its June 4th memorandum which was not given wide publicity in the United States, the Soviet Union explained that ". . . on-the-spot inspections within the limits of the agreed quotas must be effected at the request of the side interested in the inspection without any voting in the control commission or any other agency. All that is needed are objective readings of instruments at control posts indicating that a phenomenon took place in some part of the given country which might be suspected as a nuclear explosion. If there is such objective reading, the Soviet proposal envisages that neither the Control Commission nor any other body of the control organization can interfere with the satisfaction of the demand of the side for an inspection. Hence, no obstacles to inspection, to which the United States representatives refer, speaking of the so-called 'veto', can be created by the Administration Council."

Suppose, for example, that the proposed nuclear test-ban organization were set up in such a way that there were an administrative determination, below the veto level, that a suspicious disturbance of seismic magnitude 4.75 or above had occurred in a designated locality which would be eligible for inspection. A Soviet veto at such a stage would provide the basis for both an adverse world reaction and responsive action by other countries. Suppose, instead, the test-ban organization were set up in such a way that no release of factual data nor official determination that a seismic event had occurred could be made without the consent of a Soviet representative. Then it would be far easier for the Soviet Union to frustrate an inspection.

The difference between requiring consent at every stage and permitting a "safety valve" veto was demonstrated in the Security Council vote to increase the UN forces in the Congo. The Soviet Union had made clear its position that the UN troops should be withdrawn. If the release of factual reports from the Congo and a decision on what to do had required Soviet consent, such consent would probably not have been forthcoming. But as it was, the Soviet Union was presented with a majority decision of the Council in support of a resolution calling for an increase of UN troops in the Congo in the light of official factual reports. At this stage the Soviet Union found that it chose not to exercise the right of veto which it had.

The veto in an international organization is thus like a safety valve on a steam boiler. If the safety valve is set to go off too quickly it will prevent the machine from accomplishing much—although such a machine may still be better than none. If there is no safety valve at all the machine may blow up. And, as with a safety valve, a veto can be designed in such a way that it will not prevent the machine from doing its job.

3. For an ingenious proposal to use a post-adjudication veto as a device to encourage greater use of the ICJ by states, see Fisher's essay, "The Veto as a Means of Making Third-Party Settlement Acceptable," *Proceedings of the American Society of International Law* (1964) p. 123. And for criticism of Fisher's position, see Leo Gross, "Problems of International Adjudication and Compliance with International Law: Some Simple Solutions," *American Journal of International Law*, vol. 59 (January, 1965) p. 48. See also the brief discussion of Fisher in Notes and Questions in Chapter 8.

Although the problem of the veto has frequently been related to the composition and possible expansion of the membership of the Security Council, the political activity within the Organization has moved in the direction of separating the two questions. As Goodrich points out on page 182, an informal gentleman's agreement has been used as the basis for selecting the non-permanent members of the Council, but this agreement, even though it includes having states share a two-year term, has not satisfied the demands of many members, especially those from Africa and Asia. With 65 new Members in the Organization since 1945, the question of the composition of the Security Council has been more and defined as a problem of expanding its membership.

Proposals for expansion and an altered composition of the membership of the Security Council have been before the General Assembly since 1956, first as a part of general considerations concerning Charter revision and then in relation to the expansion of other bodies of the United Nations. In December, 1963, the General Assembly adopted three proposals submitted by the Special Political Committee that called for the expansion of the Security Council from 11 to 15 members, of the Economic and Social Council from 18 to 27, and of the General Committee of the General Assembly from 21 to 24; the proposals also contained the criteria and manner for selecting members to these bodies. These proposals concerning the Security Council and Economic and Social Council will come into effect only when all the permanent members of the Security Council and two-thirds of the General Assembly ratify them. (The recommendation to enlarge the General Committee of the General Assembly was treated as a change in the rules of procedure of the General Assembly and therefore did not necessitate formal amendment of the Charter. It was adopted by a unanimous vote of the Membership of the United Nations. It is interesting to note that none of the veto powers voted against the recommendation despite some reluctance to vote for expansion of the two organs.) The process of ratification was to have been completed by September, 1965, or the proposals lapse. Whatever the formal outcome, excerpts from the debates dealing with this proposal make it clear that the questions relating to structure, membership, composition, and voting within the various parts of the Organization offer us an image of contemporary political processes and indicate some of the extent to which an international organization may have an impact upon the international political system, and vice versa. These materials also offer insight into the political preconditions of transition to a less war-prone world. A portion of the debates that took place in the Special Political Committee are reproduced below. Before reading them, however, there is another excerpt from the 1960 Report of the Commission to Study the Organization of Peace that enumerates the range of criteria and alternative proposals that the Assembly might have used in dealing with the question of expansion. This is useful as a frame of reference for evaluating the various positions taken during the debates.

A larger Security Council is urgently needed. The membership of the United Nations grew from fifty-one at its foundation to ninety-nine, in late 1960, and further enlargement is expected as the liquidation of colonial empires proceeds to its conclusion. Six elective members of the Security Council barely sufficed to represent adequately the states making the largest contributions to the keeping of the peace and to the other purposes of the United Nations, when the Organization was much smaller than it is now. There has always been difficulty in filling the nonpermanent seats so as to satisfy the additional requirement of equitable geographical distribution.

If the Security Council of the future is to be a vital political organ, its elective contingent must be sufficiently enlarged to permit adequate representation (1) of the "middle powers" capable of contributing most significantly to the work of the Organization, (2) of the major geographical and cultural regions of the world, and (3) of the leading political groupings. At the very least, provision must be made for giving assured representation in the Security Council to the African states, and to the states of Asia which are uncommitted in the cold war.

It is no easy matter to divide the members of the United Nations into neat categories for representative purposes. Geographical regions are at best vaguely defined, and regional boundaries do not always coincide with cultural or political dividing lines. It would hardly be valid to assume, for instance, that a "member for the Middle East" could speak for both Israel and the Arab states—or, indeed, for all the states in the region other than Israel. Moreover, there are legitimate objections to bestowing formal recognition upon political blocs. These groupings are, in most instances, relatively informal and fluid, and it would be most unfortunate if they were formalized in such manner as to encourage their rigidification. Khrushchev's proposal for a "triumvirate" at the head of the Secretariat is unacceptable for the reason, among others, that it postulates a clear-cut division among Eastern, Western, and neutralist blocs which is not, and ought not to become, characteristic of the United Nations.

Nevertheless, it is clear that the Member States of the United Nations do fall into a number of roughly-defined groupings, which are significant despite the indistinctness of their dividing lines. Realistically, these must be taken into account; a balance must be found between the extremes of pretending that they do not exist and of recognizing them in such fashion as to promote the hardening of their boundaries.

There is nothing wrong in allowing "politics" to influence elections to the Security Council. On the contrary, political considerations are indispensable if the composition of the Council is to reflect the realities of world politics. The General Assembly did well to recognize the claim of the British Commonwealth to one of the non-permanent seats, despite the geographical dispersion of its members, since the Commonwealth as a whole made a specially important contribution to the purposes of the Organization. But the same reasoning leads to the conclusion that every important political group should also be equitably represented in an organ which is designed primarily to furnish facilities for parliamentary diplomacy and needs therefore to represent all the major interests in world affairs. In fact, the two standards for the election of non-permanent members of the Security Council which are prescribed in the Charter are flexible enough to permit due allowance for political considerations, if there were a sufficient number of non-permanent seats.

One possible approach to the objective of making the Security Council a more satisfactory representative body would be simply to amend the Charter to provide for a larger Council, thereby making more elective seats available, and to trust in the good sense of members of the Assembly to exercise their choice so as to create a reasonable and politically realistic balance in the composition of the Council. This is certainly the simplest method, and it has the merit of recognizing that states can be only advised, not commanded, as to the use which they make of their voting rights. Its demerit is that it offers no guarantee that additional seats will be distributed in accordance with the essential criterion of representativeness. If this plan were adopted, we would suggest that not more than six elective seats be added to the present six, and that the number of votes required for decision be correspondingly increased.

As a variation on the scheme just described, it might be proposed that an informal "gentlemen's agreement" be worked out among members of the United Nations as to the allocation of an enlarged bloc of elective seats in the Security Council. This would call for a modification and supplementation of the informal understandings which have had considerable influence upon elections to the Council in the past. By this device, a system of precedents might be developed which would provide reasonable assurance that the Assembly's electoral process would regularly produce a realistically proportioned Security Council.

Another variant which might be considered would be to have the Assembly establish a formal set of categories, leaving it to each Member State to opt for inclusion in the group which it desires, and determining the allocation of Council seats among the groups thus formed. This might be accomplished by adopting a new rule of procedure, whereby the Assembly would be, in effect, regulating its own performance of the electoral function. Under such a scheme, it might be desirable to provide that the members of a given group should have effective choice of the state or states to fill that group's Council quota, restricting the full Assembly to ratification of the choices thus made.

Still another possiblity would be to reserve the six existing elective seats in the Security Council for the representation of regional groupings, that representation to be worked out by one of the methods suggested above, and to create a number of additional seats to be filled by "election at large." In that case, it might be hoped that Member States, having satisfied their urge for geographical-political distribution in the election of the former group of members, would tend to choose the "members at large" from the ranks of those states which are willing and able to make particularly significant contributions to the work of the United Nations.

It is vitally important to secure adequate representation in the Security Council for states which are "principal contributors," even though it is difficult to define and measure the contributions which are involved, and it probably would be impossible to secure general agreement on a formal scheme for designating the "principal contributors" and giving them a special status in the Security Council. The criteria of importance would include population, economic significance, financial contribution to the United Nations, and capacity to assist the United Nations in military or quasi-military operations. It must be recognized, however, that the smaller, weaker, and poorer states may contribute imponderable political and moral values which in fact outweigh the tangible contributions made by their more impressive fellow members of the United Nations.

Consider, for example, the kind of contribution that may be described as moral. The strength of a Member State's devotion to the purposes of the United Nations and of its faith in the principles on which the Organization is founded may be great or little. A Member State of small population, limited natural resources, and little military power, but strongly devoted to the purposes and principles embodied in the United Nations Charter, may send able and useful representatives to meetings of the General Assembly, supply to that body an occasional president of high distinction and practical capacity for leadership in its affairs, and exert a constructive influence at every crisis in world politics. Thus it may make a more valuable contribution than another Member State of larger population, greater wealth, and superior military power, which drags its feet in every emergency and seems to have little faith in systematic and purposeful efforts to establish a better world order. Moral contributions to the purposes of the United Nations are impossible to measure, but a good reputation for respecting the obligations of membership, regardless of military power or wealth, may be the best of qualifications for election to the Security Council.

The importance of sturdy moral contributors is manifest even in operations designed to deal with threats to the peace and acts of aggression by important military powers. There have been three outstanding tests of the willingness and practical capacity of Member States to give effective aid in connection with such operations: the case of Korea in 1950, that of Suez in 1956, and that of the Congo in 1960. In each case the response of some of the Member States was immediate and impressive, though only token military contributions were accepted from the weaker contributors. But the moral force of the token contributions strengthened the morale of the Organization, enhanced its prestige, and immeasurably added to the impact of the operations in the field. The contributors of contingents to the action in Korea are commemorated by a memorial plaque in the vestibule of the General Assembly building in New York. Included among them are both important and unimportant military powers as well as both large and small financial contributors to the Organization. The same lack of relationship between actual contributions and measurable capacity to contribute appears again in the operations at Suez. In the latter case, indeed, military contributions by the major powers were deliberately excluded in order to prevent conflict between them for control of the situation. The expenses of the operation were defrayed from a special fund, contributions to which bore little relation to the established scale of assessment for the regular expenses of the Organization. It is obvious that the military power and financial capacity of the Member States constitute a very imperfect measure of their contributions to the purposes of the United Nations.

The operations in the Congo demonstrate further how useful the smallest and weakest contributors may be, when men and money are needed to accomplish the purposes of the United Nations. In this case only three states of European population, Canada, Sweden and Ireland, were called upon to furnish military contingents. The main military burden of the peace-keeping operations fell upon African Member States, most of which are both militarily and financially weak. While some of them may have had political axes of their own which they wished to grind, their initial response indicated, for the most part, a strong determination to support the authority of the United Nations with a minimum of aid from outside the Continent. Additional help, when needed was furnished by Asian Member States, regardless of their distance from the scene of action. The principal test of ability to contribute was political. The basic qualification for a helpful contributor was active sympathy with the main purpose of the United Nations in intervening in the Congo, and practical capacity to give military aid of a kind that would be acceptable to the people of the newly liberated Congo Republic.

Most of the actual contributors to the purposes of the United Nations in these cases were small states, measured by population, wealth, or military power. The greatest potential contributors to the maintenance of international peace and security are doubtless the major powers. It is regrettable that the Charter undertook to specify the states whose importance should entitle them to permanent seats in the Security Council, since the brief history of the United Nations has already confirmed the proposition that such a list becomes outmoded with the passage of time. Ideally, the list of privileged members should be revised and made flexible enough to register future changes in the status of Member States, but this hardly seems politically feasible at the present time. In any event, experience up to now shows the great importance of the military contributions by the lesser powers and ordinary Member States. Still more it shows the great importance of the moral contributions of all those, regardless of size, wealth, or geographical situation, who strongly believe in the purposes of the United Nations and freely contribute according to their means to the actions that may be deemed necessary and proper for dealings with recurrent emergencies and crises.

Moral contributions to the purposes of the United Nations may take the form of furnishing wise councillors and other leaders in the work of the Organization. Outstanding among such contributions have been the successive holders of the office of Secretary-General and the presiding officers of the General Assembly. Scandinavian Member States have supplied spirited and skillful leadership in the former office and all the General Assembly Presidents have come from other Middle Powers or lesser states. The wisest and most useful international statesmen may hail from states of lesser military or economic importance. It is evident that the selection of members of the Security Council on account of their contributions to the purposes of the United

Nations involves the weighing of many factors in the making of an international organization that will be equal to its growing responsibilities under the difficult conditions of the nuclear age.

Despite the complexities and difficulties of measurement which we have noted, no one can doubt that there is in fact a group of Member States which make outstanding contributions to the United Nations, and that the liberal representation of this group in the membership of the Security Council would do much to strengthen the political significance of that body. No scheme can guarantee the selection of the best qualified states for membership in the Security Council, but the provision of separate blocks of seats for regional representatives and for "members at large" might enhance the prospect that principal contributors would be given the prominent role in the Security Council to which their importance entitles them.

The alternative schemes which we have described represent more or less elaborately detailed approaches to a common objective: making the Security Council a more broadly representative body and thus, hopefully, a more useful instrument for the adjustment of political differences among states. We put them forward for illustrative purposes. Our aim is not to advocate a particular solution, but to stress our conviction that it is urgently necessary to remodel the Security Council so as to enhance its political usefulness, and to stimulate thought and effort toward that end.

The adoption of a well-considered plan for rehabilitating the Security Council through enlarging and balancing its membership should enable it to reflect in due measure all the important interests in world politics, and ensure that its consent to any controversial proposal would carry with it general international support. Thus, the Council would become an attractive locus for international negotiations looking toward generally acceptable solutions of the bigger problems which nations have heretofore too often sought to settle by the use or threat of armed force.

With the Commission's Report as background, we turn now to the action in the United Nations on expansion. At the 18th Meeting of the Organization, the Special Committee of the General Assembly had before it various draft proposals for the expansion of the Security Council, the Economic and Social Council and the General Committee of the General Assembly. Although our main interest here is in the first of these organs, the discussion in the Political Committee concerned all three. This creates some opportunity to become acquainted with the working of the Economic and Social Council, as well as with the committee system of the General Assembly.

In these materials a number of political elements are manifest. Perhaps the most significant of these from the viewpoint of world order is the extent to which regionalism appears to be a viable basis for building, in the future, a more peaceful international system. In essence, the Political Committee adopted proposals based on fixed geographical representation that involved dividing the world into several regions. Several classes of states were opposed to the use of regional criteria. The most intense opposition occurred on the part of states that are situated in a region that is controlled by states hostile to it, e.g., Israel, Cuba, South Africa. Other more subtle opposition was provoked because some states felt that they had political and cultural ties that transcended geographical regions and were thus entitled to representation on this basis, e.g., the members of the British Commonwealth. Still another trouble point involved a group of states that claimed common political and cultural interests in more than one region—the Arab states of the Middle East being either their own region or a part of both Asia and Africa. Although all these matters were resolved, it should be noted that the authority and competence of the Security Council is not altered by the resolutions. Of course, the operations of the Council may be different with an expanded membership based on regional composition; at any rate it is highly conjectural, however, whether net tension will increase or decrease, if the Security Council or some other international body with membership based upon geographical representation is given greatly enhanced authority over matters of peace and security.

Additional features of contemporary international politics infiltrated the debates on expansion. Among the most interesting and incendiary of these is the wisdom of excluding the Chinese People's Republic from the United Nations. Other features that are represented in the debates include the cold war, the Sino-Soviet dispute (see below, the exchange between the Soviet and Albanian delegates on the attitude of China toward the expansion proposal), and the strong Afro-Asian opposition to colonialism and neo-colonialism.

Finally it should be noted that Charter revision is a constitutional matter and that many of the arguments relied upon by the diplomats combine evaluation of contemporary international political processes with appeals to previous acts of the Organization (precedent) and to other provisions in the Charter. Recall here the discussions in Chapter 2 concerning the relationship of political and legal processes in the Organization.

United Nations
GENERAL ASSEMBLY
EIGHTEENTH SESSION
Official Records

SPECIAL POLITICAL COMMITTEE, 419th MEETING

Thursday, 5 December 1963

NEW YORK

CONTENTS

Chairman: Mr. Mihail HASEGANU (Romania).

AGENDA ITEMS 81, 82 AND 12

Question of the composition of the General Committee of the General Assembly (A/5519) (continued)

Question of equitable representation on the Security Council and the Economic and Social Council (A/5520 and Corr.1) (continued)

Report of the Economic and Social Council (chapter XIII (section VI)) (A/5503) (continued)

1. Mr. M'BALE (Congo, Leopoldville), on behalf of the Congolese people and Government, paid a tribute to the memory of President Kennedy, a great statesman who had upheld the principles of equality and justice, and had fought for the complete emancipation of the Negroes of the United States of America.

2. The Congo was one of forty-eight Asian and African countries which, taking as a basis paragraphs 1 and 2 of Article 2 of the Charter, had requested the inclusion in the agenda of the present session of the question of the composition of the General Committee of the General Assembly. He recalled that the question had already come up in resolution 791 (VIII) of 23 October 1953, by which the Assembly amended rules 38 and 39 of its rules of procedure; that at its eleventh session the Assembly had decided (resolution 1104 (XI)) to establish an eighth Vice-Presidency; and that at the following session it had decided, in resolution 1192 (XII) to increase the number of Vice-Presidencies to thirteen. Discussion of that resolution had raised issues which were still not settled in 1963. At that time the Asian and African countries formed a little over one third of the Member States. Currently they accounted for more than half, and their increase in numbers was not reflected in the present composition of the General Committee, which no longer had the "representative character" specified in rule 38 of the rules of procedure. The explanatory memorandum (A/5519) left no doubt on that subject. Even at the twelfth session the question of principle had not been at issue, as had been stressed by the United Kingdom representative in his statement at the 728th plenary meeting, that "the aims of this discussion are not really in any doubt". But in 1963 th question had become urgent and revision was essentia Of the twenty-one seats in the General Committee on six were held by the Asian and African countries. Th very effectiveness of the General Committee wa imperilled by the inadequate participation of the tw continents in its work. Far from sharing the view expressed by certain Powers, such as the Unite Kingdom and the United States, which at the twelft session had contended that the General Committe would be more effective if its membership wa limited, he could not see how its work could be impede by an equitable representation. The text of resolutic 1192 (XII), which provided that the General Committe should be so constituted as to ensure its representativ character on the basis of a balanced geographica distribution among its members, was sufficient clear and precise on that point. It was therefore t be hoped that the Committee would avoid the type discussion it had embarked upon at the twelfth sessic regarding the concepts of "representative character and "geographical distribution" and would keep to mor precise and enduring principles than political uncertainties. It was true that rule 38 of the rules of prc cedure specified "representative character" and di not mention geographical distribution, but the resolution itself clearly established that the composition the General Committee must be revised on the bas of the principle of geographical distribution.

3. The annex to resolution 1192 (XII) contained number of shortcomings which must be avoided the present session. For instance the expressic "other States" in paragraph 1 (d) of the annex wa as the United Kingdom representative had stated the twelfth session, vague and imprecise, although referred to certain members of the Commonwealt He did not propose to linger over the question of t division of Europe into two, which was a pure political matter and for which it must certainly b possible to find a solution within the framework peaceful coexistence. His delegation was not oppose to maintaining the five Vice-Presidencies allocate to the five permanent members of the Security Counci But in changing the composition of the General Con mittee, account must be taken not only of the numbe of Vice-Presidencies but also of the distribution the Committee chairmanships, since Europe and t "other States" had three chairmanships, whereas t African and Asian countries had only two. In his vie a stricter geographical distribution was essential, a countries which clearly belonged to a given contine must be included within that geographical unit. T geographical, not the political, criterion must preva and on that basis the Congolese delegation wa requesting equitable representation for Africa a Asia.

4. Turning to the question of the composition of t Security Council, he said that the body which had t main responsibility for the maintenance of inte

national peace and security had become unfit to fulfil its high mission, since it no longer represented the real situation in the United Nations in 1963. Distribution of the non-permanent seats was based on political, economic or other criteria. The Congo wished to revert to an equitable geographical distribution in accordance with Article 23, paragraph 1 of the Charter. Hitherto, distribution had been based on a gentleman's agreement concluded in 1946. The anachronism of the present distribution needed no further demonstration. The Organization had frequently found itself unable to choose a non-permanent member of the Council and had been forced to divide the normal two-year term of office between two countries. The illegality of such a decision had been condemned by a number of delegations.

5. The attitude adopted by a permanent member of the Council, which made any revision of the Charter conditional upon the admission of a certain State, seemed not only an impediment to the desire of the majority of Members to see the Council fulfil its functions as it ought to, but also contrary to the spirit of the Charter. The only possible solution, and the only one appropriate to present circumstances, was to enlarge the Security Council and to allocate the seats according to the principle of equitable geographical distribution.

6. The question of representation on the Economic and Social Council was still older than that concerning the General Committee of the Assembly. The composition of the Economic and Social Council had been fixed in 1946 at a time when the Organization had only fifty-one Members. Yet even then the question of the number of members of the Council had been debated at length and the number fixed had not been deemed satisfactory. Indeed, as early as the second session there had been a proposal to increase the membership to twenty-four.

7. With its eighteen members the Economic and Social Council could not carry out its duties to the best of its abilities. That was a point which the Latin American countries had emphasized for a long time. The unrepresentative character of the Council was particularly apparent in the fact that one of its special concerns was with the economic and social development of the developing countries and that those very countries had the smallest representation on it. A revision of its composition was thus a basic necessity in the interests of the effectiveness of its work.

8. With regard to the procedure to be followed in order to attain that end, it was necessary to ensure that, whatever happened, the Committee was not led by political considerations into the sterile discussions of previous years. Some delegations expressed readiness to meet the needs of the African and Asian countries but then found excuses for voting against what they asked for. If the principles contained in the Charter were not applied, the Economic and Social Council would end by losing all authority and all value at the very time when the Organization was trying energetically to tackle the basic problems of underdevelopment.

9. The urgent need for a revision had in any case been brought up as far back as the tenth session, when the Assembly had examined the question of convening a general conference of the Members of the United Nations for the purposes of reviewing the Charter. Most speakers had then considered that a change in the composition of the Council would be generally acceptable.

10. The following year seventeen Latin American States and one European State had proposed, in a letter dated 19 June 1956,[1] that the provisional agenda of the eleventh session should include the question of amending the Charter to increase the membership of the Economic and Social Council. Consideration of that question, which had been included in the agenda for 1957, had been postponed to the thirteenth session and then to the fourteenth. When it was taken up in 1959 the question had been dealt with in an equally disappointing resolution—resolution 1404 (XIV)—in which the Assembly had confined itself to "realizing"—instead of "taking note" as it had done at the thirteenth session—that many delegations had expressed the opinion that there should be an increase in the membership of certain bodies. Nevertheless, operative paragraph 2 of resolution 1404 (XIV) marked some slight progress, since it read: "... if progress is not made during the fifteenth session of the General Assembly towards the achievement of an increase in the membership of ... the Economic and Social Council, the Assembly should set up at that session a committee to study the possibilities of arriving at an agreement which will facilitate the amendment of the Charter ...". At the fifteenth session the Special Political Committee had been forced to state in its report that it had no recommendations to submit to the Assembly.[2] In other words, certain Member States had had no wish to increase the membership of the Economic and Social Council, and for reasons that were neither economic nor social.

11. As to the views of the Economic and Social Council itself on that matter, in its resolution 690 B (XXVI) it had called for an increase in its own membership and it had reiterated that appeal in resolution 974 C (XXXVI). In addition, it had enlarged the membership of its own subsidiary bodies. How could certain countries believe that the Council could work effectively with only eighteen members when the Technical Assistance Committee and the Committee on Industrial Development needed thirty members? In 1960 those two committees had had a membership of only twenty-four, i.e., the same number which the Asian and African countries were now asking for the Council.

12. The United Nations was a living organization and must keep in step with the times. The constant increase in the number of Members itself implied a renewal of its organs. An organization which tried to carry out its task with bodies whose composition had been fixed in 1946 was bound to lack balance and to be weak.

13. The need for revision had been recognized. The Committee was confronted with a technical problem which certain Powers wanted to make political. It was no longer possible to submit to the General Assembly a report containing no recommendations. The only thing needed for the adoption of a resolution was the agreement of the five permanent members of the Security Council. Any opposition in that respect would be regarded by his delegation as a flagrant attack on the proper conduct of the Organization's work and as

---

1/ Official Records of the General Assembly, Eleventh Session, Annexes, agenda items 56, 57 and 58, document A/3139.

2/ Ibid., Fifteenth Session, Annexes, agenda item 23, document A/4626, para. 15.

directed against the development of the African and Asian countries. The delegation of the Congo (Leopoldville) would support any draft resolution proposing a reasonable increase in the membership of the Economic and Social Council and was ready to co-sponsor such a resolution. Any such increase must be based on equitable geographical distribution and on nothing else. All must co-operate to ensure that the African and Asian countries were given the representation to which they were entitled.

420th
MEETING

Friday, 6 December 1963,

1. Mr. NAVIA (Colombia) thought that, in view of the importance of the three items under study, the General Assembly would probably have to take concrete decisions which would not be mere recommendations. Recognition must be given to the growth of the Organization, as a result of which certain States had acquired the undeniable right to equitable representation, since they were fully-fledged Members of the Organization.

2. He would not confine himself to stating the position of his delegation but would give an over-all view of United Nations law. The Charter provided two different procedures for making changes in it. Analysing the two procedures provided for under Articles 108 and 109, he noted that Article 108 was concerned with amendments and Article 109 with review of the Charter. In view of the difference in meaning between amendment and review, it was evident that the procedure to be followed in the present case was that laid down in Article 108. The alterations would, in fact, be partial and would be concerned expressly with the wording of the Charter; thus, amendments were involved, rather than review. Article 108 provided, in addition, that amendments to the Charter would come into force when they had been adopted by a vote of two thirds of the Members of the General Assembly and ratified by two thirds of the Members of the United Nations, including all the permanent members of the Security Council. On the other hand, Article 109 provided for the holding of a General Conference of the Members of the United Nations for the purpose of reviewing the Charter, at a date and place to be fixed by a two-thirds vote of the General Assembly and by a vote of any seven members of the Security Council. From the legal point of view, it was completely justifiable to increase the membership of the Councils on the basis of the provisions of Article 108.

3. The General Assembly had always displayed prudence in the defence of the Charter, and it must maintain that attitude. Reviewing the history of the Charter, he recalled that his country had been among the founders of the United Nations.

4. One of the most desirable characteristics of national constitutions was the stability of their principles. Indeed, all politically responsible peoples desired their institutions to be as lasting as possible and to reflect the social, political and economic situation. It had been said that the form the State should take was the principal concern of politicians a legislators. The purpose of the law was to ensure t common good; that was a universally accepted co cept. Thus, constitutions were living entities whi affected the social situation and were affected by and which represented a perfect political instrume suited to the most unforeseeable events. The Chart of the United Nations was a felicitous synthesis the most ambitious legal and political theories. purposes and principles constituted an expression the enormous advance in political ideas and the d velopment of law.

5. A Colombian statesman who had formulated n theories on international law in Latin America h written in 1920 that the law of nations was the bas of relations between States and a prerequisite f their prosperity. That law embraced the lasting pri ciples of justice and human dignity and the positi obligations deriving from legislation and treaties.

6. The Secretary-General of the Organization American States, José Antonio Mora, had written t during the nineteenth century and until the First Wo War the political centre of the world had been situa in the North Atlantic area, namely, for practic purposes, in Europe. After the Second World W all the countries of the world had had to be taken i account. For that reason it was important to establi rules with a view to decolonization and assistan to under-developed countries—questions which h come to occupy a dominant place among the matte of concern to the world.

7. Jurists gave priority to international law, reason of its universal applicability. Its rules g erned relations not only between States but betw the regions of the world. Its principles were bind when legal instruments were drawn up, within system of legal equality among States, to solve cert problems of common interest. In municipal law principles enunciated in treaties had priority beca they could not be ignored unilaterally. That was principle accepted by national courts and by speci ists in international law.

8. Regional organizations had played an import part in that expansion of the law of nations. Amer had been a pioneer in that regard. As early as 18 Simon Bolivar had invited the Governments of La American countries to form a confederation and convene at Panama an assembly of plenipotentiar which would serve as a consultative body in dispu and would interpret treaties in case of disagreeme

9. The peoples that had joined in alliance during Second World War had set as their ideal the esta lishment of freedom and democracy in all continen The founders of the Organization had drawn th inspiration from those great principles. Thus, Charter was the expression of the individual collective conscience of peoples. Freedom, law democracy were the three pillars of the Uni Nations, whose supreme ideal was the defence peace. Any deviation from that idea was harmfu the interests of the international community. Thro the assertion of that principle the Organization won great victories in its struggle against coloniali and all forms of discrimination, in its efforts to sec the conclusion of disarmament and denuclearizat agreements and peaceful coexistence and co-operat between States, to find just solutions for disputes to create the necessary instruments for resear

the dissemination of knowledge, for planning, for application of technology and for economic and cial advancement. All those efforts had led to the rease in the number of States Members of the ited Nations and the practical results achieved by Organization in all areas of the world.

. In view of those accomplishments, in view of political, economic and social integration of the tire world, which had advanced at an exceptionally oid rate during the past eighteen years, the Organi-tion, created by free and sovereign States on the sis of the equality of all countries, large and small, ould seek a formula which would respect the prin-le of representation by continents, according to number of States in those continents. The question d therefore arisen whether circumstances did not mand a review of the Charter. He recalled that in 55 the General Assembly had decided in resolution 2 (X)—and had been supported in its decision by Security Council[1]—that a General Conference review the Charter would be held at an appropriate ne; it had further decided to appoint a Committee consider the arrangements for a conference for review of the Charter. In 1957 the General As-mbly, having examined the report of that Com-ttee,[2] had decided in resolution 1136 (XII) to keep Committee in being. In fact, the question of a ssible review of the Charter had been raised as rly as 1946 by the General Assembly, which had structed the First Committee to study the system voting in the Security Council and, if the need arose, study the possibility of convening a general con-ence, within the meaning of Article 109, in order eliminate the privilege of the veto and interpret application of Article 27. Later, in 1953, it had en decided (resolution 796 (VIII)), to assemble the oper documentation, and the Members had been ited to state their preliminary views on a possible view of the Charter.

. Referring next to chapter XIII, section VI, of the port of the Economic and Social Council (A/5503), read out paragraphs 619, 620 and 621. In para-aph 619 reference was made to resolution 974 B XXVI), in which the Council recommended the Gen-al Assembly to take all measures to ensure adequate presentation of Africa in the Council on the basis equitable geographical distribution. Paragraph 620 ed resolution 974 C (XXXVI), in which the Council d urged the General Assembly, in the light of the ditional increase in the membership of the United tions, to take the necessary action at its eighteenth ssion to bring about an appropriate increase in the mbership of the Council, in order to enable it to main the effective and representative organ en-aged in Chapters IX and X of the Charter.

. Paragraph 621 pointed out that during the debates delegation had reiterated its opinion that any rease in the membership of the Council required revision of the Charter—a measure which could be taken until the People's Republic of China was cupying its rightful place among the permanent mbers of the Security Council; and that in the antime the only equitable solution would be to listribute the existing seats at the expense of the stern Powers. However, most members of the Council had spoken in favour of an increase in the number of its members.

13. There were two lines of thought. Some members had proposed a redistribution of the seats without an increase in their number. Others considered that the membership of the Security Council and the Economic and Social Council was much too small not merely to provide a satisfactory representation but even to enable them to fulfil their functions. Consequently, a mere redistribution of the seats was to be rejected, since it was untimely as well as against the interests of the United Nations and its Members and contrary to justice and equity. On the other hand, an increase in the number of members of those organs would be highly advisable. It would round off a long series of efforts by the Assembly; it would strengthen the working possibilities of the two Councils and would make it easier to find speedy answers to the problems entrusted to them. Such an expansion of the membership of the Councils was particularly desirable because it would meet the legitimate desires of States which were anxious to contribute to the cause of peace and therefore asked only for equitable geographical representation.

14. The question of the composition of the General Committee was not so urgent as that of equitable representation on the Security Council and the Economic and Social Council. The thirteen Vice-Presidencies were enough to meet the legitimate desires of States. And to that must be added the great honour done to a State when it was elected to the Presidency or Vice-Presidency of the Assembly. Nor must it be forgotten that the Chairmen of the Main Committees were usually elected in rotation on the basis of equitable geographical representation. He did not feel that a partial decision was enough, nor that consideration of the question of revising the Charter should be taken up anew at every session. That would be a mistake which would undermine the stability of the institutions and would be an obstacle to the continued progress of the Organization. What was necessary was a comprehensive solution. For the same reasons a redistribution of the seats on the General Committee and the Councils must be envisaged. Instead of being content once again with some more or less unofficial gentleman's agreement, there must be friendly consultations leading to a set of resolutions forming a whole and laying down the rights of the groups into which the States were traditionally divided for purposes of distributing seats.

15. The Colombian delegation was therefore ready to examine any agreement which might be envisaged for a blanket solution of the problem. It would be glad to co-operate in seeing that all such plans or proposals became an integral part of the Charter, provided, of course, that they were in accord with the criteria which he had just set out, namely that the various interests of the international community should first be defined and then set out in definitive rules and agreements.

16. While he had wished to take advantage of the general discussion to outline certain legal arguments on the question, his delegation reserved the right to speak again if necessary. In making his statement he had conformed to the already well-established tradition of the United Nations regarding attempts to review the Charter and, in particular, to enlarge the principal organs. That showed that there was in process of formation a trend of opinion favouring a review

[1] Official Records of the Security Council, Tenth Year, Supplement October, November and December 1955, document S/3504.

[2] Official Records of the General Assembly, Twelfth Session, An-es, agenda item 22, document A/3593.

of the Charter with a view to adapting it to the hard facts of a new world. It must be universally recognized that the time had come to take decisions based on the principle of equity in order to provide fair representation for the Member States. To seek cover behind certain privileges or to refuse to accept reality would seriously endanger the Organization. It was not a question of imposing a code; it was above all a question of appealing to the good sense of Governments to recognize their vital needs and to respect their aspirations. The position of the Colombian delegation was not a new one. It was based on a clear-cut sense of justice, since Colombia considered that the wishes of all continents must be recognized, as the head of the Colombian delegation had again stated at the 1223rd plenary meeting of the General Assembly. Colombia had always professed that conviction unhesitatingly and had always upheld the independence of States in their fight against colonialism. It was now ready to support the African-Asian group to ensure that it enjoyed to the full all its rights within the Organization. He recalled in that connexion the solidarity of the Latin American States, which had always been among the first to promote the principle of universality. In that same spirit he appealed to the five great Powers to help to bring about the necessary amendments to the Charter. The measures to be taken would not endanger their privileges, since the Organization, which was based on equality, was protected by its very apostolic and civilizing mission. They would also show that the United Nations was drawing closer to the ideals it proclaimed. He hoped that the analysis he had just made would facilitate co-operation between the Member States which would be crystallized in a unanimous vote on such specific amendments as might be submitted. If that goal was attained, it would be possible to say that the States had acquired a greater understanding of their responsibilities in the exercise of their rights and in the accomplishment of their duties for the greater benefit of the international community.

17. Mr. DE BEUS (Netherlands) said he would confine his remarks mainly to the question of equitable representation on the Security Council and the Economic and Social Council, an important and urgent question the background of which he would first outline.

18. A first attempt to increase the membership of the Economic and Social Council and the Security Council had been made at the eleventh session—shortly after the admission of sixteen new Members—by seventeen Latin American countries, with the strong support of the Western European countries. The Soviet Union and its friends, on the other hand, had strongly opposed that attempt, since they felt that the two Councils should not be enlarged until the People's Republic of China had been admitted to take the seat of China. In 1958, the Netherlands had brought the matter before the Economic and Social Council on the grounds that the Council, owing to the inadequacy of its membership in relation to the increased membership of the United Nations, could not properly fulfil its obligations. That same year the Economic and Social Council had adopted resolution 690 B (XXVI) inviting the General Assembly to give favourable consideration at its thirteenth session to an increase in the Council's membership. The Netherlands at that time had favoured an increase of six members.

19. The question had again been discussed at the thirteenth and fourteenth sessions, when about fifty delegations had voted in favour of enlarging the Economic and Social Council. However, about ten cou tries had opposed that view and no agreed soluti could be found.

20. At the fifteenth session, seventeen new Membe had been admitted to the United Nations, includi sixteen African States. It was at that session t forty-six delegations introduced a draft resolutio for the amendment of Article 61 of the Charter. Mc than two thirds of the delegations had voted in favc of the operative part of that resolution, which aim at increasing the membership of the Economic a Social Council by revising the Charter.

21. In May 1963, the Summit Conference of Indepe dent African States, meeting at Addis Ababa, l adopted unanimously a resolution insisting on a j and equitable representation of Africa in the princi organs of the United Nations. Previously, the Ec nomic Commission for Africa had adopted unanimou resolution 81 (V) urging the General Assembly, throu the Economic and Social Council, to take the nece sary measures to ensure the adequate representat of Africa in the Economic and Social Council on basis of equitable geographical representation. T resolution had been endorsed by the Economic a Social Council by an overwhelming majority and w now before the Special Political Committee. Final the Committee on Arrangements for a Conference the Purpose of Reviewing the Charter had held special session in July 1963 to discuss the matter. that session, again, it had become evident that vast majority of the Members of the Organizat were in favour of amending the Charter in accordar with Article 108. That fact had been made even clea during the proceedings in the Sub-Committee of Ni all the geographical groups except one had genera favoured the enlargement both of the Security Coun and of the Economic and Social Council.

22. Two thirds of the Members of the United Natio therefore, wished to expand the membership of b Councils by amending the Charter. Moreover, so thirty or forty countries in that group wished existing seats to be reallocated pending the amendm of the Charter. However, an equally large group countries was opposed to such an interim measu considering that it would be unfair to certain ot groups of Member States. Finally, certain countr in principle favoured enlarging the membership both Councils but opposed any revision of the Char as long as China's seat was not occupied by People's Republic of China. That aspect of the mat was a crucial one. Politically, the question of representation of China had been settled by Assembly a few weeks previously and actually l nothing to do with the question under considerati However, a legal problem was also involved, for a amendment to the Charter required to be ratified the five permanent members of the Security Counc The Soviet Union was understood to argue that it co not recognize the validity of a ratification by Republic of China, because it did not recognize Government of that Republic as representing Chinese people. The Netherlands, which had recc nized the People's Republic of China, considered t an attempt should be made to understand the positi in which the Soviet Union found itself and to ad a constructive approach towards it in order to f an acceptable solution. On the other hand, unde

3/ Ibid., Fifteenth Session, Annexes, agenda item 23, docum A/4626, para. 12.

tandable though the attitude of the Soviet Union might e, it should not go so far as to block arrangements which were desired by an overwhelming majority or the common good. He wondered, for instance, what people would think of a country that refused to atify the Treaty banning nuclear weapon tests in the tmosphere, in outer space and under water, signed t Moscow, simply because it did not recognize one f the co-signatories. It would be easy for the Soviet nion to make it clear that its assent did not imply ny recognition. Moreover, although the Republic f China had occupied China's seat in the Security ouncil since 1945, the Soviet Union had apparntly never disputed the validity of the voting in e Council, and no one had attempted to interpret at fact as implying Soviet acquiescence in the ocupation of China's seat by the Republic of China.

3. His delegation had consistently advocated the mmediate enlargement of both Councils, in all fairess and justice towards the new Members. However, e same principle of fairness demanded that countries r groups of countries which had been Members of e United Nations before other countries should not their turn be treated unfairly and deprived of a epresentation they had consistently enjoyed. All roups should and could be equitably represented. frica was the most under-represented group, but was not the only one under-represented. Western urope, for example, also had a claim to better repreentation on the Economic and Social Council, since 1961 it had voluntarily relinquished a seat in favour the African-Asian group. That seat should in fairess be given back to it if the membership of the ouncil was to be expanded. In order to secure an quitable representation, it would be best to increase e membership of the Security Council by two seats nd that of the Economic and Social Council by six eats.

4. The same reasons also rendered an increase in e membership of the Assembly's General Committee ghly desirable. His delegation would support such an crease provided it took place as part of an over-all ecision to extend the membership of all three bodies. he geographic distribution to be agreed upon should e laid down in a resolution, as had been done in the ase of the General Committee in resolution 1192 XII).

5. The time had come to reach a solution in the ay that had been indicated. That approach was fair the African and Asian countries, because they ould at last have the representation to which they ere entitled, to the Western European and Latin merican countries, because they would not have to ve up a representation that they had enjoyed so far, d finally towards the group of Communist States, ecause it did not prejudice their position with regard China.

6. His delegation strongly favoured the adoption as oon as possible, during the current session, of an mendment to the Charter increasing the membership the Security Council and of the Economic and Social ouncil. It hoped that if such a resolution was adopted a large majority, such an expression of the general sh of the Assembly would not be thwarted by any of e permanent members of the Security Council.

7. Mr. EL SANOUSI (Sudan) said that at that stage was his intention not to enter into details but to ncentrate on the principles involved.

28. The members of the African-Asian group had been under-represented for years, in fact since the inception of the United Nations. As long as those countries had not been represented in the Organization, their interests had been defended by friendly countries, particularly by the Latin American countries. Now that the African-Asian countries were participating directly in the work of the Organization, it was their duty to do so as effectively as possible. His delegation was anxiously awaiting the time when all peoples would have obtained their release from colonialism and joined the other Members of the Organization. Similarly, his Government had always maintained that the exclusion of the People's Republic of China hampered the work of the Organization and could even be detrimental to it.

29. All those aspects of the question, moreover, were complementary and not contradictory. It was possible to accept whatever could be obtained immediately, while continuing to strive for later gains. The main thing was that the representative character of the Organization should be preserved. As an eminent British historian had said, liberty provoked diversity and diversity preserved liberty. What was involved was not the predominance of one group over the others. The African-Asian countries were claiming only what was due to them, and they were ready to discuss the matter with all friendly countries or groups of countries.

421st MEETING

Monday, 9 December 1963,

21. Mr. QUARM (Ghana) said that the majority of delegations, in their statements in the general debate in the Assembly, had openly expressed themselves in favour of enlarging the Security Council, the Economic and Social Council and the General Committee. All delegations unquestionably agreed that Africa and Asia were grossly under-represented in the principal organs, while the Summit Conference of Independent African States, held at Addis Ababa in May 1963, had adopted a resolution declaring that Africa, as a geographical region, should have equitable representation in the principal organs of the United Nations, particularly the Security Council, the Economic and Social Council and the specialized agencies.

22. What was needed was a permanent solution which would correctly reflect the character of the United Nations as it stood today. For that reason the Ghanaian delegation did not favour any half measures, such as a redistribution of existing seats, which would merely entail taking seats away from certain regions, as though the Organization had lost and not gained Members. For that reason, too, his delegation had co-sponsored draft resolution A/SPC/L.101 on the composition of the General Committee. The formula proposed in that draft was the best one that could be devised and had only been submitted after consultation with all the delegations. He therefore urged that it be adopted by the Committee.

23. The delegation of Ghana could see no reason for the view taken by some delegations that the questions of the composition of the General Committee, the

Security Council and the Economic and Social Council should be considered together and solutions found as part of a package deal. If only one of those questions was resolved, the Organization's interests would be better served. As the representative of the Sudan had pointed out (420th meeting), the question was not one of interregional rivalry, but of upholding the Charter and the principle of equitable and balanced geographical distribution in order to ensure that the membership of the Organization was reflected properly in its organs. He therefore appealed to delegations not to insist on a package deal, which would deny the African-Asian countries their rightful representation even on the least controversial of the organs under consideration, namely the General Committee.

24. The remarks he had just made applied equally to the expansion of the Security Council and of the Economic and Social Council. The Charter should be amended to permit an expansion of the two bodies. In that connexion it was worth remembering that two more African countries were likely to join the Organization during the current week and that still more could be expected in the near future.

25. The Ghanaian delegation sympathized with the concern expressed by the Soviet Union and other Eastern European States regarding attempts to expand the Security Council and the Economic and Social Council before the People's Republic of China had taken its legitimate seat in the United Nations. Ghana had always maintained that the exclusion of the People's Republic of China from the United Nations was a mistake which must be corrected. That, however, was a political question, whereas the present issue was solely one of equitable geographical distribution, into which no political consideration should enter. The African and Asian countries were already Members of the United Nations and their presence would lose meaning if they were unable to participate fully in the life of all its organs. He therefore appealed to the Soviet Union, the Eastern European countries and the People's Republic of China to refrain from considering the question of Chinese representation and the expansion of the Councils as one and inseparable. The United Nations, being a living organism, must always reflect in reality the evolution it had undergone. He therefore hoped that draft resolution A/SPC/L.101 would be adopted unanimously.

• • •

35. Mr. EL-ZAYYAT (United Arab Republic), clarifying his earlier statement, said that the fact that draft resolution A/SPC/L.101 referred only to the composition of the General Committee did not mean that the sponsors wished to neglect the other two issues. On the contrary, they wished to dispose of that first item so as to pass on to the others. At the same time it had to be remembered that the composition of the General Committee could be changed through a mere modification to the rules of procedure, which could be done by the adoption of a suitable resolution by the General Assembly, whereas the question of equitable representation on the Security Council and the Economic and Social Council involved an amendment to Article 108 of the Charter, and that called for entirely different legal procedures. In fact, the Committee could do nothing to change the composition of the Security Council and the Economic and Social Council; it could only take the first step by adopting the necessary resolution—and the co-sponsors of draft resolution A/SPC/L.101 intende to introduce such a resolution—which would then hav to be ratified by all Member States, including the fiv permanent members of the Security Council.

36. While the African-Asian countries felt that the were entitled to half, or more than half, of the seat on the Security Council and the Economic and Socia Council in order to reflect their numbers in the General Assembly, they were also aware of the realitie of the political world and were only trying to obtai half the number of seats minus the five occupied b the permanent members of the Security Council That, in his view, was the only connexion betwee the first item under discussion and the following tw items on the agenda. He therefore hoped that th Committee would adopt draft resolution A/SPC/L.101

37. Mr. MALHOTRA (Nepal) expressed agreemen with the representative of the United Arab Republic The sponsors of draft resolution A/SPC/L.101 woul have liked to submit two other draft resolutions dealing with the Security Council and the Economic an Social Council at the same time; but owing to lac of time that had not been possible. However, ther seemed no reason why delegations should refrai from commenting on the substance of draft resolutio A/SPC/L.101 merely because the other two draft had not yet been submitted.

38. Mr. MISHRA (India) observed that although th three issues to which the representatives of Italy Brazil and France had referred were interrelate they were not inseparable. There was a closer connexion between the expansion of the Economic an Social Council and that of the Security Council tha there was between the question of expanding thos two and the question of expanding the General Committee. That was indicated by the fact that the expansion of the two Councils was the subject of a singl agenda item. The distinction was also pointed u by the fact that whereas two draft resolutions wit respect to agenda item 82 had been circulated informally during the past three weeks there had bee no such informal draft resolution with respect t item 81. To delay consideration of the draft resolutio on the General Committee would be to waste mor of what little time was left and might result in th postponement of a solution of all three issues at leas until the nineteenth session. There was no questio of delaying the submission of the other two draf resolutions; he was simply appealing to those representatives who wished to consider the three draf resolutions as a single package not to insist but t allow the Committee to proceed at once with the draf resolution already before it.

422nd MEETING

Tuesday, 10 December 1963,

7. Mr. ROWLAND (Australia) said that his delegatio believed that certain changes were required in th structure of the United Nations to take account of th greatly increased membership, particularly that o the African and Asian States. The Security Council an the Economic and Social Council should be enlarged but not to the point of making either Council unwield in relation to its purposes. It was important that in the

:ocess of expansion certain countries or groups ould not be deprived of their present opportunities of :cess to the Councils, and in particular, the principle Commonwealth representation must be preserved. ne same applied to the General Committee. The ghteenth session of the General Assembly provided e occasion for a major effort to enlarge the three dies, and a mere re-allocation of existing seats was solution.

His delegation paid a tribute to the unremitting forts made to achieve wide agreement on the extent which the three United Nations organs should be larged, and while, in his delegation's view, that aim d not yet been achieved, it was desirable that conltations should continue, taking into account the terests of all sections of the membership of the nited Nations.

The Security Council, though it should be properly presentative, did not require much enlargement. It d never been intended as a large body, and its nctions were such that a large membership was not propriate. Not only must it avoid the danger of uneldiness if it was to be capable of swift action, but so its membership had to comply with the requireents of Article 23 of the Charter, which stated that the election of the Council's non-permanent mem-rs due regard should be paid in the first instance to embers' contribution to the maintenance of internaonal peace and security and to the other purposes of e Organization and also to equitable geographical stribution. There was no doubt that the Security ouncil should be enlarged and in particular should ovide, with due regard to the criteria laid down in rticle 23, for the adequate representation of the counies of Asia and Africa in addition to the groups and e interests traditionally represented in the nonrmanent seats of the Council.

). The Economic and Social Council presented a mewhat different problem from that of the Security ouncil: the nature of its work was different, and the harter did not lay down specific qualifications for embership. In determining what the desirable mem-rship of the Economic and Social Council should be, t only the increase in the United Nations membership t also the nature of the Council's present work had to considered. For example, in the economic field, ere had been a marked change of emphasis from the oblems of full employment, with which the Council d been preoccupied in its early years, to the probms of development and economic growth, particularly the developing countries. That change was not adeately reflected in the present composition of the :onomic and Social Council, which should be more presentative of the developing countries, and should so provide representation for countries such as stralia, Canada and New Zealand which were at an termediate stage of development and had a particular ntribution to make to the Council's economic work cause of their special experience of the problems of :h the highly developed and the developing countries. stralia, for example, had been a leading advocate of ernational commodity agreements designed to tionalize and introduce some order into the vital oblem of world food supplies. It had taken the initiae in proposing the United Nations Conference on the plication of Science and Technology for the Benefit the Less Developed Areas. It had played a leading e in drafting the economic and social provisions of Charter and in developing the technical assistance tivities of the United Nations.

11. The Committee should keep several other factors in mind in determining the criteria on which membership of an expanded Council should be based. Those included the need to give adequate representation to areas containing larger countries, which though perhaps few in number, had special problems of population growth and food supply the significance of which went far beyond the immediate region in which those countries were situated; the need to represent countries of different economic and social systems; the special experience and knowledge of technical assistance programmes possessed by certain countries; and the claims of countries which, though not falling clearly within the usually accepted regional areas, had already played a valuable part in the United Nations and its Councils.

12. For the above reasons his delegation was convinced that the wide variety of countries possessing different economic interests and points of view on economic and social questions should be adequately represented in the Economic and Social Council, and it was therefore necessary to consider other factors besides equitable geographical distribution. Important as regional groupings were, it would be a great pity if the United Nations crystallized into an exclusively regional pattern—whether in the Security Council, in the Economic and Social Council or in other organs. Explicit recognition of factors other than mere geography was already an established practice in many United Nations bodies. The Special Fund, for example, divided its members into "donors" and "recipients", the principle of representation taking precedence over that of geography. Similar practices were found in the International Labour Organisation, the Food and Agriculture Organization of the United Nations, the Inter-Governmental Maritime Consultative Organization and the International Atomic Energy Agency.

13. It was widely agreed that eighteen was too small a membership for the Economic and Social Council if it was to accommodate the various interests of the Member States. His delegation was not convinced that enlargement to twenty-four was sufficient for the purpose. The original membership of the United Nations had been fifty-one and that of the Economic and Social Council eighteen. A Council of thirty would give a slightly lower proportion of seats to Members, while providing sufficient room for the equitable representation of all groups and interests. He might wish to return to that subject at a later stage.

14. His delegation believed that the traditional regional groupings alone did not offer a satisfactory basis for the distribution of seats in United Nations bodies. While regional groupings were of great importance, they did not represent, as was sometimes suggested, an immutable principle based on geography alone. Although in appearance geographical, they had in fact a large political content. Why else, for example, was Europe traditionally divided into western Europe and eastern Europe for purposes of representation? Furthermore, regional groups did not equitably cover the case of certain countries, and there was a risk of doing them an injustice if that fact was not taken into account.

15. The Commonwealth, as a world-wide multiracial association, representative of many interests and peoples and transcending regionalism, had been represented and recognized in the United Nations from the beginning, and had made an important contribution to United Nations activities. The Commonwealth was not based on mere geography; its essence lay in a variety

of links, intangible but none the less real, of language, culture, history, education, law, administrative practices and governmental and non-governmental institutions. The Commonwealth was indeed a model for the United Nations, a model of the harmonious co-operation of different groups and differing interests within a common family. Moreover, Commonwealth membership was increasing; it would soon number eighteen and more in the near future. Commonwealth countries had contributed to the United Nations in a wide variety of ways: for example, in offering constructive ideas and suggestions, and in the field of peace-keeping operations. Commonwealth countries also had a better record than most other groups in the payment of their budget contributions and their share of the cost of essential operations.

16. For all those reasons the practice of maintaining Commonwealth representation in the principal organs of the United Nations had amply justified its value and an adequate place for it would surely be found in any decision taken on that matter by the General Assembly.

17. The General Committee did not reflect the changes in the over-all composition of the United Nations. His delegation welcomed in principle any resolution aimed at correcting the imbalance but considered that the proposal before the Committee required careful examination. The Australian delegation would wish to take into account the views of other delegations. There was also the question whether the composition of the General Committee could be suitably determined except in relation to that of the other United Nations organs. His delegation was disturbed by the omission from draft resolution A/SPC/L.101 and Add.1 of paragraph 3 of the annex to General Assembly resolution 1192 (XII) providing for Commonwealth representation, and hoped that the sponsors would agree to restore the missing provision as proposed in the amendment (A/SPC/L.106) submitted by Australia, Canada and New Zealand. To do so would in no way prejudice the actual allocation of seats in the General Committee or deprive any country or group of its chance to serve on the Committee, for the very size of the Commonwealth group and the importance of the countries comprising it meant that one could scarcely imagine a General Committee elected which did not include at least one member of the Commonwealth. Rule 31 as amended by resolution 1192 (XII) specified that the General Committee would include at least one Commonwealth member without altering the geographical distribution of seats. It would be unjust to deny the Commonwealth group, the recognition it had long received, and deserved to receive, in the United Nations.

423rd MEETING

Tuesday, 10 December 1963,

41. Mr. FEDORENKO (Union of Soviet Socialist Republics) said that the request by the Asian and African States which had led to the inclusion of the present item in the Assembly's agenda had been a natural continuation of the struggle of those States to consolidate their independence after decades and even centuries during which their wishes had been suppressed by foreign colonialists. The Soviet Union understood and sympathized with their aspirations for equitable representa tion on the principal organs of the United Nations. A the General Assembly's fifteenth session it had take the initiative resulting in the adoption of the Declara tion on the granting of independence to colonial cou tries and peoples (resolution 1514 (XV)). At the san time it had called for a radical change in the structu of United Nations organs, including the Security Cou cil, so as to secure equitable representation in tho organs for three groups of States—the socialist cou tries, the neutral countries and the countries belongi to Western military blocs. The adoption of that prop sal would have given Africa and Asia truly equitab representation and a greater role in the United Nation he drew the Committee's attention to the stateme made in that connexion by the Chairman of the Coun of Ministers of the USSR at the 869th plenary meeti of the General Assembly. The Soviet Union would co tinue to work for changes in the composition of Unit Nations organs which would make the Organization r flect the interests of the three main groups of Stat and enable it to protect the interests of all Memb States.

42. The need for such changes had become se evident, and it was only fair that the new African a Asian States should be properly represented in Unit Nations organs; recognition of that fact was an integr part of the Soviet Union's well-known policy of suppor ing the struggle of peoples to win and strengthen the independence. In the circumstances it was surprisi to hear the representatives of some Powers sugge that the Soviet Union did not agree on the need to set the question of such representation. The present pr ferential position of the Western Powers in the Unit Nations structure operated to the disadvantage r only of the neutral countries, but of the socialist cou tries as well. No representative of any socialist count had ever been permitted to hold the office of Preside of the General Assembly; and for nine of the eighte years of the Organization's existence the countries Eastern Europe had been denied their elective seat the Security Council. Lastly, the settlement of t important question of restoring the lawful rights of t People's Republic of China in the United Nations h thus far been sabotaged; because the Soviet Union, li the other socialist countries, had been working co sistently to improve the structure of the princi United Nations organs through recognition of principle of equal treatment of all States, it could agree to any further delay in settling that question was evident that on the question of representation the United Nations the vital interests of the social countries and the neutral States fully coincided.

43. In the Soviet view, the proposal made by neutral States and supported by the Soviet Union at fifteenth session for redistribution of the exist elective seats in the Security Council still offe real possibilities for meeting the wishes of t African-Asian countries for more adequate rep sentation in that Council and in the Economic and Soc Council. Since the conclusion of the 1946 agreem on the distribution of the elective seats in the Secu Council, the number of Asian and African Mem States had greatly increased and that of social Member States had doubled, while the number of La American Member States had remained the same, that of Western European Member States almost same as before. The 1946 agreement should theref be superseded by a new agreement assigning elective seat in the Security Council to each of the

ıain geographical areas of the world—Africa, Asia, astern Europe, Western Europe, Latin America and ıe Middle East. The question of a redistribution of eats in the Economic and Social Council could also be ppropriately settled on that basis. He reaffirmed the oviet position in that regard, as stated in the letter ated 5 September 1963 from the representative of the nion of Soviet Socialist Republics to the Chairman of ıe Sub-Committee of the Committee on arrangements ɔr a conference for the purpose of reviewing the Char-ɹr (A/AC.81/SC.1/4/Add.11), and its willingness to elp work out an agreement on that basis.

4. The Soviet Union also sympathized with the frican-Asian countries' desire to obtain wider repre-entation in the principal organs of the United Nations ırough an increase in the membership of those organs. owever, in the case of the Security Council and the conomic and Social Council, such an increase would ntail revision of the Charter, which in turn required ıe approval of all five permanent members of the ecurity Council. That meant that the lawful rights of ıe People's Republic of China in the United Nations ıust be recognized before the Charter could be mended in keeping with its letter and spirit. In view f the desire of the independent African and Asian coun-ːies for immediate action, the Soviet Government had onsulted the Government of the People's Republic of hina, which was the only legal representative of China nd a permanent member of the Security Council. The ıtter Government had replied that, since China was till barred from participation in the Organization's ork, it would make no commitments on any amend-ıents of the Charter relating to the total number of eats in the principal United Nations organs, and that greement on its part to revision of the Charter while ıe Chiang Kai-shek representative was present in the nited Nations might lead to the creation of a "two-hina situation". The Government of the People's Re-ıblic of China had thus made it plain that it did not pprove of any attempt to settle the question of equit-ble representation by increasing the membership of ıe organs in question, and that it favoured instead an quitable distribution of the existing seats in those rgans. It was consequently difficult to understand why ertain African-Asian delegations should claim to have s support for their proposals to increase the member-hip of the Councils before the question of restoring ıe lawful rights of the People's Republic of China in ıe United Nations had been settled.

5. The Soviet Union supported the demand of the overnment of the People's Republic of China for the estoration of those rights and therefore could not vote ɔr any proposal to amend the Charter of the United ations in the absence of a representative of that overnment as a permanent member of the Security ouncil. If the African-Asian Member States would ive that demand their unanimous support, that would emove the main obstacle to increasing the member-hip of the two Councils so as to give those States roper representation. Under the present circum-tances, however, the only practical way to increase ıeir representation was to redistribute the existing eats. His delegation hoped that, in the light of those onsiderations, an equitable solution to the problem f representation on the Councils could be found.

6. The Soviet delegation agreed with those African nd Asian representatives who had pointed out that the uestion of the composition of the General Committee id not involve revision of the Charter and could there-ɔre be settled by the General Assembly without delay. However, the principle of equitable representation embodied in the relevant draft resolution (A/SPC/L.101) should be extended to apply to the President of the General Assembly. In order to settle a long-standing issue, agreement should be reached at the present session on the establishment of a system of geographical rotation in the election of Presidents of the General Assembly. Since an Asian and a Latin American had presided over the Assembly at its seventeenth and eighteenth sessions respectively, the Presidents at the next four sessions should come in turn from Africa, Eastern Europe, the Middle East and Western Europe, and the rotation should then begin again. His delegation was, however, sufficiently opti-mistic to believe that if the principle of equitable representation was approved by the General Assembly for application to the composition of the General Com-mittee, as proposed in draft resolution A/SPC/L.101, it would be firmly entrenched in United Nations prac-tice. The purpose of his delegation's proposal at the fifteenth session to reconstruct the organs of the United Nations had been to give truly universal scope to the principle of the equality of States and groups of States. That principle was in the interests of a vast majority of the States Members of the United Nations and of all peoples; he was sure that it would triumph.

47. Mr. DIALLO Telli (Guinea), speaking on a motion of order, stated that all members of the Committee, and particularly those from Africa and Asia, had listened with all due attention to the Soviet representa-tive's statement, which ruined all hope of achieving adequate representation of the States of Africa and Asia at the present session. He moved formally that the text of the Soviet representative's statement should be published in full as a document of the Committee. In addition, since the Soviet representative had re-ferred to statements by certain African and Asian representatives, he reminded the Committee that on 30 September 1963 the Minister for Foreign Affairs of the Republic of Guinea had said in the General As-sembly (1220th plenary meeting) that the restitution to the People's Republic of China of its legitimate rights and the just representation claimed by the countries of Africa and Asia were two different questions, which the Peking leaders had had the wisdom and foresight not to bind together. The Guinean Government had since been informed from an official source that that was in fact the position of the Peking leaders. It had also been informed publicly and solemnly that they were abso-lutely opposed to the injustice done to the countries of Africa and Asia by their present representation in the different organs of the United Nations. It was perfectly understandable that the Peking Government, not being a Member of the United Nations, could not in the present circumstances enter into any commitment con-cerning enlargement of the membership of the Councils by amendment. But the Soviet representative seemed to conclude that the Peking Government did not at present accept the idea of enlarging the two Councils by amending the Charter. That was an extremely im-portant statement of position, which the African States wished to examine very carefully so that they could take informed decisions and make representations to the authorities who could play a decisive part in the matter.

The Guinean representative's motion that the full text of the Soviet representative's statement should be circulated was adopted. [3]

[3] The complete text of the statement was subsequently circulated as document A/SPC/96.

48. Mr. BINDZI (Cameroon), speaking on a point of order, said that the Committee had just witnessed yet another use of the veto, which the small countries had never ceased to denounce. Once again it had seen a great Power block a move towards what had always been a legitimate aspiration and a legitimate claim for the countries of Africa and Asia. But that Power's arguments had not convinced those countries. In order that delegations might study the statement at leisure and informal groups reach an understanding on the new situation, he formally moved that there should be no meeting before the following afternoon.

49. Mr. CHAI (Secretary of the Committee), replying to a question from Mr. DIALLO Telli (Guinea), said that the text of the Soviet representative's statement could be circulated in the working languages by noon on Wednesday, 11 December 1963.

50. Mr. DIALLO Telli (Guinea) said that if no decision had been taken by 20 December, it might be necessary to postpone closure of the session so that the discussion could continue until the injustices done to the States of Africa and Asia were remedied.

51. Mr. BINDZI (Cameroon) formally proposed that the Committee should not meet until the afternoon of 12 December 1963.

It was so decided.

424th
MEETING

Thursday, 12 December 1963,

Mr. CHAPDELAINE (Canada)

14. Since the expansion of the Councils required amendment of the Charter, that was not an exercise to be undertaken lightly. The Committee should consider carefully the adequacy of proposed alterations and should judge them by the extent to which they met existing and future pressure for representation. In his delegation's opinion, expansion of the Councils by two and six seats respectively was insufficient to permit justice to be done to the under-represented newer Members without doing injustice to some of the older Members, including New Zealand and some other Commonwealth countries.

15. When the United Nations was founded, there had been six elective seats in the Security Council available for forty-six States, a ratio of about one to eight. With the doubling of membership in under twenty years, some increase in the ratio of seats to membership had to be accepted. Otherwise, governing bodies would become unwieldy, and the Security Council in particular would lose its essential quality of being able to act with speed in an emergency. On the other hand, Member States should have some prospect of election to the governing bodies. Otherwise, it might be difficult for them to sustain their interest in the work and purposes of the United Nations.

16. In his delegation's view, Member States wishing to serve on the Security Council and other bodies should have some prospect of serving at least once in every fifteen to twenty years. A shorter interval did not seem practicable for the majority of Member States, and a longer interval would be undesirable. The six elective seats in the Security Council wer now available for 106 Member States, a ratio (nearly one to eighteen. On that basis an opportuni for election to the Council would occur on averag once every thirty-four years, or only three times i each century. With the growing membership of th United Nations, that situation would worsen if th Security Council was not enlarged.

17. His delegation had initially favoured an increas of six elective seats so as to make twelve electiv seats in the Security Council available to an estimate total membership of 126 in the near future, or a rati of one to ten, which would improve the average re currence of the opportunity to serve to once ever eighteen years, or five times each century.

18. From the informal discussions which had bee going on for some weeks, his delegation had come t realize that there was little support for an increas on that scale. There was, however, a growing bod of opinion in favour of adding four seats to the Secu rity Council, and his delegation shared that opinio

19. His delegation did not favour an increase (only two seats in the Security Council because th would not permit of an equitable distribution (elective seats among the regions and groups entitle to be represented. According to one distributic proposal, two seats would be available to the Lati American group of twenty States, giving a ratio (one to ten; one to the Eastern Europe group, givir a ratio of one to nine; four to the fifty-six Africa and Asian States, giving a ratio of one to fourtee and one to the Western Europe and "other States presumably including the displaced Commonweal nations, giving a ratio of roughly one to twenty. C the existing pattern of groupings in the Assembly ar so long as there were only eight elective seats tl injustice thus done to Western Europe and "othe States" could only be remedied by doing injustice t some other group.

20. An increase of four seats, however, to give total of ten elective seats permitted a more equitab distribution. It had been suggested that five shou be given to African and Asian States; two to Lat American States; two to Western Europe and othe States; and one to Eastern Europe. That would repre sent a ratio of approximately one seat to ten Membe for all groups, which, in his delegation's opinion, w an acceptable distribution.

21. Similar arguments applied to the Economic a Social Council, the particular requirements of whi had been thoroughly analysed at the 422nd meeting b the representative of Australia. His delegation ful supported the Australian proposal that considerati be given to enlarging the Economic and Social Counc by more than six members and agreed with the co sensus of opinion that the Council should be enlarg to a total of twenty-seven members. That numb would be more in keeping with the need for the Counc to reflect adequately not only the different regions b also a balanced representation of donor and recipier industrial and developing countries. A formula for fair distribution of seats could be arrived at by co tinuing informal negotiations.

22. His delegation had wished to take an ear opportunity to put its views on record because h country, like Canada, Australia and others, did r easily fit into any of the geographic regions usual invoked in all informal discussions on the distributi of elective seats.

427th
MEETING.

Saturday, 14 December 1963.

2. Mr. PLIMPTON (United States of America) said hat his delegation regarded draft resolution A/SPC/ ..101 and Add.1 and 2 as a sensible effort to bring he composition of the General Committee into line rith the current realities of General Assembly mem- ership.

3. As far as the amendment in document A/SPC/ ..106 was concerned, his delegation felt that the rinciple of Commonwealth representation, even hough it would not appear to be jeopardized in any ractical sense by the annex to draft resolution ./SPC/L.101 and Add.1 and 2, should be specifically eiterated, for the Commonwealth had made important ontributions to the United Nations, particularly in onnexion with its peace-keeping operations. It was unique association transcending but not replacing egional affiliations, and the Assembly should recog- ize that fact by ensuring its representation in any odies in which the principle of geographical repre- entation was applied, particularly since several of he largest Commonwealth countries could not easily e identified with the major regional groupings.

4. Turning to the amendment in document A/SPC/ ..107 concerning the election of the President of the ssembly, he observed that that office was in a ategory by itself. The Charter left the Members of ie Assembly entirely free to choose the person who as to preside over them, with no reference to quitable geographical distribution. The Assembly ad decided at its first session that the election of e President should be made on the basis of qualifica- ons and experience. It should not now tie its own ands by specifying a rigid course of action with espect to the election of the President but should reserve the flexibility which would enable it at all mes to make a judicious choice in the light of the revailing circumstances. The President of the Gen- ral Assembly should be an international figure, a pokesman for the United Nations as a whole rather an for national or regional issues. Under the existing ystem a series of competent and distinguished pre- iding officers had been elected and his delegation lt strongly that the tradition of high quality which ad marked the history of the Presidence should be aintained. To confer the Presidency on the chosen andidate of a specified region would not serve to aintain that high tradition nearly as well as did the xisting practice. Certainly no candidate from any eographical region should be omitted from con- ideration if he had the qualities of impartiality, tegrity and disinterestedness which were essential a President of the General Assembly. During his rm of office the President was detached from his elegation and must command the confidence of the ssembly as an individual. If the regional origin of e candidate were to be the governing factor, the andidate put forward would in all likelihood be the an who had most identified himself with the region ther than one whose commitment to the advancement the interests of the entire United Nations would ppeal to all regions. Moreover, once the principle of gid, automatic regional rotation was established it ould take the form of rotation within each region, e candidacy being assigned first to one and then to another country, so that the principle of election on the basis of high personal qualifications would be further vitiated. Finally, it might also lead to the choice of a candidate who was clearly inappropriate because of the particular problems confronting the Assembly in a given year.

15. In practice, account had been taken of the desirability of balanced geographical representation and his delegation felt that the regional origin of the candidate should not be ignored. In the event of a choice between several highly qualified candidates, it would be natural to give the preference to the one whose region had been less recently represented in the Presidency.

16. His delegation would vote against the amendments in document A/SPC/L.107 and hoped that it would be decisively defeated.

17. As far as the two Councils were concerned, his delegation had consistently favoured enlargement with a view to giving adequate representation to the newer Members of the United Nations, particularly those from Africa and Asia, since the original membership of the Organization had included relatively few States from those two areas. A mere reallocation of the existing seats would not provide a solution but would only leave all areas dissatisfied and arouse resentment, since it would mean trying to redistribute too few seats among too many Members at the expense of some which so far had enjoyed adequate representation. Enlargement of the Councils required amendment of the Charter, and action by the Assembly had so far been discouraged by the attitude of one of the permanent members of the Security Council, whose ratification would be required before any amendment could become effective. It had been hoped that at the current session that member might at last be prepared to acquiesce in the strong desire of the great majority to see the Council enlarged. Unfortunately the statement of the representative of the Soviet Union at the 423rd meeting had been disappointing. Nevertheless, the General Assembly should not be discouraged by the Soviet Union's attitude, for if proposals to enlarge the Councils were adopted by an overwhelming majority it was conceivable that the Soviet Union might be persuaded to reconsider its position.

18. While the United States supported enlargement of the Councils it was also concerned that they should not become unwieldy in size. The membership of the Security Council should not only provide equitable geographical distribution but also, in the words of the Charter, reflect the contribution of Members for the maintenance of international peace and security. His delegation was also convinced that in the interests of effectiveness the Security Council should be kept as small as possible consistent with those principles. A membership of thirteen would permit the African and Asian States to hold four of the elective seats, which would be a fair division, since they constituted about half the total membership of the Organization, and it would at the same time continue to take into account the ability of its members to contribute to the attainment of the purposes of the United Nations.

19. The Economic and Social Council should be sufficiently representative to carry weight with the whole United Nations membership. At the same time, if its recommendations were to be meaningful a balance should be maintained among its members between developed and developing States.

20. As far as the draft resolutions were concerned, his delegation was authorized to vote in favour of amendments to the Charter providing for a thirteen-seat Security Council and a twenty-four-seat Economic and Social Council. It had no authority to support any other proposals for amendments to the Charter and if such other proposals were put to a vote it would have to vote against them.

21. Under Article 108 of the Charter no amendment to that instrument could be adopted unless it received two-thirds of the votes of the total membership. If the Committee went ahead with proposals for a Charter amendment which could not receive the support of a two-thirds majority it would not even be possible to recommend the amendment for ratification by the members of the Assembly and the present division of opinion with respect to the exact size of the increases would be perpetuated. That would be extremely unfortunate, for it appeared that all members of the Assembly except those belonging to the Soviet bloc were now ready to go ahead and increase the membership of the two Councils. Thus voting at the present stage would do no more than record known differences of opinion. It might be better for all concerned if the issue were held over for intensive discussion and negotiation which could result in agreement well before the opening of the nineteenth session on formulas equitable to all States and groups. If that course of action was taken, his delegation would pledge itself to do its utmost to bring about such solutions.

22. Mr. QUAISON-SACKEY (Ghana) introduced draft resolutions A/SPC/L.109 and A/SPC/L.110 on behalf of his own and thirty-six other delegations. The African and Asian Members of the United Nations, shortly to number fifty-eight out of a total of 111, demanded full acceptance by the Organization. If justice was denied them, they might be forced to ask for a redistribution of seats in the Security Council and the Economic and Social Council.

23. Draft resolution A/SPC/L.109 called for increasing the membership of the Security Council to fifteen rather than thirteen because the sponsors felt that fifteen represented a maximum figure as well as a minimum and that its adoption now would therefore obviate the need for a further readjustment at some future date because of further increases in the membership of the United Nations. It had been suggested that, if the membership of the Council was increased to thirteen, Africa would receive two seats. However, the sponsors of the present draft resolution felt that that would represent a gross injustice, and they hoped that an increase in the Council's membership to fifteen would result in the allocation of three seats to Africa and two to Asia. They requested that draft resolution A/SPC/L.109 be given priority over draft resolution A/SPC/L.104/Rev.1 dealing with the same subject.

24. Likewise in the case of draft resolution A/SPC/L.110, which called for increasing the membership of the Economic and Social Council to twenty-seven rather than twenty-four, as originally proposed, the sponsors requested that it be given priority over draft resolution A/SPC/L.105 dealing with the same subject since, like draft resolution A/SPC/L.109, it sought to assert the rights of the African and Asian Members of the United Nations without depriving the Latin American countries of the seats they had held since the founding of the Organization.

25. Since the talks now under way concerning the amendments in document A/SPC/L.108 to the draft resolution on the composition of the General Committee (A/SPC/L.101 and Add.1 and 2) would affec the vote on the two draft resolutions which he ha just introduced, he requested that the Committe should not take a vote on draft resolution A/SPC L.101 and Add.1 and 2 at the present meeting.

26. The sponsors of the African-Asian draft resolutions sympathized with the motives which ha prompted the Australian, Canadian and New Zealan delegations to put forward their amendment (A/SPC L.106) to draft resolution A/SPC/L.101 and Add. and 2. However, they did not feel that the issue Commonwealth representation should be brought up connexion with the question of geographical distribution and therefore hoped that the amendment woul not be pressed to a vote. In appealing for the withdrawal of the amendment, he wished to make it clea that the African and Asian delegations appreciate the active role which the Australian, Canadian an New Zealand delegations had long played in the Unite Nations.

27. The sponsors of the African-Asian draft resolu tions also sympathized with the desire of the Czecho slovak and Polish delegations that Eastern Europ should be reckoned as a factor in the election Presidents of the General Assembly. However, the would suggest the deletion of the words "every yea from the amendments to draft resolution A/SPC/L.1(and Add.1 and 2 submitted by Czechoslovakia ar Poland (A/SPC/L.107). They also considered that tl Middle East should be omitted from the list of region since it was part of Asia. He felt that those change would be in keeping with the observations just ma by the United States representative who would not, was certain, oppose the inclusion of Eastern Euro as a region.

428th MEETING

Saturday, 14 December 1963,

16. Mr. FUKUSHIMA (Japan) said that the countri of Africa and Asia were shamefully under-repre sented in the Security Council and the Economic a Social Council. The best answer would be the e largement of those bodies. Although Japan did n figure among the sponsors of draft resolutions SPC/L.109 and A/SPC/L.110, his delegation co sidered itself virtually a co-sponsor. Certain ci cumstances had caused it to wait before taking t step of joining with the other sponsors, but on t question concerning the Security Council and t Economic and Social Council his delegation wou vote as if it had been one of the sponsors of the dra resolutions which sought to raise the membersh of the Security Council to fifteen and that of the Ec nomic and Social Council to twenty-seven.

17. His delegation was a co-sponsor of the dra resolution concerning the composition of the Gener Committee (A/SPC/L.101 and Add.1 and 2). He wou have voted against the amendments submitted Czechoslovakia and Poland (A/SPC/L.107) had th not been revised as suggested by the representati of Nigeria. He would not oppose the revised amen ments.

18. Mr. BUDO (Albania), after referring to t changes that had occurred in the world in rece

years, and especially the anti-colonialist victories won by the peoples' liberation movement which had shaken the very foundations of the imperialist system of colonial domination, said that the Albanian people and Government had always firmly supported the right of peoples to liberty and independence.

19. Many new countries had been admitted to the United Nations since 1945, so that its membership had more than doubled. That change should be reflected in the structure and activities of the Organization. The demands of the countries of Africa and Asia were therefore fully justified. They could have been satisfied long ago by an equitable distribution of the existing seats. That had not been possible because of the unjustified refusal of certain Western Powers.

20. His delegation supported the demand of the countries of Africa and Asia for an increase in the number of seats in the Security Council and the Economic and Social Council and the redistribution of those seats on an equitable basis.

21. The question of the equitable representation of the countries of Africa and Asia was intrinsically different from that of the restoration of the legitimate rights of the People's Republic of China. The representatives of the Chiang Kai-shek clique represented nothing, and should therefore be expelled without delay from the Organization. The settlement of the great problems of our times demanded that action. In particular, it was evident that so long as China's seat was occupied by the representatives of the venal Chiang Kai-shek clique, the People's Republic of China would not be able to assume any responsibility in the activities of the United Nations, decisions to amend the Charter not excepted. The position of the People's Republic of China on that question had been clearly stated on many occasions by the Government of that country and was in keeping with the principles of the sovereignty and equality of States. It had been affirmed once again in the statement issued on 12 December 1963 by the Minister for Foreign Affairs of the People's Republic of China.

22. The Albanian delegation did not think it fair that a Member should invoke the People's Republic of China to justify its own position in the present debate. Why should the People's Republic of China be saddled with a responsibility which was not its own, save that it was kept out of the Organization's work? If, on the other hand, the Government of the People's Republic gave its official assent from Peking to such and such a solution while representatives of Chiang Kai-shek could make themselves heard in the United Nations, that would acknowledge the false imperialistic theory of the existence of two Chinas. In the eyes of the People's Republic of China, such a situation was inadmissible.

23. No one could doubt the attitude of the People's Republic of China to the peoples' struggle for national liberation. Everyone knew the great part it had played in support of the national liberation and independence movment. His delegation believed that each Member State should define its position on the basis of the facts of the question without introducing considerations relating to the People's Republic of China, which, owing to United States pressure, was denied the right to take part in the work of the United Nations. Each country should accept its responsibility and decide whether the question should be resolved by granting the just demands of the countries of Asia and Africa or whether to let it drag on, thus playing the imperialist game.

24. In conclusion, he repeated that his delegation would support all appropriate measures to satisfy the just demands of the countries of Africa and Asia by expanding the membership of the Security Council and the Economic and Social Council and by an equitable distribution of seats in those organs.

• • •

47. Mr. TARAZI (Syria) said that he endorsed the statements made by the representative of Iraq (427th meeting) regarding draft resolutions A/SPC/L.109 and A/SPC/L.110, particularly the idea that the Arab countries should have a seat in the Security Council. His delegation would therefore vote for those draft resolutions.

48. However, since his Government recognized the Government of the People's Republic of China as the sole representative of China in the United Nations, and since the Government's rights in the Organization should be restored to it, his delegation would have very serious reservations regarding any ratification not given by the People's Republic of China.

49. His delegation would vote for draft resolution A/SPC/L.101 and Add.1 and 2, of which it was a co-sponsor; it accepted the idea expressed in the amendments submitted by Czechoslovakia and Poland (A/SPC/L.107), for all the regions listed therein should be in a position to furnish Presidents for the General Assembly. His delegation would therefore vote for those amendments in their final form.

• • •

53. Mr. BUDO (Albania) said that he had no objection to the Canadian representative's proposal but thought that it would be fairer to issue the verbatim text of all the statements that had been made both at the morning and at the afternoon meeting.

54. Mr. CHAPDELAINE (Canada) said that he supported the Albanian representative's proposal.

It was so decided.

55. Mr. PACHACHI (Iraq), speaking in exercise of his right of reply, said that the Ivory Coast representative seemed to have misunderstood the remarks that he had made at the 427th meeting. He himself had expressed some doubts about the advisability of including in a resolution a specific reference to a non-geographical group such as the Commonwealth. He had added that, in practice, at least one Commonwealth country would no doubt be represented on the General Committee and that the same should apply to the representation of the Arab States on the Security Council. He had not advocated a specific reference to the Arab States in the draft resolution calling for the enlargement of the membership of the Security Council (/SPC/L.109), although, in contrast to the Commonwealth, the Arab States formed a distinct, homogeneous geographic entity, and were bound together by legal, political, historical and cultural ties. He had merely expressed the opinion that at least one Arab State from Africa or Asia should occupy one of the five seats to be given to the countries of Africa and Asia in the Security Council. It was true that the Arab States were situated in both Asia and Africa, but that need not be a deterrent.

56. Furthermore, the gentleman's agreement reached in 1946 was reaffirmed in draft resolution A/SPC/

L.109. Under that agreement, two non-permanent seats were reserved for Latin America, and one each for Eastern Europe, Western Europe, the Commonwealth —which was referred to in draft resolution A/SPC/L.109 as "other States"—and the Middle East. However, the Middle East seat was not provided for in draft resolution A/SPC/L.109. It would therefore be logical to ask that the seat reserved for the Middle East in 1946 should be recognized in the same way as the other seats that had been allocated to the various regions. The Arab States had nevertheless refrained from making such a request in order to preserve the solidarity of the countries of Asia and Africa and had confined themselves to agreeing that the Middle East's seat should be included among the five seats reserved for African and Asian States. The seven Arab States could hardly be criticized for having made a formal declaration to that effect.

429th
MEETING

Monday, 16 December 1963,

1. Mr. FEDORENKO (Union of Soviet Socialist Republics) said that the Soviet Union had always been and continued to be in favour of proper representation for the African and Asian countries in the Security Council and the Economic and Social Council by means which included the expansion of the membership of those bodies. That was impossible at the present time, however, owing exclusively to the position of the Western Powers, which had prevented the restoration of the rights of the People's Republic of China in the United Nations. That was the essence of the problem. In the circumstances his delegation thought that a vote on the draft resolutions proposing the expansion of the membership of the Councils should be deferred to allow for consultations which might result in a solution acceptable to all. If, on the other hand, the draft resolutions in question were put to the vote, his delegation would have no choice but to vote against them.

• • •

11. Mr. JUARBE Y JUARBE (Cuba) explained that the Cuban delegation would vote in favour of the amendment in document A/SPC/L.108 to the joint draft resolution concerning the composition of the General Committee (A/SPC/L.101 and Add.1 and 2). It would do so as a gesture of solidarity with the States of the Latin American region, although the increase in the number of Latin American seats could hardly benefit his country owing to a special policy being pursued by the Latin American group in the United Nations.

12. Mr. BLAKE (United States of America) observed that certain consultations were continuing and suggested another short suspension of the meeting.

It was so agreed.

The meeting was suspended at 6.35 p.m. and resumed at 6.45 p.m.

13. Mr. EL-ZAYYAT (United Arab Republic) welcomed the restatement of the Soviet Union's position made by the representative of the USSR at the beginning of the meeting. He noted that the Soviet Union had been and was still in favour of ensuring equitable representation of Asia and Africa in the two major Councils of the United Nations by methods which included enlargement of the Councils, and therefore, amendment of the Charter. However, the USSR's position was that an amendment to the Charter could not be ratified until a solution had been found to the question of the representation of China.

14. It seemed to him that inasmuch as the difficulty lay in the ratification of the proposed amendments the Soviet Union might be able to withhold its objection to their adoption by the General Assembly, in view of the possibility of a situation arising during the two-year period allowed for ratification that would enable it to ratify the amendments.

15. He appealed to the members of the Committee and in particular to the permanent members of the Security Council, to adopt the necessary amendments to the Charter unanimously, pending a solution of the problem of ratification at a later stage.

16. Mr. QUAISON-SACKEY (Ghana) announced that an agreement had been reached between the African-Asian and the Latin American groups to fuse the four draft resolutions relating to equitable representation on the Security Council and the Economic and Social Council by amending the two draft resolutions sponsored by Latin American countries (A/SPC/L.104/Rev.1 and A/SPC/L.105). The amendments in question would be read out by the representative of India.

• • •

27. Mr. PLIMPTON (United States of America) explained that his delegation would abstain from the vote on the two revised draft resolutions. It had repeatedly made it clear that the United States was strongly in favour of increasing the membership of the Security Council and the Economic and Social Council in order to permit adequate representation of the African-Asian States. It had deeply regretted that one of the members of the Security Council, the Soviet Union, had prevented such a solution. His delegation had been prepared to vote for the earlier draft resolutions which would have had the effect of increasing the membership of the Security Council from eleven to thirteen and that of the Economic and Social Council from eighteen to twenty-four.

28. The proposals to increase the membership of the Security Council to fifteen and that of the Economic and Social Council to twenty-seven had been very recent and if they had been put to the vote at the 428th meeting of the Committee, his delegation would have had to vote against them because of the lack of complete unanimity among those who favoured immediate increases in the two Councils. Since then, a wider measure of agreement had developed as a result of further consultations and, as a consequence, the United States delegation had been authorized to abstain. It took that position without prejudice to the final position of its Government on the proposed amendments to the Charter, which would be determined after further consultations with other Member States and in accordance with his country's administrative and constitutional processes.

29. In conclusion, he noted that the suggestion had been made informally that the final paragraph of the revised draft resolution concerning the composition of the Security Council (A/SPC/L.104/Rev.1) which prescribed the distribution of the ten non-permanent seats among the various regions, should be incorporated directly into the proposed amendment to the Charter. His delegation took no position with respect to that suggestion but thought that it ought to be borne in mind in view of the possibility that it might be put forward as a formal amendment when the items under discussion were considered in the plenary meeting of the General Assembly.

ACTION TAKEN BY THE GENERAL ASSEMBLY

At its 1285th plenary meeting on 17 December 1963, the General Assembly adopted draft resolutions I and II submitted by the Special Political Committee (A/5675, para. 21). For the final texts, see resolutions 1990 (XVIII) and 1991 (XVIII) below.

Resolutions adopted by the General Assembly

1990 (XVIII). Question of the composition of the General Committee of the General Assembly: amendments to rules 31 and 38 of the Assembly's rules of procedure

The General Assembly,

Taking into account the considerable increase in the membership of the United Nations,

Taking also into account that the General Committee of the General Assembly should be so constituted as to ensure its representative character on the basis of a balanced geographical distribution among its members,

Believing that for those reasons it is desirable to enlarge the composition of the General Committee,

Noting that the General Committee is composed of the President of the General Assembly, the Vice-Presidents of the Assembly and the Chairmen of the Main Committees,

1. *Decides* to amend rules 31 and 38 of its rules of procedure as follows:

"Rule 31

"The General Assembly shall elect a President and seventeen Vice-Presidents, who shall hold office until the close of the session at which they are elected. The Vice-Presidents shall be elected, after the election of the Chairmen of the seven Main Committees referred to in rule 101, on the basis of ensuring the representative character of the General Committee."

"Rule 38

"The General Committee shall comprise the President of the General Assembly, who shall preside, the seventeen Vice-Presidents and the Chairmen of the seven Main Committees. No two members of the General Committee shall be members of the same delegation, and it shall be so constituted as to ensure its representative character. Chairmen of other committees upon which all Members have the right to be represented and which are established by the General Assembly to meet during the session, shall be entitled to attend meetings of the General Committee and may participate without vote in the discussions."

2. *Decides* that the President of the General Assembly, the seventeen Vice-Presidents of the Assembly and the seven Chairmen of the Main Committees shall be elected as provided in the annex to the present resolution;

3. *Decides* to cancel all previous resolutions and stipulations in connexion with the composition of the General Committee and to modify all related provisions in its rules of procedure.

1285th plenary meeting,
17 December 1963.

Annex

1. In the election of the President of the General Assembly, regard shall be had for equitable geographical rotation of this office among the regions mentioned in paragraph 4 below.

2. The seventeen Vice-Presidents of the General Assembly shall be elected according to the following pattern, subject to paragraph 3 below:

(*a*) Seven representatives from African and Asian States;

(*b*) One representative from an Eastern European State;

(*c*) Three representatives from Latin American States;

(*d*) Two representatives from Western European and other States;

(*e*) Five representatives from the permanent members of the Security Council.

3. The election of the President of the General Assembly will, however, have the effect of reducing by one the number of vice-presidencies allocated to the region from which the President is elected in accordance with paragraph 2 above.

4. The seven Chairmen of the Main Committees shall be elected according to the following pattern:

(*a*) Three representatives from African and Asian States;

(*b*) One representative from an Eastern European State;

(*c*) One representative from a Latin American State;

(*d*) One representative from a Western European or other State;

(*e*) The seventh chairmanship shall rotate every alternate year among representatives of States mentioned in sub-paragraphs (*c*) and (*d*) above.

1991 (XVIII). Question of equitable representation on the Security Council and the Economic and Social Council

A

The General Assembly,

Considering that the present composition of the Security Council is inequitable and unbalanced,

Recognizing that the increase in the membership of the United Nations makes it necessary to enlarge the membership of the Security Council, thus providing for a more adequate geographical representation of non-permanent members and making it a more effective organ for carrying out its functions under the Charter of the United Nations,

Bearing in mind the conclusions and recommendations of the Committee on arrangements for a conference for the purpose of reviewing the Charter (A/5487, para. 9),

1. *Decides* to adopt, in accordance with Article 108 of the Charter of the United Nations, the following amendments to the Charter and to submit them for ratification by the States Members of the United Nations:

(*a*) In Article 23, paragraph 1, the word "eleven" in the first sentence shall be replaced by the word "fifteen", and the word "six" in the third sentence by the word "ten";

(*b*) In Article 23, paragraph 2, the second sentence shall then be reworded as follows:

"In the first election of the non-permanent members after the increase of the membership of the Security Council from eleven to fifteen, two of the four additional members shall be chosen for a term of one year";

(*c*) In Article 27, paragraph 2, the word "seven" shall be replaced by the word "nine";

(*d*) In Article 27, paragraph 3, the word "seven" shall be replaced by the word "nine";

2. *Calls upon* all Member States to ratify the above amendments, in accordance with their respective constitutional processes, by 1 September 1965;

3. *Further decides* that the ten non-permanent members of the Security Council shall be elected according to the following pattern:

(*a*) Five from African and Asian States;

(*b*) One from Eastern European States;

(*c*) Two from Latin American States;

(*d*) Two from Western European and other States.

1285th plenary meeting,
17 December 1963.

B

The General Assembly,

Recognizing that the increase in the membership of the United Nations makes it necessary to enlarge the membership of the Economic and Social Council, with a view to providing for a more adequate geographical representation therein, and making it a more effective organ for carrying out its functions under Chapters IX and X of the Charter of the United Nations,

Recalling Economic and Social Council resolutions 974 B and C (XXXVI) of 22 July 1963,

Bearing in mind the conclusions and recommendations of the Committee on arrangements for a conference for the purpose of reviewing the Charter (A/5487, para. 9).

1. *Decides* to adopt, in accordance with Article 108 of the Charter of the United Nations, the following amendment to the Charter and to submit it for ratification by the States Members of the United Nations:

"Article 61

"1. The Economic and Social Council shall consist of twenty-seven Members of the United Nations elected by the General Assembly.

"2. Subject to the provisions of paragraph 3, nine members of the Economic and Social Council shall be elected each year for a term of three years. A retiring member shall be eligible for immediate re-election.

"3. At the first election after the increase in the membership of the Economic and Social Council from eighteen to twenty-seven members, in addition to the members elected in place of the six members whose term of office expires at the end of that year, nine additional members shall be elected. Of these nine additional members, the term of office of three members so elected shall expire at the end of one year, and of three other members at the end of two years, in accordance with arrangements made by the General Assembly.

"4. Each member of the Economic and Social Council shall have one representative";

2. *Calls upon* all Member States to ratify the above amendment, in accordance with their respective constitutional processes, by 1 September 1965;

3. *Further decides* that, without prejudice to the present distribution of seats in the Economic and Social Council, the nine additional members shall be elected according to the following pattern:

(*a*) Seven from African and Asian States;

(*b*) One from Latin American States;

(*c*) One from Western European and other States.

1285th plenary meeting,
17 December 1963.

NOTES AND QUESTIONS

1. On the basis of the debates how seriously do you think the various states are taking the matter of the expansion of these bodies? Is this a very important matter either for the satisfaction of narrowly defined national interests, or for the realization of the more universal interests in preventing nuclear war? Are the debates a mere exercise in rhetoric? Do you suspect that the real issues are being thrashed out in other forums? Is a successful settlement of the expansion issue likely to make a significant difference in the authority and practices of the Security Council?
2. Is there any system of representation that might conceivably be considered sufficiently adequate so that all states would agree to vest an international organ with the authority to meet its responsibility for maintaining the peace? Is dissatisfaction with the system of representation a primary explanation of the ineffectiveness of the Security Council?
3. Articles 108 and 109 of the present Charter provide for amendment to the Charter and for the calling of a conference to review the Charter within ten years after the Organization's inception; if the conference was not held by that time, the matter was to be put on the agenda of the General Assembly. The conference was not

held and an item labelled Charter Review was automatically placed on the agenda in 1954 and, as already indicated, served as the basis for the discussion and action pertaining to the expansion of the Security Council. The difficulty of achieving a full scale Charter review, as well as the intense negotiations that took place prior to the adoption of the proposals on expansion, suggest that many, at least, of the Member States considered this question to be quite significant. Certainly, if the Security Council is to become an important force in determining the response of the international community to matters threatening international peace and security, no state could fail to be unconcerned about its composition.

4. These debates also offer clues about the process of Charter revision in general and have broad implications for a major concern of this book, that is, whether it is possible to change the international system by the adoption of a new constitutional structure. This, in essence, is the Clark-Sohn plan; it is a scheme for drastic consitutional revision of the United Nations. What can be learned about the Clark-Sohn proposals by reading the debates on the expansion of the Security Council? What are the limits set by international political processes upon the opportunities for constitutional reform? What alternatives to constitutional reform exist for those eager to bring about a system change in international politics for purposes of war prevention?
5. Compare the proposals adopted by the General Assembly for the expansion and composition of the Security Council with those embodied in the Clark-Sohn plan. Given the fact that Clark and Sohn distinguish two groups of states on the basis of population, there will be a wide variety of states in terms of geography, political ideology, military power, as well as other criteria that will feel disadvantaged. Would it have been more sensible to freeze the idea of geographical representation into the Clark-Sohn plan than to adopt population as the primary criterion? Given present regional groupings, to what extent are some members likely to find that the selection for the Council is so narrowly constricted as to be no longer "representative"? On regionalism as a basis for world order, see Yalem, **I-3A**. Does population as a criterion always assure representation on the basis of criteria of relative influence as it emerges within new political settings?
6. Do you feel that the proposals adopted by the General Assembly on expansion and composition of the Security Council are fair? Do the changes take into account, or can they be used to take account of the general principles for expansion as they are set forth in the Commission's Report? Are there any other criteria in the Commission's Report or any alternative plan that you think should have also been presented to the political organs working on these issues of expansion and composition?
7. On August 31, 1965 these resolutions were formally adopted as Amendments to the Charter, all five permanent members of the Security Council and eighty-eight other Members of the Organization having deposited ratification notices. Voting for new members of the expanded Councils is expected to take place in late 1965.

The General Assembly 5

A. The Effectiveness of General Assembly Resolutions

The most significant structural revision of the United Nations contemplated by the Clark-Sohn plan is to deprive the Security Council of primary responsibility for international peace and security and to give it to the General Assembly. The Assembly is, in fact, given *legislative* authority by Clark and Sohn in "the limited field of war prevention." The capacity of an international organization to enact and enforce laws that are binding on states and individuals in the area of international security entails an entirely new system of international relations.

The first two readings provide a basis for evaluating the Clark-Sohn proposals by focusing on the extent to which the General Assembly influences nation-states with the much more limited powers presently at its disposal. It is difficult to measure the extent of this influence, and it varies from context to context. Nevertheless, the network of powers given to the General Assembly does, as a formal matter at least, make that organ potentially a significant participant in international political processes.

The General Assembly is given the authority in Article 10 to *discuss* "any matter of international concern." At the same time, states have frequently disputed the inclusion of an item on the agenda on the ground that even discussion violates Article 2(7), the provision that requires the United Nations to refrain from intervening in matters which are essentially within the domestic jurisdiction of Member States. This jurisdictional argument is frequently motivated by the desire to avoid a precedent for action by the Organization. Part of the objection to discussion also seems to rest upon the judgment of the objecting government that discussion in the United Nations might have an adverse effect upon the state's capacity to act as it sees fit, thereby acknowledging the reality of General Assembly influence.

In addition to the power to discuss, the Assembly has the authority to investigate a wide range of matters, to set up subcommittees, to make recommendations and pass resolutions, and to arrive at certain decisions binding upon all members, especially where the operations and proceedings of the Assembly itself are concerned.

The first selection in this chapter is an article by Gabriella R. Lande, "The Changing Effectiveness of General Assembly Resolution," *Proceedings of the American Society of International Law* (1964) pp. 162–173. It attempts to develop a method for studying General Assembly influence, and focuses on the power of the General Assembly to recommend and pass resolutions. Mrs. Lande's article reveals a broad range of matters that have been acted upon by the Assembly. The identification of a set of "variables" for analyzing the effectiveness of recommendations and resolutions is an attempt to achieve some understanding of the interaction of nation-states and the United Nations. It is one aspect of the very tenuous inquiry into what would have been the history of international relations after World War II, if there had been no United Nations or other general international organization. See Ernst B. Haas, *Beyond the Nation-State* (Stanford University Press, 1964), in which Haas sets out the theoretical basis for such an inquiry.

The use of a set of variables to study the influence of resolutions upon nation-states is a way to begin to find out under what conditions, by what techniques, and with respect to which subjects the authority of the General Assembly seems to matter most. It is difficult to undertake this study because it is hard to differentiate the influence of the General Assembly from other domestic and international influences that work toward compliance or noncompliance by a nation-state. Mrs. Lande seeks, of course, an index of *independent influence* by the General Assembly. To the extent that one begins to develop a satisfactory index, one may identify those areas where it makes most sense to seek an expansion of the role of the General Assembly.

THE CHANGING EFFECTIVENESS OF GENERAL ASSEMBLY RESOLUTIONS

By Gabriella Rosner Lande

The General Assembly of the United Nations has become over the years the predominant political body of the world organization. The frequent inability of the Security Council to discharge the functions assigned to it by the Charter has brought about a change in the relative powers of the Council and the General Assembly. Member states have increasingly extended the Assembly's rôle in questions involving the maintenance or restoration of international peace and security and many of them have looked with ever widening hope to this organ for a solution to their problems. Assembly resolutions, moreover, while technically only recommendations, have been viewed by some Member countries, with regard to certain matters and within certain limits, as legally binding decisions.

These developments seem to indicate that the influence of the General Assembly has increased. The nature of this influence and its meaning for Member states and the United Nations Organization might be usefully assessed by examining the effect of the Assembly's resolutions.

The General Assembly is not a world parliament. In regard to most political matters, it cannot legislate; it can only recommend. The Assembly is empowered to do no more than to issue political or socio-economic recommendations of a general or specific character which themselves lack obligatory force. It differs from the parliament of a sovereign democratic state, for the latter presupposes a certain political agreement as to ends and means which does not exist in the United Nations forum. Majority voting in a national parliament is predicated upon an implicit ability and willingness to come to terms on certain points of issue and an implicit agreement on "fundamentals," whereas in the General Assembly there is often serious contention between the Western Powers and the Soviet Union over the nature and significance of the assumptions underlying the United Nations. Serious contention exists as well between some of the colonial and anti-colonial nations in the Assembly.

Moreover, the dissentient minority within the democratic state is constitutionally compellable. It may continue to struggle for the adoption of its view, but, if necessary, it is made to conform, since the state has a near monopoly of the means of coercion. But this is manifestly not the situation of the United Nations. Yet upon close consideration we find that General Assembly resolutions do exert considerable influence. This influence is manifested not only by the degree of compliance Member states give to Assembly resolutions, but by the general political effects which resolutions may produce in a Member state or in the relations among nations.

Let us look for a few moments at the general effects on Member states of the Assembly's political resolutions. These have been many and diverse. Some resolutions have influenced national behavior or the choice of foreign policy alternatives of Member states. The General Assembly's resolutions during the Suez crisis of 1956 were surely influential in obtaining a cease-fire and the retreat of Anglo-French forces from Egypt. After Chinese Communist intervention in the Korean War in November, 1950, General Assembly opinion and resolutions may be said to have had a restraining influence upon United States policy in Korea. They may even have helped to prevent the extension of the area of military operation close to or into Manchurian territory. Certainly, they resulted in United States acceptance of various principles as a basis for negotiating a cease-fire with the Chinese in January, 1951.

A number of Assembly resolutions have had the effect of setting standards of state behavior and have resulted in their national endorsement, at least in principle. These resolutions have crystallized elements of a new international legitimacy which at times may be hardly distinguishable from morality and justice, but which, by their constant reaffirmation, do not get lost. U.N. resolutions have defined a kind of consensus on principles—avoidance of the use of force, the right to self-determination, the right to economic development and so on. Within this category falls the Universal Declaration of Human Rights which has become a yardstick to measure the compliance by governments with international standards of human rights. It has promoted the adoption of more specific agreements along the same lines, stimulated other declarations whose purpose is the solution of international problems, and influenced legal institutions in individual countries, particularly new constitutions or constitutional amendments.

Some Assembly resolutions have affected the means at the disposal of states in their relations, particularly by creating new peace-keeping techniques to isolate clashes between smaller nations or within a smaller nation from the larger East-West struggle. The Communist retreat from South Korea in 1951, French and British evacuation of Egypt in 1956, the U. S. withdrawal from Lebanon in 1958 and the Soviet retreat from the Congo after the fall of Lumumba were surely furthered by these techniques.

A number of resolutions have put Members in the position of losing or gaining (depending on whether or not they accepted the resolutions) political friendships or understanding. A few resolutions have bound states to certain courses of action, interpreted the principle of domestic jurisdiction, or narrowed the areas traditionally considered within the exclusive realm of the national sovereign. They have had the effect of accelerating the increase in the number of states and furthering activities of peaceful change within nations.

In regard to the United Nations system, some resolutions have had the effect of providing organs with additional tools with which to perform necessary functions, enlarged the number of "world tasks" of the Organization, interpreted the meaning of Charter principles. A number of resolutions have clarified the legal rights and duties of Member states and of the Organization. Assembly resolutions have set precedents, and even institutionalized common interests.

These, then, are the very general and far-flung consequences which Assembly resolutions may have. Their effect, however, must also be analyzed with respect to Member states' compliance with them.

Roger Fisher has written that governments, in both their domestic and foreign operations, are under heavy pressure from various sources to conform, or appear to conform, to accepted standards of behavior.[1] I believe that this is true as well in regard to conformity with United Nations resolutions. Professor Fisher identifies four sources of pressure: (1) the possibility of direct retaliation by the governments directly affected; (2) the likelihood of an adverse reaction among allies and the nations less closely involved in the issue at hand; (3) political criticism from a government's own constituents; and (4) the deeply rooted moral nature of the individual decision-makers, the "law habit."

Hence, even in the absence of an organized superior sovereign power to compel obedience, a government in the General Assembly forum will not easily ignore the conduct and attitudes of the majority of U.N. Members. It must consider with care the possible reaction of other states to a defiance of an Assembly resolution. It must weigh not only the immediate reaction of the nations which would be most affected by such a breach, but also the effect on world public opinion.

A U.N. resolution may *mobilize* opinion in support of its tenets. Moreover, the Assembly sometimes is able, in the resolutions themselves, to focus and crystallize, formulate and *express* world opinion. As F. Blaine Sloan declares,

> the force of a recommendation is not derived from a judgment made in an internal court of conscience, but from a judgment made by an organ of the world community and supported by many of the same considerations which support positive international law. The judgment made by the General Assembly as a collective world conscience is itself a force external to the individual conscience of any given state.

Sloan submits that, in view of these considerations, the Assembly's moral force "is in fact a nascent legal force which may enjoy, in the rounded words of Judge Cardozo, a twilight existence hardly distinguishable from morality and justice until the time when the *imprimatur* of the world community will attest its jural quality."[2]

[1] "Bringing Law to Bear on Governments," 74 Harvard Law Rev. 1134–1135 (1961).

[2] "The Binding Force of a 'Recommendation' of the General Assembly of the United Nations," 25 Brit. Yr. Bk. Int. Law 32–33 (1948).

Actually, the nascent legal force of the Assembly has already begun to develop. In certain respects, the distinction between the status of resolutions as recommendations and resolutions as legislation may have become rather thin. The Assembly's decisions, said Dag Hammarskjöld, "introduce an important element by expressing a majority consensus on the issue under consideration." This element

> leaves scope for a gradual development in practice of the weight of the decisions. To the extent that mere respect, in fact, is shown to General Assembly recommendations by the Member States, they may come more and more close to being recognized as decisions having a binding effect on those concerned, particularly when they involve the application of the binding principles of the Charter and of international law.[3]

Majority consensus and world opinion will not of course always cause compliance; but these forces do exert an influence and sometimes even exert considerable pressure.

World opinion reacted with shock to Soviet denial of human rights in the countries under its direct influence and to Soviet action in Hungary, and was reflected in the United Nations' resolutions regarding these questions. It is improbable that the resolutions affected the conscience of Soviet leaders—they did not spur modification of Soviet action at the time—but at least total disregard of these resolutions threatened the U.S.S.R. with diplomatic isolation and helped to impress on the non-Soviet world the extent to which Communist leaders violated the fundamental rights of the individual.

At the time of the British and French inroad into Egypt in 1956, public and official concern in the United States that we would alienate and antagonize the peoples and governments of Asia and Africa were we not to criticize strongly what the majority of nations considered an illegal resort to force, certainly influenced our stand vis-à-vis Britain and France. Indeed the strong consensus of the majority of U.N. Members that the Anglo-French-Israeli attack violated the fundamental rules of international conduct, did much to bring about the cease-fire and ultimate withdrawal of troops from Egypt. Domestic opinion, especially in Britain, was also influential in modifying that government's policy.

The danger of external consequences, the reaction of other states, and the pressures of domestic and world opinion are thus important factors influencing governmental compliance with the Assembly's resolutions. In studying the changing effectiveness of U.N. resolutions and Member states' compliance with these resolutions, one might, however, consider six additional important variables. These are (1) the *time* at which the resolutions were passed; (2) the fundamental *issues* lying at the root of the resolutions; (3) the *vote* taken on the resolutions; (4) the *language* of the resolutions; (5) the *methods* and *means* used by the Assembly to

[3] Introduction to the Annual Report of the Secretary-General on the Work of the Organization, 16 June 1960–15 June 1961, General Assembly, 16th Sess., Official Records, Supp. No. 1A, p. 3.

implement its resolutions; and (6) the *expectations* of Member states in regard to the resolutions.

First, General Assembly resolutions might be analyzed at different points of postwar history in order to determine whether their effect has varied with the years. The foreign policies of Member states may in time incorporate the behavior patterns developed at the United Nations. National aims and expectations may be reconstituted and special attention may come to be paid to what is considered "legitimate" by the General Assembly, or what the effect will be of U.N. pressures and possible interventions. Hence attention must be bestowed upon the evolution of national policies as the Member nations "learned" from the U.N. encounter.

By tracing the Assembly's resolutions and Member states' response to them through the years, one might for example show that direct attempts by the Soviet Union to extend its authority into areas outside of its direct influence has been ever more strongly resisted by other U.N. Members. This resistance may well have contributed materially to a Soviet retreat in some of these areas. Greece, Yugoslavia and South Korea are eloquent examples. Could it be demonstrated that the Soviet Union "learned" from its encounter with the U.N. and modified its behavior accordingly in subsequent years? Certainly, it accepted to stay removed from such potential cold-war areas as the Middle East and the Congo. The Kremlin will probably remain far less influenced by the U.N.'s resolutions than by its own strategic decisions arrived at on the basis of evidence regarding power relations, internal stresses and the like. But its decisions will have to take past U.N. action, as expressed by resolutions, into account. Even limited U.N. action, such as an Assembly consensus condemnatory of Soviet maneuvers in Hungary, can embarrass the Soviet Union, while investigatory and fact-finding commissions instituted by an Assembly resolution may expose vulnerabilities and failures of the Communist system, and these matters will have to be weighed.

Turning to our second variable, we might seek to discover under which *conditions* there is an increase in effectiveness of Assembly resolutions and under what *circumstances* a diminution. The fundamental *issues* lying at the root of a resolution—the cold-war conflict, nationalist aspirations, developments in nuclear technology—may prove important in this respect. It has often been said, for example, that U.N. resolutions have proved most effective in dealing with issues outside or on the periphery of the cold-war conflict, issues which do not engender major political dissension between the super-Powers. Secretary General Hammarskjöld, in his classic statement of the theory of preventive diplomacy, virtually discarded the idea that the United Nations could usefully or safely intervene in "problems which are clearly and definitely within the orbit of present day conflicts between power blocs."[4] He drew the conclusion that the main field of useful activity of the United Nations in its efforts to prevent or solve

[4] Introduction to the Annual Report of the Secretary-General on the Work of the Organization, 16 June 1959–15 June 1960, General Assembly, 15th Sess., Official Records, Supp. No. 1A, pp. 4–5.

conflicts should be action to fill vacuums in areas of conflict outside or marginal to the zones already involved in the cold-war struggle. This would minimize the tendency or diminish the incentive of great Powers to move competitively into those situations. Thus, he hoped, the United Nations might prevent the widening and aggravation of the bloc conflicts.

The effectiveness of U.N. resolutions probably depends a good deal upon the basic issue to which a resolution relates.

The source of a resolution and the *vote* taken on it is another dimension of interest: From which nation or nations did the resolution in question spring and gain support? What were the aims of these nations and their influence? Did a nation's response to a resolution after its passage differ from its vote?

In his theory and practice of preventive diplomacy Hammarskjöld strongly implied that the United Nations' resolutions in the political and security field would not be effective in the absence of agreement between the super-Powers. Certainly, the fact that the votes of influential delegates "weigh more" than others in terms of their political influence may have a very direct bearing upon the relative effectiveness of various resolutions. The quality, quantity and intensity of the community support which stands behind a resolution may also determine what impact that resolution will have.

A powerful majority, including many influential Member states, passed the "Uniting for Peace" resolution in 1950. It was heralded immediately as a resolution carrying tremendous weight and certainly has had profound repercussions for the United Nations and the development of the General Assembly. The Assembly's decision to internationalize Jerusalem, taken at the same session, mustered a much weaker majority, lacked the support of the most influential nations, and "was discredited from the beginning."[5]

Resolutions adopted by a two-thirds majority do not, however, always represent the opinion of mankind. It would be wise to be wary of such judgments in evaluating the vote. What is important is to try to specify the ingredients of the compromise in each resolution and the power alignments involved. A comparison of the alignments on various issues, reflecting as they do national aims in conflict, will yield the lines of influence and pressure which are vital to a study of why some resolutions are more effective than others.

The language of the resolution is a fourth variable to be considered in analyzing compliance and effect. One may find, for example, that resolutions which regret, deplore or condemn, repeated year after year, in some cases do not have a consistently beneficial influence. Repetition may be vain. Restraint of language may be important. In examining those resolutions of the Assembly which have not been complied with, one may wonder whether in every case it was wise to formulate the decision in such blunt language. For example, the Assembly's strongly condemnatory resolution against Communist China in February, 1951, may well have

[5] H. Field Haviland, The Political Role of the General Assembly 79–80 (New York, Carnegie Endowment for International Peace, 1951).

had the negative effect of increasing Chinese intransigence and postponing Korean truce talks, rather than the beneficent effect of inducing the Chinese to conform to the Assembly's will. Maximum effectiveness requires the framing of the Assembly's decisions in such a way that they exert pressure without increasing intransigence.

The language of a resolution may have other effects as well. In the "new United Nations diplomacy" of the General Assembly, where measures must be presented in terms acceptable to a two-thirds majority of the membership, the resolutions themselves may express a modification of a particular national policy. The divergence of interests in a political body representing over one hundred states is reflected in the course of negotiation and debate and must somehow be accommodated. Hence the necessary search for a common denominator often transforms a measure from what had been originally intended by the sponsor. Most frequently, it will in the end fall short of the maximum desired by its originator. Hans Morgenthau declares that

> the constant use of a certain terminology not only for the purposes of propaganda, but in the give and take of political transactions, may well exert a subtle influence upon the substance of the transactions themselves. . . . It may well result in the blunting of the sharp edges of a national policy, in its retreat from an advanced position, its reformulation and adaptation in the light of the supranational principle embodied in the language of the resolution.[6]

The various instruments of policy, the *methods and means* used by the Assembly to implement its resolutions and the response of Member states to these methods are also significant in evaluating the effectiveness of resolutions. First, the Assembly, to promote compliance, has sometimes simply utilized a formal recommendation in the name of the United Nations. These are resolutions of publicity, appeal or admonition in which Members are reminded that they assumed certain solemn obligations with respect to U.N. recommendations when they ratified the Charter. Secondly, the technique of international surveillance and investigation is a means of promoting compliance. Philip Jessup has pointed out that this technique may be especially useful as an instrument for "mobilizing world public opinion and making it articulate to the point at which it becomes a factor in the power situation."[7] Indeed, the Assembly's agents in Greece, Korea and Palestine have performed a type of "watchdog function" to good advantage. Moreover, the Assembly has used various field agents to supervise the carrying out of particular recommendations or agreements, such as the Palestine Mediator, the United Nations Truce Supervision Organization in the Middle East, and the Temporary Executive Authority in West New Guinea. Thirdly, the Secretary General plays a central rôle in implementing all Assembly recommendations, and the Assembly has strengthened his hand in this regard during the last few years.

[6] "The New United Nations and the Revision of the Charter," 16 Review of Politics 12 (1954).

[7] "The U.N. Begins to Show Power against Power," New York Times Magazine, Oct. 23, 1949, p. 12.

Most importantly, the General Assembly has on a number of occasions attempted to organize diplomatic, economic and para-military measures as means of gaining compliance with its recommendations or with what it considered the basic postulates of the Charter. The Assembly requested Member states to break off diplomatic relations with Spain in 1946 and with the Government of South Africa in 1962. Resort to economic pressure, mostly in the form of embargoes, was authorized by the Assembly against Albania and Bulgaria during the Greek civil war in 1949, against the aggressors in Korea in 1951, and against the Union of South Africa in 1962. United Nations military or para-military forces were of course used to help implement U.N. resolutions in regard to Korea, Suez and the Congo.

During the past eight years there has been a development in the Assembly of new and more effective instruments to deal with disputes which threaten the maintenance of international peace and security. During the crisis in Greece in 1947 and 1948, the Assembly was willing merely to pass formal recommendations calling upon the offending states to desist from what it considered illegal activities, established a commission of investigation and imposed an embargo which had in effect already been in existence. Again, during the early years of the United Nations, when the Assembly recommended a partition plan for Palestine, few Member states were willing to face realistically the problem of implementing their resolution, and rather forlornly requested the Security Council to undertake this task, which the Council refused to do. With time, U.N. organs developed new techniques of peace-keeping forces, U.N. presences, or observer groups which not only had the effect of exerting pressure upon states to comply with U.N. recommendations, but also of providing an impartial mechanism for removing elements of violence and allowing states "to be taken off the hook." The most precedent-setting of these has been the United Nations Emergency Force, the success of which stimulated the creation by the Assembly or Council of other observer and para-military units, notably the U.N. Observer Group in Lebanon, the U.N. Operation in the Congo and the U.N. Force in Cyprus. The Assembly seems to be moving ever closer toward providing "teeth" for its recommendations.

The United Nations' difficulty in solving the very real financial problem which has confronted it since the inception of the Congo operation engendered the use of a number of techniques designed to promote compliance with the Assembly's financial resolutions. The General Assembly asked the International Court of Justice whether the expenses incurred for U.N.E.F. and O.N.U.C. legally constituted "Expenses of the Organization" within the meaning of Article 17, paragraph 2, of the Charter. The Court's affirmative answer to this question upheld the Assembly's right to assess all Member states for the costs of the two peace-keeping forces. The Court's opinion, being advisory, lacks compelling binding force, but it certainly carries great weight. It was accepted by the General Assembly on December 19, 1962, by a vote of 76 to 17 with 8 abstentions. Presumably, a resolution of the Assembly which itself appears to be proper and legitimate can alter the views of others as to what is legitimate. The General Assembly's political power depends in part upon its acting within the area where it is understood to have authority.

In order to influence Members to support financial resolutions relating to U.N.E.F. and O.N.U.C., the Assembly has, moreover, adopted the practice of reducing the assessments for a substantial number of states and applying voluntary contributions to offset the deficits remaining after these deductions. Finally, the sanction against delinquent states contained in Article 19 of the Charter hovers over all negotiations and deliberations regarding the financing of the peace-keeping operations.

Member states have reacted in various ways to the different forms of pressure applied by the Assembly. Consideration of these reactions leads to our last variable, that is, national *expectations* and the *satisfaction or disappointment* experienced by Member states in regard to U.N. resolutions. Surely the effect of the Court's opinion and the Assembly's resolutions on the financing of the peace-keeping operations depends ultimately upon how Members view these operations and the U.N.'s authority to establish them. It depends upon whether a Member state views the increased activities of the General Assembly as a desirable or a dangerous development. It depends on the hopes and expectations entertained by a government and its people in regard to the United Nations. In a larger respect, a Member state's response to the U.N.'s resolutions depends on whether it considers the world organization as merely a diplomatic or parliamentary meeting ground or as a dynamic instrument of governments carrying out executive action.

The Carnegie Endowment's national studies on the United Nations [8] indicate that in reacting to the U.N.'s work, many nations have passed through four distinct phases. This evolution may be roughly summarized as follows: (1) The phase of faith, hope and expectation—approximating the years 1945 to 1947; (2) The phase of disappointment and indifference—1948–1950; (3) The phase of self-reliance and co-operation with nations outside the U.N. context—1951 to 1955; and (4) The phase of limited confidence, beginning in 1956.

Let us hope that phase number five will be not one of limited confidence but of extended trust.

[8] The series of expert studies from some twenty-four countries prepared for the Carnegie Endowment for International Peace and published by the Manhattan Publishing Co., N.Y.: National Studies on International Organization.

NOTES AND QUESTIONS

1. On page 230 Mrs. Lande writes, "actually the nascent legal force of the Assembly has already begun to develop. In certain respects, the distinction between the status of resolutions as recommendations and resolutions as legislation may have become rather thin." In what respect are actions taken by the General Assembly comparable to the kinds of legislative action we find in national societies? Are there any procedures of domestic legislation that are the outcome of procedures resembling the traditional sources of international law, custom and treaties? How does a legislative standard emerge from the social life of a group? Is the formal process of enactment dependent upon some earlier forms of "preparation"?
2. Some observers have argued that the ability of the General Assembly to act in the Suez crisis was solely a result of the fact that the Soviet Union and the United States had reached an agreement with regard to the United Nations' action on that occasion, and that without this agreement there would have been no United Nations' action. Lande submits that the General Assembly's action did have an influence upon the Suez crisis. See Mrs. Lande's book, written under her maiden name, Gabriella Rosner, *The United Nations Emergency Force* (Columbia University Press, 1963). Is there any sense in which it might be meaningfully said that the General Assembly as an organ, or as a separate entity, acted in a fashion that the two major powers did not directly control, even if the original agreement of those powers defined its mission? Sociological writing on the so-called "serendipity effect" is relevant—that is, the tendency for the actual voyage to achieve a destination that is quite independent of the aims of those who launched the vessel at the outset and even of those who man the helm throughout. See Robert Merton, *Social Theory and Social Structure* (rev. ed., Free Press of Glencoe, New York, 1957). Sir Hersch Lauterpacht has made a parallel point with regard to the International Court of Justice by suggesting that it was set up primarily as a procedure for dispute settlement, but that its important role has been to foster the development of international law doctrine. See Sir Hersch Lauterpacht, *The Development of International Law by the International Court of Justice* (Stevens, London, 1958).
3. Which of the six variables enumerated by Mrs. Lande as relevant to effectiveness is most important? Can any one answer be given? Does it depend on the setting? Would you add any variables useful for the appraisal of the influence of General Assembly action? Does the Clark-Sohn model take account of the findings made by Mrs. Lande as to conditions of maximum effectiveness? Is it useful for the constitutional approach to world order to study the sociological circumstances that induce an organization to carry out its tasks most successfully? See material on organization theory cited by Ernst B. Haas, *Beyond the Nation-State* (Stanford University Press, 1964).

The next selection is written by a Polish international lawyer —Krzysztof Skubiszewski, "The General Assembly of the United Nations and its Power to Influence National Action," *Proceedings of the American Society of International Law* (1964) pp. 153–162. Skubiszewski continues the investigation of the influence of the General Assembly upon international political processes. The scope of his selection is broader than that of the previous article; it covers the full range of powers available to the General Assembly for purposes of influencing nation-state behavior and is not restricted to resolutions and recommendations. At the same time, Skubiszewski's focus is narrower, concerned almost exclusively with specifying the grounds of legal authority possessed by the Assembly to carry on these activities.

Two other important differences between this article and the previous one by Mrs. Lande should be noted. In the first place, Skubiszewski distinguishes sharply between the legislative and executive activity of the Assembly. It is his major thesis that the inability of the General Assembly to carry on executive functions is the major constraint upon its capacity to influence the behavior of nation-states. Secondly, the article is written by a Polish jurist and, although it covers much of the same substantive material discussed in the previous article, it bears down more heavily upon decolonialization and the legitimacy of peace-keeping in Suez. Does this suggest the identification of the author with the views of his government?—— to any greater extent than in the piece by Mrs. Lande? Is there any difference in the style of political analysis? Compare the discussion of Dyson (U.S.) and Talensky (U.S.S.R.) on missile defense systems in **IV-1**.

THE GENERAL ASSEMBLY OF THE UNITED NATIONS AND ITS POWER TO INFLUENCE NATIONAL ACTION

By Krzysztof Skubiszewski

In one of his dissenting opinions, Judge Alejandro Alvarez of the International Court of Justice, referring to the declarations and resolutions passed by the General Assembly of the United Nations, made the following observation:

> [T]hey have not yet acquired a binding character, but they may acquire it if they receive the support of public opinion, which in several cases has condemned an act contrary to a Declaration with more force than if it had been a mere breach of a convention of minor importance.[1]

The history of the United Nations shows that the support of public opinion does not necessarily increase the rôle and influence of the Assembly resolutions in the sphere of national policies and action. The resolutions are addressed to Member states and governments and, therefore, it is rather the backing and compliance of the latter that remain decisive for the effectiveness of any steps taken by the General Assembly.

No full exposition of the subject is attempted by the present report. The focus of the report is on the legal aspects of legislative and executive activity as a means of exerting influence on national policies—whether and to what extent the General Assembly possesses powers of legislation and executive action, and how they supplement the traditional techniques of conference diplomacy within the United Nations.

I

The enactment by an international organization of law addressed to states and creating direct rights and duties for them constitutes the most advanced form of international legislation instrumental in affecting policies of states. Only enactment of law that takes place on the basis of majority decisions binding for the outvoted minority can be said to direct and influence national action. The requirement of majority decision is met by the General Assembly (Article 18 of the Charter), but the Assembly does not fulfill other requirements for legislation in the above sense. We know both from the reading of the Charter and the history of its drafting (the defeat of the Philippine proposal presented at the Conference in San Francisco) [2] that no power to make law for states has been conferred on the General Assembly or any other organ of the United Nations. For such power, whether comprising legislation by virtue of unanimous vote, or by majority decision with the guarantees of the system of contracting-out,

[1] Reservations to the Convention on Genocide, Dissenting Opinion of M. Alvarez, [1951] I.C.J. Rep. 49, 52.

[2] 9 U.N.C.I.O. Docs. 70 (1945).

or by majority decision binding for all, must always be based on an explicit and unequivocal treaty authorization.

On the other hand, the Assembly certainly possesses the competence to make the internal law of the United Nations, *i.e.*, the law relating to the structure, functioning, or procedure of the Organization, and addressed not to its Members but to its organs, representatives, or employees. In fact, however, such law often regulates the conduct of states and constitutes a source of their rights and duties whenever they act in the framework of the Organization and in the area covered by its internal law. For instance, the application or non-application of a rule of procedure often is of importance and has influence on the merits of interests which the Members happen to espouse and defend on the United Nations platform. The General Assembly can enact internal law of the Organization not only when a specific authorization to do so has been granted to it by the Charter (Articles 21, 22, 62, paragraph 4, and 101, paragraph 1). The power of the Assembly to make its internal law can be implied, in contradistinction to creating other law.[3] But are internal regulations a kind of law that is helpful in exercising influence on the policies of states, and does the Assembly avail itself of this instrumentality? In answering this question, two sets of internal regulations should be considered.

First, there are the resolutions whereby the Assembly created the operational agencies and regulated their terms of reference and procedure. An operational agency of the United Nations administers the latter's program of assistance: United Nations International Children's Emergency Fund, United Nations Relief and Works Agency for Palestine Refugees in the Near East, United Nations Korean Reconstruction Agency, and the Office of the United Nations High Commissioner for Refugees.[4] In contrast to other subsidiary bodies, the operational agencies have the power to arrive at final decisions within their competence, including the capacity to participate in certain legal transactions (entering into contracts, suing in courts, et cetera). Their power of decision includes especially the disposal of funds. The funds, however, are acquired from voluntary contributions, and this, together with the fundamental feature of their task —they co-operate with and help governments, and do not direct the latter's actions—is a limitation on the agencies' ability to influence national policies. Still, each operational agency works on the basis of its own program, which is not necessarily identical with all the changing and fluctuating wishes and aspirations of the countries where the agency conducts its activities. During the discussion on the proposal to set up the Korean Reconstruction Agency, some Member states expressed fears with respect to the extent of the powers to be granted to the Agent General.

[3] See the following Advisory Opinions of the International Court of Justice: Reparations for Injuries Suffered in the Service of the United Nations, [1949] I.C.J. Rep. 174, 179; Effect of Awards of Compensation made by the U.N. Administrative Tribunal, [1954] *ibid.* 47, 56, 57; Certain Expenses of the United Nations (Article 17, paragraph 2, of the Charter), [1962] *ibid.* 151, 168.

[4] The Technical Assistance Board was created by the Economic and Social Council.

These doubts reflect the awareness on the part of the Members that operational agencies may lawfully become an instrumentality of influencing national policies in the area concerned.

Secondly, there are internal regulations creating machinery for compliance with the Assembly's resolutions in fields other than relief and rehabilitation programs. We are not concerned here for the time being with organs dealing with collective measures, in particular peace-keeping or peace-restoring operations. The view was rightly expressed that "often in international affairs the creation of machinery is just as vital as the adoption of substantive solutions." [5]

Thus the Assembly sets up organs that study and consider information which Members are obliged to submit. Here the Assembly lays down the basis for a next stage in handling the subject matter of the information transmitted. It creates machinery that permits the Organization to study the information and facilitates the adoption of procedural or substantive recommendations. The case in point was the establishment of a special committee on information transmitted under Article 73 e of the Charter. There was some opposition on constitutional grounds to the setting up of the committee. In the words of the French delegate, "certain representatives were trying to perform a creative and almost constitutional task by establishing fresh machinery." "Chapter XI [of the Charter] was a declaration involving an obligation but not providing for a medium of implementation." [6] The philosophy behind this attitude has not been accepted by the Assembly either in this or in other cases.

Further, there is inquiry and investigation machinery in fields where Members have no duty to transmit the information sought by the Assembly. The lack of obligation is a weakness from which this pattern of activity obviously suffers: the success and, consequently, the effectiveness of investigation depend on the co-operation of Members. Commissions of inquiry that conduct investigations in relation to disputes which are being settled under Chapter VI of the Charter are less relevant for the purposes of our problem. An activity of more interest here is the practice of setting up subsidiary bodies which investigate facts and occurrences that are not limited to or connected with a dispute in the strict sense of the term. One of the first organs falling under that category was the Special Committee on Palestine. Another body, the Special Committee on the Problem of Hungary, though vested with wide powers of investigation, had a rather limited function and purpose. In the Hungarian question, the Assembly itself considered investigation as the only and final measure to be applied, and implicitly excluded the taking of any steps on the basis of the facts that were established and assessed through such investigation. Here the Assembly in advance relinquished any serious attempt to exert

[5] Vallat, "The Competence of the United Nations General Assembly," 97 Hague Academy Recueil des Cours 203, 228 (1959).

[6] U. N. General Assembly, 1st Sess., Official Records, 2nd Part, 4th Commission (Part III) 27 (1946). French opposition is referred to by Higgins, The Development of International Law through the Political Organs of the United Nations 114 (1963).

an influence on the national policy in question. On the other hand, numerous studies of and investigations into the racial policies and legislation of the Union (now Republic) of South Africa that were made by different bodies from almost the start of the United Nations permitted information to accumulate that was meant to serve as the factual basis of the action that went beyond mere expression of disapproval and wishes on the part of the Assembly.

Finally, there are provisions of internal law enacted by the Assembly that deal with subsidiary organs, the task of which is to observe and look into the implementation of the Assembly's recommendations. The problem raises some constitutional issues, but as long as the Assembly acts within the framework of its substantive competence (which involves, *inter alia,* respect for the exclusive jurisdiction of the Security Council), the enactment of the said regulations and the ensuing activity of the Assembly and its organs are lawful. They are, however, not very effective. The basic restriction on those organs' ability to influence national action is the fact that they can perform their functions in the territories of Members only with the latter's consent. Hence the rather limited results obtained by bodies where activity was contested or at least not looked upon favorably by the states where such bodies should have exercised their functions of observation and surveillance. The Special Committee on the Balkans, the Commissions on Korea or the Peace Observation Commission are examples of bodies that were not successful in influencing national policies. Nonetheless, it has been suggested that "the fact that the Assembly has had its own eyes and ears at the scene of the difficulty has exerted an important controlling influence. . . ."[7] The delegate of a major Member of the United Nations contended that "in Greece and Korea, commissions of the Assembly had in the one case perhaps prevented open war and in the other case made prompt action possible."[8] It cannot be denied that the Korean Commission's report in 1950, at the outbreak of hostilities in Korea, facilitated, from the procedural point of view, the decisions of the Security Council. But the main task of the two Korean Commissions remained unfulfilled, while the end of the dangerous friction between Greece and her neighbors, and the end of civil war in the former country were not brought about through the influence of the Assembly but by developments extraneous to the United Nations efforts (British military support for Greece, Truman doctrine and its application, withdrawal of backing for Greek guerrillas by Yugoslavia).

When discussing the making of law as the instrumentality whereby the Assembly tries to affect national policies, a word or two should be said of one category of the Assembly's resolutions, *viz.,* resolutions which recite general rules of conduct destined to govern an unlimited number of situations and addressed to an unrestricted number of Members. There are resolutions which elucidate and define in a non-binding form the

[7] Haviland, The Political Role of the General Assembly 98 (1951).

[8] United States of America, U.N. General Assembly, 5th Sess., Official Records, 1st Commission 64, par. 14.

provisions of customary law or deduce more detailed rules from a general principle or principles of treaty law, including the law of the Charter. Examples of resolutions belonging to this class are the Draft Declaration of Rights and Duties of States annexed to Resolution 375 (IV), Resolution 217 (III), containing the Universal Declaration of Human Rights, Resolution 637 (VII) regarding the Right to Self-Determination, Resolution 1803 (XVII) on Permanent Sovereignty over Natural Resources, or the Draft Declaration of Legal Principles Governing the Activities of States in the Exploration and Use of Outer Space which is embodied in Resolution 1962 (XVIII). Where the term "draft" has been used one is tempted to argue that no legislation was implied. Instruments that purport to simply restate or interpret the law in force, on the other hand, always contain the element of law-making, as the processes of interpretation and creation of law are frequently interwoven. The resolutions under consideration are acts by means of which the juridical conscience of nations or at least of their majority finds expression; and therefore they are, to use the words of Article 38, paragraph 1(d) of the Statute of the International Court of Justice, "subsidiary means for the determination of rules of law."[9]

This is not much in terms of actual influence on the behavior of Member states. But there are also other resolutions. While they have the characteristics of the acts just mentioned, they are in a more conspicuous and definite way attempts at law-creating and at making Members comply with that law. For instance, Resolution 378 (V)A on Duties of States in the Event of the Outbreak of Hostilities contains rules which, if accepted as binding, would add to the duties of states engaged in an armed conflict. Also, it has been provided in the said resolution that compliance or non-compliance with the Assembly's recommendations there embodied "be taken into account in any determination of responsibility for the breach of the peace or act of aggression. . . ." Thus we observe here the appearance of a sanction that stands behind the Assembly's recommendation.

The tendency of making new law and imposing it on Members becomes more visible in the case of the Declaration on the Granting of Independence to Colonial Countries and Peoples (Resolution 1514 (XV)). Some of the principles formulated in the Declaration are new law, not to be found in the Charter or the remaining international law. Paragraphs 3 and 4, and paragraph 5 in part can be regarded as revising Article 2, paragraph 7, Article 73 (b), and Article 76 (b) of the Charter. We also find in the Declaration a paragraph which unequivocally states that all countries must "observe faithfully and strictly . . . the present Declaration." Rather soon, however, the Assembly had to note that the provisions of the Declaration, "with a few exceptions" only, had not been carried out (Resolution 1654 (XVI)). Judging from the information assembled by the Special Committee that watches over the implementation of the Declara-

[9] Johnson, "The Effect of Resolutions of the General Assembly of the United Nations," 32 Brit. Yr. Bk. Int. Law 97, 116, 118–119 (1955–1956).

tion, and from Resolutions 1810 and 1956 adopted at the XVIIth and XVIIIth sessions respectively, the non-compliance with the Declaration persists. By adopting the Declaration the Assembly committed itself to seeking changes in title to territory or, to use another term, to initiating "a process of quasi-legislation in the matter of sovereignty over territory."[10] This was a rather bold attempt at both modifying the present law on acquisition and loss of territory and instituting United Nations supervision and guidance, that is, giving the Organization legislative powers with respect to colonial territories. The failure of the Organization to impose its will on recalcitrant Members shows the ineffectiveness of resolutions in fields where only the application of some executive measures could guarantee that the policies of Members would conform to the "will" of the Assembly. This observation brings us to the problem of the executive powers of the General Assembly.

II

The lack of full-fledged legislative powers on the part of the General Assembly can be explained by two reasons. First, states are still reluctant to bestow regulative competences on international organizations. Secondly, to achieve its purposes the United Nations is more in need of executive powers, especially powers which enable the Organization to initiate and maintain peace-restoring and peace-keeping operations. Can the Assembly undertake such operations and, generally, has it the competence to take measures in order to induce states to conform to a certain policy? If so, was the Assembly successful in exercising an influence on national action through the instrumentality of the measures of an executive character?

In some matters—they are enumerated in the several provisions of the Charter—the Assembly has powers of decision and the Members are obliged to abide by the decisions of the Assembly. But very few of these matters offer opportunity for exerting an influence on states' policies. Thus, for instance, the act of admitting a new Member did not, as a rule, affect the problems of recognition or normal relations between the admitted state and the Members which did not recognize it or maintain normal relations with it. The Assembly's decisions on the representation of the Member, where two governments competed for the function, were politically important for the winning party but less influential on extra-United Nations relations involving that government.

To give another example of a binding decision, the Assembly adopts the budget of the Organization and imposes on the Members the duty to pay their contributions as assessed by the Assembly. If they do not pay, they run the danger of being deprived of their vote in the Assembly (but not in other organs) in accordance with Article 19. But provision of money strengthens those recommendations alone where machinery financed by the United Nations has been set up to implement the recommendations. This

[10] Jennings, The Acquisition of Territory in International Law 79 (1963).

is the case of the peace-keeping or peace-restoring apparatus created by the Assembly. Measures that are to be taken through other means, especially through action by individual Members, lie beyond the activating effect of Article 19. Besides, if a Member refuses to pay and is, consequently, deprived of its vote in the Assembly, the operation that is financed by the Organization does not gain anything from the application of the sanction.

We are not concerned here with executive action and decisions which the Assembly takes by virtue of a special delegation of powers granted *ad hoc* by states having jurisdiction over the question. An example of this kind of activity is the decision and implementing measures taken by the Assembly on the disposition of the former Italian colonies in Africa. What we are interested in is the powers of the Assembly in the executive field under the Charter—Can the Assembly, apart from wishes, exhortations and expressions of opinion, take or recommend measures that are instrumental in shaping and influencing the Members' policies?

In paragraph 1 of the Uniting for Peace Resolution (Part A) the General Assembly interpreted the provisions of the Charter on the application of collective measures by the Assembly. The powers of the Assembly stated in that resolution are to be exercised when "there appears to be a threat to the peace, breach of the peace, or act of aggression." It is submitted that the competence of the Assembly to make recommendations on executive action in political matters is not limited to those cases. On the other hand, where there appeared to exist one of the factual situations described in the Uniting for Peace Resolution, the Assembly, until now, never went to the maximum limit of its own interpretation and did not recommend the use of force for the purpose of securing compliance with its resolutions. This, together with certain rules of the Charter, suggests an interpretation in some respects more restrictive than that contained in Resolution 377 (V) A.

Our formula for the exercise of executive powers by the General Assembly is couched in the following terms:

Whenever the Security Council fails to act in cases where it has competence—and failure to act also includes mere passivity on the part of the Council—and subject to the substantive limitation of Article 2, paragraph 7, and the procedural limitation of Article 12, the Assembly has the power to recommend any measure except measures that consist of the use of military force against a state or states. In particular, the Assembly can recommend measures short of the use of military force that would be applicable against a Member or Members, and equally it can adopt resolutions on the use and deployment of military force in a territory, not against any state but for purposes of peace-restoring and peace-keeping. The core of the interpretation here put forward is that the Assembly, by recommending measures short of the use of force against a state, becomes responsible for and initiates steps that in law, especially in view of the limitations imposed by Article 51, could never be met with armed force, while in fact a forcible reaction would be highly improbable. Also, when military force is used in the territory of a state, not against that state but to keep or restore peace, the force is so used only with the consent of the sovereign. This leaves no room for a response involving use of armed force by states that happen to be dissatisfied with the measures taken by the Assembly. Thus the Assembly moves on a plane where sanctions are recommended and possibly applied, and still, reasonably, there is no danger of escalating the conflict.

The possibility of the reaction to the Assembly's measures should be considered because resolutions on executive measures are recommendations. Members are not bound by them in the sense that they are under a legal duty to conform their action to the recommendation. To quote the opinion of an eminent authority expressed, however, in a different context, a Member, "while not bound to accept the recommendation, is bound to give it due consideration in good faith. If . . . it decides to disregard it, it is bound to explain the reasons for its decision." [11] Non-compliance with the recommendations of the General Assembly may lead to the finding that the Member in question "persistently violated the Principles contained in the . . . Charter" (Article 6), and the Member may thus face the danger of expulsion from the Organization or other sanctions. Depending on the character and contents of the recommendation, even non-compliance with a single resolution may amount to a breach of the obligations flowing from the Charter. For the recommendation may spell out in detail the particular duties of Members under the Charter in a specific contingency. But as long as a formal finding to that effect is not made, it remains a *praesumptio iuris et de iure* that the Member is not obliged to follow the Assembly's recommendation. Therefore a Member state against which measures have been recommended by the General Assembly may resist them. In its opposition it is bound to conform to the principle of proportionality. Measures not consisting of the use of military force cannot lawfully be met with such force. If the Assembly had the right to recommend the use of military force by one state against another, and if it in fact made such a recommendation, the result could easily be a rather general war. If a major conflagration becomes unavoidable—an occurrence which in 1964 seems more unlikely than in the previous years—it is politically more desirable and legally in conformity with the Charter not to have the United Nations involved in such conflagration, on one side, through an act of the General Assembly. The Charter bestowed on the Security Council the exclusive competence to order any operation "by air, sea, or land forces of Members of the United Nations" (Article 42). Certainly, recommending such operations, which could lie in the domain of the Assembly, is not equal to ordering them. But apparently a basic rule of the Charter is that risks involved in the use of military force, whether ordered or recommended, should be taken by the Security Council alone and that any decision regarding the use of such force should be taken without definite opposition, explicit or implicit, of any of the great Powers permanently represented on the Security Council, or at least in

[11] Voting Procedure on Questions Relating to Reports and Petitions Concerning the Territory of South-West Africa, Separate Opinion of Judge Lauterpacht, [1955] I.C.J. Rep. 90, 119.

circumstances where a great Power could prevent the use of force. The Charter, as a treaty establishing and organizing relations among states, still makes rather significant allowances for the balance-of-power system, and it did not go very far in setting up an opposite system, *i.e.*, the collective security system.[12] The development of the latter system should be sought. This process, however, should evolve slowly and through co-operation rather than through attempts at too radical action on the part of the Assembly.

On several occasions the General Assembly has recommended that measures be taken against a state. In 1946 it recommended that Spain be debarred from membership in the specialized agencies and from participation in certain conferences, and that Members recall from Madrid their ambassadors and ministers plenipotentiary. The latter recommendation was not followed without exception. The measures proved unsuccessful in bringing about a change of the Spanish domestic regime and were revoked. In 1949 the Assembly recommended—in connection with the Greek problem—that Members refrain from the direct or indirect provision of arms or other materials of war to Albania and Bulgaria. A more extensive embargo was applied in 1951 with respect to "areas under the control of the Central People's Government of the People's Republic of China and of the North Korean authorities." In both cases the Assembly's prohibitions were not followed by those Members who were the principal and regular suppliers of war equipment and related material to the countries involved. In 1962 the Assembly requested Members to apply several measures to the Republic of South Africa and it also requested them to end the supply of arms to Portugal. In neither case could an overwhelming compliance by Members be noted, and therefore the effectiveness of the measures on the policies of *apartheid* in South Africa and the policies in Angola could not even be tested. They are all examples of unsuccessful recommendations of the Assembly in the sphere of executive action. On the other hand, the Assembly succeeded in restoring and keeping peace in the Suez conflict of 1956 and created an effective machinery for that purpose in the form of the United Nations Emergency Force. This operation could be brought about through a combination of consent and co-operation of the states directly concerned and the efforts of the Organization.

It may be said that what is probably more significant at the present stage of development of international organization is not so much a series of spectacular achievements, or rather their absence, in the executive field, but the persistent and constant effort to "conceive of the Organization primarily as a dynamic instrument of governments."[13] The present modest degree to which the General Assembly is in a position to influence national policies, and the rather restricted rôle of public opinion in increasing the Assembly's influence, make the lawyer repeat, in conclusion, the words of the late Secretary General of the United Nations that "the real limitations upon action by the Organization do not derive from the

[12] Claude, Power and International Relations 155–190 and 278–285 (1962).

[13] U.N. General Assembly, 16th Sess., Official Records, Supp. No. 1A, at 1 (1961).

provisions of the Charter. They result from facts of international life in our age which are not likely to be by-passed by a different approach or surmounted by attempts at merely constitutional reform." [14]

[14] *Ibid.*, 12th Sess., Supp. No. 1A, at 3 (1957).

NOTES AND QUESTIONS

1. Unlike Fisher (see **II-1**), Schachter (see Chapter 2) and Lande, it is Skubiszewski's view that public opinion is not an important element in producing conforming behavior on the part of the public officials of nation-states in response to Assembly action. He states that "the history of the United Nations shows that the support of public opinion does not necessarily increase the role and influence of the Assembly resolutions in the spheres of national policies and action. The resolutions are addressed to Member States and governments, and therefore it is the backing and compliance of the latter that remain decisive for the effectiveness of any steps taken by the General Assembly." Although it is clear that in certain states public opinion has a very limited role in connection with the foreign policy of the state, even totalitarian governments exhibit some responsiveness to the opinion of their constituency, although their control of public media is such that often the issue of responsiveness can be avoided altogether. The importance of public opinion should not be over-estimated, but it is certainly an element that must be considered when evaluating tactics for achieveing greater consensus on world order principles. See James N. Rosenau, *Public Opinion and Foreign Policy* (Random House, New York, 1961); and Bernard C. Cohen, *The Press and Foreign Policy* (Princeton University Press, 1963).
2. The authority to discuss, investigate, set up subcommittees, recommend, enact legislation and make implementing executive decisions suggests a series of progressive steps leading from the most minimal aspects of governmental process to the kind of authority that we ordinarily associate with domestic government in a well-ordered society. It should be clear from the discussion here that these steps, rather than being discrete, are processes that unfold in interrelation to one another. Furthermore, the extent to which one kind of authoritative technique rather than another is better for achieving effective results within a particular situation does not necessarily follow the sequence outlined above. There are, in fact, a series of complex factors operating in any particular context; they suggest what governmental technique or combination of techniques is most effective within a given situation.

   In view of the very limited *formal* authority of the General Assembly to legislate and execute its policies, it is important to realize the extent of its *actual* power to govern—that is, to set standards for state behavior that will be complied with by the designated actors. Patterns of behavior develop in a social system and tend to place normative restraints upon what is perceived as acceptable behavior. In effect, then, without any formal basis, community expectations, once crystallized in the General Assembly have a limited, albeit variable, law-making character and impact. Review Chapter 2, especially Higgins and Schachter.
3. One of the more difficult theoretical questions of international law has been the extent to which resolutions and recommendations of the General Assembly are to be considered legally binding upon Member States. Skubiszewski, like Schachter, answers that resolutions dealing with the internal operations of the United Nations

do have the status of law and then discusses the legal character of resolutions and recommendations that seek to regulate the behavior of states going on outside of the operations of the Organization.

Most jurists have argued that the resolutions and recommendations of the General Assembly are merely hortatory and do not impose legal obligations upon Member States, but a few legal experts contend that these resolutions do have some of the impact of law. Skubiszewski takes a middle position by distinguishing between kinds of resolutions. He finds one set of resolutions that are intended to be merely recommendatory and another set which, as he puts it, are "attempts at law-creating and at making members comply with that law." His brief discussion is interesting for its technical expertness and for the way he goes about deciding whether resolutions belong in his first or second category.

Skubiszewski quotes Judge Lauterpacht in the *South West Africa Voting Petitioners' Case*. Judge Lauterpacht wrote that a member, "while not bound to accept the recommendation, is bound to give it due consideration in good faith. If . . . it decides to disregard it, it is bound to explain the reasons for its decision." The extent of a nation's obligation is to give a public explanation for its refusal to comply with the directive clauses in an Assembly resolution. See D. H. N. Johnson, "The Effect of Resolutions of the General Assembly of the United Nations," *The British Yearbook of International Law,* vol. 32 (Oxford University Press, London-New York, 1957) p. 97. See also, F. A. Vallat, "The Competence of the United Nations General Assembly," *Recueil des Cours,* vol. 97–II (A. W. Sijthoff, Leyden, 1959) pp. 203–291; Blaine F. Sloan, "The Binding Force of a Recommendation of the General Assembly of the United Nations," *The British Yearbook of International Law,* vol. 25 (1948) p. 1; and 'Pollux,' "The Interpretation of the Charter of the United Nations," *The British Yearbook of International Law,* vol. 23 (1964) p. 54.

4. Note that there are two separate kinds of issues here: first, to what extent does the passage of a resolution influence national behavior; this might be called *the behavioral question.* And second, to what extent does the passage of a resolution, or a series of resolutions, constitute a law-making act; this might be called *the juridical question.* An answer to the juridical question is dependent upon one's jurisprudential orientation. What is law? What makes a behavioral standard a legal standard? These issues are clarified by H. L. A. Hart in *The Concept of Law* (Clarendon Press, Oxford, 1961). See especially the final chapter on international law. Myres S. McDougal is foremost among contemporary international lawyers who reject any sharp distinction between law and fact and refuse to restrict the designation, law, to standards created by formal procedures or to standards that are posited as obligatory. In the present context this means that just because the General Assembly acts through "non-binding recommendations" rather than "binding decisions" is not *necessarily* reason to deny its acts the status of law. McDougal suggests that reasonable community expectations with respect to behavior are a much more important indication of the existence of law than is the formal language accompanying the standard-setting act. We must look then at what is expected and what happens when resolutions of the General Assembly call upon states to act or refrain from acting in a certain way. Mrs. Lande's set of variables for an analysis is one strategy for putting McDougal's approach to work. See **II-1**.

B. The Uniting for Peace Resolution

We have been concerned with the changing authority and influence of the General Assembly over the past twenty years. It seems reasonable to conclude that the Assembly has played a modest, although occasionally important role in the events of international political life during its time of existence. In dealing with questions of international peace and security and the relative role of the General Assembly vis-à-vis the Security Council, both Lande and Skubiszewski, as well as Claude (**II-3**) and Goodrich (Chapter 4) attach great importance to the Uniting for Peace Resolution. The constitutional validity of the Resolution, the invocation of its various provisions within specific contexts, and the usefulness of the actions taken under the authority of the Resolution have been debated vigorously and often by statesman and scholars. In very large measure the United Nations financial crisis arose from its role in peace-keeping operations carried out, in whole or in part, under Assembly auspices.

France and the Soviet Union were both strongly opposed to augmenting the role of the Assembly in the peace-keeping context and have refused to pay their share of the Suez and Congo operations (through June of 1965).

The extent to which the Resolution has enlarged, if at all, the functions and competence of the General Assembly, and perhaps that of the Organization as a whole, remains subject to controversy. Certainly the Resolution has neither realized the dreams of its sponsors nor enacted the nightmares of its adversaries. It has failed in its objective to ensure that the Organization would have the capacity to act swiftly and effectively in the event that armed force or other sanctioning techniques were needed to safeguard the peace. The United Nations continues to lack that capacity except when Great Power unanimity is present. At the same time the Resolution did signal and legitimate a temporary shift in matters of international peace and security, from the Security Council to the General Assembly. In this respect, it anticipated to a degree the pattern of responsibility contemplated in the Clark-Sohn plan. The Resolution is reprinted from the *United Nations Bulletin*, vol. IX, no. 10 (1950) pp. 508–509.

UNITING FOR PEACE

Resolution 377A (V) of the General Assembly, 3 November 1950. GAOR, V, Supp. 20 (A/1775), pp. 10–12. With respect to questions which have arisen in connection with this Resolution, see SOHN, UN Law, pp. 229–47.

The General Assembly,

Recognizing that the first two stated Purposes of the United Nations are:

"To maintain international peace and security, and to that end: to take effective collective measures for the prevention and removal of threats to the peace, and for the suppression of acts of aggression or other breaches of the peace, and to bring about by peaceful means, and in conformity with the principles of justice and international law, adjustment or settlement of international disputes or situations which might lead to a breach of the peace," and

"To develop friendly relations among nations based on respect for the principle of equal rights and self-determination of peoples, and to take other appropriate measures to strengthen universal peace",

Reaffirming that it remains the primary duty of all Members of the United Nations, when involved in an international dispute, to seek settlement of such a dispute by peaceful means through the procedures laid down in Chapter VI of the Charter, and recalling the successful achievements of the United Nations in this regard on a number of previous occasions,

Finding that international tension exists on a dangerous scale,

Recalling its resolution 290 (IV) entitled "Essentials of Peace", which states that disregard of the Principles of the Charter of the United Nations is primarily responsible for the continuance of international tension, and desiring to contribute further to the objectives of that resolution,

Reaffirming the importance of the exercise by the Security Council of its primary responsibility for the maintenance of international peace and security, and the duty of the permanent members to seek unanimity and to exercise restraint in the use of the veto,

Reaffirming that the initiative in negotiating the agreements for armed forces provided for in Article 43 of the Charter belongs to the Security Council, and desiring to ensure that, pending the conclusion of such agreements, the United Nations has at its disposal means for maintaining international peace and security,

Conscious that failure of the Security Council to discharge its responsibilities on behalf of all the Member States, particularly those responsibilities referred to in the two preceding paragraphs, does not relieve Member States of their obligations or the United Nations of its responsibility under the Charter to maintain international peace and security,

Recognizing in particular that such failure does not deprive the General Assembly of its rights or relieve it of its responsibilities under the Charter in regard to the maintenance of international peace and security,

Recognizing that discharge by the General Assembly of its responsibilities in these respects calls for possibilities of observation which would ascertain the facts and expose aggressors; for the existence of armed forces which could be used collectively; and for the possibility of timely recommendation by the General Assembly to Members of the United Nations for collective action which, to be effective, should be prompt,

A.

1. Resolves that if the Security Council, because of lack of unanimity of the permanent members, fails to exercise its primary responsibility for the maintenance of international peace and security in any case where there appears to be a threat to the peace, breach of the peace or act of aggression, the General Assembly shall consider the matter immediately with a view to making appropriate recommendations to Members for collective measures, including in the case of a breach of the peace or act of aggression the use of armed force when necessary, to maintain or restore international peace and security. If not in session at the time, the General Assembly may meet in an emergency special session within twenty-four hours of the request therefor. Such emergency special session shall be called if requested by the Security Council on the vote of any seven members, or by a majority of the Members of the United Nations;

2. Adopts for this purpose the amendments to its rules of procedure set forth in the annex to this resolution;

B.

3. Establishes a Peace Observation Commission, which for the calendar years 1951 and 1952 shall be composed of fourteen Members, namely: China Colombia, Czechoslovakia, France, India, Iraq, Israel, New Zealand, Pakistan, Sweden, the Union of Soviet Socialist Republics, the United Kingdom of Great Britain and Northern Ireland, the United States of America and Uruguay, and which could observe and report on the situation in any area where there exists international tension the continuance of which is likely to endanger the maintenance of international peace and security. Upon the invitation or with the consent of the State into whose territory the Commission would go, the General Assembly, or the Interim Committee when the Assembly is not in session, may utilize the Commission if the Security Council is not exercising the functions assigned to it by the Charter with respect to the matter in question. Decisions to utilize the Commission shall be made on the affirmative vote of two-thirds of the members present and voting. The Security Council may also utilize the Commission in accordance with its authority under the Charter;

4. Decides that the Commission shall have authority in its discretion to appoint sub-commissions and to utilize the services of observers to assist it in the performance of it functions;

5. Recommends to all governments and authorities that they cooperate with the Commission and assist it in the performance of its functions;

6. Requests the Secretary-General to provide the necessary staff and facilities, utilizing, where directed by the Commission, the United Nations Panel of Field Observers envisaged in resolution 297 B (IV);

C.

7. Invites each Member of the United Nations to survey its resources in order to determine the nature and scope of the assistance it may be in a position to render in support of any recommendations of the Security Council or of the General Assembly for the restoration of international peace and security;

8. Recommends to the Members of the United Nations that each Member maintain within its national armed forces elements so trained, organized and equipped that they could promptly be made available, in accordance with its constitutional processes, for service as a United Nations unit or units, upon recommendation by the Security Council or General Assembly, without prejudice to the use of such elements in exercise of the right of individual or collective self-defence recognized in Article 51 of the Charter;

9. Invites the Members of the United Nations to inform the Collective Measures Committee provided for in paragraph 11 as soon as possible of the measures taken in implementation of the preceding paragraph;

10. Requests the Secretary-General to appoint, with the approval of the Committee provided for in paragraph 11, a panel of military experts who could be made available, on request, to Member States wishing to obtain technical advice regarding the organization, training, and equipment for prompt service as United Nations units of the elements referred to in paragraph 8;

Sohn Basic Documents F.P.Inc.—7

D.

11. Establishes a Collective Measures Committee consisting of fourteen Members, namely: Australia, Belgium, Brazil, Burma, Canada, Egypt, France, Mexico, Philippines, Turkey, the United Kingdom of Great Britain and Northern Ireland, the United States of America, Venezuela and Yugoslavia, and directs the Committee, in consultation with the Secretary-General and with such Member States as the Committee finds appropriate, to study and make a report to the Security Council and the General Assembly, not later than 1 September 1951, on methods, including those of section C of the present resolution, which might be used to maintain and strengthen international peace and security in accordance with the Purposes and Principles of the Charter, taking account of collective self-defence and regional arrangements (Articles 51 and 52 of the Charter);

12. Recommends to all Member States that they co-operate with the Committee and assist it in the performance of its functions;

13. Requests the Secretary-General to furnish the staff and facilities necessary for the effective accomplishment of the purposes set forth in sections C and D of the present resolution;

E.

14. Is fully conscious that, in adopting the proposals set forth above, enduring peace will not be secured solely by collective security arrangements against breaches of international peace and acts of aggression, but that a genuine and lasting peace depends also upon the observance of all the Principles and Purposes established in the Charter of the United Nations, upon the implementation of the resolutions of the Security Council, the General Assembly and other principal organs of the United Nations intended to achieve the maintenance of international peace and security, and especially upon respect for and observance of human rights and fundamental freedoms for all and on the establishment and maintenance of conditions of economic and social well-being in all countries; and accordingly

15. Urges Member States to respect fully, and to intensify, joint action, in co-operation with the United Nations, to develop and stimulate universal respect for an observance of human rights and fundamental freedoms, and to intensify individual and collective efforts to achieve conditions of economic stability and social progress, particularly through the development of underdeveloped countries and areas.

ANNEX

[For the amended text of the rules of procedure of the General Assembly see Rules 8(b), 9(b), 10, 16, 19 and 65, pp. 38, 40, 47, above.]

The next selection by Keith S. Petersen, "The Uses of the Uniting for Peace Resolution Since 1950," *International Organization*, vol. XIII (World Peace Foundation, Boston, 1959) pp. 219–232, analyzes the various provisions of the Resolution and discusses some of the positions taken by various states. This presentation provides additional data for understanding the extent to which the norms of the Charter, practices of the Organization, and debating positions adopted by various states in a series of situations, combine to produce some normative and institutional restraints on what Members do within the Organization. The emphasis here is not upon the effectiveness of the actual peace-restoring or peace-keeping action as such, but upon the way in which political and legal processes within the Organization are fed into particular decisions or recommendations of the United Nations.

The interesting point is that the *unintended* consequence of a political response by a state in one situation creates a precedent for action by the Organization in quite another, and that support for action in one context builds a basis for action in another where the political equities might be quite reversed. For an illuminating discussion of this phenomenon as it bears on the experience of the International Labor Organization, see Ernst Haas, *Beyond the Nation-State* (Stanford University Press, 1964).

In evaluating the issues that have been raised by the Uniting for Peace Resolution, it is useful to bear in mind that Clark and Sohn would revise the Charter to provide the General Assembly with far more authority than is stated in or has been practiced under the Resolution. In order to enrich the perspective available for evaluating events that have taken place in connection with the Uniting for Peace Resolution, as well as to provide another basis for comparing the proposals that have been made for strengthening the authority of the General Assembly, it is useful to become familiar with this portion of their scheme. In particular, assess the extent to which Clark and Sohn would provide the Assembly with the capacity to make binding decisions, to enact legislation, and to make recommendations in the area of international peace and security. See WPTWL, pp. 34–66.

THE USES OF THE UNITING FOR PEACE RESOLUTION SINCE 1950

Keith S. Petersen

The Uniting for Peace Resolution—or the Acheson Plan, as it was once popularly called—was adopted by the UN General Assembly on November 3, 1950. It is commonly conceded that its procedures were designed to help surmount an apparently major obstacle to the operation of the UN: the Soviet veto or its alleged abuse, and the concomitant stagnation of the Security Council. Its particulars were the product, at least in part, of both the accidents and the demands of the Korean War—for example, that the Security Council could and did adopt resolutions of substance pertaining to Korea up until the time (August 1, 1950) the Soviet delegate returned, after which it adopted no other; or that there was a UN commission already stationed in Korea which could and did report to the Security Council immediately upon the outbreak of hostilities in June of 1950. The resolution belonged to a longer evolutionary history, too: the general shift in emphasis away from the Security Council was manifested even before the Korean War by the creation in 1947 of an "Interim Committee" of the General Assembly. The Uniting for Peace Resolution was more or less a reflection of the immediate environment of the Korean crisis, but it was also part of the main stream of basic institutional change to which it at the same time contributed.

The intent and design of the original Charter were that disputes endangering international peace and security should be taken care of by action of the Security Council through the method, if finally necessary, of dispatching UN military forces against the offending state or states. The Security Council, however, had for the most part proven incompetent in this respect; and there were no UN military forces at all. The Uniting for Peace Resolution would rectify this situation by providing for the following six changes in organization and procedure: 1) the authority to transfer a peace-and-security issue to the General Assembly if the Security Council was blocked by veto; 2) the capacity to call emergency sessions of the Assembly, if necessary, for this purpose; 3) a recommendation that Member States maintain special UN-designated units in their respective national armed forces; the creation of 4) a Peace Observation Commission; 5) a panel of military experts; and 6) a Collective Measures Committee.[1] Thus would the central problems of maintain-

[1] General Assembly Resolution 377(V), November 3, 1950. General Assembly *Official Records* (hereafter cited as GAOR) (5th session), Supplement No. 20, p. 10–12. The summary given here follows closely that which appears in Leland Goodrich, "Development of the General Assembly," *International Conciliation*, May 1951 (No. 471), p. 272–273. The first point of these six—having to do with "transfer"—specifically includes mention of the Assembly's self-proclaimed capacity, in considering a matter so "transferred", to make "appropriate recommendations, including in the case of a breach of the peace or act of aggression the use of armed force when necessary". Quoted in *ibid.*, p. 272. See also the same author's "The UN Security Council," *International Organization*, Summer 1958 (Vol. 12, No. 3), p. 279. It is, however, dubious at best that this provision "adds" any "power"

ing international peace and security be solved: by advance warning through the Peace Observation Commission, by expeditious shifting of the dispute from the stymied Council to the veto-less Assembly, by use if necessary of voluntarily and unilaterally earmarked forces, and by further long-range planning through the Collective Measures Committee.

What use has since been made of these additional paraphernalia and procedures? The answer is simply given: some, but not much. It is the purpose of this article to investigate these uses and their possibly lasting effects on the development of the peace-and-security machinery of the UN. The conclusions may be briefly stated at the outset that the "transfer" and "emergency session" aspects of the Resolution have been recently revived and now are probably an integral part of the UN system, but that the other elements of Uniting for Peace are now more or less inactive because of an early decline in their use or lack of any practical use at all.

I. Dormant Provisions

The relatively dormant provisions may be disposed of first. The Collective Measures Committee, to begin with, has delivered itself of three separate reports, the recommendations of which have not been much followed.[2] Although the committee has now been put indefinitely on a stand-by basis,[3] it has produced little of consequence in recent years,[4] and it contributed nothing to the handling of the Egyptian and Hungarian crises in 1956.[5] Technically alive, it remains practically inactive. Secondly, the provisions which recommend the maintenance of UN-designated units in national armed forces and which authorize the establishment of a panel of military experts have become moribund together. All Member States (60 at that time) were circularized at the request of the Collective Measures Committee on what they intended to do about this recommendation to earmark troops. Out of 43 governments replying, only four (Thailand, Denmark, Norway, and Greece) made relatively unconditional offers of contingents, and these came to the grand total of 6,000 men.[6] The panel of military experts, designed to give technical advice to Members on the setting up of such UN-designated units, gave none at all—whether to these four governments or any others. The second report of the Collective Measures Committee (1952) simply noted that since the services of the members of the panel had not as yet been requested, the Committee's earlier report on the nature and func-

to the General Assembly that it would not have had under Article 10 anyway and/or had not already used, regardless of authority. See the brief but comprehensive discussion of the "Competence of the Security Council and the General Assembly" in Leland Goodrich and Anne Simons, *The United Nations and the Maintenance of International Peace and Security,* Washington, D. C., The Brookings Institution, 1955, p. 427–433.

[2] For discussion of the first two reports and their consequences see Goodrich and Simons, *op. cit.,* p. 408–414. A third report was presented in 1954. Document A/2713, GAOR (9th session), Annexes, Agenda Item 19, p. 1–4. This was "noted with approval" by the Assembly in its Resolution 809 (IX) of November 4, 1954. GAOR (9th session), Supplement No. 21, p. 4.

The "additional measures committee" is not to be confused with the Collective Measures Committee with which it is identical in membership. The additional measures committee did take a direct hand in the making of United Nations policy in respect to Korea, but it had not been established by the Uniting for Peace Resolution.

[3] In 1954 the Assembly "directed" the committee "to remain in a position to pursue such further studies as it may deem desirable . . . " Resolutoin 809 (IX), cited above (footnote 2).

[4] See, for example, the brief evaluative summary of its work, including a doleful account of the abortive efforts to create, successively, a "United Nations Guard Force" and a "United Nations Legion" in William R. Frye, *A United Nations Peace Force,* New York, Oceana Publications, Inc., 1957, p. 62–64.

[5] Stanley Hoffmann, "Sisyphus and the Avalanche: the United Nations, Egypt and Hungary," *International Organization,* Summer 1957 (Vol. 11, No. 3), p. 450–451.

[6] Frye, *op. cit.,* p. 59.

tions of the panel "would constitute sufficient guidance in the initial stages".[7] The "initial stages" have not yet been passed.[8]

The Peace Observation Commission has had a somewhat more varied, and originally more hopeful, history. But it, too, has descended into a state of more or less unanimated suspension. Two official attempts have been made to use it, one of them successful. Even this use, however, was not significant and no other official attempt, beyond these two, has ever been made at all.

The first, and only successful, attempt came in Greece in 1951. The problem of "threats to . . . Greece" had been on the agendas of successive General Assemblies since the removal of that item from the agenda of the Security Council in September 1947. The problem was concerned with the alleged fomenting and maintenance of armed rebellion in Greece on the part of its three northern neighbors, Albania, Yugoslavia, and Bulgaria. In its 1947 session the Assembly established a UN Special Committee on the Balkans (UNSCOB) whose main function was to "assist" the four neighboring parties in "the implementation of recommendations" addressed to them by the Assembly.[9] Another part of the Committee's function was observation, and report to the Assembly, of what was taking place in Greece. By the 1951 session of the General Assembly the Greek civil war had died out, and the Special Committee was replaced by a Balkan subcommission of the Peace Observation Commission.

That it was specifically this Commission and that the authority for using it could only be the Uniting for Peace Resolution were made completely clear. When the matter first arose in the Assembly's *Ad Hoc* Political Committee on November 20, 1951, United States delegate Benjamin Cohen contended that "the United Nations would be well advised to set up a subcommission under the terms of resolution 377B(V) entitled 'Uniting for Peace' of the previous year. . . ."[10] Other speakers were equally explicit. Even the opposition, although it protested the procedure of replacement, did not dispute either its legality or its actuality. The Czechoslovak representative, Dr. Vladimir Prochazka, could charge that this "system of collective measures imposed upon the United Nations was only an attempt to transform the Organization into an aggressive body".[11] But he did not contest that this "system" was being used, or deny that it could be.

Why did the Assembly wish to substitute a new subcommission for the Special Committee which already existed? There appear to be two answers. First of all, the Committee itself had recommended that "the General Assembly consider the advisability of maintaining United Nations vigilance over the Balkans in light of the present nature of the threat to peace in that area".[12] And "the nature of the threat to Greece had changed. . . . It was now part of the

[7] GAOR (7th session), Supplement No. 17, p. 13. The list of 22 members originally appointed to the panel is contained in Annex D of this second report. *Ibid.*, p. 19.

[8] The Committee's third report (August 1954) noted that two replacements had been made on the panel, which still consisted of 22 members; no action by this group was reported. Document A/2713, cited above (footnote 2).

[9] General Assembly Resolution 109 (II), October 21, 1947. GAOR (2d session), Resolutions, p. 13.

[10] GAOR (6th session), *Ad Hoc* Political Committee, Summary Records, 2d Meeting, November 20, 1951, p. 9.

[11] *Ibid.*, p. 18.

[12] *Ibid.*, p. 8, quoting UNSCOB's report.

general tension of the Balkan area."[13] So a new kind of observation group was needed, one that could go anywhere in the Balkans that it was invited. This was the obvious, official explanation. The records of the *Ad Hoc* Political Committee suggest, in addition, that some delegations may have been anxious to get about the business of using, partly for its own sake, "the collective security system which the Organization was slowly and determinedly building".[14] For Mr. Salvador P. López of the Philippines, for example, it was the necessary and desirable beginning of the activation of the Peace Observation Commission on a permanently ready, world-wide basis.[15] With these grandiose overtones, the substitution of the new subcommission for the old Special Committee was voted by the *Ad Hoc* Political Committee on November 23 and by the General Assembly on December 7, 1951.

Only on one other occasion has the presence of such a group even been officially requested. The request was made by the government of Thailand, in 1954. Thailand was disturbed at that time by the increasing tempo of civil war, then reaching its climax, in neighboring Indo-China. On May 29, 1954, it presented to the Security Council a suggestion that a UN observation group—"under the Peace Observation Commission"—be sent to its allegedly threatened border areas.[16] In a subsequent resolution before the Council this became a request to "the Peace Observation Commission to establish a sub-commission composed of not less than three or more than five members" to be sent to Thailand.[17] On June 18, 1954, this resolution was defeated (9-1-1) by negative vote of the Soviet Union.[18] But the end was not yet. In the period of explanations of vote which followed, Mr. Henry Cabot Lodge of the United States observed officially: "Thailand will undoubtedly seek a remedy elsewhere in the United Nations, and it will have our support when it does so".[19] Or as he put it, more colorfully and less obscurely, to the press: "Thank heaven we can still go on to the Assembly".[20] Thus was presaged not only a further attempt to employ the peace observation machinery of the Uniting for Peace Resolution but also its transfer, and possibly even its emergency session, devices.

These potentialities were never realized. Thailand did propose, on July 7, 1954, the addition of an observer item to the agenda of the eighth regular session (1953) of the General Assembly, which had been "recessed" since the previous December. But it asked delay until further notice of any effort toward "ascertaining the concurrence of the majority of Member States in the reconvening of the session for the consideration of the proposed additional item".[21] No further notice was ever given. Three weeks later, on July 28, the proposal was abandoned altogether.[22] Nor has any similar item ever appeared on the agenda of any subsequent session—regular, special, or emergency—of the General Assembly.

In no instance since then has such a commission been officially even asked

[13] *Ibid.*
[14] *Ibid.*, p. 11.
[15] *Ibid.*, p. 13–14.
[16] Document S/3220. Security Council *Official Records* (hereafter cited as SCOR) (9th year), Supplement for April, May, and June 1954, p. 10.
[17] SCOR (9th year), 673d Meeting, June 16, 1954, p. 3.
[18] SCOR (9th year), 674th Meeting, p. 13. Lebanon abstained.
[19] *Ibid.*, p. 16.
[20] *The New York Times*, June 19, 1954.
[21] Document A/2665, July 7, 1954, p. 3.
[22] *The New York Times*, July 29, 1954.

for. In the Syrian complaint against Turkey, in October 1957, a certain amount of "private" consideration was apparently given to the possibility of sending a selected subcommission of the Peace Observation Commission to the area, but no formal proposal on this was ever made.[23] In June of 1958, when the Security Council was just about to establish an observer group in Lebanon (UNOGIL), it was suggested by one of the members of the Council that the "characteristics" of the proposed group were "close to those of the Peace Observation Commission".[24] But no conclusions were drawn from this; no effort was made to substitute the formally established arrangement for the *ad hoc* one. These actions are as close as the UN has come since 1954 to considering the matter very seriously. There is thus an apparent inclination not to use the Peace Observation Commission even when it would seem both logical and possible to do so. The great pretensions of its employment in the Greek case in 1951 have been long since abandoned. Like the Collective Measures Committee, the earmarking of forces as UN units, and the panel of military experts, the Peace Observation Commission has also become, for all practical purposes, another dead letter of the Uniting for Peace Resolution.

II. "Transfer" and "Emergency Session" Devices

The two other major provisions of the resolution are very much alive. These are its "transfer" and "emergency session" devices: "that if the Security Council, because of lack of unanimity of the permanent members, fails to exercise its primary responsibility for the maintenance of international peace and security in any case where there appears to be a threat to the peace, breach of the peace, or act of aggression, the General Assembly shall consider the matter immediately with a view to making appropriate recommendations to Members for collective measures. . . . If not in session at the time, the General Assembly may meet in emergency special session within twenty-four hours of the request therefor"; such a session can be summoned by a vote of any seven of the members of the Council, or a simple majority of the Assembly.[25] These provisions were themselves virtually inactive for the first six years. The only possible exception to this statement arises from the UN's Korean experience. Was the "transfer" device, as specified in the Uniting for Peace Resolution, invoked and employed in connection with that dispute? The answer must be "no", but with reservations.

These reservations arise from the adoption by the General Assembly of its resolution of February 1, 1951, which, among other things, made a finding of Chinese communist "aggression in Korea". This United States proposal, as originally introduced into the Assembly's First Committee on January 20, 1951, began by "noting that the Security Council, because of the lack of unanimity of its permanent members, has failed to exercise its primary responsibility for the maintenance of international peace and security in regard to Chinese communist intervention in Korea".[26] With the exception of the concluding phrase,

[23] *Ibid.*, October 18, 1957.
[24] S/PV.825, p. 7. The observation was made by Dr. Jorge Illueca of Panama.

[25] General Assembly Resolution 377(V). (Cited above, see footnote 1.)
[26] Document A/C.1/654. GAOR (5th session), Annexes, Vol. II, agenda item 76, p. 15.

this was an almost verbatim quotation from the Uniting for Peace Resolution. This was no mere coincidence. The Security Council, with its returned Soviet member, had been considering the new Chinese phase of the Korean War since early November 1950. A six-Power draft resolution pertaining to the Chinese "intervention" had been vetoed by the Soviet Union on November 30.[27] On December 4 the six sponsoring powers thereupon requested that the Assembly take up the matter.[28] Two days later the Assembly voted to do so.[29]

All the elements of Uniting for Peace are here: the Council was considering an act of military intervention; it was prevented from exercising its "primary responsibility" to deal with it by veto of one of its permanent members; the Assembly had taken up "consideration" of the same matter "immediately" and was now adopting a resolution pertaining to it. But there was at least one major flaw. One day before the passage of the Assembly resolution (that is, on January 31, 1951) the Security Council had voted to remove its own "Korean" item from its own agenda.[30] Furthermore, the item was removed at least in part "to remove any technical doubts which might be cast on the validity of any resolution adopted by the General Assembly which contains recommendations to Members".[31] Nothing therefore had been "transferred"; an item had simply been dropped. The Assembly can pick up and act on a dropped item whenever it wants to (it had done so in the Greek case in 1947, for example), for which it obviously needs no "transfer" procedure at all. It is this strange denouement which casts doubt on either the legal validity or the practical necessity—or both—of the application of Uniting for Peace procedures in the Korean War. After January 31, 1951, of course, it did not matter any longer: there was no item left to transfer.[32]

Thus the Korean experience with the Uniting for Peace transfer mechanism was at best equivocal. For the next five and one-half years no other use of this procedure, even as dubious as this one, was attempted. The abortive Thai complaint in 1954 was as close as the UN came to considering it. The transfer and emergency session devices therefore seemed to be going the way of all other provisions of the Uniting for Peace Resolution. The Egyptian and Hungarian cases reversed this prospect, suddenly and dramatically, in the fall of 1956. The complaints of Lebanon and Jordan (taken together) in 1958 have sustained the new reversal. In all three instances both the transfer and emergency session procedures were involved. This recent record portends a future place of some significance for these devices in the evolving UN system.

III. The Egyptian Case

The record is, in various ways, cumulative. It begins, as far as the application of Uniting for Peace procedures is concerned, with the Israeli invasion of Egypt on October 29, 1956. The Security Council met to consider the matter almost immediately, four times in the

[27] SCOR (5th year), No. 72, p. 22–23.

[28] Document A/1618. GAOR (5th session), Annexes, Vol. II, agenda item 76, p. 2.

[29] By adopting a new agenda item (No. 76): "Intervention of the Central People's Government of the People's Republic of China in Korea".

[30] SCOR (6th year), 531st Meeting.

[31] Document S/1992. SCOR (6th year), Supplement for January, February, and March, 1951, p. 10–11.

[32] These complexities are considered much more extensively in my unpublished manuscript, "The United Nations, the Uniting for Peace Resolution, and the Korean War".

ext two days; substantive resolutions vere vetoed; references were made to he Uniting for Peace Resolution; an mergency session of the Assembly was alled. But the procedural niceties are ot as clear as these superficial facts night suggest. It is not possible to be ompletely certain that the resolution's ransfer mechanism was in fact employed r that, accurately, it ought to have been. 'o understand the doubts involved here, will be necessary to consider the chro- ology of events in some detail.

Immediately after the Israeli invasion, he United States requested a meeting f the Security Council for the purpose f considering "steps for the immediate essation of military action of Israel in gypt".[33] The Council met the next orning, October 30, and voted to place is item on its agenda.[34] No other action f any consequence was taken at this eeting. On the same day, the Council et again in the afternoon and still gain at night.[35] Here is where the oubts arose. In the afternoon meeting e United Kingdom representative, Sir ierson Dixon, began by informing the ouncil of the twelve-hour "ultimatum" hich his government and France had st delivered to the two belligerents srael and Egypt) either to cease fire to bring on the allegedly protective cupation of certain points in the Suez anal zone by British and French forces. he Council then turned to the consid- ation of a United States draft resolu- on which, among other things, would ve called upon Israel to withdraw its rces and upon "all Members" to re- ain from the use or threat of force "in the area in any manner inconsistent with the purposes of the United Nations".[36] This draft resolution was defeated (7-2, with 2 abstentions) by the negative votes of the United Kingdom and France. A shorter version of the same proposal was then put forth by the Soviet Union. After a brief further debate on this, the meeting was adjourned.

Reconvening that night, the Council considered and adopted an additional agenda item. This was in the form of a letter from the Egyptian government which referred to the same ultimatum that the United Kingdom delegate had himself described to the Council that afternoon, and to the consequently "imminent" occupation of Egyptian territory. The letter requested that the Council "be immediately convened to consider this act of aggression by the United Kingdom and France".[37] The addition of this item was objected to, and the objection became important. The Australian delegate, E. Ronald Walker, among others, protested that it was unnecessary to add it since "the substance of the matter has already been before the Council in the statement of the United Kingdom representative" made at the previous meeting that afternoon.[38] The new item was nevertheless adopted. It should be noted that it did not replace the item with which the Council was already seized, having to do with "the military action of Israel in Egypt"; it was merely added. And the order was likewise important. On the agenda for this meeting the Israeli item was number 2 and the United Kingdom and French "aggression" was number 3. Hav-

[33] Letter dated October 29, 1956. Document S/3706. OR (11th year), Supplement for October, November, d December 1956, p. 108.
[34] SCOR (11th year), 748th Meeting.
[35] *Ibid.*, 749th and 750th Meetings.
[36] Document S/3710. SCOR (11th year), Supplement for October, November, and December 1956, p. 110.
[37] Document S/3712. SCOR (11th year), Supplement for October, November, and December 1956, p. 111–112.
[38] SCOR (11th year), 750th Meeting, p. 3.

ing adopted its agenda (this was item 1), the Council thereupon proceeded to its unfinished business from the preceding meeting—agenda item 2. The only business to be completed hereunder was the Soviet draft resolution (a version of the United States proposal) which had been introduced that afternoon. It was defeated, and by a similar vote of 7 to 2 (the United Kingdom and France), with 2 abstentions. After explanations of vote by some members, the Council President, M. Louis De Guiringaud of France, then pronounced "that the Council has completed its discussion of item 2 of the agenda. We shall therefore go on to item 3."[39]

The Council now seemed at a loss. There were no other substantive proposals. Just before adjournment the Yugoslav delegate merely "suggested" to the members—he did not formally move—"that they might find time to consider the possibility of calling an emergency session of the General Assembly under the terms of General Assembly resolution 377(V), entitled 'Uniting for Peace' ".[40] When the Council met again the next afternoon (October 31), he presented this proposal in the form of a motion. Although the United Kingdom delegate contended that the Yugoslav motion was out of order, it was adopted. But the debate that preceded adoption raised serious questions concerning the propriety of the procedure and went to the heart of the Uniting for Peace transfer device.

The debate ran substantially as follows.[41] The Uniting for Peace Resolution required that the Security Council fail to exercise its responsibility in a given "case" due to the "lack of unanimity of the permanent members"—that is, because of a "veto"—before "the matter" could be transferred to the Assembly. But "on the item now under discussion" (item 3, the Egyptian letter), Sir Pierson Dixon argued, no resolution had been presented, let alone vetoed. The Yugoslav rejoinder to this was that all of the "aspects" of the matter which needed to be transferred had been included in paragraph 2a of the United States draft resolution (calling upon "all Members" to refrain from the threat or use of force), which had been vetoed. Furthermore, both the United Kingdom and Australian representatives had previously contended, in protesting the addition of item 3 to the agenda, that its "substance" was, and could be, included under the listing of item 2 anyway. True, the Australian delegate answered, that had been his view. But the Council, with the Yugoslav representative voting with the majority, had overridden him. Therefore it was not the Council's view. China's Dr. T. F. Tsiang observed that United Kingdom objections were "technical": "If pressed too far, they would be tantamount to an invitation to put before the Council such a draft resolution [under item 3], to put it to a vote and then to bring about the failure [by vetoing it] that would fulfill the technical requirements advanced by Sir Pierson and Mr. Walker". The French response, if true, was devastating: "If a draft resolution of the kind to which he [Tsiang] alluded were put to a vote, it could not obtain the seven votes needed for adoption. . . . " Here was a factor which would become both obvious and important in the Lebanon-Jordan case two years later: if the transfer mechanism is to be involved, a resolution must

[39] *Ibid.*, p. 7.
[40] *Ibid.*, p. 14.

[41] All of the following quotations from this debate are taken from SCOR (11th year), 751st Meeting, *passim*.

not only have been defeated in the Council, it must have been defeated by veto.

It was a losing battle. The United Kingdom motion that would have ruled the Yugoslav motion out of order was defeated. The latter was then passed. The first emergency special session of the General Assembly accordingly met the next day (November 1) to take up the "Question considered by the Security Council at its 749th and 750th meetings, held on 30 October 1956".[42] Before the vote was taken in the Council, however, Sir Pierson Dixon closed the case for the opposition by noting that "the only argument that has been advanced is that my objections have been founded on technical grounds. This, I suppose, means that I may be right in my interpretation of this important document on [the basis of] which we are asked to take certain action, but that this is a consideration which we need not take into account. This is not a good position for the Council to adopt towards its constitution. . . . "

Procedural accuracy had been sacrificed to political expediency. There was a sufficient majority for transfer—albeit a minimal one—and transfer was accomplished. But Sir Pierson's objections were of central significance. What they came down to was the meaning of the word "case" in the Uniting for Peace Resolution: the Council had to be stymied by veto in a given "case" before "the matter" could be taken over by the Assembly. The implicit United Kingdom argument here was that a "case" was the same thing as an agenda item; the Yugoslav view, apparently, was that it was (or could be) embodied in the substance of a resolution. The majority did not seem to care. Nor did the official transfer actions of either the Council or the Assembly resolve the issue. The Yugoslav resolution merely had the Council "taking account" of "the lack of unanimity of its permanent members" at its 749th and 750th meetings and therefore calling the Assembly "to make appropriate recommendations";[43] and the Assembly's agenda, as noted above, listed in like fashion the "Question [singular] considered by the Security Council" at these same two meetings. In other words, as between the arguments and the items: take your choice. The UN had therefore not yet made accurate and legitimate use of either its transfer or its emergency session mechanisms.

IV. The Hungarian Case

In the Hungarian case it did. The almost simultaneous shifting of that crisis to the second emergency special session of the General Assembly remains to date the most precise and undisputed employment of these Uniting for Peace procedures in UN experience. The eventually abortive Hungarian revolt began on October 23, 1956. Five days later, on October 28, the Security Council met to consider an item proposed by France, the United Kingdom, and the United States: "the situation in Hungary".[44] The item was adopted, over Soviet protest.[45] On November 3 the United States introduced, under this item, a draft resolution which would have called upon the Soviet Union to "desist forthwith from any kind of intervention" in Hungary, and to withdraw its armed forces "without

[42] GAOR (1st emergency special session), Plenary Meetings, p. 1.

[43] SCOR (11th year), 751st Meeting, p. 12.

[44] Document S/3690. SCOR (11th year), Supplement for October, November, and December 1956, p. 100.

[45] SCOR (11th year), 746th Meeting, p. 7.

delay".[46] In the extraordinary meeting following—from 3:00 to 5:25 a.m., Sunday, November 4—this draft resolution was defeated (9-1-1) by negative vote of the Soviet Union.[47] The United States thereupon introduced another draft resolution to call an emergency session of the Assembly "in order to make appropriate recommendations concerning the situation in Hungary".[48] This draft resolution was adopted by 10-1. The (second) emergency Assembly opened the same afternoon; the only matter of substance on its agenda bore the consistent and identical title: "The Situation in Hungary".[49]

All of this was as clear as the application of procedural law can ever be to the substance of politics. The Soviet Union, of course, protested both the original inscription of the Hungarian item on the agenda of the Security Council and its subsequent transfer to the Assembly. So, from time to time, did the Hungarian government—depending on which Hungarian goverment, and when. But the essence of protest from both quarters was in the repeated reference to Article 2, paragraph 7, of the UN Charter: "Nothing contained in the present Charter shall authorize the United Nations to intervene in matters which are essentially within the domestic jurisdiction of any state. . . ."[50] No complaint was ever made concerning the legitimacy or appropriateness of the transfer and emergency session devices of the Uniting for Peace Resolution, perhaps because no complaint could have been sustained. This was a perfect case. Conceivably, also, the Soviet delegate was embarrassed by his having voted in the affirmative majority on the same kind of resolution (pertaining to Egypt) only five days before. In the Egyptian instance the Soviet bloc found for the first time that these Uniting for Peace mechanisms—which it had voted against, condemned, and always opposed—might be useful after all. On that occasion, nobody had bothered to badger the Soviet delegate about the obvious conflict between his vote and his principles: the majority was too thin to quarrel with itself.

V. Lebanon and Jordan

Two years later—in the Lebanon-Jordan crisis of 1958—the issue arose again. This time it was debated openly. Out of these debates, for better or worse, the transfer and emergency session provisions of the Uniting for Peace Resolution have emerged stronger than ever. The Lebanon-Jordan crisis of 1958 was before different UN organs off and on for three full months, and one of the procedures involved was the transfer of a "case" from the Security Council to an emergency session of the Assembly. Because UN consideration of the matter was both protracted and complex, it may be well to start at the point of transfer itself and work backwards (or forwards) into the explanatory details as necessary.

On August 7, 1958, the Security Council had before it two draft resolutions—one Soviet and one American—for call-

[46] SCOR (11th year), 753d Meeting, p. 4. The draft resolution is Document S/3730. SCOR (11th year), Supplement for October, November, and December 1956, p. 126. This was subsequently slightly revised in Document S/3730/Rev.1. SCOR, *ibid.*

[47] SCOR (11th year), 754th Meeting, p. 12.

[48] *Ibid.*, p. 13.

[49] GAOR (2d emergency special session), Plenary Meetings, p. viii.

[50] See, for example, SCOR (11th year), 746th Meeting, p. 1–7, where Soviet delegate Arkady A. Sobolev both quotes and supports the Hungarian disclaimer to this effect, before the item was first inscribed by the Security Council. When the Council voted, on November 4, to call the Assembly, Sobolev simply repeated the "same criticism" of transfer as of the original inscription of the item. SCOR (11th year), 754th Meeting, p. 13.

ing an emergency session of the Assembly. The Soviet proposal stated that the Security Council had "considered the situation in the Near and Middle East resulting from the introduction of United States armed forces into Lebanon and of United Kingdom armed forces into Jordan"; it noted that the Council had "proved unable to exercise its primary responsibility for the maintenance of international peace and security"; and that the Council decided therefore "to call an emergency special session of the General Assembly in order to consider the question of the immediate withdrawal of United States troops from Lebanon and of United Kingdom troops from Jordan".[51] The United States alternative declared that the Council had "considered the complaints of Lebanon and the Hashemite Kingdom of Jordan"; it took into account "that the lack of unanimity of its permanent members at the 834th and 837th meetings of the Security Council" had "prevented it from exercising its primary responsibility for the maintenance of international peace and security"; and decided therefore "to call an emergency special session of the General Assembly, as provided in General Assembly Resolution 377(V)".[52]

The Security Council adopted neither one of these proposals in its original form. The Soviet draft was not even voted on—and would have been rejected out of hand if it had been—because, among other reasons, it clearly did not fulfill the technical requirements of the Uniting for Peace machinery. In order to obtain Soviet concurrence, the Council accepted only a "cut-down" version of the United States draft resolution, the final language of which tried hard to ignore, if it did not violate, these same technical requirements. But in the debate preceding what was in effect the adoption of the one proposal and the rejection of the other, the full meaning of these technicalities was not only upheld but even sharpened. Despite the semantic concessions to him in the language of the final draft, even the Soviet delegate was aware of this, and acquiesced in it.

The differences between the two drafts lay at the heart of the problem of transfer: what was a case? how could it be transferred? The Soviet draft resolution did not provide a legitimate answer to either one of these questions. The "introduction" of United States and United Kingdom forces into Lebanon and Jordan, respectively, was not the issue—the "case"—before the Security Council, and it never had been. Even if the Council, in respect to these actions, had "proved unable to exercise its primary responsibility for the maintenance of international peace and security", this was not enough. The Uniting for Peace Resolution, as was briefly noted above in respect to Egypt, requires that this "inability" arise from the "lack of unanimity of the permanent members". But this was not the case.

The Soviet argument was as good as the facts permitted. On May 23, 1958, the Security Council had received a request for addition to its agenda of a "Complaint by Lebanon in respect of a situation arising from the intervention of the United Arab Republic in the internal affairs of Lebanon . . . "[53] The Council adopted this item on May 27.[54] The same item was still before the Council when the United States sent its ma-

[51] Document S/4057/Rev.1, August 6, 1958.
[52] Document S/4056/Rev.1, August 7, 1958.
[53] Document S/4007. Letter dated May 22, 1958.
[54] S/PV.818, May 27, 1958.

rines into Lebanon on July 14. The next day in the Council the Soviet delegate introduced a draft resolution calling for the withdrawal of these troops, but no vote was taken on it at that time.[55] On July 17 United Kingdom paratroopers landed in Jordan, which simultaneously requested the Council to add to its agenda the "Complaint by the Hashemite Kingdom of Jordan of interference in its domestic affairs by the United Arab Republic".[56] The Council did so immediately.[57] The Soviet Union thereupon revised its draft resolution of July 15 to call upon not only the United States but also the United Kingdom to withdraw its forces.[58] In the Council meeting on the afternoon of the 18th this draft resolution, as revised, was defeated by a vote of 1-8, with two abstentions.[59] Thus, in the Soviet contention, had the Council "proved unable to exercise its primary responsibility . . . "

The Soviet argument rested also in part, as a good debater's should, on the weakness of its opponent's. The United States draft asserted in effect that the Council had been "prevented . . . from exercising its responsibility" in respect to the "complaints of Lebanon and the Hashemite Kingdom of Jordan". Had it? On the same day (July 18) that the Soviet resolution demanding United Kingdom and United States withdrawal had been lost in the Security Council, a long and tortuously worded United States draft resolution pertaining to the Lebanese complaint[60] was also defeated, and by Soviet veto. This was at the 834th meeting of the Council. On July 22, at its 837th meeting, the Council also failed to adopt, and again by negative vote of the Soviet Union, a Japanese draft resolution which was simply an abbreviated version of the previously defeated United States draft.[61] So, in the view of the United States, had the Council been "prevented" from acting on the "complaints of Lebanon and . . . Jordan" by virtue of "the lack of unanimity of its permanent members at the 834th and 837th meetings".

But there were two things wrong with this conclusion. In the first place, neither one of these resolutions related to Jordan, nor as much as mentioned the Jordanian complaint. Thus it might be argued that the Council had not been "prevented" from acting in respect to this matter but had been given nothing to act on. Soviet delegate Arkady A. Sobolev overlooked this first point, but he did not overlook the second. The Council had in fact acted earlier on the Lebanese complaint (which was all that the vetoed United States and Japanese draft resolutions pertained to) by deciding, on June 11, 1958, to "dispatch urgently an observation group to proceed to Lebanon" (UNOGIL) in order to "ensure that there is no illegal infiltration of personnel or supply of arms or other material across the Lebanese borders".[62] This was, after all, what the Lebanese "complaint" was all about: alleged interference by the United Arab Republic in its domestic affairs. UNOGIL was already in the field, and reporting. What the Council had, on the other hand, "proved unable" to do anything about was the "introduction" of United States and United Kingdom

55 S/PV.827, July 15, 1958.
56 Document S/4053, July 17, 1958.
57 S/PV.831, same date.
58 Document S/4047/Rev.1, same date. See S/PV.831, p. 47.
59 S/PV.834, p. 46.
60 Document S/4050/Rev.1, July 17, 1958.
61 Document S/4055/Rev.1, July 21, 1958. For vote on this resolution, which was 10–1, see S/PV.837, p. 7–10.
62 This was a Swedish resolution, Document S/4022, June 10, 1958. For the vote, see S/PV.825, p. 46.

troops into the Near East. "Therein lies the impotence of the Security Council."[63] It was a good rebuttal, but it did not conceal the greater weaknesses of the Soviet Union's position. The gaps still remained: the "troops" question had never been on the Council's agenda; no resolution pertaining to it had been vetoed.[64]

The American draft resolution, in significantly revised form, was finally accepted by the Council. United States delegate Henry Cabot Lodge read out the final version, just before adoption:

> The Security Council,
>
> Having considered items 2 and 3 on the agenda of document S/[Agenda/] 838,
>
> Taking into account that the lack of unanimity of its permanent members at the 834th and 837th meetings of the Security Council has prevented it from exercising its primary responsibility for the maintenance of international peace and security,
>
> Decides to call an emergency special session of the General Assembly[65]

The revisions were obvious, and the reasons for them were not far to seek. In the first place, the Soviet Union apparently preferred numbers to names. The "lack of unanimity" paragraph remained unchanged, since it referred only to "the 834th and 837th meetings" of the Council. These, of course, as noted above, were the ones in which the American and Japanese draft resolutions pertaining to Lebanon were vetoed. "Items 2 and 3" of the document cited in the previous paragraph were simply the Lebanese and Jordanian complaints. This kind of purposeful obfuscation was acceptable to the Council since it preserved the full meaning of the relevant technical requirements.

In the second place, the concluding phrase in the original draft—"as provided in General Assembly Resolution 377(V)"—had been dropped. Mr. Sobolev had been quite frank about this. He had earlier offered an amendment which would have substituted "rule 8(b) of the rules of procedure of the General Assembly" for "General Assembly resolution 377(V)", and explained: "my proposal is expressly designed to exclude from the draft resolution any mention of resolution 377(V). The reason for that is clear. There is no need to delve into history . . . ."[66] This proposal was acceptable to the United States, but not to the United Kingdom. It was Sir Pierson Dixon who suggested that the last paragraph read: " 'Decides to call an emergency special session of the General Assembly'—full stop".[67] Mr. Sobolev agreed: "as far as the Soviet delegation is concerned, the proposal of the United Kingdom is completely acceptable".[68] This is the way it was done. Almost all the procedural points were clear. The only real anomaly was the transfer of the Jordanian "case", concerning which no resolution had been either vetoed or even presented. Otherwise the Security Council had made its decision in strict accordance with the Uniting for Peace Resolution, and every member of the Council knew it. Perhaps the evidence of such consciousness arose from what in law are called *obiter dicta,* but these

[63] Mr. Sobolev's statement, S/PV.838, August 7, 1958, p. 81.

[64] For an excellent brief analysis of these deficiencies, see the argument in this debate by Dr. Illueca of Panama. S/PV.838, p. 91–95.

[65] *Ibid.*, p. 139–140.

[66] *Ibid.*, p. 121.

[67] *Ibid.*, p. 132–135.

[68] *Ibid.*, p. 136–138.

nonetheless revealed the sense and meaning of the Council's action quite distinctly.

The transfer and emergency session mechanics of this resolution are now more precisely defined than ever before, and the definition has been accepted in effect on all sides, including the Soviet. Of all the main provisions of the original resolution, these two alone, for all practical purposes, survive. For better or for worse—and it is by no means clear which—they will have to be reckoned with in the future.

NOTES AND QUESTIONS

1. Petersen's conclusion that the transfer and emergency provisions of the Uniting for Peace Resolution retain validity is probably accurate, although France and the Soviet Union remain in a position to contest those provisions. For a painstaking and skillful legal analysis that maintains that all the provisions of the Uniting for Peace Resolution are valid, see Jura Andrássy, "Uniting for Peace," *American Journal of International Law*, vol. 50 (1956) p. 563. Andrassy, who is Professor of International Law at the University of Zagreb, wrote this analysis in 1953, at a time when Yugoslavia and the Soviet Union were quite hostile to one another, and one could attribute the position taken in his article to the state of relationships between the two states. However, Andrassy's emphasis upon the necessity of giving the Organization the authority to deal successfully with matters of international peace and security is a position persuasive to many jurists concerned with strengthening the United Nations. A close reading of Skubiszewski seems to indicate that he does not attack the validity of the Resolution. His arguments are more concerned with the political advisability of such an approach to peace-keeping, given the rivalry between the Soviet Union and the United States.
2. In the instances where the Uniting for Peace Resolution has been invoked, the votes of the medium and small-sized nations have been needed to obtain a two-thirds majority. However, it is now widely acknowledged that some arrangement must be devised that takes special account of the heavier interests and responsibilities of the powerful states. The biggest states are expected to pay most of the costs of peace-keeping operations, and they must be persuaded that it is in their interest to do so. As this book goes to print, discussions dealing with the various phases of the peace-keeping operations are taking place in the Special Committee on Peace-Keeping Operations of the General Assembly.
3. In their proposed revisions of Chapter VI and Chapter VII of the United Nations Charter, Clark and Sohn make it clear that the Assembly would function both as a legislative organ in the field of war prevention and as the major executive organ for determining whether there had been a breach of Charter provisions or a threat to peace and security that demanded enforcement action or peace-keeping activities by the Organization. Skubiszewski, it should be recalled, placed a good deal of emphasis upon the need of the General Assembly to achieve executive capacity, but warned that, given contemporary international tensions, the Assembly should not act in these areas until a far greater degree of political agreement exists among the big powers than is the case today.

   Is it sensible to give a particular organ of the United Nations the authority to make both the substantive rules for guiding and controlling the behavior of the Organization, of Member States, and of individuals and, at the same time, provide that organ with the executive capacity to initiate and control peace-keeping operations? Are there any national legislatures or parliaments that assume executive functions to assure the realization of legislative policy? Undoubtedly, one of the motivations for the allocation of functions in the Clark-Sohn plan is a desire to make their proposal as acceptable as possible to a maximum number of governments. The establishment of, and the power to invoke and make use of the international police forces are, understandably enough, matters of vital concern to the officials in each nation-state. To achieve agreement it might prove necessary to assure all or most states that their representatives would participate in the judgements about when and where an international police force would be used.

4. This approach to peace-keeping obviously runs contrary to the original thinking of the Charter. There the permanent five members, if supplemented by the votes of any two non-permanent members of the Security Council, were authorized to control international policing. Which of these two approaches is more likely to satisfy the test of acceptability? For nations of what size, what stage of development, and with which ideology?

C. Representation and Voting

Considerable research and discussion on possible revisions in representation and voting has gone on within various international organizations. Nevertheless, there is a widespread feeling that the issues raised by these matters are only marginally relevant to the more fundamental political problems of world order, at least at this stage in the development of world community sentiments and considering the limits upon the effective and comprehensive exercise of authority by international organizations. Most often, matters of representation and voting in international organizations are regarded as dependent variables in the contemporary international political system.

Although the materials in this section may be viewed as arguing for, in a very modest way, a more important role for these elements of formal international organization, the purpose is not to establish their causal relation to contemporary international events nor to offer an evaluation of the efficiency of the formal structures of international organization. Rather, as the materials on expansion of the Security Council illustrated, questions of voting and representation are convenient ways to perceive the fundamental political problems of contemporary international life in terms of the accommodations that differing ideological blocs, political entities and alliances will have to make to move toward a more orderly, just and stable international system that is less war-prone. Thus, questions relevant to representation and voting are, as it were, the prism through which to view the fissures and frictions of the international political system. Political and constitutional problems of world order are here concerned with determining which substantive issues, procedural devices and sanctioning processes are, or should become, available to international organization. Insights emerging from questions concerning voting and representation are surprisingly helpful for an understanding of contemporary international events and as a way to get suggestive leads on what transition steps can be taken.

Furthermore, if we are to give serious study to the possibility of a radical system change such as Clark and Sohn propose, it is insufficient to evaluate this scheme or any other in terms of only general principles. To study a transition to a warless world and the manner in which a law-government would operate in that world, it is essential to come to grips with the detailed issues that arise when efforts are made to restructure the ways in which international organizations function. To bring to the level of intelligent and critical awareness the details of a projected legislative scheme for world authority is to invite others who desire world order, but find this particular scheme deficient, to suggest with the same degree of specificity not only the character of their preferred model of world order, but also their conception of the way in which the rules for world order would be generated and sustained.

Clark and Sohn give the General Assembly authority to enact binding legislation in the area of war prevention. This authority would make the Assembly into an extremely important and powerful instrument of world politics. Their scheme for weighted representation by the Assembly based on population is properly viewed as both a method for achieving transition, that is, a way to make the proposed system acceptable to Member States, and also as a demonstration of an effective way to carry on the operations once the authority is granted. Essentially their proposals are an attempt to modify the traditional notions of sovereignty of one-state-one-vote with an appeal to the ethical and moral attributes that have come to be attached to representation based on population in many states of the world. Note that other institutions, such as the World Bank, use successfully a system of weighted voting. Clark and Sohn evidently feel that their scheme of weighted voting would avoid many of the disputes that arise when criteria other than population are put forward as a basis for representation in a strengthened United Nations. Whether this effort to depoliticize the criteria is possible or desirable is something to consider carefully. In this connection, read the section of *World Peace through World Law* that sets forth the principles upon which their proposal for weighted voting is based. See WPTWL, pp. 20–34.

The Clark-Sohn proposal is one of several suggestions that have been made as to how to change the present system of one-state-one-vote; all of the proposed changes are based on the view that the existing formula does not adequately reflect certain important elements in contemporary international political processes. In this next article by Francis O. Wilcox, "Representation and Voting in the United Nations General Assembly," *Staff Study No. 4, Subcommittee on the United Nations Charter* (1954) pp. 1–23, we shall read a summary of the various proposals that have been made for revising the voting procedures in the General Assembly. In evaluating these proposals, keep in mind the underlying question of what authority should be granted to the Assembly. The extent of authority consists of the range of substantive issues placed within the competence of the Assembly and the procedural devices and sanctioning processes put at the disposal of the Assembly.

FRANCIS O. WILCOX

REPRESENTATION AND VOTING IN THE UNITED NATIONS GENERAL ASSEMBLY

I. Introductory Comments

It is a curious fact that while public opinion in the United States has been deeply disturbed over the veto and the problem of voting in the U. N. Security Council, there has been relatively little interest in the problem of voting in the General Assembly. This remains true in spite of the fact that the prestige and influence of the Security Council have been on the wane and the star of the General Assembly has been rising.

As the charter was drafted, voting power in the Security Council, where decisions on all substantive questions require the concurring votes of the five permanent members, is heavily weighted in favor of the great powers. In the General Assembly, where all states have an equal voice, the scales are balanced in favor of the smaller nations. The great powers were willing to accept such an arrangement at the San Francisco Conference because they believed their interests would be adequately protected by their right of veto in the Security Council. At the time this seemed a reasonable assumption. The Security Council was charged with the primary responsibility for the maintenance of peace and it was in that body that the really important decisions of the U. N. were to be taken. The General Assembly, which possessed only the power of recommendation, was destined, they believed, to be an organ of lesser political significance.

This estimate of the situation proved wrong. Gradually, as the tension between the Soviet bloc and the free world has increased, the importance of the Security Council—when compared with that of the General Assembly—has declined. During the past few years that organ has been greatly handicapped by the excessive use of the veto on the part of the Soviet Union.

The table below shows in a quantitative way, the extent to which the General Assembly has displaced the Security Council as a forum for the handling of international political issues. During the early years of the U. N., as the framers of the charter intended, the Security Council functioned as the principal political organ of the U. N. Beginning in 1948, however, its importance has steadily declined. By July 1951, Security Council activity reached a disturbingly low point and has continued on the decline since that time.

Political issues considered by General Assembly and Security Council—Jan. 1, 1946, to June 30, 1953[1]

Period	General Assembly	Security Council
Jan. 1–June 30, 1946	2	8
July 1, 1946–June 30, 1947	6	8
July 1, 1947–June 30, 1948	9	14
July 1, 1948–June 30, 1949	15	10
July 1, 1949–June 30, 1950	13	12
July 1, 1950–June 30, 1951	24	12
July 1, 1951–June 30, 1952	17	9
July 1, 1952–June 30, 1953	18	5
Total	104	78

[1] Table from H. J. Morgenthau, The United Nations and the Revision of the Charter, The Review of Politics, January 1954, p. 4.

Over the years there has been a comparable reduction in the number of meetings of the Security Council. In 1946, 88 meetings were held; in 1947, 137; in 1948, 168; in 1949, 62; in 1950, 73; in 1951, 39; in 1952, 42. In 1953, the Council met only 43 times. During the first 7 months of the year it dealt primarily with one subject, the election of a Secretary-General.

Given this shift of power within the U. N. structure, the importance of a reconsideration of the voting procedures in the General Assembly becomes apparent. Thus far relatively few suggestions for changes in the existing system have been made. In any event, it will be helpful to examine briefly present voting practices in the General Assembly and then turn to the proposals that have been advanced to amend the charter in this regard.

II. Present Voting Practices in the General Assembly

In the past, international organizations ordinarily have been based on two fundamental principles: the legal equality of states and unanimity in voting. In practice this has meant that nations like Luxembourg and Iceland, with very small populations, have participated in international assemblies on a basis of legal equality with large nations like the United States, China, and India. "Russia and Geneva have equal rights," declared Chief Justice Marshall in 1825, and this principle of state equality applied to international conferences (as well as to international commerce).

It has meant, too, that whenever the decision stage has been reached at an international conference, any small state, as well as any large one, has been in a position to block action on substantive questions by casting a negative vote. Sometimes little countries have responded to the pressure of other states and have abandoned their opposition; at other times they have prevented conferences from arriving at decisions which, but for their opposition, might have been unanimously approved.

Article 18

At the San Francisco Conference the framers of the U. N. Charter accepted the first of these principles but rejected the second. Article 18, which lays down the procedure for voting in the General Assembly, reads as follows:

1. Each member of the General Assembly shall have one vote.
2. Decisions of the General Assembly on important questions shall be made by a two-thirds majority of the members present and voting. These questions shall include: recommendations with respect to the maintenance of international peace and security, the election of the nonpermanent members of the Security Council, the election of the members of the Economic and Social Council, the election of members of the Trusteeship Council in accordance with paragraph 1 (c) of Article 86, the admission of new Members to the United Nations, the suspension of the rights and privileges of membership, the expulsion of Members, questions relating to the operation of the trusteeship system, and budgetary questions.
3. Decisions on other questions, including the determination of additional categories of questions to be decided by a two-thirds majority, shall be made by a majority of the members present and voting.

The fundamental proposition, expressed in article 2, that the U. N. is based on the sovereign equality of all its members is reiterated in article 18. Each member is given one vote. Theoretically, at least, it would have been possible to devise a system of weighted voting which would accord member nations a number of votes more commensurate with their relative importance in world affairs. But the practical difficulties involved in building a formula that would take account of the various factors that need to be measured were so great, and traditional concepts of sovereign equality of states so strong, that the matter was not given serious consideration either at Dumbarton Oaks or San Francisco. The time-honored doctrine of one-state-one-vote became part and parcel of the U. N. system.[2]

The only exception to this principle is to be found in the privileged position of the Soviet Union. At the San Francisco Conference, in accordance with an arrangement made at the Yalta Conference, Byelorussia and the Ukraine—which are constituent republics of the U. S. S. R. and do not qualify as "states" in the strict sense of that term—were admitted as U. N. members. They each have 1 vote which, combined with that of the Soviet Union, make a total of 3 votes for 1 country.

Actually, this arrangement involves far more than two additional votes for the Soviet Union. She is also entitled to two additional delegations. This not only triples her voting power, it triples her speaking power as well.

With respect to the principle of unanimity, the charter turns its back upon the past. No doubt the experience of the League of Nations was, in large part, responsible for this departure. Article 5 of the League Covenant, in effect, gave every member of the League a veto by providing that, with certain exceptions, "decisions at any meeting of the Assembly or of the Council shall require the agreement of all the members of the League represented at the meeting." This requirement by no means paralyzed the League Assembly. It did, however, hamper its activity and on some occasions prevented it from reaching important decisions strongly advocated by a majority of the members.

Article 18 of the charter provides for votes on two types of questions. The first category includes the so-called important questions which require a two-thirds majority. The second category includes all other questions and these call for a simple majority. It will be noted that the majority required under the article is a majority of the members

[2] Goodrich and Hambro, Charter of the United Nations: Commentary and Documents, 1949, p. 188.

50227—54——2

"present and voting." Members abstaining from the vote are considered as not voting.

By a simple majority the General Assembly may decide that further categories of questions—in addition to those enumerated in article 18—are of sufficient importance to require a two-thirds vote. It can also modify or abolish these additional categories by a majority of the members present and voting.

The two-thirds majority for the handling of important questions seems to have worked fairly well in practice. No doubt it has served as a deterrent to hasty and ill-considered action by the General Assembly. On the other hand, it has not prevented action on any measure desired by a large majority of U. N. members. During the first 6 years of the United Nations, there were some 18 instances in which draft resolutions (or portions of resolutions), received a simple majority in the committees of the General Assembly but were not adopted because they failed to secure the necessary two-thirds vote in the Assembly itself.

The principal effect of article 18 is to reject the veto with respect to General Assembly votes. This is a move in the direction of democracy in world affairs in that it decreases the negative power of individual states. At the same time it increases the positive power of groups of states which may wish to band together to accomplish their objectives within the U. N. system.

THE POWER OF THE GENERAL ASSEMBLY

At this point it may be helpful to keep in mind the fact that the General Assembly does not possess international legislative authority. It can study, it can debate, it can recommend but it cannot legislate. In general, it cannot make decisions that are binding upon the members of the United Nations.

Within its limitations, however, the scope of activity of the General Assembly is far broader than that of the Security Council. It may discuss and make recommendations on any matter within the scope of the charter or relating to the functions and powers of any U. N. organs (art. 10). Similarly, it may make recommendations concerning the general principles of cooperation in the maintenance of peace and security, including the problem of disarmament (art. 11). It may promote international cooperation in the economic, social, cultural, education, and health fields (art. 13). And it may recommend measures for the peaceful adjustment of any situation likely to impair the general welfare or friendly relations among nations (art. 14).

It is true that General Assembly votes on these matters do not carry compulsion in their wake. But there can be little doubt that many General Assembly resolutions such as those relating to Spain, Korea, Palestine, Communist China, and atomic energy, have had a fateful impact upon the course of world events. Recommendations with wide support may be more effective than half-hearted decisions, supposedly binding on member states.

INEQUALITIES RESULTING FROM ONE-STATE-ONE-VOTE CONCEPT

The principle of one-state-one-vote results in glaring inequalities in the General Assembly. Only 9 states can boast a population of 40 million or more. Some 26 states have a population of 5 million or under, including Iceland with 146,000 and Luxembourg with 300,000. Three countries—China, India and the Soviet Union—contain more than half the total U. N. population of roughly 1,800 million.

Under the circumstances, it is theoretically possible to secure a majority of 31 votes which represent only a little over 5 percent of the population of U. N. members. A vote of the 21 smallest countries—representing only about 2.3 percent of the U. N. population—could prevent the two-thirds majority needed for the approval of "important" resolutions. On the other hand, if a contest should arise between the large and small states, a two-thirds majority could be rolled up by 40 of the smallest nations with a population of only about 11 percent.[3]

Clearly, this is a hypothetical danger which probably will never arise in practice in the extreme form referred to above. U. N. members are unlikely ever to divide on important issues merely because of population differences. Even so, these figures illustrate the lack of balance which exists between population and voting strength; a very small minority of the U. N. population is in a position to control decisive votes and to frustrate the will of the majority.

Similar inequalities exist with respect to national wealth, productivity, national territory, and other factors. The U. S. S. R., for example, has a total area of 8,700,000 square miles. This is more than 1,000 times the area of El Salvador. An even greater margin of difference exists with respect to the gross national product. According to the best estimates available some 6 U. N. members had a gross national product of less than $200 million in 1952 or 1953. In contrast, the gross national product of the United States is estimated at $363 billion for 1953. The comparable figure for the Soviet Union is $100 billion, for the United Kingdom, $45 billion, and for France, $39 billion.

BLOC VOTING IN THE GENERAL ASSEMBLY

The situation has been complicated further by the development of what has come to be known as bloc voting in the General Assembly. By pooling or combining their voting strength on particular issues groups of small states are able to exert an influence far out of proportion to either their population or their political importance.

While this tendency toward bloc voting has developed considerably since 1945, the lineup in the General Assembly varies a great deal depending upon the issue. The five Communist states will invariably be found on the same side. The seven Arab countries often vote as a unit particularly with respect to Israeli-Arab problems and resolutions having to do with dependent areas. In most cases two-thirds of the 20 Latin American states will be found in the same camp.[4]

On the other hand, there is no predictable solidarity among the countries of Western Europe. The Benelux states (Luxembourg, Belgium, and the Netherlands) vote together on some issues as do the Scandinavian countries. The seven British Commonwealth nations rarely vote as a unit. Nevertheless, during the past few years, the free world countries have demonstrated a remarkable unity whenever

[3] See Vandenbosch and Hogan, The United Nations: Background, Organization, Functions, Activities, 1952, p. 116.

[4] On this subject see Margaret Ball, Bloc Voting in the General Assembly, International Organization, February 1951.

the most vital issues are up for a vote. The 52 to 5 vote on the Uniting for Peace Resolution in 1950 is a case in point.

An interesting example of what the small states can do when they are effectively organized emerged during the third session of the General Assembly when the resolution providing for the use of Spanish as one of the working languages of the U. N. was approved by a vote of 32–20 with 5 abstentions. In that case, the small states successfully opposed the permanent members. Latin America and the Arab countries, with a few supporting votes, outvoted the United States, China, three of the British Commonwealth nations, and all of Europe, including the United Kingdom.

Sir Carl Berendsen of New Zealand called attention to this problem in the plenary session of the General Assembly in 1947. "Another analogous source of irresponsibility," he said:

> is the system of bloc voting that has grown up. Let no one tell me that what we have seen at this session and on many occasions, of groups of powers voting as one, is a good system. Some of these blocs are large; indeed, they can become so large as, in effect, to constitute a veto with regard to any question of importance requiring a two-thirds majority. That is not a proper exercise of responsibility.[5]

Thus far, this problem has not proved serious so far as the United States is concerned. There has been some "bloc" voting, just as there has been some "huckstering of votes in the market place," as Sir Carl pointed out. But generally—with some few exceptions—the democratic processes in the General Assembly have worked fairly well and the United States has received the kind of cooperation that has enabled us to achieve our policy objectives in the United Nations, especially in the political field.

On the other hand, we should keep in mind the fact that the U. N. by no means has reached its outer limits with respect to membership. There are now pending 19 applications for membership including 14 countries approved by the General Assembly as qualified under the charter. If the organization continues to expand, and particularly if a number of small states are admitted, a reconsideration of the voting procedures in the General Assembly might become a more pressing issue.

III. Attempts in Past to Change Methods of Voting and Representation

For a long time the states of the international community have been groping for a satisfactory voting formula that will prove more workable in practice and still be compatible with the principle of state sovereignty. The real need is to find a measuring stick which will reflect in terms of voting power the glaring inequalities in power and importance which now exist among the nations of the world. A brief review of experience to date may be helpful in determining whether a more effective formula can now be developed.[6]

In a number of international organizations extra voting power has been given to states with colonial possessions. This practice was adopted early in the life of the Universal Postal Union and persists today. Thus for voting purposes Portuguese colonies in West Africa form a separate country as do the Portuguese colonies in East Africa,

[5] GA. II. 1947. Official Records Plenary, pp. 694–695.

[6] On this general question see the articles in Louis B. Sohn, Cases and Other Materials on World Law, 1950, pp. 316–347.

Asia, and Oceania.[7] Such an arrangement may have its commendable features in granting some voting power to people who have not yet attained their independence. No one would argue, however, that a formula which gives more votes to Portugal than to India and China together is a very good index of the relative importance of the members.

In some cases, also, attempts have been made to relate the financial contributions of members to their voting power. This was true of the former International Institute of Agriculture established in Rome in 1905. The convention setting up the Institute created five classes of membership with the number of votes allotted to states in each category increasing in arithmetical progression. The contributions of states in the various categories increased in geometric progression.

Article 10 established the various categories as follows:[8]

Groups of nations	Number of votes	Units of assessment
I	5	16
II	4	8
III	3	4
IV	2	2
V	1	1

More successful perhaps are the attempts which have been made to relate voting power to the varying interests of states in a particular problem. The International Sugar Council[9] and the International Wheat Council[10] are cases in point. The new International Sugar Agreement (1953), for example, provides that a total of 2,000 votes are to be apportioned among the Council members, divided equally between the exporting and importing countries. In general, the number of votes assigned to each import ng state is related to that state's average imports. Countries like Saudi Arabia and Jordan, with relatively small imports, have 15 votes. The largest importing countries, the United Kingdom and the United States, have 245 votes each. The 1,000 votes allocated to the exporting countries are assigned in much the same fashion.

Decisions of the Sugar Council, in general, are taken by a majority of the votes cast by the exporting states and a majority of the votes cast by the importing states. In all voting, decisions taken by a majority of the importing countries must include the votes of at least one-third of the importing states present and voting. This special proviso results in increasing the voting power of the smaller importing nations whose total votes are only slightly larger than the combined total assigned to the United States and the United Kingdom.

Of a somewhat similar character are the complicated voting procedures used by the International Bank for Reconstruction and Development[11] and the International Monetary Fund.[12] In these organizations, the voting power of each member reflects its proportion-

[7] See U. S. Senate, Committee on Foreign Relations. A Decade of American Foreign Policy. S. Doc. 123, 81st Cong., 1st sess., p. 201. In the International Telecommunications Union (1932) the International Wine Office (1924), and the International Office of Chemistry, votes were awarded for colonial possessions.
[8] Malloy, compiler. Treaties, Conventions, International Acts, Protocols and Agreements between the United States of America and other powers. S. Doc. 357, 61st Cong., 2d sess., vol. II, p. 2143.
[9] See S. Ex. B, 83d Cong., 2d sess., pp. 28–29.
[10] See S. Ex. H, 83d Cong., 1st sess., pp. 20–24.
[11] U. S. Senate, Committee on Foreign Relations, op. cit., pp. 251–272.
[12] Ibid, pp. 273–304.

ate share of the total capital to which the members as a whole have subscribed. As of June 30, 1953, for example, Panama had subscribed to less than 0.005 percent of the bank's capital and was entitled to 252 votes out of a total of 103,865. The United States, on the other end of the spectrum, having subscribed to 35.13 percent of the capital was assigned 32,000 votes, or approximately one-third of the total.

Up to the present time, population has been rarely used in international organizations as a factor in determining voting strength. The new European Consultative Assembly, which is the deliberative organ of the Council of Europe, appears to be one of the few current exceptions to the rule. Article 26 of the Statute of the Council of Europe[13] provides that member states shall be entitled to the number of representatives given below:

Belgium	6	Netherlands	6
Denmark	4	Norway	4
France	18	Sweden	6
Irish Republic	4	United Kingdom	18
Italy	18		
Luxembourg	3	Total	87

It will be seen that while voting strength in the Consultative Assembly is based roughly on population, the scale nevertheless remains weighted in favor of the small states. Thus, Luxembourg with population of less than one one-hundredth that of France nevertheless has one-sixth the number of votes. Moreover, a two-thirds vote is required for all resolutions approved by the Assembly. This means that even if the three largest states—France, Italy, and the United Kingdom—supported a proposal, their combined votes (54) would still be short of the total of 58 necessary for approval.

On the whole it has not been easy to induce states to depart from the principle of one-state-one-vote. It has been done in a few cases where international organizations have been set up to deal with special problems. It remains for the future, however, to develop a satisfactory voting formula that will be workable in the General Assembly and at the same time acceptable to the members of the U. N.

IV. Mr. Dulles' Proposal for Weighted Voting

In 1950, in his book entitled War or Peace, John Foster Dulles set forth a proposal for weighted voting in the General Assembly. While his suggestions were general in character they merit careful study, first because they embrace some interesting possibilities, and second because his is the only proposal of its kind which has emerged from official or semiofficial sources.

Mr. Dulles points out that in the Congress we have two ways of voting. In the Senate each State, regardless of size, has two votes. New York with its 15 million people, and Nevada with its 150,000, have equal voting strength. In the House of Representatives, however, where representation is based on population, New York has 45 votes to Nevada's 1.

"I would not abolish in the United Nations," he writes,

> an Assembly vote which, like that of our Senate, reflects the sovereign equality of all nations and gives them all an equal vote. But there might be introduced, in addition, a system of "weighted" voting so that the result would indicate,

[13] Published by the Council of Europe, May 5, 1949, p. 8. See also the Statute for the European Community (articles 16–17) which provide for a 2-house parliament with representation based, in part, on population.

roughly, a verdict in terms also of ability to play a part in world affairs. Then it should be provided that decisions on important matters would require a simple majority, rather than two-thirds, under each of the two voting procedures." [14]

Mr. Dulles apparently has in mind other factors in addition to population. The weight of the General Assembly's recommendations, he contends, would be far greater than they are at present if votes reflected "not merely numbers but also ability to contribute to the maintenance of international peace and security."

This point he stressed again on January 18, 1954, in his statement before the Senate Foreign Relations Committee's special subcommittee on the U. N. Charter. "If the General Assembly is to assume greater responsibilities," he said,

then should there not be some form of weighted voting, so that nations which are themselves unable to assume serious military or financial responsibilities cannot put those responsibilities on other nations? Should there be, in some matters, a combination vote whereby affirmative action requires both a majority of all the members, on the basis of sovereign equality, and also a majority vote, on some weighted basis, which takes into account population, resources, and so forth? [15]

Mr. Dulles' proposal has a great deal of merit. In the first place, it would not disturb existing machinery. It is designed to fit into the present organization without any major alterations or adjustments. Mr. Dulles does not suggest the creation of a second Assembly, nor even the need for additional delegates. He merely proposes that each vote in the General Assembly be tallied twice; the first tally would correspond to the present sovereign-state arrangement with each state casting one vote; in the second tally additional votes would be awarded to states depending upon their ability—because of population, productive capacity, armed strength, etc.—to contribute to the maintenance of world peace. A simple majority under each of the two procedures would be necessary for the General Assembly to reach a decision.

This double-barreled vote would have a double-barreled effect. It would not take away from the small nations their ability to protect their vital interests in the United Nations. So long as they could command a simple majority of the votes—and the large majority of U. N. members are relatively small nations—they could prevent decisions which might prove inimical to them. At the same time it would place in the hands of the larger states a potential veto which they could exercise in order to block what they might consider irresponsible action on the part of the smaller countries.

Moreover, if this kind of balanced-weighted voting were introduced, it would equip the General Assembly to assume full responsibility for such organizational matters as the selection of the Secretary General and the admission of new members to the U. N. As things stand now, this responsibility is shared with the Security Council where the negative vote of a permanent member has often blocked action for long periods of time.

Few people would question the logic of bestowing upon the permanent members added weight in connection with important organizational decisions. But it is certainly not logical to permit any single state, by the use of the veto, to tie the hands of the United Nations with respect to such issues. This dilemma could be resolved if the

[14] John Foster Dulles, War or Peace, 1950, pp. 191–194.
[15] U. S. Senate Committee on Foreign Relations, Subcommittee on the United Nations. **Review of the** United Nations Charter. Hearings pt. I, 1954, p. 7.

interests of the great powers were reflected by an appropriate system of weighted voting in the General Assembly. In such an event the responsibility of the Security Council with respect to such matters might well be brought to an end.

As ingenious as Mr. Dulles' plan is, it raises certain extremely difficult questions. Would the smaller nations agree to any proposal which reduces the relative importance of their role in the General Assembly? At the San Francisco Conference they bitterly resented the privileged position given to the great powers in the United Nations. By the same token would they not now resist any adverse readjustment in the balance of power that was so carefully worked out at San Francisco?

More important still, what criteria would be used in computing the voting strength of the different members? Population? Literacy? Territorial possessions? National wealth? Productive capacity? Financial contribution to the U. N.? World trade? Military strength? Willingness to contribute to the maintenance of world peace? And if several of these factors should be used, how much importance should be attached to each?

It is here that we encounter the crux of the problem of weighted voting. From a mathematical point of view, it would be far simpler to use a single criterion, such as population, and apportion the votes accordingly. But the differences between the states are so vast that any single factor would result in a false picture of the relative importance of various countries in the world and would concentrate voting power in the hands of a few states in an unrealistic way.

If, for example, an attempt is made to award votes directly in proportion to total population then we find that two states, India and China, would be entitled to nearly one-half the voting power in the General Assembly, and Burma would have six times as many votes as Norway. If military strength is our standard, considerably more than half the votes would go to the United States and the Soviet Union. On the other hand, if world trade is the measuring stick, Great Britain would receive a relatively large number of votes and the Soviet Union would be rather far down the scale.

The problem of weighted voting must be approached realistically. Clearly the small countries, which have been used to the principle of legal equality, are not going to underwrite any system of voting which gives the great powers 50 or 100 votes to their 1. They might, however, agree to a system which is far less discriminatory from their point of view.

The problem then, would seem to be one of agreeing upon two or three criteria—such as population, national production and contribution to the U. N.—and balancing them in such a way as to reflect, on a considerably reduced scale, the relative importance of the various countries in the organization. It might then be possible to set up 4 or 5 categories of states, as in the case of the International Institute of Agriculture, with each state receiving from 1 to 5 votes, depending upon its importance.

Any proposal for weighted voting in the General Assembly should also take into consideration the unique position of the Soviet Union which, together with its two constituent republics, Byelorussia and the Ukraine, already possesses three votes. The difficulty of removing voting power which has already been granted is apparent. Nevertheless, before any new formula is fixed, it would seem desirable to offset, insofar as that is possible, the initial advantage given to the Soviet Union at San Francisco.

At present, the chief weakness of Mr. Dulles' proposal is at once its greatest strength. If it were spelled out in detail it might stir up a hornet's nest of opposition. So long as it remains couched in general terms, it will probably command the support of a great many people.

V. United Nations Contributions and Voting Power

It has been suggested by at least one delegation that voting power should be directly related to a state's contribution to the U. N. budget. In 1950, the New Zealand delegate to the First Committee of the General Assembly (Mr. Doidge) called attention to the "obvious elements of absurdity" that are involved in according to a small nation the same voting power accorded a country with a population of 200 million.

Equally—

he said—

> there is much unreality in giving to a member without armed forces and one without any desire or willingness to supply armed forces even for common defense the same voting power as to those which do possess armed forces and have from time to time, by the devotion of the lives of their citizens, proved their willingess to undertake those international duties which are correlative to all international rights.

Mr. Doidge then went on to point up the complexity of the problem, suggesting that "voting must be based on many considerations and not on population alone." "Perhaps," he remarked—

> a voting power to each member roughly equal to the proportion which its financial contribution to the funds of the United Nations bears to the total contribution would provide a system of rough justice and efficiency.[16]

Since the United Nations is based upon the principle of sovereign equality—which implies equal obligations as well as equal rights—there would seem to be some logic in Mr. Doidge's suggestion. In some organizations with small expenditures, members contribute to the budget on an equal or nearly equal basis. No member of the International Telecommunications Union, for example, pays more than 5 percent of the budget, and the highest contribution in the Universal Postal Union is approximately 8 percent.

But the United Nations, with a much larger budget than any other international organization, constitutes a special case. In 1954 only 16 states contributed more than 1 percent each of the budget. Nine countries contributed as little as 0.04 percent each. The 5 permanent members contributed nearly 70 percent of the total with the United States assessed for 33.33 percent, the Soviet Union roughly 14 percent, the United Kingdom 10 percent, France and China approximately 5.5 percent each.[17]

If these figures were translated into proportional voting terms, they would mean that the United States, with one-third of the votes, would be in a position to block any important resolution proposed in the

[16] Statement made on October 11, 1950, during the Fifth General Assembly.

[17] U. S. Senate. Committee on Foreign Relations, Subcommittee on the United Nations Charter. Review of the United Nations Charter. S. Doc. 87, 83d Cong., 2d sess. p. 719–720.

General Assembly. They would mean that the five permanent members—assuming they were in agreement to do so—could always command a two-thirds majority. They would mean that the United States, the United Kingdom, and France would have a simple majority of the votes in their pockets before any voting began.

Such an arrangement would be open to serious objection. It would draw an invidious distinction between rich and poor countries. Even more important, as the United States delegation to the U. N. has repeatedly pointed out, it would be most unfortunate if any single state were to be placed in a position where it could exert undue influence over the organization. Given the tremendous differences that exist among U. N. members with respect to their capacity to pay, the contributions scale would seem to be an even less reliable criterion than population for determining voting strength.

On the other hand, from the point of view of the United States, if any reshuffling of voting power is contemplated, the financial angle certainly should not be ignored. It is a well-known fact that some of the loudest advocates of state equality show much less enthusiasm for that principle when it comes to the question of apportioning the expenses of an international organization. The Latin American countries, for example, are strong supporters of the principle of the legal equality of all states. Yet the United States, which has only 1 vote out of 21 in the inter-American system, bears more than half the expenses of the Organization of American States.

Perhaps the relationship between legal equality and financial responsibility has not been stressed enough in the United Nations. It is suggested that if an arrangement can be worked out to give some additional voting strength to states which do their best to meet their financial responsibilities it might have at least one salutary effect; it might encourage some states to increase their contributions and thus make possible a revision of the contributions scale.

In this connection consideration should also be given to certain special U. N. programs, like those dealing with Korean reconstruction and Palestine refugees, which are financed by voluntary contributions. In such instances, even more than in the regular U. N. budget, the main burden has fallen upon the United States. While the figures vary somewhat from year to year, our Government has contributed over 65 percent of the total for the U. N. Children's Fund, some 60 percent of the funds for the U. N. technical assistance program, 61 percent of the Palestine refugee program, and more than 65 percent of the funds going to the Korean Reconstruction Agency.

If it is not possible to work out a general voting formula that would take into account the contribution of members to the regular U. N. budget, it might still be feasible to accord additional voting power of an ad hoc nature to states contributing heavily to these special programs. This could be done by devising a weighted voting formula for the Executive Board of the Children's Fund, for example, which is charged with the general supervision of that particular program. It would seem logical that those governments which volunteer heavy contributions to extracurricular activities should be given additional control over the expenditure of the funds.

VI. Population and Voting Strength

In addition to the suggestions outlined above, a number of proposals have been advanced relating to representation and voting by organizations that advocate the establishment of some kind of supranational agency endowed with additional authority to meet present-day world problems. For the most part, these proposals would make drastic inroads upon the concept of national sovereignty. They would either subject the United Nations to a thorough overhaul or else replace it altogether.

Many people feel that, under present circumstances, these far-reaching proposals have no chance whatsoever of receiving the necessary support in U. N. circles to put them into effect. Nevertheless, most of these proposals represent the thinking of a substantial number of people and it may be worthwhile to review them briefly for whatever light they may shed upon the problem under consideration.

In the General Assembly, in line with the principle of sovereign equality, each state is represented by 5 delegates and 5 alternates and each delegation has 1 vote. The supranational proposals, for the most part, would abandon the principle of state sovereignty by suggesting fundamental changes in the size and character of the representation to which each country is entitled. Most of them advocate some form of weighted or proportionate representation the net effect of which would be a system of weighted voting.

THE CLARK-SOHN PROPOSALS

The most fully developed of these plans are the so-called Clark-Sohn proposals.[18] These proposals call for the creation of a United Nations peace force and would delegate to the General Assembly certain legislative authority particularly with respect to the enforcement of universal disarmament and the control of atomic energy.

Representation in the General Assembly, under the Clark-Sohn plans would be based solely on population. Each member of the U. N. would be entitled to 1 representative for each 5 million population or major fraction thereof. Small states with a population of more than 100,000 and not more than 2,500,000 would be entitled to 1 representative and members with large populations would be limited to 30 representatives. Nations with a population of 100,000 or less—such as San Marino and Monaco—would be entitled to a delegate with the right to participate in the discussion but without the right to vote. The formula would be adjusted from time to time, taking account of world population increases, in order to insure that the number of representatives should never exceed 400. The net effect of the plan would be to create a General Assembly of 382 representatives and 3 delegates to represent a world population of 2,400 million.

The authors specifically reject any system of weighted representation based on economic resources, productive capacity, literacy, trade, national income, or related factors.

[18] Grenville Clark and Louis B. Sohn. Peace Through Disarmament and Charter Revision. July 1953.

They believe that all such plans, which necessarily give weight to wealth and other economic factors that are largely the result of geography and history, involve an anachronistic discrimination. Such a discrimination would run counter to the inherent equality of all individuals, which in the modern world should not and cannot be denied. They have, therefore, come to the conclusion that the true solution lies in an apportionment based fundamentally on population. It is for reasons of workability only that in the foregoing proposal upper and lower limits have been placed on the representation of any nation.[19]

By limiting to 30 the maximum number of representatives the largest countries may have, and by counting the people of the non-self-governing territories for purposes of representation, the authors of the plan would keep fairly even the voting strength of the great powers. China, the U. S. S. R., the United States, and India would be given 30 representatives, the United Kingdom 25, and France 19. On the other hand, Germany would be entitled to only 14, Italy to 9, Japan to 17, and Indonesia and Pakistan to 15 each. Some 40 nations would have only 1 representative.

With such a wide spread in voting power, the more populous nations would be given a dominant position in the General Assembly. As a practical matter, it is extremely doubtful, at best, that the smaller countries would be willing to accept any system in which India or China would be allotted almost as many votes as the 20 Latin American States combined.

In one other important respect, the Clark-Sohn proposal departs from the principle of state sovereignty. The authors suggest that representatives to the General Assembly be chosen in national elections or by vote of the national legislatures. This, they argue, would "stress the desirability that the representatives shall receive their mandate directly from the peoples of the respective nations." [20]

Since the idea is advanced by other proponents of supranational government, and since it would drastically alter the role of national governments in the organization, it will be discussed in some detail in a later section of this study.

BRITISH PARLIAMENTARY GROUP FOR WORLD GOVERNMENT

Somewhat similar to the Clark-Sohn proposals are the recommendations of the British Parliamentary Group for World Government. In their so-called plan A [21] they call for the creation of a world legislative body made up of two chambers, the upper chamber consisting of "one representative of each nation state appointed in a manner to be determined by that state." The intention here apparently is to provide for some continuity with the present General Assembly. The group also argues that such an arrangement would "tend to secure the representation of some valuable men and women who were not willing to submit themselves to popular suffrages." [22]

In contrast to the upper house, the lower chamber would consist of representatives of member states "in numbers proportionate to population." This would reflect in some degree the balance achieved by the Senate and the House in the Congress of the United States. While the British Parliamentary Group does not spell out their plan in any detail, they evidently contemplate placing an upper limit upon the

[19] Ibid., p. 21.
[20] Ibid., p. 23.
[21] Report of the Second London Parliamentary Conference on World Government, pp. 101–107.
[22] Ibid., p. 105.

number of representatives from any state. In a note dealing with the lower chamber they point out that—

the reason for weighting the representation is to avoid the overwhelming preponderance of the nations with the largest population, and thus make it more attractive to join.

In suggesting a double-vote system based on the sovereign equality of states and some form of weighted representation, the British Parlia mentary Group approach somewhat the proposal of Mr. Dulles. The principal difference would seem to be that Mr. Dulles does not suggest changing the simple unicameral character of, or the method of representation in, the present General Assembly. He would secure his double vote by mathematical rather than physical changes.

FEDERAL UNION AND ATLANTIC UNION

Supporters of the Federal Union and Atlantic Union movements have advocated a two-house Union legislature comparable, with some variations, to our House and Senate. As Clarence Streit put it in his book Union Now,[23] the lower house would be "based completely on the population and the other modifying this principle of equal men in favor of equal states." This body would exercise the legislative authority granted to it, within a limited geographical area, for the 15 democracies first suggested for membership in the Union.

According to the formula for representation presented in Union Now—which was for illustrative purposes only—one representative would be allotted in the House for every million inhabitants. On this basis the United States would have received 129 of the 280 seats, in accordance with the population statistics then available. In the Senate, where it was proposed that each self-governing nation with less than 25 million inhabitants should be given 2 senators, with 2 additional senators for every population increment of 25 million or major portion thereof up to 100 million, the United States would have been allotted 8 of the 40 seats.

Under this plan the three largest countries (France, 42; Great Britain, 47; the United States, 129) would have 218 out of 280 representatives in the House and 16 out of 40 in the Senate. Thus, an equitable balance would be achieved, with the small states holding a substantial majority in the Senate and the large states commanding a majority in the House. No one member could possibly control either house, and the voting strength of each member would diminish relatively as other states entered the Union.

Since the suggested membership of the Union has varied somewhat, the supporters of Federal Union and Atlantic Union have deliberately refrained from developing their formula for representation in any detail. The exact number and distribution of seats would depend upon the list of participating states. Under their proposal, however, representatives in the Union legislature would be elected by popular vote, would vote as individuals, and would be responsible to the people rather than to their governments.

With respect to voting, the Atlantic Union Committee has this to say:

It is likely * * * that the constitution of an Atlantic Union would provide for a two-thirds or even three-fourths vote on questions of particular concern to its

[23] Clarence Streit, Union Now, 1940, p. 142.

constituent peoples. This, together with provision for two houses in the Union's legislature, would afford protection to minority interests. Such protection, which could be carried as far as the people forming the Union believed desirable, would have to satisfy the American people in order to secure their ratification of the Union's constitution.[24]

VII. Regionalism and Voting Strength

Still another approach to the problem emerged in 1948 from the Committee to Frame a World Constitution. This committee, which conducted its studies at the University of Chicago, used the concept of regionalism as a basis for representation in a world assembly. The formula which they devised was designed to accomplish two major objectives: (1) To deemphasize national boundary lines and minimize the importance of the nation state; and (2) to develop a method of representation based on population, yet weighted in favor of those countries with the richest experience in democratic government.[25]

Under the committee's proposal a Federal convention would be convened consisting of delegates elected directly by the member states, one delegate for each million of population or major fraction thereof. This body would then subdivide into 9 electoral colleges, corresponding to 9 regions of the world, for the purpose of nominating and electing a President and the members of the world council or legislature. The council would be made up of 9 members from each region with 18 elected at large, or a total of 99. Representatives would vote as individuals rather than as members of instructed delegations.

The nine regions are delineated in the draft constitution as follows: [26]

(1) The continent of Europe and its islands outside the Russian area, together with the United Kingdom if the latter so decides, and with such overseas English- or French- or Cape Dutch-speaking communities of the British Commonwealth of Nations or the French Union as decide to associate (this whole area here tentatively denominated "Europa");

(2) The United States of America, with the United Kingdom if the latter so decides, and such kindred communities of British, or Franco-British, or Dutch-British or Irish civilization and lineage as decide to associate (Atlantis);

(3) Russia, European and Asiatic, with such east Baltic or Slavic or south Danubian nations as associate with Russia (Eurasia);

(4) The Near and Middle East, with the states of north Africa, and Pakistan if the latter so decides (Afrasia);

(5) Africa, south of the Sahara, with or without the South African Union as the latter may decide;

(6) India, with Pakistan if the latter so decides;

(7) China, Korea, Japan, with the associate archipelagoes of the north- and mid-Pacific (Asia Major);

(8) Indochina and Indonesia, with Pakistan if the latter so decides, and with such other mid- and south-Pacific lands and islands as decide to associate (Austrasia);

(9) The Western Hemisphere south of the United States (Columbia).

---

[24] Atlantic Union Committee, 20 Questions on Atlantic Union, pp. 14–15.
[25] Preliminary draft of a World Constitution, University of Chicago, 1948.
[26] Ibid. art. V.

It will be noted that some of these regions would have a greater representation in proportion to population than others. Thus Asia Major (China, Japan, Korea), with about 25 percent of the world's population, would receive 11 percent of the total representation, while Columbia (Latin America) would have the same number of representatives with only about 7 percent of the population. The three regions of the Western World—Europa, Atlantis, and Columbia—with about a fifth of the world's population, would be given one-third of the representation.

Admittedly, this device of grouping kindred nations or cultures together into regions for representation and voting purposes would have certain theoretical advantages which some of the other proposals would not have. Certainly no single region, and no bloc of 2 or 3 regions, could dominate the world assembly or prevent the approval of desirable measures. Moreover, the formula provides a basis for representation other than mere population statistics without undue discrimination against any area of the world.

Space will not permit an analysis of the plan's weak points. Obviously it is a very complex proposal which assumes that people and governments are willing to move much further in the direction of world government and regionalism than is probably the case. There is little in the experience of the United Nations to date that would indicate that states are ready to pool their voting power with their neighbors on a purely regional basis. Proximity does not necessarily result in compatibility between states.

VIII. Other Proposals

Certain groups have also suggested that representation and voting be weighted on the basis of population and other factors. For the most part, they do not explain in any detail the procedure by which this might be accomplished.

The United World Federalists have long favored a system of "balanced representation" in their projected world legislative assembly. In 1949, Alan Cranston, speaking for the UWF stated:

> It is unlikely that a system of representation based solely upon population, with no upper or lower limits, would be more acceptable or desirable, for then India and China, with their vast millions, would receive a voting power out of proportion to their present role in the world.
>
> Again, we do not seek to provide a precise formula, but we suggest that in addition to population other factors might be taken into account, such as economic development and education.[27]

In 1950, in his testimony before the Senate Foreign Relations Committee, Mr. Cranston suggested that such factors as population, industrial capacity, monetary contribution and regional formulas ought to be taken into account. Other representatives of UWF have expressed, in general terms, the same point of view.[28]

In their so-called plan B, which is designed to remove what they regard as certain imperfections in the U. N. Charter, the British Parliamentary Group for World Government arrive at the same con-

[27] U. S. House of Representatives, Committee on Foreign Affairs, To Seek Development of the United Nations into a World Federation, hearings on H. Con Res. 64, 1949, p. 163.

[28] U. S. Senate, Committee on Foreign Relations, Revision of the United Nations Charter, hearings, 1950, pp. 523 and 127.

clusion. Plan B recommends that the governments of member states of the U. N. take action—

to improve the representative character of the Assembly, by, for example, introducing the principle of weighted voting possibly by establishing a bicameral Assembly and relating representation in one of the chambers to economic and/or population factors.[29]

The means for implementing the proposal are not indicated in the plan.

IX. Representatives Voting as Individuals

One common feature of the so-called supranational proposals is the proposition that representatives to a world assembly should be popularly elected and should cast their votes as individuals. While such a recommendation might be considered essential in any scheme of world government where state sovereignty is relegated to the background, if it were transplanted to the General Assembly, as suggested in the Clark-Sohn proposals, it would involve a fundamental change in the character of the United Nations.

If some kind of weighted representation should be considered for the General Assembly, it will be particularly important to keep the problem of responsibility in mind. At present our delegation to the General Assembly is appointed by the Government, is responsible to the Government, and votes in accordance with instructions issued by the Government. The lines of responsibility are clear and direct. Any other arrangement might well result in an unmanageable dispersal of power that would prove embarrassing both to the member states and to the U. N.

Advocates of world government pointed out that in the beginning elected delegates probably would vote in national blocs but as time goes on this tendency would be overcome. "It is true," state the Clark-Sohn proposals:

that the representatives of a particular nation would tend to vote the same way on issues of great importance to that nation * * *. It can, however, be expected that there would develop in the course of time a spirit of representing the interests of the world as a whole rather than those of individual nations; and that the representatives would more and more tend to vote in accordance with their judgment as to the best interests of all the peoples as in the case of national parliaments where the interests of the whole nation have become of no less importance than the interests of a particular section or group.[30]

The arguments against such an arrangement in an organization of sovereign states are apparent. The first has to do with the relations between democratic countries and totalitarian systems. Democratic delegates might possibly vote as individuals but it is inconceivable that the representatives of totalitarian states would ever be in a position to do so.

In the second place, the lack of discipline would be harmful to United Nations programs. What good would come from our delegation voting for a General Assembly resolution if, after it was passed, our Government refused to support it?

Finally, with the conduct of diplomacy as complicated as it is, states find it extremely difficult to develop a unified, cohesive foreign

---

[29] Report of the Second London Parliamentary Conference on World Government, p. 108.
[30] Clark and Sohn, op. cit., pp. 47–48.

policy even under the best of conditions. It would seem unlikely that most governments and the people they represent would want to abdicate their responsibility for the conduct of foreign relations to persons voting as "individuals" and thus beyond their control in an international organization.

X. Concluding Comments

In spite of the growing importance of voting in the General Assembly, this remains one of the great unexplored areas of the charter. Very little research has been done on this problem; very few practical suggestions have been made for improving the present situation. Nor does the experience of international organizations in the past shed much helpful light on the subject. It is apparent that the whole question needs very careful analysis before our Government can be in a position to consider seriously any specific proposals for changing the present charter provisions.

Summarizing what has been said above, however, two conclusions seem inescapable. In the first place, there are striking inequalities among the 60 U. N. members with respect to population, armed strength, national income, territory, contribution to the U. N. and other factors. The present system of awarding one vote to each state thus confers upon the smaller countries a voting strength far out of proportion to their influence in world affairs.

In the second place, if any departure is made from the principle of one-state-one-vote it will have to be a modest one with a relatively low ceiling placed on the voting power of the great nations. For the small states, having been in a favorable voting position for many years, can be expected to put up a vigorous fight to block any proposal which would seriously alter what is in effect their privileged status in the General Assembly.

This does not mean that a satisfactory quid pro quo could not be arranged. It would appear that the problem of weighted voting is closely related to the further revision of the charter. The small states, in other words, might be persuaded to make significant concessions in this respect if the General Assembly is given sufficient authority to take vigorous and effective action on behalf of world peace.

There is presented below, by way of illustration, an approach to the problem of weighted voting which is based, in part, on past experience and which does not constitute a drastic departure from present procedures. The idea is not final in form; rather it is presented as a tentative suggestion in order to stimulate further discussion of an important issue.

It is suggested in this illustration, in line with Mr. Dulles' proposal outlined above, that the vote of each state in the General Assembly be counted twice; once on the basis of one vote for each state and the second time on the basis of a weighted formula. A majority of each of the votes would be required for the General Assembly to reach a decision.

ILLUSTRATIVE WEIGHTED VOTING FORMULA—UNITED NATIONS GENERAL ASSEMBLY VOTING STRENGTH IN ORDER OF POPULATION, FINANCIAL CONTRIBUTION, AND COMBINED WEIGHTED VOTES

Population vote

Rank	Country	Population [31] (thousands)	Vote	Percent of population vote
1	China	463,493	5	
2	India	367,000	5	
3	United States	156,981	5	2.87
4	U. S. S. R.	151,663	5	
5	United Kingdom	[33] 122,537	5	
6	France	[33] 91,128	5	
7	Indonesia	78,163	4	
8	Pakistan	75,842	4	
9	Brazil	54,477	4	
10	Ukraine	30,960	4	2.30
11	Mexico	26,922	4	
12	Poland	24,977	4	
13	Egypt	21,425	4	
14	Turkey	20,934	4	
15	Philippines	20,631	4	
16	Iran	19,798	3	
17	Thailand	19,193	3	
18	Burma	18,859	3	
19	Argentina	18,054	3	
20	Yugoslavia	16,729	3	
21	Ethiopia	15,000	3	
22	Canada	14,430	3	
23	Union of South Africa	12,912	3	
24	Czechoslovakia	12,340	3	
25	Afghanistan	12,000	3	1.73
26	Colombia	11,768	3	
27	Netherlands	10,377	3	
28	Peru	8,864	3	
29	Belgium	8,706	3	
30	Australia	8,649	3	
31	Greece	7,761	3	
32	Sweden	7,125	3	
33	Saudi Arabia	7,000	3	
34	Chile	5,932	3	
35	Cuba	5,927	3	
36	Byelorussia	5,568	3	
37	Venezuela	5,280	3	
38	Iraq	5,100	3	

Contribution vote

Rank	Country	Contribution [32] (dollars)	Vote	Percent of contribution vote
1	United States	13,765,290	5	
2	U. S. S. R.	5,84[illegible],950	5	
3	United Kingdom	4,047,400	5	3.05
4	France	2,374,750	5	
5	China	2,321,060	5	
6	India	1,404,200	4	
7	Canada	1,362,900	4	
8	Ukraine	776,440	4	
9	Australia	722,750	4	
10	Poland	714,490	4	2.44
11	Sweden	681,450	4	
12	Brazil	578,200	4	
13	Argentina	578,200	4	
14	Belgium	569,940	4	
15	Netherlands	516,250	4	
16	Czechoslovakia	433,650	3	
17	Denmark	322,140	3	
18	Union of South Africa	322,140	3	
19	Mexico	309,750	3	
20	Pakistan	309,750	3	
21	Turkey	268,450	3	
22	Indonesia	247,800	3	
23	Byelorussia	206,500	3	
24	Norway	206,500	3	
25	New Zealand	198,240	3	1.83
26	Egypt	194,110	3	
27	Philippines	185,850	3	
28	Yugoslavia	181,720	3	
29	Colombia	169,330	3	
30	Venezuela	161,070	3	
31	Cuba	140,420	3	
32	Chile	136,290	3	
33	Iran	115,640	3	
34	Greece	86,730	2	
35	Peru	74,340	2	
36	Thailand	74,340	2	
37	Uruguay	74,340	2	

Combined vote

Rank	Country	Vote	Percent of combined vote
	China	10	
	U. S. S. R.	10	
1	United Kingdom	10	2.96
	United States	10	
	France	10	
2	India	9	2.66
	Brazil	8	
3	Poland	8	2.37
	Ukraine	8	
	Argentina	7	
	Australia	7	
	Belgium	7	
	Canada	7	
	Egypt	7	
	Indonesia	7	
4	Mexico	7	2.07
	Netherlands	7	
	Pakistan	7	
	Philippines	7	
	Sweden	7	
	Turkey	7	
	Byelorussia	6	
	Chile	6	
	Colombia	6	
	Cuba	6	
5	Czechoslovakia	6	1.78
	Iran	6	
	Union of South Africa	6	
	Venezuela	6	
	Yugoslavia	6	
	Afghanistan	5	
	Burma	5	
	Denmark	5	
	Ethiopia	5	
	Greece	5	

39	Yemen	4,500	2	1.15
40	Denmark	4,334	2	
41	Syria	3,381	2	
42	Ecuador	3,350	2	
43	Norway	3,327	2	
44	Haiti	3,200	2	
45	Bolivia	3,089	2	
46	Guatemala	2,938	2	
47	Uruguay	2,365	2	
48	Domican Republic	2,236	2	
49	New Zealand	1,995	2	
50	El Salvador	1,986	2	
51	Liberia	1,648	2	
52	Israel	1,607	2	
53	Honduras	1,513	2	
54	Paraguay	1,464	2	
55	Lebanon	1,320	2	
56	Nicaragua	1,128	2	
57	Costa Rica	850	1	.57
58	Panama	841	1	
59	Luxembourg	301	1	
60	Iceland	148	1	
	Total	2,012,026	175	--------

38	Israel	70,210	2	1.22
39	Burma	53,690	2	
40	Iraq	49,560	2	
41	Ethiopia	41,300	2	
42	Afghanistan	33,040	2	
43	Syria	33,040	2	
44	Saudi Arabia	28,910	2	
45	Guatemala	28,910	2	
46	Bolivia	24,780	2	
47	El Salvador	24,780	2	
48	Luxembourg	24,780	2	
49	Dominican Republic	20,650	2	
50	Lebanon	20,650	2	
51	Panama	20,650	2	
52	Costa Rica	16,520	1	.61
53	Ecuador	16,520	1	
54	Haiti	16,520	1	
55	Honduras	16,520	1	
56	Iceland	16,520	1	
57	Liberia	16,520	1	
58	Paraguay	16,520	1	
59	Nicaragua	16,520	1	
60	Yemen	16,520	1	
	Total	41,300,000	164	

6	**Iraq**	**5**	**1.48**
	New Zealand	**5**	
	Norway	**5**	
	Peru	**5**	
	Saudi Arabia	**5**	
	Thailand	**5**	
7	**Bolivia**	**4**	**1.18**
	Dominican Republic	**4**	
	El Salvador	**4**	
	Guatemala	**4**	
	Israel	**4**	
	Lebanon	**4**	
	Syria	**4**	
	Uruguay	**4**	
8	**Ecuador**	**3**	**.89**
	Haiti	**3**	
	Honduras	**3**	
	Liberia	**3**	
	Luxembourg	**3**	
	Nicaragua	**3**	
	Panama	**3**	
	Paraguay	**3**	
	Yemen	**3**	
9	**Costa Rica**	**2**	**.59**
	Iceland	**2**	
	Total	339	

[31] Statistical Office of the U. N., Population and Vital Statistics Reports, Series A, vol. VI, No. 2, New York, April 1954.

[32] U. S. Senate Subcommittee on the United Nations, Review of the United Nations Charter, 83d Cong., 2d sess., Doc. No. 87, Washington, 1954, pp. 719–720.

[33] Aggregate figure, including non-self-governing territories and dependencies. In this illustrative formula, France, a permanent member of the Security Council is awarded 5 votes even though her total population falls below the 100 million suggested for the first category of states.

In the weighted voting formula here presented, only two criteria are taken into account; a state's population and its contribution to the United Nations. Each state would be awarded from 2 to 10 votes with the scale running from 1 to 5 for each criterion. Votes would be awarded for population in accordance with the following scale: States under 1 million would receive 1 vote; 1 to 5 million, 2 votes; 5 to 20 million, 3 votes; 20 to 100 million, 4 votes; and over 100 million, 5 votes. For U. N. contributions the scale would be: States contributing less than $20,000 to the regular U. N. budget would receive 1 vote; $20,000 to $100,000, 2 votes; $100,000 to $500,000, 3 votes; $500,000 to $2 million, 4 votes; and all over $2 million, 5 votes.

Several observations may be made about this kind of illustrative weighted voting system.

1. It would increase the relative voting strength of certain countries—particularly the great nations—but it would not materially alter the balance of power in the General Assembly.

2. The Latin American and the Arab States would lose somewhat, as indeed they would in almost any system of weighted voting that could be devised. Thus, the 20 Latin American states, with a total of 91 out of the 338 votes in the General Assembly, would command only 27 percent of the votes instead of the strategic one-third they now control. The 6 Arab States would drop from 10 percent to roughly 8 percent.

3. Unless the votes of the Ukraine and Byelorussia were discounted somewhat, as suggested earlier in this study, the Soviet bloc would pick up voting strength. The 5 Communist states now control 8 percent of the votes; under the illustrative schedule they would claim 11 percent. The so-called neutralist states of India, Indonesia, and Burma would also add slightly to their voting power.

4. Two other groups of states, generally inclined to support American policy, would either hold their own or else gain voting strength. The 12 NATO states in the U. N. would continue to hold roughly one-fifth of the votes. The seven British Commonwealth countries would increase their total from 11.6 percent to 15 percent.

5. If other criteria, such as national income, productivity and foreign trade, are taken into account, the states of Western Europe and the British Commonwealth countries would improve their relative standings somewhat. The more complicated the formula, however, the more opposition it is likely to encounter.

6. In this chart the votes are calculated on the basis of the contribution of each member to the *regular* U. N. budget. Clearly, this is not the most satisfactory measuring stick. It would be far better—though perhaps not very practical—if a schedule could be devised that would reflect the ability and the willingness of U. N. members to contribute manpower, military equipment and supplies, as well as bases and other facilities toward the maintenance of world peace.

Thus far there has been little congressional comment on the concept of weighted voting. Two Senators, however, have declared themselves in opposition. Senator Guy M. Gillette, a member of the Special Subcommittee on the U. N. Charter, told the American Society of International Law in April 1954 that he was strongly against it. Senator John Bricker of Ohio in a speech before the Iowa Bar Association in Des Moines on June 4, 1954, said he would oppose weighted voting because it "paves the way for vesting the General Assembly with legislative authority" and is a move in the direction of transforming the U. N. "into a limited or full world government." Additional comment can be expected as the issue becomes sharper in the public mind.

Voting in the General Assembly is grimly serious business. Any significant realinement of votes might have an adverse impact upon our policy—either now or at some time in the unpredictable future.

Before we urge the principle of weighted voting, therefore, we must make certain, through a careful analysis of the facts, that such a move is in our national interest. We must make sure that we are not opening a Pandora's box from which a host of unpleasant results might flow to plague us in the years to come.

Clearly, any formula that would result in a substantial decrease in voting power for the 20 Latin American countries would be open to grave objections on our part. Generally speaking, these nations have been the most consistent supporters of our policy in the United Nations and we hope they will remain so.

Our national position on this issue must also be conditioned by the probability that a number of states—including the relatively great powers of Germany, Japan, and Italy—may be admitted to the U. N. within the next few years. With a possible increase in membership that may run as high as 30 percent, Assembly voting patterns could undergo drastic changes.

Up to the present time, the United States has been able to retain its position of leadership in the General Assembly through the logic of its argument and the justice of its cause. In a political organization where each state has one vote, we have been able to rally the small countries to the cause of the free world.

Theoretically, there may be logical reasons for supporting a system of weighted voting for the General Assembly. From a practical point of view, however, it might be better to let well enough alone.

One of the popular arguments in favor of revising the system of voting in the General Assembly has to do with the extent to which bloc voting has emerged in the Assembly. Complaints about bloc voting are often directed at the so-called African Bloc. The following excerpts from a book on African voting patterns in the General Assembly—Thomas Hovet, Jr., "How the African Bloc Uses its Votes," *Current* (March, 1964) pp. 26–27—addresses itself to this question. In addition to suggesting that the African Bloc is not nearly as cohesive as is generally supposed, Hovet emphasizes the role of negotiations in the pursuit of political goals. Negotiations more than voting seem to determine political outcomes in the United Nations today and this might also be expected to be true in the revised system as suggested by Clark and Sohn. It is obvious, as well, that if there is to be a change in the weight of various national votes this would have to come about through the process of negotiation. This is another way to talk about the practice of Parliamentary Diplomacy in the life of the Assembly.

THOMAS HOVET, JR.

How the African Bloc Uses Its Vote

"Our analysis of the voting indicates that the African group does not present a completely united front on even African issues, though it does reach a high degree of cohesion on them. Moreover, its policy of confining itself primarily to African issues gives the group a basis for negotiation in the Assembly. The fact that it appears to use its solidarity for negotiating agreements on resolutions shows a realistic approach, which recognizes actual power relationships within the United Nations.

"True, the group sometimes attempts to pass resolutions through its sheer number of votes—resolutions that clash with the policies of the major powers in the United Nations. But if it did this oftener, its influence would be more fictional than real. On the other hand if the group continues to use its potential votes to negotiate support for resolutions of primary concern to Africa, by offering its support on non-African issues of primary concern to other states, its influence in the United Nations can be considerable.

"One difficulty encountered by the African states in such processes of negotiation is a reflection of their sudden emergence as independent states. Their fight for independence had so preoccupied them that, once they achieved it and became U.N. members, they were often uninformed or unprepared to take policy positions on U.N. issues not immediately comparable with their experiences.

"In 1960, for example, many of the newly independent African states were not prepared to take a stand on the question of the representation of China. In many instances their delegations did not even have instructions on this issue, although there could have been no question that the issue would be on the agenda of the General Assembly. When asked by other states either to support or to oppose a particular action on this question, the representatives of these newly independent states could only plead ignorance. . . .

"Charges of irresponsibility, then, can be leveled against the African states when it is evident that they are uninformed on issues that they are willing to support in exchange for support on issues of concern to them. Their constant argument is that their position on any African issue will be supported by all states who understand it and therefore recognize the logic of the African viewpoint. But for responsible negotiation most states do not expect to get voting support simply by crass bargaining on the principle of 'you vote for me; I'll vote for you.' Thus if the policy positions of the African states are to be respected, they must show respect for the policy positions of other states. And resolutions of the General Assembly will not have an impact or be implemented unless they are passed in an atmosphere of responsibility.

"The representatives of the African states do not always feel a responsibility to become informed on non-African issues before the United Nations. It comes as a shock when one learns in a luncheon conversation in the delegates' dining room that an African delegate is not aware that Korea is divided into North and South Korea. It is even more shocking to realize that this delegate represents an African state which has been a member of the United Nations for several years and that he normally holds an important policy position in his government. Still more important is the fact that he represents his delegation on the main committee concerned with discussion of the Korean question. Such an experience may not be typical, of course, but that it could happen at all creates doubts about the ability of the African states to play a responsible part in the United Nations.

"Clearly, therefore, if the United Nations, and especially the General Assembly, [is] to perform a role in diplomacy, it is very important that all states be informed on all issues or at least make an effort to become informed. Since each state has one vote in the General Assembly, regardless of its actual power or influence in international politics, and since resolutions can be passed by a simple or two-thirds majority vote, there is always the danger of passing resolutions that are wholly unrealistic. If such irresponsibility should prevail, the General Assembly could be eliminated as a factor in international relations.

"Yet for the African states, concerned as they are with issues of racial prejudice and colonial excesses, the General Assembly provides a diplomatic instrument that can be used to raise moral indignation and cultivate the support of public opinion. If the Assembly were reduced to a facade in international relations, its importance to Africa as an effective instrument of public diplomacy would be appreciably diminished. Thus the African states have a real stake in making sure that the Assembly reflects responsibly and realistically the existing power relationships.

Finally, in an official statement issued by the Department of State with the title "Would Weighted Voting Help the U.S.?" reprinted in *Current* (September, 1963) pp. 28–29—we look at the question of voting in the General Assembly as it is now officially viewed by the United States. Somewhat surprisingly, after a study involving an analysis of UN votes on various issues, the State Department concluded that it preferred to retain the present one-state-one-vote procedure because it worked out better for the United States than did any alternative scheme. It should be emphasized, however, that the State Department conclusion assumes that the General Assembly will not be given any substantial legislative authority within the immediate future. If the Assembly were to assume legislative responsibilities then it is quite possible that the State Department would revert to some scheme such as that suggested by Dulles in 1955 (see Wilcox above) or perhaps even to a set-up resembling that suggested by Clark and Sohn.

United States Department of State

WOULD WEIGHTED VOTING HELP THE U. S.?

Because of the wide disparity in size and resources among U.N. member states, the suggestion is often made that these differences be considered in voting procedures. How such a change would affect U.S. national interests is examined in a State Department report directed by Harlan Cleveland, Assistant Secretary of State for International Organization Affairs. The report was based on a computer study made by David Wainhouse, a former Deputy Assistant Secretary for United Nations Affairs. (See also Current, *June 1961, page 36.)*

"Among the proposals for changes in the United Nations are various suggestions for the introduction of some form of weighted voting in the General Assembly. Interest in this idea has increased as the membership of the United Nations has grown, changing its composition from that of a predominantly Western organization to one in which roughly half the members are from Africa and Asia. This, together with the shift of emphasis from the Security Council, where the great powers have a veto, to the General Assembly which operates on the one state-one vote principle, has aroused concern over the U.S. position in the U.N. . . .

"It has therefore been suggested that some form of weighted voting be instituted in the Assembly in order more accurately to reflect the varying ability of member states to carry out their international obligations under the Charter.

"The great powers recognized when the Charter was drafted that as a minority their position would have to be protected. This protection took the form of the veto in the Security Council, which alone has the power to take decisions binding on the members, except for the General Assembly's power to assess members under Article 17, and of the requirement of a two-thirds vote in the General Assembly for the adoption of recommendations on any important question.

"Over the years the position of the majority has generally coincided with that of the U.S. We have also been generally successful in securing the necessary two-thirds majority for recommendations that we could accept and in preventing a two-thirds majority for those we could not accept. The record is, in fact, remarkably good. However, there have been exceptions and it is reasonable to ask whether we would have done better under some form of weighted voting.

"We have therefore considered fifteen possible voting arrangements designed to reflect national power [and], . . . either separately or in combination, the factors of national income, the U.N. scale of assessment which is based on several selected factors, and population.

"When applied against a sampling of 178 major roll-call votes on a varied range of issues beginning in 1954, when there were sixty U.N. members, and ending in 1961, when there were 104 members, none of the weighted arrangements produced general results as favorable to U.S. interests as the one state-one vote principle. This is because the over-all success of U.S. policies in the U.N. has in very large measure depended upon the support of the smaller states and it is these smaller states whose voting power is heavily reduced under any weighted voting system.

"On issues requiring a simple majority on which the United States has voted in the affirmative, weighted voting on the average reduces the 'yes' to 'no' ratio from 4:1 to 3:1—a reduction of roughly 25 per cent.

"On issues requiring a two-thirds majority on which the United States has voted in the affirmative, weighted voting on the average reduces the 'yes' to 'no' ratio from 6:1 to 4:1—a reduction of roughly 33 and one-third per cent.

"On issues requiring a simple majority on which the United States has voted in the negative, the 'yes' to 'no' ratio is reduced on the average by weighted voting from 1½:1 to 1:1—a reduction of roughly 33 and one-third per cent.

"On issues requiring a two-thirds majority on which the United States voted in the negative, the 'yes' to 'no' ratio is reduced on the average by weighed voting from 1½:1 to 1:1. While this reduction is the same as the reduction in cases where a simple majority is required, it is not of much significance in this instance since a 2:1 ratio would be needed for the issue to pass.

"Thus while there would appear to be some advantages to the United States in weighted voting in the case of issues on which it votes negatively, in contrast to those on which the United States votes affirmatively, there is no over-all advantage since on the issues tested (excluding abstentions) the United States voted negatively only 35 per cent of the time.

"In each of the plans tested, the United States and its NATO allies gain in voting strength as does the Soviet Union with the other Communist states. In each of the plans, the gains of the United States and its NATO allies and the gains of the Communist states are at the expense of the Latin-American and the smaller Afro-Asian states. The former and some of the latter are our treaty allies and many others among the latter support the United States position on issues crucial to the West.

"Any change in the voting arrangements in the General Assembly would require amendment of the Charter which, in turn, requires approval of two-thirds of the members of the United Nations, including the five permanent members of the Security Council. A two-thirds vote is highly unlikely since the Latin Americans and Afro-Asians, the principal losers under any one of the fifteen plans, constitute well over half of the total U.N. membership.

"This fact and the fact that any initiative on our part to bring about a departure from the one state-one vote principle would arouse widespread resistance and resentment among the losing states point clearly to the conclusion that it is not in the United States' interest to raise the issue in the absence of any clear and overriding advantage to the United States in making the attempt." ("Weighted Voting," Study, U. S. State Department, June 2, 1963)

NOTES AND QUESTIONS

1. Schemes for weighted voting are especially relevant to the workability of the Uniting for Peace Resolution and other peace-keeping approaches. Those who contribute most of the materials, men and money are likely to want to have a greater say in how the operation is set up and carried out. To the extent that the superpowers are now heavily populated and do or will contribute to peace-keeping, the Clark-Sohn proposal for weighted voting may mean that they would find the scheme acceptable. Smaller states that retain some voting power and that are not faced by a veto might also be willing to accept such a scheme, especially if they were given a real stake in the venture, such as significant relief in the terms of international trade or greatly increased help with economic development. To proceed by constitutional reform, as Clark and Sohn propose, it is not enough to make the undertaking acceptable to the superpowers. Almost every state must be convinced, enough so as to overcome political inertia, that their total interests, and not just their special interest in a peaceful world, will be significantly benefited by the ratification of the proposal. The Clark-Sohn plan rejects the notion that a stable peace system can arise if the interests of the Great Powers are taken care of. The major emphasis on the World Development Authority is indicative of their

concern for all states. The use of population rather than some criterion of relative power, such as gross national product, suggests perhaps that they regard other criteria as too invidious, and that they seek to bring into being an international system in which the relative power of states would be a less significant variable.

2. What is the importance of relative power in a world where neither violence nor its threat can be employed? What about wealthy states with relatively small populations—those of Europe or Canada? What does Canada gain by the adoption of the Clark-Sohn plan?——or Sweden? What do they lose?
3. A long review of *World Peace through World Law* by a Soviet author, O. Vahsilyef, published in 1961 in the periodical, *Soviet State and Law*, included the following comment on the weighted representation proposals of Clark and Sohn: "In all, the Assembly, according to the author's count, would be composed of approximately 600 representatives with the right to vote. Here the circumstances attract our attention that in the majority of these six groups the predominant position is assured to the countries of the Western-military political bloc. That is, the situation in the second (with such countries), the third, the fifth, and the sixth groups. In light of this, it is obvious that the criterion put forward by the Office of Representation in the General Assembly does not reflect realistically the present alignment of forces in the world arena."

   Assuming that the principles suggested by Clark and Sohn should be operative in the long run, is it possible to devise some transition voting proposal that would meet the objection made by Vahsilyef and would, at the same time, move toward the eventual adoption of the Clark-Sohn principles? Is Vahsilyef making a legitimate objection? What is the present alignment of forces?
4. Do you think that Britain and France are likely to accept a representation scheme that places them on a par with Brazil, Indonesia and Pakistan, but below China, India, the United States and the U.S.S.R.? Will the small powers who now have an equal vote be willing to give up their present strength? Are there any governments that are likely to feel that they are not being given sufficient voting influence? Is there anything which can be done to satisfy them?
5. Compare the regions that were designated in the Draft World Constitution in *Common Cause*, vol. I, no. 9 (Committee to Form a World Constitution, Chicago, March, 1948) pp. 332–333, with those used in proposals for expanding the Security Council. What differences are there between them? Which do you prefer? Why?
6. Which scheme of representation and voting would you support now? Assuming that the General Assembly may be increasingly acting in a legislative capacity, which scheme would you prefer?
7. Clark and Sohn present reasons for taking a series of transition steps from the present system in which delegates to the Assembly are appointed by the executive in each Member State to the eventual election of representatives either by national legislatures or by direct popular vote. See WPTWL, pp. 32–33. Wilcox is critical of this proposal. Does the proposal seem sound to you? What problems or dangers do you see in the Clark-Sohn proposal? Can it be strengthened? Can you think of a better one?——better for what sort of reasons?

The Secretariat and the Secretary-General

6

In addition to the Security Council and the General Assembly, the other organ of the United Nations with direct responsibility and some independent authority in the area of international peace and security is the Secretariat. Unlike either the General Assembly or the Security Council, however, this authority is vested in an office held by an individual whose ultimate obligations are to the Organization rather than to a political organ made up of representatives from Member States. Controversy about the nature of the independent authority of the Secretary-General and about his ability to act as an impartial official of the Organization has precipitated major political and legal issues concerning this Office.

Appointed by the General Assembly upon recommendation of the Security Council, the Secretary-General, in addition to being the chief administrative officer of the Organization, is empowered under Article 99 to "bring to the attention of the Security Council any matters which, in his opinion, threaten the maintenance of international peace and security." Many, including the authors represented in this chapter, have argued that this language supports the view that the founders of the Organization intended an independent executive capable of acting on behalf of the Organization. The contrary view contends that this authority is very narrowly circumscribed in Article 99.

Although acknowledging that many specialized international organizations—most notably the International Labor Organization under Albert Thomas—have had vigorous executives who were permitted and even encouraged to assume individual policy initiatives, those who argue that Article 99 restricts the authority of the Secretary-General point to the exclusively administrative role of Sir Edward Drummond during his tenure as the Secretary-General of the League of Nations. Sir Edward's behavior in this Office is considered a precedent for an administrative officer in a general international organization which has competence in the area of international peace and security. A primary focus of the investigation in this chapter will be to discover the extent to which the Office of the Secretary-General is and might continue to be a source of executive leadership in the world community, and, on this basis, to assess the opposing positions in the cold war controversy that has been carried on about this subject.

It is difficult to know what effect the presence of Article 99 has had on the rather remarkable role played by those who have held the position of Secretary-General. As will be made clear in the selections, Article 99 has been actually invoked on only a few occasions, and at first sight, the initiatives permitted by the provision are quite limited. The *right* to demand a hearing before the Security Council does constitute, however, a considerable measure of political status since, with this single exception, only Member States are granted this right. Furthermore, the implied power to investigate situations to enable the Secretary-General to make a judgment as to applicability of Article 99 permits a latitude of action without requiring actual invocation. Certainly, too, the men who held the position—Trygve Lie, Dag Hammarskjöld, and U Thant—have each been acutely aware of the fact that they possessed authority that emanated from a specific provision in the Charter; and they have felt it to be their duty and responsibility to speak and act whenever appropriate.

The other occasions of executive leadership by the Office arose as a consequence of a series of peace-keeping tasks given to the Secretary-General by the Security Council and General Assembly. It is in connection with these tasks that the issues connected with independent authority and capacity to act impartially have been joined. Whatever the merits of the contention that it is impossible for an international official to be neutral in a political system where there exist basic ideological and political issues between major units of the system, it seems clear that the original conception of the Office of Secretary-General was that of an international public servant owing primary loyalty and allegiance to the United Nations and not to an individual state or ideological bloc. The proposal for a troika administration made by Nikita Khrushchev in 1961 reflected the view that this original conception had proven impossible in practice. Although there is presently no challenge directed at the Office of the Secretary-General, is seems useful to review the arguments that arose in this controversy, for they recur again in the context of discussions about the organization and command of peace-keeping activities. Furthermore, these problems have cropped up even in the so-called administrative and technical activities of the Secretariat. In fact, the question as to what constitutes equitable representation by the Member

States in the Secretariat and in various special agencies connected with it, has been a constant source of discontent and complaint. This situation may continue for some time.

Finally, by way of introduction, it should be noted that Clark and Sohn suggest no major changes in the provisions of the Charter dealing with the Secretariat. Given the authority that they provide for the General Assembly and Security Council, this must be interpreted as a judgment on their part that the executive capacity needed in the world community should not, or will probably not evolve, in the main, from the Secretary-General. See WPTWL, pp. 183–186.

The following two readings intend to clarify the issues raised by this judgment on the part of Clark and Sohn, for they are concerned with the Charter definition of the Office of Secretary-General and with describing some of the prominent activities of this Office during the first seventeen years of the United Nations. The first selection—Charles H. Alexandrowicz' "The Secretary-General of the United Nations," *International and Comparative Law Quarterly,* vol. XI (British Institute of International and Comparative Law, 1962) pp. 1109–1130—consists of a thoughtful and lucid analysis of the provisions of the Charter relevant to the authority of the Office and to the practice that has given specific meaning or raised issues about the exercise of this authority. Written by a distinguished scholar, the article contains several concepts that are useful for evaluations of the authority of the Office.

THE SECRETARY-GENERAL OF THE UNITED NATIONS

By

CHARLES HENRY ALEXANDROWICZ

I. THE ADMINISTRATIVE AND POLITICAL THEORIES

IN an address delivered at Oxford University a few months before his death, Dag Hammarskjold referred to an interview which Walter Lippmann had had with Mr. Khrushchev in Moscow, and in which the latter stated that " while there are neutral countries, there are no neutral men." The interviewer drew from this statement the conclusion that it is now the view of the Soviet Government " that there can be no such thing as an impartial civil servant in this deeply divided world, and that the kind of political celibacy which the British theory of the civil servant calls for, is in international affairs a fiction." Mr. Hammarskjold's address contains an illuminating comment on the above conclusion and some of his arguments deserve to be briefly considered.[1] They also throw significant light on the position of the Secretary-General of the League of Nations and of the United Nations from the historical point of view.[2]

At the time when the Covenant of the League of Nations was being drafted, two divergent views on the conception of the Secretary-General appeared. One, represented by Lord Cecil, advocated the establishment apart from the two representative organs of the League (the Assembly and the Council), of a Chancellor as a statesman endowed with political powers and acting as the spokesman of international interests, and it was originally thought that Mr. Venizelos, the Greek Prime Minister, would be the best

[1] D. Hammarskjold, *The International Civil Servant in Law and in Fact* (Oxford U.P., 1961). The present article is primarily concerned with the administrative, political and constitutional concepts relating to the position of the Secretary-General in theory and practice (Articles 97, 98 and 99 of the U.N. Charter). It may be noted that the Soviet view (as stated by Mr. Lippmann) implies the classification of functions of the U.N. Secretariat into administrative and political functions, and it is obviously connected with the Soviet proposal to introduce the " troika " headship of the Secretariat in place of one Secretary-General, the extension of whose powers from the administrative to the political field has been heavily criticised.

[2] Ranshofen-Wertheimer, *The International Secretariat* (1945); J. L. Kunz, " The Legal Position of the Secretary-General of the United Nations " (1946) 40 Am.J.Int.L. 786.

candidate for the position. Adherents to the other view tended to discard the political element and proposed instead a purely administrative conception of the Secretary-General. In his address Mr. Hammarskjold draws our attention to a plan proposed by Sir Maurice (now Lord) Hankey who had been offered the post of Secretary-General of the League by the Allied Powers. This plan followed to a great extent the precedents established by the secretariats of the various public international unions created before World War I which were conceived on a purely administrative basis.[3]

The founder fathers of the League of Nations incorporated neither the political nor the administrative conception of the Secretary-General in the Covenant. Article 6 of the Covenant stated that the permanent Secretariat " shall comprise a Secretary-General and such secretaries and staff as may be required." The first Secretary-General was to be the person named in the annex to the Covenant. Article 7 (4) conferred on the Secretary-General and his staff diplomatic privileges and immunities but no reference was made to their international responsibility. In these circumstances all depended on the personality of the first Secretary-General who had not been tied constitutionally to any conception of his office. As is generally known, Sir Eric Drummond, the first Secretary-General, adhered throughout his term of service with the League to the administrative conception and never contemplated any significant extension of his secretarial functions to the political field. He never acted as a politician or statesman but remained within the limits of the functions of a permanent Under-Secretary of State exercising self-restraint and self-effacement and dealing with political matters only exceptionally behind the scenes. He never addressed the League Assembly, and in the Council he spoke as Secretary of a Committee only. Moreover, even in the application of the administrative conception to his office, he confined himself predominantly to ministerial functions and in fact the League of Nations (unlike the U.N.) rarely engaged in administrative activities of an operational character such as, for instance, technical assistance. On the other hand, Sir Eric Drummond must be considered the organiser of the first truly international secretariat and civil service. He recruited his staff on a purely international basis and introduced the principles of its international composition and international responsibility combined with the protection of the secretariat members by privileges and immunities on functional lines.

[3] *e.g.*, the UPU or ITU. These Secretariats were not operating on the basis of international responsibility.

Exclusive loyalty to the Organisation with the rejection of any extraneous instructions or influence was the most constructive legacy which the League Secretariat left to the United Nations.[4]

While the impact of Sir Eric Drummond's personality on the League Secretariat reflected the administrative (ministerial) conception of the Secretary-General, the influence of Albert Thomas, the first Director of the International Labour Office, led to the establishment of a position of active leadership within the I.L.O. Albert Thomas acted throughout his term of office as a mediator in great issues, remained in constant touch with member governments, to whom he wrote letters of principle (suggesting methods of implementation of duties under the I.L.O. constitution), and addressed the representative bodies of the I.L.O., making proposals to them and defending his policies. While Sir Eric Drummond and M. Avenol, his successor in the League of Nations, created the pattern of Chief Administrative Officer of the World Organisation, Albert Thomas appeared as an international statesman and as a spokesman of world interests and there is room to suppose that, had he been the Secretary-General of the League of Nations, he would have reacted in a statesmanlike manner to the dramatic events leading to the outbreak of World War II. Without entering into undue speculations on this point, it is fair to stress that the League of Nations and the I.L.O. practice created two separate patterns which had an impact on the drafting of the U.N. Charter and which continue to exercise an influence on developments within the U.N. For the administrative ("Drummond") theory constitutes even today a minimum basis on which a Secretary-General may rely or fall back if adverse circumstances connected with the dissent between the big Powers compel him to exercise restraint. The U.N. Charter, as we shall see, extended the administrative functions of the Secretary-General to the political field, no doubt enabling him (in the spirit of the "Albert Thomas" precedent) to act over and above his functions as Chief Administrative Officer.[5] But, though the Charter has institutionalised this extension of power, its exercise in practice remains one of the most controversial questions. A discussion of the relevant problems will be attempted by a comparative examination of Articles 97, 98 and 99 of the Charter with reference to U.N. theory and practice.

4 The League Secretariat also became a repository of expert knowledge which helped the Secretary-General to offer technical advice to member countries. The staff of the League developed great skill in preparing drafts of decisions and conventions and in applying formulas for the solution of conflicts.

5 *The United Nations Secretary-General, his Role in World Politics* (Fourteenth Report of the Commission to Study the Organisation of Peace, December 1961).

II. The Secretary-General as a Principal Organ of the U.N. and his Constitutional Powers

Before inquiring in some detail into the circumstances surrounding the adoption and operation of Articles 97, 98 and 99, it would be relevant to recall that the Secretary-General is one of the principal organs of the U.N. This statement is perhaps not quite correct as Article 7 (enumerating the principal organs) refers to the Secretariat and not to the Secretary-General. However, according to Article 97 the Secretariat is composed of the Secretary-General and the staff, and as the latter is appointed by the former and as the Secretary-General is alone responsible to the Organisation for the work of the Secretariat, he may rightly be considered a principal organ in the meaning of Article 7. The acquisition of such a status must entail significant consequences, for it is the principal organs which are primarily responsible for the attainment of the objectives of the Organisation and for the observance of the principles of the Charter and, if so, the Secretary-General appears as one of the organisational elements shouldering and sharing the responsibility for the constitutional behaviour of Member States. In this connection we shall later discuss the question whether it would be possible to conceive, apart from the administrative and political theories, a constitutional theory in the interpretation of the Secretary-General's position.

Article 97 defines the Secretary-General as the Chief Administrative Officer of the Organisation thus following the administrative conception. However Article 97 is followed by the provisions of Articles 98 and 99 which extend his jurisdiction to a wider field. Article 98 states that the Secretary-General " shall act in that capacity " (*i.e.*, as Chief Administrative Officer) in all meetings of the representative organs, *i.e.*, the General Assembly, the Security Council, the Economic and Social Council and the Trusteeship Council. Moreover, he " shall perform such other functions as are entrusted to him " by the representative organs. In this way the Secretary-General may receive, in addition to his administrative powers, also political powers. While these powers under Article 98 are *delegated*, he can act independently of any other organ under Article 99 which authorises him to " bring to the attention of the Security Council any matter which in his opinion may threaten the maintenance of international peace and security." Thus he may enter the scene as a spokesman of international interests and take action in the spirit of what has been tentatively called the " Thomas " doctrine.

Irrespective of the interaction of the administrative and political conceptions in the formulation of Articles 97, 98 and 99, the San

Francisco Conference was confronted with the question whether the Secretariat should be headed by the Secretary-General alone or by him and additional Deputy Secretaries-General. Originally the addition of four Deputies was suggested and the mode of their election (appointment) was to be the same as that of the Secretary-General, *i.e.*, by the General Assembly on the recommendation of the Security Council. The U.S.S.R. proposed five Deputies, *i.e.*, one to act as alternate to the Secretary-General, and the others to serve with the four representative organs. The objection raised by the opponents of this proposal was that its acceptance would jeopardise the international character of the Secretariat. Each of the Deputies elected in the same way as the Secretary-General and drawn from one or other of the power groups was likely to remain loyal to his supporting group instead of being truly internationally responsible as the Secretary-General who is elected (appointed) by the consensus of the big Powers. The Committee considering the problem voted by fifteen votes to thirteen in favour of referring to Deputies in the Charter but, as there was no two-thirds majority (required for the acceptance of the proposal), the matter was dropped.[6] Thus the founder fathers of the U.N. made it clear in Article 97 that the Secretary-General is the sole head of the Secretariat and that the idea of any collective headship would not be tolerable. The U.S.S.R., following their view that there are no neutral men and no impartial international civil servants, reiterated recently their proposal for a " troika " in the Secretariat, *i.e.*, the replacement of one Secretary-General by a committee of three members. This proposal is not reconcilable with the provisions of the Charter and would no doubt be turned down if ever an amendment of the Charter were to be sought for the establishment of a secretarial triumvirate. We shall return to this question later.

III. The Formal and Informal Application of Powers under Article 99

While the two Secretaries-General of the League of Nations had fallen short of international leadership, Mr. Trygve Lie, the first U.N. Secretary-General, extended his administrative functions significantly to the political field, acting partly under Article 98 and partly under Article 99 of the U.N. Charter.[7] Article 98 refers, apart from delegated political functions, to annual reports which the Secretary-General has to submit to the General Assembly. In

[6] In the next voting the proposal introduced by the U.S.S.R. was entirely defeated. As to the relevant documents see: *Documents of the U.N. Conference on International Organisation*, San Francisco, 1945, particularly Vol. VII. Commission I (General Provisions).

[7] S. M. Schwebel, *The Secretary-General of the United Nations* (1952).

these reports Mr. Trygve Lie never confined himself to giving a mere chronology of events or to a bureaucratic description of the work of the U.N. Quite to the contrary, in course of time the annual reports became balance sheets of the successes and failures of the Organisation, and Mr. Trygve Lie recorded his reactions to major problems of world politics.

The annual reports contain, apart from the detailed report (second part), an Introduction in which the Secretary-General pronounces his judgment and opinion on international conflicts and on economic and social problems. Particular attention may be drawn to Mr. Hammarskjold's reports in which he went one step further and started outlining a U.N. doctrine. Details of this doctrine, particularly the development of a theory of U.N. multilateral diplomacy, can also be found in his numerous addresses given in various centres in Europe and in the U.S.A.,[8] of which the last and most significant was his address at Oxford University given on May 30, 1961. In this way the first and second Secretaries-General of the U.N. committed themselves to definite views on the work of the U.N. As stated above, they also carried out delegated political functions under Article 98 and exercised independent political initiative under Article 99.

The discussion of the two Articles cannot be undertaken separately as there is a constant interaction of the two in U.N. practice. However the examination of Article 99 raises a number of controversial problems which deserve our special attention.[9] It may be recalled that the original drafts of the U.N. Charter (submitted by the State Department) proposed, first, a Secretary-General as permanent Chairman of the Executive Committee and the Council, endowed with political initiative. Some of the later drafts proposed a separate Secretary-General (Director-General) in charge of administrative affairs only and a President of the U.N. who would preside over the Council and exercise extensive political functions. When the idea of a political President was ultimately dropped, the right to political initiative devolved on the Secretary-General who thus combined administrative (Article 97) and independent political

[8] See *Three University Addresses on Service to the Community of Nations*, (U.N. June 1955); "The Vital Role of the U.N. in a Diplomacy of Reconciliation," *U.N. Review*, May 1958; "Do we Need the U.N.?" *U.N. Review*, June 1959; "The Development of a Constitutional Framework for International Co-operation," *U.N. Review*, June 1960. See also: The Vital Role of the U.N. in a Diplomacy of Reconciliation; The U.N. and the Major Problems which face the World Community; Why the U.N.?—An Answer; Man's Greatest Challenge (Four Addresses by D. Hammarskjold (U.N., 1958)).

[9] S. M. Schwebel, "The Origins and Development of Article 99 of the Charter' (1951) 28 Brit. Year Book Int.L. 371; Eric Stein, "Mr. Hammarskjold, the Charter Law and the Future Role of the U.N. Secretary-General" (1962) 56 Am.J.Int.L. 1.

functions (Article 99), apart from delegated political functions (Article 98). It is in relation to the prerogatives under Article 99 that Sir Eric Drummond (Lord Perth) once remarked that, had he had Article 99 at his disposal, the position of the Secretary-General of the League of Nations would have developed differently.

It has been stated above that, according to Article 99, the Secretary-General *may* bring to the attention of the Security Council any matter which *in his opinion* may threaten the maintenance of international peace and security. Thus he is given a double discretion. Before going to the Security Council, he has to decide whether *in his opinion* the matter would be eligible to be put on the Agenda of the Council. But, even if he comes to the conclusion that this is the case, he need not necessarily submit the matter to the Council. Article 99 makes it clear that he may do so, but that there is no duty on him to go so far. At the San Francisco Conference the problem of the right or duty of the Secretary-General to act under Article 99 was ventilated, but the idea of imposing a duty on him was definitely abandoned. It will be seen later that the consequences of the above formulation of Article 99 proved far reaching.

The first Secretary-General of the U.N. only once invoked *formally* Article 99, *i.e.*, in the Korean crisis. The reluctance of Mr. Trygve Lie to resort more often to the provisions of this Article in practice is quite understandable if it is kept in mind that if the Secretary-General takes the initiative (on the basis of an opinion formed by him in case of emergency) and asks the Security Council to put the matter on its Agenda, and if the Security Council subsequently rejects his initiative and pronounces a different opinion in the matter, his prestige would be badly affected. Except in extreme emergency cases when he would take action even at the risk of not seeing eye to eye with the Security Council, the Secretary-General is not likely to take formally the initiative in isolation from the prevailing opinion of the Council. However, the Secretary-General, prior to forming an opinion, has an implied right to collect information, to make investigations and even to engage in negotiations. Thus Article 99 gives him an investigating and exploratory power, though its exercise does not impose a duty on him to invoke it formally and to go to the Security Council. If so, the Secretary-General may combine the above investigating and exploratory powers with suggesting courses of action, proposing solutions, endorsing policies, etc. In this respect there is an essential difference between United Nations practice as initiated by its first and second Secretaries-General, for while Mr. Trygve Lie acted on Article 99 in a statesmanlike way, mostly in the framework of

U.N. " parliamentary " (public) diplomacy, Mr. Hammarskjold appeared as the architect of a new conception, that of combined public and private multilateral diplomacy which he put into practice with the utmost skill and ingenuity.

The first test case relating to the informal use of Article 99 was that of the conflict between the U.S.S.R. and Iran (1946) when Mr. Trygve Lie submitted to the Security Council a legal opinion advocating, in view of the understanding reached by the parties, withdrawal of the matter from the Agenda. In this move the Secretary-General enjoyed the support of the U.S.S.R. and incurred criticism from the U.S.A. Even more characteristic was his intervention in the Greek question when the U.S.A. proposed that the Security Council should establish a Commission composed of three members nominated by the Secretary-General to investigate the Greek frontier situation. This was obviously a case of suggested delegation of political functions under Article 98. At this stage the Secretary-General intervened by stating that, should the proposal not be carried by the Security Council, he would still reserve his right to act under Article 99. Again he was supported by the U.S.S.R. This case is a characteristic illustration of the possible interaction of the provisions of Article 98 and Article 99. It is obviously one of the constitutional prerogatives of the Secretary-General to act under Article 99, in the same way as he has under Article 97 the sole right to act as Chief Administrative Officer. His constitutional rights cannot be taken away from him, neither can he renounce them whenever it is his duty to function as one of the principal organs of the U.N. Thus no delegation of powers under Article 98 can change his prerogatives as head of the U.N. Secretariat, and neither the adoption nor rejection of a proposal for delegation of powers to him can affect his prerogatives under Article 99. The question may arise what are the rights and duties of the Secretary-General, in case of an inconsistency of the terms of his delegation with his constitutionally guaranteed powers. Has the Secretary-General the right to seek for himself a solution of the ensuing conflict? No doubt he has, in so far as it is necessary for him to reconcile his rights and duties under Articles 99 and 97 with those under Article 98. Should he be unable to find a solution, the obvious way out of the dilemma would be a request to the International Court of Justice for an Advisory Opinion (submitted by one of the representative organs), as conflicts as to competence between the principal organs of the U.N. cannot be solved by any one of them alone.

It will be seen later that Mr. Hammarskjold had to face a further problem, that of gaps in the delegation of powers and the ensuing question of filling these gaps in the absence of guidance from the Security Council. Whatever the developments during Mr. Hammarskjold's term of office, it would be relevant to state that already during the period of Mr. Trygve Lie's Secretaryship a fairly clear pattern of operation of Article 99 (as combined with Articles 98 and 97) emerged in practice. Apart from its formal invocation in the Korean crisis in 1950, which badly affected the Secretary-General's relations with the U.S.S.R. and gained him the confidence of the U.S.A., Article 99 was relied on by him in an informal way in the Iranian or Greek questions in 1946 and later in the matter of the Statute of Trieste in 1947, and also in the questions of the partition of Palestine in 1948 and of the representation of China in the U.N. in 1950, in which the Secretary-General advocated the admission of the Peking Government to the U.N. In a number of cases the Secretary-General's intervention took the form of submission of legal memoranda and towards the end of his term of office Mr. Trygve Lie laid before the General Assembly a Ten Point Memorandum in which he proposed *inter alia* a twenty years' programme for achieving peace through the U.N., special periodical meetings of the Security Council attended by Foreign Ministers or Heads of Governments, control of atomic energy, universality of membership of the U.N., expansion of technical assistance, a more vigorous use of the service of the Specialised Agencies, the ratification of the Havana Charter and the establishment of an International Trade Organisation. In the preparation and submission of the Memorandum the Secretary-General acted no doubt as one of the principal organs of the U.N., but he relied particularly on the employment of his discretionary powers under Article 99 in an informal way.

IV. U.N. Multilateral Diplomacy (Public and Private)

While Mr. Trygve Lie conceived the office of the Secretary-General in a statesmanlike way, Mr. Hammarskjold must be considered the originator and formulator of a *sui generis* U.N. multilateral diplomacy.[10] It is his merit to have combined public with private (traditional) diplomacy within the framework of the U.N. on an unprecedented scale. Before discussing some of the most characteristic cases involving intervention of a preventive character, it would be relevant to recall that among the traditional methods of settling international disputes (outside the domain of judicial proceedings) are diplomatic negotiation, good offices, mediation and conciliation. It has been maintained that traditional diplomatic negotiation is a

[10] Michel Virally, "Le rôle politique du Secretaire-Général des Nations-Unies" (1958) *Annuaire Français de Droit International* 360.

deficient method for various reasons [11]: it may not be suitable for settling a dispute objectively; in the absence of a third party the negotiators tend to bargain; if bargaining power is unequal, the weaker State is in an unfavourable position; there is a danger of deadlock in negotiations; and if complex problems arise, they may be beyond the capacity of diplomatic negotiators. It may, however, be submitted that, if diplomatic negotiations are transferred to the U.N. forum and carried out with the assistance of the Secretary-General, it is possible to attempt an objective settlement because the negotiators will act within the framework of the U.N. Charter and its principles; their bargaining discretion will be reduced by a multilateral approach to problems in which all members of the Organisation have a direct or indirect influence; the unfavourable position of weaker States can be improved by bargaining against the background of wider U.N. interests; the danger of a deadlock can be overcome with the help of the Secretary-General and the complexity of problems can be reduced with the assistance of the Secretariat which can put its expert knowledge at the disposal of the negotiating parties.

In connection with the above it may further be recalled that, according to Article 33 of the U.N. Charter " the parties to any dispute, the continuance of which is likely to endanger the maintenance of international peace and security, shall first of all seek a solution by negotiation, enquiry, mediation, conciliation, . . ." How can the Secretary-General intervene in negotiations or assist the parties by his good offices or as a mediator or conciliator under Article 33? We have seen that under Article 99, whenever a matter is likely to threaten the maintenance of international peace and security, he will engage in fact finding or start investigations or take other steps of an exploratory nature in order to form an opinion in the matter. If so, his action under Article 99 may coincide with the endeavour of the parties under Article 33 to settle a conflict by traditional methods and he may take the initiative of offering them assistance or, as has happened in several cases, he may be asked by the parties to help. But whenever asked to intervene as a " third party " (as negotiator, good offices bearer or mediator), his participation in the conflict and the transfer of the matter to the forum of the United Nations Secretariat entails the application of methods of multilateral diplomacy. In this respect a significant development has taken place within the U.N. which proved to be instrumental in the promotion of multilateral private diplomacy on top of the existing " parliamentary " U.N. proceedings which operate through public debate and voting and frequently proved

11 Julius Stone, *Legal Controls of International Conflict* (1954), pp. 67–72.

insufficient for the solution of conflicts.[12] This new development originates from the assumption by the U.N. of the active and passive right of legation. The exercise of this right in practice (together with the participation of the U.N. in treaties and international agreements) testifies to its international personality which, unlike its personality in the municipal laws of member countries, has not been stipulated in the Charter. The International Court of Justice has made reference to this development in the *Reparation for Injuries* case [13] and has gone so far as to consider the international personality of the U.N. as an objective one, having validity *erga omnes* and not confined to member countries only. The exercise of the right of legation of the U.N. is no doubt one of the significant elements in the development of the juridical status of the Organisation in international law. It also has led to the establishment of a permanent diplomatic corps at U.N. headquarters which enables the Secretary-General to remain constantly in touch with the representatives (usually of ambassadorial rank) of member countries. Before the impact of this development on U.N. practice is discussed the following remarks would be relevant.

The passive right of legation (as well as the active right of sending U.N. representatives) is exercised on behalf of the U.N. by the Secretary-General who receives the credentials of the members of the Corps Diplomatique accredited to the Organisation. The handling of U.N. external relations by the Secretary-General is in principle not based on his delegated powers under Article 98 [14] but is carried out on the basis of authority assigned constitutionally to his office. The administration of external relations may be deemed to be part of his general rights and duties as Chief Administrative Officer. If this conclusion were not acceptable, the alternative juridical basis would be the domain of his inherent powers. It may however be stressed that, while the administration of the active and passive right of legation must be handled by the Secretary-General on one or other basis, treaty-making (as part of U.N. external affairs) would be carried out by the Secretary-General under Article 98 only, *i.e.*, on the basis of delegation of powers. The external affairs activities of the Secretary-General are therefore a complex of heterogeneous functions. Whenever he receives the credentials of envoys accredited to the U.N., he acts like the head of a State. Whenever he negotiates and signs treaties, he acts (with

[12] One of the drawbacks of public negotiations is the tendency of the parties to score propaganda points instead of concentrating on the effort of narrowing down the issues.

[13] (1949) *I.C.J. Reports*, 174.

[14] Though of course the overall direction of U.N. policy is the concern of the General Assembly and the Security Council.

the exception of certain administrative arrangements) on instructions of the representative bodies. But like the head of a foreign office he enjoys a good deal of autonomy in the conduct of current negotiations with the permanent representatives at U.N. headquarters.

In spite of these analogies it would be difficult to define the diplomatic activities of the Secretary-General with absolute precision. The proportional measure of his dependence or independence of action could perhaps best be assessed by a joint reading of Articles 97, 98, 99 and 33 of the Charter. We have seen that Article 97 provides him with the administrative machinery which enables him to carry out executive functions in the internal and external spheres—functions which cumbrous representative bodies, similar to legislatures in the municipal field, cannot assume. On the other hand Article 98 makes him the bearer of powers which he could not assume without delegation. Finally, the joint application of Articles 33 and 99 frequently enables him to take the initiative under Article 99 and to use informally his powers of fact-finding and inquiry and at the same time to assist the parties seeking under Article 33 a solution of conflicts by methods of traditional diplomacy.

The transfer of a matter to the U.N. Secretariat thus often helps to handle it in an informal manner without losing the benefits of multilateral diplomacy. Traditional diplomacy by itself cannot produce the beneficial results which multilateral negotiations are able to offer. In an address given to the United Nations Association in Oslo in 1958 the Secretary-General stressed the insufficiency of the classical forms of bilateral diplomacy. The creation of public (parliamentary) diplomacy within the constitutional framework of the League of Nations and the United Nations was an important step forward in the methods of solving international conflicts. However, in the process of public debate and voting, the benefits of classic informal ways and means are often lost. It is no doubt Dag Hammarskjold's great achievement to have supplemented public U.N. processes by the application of methods of private diplomacy on a multilateral basis.[15] The Secretary-General, while remaining in constant touch with the representatives of Member States of the U.N., was able to conduct negotiations with the parties to an issue with the employment of the maximum available factors

[15] In an address given to the Students' Association in Copenhagen in 1959 Mr. Hammarskjold stated that the Secretary-General "must accept the limitation of acting mainly on inner lines without publicity. In nine cases out of ten the Secretary-General would destroy his chances by exerting an independent influence on developments by publicly appealing to opinion over the heads of governments."

which could remove misunderstandings and bring about solutions. His mission to Peking, aiming at the release of the detained U.S. airmen, was an example of diplomatic action undertaken without delegation under Article 98 (though the Peking Government is not represented at the U.N.). In his annual report for 1958–59 the Secretary-General referred to the Cambodia-Thailand border dispute which had led to the suspension of diplomatic relations between the two countries. The Secretary-General stated that the two governments invited him to assist in the settlement of the conflict and that, after *informal* consultations with representatives of member countries holding seats in the Security Council, he accepted the invitation.[16] The Secretary-General also acted on the invitation of the Government of South Africa, which refused to submit to the intervention of the Security Council in the matter of segregation policies but agreed to consultations with the Secretary-General. He acted on the invitation of the Government of Laos and applied methods of preventive diplomacy though this attracted the criticism of the U.S.S.R. as to the alleged unconstitutionality of his action.[17]

Methods of private diplomacy used in conjunction with U.N. parliamentary procedures were applied by the Secretary-General in connection with the adoption by the General Assembly of the Atoms-for-Peace plan (1954). One part of this plan was to bring scientists together to discuss the peaceful use of atomic energy as distinct from its military application. The General Assembly established an Advisory Committee to advise the Secretary-General which sat in private under his chairmanship and contributed greatly to the success of the Geneva Conference of 1955 on the peaceful use of atomic energy. The Secretary-General stressed in an address given to both Houses of Parliament of the U.K. in 1958 that to achieve agreement of the powers in the Committee no vote was ever taken. Instead he applied the practice of summing up the conclusions from the debate and any member of the Committee was free to go on record with objections to the summing-up. The Secretary-General remarked that " Never in the course of these years has any such observation been put on record in the Committee." As a further example of the same procedures, the Secretary-General also quoted the meetings of the U.N. Radiation Committee.

[16] Also in his intervention in Lebanon the Secretary-General was able to take such supplementary measures after informal communication with members of the Security Council.

[17] See Appendix to the Report of the Committee of Experts appointed under the General Assembly Resolution 1446/XIV (A/4776, June 14, 1961), in which Mr. Roshchin criticised the dispatch of the mission to Laos by the Secretary-General without formal agreement of the Security Council or General Assembly.

Mr. Hammarskjold referred in his annual report for 1958–59 to the employment of informal methods of multilateral diplomacy as a " common law " development in the sphere of international co-operation. Even if such an analogy is not quite acceptable from the point of view of international law-making, it is obvious that the development heralds the establishment of new *usages* in U.N. practice.

V. Issues Relating to Delegation of Powers (The Constitutional Theory)

Reference has been made to Mr. Hammarskjold's address at Oxford University in which he spoke of the U.N. Secretariat in law and in fact. Apart from discussing cases under Article 99, he extended his analysis to another category of conflicts which confronted him with one of the most acute problems, that of the exercise of delegated powers in case of gaps in the original delegation under Article 98 particularly to the case of the Republic of the Congo. Before discussing this case in more detail, he referred to earlier cases [17a] of delegation of powers such as the Palestine Armistice problem when the Security Council asked him " to arrange with the parties for adoption of any measures " which in his opinion " would reduce existing tension along the Armistice demarcation lines." After the outbreak of hostilities in Egypt, the General Assembly authorised the Secretary-General to " obtain compliance of the withdrawal of foreign forces." He was requested to submit a plan for a United Nations Emergency Force (U.N.E.F.) to " secure and supervise the cessation of hostilities " and he was also requested to take the necessary measures to organise the Force and dispatch it to Egypt. The negotiations by the Secretary-General of the preliminary understandings between the parties to the issue and of the relevant agreements leading to the successful operation of the U.N.E.F.[18] must be considered a masterpiece of private diplomacy within the framework of his delegated functions.[19] Some of the significant problems confronting the Secretary-General were the conclusion of the agreement with the Government of Egypt for entry of the U.N.E.F. into Egyptian territory, the recognition of the proper juridical status of

17a The following extracts from the U.N. decisions are quoted from the Oxford address, *cit. supra*, n. 1.

18 A useful collection of Basic Documents relating to UNEF has been prepared by Mr. E. Lauterpacht under the title, *The United Nations Emergency Force, Basic Documents* (the British Institute of International and Comparative Law (1960)).

19 The General Assembly also requested the Secretary-General to issue all regulations and restrictions for the effective functioning of the Force as a subsidiary organ of the U.N. This would be an example of delegation to the Secretary-General of power to pass administrative legislation.

the Force in Egypt with reference to its privileges and immunities under Article 105 of the U.N. Charter (which was achieved by exchange of letters amounting to an agreement between the U.N. and the Government of Egypt), the application of the U.N. flag code and the conclusion of agreements with governments contributing to the formation of the U.N.E.F. The ensuing developments relating to the operations of U.N.E.F. are examined in the annual reports of the Secretary-General for 1956–57 and 1957–58. These reports also refer to the U.N.E.F. Advisory Committee established by the General Assembly and to the Suez Canal clearance operations.

In 1958, the Secretary-General was asked to dispatch an Observation Group to Lebanon " so as to ensure that there is no illegal infiltration of personnel or supply of arms or other material across the Lebanese border." Subsequently he was requested to make " such practical arrangements as would adequately help in upholding the purposes and principles of the Charter in relation to Lebanon and Jordan."

Finally, in 1960 the Secretary-General was asked to organise a U.N. operation in the Republic of the Congo. In the basic mandate given to the Secretary-General the Security Council authorised him " to take the necessary steps, in consultation with the Government of the Republic of the Congo, to provide the Government with such military assistance as may be necessary, until, through the efforts of the Congolese Government with the technical assistance of the U.N., the national security forces may be able, in the opinion of the Government, to meet fully their task." Additional guidance was provided by the principles relating to the employment of the U.N.E.F. as earlier developed. The Secretary-General informed the Security Council that he would base his action on these principles subject to their further elaboration as applicable to the Congo operation. A report on the matter was approved by the Security Council but " it proved to leave wide gaps." In these circumstances the Secretary-General asked the Council for an interpretation of his mandate (delegated powers) in the light of unforeseen events in the Congo. In the absence of further guidance, he was left with the question how to proceed further, particularly whether to terminate the Congo operation or to fill the gap in his mandate by reliance on legal factors which would allow him to answer outstanding questions and to implement the mandate in spite of no guidance.[20]

Before an examination of these legal factors is attempted it would be relevant to emphasise that, as stated in the annual report

[20] See Oxford address, 1961, *cit. supra*, note 1.

of the Secretary-General for 1959–60, the Congo operation was (and still is) one beyond the existing U.N. machinery. It involved from the beginning an interplay between parliamentary U.N. operations, political action, diplomatic negotiations and military and administrative measures.[21] A report of the special representative of the Secretary-General in the Congo, written in September 1960, brought home the stark facts of the situation which had arisen after the breakdown of law and order in the newly independent African republic. The representative wrote about " complete failure to arrange for any organised hand-over to the Congolese of the administrative machinery of government or of essential services. . . ." Powerless to restore order and to maintain normal life in the country the Government appealed to the U.N. for military and technical assistance. The U.N. moved in to fill the power vacuum in the hope of isolating the area of tension from the great power *bloc* conflicts; it engaged in the largest operation ever undertaken since its establishment. Within the Republic of the Congo three rival political groups had started competing with each other, the Presidential group, Prime Minister Lumumba's group, and the army led by the Chief of Staff. President and Prime Minister declared each other deprived of legitimate power, and in addition to the two rival governments the Chief of Staff created a third one. On top of this came the secession of Katanga led by Mr. Tshombe. In these circumstances the Secretary-General was confronted with the problem of how to implement his mandate and to whom to give the assistance stipulated in the decisions of the Security Council.[22] The original consensus of opinion within the Council as to the conduct of the Congo operation had meanwhile disintegrated, and the Secretary-General, not being able to obtain guidance as to questions which were not foreseen in the delegation of powers, had to fall back

21 There was, in particular, lack of expert personnel capable of assisting the Secretary-General at the secretarial top level. A Committee of Experts appointed under the General Assembly Resolution 1446/XIV (U.N. Gen. A/4776, June 14, 1961) issued a report in which it advocated the reorganisation of the Secretariat at the top level by the addition of more officials having political and diplomatic experience. The Committee also stated that it was impressed by the "unbalance and inequality in geographical distribution of staff." This problem is bound to become even more acute with the constantly rising number of Member States of the U.N. See also report to the Secretary-General of three past Presidents of the General Assembly (1960) (Annex I A/4776) and Appendix containing the separate opinion of Mr. Rospchin, the U.S.S.R. delegate. U-Thant, the acting Secretary-General, appointed recently a number of Principal Advisers (*U.N. Review*, March 1962). See also E. Jackson, "The Developing Role of the Secretary-General" (1957) XI *International Organisation* 431.

22 Progress Report to the Secretary-General from the special representative in the Congo (*U.N. Review*, November 1960).

on non-delegated powers. This is how he himself formulated the position [23]:

> " A simple solution for the dilemmas thus posed for the Secretary-General might seem to be for him to refer the problem to the political organ. . . . Under a national *parliamentary* régime, this would often be the obvious course of action for the executive to take. Indeed, this is what the Secretary-General must do whenever it is feasible." [24]

Mr. Hammarskjold further argued that, if the above parliamentary procedure (applied by analogy) is not capable of giving a positive result because of a deadlock in the representative organ, the Secretary-General had two alternatives. One would be to refrain from action and this, he stated, " may be tempting; it enables him to avoid criticism by refusing to act until other political organs resolve the dilemma." The other alternative would be for him to undertake independently a solution of the outstanding problems " on his own risk but with as faithful an interpretation of the instructions, rights and obligations of the Organisation as possible in view of international law and the decisions already taken." Mr. Hammarskjold had no doubt as to his choice of one or the other alternative. He said:

> " The answer seems clear enough in law; the responsibilities of the Secretary-General under the Charter cannot be laid aside merely because the execution of decisions by him is likely to be politically controversial. The Secretary-General remains under the obligation to carry out the policies as adopted by the organs; the essential requirement is that he does this on the basis of his exclusively international responsibility (Article 100) and not in the interest of any State or group of States.
>
> " This presents us with this crucial problem: is it possible for the Secretary-General to resolve controversial issues on a truly international basis without obtaining the formal decision of the organs? In my opinion and on the basis of my experience the answer is in the affirmative. . . .
>
> " Of primary importance [in the independent solution of problems by the Secretary-General] are the principles and purposes of the Charter which are the fundamental law accepted by and binding on all States. . . . The principles of the Charter are moreover supplemented by the body of legal

23 See Oxford address, 1961, *cit. supra*, note 1.

24 Oxford address, 1961, *cit. supra*, note 1 at p. 23. Italics are mine.

doctrine" [as well as precepts and precedents in U.N. practice].[25]

The following remarks may be offered in connection with this fundamental statement: first of all, if a solution of problems connected with gaps in the delegation of powers is not obtainable by a process analogous to that applied under a parliamentary system, *i.e.*, by ultimate guidance from the representative organ, a solution may be sought on the lines of practices analogous to those under the presidential régime as prevailing in the U.S.A. In this respect the Secretary-General referred again to Article 99 which gives him (irrespective of the submission by him of a case to the Security Council) the initiative of acting independently by fact-finding, inquiry, investigation and, generally speaking, by acting at his discretion, provided he does not act *ultra vires* the Charter or inconsistently with a mandate obtained from a representative organ. Mr. Hammarskjold, referring to the conferment (in the Charter) on the Secretary-General of political powers, said [26]:

> "This is a reflection in some measure, of the American political system which places authority in a chief executive officer who is not simply subordinated to the legislative [representative] organs and who is constitutionally responsible alone for the execution of legislation and in some respects for carrying out the authority derived from the constitutional instrument directly."

There is no doubt some force in the argument that the legal position of the Secretary-General is *mutatis mutandis* analogous to that of the bearer of presidential powers. There are, however, essential differences between the two which are connected with the election (appointment) of the Secretary-General by, and his dependence on, the representative organs of the U.N.[27] The Secretary-General has no direct appeal to the electorate (*i.e.*, to Member States) and his international responsibility to the Organisation as stipulated in Article 100 does not allow him to rise, with the help of independent constitutional powers, above the representative organs. However, there is no doctrine of "parliamentary" supremacy inscribed in the U.N. Charter which would reserve to any one of the principal organs a paramount position. The Secretary-General is one of the principal organs and, in the light of the administrative

[25] *Ibid.* at pp. 24–25. In this way Mr. Hammarskjold gave an answer to Mr. Krushchev's denial of the possible existence of a truly international civil service.

[26] See Oxford address, 1961, *cit. supra*, note 1, at p. 11.

[27] Apart from those connected with the general differences between a State and an Inter-State Organisation.

as well as the political theory, there is room for assuming that he bears an independent co-responsibility (with other organs) for the management of U.N. affairs.

Moreover, as a permanent and exclusively internationally responsible organ, he may be presumed to be the *constitutional* guardian of the principles of the U.N. Charter, which may enable us to conceive (apart from the administrative and political theories) a constitutional theory imposing a sacred trust on the Secretary-General to secure within the limits of his powers the observance of United Nations principles by the member countries. Mr. Hammarskjold's well-known statement in the Security Council (made on October 31, 1956) that " the principles of the Charter are by far greater than the Organisation in which they are embodied, and the aims which they are to safeguard are holier than the policies of any single nation or people," testify to the possibility of conceiving a constitutional theory of the Secretary-General's position. There are many instances in U.N. practice which may be quoted in support of the tentative formulation of such a theory.

We have seen that the task of reminding the Member States of an organisation of the need for scrupulous fulfilment of the duties stipulated in its constitution was undertaken by Albert Thomas, the first Director of I.L.O. Mr. Trygve Lie followed the same practice when he proposed that the problem of the admission of the Peking Government to the U.N. should be settled on a constitutional basis, and in the Korean crisis of 1950 his vigorous action was a vindication of the principles of the Charter. In his address to the Students' Association in Copenhagen in 1959 Mr. Hammarskjold referred to the duty of the Secretary-General to take a stand in international conflicts, always based on the principles of the Charter. The possible use of the constitutional conception for enabling the Secretary-General to act as the guardian of the principles of the Charter had been considered by the founder fathers of the U.N. at San Francisco when they dealt with the Uruguayan proposal to give Article 99 a much wider meaning. Instead of limiting the Secretary-General only to the right to draw the attention of the Security Council to any matter which may threaten the maintenance of international peace and security, this proposal authorised him to lay before the Council " any matters which constitute an infringement or violation of the principles of the Charter." [28] This proposal was rejected by a vote of 16 to 13 but, though rejected, its basic idea remains inherent in the provisions of Article 99, as evidenced in U.N. practice. The rise of the

[28] *Documents of the U.N. Conference on International Organisation* (see above).

Secretary-General to the level of an international spokesman made him at the same time the guardian of the *pacta sunt servanda* principle in relation to the U.N. Charter. The constitutional theory found its expression in the annual report of August 31, 1960, where the Secretary-General states:

> " If the U.N. firmly adheres to its principles and purposes, with flexibility and intelligent adjustment to needs as regards proceedings, members engaged in this co-operation will increasingly turn to the Organisation for assistance. Therefore they will find it increasingly necessary to maintain its strength as an instrument for the world community. . . ."

To answer again Mr. Hammarskjold's " crucial " question whether the Secretary-General can (in case of emergency) resolve controversial issues without guidance from the representative organs, there are situations in which he would be advised to interpret his task in the spirit of the constitution (Charter) and to act on the *consensus praesumptus* of the family of nations. It pertains to the quality of international statesmanship of the Secretary-General to anticipate events and to speak for the community of nations even if in the absence of their express consent he cannot immediately obtain their guidance. By reading his constitutional trust into Articles 97, 98 and 99, the Secretary-General can subject to the limitation of power politics help to cement their presumed co-operation. Even if measures taken by him are not *prima facie* related to international law, they are bound to have an impact on the development of new standards of international behaviour.[29]

VI. The Secretary-General and the Proposal for a " Troika "

Before concluding this brief inquiry it would be relevant to consider the situation created after Mr. Hammarskjold's death by the appointment of an Acting Secretary-General as the result of a compromise reached by the opposing power *blocs*. The question arises whether at the termination of the present provisional arrangement the U.S.S.R. will still insist on the appointment of three Secretaries-General.[30] If they do, an amendment of the U.N. Charter would be required (to bring the proposal into line with the

[29] Oscar Schachter, " Dag Hammarskjold and the Relation of Law to Politics " (1962) 56 Am.J.Int.L. 1. (See reference to U.N. usages, above.)

[30] At the 15th Session of the General Assembly the U.S.S.R. proposed the replacement of the Secretary-General by a Committee of three elected officials. Mr. Nehru opposed the proposal and expressed the view that its adoption would weaken the U.N. Executive. It may be noted that U.N. membership has now risen to 105 with increasing influence of the Afro-Asian group. The expansion of the General Assembly (without a simultaneous change in the Security Council) poses new problems, and the former in many respects looks to the Secretary-General for efficient leadership.

Charter) and such amendment is likely to be vetoed by the Western Powers. The idea of a composite secretarial headship (proposed at San Francisco by the addition of deputy secretaries-general appointed in the same way as the Secretary-General) was not found reconcilable with the international responsibility of the Secretariat. It would be difficult to preserve the Secretary-General's, and his subordinate staff's, international immunity if his position were diluted within a collective agency whose members would not be able to resist the pressure of their political supporters (Communist, non-Communist, or neutral).[31]

On the other hand the U.S.S.R. would be able to block the appointment of any of the candidates proposed by the Western Powers. If there is no apparent way out of the deadlock, is it possible to argue that the absence of a Secretary-General within the Organisation is unconstitutional as the Secretariat is one of its principal organs (Article 7) and must be composed of the Secretary-General and the staff (Article 97)? If the necessary recommendation of the Security Council were not forthcoming, could the General Assembly appoint a Secretary-General without it, so as to satisfy the constitutional requirement of providing for a fully constituted principal organ without which the Organisation could not function? U.N. practice records a precedent in this respect, particularly the action of the General Assembly at its 298th plenary meeting on November 1, 1950 (by 46 votes in favour, 5 votes against and with 8 abstentions) in adopting a resolution to continue the Secretary-General (Mr. Trygve Lie who had completed a term of five years) in office for three more years. This resolution was adopted without a recommendation by the Security Council, which had been unable to reach a decision. Extension of office must be considered as reappointment and the action of the General Assembly can therefore hardly be considered as constitutional. At the 296th plenary meeting of the General Assembly the representative of the U.S.S.R. had declared that, if the Secretary-General were to be reappointed without recommendation by the Security Council the Government of the U.S.S.R. would refuse to regard him as Secretary-General.[32] However, in spite of opposition and subsequent criticism it gave no effect to refusal of his recognition as Secretary-General in practice, and it might be argued that a precedent (constitutional convention) has been established enabling the

[31] It may also be noted that the proposal of establishing a secretarial "troika" is not justified by the existence of three equal power groups (Communist, non-Communist and neutral). There is neither any measurable equality between the three groups nor is the composition of the neutral group stable.

[32] H. Kelsen, *The Law of the United Nations* (Supplement, 1951).

General Assembly to act alone in the event of a deadlock in the Security Council. Would it be possible to suggest that the General Assembly could again take action in reliance on this precedent? It may not be possible to offer a positive answer to this question from the legal point of view, but it is fairly certain that any such course of action taken by the Assembly would encounter the definite opposition of those who adhere to express constitutional provision and require a recommendation of the Security Council for a valid appointment of the Secretary-General. A commendable way out of the dilemma, if ever it should occur, would be for the General Assembly or the Security Council, in accordance with Article 96 of the U.N. Charter to request the International Court of Justice to give an Advisory Opinion on the question.

The second reading by a long-time official observer in the United Nations, Sydney D. Bailey, "The Troika and the Future of the United Nations: The Secretary-General," *The Secretariat of the United Nations* (rev. ed., Praeger, New York, 1962) pp. 37–59, is an excerpt from a larger study of the Secretary-General. Sensitive to the language of the Charter, to the legal issues raised by it, and to their relationship to the political processes of the Organization, Bailey's account is placed here because it reports as well on several main instances in which the Secretary-General has acted. This is helpful for an understanding of the various tensions and opportunities inherent in the Office. Bailey's analysis of the troika proposals and the development of an independent Secretariat will also be of concern.

SYDNEY D. BAILEY

The Troika and the Future of the United Nations: The Secretary-General

. . . . . perhaps the most important development in the role of the Secretary-General has related to functions exercised without the express authority of a policy-making body. Hammarskjold always distinguished between those specific responsibilities conferred on him by policy-making organs and those general responsibilities which, explicitly or implicitly, attached to the Office of Secretary-General. When he visited Peking in 1955, following a General Assembly resolution that requested him to seek the release of captured personnel, he was able, in his capacity as Secretary-General of the United Nations and apart from functions entrusted to him by the Assembly, to exchange views with Chinese officials. When in 1956 he was asked by the Security Council to survey various aspects of compliance with the general armistice agreements in the Middle East, he insisted not only that this request did not detract from his authority under the Charter, but also that it did not add to it. On the occasion of his reappointment in 1957, he stated that the Secretary-General should act not only when guidance could be found in the Charter or in the decisions of the main organs, but also without such guidance 'should this appear to him necessary in order to help in filling any vacuum that may appear in the systems which the Charter and traditional diplomacy provide for the safeguarding of peace and security'.[47]

Within a year of his reappointment, his interpretation was put to the test. Lebanon had complained to the Security

Council of intervention in its internal affairs by the United Arab Republic. The Council, acting on a proposal by Sweden, decided to send an observation group to the area in order to ensure that there was no illegal infiltration across the Lebanese borders. A month later, the Lebanese government requested the United States to send forces to help preserve the country's integrity and independence, and the United States complied with the request.

The resulting situation was thereupon considered by the Security Council. A Soviet proposal calling for the immediate withdrawal of United States troops from Lebanon (as well as British troops from Jordan) was defeated, as was a Swedish proposal to suspend the activities of the United Nations Observation Group. The United States proposed that the Secretary-General should make additional arrangements to ensure the independence and integrity of Lebanon, but this was blocked by a Soviet veto.

In this confused and grave situation, Japan submitted what was intended to be a compromise proposal, cxpressed in the most general terms. This asked the Secretary-General to make arrangements forthwith for such measures as he might consider necessary with a view to ensuring the integrity and independence of Lebanon, thus making possible the withdrawal of United States forces from that country. This received ten affirmative votes, but the negative Soviet vote constituted a veto.

Here was a vacuum *par excellence*, and Hammarskjold had no hesitation in acting. His statement to the Security Council conveys most vividly his sense of responsibility.

> The Security Council has just failed to take additional action in the grave emergency facing us. However, the responsibility of the United Nations to make all efforts to live up to the purposes and principles of the Charter remains. . . .

In a statement before this Council on 31 October 1956, I said that the discretion and impartiality imposed on the Secretary-General by the character of his immediate task must not degenerate into a policy of expediency. On a later occasion—it was 26 September 1957—I said in a statement before the General Assembly that I believed it to be the duty of the Secretary-General 'to use his office and, indeed, the machinery of the Organization to its utmost capacity and to the full extent permitted at each stage by practical circumstances.' I added that I believed that it is in keeping with the philosophy of the Charter that the Secretary-General also should be expected to act without any guidance from the Assembly or the Security Council should this appear to him necessary towards helping to fill any vacuum that may appear in the systems which the Charter and traditional diplomacy provide for the safeguarding of peace and security. . . .

I am sure that I will be acting in accordance with the wishes of the members of the Council if I, therefore, use all opportunities offered to the Secretary-General, within the limits set by the Charter and towards developing the United Nations effort, so as to help to prevent a further deterioration of the situation in the Middle East. . . .

First of all . . . this will mean the further development of the Observation Group [in Lebanon]. The Council will excuse me for not being able to spell out at this moment what it may mean beyond that. . . .[48]

Limits of Parliamentary Diplomacy

The fact is that policy-making organs do not always respond to a crisis smoothly or swiftly; parliamentary diplomacy has its limitations. When tension arose between Cambodia and Thailand in 1958, the two governments agreed that the dispute should not go to a policy-making organ in the first instance. They asked the Secretary-General to designate a representative to help them in finding a solution. This was done without the formal approval of the Security Council, though with the knowledge of its members.* 'Such actions by the Secretary-General', reported Hammarskjold, 'fall within the competence of his Office and are . . . in other respects also in strict accordance with the Charter, when they serve its purpose'. The method he had used, he said, avoided public debate in a policy-making organ which might have increased the difficulties. Member States might well have been hesitant to give explicit prior approval to an action without fuller knowledge of the facts. The evolution of the Office of Secretary-General represented 'an intensification and a broadening of the interplay' between the policy-making organs and the Secretariat, while maintaining the principle that the activities of the United Nations are 'wholly dependent on decisions of the Governments'.[49]

In 1959, Hammarskjold again took action on his own responsibility in a difficult situation, even though the matter had come before the Security Council. The Laotian government requested that a United Nations force be sent to Laos to halt aggression. The Security Council met at Hammarskjold's request and decided to appoint a sub-committee to inquire into the situation.† The sub-committee reported on 5 November 1959, and three days later Hammarskjold announced that, 'taking into account his duties under the Charter, and all the information at present available', he had decided to pay a personal visit to Laos.[50] Later, within the framework

* In 1962, Cambodia and Thailand asked U Thant to appoint a personal representative to assist them regarding further differences which had arisen; U Thant complied with the request.

† The Soviet Union regarded this as a substantive rather than a procedural question, and therefore as subject to the veto. The Council decided by 10 votes to 1 (the Soviet Union) that the decision was only procedural, but the Soviet Union argued that this preliminary question should also be subject to the veto, in accordance with the four-power statement at San Francisco of 7 June 1945. The President of the Council ruled, however, that the resolution had been validly adopted.

of the United Nations technical assistance program, he appointed a special consultant for the co-ordination of United Nations activities in Laos. The Soviet government took the position that Hammarskjold's visit and his subsequent actions were 'designed to cover by the name of the United Nations further interference of the Western powers in Laos. . . .'[51]

U Thant has continued the policy of taking diplomatic and political initiatives. In 1962, on his own responsibility, he acceded to a request from the Netherlands and Indonesia that the United Nations should establish a temporary executive authority for West New Guinea (West Irian).[52] The following year he agreed to the despatch of United Nations observers to the Yemen, and the matter was discussed and approved by the Security Council only as a result of a request from the Soviet government.[53] Also in 1963, at the request of Malaya, Indonesia, and the Philippines, he agreed to 'ascertain the wishes' of the people of Sabah (North Borneo) and Sarawak regarding the future status of the two territories.[54]

There have been, then, two parallel and related trends. First, policy-making organs have increasingly entrusted the Secretary-General with broad diplomatic and operational functions; secondly, the Secretaries-General have used to the full the resources of the Office in the exercise of independent initiatives designed to further the purposes and principles of the Charter. And it cannot be denied that the totality of these developments has given to the Office of Secretary-General a character that had not been foreseen by the founders of the Organization. Indeed, Hammarskjold had gone so far as to describe the office as 'a one-man "executive", with explicit authority in the administrative field, supplementary to, but not overlapping the authority of either the [Security] Council or the Assembly'.[55] In his speech at Oxford in 1961, he stated that the conception of the office of Secretary-General originated in the United States.

> The United States gave serious consideration to the idea that the Organization should have a President as well as a Secretary-General. Subsequently, it was decided to propose only a single officer, but one in whom there would be combined both the political and executive functions of a President with the internal administrative functions that were previously accorded to a Secretary-General.[56]

The Secretary-General is, of course, appointed by the will of Member States, and his independence is guaranteed by the Charter stipulation that he shall neither seek nor receive instructions from any source external to the United Nations. If Member States had wished to prevent the strengthening of the office of Secretary-General, they could have done so. They were, however, glad to leave things to the Secretary-General when parliamentary diplomacy was not enough.

The trouble was that parliamentary diplomacy had been becoming more and more parliamentary, and less and less diplomatic. Delegates were sometimes in danger of forgetting the purposes of the United Nations, so admirably set forth in the first Article of the Charter; attention, instead, was increasingly directed, not to purposes, but to methods. Debate was coming to be thought of as an end in itself; a vote was mistaken for action.

The chief purpose of parliamentary diplomacy (though not always the only one) is to cause a reassessment of national interests in the light of the national interests of others. The various elements that together constitute parliamentary diplomacy are occasionally sufficient in themselves to bring the actions of nations into harmony. This seems to have been the case, for example, in the General Assembly's consideration of the Syrian-Turkish tension in 1957 and in the Security Council's consideration of the Sudan-Egyptian border dispute in 1958. But sometimes more is needed. In a variety of circumstances, it has been found useful to go further, and to inject the physical presence of the United Nations into situations of difficulty or tension. Such a United Nations presence symbolizes the concern of the international community, but it may do more than that. A government may refuse to comply with a decision of a policy-making organ but would think twice before taking action which would bring it into direct, on-the-spot conflict with representatives of the international community. A United Nations presence creates conditions in which it is difficult to assault the principles of the United Nations without at the same time assaulting its representatives.

The 'presence' of the United Nations may consist of the Secretary-General, or one or more representatives appointed by him, or by a policy-making organ; it may consist of an inter-governmental committee; it may consist of persons or contingents, loaned by governments, for observation or police duties; it may consist of a section of the Secretariat with special regional or functional responsibilities. The form of the presence has to be tailored to the needs of each situation.

In practice there are, naturally, limits to what a United Nations 'presence' can do under Chapter VI of the Charter. It cannot enter territory without the consent of the government concerned. It must have the freedom of movement and the facilities necessary to undertake the tasks committed to it. It must to some extent operate independently of the host government, and yet without becoming a rival authority. It must abstain from actions taken to influence the internal political situation.

The United Nations operations initiated in the Middle East following the crises of 1956 and 1958 created important precedents. In both cases, considerable discretion was given to the Secretary-General in implementing the decisions of policy-making organs. The 'presences' were established in accordance with his proposals, and he was made the agent of the Organization in attempting to secure certain objectives.

The Congo

The Congo case has been the most intricate and intractable in which the United Nations has been involved. The lack of preparation for independence and the unexpected speed of the transfer of sovereignty resulted in a vacuum that Congolese nationalists were not in a position to fill. The question in July 1960 was whether the United Nations could stabilize and insulate the situation for an interim period until adequate and united Congolese leadership had emerged. The Congo operation has been criticized from almost every conceivable point of view, but the critics should bear in mind that the operation had to be conducted in conformity with principles that had been accepted as valid in earlier and very different operations, and that actions taken in the Congo would become precedents for the future. It is easier to complain that this or that political result was not achieved than to lay down an acceptable code for United Nations action, particularly in relation to the internal affairs of a State.

Moreover, the decisions of the Security Council and the General Assembly regarding the Congo did not always give clear guidance to those on the spot. How was the Secretary-General to interpret the mandate to assist the Government of the Congo if more than one authority claimed to be that government? How was it possible for the United Nations both to safeguard the unity of the Congo in the face of secessionist activities and at the same time to abstain from any action that would influence any internal conflict? Did the United Nations mandate to prevent civil war extend to resisting by force Central Government troops which might try to enter secessionist areas if their declared purpose was to restore the territorial integrity and unity of the Congo? At what point did the use of force, as a last resort, become necessary? Nor should it be forgotten that many Member States were content to give instructions to the Secretary-General (and, indeed, to complain at the way he carried them out) while denying him the material resources and diplomatic backing he was entitled to expect.

It was the course of events in the Congo that sparked off the Soviet onslaught on Hammarskjold. Until 1959, the Soviet Union appeared to trust and respect him. In spite of Hammarskjold's support for the idea of a committee to investigate the situation following the Hungarian revolt in 1956, Khrushchev proposed in 1958 that the Secretary-General should participate in a meeting of heads of government on the Middle East. Although there was some Soviet criticism of Hammarskjold's activities in connection with the Laotian appeal for a United Nations force, the attack was relatively muted, and after Hammarskjold had invoked Article 99 of the Charter in connection with the Congo in July 1960, the Soviet Union supported the first three resolutions asking the Secretary-General to implement the Security Council's decisions. Within a few weeks, however, the Soviet government had launched a bitter personal attack on Hammarskjold. Khrushchev complained, first, that Hammarskjold had disregarded decisions of United Nations organs; second, and more generally, that he had supported the colonialist and capitalist States in the Congo and was biased against the Soviet Union and its allies. Khrushchev said bluntly that the countries of the Soviet bloc no longer trusted Hammarskjold and called on him to resign. Later, the Soviet government went even further and demanded that Hammarskjold be dismissed from his post.[57]

But the Soviet government wanted more than simply the removal of Hammarskjold. Khrushchev maintained that there were basic faults in the structure of the United Nations. The concrete reality of the present world, he said, is that it comprises three groups of States: the communist States; the neutralist, unaligned, or uncommitted States; and States which he described as belonging to Western military blocs. The post of Secretary-General should be abolished, he said; 'the executive organ of the United Nations should reflect the real situation that obtains in the world today'. In place of a single Secretary-General there should be a collective executive organ consisting of 'persons representing the States belonging to the three basic groups'. The crux of the matter, said Khrushchev, is not what should be the name of the new executive body but that this executive organ should 'represent' the States belonging to the three groups, thus guaranteeing that the executive work of the United Nations 'would not be carried out to the detriment of any one of these groups of States'.[58]

What had happened between 9 August 1960, when the Soviet delegation voted for the resolution confirming the authority already given to the Secretary-General in the Congo and entrusting additional responsibilities to him, and 23 September, when Khrushchev attacked Hammarskjold from the rostrum of the General Assembly? Was the 'troika' proposal a hasty and petulant response to particular United Nations actions in the Congo which had displeased the Soviet government, or did it represent a premeditated demand based on a long-term Soviet interpretation of general trends in world affairs?

It is not in dispute that the Soviet government suffered a setback in the Congo, but it is significant that the 'troika' idea was linked closely to possible future developments in relation to disarmament and the peace-keeping functions of the United Nations. The particular form the proposal took was probably based on the following considerations. First, in the light of the growth of the Secretary-General's independent exercise of those functions which the Soviet Union regarded as the sole responsibility of the Security Council, the Soviet government wished to have means to prevent action by the Secretariat which it regarded as inimical to its interests. Secondly, the Soviet government had for some years claimed that the Soviet bloc should have a position of parity with the Western group in United Nations organs. Finally, the Soviet government considered that the concept of impartiality was merely a mask to conceal the fact that the Secretariat promoted Western policies.[59]

This is not the occasion to attempt to write an account of the United Nations operation in the Congo[60] or of Hammarskjold's service as Secretary-General of the United Nations, but I am convinced that no man could have acted with greater independence, integrity, and impartiality than Hammarskjold, that no man could have shown a higher sense of international responsibility.

The United Nations responded to the request from the government of the Congo on the basis of complete impartiality and neutrality regarding internal political differences. The United Nations Emergency Force in the Middle East had been based on the same principle that it would never be used to enforce any particular political solution or to influence the political balance in any way.[61] The United Nations Observation Group in Lebanon similarly sought to avoid any partisan act, even during conditions of civil war. The Security Council's resolution of 9 August 1960 regarding the Congo reaffirmed that 'the United Nations Force in the Congo will not be a party to or in any way intervene or be used to influence the outcome of any internal conflict, constitutional or otherwise'.[62]

It was not possible, at the time the Congo operation was launched by the Security Council, to foresee how difficult it would become to interpret the original mandate. The United Nations was sending a force to the Congo, not to secure and supervise the cessation of hostilities as had been the task of UNEF in the Middle East, nor to prevent infiltration across borders as had been the case with the Observation Group in Lebanon. The Security Council decided in its first resolution to furnish military assistance to the government of the Congo, and called for the withdrawal of Belgian forces. The United Nations Force was to provide the government of an independent State with military aid. The principle that the United

Nations Force would not influence internal conflicts in the Congo became increasingly difficult to interpret and implement, particularly when secessionist and other groups in the Congo received encouragement and support from outside.

The crisis leading to the events of which the Soviet Union complained broke on 5 September. The Congo was on the verge of economic and political collapse. The Prime Minister, Patrice Lumumba, had clashed with Hammarskjold about the way the United Nations had handled the Katanga problem, and had then openly taken military help from the Soviet Union and other non-UN sources. This brought to a head differences within the Congolese government, and on the evening of 5 September, President Kasavubu declared over the radio that he had dismissed the government of Lumumba and had invited Joseph Iléo to form a new government. Lumumba thereupon called a meeting of the Council of Ministers, which decided to depose Kasavubu.

Léopoldville was in an explosive and tense condition, with two rival groups trying to mobilize support among the population. The attempt to insulate the Congo from disruptive external forces was being impeded by the fact that Belgium was openly supporting one faction in the Congo and the Soviet Union another. On the day of Lumumba's dismissal, Hammarskjold had addressed a blunt communication to the Belgian Delegation in New York on the delay in the evacuation of Belgian troops from the Congo and an equally blunt communication to the Soviet Delegation about the arrival in the Congo of Soviet Ilyushin planes, in defiance of the Security Council's resolutions.[63]

United Nations representatives in the Congo had been instructed to avoid any action by which, directly or indirectly, openly or by implication, they might pass judgment on any internal conflict, and they found themselves in a situation in which inaction as well as action was likely to be interpreted by one side or the other as contravening this principle. In an effort to prevent an outbreak of violence in Léopoldville, the United Nations Special Representative temporarily closed the radio station and the airport. It was his intention that the action would be impartial in its consequences; Kasavubu and Lumumba were to be equally affected by it, although in the event the action worked against Lumumba. These emergency measures were taken without consulting Hammarskjold, who was at Headquarters in New York.

Hammarskjold clearly faced a painful dilemma. While he could hardly disavow a decision taken in good faith by a trusted colleague at a time of acute difficulty, to endorse the action would risk bringing him into open conflict with influential Member States. Hammarskjold did not hesitate to take that risk and stated plainly that he fully endorsed the action.

After his dismissal, Lumumba sought and was granted United Nations protection in Léopoldville. At the end of November, Lumumba left the residence in which he had been guarded by the United Nations, and some days later he was arrested by the Congolese National Army. In the middle of January 1961, Lumumba was transferred to Elisabethville; on 10 February it was announced by the authorities in Katanga that Lumumba had 'escaped', and shortly afterward it became known that he had been killed.

After Lumumba's arrest, United Nations representatives in the Congo had tried to secure all possible legal and humanitarian protection for him. When he was transferred to Elisabethville, the Secretary-General and his representative in the Congo exercised all the influence possible for his return to Léopoldville and for the application of normal legal rules in the protection of his interests. No attempt was made by the United Nations to obtain his release by forcible means, since such action was considered to have been beyond the mandate conferred by the Security Council at that time.

The murder of Lumumba was—to use Hammarskjold's words—a revolting crime; it was also a political tragedy. But when Khrushchev first attacked Hammarskjold, Lumumba was still alive, enjoying the protection of United Nations forces. The launching of the 'troika' proposal preceded the assassination of Lumumba by about four months.

The Security Council met in September 1960, but by now the unanimity of the great powers could no longer be obtained. Following the veto of a resolution sponsored by Tunisia and Ceylon, an emergency special session of the General Assembly was called under the Uniting for Peace procedure. The countries of the Soviet bloc attacked Hammarskjold's handling of the Congo operation, but the Assembly voted by 70 votes to none (the Soviet bloc, France, and South Africa abstaining) to confirm and strengthen the Secretary-General's mandate. The break with Hammarskjold was to come three days later.

The Troika

Khrushchev attacked Hammarskjold for his conduct of the Congo operation, but it is significant that whenever he addressed the General Assembly on the subject of tripartite administration in 1960, he immediately proceeded to discuss disarmament and the use of international forces for maintaining peace.

> The United Nations Secretariat must therefore be adapted even now to the conditions which will come into being as disarmament decisions are implemented. An identical point of view has emerged . . . regarding the necessity of following up an agreement on disarmament with the establishment of armed forces of all countries, under international control, to be used by the United Nations in accordance with the decision of the Security Council.[64]
>
> It has been said that, after an agreement on disarmament has been reached, international armed forces should be formed. We are, in principle, in agreement with this.

> But the question arises, who will command these forces? The United Nations Secretary-General? . . . Is it really permissible for the fate of millions to be dependent on the actions of the one man occupying that post? . . . There can be no disarmament, there can be no international armed forces, in the absence of guarantees for all three groups [of States] against the misuse of these armed forces.[65]

To demand guarantees against misuse is legitimate; the Soviet government is not alone in making this demand. But the proposal for a collective executive body, in the form in which it was presented, went much further. Each member of the proposed triumvirate would be able, in certain circumstances, to prevent the decisions of policy-making organs from being implemented, either by outright veto or by the use of delaying tactics. What other interpretation can there be of the following extract from Khrushchev's first statement on the subject?

> We consider it advisable to set up, in the place of a Secretary-General who is at present the interpreter and executor of the decisions of the General Assembly and the Security Council, a collective executive organ of the United Nations consisting of three persons each of whom would represent a certain group of States. That would provide a definite guarantee that the work of the United Nations executive organ would not be carried on to the detriment of any one of these groups of States. The United Nations executive organ would then be a genuinely democratic organ; it would really guard the interests of all States Members of the United Nations. . . .[66]

It is true that the Soviet government never formally stated that each member of a three-man executive would in all circumstances have the right of veto, but it is a reasonable assumption and will no doubt be generally accepted until it is expressly denied. Indeed, in an official elaboration of its views, the Soviet government did not challenge an allegation by the United States that the 'troika' proposal would be tantamount to the introduction of the right of veto into the administrative realm.[67]

The veto, even if it is called the rule of unanimity, is essentially negative. Its effect is not to foster cooperation; it is to prevent action. Indeed, if the problem were simply to prevent the United Nations from acting to the detriment of any State or group of States, the solution would be to extend the veto to all Members in all organs of the United Nations. The heart of the matter is whether we will advance toward the goal of a secure international order by limiting or by extending the right of States to act arbitrarily in pursuit of objectives they regard as legitimate.

The veto in the Security Council can prevent the initiation of action, but it cannot ensure its termination. Although a policy-making organ of the United Nations can withdraw a mandate as easily as it can confer it, once a decision has been taken, it is valid until rescinded. An operation authorized by the Security Council cannot be stopped by a veto if one of the permanent members later finds the course of events not to its liking. The return of the Soviet representative to the Security Council after the boycott in 1950 could not lead to the cancellation of the earlier decisions to resist aggression in Korea. In the Lebanon operation of 1958, the veto of a proposal that the Secretary-General should make arrangements for such measures as he might consider necessary to ensure the integrity and independence of the Lebanon did not annul the original decision to send an observation group to ensure that there was no illegal infiltration across the Lebanese borders. When the Soviet Union became displeased with events in the Congo, it was unable to use its veto to terminate the United Nations operation.

The situation in the General Assembly is similar. An

operation may be launched by a two-thirds majority of those Member States present and voting; one-third of the Members plus one can prevent a decision. But an operation, once under way, can be halted only by an express decision by a two-thirds majority.

Interpreting the Mandate

Difficulties undoubtedly arise when resolutions entrusting the Secretary-General with broad responsibilities are expressed in vague general terms. It is, of course, impossible to foresee all eventualities; some matters must be left for later interpretation or decision. But there is all the difference in the world between a prudent avoidance of precision when all the circumstances cannot be foreseen and the transfer of total responsibility for decision and action to the Secretary-General because a policy-making organ has failed to agree on what should be done.

Agreement depends on negotiation, and negotiation takes time. The General Assembly, in particular, now tries to do more than it can do well. Time can be saved for the more important matters only by the exercise of greater discrimination regarding the agenda and a decrease of what in the British House of Commons is called 'irrelevance or tedious repetition'.

Public debate is an essential part of parliamentary diplomacy, but its limitations must be recognized. After the parties to a dispute have made initial statements in a public session of a policy-making organ, efforts to narrow the differences can be undertaken in private. The use of special rapporteurs, both to elucidate the issues and to make proposals for a solution, was one of the more successful practices of the League of Nations, and it is a pity that United Nations organs have not adopted the practice. Individuals can nearly always perform this function more effectively than committees.[68] This is not to say that there is some magic formula for ensuring the sort of agreement that can be embodied in an unambiguous resolution, but there are some methods that tend toward this result and some that do not.

Even when resolutions are fairly precise, later developments may pose problems for the Secretariat which were not foreseen when the resolution was adopted. In some cases, the Secretary-General may be able to consult an advisory committee of Member States; in other cases, he may refer the matter to the policy-making organ for clarification or extension of the original mandate. When differences arose between Hammarskjold and Lumumba in August 1960, Hammarskjold called for a meeting of the Security Council to clarify its attitude.[69] At a later stage in the Congo operation, Hammarskjold made it clear that fresh decisions by the Council were needed. 'It cannot shirk its responsibilities by expecting from the Secretariat action on which it is not prepared to take decisions itself.'[70] The Council, after debate, adopted a resolution authorizing the use of force, if necessary, in the last resort, in order to prevent civil war in the Congo.

The Secretary-General, however, may occasionally be confronted with issues regarding which it will be impossible to secure a clear judgment from an advisory committee or a policy-making organ. In such circumstances, Hammarskjold was prepared to act 'on his own risk, but with as faithful an interpretation of the instructions, rights and obligations of the Organization as possible in view of international law and the decisions already taken'.[71] It is no criticism of Hammarskjold to suggest that no Secretary-General should, in present circumstances, be expected to decide such questions 'on his own risk'.

The fact that it is difficult to delineate the scope within which a Secretary-General may properly exercise initiative should not be a reason for replacing a single, independent, and impartial officer by a triumvirate of ideological representatives. Although there was a widespread sentiment in 1960 that some organizational changes in the Secretariat were desirable, the Soviet proposal for a tripartite executive evoked virtually no support outside the Soviet bloc. What amounted to a vote of confidence in Hammarskjold took place at the fourth emergency special session of the Assembly in September 1960, and this was confirmed the following April. It had been proposed to omit the words 'by the Secretary-General' from a draft resolution asking that 'necessary and effective measures be taken' to prevent the introduction of arms and supplies to the Congo. A roll-call vote was requested by Guinea, and the proposal not to refer to the Secretary-General was rejected by 83 votes to 11, with 5 abstentions. The minority comprised the nine Soviet bloc States of Eastern Europe, together with Cuba and Guinea. This was a striking expression of confidence in Hammarskjold.

When Hammarskjold died, the Soviet Union could have proposed that a three-man executive organ be created, and it could have threatened to veto in the Security Council any attempt to appoint a single successor. One reason why the Soviet Union was prepared to agree to the appointment of U Thant was presumably the knowledge that the 'troika' idea would have received no more than a dozen or so votes in the General Assembly. Soviet protests about decisions taken in the Secretariat in the interval between the death of Hammarskjold and the appointment of U Thant were relatively perfunctory.[72]

The terms of U Thant's appointment do not derogate from the principles of the Charter. The text of his speech of acceptance may have been known in advance to a number of people, but the speech was naturally not delivered until after he had been appointed. His reference to Article 101 of the Charter and to his intention to designate a limited number of advisers maintained the important principle that it is the Secretary-General who appoints the staff. U Thant emphasized that the arrangement was without prejudice to such future changes as might be necessary.

U Thant has shown himself a worthy successor to Lie and Hammarskjold—courteous, fair-minded, and firm. His task is not easy. In addition to the normally heavy responsibilities of the Office, he must guide and inspire the Secretariat during a difficult process of reorganization, and at a time when the United Nations as a whole faces serious political and financial problems. He must establish an effective system of consultation at the top level of the Secretariat.

Hammarskjold never succeeded in creating a satisfactory system of consultation and collaboration at the senior level of the Secretariat. He handled much of the political work himself, with the help of a few colleagues on the thirty-eighth floor; the Department of Political and Security Council Affairs tended to lack drive and purpose. The meetings of Under-Secretaries, held on Friday mornings, were primarily occasions for reporting information rather than for resolving issues. Hammarskjold dealt with difficulties by direct discussion with the officials concerned.

A similar problem had beset the League of Nations, and the idea of constituting an advisory group for the Secretary-General of the League was frequently mooted. A former League official, after referring to certain 'arbitrary measures taken by the second Secretary-General during the critical months of 1940', comments as follows:

> It is the almost generally accepted opinion of persons with inside experience that, basically, the head of the international administration must retain the sole and final responsibility but that his relationship to his principal collaborators should be formalized by the creation of an advisory body. . . . Such an advisory body would . . . fulfill an important function without hampering the unity of control and moment.[73]

It is clear from the Charter that it is for the Secretary-General to decide a matter of this kind. Every Secretary-General will take account of both legal and political considerations, and will be influenced by his own temperament and by the personalities of his senior colleagues. Some tasks can be delegated; some responsibilities can be shared; but in the last resort, there are duties that have been expressly conferred on the Secretary-General, who is the only official of the Secretariat appointed by Member States.

Relations with Member States

Apart from his varied internal responsibilities of an administrative and related character, the Secretary-General must seek to establish relations of trust with Member States. We take it for granted nowadays that this means, in the first place, relations with permanent missions at Headquarters, but this would have shocked Sir Eric Drummond. Drummond was very much opposed to permanent diplomatic missions attached to the League of Nations, as he considered it essential that the League Secretariat should have direct access to governments and should not have to go through intermediaries. He also feared that the staff of permanent missions would be used to represent governments on League organs on matters for which they were not technically qualified.[74] The first of Drummond's anxieties has not, in the event, proved to be well founded; indeed, the institution of permanent missions has, in important respects, facilitated contacts between the Secretariat and Member States.

Relations between the Secretary-General and the permanent missions are largely of an informal kind, but formal institutions of consultation are also needed. Because the General Assembly is so large, select committees of Member States have proved useful in connection with some of the functions entrusted to the Secretary-General. Advisory committees exist for the operations in the Middle East and the Congo, and there is also an advisory committee on scientific questions. Certain principles regarding the composition and working of these committees may be suggested.

(1) They should be as representative as possible of the States providing the operation in question with the men, materials, logistical support, finance, and diplomatic backing.
(2) In order to facilitate effective working, such committees should be kept small; fifteen should normally be regarded as the maximum size.
(3) They should meet in private; there should normally be no voting; the chairman should sum up the feeling of the meeting, and any member should have the right to place a dissenting opinion on the record or, in the case of acute dissatisfaction, to request a meeting of the appropriate policy-making organ to resolve the issue.

When broad responsibilities are committed to the Secretary-General by the policy-making organs and unforeseen questions of interpretation are possible, it might be useful to have some procedure analogous to that used in a number of national political systems for the scrutiny of delegated legislation. In the United Kingdom, a representative committee of the House of Commons examines each exercise of delegated legislation with a view to determining whether the attention of the House should be drawn to it on any one of a number of grounds. These include:

(1) that it has financial implications;
(2) that it appears to make some unusual or unexpected use of the powers conferred;
(3) that there appears to have been an unjustifiable delay in publishing the relevant documents;
(4) that for any special reason the form or purport calls for elucidation.[75]

Such a scrutinizing procedure does not require that the merits of the original decision should be reviewed, only that the body conferring the mandate should be informed if the authority appears to have been improperly exercised.

The United Nations is an instrument, admittedly imperfect, with which Member States seek to mitigate the hazards of what would otherwise be international anarchy—if by anarchy is meant the absence of government. No particular form of machinery will ensure that a consensus will emerge among the States of which the Organization is composed; but when a consensus does emerge, when a policy-making organ is able to make a clear decision, it is essential that it be carried out by the Secretary-General and staff in a spirit of independence, impartiality, and integrity. To replace a single, independent Secretary-General by a political triumvirate, each member armed with a veto on administrative or executive action, would render the United Nations helpless in any situation in which one of the triumvirs considered that, in order to 'represent' a group of States, he had to block a particular action—and what situation can be conceived in which this possibility would not exist? The 'troika' would confine the Organization to being a forum for conference diplomacy and could bring to a halt a wide range of operational activities, first in the political field and later in the economic and social fields also. It would be the medium and smaller nations whose interests would be most adversely affected.

35. G.A.O.R., 18th Session, Annexes, Agenda item 66, A/C. 5/987 (11 October 1963), para. 18.
36. Report of the Preparatory Commission of the United Nations, PC/20 (23 December 1945), Chap. VIII, Sec. 2, para. 16, pp. 86–87.
37. Lie, *In the Cause of Peace*, p. 39.
38. *The International Secretariat of the Future*, p. 8.
39. Report of the Preparatory Commission of the United Nations, PC/20 (23 December 1945), Chap. VIII, Sec. 2, para. 16, pp. 86–87.
40. G.A.O.R., 5th Session, 289th plenary meeting (28 September 1950), para. 40.
41. S.C.O.R., 11th year, 751st meeting (31 October 1956), para. 1.
42. S.C.O.R., 14th year, 847th meeting (7 September 1959), para. 12.

43. S.C.O.R., 15th year, 873rd meeting (13/14 July 1960), para. 26.
44. Michel Virally, 'Le rôle politique du Secrétaire-Général des Nations Unies', Annuaire Français de Droit International, Paris, Centre National de la Recherche Scientifique, 1958, pp. 369–70.
45. S.C.O.R., 16th year, 964th meeting (28 July 1961), para. 86.
46. In 1958, for example, when the General Assembly was considering the future of United Nations assistance to Palestine refugees, a specific request that the Secretary-General should submit proposals on the matter was withdrawn on the understanding that the Secretary-General would, 'as part of his regular duties, look into the technical operation of UNRWA in preparation of such proposals as he might consider helpful or necessary to bring forward to the General Assembly. . . .' G.A.O.R., 13th Session, Special Political Committee, 125th meeting (10 December 1958), para. 5.
47. G.A.O.R., 12th Session, 690th plenary meeting (26 September 1957), paras. 72–73.
48. S.C.O.R., 13th year, 837th meeting (22 July 1958), paras. 10–16.
49. G.A.O.R., 14th Session, Supplement No. 1A, p. 3.
50. U.N. doc. SG/868, 8 November 1959.
51. Soviet Mission to the U.N., Press Release, 16 November 1959.
52. G.A.O.R., 17th Session, Annexes, Agenda item 89, A/5170 (20 August 1962).
53. U.N. docs. S/5298 (29 April 1963), S/5321 (27 May 1963), S/5326 (8 June 1963).
54. U.N. doc. SG/1583, 13 September 1963.
55. Speech in Chicago, U.N. doc. SG/910, 1 May 1960, p. 6.
56. Hammarskjold, *The International Civil Service in Law and in Fact*, p. 11.
57. The main statements of the Soviet position are to be found in Khrushchev's speeches in plenary meetings of the General Assembly, G.A.O.R., 15th Session, 869th, 882nd, and 904th plenary meetings (23 September, 3 October, and 13 October 1960); in part of a draft resolution on disarmament submitted to the First Committee, G.A.O.R., 15th Session, Annexes, Agenda items 67, 86, 69 and 73, A/C.1/L.249 (13 October 1960); in the state-

ment of the Soviet Government that it would 'not maintain any relations with Hammarskjold and . . . not recognize him as an official of the United Nations . . .', S.C.O.R., 16th year, Supplement for January, February and March, S/4704 (14 February 1961); and in the views expressed by the Soviet member of the Committee of Experts on the Activities and Organization of the Secretariat, G.A.O.R., 16th Session, Annexes, Agenda item 61, A/4776 (14 June 1961), pp. 41–42.

58. G.A.O.R., 15th Session, 869th plenary meeting (23 September 1960), paras. 283–5.
59. See, for example, G.A.O.R., 16th Session, 5th Committee, 874th meeting (8 November 1961), paras. 27, 29, 32.
60. See King Gordon, *The United Nations in the Congo*, New York, Carnegie Endowment for International Peace, 1962.
61. G.A.O.R., 1st Emergency Special Session, Agenda item 5, A/3302 (6 November 1956), para. 8; 13th Session, Annexes, Agenda item 65, A/3943 (9 October 1958), paras. 166–7.
62. S.C.O.R., 15th year, Supplement for July, August and September, S/4426 (9 August 1960), para. 4.
63. S.C.O.R., 15th year, Supplement for July, August and September, S/4503 and S/4475/Add. 2.
64. G.A.O.R., 15th Session, 869th plenary meeting (23 September 1960), paras. 278–9.
65. G.A.O.R., 15th Session, 882nd plenary meeting (3 October 1960), paras. 48–49. Khrushchev told C. L. Sulzberger that 'The "troika" principle will be necessary only in the event that international forces are set up. The command of these forces should be based on that principle. This would be necessary to guarantee that no state or group of states could use international United Nations forces to the detriment of any other state of group of states.' *The New York Times*, 8 September 1961.
66. G.A.O.R., 15th Session, 869th plenary meeting (23 September 1960), para. 285.
67. U.N. doc. A/4797 (7 July 1961), p. 8.
68. See the statement by the Rapporteur in Report of the Committee of Experts . . ., Appendix 2.
69. S.C.O.R., 15th year, 887th meeting (21 August 1960).
70. S.C.O.R., 16th year, 935th meeting (15 February 1961), para. 35.
71. Hammarskjold, *The International Civil Servant in Law and*

in Fact, p. 23; see also G.A.O.R., 16th Session, Supplement No. 1A, p. 5.

72. See, for example, S.C.O.R., 16th year, Supplement for October, November and December, S/5003 (27 November, 1961).

73. Egon F. Ranshofen-Wertheimer, *The International Secretariat: a Great Experiment in International Administration*, Washington, Carnegie Endowment for International Peace, 1945, pp. 73–74.

74. *Proceedings of the Exploratory Conference on the Experience of the League of Nations*, pp. 40, 41, 45.

NOTES AND QUESTIONS

1. From the viewpoint of authoritative action, the most important change introduced by Clark and Sohn in the Office of the Secretary-General is found in Article 99 where the word "may" is replaced by "shall." The purpose of the change is to make it a positive duty, rather than a discretionary choice for the Secretary-General to bring matters concerning international peace and security to the attention of the Security Council. In view of the overwhelming concern that all nations would be expected to have in raising these matters under the Clark-Sohn scheme, and as a result of the fact that the element of discretion necessarily remains even if the phrase, "in his opinion," in Article 99 were to be deleted, the Clark-Sohn revision would probably be of little consequence. As Alexandrowicz suggests above, if the same change were made in the present context, however, it would undoubtedly have greater meaning.
2. As was noted in the introduction to this section, Clark and Sohn do not envision enlarging the executive capacity of the Secretary-General. Given the fact that the Secretary-General's Office has operated in the peace-keeping areas, would it not be sensible for those who desire to enlarge the peace-keeping capacities and actual forces of the United Nations to attempt to do so through the further development of this Office? Perhaps it will be easier to initiate a standing international police force through this Office than through the use of either Article 43 of the Charter, or the General Assembly recommendations, or by creating some newly established organization. For the legal argument that an international police force can be established directly under the Secretary-General without Charter revision, see Louis B. Sohn, "The Authority of the United Nations to Establish and Maintain a Permanent United Nations Force," *The American Journal of International Law*, vol. 52 (April, 1958) pp. 323–329.

   It would be instructive in this connection to investigate the recent role of the Secretary-General in connection with the Yemen and Cyprus peace-keeping operations of the United Nations.
3. Bailey states a very persuasive case that once the United Nations starts to operate in the peace-keeping area and the Secretary-General has been given the responsibility for administering the Organization's activities, it is extremely difficult for Member States to persuade the political organs to terminate peace-keeping operations. This fact may make many states sufficiently cautious that, before soliciting action by the United Nations, they will insist on providing for explicit instructions for the Secretary-General and for the forces in the field. It may be that a recognition of the need for this explicitness will lead to the establishment of a set of rules to be generally applied wherever UN forces are operating. On the need for such rules, see McVitty, Chapter 9B.
4. The present Charter does not specify a fixed term of years for the Office of Secretary-General, although appointments are generally made for five-year periods. This has caused some difficulty. It was impossible to agree upon the successor to Trygve Lie in 1950, and he remained in office for three years beyond his original period of appointment on the ground that his position did not terminate until a new Secretary-General was appointed. Clark and Sohn have incorporated this practice in their revision of Article 97 and have, in addition, provided for a term of six years. They have also given the Assembly authority to remove the Secretary-General by a two-thirds vote.

5. In "Should We Veto the Troika?" (see Notes and Questions, Chapter 4, p. 197), Roger Fisher points out that the Troika proposal has two elements that are frequently confused: (1) the decision should be made by a group representing different points of view, rather than by a single individual and, (2) the right to veto. In our discussion of the Security Council we have already looked at some of the problems of the veto. With regard to the Troika as a device to require a group decision, Fisher suggests that there are two problems. One is impartiality and the other is effectiveness of administration. He has the following to say on those matters:

> In the case of the nuclear test ban, the Soviets have proposed that there be 'an Administrative Council of three equal representatives, one each from the principal groups of states—the Socialist states, the countries belonging to Western military blocs and the neutralist states.' The theory underlying this proposal was summarized in the Soviet memorandum given President Kennedy in Vienna:
>
>> The control commission, on which all principal groups of states will be represented, can adopt sound, just decisions, taking into consideration the interests of all states. However, it is not enough to take such decisions. It is imperative to guarantee their impartial implementation. Impartiality cannot be guaranteed if the implementation of the decisions is left to one man alone.
>
> Now, in suggesting that important decisions should be made by a group rather than by an individual Mr. Khrushchev has said nothing new or controversial. Americans are familiar with the device of giving a group rather than an individual responsibility both for formulating policy and for carrying it out. After Congress has decided what policy should be and has adopted appropriate legislation, it is often reluctant to leave its implementation to a single person, as is illustrated by the Atomic Energy Commission, the Federal Trade Commission and other regulatory agencies. Policy decisions in our private corporations are made by boards of directors, and even at the level of execution, the executive committee is common. Military policy in the Defense Department is implemented by the Joint Chiefs of Staff. No clear line can be drawn between the forming of policy, where it is generally recognized that joint wisdom is best, and the carrying out of policy, where the efficiency of a single responsible officer is usually desired. If we, without common bonds, interests, and law are unwilling to trust a single official we should understand better than we do the concern which the Soviet proposal reflects.
>
> Where the views of different representatives in a group are sharply divided, as might be the case between representatives of East and West, the produce of the group will tend to be less a collective judgment and more a collective bargain. But where interests sharply conflict, the group process can nonetheless be a useful means of arriving at an acceptable accommodation.
>
> Having said this, I must add that the particular three-headed monster proposed by Mr. Khrushchev would seem to be ill-designed. There is little value in assuming, and thereby accentuating, a division of the world into three defined camps, each of which can theoretically be represented by one point of view. Moreover, if neutrals are to exert a moderating influence upon representatives of the United States and the Soviet Union, it would be better to have several of them rather than one. There is enormous pressure on a single neutral whatever the merits of particular issues may be. However, Mr. Khrushchev is certainly less concerned with giving the neutrals a vote than in getting a veto for himself. The group-decision feature of the troika proposal thus raises a question of degree: how far down toward the details of administration do the benefits of collective judgments and bargaining outweigh the drawbacks? This is a matter which can be discussed and for which any solution, inherently, requires balance and compromise. To repeat, the group-decision feature of the troika proposal is not something to which we should object on principle.

6. Bailey makes the point that the notion of Troika was advanced prior to Patrice Lumumba's death and was connected with problems of peace-keeping and disarmament. Bailey argues, therefore, that it is an important part of the perspective that the Soviet Union brings to world organization. It must be acknowledged that there is considerable difficulty in achieving an objective or neutral image for an international public servant, at least in the continuing absence of a set of mutually agreed upon norms or common interests to which the official of an international organization might refer. At the same time it seems that the Secretary-General, sensitive as he is to the problems of developing common interests and mutually acceptable principles, can do a great deal to foster a neutral image. An awareness of the role of law, it should be added, may be a most significant aspect of this process. Alexandrowicz' analysis of the constitutional powers of the Secretary-General are germane.
7. Thus far we have been discussing mainly the position of the Secretary-General. This Office is, however, the apex of an organ, the Secretariat. As Bailey points out, there has been difficulty connected with the staffing of the top policy posts in the Secretariat, especially as they relate to the Office of the Secretary-General itself. Each Secretary-General has found it convenient to have a different number of positions at the top policy level, that number running from four to seven, and, furthermore, each has acted differently with regard to them. Some of the individuals in these posts have attempted to operate as international public servants. Others have more or less tended to represent their respective governments.

   It is not merely, however, at the top policy level that the Secretariat is faced with problems of organizing and staffing. There is the problem of an equitable distribution of staff in terms of geographical distribution at all levels. While there have been some disputes concerning what constitutes equitable representation, the fact is that much of the problem of staffing this Organization of six thousand is caused by Member States who are unwilling to provide permanent and competent international public servants, or who do not have at their disposal a sufficient number of nationals capable of doing the job or who cannot spare skilled people because of the pressing needs for skilled bureaucrats in their own society. For an illuminating discussion of these matters, see Commission to Study the Organization of Peace, "Problems of Organizing and Staffing the Secretariat," *The U.N. Secretary-General—His Role in World Politics,* Fourteenth Report, Part IV (American Association for the United Nations, 1962).
8. For a major study of the evolving role of the Secretary-General, see the forthcoming study by Leon Gordenker, entitled *The Secretary-General,* to be published by Columbia University Press. See also Sidney D. Bailey, *The Secretariat of the United Nations* (rev. ed., Praeger, New York, 1962) Chapter IV.

7

The Limitations on the Authority of the United Nations: Article 2(7) and Apartheid in the Republic of South Africa

The most pervasive question that arises in connection with the United Nations and its constituent organs is the extent to which the Organization may act on behalf of the world community to establish and enforce rules of conduct upon nation-states. The study of the Security Council, General Assembly and Secretariat in prior chapters revealed that the major political and legal problems of these organs were related to differing interpretations of the scope and extent of this capacity. Since this question permeates all matters relevant to the establishment of a formal international organization capable of dealing with war prevention, much of the material already considered has either implicitly or explicitly been concerned with this problem. However, in order to provide a frame of reference for dealing directly with the extent of United Nations authority over states, this chapter examines directly the norm that prohibits the Organization from interfering in the reserved domain of domestic jurisdiction.

In terms of the present United Nations Charter this undertaking is best accomplished through an appreciation of Article 2(7) which reads: "Nothing contained in the present Charter shall authorize the United Nations to intervene within matters which are essentially within the domestic jurisdiction of any state or shall require the members to submit such matters to settlement under the present Charter; but this principle shall not prejudice the application of enforcement measures under Chapter VII." Given the obvious reluctance of officials of nation-states to surrender sovereignty to a supranational organization, it should be no surprise that this provision can be interpreted to contain both the most severe limitation upon United Nations activity and its broadest grant of authority. That is, if the prohibition against intervening within the domestic jurisdiction of states is defined broadly, then it might well be that the Organization will have few matters that it is authorized even to discuss, let alone to take action upon; yet there is the significant exception to the prohibition that, in the event that the five permanent members of the Security Council with concurrence of any two nonpermanent members make the decision under Chapter VII of the Charter that there is a threat to the peace, breach of the peace, or act of aggression, then the Council without further consultation, possesses the authority to make legally binding demands upon other Member States. The Security Council could order a state to desist from military action, even where its use of force was alleged to be in the exercise of the right of self-defense, or the Council could call upon Member States to cease all diplomatic and economic relations with another state, or it could call into being an international military and police force to coerce states to comply with its decision. The obvious tension between the separate clauses of Article 2(7) has been a focal point for much of the discussion of the supranational quality of the United Nations. A good deal of the debate has centered upon the capacity of the Organization to operate in situations where a direct threat to international peace existed. At the same time, the authority to act in other substantive areas has been a source of considerable difficulty. This difficulty reflects the uncertain content of domestic jurisdiction, an uncertainty evident whenever the Organization proposes to act with respect to subject matter that appears, in certain senses, to be a matter of domestic concern.

To help understand the general dimension of the problems which arise when the Organization attempts, through votes of its Membership, to discuss or act upon a matter that a state feels is essentially within its domestic jurisdiction, we have selected for study one particular situation: the efforts of the United Nations to induce the Government of the Republic of South Africa to cease the practice of apartheid. At least three reasons account for selecting this particular interaction between the Organization and one of its Members.

First of all, the problem of dealing with apartheid raises a fundamental question about achieving a peaceful world order through formal international organization; it asks that we determine what kinds of social matters must be made part of the proper concern of the Organization if international violence is to be prevented. If we look at the Clark-Sohn model for world order and at their revision of Article 2(7), it becomes clear that Clark and Sohn feel it is necessary for the Organization to exercise comprehensive control over military power, to have pacific settlement procedures at its disposal that provide appropriate tribunals with compulsory jurisdiction over international disputes, and to administer a world development authority that can provide the material means to enable poorer states both to sustain a rate of economic growth and to raise the living standards of their populations. One could summarize the relation between the authority of states and that of the United Nations by saying that Clark and Sohn confer substantial supranational authority upon their world organization in the areas of security and welfare, but not in the area of human rights. To be sure, Clark and Sohn show *some* concern for the international protection of human rights, and in Annex VII they give the outline of a Bill of Rights; but they make it clear that these rights are limitations upon the competence of the United Nations rather than being attempts to protect the rights of individuals by enlisting the authority and power of the Organization against states guilty of abusing human rights. Clark and Sohn give their United Nations approximately the same competence to discuss and act with respect to human rights as that which exists under the present Charter. For the Clark-Sohn view on the matters discussed here, see their revision of Article 2(7), pp. 7–9, their proposals for a World Development Authority, pp. 345–348, and their outline for a proposed Bill of Rights, pp. 365–370.

The Clark-Sohn position on human rights reflects their view that any treatment of the subject which is less conservative would lessen the acceptability of their overall proposals by posing too direct a challenge to the control of governments over their own nationals, and thereby squarely challenge prevailing attitudes toward what is within the reserved domain of national sovereignty. Clark and Sohn apparently assume that the Organization can handle the tasks of war prevention without extending its control beyond present limits in the area of human rights. Some analysts feel that even aside from challenging prevailing notions of sovereignty, it would be dangerous to place so much authority in the hands of a central world organization, since it would increase the risk that a totalitarian world state might emerge; thus, in terms of separation of powers or of allocating and distributing authority to avoid the control of the Organization by tyrannical forces it would, the argument goes, be best to omit this area from the competence of the Organization. The excerpt from Hutchins in **I-1D** and the encyclical, *Pacem in Terris*, in **I-1F** imply a position contrary to the Clark-Sohn view, for both express the view that until matters of human rights are dealt with and protected by a supranational organization, it would be unfortunate (as it might freeze abuse into the system) and perhaps even impossible (as the perception of abuse breeds violence) to achieve a peaceful world order.

Within the area of human rights there exists an overwhelming consensus of states that insists upon coercive action by the United Nations. This social fact might indicate that unless a world organization undertakes to uphold minimal standards for human rights it will be unable to attract and retain the support of the peoples of the world for such other of its purposes as war prevention. The acceptability of the Clark-Sohn world may depend for certain states more upon its likely ability to combat racial discrimination than to reduce the risk of major war. It may, in fact, be a form of provincialism to project upon the world, especially in view of the large Afro-Asian portion, the over riding identification in the West of world order with world peace. Many of these newly independent states may, for instance, prefer to accept higher risks of major war in exchange for the great prospect of ending the practice of apartheid.

Although other substantive areas will not be discussed here (see, however, **IV-6**), the point goes beyond apartheid to the more general problem of the degree to which it becomes necessary for the United Nations to overcome the domestic jurisdiction prohibition in the interest of world order. We might in general ask whether Clark and Sohn give sufficient authority to the United Nations to enable it to impose social and economic reforms on Member States. Suppose, for example, that changes in the fiscal and tax policy or in an agricultural program within a particular state would bring about increased benefits for the population of that state, and that without these changes the society would remain stagnant and would have to rely either upon monies from other states, or upon the generosity of the World Development Authority. Should the Organization permit such inefficient, and perhaps, inhumane practices to continue out of deference to the notions of national sovereignty and domestic jurisdiction? How should the will of the international community be balanced against these patterns of deference? Or, put another way, is it really possible to set up the machinery for effective war prevention and not become involved in the tensions generated in connection with trade, immigration, monetary, fiscal and agricultural policies adopted by the individual states? To make any world order scheme work, is it necessary to include these matters in the authority of the Organization?

A second reason for dealing with apartheid is to see the meaning that has been given to Article 2(7) in the practices of the United Nations. This history of the apartheid question is particularly revealing because it has proceeded through all the phases of what is meant by "intervention" in domestic jurisdiction—both in terms of procedure and substance. From the viewpoint of procedure of the Organization a series of steps can be taken: the matter can be placed on the provisional agenda or it can be inscribed on the permanent agenda, a discussion can take place within an organ or any agency of the Organization commissioned to study the problem, resolutions can be passed by the Assembly announcing a policy of the United Nations, general recommendations can be made to the states on various policies, specific recommendations either directly mentioning particular states or identifying specific policies can be put forward, recommendations that states impose sanctions upon another state can be made, decisions can be taken that are obligatory upon Member States, and finally, the imposition of sanctions through decisions can be launched. Each of these steps may at one point or another be opposed on the ground that it is a violation of the domestic jurisdiction of a state. As United Nations action concerning South Africa's practice of apartheid has occurred, the relationship between Charter provisions that serve as the basis for these procedures necessarily also discloses the processes whereby constitutional authority is allocated among the various units of the Organization, as well as the relationship of such a pattern of allocation to the degree and content of world community consensus.

The elucidation of the relevance of consensus to the authority of the United Nations provides our final reason for selecting apartheid as the substantive topic that is most illuminating in the study of domestic jurisdiction. For the subject provides an opportunity for exploring the interaction of the traditional processes by which international law has developed with the law-creating processes operative within the United Nations, and thereby to resume the inquiry initiated in Chapter 2. Customary international law, it will be recalled, develops as the practice of nation-states form patterns of behavior that solicit the general acquiescence of other states in the international community. This process of unfolding law through time has contributed many of the rules and standards that are accepted as law. Racial prejudice resulting in official policies of political and legal discrimination and social segregation has been subjected to increasing moral and political attacks throughout the world. The presence of a central international forum in which to dramatize the charges of oppressive discrimination has given great importance to this process of denunciation. This importance is vividly illustrated by the role of the United Nations vis-à-vis South Africa. Years full of debate were followed by virtually unanimous approval by Member States of positions condemning apartheid as a policy and demonstrating the capacity of the Organization to mobilize universal sentiments. The United Nations has almost certainly hastened the development of a minimum international standard of non-discrimination in the area of human rights; no nation can now flaunt this standard without anticipating very nearly universal disapproval and may also soon find itself under significant pressure to adapt its policies to accord with the global consensus. A study of apartheid casts some light on the intricate problems of the impact of General Assembly resolutions and recommendations upon state behavior and upon an appraisal of the extent to which these formal acts acquire the character of legally binding and effective obligations.

The question of the policy of South Africa in connection with its treatment of racial groups has actually been on the agenda of the United Nations in some form since its founding in 1945, the earliest item being "Treatment of Indians in the Union of South Africa." Resolutions condemning racial persecution and racial discrimination in the General Assembly were passed as early as 1946; the adoption of the Universal Declaration of Human Rights in 1948 helped crystallize world sentiments on the subject; thereafter, the specific identification of apartheid as a policy officially announced by the South African government to deal with its different racial and tribal groups and as incorporated in the Group Areas Act of 1950 that set up a complicated arrangement of separate geographical areas for the various races in their nonworking hours and provided for strict supervision during working hours, was denounced in General Assembly Resolutions of 1950 and 1952. To grasp the character of this specific denunciation, it is helpful to examine the political and legal context within which it evolved.

Throughout this early period the South African government argued strenuously that all these matters bearing on its racial policies were essentially within its domestic jurisdiction and that, therefore, the General Assembly lacked even the competence to place the subject on the agenda, let alone discuss it. While only a few states supported the South African government in this position, there were a large number of states that felt that a discussion and study of the subject intended to produce recommendations of even a general nature should be approached very cautiously in so far as such an undertaking might reasonably be interpreted as intervening in the domestic jurisdiction of Member States. There was an even stronger sentiment in this early period for not passing resolutions that would identify specific states as wrongdoers since it was believed that such explicitness would certainly be contrary to the prohibition of Article 2(7). Yet, despite these rather widely-held attitudes, the Assembly not only adopted the resolutions of 1950 and 1952, but placed on the agenda an item in 1952 entitled "The Question of Race Conflict in South Africa Resulting from the Policies of Apartheid of the Government of the Union of South Africa." As might be expected, the South African government protested vehemently against the inscription of this item on the agenda. Some excerpts from the debates that arose are reproduced to illustrate the opposing points of view on the matter.

In reading these debates special attention should be given to the ways in which various provisions of the Charter are invoked by the parties. It is difficult to evaluate whether the reference to these provisions was significant in persuading states to vote one way or another on different occasions; but that representatives in the political organs of the Organization felt compelled to find a justification for their positions in Charter language, that positions taken in one situation may exert an influence in other circumstances as yet unforeseen, and that there may even be the possibility that the Charter language provides both some direction and certain constraints seems clear from the transcript of the debates. An appreciation of the behavior of Member States helps with an understanding of the manner in which law and politics interact in an international organization to produce standards and rules of conduct that guide international behavior, as well as set a tone of orderly government process. For a more detailed explanation of this point, see Chapter 2, and **II-1**.

There is such a natural convergence of political and legal attitudes with regard to many of the issues raised whenever the subject of domestic jurisdiction is discussed, that the articulation of explicit views on the character of policy underlying relevant legal doctrine is, at once, of immense importance and almost inevitable. Although there exists no definitive view of what constitutes the policy controlling an interpretation of domestic jurisdiction, it may help a reader approach the somewhat discursive materials that follow to consider one coherent conception of the policy that should guide the organs of the United Nations when confronted by the need to interpret domestic jurisdiction. This is the conception worked out by Mrs. Rosalyn Higgins in the following statement from her book,

Development of International Law Through the Political Organs of the United Nations (Oxford University Press, London, 1963) pp. 61–62.

The legal principle of domestic jurisdiction is, for various reasons, singularly susceptible to development by the process of interpretation by political bodies. Article 2(7) is far from unambiguous, and by its very nature the concept of domestic jurisdiction is incapable of capture and crystallization for all time. What is truly domestic today will not necessarily be so in five years' time. Problems of prostitution and narcotics were once the sole concern of sovereign states; they are now acknowledged to be matters of international concern. Until very recently it has been assumed that the regard for human rights which a state shows in the treatment of its own citizens was a question of domestic jurisdiction; today this assumption is open to serious doubts. In deeming Article 2(7) applicable or inapplicable to any given situation, organs of the United Nations must decide, in good faith, whether the matter under discussion is one which, at the present time, can be said to be 'essentially within the domestic jurisdiction' of the state. They must also decide whether the action proposed by the United Nations—be it the mere placing of the matter on the agenda, or discussion, or establishing a means of inquiry, or a resolution—constitutes 'intervention'. And they must consider whether the only exception to the principle is the one explicitly mentioned in Article 2(7)—namely, enforcement measures—or whether the integrity of other obligations in the Charter would be impaired if Article 2(7) were interpreted in this manner.

It is undeniable that in attempting to find the answer to these complex points of law, an interpretive element is introduced. Equally, it is essential that this interpretation be in accordance with a well considered policy based on desirable objectives, and not merely in accordance with political convenience, propaganda purposes, and habits of bloc-voting. What, then, should this basic policy be? In other words, for what purposes, in what degree, and by what methods, should international organizations be permitted to concern themselves with the affairs of sovereign states? Any legalistic interpretations of Article 2(7) which do not consider these questions will be but specious. Given the mutable and developing nature of the concept of domestic jurisdiction, a flexible approach is desirable, based on the principle that states must be made responsible to the international community when their actions cause substantial international effects. This principle would seem to be especially true of those fields which are the subject of natural concern to the United Nations, as exemplified by the Principles of the Charter. To be guided in one's interpretive tasks by such a policy is not to deny all efficacy to the reservation of domestic jurisdiction; nor is it to insist upon the intrusion of the international Organization into areas which by general consensus nations regard as more properly dealt with by themselves. The right of a people freely to choose its own government is such a right, and to subject that choice to international review is both illegal and undesirable, though even here it may be asked if the matter remains within the domestic jurisdiction if the choice of a particular government is a threat to the peace. Moreover, the interpretation of what may be reserved to the domestic domain must not be so severely limited that the confidence of the member states is forfeited, for this would ultimately discourage participation and goodwill in an Organization that must aim at near-universality of membership if is is to function sucessfully in its stated aims. Within the limits of this proviso, interpretation should be in favour of the efficacy of the Organization, and in favour of rendering states accountable for their behaviour in areas of international concern. It must therefore be a cardinal principle that a state may not judge for itself what falls within its own domestic jurisdiction. In so far as the political organs of the United Nations are concerned,[16] this must mean that the question of whether or not a matter is in fact one of domestic jurisdiction must be open for discussion and vote, and so must the issue of whether it should be inscribed upon the agenda. The analysis which follows of past practice and the trend of decision endeavours to bear these policy objectives in mind.

[16] In relation to the legal organ, the ICJ, this principle arises in the form of the so-called 'Connolly amendment'.

We turn now to one of the early arguments on the legal propriety of placing the matter of apartheid on the agenda of the General Assembly.

Debate in the General Assembly on Inclusion of Agenda Item "Treatment of People of Indian Origin in the Union of South Africa: report of the United Nations Good Offices Commission."

U.N.G.A. Official records, 8th sess. Plenary meetings, 435th meeting, 17 September 1953. pp. 23–27 (A/PV.435).

Adoption of the agenda: report of the General Committee (A/2477)

[Agenda item 8]

PART I

2. The PRESIDENT: The report of the General Committee [*A/2477*] has been circulated. I propose to place the matters contained in the report before the General Assembly for its consideration in the order in which they appear in the report. If there is no objection, I invite the attention of the General Assembly to the items recommended for inclusion as set out in Part I of that document. At this time, the General Assembly is concerned only with the question of the inclusion of items. The question of their allocation to Committees will be open for consideration after the adoption of the agenda. Before beginning the consideration of the proposed agenda, I wish to draw the attention of members to rule 23 of the rules of procedure. This reads:

> "Debate on the inclusion of an item in the agenda, when that item has been recommended for inclusion by the General Committee, shall be limited to three speakers in favour of and three against the inclusion. The President may limit the time to be allowed to speakers under this rule."

3. It will be observed that the General Committee has recommended the inclusion in the agenda of all the items on the provisional agenda [*A/2416*] and on the supplementary list [*A/2443*], as well as the proposed additional item [*A/2466*]. There are no recommendations from the General Committee for the exclusion or postponement of any item.

4. The General Assembly will now consider th inclusion of items 1 to 17 inclusive.

Items 1 to 17 inclusive were placed on the agend without discussion.

5. The PRESIDENT: Are there any objections t the inclusion of items 18 to 25 inclusive?

6. Mr. JOOSTE (Union of South Africa): I sha deal at this stage, of course, only with item 20. It wi be recalled that when the General Committee yesterda considered the provisional agenda, I again placed o record my Government's objection to and protest against the inclusion of item 20, entitled "Treatmer of people of Indian origin in the Union of South Africa report of the United Nations Good Offices Com mission".

7. I do not have to remind this Assembly of th history of this matter, the long history to whic reference was made yesterday by the representative c India. Nor do I have to remind the General Assembl of the attitude which my Government has taken wit regard to it. It is, therefore, not my intention to g further than merely to state once again that the ques tion of the treatment or the allegations with regard t such treatment of people of Indian origin in Sout Africa is one which falls essentially within the domesti jurisdiction of the South African Government and tha the United Nations is explicitly debarred by the pro visions of Article 2, paragraph 7, of the Charter fror dealing with it.

8. It may be recalled that when I raised this matte in the General Committee, merely for purposes of th record, the representative of India took issue with m and reminded the Committee that the General As sembly had on previous ocasions pronounced itself o the question of competence with regard to this matte when it had held that the United Nations had th authority to deal with this particular item. He als reminded the Committee that on the present issue th Assembly would be required to deal with the report c the Good Offices Commission which had been set u last year [*resolution 615 (VII)*].

9. As regards the first point, that is, previous decision by the General Assembly and its Committees on th question of competence, let me repeat what we hav so often stated before, namely, that in our view ther can be no doubt whatsoever that Article 2, paragrap 7, of the Charter does in fact prohibit this Organizatio from intervening in the domestic affairs of Membe States. We have often indicated our reasons for thi view and we have never yet heard an adequate leg argument to the contrary. In any case, our argumen are well known and I am not going to take up th time of the Assembly to repeat them, not now at a events. This item is clearly related to a matter whic

one of essentially domestic concern, and in terms Article 2, paragraph 7, of the Charter, the Organiza-on has no authority to deal with it in any way hatsoever.

. As regards the second point, namely, that the ssembly is required to receive a report from its Good ffices Commission—a body which it set up itself— t me repeat what I have said before, that from the rictly legal point of view, which is the only valid pproach to this matter, this consideration does not in y way affect the fundamental principle involved, that , that this Organization cannot, constitutionally, deal ith this item. I repeat, therefore, that the present em is one with which the General Assembly, in con-quence of the explicit provisions of Article 2, para-aph 7, of the Charter, cannot properly deal.

. I am turning now to another aspect of the matter. ay I remind the Assembly that Article 2, paragraph of the Charter stipulates also, in the clearest possible nguage, that nothing contained in the Charter shall quire Members to submit such matters to settle-ent under the Charter. My Government has con-stently made it quite clear that it is not prepared to bmit the matter to settlement under the Charter. This a right which, as I have pointed out, is safeguarded the Charter itself. My Government continues to here to this attitude.

. It is for these reasons that I again ask the eneral Assembly not to include the present item in agenda.

. Mr. DAYAL (India): This is the seventh casion on which the question of the treatment of ople of Indian origin in the Union of South Africa s come up before the General Assembly. It gives no pleasure to have this matter discussed here year er year. But the attitude of the Government of the nion of South Africa towards the resolutions of the neral Assembly, adopted year after year, makes ch a discussion inevitable. The representative of the nion of South Africa has, for the seventh time, chal-ged the inclusion of this item in the agenda. At six the previous sessions of the General Assembly a nilar objection was made. On all six occasions the neral Assembly rejected the objection and included e item in its agenda.

. It seems somewhat superfluous to us to contest ain the question of competence, when the Assembly s repeatedly declared itself in favour of its inclusion. is is of course not the time nor the place to raise question of competence, which in any event cannot decided until the item is placed on the agenda and Assembly has had an opportunity of studying the ts.

. It will be recalled that at its seventh session the neral Assembly adopted resolution 615 (VII), ablishing a Good Offices Commission for the purpose arranging and assisting in negotiations between the vernment of the Union of South Africa and the vernments of India and Pakistan. That resolution quested this Commission to report the results of its orts to the eighth session. Further, in order to sure proper consideration of its report, the Assembly cided to place the item on the provisional agenda of eighth session.

The report of the Good Offices Commission is, I derstand, shortly expected, and under the terms of resolution which I have just mentioned, the General Assembly will be required to consider it. The previous decisions of the Assembly and the resolution of last year clearly require the Assembly to discuss the item and I therefore earnestly hope that the General Assembly will decide to place it on its agenda.

17. The PRESIDENT: As there are no other speakers on item 20, the General Assembly will proceed to a vote.

Item 20 was placed on the agenda by 45 votes to 1, with 11 abstentions.

18. The PRESIDENT: I call on the representative of the Union of South Africa, who wishes to speak on item 21.

19. Mr. JOOSTE (Union of South Africa): When the General Committee considered the provisional agenda for this session, I, in this case as well, appeared before it and placed on record my Government's protest against the inclusion of the present item. I then gave notice that as the final decision on items to be included in the agenda was a matter for the General Assembly, where all Member Governments are represented, I would again raise our objection at this stage.

20. The Assembly may recall that this procedure was followed by the South African delegation at the previous session. However, it will also be remembered that at that time, when the General Committee's report was submitted to the Assembly, my delegation intervened and invoked rule 80 of our rules of procedure and asked that the question of competence be decided prior to a decision on inscription.

21 Unfortunately, after we had been permitted by the President, without any objection from any delegation present, to argue our case, a procedural difference developed in consequence of which my delegation was denied the opportunity of obtaining a clear-cut decision on whether or not the Assembly was competent to deal with this matter. It was in these circumstances that a vote was taken not in terms of rule 80 but merely on the question of inscription. The history of this unhappy incident is reflected in our records, and I shall say no more about it.

22. This year, having regard to our experience last year, my delegation has decided to deal directly with the question of inscription and to ask the General Assembly not to include this item in its agenda.

23. On what grounds do I ask the Assembly to reject the recommendation of the General Committee to inscribe the present item? I do so for reasons which were fully set out in my argument last year, an argument which is on record and which, I believe, is known to most delegations present—a legal argument of which, I submit, there has been no rebuttal, and which, I also submit, continues to be valid. It is not my intention today to repeat that argument in detail. I shall merely remind the Assembly of the main features of the case on which, last year, I asked that the matter should not be inscribed on the agenda.

24. We expect, of course—as I indicated in the General Committee, and as actually happened—that it will be contended that this year the General Assembly is being asked to give consideration to a report for which the Assembly itself had asked and that it could hardly be held that the Assembly should be prevented from considering, or is not properly entitled to consider, the report, coming as it does from one of its own creatures.

25. This argument which I am anticipating is not unknown to us. We have been faced with it before in the United Nations. It is the type of argument which, when viewed superficially, is not without effect. On careful reflection, however, its fallacious character is readily discernible. For surely it cannot be denied that, if perchance the Organization is debarred by the explicit provisions of the Charter from dealing with any particular matter, then also it is debarred from dealing with any report on such a matter, whether that report is submitted to it by a body of its own creation or not. A matter excluded by the explicit provisions of the Charter from the competence of the United Nations can be brought within the Organization's competence only by an appropriate amendment of the Charter. No unilateral act on its part can therefore render the Assembly competent with regard to such a matter. Consequently, any assumption of competence in violation of the Charter is without legal force and therefore unconstitutional.

26. It was on these grounds that my Government contended, and still contends, that the Commision set up last year to study South Africa's racial policies was set up unconstitutionally. Any report emanating from that Commission on my Government's internal policies must consequently also be regarded as without legal status. I therefore repeat that the report in question cannot constitute a valid means of rendering the General Assembly competent to intervene in the domestic affairs of South Africa—unless, of course, such intervention is legally possible in terms of the explicit provisions of the Charter.

27. The question is therefore reduced to this: is the subject matter of the present item one with which this Organization can deal in consequence of competence which it derives from the Charter? And let me state, as emphatically as I can, that it is my Government's submission that it is not.

28. As I have already stated, my delegation last year submitted a detailed argument on this point to the Assembly, an argument the validity of which has not yet been disproved. I have also said that it is not my intention to repeat that argument in detail today. I shall, however, indicate in broad outline the legal basis for my Government's contention. Before doing so, however, it is necessary that I remind the Assembly of the exact nature of the present item. In order to do so it is necessary to look at the explanatory memorandum [*A/2183*] which accompanied the original request in 1952 for the inclusion of this item. In that memorandum the sponsors declared in very clear and very strong language that the racial policies and laws of the Government of the Union of South Africa were in violation of the human rights provisions of the Charter and that they constituted a threat to international peace. The sponsors also listed the specific matters in respect of which my country's policies and laws allegedly violated the Charter provisions in question and threatened world peace. With this clearly in mind, let me now proceed briefly with the legal basis for my Government's contention that the Organization is not competent in the matter.

29. It is our submission that every item listed in the charges brought against the Union of South Africa relates to matters which in every country fall within the domestic jurisdiction of the State. In respect of such matters, Article 2, paragraph 7, of the Charter states:

> "Nothing contained in the present Charter sha authorize the United Nations to intervene in matter which are essentially within the domestic jurisdictio of any State or shall require the Members to subm such matters to settlement under the present Charter but this principle shall not prejudice the applicatio of enforcement measures under Chapter VII."

30. Last year, I exhaustively analysed the meanin and scope of this paragraph. I need not do so agai I would merely remind the Assembly that the element of that analysis were as follows.

31. First, the word "nothing" in the initial phrase c Article 2, paragraph 7, has an overriding effect an forbids any activity which takes the form of an inte vention in the domestic affairs of any State, regardles of any other provision of the Charter—except enforce ment measures, with which, in any case, the Gener Assembly is not competent to deal.

32. Secondly, the word "intervene" in the paragrap which we are examining has its ordinary dictionar meaning and includes interference. It cannot mea dictatorial interference, as has repeatedly been allege since only the Security Council can interfere dict torially when it concerns a question of enforcemer measures under Chapter VII of the Charter. Sinc the General Assembly has no competence in this regar the prohibition not to intervene in a country's domest affairs would be tantamount to prohibiting the Asser bly from doing something which in any case it ha no competence to do, namely, interfering dictatoriall

33. Thirdly, the word "essentially" in the phras "essentially within the domestic jurisdiction of an State" was used in order to widen, and not to narrov the scope of domestic jurisdiction. This much abundantly clear from the records of the San Francisc Conference, from which I quoted in support of m contention during our last session.

34. The words "domestic jurisdiction", according international law, concern the relationship between State and its nationals, including the treatment of i nationals, which is universally recognized as a matt of exclusive domestic jurisdiction allowing of no inte ference by another State or by any external organiz tion, subject only to treaty obligations in terms which a State may have waived its inherent rights sovereignty.

35. So much for the meaning of Article 2, paragrap 7, of the Charter. But it has been argued that Artic 2, paragraph 7 does not apply when there is an allege question of human rights. I need merely mention th there was a very full discussion at San Francisco c the question of fundamental human rights in relatic to Article 2, paragraph 7. The outcome of that di cussion was the adoption by Commission II and su sequently by the plenary meeting of the Conferen of the following statement:

> "The members of Committee 3 of Commission are in full agreement that nothing contained Chapter IX can be construed as giving authority the Organization to intervene in the domestic affai of Member States." [1]

36. This wording, I submit, could not be clearer. should be noted that if the United Nations were to b permitted to intervene under Article 55 c, which, inc

[1] See *United Nations Conference on International Organiz tion*, II/3/55 (1), p. 271.

ıntally, concerns the promotion of human rights, on ıe ground that the matters contained therein were ɔt covered by the prohibition against intervention ɔntained in Article 2, paragraph 7, then the Assembly ould be equally permitted to intervene in regard to atters set out in Article 55 a and b, that is, economic ıd social matters, higher standards of living, full nployment, health legislation, etc. And I submit that ɔ State on earth would tolerate this.

'. But it was argued again and again that if the eneral Assembly could not discuss and make recom- endations in regard to the promotion of human rights, ɔw was the pledge contained in Article 56 to be rried out? Articles 55 and 56, read with Article 13 the Charter, provide the answer. There are the nctions of the Economic and Social Council in the cial and economic fields, the establishment of special- ed agencies, reports by governments, the making of ıdies and general recommendations, etc. There is the ommission on Human Rights which drafted the niversal Declaration of Human Rights and is now afting covenants on human rights which would define ıman rights and have internationally binding force respect of all signatory States. All these things may done without interfering in the domestic affairs of State.

. In conclusion, on this point, I should draw atten- ɔn to the fact that neither the Charter nor any other ternationally binding instrument contains any defini- ɔn of fundamental human rights. If they had, there ɔuld have been no need to set up the Commission frame the proposed covenant on human rights.

. This concludes what I have to say today on the egation that our laws and policies violate the Charter ovisions in question. Let me now turn briefly to e allegation that what is happening in South Africa nstitutes a threat to the peace. This is, of course, a ɔst reprehensible and mischievous allegation since ere can be a threat to the peace only when the terri- rial integrity or political independence of another ate is threatened. Can any State be accused of threat- ing the territorial integrity and political independence another because it makes laws of a purely domestic ture in the interests of good government? No single ate can claim that its sovereignty and security have en threatened by the Union of South Africa. None the charges listed against South Africa involves any atter which, in any way, affects the legitimate rights another State. If they had, we would have to concede at such other States enjoyed legitimate rights and thority with regard to our internal affairs and, erefore, that we had yielded our sovereignty with gard to the matters in question. The absurdity of ch a contention can easily be demonstrated by merely urning to the original explanatory memorandum and utinizing the nature of the specific matters listed erein. As the Assembly will note, these matters are, st, the regulation of the occupation of land and emises in South Africa by South African nationals; condly, public service facilities on our railways and r buses and post offices; thirdly, the means employed South Africa to repress communism; fourthly, the nposition of our armed forces; fifthly, voting rights our citizens; sixthly, educational and housing facil- es for the non-European citizens of South Africa.

Apart from the obviously hostile and distorted esentation of facts concerned, I would ask in all sincerity: by what stretch of imagination can it be contended legitimately that these matters do not fall exclusively within the domestic jurisdiction of my coun- try? Or how can it possibly be contended that they can be held to constitute a threat to the peace? Surely this is preposterous in the extreme. In fact, it is a most mischievous attempt to attract support for the ven- detta which the Government of India initiated against the Union of South Africa in the United Nations.

41. These are domestic matters which fall within the exclusive jurisdiction of any sovereign Member State. If they do not, then it is indeed difficult to conceive of any matter which could possibly fall within that category.

42. It is most interesting to note that, in this con- nexion, the representative of Pakistan, on 26 August of this year, speaking in the Security Council [*619th meeting*] on the question of Morocco, I believe, attempted to give a definition of what should be regarded as matters of domestic concern within the meaning and scope of Article 2, paragraph 7. He then stated that, in the view of his delegation, a matter was within the domestic jurisdiction of a Member State when it "pertains to the affairs of the subjects and the territories of that State, and [*is*] one over which that State has powers of direct legislation". I shall not endeavour to assess the validity of this defini- tion although it at least approximates to what we hold to be correct. But coming as it does from the repre- sentative of Pakistan, who is one of our accusers, it merits our close attention in so far as it can be related to the present item.

43. Can it be contended fairly and justly that the matters to which this item relates and which are listed in the memorandum to which I have referred, are not matters which fall within the scope of the definition attempted by the representative of Pakistan? I do not believe that I would be unfair in saying that, holding the views he does, at least the representative of Pakistan should be fully satisfied that the matters listed in the explanatory memorandum are of purely domestic con- cern and cannot properly and legally be dealt with by this Organization.

44. In any case, as I have stated, if these matters are not within the meaning and scope of Article 2, para- graph 7, of the Charter, then it is difficult to imagine how any matter can be so regarded. And, in that case, Article 2, paragraph 7, of the Charter becomes purpose- less and affords to no Member State any protection against intervention in its internal affairs.

45. I believe that it would be well for this Assembly to turn back the pages of history and look once again at the records of the San Francisco Conference. The statements made on this very point by statesmen such as Mr. Dulles and Mr. Evatt would prove most enlight- ening and perhaps serve as a clear reminder as to what precisely those responsible for this all-important pro- vision had in mind, a provision without which few if any of the smaller States would have found it possible to sign or ratify the Charter. My own country would not have been able to do so. It is the contention of my dele- gation, therefore, that the matters to which the present item relates are matters which fall essentially within the domestic jurisdiction of my country and that this Organization is specifically precluded by the provisions of Article 2, paragraph 7, from dealing with the item under discussion.

46. This brings me to one last point, namely, whether inclusion of the item can reasonably be opposed on the basis of the arguments I have placed before the Assembly. In this connexion we are only too well aware of the contention on the part of some that an item must be placed on the agenda in order to determine the competence or lack of competence of the Organization with regard thereto. This is a contention which my delegation rejects. We have often dealt with it before and last year again fully explained the legal basis and considerations which govern our attitude. I will not now recapitulate our arguments in detail; let me merely remind the Assembly of the fact that this matter has been discussed and that there can be no question any longer in the mind of any representative as to what precisely is the burden of the complaint against us. In any case, my Government holds that discussion of an argument constitutes intervention in the sense in which that term is used in Article 2, paragraph 7, where it bears the ordinary dictionary meaning and where it cannot but include the concept of interference in every sense of the word.

47. In that connexion it may also be as well if I remind members of the Assembly of the true nature of discussion: what is meant by discussion, what is entailed by discussion. In the United Nations there are few whose experience will not bear me out that discussion in the United Nations often constitutes what is perhaps one of the most insidious and effective forms of intervention of which this Organization is capable. My country has had considerable experience of this and we cannot but resist every effort on the part of the United Nations to discuss affairs which fall within our domestic jurisdiction.

48. It is in these circumstances that I ask the Assembly to reflect carefully on this matter and to exclude the present item from its agenda.

49. Mr. DAYAL (India): My delegation had hoped that it would not find it necessary to take up the time of the General Assembly today in making a statement on the matter before us, but since the representative of the Union of South Africa has decided to challenge the competence of this Assembly, even to place the question on its agenda, I consider it necessary to draw a few relevant considerations to the notice of the Assembly.

50. In our view this is not the right time or place to raise the question of the General Assembly's competence to discuss this item. We are at this stage concerned only with the question of the inclusion of the item in the agenda. I propose, therefore, not to deal with the various arguments which the representative of the Union of South Africa has advanced in support of his contention as to the incompetence of this Assembly, and I reserve the right to do so at the appropriate stage of the discussion.

51. It will be recalled that when the report of the General Committee was being considered last year in the Assembly, the representative of the Union of South Africa raised the question of the Assembly's competence and actually sought to move a resolution challenging it. By an overwhelming vote the General Assembly decided [*381st meeting*] that that was not the occasion to take up the matter of competence as the Assembly was merely concerned with the question of the inclusion of the item in its agenda. That was, of course, an entirely appropriate decision, fully in accord with our rules of procedure and the practice of th Assembly.

52. If the representative of the Union of South Afri again wishes to challenge the Assembly's competen to discuss this item, he can do so at the appropria stage after its inclusion in the agenda. Obviousl before we can discuss the question of competence, it essential first to place the item on the agenda.

53. Members of this Assembly will recall that t question of competence was deliberated upon at leng at the seventh session, both in committee and in t Assembly. The delegation of the Union of South Afri introduced motions to the effect that the *Ad H* Political Committee and the General Assembly had competence to consider the item. Both in the *Ad H* Political Committee [*21st meeting*] and in the Gener Assembly [*401st meeting*], the motion was rejected b overwhelming majorities of 45 votes and 43 vot respectively. The Assembly having already taken firm decision in the matter of competence, it seem unnecessary for this session to cover the same groun again.

54. The General Assembly last year adopted resol tion 616 (VII), to which the representative of t Union of South Africa has just referred, which esta lished a United Nations commission to study the raci situation in the Union of South Africa in the lig of the Purposes and Principles of the Charter. Th resolution enjoined upon the Commission to repo its conclusions to the General Assembly at its eigh session. It further decided to retain the question o the provisional agenda of the General Assembly present session. The report of that Commission will, trust, shortly be available and it is obvious that it mu come before this Assembly for consideration under t terms of last year's resolution.

55. If the contention of the representative of Sou Africa is to be accepted, and I earnestly hope that will not be accepted, it would be tantamount to th Assembly acting in a manner contrary to the expre decision taken at its seventh session. Such a cour I am confident this Assembly will not be prepared take and I feel sure that it will decide, as it di last year by an impressive majority, to place the ite on the agenda.

The report to which Mr. Jooste made reference was submitted in October of 1953 by a Commission that had been established by a resolution of the General Assembly in 1952 "to study the racial situation in the Union of South Africa in the light of the Purposes and Principles of the Charter, with due regard to the provisions of Article 2, paragraph 7, . . . Article 1, paragraphs 2 and 3, Article 13, paragraph 1(b), Article 55(c) and Article 56 of the Charter, and the resolution of the United Nations on racial persecution and discrimination, and to report its conclusions to the General Assembly at its eighth session." In this report the Commission answers each of the points raised by Mr. Jooste and in so doing covers many of the legal issues that have been raised vis-à-vis Article 2(7). Although the report does not discuss the specific political contexts in which the various positions on domestic jurisdiction arose, it is clear, nevertheless, that the Commission's policy is firmly in accord with scholarly writing on the subject and that it also reflects accurately the prevailing patterns of practices and attitudes of state officials.

Discussion of Article 2(7) by the Commission on the Racial Situation in the Union of South Africa.

U.N.G.A. Official records, 8th sess. Suppl. no. 16, 1953, pp. 15–23, 34. (A/2505 and A/2505/Add. 1).

V. Article 2, paragraph 7, of the Charter

117. At this stage of the report the Commission does not propose to analyse the force of the restrictive clause in Article 2, paragraph 7, of the Charter in relation to the powers of the General Assembly and the Economic and Social Council to implement the Purposes and Principles of the Charter. That general analysis will be carried out later. For the moment the Commission proposes to complete this analytical study of the Charter provisions referred to in resolution 616 A (VII) by a reference to Article 2, paragraph 7, in order to facilitate the general study which will be made in a later section of the chapter.

The paragraph in question reads as follows:

"7. Nothing contained in the present Charter shall authorize the United Nations to intervene in matters which are essentially within the domestic jurisdiction of any state or shall require the Members to submit such matters to settlement under the present Charter; but this principle shall not prejudice the application of enforcement measures under Chapter VII."

118. Among the Dumbarton Oaks proposals there was one provision which differed appreciably from the text adopted at San Francisco. Chapter VIII, section A, paragraph 7 of the proposals stated that the provisions of the six preceding paragraphs relating to the pacific settlement of disputes "should not apply to situations or disputes arising out of matters which by international law are solely within the domestic jurisdiction of the state concerned".

119. The Covenant of the League of Nations contained a similar provision, which read as follows:

"If the dispute between the parties is claimed by one of them, and is found by the Council, to arise out of a matter which by international law is solely within the domestic jurisdiction of that party, the Council shall so report, and shall make no recon mendation as to its settlement."

120. The history of the drafting of Article 2, par graph 7, at San Francisco shows that the text final adopted was, apart from some slight alterations its final part as a result of an Australian amendmen the joint work of the countries which drafted th Dumbarton Oaks proposals, namely, China, the Unic of Soviet Socialist Republics, the United Kingdom an the United States. The United States representativ explained, at the request of the Committee concerned, the scope of the proposed amendments. According the Summary Report, Mr. Dulles observed, *inter ali* that:

". . . The scope of the Organization was no broadened to include functions which would enab the Organization to eradicate the underlying caus of war as well as to deal with crises leading to wa Under the Economic and Social Council the Orga ization will deal with economic and social problem This broadening of the scope of the Organizatio constituted a great advance, but it also engendere special problems.

"For instance, the question had been raised a to what would be the basic relation of the Organiza tion to member states: would the Organization de with the governments of the member states, or woul the Organization penetrate directly into the domesti life and social economy of the member states As provided in the amendment of the sponsorin governments, Mr. Dulles pointed out that this princi ple would require the Organization to deal wit the governments. Under the Economic and Soci Council the Organization had a mandate to rais the standards of living and foster employment, etc but no one in the 10-member Council would g behind the governments in order to impose it desires."[45]

121. It is also interesting to note that during th discussion on this Article an amendment[46] was sub mitted to the effect that it should be left to the Inter national Court of Justice at the request of a party t decide whether or not a situation or dispute arose ou of matters that under international law fell within th domestic jurisdiction of the State concerned. In tha connexion, Mr. Dulles, in opposing the amendment pointed out

". . . that international law was subject to con stant change and therefore escaped definition. I would, in any case, be difficult to define whether o not a given situation came within the domestic juris diction of a state. In this era the whole internal lif of a country was affected by foreign conditions. H did not consider that it would be practicable to pro vide that the World Court determine the limita tions of domestic jurisdiction or that it should b called upon to give advisory opinions since som countries would probably not accept the compulsor jurisdiction clause.

". . . Moreover, this principle was subject t evolution. The United States had had long expe rience in dealing with a parallel problem, i.e., th relationship between the forty-eight states and th Federal Government. Today, the Federal Govern

---

[44] Documents, vol. VI, page 507.

[45] Documents, vol. VI, pages 507-508.

[46] Documents, vol. VI, page 509.

ment of the United States exercised an authority undreamed of when the Constitution was formed, and the people of the United States were grateful for the simple conceptions contained in their Constitution. In like manner, Mr. Dulles foresaw that if the Charter contained simple and broad principles future generations would be thankful to the men at San Francisco who had drafted it."

122. Thus, the authors of the Charter expressly ıanifested the intention that organs of the United Iations should themselves be called upon to interpret he scope of that Article in every individual case nd to determine in each case whether or not a given ituation was within the domestic jurisdiction of a tate. As will be shown later, the General Assembly as used this power whenever its competence under hat Article has been questioned. Moreover, it has ystematically rejected proposals to seek the opinion f the International Court of Justice on such compe- nce.

123. Other controversial aspects of the interpreta- on of the terms of the Article, such as the words essentially" and "intervene", will be examined subse- uently in the general study in section VI of this hapter.[47]

VI. Competence of the United Nations

124. At this stage the various provisions of the harter should be examined together, in order to deter- ine the extent of the United Nations competence, in specific case of this kind where fundamental human ghts are violated as a result of racial discrimination.

125. Four principal arguments have been put for- ard regarding the competence of the United Nations rgans (General Assembly and Economic and Social ouncil) to examine allegations made against any given tate that it is not respecting, or is violating human ghts, and subsequently to address its recommenda- ons to that State.

These arguments may be summarized as follows:

(*a*) The first, and most restrictive argument is to aintain that the organs of the United Nations have o competence whatsoever in this sphere, and that con- quently the Assembly cannot deal with any such al- gations, either by examining them or, *a fortiori,* by ddressing any recommendations;

(*b*) The second argument, while generally uphold- g the same point of view as the first, nevertheless lows of an exception in the case where the allegation oncerns a violation of the principle of non-discrimina- on, particularly on ethnical grounds; in such an event, e General Assembly is regarded as fully competent;

(*c*) The third argument seeks to differentiate be- veen the examination of the allegations, which it al- ws and the addressing of recommendations, which rejects. A general statement of principles may be ade on the subject, in the form of recommendations ddressed to all the Member States after the examina- on;

(*d*) Finally, the fourth argument, based on the idest view of the matter, recognizes that in prin- ple the organs of the United Nations are competent deal with allegations against a State and to address irect recommendations. As will be seen, however, this rgument may be developed in a number of ways.

[47] See paragraphs 126 *et seq.*

(a) *First argument concerning the competence of the United Nations*

126. The Commission considers that a detailed examination of the first of these arguments, that of complete lack of competence, necessarily involves also the second and the third. In this examination, the Commission will adopt as its basis the speech delivered by the South African representative, Mr. Jooste, at the eighth session of the Assembly when the discussion turned on the inscription on the agenda of the question submitted to the Commission.[48] The Commission regards the South African representative's statement of his thesis as complete and logical.

127. South Africa's argument is that the General Assembly is not competent to deal with the question of the racial situation in that country for a number of reasons, some based on Article 2 (7) of the Charter and the relevant preparatory work at San Francisco, others on Articles 55 and 56.

128. The South African representative advanced three points based on the wording of Article 2, (7), of the Charter:

(i) "The word 'nothing' in the initial phrase of Article 2, (7), has an overriding effect and forbids any activity which takes the form of an intervention in the domestic affairs of any State, regardless of any other provision of the Charter, except enforcement measures, with which, in any case, the Assembly is not competent to deal.

(ii) "The word 'intervene' in the paragraph which we are examining has its ordinary dictionary meaning and includes interference. It cannot mean dictatorial interference, as has repeatedly been alleged, since only the Security Council can interfere dictatorially when it concerns a question of enforcement measures under Chapter VII of the Charter. Since the Assembly has no competence in this regard, the prohibition not to intervene in a country's domestic affairs would be tantamount to prohibiting the Assembly from doing something which in any case it has no competence to do, namely, interfering dictatorially.

(iii) "The word 'essentially' in the phrase 'essentially within the domestic jurisdiction of any State' was used in order to widen, and not to narrow, the scope of domestic jurisdiction. This much is abundantly clear from the records of San Francisco, from which I quoted in supfort of my contention during our last session."

129. (iv) Dealing next with the history of Article 2 (7), the South African representative referred to the view that this paragraph is not applicable when there is an alleged question of human rights, and made the following comment:

> "I need merely mention that there was a very full discussion at San Francisco on the question of fundamental human rights in relation to Article 2, (7). The outcome of that discussion was the adoption by Commission II and subsequently by the plenary meeting of the Conference of the following statement:
>
> " 'The Members of Committee 3 of Commission II are in full agreement that nothing in Chapter IX can be construed as giving full authority to the

[48] See *Official Records of the General Assembly, Eighth Session, Plenary Meetings,* 435th meeting.

Organization to interfere in the domestic affairs of Member States'."

130. Mr. Jooste then referred to the wording of Articles 55 and 56, and made the two following comments on the subject:

(v) "If the United Nations were to be permitted to intervene in regard to paragraph c of Article 55, which incidentally concerns the promotion of human rights, on the ground that the matters contained therein were not covered by the prohibition against intervention contained in Article 2 (7), then the Assembly would be equally permitted to intervene in regard to matters set out in paragraphs a and b of Article 55; that is, economic and social matters, higher standards of living, full employment, health legislation, etc. And I submit that no State on earth would tolerate this.

(vi) "In conclusion, on this point, I should draw attention to the fact that neither the Charter nor any other internationally binding instrument contains any definition of fundamental human rights. If they had, there would have been no need to set up the Commission to frame the proposed covenant on human rights."

131. The Commission will first examine the arguments concerning the wording of Article 2 (7), and the relevant preparatory work at San Francisco.

(i) THE WORD "NOTHING"

132. It is clear, as South Africa maintains, that the use of the word "nothing" at the opening of Article 2 (7) leads to the conclusion that this provision extends to all other provisions of the Charter, but the Commission feels that the exact scope of the prohibition contained therein can be assessed only in the light of the proper interpretation of the two other words, "intervene" and "essentially" which follow. Therefore this first argument is not absolutely valid *per se*, but only in relation to the interpretation placed on the other two words.

(ii) THE WORD "INTERVENE"

133. The interpretation of the word "intervene" is, of course, one of the keys to the interpretation of the scope of the provisions of Article 2 (7). According to the Union of South Africa, this word has here its ordinary dictionary meaning, and includes "interference." It simply means to "meddle". The same interpretation has been upheld by other countries to support the argument that the United Nations is not competent.

134. The contrary view, defended by the majority of the Member States, maintains that the word "intervene" means "dictatorial interference". The discussion of a matter by the Assembly and the drafting of recommendations do not amount to "dictatorial interference", and hence they do not constitute "interference" within the meaning which according to the intentions of the San Francisco Conference should be attributed to that word.

135. It should be noted that this latter interpretation has the support of two distinguished jurists, Professor H. Lauterpacht, member of the International Law Commission of the United Nations, and Professor René Cassin, member of the Human Rights Commission, both of whom are experts not only on human rights but also on the interpretation of the Charter.

136. In his book *International Law and Human Rights* Professor Lauterpacht expresses the opinion that "intervention is a technical term on the whole, unequivocal connotation. It signifies dictatorial interference in the sense of action amounting to a denial of the independence of the State". This implies "a peremptory demand for positive conduct or abstention —a demand which, if not complied with, involves a threat of or recourse to compulsion, though not necessarily physical compulsion in some form". "In order to justify the use of the term intervention there must be an attempt to 'impose the will' of one or more States upon another State in an 'imperative form'." That interpretation supplies an answer to the question of the limits of the action of the United Nations in the field of human rights. The General Assembly, or any other competent organ is authorized to discuss human rights, address recommendations of a specific nature to the State directly concerned, and undertake or initiate a study of the problem. There is, however, no legal obligation to accept any such recommendation. The prohibition in Article 2 (7) refers therefore only to direct intervention in the domestic economy, social structure, or cultural arrangements of the State concerned but does not in any way preclude recommendations, or even inquiries conducted outside the territory of such State.

On the basis of these considerations, Professor Lauterpacht concludes that Article 2 (7) can in no event exclude the study of a problem brought before the United Nations, the submission of the relevant reports, and the formulation of recommendations, since none of these acts constitutes intervention in the strictly technical sense. Any interpretation withholding human rights from the United Nations' field of action by reason of Article 2 (7) would render altogether nugatory the relevant provisions of the Charter concerning human rights and fundamental freedoms.

137. Professor Cassin, considers that in the field of human rights Article 2 (7) only forbids "intervention", that is to say interference in the technical sense, the imperative nature of such action taking the onward form of injunctions or orders.[49]

138. Professors Norman Bentwich and Andrew Martin, in their book *Commentary of the Charter of the United Nations*, gave a similar interpretation of the word "intervene". They consider that it must be interpreted according to its strictly technical meaning, that is to say "dictatorial interference by a State in the affairs of another State", and consequently that the study of a problem, or an inquiry into it, or even a formal recommendation, cannot be regarded as "intervention".

139. As we have seen, South Africa relies, in support of its thesis, on the argument that since the Assembly is in any event not competent to take enforcement action, the prohibition contained in Article 2 (7) is meaningless in the Assembly's case if the word "intervention" is taken as meaning "dictatorial interference".

140. In this connexion, the Commission points out that the Assembly is not precluded from "dictatorial interference", since it may use measures of coercion or enforcement by way of recommendations to the Member States, when a matter is not essentially within the

[49] See "La Déclaration universelle et la mise en œuvre des droits de l'homme", Académie de droit international. Extract from *Recueil des cours 1951*, pages 1 and 2.

domestic jurisdiction of any State, as is witnessed by General Assembly resolution 39 (I), concerning the relations of Members of the United Nations with Spain. In any event, the doctrine set forth above was firmly established by the Assembly through the adoption of resolution 377 (V), "Uniting for peace".

141. The effect of Article 2 (7) seems, therefore, to prohibit "dictatorial interference" by the United Nations in matters which are essentially within the domestic jurisdiction of any State.

(iii) THE PHRASE "ESSENTIALLY WITHIN THE DOMESTIC JURISDICTION OF ANY STATE"

142. The interpretation of the words "essentially within the jurisdiction of any State" is at least of equal importance to that of the word "intervene". That was the most keenly disputed point during the discussions in the Assembly, when most Member States again expressed views in opposition to those advanced by the Union of South Africa.

The opinion of certain jurists and experts may be worth quoting.

143. Professor Cassin, in the book already mentioned, states that the word "essentially" cannot be taken to mean "principally, or even preponderatingly". According to him, the Charter is to be interpreted as having brought within the international field all human rights and fundamental freedoms, only those for which the United Nations does not call for the co-operation of its Members under Articles 55 and 56 of the Charter being excepted and classified as reserved.[50] The author claims that this interpretation is confirmed by the San Francisco records. In rejecting an amendment to vest in the International Court of Justice power to decide whether a situation or dispute arises out of matters solely within domestic jurisdiction, the United Nations took, in his opinion, the view that the competent organ of the United Nations, including, when appropriate, the Court, should be left with authority to decide, with regard to the actual circumstances in each disputed case, whether the subject matter falls essentially within a State's national jurisdiction or not.[51]

144. Professor Cassin had previously supported the same thesis, in his capacity as French representative to the General Assembly. During the discussions in the Assembly's Third Committee (first part of the third session) on the draft Universal Declaration of Human Rights, he expressed the following opinion reported in the summary records:[52]

"In his country's opinion, the competence of the United Nations on the question of human rights was positive, and the provisions of Article 2, paragraph 7, of the Charter, relating to domestic jurisdiction of Member States, could not be invoked against such competence when, by adoption of the Declaration, the question of human rights was a matter no longer of domestic but of international concern."

145. In considering the meaning of the phrase "matters which are essentially within the domestic jurisdiction of any State", Professor Lauterpacht, in the book already cited,[53] contends that this is a question of fact. Each specific problem that arises has to be studied in the light of the "Purposes and Principles" of the Charter as a whole. In no event may such a study lead to the extinction of any legally binding obligation imposed by that document.

146. Professor Lauterpacht says that there is no technical or immutable sense attaching to the term "essentially". He does not consider that the change of phraseology in the Charter, as compared with the corresponding Articles of the Covenant of the League of Nations which used the word "exclusively" *(sic)*, implies a restriction of the United Nations' competence more drastic than that which Article 15 (8) of the Covenant imposed on the League; he is, on the contrary, of opinion that the United Nations has greater freedom than that enjoyed by the League to discuss matters normally within domestic jurisdiction, particularly where human rights are concerned, in view of the prominence given to such rights in the Charter. Conversely, he thinks that there is little cogency in the argument that "essentially" means that any matter, even though governed by international treaty, is within the domestic jurisdiction of a State provided only that it is, by its nature, essentially of domestic concern. According to him, it could be said with equal justification that a matter is essentially within the domestic jurisdiction of a State only if it is not regulated by international law, or if it is not capable of being so regulated.

The power to decide whether Article 2 (7) is applicable, belongs in principle, according to Professor Lauterpacht, to the organ responsible for the implementation of the relevant chapter of the Charter in each particular case.

147. The study summarized above leads Professor Lauterpacht to the following conclusions:

(*a*) "Matters essentially within the domestic jurisdiction of a State" do not comprise questions which could become the subject of international obligations, by custom or treaty, or which have become of international concern by virtue of constituting an actual or a potential threat to international peace and security;

(*b*) Human rights are no longer a reserved question.

148. Professor R. Brunet's treatise on *La garantie internationale des droits de l'homme d'après la Charte de San-Francisco* contains an exhaustive study of this point. His opinion agrees with those mentioned above. Thus, for instance, in one passage he suggests that Article 62 (2) of the Charter, which authorizes the Economic and Social Council to make recommendations "for the purpose of promoting respect for, and observance of, human rights and fundamental freedoms for all", must, unless it is quite meaningless, imply that: "respect for and observance of human rights and fundamental freedoms are an international question, and have ceased to be a matter of domestic jurisdiction". According to Professor Brunet, Article 62 (2) confirms that "all matters connected with the protection of human rights have been removed by the Charter from the reserved class of national questions, and placed under the direct gaurantee of the United Nations".

149. How can this interpretation be reconciled with the provisions of Article 2 (7)? Professor Brunet considers that the States which drafted the San Francisco Charter intended to effect "only one breach" in the fortifications protecting the reserved class, the breach made in favour of the respect for human rights. They had either to acquiesce in the protection of human rights

[50] *Ibid.* page 18.

[51] *Ibid.* pages 18 and 19.

[52] See *Official Records of the General Assembly, Third Session, Part I, Third Committee,* 92nd meeting.

[53] *International Law and Human Rights.*

and to relinquish a fraction of their sovereignty to that end or to forego the inclusion of that principle in the Charter. They chose the first alternative because the pressure of public opinion at the time was stronger than their will to resist.

150. Professor Georges Scelle, in his book *Droit international public*,[54] briefly surveys the problem raised by Article 2 (7). He considers that the substitution in the Charter of the word "essentially" for the term "exclusively" used in Article 15 (8) of the League Covenant, was a retrograde step, all the more serious in that "the notion of exclusive jurisdiction, instead of remaining a simple demurrer, now becomes a fundamental principle of the law of nations".

151. This defect is, however, offset by the fact that "essentially domestic jurisdiction" can only be pleaded before the organ dealing with the matter, which has sole authority to decide whether the demurrer is well founded. Thus, the meaning of the phrase "matters essentially within the domestic jurisdiction of any State" will be little by little determined by the jurisprudence in the discussions in its competent organs.

152. In an article published in 1949, Mr. Lawrence Preuss, Professor of Political Science in the University of Michigan, examines the problem of Article 2 (7).[55] The author concludes from the preparatory work in the San Francisco Conference, that the governments represented at the Conference had intended to restrict so far as possible the Organization's power to intervene in the internal affairs of any State. But, notwithstanding this trend towards strict limitation, the Organization was even then invested with competence to determine in each individual case whether Article 2 (7) applied. And the writer finds that in interpreting that clause the United Nations accepted the view that "intervention" means an act implying a refusal to recognize the independence of a State and a threat of coercion. Article 2 (7) would not therefore in any way preclude "discussion, study, investigation and recommendation".

153. He ends up with the statement that the provisions of Article 2 (7) have not proved to be a substantial obstacle to the expansion of the activities of the United Nations in fields which have hitherto been inviolable and sacrosanct. He goes on to say: "The framers of the Charter undoubtedly intended, through the novel formulation which they gave to the domestic jurisdiction clause, to place narrow limits upon the powers of the United Nations, but the very elasticity of the terminology which they employed has permitted a degree of interference by the United Nations in internal matters which would not have been possible under such a provision as Article 15 (8) of the Covenant. The concept of 'international concern', applied by the political organs of the United Nations in the exercise of a virtually unlimited discretion, has removed from the domestic sphere any situation which presents a potential threat to the peace, or even a threat to the good understanding among nations".

154. Professor H. Kelsen[56] is in almost entire agreement with Professor Preuss. He too considers that the intention of the legislators at San Francisco was generally to place limitations on the Organization's actions, and that Article 2 (7) applies to the subjec matter of Chapters IX and X of the Charter, as i evident from a study of the preparatory work at Sar Francisco. But he further maintains that a State is no thereby precluded from submitting to the competen organs of the United Nations any matter which anothe State claims to fall within its domestic jurisdiction. I this connexion, Professor Kelsen thinks that the replace ment of the word "solely" which appeared in Articl 15 (8) by "essentially" is not an improvement. In hi view there are no matters "essentially" within domesti jurisdiction. A matter which is not expressly regulate in one way or another by international custom o treaty belongs "solely" within the internal jurisdictio of a State, but never "essentially"; and the questio whether a matter falls within the reserved class o questions can only be answered by reference to interna tional law. Therefore, the new wording of the claus relating to the reserved class does not represent a advance from the position in the past. In the first place it might be supposed that a matter falls "essentially within domestic jurisdiction if it is "essential" to th sovereignty of the State concerned. Such State coul therefore refuse to submit any matter of this nature t international settlement, if it considered such submissio incompatible with its sovereignty. The fact that Mem bers are not bound to submit matters within thei domestic jurisdiction to international settlement i terms of the Charter, could likewise relieve them c their obligations under Article 37, or even of the dut of settling their disputes by peaceful means, since unde Article 2 (3) Members need only seek peaceful mear in the case of an "international dispute", which woul seem to exclude disputes arising from matters othe than those having an international character, that is t say those within domestic jurisdiction. In any even the importance to be attributed to Article 2 (7) large depends on "the answer to the question as to who competent to decide whether a matter is essential within the jurisdiction of a State". On the wording Article 2 (7), it is arguable that the State concerne is free to indicate that authority; but the State whic demurs to the contention that the matter falls with the domestic jurisdiction of the government again which the complaint is brought, is obliged to bring th dispute before the competent organ of the United N tions. Thus it will be that organ which will in eve instance finally decide whether the matter falls with the reserved class. In his conclusion, Professor Kels affirms that the wording of Article 2 (7) probably go farther than was intended by those who framed it. is very likely that the authors of the Charter did n intend to release by Article 2 (7) any Member fro the obligation to refrain from the threat or use of for in the settlement of a conflict arising out of a matt which, in the opinion of that Member, is essential within its domestic jurisdiction.

155. Professor Ross of the University of Cope hagen,[57] considers that it is sufficient if a matter is its nature (essentially) within the domestic jurisdicti of a State, for the provision to be applicable in pri ciple; but far from specifying when and in what c cumstances such a situation may arise, the Article leav that question completely unanswered.

In any event, it must be the competent organ its which finally decides whether or not any matter su

54 See Section III: "Théorie de la compétence exclusive".

55 See "Article 2, paragraph 7, of the Charter and matters of domestic jurisdiction", by Lawrence Preuss, Professor of Political Science, University of Michigan. *Recueil des cours 1949*, 1, Académie de droit international.

56 *The Law of the United Nations.*

57 *Constitution of the United Nations.*

tted to the United Nations is within its competence. ıat, in Professor Ross's view, will increasingly tend restrict the reserved class of question, and favour ever more pronounced interference by the Organiza-n in matters which normally fall within domestic risdiction.

From the economic and social point of view, Article (7), literally interpreted, seems to paralyse the ganization, but that could not have been the object the authors of that provision. Professor Ross feels, erefore, that in these spheres the Article refers only recommendations addressed to a specified country, thout prohibiting recommendations of a general aracter.

156. Summing up his views, he stresses the vague-ss of Article 2 (7). He is unable to accept that there ist certain matters that by their nature are outside competence of international law. As drafted, the ovision is hostile to progress and can only lead to the rpetuation of the chaotic condition of international v. The introduction of the essentiality qualification d the omission of a reference to international law as a sis of judgment, tend to replace legal judgment by itical judgment. The practical scope of the provision however, greatly limited by the power of the Organ-tion itself to decide whether or not the plea of mestic jurisdiction is justified.

157. Professors N. Bentwich and A. Martin, in their ok on the Charter of the United Nations,[58] after list- a certain number of matters such as nationality, toms tariffs, immigration laws and so forth, which ditionally come within domestic jurisdiction, submit view that even such problems may, in certain cir-ıstances, assume an international character. The way which racial minorities are treated in one State y have serious repercussions in another; the im-gration laws of one country may create difficult prob-ıs for others which are forced by the lack of national ources to encourage their surplus population to igrate; the customs and tariff policy of an importing te is of the utmost concern to States with large ex-ts to sell. As a result, the border-line between nestic jurisdiction and international regulation has ome fluid. And while the existence of a border-line recognized by the Charter in Article 2 (7), no at-pt is or could be made to define the two fields it arates. The authors believe that the present wording Article 2 (7) makes it a question of fact and not of whether any particular matter justifies intervention the Organization, since the omission of all reference international law has removed the only reliable oretical standard. But, from the legal point of view, Article must not be allowed to bar the way to action the United Nations if the latter has come to the clusion that an issue, though domestic in appearance, s for international action.

58. It will be seen from the foregoing that jurists not in full agreement upon the interpretation of the ase "matters essentially within the domestic juris-ion of a State". Authorities with an exceptional wledge and experience of the United Nations, such Professors Cassin and Lauterpacht, maintain cate-ically that, as a result of the adoption of the Charter, fundamental human rights have become part of international law and no longer fall essentially within domestic jurisdiction. Others like Professor Kelsen consider that the provisions of the Charter do not suffice for assessing which matters fall essentially within and which outside domestic jurisdiction, since the Charter is silent on the exact criterion to be applied. But the important point to note is that the supporters of the latter argument agree with the other school of thought that the Charter, both in the letter and the spirit, empowers the principal United Nations organs, within the sphere of their respective jurisdictions, to decide in every specific instance referred to them whether or not the matter falls within the domestic jurisdiction of a State. On this point, therefore, there is no disagreement between the authorities. In brief, all the jurists agree that such organs are the sole judges in deciding their own competence for the purposes of Article 2 (7) of the Charter.

159. It would obviously be wrong to suppose that the organs concerned may abuse this discretionary power, through addiction to some arbitrary criterion. In each case they will weigh the question whether the international aspect of the matter has sufficient validity or gravity to warrant the consideration of it. The General Assembly and the Economic and Social Council will naturally act cautiously and with a clear sense of the responsibility conferred on them by the Charter. Thus, for example, if an isolated instance of violation of fundamental human rights should arise in a country where the citizens enjoy legal facilities for seeking and obtaining redress, there would be no case for making it an international question. The United Nations organs would be failing to perform their duties under the Charter in a responsible and cautious manner were they to interfere in a domestic situation which, though incompatible with the principles of the Charter, is due to certain well-defined historical conditions and circumstances which cannot be changed overnight but which the State concerned is endeavouring gradually to eliminate. On the other hand, to go to the opposite extreme, the United Nations is unquestionably justified in deciding that a matter is outside the essentially domestic jurisdiction of a State when it involves systematic violation of the Charter's principles concerning human rights, and more especially that of non-discrimination, above all when such actions affect millions of human beings, and have provoked grave international alarm, and when the State concerned clearly displays an intention to aggravate the position.

160. The Commission finds no justification for the excessive apprehension of certain States regarding what they term a flagrant attack on their sovereignty, for it is agreed that the Assembly has authority to decide whether or not it is competent to deal with any matter affecting human rights in a given State solely for the purposes of discussion, investigation, and, according to circumstances, the formulation of recommendations to the State concerned. A point to be noted is that the two-thirds majority rule has hitherto always been imposed by a majority of the Members present and voting in contentious matters concerning human rights. That rule protects those countries which fear excessive interference in matters which they regard as falling within their domestic jurisdiction. It will be recalled that during the discussions on the question of "the treatment of persons of Indian origin in the Union of South Africa", during the fourth session of the

---

A Commentary on the Charter of the United Nations by man Bentwich, LL.D., Barrister-at-Law, and Andrew tin, Ph.D., Barrister-at-Law.

Assembly[59] it was decided that the question of competence should be settled by a two-thirds majority. It is almost impossible to imagine two-thirds of the Member States failing to display a proper sense of responsibility or acting frivolously or at the dictate of prejudice against another Member State.

We need only remember that, in accordance with the provisions of the Charter and with the resolutions which the Assembly has itself adopted, that body is very properly called upon to show an exceptionally serious mind in deciding upon matters affecting Member States.

161. For instance, Article 11 (2) of the Charter authorizes the General Assembly to:

> "Discuss any questions concerning the maintenance of international peace and security brought before it by any Member of the United Nations, or by the Security Council, or by a State which is not a Member of the United Nations in accordance with Article 35, paragraph 2, and, except as provided in Article 12, may make recommendations with regard to any such question to the State or States concerned or to the Security Council or to both."

On the basis of this Article, the Assembly adopted, in 1950, resolution 377 (V), "Uniting for peace", prescribing a whole series of collective measures which the Assembly is to recommend to the Member States in cases where:

> "The Security Council, because of lack of unanimity of the permanent members, fails to exercise its primary responsibility for the maintenance of international peace and security in any case where there appears to be a threat to the peace, breach of the peace, or act of aggression."

These collective measures may, according to the resolution, include:

> "In the case of a breach of the peace or act of aggression, the use of armed force when necessary, to maintain or restore international peace and security."

162. Now the Charter has not defined the meaning of "threat to the peace", "breach of the peace" or "act of aggression". It is for the Assembly to determine whether any such situation has arisen. The Assembly possesses a Peace Observation Commission, responsible for assisting it in this matter. But the Assembly may, even without the advice of that Commission, declare that there exists a "threat of aggression", a "breach of the peace" or an "act of aggression", and consequently recommend to its Members any of the collective measures prescribed by the Charter and developed in resolution 377 (V), including economic sanctions and the use of armed force. *A fortiori,* therefore, it is logical to suppose that the Assembly may, by the same two-thirds majority, judge whether a violation of fundamental human rights in a particular country falls essentially within its domestic jurisdiction or not, since the only point then at issue is that of affording the Assembly an opportunity to discuss, investigate, and report, and, if necessary, address a recommendation to Member States inviting them to liquidate the position in question.

(iv) DRAFTING OF ARTICLE 2, PARAGRAPH 7, OF THE CHARTER

163. In support of its contention the Union of South Africa also refers to the argument based on the drafting of Article 2, paragraph 7 and, in particular, to the e[xtract] reproduced above[60] from the report of the Ra[p]porteur of Committee II/3 of the San Francisco Co[n]ference.

The Commission comments that this argument ad[ds] nothing to that based on the presence of the wo[rd] "intervene" in the paragraph in question since the sa[me] term recurs in the report; consequently, everythi[ng] depends on the construction placed on this term. T[he] Committee itself stated its view on that point earl[ier] in this document.[61]

(v) ARTICLE 55 A AND B OF THE CHARTER

164. With regard to the Union's argument conce[rn]ing the powers of the Organization to "intervene" [in] the case of the questions mentioned in Article 55 a a[nd] b,[62] the Commission, in the light of its interpretati[on] of the term "intervene"[63] and for the reasons sta[ted] earlier, considers that the exercise by the United N[a]tions of the functions referred to in these provisi[ons] cannot in any way constitute an "intervention".

165. Furthermore, Article 55 b provides that [the] Organization shall promote "solutions of internatio[nal] economic, social health, and related problems; and [in]ternational cultural and educational co-operatio[n]". Hence the Union's argument leads to a conclusion wh[ich] is diametrically opposed to what it is trying to pro[ve] since the Charter itself recognizes the internatio[nal] nature of certain economic and social problems wh[ich] are to be solved by means of "international co-ope[ra]tion".

166. Since by virtue of Article 55 a the Uni[ted] Nations is under a duty to promote "higher standa[rds] of living, full employment and conditions of econo[mic] and social progress", it is contended that its m[ost] competent organs are authorized to discuss the situat[ion] existing in each of the Member and non-mem[ber] States and to address either collective or individ[ual] recommendations to these States.

167. This has, in fact, been a constant practice [on] the part of the Assembly and Economic and So[cial] Council from their earliest days. The Organizat[ion] has been continuously studying the economic sit[ua]tion, food conditions, employment, unemployment, so[cial] and health conditions, etc., in all the Member Stat[es]; it has discussed these situations and conditions [at] length and in detail and made recommendations wh[ich] were not perhaps addressed to a single State in par[tic]ular, but to a relatively small group of the Memb[ers] of the Organization, which for the purposes of [the] present study comes to the same thing.

(vi) THE DEFINITION OF HUMAN RIGHTS

168. Because neither the Charter nor any other bi[nd]ing international instrument defines the term "fun[da]mental human rights", therefore the Union of So[uth] Africa argues that Article 56 does not create a le[gal] obligation for States. The Commission points out, fi[rst]ly, that other terms, which certainly do involve obl[iga]tions on the part of Member States, are also not defi[ned] in the Charter; this is true of such terms as "inter[na]tional peace and security", "threats to the pea[ce]"

[59] See *Official Records of the General Assembly, Second Part of the First Session, Plenary Meetings,* 52nd meeting.

[60] See paragraph 129.

[61] See paragraph 141.

[62] See paragraph 130.

[63] See paragraph 141.

"breaches of the peace", and "acts of aggression", as mentioned before.

169. Secondly, the idea of "human rights and fundamental freedoms" does not date from the Charter but goes back at least to the Declaration of the Rights of Man and the Citizen of 1789 and to the American Declaration of Independence. Since that time nearly two centuries ago, this idea has become an integral part of the public law of most civilized States in Europe, America and elsewhere. Nothing proves better that the authors of the Charter meant to refer to this time-hallowed idea than the passage in the Preamble of the Charter: "the peoples of the United Nations determined . . . . to reaffirm faith in the fundamental human rights".

The notion was therefore sufficiently familiar in 1945 that it could become the subject of an express legal obligation. What the Charter did was to introduce this principle of municipal law into international relations. The principle was later affirmed afresh, in more precise terms, in the Universal Declaration of Human Rights which the General Assembly adopted on 10 December 1948.

In this connexion, particularly as regards the weight of the Universal Declaration as an instrument defining the human rights mentioned in the Charter, the Commission refers to the comments made in sections II and III of this chapter, and, in particular, to the authoritative views quoted there.[64]

170. The Commission would also like to quote from the remarks of Mr. Charles Malik (Lebanon), one of the drafters of the Declaration and the Chairman of the Third Committee of the Assembly at which the final discussions of the draft Declaration took place:[65]

"Finally, Mr. Malik felt that the Universal Declaration of Human Rights was essentially different from any other resolution adopted by the General Assembly. The other resolutions were consistent with the Charter only from a formal point of view, whereas the very substance of the Declaration of Human Rights was contained in the Charter and was governed by specific provisions. The Declarations continued and, in a way supplemented the Charter, and could not therefore be considered a mere resolution."

171. Furthermore, in a case of racial discrimination, one need not rely on a definition or legal clause contained in some instrument other than the Charter for the purpose of proving that there is a binding pledge.

As stated earlier, the principle of non-discrimination is laid down in the Charter itself, which in its Preamble, in its Purposes and Principles, in Article 13 and in Article 55, condemns implicitly and explicitly, "distinction as to race, sex, language or religion." The principle of non-discrimination is a fundamental principle of the Charter, introduced as a reaction against misconceived racial theories, as pointed out elsewhere in this report.[66]

(b) *Second and third arguments concerning the competence of the United Nations*

172. The second argument is identical with the first, except in that it concedes that the rule of the non-competence of the Assembly is subject to an exception in cases where the allegation involves the Purposes of the Charter as defined in Article 1, paragraphs 2 and 3 and, in particular, the principle of non-discrimination. The Commission takes the view that the situation which it was asked to study by the Assembly involves precisely this principle: hence, even according to the supporters of this argument, the United Nations is competent in the matter.

173. The third argument admits the Assembly's competence to discuss a matter concerning human rights in a particular State but denies it the right to address recommendations to that State.

Actually, the Articles of the Charter cited to prove the Assembly's competence in this matter (Articles 10 and 13) speak simultaneously of the competence to discuss (or initiate studies) and to make recommendations. The only Article (Article 14) which mentions only one of these twin terms does not mention the competence to discuss but does speak of the competence to recommend. Hence it is difficult to see on what the above argument can be based, unless it be the inferences drawn from Article 2, paragraph 7, of which the Commission has already disposed.

(c) *Fourth argument concerning the competence of the United Nations*

174. These three arguments having been disposed of, the conclusion reached is that the fourth argument[67] is correct. This does not, of course, in any way invalidate the earlier affirmation that the organs of the United Nations take the final decision on competence, on whether, from a political standpoint, the question before them is or is not within the domestic jurisdiction of the State and whether it is sufficiently serious and important to arouse international concern and justify a discussion, inquiry or even a recommendation by the organ concerned.

The racial situation in the Union of South Africa is clearly one which the Assembly wished to discuss. As mentioned before, it rejected, by a heavy majority, a motion of non-competence submitted to the *Ad Hoc* Political Committee, and again at a plenary session of the Assembly. Moreover, simultaneously with setting up this Commission, the Assembly adopted resolution 616 B (VII) which states:

"In a multiracial society, harmony and respect for human rights and freedoms and the peaceful development of a unified community are best assured when patterns of legislation and practice are directed towards ensuring equality before the law of all persons regardless of race, creed or colour, and when economic, social, cultural and political participation of all racial groups is on the basis of equality";

and affirms that:

"Governmental policies of Member States which are not directed towards these goals, but which are designed to perpetuate or increase discrimination, are inconsistent with the pledges of the Members under Article 56 of the Charter."

There is no doubt that in this resolution the Assembly reaffirmed its competence.

The next section of this report deals with the case-law built up by the United Nations in considering questions similar to those studied by the Commission

[64] See paras. 101-104, and 144.

[65] See *Official Records of the General Assembly, Third Session, Part II, General Committee,* 59th meeting.

[66] See paragraphs 81 and 82.

[67] See paragraph 125 (*d*).

VIII. Conclusions on the Commission's terms of reference in the light of the provisions of the Charter and the General Assembly resolutions

254. The Commission reached the following conclusions on the terms of reference with which it had been endowed by the General Assembly.

1. By establishing the Commission and giving it its terms of reference, the Assembly reached an affirmative decision on the principle of its own competence to consider "the question of race conflict in South Africa resulting from the policies of *apartheid* of the Government of the Union of South Africa" and the Commission's competence "to study the racial situation in the Union of South Africa" and "to report its conclusions" to the General Assembly.

2. A general study of the provisions relating to the Purposes and Principles of the Charter and the powers and limitations of principal organs of the United Nations in carrying them out leaves no room for doubt that, under the Charter, the Assembly is empowered to undertake any investigations and make any recommendations to Member States that it deems desirable concerning the application and enforcement of the Purposes and Principles of the Charter, among which the respect of human rights and fundamental freedoms is outstanding. The exercise of the powers and functions devolving on the Assembly in such matters does not constitute an intervention within the meaning of Article 2, paragraph 7, of the Charter. Hence, since the Commission is a subsidiary body of the Assembly it too is not restricted by these provisions in its activities, which are to carry out a study for the Assembly and report its conclusions to that body.

3. That conclusion is particularly important when the activities of the General Assembly and its Commission relate to violations of the principle of non-discrimination, which is explicitly included in the Charter in several places, and more particularly when the discrimination is systematic and is based on a doctrine of racial inequality. It is precisely such situations that the authors of the Charter wished to prohibit when they included in the Charter the principle of non-discrimination on grounds of race, thereby giving expression to mankind's deepest aspirations.

4. The above conclusions are fully borne out by the jurisprudence established by the principal organs of the United Nations in cases relating to violations of human rights and fundamental freedoms.

The next significant development that took place from the viewpoint of United Nations authority to deal with these matters was a resolution passed in 1954 continuing the work of the Commission and referring to Article 14 of the Charter. This set the framework for recommendations on the part of the Assembly by calling for the peaceful adjustment of "any situation, regardless of origin" which might impair "friendly relations among nations, including situations resulting from a violation of the provisions of the present Charter setting forth the Purposes and Principles of the United Nations." Following a second report by the Commission that surveyed the techniques for resolving racial differences and that faced squarely the question of whether United Nations intervention in South Africa might not exacerbate tensions in South Africa, the Assembly and various committees continued to investigate and pass more strongly-worded resolutions condemning the racial policies pursued by the government of South Africa and calling upon that government to eliminate the political and legal structure implementing apartheid. A third report resulted in still more resolutions, but the Commission was disbanded in 1955 when it failed to receive the necessary two-thirds vote to continue.

In the period between 1956–1960 the matter of apartheid was discussed in several bodies of the United Nations with the consequent passage of more resolutions. Most of the discussion about the Assembly's competence took for granted the propriety of being concerned about apartheid, and centered instead on the development of appropriate procedures for inquiry and pressure with the object of rectifying what many states came to regard as an intolerable situation. The Charter bases of early United Nations action are to be found in Articles 10 and 14; however, a turning point in the grounds of organizational competence to deal with the matter was reached in 1960 when the riots in Sharpesville took place and seventy to eighty people were killed. At this time the so-called Afro-Asian bloc had become numerically strong, and twenty-nine of them requested an urgent meeting of the Security Council on the grounds that this was "a situation with grave potentialities for international friction, which endangers the maintenance of international peace and security." The following material is a portion of the debate that took place following the Sharpsville Riots. (Throughout the remainder of these materials the editors have borrowed liberally from Louis B. Sohn's *Cases and Materials on International Law and World Organization,* July 20–August 1, 1964.)

Debate in the Security Council on Disturbances in Sharpesville in 1960.

U.N.S.C. Official records, 15th sess. 851st – 855th meetings. 30 March 1960 – 1 April 1960. (S/PV. 851 – S/PV. 855) and Suppl. for April, May and June 1960. (S/4300)

10. Sir Pierson DIXON (United Kingdom): Her Majesty's Government in the United Kingdom has not objected to the adoption of the agenda. Nevertheless, it maintains its strong view that nothing in the Charter authorizes the United Nations to intervene in matters which are essentially within the domestic jurisdiction of any State. I must inform the members of the Council that the United Kingdom Government will approach the discussion in the Security Council of these tragic incidents with that point in mind.

11. Mr. BERARD (France) (translated from French): The French Government's position on the scope and jurisdiction of the United Nations is too well known for there to be any need for me to explain it again at length. It is based on Article 2, paragraph 7, of the Charter which states categorically that "nothing contained in the present Charter shall authorize the United Nations to intervene in matters which are essentially within the domestic jurisdiction of any state".

12. The authority which the United Nations enjoys in the world depends, we believe, on respect for this rule and for the principle of non-intervention in matters over which the individual State has sole jurisdiction. The fact that my delegation did not oppose the adoption of the agenda in no sense means that it is abandoning a traditional stand which, on the contrary, it continues steadfastly to uphold.

13. French opinion was deeply moved by the news of the tragic incidents at Sharpeville and Langa. It has always strongly disapproved of the practices of racial discrimination and segregation and fervently hopes that there will be no recurrence of such unfortunate incidents.

14. My delegation none the less has serious doubts regarding the legal merits of the case which has been submitted to the Council and regarding the competence of the Council to deal with this question.

24. The PRESIDENT: If no other member of the Council wishes to speak at this time, I shall speak as representative of the UNITED STATES OF AMERICA.

25. The United States supported the adoption of th agenda, and I should like to set forth our reasons fo so doing. Our position on this question was expresse clearly in Washington by Secretary of State Herte last Friday. At that time he said that the Unite States favoured Security Council discussion of thi question. In so doing, he pointed out that the Unite States has followed the same policy in the discussio on "apartheid" in the General Assembly over th last five years.

26. Since various comments have been made on th question of competence, let me state briefly our vie on this matter. The United States views on the interpretation and application of Article 2, paragraph 7 of the Charter have been clearly established. I mysel stated, in the discussion of the question of Tibet a the Fourteenth session of the General Assembly:

"In the years since the establishment of th United Nations certain principles and rules concerning the application of Article 2, paragraph 7 have emerged. It has become established, fo example, that inscription and then discussion o an agenda item do not constitute intervention i matters which lie essentially within domestic jurisdiction."[1/]

27. We hold the same views with respect to th Security Council that we do in the General Assembly When a question such as the present one is involve Article 2, paragraph 7, must be read in the light c Articles 55 and 56. Under Articles 55 and 56 of th Charter, all Members of the United Nations hav pledged themselves to promote "universal respe for, and observance of, human rights and fundament freedoms for all without distinction as to race, se language or religion."

28. During the thirteenth session of the Gener Assembly, Mr. George Harrison, the United State representative in the Special Political Committe expressed the United States policy on these Article in connexion with the discussion on "apartheid He said:

"No Member of this Organization could justifiab seek purposely to escape its pledge. No Membe could justifiably be excused from endeavouring t fulfil its pledge. We believe that the United Natior can legitimately call attention to the policies Member Governments which appear to be in consistent with their obligations under the Charte and earnestly to ask Members to abide by th undertakings that they have accepted in signing th Charter.

We all recognize that every nation has a right o regulate its own internal affairs. This is a right ıcknowledged by Article 2, paragraph 7, of the Charter. At the same time, we must recognize the ight — and the obligation — of the United Nations o be concerned with national policies in so far as hey affect the world community. This is partic- ılarly so in cases where international obligations mbodied in the Charter are concerned."[2/]

9. The United States profoundly regrets the tragic oss of life in South Africa. Twenty-nine Member States have brought this situation before the Security Council, stating that they consider it to have "grave otentialities for international friction, which en- langers the maintenance of international peace and ecurity" [S/4279 and Add.1]. What this means is hat in their view this situation is not only within he scope of Articles 55 and 56, but also of Articles 4 and 35. Such wide-spread concern testifies to the lesirability of the Council considering the problem.

0. Let me say that the United States approaches his question with no false pride at all. We recognize hat many countries, and the United States must be ncluded in the list, cannot be content with the progress which they have made in the field of human rights nd that we must continue our efforts, as we have, o provide full equality of opportunity for all our itizens. In many countries, unsanctioned violations f human rights continue to occur, but we think there s an important distinction between situations where overnments are actively promoting human rights nd fundamental freedoms for all without distinction s to race, sex, language or religion, and situations here governmental policies run counter to this.

1. The question we are asked to consider today as its own particular background of geography, acial composition, cultural diversity and economic elationships, but even difficulties of this sort do not elieve a government of its obligations, nor can hey relieve the United Nations of its responsibilities. Ve think this question is a proper one for United lations consideration, and we therefore supported he adoption of the agenda.

3. Mr. FOURIE (Union of South Africa):

5. The South African Government's objection to ne consideration of this matter by the Security ouncil is, in the first instance, based on two legal rounds, namely:

6. First, that the inclusion of this item in the genda and any subsequent discussion or resolution regard thereto is in violation of a basic principle f the Charter upon which the United Nations was ounded. This basic principle is enshrined in Article 2, aragraph 7, of the Charter which has an overriding ffect in regard to all the other Articles of the Charter.

7. Second, the Union's objection is based on the round that such action is in conflict with the terms f a decision unanimously taken and recorded by a enary session of the San Francisco Conference of 945. That decision read as follows: "nothing con- ained in Chapter IX of the Charter can be construed s giving authority to the Organization to intervene ı the domestic affairs of Member States".[3/] And I ay add that Chapter IX includes, inter alia, Articles 5 and 56.

48. In the past some Members of the United Nations have, however, considered Article 2, paragraph 7, not as excluding debate, but as excluding what is called "intervention". I shall refer to only a few expressions of opinion on this point, taken from the summary records of the Special Political Committee.

49. On 23 October 1957, the representative of Iraq made a statement on the question before the Special Political Committee. I shall read a portion of the summary record:

"... there was nothing in Article 2, paragraph 7, of the Charter to prevent the United Nations from discussing any question which it judged to be within its competence or from adopting any resolutions it thought fit on such questions. No one had suggested, of course, or was suggesting that the United Nations should intervene directly to put an end to the policies of "apartheid" of the Union Government. Only the people of the Union could do that".[4/]

50. On 29 October 1957 the representative of Argentina made a statement, the summary record of which read as follows:

"Many delegations wondered whether the Assembly had not gone too far, and likewise recognized that, having established a precedent, it would find it hard to decide where to draw the line in intervening in the domestic affairs of States. There were many instances in which it could be claimed that States were violating human rights in their domestic affairs. That explained the opposition of many States which abhorred racial segregation and them- selves respected all the provisions of the Charter, to intervention by the United Nations in any matter which they considered fell within the domestic jurisdiction of States. Article 2, paragraph 7, of the Charter provided a fundamental guarantee which Member States should not sacrifice and was of vital importance to those among them that were not en- titled to exercise the veto. Its existence had been of far greater value in the maintenance of peace than had over-liberal interpretations of the scope of the Organization's activities, however worthy the purpose of such interpretations might have been.

"Although it was right that the United Nations should do its utmost to promote respect for human rights and fundamental freedoms for all without regard to race, it was equally true that in doing so it could not make itself into a supra-national authority. Any attempt on its part to intervene in the domestic affairs of its Members weakened its authority and prestige."[5/]

51. In 1952, the representative of Canada also clearly stated the case in the context of this particular matter. I shall read from the summary record.

"[The representative of Canada] did not believe that the Charter should be interpreted in such a way as to exclude discussion of an item once it had been placed on the agenda. The Canadian dele- gation had no intention of ignoring Article 2, paragraph 7, of the Charter, or dismissing it as a legal technicality. It felt, however, that a dis- tinction should be drawn between intervention and the right of the General Assembly to discuss any matters within the scope of the Charter."[6/]

52. In November 1955 the representative of India said that his delegation did not consider that the discussion of the matter by the General Assembly involved any intervention in matters essentially within the domestic jurisdiction of the Union of South Africa; if it did, his delegation would be opposed to such discussion.[7]

53. In November 1952, the representative of Sweden said that a commentary had been made on the Charter with which he was inclined to agree, that the word "intervention", as used in that paragraph, was not to be given a narrow, technical interpretation since discussion did not necessarily amount to intervention.[8]

54. However, in relation to the matter now before the Council, I do not think that anybody can deny that by placing this question on the agenda "intervention" in the domestic affairs of South Africa, even in the narrower sense of that term, is contemplated. This attempt is being made by reference to Article 35 of the Charter.

55. The scope of that Article is, however, circumscribed by Article 34, which reads:

> "The Security Council may investigate any dispute, or any situation which might lead to international friction or give rise to a dispute, in order to determine whether the continuance of the dispute or situation is likely to endanger the maintenance of international peace and security."

It has been argued that recent events in South Africa constitute a situation "which might lead to international friction or give rise to a dispute likely to endanger international peace and security".

56. The question arises, therefore, how these possibilities can eventuate. Clearly there must be at least two parties if there is to be a dispute or if such a situation is to exist. Furthermore, within the framework of the Charter these parties must be sovereign independent States.

57. I assure the Council that the Union has no intention, or the least desire, of provoking such a dispute or creating such a situation. If, therefore, such a danger does in fact exist, then I submit that the Council should focus its considerations on the actions of the other party or parties trying to create an international dispute and thereby to endanger international peace and security.

58. I do not wish to engage in any exhaustive legal arguments on the implications of Article 2, paragraph 7, of the Charter. Members of the Council are well aware of all the arguments stated and restated through the years. The South African Government continues to adhere to the views it has so often expressed and continues to maintain its position on the meaning and scope of this Article of the Charter. However, leaving aside for the moment the legal objections to the consideration of this subject, the question arises immediately why the anxiety to pick on South Africa? How many disturbances and riots, leading to a serious loss of life, have occurred during the last twelve months throughout the world, including Africa?

59. On what grounds is it now proposed to single out the Union of South Africa? Or am I to assume that all Members favouring the placing of this item on the Council's agenda will, when their turn comes, willingly submit to the consideration in this Council of their efforts to maintain law and order in their own countries? If it is to be done in the case of South Africa, it can be done in the case of all violent disturbances against the authority of all Member States. Are Members prepared to accept that sort of future for themselves and for the United Nations? Or, if they are not willing so to submit themselves, must one then assume that it is simply a case of South Africa being made the whipping boy?

78. One of the most important principles involved in this matter is the question of the observance of the law of the land. The point at issue is not whether there is agreement or disagreement with any particular law. The point at issue is that the law must be enforced despite disagreement, and no Government worthy of the name could abdicate from or share its responsibility in such enforcement. If such abdication or sharing does take place chaos will undoubtedly result and rule by the mob will take the place of rule by the Government. The Government itself is the arbiter of the measures it deems necessary to secure obedience to the law, and interference, from any source whatsoever, in this prime responsibility of any sovereign government, cannot be countenanced. Indeed, any such interference, or attempt at interference, could only have a most deleterious effect on the observance of the rule of law—and this applies not only to South Africa. It is equally applicable to all countries and to all the Governments of the world.

79. Therefore, if by word or deed, or even gesture, this Council disassociates itself from this vital principle of constitutional government, namely the enforcement of the law of the land, a step will have been taken the consequences of which cannot be foreseen.

80. It is my Government's belief that the annual discussion of the racial problems of South Africa since 1946 has helped to inflame the situation there. It would be even more serious if the present discussion in the Council were to embolden the agitators or serve as incitement to further demonstrations and rioting in South Africa, with subsequent attacks by rioters not only on members of the police, but also the mass of peaceful citizens of all races trying to carry on a normal life. I am instructed to say that if this were to be the result the blame will rest squarely on the shoulders of the Security Council. I am sure that members of the Council would not wish to accept such a heavy responsibility. This question now having been placed on the Council's agenda, it is incumbent on me to report to my Government for instructions.

83. Mr. SLIM (Tunisia)

116. My delegation considers that the Council cannot shirk the responsibility incumbent upon it under Article 24, paragraph 1, in particular, which authorizes it to act on behalf of the Members of the United Nations, the more so since more than one third of those Members have drawn its attention to the situation in South Africa as one likely to endanger international peace and security. In agreeing that in carrying out its duties the Council acts on their behalf, all th

Members have implicitly undertaken to abide by its decisions, in accordance with the Charter. It is only logical that the Council, for its part, cannot avoid studying a situation brought before it by a large number of Members of the Organization, especially in view of the various resolutions in which the General Assembly has already, and in vain, made recommendations designed to prevent a dangerous situation like the one which we now deplore. In our opinion it is useless to invoke Article 2, paragraph 7, and to say that the matter is essentially within the domestic jurisdiction of a Member State. In the first place, the eight sessions of the General Assembly which dealt with racial discrimination in South Africa and the many resolutions which have been adopted, by majorities of over two-thirds, make such an argument untenable. Moreover, it has been recognized many times that there are situations in which the violation of human rights is so serious that the United Nations could not disregard them without running the risk of failing in its mission, as defined in Chapter I setting forth the purposes and principles of the Charter. When a State sets up the supremacy of one race over another as a fundamental principle of its public life and devises every means of coercion to apply it rigorously, it incontestably creates a dangerous situation not only within its own territory but also for the peace and security of the continent where it is situated and, consequently, of the whole world.

117. I have said that one cannot help comparing the racial policy practised in South Africa with regard to the African majority in that country to the policy practised by the Nazis with regard to the Jewish minority in their country. In both cases an inhuman policy was carried out by the Government. The Africans in the Union of South Africa have only this advantage over the Jews during the Nazi régime: that the colour of their skin absolves them from the obligation to wear some visible sign. Our generation has not yet forgotten the disastrous consequences which the Nazi methods entailed for the world.

118. One of the fundamental reasons for the establishment of the United Nations was precisely that it should endeavour to guarantee the fundamental rights of man in equality, dignity and justice. Its efforts to do so during the various debates of the General Assembly on the racial policy of South Africa have been in vain. Now, and especially since 21 March 1960, it is the duty of the Security Council to find the best solution to a situation which is becoming increasingly dangerous, for we are no longer confronted with a situation that is merely contrary to morality and law; we are confronted with a situation which endangers peace on the whole African continent. When there is a threat to peace, the Council is in duty bound to intervene.

119. May I recall that in 1946, during its discussion of the Spanish question, the Security Council gave very serious attention to what might seem to be a purely domestic situation. It considered, however, that the situation was a sufficiently serious threat to the maintenance of peace to warrant its taking the matter up very actively. In our opinion the state of affairs now prevailing in South Africa creates a much more serious situation than did the Spanish question.

120. First of all, I should like to emphasize how peaceful we Africans are and what a feeling of deep friendship we have for all the foreigners who have settled in our continent, especially when they cease to define their relations with us as those between the dominating and the dominated. We are seriously afraid that the brutality with which on 21 March last the Government of the Union of South Africa put down a movement of peaceful and legitimate protest against one of the manifestations of its racial policy—that of not being able to move from place to place without a pass—we fear, I say, that the situation thus created will engender throughout Africa unfortunate resentments which will jeopardize co-operation, concord and harmony on the African continent.

121. I venture to hope that the Africans of the Union will be able to remain sufficiently calm and composed in the face of the repression which the Government of the Union of South Africa has unfortunately undertaken. From this point of view it is indeed reassuring that on 22 March one of the African leaders, Mr. Albert Luthuli, President of the African National Congress, who has been ordered to live in Zululand, sent a message to the Europeans. After asserting that the Africans had no intention of driving the whites out of the country but were simply claiming the right to just treatment, he stated that there would be no solution until the races reached an understanding. Thus, it is reassuring to see that the Africans are thinking only of peace and agreement. But it would be dangerous if the Security Council did not take the situation seriously in hand with a view to finding an adequate solution for it.

122. At this stage of the debate, the Tunisian delegation wishes to make the following observations.

123. The request that we addressed to the Security Council does not concern the problem of racial discrimination _per se_, as a question involving the universal principles of human rights, since in our opinion this question is still within the competence of the General Assembly, which has already dealt with it in the course of eight consecutive sessions. We can only regret that the various resolutions adopted in that respect have not been accepted by the Government of the Union of South Africa.

124. What the request brought before the Council by the twenty-nine nations concerns is the bloody repression undertaken by the Union Government, especially since 21 March 1960, as an inevitable consequence of its racial policy. The present situation is likely to produce complications both inside and outside the Union, thus creating a latent threat to international peace and security. We hold that the Council is in duty bound to take prompt and energetic action in accordance with its responsibilities. It seems to us that the General Assembly's various resolutions have exhausted all possible means of conciliation; we can only regret that they have been unsuccessful.

125. It is now the Council's duty to take really effective action to bring the situation before it to an end, with a view to the maintenance of a genuine and lasting peace, which according to resolution 377 (V), entitled "Uniting for peace", "depends... especially upon respect for and observance of human rights and fundamental freedoms for all ...".

38. Mr. JHA (India):

60. International opinion, both inside and outside the United Nations, recognizes that the racial problem, particularly in Africa, is now a concern of the entire international community. The intensity and the sustained character of the United Nations concern in this question since 1946, when India brought to the attention of the General Assembly the item entitled "Treatment of Indians in the Union of South Africa", the fact that racial discrimination anywhere and particularly in South Africa stirs to the innermost depths tremendous masses of men, not only on the continent of Africa but elsewhere the emergence of a strong sense of African nationalism and African personality which is not prepared to tolerate the slightest manifestation of racialism and assumption of superiority by any other people, are among the most striking events of our time. These are now a part of the ethos of the United Nations and represent currents and forces which the the world can only ignore at its peril.

61. The shooting down of large numbers of unarmed men and women would have been regrettable in any case; world opinion was bound to be moved by the killing of peaceful and defenceless demonstrators. But the killings in South Africa do not stand out in isolation. They are intimately concerned with and are indeed a culmination of the cult of racism in South Africa which the United Nations has deplored and condemned over the years. The events in South Africa can no longer be an exercise in academic discussion on human rights. They cut much deeper than that; and if international peace has any relation to the state of feeling of millions of people inhabiting vast geographical areas in Africa and Asia—and may I add here that they constitute well above half the world's population—it is clear that seen against the background of the current forces in Africa they constitute a serious threat to international peace and have grave potentialities for international friction. Peace does not mean the mere avoidance of war; the threat to international peace does not merely connote a threatening war situation between two or more nations. Any issue which threatens to divide humanity as deeply as the present one is a threat to international peace.

62. Here, if I may digress a moment, I must point out that the interpretation given by the representative of South Africa—I do not see him, to my great regret and misfortune, at the table, but I hope he will hear my voice somewhere—that there are no two parties in the present dispute facing each other for a war, is much too narrow and unacceptable as it does not conform to the concepts embodied in the Charter. Let me remind our South African colleague of what a great countryman of his, add one of the architects of the Charter, Prime Minister Field Marshal Smuts, said at a plenary meeting of the San Francisco Conference. I quote excerpts from Field Marshal Smuts' statement:

> "The new Charter should not be a mere legalistic document for the prevention of war. I would suggest that the Charter should contain at its very outset and in its preamble, a declaration of human rights and of the common faith which has sustained the Allied peoples in their bitter and prolonged struggle for the vindication of those rights and that faith.
>
> " ...
>
> "Let us, in this new Charter of humanity, give expression to this faith in us, and thus proclaim to the world and to posterity, that this was not a mere brute struggle of force between the nations but that for us, behind the mortal struggle, was the moral struggle, was the vision of the ideal, the faith in justice and the resolve to vindicate the fundamental rights of man, and on that basis to found a better, freer world for the future.
>
> " ...
>
> "The peace we are striving for, and are taking such pains to safeguard, is a peace of justice and honor and fair-dealing as between man and man, as between nation and nation. No other peace would be worth the sacrifices we have made and are prepared to make again and the heavy responsibilities we are prepared to take under this Charter." 4/

63. This, I submit, is the true spirit of the Charter and this is the background of faith and high moral principles against which we must interpret not only Article 34 but every other Article of the Charter. I have taken the liberty of quoting this statement to show that the contention that there must be two parties armed with guns or sticks, or whatever it may be, facing each other for an open conflict, as the only situation in which Article 34 applies, is totally irrelevant and unacceptable.

97. We stand by Article 2, paragraph 7, of the Charter, but we do not agree that that paragraph can be a cover for acts which amount to a patent violation of the United Nations Charter, whether it be an Article in Chapter IX or in any other Chapter of the Charter. Events which cause world-wide concern, which have potentialities for international friction and disharmony, and which are directly opposed to the spirit and letter of the Charter cannot be brought within the straitjacket of Article 2, paragraph 7.

99. The Council has faced many issues; it has discussed many situations endangering international peace; but none of the issues brought before the Council measures up, in extent and in far-reaching implications, to the danger to international peace posed by the situation in South Africa. It has been said that the seeds of war lie in the minds of men. How well the United Nations Educational, Scientific and Cultural Organization has put it in the preamble to its constitution: "That since wars begin in the minds of men, it is in the minds of men that the defences of peace must be constructed."

100. The mind is far stronger than matter; far stronger, indeed, than the most powerful nuclear weapon; and it is the minds of men that have been deeply stirred on the continent of Africa and elsewhere by the large-scale killings and ruthless and violent suppression of the African people in the Union of South Africa in pursuit of racial policies which are totally contrary to the Charter of the United Nations. The cult of the master race, which is being practised in all its nakedness in South Africa, is a dangerous one. One has only to look back on the history of our own times, thirty years ago or less. Those who ignored the racial policies, the cult of racism and race superiority practised in Hitler's Germany did so at the cost of a world war. Let not the same mistake be committed again. The Security Council owes it to itself and to humanity to pool the wisdom and statesmanship of its members and to act and act decisively to save the world from the grave danger of a conflagration.

3. Mr. COX (Liberia):

5. There would seem to be little doubt that the situ-
ion before the Council is one urgently requiring
tion. It is clearly a situation which has already led
international friction and the continuance of which
clearly likely to endanger the maintenance of inter-
tional peace and security as envisaged in Articles
and 35 of the Charter. It would seem beyond argu-
ent that if the continuance of a situation is likely to
danger the maintenance of international peace and
curity, it cannot possibly be essentially within the
mestic jurisdiction of any one nation but is, on the
ntrary, an international question. Here I am quoting
passage from the book by Goodrich and Simons. The
ited Nations and the Maintenance of International
ace and Security, referring to the Spanish question
ich was before the Security Council, 18 April 1946.

6. It has sometimes been argued that only enforce-
ent measures under Chapter VII may be taken in the
ce of the domestic jurisdiction provision. The dis-
ction between a situation likely to endanger the
aintenance of international peace and security and a
reat to peace is obviously one of degree only, that
, of immediacy and seriousness of the danger to
ace. To hold that enforcement measures only may
taken would constitute an abdication of the functions
the Security Council and an invitation to permit the
uation to deteriorate. It would be most difficult to
cept this point of view which, as has been pointed
t, suggests the rather disturbing thesis that the
ited Nations has no authority to deal with certain
estions unless and until peace is directly and im-
ediately threatened, when it may be too late to take
ective preventive measures.

7. There is something profoundly disturbing in the
ion that this organ of the United Nations must sit
supinely while the whole civilized world is united
protest and is determined to mobilize all the resour-
s of humanity not only to prevent the repetition of
s violent outrage but to eradicate the conditions of
gregation and suppression which are the breeding
ound for the tragic events of the past week. There
not and there cannot be any reasonable interpreta-
n of any provision of the United Nations Charter
ich requires this organ charged with the primary
sponsibility for the maintenance of international
ace and security to stand aloof until the tinder is
own into the dynamite. The Security Council has the
wer to stay the hand that is about to initiate the
nflagration. If it is possible, by any conceivable
erpretation of the language and spirit of the United
tions Charter, to avoid the stultification of the Se-
rity Council, then such an interpretation must be
opted. The people of the world will not understand
y other course, for they have no other recourse
n the Security Council if they are to seek peaceful
dress of this most grievous assault against the
man spirit.

. Mr. SOBOLEV (Union of Soviet Socialist Re-
blics) (translated from Russian):

. The crux of the matter lies not only and not
much in the fact that the Government of the Union
South Africa is flagrantly defying the provisions
Articles 1, 55 and 56 of the United Nations Charter,
ich require respect for and observance of human
hts and fundamental freedoms for all without
distinction as to race, sex, language, or religion.
It is now something far more serious: the latest
actions of the South African authorities, which have
embarked on the mass destruction of people of other
races, are threatening the preservation of peace on
the African continent.

38. It is precisely to this that the twenty-nine Asian
and African States refer in their letter to the Security Council [S/4297 and Add.1], rightly pointing
our that as a result of the actions of the South African
authorities a situation has arisen which is pregnant
with grave potentialities for international friction
and endangers the maintenance of international peace
and security.

40. The Security Council must heed the views of
more than a third of the States Members of the
United Nations; it must carefully weigh the material
placed before it, and attentively examine the alarm-
ing situation which has arisen and fulfil its task
under the Charter in maintaining peace and security.

50. The Security Council must take immediate measures to put a stop to and prevent the recurrence
of such acts of violence and despotism against the
African people and endow them with full rights in
accordance with the requirements of the United
Nations Charter and the Universal Declaration of
Human Rights.

51. The Security Council should show the African
peoples that the United Nations is on their side in
their struggle for freedom and independence and
for the basic human and civil rights, as, indeed,
are world public opinion and all the peoples of the
world.

81. Mr. CORREA (Ecuador)

85. My delegation proposes to examine the situation
without losing sight of the framework of juridical
limitations established in the United Nations Charter,
or of the duties of the Council and its members
under the Charter, or of the constructive approach
which our obligation to guard the peace compels us
to take, and without, on the other hand, ignoring
our humanitarian feelings as representatives of peoples whose futures and destinies are inextricably
linked.

86. From the legal point of view, the objection to
the Council's competence on the basis of Article 2,
paragraph 7, as raised once again by the Union of
South Africa, is to our mind unacceptable. The fact
that the General Assembly has dealt with this problem at various sessions, that it has established a
subsidiary organ to study the question and that it has
made recommendations to the Union Government
which express its disapproval of the policy of racial
discrimination and segregation, constitutes an undeniable precedent that the principle of non-intervention
laid down in Article 2, paragraph 7, cannot be used
to prevent United Nations organs from fulfilling their
duties under Articles 55 and 56 of the Charter, and
specifically the duties associated with promoting
universal respect for, and observance of, human
rights and fundamental freedoms for all without distinction as to race, sex, language, or religion.

87. The duties stated in Articles 55 and 56 pertain
to the General Assembly and the Economic and Social

Council. One of them is to see that Member States respect and fulfil the contractual commitment—a fully binding commitment freely entered into upon signature of and accession to the Charter—to respect and promote the observance of human rights. This is the situation as far as Articles 55 and 56 are concerned.

88. Article 34 of the Charter, on the other hand, provides that the Security Council may investigate any situation which might lead to international friction or give rise to a dispute, in order to determine whether the continuance of the dispute or situation is likely to endanger the maintenance of international peace and security. If, therefore, the Assembly's practice precludes the use of Article 2, paragraph 7, to nullify Articles 55 and 56, we can hardly conceive that the power of investigation vested in the Council under Article 34 of the Charter might be rendered ineffective or inoperative by that paragraph.

89. We have heard voiced in the Assembly the idealistic thesis that the peace which the Security Council is called upon to preserve is not simply the negative condition represented by the absence of armed conflict, but rather a positive peace having as one of its essential elements the universal observance of human rights, and that consequently any case of systematic violation of human rights must be viewed as a threat to the peace.

90. I cannot claim to follow this line of argument, however logical it may be and however popular it may have become among the people of many of our countries. In the present case, I prefer to view the matter from a standpoint of greater immediate realism. We must admit that while every violation of human rights perpetrated by a State as a matter of State policy constitutes a violation of obligations assumed under the Charter, it does not necessarily and in every case constitute an immediate danger to international peace and security. In some cases, on the other hand, the violation of human rights may be surrounded by circumstances such that the maintenance of international peace and security is endangered, with the result that the situation becomes open to Security Council action. It rests with the Council to determine whether such a situation has arisen.

91. Having thus stated our position on the question of competence, I must now refer to the events in South Africa. I should like to be able to do so without becoming dramatic or adding a tragic colour to my words, but the facts themselves are so tragic that they call forth an emotional reaction. According to the available evidence, we are faced, in short, with the large-scale killing, imprisonment and repression of a people in rebellion against an unjustified and odious policy of discrimination imposed upon them against their will and condemned by the world conscience.

95. The Security Council cannot remain indifferent before these happenings. The sole fact that twenty-nine States Members of the United Nations have expressed their concern to the Council is a clear indication that we are faced with a situation which may well endanger international peace and security. The emotion with which people have responded in almost every corner of the globe bears out this contention.

96. There is, in our view, ample justification f the request made by various speakers that the Cou cil should take effective action to stem the tide events in the Union of South Africa. It rests wi the members of the Council to seek the most a visable course of action, sincerely and in good faith

17. Mr. FOURIE (Union of South Africa):

18. Since my original statement, a great deal has be said about the scope of Article 2, paragraph 7. None the arguments used in any way invalidates the So African Government's contention that the Council precluded by this Article from considering the Sou African Government's efforts to maintain internal l and order. I am therefore instructed to record on again our protest against this disregard of Article paragraph 7.

19. It has been argued that the Council is justified, accordance with Articles 34 and 35, in considering th question. It will be recalled that I dealt with this aspe in my opening statement. I do not wish to reiterate wh I then stated. I wish to emphasize, however, that it clear from Chapters VI and VII of the Charter that t Council is empowered to deal only with disputes situations the continuance of which is likely to endang the maintenance of international peace and securi Furthermore, Article 33 makes it clear that there mu be more than one party to a dispute, and there can no doubt at all that the relevant Articles of the Chart envisage disputes or situations arising between Stat and countries, and that purely internal situations a excluded.

20. If this were not so, any State would be enable simply by claiming that internal disturbances in a other State are likely to create a situation endangeri international peace, to bring such domestic matte before the Council. Such a procedure will leave State immune to outside intervention in its intern affairs and can lead to chaos in international life.

21. I cannot see how, if a State or a group of Stat disapprove of the internal policy of another State, th can be used as an argument that a threat to inte national peace, as envisaged in the Charter, does exi It is hardly possible for any State not to disagree wi some aspects of the internal policies of other State Such disagreement might exist even between maj Powers. Such disagreement could extend to most in portant and serious matters of policy. Must this henc forth be interpreted to mean that Council action can instituted on the grounds that such disagreement co stitutes a dispute likely to endanger the maintenance international peace and security?

22. No, the way the functions of the Security Coun are defined in Articles 34 and 35 makes it obvious th the Council has the right to discuss only disturbanc and situations arising directly between soverei States themselves.

54. Mr. JHA (India):

58. Article 2, paragraph 7, of the Charter has been i voked in this case by the Union of South Africa, a this plea has received support from the United Kingd and France. This is not the first time that this pr vision of the Charter has been cited to bar discussi and consideration of a matter by the Security Coun and the General Assembly. The Repertory of Practi

United Nations Organs 1/ lists, for the period up to 55, twenty-three instances, including eight in the curity Council, in which Article 2, paragraph 7, was voked, mostly in cases involving gross violations of man rights. Since then, there have been, I imagine, least half a dozen occasions when the same Article is relied upon. In no single instance has the plea been cepted by any organ of the United Nations. Indeed, the ited Nations bodies, with vast majorities, have held at although intervention in the sense of dictatorial terference and direct action in matters essentially thin the domestic jurisdiction of a country is not rmissible, except in respect of action under Chapter I of the Charter, consideration, discussion and appropriate recommendation are within the rights and mpetence of the United Nations where a country does t live up to its obligations under the Charter.

. I will refrain from going into a theoretical discussion of the implications of Article 2, paragraph 7, the Charter. In the very able presentations made by e representatives of Argentina, Ecuador and other untries, not to mention the representatives of Tunisia d Ceylon, the argument about the applicability of ticle 2, paragraph 7, has been more than adequately et. I will, however, claim your indulgence to quote om a remarkable analysis by the Indian representa-ve, Mr. A. K. Sen, an eminent lawyer who is now the nister of Law in the Government of India. This alysis was made on 30 September 1955 before the neral Assembly:

"The expression 'essentially within the domestic urisdiction of any State' proprio vigore emphasized he coexistence of a jurisdiction assigned under the Charter to the United Nations. Otherwise it would not have been necessary to emphasize the prohibition in egard to matters 'essentially within the domestic urisdiction of any State'. It must necessarily mean hat a special jurisdiction has been created for the Jnited Nations by the States subscribing to the Charter.

"I suppose everyone will agree that no international obligation can live apart from the domestic phere. International obligations are imperceptibly nterwoven in the domestic texture of any State, for t is only through municipal action and legislation hat international obligations are enforced and adhered to. Similarly, it is only through municipal ction and law that international obligations are roken. The two sets of obligations do not live apart; hey do not fall easily within rigid, watertight compartments...

"... Take any problem—the problem of labour, the problem of factories, the problem of franchise for vomen or various other problems which have been lebated, discussed and which have even formed the ubject matter of various resolutions of this General Assembly. None of these matters can be discussed or lecided upon without bringing about some sort of ndirect effect on the national policies or affairs of Member States.

"That is made clear when we refer to the words essentially within the domestic jurisdiction of any State'. That means that matters which are decided or discussed here are necessarily connected with domestic affairs of the Members and will necessarily have effect on the domestic affairs but they do not necessarily become matters which are essentially domestic." 2/

64. I do not wish to say anything more on the question of Article 2, paragraph 7. However, there were one or two statements made by the representative of the Union of South Africa to which I should like to reply.

65. He stated—and I must say that he argued very ably the case that has been given to him—that a purely internal situation must be excluded from the jurisdiction of the Council and that the situation in South Africa is merely a matter of maintaining law and order. We would entirely agree with him that there are civil disturbances in many countries and that it is the task of government everywhere to apply the law and to maintain law and order. But the situation in South Africa is different. The situation that has arisen there is inextricably connected with the internal policies, racial policies, which are an infraction of the Charter of the United Nations, and it is for that reason that the situation attracts the attention of the United Nations—the General Assembly or the Security Council or any other organ. If it were a purely civil disturbance, if South Africa had been following a policy entirely in consonance with Articles 55 and 56 of the Charter, we would have had nothing to say. It would be a regrettable thing indeed, but we would have nothing to say. But this is the culmination, this is the apex, this represents the fulfilment of the policy adopted by the Union of South Africa, a policy which has repeatedly been found by the United Nations to be contrary to the Purposes and Principles of the Charter and which is an infringement of the very obligations undertaken by the Union of South Africa.

66. That is why we are here. That is why the United Nations has the competence, the right, to discuss this matter, apart from the question of its being a threat to peace. That is proved by the statements of Government leaders, by the statements in the Press, a great number of which I took the liberty of quoting in my last statement [852nd meeting]. It is proved that this is a matter of grave international concern and that it must necessarily receive the attention of the Security Council.

67. Secondly, the draft resolution that is before the Security Council—and we very much hope that it will be adopted—cannot be said to represent any dictatorial interference in the internal affairs of South Africa. It is simply a recommendation. Perhaps it is a recommendation couched in strong terms, but the terms of the recommendation are a matter to be judged entirely by the Security Council, or by whatever body of the United Nations is making the recommendation. But this draft does not seek to interfere with the legal and constitutional processes by which the recommendation should be given effect. There is no intention on the part of the Security Council to arrogate to itself, and there is no implication in the draft that the Security Council will arrogate to itself, either by direct action or by subversion of any constitutional machinery in the Union of South Africa, the task of giving effect to this. It represents the pressure that we want to put on the Union of South Africa. We are entirely justified in wanting to apply that pressure. Of course, the measure of pressure is probably great. It has to be great in the circumstances because we are facing a catastrophic situation.

68. That is all we are trying to do. There is no question of dictatorial interference in the internal machinery of the Union of South Africa. But we have every right, I submit, to tell the Union of South Africa that the United Nations, the Security Council and other organs, do not approve of this policy, that we think it is a danger to peace, and we have every right to ask the Union of South Africa to revise its policies, to modify them, and to change its laws and regulations to conform with the Charter of the United Nations.

On the basis of a proposal by the Ecuadorian delegation, the Council adopted the following resolution on 1 April 1960 (UN Doc. S/4300; SCOR, XV, Suppl. for April–June 1960, p. 1):

The Security Council,

Having considered the complaint of twenty-nine Member States contained in document S/4279 and Add.1 concerning "the situation arising out of the large-scale killings of unarmed and peaceful demonstrators against racial discrimination and segregation in the Union of South Africa",

Recognizing that such a situation has been brought about by the racial policies of the Government of the Union of South Africa and the continued disregard by that Government of the resolutions of the Gene Assembly calling upon it to revise its policies and bri them into conformity with its obligations and respo sibilities under the Charter of the United Nations,

Taking into account the strong feelings and gra concern aroused among Governments and peoples the world by the happenings in the Union of Sou Africa,

1. *Recognizes* that the situation in the Union South Africa is one that has led to international fricti and if continued might endanger international peace a security;

2. *Deplores* that the recent disturbances in the Uni of South Africa should have led to the loss of life of many Africans and extends to the families of the victi its deepest sympathies;

3. *Deplores* the policies and actions of the Gove ment of the Union of South Africa which have giv rise to the present situation;

4. *Calls upon* the Government of the Union of Sou Africa to initiate measures aimed at bringing abo racial harmony based on equality in order to ensu that the present situation does not continue or rec and to abandon its policies of *apartheid* and racial d crimination;

5. *Requests* the Secretary-General, in consultati with the Government of the Union of South Afri to make such arrangements as would adequately help upholding the purposes and principles of the Chart and to report to the Security Council whenever nec sary and appropriate.

While previous General Assembly discussions and resolutions had made mention of the danger of apartheid to peaceful international relations—the 1953 Commission report stated, for example, that the continuance of apartheid would "endanger friendly relations among states"—the fact that the Security Council had now become involved opened up the possibility that the entire dispute-resolving machinery of Chapter VI and, even more strikingly, that the enforcement provisions of Chapter VII of the Charter might now be available to deal with South Africa's unwillingness to comply with the numerous resolutions and recommendations that had been directed at it by the Organization over the years. Viewed from the perspective of the early debates on the matter, and the admonitions of caution by France and Great Britain to the effect that even placing the matter on the agenda must be carefully scrutinized for possible violations of Article 2(7), this involvement by the Security Council amounted to a very radical step.

Yet it should be noted that this Resolution of the Security Council also represents just one further step in an evolutionary development in which there has been a gradual, but steady, erosion of the inhibitions imposed by Article 2(7); in their place there is an emerging sense of responsibility on the part of the Organization to act as if some minimal standards concerning human rights for the world community existed that all nations are obliged to maintain. The use of the provisions concerning the threat to international peace and security may be viewed either as a legalistic device to provide the Security Council with the necessary competence to act, or as an expression of the fact that a violation of these standards was so repugnant to the vast majority of the governments of the world that their violation does in fact produce antagonisms and tensions that threaten international peace and security.

Nevertheless, throughout this entire period the government of South Africa has refused adamantly to change its policy of apartheid and, while it did meet on occasion with representatives of the United Nations to discuss the resolutions, the government has also ordered its representatives to boycott meetings and has threatened to withdraw from the Organization. By 1962 the continuing inability of the United Nations to effect change through recommendations and resolutions of the various organs had persuaded a number of states to demand that some kind of enforcement procedures be undertaken to coerce compliance. The following materials are indicative of the type of debate that ensued, and they reveal the kind of enforcement procedures that have been discussed and actually put into operation. Recall also the excerpt in Chapter 2 from the *South West Africa Cases*.

Discussion in the Special Political Committee of the General Assembly on the Policies of Apartheid of the Government of the Republic of South Africa.

U.N. G.A. Official records, 17th sess. Summary Records of meetings, 19 September 1962 – 18 December 1962. pp. 5–7, 18, 37–38, 69–70. (A/SPC/SR. 325–376)

Mr. JANTUAH (Ghana)

8. South Africa had violated the principles of the Charter by erecting racial discrimination into a system of government, and it was time for the United Nations to decide whether any country or group of countries which helped South Africa to maintain that form of government was not itself an accomplice in the violation of the Charter. There was a startling contradiction betweeen the public professions of those NATO Powers in regard to South Africa's racial policies, and their surreptitious supply of arms and equipment to assist it in maintaining its defiance of the Charter. That duplicity seriously impaired the favourable impression which the leading NATO Powers, the United States, the United Kingdom and France, had been making in their stand against racial bigotry and persecution. The comparatively creditable record of achievement of the United Kingdom and France with regard to decolonization was being spoilt by their assistance to South Africa. The other Members of the United Nations had a right and a duty to warm those countries of the danger of their activities and to demand that they should refrain forthwith from actions which sabotaged the efforts and the determination of the Organization.

9. South Africa's military ambitions were not confined within its bòrders. The Minister of Defence had spoken of developing rockets to carry bombs, and a member of the South African Atomic Energy Board had announced that South Africa might soon begin the manufacture of atomic bombs as a weapon against "loud-mouthed African-Asian States". Munitions factories were being built with technical assistance from Belgium, Britain and France, and a French armament firm producing rocket missile components for NATO had established a factory in the Rand. The evidence of South Africa's aggressive intentions was overwhelming and the United Nations must act quickly and decisively to prevent it from starting an atomic [illegible]

10. The military build-up of South Africa had reach a stage at which it was a threat to the peace of t whole African continent, and those countries whi were lending it military assistance would share t responsibility for the consequences. An unholy a liance was being formed to perpetuate and expand t rule of white racist minority governments in Afric The Governments of South Africa, Portugal and t Federation of the Rhodesias and Nyasaland were n in league to perpetuate racial discrimination throug out the whole of the southern part of the Afric continent. There were reports that a secret defer agreement had been signed, and Southern Rhodes army units had taken part in training exercises South Africa while military missions from both So Africa and the Federation had visited the Portugue colony of Lourenço Marques and taken part in traini exercises there. The South African authorities h been pressed to assist the Portuguese in Angola, a there were reports that the airstrip at Caprivi h been used by both the South African and the Portugue air forces against the Angolan people. The Territo of South West Africa was being administered by So Africa in violation of the Purposes and Principles the Charter. General Assembly resolution 1702 (X had noted the progressive deterioration of the situat there, which would, if allowed to continue, endan international peace and security.

11. Apart from the threat to international peace a security, the Ghanaian delegation also believed t the arming of a minority racial group against a m jority of African, Indian and Indo-Pakistan ori constituted a serious tendency leading to genoc in South Africa. Article II (c) of the Convention on Prevention and Punishment of the Crime of Genoc (General Assembly resolution 260 III) said that form of genocide was "deliberately inflicting on group conditions of life calculated to bring about physical destruction in whole or in part". It was coincidence that the Republic of South Africa was a signatory to that Convention.

12. It was obvious that the South African Governm had no intention of mending its ways. Its policy racial discrimination, masquerading as separate velopment for the various races in South Africa, been intensified and it had turned a deaf ear to pleas of world opinion. Clearly, therefore, the is could not be solved by appeasement or entreat The time had come for blunt political, diploma

d economic action against South Africa, on a world-de scale. It had become apparent at the sixteenth ssion of the General Assembly that there were a mber of countries which, though prepared to con-mn the actions of the South African Government, re not prepared to support any positive measures force the ending of apartheid. There was no point merely deploring apartheid, year after year, when Charter gave a mandate for positive action. Even ough the Republic of South Africa was violating Charter, it had neither the will nor the courage leave the Organization. Obviously, however, any ember of an organization that refused to comply h that organization's rules automatically forfeited right to membership. The United Nations would condoning the violation of its own Charter if it not consider expelling the Republic of South Africa. e Ghanaian delegation once again called upon the mmittee to consider whether the Security Council ould not be invited to consider the expulsion of ıth Africa from the Organization.

There were some Members of the Organization ich did not wish to see South Africa expelled and ıth Africa itself did not wish to be expelled. That, doubt, was why the South African Foreign Minister ne every year in person to the General Assembly plead the cause of his country, though it was riddled h policies which the United Nations condemned.

The Ghanaian delegation also wished to recom-nd the establishment of a small committee of mber States to keep the South African situation manently in view while the General Assembly was in session. Such a committee should be empowered visit South Africa and to report either to the Gen-l Assembly or to the Security Council as appro-ate from time to time.

The General Assembly had already called upon mber States in its resolution 1663 (XVI) to take ividual or collective measures against South Africa, the Ghanaian delegation would like to know what ividual Member States had done in the past year. President of Ghana had said in a speech to the ional Assembly that the application of economic ctions would seem to be the most direct method oringing South Africa to heel. He proposed, there-, that the following sanctions should be imposed: diplomatic relations with the Government of the ublic of South Africa should be broken off; the ts of the world should be closed to all vessels ng the South African flag; legislation should be cted prohibiting the ships of Member States from ring South African ports; all South African goods ld be boycotted; landing and passage facilities ld be refused to aircraft belonging to the Govern-t and to companies registered under the laws of Republic of South Africa; air, postal, telegraphic, o and other means of communication with the ublic of South Africa should be interrupted.

The United Nations had already adopted many lutions on the South African problem but they had achieved their purpose because they lacked the ired bite. The South African Government had d it safe to ignore them. The prestige of the nization was at stake, and the time had now come ke decisive action. Many African delegations had e to the current session with an uncompromising date from their Governments to vote for the stern-neasures against South Africa. The African States were now more than ever determined to demonstrate their solidarity and singleness of purpose. It was to be hoped that a great majority of Members would be able to support the determination of the African States. It was also to be hoped that no attempt would be made to impair that solidarity and unity of purpose through the introduction of tame and spurious resolutions as had happened in the past. The situation in South Africa today was too explosive for diplomatic legerdemain.

7. Mr. VASQUEZ (Colombia)

8. The problem of apartheid in the Republic of South Africa seemed insoluble. The two most recent resolutions adopted by the General Assembly had failed to bring about the desired result. Not in Africa alone, but all over the world, racial discrimination was a contradiction of the elementary principles of democracy and international law. It was so clearly a negation of democracy that to impose it as a permanent system in the case of Nazi Germany it had been necessary to construct a police State.

9. There were three possible methods of solving international disputes by peaceful means: the repetition of statements and admonitions by the General Assembly, the course previously adopted in the South African case, though without success; the application of sanctions; and recourse to the International Court of Justice. So far as sanctions were concerned, in the absence of specific proposals it was not clear what the advocates of such measures had in mind, or whether the General Assembly would be entitled to impose such sanctions without the intervention of the Security Council. Colombia inclined, therefore, to the third course. It believed that the International Court of Justice should be strengthened and allowed to act in cases involving a conflict of standards as well as in cases of political disputes. Colombia had given an example of that attitude when it had agreed with the Government of Peru in 1949 to have the question of asylum submitted to the International Court of Justice.[1] The International Court should be called upon to establish the duty of the Republic of South Africa in regard to racial discrimination and human rights. The ineffectiveness of the General Assembly's resolutions on apartheid in South Africa had given rise to what was obviously a legal question: the conflict of standards between the principle of national sovereignty and that of respect for human rights. There were certain apparent contradictions betweeen Article 2, paragraph 7 and Article 55 of the Charter, which its authors had perhaps not foreseen. It would be desirable to determine whether the first provision, which prohibited the Organization from intervening in matters which were essentially within the domestic jurisdiction of States, took precedence over the obligation to comply with resolutions relating to human rights. It would be useful, therefore, to refer the question at issue to the International Court of Justice so that it could clarify certain points of law.

10. In any event, Colombia wished to reiterate its support for human rights, human dignity and non-discrimination. It believed that racism was incompatible with the provisions of the Charter and of the Universal Declaration of Human Rights. In adopting that position, Colombia was following the tradition of Latin America from its earliest times. Moreover,

[1] Columbian-Peruvian asylum case, Order of October 20th 1949: I.C.J. Reports 1949, p. 225.

American law specifically prohibited racial discrimination, as was shown by various resolutions adopted at conferences of American States. In keeping with its convictions and its practice, therefore, Colombia was in favour of measures which would impose respect for human rights on South Africa. It would examine any proposals that were made in the light of those convictions and of the provisions of the Charter.

22. Mr. PLIMPTON (United States of America) considered that no more important question faced the Assembly than the assurance to all men and women of their full rights and dignities as human beings. Since its birth as a nation, the United States had been committed to the belief that all men were created equal—a belief that was proclaimed as a self-evident truth in the Declaration of Independence. It was true that the problem of racial discrimination still existed in the United States, but the fight to establish equality—which had begun with the Civil War—was still being fought, and the United States Government was making determined efforts to bring discrimination to an end in the pockets where it still lingered. Similarly, the United States would use its influence to win acceptance for the principles of human equality elsewhere in the world. It was a matter of universal shame that several Member States, in complete disregard of their pledges under the Charter, continued to proscribe or penalize those whose race, religion or conscience was unacceptable to the ruling Government.

23. In view of its traditions, the United States was inevitably and irrevocably opposed to apartheid in all its aspects. In the firm belief that the continuation of such a policy could only lead to profound human tragedy for all races in South Africa, it would use its best efforts to encourage the South African Government to abandon it and to live up to its obligations under the Charter. But above all, the United States—and the United Nations—could not but feel the deepest anxiety, for by the harsh policy of apartheid the lives of millions of people were thwarted.

24. The arguments used to justify apartheid were depressingly familiar. They had been used a century earlier in the United States to justify a system of human bondage. But they were refuted equally by advances in ethical teachings and in scientific knowledge. During the past year two leading scientific organizations in the United States had passed resolutions categorically repudiating claims concerning biological inequalities between different races, which were used as grounds for the denial of rights. The Government of the United States and the majority of its people supported those conclusions in the conviction that partnership and not separation of races was the key to a harmonious multi-racial society.

25. Regrettably, the situation in South Africa had not improved during the past year, and the passage of the Sabotage Act could only aggravate the prospects for progress. However, despite the large number of arrests under that Act, the voice of protest had not been stilled in South Africa and, in the end, it would be the South Africans themselves who would bring about the change that would allow all races to live together in amity. The United States offered its sympathy to those courageous persons who continued peacefully to affirm basic human rights in South Africa.

26. But more than sympathy was required, and all Members of the United Nations would have to consider how best to convince the South African Governme that apartheid was both wrong and useless and mu be abandoned for the good of all the peoples of Sou Africa. Indeed its abandonment would aid the contin as a whole, for apartheid not only separated the rac within South Africa, but it separated that nation fr the rest of Africa and denied it the opportunity contribute to African progress.

27. The Assembly should begin by reaffirming condemnation of apartheid and declaring that So Africa had a solemn duty to bring its racial polic into conformity with the Charter. Then it must or again urge the South African Government to meet obligations with respect to the treatment of peop of Indian and Indo-Pakistan origin. Furthermore, resolution to be adopted must call on individual Sta to exert the utmost influence on the South Afri Government to abandon its regressive policies, Member States should be instructed to report back the Assembly at its eighteenth session concern the specific measures taken towards that end. S reports would enable the Assembly to assess effects of various means that might be used to has the end of apartheid. Finally, the Security Cour might be requested to maintain a close and continu watch on the situation, as one that might precipit a serious threat to world peace and security.

28. The United States delegation feared that a re lution recommending the application of sanctions South Africa would not achieve the practical res desired. The adoption of a draft resolution calling measures that could easily be evaded, would serve to cast doubt on the efficacy of the sanc process. Also, the sense of frustration that prom such measures would only be heightened by t failure. Then again, dissension might arise betw various Member States as to the extent of their c pliance with the resolution and, finally, the failur such a resolution could seriously weaken the autho of the United Nations—a consequence which all M bers, and particularly the smaller nations, would v to avoid. It would be recalled that the decline of League of Nations had been largely precipitated that body's inability to enforce sanctions.

29. As for the suggestion that South Africa shoul expelled from the United Nations, the practical re of such a course would be to remove the South Afr Government from the one place where the full we of world opinion could be brought to bear o Apartheid could be ended not by diminishing S Africa's contacts with the rest of the world b expanding them. The steady and repeated impac the conscience of the world community would be o more use than any dramatic action.

32. Mrs. SOLOMON (Trinidad and Tobago) said there seemed to be a general determination ir face of the increasingly critical situation in S Africa and despite the inherent difficulties to precise and decisive steps at the current sessi the General Assembly. Her delegation shared determination.

35. The Organization was faced with the proble avoiding recommendations which were too extrer be feasible and those which were too mild effective. One course would be to continue its ef to mobilize world opinion against the racial pol

of the South African Government. Since the Government itself was clearly impervious to such approaches, the renewed efforts would have to be directed towards the liberal opinion that still existed in South Africa. Yet, even if the United Nations succeeded in increasing opposition to the Government in South Africa, it was unlikely that the present Government could be defeated by constitutional means. Electoral arrangements in South Africa were such that it could probably maintain itself in power indefinitely.

36. A second, less conventional, course would be the imposition of economic sanctions. True, there were a number of formidable difficulties in the way but they need not prove insurmountable. With regard to the fear of creating an undesirable precedent, she noted that the principle of sanctions had been recognized by the League of Nations, although in most cases the League had found them unenforceable in practice. It was surely desirable for the United Nations to try to set precedents rather than avoid them in such matters, with a view to preventing similar phenomena in the future. Of course, if the scope of the sanctions was made too great, countries would find it difficult, on purely technical grounds, to enforce them strictly. Moreover, if South Africa's major trading partners failed to carry them out, there was no way of compelling them to do so. To be effective, therefore, sanctions must be both manageable in scope and applied with the willing co-operation of the major trading partners. The aim of sanctions could obviously not be to cripple the economy of the countries imposing them, but the world was entitled to expect such countries to impose certain agreed sanctions which would cause comparatively little disruption in their own economies.

37. Her delegation suggested as a basis for discussion a total ban by all countries on imports from South Africa of all goods in the categories of animal and agricultural products and also ales, wines, spirits and beverages and tobacco and tobacco manufactures.

38. In 1960 approximately one-quarter of South Africa's export trade, including bullion, came from the export of those commodities. Countries would probably find it technically easier and economically more acceptable to ban imports from South Africa rather than their own exports. South Africa would probably in turn attempt to restrict its imports, but such restrictions could not be complete or confined to the goods of any one nation. The categories proposed consisted of products which could be obtained from alternative suppliers and it should not be impossible to rearrange the pattern of trade.

39. The initial impact of the ban on imports from South Africa would be upon the South African farmers, who were the most rabid supporters of the Government's racial policy. South Africa already possessed an agricultural surplus problem and the ban would seriously aggravate that situation. The pressure of world opinion, expressed in those economic terms, might well serve to make more elements of South African opinion, perhaps within Government circles themselves, question the wisdom of the Government's policies, on economic if not on racial grounds.

40. Countries which considered even the measures she proposed to be too extreme should note that neither their own exports nor their investments would be directly or immediately affected. As to the long-term effect on investment, no country whose Government relied upon military strength and oppression to protect itself from revolution could be regarded as a satisfactory field for investment. Countries which considered the suggested measures too mild should note that those limited economic sanctions were only a minimum which all nations would be expected to impose. Individual countries could extend the range as they chose.

After the Committee, by 46 votes to 39, with 11 abstentions, refused to allow a separate vote on a paragraph of a proposed resolution that related to sanctions, it adopted the draft resolution as a whole by 60 votes to 16, with 21 abstentions. A similar procedure was resorted to at the plenary session and the General Assembly adopted the resolution by 67 votes to 16, with 23 abstentions. For text of the resolution, see below.

Resolution 1761 (XVII) of the General Assembly, 6 November 1962

U.N. G.A. Official records, 17th sess. 1962. Annexes XVII 87: agenda item 87 pp. 8–9 (A/5276)

1761 (XVII). THE POLICIES OF *apartheid* OF THE GOVERNMENT OF THE REPUBLIC OF SOUTH AFRICA

The General Assembly,

Recalling its previous resolutions on the question of race conflict in South Africa resulting from the policies of *apartheid* of the Government of the Republic of South Africa,

Further recalling its resolutions 44 (I) of 8 December 1946, 395 (V) of 2 December 1950, 615 (VII) of 5 December 1952, 1179 (XII) of 26 November 1957, 1302 (XIII) of 10 December 1958, 1460 (XIV) of 10 December 1959, 1597 (XV) of 13 April 1961 and 1662 (XVI) of 28 November 1961, on the question of the treatment of peoples of Indian and Indo-Pakistan origin,

Noting the reports of the Governments of India (A/5166) and Pakistan (A/5173) on that subject,

Recalling that the Security Council in its resolution of 1 April 1960[3] recognized that the situation in South Africa was one that had led to international friction and, if continued, might endanger international peace and security,

Recalling further that the Security Council in its aforesaid resolution called upon the Government of South Africa to initiate measures aimed at bringing about racial harmony based on equality in order to ensure that the present situation does not continue or recur, and to abandon its policies of *apartheid* and racial discrimination,

Regretting that the actions of some Member States indirectly provide encouragement to the Government of South Africa to perpetuate its policy of racial segregation, which has been rejected by the majority of that country's population,

1. *Deplores* the failure of the Government of the Republic of South Africa to comply with the repeated requests and demands of the General Assembly and of the Security Council and its flouting of world public opinion by refusing to abandon its racial policies:

2. *Strongly deprecates* the continued and total disregard by the Government of South Africa of its obligations under the Charter of the United Nations and, furthermore, its determined aggravation of racial issues by enforcing measures of increasing ruthlessness involving violence and bloodshed;

3. *Reaffirms* that the continuance of those policies seriously endangers international peace and security;

4. *Requests* Member States to take the following measures, separately or collectively, in conformity with the Charter, to bring about the abandonment of those policies:

(*a*) Breaking off diplomatic relations with the Government of the Republic of South Africa or refraining from establishing such relations;

(*b*) Closing their ports to all vessels flying the South African flag;

(*c*) Enacting legislation prohibiting their ships from entering South African ports;

(*d*) Boycotting all South African goods and refraining from exporting goods, including all arms and ammunition, to South Africa;

(*e*) Refusing landing and passage facilities to all aircraft belonging to the Government of South Africa and companies registered under the laws of South Africa;

5. *Decides* to establish a Special Committee consisting of representatives of Member States nominated by the President of the General Assembly, with the following terms of reference:

(*a*) To keep the racial policies of the Government of South Africa under review when the Assembly is not in session;

(*b*) To report either to the Assembly or to the Security Council or to both, as may be appropriate, from time to time;

6. *Requests* all Member States:

(*a*) To do everything in their power to help the Special Committee to accomplish its task;

(*b*) To refrain from any act likely to delay or hinder the implementation of the present resolution;

7. *Invites* Member States to inform the General Assembly at its eighteenth session regarding actions taken, separately or collectively, in dissuading the Government of South Africa from pursuing its policies of *apartheid*.

8. *Requests* the Security Council to take appropriate measures, including sanctions, to secure South Africa's compliance with the resolutions of the General Assembly and of the Security Council on this subject and, if necessary, to consider action under Article 6 of the Charter.

[3] *Ibid.*

On 7 August 1963, the Security Council noted "with concern the recent arms build-up by the Government of South Africa, some of which arms are being used in furtherance of that Government's racial policies"; strongly deprecated "the policies of South Africa in its perpetuation of racial discrimination as being inconsistent with the principles contained in the Charter of the United Nations and contrary to its obligations as a State Member of the United Nations"; called upon "the Government of South Africa to abandon the policies of *apartheid* and discrimination as called for in the previous Security Council resolution of 1 April 1960, and to liberate all persons imprisoned, interned or subjected to other restrictions for having opposed the policy of *apartheid*"; and solemnly called "upon the States to cease forthwith the sale and shipment of arms, ammunition of all types and military vehicles to South Africa." UN Docs. S/5385 and A/5497, p. 28. At the same time, a proposal that the Council call upon "all States to boycott all South African goods and to refrain from exporting to South Africa strategic materials of direct military value," failed to obtain the required majority.

Concern for these matters shifted back to the General Assembly, and the demand for sanctions against the Republic of South Africa grew in intensity. The Special Committee on the Policies of Apartheid of the Republic of South Africa submitted a report to the General Assembly, portions of which are reproduced below.

Report of the Special Committee on the Policies of Aparthied of the Government of the Republic of South Africa: Recommendations

U.N. G.A. Official records, 18th sess. 1963. Annexes XVII 30/Add.1: agenda item 30. pp. 48–9 (A/5497 and Add. 1)

509. First, in view of the non-compliance of the Government of the Republic of South Africa with the provisions of General Assembly resolution 1761 (XVII) and its defiance of the Security Council resolutions of 1 April 1960 (see annex II) and 7 August 1963 (see paragraph 57), the Special Committee feels that the situation should be considered without delay and with particular reference to the obligations of the Republic of South Africa under Article 25 of the Charter.

510. Second, the Special Committee deems it essential that the General Assembly and the Security Council should: (*a*) take note of the continued deterioration of the situation in the Republic of South Africa, in consequence of the continued imposition of discriminatory and repressive measures by its Government in violation of its obligations under the United Nations Charter, the provisions of the Universal Declaration of Human Rights and the resolutions of the General Assembly and the Security Council; (*b*) affirm that the policies and actions of the Republic of South Africa are incompatible with membership in the United Nations; (*c*) declare the determination of the Organization to take all requisite measures provided in the Charter to bring to an end the serious danger to the maintenance of international peace and security; (*d*) call upon all United Nations organs and agencies and all States to take appropriate steps to dissuade the Republic of South Africa from its present racial policies.

511. Third, the Special Committee deems it essential that all Member States be called upon to take requisite measures speedily to implement the relevant provisions of General Assembly resolution 1761 (XVII) and the Security Council resolution of 7 August 1963. It feels that Member States which have taken effective measures in this respect should be commended, and that an urgent invitation should be addressed to all others to take action and report without delay. It feels, moreover, that the General Assembly and the Security Council should express disapproval at the actions of certain States which have taken measures contrary t the provisions of the resolutions of the General A sembly and the Security Council on the policies *apartheid* of the Government of the Republic of Sout Africa (see paragraphs 472-478 and 492-505).

512. Fourth, the Special Committee feels that th States responsible for the administration of territori adjacent to the Republic of South Africa should b called upon to provide asylum and relief to Sout African nationals who are obliged to seek refuge b cause of the policies of *apartheid* and to refrain fro any action which may assist the South African author ties in the continued pursuit of their present raci policies (see paragraphs 495-503).

513. Fifth, in view of the persecution of thousan of South African nationals for their opposition to th policies of *apartheid* and the serious hardship fac by their families, the Special Committee considers th the international community, for humanitarian reason should provide them with relief and other assistanc It recommends that the Secretary-General should b requested, in consultation with the Special Committe to find ways and means to provide such relief an assistance through appropriate international agenci (see paragraph 451).

514. Sixth, with regard to the request to the Mem ber States by the General Assembly that they refra from exporting all arms and ammunition to Sou Africa, and by the Security Council that they cea forthwith the sale and shipment of arms, ammunitic of all types and military vehicles to South Africa, t Special Committee submits the following supplementa recommendations: (*a*) Member States should be r quested not to provide any assistance, directly indirectly, in the manufacture of arms, ammunitic and military vehicles in South Africa, including t supply of strategic materials, provision of technic assistance, or the granting of licenses; (*b*) Memb States should be requested to refrain from providi training for South African military personnel; ar (*c*) Member States should be requested to refrain fro any form of co-operation with South African milita and police forces.

515. Seventh, the Special Committee suggests th the General Assembly and the Security Council giv consideration to additional measures, including t following, to dissuade the Government of the Republ

f South Africa from its racial policies: (*a*) recom-nendation to all international agencies to take all nec-ssary steps to deny economic or technical assistance o the Government of the Republic of South Africa, vithout precluding, however, humanitarian assistance o the victims of the policies of *apartheid*; (*b*) recom-nendation to Member States to take steps to prohibit r discourage foreign investments in South Africa and oans to the Government of the Republic of South Africa or to South African companies; (*c*) recom-nendation to Member States to consider denial of acilities for all ships and aircraft destined to or return-ng from the Republic of South Africa; (*d*) recom-nendation to Member States to take measures to rohibit, or at least discourage, emigration of their ationals to the Republic of South Africa, as immigrants re sought by it to reinforce its policies of *apartheid*; nd (*e*) study of means to ensure an effective embargo n the supply of arms and ammunition, as well as etroleum, to the Republic of South Africa, including blockade, if necessary, under the aegis of the United Nations.

516. Finally, the Special Committee feels that Mem-er States should be urged to give maximum publicity o the efforts of the United Nations with respect to this question and take effective steps to discourage and counteract propaganda by the Government of the Republic of South Africa, its agencies and various other bodies which seek to justify and defend its policies.

517. Considering the extreme gravity of the situation in the Republic of South Africa, and its serious international repercussions, the Special Committee deems it essential that the General Assembly and the Security Council should keep the matter under active consideration in order to take timely and effective measures to ensure the fulfilment of the purposes of the Charter in the Republic of South Africa. The Special Committee feels that they should consider, with no further delay, possible new measures in accordance with the Charter, which provides for stronger political, diplomatic and economic sanctions, suspension of rights and privileges of the Republic of South Africa as a Member State, and expulsion from the United Nations and its specialized agencies. The Special Committee will actively pursue its task of assisting the principal organs in connexion with this problem, and to this end invites the continued co-operation of the Member States and the specialized agencies, as well as all organizations and individuals devoted to the principles of the Charter.

At its Eighteenth Session the General Assembly adopted three resolutions concerning apartheid in South Africa. In the first one the General Assembly condemned "the Government of the Republic of South Africa for its failure to comply with the repeated resolutions of the General Assembly and of the Security Council calling for an end to the repression of persons opposing *apartheid*"; and, considering the arrangements being made in South Africa for a "trial of a large number of political prisoners under arbitrary laws prescribing the death sentence," requested the government of South Africa to abandon that trial "and forthwith to grant unconditional release to all political prisoners and to all persons imprisoned, interned or subjected to other restrictions for having opposed the policy of *apartheid*." GA Resolution 1881 (XVIII), 11 October 1963; GAOR, XVIII, Suppl. 15 (A/5515), p. 19. In the second one, the General Assembly requested the Special Committee on Apartheid "to continue to follow constantly the various aspects of this question"; and appealed "to all States to take appropriate measures and intensify their efforts, separately and collectively, with a view to dissuading the Government of the Republic of South Africa from pursuing its policies of *apartheid*, and requests them, in particular, to implement fully the Security Council resolution of 4 December 1963." In the third one, the General Assembly requested the Secretary-General "to seek ways and means of providing relief and assistance, through the appropriate international agencies, to the families of all persons persecuted by the Government of the Republic of South Africa for their opposition to the policies of *apartheid*." GA Resolutions 1978 A and B (XVIII), 16 December 1963; *idem,* at pp. 20–21.

The Special Committee made a new report on 25 March 1964, noting that the South African Government "has intensified its ruthless repression of all political activity in favour of racial equality" and that some political prisoners opposed to apartheid have been condemmed to death. It recommended that the Security Council should demand that the South African Government should:

"(a) Refrain from the execution of persons sentenced to death under arbitrary laws providing the death sentence for offenses arising from opposition to the Government's racial policies;

"(b) End immediately trials now proceeding under these arbitrary laws, and grant an amnesty to all political prisoners whose only crime is their opposition to the Government's racial policies;

"(c) Refrain from all other actions likely to aggravate the present situation."

The Committee considered it essential that the Security Council should set a strict time-limit for South African compliance, and that in case of non-compliance the Council should take "new mandatory steps to compel the South African Government to comply with the decisions of the Council." UN Doc. A/5692, p. 6.

At the same time, pursuant to the Security Council Resolution of 4 September 1963, the Secretary-General had appointed a group of experts "to examine methods of resolving the present situation in South Africa through full, peaceful and orderly application of human rights and fundamental freedoms to all inhabitants of the territory as a whole, regardless of race, colour or creed, and to consider what part the United Nations might play in the achievement of that end." This group submitted its report on April 20, 1964, relevant portions of which are reproduced below.

(Excerpt from)

Report of a Group of Experts appointed by Secretary-General, 20 April 1964

(To be found in U.N.S.C. (S/5658))

V. The Role of the United Nations

80. In accordance with the Security Council resolution of 4 December 1963, setting out our terms of reference, we were required to consider what part the United Nations might play "in resolving the present situation in South Africa through full, peaceful and orderly application of human rights and fundamental freedoms".

81. We are limiting our comments to the early stages of the "peaceful and orderly" transformation; we are confident that when the transformation is started and a fully representative system of government is introduced a wide range of international assistance can be readily made available at the request of the Government of South Africa.

82. In the immediate task of initiating the transformation, how can the United Nations assist a new effort of constructive co-operation, and how, more particularly, can United Nations action facilitate the new start to be made through a National Convention?

83. We have already proposed that the United Nations should initiate action by inviting the South African Government to send representatives to the United Nations to carry out discussions on the formation of and the agenda for a National Convention, and that a special body should be appointed for these discussions. In these discussions the good offices of the United Nations could assist in several ways, and at the Convention itself the United Nations could, if so requested, provide expert advice on constitutional, economic and social problems.

84. At a later stage, the United Nations could help in administrative reorganization and in particular could help to meet any request for the organization and supervision of elections. If the necessity should arise, the United Nations could also, as suggested by the Danish Foreign Minister in his speech to the General Assembly on 25 September 1963, "contribute to the maintenance of law and order and the protection of life and civil rights" and thus both allay fears and secure confidence.

85. There is one important task which could be put in hand by the United Nations and its specialized agencies at once. This would be

in the vital field of education and training. The need for very large numbers of non-Whites to be qualified for the professions and for the civil service and for teaching is acute now. It will become quickly far greater. We consequently recommend that a United Nations South African Education and Training Programme should be prepared in consultation with the United Nations specialized agencies, the first purpose being to plan educational and training scholarship schemes and then to supervise and administer these schemes. UNESCO might accept responsibility for the project in co-operation with other specialized agencies (in particular the ILO), or it might be considered preferable to set up new and separate machinery for the administration of the programme including the control of funds provided by contributing nations and dealings with students and colleges and training centres participating in the programme. Useful experience in planning such assistance for South African students can be gained from the training schemes initiated by Scandinavian Governments.[3]

86. Once preliminary plans have been drawn up we suggest that the United Nations should call on all Member States to make financial contributions to this programme for training abroad of a large number of South African lawyers, engineers, agronomists, public administrators, teachers at all levels and skilled workers, as well as training in such fields as labour education and business and industrial management. Much of the education and training programme could be undertaken in other African States. The purpose will be to enable as many South Africans as possible to play a full part as quickly as possible in the political, economic and social advance of their country.

87. This is a task to which the Member States can contribute and in which the specialized agencies can participate. It also offers a wider opportunity for concerted action by international organizations and other foundations whether associated with the United Nations or not. Each in its own field can play a part in helping South Africans who have been deprived of their rights and denied opportunities of education and professional, vocational and scientific training. Thus governments, specialized agencies of the United Nations, universities and training colleges and public and private organizations throughout the world can come together to assist in bringing influence to bear on the South African Government by positive action. An international effort of this constructive kind will at the same time illustrate international concern, show the general desire to give immediate practical assistance and give new hope to people who want to see some immediate evidence of a new start.

[3] These are schemes under which funds have been provided for "assistance to young South Africans in exile" covering an educational programme for South African students and support for their studies in schools and colleges outside South Africa at the primary, secondary and higher levels. Other considerable sums have been allocated by African States for vocational training and scholarships for higher studies in African, European, Asian and American universities.

88. This would be a practical means of giving expression to world opinion, and we reaffirm our conviction that only by concerted international pressure can the new start be made. Every country and every organization and every individual who realizes the suffering which the present situation causes and the dangers which now threaten has an opportunity and an obligation to participate in that pressure. Nations can increase diplomatic pressure; churches can do more to make their views known and felt. Organizations and groups of many kinds, both international and national, can exert their influence in the closing circle of world opinion.

89. We emphasize the special importance of world opinion. Many countries, particularly African countries, are directly identifying themselves with the cause of the oppressed people of South Africa, but there is a wider international concern. The conscience of the world has been stirred, and there is a recognition in world opinion generally that the South African problem is unique, demanding exceptional treatment. There is an international crisis of conscience; it arises from the fact that in South Africa there is a government professing to speak in the name of Christianity and the "European race" which is the only government in the world which chooses as its guiding policy not a striving to attain justice, equality and safeguards for human rights, but a determination to preserve privileges, defend discrimination and extend domination to such a degree that it amounts to the organization of a society on principles of slavery. In South Africa the denial of human rights and fundamental freedoms is openly pursued as an avowed policy. There are many in the Christian Churches and amongst those who can claim to speak for European civilization who can be expected to feel an exceptional responsibility in regard to developments in South Africa. Their influence in many ways and through many channels might be more effectively deployed.

90. There is another major international interest involved. That is the interest of commerce, industry and banking, often acting through great business concerns and organized on an international basis, which draws high profits and special benefits from investments in and trade with South Africa. They too should feel an exceptional responsibility, for it is largely from the cheap labour maintained by the policies of *apartheid* that their profits derive. These business interests and financial houses together with Chambers of Commerce and industrial trading concerns and associations could exercise effective influence on the South African Government, and specially might make a constructive contribution by demanding and putting into effect a "fair employment policy".

91. The situation can also be influenced by voluntary action undertaken by trade unions and other such co-operative groups in many countries. The protests of these groups have occasionally been expressed in

the form of boycott of South African goods. Though the direct economic results of such boycotts have been limited, their psychological effect is valuable.

92. While we emphasize the great and growing importance of international opinion, and while we recognize too that diplomatic pressure should be consistently maintained and increased, we also recognize that in the sphere of pressure for achieving a new start in South Africa in consultation and co-operation the United Nations itself should have a vital and central role of initiative and leadership.

93. We have consequently studied what has been said and written in the records of United Nations discussions and elsewhere about various forms of strategic and economic pressure.

94. The case for economic sanctions against South Africa has often been stated in the United Nations and on 6 November 1962 the resolution (A/RES/1761 (XVII)), calling for sanctions, was passed by a majority of more than two thirds in the General Assembly. We have also taken into account the resolution adopted in Addis Ababa by the African Heads of State on 25 May 1963, which decided to concert and co-ordinate their efforts to put an end to the South African Government's policy of *apartheid,* including measures of sanction; and appealed to all States, and more particularly to those which have traditional relations and co-operate with the Government of South Africa, to apply the United Nations resolution of sanctions of 6 November 1962. This has been followed up by the resolution of the African Foreign Ministers at their meeting held in Lagos in February 1964, in which *inter alia* they decided to recommend to the Organization of African Unity:

> "That it should renew its appeal to all States to apply strictly the economic, diplomatic, political and military sanctions already decided upon by the United Nations General Assembly and Security Council;
> "That it should address a special appeal to the major trading partners of the Government of South Africa to desist from the encouragement they are giving to *apartheid* through their investments and their trade relations with the Pretoria Government;
> "That it should decide to take all necessary steps to deny the right of overflight, landing and docking, and all other facilities to aircraft and ships coming from or bound for South Africa;"

95. These resolutions provide ample proof, if such is necessary, of the determination of all African States to pursue the cause of South African emancipation and to make sacrifices in that cause.

96. But while many African and other States have responded to the call of the General Assembly for sanctions, the hard fact remains that the South African economy is not seriously affected by the sanctions so far undertaken. Even if full sanctions were imposed by all the States whose representatives voted for the resolution of the General

Assembly, the effect on the economy of South Africa would still be entirely inadequate. It is on the trading relations of South Africa with a few main trading partners that the strength of its economy rests. Nearly 40 per cent of South Africa's exports go to the United Kingdom and the United States, and nearly 50 per cent of her imports are drawn from these two countries. As Mr. Eric Louw pointed out in referring to the vote in the General Assembly in 1962, "The nations not supporting sanctions absorb 79.6 per cent of South Africa's exports and send her 63.7 per cent of her imports".

97. Without the co-operation of the main trading partners of South Africa, no move to impose sanctions can be effective. This being so, and since the United Kingdom is both the principal supplier of South Africa's imports and the principal purchaser of South Africa's exports, we have studied the papers presented to the International Conference on Economic Sanctions held in London in April 1964.

98. We shall not attempt to summarize the papers of the Conference, but we invite special attention to the following contributions:

99. Firstly, the paper presented by G. D. N. Worswick, Fellow of Magdalen College, Oxford, on the "Impact of Sanctions on the British Economy", was concluded with the following comment about the position of the United Kingdom:

> "Thus there is no simple answer to the question—what would be the effect of economic sanctions on the U.K. economy itself. If Britain acted unilaterally, and then proceeded to cope with consequential balance of payments problems by the wrong means, the outcome might mean a sacrifice of 2½ per cent of national product. But if an optimal policy were followed, a combined operation of all the nations, the overall loss would be imperceptible, especially in economies which are growing at a reasonable rate. Britain's position with regard to sanctions is a strategic one. On the one hand, if Britain were to go it alone, and were obliged to cope with consequential balance of payments problems single-handed, she might run into rough water. Thus Britain, if she supports sanctions, has a strong case for asking that they should take the form of a combined United Nations operation, in which event the burden would be light".

100. The paper presented by Roger Opie, Fellow of New College, Oxford, stated the following with regard to South African gold exports:

> "Thus the conclusions emerge: (i) that a ban on the purchases of South African gold could severely damage the South African economy; (ii) that such a ban need do no more than the most trifling damage to the international monetary system (and might just precipitate a much needed series of reforms therein); (iii) that, equally, the damage to the U.K. would be small although the damage to a very small number of City firms could be serious. But the policing problems would be great—gold is in demand anywhere in the world, and many private persons would no doubt be prepared to buy and hold South African gold if it were sold at a discount now, but with the certainty that the ban would soon be

lifted. Nonetheless, merely a refusal by the Central banks of the Western world to buy South African gold would harm themselves little but South African gold producers much."

101. The paper presented by William F. Gutteridge, of the Lancaster College of Technology, Coventry, stated:

> ". . . Thus a blockade which concentrated on oil and rubber and in particular, shut off supplies from the Persian Gulf, would have a substantial chance of bringing the South African Government to its knees, because it would, within a matter of months, restrict internal security patrols and, above all, reduce the capacity of the security forces to move rapidly to meet an emergency."

102. A. Maizels of the National Institute of Economic and Social Research, London, said:

> "The concentration of South African foreign trade on a limited number of industrialised countries implies that no attempt by the United Nations to impose sanctions on South Africa could succeed without the full agreement and participation of these countries, among which Britain and the United States are the most important.
>
> "Sanctions limited to a few 'key' commodities (petroleum, capital equipment and gold) would have severe adverse repercussions on the South African economy, without putting that economy under 'siege' conditions.
>
> "Some form of 'policing' of trade with countries not conforming with a general United Nations sanctions scheme would have to be instituted to prevent any substantial evasion by way of trade diversion.
>
> "Finally, the countries imposing sanctions would suffer an economic loss, since they would have to switch their trade to less profitable markets, or buy from more expensive sources of supply. Such losses would, however, be marginal for most countries, and there seems little case for proposing a special scheme of compensation from international funds, particularly as the majority of countries likely to be most affected (relatively to their total trade) have already banned trade with South Africa."

103. We do not propose in this report to pursue a discussion on the economic and strategic aspects of sanctions, but we wish to record certain general conclusions which arise from our study of this problem.

104. As to the argument that sanctions should not be imposed because they would harm the non-White population of South Africa, it should be noted that the African leaders have vigorously rejected any such contention. As Oliver Tambo of the African National Congress said when he was making his statement in the United Nations on 29 October 1963:

> "This is a type of pity and paternalism which hurts us even more than sanctions would hurt us."

105. It is true that sanctions would cause hardship to all sections of the population, particularly if they had to be long maintained, but for the supporters of *apartheid* to use this argument to oppose sanctions

would lay them open to a charge of hypocrisy.

106. Secondly, it is clear that if sanctions are to be effective they must be put into effect with the co-operation of South Africa's principal trading partners, particularly the United Kingdom and the United States.

107. Thirdly, as South Africa is specially dependent on imports of petroleum and rubber there is a case for a ban on exporting these products to South Africa, on the ground that an embargo on these supplies could be more easily and quickly decided and enforced than a general ban on all imports into South Africa. The application of economic sanctions even if limited to petroleum (and possibly rubber) might act as a sufficient warning and deterrent.

108. On the other hand, we recognize the force of the argument that any concerted plan for sanctions would be better directed not to one or two commodities but to all; that piecemeal and progressive application of sanctions might defeat its purpose and lead to a hardening of South Africa's determination to resist pressure from the outside world, whereas the object is of course to achieve a change in South African policy.

109. Fourthly, the tests to be applied in deciding these questions are the tests of speedy decision, full co-operation and effective implementation, the overriding purpose being to achieve a rapid transformation with the minimum of suffering and dislocation.

110. With these considerations in view we recommend that use should be made of the interval before a final reply is required from the South African Government on the proposal for a National Convention to enable an expert examination to be made of the economic and strategic aspects of sanctions. There seems to us to be an urgent need for a further practical and technical study of the "logistics" of sanctions by experts in the economic and strategic field, particularly in international trade and transport.

111. It is obviously of great importance to keep constantly in mind the purpose of sanctions. That purpose is not to cripple the South African economy, but to save it. If the decision to impose sanctions is universal then the threat of sanctions will be compelling. The period of imposition will be reduced thus lessening hardship, and indeed if the threat is universal and complete the actual imposition of sanctions might in fact become unnecessary.

112. Our conclusion is that it can only be by United Nations action, in the form of a unanimous decision of the Security Council, that the weapon of sanctions can be rapidly effective. Only if action is agreed and complete can the threat of sanctions achieve its purpose. Only by this drastic means can material loss and trade dislocation and hardship to many innocent people both in South Africa and elsewhere be avoided.

VI. Recommendations for Action by the Security Council

113. Our conclusion is that all efforts should be urgently directed to the formation of a National Convention fully representative of all the people of South Africa, and we therefore urge that, as a first step, our recommendation for such a Convention should be endorsed by the Security Council.

114. We propose that, at the same time, support be given to our recommendation in regard to the establishment of a United Nations South African Education and Training Programme.

115. We further propose that these decisions be referred to the South African Government, with an invitation to send its representatives to take part in discussions under the auspices of the United Nations on the formation of the National Convention.

116. We emphasize the need for a renewed and urgent appeal for an immediate amnesty for opponents of *apartheid*.

117. We recommend that the Security Council should fix an early date by which a reply to the invitation would be required from the South African Government.

118. We recommend, moreover, that the Security Council should invite all concerned to communicate their views on the agenda for the Convention before the date for the reply of the South African Government.

119. Such an invitation should be addressed to all representative groups including political parties, Congresses at present banned under the Unlawful Organizations Act, and other South African organizations such as the Churches, Universities, Trade Unions, Associations of Employers, Chambers of Commerce, Bar Associations, Institutes of Race Relations, the Press and all other representative groups.

120. We recommend that the interval pending the reply of the South African Government should be utilized by the Security Council for the urgent examination of the logistics of sanctions which we have recommended in paragraph 110 above.

121. The Security Council in December 1963 expressed its strong conviction that "the situation in South Africa is seriously disturbing international peace and security". This situation has deteriorated further due to the actions of the South African Government. If no satisfactory reply is received from the South African Government by the stipulated date, the Security Council, in our view, would be left with no effective peaceful means for assisting to resolve the situation, except to apply economic sanctions. Consequently, we recommend that the Security Council should then take the decision to apply economic sanctions in the light of the result of the examination recommended in paragraphs 110 and 120 above.

NOTES AND QUESTIONS

1. One of the most troublesome aspects of contemporary international life is the frequency and intensity with which states intervene in one another's affairs. The traditional image of world order in the centuries between the Middle Ages and the League of Nations was based upon the mutual respect of states for the exercise of complete territorial sovereignty. Ideas of domestic jurisdiction, sovereign equality, and nonintervention express aspects of this traditional image. Whenever a revolutionary actor emerged in international society, interventionary patterns of behavior emerged as the revolutionary flames were spread from one country to another and as the counter-revolutionary forces acted to destroy the danger of revolution. In the period following the French Revolution of 1789 until the Congress of Vienna, the forces of revolution and counter-revolution engaged in competitive interventions throughout Europe. For reasons too obvious to dwell on, the existing international society exhibits interventionary patterns which arise from a revolutionary confrontation.

In the materials in this chapter the discussion centered upon whether the response of the United Nations to the practice of apartheid by South Africa was "intervention" within the meaning of Article 2(7) of the Charter. It is very important to distinguish the control of interventionary conduct by states from that of international institutions, whether they be of a regional or global character. For institutional interventions are carried out in behalf of the values and policies of the relevant community (whether regional or global), whereas national interventions are more properly conceived of as a part of power politics and are, at best, an expression of national values and policies. At the root of the issue here is the proper locus of *authoritative decision-making—who decides* to intervene for what *purposes*, by what *means*, for what *objectives*. The perception of the "interventionary" undertaking as supportive, rather than destructive of international order depends, in large part, upon the extent to which community decision-making procedures, policies, and resources are brought to bear upon the domestic circumstance that gives rise to the interventionary response. Thus it is misleading to equate the intervention of the United Nations in Congolese or South African domestic affairs with say, the Soviet intervention in Hungary in 1956 or the various United States interventions in Cuban affairs since Castro took over.

Regional interventions stand midway between national and global interventions. Somewhat greater legitimacy attaches to regional intervention, although this is mostly lost if the regional actor merely acts as a cover for the fulfillment of the policies of the state dominant in the region. For instance, it has been suggested that the Organization of American States must expel the United States if it wants to become a genuine regional actor. For a general discussion of regionalism as a basis for world order, see Yalem, **I-3A** and his book, *Regionalism and World Order* (Public Affairs Press, Washington, D.C., 1965).

Procedures for Pacific Settlement 8

Clark and Sohn emphasize the need to find substitutes for violence in international relations. They argue that one reason for recourse to violence in the past has been the absence of effective procedure for the nonviolent settlement of international disputes. They go so far as to maintain that if "comprehensive and flexible world machinery for peaceful settlements on the basis of fair hearing, law, and equity" existed, then "no nation could any longer have even a plausible reason to plead the lack of such machinery as an excuse for violence." See WPTWL, p. 106. Their conception of flexible and adequate machinery is a sophisticated one that acknowledges that the procedure for settlement must be suited to the character of the dispute, that some disputes call for mediation between the parties in the search for a compromise, that others call for adjudication to assess relative rights, and that still others call for a legislative solution. That is, they call for a solution in accord with some prevailing concept of policy that may be inconsistent with the relative legal rights of the parties and unacceptable to one or both through conciliation or by the methods of diplomacy.

To accommodate these alternative routes to pacific settlement Clark and Sohn propose what they call a Judicial and Conciliation System. See WPTWL, pp. 335–344. This system consists of four main units; first, the International Court of Justice to resolve legal disputes; second, a World Equity Tribunal capable of reaching legislative solutions; third, a World Conciliation Board designed to facilitate conciliatory solutions; and fourth, the establishment of a system of regional courts, inferior to the ICJ, with competence mainly "for the trial of individuals and private organizations accused of violating the revised Charter or any law or regulation enacted thereunder" (p. 341). The last three units are new additions with no counterpart in the existing framework of the United Nations.

The main description of how this system of judicial conciliation might be expected to function is found in the revised provisions of Chapter VI of the Charter. See WPTWL, pp. 89–110. The central idea is to give the United Nations the authority to insist that pacific settlement procedures be used whenever a dispute is found to be dangerous. Such authority can be exerted before violence has taken place and to forestall the temptation to have recourse to violence. It might facilitate an understanding of this rather complicated set-up for pacific settlement to explore in some detail the Clark-Sohn model to see how it promotes the goals of war prevention.

The scheme achieves a delicate mixture of political authority by the organs of the United Nations and respect for the sovereignty of the disputant states. But the maintenance of peace takes precedence, and if the states cannot agree on what procedure of pacific settlement to use, then the General Assembly or the Executive Council may determine the appropriate procedure. See Articles 33 and 36. But what if the organs of the United Nations, as well as the states in dispute, are unable to decide?——or suppose the determination is unpopular? Article 36 (8), (9) and (10), and the Notes and Questions that follow discuss this possibility in the setting of the recommendations made by the World Equity Tribunal. Clark and Sohn introduce a post-determination political check on the acceptability of the outcome of this form of pacific settlement; Article 36 provides for full approval, partial approval, or rejection of the Tribunal's finding. But what if the nation that feels dissatisfied with the conclusions reached by the World Equity Tribunal refuses to comply? According to Article 36 (9), if three-fourths of the Representatives of the General Assembly, including two-thirds of those Representatives voting on behalf of the twelve states with fifteen or more Representatives, vote to approve the recommendations of the Tribunal, then a failure to comply makes applicable the enforcement provisions of Article 94. By this rather complicated formula Clark and Sohn want to obtain a real consensus among both the membership at large of the Assembly and the membership of the most populous states. But suppose the requisite majorities cannot be obtained? Article 37 authorizes the Assembly or the Executive Council to make binding provisional measures. But suppose agreement cannot be reached on provisional measures either? What happens in the Clark-Sohn system when the political organs of the United Nations are unable to agree? What happens in a domestic political system in comparable situations?

In addition, it should be noted that Clark and Sohn retain a hierarchy of procedures to deal with dangers to world peace. A failure to resolve the dispute by the machinery of pacific settlement can lead to the use of the machinery of coercive settlement (action with respect to threats to the peace, breaches of the peace, and acts of aggression) set out in their revisions to Chapter VII of the Charter and backed up by the United

Nations Peace Force. That is, in the event of international friction arising out of an unresolved dispute, Clark and Sohn place an initial reliance upon the settlement capacity of traditional diplomacy. If traditional diplomacy is unsuccessful, then this range of procedures is available to the parties for pacific settlement. If the parties are unable to agree on the appropriate procedures, and the political organs regard the dispute as dangerous to international peace, Article 36 allows the Assembly or the Executive Council to determine by a special majority the appropriate procedure and to require the parties to use it. In Annex III Clark and Sohn give the ICJ "compulsory jurisdiction" over a wide category of legal disputes. This means that the complaining party, the plaintiff state, may, if it wishes, require its adversary to accept recourse to the ICJ. See the list of disputes that Clark and Sohn give to the ICJ on p. 337. What makes a dispute a legal issue?—who decides?

As these questions suggest, the Clark-Sohn scheme is a complicated and ingenious arrangement of techniques, competencies, and powers that tries to achieve a flexible balance. It recognizes that there are various kinds of disputes, that some choice must be left to the disputants as to the means of settlement, that some authority must be given to the political organs to choose the means of settlement and to compel its use in the event the parties cannot agree among themselves. The whole process is backed up by the authority in Article 94 to decide upon enforcement measures, including the invocation of the sanctioning processes of Articles 41 and 42. Nowhere does one get a better sense of the intricacy of the institutional framework that Clark and Sohn have created to deal with conflict in a disarmed world than in this area of pacific settlement. Many types of contingency have been anticipated and dealt with in accord with the overriding principle of using the minimum amount of supranational coercion compatible with upholding international peace. Deference to national sovereignty is maintained, subject only to the needs of war prevention, and the parties are given an elaborate and flexible apparatus that reinforces every reasonable incentive to find a peaceful solution.

Despite the ingenuity of the Judicial and Conciliation System, its adequacy in a disarmed world depends considerably upon one's image of the nature of political conflict. Note the discussion of this issue in the Clark-Sohn Comment on Article 36, pp. 103–107. Is it realistic to think that Israel or the United Arab Republic could be persuaded to accept an adverse judgment regardless of the weight of world public opinion? If, in fact, there existed the prospect that "pacific settlement" might be "enforced" against an adversary in one of the outstanding international disputes of the day (see their list of such disputes on p. 103), would not the states involved be well advised to resist the adoption of the Clark-Sohn plan? Is the avoidance of a major war on the strategic level as important to, say, Israel or to the Republic of South Africa as maximum assurance that the international challenges directed against them are not allowed to prevail? This seems to be a major transition hurdle. Why should Israel, South Africa, Malaysia, East Germany, and others take the risk of a warless world? In the world as it now exists, especially given the fact that the dangers of nuclear war inhibit recourse to violence, the chances of these countries to uphold their *status quo*, even a *status quo* that is highly unpopular in the world community (e.g., South Africa) appear excellent. But what would be their prospect in a Clark-Sohn world? Do these questions suggest that all, or at least most, of the festering international disputes must be settled before the Clark-Sohn plan becomes politically acceptable? Clark and Sohn obviously do not think so (see the important Comment attached to Article 36), but what reasons have they given to convince us? These issues are stressed here because this seems to be an area where the assurances about life in the world projected by Clark and Sohn would seem to be very threatening to a substantial body of states, and to just those states which, because of their strong involvement in an international dispute, are, at present, least responsive to the directives of the organized world community.

In view of this aspect of the transition problem, it is crucial to engage in discussion at a level of concreteness, and to make evident, at least, what needs to be done. This permits intelligent and responsible action by those seeking to avoid major war, even those situated in countries where the cause of war prevention receives lowest priority. Perhaps, from the depth of their engagement in the situation itself, useful thoughts on conflict resolution in a disarmed world may begin to emerge. See Knorr's article in **IV-4** for insight into ways of thinking about these problems.

The selections in this chapter depict the framework for pacific settlement that operates within the existing international system. We begin with a politically sophisticated presentation by Morton A. Kaplan and Nicholas deB. Katzenbach, "The Institutions of International Decision Making," *The Political Foundations of International Order* (Wiley, New York, 1961) pp. 265–283. This account is valuable to survey the range of what is available and to explain the limits of pacific settlement procedures, in view of the character of world political processes. It is valuable also because it uses a definition of the international legal system that is wide enough to embrace *national* institutions. As Kaplan and Katzenbach point out, national courts, although a step removed from state-to-state relations, resolve many disputes on the basis of norms of international law. National courts are arenas for dispute settlement and resolve certain controversies that might otherwise generate international friction. Clark and Sohn, too, are sensitive to the potential role of national officials and institutions in discharging the functions of an integrated world peace system. This corrects the widespread fallacy of assuming that progress in international dispute settlement consists only in getting states to use the ICJ. This is fallacious because it is not always appropriate to use the ICJ (see Fuller in this chapter), and it is fallacious because it overlooks the range of alternatives to adjudication in the search for improved procedures of pacific settlement. At the same time the acceptance of jurisdiction of the ICJ does signalize a willingness to substitute the judgment of an impartial decision-making body for the power-laden processes of diplomatic negotiation and self-help. Thus it is reasonable to treat the issue of the extent of compulsory jurisdiction possessed by the ICJ as symbolic of the degree to which a state is prepared to endorse the role of law in international affairs. For this reason it is worth paying attention to the Kaplan-Katzenbach references to the Connally reservation as a "fraud" and to Louis Sohn's suggestions (in the next selection) for mitigating its effects without an outright repeal.

THE INSTITUTIONS OF INTERNATIONAL DECISION MAKING

by

MORTON A. KAPLAN
and
NICHOLAS deB. KATZENBACH

In the previous chapter our emphasis was upon the techniques of the international legal process and the limitations upon the discretion of officials imposed by legal methodology—at least whenever the decision maker is concerned with providing a convincing legal justification for action taken or protested. Here we wish to pursue another facet of the process: Who invokes international law, in what arenas, and with what effects? Our points of attention in this chapter are, then, the ways in which the decision-making process is organized and the roles of the various participants.

In general theory and broad outline, the organization of the international legal process is underdeveloped and uncomplicated. As we have seen, international law is viewed as a body of rules binding upon states as entities, or "subjects." States are legally obligated, by whatever means they elect, to insure that state officials comply with international norms, but (at least, up until the Nuernberg trials) the obligation is not conceived as being imposed directly upon the officials themselves. Acts taken by state officials that violate international norms may be protested, through diplomatic channels, by an injured state, the protest being accompanied by a demand that the wrong be righted in some appropriate way. Diplomatic correspondence cast in terms of legal argumentation ordinarily follows such a protest. If disagreement persists at any level—as to the facts, the relevant norms, or the application of the norms to facts—the matter may be settled by the parties, mediated by a disinterested party, referred to an arbitrator or international tribunal, put before an international or supranational body, or simply left unresolved. The offended state may, if other means of resolution are frustrated, resort to appropriate sanctions by way of reprisal if this possibility is technically feasible and politically possible.

Relatively few disputes are resolved by impartial judges. If the states involved desire adjudication, either of existing disputes or prospectively with regard to categories of questions, there is no difficulty in securing the services of objective and impartial observers who can employ the techniques described in the previous chapter to resolve the dispute. The services of the International Court of Justice are, of course, always available to states. The failure of states generally to resort to judicial resolution is attributable not to the lack of a mechanism for handling the dispute, but, rather, to a preference, in most instances, not to use this method of dispute settlement.

Our primary concern here is not with the reasons that underlie this preference, but rather with the fact of its existence. Nonetheless, it may be helpful to suggest at least some of the considerations that lead states to reject a judicial method of dispute resolution.

We must, first, bear in mind that, although all disputes involving normative standards can be decided by impartial reference to authoritative declarations and past practices, even a developed and comprehensive legal system does not attempt to resolve all disputes in this fashion. Although authoritative norms may be and are derived and abstracted from past experience, not all norms are created in this way. We would not ordinarily claim that a disagreement among interest groups as to a desirable general rule could best be resolved by reference to a referee who would determine which proposal more nearly complied with precedent and past practice; yet each group might, as part of its effort to gain political support, invoke precedent from sources analogous to those discussed in the prior chapter.

One factor, then, which influences states to refrain from any comprehensive acquiescence to adjudication is the belief that adjudication is inappropriate, at least until a more satisfactory international legislative system is evolved. The present system of international legislation, whether by multilateral treaty, United Nations vote, or otherwise, requires formal assent by others, and is, to say the least, a tedious process, the more so because the individuals involved operate under limited instructions from the states they represent. The clumsiness of this arrangement is compensated for within the system of international law by a looser technique of doctrinal innovation than exists in a more developed governmental system, by a failure to resolve definitively doctrinal issues, and by legitimizing retroactively, in a variety of ways, a great amount of unilateral policy, including the application of national laws to transnational events and interests. The reliance is upon informal—or political—restraints as well as the doctrine that has existed to enforce moderation. So long as prescribing and adjudicating functions are not embedded in separate institutional structures in the international system, reference to impartial adjudication will be limited.

Not all disputes are best resolved by the judicial process. We may agree that the Constitutional power of the President of the United States to send troops to participate in the UN action in Korea is a legal question. Yet we may doubt that the question would be best resolved by reference to the Supreme Court. Similarly, there are questions of law that courts decline to resolve on the grounds that the issue is "non-justiciable," or "political"; and these are better resolved in other arenas.

Also, disputes that affect the security or continued existence of a state cannot easily be put in the hands of a third party, however impartial, if any alternative is feasible. Even if the risk of unfavorable adjudication is slight, states are understandably reluctant to take any unnecessary risk on fundamental questions.

But basic to these reasons, and to others, is the simple fact that national identification still dominates, and there are no widespread ties of sentiment to the international community, or, though we are in a state of transition, to supranational entities. An important conviction as to the importance of preserving the group and a sense of group solidarity is a necessary condition to the establishment of comprehensive dispute-resolving mechanisms in the present period. Although we can see the growth of this identification in many areas, both geographical and functional, there is no indication that such supranational communities presently exist in any comprehensive way.

As a result of these conditions and of this organizational scheme, the international legal process, unlike its municipal counterpart, is not designed to operate primarily by means of judicial settlement; and international law is typically invoked in arenas other than international judicial arenas. The techniques described in the previous chapter may be employed by an impartial arbiter to decide a dispute, and sometimes are; but they are customarily employed in other contexts by persons who, in various degrees, have partisan political roles. This circumstance is of the utmost importance in understanding the process. It does not by any means defeat the existence of an operative normative order; it does, however, mean that the international process differs importantly from one that includes the operations of an impartial judiciary. State officials may both act differently and conceive their roles differently with respect to international matters from the ways they act or conceive their roles with respect to national matters.

Let us consider the traditional arenas in which international law has been invoked—national courts and diplomatic intercourse—and proceed thereafter to the important institutional modifications resulting from the growth of international procedures and organizations.

National courts. In traditional theory, national courts apply national law—even when they apply international standards. National courts, it is said, apply international law only because the latter has been received into, or incorporated within, national law. There is a reason for this otherwise awkward theory, and that lies in the relationship of the judiciary to other branches of the municipal government. There is international law doctrine which requires a state to adhere to rules of international law, but there is no international requirement that a state take its judiciary's view of what the international norm is or how it applies. The international obligation is that of the state, and it may implement it internally in any way that it sees fit.

Issues of international law arise in national courts indirectly, and not as disputes between states; they are at one remove from diplomatic representation. For example, state officials may attach property and be faced with a claim that the property belongs to another sovereign entitled, under international law, to immunity from local process; a seaman may be apprehended for a minor crime committed on a foreign flagship in a local port and claim that he is immune from prosecution under customary international law; goods may be seized during wartime as contraband and the owner may claim the seizure is in violation of his rights as a neutral; property may be nationalized and the owner may claim that the compensation offered is inadequate under international standards; and so forth.

One primary function of courts, and the *raison d'etre* of an independent judiciary, is to insure that government officials do not exceed their lawful authority. A decision of the executive to take certain action does not automatically establish its lawfulness, and may be tested by impartial judicial review. If international law is a part of the national law, the court is acting on questions raising international standards exactly as it would if only local issues and local law (in a restricted sense) were involved. International law, for a national court, does not assume priority over national law; in fact, the latter almost always supersedes the former if there is unavoidable conflict. A statute in conflict with a prior treaty provision or customary international law will be applied nonetheless in most countries by national courts.

The result of this theory, then, is that the national judiciary must take the views of the political branches as to what international law requires whenever these views are enacted as formal municipal law; otherwise, courts determine independently what the international standard is and what it requires in the case at hand. Thus although national courts, in performing this latter function, develop a good many international standards, they cannot be regarded as independent and faithful custodians of international law doctrine. They may, in this respect, be contrasted rather sharply with state courts in our federal system which do have an independent obligation to uphold the federal Constitution. It hardly requires argument that this difference of role has considerable impact upon the development of the international law process.

The task of developing international law norms on the one hand and deferring to formal national policy on the other can make for awkward situations. A court in State *X* determines that international law prohibits a certain act, or requires a certain procedure; once this determination is made it is extremely difficult for the state's foreign office, or legislature, to arrive at a different formulation of the international rule without the considerable embarrassment of having its own judiciary cited to the contrary. For this reason, the state may be forced to reverse its judiciary by the tedious process of international agreement, even though, for local purposes, it could do so by simple legislative act.

This same difficulty—in part due to a semantic confusion and failure to clarify issues—often follows from the fact that a number of countries, including the United States, have taken the view that questions of law (what the international standard is) are questions for the judiciary, and that as a result the courts are not bound by foreign office views unless formally a part of municipal law. In the United States, the Constitution specifically describes treaties as "supreme law," and inferentially assigns courts the task of their interpretation. There is, of course, some justification for judicial supremacy where the issue has arisen and the interpretations could retroactively affect private parties in an existing suit. But, at least prospectively, it is difficult to justify anything but the greatest deference of municipal courts to their respective foreign offices.

In practice, courts are extremely sensitive to political involvement, particularly in recent years when it has been increasingly obvious that much traditional doctrine needs modification. Though troubled by the seeming intrusion on independence, courts have been desirous of getting political guidance on policy matters. In the United States, at least, it is not uncommon to see courts and State Department playing Alphonse and Gaston roles, the one saying a question of policy has arisen on which the court should have political guidance, and the other maintaining a discreet silence on the same issue, characterizing it as one of law. In this regard, we are conscious of a change of attitude over time. A century or more ago, courts played far more important roles in law development than they do in the present day. In the early nineteenth century, there was great confidence in a process of law development by the judiciary. As law has come to be thought of more and more in terms of a conscious community policy, initiative has shifted to political bodies. Norms previously conceived as derived from universal reason or practice or custom are now thought of as conscious community policy. With this in mind, courts have lost their confidence to prescribe in the international area, becoming sensitive to both the policy and political issues which may be involved. Often in cases where international law is invoked, American courts, at least, have tended to test the contention as much against foreign policy objectives—the norms the United States would like to see universally established—as against anything that could fairly be said to be derived wholly from any universal practice.

Thus, in the world today, there is relatively little effort by national courts to play what seems to be an overcomplex and difficult task of creating universal norms. This task is left to political officials, whose leads courts are desirous to follow. We might almost say that the theory which led national courts to be subservient to formal national policy has been greatly extended, and that courts are today subservient to even a whisper of national policy. Therefore, rather than playing important creative roles in determining common international standards, national courts have more and more become apologists for national policies determined by political arms of government.

This does not mean that national courts do not continue to play an important moderating role and to invoke international law to assist them in this function. But it suggests that national courts are less important to the performance of this task than in the past, and that the creative use of method and technique to establish new norms has passed to other branches of the government, and to supranational bodies.

Foreign office: diplomatic intercourse. The traditional method of maintaining the integrity of international norms has been through diplomatic protest by the offended state, or states, of action that in its view was incompatible with existing law.

But before a state reaches the point of formal protest, it is subjected to the moderating influence that arises from the self-restraint most states exercise in order to encourage self-restraint on the part of others. As we stated above, the incorporation of international norms into national law permits recourse to legal action by private citizens to insure the compatibility with international law of administrative actions taken by state officials. Municipal officials are thus subjected to judicial restraint in matters litigable in local courts. In addition, all govenments go to considerable lengths to make sure that administrative and military officers respect international norms, at least as set forth by the state involved. In the United States we find manuals prepared for the Armed Services setting forth what is permitted and prohibited in all likely situations, and this is supplemented by a network of competent legal officers whose advice can be sought to clarify close cases. In the Department of State, personnel trained in law check and coordinate policies and programs to insure that they do not violate treaties or customary law. In all aspects of government, and in all governments, there exist similar internal checks on official action to ascertain that it is consistent with international law at least as exposited by the state involved.

The fact that there may be different formulations of rules and different interpretations of doctrine does not invalidate the broad area of agreement thus achieved. Further, many differences are of marginal significance and well within a discretion which other states can tolerate. The important point is that before a state departs consciously and abruptly from norms strongly supported by others, there must be an authorization at a quite high level of government, a policy decision near the top echelon. There is a question of both timing and substance involved and of willingness to take political risks.

A similar judgment must be made by other states in a position to protest, or at least dissent from, the suggested departure. Among friendly nations there is caution. Clarification of the change is often requested, and typically there is an effort to explore and expand points of agreement and narrow as far as possible the area of dispute. Formal protests as to illegality are relatively rare, and are becoming much rarer today among bloc members though perhaps more frequent between blocs. There is, after all, little service to bloc interests in accusing bloc partners of disrespect for international law, although such accusations between blocs may actually help create a politically desired image.

Now, diplomatic negotiation involves techniques which are flexible and range widely in the process of accommodation. Legal doctrine and methods of argumentation may help to clarify issues, but the diplomat is by no means confined, as is the judge, to rendering an opinion based exclusively upon existing doctrine. He employs law more in the fashion of advocate and legislator, with the important qualification that he has to be circumspect in statements which enter into the law process as future sources. He is desirous to preserve certain norms and support them as strongly as he is able. Yet he must weigh the consequences of the immediate controversy in terms of other objectives as well. Finally, of course, he has a domestic public to satisfy.

The diplomat, then, is not using law to decide cases, as is the judge, but to support policies. Although his method may be similar, he is subject to different constraints and has different objectives.

Let us reflect for a minute on the considerations we discussed at the outset. If the decision makers of two states feel that the norm each state espouses involves a really important issue of principle, at least one state, and perhaps both, will refuse adjudication by an impartial tribunal. Each will present its case as strongly as possible and then, almost by an unspoken mutual assent, leave it undecided. If, however, the controversy has to be compromised, each will prefer a non-doctrinal horse-trade to a solution that in any way weakens its doctrinal claim. Yugoslavia and the United States were quite unable to agree on the right of a state to nationalize property of foreigners without compensation, but were able to agree on a lump sum settlement in which neither sacrificed its position. If the controversy is one in which only a doctrinal compromise will suffice because it will apply frequently in like situations affecting both states, then the basic question of whether the doctrine or the relationship is more important must be asked.

INTERNATIONAL PROCEDURES

Good offices, mediation, and conciliation. Good offices, mediation, and conciliation techniques, which make use of "third parties" not directly concerned in the dispute, are, like diplomacy, intended primarily to compose differences. Intervention by a third party, even if not in the form of a court or arbitral tribunal, usually compels the disputing parties, in order to appeal to the third party, to phrase their demands in terms of rules that could be applied universally to all similar cases. It must be added that this fact does not automatically guarantee the success of third-party efforts. Each party to a dispute may enunciate a seemingly reasonable general rule to support its position. The parties to a dispute may differ on the facts, the interpretation of the facts, or the rule to be applied to a particular case.

Nonetheless, the fact that reference to universal standards is facilitated explains in part the usefulness of third-party efforts. Good offices, mediation, and conciliation are variant forms of a common technique. Technically good offices are restricted to interceding with the parties to get them to use diplomacy to settle their quarrel; mediation occurs when the mediator aids in the discussion of the substantive issues; and conciliation occurs when the conciliator proposes for the consideration of the parties either the rules that ought to govern the settlement or the actual terms of the settlement. Despite the seeming distinctions, the lines between good offices, mediation, and conciliation are rather difficult to draw. The use of good offices may founder if completely unresponsive to the substantive issues that led to the quarrel, for the willingness of the parties to accede to the services of those performing the good offices role depends in part upon the relationship of negotiation to an acceptable settlement of the substantive issues.

For instance, in the Franco-Tunisian dispute of 1958, France would have been willing to discuss the question of indemnities for the bombing, but not the question of the right of French troops to remain in Tunisia, and particularly not any aspect of Algerian hostilities. Yet some extension of the discussion was necessary from the Tunisian point of view both for reasons of public demand and because Tunisia believed the issues to be inextricably related. Therefore it was not really possible for the United States to use its good offices to bring about discussions unless it used its influence to affect the agenda of the discussions. Yet it could hardly have done this without some discussion of whether the issues were in fact related. The American representative, Mr. Murphy, was presumably able to discuss whether the issues were related and whether it was advisable to link them in these particular negotiations without prescribing the outcomes of the negotiations on the issues or even the rules that were to govern the settlements. But Mr. Murphy's intervention nonetheless affected the substantive issues. Persuasion of France to discuss Algeria inevitably would have affected the position of France in Algeria.

The use of good offices occurs when the negotiator meets with the contending states separately. The mediator or conciliator may meet with the parties either separately or jointly. In the past, it was generally regarded as a friendly act for a state to offer its services in one of the three roles. Today, it is extremely dubious that such an offer would be regarded as friendly unless the circumstances made it appropriate for that particular state to offer its services. For instance, an offer by the Soviet Union to mediate between France and Tunisia would be regarded—and rightly so—as an effort further to injure relations rather than to ease them. The United States offer of good offices (although made inadvertently) was acceptable to both sides because the United States had a real interest in finding some way to ease the problem. The French could not afford to allow conditions to deteriorate further and therefore welcomed the good offices of a friendly state. The Tunisians desired to remain friendly to the West and hoped that the United States would be forced to link the Algerian and Tunisian situations to prevent the North African position of the NATO states from crumbling.

The peculiarly long-term character of bloc alignment during the loose bipolar period, therefore, specializes the role of negotiator. In the "balance of power" system a state not directly involved in the controversy usually was sufficiently neutral to serve as a mediator. In the loose bipolar system, most conflicts indirectly affect bloc affairs and the blocs have an interest in influencing their course. Finding an appropriate mediator for a dispute becomes enormously difficult under these circumstances. The leading member of a bloc may be the appropriate mediator between two other members of the bloc. But who can mediate between the leading member and another member of the bloc? Even in the first case, less formal diplomacy may be more appropriate than formal good offices or mediation. Who can mediate between the leading members of the two blocs? A single uncommitted state would not have sufficient strength or prestige. Moreover, on any number of issues, many uncommitted states would not genuinely be neutral—for instance, on any issue involving colonialism or thermonuclear tests. If no single uncommitted state is likely to be an acceptable mediator in bloc disputes, large numbers of uncommitted states may have to play such a role through the United Nations or by means of joint political influence exercised informally. Conflicts between uncommitted states can probably be mediated by still other uncommitted states in an effort to keep the dispute from becoming involved in the bloc conflicts. These are not, however, exclusively techniques for law resolution, although their effective use may be responsive to precedent and norms and may, in turn, serve as precedent for future cases.

International arbitration and international courts. International arbitration and judicial settlement are virtually identical procedures. In neither procedure may the judge or arbitrator decide the case with a view primarily to the accommodation or compromise of the conflicting interests, although decisions that fail to take such conflicts of interest into account are unlikely to prove effective. In each case, the settlement must be made according to rules that could be applied with equal validity to all other cases involving the same issues of law and of fact. There is an important difference, however. In arbitration, the arbitration agreement (or special submission to an International Court) may specify the issues that are to be decided and the facts that are to be taken into account. The contending parties may, if they wish, instruct the tribunal to accept an interpretation of the law to which the parties agree or a special rule that is to be applied to the particular case. For these reasons, the norm-creating power of the decision is somewhat limited.

Arbitration may proceed by means of *ad hoc* tribunals or individual arbitrators may be used. Finally, the parties involved may establish a continuing panel to arbitrate specific or general issues between them or recourse may be had to a tribunal open to all parties, such as the Permanent Court of Arbitration created by the Hague Convention of 1899. Arbitration agreements that are general usually exclude the vital interests of the nation, matters of honor, and matters that affect the interests of third parties. Although these limitations are sometimes viewed as defects of the arbitral systems, they actually are necessary if the systems are to be workable. Any system must have political methods for settling important conflicts of interest as well as juridical methods. In the present state of the international society direct negotiations between the disputants, the intervention of third parties, the application of the political machinery of international organizations, or perhaps the use of force constitute political techniques open to the parties.

Ad hoc tribunals, as a general rule, have their members selected by the parties to the dispute. Two disputants, for instance, may each select an arbitrator, and the two arbitrators may then select a third, in order to avoid the possibility of a tie vote. It is usually easier for the two arbitrators to agree upon the third than for the parties to the dispute to select directly an individual whom they can agree will apply the law impartially to the points at issue. The arbitrators selected by the parties usually find for the party who selected them. This somewhat diminishes the impartiality of these arbitrators. But it remains true that the arbitral award must be couched in normative language and not in the language of political negotiations.

The Permanent Court of International Justice, established by the Statute of the Court in 1921, and associated with the League of Nations, has now been replaced by the International Court of Justice as part of the general framework or organization established by the Charter of the United Nations. The judges are appointed to the International Court of Justice by a complicated procedure. Each of the national groups represented on the Permanent Court of Arbitration, and still functioning under the Charter, may nominate up to four judges not more than two of whom may come from their own nation. From this list the General Assembly and the Security Council each choose fifteen persons. Each person receiving a majority vote in both organs is elected, except that if two or more are elected from the same nation, only the elder receives the position. If a deadlock occurs, the sitting judges are empowered, as a last resort, to elect the remaining members of the bench. Five judges are elected every three years for nine-year terms. Judges cannot be dismissed unless their colleagues unanimously agree that they have ceased to satisfy the requirements of the position. Nine judges constitute a quorum, although a smaller bench is provided for when the parties desire a summary decision. If no judge of the nationality of one of the disputing parties is sitting, that party may nominate a judge for the case.

The judges of the International Court of Justice occupy a role of greater impartiality than do the judges of arbitral tribunals despite the provision in the Statute of the International Court of Justice for judges who are nationals of the parties to the dispute. Disputes may be submitted to the Court by all states which have signed its statute and to other states under conditions established by the Security Council. The Court may hear any matter submitted to it by states party to a dispute, and may hear all matters arising from the provisions of treaties or conventions that provide for compulsory jurisdiction. Whether the Court has jurisdiction is determined by the Court. Theoretically, therefore, in the areas where the parties have accepted compulsory jurisdiction, either by acceding to the Court Statute under the "Optional Clause," or by entering into bilateral or multilateral agreements to this effect, one party to the dispute may bring the matter before the Court without the agreement of the other party.

The "Optional Clause" of the Statute of the International Court of Justice provides for compulsory jurisdiction between states that have accepted the clause in all legal disputes over the interpretation of a treaty, questions of international law, the existence of facts that, if established, would constitute a breach of an international obligation, or the kind or extent of reparation to be made for a breach of an international obligation. Although most signers of the Court Statute have also accepted the "Optional Clause," most of these have made reservations that diminish the significance of that action. The United States has excluded from the jurisdiction of the Court matters essentially with its domestic jurisdiction, as determined by the United States rather than by the Court, and disputes arising under a multilateral treaty unless either all the parties to the agreement affected by the dispute are parties to the action or the United States agrees to jurisdiction.

The idea of expanding the jurisdiction of the World Court is currently a very popular one in the United States. As a first step, the highest political circles have come to support a broader form of United States submission, although considerable Senate opposition appears to remain. To date, the Court has been very little used by Members, and there are few submissions to compulsory jurisdiction that are not qualified heavily. The reasons for this refusal to make use of the Court are worth examination.

It has already been noted that disputes about treaty interpretation or the application of rules of customary law are often a means of asserting what is really a desire for legislative reform; that is, for changing the content of the rules. To the extent that this is true disputes about the law are not *bona fide* legal disputes, but rather an aspect of political maneuver. In such cases at least one party does not want resolution by any third party institution, and particularly one employing the relatively narrow legal procedures of a court. A basic precondition to any voluntary submission to judicial resolution would seem to be agreement about the rules that will be applied. This is particularly true when there is no ready alternative to modify the rules except diplomatic negotiation. The unresolved dispute has a legislative impact, for the contentions of both parties enter into the stream of available precedent for others in like situations and for future decision makers to draw upon. This potential legislative power is important to states, and they are hesitant to entrust it to third parties, particularly if they believe, as do the smaller states, that their voice in world affairs is becoming more powerful.

Related to the foregoing is the fact that many disputes which appear to be disputes about the correct interpretation of a treaty or customary law have hidden motivation. Judicial resolution in terms of the legal issues presented would not touch the real source of difficulty, the real problems and policies that are involved. The recent dispute between Iceland and the United Kingdom as to the permissible breadth of the territorial sea is an example in point. Iceland wished to extend her sea to a breadth of twelve miles in order to protect her local fishing industry from foreign, particularly British, competition. Fishing is one of Iceland's most important industries, and the greater efficiency of British trawlers resulted in great loss of income to Icelandic fisherman. The government was under heavy pressure to protect the industry against more efficient foreign competition.

Great Britain wanted to protect its fishing industry from exclusion from Icelandic fishing grounds merely because it was more efficient. But, in addition, the three-mile limit to territorial waters was (and is) an extremely important principle to maintain for any country with extensive maritime interests throughout the world. For Great Britain, then, far more than Icelandic fish were in issue. If this question were submitted to the Court, as, surprisingly, the United Kingdom proposed, the Court could have decided either way, but it could not (unless specially empowered by the parties) have explored any other means of resolution, such as a subsidy to Icelandic fisherman. Its decision would have left unresolved basic problems for one party or the other, and would have been operative not to resolve the dispute but merely to change the bargaining positions of the parties.

Furthermore, for the Court to have decided this dispute would have had worldwide repercussions affecting the interests of other countries. The breadth of the territorial sea has been hotly debated by many countries; the International Law Commission failed to resolve the problem; it was not possible to find a two-thirds majority from among the eighty nations represented at the Geneva Conference on the Law of the High Seas for any specific proposal governing the width of territorial seas. Would the Court's imprimatur on one breadth or another have been the end of dispute? Indeed, could it have risked such a decision? A good guess is that it would have been forced to say that the matter was in such doubt that it could not find any rule of international law prohibiting a state from claiming as much as twelve miles. Yet, even this decision would have been, as decisions cannot avoid being, favorable to one party at the expense of the other. More importantly, it could not have overtly weighed, because neither its method nor its prestige would permit, the better rule from the viewpoint of the international community.

This controversy illustrates two other shortcomings of reference to the ICJ that should be noted. First, the Court, in deciding a particular dispute must almost inevitably lay down general principles of international law that are of considerable interest and concern to states not parties to the particular dispute. The Court is, after all, the highest existing authority on international law, and any statements it makes in clarification of existing doctrine must be taken accordingly as authoritative. It is no answer to say—as does the Charter—that decisions of the Court have no precedential authority. They cannot help but have, whatever the theories of precedent may be. The Court must pay deference to its prior decisions if it is to avoid attack on grounds of partisanship among litigants. In addition, the opinions of the Court are taken most seriously, by scholars and by foreign offices alike, and treated as authoritative on the points decided and, indeed, on those merely discussed. Given this situation, we should ask whether or not it is really desirable to use the Court as the most important instrumentality for restating general principles of international law. Even if we concede the wisdom of clarifying rules (and this should not invariably be conceded), is the litigated case preferable to other alternatives? Examples of other alternatives are the International Law Commission, and various forms of multilateral treaty. It may be easier and more generally satisfactory to negotiate treaties restating and codifying general principles of international law if the rules themselves are still moot rather than after the Court has ruled on disputed points.

A second major shortcoming rests with the underdeveloped state of international law. When the Court deals with "customary" rules, it adopts the position that states are free to take unilateral action in the absence of a clear rule prohibiting the action taken. To a lesser extent, the Court takes the same view of treaty interpretation, allowing either party to interpret its obligations within the bounds of reason. Although those who profess a fear of too much interference by the Court with "sovereign" prerogatives might take comfort from this traditional judicial conservatism, we should also be aware that the basic causes of disputes remain relatively untouched. In almost every case, the complainant is seeking to formulate a rule that suggests that matters of mutual concern should be subject to joint regulation, not unilateral decision. Yet the state of international law doctrine, and the Court's jurisprudence, tends to leave the dispute where it was by declining to curb unilateral action. Indeed, those who point with pride to the fact that the Court's judgments have almost invariably been complied with should not neglect to point out that with very few exceptions the present Court has left the parties precisely where they were when they came to Court.

These observations should not be taken as criticisms of the Court. Quite the contrary, for judicial institutions must essentially preserve the status quo. Neither the methodology nor the function really permits otherwise. Courts must make new rules slowly, conservatively, and, of necessity, interstitially; a court is ill-equipped to rewrite a whole area of law within the limits of a single narrow controversy. For these reasons the ICJ cannot really contribute greatly to relieving international tensions even should its jurisdiction be expanded; it can seldom get at the basic causes of which the particular dispute is merely symptomatic. Today, for example there is considerable controversy over whether or not a state can confiscate, without compensation, foreign-owned enterprises on a non-discriminatory basis. Would a decision on this issue by the Court be helpful? Would it reduce international tensions, whichever way it was decided?

Both the geographical composition and mode of selection of judges create some problems. It is difficult to do much about giving the Communist countries and Afro-Asia more representation without offending other nations, particularly Europe and Latin America at whose expense the seats would probably shift. Furthermore, contentions that the present distribution of seats is unfair does not represent, as it might in this country when geographical areas or minority groups demand Supreme Court representation, merely a local pride and desire for status. It is founded on the notion that the Court does play a political role and is not really non-partisan. To acknowledge these demands might be to destroy the tradition of impartial role that the Court, with great difficulty, is seeking to build. That the Court, with seven members from the Western bloc, plus three Latin Americans, a Russian, a Pole, a Pakistani, and an Egyptian, is not a suitable mechanism for determining inter-bloc disputes is obvious. Shift the seven from West to East and envision the United States' attitude toward it. The tradition of impartial administration is by all evidence far stronger in the Western world, and in those areas of Afro-Asia which have preserved the British common law, than it is among the members of the Communist bloc. A major shift in its composition would greatly affect the attitude of Americans and Europeans toward the Court.

The Court is a useful and probably necessary, though not yet very important or powerful, part of the UN organizational complex. It can offer advisory opinions on the Charter. In addition, it can provide opinions on other basic UN documents to other UN agencies and help to clarify the growing area of international administrative law. These latter functions seldom raise very hot political questions, and the present composition of the Court reflects reasonably well the membership of specialized UN agencies, although slight modifications might not affect this consideration.

But the utility of the Court, by reason of its pretension to universality, to decide disputes between Member states is more questionable. Quite apart from the difficulties of any third-party adjudication in many disputes, adjudication by the highest judicial authority raises further difficulties. We have already noted that clarification of a theoretically universal "customary" law by virtue of pronouncement in two-party litigation is problematic, and that decision by this Court cannot help but freeze rules at a time when new problems require a more flexible approach. In addition, there is some doubt of the utility of an interbloc court to resolve intrabloc differences, of the need for fifteen judges and an expensive litigation process to clarify minor technical differences of interpretation, and of the wisdom of selecting to interpret a particular bilateral arrangement a Court that, because of its composition and prestige, must look to the impact of its decision on a variety of other agreements among other parties using similar language. Although any impartial decision maker would take these considerations into account, the authority of other decision makers and the impact of their decisions on non-litigating states would be less than that of the Court, and their decisions would consequently be more responsive to the problems raised by the litigating states.

Many of these difficulties could be met by having the Court sit in smaller panels (as the Charter permits) in a more convenient location. Decisions rendered by panels composed of judges whose impartiality between the litigants would be less subject to attack, and whose opinions would be less finally determinative of the general rule of international law are a feasible alternative. But even here it is difficult to envision extensive resort to the adjudicative process. Insofar as the process of adjudication also involves the restatement and clarification of rules that have future impact on the participants, the process has a "political" element, and it is by no means clear that the participants really wish to delegate this kind of authority to third parties, no matter how impartial, at least in the absence of an alternative mechanism to which appeal can be made. This is particularly true today because the classical rules and processes of international law are strongly tinted by Western jurisprudence and by rules derived from a period of laissez-faire economics. Many were in effect legislated by the great nations of yesteryear. Recognition of these difficulties is conceded by those who propose a Court of Equity and review of its decisions by the General Assembly. But again, the clarification of important rules in the context of particular disputes is a questionable device. It has the difficulties of an interstitial approach, and lacks the moderating influence that can come from more flexible institutions capable of broadening the area of negotiation and compromise, and of recommending more comprehensive solutions.

Finally, it should be added that none of what has been said above is particularly relevant to the proposal current in the United States to remove the Connally amendment to the United States reservation with regard to compulsory jurisdiction of the World Court. The reservation states that the U.S. will not submit disputes "essentially within the domestic jurisdiction of the United States of America *as determined by the United States of America.*" (The italicized words are the so-called Connally Amendment.) Obviously, this submission, as qualified above, is a fraud, and on that ground alone should be withdrawn. The United States should be the more embarrassed that this form of submission has been widely copied by others.

There is little danger to the United States in submitting to compulsory jurisdiction of the Court reciprocally with all other states who are willing to do so. The United States has infinitely more to gain than to lose from such a submission. It is consistent with the faith professed by the United States in peaceful and legal means of settlement of disputes, and with the image that the U.S. has of itself and wishes to project into the world community. The existing state of international "customary" law, and the treaties the United States is party to, seem generally favorable to the values that the United States is trying to promote in the world today and to the position of the United States in the international system, although it would require much more prevision than any of us have to know this with certainty. And, finally, the composition of the Court could not be more favorable to the American position on virtually any important issue.

NOTES AND QUESTIONS

1. Is the sense of political context provided by Kaplan and Katzenbach consistent with that provided by Clark and Sohn in their Comment to Article 36? How do Kaplan and Katzenbach approach the issue of specifying the limits of pacific settlement? To what extent do they consider that these limits are a reflection of deficient institutional structure? Do they foresee a role for institutions like the World Conciliation Board or the World Equity Tribunal? Is this a deficiency in their analysis?
2. What is the relevance of diplomacy to pacific settlement?
3. What is the relevance of the Optional Clause of the Statute to the ICJ? What is the so-called Connally Amendment? Should the United States accept more, less, or the same amount of compulsory jurisdiction as the Soviet Union? Why? Are their positions vis-à-vis the ICJ symmetrical in the sense that both states have as much reason to participate fully on a compulsory basis?

4. How are decisions by the ICJ enforced under the Charter at present? How are other kinds of settlements of international disputes enforced? For full discussion, see Oscar Schachter, "Enforcement of International Judicial and Arbitral Decisions," *The American Journal of International Law*, vol. 54 (1960) p. 1.

The next selection, by Louis B. Sohn, "Step by Step Acceptance of Jurisdiction of the International Court of Justice," *Proceedings of the American Society of International Law* (1964) pp. 131–136, is included as an example of a transition step in the area of pacific settlement. It illustrates the kind of proposal which might be immediately acceptable and which, if accepted, could be expected to make a modest contribution to the expansion of compulsory adjudication. By putting it forward, Sohn, in effect, acknowledges the need to compromise the obvious objective of persuading states (especially the United States) to accept the compulsory jurisdiction of the ICJ for *all* disputes involving international law. For presentation of this maximalist position, see Arthur Larson, *When Nations Disagree* (Louisiana State University Press, 1960). Sohn's proposal is an attempt to introduce a middle alternative between the pro and con debate on the acceptance of compulsory jurisdiction. Sohn's proposal results in getting as much compulsory jurisdiction as possible, given the present mix of commitments to sovereign prerogatives and international law.

STEP-BY-STEP ACCEPTANCE OF THE JURISDICTION OF THE INTERNATIONAL COURT OF JUSTICE

By Louis B. Sohn

It is a tragic fact of international life that the International Court of Justice is sidestepped in most international disputes and is, consequently, under-employed. This situation cannot be remedied merely by repetitious insistence that important questions of international law should be immediately sent to the Court, including such questions as Berlin, Vietnam or Formosa. Nor can the fact that only one third of the Members of the United Nations have accepted the jurisdiction of the Court be remedied by an exhortation that the other Members of the United Nations should accept that jurisdiction quickly and without any reservations. Instead, it might be more realistic to follow a wise saying that we should "elevate our sights a little lower," perhaps much lower. Instead of adopting an all-or-nothing attitude, we might explore a step-by-step approach which would gradually increase the Court's permanent jurisdiction. Four lines of approach might be explored in this connection:

1. Acceptance of the jurisdiction of the International Court of Justice over disputes relating to the interpretation and application of treaties.
2. Acceptance of the jurisdiction of the International Court of Justice over specified areas of international law.
3. Acceptance of the jurisdiction of the Court through regional arrangements.
4. Granting to the United Nations the power to make a binding request that parties to a dispute refer the matter to the International Court of Justice.

All these steps can be taken outside the framework of the optional clause in Article 36 of the Statute of the International Court of Justice, and the agreement of states to take these steps might be embodied in a General Act on the Judicial Settlement of International Disputes similar to the Geneva General Act of 1928 on the Pacific Settlement of International Disputes, which was revised by the United Nations in 1949. The proposed Act would permit ratifying states to accept all four obligations mentioned above, or only one or two or three of them, at the discretion of each state. Each of the obligations might, in turn, be subdivided, thus permitting additional options. Such rampant gradualism should permit even the most recalcitrant state to accept something and in this manner to take the first hesitating step toward broader acceptance in the future. Once states find that the first steps did not prove disastrous, they might become more venturesome and start taking several steps in quick succession.

Slowly, but surely, the jurisdiction of the Court would expand and, hopefully, the number of cases presented to the Court would increase, and one day we might discover that the problem which seems to be so intractable today has been solved by the process of gradual accretion.

Returning to the four proposals made previously, it might be useful to make some comments on each one in turn.

1. *Disputes relating to the interpretation and application of treaties.* The idea that disputes relating to treaties are especially suitable to international adjudication is not a new one. The First International Conference of American States, meeting in Washington in 1890, was one of the pioneers in proposing that arbitration should be obligatory in all controversies concerning "the validity, construction and enforcement of treaties." In many arbitration treaties states have actually committed themselves to submit such disputes first to arbitration and later to adjudication. In addition, many hundreds of treaties on a large variety of subjects contain so-called compromissary clauses conferring on the International Court of Justice jurisdiction to decide disputes relating to their interpretation or application. There is probably no state in the world which has not accepted at least a few of these treaties and has thus conferred on the Court jurisdiction to interpret them.

It might be possible, therefore, to persuade most of the states of the world to accept the jurisdiction of the Court to interpret all treaties binding upon them. States might be given several options here; for instance, their acceptance might apply: to all treaties or only to treaties registered with the United Nations (of which there were more than 7,000 on January 1, 1964), or to interpretation of treaties only, or to both their interpretation and application. States might also be permitted to exclude a specific number of treaties from their acceptance, but no other reservations should be allowed.

2. *Disputes relating to specified areas of international law.* At the Second Hague Conference in 1907, a joint Anglo-American proposal was discussed in which more than twenty specified subjects were listed, and states were invited to accept the obligation to submit disputes relating to them to arbitration, each state selecting one or more of these subjects. Similar proposals were advocated for many years by Sir Thomas Barclay, but were considered premature. In the Statute of the Permanent Court of International Justice in 1920 the bold step was taken of asking states to accept the jurisdiction of the Court over disputes relating to "any question of international law." It is undoubtedly this provision that scared so many states away from the Court and caused others to make far-reaching reservations. Perhaps we should retrace our steps and return to the more modest proposals of the 1907 vintage. One can easily prepare a list of many subjects of international law, and provide states with an

option to accept the jurisdiction of the Court with respect to those areas which they consider least controversial. Such a list might look as follows:

	Afghanistan	Albania	Algeria	Argentina	Australia	Austria	Belgium	Bolivia	Brazil	Bulgaria	Burma	Burundi	etc.
1. Recognition of states													
2. Recognition of governments													
3. Succession of states													
4. Succession of governments													
5. Acquisition of territory													
6. Boundaries of states													
7. Leased territories													
8. International servitudes													
9. Inviolability of national territory													
10. Ports and inland waters													
11. International rivers and lakes													
12. Territorial waters													
13. Contiguous zones													
14. Continental shelf													
15. International canals and straits													
16. Regime of the high seas													
17. Fisheries													
18. Whaling and sealing													
19. Air navigation													
20. Polar regions													
21. Regime of outer space													
22. Nationality and status of ships													
23. Piracy													
24. Slavery													
25. International traffic in women and children													
26. International traffic in narcotic drugs													
27. Nationality and statelessness													
28. Admission of aliens													
29. Position of aliens													
30. Expulsion of aliens													
etc.													

States might again be given several options: for instance, they might agree to accept at the time of ratification at least ten subjects, or they might agree to accept the minimum of ten and at least ten more in each ten-year period thereafter. States would thus have a chance to select at the beginning only subjects which are least likely to involve a danger to their vital interests, and to postpone more difficult areas until later. But once more than one state should accept the Court's jurisdiction over a particular subject, each of these states would be bound with respect to all other states accepting the jurisdiction of the Court over that subject and after a while a network of international commitments would be woven broadening the jurisdiction of the Court over a multitude of subjects.

3. *Acceptance of the jurisdiction of the Court through regional arrangements.* In anticipating "dangerous" international disputes, governments worry not only about the subject-matter of the possible disputes, but also about the parties to them. It is relatively easy to contemplate going to the International Court of Justice in a dispute with a friendly state, and a government does not mind being able to bring to the Court a good case against an adversary. It is the other side of the coin that scares governments: the possibility that an unfriendly state would use the Court to harass the government which has accepted the Court's jurisdiction *erga omnes,* without excluding in some way all potential enemies. Some states might prefer, therefore, to limit their commitments to go to the Court to states with which they have long-standing ties of friendship and as to which no bitter disputes should be anticipated. Thus, the members of the Council of Europe could easily agree to submit any legal dispute between them to the International Court of Justice, and the European Convention for the Peaceful Settlement of Disputes in 1957 conferred a large amount of jurisdiction on the Court. Similarly, certain American States (though not the United States) found it possible to accept the jurisdiction of the Court through ratifying the American Treaty on Pacific Settlement (the Pact of Bogotá) of 1948. A regional agreement on pacific settlement is also contemplated by the Charter of the Organization of African Unity (1963).

One might think that when methods are being sought to restore the unity of the Atlantic community, some attention would be paid to the possibility of strengthening the juridical link by an Atlantic Convention on Pacific Settlement which would, *inter alia,* confer on the Court jurisdiction to deal with legal disputes between the parties to the North Atlantic Pact. If all professions of amity are not mere propaganda, at least these nations should be able to agree that legal disputes between them should be referred to the International Court of Justice.

While the United States might be afraid to have disputes brought to the Court against it by Communist nations (assuming they ever accept the Court's jurisdiction), it cannot in good conscience object to a decision by the Court in a case involving one of its closest allies. The only thing which is necessary here is to forget the old-fashioned notion that it might endanger our relations with our friends if we bring cases against them, or if they bring cases against us, to the Court. In most legal disputes, the points involved do not concern any vital interests of either side, but both sides believe that they have a valid legal point which they do not want to give up in bilateral negotiations. For instance, neither the Congress nor the people of the United States would rise in arms if the United States and the United Kingdom should submit the long-standing dispute about Christmas Island in the Pacific to the Court for final decision; or if the United States and Canada would submit a question of interpretation of an extradition treaty to the Court.

It is amazing, in fact, that despite the close relations between the United States and Canada, and between the United States and the United Kingdom, there is no clear obligation, not hedged with far-reaching reservations, to submit disputes between the United States and those states to the Court for decision. Before tackling the slightly more difficult task of preparing an Atlantic Treaty for pacific settlement of disputes, it might be useful to have bilateral treaties concluded immediately with all the members of the alliance which are willing to do it. Perhaps, more generally, there should be a revival of the bilateral treaties for the pacific (or at least judicial) settlement of international disputes. Despite the great increase in the number cf states, only a few such treaties have been concluded in recent years. When Sweden expressed her willingness to conclude bilateral treaties accepting the Court's jurisdiction over legal disputes, only Greece took up this offer in 1956. Perhaps a prize should be made available by the Nobel Peace Institute to the Foreign Minister of the country which concludes the largest number of such treaties in a specified period. There is no excuse for doing nothing in this area for so many years. Some energetic efforts by a few countries could easily change the climate and, thanks to the general tendency to imitate which prevails among the Foreign Offices, a stampede to accept the Court's jurisdiction might quickly follow.

In any case, it might be useful to give states an option to accept the jurisdiction of the Court over all (or some) legal disputes, not with respect to everybody but with respect to selected groups of states (for instance, partners in various alliances or parties to certain treaties) or with respect to specified states only. Each state accepting this obligation might be bound to list at least ten states to which this obligation would apply, and there might be the additional option of agreeing in advance to increase the list by at least ten more states every ten years after the original acceptance. In this way, the circle of states with respect to which the obligation will be binding would extend slowly to most of them. Of course, such an obligation would apply only to states accepting the same obligation, and, to confer jurisdiction, it would be necessary that the names of the parties to a particular dispute appear, respectively, on the lists of both parties to that dispute.

4. *Increase in the power of the United Nations to refer disputes to the Court.* Article 36, paragraph 3, of the Charter already provides that in recommending appropriate procedures for the settlement of a dispute referred to it, the Security Council "should also take into consideration

that legal disputes should as a general rule be referred by the parties to the International Court of Justice.'' Such a recommendation was in fact made by the Security Council in the *Corfu Channel* case, and that recommendation seems to have contributed to the acceptance by Albania of the jurisdiction of the Court. There is, however, no general obligation to accept such a recommendation of the Security Council, or a similar recommendation of the General Assembly under Articles 11 and 35.

Some states might be willing to accept in advance an obligation to go to the Court if the Security Council (or the General Assembly) should request them to submit a legal question to the Court. In the Italian Peace Treaty the parties agreed to accept as binding a decision by the General Assembly on the disposition of Italian colonies. It should be even easier to accept as binding a merely procedural decision requiring the parties to solve a particular dispute by recourse to the Court. It need not be feared that the Security Council or the General Assembly would abuse such a power. In each case the Security Council or the General Assembly would, in accordance with Chapter VI of the Charter, have to determine in the first place that the continuance of the dispute is likely to endanger international peace and security; and, secondly, that important issues are involved in the dispute the solution of which would assist in the settlement of the remainder of the dispute. After a while, a line of precedents would be established, indicating in a foreseeable manner which types of cases are likely to be referred to the Court and in what situations such reference is apt to be most fruitful.

As in the previous instances, a state might be given several options. For instance, states could be permitted to choose between accepting as binding the request of the Security Council to go to the Court, or of the General Assembly, or of both of them. Other limitations might also be included.

In conclusion, it might be useful to emphasize that the proposals made here are purely illustrative, and that many other ways of fractionating the obligation to go to the Court can probably be devised. It is the duty of the international legal profession to increase the number of ways in which states should be able to accept the Court's jurisdiction. Once a rich smorgasbord is placed before the states, only the most strong-minded will be able to resist the temptation of nibbling here and there. As is well known, *l'appétit vient en mangeant,* and once they start sampling the available methods, they might be easily carried away.

After the acceptance of the Court's jurisdiction by many more states in many more ways, time would come to try to persuade the states to utilize the new opportunity and to start actually going to the Court. After a few minor cases are decided without disastrous results, more important cases would be submitted, and jurisdiction would be further broadened. If we don't dare to try, we shall never find out whether present obstacles to the Court's jurisdiction can be overcome. As Amelia Earhart Putnam said, "Courage is the price that life exacts for granting peace."

NOTES AND QUESTIONS

1. Which categories of disputes would you think most suitable for compulsory jurisdiction? Which categories are least suitable? In general, what factors make a state reluctant to accept compulsory jurisdiction? Even if a state accepted the *general* desirability of compulsory jurisdiction, are there any considerations that might explain a reluctance to accept it for a *particular* category of disputes? For instance, a state may feel dissatisfied with international legal standards in an area that is important to it; thus a newly independent state may not want to entrust the ICJ with competence to decide the extent to which it succeeds to obligations inherited from its period of colonial servitude. See D. P. O'Connell, *The Law of State Succession* (University Press, Cambridge, England, 1956). The United States may not want to face a legal challenge directed at its sovereign rights in the Panama Canal Zone.
2. The issue of unlimited compulsory jurisdiction is linked to the problem of legislative change. Without a legislative organ in being, how does a social system repudiate old rules and create new ones? This issue is connected with the attempt in the Clark-Sohn plan to allow legislative considerations to enter into the pacific settlement procedure; first, by creating the World Equity Tribunal; second, by giving the General Assembly some authority to determine when it shall be used; and third, by giving the Assembly the authority to accept or reject the recommendation of the Tribunal. In effect, this allows the Assembly to play some role in deciding which disputes warrant a "legislative" solution and some control over the character of acceptable legislation.
3. For an analysis of the use of a national post-adjudicative veto as a way to induce states to accept jurisdiction of the Court, see Roger Fisher, "The Veto as a Means of Making Third-Party Settlement Acceptable," *Proceedings of the American Society of International Law* (1964) pp. 123. For a criticism of this approach, see Leo Gross, "Problems of International Adjudication and Compliance with International Law: Some Simple Solutions," *American Journal of International Law*, vol. 59 (January, 1965) p. 48.

The final selection is a provocative essay by Lon Fuller on the limits and nature of adjudication—"Adjudication and the Rule of Law," *Proceedings of the American Society of International Law* (1960) pp. 1–8. Fuller's approach helps to identify the kind of legal disputes that are ripe for adjudicative settlement and manages to penetrate beneath the over-generalized distinction between legal and political disputes that is often invoked in such discussions. What makes a dispute "political"—the nature of the issues in contention, the attitudes of the parties toward their proper mode of settlement, or the scope of the conflict? Fuller not only helps us to think about this complicated question, but also challenges the conventional wisdom that regards adjudication as the appropriate way to resolve all legal disputes. Fuller points to the intrinsic limits of the adjudicative method, limits that have nothing to do with difficulties of enforcement or the character of international society, but which derive from the way in which courts decide. This is very important because often progress in expanding the role of law in world affairs is measured almost exclusively by the extent to which national governments can be persuaded to settle international disputes in courts. As Fuller notes, adjudication reaches the kind of either/or conclusions that are usually quite inappropriate for the solution of what he calls polycentric problems. Most of the salient international controversies of the day, no matter how much they are embedded in disagreements about relative legal rights, are "polycentric," and in Fuller's view, inappropriate for adjudicative settlement.

ADJUDICATION AND THE RULE OF LAW

By Lon L. Fuller

I

The analysis that underlies this essay originated partly in a concern with the conventional problems of legal philosophy, including the perennial favorite: "What is law?" This analysis also had another source that lay in a concern with the practical problems of labor relations and administrative law. These two areas share with international law the characteristic that in them if law exists at all, it exists imperfectly—it is still in process of being born. The reflections prompted by these concerns ran along two converging lines, the first having to do with what I have called "the limits of adjudication," the second with clarifying what is meant by "the rule of law."

By speaking of "the limits of adjudication" I mean to indicate the very simple and familiar idea that there are certain kinds of social tasks that are not suitable raw material for the adjudicative process. We cannot solve all of our problems and disputes by referring them to judges or arbitrators. Anyone who discharges a judicial function works within a particular institutional framework. That framework is like a specialized tool; the very qualities which make it apt and efficient for one purpose make it useless for another. A sledge-hammer is a fine thing for driving stakes. It is a cumbersome device for cracking nuts, though it can be used for that purpose in a pinch. It is hopeless as a substitute for a can-opener. So it is with adjudication. Some social tasks confront it with an opportunity to display its fullest powers. For others it can be at best a *pis aller*. For still others it is completely useless.

When the question is thus stated, one is faced with the problem of clarifying the concept of adjudication itself. This is no easy task, for adjudication presents itself in many mixed forms. Sometimes, for example, it verges on mediation directed toward compromise. In this form it tends to merge with the concept of contract. At other times, when the members of a tribunal are selected in such a way as to make them representative of the various interests affected by the tribunal's decisions, adjudication verges on representative government.

One line of my thought was, then, directed toward some definition of adjudication in what might be called its unmixed manifestations; when it presents itself *simpliciter* and does not borrow its forms and methods from some other process of social decision.

The other line of thought was, as I have said, directed toward clarifying the meaning of "the rule of law." In the literature we find the rule of law identified with ideas that not only seem quite different from one another but actually opposed in meaning. It can be said—and it has been said with varying degrees of explicitness—that the rule of law exists, *first,* where there is respect for justice and human dignity; *second,* where there is constituted a law-making authority whose decrees will be obeyed even when they are unjust; *third,* where the rules established by authority are faithfully enforced by judicial processes; *fourth,* where there is an independent judiciary ready to protect the affected party against the arbitrary acts of established power, *et cetera.*

I suggest that one way of bringing coherence into this confused area is to emphasize one aspect of the process by which a state of anarchy or despotism is converted into something we can call "the rule of law." The aspect I have in mind is the process by which the party affected by a decision is granted a formally defined participation in that decision. Thus we may oppose against anarchy and naked power a society in which there are recognized voting procedures, for voting is an ancient and cherished device by which the individual is accorded a participation in decisions which affect his interests. Again, we may oppose against anarchy and untrammeled power a society organized by the principle of contract, for negotiation (directly or through representatives) is a procedure by which the affected party is granted a participation in the settlement which governs his future conduct.

Continuing along the same line of thought, we may arrive at the conclusion that the fundamental characteristic of adjudication also lies in the particular form of participation it accords to the affected party. That participation consists in the institutionally protected opportunity to present proofs and arguments for a decision in his favor. This is, in effect, nothing more than an unfamiliar formulation of a very familiar conception, that of giving the affected party "his day in court." The formulation I am offering has the advantage, I believe, of clarifying what is necessary to make the party's day in court meaningful. For one thing, he must have some conception of the issues toward which his proofs and arguments are to be directed, if his opportunity to present proofs and arguments is to be meaningful. This is a truth that has been recognized in writings as far apart as Kafka's *The Trial* and Lewis Carroll's account of the Mad Hatter's attempt to testify before the King of Hearts. It is a truth that is, however, often forgotten, I am afraid, by uncritical enthusiasts for "judicializing" every kind of social decision.

To recapitulate, the analysis presented here regards adjudication as a process of social decision characterized by the peculiar form of participation it accords to the affected party, that of presenting proofs and arguments for a decision in his favor. This conception is, I believe, capable of bringing into some kind of order notions about the proper rôle of adjudication that otherwise remain merely enumerative and disjunctive. I do not have time here to trace, or even to suggest, all the implications that seem to me to flow from this conception. I shall have to content myself with two.

II

The first of these has to do with the concept of the polycentric task. This is a term I have borrowed from Michael Polanyi's profound and much neglected work, *The Logic of Liberty* (1951). To anticipate my conclusion I shall assert that adjudication is a process of decision badly suited to the solution of polycentric problems.

What is a polycentric problem? Fortunately I am in a position to borrow a recent illustration from the newspapers. Some months ago a wealthy lady by the name of Timken died in New York leaving a valuable, but somewhat miscellaneous, collection of paintings to the Metropolitan Museum and the National Gallery "in equal shares," her will indicating no particular apportionment. When the will was probated the judge remarked something to the effect that the parties seemed to be confronted with a real problem. The attorney for one of the museums spoke up and said, "We are good friends. We will work it out somehow or other." What makes this problem of effecting an equal division of the paintings a polycentric task? It lies in the fact that the disposition of any single painting has implications for the proper disposition of every other painting. If it gets the Renoir, the Gallery may be less eager for the Cezanne, but all the more eager for the Bellows, *et cetera*. If the proper apportionment were set for argument, there would be no clear issue to which either side could direct its proofs and contentions. Any judge assigned to hear such an argument would be tempted to assume the rôle of mediator, or to adopt the classical solution: Let the older brother (here the Metropolitan) divide the estate into what he regards as equal shares, let the younger brother (the National Gallery) take his pick.

Let me now give a series of illustrations of polycentric problems, some of which have been assigned, with poor success, to adjudicative treatment, some of which have been proposed for adjudicative treatment, and some of which are so obviously unsuited for adjudicative decision that no one has dreamed of subjecting them to it: setting prices and wages within a managed economy to produce a proper flow of goods; redrawing the boundaries of election districts to make them correspond to shifts in population; assigning the players of a football team to their respective positions; designing a system of throughways into a metropolitan area; allocating scarce funds for projects of scientific research; allocating air routes among our various cities; drawing an international boundary across terrain that is complicated in terms of geography, natural resources, and ethnology; allocating radio and television channels to make balanced programs as accessible to the population as possible.

For problems like these it is clear that adjudication can at best be an unsatisfactory mode of decision. There is and can be no single solution or issue toward which the affected party may direct his proofs and arguments. The mode of participation in the decision accorded to him, that is, the opportunity to present proofs and arguments for a decision in his favor, therefore loses most of its meaning. If he is nevertheless "given his day in court," this concession cannot have the meaning it does for the ordinary litigant, since the deciding agency must direct its mind toward considerations much more important than those contained in the fragmentary presentation open to any single party.

To avoid misunderstanding, let me present briefly a series of clarifications and qualifications.

First, polycentricity is not merely a matter of the complexity of the issues presented to the deciding tribunal. A suit by *A* against *B* on a promissory note for $100 may present extremely complex issues, where, for example, the note was given as part of some complicated deal between the parties. It is not complexity of issues but of patterns of decision that characterizes the polycentric problem. In the case of the promissory note the court can decide that *A* wins over *B,* without having to move *C*'s position, or to exchange *C*'s position for that of *D*. Contrast this with the football coach who, when he put A in as quarterback, has to move B from halfback to end, to retain C as a center, *et cetera.*

Second, polycentricity is not a matter merely of a multiplicity of affected parties. Indeed, as I have indicated, a polycentric problem can arise between two parties, as in the case of Mrs. Timken's will. On the other hand, if an award were offered for information leading to the capture of a particular criminal, the fact that ten claimants might appear would make for a cumbersome hearing; it would not make the problem polycentric.

Third, I am not asserting that polycentric problems are problems without rational solution. There are rational principles for building bridges of structural steel. But there is no rational principle which states, for example, that the angle between girder *A* and girder *B* must always be 45 degrees. This depends on the bridge as a whole. One cannot construct a bridge by conducting successive arguments on the angle of every pair of intersecting girders. One must deal with the whole structure at once.

Fourth, the fact that an adjunctive decision affects and enters into a polycentric relationship does not of itself mean that the adjudicative tribunal is moving out of its proper sphere. On the contrary, there is no better illustration of a polycentric relationship than an economic market, and yet the laying down of rules that will make a market function properly is one for which adjudication is generally well suited. The working out of our common law of contracts case by case has proceeded through adjudication, yet the basic principle underlying the rules thus developed is that they should promote the free exchange of goods on a polycentric market. The court gets into difficulty, not when it lays down rules about contracting, but when it attempts to write contracts.

Fifth, the polycentricity of any given problem is a matter of degree, though we need to recall Holmes' remark that a distinction may be a matter of degree and none the worse for that. For example, in the evolution of the rules of contract law, our courts often had to backtrack when they discovered that a rule that seemed proper in *Situation X* worked an injustice when applied to *Situation Y*. The problem of the unexpected side effects of a precedent is one that plagues all systems of law, including those which interpret contracts as well as those which lay down the rules for contracting. But the difficulties of this problem furnish no argument for abandoning any concern for the limits of adjudication. On the contrary, they warn us eloquently where adjudication will land if it decides it might as well quit the frying pan for the fire.

To recapitulate: When we move from a condition of anarchy to despotism toward something deserving the name of "the rule of law," one of the most important aspects of that transition lies in the fact that formal institutions are established guaranteeing to the members of the community some participation in the decisions by which their interests are affected. Adjudication is a form of social decision which is characterized by a peculiar mode of participation accorded to the affected party, this participation consisting in the opportunity to present proofs and arguments for a decision in his favor. Whatever impairs the meaning and force of that participation impairs the integrity of adjudication itself. This participation is seriously impaired where an attempt is made to deal with problems where the polycentric element, as here defined, is important and significant. Adjudication is a mode of decision badly suited for the solution of polycentric problems. When it is seriously misused in this direction the rule of law is itself impaired.

What measures, then, are open for the solution of polycentric problems? I can see only two: *contract* and *managerial authority*. The first is illustrated by an economic market; the second by a football coach who assigns his players to their appropriate positions.

The majority principle is itself incompetent to deal with polycentric tasks; at least it would be incompetent if it were not so commonly supplemented by contract in the form of the political deal. Perhaps studies in voting forms (such as those of Kenneth Arrow, Duncan Black and Gordon Tullock) may yield methods of voting that will accommodate the machinery of elections to the solution of polycentric tasks.

III

The second main implication of my analysis is one that I have already mentioned, and that is that adjudication must take place within a framework of accepted or imposed standards of decision before the litigant's participation in the decision can be meaningful. If the litigant has no idea on what basis the tribunal will decide the case, his day in court—his opportunity to present proofs and arguments—becomes useless. Just as the judge cannot be impartial in a vacuum, so the litigant cannot join issue with his opponent in a vacuum. Communication and persuasion presuppose some shared context of principle.

Those who regard the judge's task as essentially deductive have considered that adjudication can function meaningfully only when rules have been formally laid down in advance for the decision of controversies. According to this view, in any situation where the rule of law is in process of being born, we must first establish rules of decision, and then set up tribunals to administer and apply those rules in particular cases. If the established rules are insufficient to cover the area of possible controversy, then to that extent adjudication must also default as an ordering principle.

Against this view stand those who contend that rules are a kind of by-product of the adjudicative process, who indeed often seem to regard rules as an unwelcome by-product of adjudication, born of the perverse human impulse toward rationality, often manifesting itself at the cost of good sense.

With considerable simplification we can divide the opponents in this dispute into those whose slogan is: "First rules, then courts," and those who adopt the opposite slogan: "First courts, then rules." Those who take the second position—that is, those who say, "First courts, then rules" —often support their argument by references to history. It is pointed out that the two great systems of law that dominate the world today—the common law and the Roman law—took their origins in a case-by-case evolution of doctrine. Even today, when developments occur in the common law, it is often only at the end of a series of cases that the governing principle becomes clear. In the civil-law countries the codes from which courts purport to derive their principles often provide little beyond a vocabulary for stating legal results. They are filled with clauses referring to "good faith," "equity," "fair practice," and the like—standards that any court could apply without the aid of a code. One of the best of modern codes, the Swiss Code of Obligations, lays down very few rules and contents itself largely with charting the range of judicial discretion and with setting forth what might be called check-lists for the judge to consult to make certain that he has overlooked no factor properly bearing on the exercise of his discretion.

Those on the opposite side of this argument reject this historical argument. To their minds it only confirms the truth of their own slogan,

"First law, then courts." In the instances mentioned there were already rules which the courts could apply. These were not, to be sure, rules of law, but they were established moral principles that were generally accepted by the litigants who came before the courts. What happens in such cases has no bearing on situations where a court attempts to project its functions into a moral and legal vacuum. Here the court will fail unless it can enter this wilderness armed with rules authoritatively laid down in advance.

It seems to me that what is needed in this dispute is some analysis of the circumstances under which rules or standards of decision can develop out of the adjudicative process without being laid down in advance; where, in other words, adjudication may reasonably be expected to produce such rules or standards as a by-product of its functioning. For we cannot assume that this will under all conditions occur. Some of our most important domestic regulative agencies were initiated in the hope that, as knowledge was gained case by case, a body of principle would emerge that would be understandable by all concerned and that would bring their decisions within the rule of law. Sometimes this has happened; sometimes our hopes that it would happen have been completely disappointed. Here is a pool of experience which ought to be tapped.

As I see it, there are two major conditions that must exist before principles of decision may be expected to emerge as a by-product of adjudication. The first is that there must be an extra-legal community, existent or in process of coming into existence, from which principles of decision may be derived. The common law of contracts developed concomitantly with the development of the economic institution of exchange. In the course of the long evolution of legal doctrine about contracts, litigants had to put up with many unpleasant manifestations of the adjudicative process—with wooden literalness, with confused analysis, with class bias, with imperfect insight and foresight. But they put up with these inconveniences because they saw that adjudication was necessary to maintain something that existed outside the courtroom that they wanted to preserve and develop. They saw also, by and large, that the principles of law laid down by the courts were themselves derived from the intrinsic demands of this extra-legal community of interest. This was just as true, I think it should be emphasized, whether the courts were laying down rules for the making of contracts, or were developing principles for the interpretation of contracts already concluded, for I believe that it is in the sphere of interpretation that the law's dependence upon extra-legal community is most direct and complete.

The first condition for the emergence of legal doctrine as a by-product of adjudication is, then, the actual or potential existence of extra-legal community. The second condition is that the adjudicative process must not, in attempting to maintain and develop extra-legal community, assume tasks for which it is radically unsuited. I hope I shall not appear to be overworking the concept of polycentricity if I say that all community is polycentric in nature, as indeed are all living relationships. Adjudication may profitably nurture extra-legal community and help it into being; it cannot create it.

It is notable that the greatest failure in American administrative law has been with respect to those agencies that were assigned, or assumed for themselves, polycentric tasks which they attempted to discharge through adjudicative forms. This has been the case with the Civil Aeronautics Board and the Federal Communications Commission. Both of these agencies have attempted to operate as adjudicative tribunals with only the guidance of very general legislative mandates. Both have failed to build up any coherent body of doctrine that can be called a system of law. Both have failed, not because there was nothing in the way of extra-legal community they could help to develop, but because they were compelled, or thought they were compelled, to create and shape that community through adjudicative procedures. The inadequacies of the community thus built, as well as the too frequent lapses from the judicial proprieties that have characterized both agencies, are alike attributable to an attempt to use adjudicative forms for the accomplishment of tasks for which they are not suited. It is as if the courts of common law, instead of laying down rules governing the making and interpretation of contracts, had from the beginning felt compelled to write contracts for the parties, and had attempted to hold a separate hearing for each clause as the contract was being written.

My final conclusion is that, like many other precious human goals, the rule of law may best be achieved by not aiming at it directly. What is perhaps most needed is not an immediate expansion of international law, but an expansion of international community, multiplying and strengthening the bonds of reciprocity among nations. When this has occurred—or rather *as* this occurs—the law can act as a kind of midwife—or, to change the figure—the law can act as a gardener who prunes an imperfectly growing tree in order to help the tree realize its own capacity for perfection. This can occur only when all concerned genuinely want the tree to grow and to grow properly. Our task is to make them want this.

NOTES AND QUESTIONS

1. There is an approach to conflict resolution that urges the fractionation of the conflict into a series of separable and technical issues. Such fractionation can then lead to the resolution of conflict on an issue-by-issue basis. See "Fractionating Conflict," *International Conflict and Behavioral Science*, edited by Roger Fisher (Basic Books, New York, 1964) p. 91. For an application of issue-splitting in the context of adjudication, see Arthur Larson, "Peace Through Law: The Role and Limits

of Adjudication—Some Contemporary Applications," *Proceedings of the American Society of International Law*, vol. 54 (1960) p. 8.

2. What is a polycentric issue? See Michael Polanyi, *The Logic of Liberty* (University of Chicago Press, 1951).

Procedures of Coercive Settlement: Sanctions, Peace-Keeping, and Police

9

Throughout the history of international relations there has been an attempt to distinguish in theory and practice between permissible and nonpermissible uses of violence by states in their relations with one another. An important insight into the character of a particular world order system is to identify who in the system makes authoritative judgments about whether a particular use of violence is permissible or not. It may deepen this insight to compare international procedures with the character of the decision-making procedures used in domestic societies to deal with these issues.

The quality of social order is considerably influenced by the degree of centralization that exists with regard to the identification of nonpermissible violence. A growth in this aspect of centralization marked the transition from feudalism to the modern bureaucratic state in domestic political organization. A similar growth in centralization may eventually take place in international society. At present, permissible uses of violence (Article 51) are complementary to nonpermissible uses (Article 2(4)) in the Charter, but there are no definitive criteria for deciding which is which (no authoritative definitions of either self-defense or aggression), and reliance is place upon the *ad hoc* procedures of the political organs of the United Nations for the classification of a particular instance.

In this chapter inquiry centers upon the implementation of Article 2(4) of the Charter, especially implementation through the invocation of police methods of law enforcement. Such an inquiry presupposes that the identification of nonpermissible violence has been made, and moves on to consider what happens next. Clark and Sohn rely heavily upon a United Nations Police Force to prevent and correct violations of Article 2(4). The reasoning behind this proposal of a police force is based on what they consider to be the necessary elements of an acceptable plan of general and complete disarmament. Clark and Sohn seem convinced that sovereign states will be unwilling to disarm if they must base their security on the goodwill and self-restraint of other states. A compulsory system for the settlement of international disputes does not provide satisfactory assurance that the commitment to renounce violence will be kept. The world community must also possess an effective police force to halt the use of violence even in a disarmed world, just as police forces are used in all modern states to provide for security against criminal elements and other individuals engaging in deviant behavior. That is, order cannot be kept merely by disarming, nor can the commitment to disarm be made until states anticipate a secure existence in a disarmed world. A world police force is, in the view of many, crucial to anticipating this sense of security. The subject is complicated because some reluctance to disarm can be traced to the fear that the world police force would itself be a military actor capable of aggression and, therefore, constitute a possible danger to national security.

Clark and Sohn conceive of a United Nations Peace Force, as they call it, that consists of 200,000 to 600,000 men (with a reserve force of 600,000 to 1,200,000) armed with the most modern military equipment available. The Peace Force would under certain circumstances and on the basis of a special vote of the General Assembly even have the authority to use, if necessary, nuclear weapons. The detailed scheme for the recruitment and composition of the Peace Force, the process for invoking its use by the political organs of the United Nations, and the command and control structure governing its operations are set out in comprehensive detail in Annex II of *World Peace through World Law*.

Many persons regard this aspect of the Clark-Sohn model as utopian in the sense that it is an unrealistic proposal within the foreseeable future. After all, the argument runs, even if one grants that the United Nations has been moderately successful in its efforts to prevent and to halt international violence, it has had a very difficult time achieving an effective collective security system, let alone a permanent police force of any size, even of token proportions. Furthermore, even if we were to overlook the contemporary ideological and political fissures and strains, the high level of existing international tensions, and the apparent unwillingness of almost all states to surrender their traditional unilateral decision-making power with respect to national defense structures, there are additional reasons why the Clark-Sohn approach to peace-keeping is vulnerable to objection. A succinct way to summarize these objections is to call attention to the supposed dilemma between efficiency and tyranny. That is to say, a responsible official of a nation-state would want to be assured that an international police force was sufficiently strong and flexible to operate swiftly and efficiently and, at the same time, have reasonable assurance that it would not become an autonomous actor that might itself pose threats to the security of his state. The Peace Force, in this view, is a potential aggressor, and paradoxically, unless it has this capability to aggress, there is no reason to rely upon its capacity to deter national aggressors.

There are several ways to diminish, if not overcome, this apparent dilemma. It can be argued, for example, that the security problems in a disarmed world under law would be much alleviated and that there would be little occasion for states to threaten or use violence to achieve their goals. It is also pointed out that the personnel of the Peace Force would be recruited and trained to emphasize their role in a system of world order. Such a system might easily be expected to produce public servants with a deep commitment and dedication to the ideals of the Charter. It is also plain that the police force would be subjected to such strict political supervision that there would be little possibility of its being able to take over any state, let alone impose its rule upon the entire world. See Fisher, **IV-5**. There are, of course contrary arguments: even assuming a disarmed world, many observers (see Millis, **I-1C**, and Waskow in Section C of this chapter) feel that intense competition among states would persist, and perhaps even increase, as a result of severe political and ideological controversies and that a relatively high amount of violence, although not with weapons of mass destruction, might well take place. Although it seems unlikely that a police force would seek or be able to impose a tryannical rule upon the world, or even a portion of it, it would be irresponsible for governmental officials to ignore this possibility. It must, accordingly, be taken seriously in evaluating any proposal to establish any world police force of military significance.

The Clark-Sohn proposal can be evaluated, we submit, by formulating a series of issues that bear upon its political acceptability to the nations. It is desirable that the Clark-Sohn plan for a world peace force be evaluated as systematically as possible to discern its strengths and weaknesses, always recognizing, of course, that such an analysis is quite conjectural, that the problems in practice would be unlikely to resemble the problems as we project them. In the rest of this chapter the effort will nevertheless be made to combine analytical and historical perspectives in the study of the problems connected with setting up and using a world peace force. The sequence of readings will begin with some material on enforcement or sanctioning procedures in general (that is, on how to coerce compliance with rules of order in world affairs), move on to consider briefly the experience of the United Nations in the peace-keeping area, examine several modest proposals for standing peace forces that are much more closely geared to what seems presently attainable than is the Clark-Sohn plan, and finally, return at the end of the chapter to a reconsideration of the prospect for and adequacy of the Clark-Sohn conception of a world police force.

A. Perspectives on Sanctioning

This section consists of three articles that examine a series of issues bearing upon the feasibility and advisability of establishing an international police force. The first article, written by the late Professor James Brierly, "The Prohibition of War by International Law," *The Basis of Obligation in International Law* (Clarendon Press, Oxford, England, 1958) pp. 280–296, was first published in the midst of World War II. It sets forth a list of principles that might be used in creating an international system capable of effectively outlawing war. Brierly's summary of customary international law doctrine on the legality of war includes a discussion of whether it is necessary or desirable to define aggression, as well as a statement of his views on the problem of enforcing rules of law in the international community and an evaluation of the question of whether a revival of the concept and practice of neutrality would contribute to a system designed to minimize international violence.

On this firm intellectual basis Brierly advances a set of operational principles that he feels should guide attempts to establish an effective collective security system. These principles reflect both Brierly's thorough understanding of the traditional doctrine of international law and his sophisticated view of international political processes. Brierly felt that the way to make collective security a workable and acceptable basis of world order was to *require* only the most *minimal* participation by a given state in any *particular* collective security action. Note that this advocacy of an obligation of minimal participation is at odds with both the present Charter and with the Clark-Sohn plan. For example, Article 2(5) of the present Charter reads: "All Members shall give the United Nations every assistance in any action it takes in accordance with the present Charter, and shall refrain from giving assistance to any state against which the United Nations is taking preventive or enforcement action."

Clark and Sohn in their Comment on revised Article 2(5), pp. 9–10, suggest that "the proposed amendments to paragraphs 3, 4 and 5 [of Article 2] would extend to all nations, whether members of the United Nations or not, the obligation to settle international disputes peacefully, to refrain from the use of force and from giving assistance to any state against which the United Nations is taking action. On the other hand, the duty, under paragraph 5, actively to assist the United Nations would continue to apply only to member Nations." A basic issue of world order is present here: What degree of mandatory participation in a collective security system is desirable and necessary? The financing crisis of the Organization expresses the unwillingness of certain states to pay for collective security actions with which they disagree or which were undertaken by procedures of which they disapprove.

It should be noted that Brierly's scheme is unrelated to and not dependent upon disarmament. This partially reflects Brierly's view that an acceptance of a collective security system is best achieved by minimum change in the ongoing system: his proposals leave intact, formally at least, the right of individual states to make unilateral decisions with regard to their national defense establishments. A number of important questions are raised by this approach that will be relevant in the remainder of these readings. Many of these questions affect the relationship between a police force and general and complete disarmament, and apply both to its attainment and its maintenance. Is it possible to achieve a police force without some measure of disarmament? Is it possible to achieve disarmament without a police force? If a police force were established, would it be necessary also to have disarmament? If disarmament were achieved, would it be necessary to have a police force? What is the correlation, if any, between the size and capability of a world police force and the size and capability of national military establishments? Should the police force increase as national forces are eliminated?——by a constant rate?——depending on security needs?

JAMES L. BRIERLY

THE PROHIBITION OF WAR BY INTERNATIONAL LAW[1]

I. *The Attitude of the Customary Law to War*

SINCE the rules of customary international law are not contained in any authentic text, the attitude of that law to war must be sought in the opinions of jurists and in the practice of states.

Unfortunately, these sources leave it uncertain whether or not a customary rule prohibiting war exists or has ever existed, for the opinions of jurists have varied and the practice of states is ambiguous. In any case the question is of no great practical importance today, for no one would suggest that a customary prohibition of war, if it can be said to exist at all, would provide a secure basis for future international order. None the less the history of theory on the question is of interest, since it throws light on the nature of the problem which the practice of war sets to the international lawyer.

The classical writers for the most part had no doubt that the law does set limits to the right of states to resort to war. They took over from the medieval theologians and canonists the doctrine that war was *justum*, that is to say, regular or lawful, only on certain conditions, and they tried to establish this doctrine as a legal, and not merely, as

[1] This paper was submitted for discussion to an inter-allied conference of lawyers held in London on 10–12 July 1943. It has a limited purpose. It attempts only to state the writer's view of the minimum of change that would have to be made in the present system of international law if a rule making it illegal for a state to resort to war is to be effectively established. One of its conclusions is that no such rule can be established in an unorganized world, but it does not discuss the form that an international organization should take; in the writer's view something on the lines of the changes set forth would have to be incorporated in *any* kind of organization of states whether of the federal or the co-operative type. Nor does the paper try to deal with the much wider question of the various measures that it may be necessary or useful to take in order to make war less probable. Members of the conference suggested, *inter alia*, that war is unlikely to be abolished unless we establish in its stead international machinery for the redress of grievances; that there ought to be procedures by which those who make wars can be made criminally responsible for their conduct; that an international police force is a *sine qua non*. These are all important questions, but they fall outside the purview of this paper.

it had hitherto been, an ethical, principle. One of the requirements of a *bellum justum* was, they held, that it must originate in a *justa causa*, a lawful reason for making war, and though different writers enumerated these causes of war in different terms, most of them, Grotius tells us, mentioned defence, recovery of property, and the punishment of wrongs. The common element in the enumerations was the condition that the state against which war was undertaken should have committed some wrongful act; 'there can be no lawful cause of making war', says Grotius, 'except *injuria*'.[2] Thus what the classical jurists taught was in effect that for war to be justified it must be used as an instrument for upholding the law.

Some of these writers saw the practical difficulties of making this principle prevail, and the passage in which Grotius summed these up under two heads is interesting because the difficulties that he mentions, though we express them now in different words, are the same that we have to meet today. One of these was that when nations go to war there are no *indicia externa*, no outward signs, to show other nations which of the belligerents has the right on his side; and the other was that it was dangerous for other nations to pronounce on the rights and wrongs of the case, since the result might be to involve them in a war with which they were not concerned. He concluded that it was better to leave the matter to the conscience of the belligerents themselves, and not to ask third states to judge between them.[3]

This was a lame conclusion, for Grotius must have known quite well that the conscience of belligerents was a frail support to rely on. But that he should have been driven to it shows the difficulty against which international legal theory has always had to contend. The attempt to import a distinction between lawful and unlawful war into the customary law has always contained an element of make-believe. The theory of the law has had to choose between two alternative doctrines of the relation between law and war, and each of these is equally unsatisfactory to the conscience of the jurist. It might on the one hand persist in maintaining that the law does really distinguish between lawful and unlawful war, but against this were the stubborn facts that the practice of states only too evidently disregarded such a distinction, and that it was not practicable for the law to enforce it. On the other hand, it was possible, but only at the cost of bringing the system into discredit and coming near to denying its claim to be a

[2] *De jure belli ac pacis*, iii. 1, 1 and 2.
[3] Ibid. iii, 4, 4.

legal system at all, to admit that international law does not make the most elementary of all legal distinctions, that between the lawful and the unlawful use of force. What happened was that, while writers continued for generations to repeat that the law did make the distinction, their treatment of the matter took on more and more the aspect of a moral aspiration or of a mere literary convention, and ceased to be the enunciation of a rule of law in the existence of which they genuinely believed. In the later nineteenth century, with the ascendancy of positivist doctrine in legal theory, most writers came to adopt the second and more realistic horn of the dilemma, and to regard war simply as an event, neither legal nor illegal, which occurs from time to time in the relations of states, and which the law tolerates because it can do nothing else about it. It accepts the making of war, for any reason or for none, as one of the prerogatives of a modern sovereign state, and it devotes itself to the secondary task of trying to control, so far as it can, the manner in which belligerents carry on the operations of their war both towards one another and towards other states not involved in the war. On this view, whatever the origin of a war may be, both sides are in the same position in the eye of the law, their rights and duties are the same, and no third state has the right to judge between them.

II. *Prohibition of War by Convention*

During the period between the two world wars two attempts of the first importance have been made to limit by international agreement the freedom which sovereign states have hitherto exercised to make war at their discretion. These are the Covenant of the League of Nations and the Pact of Paris. Neither of these attempts has been successful, but the experience which they have afforded must inevitably be the foundation of any future attempt to solve the problem of the relation of war to the law. That experience contains both encouragement and warning.

The Covenant did not require the member states of the League to renounce their freedom to make war in all circumstances; it required them to accept (in the French version of the text, which on this point is clearer than the English) 'certaines obligations de ne pas recourir à la guerre'. These obligations related to wars of a specially inexcusable kind; in effect, to wars entered on in circumstances where a reasonable settlement would have been possible if the aggressor had been content with that. Thus a state might resort to war without breaking any of its obligations under the Covenant, if it first submitted the dispute to arbitration, to judicial settlement, or to inquiry by the Council, if it waited for three months after the arbitrators' award, the court's decision, or the Council's report, as the case might be, and if it did not make war on a state complying with the award, the decision, or the report, provided in the last case that the Council had been unanimous apart from the parties to the dispute. But these provisions were not the whole of the Covenant's scheme against war; the Covenant did not contemplate that the League should simply stand aside if a state should resort to war even though it should do so without breaking its express obligations. On the contrary Article 11 declared that 'any war or threat of war' (including, that is to say, a war which did not involve a breach of Covenant obligations) was to be a matter of concern to the whole League, and that the League was to take 'any action that may be deemed wise and effectual to safeguard the peace of nations'.

It is necessary to emphasize this point and to insist that the Covenant provisions against war ought to be judged as a whole because the existence of these so-called 'gaps' in them has often been unfairly criticized, and interminable debates have taken place at Geneva and elsewhere which have assumed it to be a matter of the highest importance that the 'gaps' should be closed. That implied that if war came, there was a real danger that the aggressor would first carefully observe his Covenant obligations, and then take advantage of one of the gaps to enter on a war not expressly prohibited; this was formally possible, but it was always politically most improbable, and in fact none of the wars that have broken out since the Covenant came into force has begun in that way. But even if the contingency had been one which it was prudent to guard against, the critics have generally failed to take the Covenant scheme as a whole. If that is done, there seem to be two dominant ideas underlying the provisions on war: the first is that no war, whatever the circumstances, can ever be a matter of indifference to the members of a collective security system, for whatever the origin of a war may be, and even if the aggressor state has some justification for resorting to war, yet its effects are so far-reaching, so difficult to foresee or to keep within bounds, that it can never be safe for the general body of states to declare beforehand that they will stand aside and do nothing about it; and the second dominant idea is that there are some wars, which it is possible to define in some such terms as are used in the Covenant, as to which states ought to be ready to go farther than this, and to announce beforehand in terms more precise the action that they will take in order to maintain or to restore the peace. Such a plan is not, as critics have sometimes accused it of being, to 'legalize' wars in certain circumstances; it is merely to take the view, which is a tenable view, that to require the members of a security system to declare in advance exactly what they will do in all cases, and to undertake to take the same measures irrespective of the circumstances in which a war has its origin, is to expose the system to a strain which in present conditions of international society it may be unable to bear.

At first sight the Pact of Paris may seem to deal with the problem of war in a bolder and more satisfying way than that taken by the Covenant. The Pact simply declared that the signatory states 'condemn recourse to war for the solution of international controversies, and renounce it as an instrument of national policy in their relations with one another', and the most probable interpretation of this rather unlawyer-like terminology is that the Pact intended to forbid all wars except wars of self-defence, and perhaps also wars undertaken in pursuance of some *international* policy. But it is a simple matter to declare that all aggressive war should be abolished if the states concerned do not intend to bind themselves to do anything about the matter if war should come in spite of the prohibition, if, that is to say, the whole difficult question of enforcement is to be left in the air as it was by the Pact of Paris. This is not to say that the Pact did nothing to promote the control of war by the law; indirectly, as the Budapest Resolutions of the International Law Association[4] have shown, it made it possible, though not obligatory, for a neutral state to judge between the parties to a war and to render assistance to the injured party against the party violating the Pact without thereby itself committing a breach of the law. The adoption of the Lease-Lend Act by the United States, while still neutral in the present war, was justly defended by members of the Administration on this very ground.

[4] 'In the event of a violation of the Pact . . . other states may, without thereby committing a breach of the Pact or of any rule of international law, do all or any of the following things: (*a*) refuse to admit the exercise by the state violating the Pact of belligerent rights, such as visit and search, blockade, etc.; (*b*) decline to observe towards the state violating the Pact the duties prescribed by international law, apart from the Pact, for a neutral in relation to a belligerent; (*c*) supply the state attacked with financial or material assistance, including munitions of war; (*d*) assist with armed forces the state attacked.'

III. *The Future Scope of a Legal Prohibition of War*

It is usual and convenient to speak of making 'war' illegal. But 'war' is a technical term, and the fact that what the Covenant forbade was 'resort to war' has made it possible for lawyers to debate such questions as whether, when Mussolini bombarded Corfu in 1923, he was 'resorting to war' against Greece and therefore breaking the Covenant, and even whether the prolonged hostilities of Japan in China constituted a 'war' until the matter was settled by the recent declaration of war by China. These were not mere quibbles, though it might be difficult to persuade the layman to take that view; for so long as war is an event producing legal results, the lawyer must have a definition of it in order to be able to say whether those results have come about or not, and hitherto he has had to work with a definition which has not covered the use of armed force in all possible circumstances. But clearly acts like the bombardment of Corfu and the invasion of China, whether or not they constitute 'war', are acts which the law should forbid. Some at least of the earlier drafts of the Covenant spoke of 'resort to armed force', and it is not clear why that wording was changed. It is submitted, therefore, that the first and fundamental provision of the law of the future should be a prohibition for any state to resort to the use of armed force except in circumstances defined by the law.

Such a prohibition, however, though a necessary first step, would be a small step in itself, no more than a clearing of the ground for measures of a more positive kind. The tragic history of the Paris Pact has surely taught us the futility of declaring war illegal and hoping that the prohibition will be self-enforcing. It is essential, therefore, to face squarely the problem of making the legal prohibition effective, and the difficulties in the way of doing that were clearly put by Grotius in the passage which has already been quoted. Our modern difficulties still fall under Grotius's two heads: (*a*) the absence of *indicia externa*, whereby other states may know, when a state uses force, whether it is doing so in breach of the law or not; or as we should say today, the difficulty of determining the 'aggressor'; and (*b*) the danger that other states incur if they assume to judge between the opposing parties to a war and to assist that which has the law in its favour.

IV. *The Determination of the Aggressor*

On this part of the problem it is believed that the experience of the League, and the continuous study which has been devoted to the question during the period between the wars, have led to some important conclusions which may be regarded as now established. One such conclusion is that all attempts to determine the aggressor by forming a judgment of the *merits* of a dispute which has led or threatens to lead to war lead to a dead-end. That is a task for historians, and one that statesmen, who have to deal with the current problems of politics, cannot make the basis of their action. It is a task, too, which cannot always be performed contemporaneously with the events, for the obvious reason that the causes of some wars are exceedingly complex; they have their roots in the past, and the relevant evidence is not always available to contemporaries. Another conclusion which emerges with almost equal clearness seems to be that the test cannot be found in an enumeration of specific acts; even such acts as the invasion of territory, or a declaration of war, are not conclusive, for it is possible to imagine circumstances in which they would be legitimate acts of self-defence.

It is unfortunate that so much recent discussion should have been concentrated on the definition of a word. 'Aggression' and 'aggressor' are popular terms and their use is often convenient, but they are not terms of art and there is no need to try to make them so. What matters is not the meaning of a word, but that the law should contain some easily recognizable means of distinguishing between the lawful and the unlawful use of force by a state. If we like to call a state that uses force unlawfully an aggressor, we may do so, but if we do, do not let us go round in a circle and proceed to look for a definition of the label that we have affixed. For the label is no more than a convenient way of designating a state which, to use the words of the Covenant, resorts to armed force 'in disregard of its covenants', and the practical question is to decide what are the covenants against the use of such force that states can reasonably be expected to make and to observe. Further, it is no easier to construct a satisfactory definition of defence than it is of aggression, and in the case of defence there is not even the possibility of using the method of enumeration as a substitute for a definition; we cannot make a list of acts which the law should regard as defensive and therefore permissible uses of force.

There is no great difficulty about the substance of the formula that we are seeking. It must allow states to use force in self-defence, it must allow them to use it in support of the law, but it must forbid them to use it, as the Pact of Paris expresses it, 'as an instrument of their national policy'. But these are all popular phrases of little use to the draftsman, whose task it is to devise a procedure supplying those *indicia externa* which, when force is used, will show promptly and with reasonable certainty whether its use is lawful or unlawful. For that the covenants of a state must go beyond the mere renunciation of force, as in the Pact; they must also be positive covenants, covenants whereby a state will undertake, before resorting to force, to supply unequivocal evidence of its willingness to accept an alternative to force if the other state concerned will agree. This positive undertaking must be such that compliance or non-compliance with it will be a matter of notoriety, a question which can be answered, without examining the motives which have induced, or are alleged to have induced, a state to resort to force, simply by asking whether or not it has followed a prescribed procedure before doing so. But a procedure of this kind depends for its working on one essential condition. It can only work in an organized world of states, for it is only in such a world that the law can offer states an alternative to force for the protection of their legitimate interests. Unless the law can do that, it is idle to suppose that its prohibition of the use of force can be made effective, for if states are powerful enough to protect their own interests by their own strength they will do so if the law cannot do it for them. In the world of his day Grotius looked in vain for the *indicia externa* of *bellum injustum*, for in an unorganized world they do not exist and they cannot be created.

This procedural test is, of course, the essence of the Covenant plan, and to have shown, as the founders of the League did, that we need not be baffled by the problem of devising a workable test for the distinction between lawful and unlawful force is one of the greatest of the achievements that they have bequeathed to us. Under the scheme of the Covenant we ask, when war breaks out, whether or not a state has 'resorted to war in disregard of its covenants', that is to say, without having been willing to submit the dispute to one or other of the methods of peaceful process already mentioned in this paper, which it has undertaken to use. We do not ask, for the question would be irrelevant, *why* a state may have acted in this way. It has put itself in the wrong by resorting to war without following the covenanted procedure.

This does not mean that the Covenant scheme does not admit of being improved in detail, and there are at least two elements in it which deserve particularly to be considered from this point of view.

One of these is whether it is desirable to close the so-called 'gaps' in the Covenant's provisions against war. It has been suggested earlier in this paper that from a practical point of view this is not a question of the first importance, since it is not at all probable than an aggressor would find it expedient to arrange his aggression so as to take advantage of one of the gaps. Still the possibility exists at any rate in theory, and probably from a psychological point of view it may be an advantage that the law should prohibit any use of armed force as an instrument of merely national policy. It is submitted, therefore, that the law should prohibit resort to armed force even in those cases where resort to war is not expressly ruled out in the Covenant, but that if this conclusion is accepted it should not be taken as involving the further consequence that all prohibited resort to force must necessarily entail the same consequences. The question of the action to be taken by other states in the event of the law being violated is one for separate consideration, and it does not follow that their action should be the same in all circumstances.

The Covenant provisions may also be criticized on the ground that they do not ensure that all states will decide in the same way the question whether a state has resorted to war in disregard of its covenants; they vest no power in any body to decide that question for the League as a whole, leaving each state free to make its own individual decision. This feature of the scheme, however, could only be avoided by some system of majority voting, which would imply an international organization very different in character from the League. This paper is not concerned with the general form of the post-war organization of the world except to the extent that the prohibition of war cannot always be discussed without some assumptions on that wider matter. Clearly, if a system ensuring that there should always be a single decision on the question of the legality or illegality of a state's use of armed force, and that this decision should be binding on all states, is practicable, it would have an advantage over the system of the Covenant with its risk of divergent decisions. On the other hand, if it is decided that such a system cannot be established, or that if it were established it could not be relied upon to work, it is submitted that a system on the lines of the Covenant need not prove a fatal flaw in the establishment of an effective rule against war. For the experience of the League shows that even when states retain the right to take their own several decisions, much can be done to increase the likelihood of their decisions being the same; and it may well be more prudent to make this our aim rather than to aim at inducing states to accept a new system giving a majority the right to impose its decision on the rest on a matter of this supreme importance. The 'rules of guidance' which were adopted by the Assembly in 1921 recognized that it was for each member of the League to decide for itself whether a breach of the Covenant had been committed, but they also provided that the Council should meet to consider all breaches or threatened breaches, and that if the Council was of opinion that a breach had occurred it should notify all the members and invite them to take appropriate action. The obvious purpose was to emphasize the collective nature of the action to be taken, and to make it likely, though not absolutely to ensure, that such action would be co-ordinated. In the only case in which the machinery was put into operation it worked well. In 1935 out of fifty-four states present in the Assembly all except four, Italy herself, Austria, Hungary, and Albania, decided that Italy had resorted to war in disregard of her covenants. No doubt this case was a particularly clear one, about which only one opinion could honestly be expressed. But so far as it goes the incident supports the view that a system relying on separate state decisions co-ordinated so far as possible is at least not unworkable. The ultimate failure of the League in the crisis of 1935–6 was in no way due to the fact that each member retained the right to decide for itself whether a breach of the Covenant had been committed.

v. *The Enforcement of a Legal Prohibition of War*

It remains to consider the second difficulty which led Grotius to conclude that the distinction between lawful and unlawful war must be left to the conscience of belligerents, namely, the danger to other states if they assume the role of judging between the parties. Like his first difficulty, this one, too, is only soluble in an organized world of states, for only in such a world can a preponderance of force be ensured for upholding the law, and only by a preponderance of force behind the law can the risk to the law-enforcing states be reduced. Between the alternatives of trusting to the conscience of states to obey the law and the enforcement of law by collective action there can therefore be no half-measures.

This paper does not attempt to fill in the details of a plan of collective security. Such a plan ought to be the concerted task of experts in many fields, of which law is only one and perhaps not the most important. But there are some aspects of the question on which those who have given special thought to the nature of law, its limitations and potentialities as a social force, and the conditions of its application to inter-state relations, may have a contribution to make.

One fact about any system of collective security that we cannot afford to neglect is that the obligations which it must inevitably impose upon states will at the best be onerous. It is curious how little attention this fact seems to have received at the time of the making of the League in some countries at least. Realization of its importance came soon afterwards, with unfortunate results; for the commitments had been made, and when it began to be suggested that perhaps they had gone too far, doubts began to be felt whether they were likely to be honoured, and a security system which does not inspire confidence is worse than useless. In the event the doubts proved to have been well founded, and in retrospect it is easy to see that the security provisions of the Covenant never had more than a paper existence. The first requisite of any future security scheme, therefore, surely is that it must be capable of inspiring confidence, and it will only do that if it is reasonably certain that the engagements which it imposes on states will be honoured.

It is essential, therefore, that the means whereby it is intended to secure the enforcement of a law against the illegal use of armed force should be founded on as careful a forecast as we can make of the kind of action that states will be willing to take to uphold the law if and when the time for doing so arrives. But it is not cynical to believe that in this matter the action of states is no more likely to be disinterested in the future than it has been in the past. We may reasonably hope that one result of the second world war in one generation will be that states will be more disposed than before to believe that the preservation of peace as such is a primary interest of each of them, but that only means that we may hope that their estimates of their interests will be more enlightened; it does not mean that we should expect them to be actuated by altruistic motives. Whether ethically it is right that states should act unselfishly, and how far the rules of individual morality ought to apply to their government, are questions which admit of more than one view; but the would-be designers of an international order which is intended to work will be wise to assume that in the present state of the world states do ordinarily act from motives of self-interest, which may be either more or less enlightened, and that they are likely to continue to do so.

VI. *Neutrality as a Possible Alternative Policy*

These considerations are particularly relevant if we compare the respective advantages of two contrasted policies between which it seems likely that states must choose in future when war breaks out, namely, a collective-security system on the one hand and a revival of neutrality on the other. It has been common recently to urge as an argument against neutrality and in favour of collective security that the former is an immoral and selfish policy, to be condemned as decisively and for the same reasons as we condemn the individual who thinks only of saving his own skin and cares nothing for the wrongs that he sees in the world around him. But it is not at all certain that that comparison is just, and even if it is, it is doubtful whether that line of criticism is likely to produce much effect. It is more likely that neutrality will only disappear if and when states come to believe that it is a short-sighted policy, one that in the modern world is not likely to lead to the result which it professes to achieve, that is to say, the protection of a state from involvement in a war with which it is not primarily concerned.

If then we would estimate the prospect of a reversion to policies of neutrality being more attractive to states in the post-war world than membership of a collective security system with all the risks that such membership must necessarily impose, the important question to ask is whether or not a policy of neutrality can in the conditions of the modern world insulate a state from the quarrels of other states. There is no doubt that, so far as the theory on which modern international law is founded goes, neutrality ought to be able to do that, for when war breaks out it is part of the prerogative of a sovereign state to determine for itself whether it will take part in it or not. But the history of war shows that the practical value of the right to be neutral has varied in different ages. On the whole such a right was well respected throughout the nineteenth century, but it was not at all well respected, and in fact it had only a rather shadowy existence even in theory, in the seventeenth and eighteenth centuries, and it has certainly not been respected so far in the twentieth. Thus the period during which it has been realistic to regard the right to be neutral as a solid protection for states when other states have chosen to go to war is a short one, and the rules of international law have had little to do with the matter one way or the other. The chances of maintaining a neutral policy successfully have always been governed by the character of warfare, and they have varied with the variations of warfare in different ages. The conditions in which wars were fought in the nineteenth century, the one period during which neutrality has seemed to be an effective and easily maintainable policy for avoiding involvement in a war, were of a very special kind. For one thing the wars of that century were wars with limited aims, undertaken for the settlement of fairly well-defined issues; they were not wars of the kind that we now call totalitarian, wars in which each side aims at the complete and unconditional submission of the other to its own will. Then again, whereas before the Napoleonic wars central Europe was split into so many small states that, if every state had been allowed to decide for itself whether it would be neutral or not, belligerents could not have waged their wars effectively, that state of things had been altered as a result of Napoleon's work; with the disappearance of the 'Kleinstaaterei' and the consequent consolidation of the map of Europe it became possible in the nineteenth century for belligerents, with the instruments of war and in the conditions of mobility then available, to carry on war and at the same time to respect the wishes of states desiring to be neutral without seriously impairing their own military efficiency. The result of these conditions was that a policy of neutrality came to be generally regarded, with some justification, as an effective means of limiting the area of war by drawing a ring round the belligerents and letting them fight out their quarrel inside it, and the special and temporary nature of the conditions which made this possible attracted little attention.

On this insecure foundation the lawyers proceeded to erect an edifice of rules regarding the neutral status which reached its culmination in the Conventions of The Hague. But the fragility of the structure was beginning to be apparent at the turn of the century. The Schlieffen Plan of the German General Staff was made in 1897, and at the very time that the lawyers were talking at The Hague the chancelleries of Europe knew that it was Germany's intention in the next war to violate the neutrality of Belgium. From a purely military point of view the Schlieffen Plan was sound enough, for the increased size of armies, the greater range of weapons, and improved conditions of mobility had made it impossible to deploy an army to the best effect if every small state that preferred to be neutral was to be allowed to be so. Obviously that is even less possible today, and in any estimate of the future of neutrality, and hence of the alternative prospect that states may be willing to seek their security by the method of collective action, that is a cardinal fact to keep in mind. No state in Europe that is neutral today is so because its neutrality is protected by international law; every one of them owes the preservation of its neutrality, either to the fact that Germany has not thought that its violation would be of military advantage to herself, or, as with Eire, to the protection of the British fleet. In effect the increased scale and speed of modern war has restored the map of Europe to its condition in pre-Napoleonic times, so that once again war cannot be waged effectively if at the same time neutrality must be respected. The would-be neutral state has constituted for Hitler the same simple problem that it did for Gustavus Adolphus, and he has dealt with it in the same ruthless, but militarily efficient, way.

Humanly speaking it seems certain that this state of things is not likely to be reversed, and that the conditions of war in the nineteenth century cannot be restored. But if that is so, it means that neutrality, at least in Europe, cannot again with any plausibility be regarded as a method of security which offers a real alternative to a collective system. On the other hand, it is also important to note the limits within which this conclusion is valid. It is not true, at any rate not yet true, that peace is 'indivisible' throughout the world as a whole; there are still circumstances in which it is possible for states to stand aside from wars without danger to themselves; even in this war that has been possible for some states. Certainly modern developments have reduced geographical distances, whether as barriers to intercourse or as safeguards of independence, but they have not yet eliminated them in either capacity, and so long as this remains true, it will follow that states will still find their interests unequally engaged in the wars of other states. That again is a fact of which it will be prudent to take account. It is a fact which the scheme of the Covenant neglected, when it was decided that in the event of a state resorting to war in disregard of its covenants the obligations of other members of the League should be uniform. For the reasons just given that was probably to go too far; it was a perfectionist policy which assumed a measure of world unity which does not yet exist.

VII. *The Content of a State's Obligation to Enforce the Law*

It may therefore be wiser that the obligations which states are asked to undertake for the maintenance of peace should be graded both according to the interest that each of them may be expected to feel in the promotion of peace in different circumstances, so far as that interest can be measured in anticipation of the event, and also according to the resources of which each can dispose.

If all men in all states were perfectly wise, it may be that they would feel that peace is everywhere and always their own highest interest, but we have to reckon with the fact that they do not yet feel in that way, and until they do we shall do well to devise a scheme which, if theoretically less perfect than one based on uniformity of obligations, is at least more likely to stand the strain to which all undertakings of the kind we are considering are inevitably exposed.

We do not yet know the shape that international organization will take after this war. But there is at least a minimum undertaking that every state, or if the organization is less than world-wide, then every member state, can fairly be expected to make, and if it makes it, to honour. This would be a negative undertaking, a promise not to assist any state found by the procedure agreed on to be violating its covenants against the use of force. It would mean that all states would be obligated at least to deny to an aggressor the rights that a neutral has traditionally accorded to a belligerent; it would create for all states in the event of aggression at least a status not unlike that which has recently come to be known as 'non-belligerency'. It would not debar a state from taking a more active part in enforcing the law if it should desire, but it would not oblige it to do so. But beyond this it would be necessary that states whose interests were more directly and obviously engaged should assume wider obligations, positive in character, and the question of designating before the event what states these would be is of course not an easy one. But one element in the solution would probably be the formation of smaller, more closely knit, associations which would be comprised within the larger association; by way of illustration it is reasonable to suppose that all the states of the Atlantic seaboard would feel their interests so closely engaged by any illegal resort to force within that area that they would be willing to undertake to join in positive action to defeat it in all events. Such restricted associations need not be mutually exclusive; many states are vitally interested in the peace of more than one region of the world, and some have world-wide or nearly world-wide interests in that matter. Nor need the basis of all the smaller associations be the same; in some it might be regional, in others, like the British Commonwealth, a community of sentiment and interests. The essential is that every co-operating state should count the cost of its commitments before it makes them, that the cost should be proportioned to its resources, and that this time no state should undertake any obligation which there is a chance that it may not be willing, or may not be able, to fulfil. A further question which needs to be considered is whether all a state's commitments should apply irrespective of the circumstances in which a war originates, or whether we should not retain in some form the distinction which the Covenant made between wars as to which states declare beforehand exactly what they will do, and other wars as to which they make no precise anticipatory commitment, but reserve the right to take 'wise and effectual action' in the light of the circumstances of the time when these are known.

VIII. *Conclusions*

The main conclusions to which the argument of this paper is intended to lead are these:

(*a*) International law should contain a rule forbidding the resort by states to the use of armed force except in circumstances defined by the law.

(*b*) In that event it will be essential that machinery should exist for distinguishing promptly and without ambiguity between the use of armed force which the law permits and that which it prohibits. The distinction therefore cannot be left to depend on a judgment of the merits of the dispute which is the occasion of a state resorting to armed force.

(*c*) The most practical test is procedural in character, and it should be declared that the use of armed force is legal only if (1) it is authorized by whatever international authority, competent for that purpose, it may be decided to create, or (2) it is preceded or accompanied by an offer to submit the dispute to some form of international consideration.

(*d*) A distinction between the legal and the illegal use of armed force can only be made good within a system of international order so constructed as to secure that preponderant force will in all probability be available to enforce the law.

(*e*) Inasmuch as any such system will necessarily impose onerous obligations on the states co-operating in it, it is vital that the commitments they undertake should not go beyond either their resources or their foreseeable willingness to honour them. No system of collective security which disregards this limiting factor will either deserve or inspire general confidence.

(*f*) It cannot yet be assumed that all states feel their interests equally threatened by every act of aggression, irrespective of the circumstances and of the region of the world in which it occurs. Accordingly if states are to make only such commitments as it is morally certain that they will honour, these ought not to be uniform, as in the Covenant of the League. They should be graded so as to correspond as accurately as possible to the interests and the capacities of each state.

(*g*) This implies a twofold form of security organization. On the one hand all the member states would undertake a minimum obligation, negative in character, to deny to a state found under agreed procedure to be an aggressor those rights which have traditionally been accorded by neutrals to belligerents, and not to impede the enforcement of the law by claiming the rights of a neutral from states taking more positive action. On the other hand the states more directly concerned, either because of the region in which the peace is threatened, or by reason of their wider interests, should be prepared to undertake whatever action is necessary in order to maintain or restore the peace.

NOTES AND QUESTIONS

1. In footnote 1 of his article, Brierly points out that his attempt here is conceived most narrowly in that he does not relate his analysis to other modes of decreasing the likelihood of violence. To what extent do you feel his analysis suffers from this limitation? To what extent does it benefit from it?
2. Which of Brierly's propositions concerning the nature of an effective system of collective security have been introduced into the present United Nations Charter? If they are present, identify the specific provisions that contain them. If they are missing, is it likely or desirable that they be incorporated into the collective security system at a later date?

Whereas the essay by Brierly introduces a set of variables encompassing a broad range of problems relevant to the study of the establishment of an effective international police force, the next selection has a more clearly delineated focus—the sanctioning system of the United Nations. Written by the eminent jurist, Hans Kelsen, only a little over eighteen months after the founding of the United Nations, this article—"Sanctions in International Law under the Charter of the United Nations," *Iowa Law Review*, vol. 31 (1946) pp. 499–543—is a painstaking and comprehensive legal analysis of all the provisions of the Charter, including their interrelationships, that in some way concern the authority of the Organization to employ sanctions.

Kelsen's concept of law, often described as "the pure theory of law," forms the basis of a distinctive school of jurisprudence, that of legal positivism, one that is quite different, for example, from the more sociological approach to the study of international law used by McDougal (**II-1C**) or Kaplan and Katzenbach (**II-1B**), or that of the author of the third selection in this chapter, Wolfgang Friedmann. Kelsen's formal definition of sanction is a cardinal feature of his jurisprudence. It seems advisable to defer judgment on the usefulness of his approach until there has been an opportunity to review other perspectives on the nature of law and sanctions. Kelsen's analysis of the provisions in Chapter VI and Chapter VII of the United Nations Charter are crucial to the study of policing activities. Kelsen's rigorous and systematic style of legal analysis uncovers, by its discussion of all plausible alternatives, many of the problems and controversies that have actually arisen concerning the effectiveness and authority of the Organization to respond to international violence. In addition, his evaluation of each sanction in terms of previous practice makes clear the extent to which the Charter introduced changes into the sanctioning procedures of the international community and underscores the fact that the United Nations was entrusted, formally at least, with greater authority than the League of Nations to reinforce the rule of order (Article 2(4)) that prohibits states from threatening or using force against the territorial integrity or political independence of another state. Finally, Kelsen's analysis of Articles 41 through 49 outlines the complex relationships between the composition of an international police force, the procedure for its invocation and the structure of its command and control.

SANCTIONS IN INTERNATIONAL LAW UNDER THE CHARTER OF THE UNITED NATIONS

Hans Kelsen

Introduction

Law is, by its very nature, a coercive order. A coercive order is a system of rules prescribing certain patterns of behavior by providing coercive measures as sanctions to be taken in case of contrary behavior, or, what amounts to the same, in case of violation of the law. "Violation" is a figurative and sometimes misleading expression. The term "delict" (wrong, illegal act) more correctly designates any kind of behavior which is made the condition of a sanction because it is considered to be undesirable.

Sanctions have the character of forcible deprivation of certain possessions, such as life, freedom, economic or other values. They are coercive in so far as they are to be taken even against the will of the subject to whom they are applied, if necessary by the employment of force. This is the way in which the law protects life, freedom, economic and other interests against delicts. Hence, sanctions are forcible interference in the sphere of interests normally protected by the law. They are legal sanctions if they shall be applied only on the condition that a delict has been committed or, what amounts to the same, that an obligation established by the law has been disregarded, and only against the delinquent or individuals who are in a legally determined relation to the delinquent, that is to the one who by his own behavior has committed the delict. Sanctions are the specific reactions of the community, constituted by the legal order, against delicts.

The fundamental legal concepts: delict, obligation, and responsibility are corollaries of the concept of sanction. A certain behavior is a delict if it is the condition of a sanction. A certain behavior is the contents of a legal obligation if the contrary behavior is the condition of a sanction and as such a delict. If the sanction is directed against the delinquent, individual responsibility, that is responsibility for an individual's own behavior, is established. If the sanction is directed against an individual or individuals other than the delinquent, responsibility for the behavior of another or others is established. If the sanction is directed against the individuals who belong to the same community—family, tribe, state—as the delinquent, collective responsibility is established.

International law is law in the true sense of the term, for its rules, regulating the mutual behavior of states, provide sanctions to be directed against the state which has committed an international delict, or, what amounts to the same, has disregarded its obligations towards another state and thus violated the right of the other state. The specific sanctions provided by general international law are: reprisals and war. Both are coercive acts, the former a limited, the latter an unlimited interference in the sphere of interests of a state. The distinction between reprisals and war rests upon the degree of interference: whether the enforcement action undertaken against the state is aimed solely at the violation of certain interests of this state, or is directed towards its complete submission or total annihilation and consequently performed by the armed forces of the opponent.

It is a generally accepted principle of international law that reprisals, i. e. limited interference in the sphere of interests of one state by another are allowed only as a reaction against a delict, that is to say, as a sanction. But, is this principle applicable also to an unlimited interference in the sphere of interests of another state, to war? As far as the answer to this question is concerned, two opposite views exist. According to one opinion, war is neither a delict nor a sanction; any state that is not bound by special treaty to refrain from warring upon another state or to resort to war only under certain definite conditions, may wage war against any other state on any ground, without violating general international law. The opposite opinion, however, holds that according to general international law war is in principle forbidden; it is permitted only as a reaction against an international delict and only when directed against the state responsible for this delict. Like reprisals, war has to be a sanction if it is not to be considered as a delict. This is the doctrine of *bellum justum,* just war.

If the doctrine of *bellum justum* is correct, then the employment of force on the part of one state against another is in principle forbidden as a delict; but it is exceptionally allowed as a reaction against a delict, that is to say, as a sanction. Only if it is possible to interpret so-called international law in this way can that order be considered as law in the true sense of the term.

General international law is characterized by a high degree of decentralization. The community constituted by this law has no central government, no court, no administrative organs. The far-going decentralization of general international law manifests itself in particular in the fact that no special organs exist to execute the sanctions against the delinquent. The international person whose right has been violated is authorized to react with reprisals or war against the international person who is responsible for the delict. Under general international law there are no courts competent to ascertain in an impartial way whether a delict has been committed and whether, therefore, a sanction should be directed against the delinquent. General international law is characterized by the principle of self-help. In this respect it is primitive law.

The primitive technique of self-help prevailing in general international law almost completely frustrates the application of the *bellum-justum* principle. For, as long as there is not established a central and impartial organ to decide whether or not a state has committed an international delict and thus violated the right of another state, this matter can be settled only by an agreement between the two states concerned. Since such agreement by which a state recognizes to have violated the right of another state is likely to be reached only by a peace treaty imposed by the victor upon the vanquished state (Art. 231 of the Peace Treaty of Versailles), the decisive question and hence also the question whether a war waged by one against another state is a just or an unjust war, remains almost always unanswerable.

The question as to whether general international law forbids war except as a reaction against a delict, has lost its importance since in the period between the two World Wars treaties have been concluded by almost all the states of the world for the purpose of outlawing war. The most important of these treaties are: the Covenant of the League of Nations (1919), the General Treaty for the Renunciation of War called the Briand-Kellogg Pact (1928), and the Charter of the United Nations (1945). The Covenant of the League of Nations did not forbid war under all circumstances. The Members of the League were allowed to resort to war against one another under certain circumstances, but only "for the maintenance of right and justice." The Briand-Kellogg Pact outlawed war as an instrument of national policy; consequently, war as an instrument of international policy and especially a war waged by one state against a state which has violated the Pact, was not forbidden.

The Charter of the United Nations goes much further than its predecessors. It obligates the Members of the United Nations not only not to resort to war against each other but to refrain from the threat or use of force and to settle their disputes by peaceful means (Art. 2, par. 3 and 4). The use of force—so-called enforcement action—is allowed by the Charter (except in case of self-defense) only as a reaction of the Organization against a threat to the peace or a breach of the peace (Art. 39). If the enforcement actions provided for by the Charter are true sanctions, the Charter is a perfect realization of the *bellum-justum* principle.

Although the Charter is a treaty concluded only by 51 states, the former enemy states in World War II and the neutrals not being contracting parties to this treaty and hence not or not yet Members of the United Nations, the Charter, in Art. 2, par. 6, claims to apply also to states not Members of the United Nations so far as may be necessary for the maintenance of international peace and security. This provision is not in conformity with general international law as prevailing at the moment the Charter came into force. According to the principles of this law treaties are binding only upon the contracting parties. Whether the provision of Art. 2, par. 6 will obtain general recognition remains to be seen. If so, the Charter of the United Nations will assume the character of general international law. Then the sanctions provided for by the Charter, in so far as they apply to all the states, are to be considered as sanctions under general international law. The procedure for the application of these sanctions is completely centralized, and thus the principle of self-help eliminated. This is the most striking difference between the old and the new general international law.

VI.

The most important sanctions provided by the Charter are considered to be the enforcement measures determined in Chapter VII of the Charter. The Charter lays particular stress on these measures in proclaiming in Art. 1, par. 1 as the first Purpose of the United Nations "to take effective collective measures for the prevention and removal of threats to the peace, and for the suppression of acts of aggression and other breaches of the peace." The "collective measures" referred to in Art. 1, par. 1 are specified in Articles 41, 42 and

45. There are two kinds of such measures: measures not involving the use of armed force, and measures involving the use of armed force. Both are "enforcement measures" or "enforcement actions" as they are sometimes called in the Charter ("measures": Art. 2, par. 7, Art. 50, "actions": Art. 5, Art. 53), although only the measures determined in Articles 42-47 involve the use of "armed" force. The measures determined in Art. 41 are especially: "complete or partial interruption of economic relations and of rail, sea, air, postal, telegraphic, radio, and other means of communication, and the severance of diplomatic relations." This purpose is defined in Art. 41 as follows: "to give effect to its [the Security Council's] decisions"; that means to enforce the decision upon a recalcitrant state. Hence these measures, too may be considered to be "enforcement measures" or "enforcement actions" referred to in various Articles of the Charter.

It has already been pointed out that it is doubtful whether the enforcement measures provided for by the Charter may be properly characterized as sanctions.

The economic and military enforcement actions stipulated by Art. 16, par. 1 and 2 of the Covenant of the League of Nations have evidently the character of sanctions (although they are not designated as such in the Covenant), since they are expressly directed against a specific violation of the Covenant. Art. 16, par. 1, dealing with the enforcement measure not involving the use of armed force, states: "Should any Member of the League resort to war in disregard of its covenants under Articles 12, 13 or 15 it shall *ipso facto* be deemed to have committed an act of war against all other Members of the League which hereby undertake immediately to subject it to, etc." And paragraph 2 of Art. 16, dealing with enforcement action involving the use of armed force, stipulates: "It shall be the duty of the Council in such case"—that is to say, in case a Member resorts to war in disregard of its obligations under the Covenant—"to recommend to the several Governments concerned what effective military, naval or air force the Members of the League shall severally contribute to the armed forces to be used to protect the covenants of the League." The use of armed force as an enforcement measure is expressly destined for the protection of the Covenant, that is for the defense of the particular law of the League.

The Charter, however, does not prescribe that the enforcement actions provided for in Chapter VII shall be taken exclusively against a Member which has violated its obligations; and the conditions under which the Security Council is authorized to take these actions are determined in a way different from that in which the obligations of the Members are formulated.[5]

Art. 39, the first Article of Chapter VII dealing with the enforcement actions, runs as follows:

> The Security Council shall determine the existence of any threat to the peace, breach of the peace, or act of aggression and shall make recommendations, or decide what measures shall be taken in accordance with Articles 41 and 42, to maintain or restore international peace and security.

None of the various obligations imposed upon the Members by the Charter is formulated as obligation to refrain from "any threat to the peace, breach of the peace, or act of aggression." The obligation the contents of which comes nearest to this is the one constituted by Principle 4 in Art. 2:

> All Members shall refrain in their international relations from the threat or use of force against the territorial integrity or political independence of any state, or in any other manner inconsistent with the Purposes of the United Nations.

The phrase "or in any other manner inconsistent with the Purposes of the United Nations" refers to the words "against the territorial integrity, etc." The meaning is: the Members shall refrain from the threat or use of force not only against the territorial integrity and political independence of any state but also in any other matter inconsistent with the Purposes of the United Nations, that is to say: with the provisions of Art. 1 of the Charter. The main import of the obligation established by Art. 2, par. 4: "to refrain from the threat or use of force" is not affected by the reference to Art. 1 of the Char-

[5] In the discussions at the San Francisco Conference the measures under Chapter VII were frequently designated as "sanctions." Cf. Doc. 134, III/3/3, May 9, 1945, pp. 10 ff; Doc. 23, III/3/9, May 11, 1945; Doc. 23, III/3/9 (1), May 22, 1945; Doc. 320, III/3/15, May 15, 1945; Doc. 577, III/3/28, May 25, 1945. The Report to the President on the Results of the San Francisco Conference by the Secretary of State, Dept. of State, Publication 2349, Conference Series 71, 1945, contains, p. 42, the following statement with reference to the obligation of the Members to refrain from giving assistance to any state against which the United Nations is taking preventive or enforcement action (Art. 2, par. 5): "It constitutes a general pledge not to strengthen the hand of a state which has violated its obligations under the Charter to the point where preventive or enforcement action has become necessary." Here the Report presupposes that enforcement action is to be directed only against a state "which has violated its obligations under the Charter," that means that the enforcement action is considered to be a sanction.

In the Hearings before the Committee on Foreign Relations, United States Senate, on the Charter of the United Nations, United States Government Printing Office, Washington, 1945, p. 252, Mr. Pasvolsky, Special Assistant to the Secretary of State, said in the discussion of Art. 14: "Sanction is provided only for breaches of the peace and threats to peace." This refers to the enforcement measures of Chapter VII. That sanctions are provided "only" for breaches of the peace or threats to peace or in other terms, that these enforcement measures are the only sanctions provided for by the Charter is certainly not true. Expulsion is—according to Art. 6—a sanction provided for persistent violation of any obligation imposed upon Members by the Charter.

ter where the main function of the Organization is defined—not exactly by the same, but almost by the same fomula as that used in Art. 39. Art. 39 speaks of "threat to the peace, breach of peace or act of aggression," whereas Art. 1, par. 1—more correctly—of "threats to the peace," "acts of aggression or other breaches of the peace." "Breaches of the peace" include "acts of aggression." It is superfluous to mention "acts of aggression" in addition to "breaches of the peace"; this all the more as the Charter does not define the very problematical concept "act of aggression."

There can be little doubt that the formula: "threat to the peace, breach of the peace, or act of aggression" as used in Art. 39, has not the same meaning as the formula "threat or use of force" adopted in Art. 2, par. 4. As "act of aggression" an act may be considered which is not a "threat or use of force." In the definition of aggression laid down e. g. in the Geneva Protocol the refusal to submit a dispute to the procedure of peaceful settlement is declared an act of "aggression." The same is true regarding the term "breach of the peace." Any serious violation of international law and especially the violation of almost any obligation imposed upon the Members by the Charter—and not only a violation of the obligation to refrain from the threat or use of force—could be interpreted as breach of the peace. The scope of Art. 39 of the Charter is much wider than that of Art. 16 of the Covenant which limits the application of enforcement measures to illegal resort to war. Of the utmost importance is the difference between the meaning of "threat of force" used in Art. 2, par. 4, and "threat to the peace" used in Art. 39. If a state refuses to execute the decision of an international tribunal or to comply with the recommendations of a commission of conciliation, its conduct may be characterized as a "threat to the peace," but not as a "threat of force" as long as its conduct does not allow the conclusion that the state intends to resort to force. As a "threat to the peace" and, consequently, as a condition of enforcement action according to Art. 39 may be interpreted: non-acceptance of the "plans" submitted under Art. 26 by the Security Council to the Members of the United Nations for the establishment of a system for the regulation of armaments; non-compliance with the provision of Art. 33, par. 1, to seek a solution of a dispute by peaceful means; non-compliance with a call of the Security Council to settle a dispute by means of the own choice of the parties in accordance with Art. 33, par. 2; non-compliance with the prescription of Art. 37, par. 1, to refer a non-settled dispute to the Security Council; non-compliance with one of the various recommendations made by the General Assembly or the

Security Council under Art. 10, Art. 11, par. 2, Art. 14, Art. 36, par. 1, Art. 37, par. 2, Art. 38, even if all these acts are not considered to be violations of "obligations" in the strict sense of the term.[6] The Charter does not only not prescribe that the enforcements actions referred to in Articles 39, 41, and 42, shall be directed only against a Member which has violated one of its obligations under the Charter, it does even not prescribe that the enforcement measures shall be directed only against a Member guilty of a threat to the peace, breach of the peace, or act of aggression. The Charter simply authorizes the Security Council to take such measures after having determined the existence of any threat to the peace, etc., without binding the Security Council with respect to the state against which these measures shall be directed.[7]

---

[6] The Report of Rapporteur on Chapter VIII, Section B (of the Dumbarton Oaks Proposals corresponding to Chapter VII of the Charter), Doc. 881, III/3/46, June 10, 1945, pp. 3 f. contains the following statements: "A number of amendments referring to paragraphs 1 and 2 were directed at limiting the very great freedom which, in the Dumbarton Oaks Proposals, is left to the Council in determining what action, if any, to take. Some of these amendments were designed to make more precise the Council's obligation to act in accordance with the purposes and principles of the Organization and the provisions of the Charter. The Committee considered that, since such specifications were already stated in Chapter VI defining the powers of the Council, it was unnecessary to make special mention of them in the present chapter. The Committee similarly put aside a proposal which would have obligated the Council to aid any party submitting the judicial settlement. It believed that this unduly restricted the Council's freedom of action and that cases might arise where a party refusing to submit to a judicial settlement might not necessarily be at fault. A more protracted discussion developed in the Committee on the possible insertion in paragraph 2, Section B, Chapter VIII, of the determination of acts of aggression. Various amendments proposed on this subject recalled the definitions written into a number of treaties concluded before this war but did not claim to specify all cases of aggression. They proposed a list of eventualities in which intervention by the Council would be automatic. At the same time they would have left to the Council the power to determine the other cases in which it should likewise intervene. Although this proposition evoked considerable support, it nevertheless became clear to a majority of the Committee that a preliminary definition of aggression went beyond the possibilities of this Conference and the purpose of the Charter. The progress of the technique of modern warfare renders very difficult the definition of all cases of aggression. It may be noted that, the list of such cases being necessarily incomplete, the Council would have a tendency to consider of less importance the acts not mentioned therein; those omissions would encourage the aggressor to distort the definition or might delay action by the Council. Furthermore, in the other cases listed, automatic action by the Council might bring about a premature application of enforcement measures. The Committee therefore decided to adhere to the text drawn up at Dumbarton Oaks and to leave to the Council the entire decision as to what constitutes a threat to peace, a breach of the peace, or an act of aggression."

[7] The Report to the President, p. 92, stresses that the action on the part of the Security Council is not "automatic"; previous determination of the existence of a threat to the peace, breach of the peace, or act of aggression is necessary. The Report states that it has been intentionally conferred upon the Security Council "ample authority to decide what constitutes a threat to the peace, a breach of peace, or an act of aggression, and to decide also which of the disputing parties has been mainly at fault." However, a decision of the Security Council with respect to the question which of the parties is right and which is

Art. 40 stipulates that the Security Council may, before deciding upon the enforcement measures, "call upon the parties concerned" to comply with certain provisional measures. This provision presupposes that the threat to the peace, breach of the peace, or act of aggression against which the enforcement measures shall be taken must be involved in the relation between two or more definite states: "the parties concerned." But it is quite possible, it is even the rule, that only one of the parties concerned is guilty of a threat to the peace, breach of the peace, or act of aggression. The Charter does not prescribe that the Security Council shall direct the enforcement action exclusively against the party guilty of such conduct. It is true that Art. 24, par. 2 of the Charter stipulates that the Security Council in discharging its duties shall act in accordance with the Purposes and Principles of the United Nations, among which "conformity with the principles of justice and international law (Art. 1, par. 1) is established. However, this postulate refers only to the Organization's Purpose to bring about settlement of disputes or adjustment of situations, not to the enforcement actions;[8] and Art. 2, par. 3 obligates only the Members to settle their disputes in a way that "justice" is not endangered. And even if it is assumed that the Security Council is bound to conform its enforcement actions with the principles of justice and international law, it has the choice between justice and law, which are not identical. Consequently it may consider it to be just to direct enforcement action against a party which legally, that is, from the point of view of international law, is not wrong, since it has not violated any obligation imposed upon it by the text of the Charter.[9]

---

wrong, is not at all mentioned in the Charter. The Security Council is not bound to decide this question at all. Cf. note 9.

[8] Committee I/1 voted 19 in favor and 15 against on the proposal that the words "in conformity with the principles of justice and international law" in Art. 1, par. 1, be placed in the first line after the words "peace and security." Since the proposal lacked a two-thirds majority it was not adopted. The Committee voted 19 in favor and 12 against on a proposal to add the word "justice" after the words "peace and security" in the first line. Since the proposal lacked a two-thirds majority it was not accepted.

The Report to the President, p. 85, mentions the request made at the San Francisco Conference to limit "the Security Council in its decisions by referring to principles of international law and justice"; it states that due observance of justice and international law was assured by Articles 1 and 2 of the Charter, and: "the Security Council should not be hampered by detailed direction of its activity."

[9] In the Hearings (p. 282), Mr. Pasvolsky interpreted Art. 39 to mean: "the Council does not have to wait until there is a determination of who is right and who is wrong. The problem is to stop the fighting or to remove the threat to the peace as soon as possible."

VII.

This situation may be interpreted in a twofold manner. It may be argued that the enforcement measures determined in Articles 39, 41, 42, and 45, are not "sanctions" since they are not established as reaction against a violation of obligations under the Charter. The only genuine sanctions provided for by the Charter are expulsion from the Organization according to Art. 6, and suspension from the right of voting in the General Assembly according to Art. 19. The enforcement actions are purely political measures to be used by the Security Council at its discretion for the purpose to maintain or restore international peace. This interpretation may be confirmed by the fact that according to Art. 39, the first Article of Chapter VII, the Security Council, after having determined the existence of a threat to the peace, breach of the peace, or act of aggression, may not only resort to enforcement action but may "make recommendations."[10] It

[10] Committee 3 to Commission II decided that the text of Art. 39 and 40 "should be interpreted in accordance with the scope of the following observations, the inclusion of which in the Report [of the Rapporteur] was unanimously approved by the Committee": "In using the word 'recommendations' in Section B [Chap. VII of the Charter], as already found in paragraph 5, Section A [Art. 36, par. 1 of the Charter] the Committee has intended to show that the action of the Council so far as it relates to the peaceful settlement of a dispute or to situations giving rise to a threat of war, a breach of the peace, or aggression, should be considered as governed by the provisions contained in Section A [Chap. VI of the Charter]. Under such an hypothesis, the Council would in reality pursue simultaneously two distinct actions, one having for its object the settlement of the dispute or the difficulty, and the other the enforcement or provisional measures, each of which is governed by appropriate section in Chapter VIII [Chap. VI and VII of the Charter]." Report of the Rapporteur on Chapter VIII, Section B (of the Dumbarton Oaks Proposals corresponding to Chapter VII of the Charter), Doc. 881, III/3/46, Pune 10, 1945, p. 6. It is difficult to understand how the Security Council can "pursue simultaneously" action under Art. 36, par. 1 and Art. 37, par. 2, that is to say, recommend appropriate procedures or methods of adjustment or terms of settlement, and action under Art. 39, that is to say, recommendations under this Article. Recommendations under Art. 39 need not necessarily be different from recommendations made under Art. 36, par. 1 or Art. 37, par. 2. In this respect the actions are not "distinct." It seems that, according to the intentions of the Charter, the conditions under which recommendations under Art. 36, par. 1 or Art. 37, par. 2, and those under which recommendations under Art. 39 may be made, are different. Recommendations under Art. 36, par. 1 and Art. 37, par. 2 may be made if the continuance of the situation or the dispute is likely to endanger the maintenance of international peace and security; recommendations under Art. 39 may be made if there exists a threat to the peace. If these two conditions are really distinguishable, then action under Art. 36, par. 1 or Art. 37, par. 2 may be taken in one case and action under Art. 39 in another case. Then it is impossible to "pursue simultantously" both. If, however, there is no difference between a situation being a "threat to the peace and the continuance of a situation (including disputes) being likely to endanger peace," the Security Codncil has the choice between making recommendations under Art. 36, par. 1 or Art. 37, par. 2 and making recommendations under Art. 39: the choice between two actions, not the possibility of pursuing simultaneously both. Action under Art. 36, par. 1 an dArt. 37, par. 2 is different from action under Art. 39 in so far as the rule excluding members of the Security Council parties to a dispute from voting applies to the former but not to the latter.

has the choice between the two different measures of which only the former could have the character of a sanction. The fact that the Charter in the Chapter entitled "Action with respect to threats to the Peace, Breaches of the Peace, and Acts of Aggression" does not only provide enforcement actions but also the making of recommendations, may allow the conclusion that this Chapter is not intended to deal particularly with sanctions. The Charter does not determine what kind of recommendation the Security Council may make under Art. 39. Hence any kind of recommendation is permissible; and if the Security Council has determined the existence of a threat to the peace involved in a dispute, it may make, under Aft. 39, the same recommendations as those it is authorized to make under Art. 37, par. 2 after having determined that the continuance of the dispute is likely to endanger the maintenance of international peace. Besides, it is hardly adequate to authorize the Security Council to make recommendations after it has determined the existence of a threat to the peace, breach of the peace or act of aggression. Such recommendation may be justifiable in case of a threat to the peace of the Security Council had no opportunity of making recommendations in an earlier stage of affairs, when the situation was only "likely to endanger the peace" (Art. 34). In case of an act of aggression or another breach of the peace, however, only enforcement action seems to be appropriate.[11] Under the Charter the Security Council may act in this way; but the Charter does not prescribe this course of action.

To interpret enforcement measures taken in accordance with Art. 39 not as sanctions, but as political measures to be used by the Security Council at its discretion, would be in conformity with the general tendency which prevailed in drafting the Charter: the predominance of the political over the legal approach. This interpretation, however, leads to the consequence that with respect to enforcement measures there is no difference between a Member which has violated its obligations under the Charter, and a Member which is not guilty of any such violation. The latter, as well as the former,

---

[11] The Commentary to Art. 39 and 40 adopted by Committee 3 to Commission III contains also the following statement: "It is the Committee's view that the power given to the Council under paragraphs 1 and 2 [Art. 39 and 40 of the Charter] not to resort to the measures contemplated in paragraphs 3 and 4 [Art. 41 and 42 of the Charter], or to resort to them only after having sought to maintain or restore peace by inviting the parties to consent to certain conservatory measures, refers above all to the presumption of a threat of war. The Committee is unanimous in the belief that, on the contrary, in the case of flagrant aggression imperiling the existence of a member of the Organization, enforcement measures should be taken without delay, and to the full extent required by circumstances, except that the Council should at the same time endeavor to persuade the aggressor to abandon its venture, by the means contemplated in Section A and by prescribing conservatory measures." Report of Rapporteur on Chapter VIII, Section B, Doc. 881, III/3/46, June 10, 1945, p. 6.

may be subjected to enforcement actions if the Security Council deems it necessary for the maintenance or restoration of peace. An enforcement action is an evil much harder than the severest sanction applicable to a violator of the Charter, namely, expulsion from the Organization.

However, the interpretation according to which the enforcement actions are merely political measures, is not the only possible one. It may be argued that in accordance with general international law a forcible interference in the sphere of interest of a state, that is reprisals or war, is permitted only as a reaction against a violation of law, that is to say, as sanction. Since the enforcement actions determined by Articles 39, 41, 42, and 45 of the Charter constitute forcible interference in the sphere of interests of a state, they must be interpreted as sanctions if the Charter is supposed to be in conformity with general international law. If the enforcement actions are sanctions, then any conduct against which the Security Council is authorized by the Charter to react with enforcement actions must have the character of a violation of the Charter. Consequently, the Members of the Organization have not only the obligations expressly formulated in the text of the Charter, but the obligation to refrain from any conduct against which the Security Council might take enforcement action, and the Security Council may take enforcement action against the state guilty of any conduct which the Security Council considers to be a threat to the peace, breach of the peace or act of aggression; this in spite of the fact that according to the wording of Art. 39 the Security Council is authorized to take enforcement action against any state whatever after having determined the existence of any threat to the peace, breach of the peace, or act of aggression. Since the Security Council is completely free in its determination of what is a threat to the peace, breach of the peace or act of aggression, it may especially determine as such any conduct of a state which constitutes non-compliance with any act of the Security Council or the General Assembly whether it is called "decision," "recommendation," "call" or "plan."[12] According to this

[12] In Art. 11 the General Assembly is authorized to make "recommendations" with regard to principles governing disarmament and the regulation of armaments." In Art. 26 the Security Council is authorized to formulate "plans to be submitted to Members of the United Nations for the establishment of a system for the regulation of armaments." These "plans" have the same character as "recommendations." In the Hearings (p. 264) Mr. Pasvolsky interpreted the term "plans" in Art. 26 to mean: "The recommendations as to the precise methods and the precise system of regulation would be made by the Security Council" (in contradistinction to the recommendation of a general "principle" to be made by the General Assembly under Art. 11, par. 1). By the phrase "for the establishment of a system for the regulation of armaments" probably international treaties concerning disarmament concluded among the Member States

interpretation, a Member may be under an obligation to act in a certain way although the wording of the Charter referring to this action does not imply the idea of an obligation. This is of particular importance with respect to the "recommendations" of the General Assembly and the Security Council. Whether such "recommendations" constitutes an obligation of the Member to which it is directed, depends upon whether the Security Council will consider, under Art. 39, non-compliance with the recommendation as a threat to the peace or breach of the peace. If it does so and takes enforcement action against the Member the latter must be considered to have been obliged to comply with the so-called "recommendation," which—according to this interpretation—is in truth a binding decision. Since it is difficult to foresee whether the Security Council will consider in a concrete case non-compliance with a recommendation or any other conduct of a state as a threat to the peace or breach of the peace and have as a condition of enforcement action, a state of uncertainty may prevail. Such undesirable effect could have been avoided by using in Art. 39 the same formula as in Art. 2, par. 4. As pointed out the words "act of aggression" in the text of Art. 39 are superfluous, since their meaning is covered by the term "breach of the peace." To use in Art. 39 the phrase "threat or use of force" instead of "threat to the peace or breach of the peace" would also have had the advantage that the enforcement actions were without any doubt conditioned by violation of the obligation imposed upon the Members in Art. 2, par. 4.

The difference between the two interpretations is rather of theoretical than of practical importance. Both, however, reveal the extraordinary power which the Charter has conferred upon the Security Council. The latter is not bound, it is only authorized, to take enforcement action under the conditions determined in Art. 39. It may, for political reasons, not be willing or, due to its voting procedure, not be able to work. Since, on the other hand, self-help is, in principle, prohibited a situation may occur under the Charter where it is impossible to enforce the law against violations other than those committed by armed attack (Art. 51). This is no improvement of the legal

are meant. This is the interpretation presented by Mr. Pasvolsky in the Hearings (p. 262). The Security Council under Art. 26 has only to recommend such treaties. What happens if the one or another Member refuses to conclude such treaty recommended by the Security Council? In the Hearings (p. 261) the Chairman of the Committee asked: "There is no compulsion whatsoever, no authority to impose disarmament unless the nations affected agree to it and sign a treaty to that effect?" and Mr. Pasvolsky answered in the affirmative. But here again the fact had been ignored that the Security Council may, under Art. 39, determine such a conduct as a threat to the peace and take enforcement action against the state concerned.

status as it existed under the Covenant and even under general international law prior to the Charter.

VIII.

The enforcement actions as well as all the other measures which may be interpreted to be sanctions under the Charter are to be directed against states as such, not against individuals. This in spite of the fact that under the Charter individuals may be appointed or elected with the effect of being directly organs of the United Nations; as, for instance, the Secretary General and the members of the staff of the Secretariat. Sanctions to be directed against states as such constitute collective, not individual responsibility. The Charter does establish only collective responsibility of states for violation of the Charter, not responsibility of the individuals who—in their capacity as organs of a state or in their capacity as organs of the United Nations—have Committed by their own conduct the violation of the Charter. This is of particular importance in respect to those violations of the Charter which have the character of an illegal use of force. In this respect the Charter remains far behind the Agreement concluded on August 8, 1945, at London, for the Prosecution of European Axis War Criminals. This treaty establishes individual criminal responsibility for "crimes against peace" committed by persons acting whether as individuals or as heads of state or as responsible officials in government departments (Art. 6 and 7 of the Charter of the International Military Tribunal, annexed to the Agreement). The individual criminal responsibility of the persons concerned is established by the Agreement authorizing an International Military Tribunal to impose upon these individuals on convicition, death or such other punishment as shall be determined by it to be just (Art. 27 of the Charter annexed to the Agreement).

The Agreement of London applies only to subjects and organs of the vanquished European Axis Powers, not to subjects or organs of the states Members of the United Nations. Hence criminal individual responsibility for violation of the rules prohibiting war, as established by the Agreement without the consent of the vanquished states, will hardly be recognized as a principle of a new international law. To achieve this effect it would have been necessary to insert the principle into the Charter as a general rule applicable to the subjects and organs of all the Members of the United Nations and—through Art. 2, par. 6—to all the other states of the world.

IX.

Enforcement actions under Chapter VII may be preceded by "provisional measures." Art. 40 stipulates:

> In order to prevent an aggravation of the situation, the Security Council may, before making the recommendations or deciding upon the measures provided for in Article 39, call upon the parties concerned to comply with such provisional measures as it deems necessary or desirable. Such provisional measures shall be without prejudice to the rights, claims, or position of the parties concerned. The Security Council shall duly take account of failure to comply with such provisional measures.

The "call" to comply with the "provisional measures" which the Security Council deems necessary or desirable is to be made after the Security Council has determined, in accordance with Art. 39, the existence of a threat to the peace, breach of the peace, or act of aggression. The Security Council has first to decide upon such provisional measures and then "call" upon the parties concerned to comply with them. In the Report to the President[13] it has been pointed out, that it is not the Security Council which takes the provisional measures, as it takes enforcement action. It is the parties themselves which are to take the provisional measures in accordance with the "call" of the Security Council. However, this interpretation is correct only, if the "call" of the Security Council is not binding upon the Members. Whether the "call" is an act constituting an obligation of the parties concerned or a simple "recommendation" depends on the consequences which the Charter attaches to a failure to comply with the call (or, as Art. 40 says, not quite correctly: with the provisional measures). The "call" stipulated in Art. 40 is the only one of the various calls provided for in the Charter with regard to which the consequence of failure to comply therewith is expressly stipulated. The Security Council "shall duly take account" of failure to comply with the call. That can mean only that failure to comply with the call shall influence the action which the Security Council is to take according to Art. 39; especially its choice between recommendations and enforcement actions, and its decision against which of the parties and what kind of enforcement action shall be taken. Hence the call according to Art. 40 is rather a command than a simple recommendation of provisional measures; and the provisional measures referred to in Art. 40 may be considered to be taken by the Security Council.

---

[13] The Report to the President, p. 92, says: "the disputing parties will be asked to undertake themselves upon recommendation of the Security Council" the provisional measures. These measures "are therefore not to be regarded as preliminary sanctions." It is interesting that the Report characterizes the "call" referred to in Art. 40 as "recommendation," and that it emphasizes that the provisional measures are not "sanctions." But are the enforcement measures "sanctions"? To this question the Report gives no clear answer.

The provisional measures may be characterized as "preventive"; for their purpose is to "prevent" an aggravation of the situation. This does not mean that the enforcement actions to be taken after the call to comply with provisional measures may not have a "preventive" character too. It has already been explained why the provisional measures taken under Art. 40 in spite of their preventive character must not be interpreted to be "preventive actions" referred to in Art. 5 (or Art. 2, par. 5, and Art. 50). Hence suspension from the exercise of the rights of membership in conformity with Art. 5 is not applicable to a Member upon which the Security Council has called under Art. 40 to comply with the provisional measures which it deems necessary or desirable.

The Charter differentiates the "provisional measures" from other measures, especially from the enforcement measures, by stipulating in Art. 40 that "provisional measures shall be without prejudice to the rights, claims, or position of the parties concerned." No such provision is made with respect to the measures taken in accordance with Articles 41, 42 and 45. This may indicate that these measures—in contradistinction to mere provisional measures—can effect a change in the legal situation of the parties concerned. This possibility may be of great importance for the interpretation of the provisions concerning the power of the Security Council in the settlement of disputes. Art. 37, par. 2 authorizes the Security Council "to recommend such terms of settlement as it may consider appropriate." According to Art. 24, par. 2 the Security Council, in discharging this duty, "shall act in accordance with the Purposes and Principles of the United Nations." Art. 1, par. 1 declares as a Purpose of the United Nations "to bring about by peaceful means, and in conformity with the principles of justice and international law, adjustment or settlement of disputes or situations which might lead to a breach of the peace." Since justice may be in conflict with international law the Security Council has the choice between both. That means that it may recommend a settlement of the dispute not in conformity with positive law, but in conformity with justice and this means: since the Charter does not define this concept, in conformity with what the Security Council considers to be justice in the case at hand. This amounts to the same as: "recommend such terms of settlement as it may consider appropriate," which is the formula used in Art. 37, par. 2. If the Security Council considers non-compliance with such recommendation a threat to the peace it may—under Art. 39—take enforcement action against the Member which refuses to comply with the recommendation. That means that the Security Council is empowered to enforce its recommendation, even if it is not in conformity with positive law. This interpretation is confirmed by Art. 40. Since the Charter stipulates only with reference to the "provisional measures" that they shall be without prejudice to the rights of the parties concerned, it is permitted to assume that enforcement measures may be prejudicial to the rights of the parties concerned. By taking enforcement measures the Security Council may create new law. If so, these measures may assume the character of legislative acts and are "political" actions—like any legislative act—only when viewed from the angle of the law existing prior to their enactment.

X.

The Charter, as pointed out, establishes two kinds of enforcement measures: measures not involving, and measures involving, the use of armed force. Measures not involving the use of armed force may, according to Art. 41, "include complete or partial interruption of economic relations and of rail, sea, air, postal, telegraphic, radio, and other means of communication, and the severance of diplomatic relations." The measures involving the use of armed force are characterized in Art. 42 as "action by air, sea, or land forces;" and "may include demonstrations, blockade, and other operations by air, sea, or land forces of the Members of the United Nations." This action may have the character of ordinary military measures. According to Art. 43, par. 1, "All Members of the United Nations" are obliged "to make available to the Security Council, on its call and in accordance with a special agreement or agreements, armed forces, assistance, and facilities, including rights of passage, necessary for the purpose of maintaining international peace and security." Art. 45 stipulates: "In order to enable the United Nations to take urgent military measures, Members"—it is not said as in Art. 43: all Members—"shall hold immediately available national air-force contingents for combined international enforcement action."

What is the nature of the act by which the Security Council takes an enforcement measure determined in Articles 41, 42 and 45? It is a "decision." According to Art. 39, the Security Council shall "decide" what measures shall be taken in accordance with Articles 41 and 42. According to Art. 41, the Security Council may "decide" what measures not involving the use of armed force are to be employed to give effect to its "decisions." Art. 42 says only, the Security Council may "take such action by air, sea, or land forces as may be necessary, etc.," without expressly authorizing the Security Council to adopt a "decision." But Art. 44 says: "When the Security Council has "decided" to use force, etc."; and Art. 48, with reference to all enforcement actions, speaks of the action required to carry out the "decisions" of the Security Council and stipulates: Such "decisions" shall be carried out, etc.

After having made this decision, the Security Council first "determines" by which Members of the United Nations the required action shall be carried out. Art. 48, par. 1 stipulates: "The action required to carry out the decision of the Security Council for the maintenance of international peace and security shall be taken by all the Members of the United Nations or by some of them, as the Security Council may determine." After having determined by which Members the action shall be carried out, the Security Council "calls" upon the Members either "to apply" measures not involving the use of armed force according to Art. 41, or—as formulated in Art. 44—"to provide armed forces in fulfillment of the obligations assumed under Art. 43." If "urgent military measures" are to be taken the Security Council calls upon some Members to provide the national air force contingents in fulfillment of the obligations assumed under Art. 45. This is not expressly provided by the Charter, but may be inferred by analogy.

These "calls" constitute obligation of the Members concerned, since they are based on "decisions" of the Security Council, and the Members are—according to Art. 25—obliged to accept and carry out the decisions of the Security Council.

In this respect there exists a striking difference between the Charter of the United Nations and the Covenant of the League of Nations. The latter is characterized by a complete decentralization of the procedure for the application of enforcement measures. Art. 16 of the Covenant leaves it to the Members of the League to decide whether another Member has violated its obligations under the Covenant and whether enforcement measures not involving the use of armed force shall be applied. With respect to these measures no intervention of the Council is provided for. With respect to the measures involving the use of armed force, the Covenant does not impose upon the Members any obligation. It only authorizes the Council to make recommendations. It is to be considered a great progress that the Charter has centralized both the decision as to the question whether there exists a threat to the peace, breach of the peace, or act of aggression and the decision as to the application of the enforcement measure whether involving or not involving the use of armed force, and has imposed upon the Members the obligation to carry out this decision.

Since the Member which by a call of the Security Council is obliged to apply enforcement measures of the one or other kind may not be a member of the Security Council, the question arises whether such Member may or shall be invited to participate in the discussion or decision of the Security Council with respect to the enforcement measure. Art. 4, par. 5 of the Covenant stipulates that "any Member of the League not represented on the Council shall be invited to send a Representative to sit as a member at any meeting of the Council during the consideration of matters specially affecting the interests of that Member of the League." That means that the Member whose interests are affected has the right to participate not only in the discussion but also in the decision of the Council. Since according to Art. 5, par. 1 decisions of the Council require the agreement of all the Members of the League represented at the meeting, no decision can be taken against the vote of the Member whose interests are affected (except the decision refers to a dispute to which the Member is a party). The Charter provides in Art. 31:

> Any Member of the United Nations which is not a member of the Security Council may participate, without vote, in the discussion of any question brought before the Security Council whenever the latter considers that the interests of that Member are specially affected.

It seems that this provision is not applicable when the Security Council's decision implies the use of armed force. For another Article regulating the participation of Members of the United Nations which are not represented on the Security Council expressly refers to the case that such a state is called upon to apply measures involving the use of armed force. It is Art. 44 which stipulates:

> When the Security Council has decided to use force it shall, before calling upon a Member not represented on it to provide armed forces in fulfillment of the obligations assumed under Article 43, invite that Member, if the Member so desires, to participate in the decisions of the Security Council concerning the employment of contingents of that Member's armed forces.

However, the interpretation is not absolutely excluded that in case a non-member of the Security Council is called upon to apply measures involving the use of armed forces, both, Article 31 and Article 44, are applicable.

In case the Security Council decides that measures not involving the use of armed force shall be employed and calls upon a certain Member to apply such measures according to Art. 41, Article 31 is applicable. This Article—in contradistinction to Art. 44—does not provide expressly for an "invitation" of the Member. It stipulates only that the Member may participate, without vote, in the discussion of the question whenever the Security Council "considers that the interests of that Member are specially affected." Since this question is to be decided by the Security Council, the Member cannot participate in the discussion without being invited by the Security Council. There was no reason to omit in Art. 31 the provision of an "invitation" of the Member. The invitation depends on the discretion of the Security Council; and the Member has no right to participate in the decision by which it is called upon to apply the enforcement measure.

In case the Security Council decides that measures involving the use of armed force shall be applied—the wording of Art. 44: to use "force" is not correct, since "force" and "armed force" are not identical—and intends to call upon a Member which is not represented in the Security Council to provide armed forces in fulfillment of the obligations assumed in Art. 43, it shall—according to Art. 44—invite that Member, if the Member so desires, "to participate in the decisions of the Security Council concerning the employment of contingents of that Member's armed forces." If one accepts the interpretation according to which in this case Art. 31 too, is applicable, then the Security Council may, if it considers the interests of that Member specifically affected, invite that Member to participate in the discussion; but if the member so desires, the Security Council shall invite it to participate in the decisions. If the invitation to participate in the decisions is interpreted as implying also the invitation to participate in the discussion, the question whether Art. 44, or both Articles 31 and 44, are applicable in case the Security Council intends to call upon a non-member of the Security Council to make available armed forces according to Articles 43 or 45, is of practical importance only insofar as the application of Art. 31 depends on the discretion of the Security Council, whereas the application of Art. 44 on the desire of the Member, which has a right to be invited under Art. 44, but no right under Art. 31. The Member may or may not exercise this right.

It is not very clear what is meant by the words "decisions of the Security Council concerning the employment of contingents of that Member's armed forces." It can not mean that the Member is allowed to participate in the decision by which it is "called," under Art. 43, "to make available" armed forces, for Art. 44 refers exber is under "obligation" to comply with the "call" to "make available" armed forces, it can not participate in the decisison to "provide armed forces," as formulated in Art. 44, since it can not have the right to vote against such decision. The right to participate can only refer to decisions concerning the manner in which the contingents of armed forces, made available to the Security Council by that Member, are to be employed; a provision which corresponds to that of Art. 47, according to which "there shall be established a Military

Staff Committee to advise and assist the Security Council on all questions relating to the Security Council's military requirements for the maintenance of international peace and security, the employment and command of forces placed at its disposal, etc.,'' and according to which ''any Member of the United Nations not permanently represented on the Committee''—only the permanent members of the Security Council are permanently represented on the Committee—''shall be invited by the Committee to be associated with it when the efficient discharge of the Committee's responsibilities requires the participation of that Member in its work.'' Since Art. 44 refers only to decisions ''concerning the employment of contingents'' of the Member, the latter is not entitled to participate in decisions not concerning the ''armed forces'' but other kinds of ''assistance, and facilities, including rights of passage,'' made available to the Security Council by the Member according to Art. 43, par. 1.[14]

---

[14] The Report of Rapporteur on Chapter VIII, Section B (of the Dumbarton Oaks Proposals corresponding to Chapter VII of the Charter), Doc. 881, III/3/46, June 10, 1945, p. 3, contains the following statement with reference to Art. 44: ''This supplementary paragraph takes into account the concern very vigorously expressed by many powers that the military forces put at the disposition of the Security Council by the special agreements might be used without the contributing nation having had a voice in the Council meetings where it is decided to use these forces. Henceforth, every member not represented on the Council may participate, with the right of voting, in the deliberations of the Council when it is a question of the utilization of its armed forces. To repeat a well chosen expression of the Delegate of the Netherlands, the principle of 'no military action without representation' was accepted by the Committee.

This decision is of such a nature as to reassure, in large measure, the middle and small powers, which might otherwise have feared that they were giving *carte blanche* to the Council in the particularly serious domain of the utilization of their military forces outside their national frontiers.

It has not appeared possible to extend the conception of *ad hoc* representation on the Council to include those instances wherein the latter discusses, not the utilization of armed forces, but rather the use of facilities and assistance to be furnished by a state not a member of the Council. As a matter of fact, it was recognized that the adoption of such a formula might unduly increase the number of Council members and delay its decisions.

Furthermore, the desire to take into consideration the well-founded observations of the Egyptian Delegation on this subject led the Committee to approve the explanations furnished by the Delegations of Great Britain, the U. S. S. R., France, and Greece. Accordingly, it was recognized that the question 'of facilities and assistance' was already covered by the special agreements contemplated in paragraph 5, Section B, Chapter VIII. Paragraph 9 of the said chapter contemplates, on the other hand, that a state not represented on the Military Staff Committee should be invited to be associated with it should the need arise. Finally, paragraph 4 of Section D, Chapter VI, formally provides for the participation in the Council discussions of any member of the Organization whose interests may be particularly affected.

In the light of these assurances, which covered its point of view, the Delegation of Egypt withdrew its amendment.''

The same Report, p. 9, contains the following statement with reference to Art. 43, par. 2: ''The new text . . . specifies . . . that the special agreements should fix the degree of readiness and the general location of the forces. It thus incorporates the substance of the amendments introduced by France to para-

The decisions of the Security Council concerning the employment of contingents of the Member invited to participate in this decision under Art. 44 requires according to Art. 27, par. 3 an affirmative vote of seven members including the concurring votes of the permanent members. In case Art. 44 is applied twelve representatives instead of eleven, may participate in the vote, so that a majority of seven opposes a minority of five instead of four. The Member invited to participate in the decision may be outvoted. This is excluded under Art. 4, par. 5 and Art. 5, par. 1 of the Covenant.

The "call" to provide armed forces according to Art. 43, par. 1, and Art. 44, or national air-force contingents held immediately available for urgent military measures according to Art. 45, is to be carried out "in accordance with a special agreement or agreements" (Art. 43, par. 1). "Such agreement or agreements shall govern the number and types of forces, their degree of readiness, and general location, and the nature of the facilitic sand assistance to be provided" (Art. 43, par. 2). With reference to the national air force contingents held immediately available for "urgent military matters," Art. 45 provides: "The strength and degree of readiness of these contingents and plans for their combined action shall be determined, within the limits laid down in the special agreement or agreements referred to in Article 43, by the Security Council with the assistance of the Military Staff Committee. This provision may be interpreted to mean that the agreement or agreements referred to in Art. 43 shall determine, with respect to the national air force contingents, nothing else but what they shall determine in conformity with Art. 43, par. 2 with respect to the contingents made available for the military enforcement action under Art. 42. The "plans for their combined action" shall not be determined by these agreements, although the wording of Art. 45 is not very clear in this point. According to Art. 43 and 45 the agreements do not refer to the question as to whether or not the Member shall provide armed forces and especially national air-force contingents; they refer to the question how these obligations established by the Charter itself shall be fulfilled on the part of the Member. It seems that they do not refer to the question as to how the Security Council shall or may use the armed force placed at its disposal by the Member state.[15] They shall govern, it is true, the "general loca-

---

graphs 5 and 6 concerning the period within which forces must be made available and the zones of occupation of the military contingents."

[15] In the Hearings (pp. 651 ff.), Senator George asked the question: "Mr. Dulles, speaking of the agreement or agreements which are to govern the numbers and types of forces and the degree of readiness and general location and the nature of the facilities and assistance to be provided, as set out in article 43, subsection 2, is it your opinion that the United States in making available to the Council military contingents could restrict the place of the use of the forces—

tion'' of the armed forces made available to the Security Council by the Member. The words ''general location,'' which have been added to the text of the corresponding provision of the Dumbarton Oaks Proposals (Chapter VIII, Section B, par. 5), are not very clear. It is doubtful whether they should be interpreted to mean the territories where the Security Council is authorized to use the contingent placed to its disposal by the Member. Besides, the provision concerning the contents of the special agreements is of problematical value. The Members cannot be compelled to conclude the agreements and, thus, are in a position to make their consent dependent upon conditions not provided by the Charter.

Art. 43, par. 3 stipulates:

> The agreement or agreements shall be negotiated as soon as possible on the initiative of the Security Council. They shall be concluded between the Security Council and Members or between the Security Council and groups of Members and shall be subject to ratification by the signatory states in accordance with their respective constitutional processes.

These agreements are international treaties. Contracting parties to such a treaty are: on the one side, the United Nations Organization represented by the Security Council, on the other side Members or ''groups of Members.'' That means that the United Nations represented by the Security Council is a juristic person of international law. It is not quite correct to state—as Art. 43, par. 3 does—that the agreements concerned shall be concluded between the Security Council and Members, etc. The Security Council can not be an international personality because it is only the organ of an international

---

aside from the question of whether we could want to?'' Whereupon Mr. Dulles answered: ''There is no doubt in my mind but what we can do that.'' In reply to a question of Senator Austin, Mr. Dulles made the following statement: ''In my opinion, Senator Austin, the phrase that they are 'to be made available in accordance with a special agreement or agreements' enables the states to make any conditions which they want to attach, and I would think it quite probable that even the great powers, while they would probably want to make some forces available for use anywhere, that there would be some understanding whereby they would at least supply the preponderant force in the areas of their proximity.'' If it was intended to leave to the special agreements to determine where the contingents placed at the disposal of the Security Council may be used by the latter, that is to say, to restrict the use of these forces, the words ''their general location'' were certainly not adequate to express this idea. But in reply to a question to Senator George, Mr. Dulles made the following statement: ''If restricted use of our military contingent were desired, Senator, I would think the wise thing to do would be to make provision for that in your basic military agreement which will come before the Senate for ratification.'' Then Senator George asked: ''But aside from where it should be made, it is your opinion that a limitation of that kind could be, consistently with the obligations assumed under the Charter, inserted?'' Whereupon Mr. Dulles stated: ''There is no doubt in my mind whatever as to that. Many of the smaller member states already are clear in their own minds that they will not agree to make contingents available except for use in relatively near areas. Whether or not a great power wants to do that is a question of policy. As to the fact that it may do it, there is no doubt whatever in my mind.''

union of states which, through its Charter, has the quality of a person of international law. Contracting party to the agreement can be only the United Nations, represented by the Security Council.[16] And the Security Council can fulfill this function only if its organization established according to Articles 29 and 30 contains a provision authorizing one of the individuals representing the Members on the Security Council—for instance, its President—to represent the Security Council in relation to the Members of the Organization and other states.

If a "group" of Members as such is to be a contracting party to the agreement it is supposed to be a juristic person too. But this is possible only if it is an organized group endowed with an organ competent to represent the "group" in relation to other persons of international law. According to Art. 52, par. 1 the Members are authorized to establish "regional arrangements or agencies" and according to Art. 53, par. 1 the Security Council "shall, where appropriate, utilize such regional arrangements or agencies for enforcement action under its authority." If the "regional arrangement" consists in the establishment of an organized union (confederacy) of states on the basis of an international treaty by which an organ is instituted competent to represent this union or confederacy of states in relation to the Security Council, the provision of Art. 43, par. 3 according to which the agreement is to be concluded between the Security Council and a "group" of Members is applicable. If, however, the "group" of the Members is not organized in this manner, the agreement can be concluded only between the Security Council and the individual members of the "group." If not organized, the group has no legal personality and cannot conclude — as a "group" — international treaties.

If an international treaty is subject to ratification at all—it can be ratified only by the contracting parties. Art. 43, par. 3, stipulates that the agreement or agreements referred to in paragraphs 1 and 2 of this Article shall be subject to ratification in accordance with the respective constitutional processes. But this provision refers only to the "signatory states"; as if the agreements were to be concluded only by states, and not by unions of states, such as the United Nations represented by the Security Council and "groups of Members" represented according to their constitution. If this provision means that the agreement concluded by the United Nations represented by

---

[16] The Report to the President, p. 96, states: "The party which will have to call for the forces and direct their use, namely the Security Council, will be the same party to which are owed the obligations to provide them." The latter party is not the Security Council but the Organization of which the Security Council is an organ.

the Security Council or by a "group of Members" is to be ratified by the states which are members of the Security Council or the "group," the agreement cannot be considered as having been concluded by the Security Council, that is to say, by the United Nations represented by the Security Council, or by the "group," but by the states which are the members of the Security Council or the group. In this case, too, the United Nations Organization represented by the Security Council, or the "group" are only "signatories" to the agreement, not contracting parties, since an international treaty—if subject to ratification—is not concluded by the acts of "signature" but by the acts of ratification. The opposite doctrine is hardly tenable. But even if the doctrine is adopted that an international treaty is "concluded" by the signatories, no ratification of the agreement on the part of the United Nations represented by the Security Council is possible since the Charter does not provide for a special process for ratification of treaties concluded by the United Nations. Ratification of the agreement—which according to the incorrect wording of Art. 43, par. 3 is concluded by the "Security Council"—on the part of the states which are the members of the Security Council is not in conformity with the text of this paragraph, which prescribes "ratification by the signatory states;" and the Security Council is not a signatory "state"; even if the Security Council—and not the United Nations represented by it—were to be considered as the "signatory." Hence Art. 43, par. 3 can be hardly interpreted in another way than by assuming that ratification of the agreement is not necessary on the part of the Security Council or the United Nations represented by it; or on the part of a "group of Members" if the latter concludes the agreement as a juristic person, but only on the part of the individual states which are signatories to the agreement.

It would have been possible to subject the agreement signed by the Security Council to ratification on the part of the states which are the members of this body, thus conferring upon these states a power similar to that of the Senate according the Constitution of the United States. If this was the intention of the Charter, its wording is certainly not adequate. But ratification on the part of the members of the Security Council in addition to the signing of the agreement on the part of the Security Council representing the United Nations, is quite superfluous, even from the point of view of the Constitution of the United States. For the decision by which the Security Council gives its consent to the conclusion of the agreement requires, according to Art. 27, an affirmative vote of seven members including the concurring votes of the permanent members; and the state which assumes obligations by the agreement has in any way to ratify it. If it is an agreement concluded with the United States it can be brought about only with the consent of the representative of the United States on the Security Council and with the consent and advice of the Senate ratifying the agreement. The situation is doubtful only if the agreement is concluded with a "group" of states of which the United States is only a member; which means that this "group" as such is a signatory to the agreement, not a single state. Since only ratification "by the signatory states" is required the agreement may, according to the Charter, come into force without ratification on the part of the single states members of the "group." Ratification by the United States—apart from its own Constitution—is necessary only if the constitution of the "group" requires such ratification for the conclusion of the agreement with the Security Council.

XI.

An international treaty presupposes the voluntary cooperation of all the parties to the treaty. There is no obligation to conclude a treaty, and the Members of the United Nations are certainly not under any obligation to conclude with the Security Council the agreements referred to in Articles 43 and 45. If such agreements cannot be brought about the provisions of Chapter VII concerning the employment of measures involving the use of armed force are not applicable. How, then, can the Purpose of the United Nations be fulfilled which the Charter places before all other Purposes: to take effective collective measures for the prevention and removal of threats to the peace, and for the suppression of acts of aggression as long as the agreements referred to in Art. 43 have not come into force? To this question Art. 106 gives an answer:

> "Pending the coming into force of such special agreements referred to in Article 43 as in the opinion of the Security Council enable it to begin the exercise of its responsibilities under Article 42, the parties to the Four Nation Declaration, signed at Moscow, October 30, 1943, and France, shall, in accordance with the provisions of paragraph 5 of the Declaration, consult with one another and as occasion requires with other Members of the United Nations with a view to such joint action on behalf of the Organization as may be necessary for the purpose of maintaining international peace and security."

Par. 5 of the Four Power Declaration runs as follows:

> "The Governments of the United States of America, the United Kingdom, the Soviet Union and China: ... jointly declare ... 5. That for the purpose of maintaining international peace and security pending the re-establishment of law and order and the inauguration of a system of general security, they will consult with one another and as occasion requires with other Members of the United Nations with a view to joint action on behalf of the community of nations."

During the period between the coming into force of the Charter and the establishment of the special agreements referred to in Art. 43

the Security Council will fulfill its function under Chapter VI and Art. 39, 40, 41 of Chapter VII, insofar as their application does not presuppose the establishment of the special agreements. "The Security Council will refrain from the performance of its responsibilities only with respect to those functions the exercise of which is suspended until the conclusion of the special agreements indicated in Article 43."[17] During this period the function of the Organization determined in Art. 42 will be exercised by the five Powers determined in Art. 106. They are identical with the powers having permanent seats in the Security Council. Art. 106 authorizes these Powers to take "joint action on behalf of the Organization" only as long as the Security Council has not expressed the opinion that enough special agreements have come into force to enable it to begin the exercise of its responsibilities under Art. 42. As soon as the Security Council declares that it is able to exercise these responsibilities, the authorization of Art. 106 ceases to be valid. Is it valid as long as the Security Council does not make such a declaration or is any joint action under Art. 106 possible only if the Security Council positively declares not yet to be able to exercise its responsibilities under Art. 42? Both interpretations are possible. What majority is required for the decision that sufficient agreements have come into force to enable the Security Council to exercise its responsibilities under Art. 42? Since this decision does not refer to a procedural matter Art. 27, par. 3 is applicable. That means that each of the five Great Powers which are authorized to take joint action and at the same time permanent members of the Security Council may prevent such a decision, and, if such a decision is required to terminate the authorization of Art. 106, to prolong this authorization *ad libitum*.[17a]

Art. 106 does not directly authorize the five Powers to take joint action. Just as Par. 5 of the Four Power Declaration, Art. 106 stipulates only that the five Powers shall "consult" with one another and,

---

[17] Cf. Report of Committee 3 to Commission III on Chapter XII (Dumb. Oaks) Doc. 1095, III/3/50, June 19, 1945, p. 3.

[17a] The Summary Report of Meetings of Subcommittee 3/A, May 31 and June 1, To Consider Redrafft of Chapter XII (Dumbarton Oaks Proposals), contains the following interpretation of paragraph 1 of Chapter XII of the Dumbarton Oaks Proposals, corresponding to Art. 106 of the Charter: "The decision to turn over the military enforcement responsibilities of the signatories of the Moscow Declaration and of France to the Security Council should be the responsibility of the signatory powers and of France and not of the Security Council." (Doc. WD 68, III/3/A.) This sentence has been changed later to read as follows: "The decision to turn over to the Security Council the responsibilities for the maintenance of peace assumed by the signatories of the Moscow Declaration and by France should be the responsibility of the signatory powers and of France." (Doc. 765, III/3/39, June 3, 1945, p. 3.) According to this interpretation, it is upon the five powers determined in Art. 106 to decide when the authority conferred upon them by Art. 106 terminates.

if necessary with other Members of the United Nations, with a view to a "joint action." Such "joint action"[18] is not obligatory and could not be made obligatory by the Charter, since such action is possible only if an agreement is reached with respect to the action. It is not very clear whether an agreement of all the five Great Powers is necessary in order that the "joint action" can be taken, or whether two or three or four of them may take such "joint action" even if the other or the others do not agree. That an agreement of the five suffices, seems to be certain; and since the "joint action" is to be taken "on behalf of the Organization" the interpretation seems to be most plausible, that all five Powers must agree in order to make "joint action" possible. Such agreement has no less voluntary character than the special agreements referred to in Art. 43. If it can not be reached, the most important function of the Organization, the function which forms the core of the Charter, can not be performed.

The purpose of Art. 106 is to make provisions for the period the Security Council is not in a position to take the military enforcement action referred to in Art. 42. Such enforcement action is—according to Art. 39—permissible only after the Security Council, by a vote of the five permanent members plus two non-permanent members, has determined the existence of threat to the peace, breach of the peace or act of aggression. Article 106, however, authorizes the five Powers, which are the permanent members of the Security Council, to take joint action, including enforcement action, on behalf of the Organization without obliging them to determine beforehand the existence of a threat to the peace, breach of the peace or act of aggression, or to act only after the Security Council has made this determination and decided according to Art. 42 that a military enforcement action is necessary. The fact that the special agreements referred to in Art. 43 are not yet in force, is no reason to suspend the just mentioned functions of the Security Council with respect to the military enforcement action to be taken by the five Powers designated in Art.

---

[18] The Report of Committee 3 to Commission III on Chapter XXI (Dumbarton Oaks Proposals, corresponding to Chapter XV of the Charter), Doc. 1095, III/3/50, June 19, 1945, p. 3, contains the following statements: "Several Delegations, especially those of Canada, Egypt and Belgium, have requested the Delegations submitting the amendment to make a declaration explaining the meaning of the words 'joint action on behalf of the Organization.' The Delegate of the United Kingdom pointed out that it was impossible to define such an action, since the powers of the Security Council would gradually develop in proportion to the forces which would be put at its disposal. The Delegate of the United States, for his part, explained that the meaning of the words, 'joint action,' might be deduced without difficulty from the first part of the paragraph, which referred to the special agreements mentioned in Chapter VIII, Section B, paragraph 5."

106. But according to this Article the five Powers in taking their joint action are completely independent from the Security Council, and their action is limited only insofar as it is, in their opinion, necessary for the purpose of maintaining international peace and security. This action is in a still lesser degree than the enforcement action of the Security Council, a sanction, that is to say a reaction of the Organization against violation of the obligations imposed upon the Members by the Charter. Art. 106 confers upon the Governments thus designated an almost unlimited power for an indefinite period of time.[19]

---

[19] The Report to the President, pp. 161 ff., contains the following statements with respect to Art. 106: "Nowhere more clearly than in the Chapter on transitional security arrangements is there manifested the intelligent realism of the architects of the United Nations. From the outset these men faced squarely the fact that the Charter could not create an Organization which would spring into being possessed from the start of full power to maintain international peace and security. They knew that if it was to succeed it must not be burdened at the outset with responsibilities which it could not immediately fulfill. They knew that it must be given time to become firmly established. . . . Armed force is the ultimate sanction in the enforcement of peace. The United Nations will have no armed force at its disposal until at least some of the agreements envisaged in Article 43 become effective. This difficulty is taken care of by Article 106, the first of the two which comprise this short Chapter. During the indefinite time which must elapse before the Security Council decides that enough of the agreements are effective for it to begin the exercise of its responsibilities for military enforcement action, the five great powers which are to be the permanent members of the Security Council undertake to exercise on behalf of the Organization, jointly and with other members of the United Nations, such security functions as may be necessary." The text of Article 106 "makes it clear that not all the special arrangements for the provision of armed forces have to be ratified—a process which might take years—before the Security Council can take military enforcement action. Only such agreements as the Security Council itself deems sufficient for the purpose need be in effect. Article 106 does not, as some delegates wished it to, define precisely the functions of the Security Council during the interim period, nor the limits of the joint action which the five powers may take. Had it done so it would have established a fixed and frozen division of responsibility, and thus defeated its own purpose, which is to provide for the orderly growth of the Security Council's functions, to permit it to take successively larger bites of responsibility. This flexibility is accomplished in two ways. First, only the power to take military enforcement action is withheld from the Security Council and that only temporarily. Secondly, the five powers which will be permanent members of the Security Council are granted authority to fill the temporary vacuum to the extent necessary by taking action on behalf of the Organization. It should be emphasized, however, that this five-power action must be joint and that consultation with other members of the United Nations is provided for. In other words, while this action may, in a formal sense, be outside the framework of the Organization, it is to be completely within the spirit of the Charter." The fact that Art. 106 authorizes military enforcement action without the precautions laid down in Art. 39 and 42 makes it very doubtful whether the Article is "completely within the spirit of the Charter." It is very dangerous to maintain that the spirit of the Charter is expressed by an Article which confers upon the five great Powers unrestricted dominance over the World.

The Report of Committee 3 to Commission III on Chapter XII (of the Dumbarton Oaks Proposals corresponding to Chapter XVII of the Charter), Doc. 1095, III/3/50, June 19, 1945, p. 2, contains the following statement: "The Delegations have not questioned the necessity, during the transitional period, of the collective responsibility of the Five Powers which derives from the obligations which they have assumed during the course of hostilities. But some delega-

XII.

One of the most important questions concerning the enforcement action involving the use of armed force is the question as to the power the Charter has conferred upon the Security Council with regard to the armed forces which the Members are obliged to make available to the Security Council according to Art. 43, and especially the national air-force contingents which certain Members are obliged to hold immediately available for urgent military measures according to Art. 45. It is the question whether there is established by the Charter an armed force of the United Nations distinct from the armed forces of the Members or whether the military enforcement actions provided for by the Charter are to be executed by the Members through their own armed forces.

There can be no doubt that the armed forces which—to have recourse to an expression used by Art. 47, par. 1 and 3—are "placed at the disposal of the Security Council" are composed of the contingents of the armed forces of several Members. Art. 42 says that the military action taken by the Security Council may include "operations by air, sea, or land forces of Members of the United Nations." Art. 48, par. 1 expressly states:

> The action required to carry out the decisions of the Security Council for the maintenance of international peace and security shall be taken by all the Members of the United Nations or by some of them, as the Security Council may determine.

And paragraph 2 of this Article stipulates:

> Such decisions shall be carried out by the Members of the United Nations directly and through their action in the appropriate international agencies of which they are members.

The provision that the decisions of the Security Council with regard to enforcement action shall be carried out by the Members "directly" seems to indicate that the enforcement action involving the use of armed force is according to the Charter decentralized to the same extent as it was according to the Covenant. But there are other pro-

---

tions, particularly the Canadian Delegation, called attention to the fact that paragraph 1 would grant temporary authority to the Five Powers for a period which might be very long, and that this authority was qualified only by the phrase, 'joint action on behalf of the Organization.' They, therefore, asked that paragraph 1 further specify the powers granted to the Five Powers during the interim period, especially with respect to responsibility for the peaceful settlement of disputes according to Section A, Chapter VIII, and the matter of ascertaining which special agreements would need to become effective before the Security Council assumes its full responsibility." The only difference between Chapter XII, par. 1 of the Dumbarton Oaks Proposals and Art. 106 of the Charter is that France has been added to the four Powers of the Moscow Declaration, and that the Security Council has been authorized to decide the question as to whether sufficient agreements have come into force to enable it to exercise its responsibilities under Art. 43. The powers granted to the five Powers are not more specified in Art. 106 than they were in the Dumbarton Oaks Proposals.

visions of the Charter which have no equivalent in the Covenant and which are not consistent with the principle stipulated in Art. 48, par. 2, that the enforcement actions shall be carried out by the Members of the United Nations "directly." The provisions confer upon the Security Council the right to "dispose" of the armed forces made available to it by the Members.

We have already mentioned the fact that the Charter expressly uses this term in Art. 47. In the same direction points the formula: the Members shall make available to the Security Council armed forces (Art. 43, par. 1). The Charter expressly states in Art. 42 that the Security Council "may take such action by air, sea, or land forces as may be necessary to maintain or restore international peace and security." The Covenant of the League of Nations carefully avoids to speak of an action of the Council or the League. Art. 16, par. 2 only authorizes the Council to "recommend to the several Governments concerned what effective military, naval or air forces the Members of the League shall severally contribute to the armed forces to be used to protect the covenants of the League." It does not say: to the armed forces of the League, or to be used by the Council. The armed forces contributed by the Members of the League are not "at the disposal" of the Council. The Security Council, however, is authorized by Art. 46 to make "plans for the application of armed force" which can mean only: for the armed forces made available to it by the Members. Finally, the Charter attaches a Military Staff Committee as an auxiliary organ to the Security Council. This indicates that the Security Council is supposed to exercise—directly or indirectly—the function of a commander-in-chief of the armed forces placed at its disposal. Art. 47, par. 1 stipulates:

> There shall be established a Military Staff Committee to advise and assist the Security Council on all questions relating to the Security Council's military requirements for the maintenance of international peace and security, the employment and command of forces placed at its disposal, the regulation of armaments, and possible disarmament.[20]

Paragraph 3 of the same Article stipulates:

> The Military Staff Committee shall be responsible under the Security Council for the strategic direction of any armed forces placed at the disposal of the Security Council. Questions relating to the command of such forces shall be worked out subsequently.

It is not expressly said that the "command" and the "strategic di-

[20] The wording of Art. 47, par. 1, "There *shall* be established a Military Staff Committee..." is not correct. The Military Staff Committee *is* established by the Charter just as the General Assembly, the Security Council and the other principal organs of the United Nations "are established" as Art. 7 correctly formulates it. No act of establishing the Military Staff Committee is necessary, and no such act is provided for by the Charter.

rection'' are to be exercised by the Security Council. This interpretation, however, is not only a possible, but the most adequate one in view of the fact that the forces are placed at the Security Council's ''disposal.''

There can be no doubt that a body composed of eleven members whose decisions require an affirmative vote of seven members including the concurring votes of the permanent members, is not a proper organ to work as a commander-in-chief of armed forces. But according to Art. 29, ''the Security Council may establish such subsidiary organs as it deems necessary for the performance of its functions.'' In conformity with this Article the Security Council may very well appoint a commander-in-chief. Whether such a commander-in-chief is appointed by the Security Council or whether the command and strategic direction of the armed forces placed at the disposal of the Security Council is exercised directly by this body, the contingents of the armed forces of the various Members are united under a unified command and may properly be characterized as the armed force of the United Nations. With reference to the ''urgent military measures'' to be taken according to Art. 45, the Charter speaks of ''combined international enforcement action.'' Since the Security Council is an organ of the United Nations any instrument used in such action is an instrument of the United Nations. ''To take effective collective measures for the prevention and removal of threats to the peace, and for the suppression of acts of aggression or other breaches of the peace''—which means enforcement actions—is declared by Art. 1, par. 1 of the Charter as one of the Purposes of the United Nations. Art. 24, par. 1 speaks of ''prompt and effective action by the United Nations.'' It is, therefore, not consistent and, in addition, not correct, if this paragraph states that in order to ensure such action by the United Nations ''its Members confer on the Security Council primary responsibility for the maintenance of international peace and security, and agree that in carrying out its duties under this responsibility the Security Council acts on their behalf.'' It is not the Members that confer on the Security Council any responsibility, it is the Charter that constitutes all duties, rights, and responsibilities of the Members as well as of the organs of the United Nations; and its organs, especially the Security Council, do not act on behalf of the Members but on behalf of the Organization. The inconsistent and incorrect construction adopted by Art. 24, par. 1 is the result of an ideology which is a typical element of the dogma of sovereignty and whose purpose is to let disappear the Organization behind its Members, to ignore the existence of the Organization in favor of its sovereign members.

That the Organization has an international character is the consequence of the fact that it is established by an international treaty and that its centralization does not exceed a certain degree. Even if "international," it is usual to consider it as an entity different from its Members especially when it has—as the United Nations have—the character of an international person capable of concluding international treaties. Any action and in particular the enforcement action of an international organization is an "international" action. That the "urgent military measures" to be taken by the United Nations are characterized in Art. 45 as "combined international enforcement action" is quite compatible with designating the armed forces placed at the disposal of the Security Council as "armed forces of the United Nations." The action is a "combined" action if the armed forces placed at the disposal of the Security Council are composed of the contingents of several Members; but it is an international action, and the armed force, are armed forces of the United Nations even if the action is performed by the Security Council through the contingent of one Member only. However, Art. 48 stipulates that the action of the Security Council for the maintenance of international peace and security "shall be taken by all the Members of the United Nations or by some of them, as the Security Council may determine." According to the wording of this provision the Security Council seems not to be authorized to call upon one Member only to apply measures not involving the use of armed force according to Art. 41; or to provide armed forces in fulfillment of the obligations assumed under Art. 43; or a national airforce contingent in accordance with Art. 45; so that the enforcement action will be always a "combined" international action although the Charter uses this term with reference only to urgent military measures.

The result of the preceding analysis is that the above raised question whether the Charter establishes an armed force of the United Nations distinct from the armed forces of the Members, or whether the enforcement actions provided for by the Charter are to be executed by the Members through their own armed forces, cannot be answered simply in one or in the other way. The Charter has created a type which is in the midst between two extremes. Regarding its composition, the armed forces by which the action of the Security Council for the maintenance or restoration of peace is performed, are the combined armed forces of all or several members. In this respect there is no armed force of the United Nations distinct from the armed forces of the Members. However, the armed forces of the Members are unified by being placed at the disposal and under the command

and the strategic direction of a single body, the Security Council assisted by a Military Staff Committee. By virtue of this unitary command the United Nations Organization has its own armed force although it is composed of the armed forces of its Members.[21]

---

[21] In his statement at the opening meeting of Committee III/3 of the San Francisco Conference the Rapporteur (Delegate of the French Republic) said: "Theoretically the international force can be conceived in several forms. A permanent army of an international nature over and above the national armies or even replacing them, national contingents under international command, which presupposes control by permanent international military staff; national contingents at the disposal of an international body, but remaining under the command of their national army." The type of armed force chosen by the Charter corresponds, according to the Rapporteur, to the second of the three plans he exposed.

He declared, that "the question of command is not settled in advance" by the Dumbarton Oaks Proposals, "it is only provided that the Military Staff Committee is responsible under the Security Council for the strategic direction of any armed forces placed at the disposal of the Security Council, and that questions of command of forces shall be worked out subsequently." The Rapporteur seems to have overseen that Chapter VIII, Section B, par. 9, of the Dumbarton Oaks Proposals which is identical with Art. 47, par. 1 of the Charter, expressly provides that the Military Staff Committee shall "advise and assist the Security Council on all questions relating to . . . the employment and command of forces placed at its disposal." Doc. 134, III/3/3, May 9, 1945.

In the Hearings (p. 301), the following discussion took place: "Senator Tunnell: Under the provisions in this Charter, is it contemplated that there be any standing force called for by the Security Council? Senator Hatch: Do you mean an international police force? Senator Tunnell: Yes. Mr. Pasvolsky: No; there would be national contingents available for combined action." The answer of Mr. Pasvolsky does not take into consideration the military command under which the national contingents are placed. The term "international police force" is quite applicable to the armed forces under the command of the Security Council, if the term is taken literally, meaning that the armed forces have an international character and are not the instrument of a super-state.

NOTES AND QUESTIONS

1. Omitted from this article is Kelsen's discussion of expulsion from membership (Article 6), withdrawal of rights and privileges (Article 5), suspension of voting rights (Article 19) and the consequences of violating the provisions of Article 102(1). These provisions, in conjunction with those of Chapters VI and VII of the Charter, comprehend the full range of sanctions authorized for use by the Organization. His discussion of these matters includes an analysis of the appropriate forums for interpreting and applying these rules. For additional discussion of Article 6, see Chapter 3.
2. Kelsen's discussion of Article 19, dealing with suspension of the voting privileges of Member States in the event of their failure to meet financial obligations to the Organization, foreshadows the controversy that has plagued the United Nations since 1961. There are other respects in which Kelsen's article anticipated problems and controversies that have arisen in the last decade. This is interesting if only to undermine those critics who have argued that Kelsen's formal method of legal analysis is sterile because it fails to consider the social and political context of law. This article on Charter sanctions shows that Kelsen's logical method of analysis discloses the ambiguities of legal prescription that emerge as political and legal problems when practice accumulates around conflict.

3. It would be useful to contrast the meanings given to the words "political" and "legal" by Kelsen with those of McDougal, and Kaplan and Katzenbach.
4. Kelsen's analysis of the sanctioning system embodied in the Charter of the United Nations suggests, for comparison and contrast, the distinctive features of sanctioning systems operative in domestic societies. The sanctions of the organized international community are geared to deal with states rather than individuals, and the measures developed are designed to persuade the decision-making elite that acts on behalf of the state to be responsive to rules of world order forbidding recourse to violence except in self-defense against an armed attack (Article 51). Recently some have argued that the United Nations is defective as a sanctioning system precisely because it seeks to deter states rather than individuals who act in their behalf. Oskar Morgenstern has maintained in general terms that the most effective deterrent upon aggressive political behavior would be "a government homing missile" that would have the peculiar property of seeking, finding, and destroying only the decision-makers responsible for initiating the violence. In Section C of this chapter, Arthur Waskow suggests directing sanctions against individuals, and Roger Fisher has developed an especially imaginative approach to solving sanctioning problems, taking special pains to *avoid* directing sanctions at states *as such*. See Fisher's essay reprinted in **IV-5B-C**. Clark and Sohn impose sanctions on individuals, as well as upon states.

   The traditional view is that international law imposes rights and duties only upon states. In time, a number of exceptions have grown up. For example, a concept of international crime grew up around the efforts of the international community *as a whole* to avoid such activities as piracy, slave-trading, the transport of narcotics, and counterfeiting of currency. The individuals apprehended for such conduct were punished on the basis of the international legal system, as well as on the basis of the national laws of the apprehending state. This experience culminated in the Nuremberg and Tokyo War Crimes Trials after World War II in which the leaders of Germany and Japan were prosecuted for, among other things, their role in planning and inciting the conduct of aggressive war. These prosecutions remain controversial both in terms of their contribution to world order and as a fulfillment of some kind of concept of international justice. Do you think that national leaders are influenced at all in their conduct of foreign policy by a fear that if a war results and is lost they may be held criminally responsible? Is it likely that the aggressor will lose all wars? Is it likely that leaders of the victorious side will be prosecuted?

   For an extreme view that the prospect of criminal responsibility will inhibit aggressive national behavior, consider the following passage by the Indian jurist, Satyavrata R. Patel: "The Nuremberg Trial constitutes a milestone in the progress of international law. Henceforward, international law is made a stronger law. It has made future world wars almost impossible. If war would come at all, commanders would hesitate to kill innocent persons. The trial marks an epoch, because no man can escape the consequences of war crimes. International law shall not tolerate any violation of the laws of warfare." Patel, *A Textbook of International Law* (Asia Publishing House, New York, 1964) p. 185.

The final paper in this section—Wolfgang Friedmann, "National Sovereignty, International Cooperation, and the Reality of International Law," *UCLA Law Review*, vol. 10 (May, 1963) pp. 739–753—adds an important dimension to our study of the establishment of an international police force. Brierly provided a set of principles useful for the establishment of a collective security system that assumed the persistence of national defense systems. Kelsen's analysis sets the stage for relating the establishment of an international police force to an entire system of sanctioning procedures for use in the organized international community. In the following paper Wolfgang Friedmann suggests that in searching for proper enforcement and sanctioning machinery to support the rule of Article 2(4) of the Charter, it is important to take advantage of the actual development of opportunities for increasing international cooperation, and to appreciate the relevance of this cooperation to the policies of diminishing the likelihood and intensity of violence in world affairs. Although Friedmann thinks that a stable world order requires strong central legal structures, his position in the following selection points to the fact that there are limitations upon the use of police forces as sanctioning devices, and that police sanctions based on punishment and deprivation need to be supplemented by a wider view of what is a sanction, so as to encompass activities in the social, economic, and welfare spheres. Friedmann is saying that force—in its military aspect —does not exhaust the possibilities for bringing effective pressure to bear upon states to refrain from violence. His line of argument is developed as part of an overall demonstration of "the reality" of international law and contributes generally to our understanding of law as a constituent aspect of contemporary world order.

It is Friedmann's view that "cooperative" law has been developing in the international community. He notes that traditional international law was mainly a collection of "don'ts" or prohibitions with coercive sanctions as appropriate remedies when the rules were violated. In view of the tremendous growth in a concern for matters of security, communication, and welfare, Friedmann suggests that "it is in the positive rules of cooperation for common interest" that new law is emerging. Friedmann's analysis, then, may be read as a proposal for encouraging the development of world order through the establishment of international machinery of a sort that would benefit the economic and welfare interests of every state, making exclusion a significant denial.

NATIONAL SOVEREIGNTY, INTERNATIONAL COOPERATION, AND THE REALITY OF INTERNATIONAL LAW

Wolfgang Friedmann

Whether, and to what extent, international law is "real law," *i.e.*, a system of rules felt to be binding and generally observed by those supposed to be subjected to it, is still one of the most debated questions of jurisprudence. It is also a matter of deep and intimate concern to the peoples of the mid-twentieth century for whom the difference between a fictitious system of international law, and one that is "real," *i.e.*, that imposes order and restraint upon the states which are the predominant, though no longer the only subjects of international law, may mean the difference between life and death.

It is the thesis of this article that the usual discussions about the reality of international law are based on a concept of law which is theoretically inadequate in its exclusive emphasis on the punitive aspects of law, and that, in contemporary international society, there is rapidly developing a new type of "cooperative international law," for which the traditional concept of sanction is largely meaningless since its effectiveness is predominantly predicated upon the privilege of participation in joint endeavors serving the common interests of mankind.

In order to understand the theoretical and practical importance of this approach to the problem of the reality of international law, and in particular of the meaning and function of sanction in contemporary international society, it will be necessary briefly to recapitulate the principal schools of thought concerning the reality of international law.

Discussions about the reality of international law have centered around three major problems: First, the question of hierarchy or supremacy. For those who cannot conceive of any legal order without a clearly defined sovereign there can be no international law unless there is an international sovereign to whose commands or threats the states are subordinate. Second, divergent conceptions of the reality of international law are linked with divergent definitions of the law. To those who, like Austin, Kelsen, and their followers, regard the sanction as an essential element of the legal norm, international law cannot be real unless it is equipped with sanctions. From this follow many divergent views as to whether and what type of sanction is at the disposal of the international society. A third and essentially different line of approach centers around the sense of obligation. In this approach the central question is whether and to what extent the states—and any other actual or potential subjects of international law—feel a sense of obligation regarding the rules of international law.

This sense of obligation derives from a variety of motives. A recognition of the predominant common interest in observing a code of conduct, a sense of moral responsibility for the observance of civilized rules of behavior freely agreed upon, habit, and, of course, a fear of the consequences of violation are all important component factors in the sense of obedience, although their respective weight varies greatly from nation to nation and from one historical period to another, and although it is greatly influenced by the particular political conditions of any particular state at a given time. The fear of punishment for nonobedience is thus present in the sense of obligation. But it is no longer the crucial element in the assessment of the reality of international law. This approach detaches the question of the reality of international law both from the presupposition of a legal hierarchy, culminating in an international sovereign, and from the requisite of a sanction, *i.e.,* the threat of a punishment inflicted for the violation of the international legal norm as an essential condition of its legal character.

Although these three basic approaches to the reality of international law have not always been kept clearly distinct from one another, there would be little point in returning to this matter unless the changing scope and dimensions of contemporary international law gave—as they most definitely do, in this writer's opinion—an essentially new aspect to the whole discussion. In order to understand why this is so it will be necessary briefly to restate the principal points of controversy.

Generally, though by no means necessarily, the views that any "real" legal norm properly speaking must be equipped with a sanction, go together. This goes back to Austin, who linked sovereignty, command, and sanction in his famous definition of law:

> Laws properly so called are a species of *commands*. But, being a *command,* every law properly so called flows from a *determinate* source. . . . [W]henever a *command* is expressed or intimated, one party signifies a wish that another shall do or forbear: and the latter is obnoxious to an evil which the former intends to inflict in case the wish be disregarded. . . . Every sanction properly so called is an eventual evil *annexed to a command.*

> Every positive law, or every law simply and strictly so called, is set by a sovereign person, or a sovereign body of persons, to a member or members of the independent political society wherein that person or body is sovereign or supreme.[1]

With a definition of laws that required both a definite sovereign and a definite sanction to back up a legal command, Austin quite logically characterized international law as "positive morality."

In the dual postulate of the hierarchy of legal norms issuing from a sovereign, and the requirement of a sanction as an indispensable element of a legal norm, Kelsen entirely agrees with Austin. The dehumanization of the legal norm from an imperative to a relation of condition and sequence is not a relevant distinction for our purposes. It is not in the basic requirements of sovereign and sanction but in the characterization of contemporary international society as containing depersonalized elements of both that Kelsen deviates from Austin, and in both respects his deviations are questionable.

Since there is no clearly defined sovereign in present-day international society comparable to the United States Constitution, the British Parliament, the Kremlin, or the Fascist government of Franco, Kelsen substitutes a kind of depersonalized sovereign, *i.e.*, the norm of general international law created by custom constituted by acts of states, which postulates that states ought to behave in conformity with the treaties they have concluded.[2] In other words, the sovereign is a general principle of conduct acknowledged by the states.

More questionable still is the characterization of war and reprisal as the sanctions of contemporary international law.[3] These paramount instruments of national policy—overwhelmingly used in the denial rather than in the implementation of international law—can, of course, be characterized as international law sanctions only insofar as they constitute reactions of the international community against a delict committed by a state. Kelsen arrives at his characterization of wars and reprisals as sanctions of international law by regarding the states as executants of international law in an international society that is, as yet, bereft of properly functioning organs

---

[1] 1 AUSTIN, LECTURES ON JURISPRUDENCE 182, 225-26 (4th ed. 1873); AUSTIN, THE PROVINCE OF JURISPRUDENCE DETERMINED 133, 193 (1954).

[2] KELSEN, PRINCIPLES OF INTERNATIONAL LAW 417-18 (1952). In this acceptance of *pacta sunt servanda* as the supreme legal norm of international conduct, Kelsen follows Anzilotti.

[3] See KELSEN, GENERAL THEORY OF LAW AND STATE 328-30 (1945); KELSEN, THE LEGAL PROCESS AND INTERNATIONAL ORDER (1934); KELSEN, REINE RECHTSLEHRE 321-28 (2d ed. 1960).

and must, therefore, devolve the affiliation of its norms upon the member states.[4] In this construction the states are both prosecutors and judges. The theoretical division of state actions into those that pursue national policy and those that execute international law obscures the fact that the international community does not dispose of sanctions of its own superior to the will of the states. Each state is exclusively competent to qualify its actions as a vindication of international law, and the usually conflicting claims of antagonists create legal anarchy, not order.[5] Only insofar as wars and reprisals were outlawed as instruments of national policy and became exclusive sanctions of the international community applied against the lawbreaker would it be justified to regard them as legal sanctions at the disposal of international society. To a limited extent, both the League of Nations Covenant and the United Nations Charter have outlawed wars, *i.e.,* wars of aggression as instruments of national policy.[6] It can accordingly be maintained that these prohibitions of international law as the higher norm invalidate inconsistent treaties of alliance or neutrality.

It cannot, however, be said that contemporary international community law, as embodied in the United Nations Charter, is equipped with sanctions against aggressive war comparable to the sanctions of municipal law as understood by Austin, Kelsen, and the great majority of positivists; namely, as a threat of punishment for violation of an order or prohibition. Under the Charter it is possible to obtain a decision—even against one of the permanent members of the Security Council—if it is involved as a party in a dispute, since any member of the Council must abstain from voting in a matter in which it is involved. But the execution of any decision, *i.e.,* punitive action against one of the permanent members, is subject to the veto; in other words, punitive action is not possible without its consent. To describe this as a sanction in the sense postulated by Austin, Kelsen, and others would be a distortion of the concept.[7]

It could, of course, be argued that the immunity of the five major powers which are the permanent members of the Security

---

[4] See KELSEN, REINE RECHTSLEHRE 323 (2d ed. 1960).

[5] For a recent criticism along the same lines, see ARON, PAIX ET GUERRE ENTRE LES NATIONS 706 (1962), which quotes Papaligouras.

[6] *Cf.* 2 OPPENHEIM, INTERNATIONAL LAW 292 (7th ed. Lauterpacht 1952).

[7] See Fitzmaurice, *The Foundations of the Authority of International Law and the Problem of Enforcement,* 19 MODERN L. REV. 1, 6 (1956): "as things are at present, neither of the main political organs of the United Nations can, in any but the most qualified sense, be regarded as an instrument for the enforcement of the legal rights of States, or the redress of legal wrongs *generally.*"

In the same sense, see HART, THE CONCEPT OF LAW 212 (1961): "We shall take it that neither Article 16 of the Covenant of the League of Nations nor Chapter VII of the United Nations Charter introduced into international law anything which can be equated with the sanctions of municipal law. "

Council[8] does not affect the legal system of the Charter, and that at worst the Big Five would be lawbreakers—violators of a system that continues to exist validly for the rest of the international community. Such a view must accept that, in terms of enforceability, there are two international legal orders, one for the five major powers, comprising some 500 million people and an overwhelming proportion of the military and industrial power of the earth, and another for the rest. Politically the maintenance of peace in such conditions depends not on legal sanctions but on the balance of power between the major states. This is, in effect, the contemporary position.

If the reality of the international legal order is to depend upon the dual requisites of a clearly defined sovereign and a punitive sanction, only the most strained construction can characterize the present system of international rules as a legal order. Austin would no doubt still view the contemporary international "law" as positive morality, as he did in his own time. And Kelsen must either strain the meaning of sovereign and sanction, or alternatively abandon his monistic approach; *i.e.*, the clear-cut alternative between international and national sovereignty which does not admit any possibility of compromise.

The great majority of contemporary international lawyers have taken the sense of obligation as the crucial test of the "reality" of international law. The general legal philosophy underlying this approach is that obedience to law does not necessarily rest upon either command or the threat of sanction but on the acceptance of a norm as binding. Within this general view, there is, however, a vast variety of approaches.

About the turn of the century, two noted German jurists attempted to formulate theoretical compromises between state sovereignty and the binding character of international law. Georg Jellinek derived the binding character of the customary rules of international law from the "self-limitation" of the states.[9] By consenting to observe the customary rules of international conduct, the states accepted these rules of conduct without abandoning their sovereignty.

---

[8] *I.e.*, the U.S.S.R., the United States, Great Britain, France, and China. Although the effective major power in China today is not the Chiang regime which represents China in the Security Council but Communist China which controls the overwhelming bulk of the Chinese territory and population, this does not alter the fact that China is among the powers exempt from the sanction processes of the United Nations. While Taiwan participates in the veto power, Communist China is altogether outside the Charter and the obligations imposed by it. The inclusion of Communist China would, of course, more than double the total population of the Big Five.

[9] JELLINEK, ALLGEMEINE STAATSLEHRE (1905).

The obvious weakness of this theory is that what states can consent to, they can also revoke. The self-limitation of states can derive normative character only from an already existing rule that a state is bound to keep its promises.[10] In other words, this theory postulates that the *pacta sunt servanda* principle, in order to constitute an effective basis of international law, must stand above the revocable consent of states.

A somewhat closer approximation to the last mentioned postulate is the theory of Triepel that agreements made between states merge into an objective body of conventions which the states are then no longer free to repudiate.[11] In this theory, the international norm of conduct does become superior to the will of the states, but only as a product, not as a presupposition of interstate agreement.

The great majority of contemporary international lawyers, who do ascribe legal character to the norms of international conduct, have abandoned these fragile constructions for the test of recognition and observance with a sense of obligation of the rules of international law. While not denying the absence of effective sanctions or the frequency of breaches of international law in the contemporary world, these writers see in the practice of states overwhelming acknowledgement of the existence of international law as an obligatory system.

> The best evidence for the existence of international law is that every actual state recognizes that it does exist and that it is itself under obligation to observe it. States may often violate international law, just as individuals often violate municipal law; but no more than individuals do states defend their violations by claiming that they are above the law. . . . States may defend their conduct in all sorts of other ways, by denying that the rule they are alleged to have broken is a rule of law, by appealing to a supposed right of self-preservation superior to the ordinary law, and by other excuses more or less sincerely believed in as the case may be; but they do not use the explanation which would obviously be the natural one if there were any doubt that international law has a real existence and that they are bound by it.[12]

---

[10] *Cf.* Fitzmaurice, *supra* note 7, at 9: "it is because international law already makes consent a source of obligation that obligations can arise from consent." See also Fitzmaurice, *The Law and Procedure of the International Court of Justice, 1954-9—General Principles and Sources of International Law*, 35 BRIT. YB. INT'L L. 183, 196 (1959): *pacta sunt servanda* "is a principle of natural law in the nature of *jus cogens* . . . a postulate of international law, giving the latter system an *objective* validity—i.e. a validity not dependent on the consent of the entities subject to the system."

[11] TRIEPEL, VÖLKERRECHT UND LANDESRECHT (1899).

[12] BRIERLY, THE OUTLOOK FOR INTERNATIONAL LAW 5 (1944). For similar points of view, see, *e.g.*, 1 HACKWORTH, DIGEST OF INTERNATIONAL LAW 12 (1940); Fitzmaurice, *supra* note 7; Jessup, *The Reality of International Law*, 18 FOREIGN AFFAIRS 244 (1940). See also Fisher, *Bringing Law To Bear on Governments*, 74 HARV. L. REV. 1130 (1961).

This view is overwhelmingly borne out by contemporary state practice. In recent times there have been some significant exceptions to the acceptance of international law as a standard of conduct. Both Mussolini, in his invasion of Ethiopia in 1935, and Hitler, in his attack on Poland, translated into practice their idea that international law should in no way derogate from the supreme freedom of national sovereignty and the implementation of national destiny through war. These attitudes eventually brought disaster to their champions.

Overwhelmingly, however, international disputes are tested and judged by reference to international law, even though, depending on a variety of factors of power and opportunity, the contestants may distort the facts or the law in their own interest. In the dispute over the legal status of occupied Berlin, both sides adduce legal arguments: the Western powers by reference to the occupation status established after the end of the war, the Soviet Union by reference to *rebus sic stantibus, i.e.,* the shattering of the foundations on which the four power regime was established. In Viet Nam, Laos, or the Congo all sides accuse each other of aggression. The difference between the former diplomacy and the contemporary references to international law lies in the existence of an organized forum of world opinion which, though often powerless to enforce even an overwhelming majority view on a strong party, is too important in the precarious balance of power to be ignored or despised. Without a rough balance of power between the major antagonists, the organized world opinion articulated in the United Nations might be more ineffective than it is at present. Coupled with the existence of such balance, this organized world opinion is an important factor. It is, of course, more potent in some situations than in others. When the U.S.S.R. bloodily suppressed the Hungarian Revolution in 1956, it rightly judged that the strength of its national interest in the preservation of the existing puppet regime, combined with her overwhelming logistic advantages vis-à-vis the forces of the West, whether organized inside or outside the United Nations, made armed intervention and violation of the Charter an acceptable risk. Similarly India, in 1961, judged that the combination of a number of favorable conditions—the almost bloodless occupation of Goa, the general distaste not only of the newer states of Asia and Africa but also of the Western democracies for Portuguese colonialism, the geographic and logistic conditions, and finally the reluctance of any major power to break openly with India—would make the venture feasible without overly adverse reactions. On the other hand, the United States, in abandoning its abortive intervention against the Castro regime in 1961, was guided in considerable measure by the reluctance to engage in what legally was an act of aggression in defiance of the Charter and organized world opinion. In 1962 the United States successfully countered an imminent danger to its security posed by the installation of medium-range Soviet missiles in Cuba by a quarantine which induced the Soviet Union to remove the missiles. Predominant opinion was that this action was justified by the right of self-defense against imminent aggression, and the unanimous support of the Organization of American States, a regional organization declared legitimate by article 52 of the United Nations Charter.

In numerous disputes which in earlier times would have led to war, the rules of international law have powerfully contributed to an attitude of restraint. To date they have at least helped to prevent such conflicts as the Korean partition, the Vietnamese or Laotian guerrilla wars, and above all, the Berlin conflict, from erupting into major war.

Analogies have often been drawn between the organization of early medieval society when states were powerless against the "overmighty subjects" and the contemporary condition of international society.[13] But there are also basic differences. Modern municipal law applies its commands and sanctions to a multitude of individuals, each of whom—with the possible exception of the giant corporations of our time— is interchangeable and relatively powerless. But the actors in the family of nations are states whose action engages the fate of hundreds of millions of individuals, and in present-day conditions, the possibility of the extinction of organized life on earth. While these are restraints of self-interest, international law today poses the only generally accepted standard of behavior by which right and wrong in provoking war and thus the almost inconceivably great responsibility for the consequences of major conflict can be judged.

In due course the international legal order will no doubt either have to be equipped with a more clearly established hierarchy of norms and more powerful sanctions, or decline and perish. The present is either an era of dawn or twilight. While the logical analyst must pose clear and irreconcilable alternatives between national and international sovereignty, there are in fact shades of each. International law today restrains sovereign states in some respects but leaves them free to act in others.[14]

If we confine our vision to the traditional system and scope of international law, we shall have to rest content with the belief and the hope that a general acceptance of international law, as the only

[13] See, *e.g.*, Jessup, *supra* note 12.
[14] *Cf.* HART, *op. cit. supra* note 7, at 218.

rational and universally acknowledged system of rules of international conduct, will by and large insure its continuity as a standard of reference and induce general observance by the family of nations, short of extreme situations in which the usual restraints would disappear and which in contemporary conditions would almost certainly spell universal disaster for mankind.

The force of these restraints imposed by the danger of obliteration is in a sense inverse to the duality of legal standards represented by the present sanctions system of the United Nations. While many of the small new states of Africa, Asia, or Latin America could engage in conflict without a general destruction of the international system, they must fear the potential imposition of the collective organized force of the United Nations—if it finds at least predominant support among the major powers—and the risk of their actions depends upon the likelihood of such sanctions being imposed. On the other hand, the major powers are legally immune from military sanctions but politically under far greater restraint, because wars in which they become involved are far more likely to lead to universal destruction. Such involvement may result not only from direct confrontation, but also from what Schwarzenberger terms "aggression by proxy," *i.e.*, assistance to a satellite, of which the war in Viet Nam is a typical illustration.

This entire approach, based on fear as the crucial factor—though still underlying all the discussions about the "reality" of international law—ignores the fundamentally different character of the developing "cooperative" law of nations—the steadily increasing scope and variety of international conventions, agreements, or, in some cases even new customs, which bind the nations, not in the traditional rules of abstention and respect, but in positive principles of cooperation for common interests. To some extent these new rules of cooperation express themselves in the growing network of permanent international organizations. In other fields they are still the subject of conventions which in time may produce permanent organizations. Be that as it may, this new and growing area of international law compels a far-reaching reconsideration of the meaning of "sanction" in contemporary international society, and through it, a reassessment of the strength of the ties that today bind nations to the observance of international rules of cooperation.

The traditional system of international law regulates the rules of coexistence between sovereign states. It is essentially a collection of "don'ts"; a vast, though far from watertight network of protective umbrellas. States must not be interfered with in their sovereignty on land and such parts of the sea as are claimed as territorial waters and in the air space above the land. They must now not be interfered with in the exclusive exploitation of the resources of the Continental Shelf. They are immune from jurisdiction by other states. Their citizens must be protected from arbitrary interference with their lives, properties, or other economic interests, even though the extent of this protection is now deeply controversial.

For the enforcement of this type of prohibitive and protective rules of conduct, the appropriate remedies are coercive sanctions, and in the absence of sanctions at the disposal of a supranational authority, the principal sanctions used by sovereign states against each other are war and reprisal, *i.e.*, the traditional instruments of national sovereignty. Reprisals may, of course, be economic as well as military.

But the immense intensification and amplification of the concerns for security, communication, and welfare are producing a different and constantly growing type of international law which develops principles and methods of cooperation. The implementation of many of these concerns is as yet in an embryonic stage. Thus the standards of labor and social welfare developed under the aegis of the International Labor Organization for the most part so far lack the universal authority—both in a legal and in a moral sense—which in many of the modern industrial democracies today would suffice to exclude a noncomplying employers' or employees' organization from the legitimate labor market and withhold from the offender the benefits of official recognition. But the day can be foreseen when the ILO conventions and directives will attain such force and when the stigma of noncompliance will mean exclusion from an international labor market. The effectiveness not only of the direct sanctions of fines and levies but of the exclusion from participation can already be much more clearly discerned in the more closely integrated and organized economic community of Western Europe. Thus an enterprise offending against the legal standards of employment will find itself excluded from potential participation in the benefits of loans or subventions, temporary import quotas, and other emergency measures that the High Authority of the European Coal and Steel Community has the power to impose in times of crisis.

The effectiveness of the sanction of nonparticipation will, at this stage of development of international society, differ greatly according to the degree of dependence of the state concerned on the activity or organization from which it may be excluded. Certainly the major states are generally better able to resist pressure of this kind than the smaller states, but it is submitted that—apart from the states that, by choice or necessity, are outside the legal nexus of international organization, such as Nazi Germany at one time and Communist China at the present—every state, large or small, is today very reluctant to abandon the benefits of participation in international organization. To begin at the most universal level, the two most powerful members of the United Nations, the United States and the Soviet Union, have been most careful not to let policy disagreements with each other or with the United Nations itself develop to the point of rupture.[15] Neither has to fear military sanction, but both attach the greatest importance to the opportunities offered by leading membership in the United Nations for the presentation of their position and the influencing of organized world opinion, as well as of informal contacts with each other, both before and behind the scenes. In the recent Budget Opinion of the International Court of Justice,[16] where the Court confirmed the power of the General Assembly to assess all Members for expenses arising out of the Congo and Middle East operations, the specter of exclusion loomed in the possibility that under article 19 of the Charter "a Member of the United Nations which is in arrears in the payment of its financial contributions to the organization shall have no vote in the General Assembly if the amount of its arrears equals or exceeds the amount of the contributions due from it for the preceding two full years." Although France and the Soviet Union, the two chief defaulters, have reiterated their refusal to pay, it is likely that both will avoid getting into the position where article 19 might be applicable, even though the chances of article 19 being applied against them are very slight.[17]

A more direct applicability of the sanction of nonparticipation for behavior contrary to international legal standards is offered by the increasingly important field of international economic development aid. The World Bank and its affiliates, which between them annually dispense well over a billion dollars worth of economic development aid, have no more or greater international sanctions in the traditional sense at their disposal than the international society at large. But if a borrowing state were to confiscate, without compensation and in a discriminatory manner, the property of foreign investors, or if it would violate the terms of the loan agreement with the international lending organization itself, it would find itself excluded from participation in further development aid. The

---

[15] On the whole this has been a more serious problem for the U.S.S.R., which for the greater part of the history of the United Nations found itself in a minority. But as the Cuban crisis of October, 1962 showed, the United States may find itself increasingly in situations of conflict between national policy and compliance with the United Nations Charter.

[16] Certain Expenses of the United Nations (Article 17, Paragraph 2, of the Charter), [1962] I.C.J. Rep. 151 (advisory opinion).

[17] For an appraisal of the various possibilities, see Hogg, *Peace-Keeping Costs and Charter Obligations—Implications of the International Court of Justice Decision on Certain Expenses of the United Nations*, 62 COLUM. L. REV. 1230 (1962).

same would be true if a government that had concluded a concession agreement with a foreign investor, containing an arbitration clause, were to repudiate the jurisdiction or the award of the arbitration tribunal in the case of a dispute. Regardless of the precise legal character of such concession agreements, the repudiation of an engagement freely and voluntarily given would comport the indirect sanction of exclusion from participation in the public international lending market—and, of course, the less significant private lending market. This fact may in part explain the record of the World Bank transactions since its inception, which do not show a single default.[18] The effectiveness of this sanction of nonparticipation, of course, depends upon the extent of the common interests at stake. As far as international financing goes, the Communist bloc is today outside the reach of the international financing agencies, though some of its most prominent members have now joined other international organizations, such as the ILO and the WHO.[19]

Again, an offender against the air navigation rules and standards established by the International Civil Aviation Organization may find himself excluded from the benefits of international air traffic regulation. If and when such international welfare organizations as the World Health Organization or the Food and Agriculture Organization attain the functions and powers that are already in an active stage of discussion, *i.e.*, a more comprehensive supervisory and regulatory authority for sanitary standards for the WHO, and the functions of a worldwide food pool and clearinghouse center in the case of the FAO, the benefits of participation, and the disabilities flowing from exclusion from participation will be obvious and drastic.

In another area of beginning cooperative organization, that of conservation of resources, it is the mutual interest in the conservation of vital human resources that will increasingly compel agree-

---

[18] It may, of course, be said that this type of sanction—by exclusion from participation in financial aid—may lead to abuse of the power of the economically strong against the economically weak. However, any sanction is an exercise of power by the stronger against the weaker and the decisive test is in whose name it is exercised. As long as the World Bank is a genuine organ of the international community there would seem to be adequate controls against an abuse of power.

[19] It is today an open issue whether the reach of international economic and financial organizations will gradually become more universal, or whether the vital political blocks will develop their own exclusive and antagonistic sets of institutions. This is part of the wider problem of coexistence in international law.

On the whole, it seems more likely that the economic development institutions of the United Nations, such as the World Bank, will remain instruments of the Western World, though their activities—and thus the sanctions of exclusion—comprise the great majority of the "noncommitted" underdeveloped countries of Asia and Africa. The Communist bloc is developing its own system of low-interest loans, coupled with the supply of machinery and technicians. This entails its own system of sanctions.

ment on fisheries and other maritime resources. It is, however, only when international agreements of this kind are buttressed by an international organization equipped with the positive dispensing powers as they are notably enjoyed by the World Bank in the field of international development financing that the sanction of non-participation will be really effective in the field of conservation of resources.

In recent jurisprudential discussions of the meaning and role of sanction in municipal law, the insufficiency of the traditional concept of the sanction has begun to be recognized. Thus, in a valuable recent study on the "Public Order," Arens and Lasswell have, in a survey of the sanctions of the legal process, pointed out the much neglected importance of the sanctions of exclusion such as unemployability caused by adverse findings or publicity as regards the loyalty of the person concerned.[20] They have in this context criticized the looseness and inadequacy of the safeguards against the imposition of this type of—often very serious—sanction as it is at the disposal of congressional committees equipped with quasi-judicial powers but not subjected to the traditional judicial safeguards of democratic systems.

In a wider juristic framework, Professor H. L. A. Hart has criticized the insufficiency of the Austinian and the Kelsenian concept of law as a coercive order backed by threats.[21] This concept "plainly approximates closer to a penal statute enacted by the legislature of a modern state than to any other variety of law."[22] But, as Professor Hart points out, there are many laws that do not impose duties or obligations.

> Instead, they provide individuals with *facilities* for realizing their wishes, by conferring legal powers upon them to create, by certain specified procedures and subject to certain conditions, structures of rights and duties within the coercive framework of the law.
>
> The power thus conferred on individuals to mould their legal relations with others by contracts, wills, marriages, &c., is one of the great contributions of law to social life; and it is a feature of law obscured by representing all law as a matter of orders backed by threats.
>
> . . . .
>
> The principal functions of the law as a means of social control are . . . to be seen in the diverse ways in which the law is used to control, to guide, and to plan life out of court.[23]

The emphasis on the law as a means of ordering social life con-

---

20 Arens & Lasswell, In Defense of Public Order (1961).
21 Hart, The Concept of Law (1961).
22 *Id.* at 24.
23 *Id.* at 27-28, 39.

structively and positively, while perhaps obvious on even a superficial survey of the many instruments and modalities of both public and private law, and of the functions exercised by courts in the matter of wills, guardianships, and adoptions, has long been obscured in legal theory by the predominance of the analytical positivism of Austin, and more recently, Kelsen, and their many followers.

Surprisingly, however, Professor Hart entirely fails to apply this important insight to international law. Nor indeed does any other contemporary writer appear to have stressed this decisive shift in the meaning and role of sanction in contemporary international law, although some modern authors have stressed the changes in the scope and dimensions of the modern law of nations.[24] It is indeed as a means to control, to guide, and to plan the life of the nations out of court—in the processes of international economic development in which public international organization and law plays a predominant part, in the means of cooperating and communicating on the seas, in the air and in the as yet unappropriated dimensions of outer space, in common efforts to rescue humanity from ruin through unlimited and uncontrolled breeding or the rapacious use of the resources of the earth, in the gradual approximation of international labor and health standards—that international law is beginning to exercise its principal function. Indeed, it may be predicted that either international society will more and more develop these positive and formative aspects of international law, or that mankind will destroy itself, whether through war, or through ruinous and destructive competition and exploitation of the resources of the earth short of war.

The quest for effective international legal sanctions in the traditional sense will, of course, remain extremely important. There is a burning and vital need for the establishment of an effective international military force—as provided for in the hitherto abortive provisions of the United Nations Charter—a force that will be able to enforce the authority of the international community against all states large and small. There is a need for the extension of the jurisdiction of the International Court of Justice, and for enforcement powers that will make the defiance of its judgments—as exemplified in the very first case considered by the new Court, the *Corfu Channel Case*[25]—impossible. There is need for the extension

[24] See, *e.g.*, Jenks, The Common Law of Mankind (1958); Jessup, Transnational Law (1956); Röling, International Law in an Expanded World (1960); Schwarzenberger, The Frontiers of International Law (1962); Friedmann, *The Changing Dimensions of International Law*, 62 Colum. L. Rev. 1147 (1962); McDougal, *International Law, Power, and Policy: A Contemporary Conception*, 82 Recueil des Cours 137 (1953).

[25] Corfu Channel Case (Merits), [1949] I.C.J. Rep. 4; Corfu Channel Case (Preliminary Objection), [1949] I.C.J. Rep. 15.

of judicial and enforcement machineries in the growing number of international economic transactions, and especially those to which governments on the one side and private corporations on the other side are parties.

What is challenged here is the exclusive emphasis on this type of international legal order. Some of the sanctions of nonparticipation that flow from the new cooperative or welfare type of international law will not be of universal scope; others will. But as the physical frontiers of mankind shrink, as the powers of mutual and universal destruction and the immense dangers of overpopulation and of the exhaustion of the resources of the earth increase at a dramatic rate, the nonpunitive aspects of the international legal order will become increasingly important. This should be a source of great encouragement to those concerned in the building of an effective law of nations. It is infinitely more difficult to establish an effective coercive and punitive international machinery of sanctions which will assert the will of the international society even against the most powerful state. We are far more advanced along the alternative road where the needs of survival and development will dictate compliance with international standards of conduct as progressively laid down in the developing international legal order.

NOTES AND QUESTIONS

1. Friedmann's analytical breakdown of the question of the reality of international law into three dimensions—hierarchy, the presence or absence of sanctions, and the extent of the sense of obligation felt by various states—should be compared with the discussions of Kaplan and Katzenbach (**II-1B**), Roger Fisher (**II-1B**) and Oscar Schachter (Chapter 3). A review of these materials just cited would be useful and relevant to an understanding of the problems raised in this chapter.

   Friedmann's analysis points to three elements that are important for a study of an international police force: the proper degree of centralization of authority and command, the appropriate attitudes regarding the compliance of states with the basic rules of order in the legal system, and the range of international responses available to deter and terminate instances of noncompliance.
2. In emphasizing the extent to which the threat of nonparticipation in an international organization may be treated as a sanction, Friedmann performs the very valuable service of broadening the ordinary notion of sanction beyond that of enforcement. This suggests a control system that deals with noncompliance and compliance in terms of rewards as well as punishments, for the right of participation acts as a positive inducement to sustain compliance.

   This line of thought concerning a response system in which positively oriented devices are used to attract compliance with rules helpfully blurs the distinction between sanctions as negative events and welfare programs designed to produce behavior in support of a social structure as positive events. The functionalist view that world order may best be achieved through the establishment of an organizational structure that meets the perceived needs of the various nation-states is embodied by Clark and Sohn in their proposal for a World Development Authority that they expect would significantly reduce poverty and underdevelopment.

3. A particularly penetrating and comprehensive analysis of the sanctioning processes and structures in the world community is to be found in Chapter IV of Myres S. McDougal's and Florentino P. Feliciano's impressive study, *Law and Minimum World Public Order* (Yale University Press, 1961). The theoretical structure underlying the approach is explained in the article by McDougal in **II-1C**. McDougal and Feliciano develop a methodology that is brilliantly conceived to permit the investigator to deal systematically with the contextual variables most relevant in international crisis situations. Their primary emphasis concerns the relationship between authoritative decision-makers and community expectations. The approach indicates the need to maximize community support for sanctioning processes.
4. It is useful to make the distinction between sanctioning systems and response systems. A sanctioning system may be thought of as a set of procedures intended to deprive individuals and other actors of valued objects or activity and is essentially punitive in character. A response system may be considered to be more comprehensive as it embraces all sanctioning processes but involves, as well, positively oriented means to secure compliance by subjects with rules. The work by Arens and Lasswell cited by Friedmann is the most original and creative contribution to the literature on sanctions in recent times; it is strongly recommended to those interested in further study.
5. Do you agree with Friedmann's analysis of the variety of motives that produce a sense of obligation to adhere to a code of conduct? Are there any other motives that you would add? What international organizations do you think can be persuaded to relate their activities to sanctioning and compliance goals?
6. Friedmann does not deny the need to create effective peace-keeping and adjudicatory machinery but contends that there is a good deal more pay-off in world order likely to result from the positive approach, from shaping the welfare activities going on in international society, so that even states alienated from the existing international system will want to participate in its formally constituted organs and activities. Which of these two approaches do you think needs to be given highest priority and why? Are they in any sense incompatible? Would it be useful to integrate the traditional idea of punitive sanctions with the more modern idea of positive inducement into a single strategy of world order? How would one go about such a task? Is it clear that the roots of violence are sufficiently rational so that proponents of violence can be dissuaded by the prospect of net loss? These questions suggest that a *deterrent* system needs to be supplemented by a *defense* system in any adequate approach to world order, that the rational appeal based on rewards and punishments may not be heeded by determined aggressors or revolutionary actors and that, in this event, effective means must be available to neutralize deviant conduct. This line of questioning brings us back from the theory underlying a compliance system to the characteristics of coercive enforcement, including the means by which the enforcement activities of the organized international community can be made more effective in the transition context.

B. Peace-Keeping by the United Nations

The central problem of world order is the extent to which the organized international community possesses the actual and potential capacity to prevent war, or, more precisely, to decrease substantially the likelihood that principal nations would, for whatever reason, have recourse to major violence. It is now generally agreed that during the past forty-five years many statesmen and people throughout the world have started to think seriously both about formulating a rule against the use of violence and creating an institutional structure that would enhance the prospects for compliance with the rule. The study of the traditional international legal processes at work outside the framework of formal international organizations reveals that some normative restraint upon the use of violence in international relations has always existed, but it also reveals that the interaction of attitudes and beliefs about the use of violence has not permitted the establishment of enduring peace within a social system as decentralized as international society. Prior materials bear on this discussion, for example, those in **II-1** and **II-6**.

In this section inquiry centers upon the role of the United Nations in preventing and controlling the scale of war, as well as its role in dealing with a situation where an imminent threat of violence exists. The objective of this inquiry is to evaluate the activities of the Organization in light of the following question: *Is it advisable and feasible to establish an international police force?*

The first selection is an address to the Harvard Alumni Association given by the present Secretary-General, U Thant, in June of 1963: "United Nations Peace Force," *International Military Forces*, edited by Lincoln P. Bloomfield (Little, Brown, Boston, 1964) pp. 259–267. Somewhat surprisingly, it might seem, U Thant answers the question posed in the preceding paragraph in the negative. That is to say, if by an international police force we mean a cadre of men hired, trained and compensated by an international organization to carry on the tasks comparable to those performed by the police in domestic societies, then the Secretary-General's answer is no. For U Thant somewhat reluctantly arrives at the conclusion that the requisite degree of world community sentiment in favor of the establishment of such a force does not presently exist. At the same time U Thant feels that the experiences of the United Nations in a number of troublesome international situations suggest that some additional steps can and should be taken at this time to give the Organization an improved peace-keeping capacity. In Section C of this chapter his views on these matters will be evaluated.

More pertinent for immediate purposes is the Secretary-General's insistence that the character of United Nations operations in situations concerned with violence are properly characterized as "peace-keeping," and that these operations should be sharply distinguished from the kind of undertaking contemplated in Chapter VII of the Charter. It will be recalled that the original conception of the Charter expected the so-called Big Five to police the world against potential aggressors. The language of Articles 43 through 49 makes clear that, should the Big Five find it necessary to use violence to maintain international peace and security, traditional military forces drawn from national establishments would be brought into operation. Along with many others, U Thant points out that the United Nations has not engaged in traditional military activities directed against states, but that the mission of the UN forces has always been to stop the fighting and establish a cease-fire. Furthermore, these activities, with the notable exception of Korea, have been executed mostly by the smaller and medium-sized powers rather than by the big powers. The long-range implications of this shift from the enforcement provisions of Chapter VII of the Charter to peace-keeping activities carried on by smaller powers will be considered in the rest of this chapter.

Finally, U Thant's enumeration and characterization of peace-keeping activities is not only a useful resumé of the history of UN actions, but serves as an introduction to the range of functions that a UN police force might be expected to perform.

UNITED NATIONS PEACE FORCE

An address to the Harvard Alumni Association,
delivered in Cambridge, Massachusetts, June 13, 1963,
by the Secretary-General of the United Nations,

U THANT

The development of an international order, enshrined in an accepted code of world law and guaranteed by an effective world police force, has long been a human aspiration. This dream is based upon the very reasonable idea of projecting the stability and orderliness of a well-governed State onto the relations between nations.

In the history of most nation-States, there came a time when the feuding of a few powerful interests or personages, in disregard of the welfare of the majority, and the ensuing chaos and disaster, became intolerable. From this situation, there was the evolution in due course of a strong central authority, based on popular representation, a sound system of law and a reliable police force. In our world, we reached a similarly intolerable situation many years ago and have twice in this century paid a terrible price for having failed to draw the necessary conclusions.

Most sensible people now agree that some reliable system of ensuring world peace is essential. But, as in most situations involving great and conflicting interests and very large numbers of people, there is all the difference in the world between the need and the practical fulfilment of the need. That fulfilment will be a long and complicated process, requiring a degree of confidence and understanding which we have not yet established in our world.

Few would deny that, if we are to look forward with confidence to the future, we have to take a great step forward in regulating the relations of nations and produce workable institutions for that purpose. One should not, however, underestimate the difficulties of such a step or the inevitable risks which attend it.

Nations and Governments, taking a great step forward, face imponderables and unknown dangers which no research or scientific test can resolve, for these unforeseeable events will be the result of the actions, reactions and interactions or hundreds of millions of human beings, and the human mind and human behaviour are still perhaps the most mysterious and awe-inspiring force in our world. Statesmen are wise, therefore, to view the future with caution and to examine proposals for fundamental change with more than usual care.

While we are making this step forward towards a new world order, we need guarantees, we need moderating influences and we need some commonly operated and accepted agency to share the risks and make the necessary tests and experiments, and even mistakes. Certainly we need an agency through which the necessary confidence and contact among nations can be built up and maintained. The United Nations is the nearest thing we have to such an agency, and I believe that it is beginning to play an important role of the kind I have just described.

It is no doubt true that there are certain great problems, such as the struggle between the greatest powers and the related problem of disarmament, which may be with us for a long time and which, perhaps, cannot be tackled head-on by the United Nations. We must, of course, do everything that we can to avoid adding fuel to the great power struggle.

There are, however, a large number of important problems and situations which *can* usefully be tackled and, if this is done, the greatest problems themselves can be isolated, if not resolved. We should, in this process, begin to develop the necessary institutions and practices by which, at a later stage, a more stable world order can be ensured.

I am going to talk today about one particular aspect of our problems, namely, peace-keeping and the use of international peace forces by the United Nations. Due partly to the lack of unanimity among the great powers ever since 1946, and partly to the radical change in the nature of war resulting from the development of atomic and hydrogen weapons, there has been a gradual change in thinking on questions of international security in the United Nations.

There has been a tacit transition from the concept of collective security, as set out in Chapter VII of the United Nations Charter, to a more realistic idea of peace-keeping. The idea that conventional military methods — or, to put it bluntly, war — can be used by or on behalf of the United Nations to counter aggression and secure the peace, seems now to be rather impractical.

There also has been a change in emphasis from the use of the military forces of the great powers, as contemplated in the Charter, to the use, in practice, of the military resources of the smaller powers, which has the advantage of not entangling United Nations actions in the antagonisms of the cold war.

Although there has been one collective action under the aegis of the United Nations — Korea — and although in 1951 the Collective Measures Committee, set up by the General Assembly under the Uniting for Peace resolution, actually published in its report a list of units earmarked by

Member States for service with the United Nations in actions to counter aggression, actual developments have in practice been in a rather different direction.

The nature of these developments is sometimes confused, wittingly or unwittingly, by an attempt to relate them to the use of force to counter aggression by the Security Council provided for in Chapter VII of the Charter. In fact, the peace-keeping forces I am about to describe are of a very different kind and have little in common with the forces foreseen in Chapter VII, but their existence is not in conflict with Chapter VII. They are essentially *peace* and not fighting forces and they operate only with the consent of the parties directly concerned.

In this context, it is worth noting that *all* of the permanent members of the Security Council have, at one time or another in the past 15 years, voted in support of the creation of one or other of these forces, and that none of them has in any case gone further than to abstain from voting on them.

Since 1950, the United Nations has been called on to deal with a number of critical situations of varying urgency. The most urgent of these have been what are sometimes called "brush-fire wars", meaning, I take it, small conflagrations which, unless controlled, may all too easily ignite very much larger ones.

If we briefly look through the United Nations experience with this kind of operation, we can see that from small and informal beginnings a useful body of precedent and practice has grown up over the years of using military personnel of Member States on peace-keeping operations. In Greece in 1947, the United Nations Special Committee on the Balkans found that professional military officers were invaluable as an observer group in assessing the highly complicated and fluctuating situation. The Security Council itself set up an observer group of military officers in India and Pakistan to watch over the Kashmir question. This observer group, which was set up in 1948, is still operating.

A much larger use of military observers by the United Nations was made when, in July 1948, the first truce agreements in the Palestine war were supervised on the ground by some 700 United Nations military observers working under the United Nations Mediator and the Chief of Staff. This team developed into the United Nations Truce Supervision Organization after the armistice agreements between Israel and her Arab neighbours were concluded in the period from February to July 1949.

This organization of officers from many countries still plays a vital role in keeping the peace in the Middle East and in reporting on and dealing with incidents which, though small in themselves, might all too easily become the cause of far larger disturbances if not dealt with. Its indefatigable members in their white jeeps are now a familiar and welcome part of the Middle Eastern landscape.

A peace-keeping organization of a different nature made its appearance as a result of the Suez crisis of October 1956. Confronted with a situation of the utmost urgency in which two of the permanent members of the Security Council were directly involved, the General Assembly voted for the urgent creation of a United Nations force. This was essentially *not* a force designed actively to fight against aggression.

It went to Egypt with the express consent of the Egyptian Government and after the other parties concerned had agreed to a cease-fire. It was designed not to fight but rather to allow those involved to disengage without further disturbance. It allowed for the peaceful resolution of one of the most dangerous crises which had faced the world since the Second World War. It also, incidentally, allowed for the clearance by the United Nations of the Suez Canal, which had been blocked during the previous military action.

The United Nations Emergency Force in the Middle East has for six years watched over the borders of Israel with the United Arab Republic in the Gaza Strip and through the Sinai Desert. It also watches over the access to the Gulf of Aqaba and to the Israeli port of Elath. What was once a most troubled and terrorized frontier has become peaceful and prosperous on both sides, and the very presence of the United Nations Force is both an insurance against a resumption of trouble and a good excuse not to engage in it. It presents us with one serious problem. To maintain an army of over 5,000 men costs money, but at present the parties concerned have no wish to see it removed.

In 1958 another very tense situation, with quite different origins, occurred in Lebanon. After the success of UNEF, there were suggestions in many quarters that another United Nations force should be collected and dispatched to that country. Here, however, the problem, though aggravated by external factors, was essentially a domestic one.

The Security Council therefore set up a three-man observer group and left the Secretary-General considerable latitude as to the methods to be employed to make this group effective in watching over the possibilities of infiltration from outside. A highly mobile group of 600 officers was quickly organized to keep watch from ground and air, while the crisis itself was resolved by negotiation and discussion. By the end of 1958, it was possible to withdraw the United Nations Observer Group from the Lebanon altogether.

The greatest and most complex challenge to the United Nations in the peacekeeping field arose a few days after the Congo gained its independence from Belgium on 30 June 1960. The general proportions of this problem are sometimes obscured by a wealth of dramatic detail and are worth restating. Harassed by mutiny, lawlessness and the collapse of public order and services from within, and afflicted by foreign military intervention as well as by ominous threats of other forms of interference from without, the new Government of the Congo appealed to the United Nations for help.

The Security Council committed the United Nations to respond to this appeal and thus made the Organization not only the guarantor of law and order and the protector of the Congo against external interference from any source, but also the adviser and helper of a newly independent State which had had virtually no preparation for its independence.

By filling, in the space of a few hours, the very dangerous vacuum which existed in the Congo in July 1960, the urgent danger of a confrontation of the great powers in the heart of Africa was avoided and the territorial integrity of the Congo preserved. The new leaders of the Congo have been given at least a short breathing-spell in which to find their feet. Despite its shortcomings, which must be judged in the light of the fearsome complexity of the problem, the United Nations Operation in the Congo is, in my opinion, a promising and encouraging experiment in international responsibility and action.

The blue helmets of the United Nations Force are known throughout the Congo as the symbol of security. Its soldiers have given protection at one time or another in the last three years to almost every Congolese public figure and almost every group, both African and non-African, when danger and violence threatened them. It is worth noting that, now that the withdrawal of the United Nations Force in the Congo is in sight, the deepest regret, and even alarm, is expressed by the very groups who used to be its most hostile critics and detractors.

In the Force, soldiers from other African countries work side by side in this vast tropical country with those from farther away. Their loyalty to the United Nations, their team spirit and comradeship have been an inspiration to all those who value the peace-keeping role of the United Nations.

I will end my catalogue with two more operations, one of which has already been successfully concluded, and which also involved an unprecedented role for the United Nations. I would like to refer first to the transfer of West Irian from Dutch rule, through a temporary period of United Nations executive authority, backed by a United Nations Security Force, to the administration of Indonesia. This entire operation has taken place with the agreement of the parties concerned, and in consultation with them.

The second is the dispatch to Yemen of an observer team as a basis for the disengagement of the United Arab Republic and Saudi Arabia from the affairs of Yemen. This operation will be paid for by the two parties concerned, and has been undertaken at their request and that of the Government of Yemen.

Although these are peace forces, service in them is hard and can be dangerous. In the Middle East, the United Nations has registered casualties not only from accidents and disease, but from mines. Both there and in

West Irian, as also in Yemen, the terrain and the climate are inhospitable. In the Congo, we have had, unfortunately, serious casualties from unwanted fighting as well as from other causes, and I very much hope that we shall have no more.

I have only mentioned here the peace-keeping activities which have involved the use, in one way or another, of military personnel. If I were to mention the many other tense situations in which the United Nations, and my office in particular, have been used as a meeting-ground and as an instrument for mediation and peaceful settlement, the list would be much longer.

To sum up, we have now had experience of three major peace-keeping forces and a variety of military observer and truce supervisory operations. Each of the three forces has been different in composition, nature and task, but they have shared certain common characteristics.

All three were improvised and called into the field at very short notice; all three were severely limited in their right to use force; all three were designed solely for the maintenance of peace and not for fighting in the military sense; all three were recruited from the smaller powers and with special reference to their acceptability in the area in which they were to serve; all three operated with the express consent and co-operation of the States or territories where they were stationed, as well as of any other parties directly concerned in the situation; and all three were under the direction and control of the Secretary-General acting on behalf of the organs of the United Nations.

These facts may now seem commonplace; it is a measure of the progress that has been made that even ten years ago they would have seemed very unusual.

By the standards of an efficient national military establishment, these forces have considerable disadvantages. Obviously, a force put together only after the emergency with which it is to deal is in full swing, will inevitably have some shortcomings. There is difficulty in recruiting at very short notice exactly the right kind of units for the work in hand, and in operating a force whose units and officers meet each other for the first time in the midst of a delicate operation. There are differences not only of language and tradition but of training, equipment and staff procedures. There are differences in pay and emoluments which, if not handled carefully, can cause considerable problems of discipline and morale. Staff-work and command are especially difficult where every decision has important political implications.

Although these contingents from Member States are under the operational control of the United Nations, disciplinary powers are still vested in the national authorities and this could be, although in fact it never has been, the cause of very serious difficulties for the United Nations Force Commander and for the Secretary-General.

The fact that the military establishments of the permanent members of the Security Council cannot be used cuts us off from the most obvious sources of equipment and personnel. The improvised nature of these operations also gives rise to various problems of logistics.

In our experience, these difficulties, which are inherent in the pioneering nature of these operations, have been offset by the enthusiastic co-operation of Member States and by the spirit and comprehension of the officers and men of the contingents which have made up the United Nations forces. It is an encouraging thought that in the military establishments of some 30 or more countries in the world there are now large numbers of officers and men who have served the United Nations with distinction in one or other of these operations and have added thereby a new dimension to their military experience.

The improvised approach also makes it possible on each occasion to make up the United Nations force from the countries which are, politically and in other ways, most suitable for the operation in hand, and at least the United Nations is not afflicted with the age-old problem of having on its hands a standing army with nothing to do.

In my opinion, a permanent United Nations force is not a practical proposition at the present time. I know that many serious people in many countries are enthusiastic about the idea, and I welcome their enthusiasm and the thought they are putting into the evolution of the institution which will eventually and surely emerge. Many difficulties still stand in the way of its evolution.

Personally, I have no doubt that the world should eventually have an international police force which will be accepted as an integral and essential part of life in the same way as national police forces are accepted. Meanwhile, we must be sure that developments are in the right direction and that we can also meet critical situations as and when they occur.

There are a number of reasons why it seems to me that the establishment of a permanent United Nations force would be premature at the present time. I doubt whether many Governments in the world would yet be prepared to accept the political implications of such an institution and, in the light of our current experience with financial problems, I am sure that they would have very serious difficulties in accepting the financial implications.

I believe that we need a number of parallel developments before we can evolve such an institution. We have to go further along the road of codification and acceptance of a workable body of international law. We have to develop a more sophisticated public opinion in the world, which can accept the transition from predominantly national thinking to international thinking.

We shall have to develop a deeper faith in international institutions as such, and a greater confidence in the possibility of a United Nations civil service whose international loyalty and objectivity are generally accepted and above suspicion. We shall have to improve the method of financing international organization. Until these conditions are met, a permanent United Nations force may not be a practical proposition.

But we have already shown that, when the situation demands it, it is possible to use the soldiers of many countries for objectives which are not national ones and that the soldiers respond magnificently to this new challenge. We have also seen that, when the situation is serious enough, Governments are prepared to waive certain of the attributes of national sovereignty in the interest of keeping the peace through the United Nations. We have demonstrated that a loyalty to international service can exist side by side with legitimate national pride.

And, perhaps most important of all, we have shown that there *can* be a practical alternative to the deadly ultimate struggle and that it is an alternative which brings out the good and generous qualities in men rather than their destructive and selfish qualities.

Although it is perhaps too early, for the reasons I have already given, to consider the establishment of a permanent United Nations force, I believe there are a number of measures which could be taken even now to improve on our present capacity for meeting dangerous situations. It would be extremely desirable, for example, if countries would, in their national military planning, make provision for suitable units which could be made available at short notice for United Nations service and thereby decrease the degree of improvisation necessary in an emergency.

I take this opportunity publicly to welcome and express my appreciation for the efforts of the Scandinavian countries in this direction. Denmark, Norway and Sweden have for some time now engaged in joint planning of a stand-by force comprising various essential components to be put at the disposal of the United Nations when necessary. It would be a very welcome development if other countries would consider following the lead of the Scandinavian countries in this matter.

At present, the activities of the United Nations are overshadowed by a very serious financial crisis, a crisis which stems directly from the costs of the special peace-keeping operations in the Middle East and the Congo and from the failure of some Members to pay their assessments for those operations. Although the sums of money involved are small in comparison to the sums spent by many countries on military budgets, they do, nonetheless, present a very serious financial and political challenge to the stability of the United Nations.

The United Nations is the sum of all its Members and, to develop in the right direction, it must maintain this global character. On the other hand, I am convinced that the Organization must maintain and develop its active role in keeping the peace. I therefore view with the gravest concern the prolongation of the financial crisis of the United Nations with its very serious political overtones, and I trust that we may see a solution of the problem before too long.

I am concerned at this financial crisis more particularly because I see, in the long run, no acceptable alternative method of keeping peace in the world to the steady and sound development of the peace-keeping functions of the United Nations. It is no longer possible to think rationally in terms of countering aggression or keeping the peace by the use of the ultimate weapons.

However improvised and fumbling the United Nations approach may be, we have to develop it to deal with the sudden antagonisms and dangers of our world, until we can evolve more permanent institutions. There has been already a great advance in the world towards co-operation, mutual responsibility and common interest. I have described some of the pioneering co-operative efforts made by the United Nations to keep the peace.

I believe that these efforts constitute vital steps towards a more mature, more acceptable, and more balanced world order. We must have the confidence and the means to sustain them and the determination to develop out of them a reliable and workable system for the future.

I am a firm believer in the organic development of institutions. I also firmly believe that, if the United Nations is to justify the hopes of its founders and of the peoples of the world, it must develop into an active and effective agency for peace and international conciliation by responding to the challenges which face it. May we have the courage, the faith, and the wisdom to make it so.

NOTES AND QUESTIONS

1. Dag Hammarskjöld, U Thant's predecessor, also felt that the United Nations was not yet ready to develop a standing international police force and, like U Thant, expressed the view that stand-by forces drawn from specified national contingents of various Member States would be the appropriate next step in the development of an effective international police force. Since the views of these two men are based on their firsthand experiences in the United Nations and reflect the difficulties of marshalling a consensus sufficient to establish, direct, and finance UN troops, their evaluation of what is feasible and necessary deserves most serious consideration. However, respect for their views should not preclude the serious investigation of other positions and, accordingly, in Section C several proposals for the establishment, at present, of a standing or permanent UN police force will be studied.

   U Thant points out that the Scandinavian countries have already acted to earmark national contingents for possible use in UN peace-keeping, and that a number of other countries, including some Commonwealth and Latin American countries, have indicated that they would be likely to do so in the near future. For a detailed and painstaking study of a United Nations stand-by force that would include a central command structure and UN training for the national troops earmarked for peace-keeping activities, see "A Proposal" in the valuable book edited by Lincoln P. Bloomfield, *International Military Forces* (Little, Brown, Boston, 1964) pp. 79–99. Envisioning a force consisting of about 25,000, Bloomfield relies upon the field and financial experiences of previous peace-keeping operations to develop his proposal.

The two most extensive policing actions undertaken by the United Nations (Korea aside) have been in connection with Suez beginning during the crisis of 1956 and continuing until the present to patrol the Gaza Strip between Israel and Egypt, and in the Congo between 1960 and 1964. In the next selection, "An Appraisal," from *International Military Forces* (see reference above) pp. 105–125, Herbert Nicholas discusses the major political problems that arose in connection with each of these two situations. Nicholas starts with an intriguing inquiry into the circumstances in which the United Nations has failed to act despite the occurrence of international violence, and then goes on to clarify the various interests and social forces that permitted the Organization, in contrast, to operate successfully in Suez and the Congo. Nicholas' essay suggests that a useful focus for the study of UN peace-keeping might be to isolate those political and social factors that enable it to act effectively and those that seem to preclude effective action. Such an analysis might facilitate thinking about how to cope with the various factors that currently inhibit effective action.

HERBERT NICHOLAS

An Appraisal

I

It is sometimes instructive, as Holmes long ago pointed out to Watson, to begin by asking a few questions about dogs that do not bark in the night. Suez and the Congo are not the only major crises which have disturbed the United Nations. Yet they are the only ones to which it has responded by creating a true United Nations force. Why?

Consider the case of Hungary. Coincident with Suez, it provoked from the General Assembly stronger verbal denunciation. While the Anglo-French attack was described colorlessly as "military operations against Egyptian territory,"[1] the Soviet move in Hungary was denounced initially as "foreign," "armed intervention," and later as a "violation of the political independence of Hungary," a deprivation of "its liberty," and a "violation of the Charter."[2] Yet the employment of a United Nations force of any kind was not even considered; it was left to the Secretary-General to "investigate" and "observe the situation directly through representatives named by him."[3]

Thus, though the United Nations' judgment was unequivocal, its actions were minimal. Vehemence stopped at words because everyone knew that to go further was to involve one's country in an outright clash with a great power in an area which the Soviet Union was obviously going to regard as vital. Nor in this regard was there any difference of degree among the critics of the Soviet Union — all, from

[1] General Assembly Resolution 997 (ES-I), November 2, 1956.
[2] General Assembly Resolution 1131 (XI), December 12, 1956.
[3] General Assembly Resolution 1004 (ES-II), November 4, 1956.

the United States down to the smallest member of the General Assembly, drew back from any action stronger than words. It was not merely the defense of Hungary that was unthinkable; even the admission into the country of the mildest form of United Nations presence, the Secretary-General's representative, could not be insisted upon in the face of Soviet refusal, and was in fact never secured.

Five years after Hungary, India invaded Goa. The issue was brought before the Security Council by Portugal on December 18, 1961, with a request for an immediate cease-fire. A Western-sponsored resolution was not only defeated by a Soviet veto but was also opposed by all three Afro-Asian members of the Council. The "Uniting for Peace" mechanism was not invoked, it is generally understood, because there seemed no prospect of obtaining a two-thirds majority in the General Assembly for any resolution along the lines of that defeated in the Security Council. However, even the defeated resolution gave no hint of the possible employment of a United Nations force; it called only for an immediate cessation of hostilities, a withdrawal of Indian forces, a solution by peaceful means, and the provision of such assistance by the Secretary-General as might be appropriate. India announced the surrender of the Goan forces on the same day that the Security Council met.

In Goa, in contrast to Hungary, no great power was directly involved. Aggression, in most ordinary senses of the term, had clearly been committed. Nevertheless, any realistic observer of the reactions in Turtle Bay to India's action must recognize that, in the present UN context, there is one crime which in certain circumstances may be judged to outweigh the crime of aggression — namely, colonialism. The failure of the United Nations to register even a verbal protest against India's behavior in Goa was basically due to the fact that Portugal had put itself outside the pale by its actions in the same year on Angola. Since the UN can assist only those who at any rate initially can themselves resist, the sheer rapidity of the Indian operation would probably have deprived any United Nations resolution of more than academic effect. But, even if time had permitted the interposition of a UN force between Goa and its attackers, a sufficient number of impartial, small powers would not have been willing to serve on it.

Lastly, let us consider Korea. Here the United Nations came nearest to establishing a fighting force. It did create a United Nations command and requested Members to make forces available to it, but this was a mere anointing of the existing United States Far East command, a sanctification, as it were, of its personnel and its commander, General MacArthur, and of whatever active units Member States might supply and place under his command. In an important sense, the action taken by MacArthur and his forces was United Nations action; this was its status in international law.[4] In terms of international politics and of international organization, however, it fell crucially short of being a real United Nations operation. It was not under the executive control of the United Nations; the Secretariat had no part in its organization or deployment; it was not financed by the United Nations, nor did the United Nations determine in any but the very broadest terms the conditions and objectives of its employment. The response to the appeal to all Member States to furnish assistance was generally poor. One Member, the United States, was the self-appointed Atlas of the operation, without whose broad shoulders all would have failed. By the end of 1950, the only foreign ground troops fighting by the Americans' side were from the United Kingdom, Australia, France, Greece, the Netherlands, the Philippines, Thailand, and Turkey.[5] South Koreans apart, the unified command in Korea consisted of about a quarter of a million Americans compared with only about 36,000 troops from all other Member States combined.

Of the three cases only Korea bears the slightest resemblance to Suez and the Congo in that here the United Nations response to a violation of the Charter took a forceful form. This was due in large part to a series of happy accidents. The fact of aggression could be quickly established, owing to the presence in Korea of the United Nations Commission on Korea. Resistance could be quickly organized, because a great power had its armed forces virtually *in situ* when the fighting broke out (and the other super power behind the aggression had made the mistake of walking out of the Security Council). Supplementary assistance was lent to the United States-United

[4] See Guenter Weissberg, *The International Status of the United Nations* (New York: Oceana, 1961), pp. 78 ff.

[5] In 1951, ground troops were also furnished by Belgium, Canada, Colombia, Ethiopia, Luxembourg, and New Zealand.

Nations command by countries who felt themselves already bound to support American action by virtue of other ties, most obviously by their common North Atlantic Treaty Organization (NATO) membership. And although the Soviet Union was wholly hostile to the United Nations action in Korea, it did not attempt to frustrate it in a manner that might cause a local police action to escalate into a direct clash between two super powers. Indeed, the Korean conflict occurred at a time when the American lead in nuclear weapons made it reasonable to suppose that the United States was, strictly speaking, the only super power.

Soon, however, countervailing considerations made themselves felt. The very predominance of United States strength which made the United Nations operation in Korea possible also diminished its United Nations appeal and reduced the crucial element of universality. This, in fact, accounted for what Mr. Lie called the "disappointing"[6] response to his appeal to Member States for further assistance. More seriously, the open intervention of Communist China transformed the nature of the conflict and greatly heightened the risks of its growing, if not into a conflict of super powers, at least into an interminable and costly war in which military advantages accruing to superior nuclear weapons would be offset by the political impossibility of using the weapon of Hiroshima in the service of the Charter. Support at the United Nations fell away from an operation which previously, however inadequate its United Nations character, was yet felt to serve United Nations objectives.

Subsequently, the emphasis fell increasingly on the search for a Korean settlement, reaching a point indeed where, in the behavior of many Members even outside the communist bloc, the United States and the North Koreans were treated as if both were in equal violation of the Charter and as if each needed in equal measure to be forced to keep the peace. Members differed in their degree of concern over the prolongation and extension of the war, but sooner or later all shared the conviction that to persist in using force, no matter how impeccable its United Nations credentials, was to frustrate the very purpose of the Organization. In this sense, as has frequently been observed, the

[6] Trygve Lie, *In the Cause of Peace* (New York: Macmillan, 1954), p. 338.

moral of Korea is not that collective security under United Nations auspices can be made to work, but that not even United Nations auspices will persuade Member States to risk military action where no vital national interest, narrowly construed, is involved, and where United Nations action may lead to hostilities with a major power.

This brings us to the two clear occasions when the dogs did bark, and the police did turn out — Suez and the Congo. In neither case can one explain United Nations action by the operation of a single factor; in both, several desperate elements combined. Let us take them in order.

II

In the first place, the complex of military events which it is convenient to call "Suez" occurred in an area long the subject of continuous United Nations concern. At the time of the Israeli attack there was actually operating at Gaza the United Nations Truce Supervision Organization (UNTSO) under its Chief of Staff, General Burns. His presence in the area served something of the same purpose in relation to the organization of the United Nations Emergency Force (UNEF) that the United Nations Commission on Korea served in relation to the alerting of the United Nations in Korea.

Secondly, Suez lay outside the zones of direct great power confrontation. But at the same time it was a key area strategically and economically which the West could not afford to lose to the Soviet bloc and which the Soviet bloc was proportionately eager to acquire. Two permanent members of the Security Council, the United Kingdom and France, regarded Nasser's nationalization of the Canal as an assault upon a vital national interest, but they always claimed that their forceful action to protect this interest was intended only to fill the void created by United Nations impotence in the face of the Israeli attack. Whether true or not, the argument made it difficult for them to refuse a United Nations force when offered, and indeed, in the case of Britain at least, reflected a profound national schizophrenia on the propriety of her violent action. Furthermore, the joint strength of Britain and France, though overwhelming against Egypt, was not sufficient to put them in the great power class, as became apparent when pressure was put on them simultaneously by the United States and the Soviet Union. This pressure was strong and potentially irresistible. Yet it was not in the United States' interest to drive her closest allies into too humiliating a retreat, and the Soviet Union's "rocket-rattling" diplomacy certainly worked both ways — stiffening Anglo-French resistance at least as much as it accelerated compliance. Nor did Nasser want to exchange British and French occupation of the Canal for Soviet tutelage. Thus a complex of considerations all led to the acceptance of Lester Pearson's UNEF as a device which would enable all parties to return to the *status quo ante* with maximum speed and minimum loss of face.

It is perhaps true that the UNEF idea owed some of its immediate acceptance to the fact that it was imperfectly understood: Britain and France in particular hoped to see the force act as the agent of the United Nations in implementing the six-point recommendations on a Canal settlement announced by Mr. Hammarskjöld on October 12, 1956, while Israel hoped to see it remedy her grievances about transit through the Canal and the Gulf of Aqaba. If true, however, this remains a marginal consideration. UNEF was created basically because no interested power could impose a solution alone, and all powers, great and small alike, preferred an internationally contrived and controlled solution to a conflict which could develop dangerously into a wider war. Negative considerations pointed the same way; neither of the two alliances, the Warsaw Pact or NATO, felt their vital interests threatened (however much, briefly, Britain and France may have), and neither Israel nor Egypt, on reflection, wanted a fight *à outrance* then and there.

To see these as the underlying factors that made UNEF possible is not to depreciate the efforts of Lester Pearson and the other representatives who came to be known at the United Nations as the "fire brigade," or the role of the Secretary-General and the Secretariat. "Factors" by themselves do not stop wars; they have to be assessed and manipulated by human beings. If courage, perseverance, diplomatic skill, imagination, and personal prestige had not existed in the right quarters at the right moment in 1956, the resulting drift and confusion would have required more than a UNEF to remedy them.

The celebrated conditions of UNEF laid down by the Secretary-General in his two reports of November 4 and 6, 1956,[7] were the necessary preconditions of its existence and also set the limits to what it might achieve. No one except the Soviet bloc states and the convicted trio of Britain, France, and Israel was willing to enlist in a United Nations force with coercive powers; no one was willing to fight Egypt or Israel, or possibly both simultaneously, in order to impose a just settlement — whatever that would have been — on these old combatants. Once this was recognized, it followed inevitably that the United Nations force could have only the function of facilitating the invaders' withdrawal, of maintaining a minimum of order in the transitional phase from war to armistice, and, finally, of keeping the local combatants, Israel and Egypt, at arms' length. The element of force was, strictly speaking, minimal. It was military only in being composed of soldiers; its functions were fewer even than those of a normal civilian police corps. Police exist to prevent crime and enforce the law as well as to preserve the peace, but UNEF has no powers to prevent anything save the most blatant frontier violations. Its role is pacific and passive. It is essential interpository in character, a moral United Nations presence given physical embodiment on a scale sufficiently extensive to guarantee that neither side can aim the slightest blow at the other without involving itself by that very act in larger, international consequences. Ever since the cease-fire and withdrawals were effected, UNEF has been in fact a larger and more physically impenetrable UNTSO.

In this capacity its success is undoubted. It has not only achieved its immediate objectives; it has also kept the peace between Egypt and Israel ever since, both in the large and obvious sense and in that of reducing to a previously unknown level the number of incidents along the border. This has been due to many factors besides the efficiency and

[7] UN Documents A/3289 and A/3302. The conditions were later codified in Document A/3943. In summary, these principles were:

(i) No permanent member of the Security Council or any "interested" government should contribute contingents.

(ii) The force should not be used to affect the military or political outcome of the dispute.

(iii) Its arms should only be used in self-defense.

(iv) It should not be stationed on a state's territory except with that state's consent.

loyalty of the force. Though the basic local antagonisms remain, nothing has occurred to provoke another 1956 flare-up, while the great power outsiders have all for various reasons been tolerably content not to stoke up the fires of Egyptain-Israeli animosity.[8] Then again there has been a simplicity, a straightforwardness about UNEF's role, rare in international affairs, which has helped it greatly. Its task is only to patrol a strip of desert, for the most part totally uninhabited, where it can exercise its simple function with a minimum risk of offending the susceptibilities of its host country or of anyone else. To adapt Tacitus, "Because it is a solitude, they can keep it at peace." The boundary it patrols is ideal for its purpose — open to view, clearly demarcated, uncomplicated by the presence of any human or economic factors more portentous than the occasional Bedouin herdsman and his flock.

Finally, the Arab-Israeli rivalry for all its intensity is basically parochial in scale. Outside the Moslem world few countries feel themselves deeply committed to one side or the other. This has made it comparatively easy to recruit for the force contingents whose nationality does not involve them in any serious risk of partisanship or even in accusations of partisanship. The Americas, Scandinavia, India — from this core it was not too difficult to construct a force which satisfied the criteria of geographical representativeness and detachment from local and great power conflicts.

In consequence, the difficulties of the force have been virtually confined to the familiar problems of finance. These, of course, reflect the fact that what was originally welcomed as a solution to an emergency has now become an apparent permanency. The fireman has turned into the lodger. The respite which UNEF provided for solving the Middle East problem has turned out to be the solution itself. It might even be argued that the existence of UNEF has relieved all the parties concerned of the need to find some other more lasting solution, but this argument would carry more force if anyone could suggest what such a solution might be. As it is, the forces of world politics and the circumstances of Middle East geography have made it possible to provide inveterate antagonisms with a mutually tolerable insulation. In so

[8] Some would list the protective blanket of the Eisenhower Doctrine among the dampening influences on the Middle East, though this seems to me more disputable

doing they have created a precedent and left a legacy of practical experience in the organizing and operating of a United Nations force.

When this legacy was drawn on in the Congo, it was in circumstances that soon made one wonder how far UNEF could properly be regarded as a precedent for the United Nations operation in the Congo (ONUC).[9] To take the simplest factor first, in place of the sealing off of a desert peninsula as in Suez, the Congo crisis required the insulation of an almost land-locked subcontinent, as well as the internal policing of that same huge area. Similarly, whereas UNEF had only to keep two organized and accountable states apart, ONUC had the double task of excluding outside intervention and creating internal viability. While UNEF could operate in an area physically free from complicating interests or inhabitants, no United Nations operation in the Congo could possibly avoid contact with Congolese life at every point — and in circumstances where any contact (or indeed no contact) inevitably involved interference. Finally, whereas it was relatively easy to construct a UNEF out of the contributions of disinterested states, disinterestedness was a much harder quality to command where the Congo was concerned. (What is more, for reasons of incipient Pan-Africanism and color consciousness it was, when discovered, by no means so obviously welcome.) At the very outset all these complications presented a formidable challenge to ONUC; before it had been long in operation, others, and worse, arose for which there was no precedent in the annals of international organization or in the records of international law.

Paradoxically — and the whole Congo operation was a jungle of paradoxes — it was easier to get ONUC established than UNEF. The whole United Nations was intensely "Africa-conscious"; the Secretary-General, then at the height of his prestige, had already established a United Nations presence in Leopoldville in the person of Dr. Bunche; and the fact that, at least in one aspect, ONUC could be viewed as a technical aid operation made its initial acceptance easier. Again, the need for the force did not immediately proceed from any actual clash of major powers which might try to bargain and prevaricate before

[9] In the interests of convenience I have used "ONUC" throughout to refer to the United Nations military force in the Congo, although strictly speaking, of course, it applies to the important civilian operation as well.

making way for it; only one power with modern armaments was involved, Belgium, and even it did not oppose the force in principle. The prize of the Congo was indeed a rich one, but no one in July 1960 was willing to be labeled a colonialist in order to win it, not even the Soviet Union. The United States in particular was content to see a neutral Congo established. The now classic rules of super-power diplomacy operated: neither side wanted to see the other gain control of the territory, but equally, neither wished to see a Congo civil war escalate into something more general. Each side no doubt gave different weight to different considerations, but initially the result was the same — a Security Council vote in which the United States and the Soviet Union voted on the same side and France, Britain, and Belgium abstained, ostensibly only because of reservations about the wording of the paragraph asking for Belgian troop withdrawals.

There was from the beginning an ambiguity about the authority and objectives of ONUC which reflected the anomalous position of the Congo itself, a state so newly independent that the *Loi Fondamentale* designed to authorize its constitution had not yet been ratified by the body appointed to do so, the Congolese parliament. In part, ONUC was a routine response to a routine request from a new state for technical assistance; what was novel was that it was for *military* assistance, a category hitherto unknown in United Nations technical aid circles. Simultaneously, however, it was an appeal for United Nations protection against the reintroduction of Belgian troops into the territory of an ex-colony now independent and also, from the United Nations point of view, a necessary safeguard against unilateral assistance pouring in from rival sides in the Cold War. ONUC's role from the outset was consequently a dual one — the provision of both internal and external security. Though the words "international peace and security" do not appear in the Security Council resolution[10] passed at its first meeting concerning the Congo on July 14, 1960, the Secretary-General later [11] stated that his authority to summon the meeting came from

[10] UN Document S/4387.

[11] Security Council *Official Records* (15th year), 884th meeting, August 8, 1960, p. 5.

Article 99 of the Charter,[12] and any such verbal deficiency was quickly made good in the following resolution of July 22.[13] Thus the force had a role closely analogous to that of UNEF — to facilitate and accelerate the withdrawal of foreign troops and to remove by its presence the justification for any other powers' interference; but it could not assume, as UNEF did, that the host country would look after internal security. Indeed ONUC's ability to restore internal security was a practical (if not a legal) condition of the successful discharge of its obligations toward international peace and security.

Nevertheless the Secretary-General took the view that the principles which he had laid down for the UNEF were equally valid for ONUC. As he told the Security Council on July 13, 1960,

> The United Nations Force would not be authorized to action beyond self-defence[14]. . . . They may not take any action which would make them a party to internal conflicts. . . . The selection of personnel should be such as to avoid complications because of the nationalities used. . . . This does not . . . exclude the use of units from African States, while . . . it does exclude . . . troops from any of the permanent members of the Security Council.[15]

In saying this, the Secretary-General could hardly have been unaware, even at this early stage of the operation, that the problems presented by the Congo were vastly different from those of Suez. His emphasis on UNEF principles in the Congo context must therefore have re-

[12] To "bring to the attention of the Security Council any matter which in his opinion may threaten the maintenance of international security."

[13] UN Document S/4405.

[14] How strictly this was originally interpreted can be seen in the wording of the leaflet distributed by Dr. Bunche and General von Horn to all members of ONUC on their arrival in the Congo:

> "You serve as members of an international force. It is a peace force, not a fighting force.
>
> The United Nations has asked you to come here in response to an appeal from the Government of the Republic of the Congo. Your task is to help in restoring order and calm in this country which has been so troubled recently. You are to be friendly to all the people of this country. Protection against acts of violence is to be given to *all* the people, white and black.
>
> You carry arms, but they are to be used *only* in self-defence. You are in the Congo to help *everyone*, to harm no one."

[15] Security Council *Official Records* (15th year), 873rd meeting, July 13, 1960, p. 5.

flected, as was surely right, a concern for the context of international politics within which the problems of the Congo would have to find their solution, if at all.

As every UN debate from the July 13 Security Council meeting onwards showed, the gravest differences of opinion existed among Member States as to what kind of settlement, what kind of Congo indeed, should be aimed at — differences, moreover, not merely between the Soviet bloc and the West but also within the West, within the Afro-Asian group, and even within the ranks of the Africans themselves. Even before Katanga's secession or the outright clash between Kasavubu and Lumumba, these differences were violent enough to guarantee that, if the United Nations attempted to formulate a positive policy for ONUC, it would not merely provoke a clash of opposites; it would reveal the lack of *any* clear majority consensus. (This was precisely what did happen in December 1960.) The only way to avert such a clash was to insist on the principle of non-interference and its corollary of no initiative in the use of force and to hope and work for conditions in which the empty formalism of the first and the acute frustrations of the second did not become too evident or impose too great a strain on those who had to apply them. Nor is it relevant to say that such a policy could not succeed unless it can be shown what other course of action would have been more successful.

Certainly, if a proving-ground for the Secretary-General's principles were desired, no more exacting one could be devised than the Congo. As might be expected, having regard to the conditions which provoked ONUC's presence, the first principle to come under strain was the ban on the use of armed force. In a country where the government was little more than an expression and where the army had no officers and was mutinous, any peace force was bound to find itself in a self-contradictory position. In Suez and Gaza there were always local police forces to whom UNEF could turn over any violators of the peace who came its way. In the Congo such entities hardly existed, yet ONUC itself had no powers to arrest or even disarm the mutineering elements of the *Force Publique*. Such a power eventually was given, and critics have argued that the biggest error of the whole Congo operation was not to have given it at the very beginning. This may be so, but two things have to be remembered. First, in a continent hypersensitive about "neo-colonialist" interference and in a country teetering on the edge of mass hysteria, it was important for the United Nations' long-term mission to preserve the image of itself as a pacific agent seeking only to help Africans to help themselves. Secondly, although some states that contributed to the force, e.g., Ghana, were willing, even eager to have their troops employed forcefully, others would have refused contributions to a force which was involved in the killing of Africans even in the best causes and even at the hands of other Africans. When, later on, resolute measures were taken, certain states did seek to withdraw in protest.

But, of course, more was involved than clashes with *Force Publique*. The issue of force or no force merged into the issue of interference or non-interference. Non-interference was even less possible in practice than abstention from force, because the mere presence of ONUC was interference. Non-interference, however, was also a more indispensable principle because there was no agreed alternative to put in its place. Even after the passage of the Security Council resolution of February 21, 1961,[16] authorizing "the use of force, if necessary, in the last resort," it was still the United Nations' position that it was not going to become a party to any internal conflict in the Congo. Similarly, when in September 1961 open fighting developed between ONUC and the Katangese forces, the United Nations' objectives (*pace* Mr. Conor C. O'Brien) were only the expulsion of "foreign mercenaries," the prevention of civil war, and the defense of its own positions. When finally, by the Security Council resolution of November 24, 1961,[17] the Secretary-General's authority was broadened to include "vigorous action, including the use of requisite measure of force if necessary," the object of this was still said to be the exclusion of foreign intruders.

It was also true that the United Nations accepted the unity of the Congo as axiomatic and secessionist activities as illegal. It explicitly rejected Katanga's claim to independence. Nevertheless, it never laid on ONUC the task of enforcing Congolese unity or ending Katangese independence. These objectives were to be secured by conciliation, moral pressure, or, at most and not until very late in the day, economic

[16] UN Document S/4741.
[17] UN Document S/5002.

and financial sanctions. Moreover, since ONUC had a positive obligation to prevent civil war, it was as opposed to the central government's forcible occupation of Katanga as to Katanga's forcible secession.

In all these senses the United Nations was impartial. Within the framework of Congolese unity it was for the Congolese to decide who should rule and how. But in almost all the actual power contests of Congo politics the United Nations could not avoid taking decisions which favored one side or the other. Seizing the radio station and closing the airports was a logical application of ONUC's duty to stop civil war and external interference, but it was also inescapably an act which, at the moment it was taken, tilted the scales in favor of Kasavubu and against Lumumba. The fact that this occurred in the Alice in Wonderland situation when the President claimed to have dismissed his prime minister and the prime minister claimed to have dismissed his President provided a further legal justification for the United Nations action but left its practical consequences unchanged.

In its external role as the United Nations' agent for relieving the Congo of Belgian interference and protecting it against all other non-UN intrusions, ONUC ran into comparable difficulties. Its early claims of success in effecting Belgian withdrawal turned out to be premature since Katanga remained a center of foreign influence and activity, hostile alike to the UN and to the central government, while ONUC's inability to restore order even in the rest of the Congo provided Belgium with an excuse for retaining or reintroducing her forces. This in turn aggravated Congolese impatience and encouraged factional leaders to seek extra-UN assistance of a kind which was only too readily available, with the result that a month or so after ONUC had come into operation massive Soviet aid was placed at the disposal of Lumumba.

The Soviet assistance came by air and, to be countered, necessitated the closure by United Nations forces of all Congolese airports. No doubt this action hampered Soviet plans for further intervention, though its legal justification and its immediate purpose were to prevent Lumumba from using the troop-carrying Ilyushin planes to launch his forces against Kasai province. Nevertheless, it is almost certainly true to say that it was Mobutu's seizure of power and his ensuing expulsion of all Soviet bloc representatives rather than any direct ONUC action which put a stop to Soviet intervention. It was on this account that no direct on-the-spot clash between the Soviet interlopers and the ONUC command occurred. No doubt the Soviet Union, in the interests of its relations with the African powers, was glad not have any such showdown. On the evidence available, however, it cannot be said that the mere presence of ONUC was adequate, as many hoped it would be, to deter great-power intervention. It is one thing to violate a clearly held United Nations patrol line; it is another thing to fly "volunteers" into a civilian airport with little or no show of military might. ONUC's experience here is a reminder that the third dimension of the air can make nonsense of the attractive concept of a United Nations buffer force whose mere physical presence on the ground serves as an adequate moral trip-wire or plate glass window.

The cross-currents set up by factional fighting inside the Congo and intervention from outside complicated the Congo operation in two other respects. In getting on to a decade of operation UNEF has had little difficulty in holding its national contingents together or in maintaining equable relations with its host government. ONUC speedily ran into trouble on both fronts. Dag Hammarskjöld's decision to make ONUC a predominantly African force was certainly a right one; no other course would have secured the indispensable moral backing in Africa or the African votes in the United Nations. But it was impossible for a force so composed to be completely disinterested. Each contributing state had strong views on every Congo issue, and every decision that ONUC had to make imposed a strain on its loyalties. Looking back over the fiercely troubled course of the Congo since July 1960 one is truly impressed to see how well in such circumstances the conglomerate ONUC held together. Nonetheless, it is instructive to notice how and where the bonds of loyalty chafed.

Thus in September 1960 ONUC's denial to Lumumba of the use of the radio station and airports provoked Guinea, Ghana, and the United Arab Republic to threaten a withdrawal of their troops and claim a right to place them at Lumumba's disposal. This led the Secretary-General to elaborate the basic principles on which a composite UN force operated, as follows:

> Were a national contingent to leave the United Nations Force, they would have to be regarded as foreign troops introduced into the

> Congo, and the Security Council would have to consider their continued presence in the Congo, as well as its consequences for the United Nations operation, in this light.[18]

This important circumscription of the conditions under which withdrawal could take place was further sharpened the following January when Morocco ordered its brigade to "cease to perform its functions" while remaining in the Congo. The Secretary-General insisted that it could remain only "as an integral part of the United Nations Force" and that any other position would be "untenable."[19] Morocco agreed to its troops remaining under the United Nations flag until repatriation could be arranged, "but if called upon to act against their conscience" they would feel bound not to accept any decision contrary to the interests of the Congo and of legality."[20] The Secretary-General's own inimitable blend of legal argument, moral authority, and diplomacy in fact prevented most of these threatening checks ever being presented for actual payment, but even so he could not eliminate the enervating effect which they had on the United Nations operation. Whereas UNEF was a force united in a common acceptance of a clearcut task, ONUC for long periods at a time lacked any agreed purpose, indeed at certain periods was sharply divided within itself. Even if the disagreements of participating governments were not fully reflected in the behavior of their contingents, they could not but impair their full cooperation.

To speak of a "host government" in the context of the anarchy which prevailed for most of 1960 and 1961 in the Congo is to bring out how remote were the realities of the United Nations operation from the language of law and diplomacy in which it had to be clothed. Repeatedly ONUC found itself not merely at odds but actually at blows with the agents of the government whom it was to "assist" and "consult with," to quote the language of repeated United Nations resolutions. Most of these incidents belong to that level of UN-Congolese relations which had more to do with bizarre bargaining and gang warfare than diplomacy, but some of them raised issues not only

[18] Security Council *Official Records* (15th year), 896th meeting, September 9, 1960, p. 20.
[19] UN Document S/4668.
[20] *Ibid.*

important at the time but having possible future significance for United Nations procedure and international law. This was conspicuously true of Kasavubu's attempts to impose impossible conditions on ONUC, particularly in connection with the use of the port of Matadi in March 1961. These led the Secretary-General to issue the following interpretation of their relations:

> The relation between the United Nations and the Government of the Republic of the Congo is not merely a contractual relationship in which the Republic can impose its conditions as host State and thereby determine the circumstances under which the United Nations operates. It is rather a relationship governed by mandatory decisions of the Security Council. . . . Only the Security Council can decide on the discontinuance of the operation and . . . therefore conditions which, by their effect on the operation, would deprive it of its necessary basis, would require direct consideration of the Security Council. . . .[21]

Here, obviously, we have a potentially far-reaching modification of the 1956 doctrine requiring the consent of the host state as a necessary precondition of the presence of a United Nations force. Partly this reflects the shift in the source of the mandate from the General Assembly to the Security Council; partly it reflects the distinctive role of a United Nations force called in to provide internal aid as well as external protection. Yet even so, a word of caution must be added. It is in the Congo context that the Secretary-General is speaking — i.e., in a political hall of mirrors, where the reality and its reflections become swiftly indistinguishable and nothing is quite what it seems. For if one seeks to establish what sanctions the Secretary-General employed to secure the cooperation of the Congolese authorities or at least to curb their obstructiveness, one finds that they amounted to nothing more or less than the threat to withdraw the presence which offends. It was in these terms that Dag Hammarskjöld wrote to Kasavubu on December 21, 1960, warning him against behavior which would lead on to civil war:

> I sincerely trust that no situation will develop which would give me no choice but to recommend to the Security Council that it authorize the withdrawal of the United Nations Force . . . thus throwing on the

[21] UN Document S/4389/Add.5.

> authorities of the Congo the full responsibility of maintaining law and order.[22]

We are back, not for the first time, in the world of the nursery where authority and prudence alike reinforce the wisdom of Hilaire Belloc's advice:

> And always keep a hold of Nurse
> For fear of finding something worse.

III

Any lessons which one may draw from these events while the Congo operation is so recent must be tentative. Even so, something can be said.

First a *caveat.* It is often said that the Congo is *sui generis.* It certainly differs from any situation the United Nations has had to tackle before, but is it so different from what may arise in the future? As long as underdeveloped countries are in ferment and communist (or other) powers prefer subversion to open aggression, variations on the Congo theme are practically bound to occur. No doubt also it is true that the United Nations is not designed to cope with such situations; as an international organization it is built on the assumption that viable states are the entities with which it has to deal. This palliates failure, but it cannot excuse inaction. Future Congos cannot be ignored simply because they were not dreamed of in the philosophy of San Francisco. This is not to say that the United Nations ought to get into every situation where internal breakdowns occur; if such crises can be settled without such intervention, so much the better. But if they threaten international peace and security, the United Nations cannot side-step them on any narrowly legalistic ground.

But it is also probable in any foreseeable future that the balance of world politics, in particular the near-deadlock rivalries of East and West and the persistent floating votes of the nonaligned, will remain much as before. If so, Suez and the Congo suggest that there are limits to what any United Nations force can, at present, achieve. UNEF represents about as successful a buffer operation between states as can be imagined — in about as propitious a set of circumstances. Happy

[22] UN Document S/4606.

the UNEF of the future which has as easy a task. In the more likely case, however, in which external clashes are accompanied by internal breakdown, some if not all the problems of ONUC seem likely to recur. There may be fewer difficulties on the ground — there could hardly be more — but there are likely to be just as many in the council chambers of the United Nations. If this is so, it seems idle to press for a United Nations force which would discard the three principles of "force only in self-defense," "non-interference," and "entry only with the consent of the host country." Of course these principles are not adequate (whatever that may mean); they are merely in the present state of the world indispensable. They may be stretched, modified, even conceivably bypassed; they cannot within the framework of the present United Nations be replaced by any positive alternatives.

If this is true, it does not follow that no improvements on ONUC are possible or that no advance planning, even perhaps advance organization, for a United Nations force, can be contemplated. On the contrary, the peculiar strains which such a role imposes on a United Nations force and its leaders make it the more desirable that everything which is politically possible should be done to train it for the discharge of its very distinctive functions. It lies outside the scope of this paper to consider how this could be best be done, but that it should be done is certainly in accordance with our conclusions.

Certain other conclusions also follow. If one asks why, despite all its difficulties, ONUC was able to function as well as it did, or — to concede everything to its critics — to function at all, the answers are threefold. First, because the West, and in particular the United States, has been willing to foot the financial bill. No doubt it is wrong — in terms of the Charter — that this burden should fall as unevenly as it does. But if, like Britain, any Member State is inclined to feel self-righteous when it pays its share or, like France, self-justified when it does not, let it pause to ask whether its national interest would be better served if the Soviet Union paid the whole. Piper-paying and tune-calling are not interchangeable terms in the United Nations — otherwise what would the Charter be for? — but they are connected. Certainly, no future ONUC can operate unless it has funds, and if it is to operate with higher efficiency than the present Congo force, it will need larger funds. These can only come from the well-to-do West — unless they are to come from the Soviet Union.

The second reason for ONUC's survival is the general willingness of most of the states variously described as "nonaligned," "neutralist," or the "fire brigades," to support the operation by their votes and often by their contributions. In this the role of the Afro-Asians has been crucial not only because of their numbers but also because of their position on the spectrum of United Nations politics. They alone could supply the disinterestedness which comes from their relative impotence and the loyalty which reflects their own dependence upon the Organization.

This dependence has often seemed to be personified in their support of the Secretary-General and has even been ascribed to a personal confidence in Dag Hammarskjöld. But to see it entirely in these terms is to mistake the man for the institution. It is not by an accident of personality that the creation and functioning of UNEF and ONUC have been linked so closely with the office of the Secretary-General. It is because any sustained executive functions, however limited, can only be discharged in an organization like the United Nations by its Secretariat, a body which the Secretary-General at once leads and personifies. Only the Council and the Assembly are capable of authorizing a United Nations force, but if the history of Suez and the Congo demonstrates anything, it is that they are utterly incapable of running it. In this more than in anything else that the Secretary-General is called upon to do, the now familiar concept of "filling a vacuum of authority" manifests and justifies itself.

There is a logical connection between the Soviet opposition to ONUC and its advocacy of the "troika." An equivalent logic dictates that no future United Nations force is conceivable for which executive authority is not delegated to a Secretary-General willing and able to act when his "parliamentary" overlords are deadlocked. An advisory committee may abate his loneliness; it cannot relieve him of his responsibility and should not seek to curb his authority. If the office seems dangerously potent, as so developed by Dag Hammarskjöld and as apparently now operated by U Thant, the weapons of negation and frustration are at hand in the Security Council, the General Assembly and, behind both, in the financial deliberations of the Fifth Committee. Those who wish to use them, however, should do so with a full awareness of the consequences. Nothing in the experience of Suez and the Congo suggests than an international force is exempt from the workings of the inexorable rule that he who wills the end must will the means as well.

NOTES AND QUESTIONS

1. Three situations other than those discussed by Nicholas should be considered in relation to an assessment of UN peace-keeping efforts. They are the minimal participation of the United Nations in the Soviet—United States confrontation arising from the Soviet attempt in 1962 to place intermediate-range missiles in Cuba, the Chinese use of armed force to press their claims for an adjustment of territorial boundaries with India, and the continuing internal war (with external involvement) in South Vietnam. Each of these situations is exceedingly complicated and only a few observations can be hazarded here.

   The use of the Organization of American States as a device for dealing with the 1962 missile crisis raises the question of the extent to which regional organizations should be given a greater or lesser responsibility for peace-keeping activity. This is a fundamental question, for it involves, among other matters, the rights of individual states like Cuba or Hungary or Israel who do not adhere to the prevailing political consensus in the region, and the extent to which the overall global community needs effective procedures by which to review coercive policies pursued by regional organizations as well as those pursued by nation-states. Some analysts of world order have thought that regional organizations might actually inhibit the growth of an adequate world community structure for dealing with international peace and security. On this, see Yalem, **I-3A** and Henkin, **II-3**.

   The role of the United Nations in a confrontation between the superpowers is dealt with by Hammarskjöld in his last annual report reprinted in Chapter 11 of this volume. For an analysis of the potential role of the United Nations in the Berlin situation which includes the recommendations that planning on the matter begin before a crisis, and for the specific suggestion that UN troops be stationed in the city as "a UN presence" that might even assume the function of patrolling the boundary lines of the various zones and the access routes to Berlin from West Germany, see Louis Henkin, *The Berlin Crisis and the United Nations* (Carnegie Endowment for International Peace, New York, 1959).

   The Chinese use of armed force against India (and it should be noted, against Tibet as well) raises the question of what the role of the United Nations can and should be toward the use of international violence by political entities that are nonmembers. Article 2(6) is relevant here, and so is the whole debate on universality of membership (Chapter 2).

   The internal war in South Vietnam is a situation in which there has been almost no United Nations action, although there have been a number of formal international conferences held outside the United Nations system. The most notable was held at Geneva in 1954.

2. Nicholas' observation that the policing difficulties encountered in the Congo may not be unique, but are in fact likely to be rather typical, is an important one that raises the question of whether we can anticipate effective action by the United

Nations in the next few decades, and when it may be called upon to act in the face of a breakdown of law and order within nation-states. The sources of this breakdown may be almost totally internal and arise from the inability of the inhabitants to deal with their social problems, and contrariwise, they may be the product of external interventions. To what extent is a United Nations peace-keeping operation more likely to succeed when the civil strife is purely internal? Is it appropriate, given the limits imposed by Article 2(7) (see Chapter 7), for the United Nations to intervene in a purely internal civil war?——on what theory?

Many students of international relations have come to the conclusion that the major form of violence in the international community is likely to be centered upon struggles for control of the government of a single country—that is, upon the phenomena of civil or internal war. The most legalistic argument for this stress on the role of civil war is the suggestion that the prohibition on force in Article 2(4) has come to have a considerable impact upon nation-state behavior, so much so that most states are now willing to cast votes of censure in the General Assembly and Security Council and sometimes to take action against states who have recourse to sustained violence across territorial boundaries. Underlying this argument is the social fact that there exists a universal interest in avoiding thermonuclear war. This interest is coupled with the recognition that when an armed attack across a state line takes place there is a greater likelihood that violence will escalate into nuclear war. There are many explanations of this apprehension, among them that traditional military alliances will be called into play, and thereby almost automatically increase the scale of conflict.

3. Nicholas suggests that the three principles of "force only in self-defense," "non-interference," and "entry only with the consent of the host country," although not adequate for purposes of world order, are indispensible, given the present state of the world. He writes that these principles "may be stretched, modified, even conceivingly by-passed; they cannot within the framework of the present United Nations be replaced by any positive alternatives." What does this mean? What is the relationship between the functional requisites of world order and the limits of political acceptability?
4. Nicholas indicates that it might be plausible to impose the burden of financing peace-keeping activities upon some basis other than the usual scale of assessment. This suggestion recalls Brierly's view that those states with the most immediate interest in a particular security venture should be willing to accept a disproportionately large share of the burdens connected with undertaking it. Such an arrangement on financing seems to have been adopted with regard to establishing a United Nations presence in Yemen.

The danger of allowing states to choose the extent of their involvement in a given peace-keeping situation is that the use of coercion by the United Nations will have the appearance of a coalition action rather than of a genuine community undertaking. If the contribution to peace-keeping was independent of a state's sympathies and interests, then it would appear to be a more universal, less provincial, system of peace and security. Perhaps some sort of compromise is feasible. The community participation could be achieved at the invoking stage when two-thirds or more of the membership would have to authorize the peace-keeping mission. However, once authorized, then the recruitment of personnel and the burden of financing could be distributed according to some set of criteria that recognized the wishes of states to be maximal or minimal participators.

5. Has the United Nations been successful in its peace-keeping activities to date? How is success to be measured? Is it a matter of stopping the fighting? Are there any considerations of justice involved? Is it a matter of upholding world community expectations—that is, performing as the authorizing majority expects? An affirmative reply implies that the authorizing states share a common set of expectations. Events, especially the Congo operation, reveal how an initial consensus built up around repelling Belgian reentry and Katanganese secession can disappear in the field. There must be a continuing consensus—and yet, once the peace-keeping action begins, it is difficult to revoke its mission or even adapt the mission to evolving circumstances.

Previous authors commenting on Suez and the Congo as peace-keeping operations include Claude, **II-3**, Lande, Chapter 5A and Skubiszewski, Chapter 5A. Among the most useful books on the subject are Arthur Lee Burns and Nina Heathcote, *Peace-Keeping by U.N. Forces—From Suez to the Congo* (Praeger, New York, 1963); Gabriella Rosner, *The United Nations Emergency Force* (Columbia University Press, 1963).

The next selection is a portion of the report written by Dag Hammarskjöld in the fall of 1958, "United Nations Emergency Force," UN Document A/3943 (October 9, 1958). It is a summary of the basic principles that he believed important for increasing the efficiency and acceptability of the peace-keeping forces of the United Nations. This report is based almost exclusively on the lessons learned from UNEF and from the use of the UN observation teams in Lebanon and Jordan in 1958. It imaginatively distills principles from rather scant UN experience and gives the impression that these principles offer suitable guidelines for future operations of the Organization in the peace-keeping area. Written in a terse style, the report covers a series of problems that seem likely to remain relevant to the effective operation of United Nations police and peace-keeping activities in the foreseeable future. Hammarskjöld's guidelines apply to the following subject-matter: the doctrine of good faith as the proper foundation for the relationship between the United Nations forces and the host state; some standards with regard to the composition of the forces; the allocation of functions between the UN forces and the security forces of the host government; reconciliation of the national loyalties of the peace-keeping personnel with continuing allegiance to the United Nations; the designation of who will make decisions with regard to field commanders; the limited capacity of the Secretary-General to call, on his own initiative, directly upon Members of the Organization to provide troops; the relationship between the Secretary-General's responsibility and authority in the peace-keeping area and that of the General Assembly and Security Council; and the permissible use of force by United Nations troops for purposes of self-defense.

UNITED NATIONS EMERGENCY FORCE

Summary study of the experience derived from
the establishment and operation of the force.
"Concluding Observations and Principles"
from the Report of the Secretary-General,

DAG HAMMARSKJÖLD

A. OBSERVATIONS

148. In the preceding pages of this report a summary has been given of the experience of the United Nations derived from the establishment and operation of the United Nations Emergency Force. In advance of the conclusions, certain observations are called for regarding the specific circumstances in which the experience with UNEF has been gained, since those circumstances definitely limit any detailed application of that experience to the general problem of United Nations operations of this character. It is useful, in this context, also to note and compare the subsequent experience with United Nations operations in relation to Lebanon and Jordan.

149. UNEF was brought into being to meet a particular situation in which a United Nations force could be interposed between regular, national military forces which were subject to a cease-fire agreed to by the opposing parties. UNEF has continued to function along the "dividing line" between the national forces. It follows that in UNEF there has never been any need for rights and responsibilities other than those necessary for such an interposed force under cease-fire conditions. The Force was not used in any way to enforce withdrawals but, in the successive stages of the withdrawals, followed the withdrawing troops to the "dividing line" of each stage. It is also to be noted that the Force has functioned under a clear-cut mandate which has entirely detached it from involvement in any internal or local problems, and also has enabled it to maintain its neutrality in relation to international political issues. The fact that UNEF was designed to meet the needs of this specific situation largely determined its military

UN Document A/3943, October 9, 1958.

components, geographical composition, deployment and status, and also its effectiveness.

150. A further factor of significance in the evaluation of the UNEF experience is that in Gaza the Force is in an area having special status under the Armistice Agreement. In Gaza and elsewhere in its area of operations, UNEF has been able to function without any question arising of its presence infringing upon sovereign rights, on the basis that, at the invitation of the Egyptian Government and in accordance with the decision of the General Assembly, the United Nations assists in maintaining quiet on the Armistice Demarcation Line around the Gaza Strip and along the international line to the south. The Government of Egypt has co-operated by taking necessary steps to facilitate the functioning of UNEF in the Gaza area. The same is true of the position of the Egyptian Government in keeping its limited military units in the Sinai Peninsula away from the area in which the UNEF chiefly functions.

151. Obviously, some of the above-mentioned circumstances are of such a nature that it could not reasonably be expected that they would often be duplicated elsewhere. Nor can it be assumed that they provide a sufficient basis to warrant indiscriminate projection of the UNEF experience in planning for future United Nations operations of this kind. Indeed, the more recent experiences in Lebanon and Jordan serve only to emphasize the uniqueness of the UNEF setting, which, in part at least, explains the success of this pioneer venture. Neither in Lebanon nor in Jordan would it have been possible to interpose a United Nations force between conflicting parties. Nor would it have been possible in either of those situations to preserve a natural distinction between the presence and functions in various areas of any United Nations force and the presence and functions of government troops. In Lebanon, it is unlikely that a United Nations force could have operated without soon becoming a party to the internal conflicts among nationals of the country. In Jordan, the presence of a United Nations force has been regarded by the Government as difficult to reconcile with its own exercise of full sovereignty over the people and territory of the country. United Nations experience with these three Middle East operations justifies the assumption that, in each new conflict situation in which the United Nations might be called upon to intervene with military personnel, the nature of the actual organization required and its paramilitary aspects would be determined by the particular needs of the situation and could not, therefore, be anticipated in advance. Thus, for example, stand-by arrangements for a force designed for a UNEF-type operation would not have been of practical value in either of the situations in Lebanon or Jordan, where conditions required an approach in all relevant aspects quite different from that employed in UNEF.

152. The foregoing leads to the obvious conclusion that, in considering general stand-by arrangements for United Nations operations of the kind

envisaged in this report, a course should be followed which would afford a considerable degree of flexibility in approaching the varying needs that may arise. This could be achieved if stand-by arrangements were to consist of an approval of those general conclusions regarding principles which can be reached in the light of the UNEF experience, and which would provide a setting within which, with the necessary variations of approach, personnel in units or otherwise could be recruited and an operation organized without delay and with full adjustment to the specific situation requiring the action.

153. Further support for the position here taken is found in that the type and rank of military personnel required, the need for specialists and for supporting units, as well as the vehicle and equipment demands, as experience has shown, also vary so much from case to case that more far-reaching and firm arrangements — as, for example, the maintenance of a nucleus United Nations force of the type generally envisaged — would be without great practical value and certainly would not warrant the substantial sacrifices involved. By way of illustration of this point UNEF has been able to use enlisted men with short military experience under the command of experienced officers; the recruitment of personnel for the United Nations Observation Group in Lebanon has been limited largely to officers, who, however, with few exceptions, did not have to be rigorously screened for the mission; while the arrangements in relation to Jordan may involve, if any, only a very limited number of military personnel, all of officer rank but individually and carefully chosen for the purpose. Similar differences are apparent as regards the need for matériel with UNEF being adequately served by, in military calculations, a quite modest number of aircraft and vehicles, while UNOGIL has had to operate with a considerably higher ratio of planes and vehicles to the men involved, because of the specific tasks with which it has been entrusted.

B. BASIC PRINCIPLES

154. In view of the impossibility of determining beforehand the specific form of a United Nations presence of the type considered in this report, which would be necessary to meet adequately the requirements of a given situation, a broad decision by the General Assembly should attempt to do no more than endorse certain basic principles and rules which would provide an adaptable framework for later operations that might be found necessary. In a practical sense, it is not feasible in advance of a known situation to do more than to provide for some helpful stand-by arrangements for a force or similar forms of a United Nations presence. In the following paragraphs, certain principles and rules are laid down in the light of the experience gathered in the past years, which, if they were to meet with the approval of the General Assembly, would provide a continuing basis on which useful contacts in a stand-by context might be established with

interested Governments, with the aim of being prepared for any requests which might arise from future decisions by the Assembly on a force or similar arrangement to deal with a specific case.

155. As the arrangements discussed in this report do not cover the type of force envisaged under Chapter VII of the Charter, it follows from international law and the Charter that the United Nations cannot undertake to implement them by stationing units on the territory of a Member State without the consent of the Government concerned. It similarly follows from the Charter that the consent of a Member nation is necessary for the United Nations to use its military personnel or matériel. These basic rules have been observed in the recent United Nations operations in the Middle East. They naturally hold valid for all similar operations in the future.

156. The fact that a United Nations operation of the type envisaged requires the consent of the Government on whose territory it takes place creates a problem, as it is normally difficult for the United Nations to engage in such an operation without guarantees against unilateral actions by the host Government which might put the United Nations in a questionable position, either administratively or in relation to contributing Governments.

157. The formula employed in relation to the Government of Egypt for UNEF seems, in the light of experience, to provide an adequate solution to this problem. The Government of Egypt declared that, when exercising its sovereign right with regard to the presence of the Force, it would be guided by good faith in the interpretation of the purposes of the Force. This declaration was balanced by a declaration by the United Nations to the effect that the maintenance of the Force by the United Nations would be determined by similar good faith in the interpretation of the purposes.

158. The consequence of such a bilateral declaration is that, were either side to act unilaterally in refusing continued presence or deciding on withdrawal, and were the other side to find that such action was contrary to a good faith interpretation of the purposes of the operation, an exchange of views would be called for towards harmonizing the positions. This does not imply any infringement on the sovereign right of the host Government, nor any restriction of the right of the United Nations to decide on termination of its own operation whenever it might see fit to do so. But it does mean a mutual recognition of the fact that the operation, being based on collaboration between the host Government and the United Nations, should be carried on in forms natural to such collaboration, and especially so with regard to the questions of presence and maintenance.

159. It is unlikely that any Government in the future would be willing to go beyond the declaration of the Government of Egypt with regard to UNEF. Nor, in my view, should the United Nations commit itself beyond the point established for UNEF in relation to the Government of Egypt. In these circumstances, I consider it reasonable to regard the formula

mentioned in paragraph 158 above as a valid basis for future arrangements of a similar kind.

160. Another point of principle which arises in relation to the question of consent refers to the composition of United Nations military elements stationed on the territory of a Member country. While the United Nations must reserve for itself the authority to decide on the composition of such elements, it is obvious that the host country, in giving its consent, cannot be indifferent to the composition of those elements. In order to limit the scope of possible difference of opinion, the United Nations in recent operations has followed two principles: not to include units from any of the permanent members of the Security Council; and not to include units from any country which, because of its geographical position or for other reasons, might be considered as possibly having a special interest in the situation which has called for the operation. I believe that these two principles also should be considered as essential to any stand-by arrangements.

161. Given the two principles mentioned in paragraph 160, in actual practice the area within which conflicting views may be expressed will in all probability be so reduced normally as to facilitate the harmonizing of the rights of the United Nations with the interests of the host country. It would seem desirable to accept the formula applied in the case of UNEF, which is to the effect that, while it is for the United Nations alone to decide on the composition of military elements sent to a country, the United Nations should, in deciding on composition, take fully into account the viewpoint of the host Government as one of the most serious factors which should guide the recruitment of the personnel. Usually, this is likely to mean that serious objections by the host country against participation by a specific contributing country in the United Nations operation will determine the action of the Organization. However, were the United Nations for good reasons to find that course inadvisable, it would remain free to pursue its own line, and any resulting conflict would have to be resolved on a political rather than on a legal basis. I would recommend that the basis thus laid in the case of UNEF be considered as the formula on composition applicable to similar operations in the future.

162. The principles indicated in the four points discussed above (paragraphs 155-161 inclusive) were either established by the General Assembly itself, elaborated in practice or in negotiations with the Government of Egypt. They have served as the basis for a status Agreement which applies to the United Nations personnel in the Force in Egypt. In its entirety, this status Agreement has stood up well to the test of experience. Its basic principles should be embodied in similar agreements in the future, and their recognition, therefore, would seem necessarily to form part of any stand-by arrangements for a force. The Agreement regarding the presence of UNOGIL in Lebanon, although much less elaborate because of the modest size of the operation and the fact that normal immunity rules

could be applied to the bulk of the personnel, also reflects the basic principles I have in mind.

163. The most important principle in the status Agreement ensures that UNEF personnel, when involved in criminal actions, come under the jurisdiction of the criminal courts of their home countries. The establishment of this principle for UNEF, in relation to Egypt, has set a most valuable precedent. Experience shows that this principle is essential to the successful recruitment by the United Nations of military personnel not otherwise under immunity rules, from its Member countries. The position established for UNEF should be maintained in future arrangements.

164. Another principle involved in the UNEF status Agreement, and which should be retained, is that the United Nations activity should have freedom of movement within its area of operations and all such facilities regarding access to that area and communications as are necessary for successful completion of the task. This also obviously involves certain rights of over-flight over the territory of the host country. These principles have been maintained in the case of UNOGIL. Their application requires an agreement on what is to be considered as the area of operations and as to what facilities of access and communications are to be considered necessary. On the assumption that, like UNEF, any similar United Nations operation in the future would be of assistance to the nation on whose territory it is stationed, it is not to be expected that the necessary process of agreement will give rise to any serious complications in the interpretation of the principle.

165. Apart from the principles thus established in negotiated agreements or formal decisions, a series of basic rules has been developed in practice. Some of these rules would appear to merit general application. This is true especially of the precept that authority granted to the United Nations group cannot be exercised within a given territory either in competition with representatives of the host Government or in co-operation with them on the basis of any joint operation. Thus, a United Nations operation must be separate and distinct from activities by national authorities. UNEF experience indicates how this rule may apply in practice. A right of detention which normally would be exercised only by local authorities is extended to UNEF units. However, this is so only within a limited area where the local authorities voluntarily abstain from exercising similar rights, whether alone or in collaboration with the United Nations. Were the underlying principle of this example not to be applied, United Nations units might run the risk of getting involved in differences with the local authorities or public or in internal conflicts which would be highly detrimental to the effectiveness of the operation and to the relations between the United Nations and the host Government.

166. A rule closely related to the one last-mentioned, and reflecting a basic Charter principle, precludes the employment of United Nations elements

in situations of an essentially internal nature. As a matter of course, the United Nations personnel cannot be permitted in any sense to be a party to internal conflicts. Their role must be limited to external aspects of the political situation as, for example, infiltration or other activities affecting international boundaries.

167. Even in the case of UNEF, where the United Nations itself had taken a stand on decisive elements in the situation which gave rise to the creation of the Force, it was explicitly stated that the Force should not be used to enforce any specific political solution of pending problems or to influence the political balance decisive to such a solution. This precept clearly imposes a serious limitation on the possible use of United Nations elements, were it to be given general application to them whenever they are not created under Chapter VII of the Charter. However, I believe its acceptance to be necessary, if the United Nations is to be in a position to draw on Member countries for contributions in men and matériel to United Nations operations of this kind.

168. Military personnel employed by the United Nations in paramilitary operations are, of course, not under the same formal obligations in relation to the Organization as staff members of the Secretariat. However, the position must be maintained that the basic rules of the United Nations for international service are applicable also to such personnel, particularly as regards full loyalty to the aims of the Organization and to abstention from acts in relation to their country of origin or to other countries which might deprive the operation of its international character and create a situation of dual loyalty. The observance of this rule is not only vital for good relations with the host country, it is also to the benefit of the contributing countries concerned, as any other attitude might involve them in responsibilities which would be undesirable in the light of the national policies pursued.

169. In setting up UNEF, the General Assembly appointed a Commander of the Force with the position of an international civil servant responsible for discharge of his task to the Assembly, but administratively integrated with the United Nations organization, and under instructions from the Secretary-General on the basis of the executive authority for the operation vested in him by the Assembly.

170. A somewhat different procedure was followed in the case of UNOGIL, where the Security Council delegated to the Secretary-General the responsibility for constituting the Observation Group. However, basically the same principle employed in UNEF is applied to UNOGIL, for the Group is responsible for the conduct of its business to the Security Council, while administratively it is under the Secretary-General, who is charged with its organization. A basically similar pattern finds reflection also in the arrangements being made by the United Nations in relation to Jordan.

171. The innovation represented by the constitutional pattern thus followed in recent United Nations field operations has, in experience, proved to be highly practical and, especially, politically of decisive importance, as it has provided for an integration giving the operation all the advantages of administrative co-ordination with the Secretariat and of the fully internationalized status of the Secretariat. As pointed out in my "Second and final report on the Emergency Force", on which the General Assembly based its decision to organize the Force, the appointment by the General Assembly of a Commander determined the legal status of the Force. The other arrangements, mentioned above, reflect the same basic concept.
172. In full recognition of the wide variety of forms which decisions on a United Nations operation may take in seeking to fit differing situations calling for such an operation, the underlying rule concerning command and authority which has been consistently applied in recent years, as set out above, should, in my view, be maintained for the future. Thus, a United Nations operation should always be under a leadership established by the General Assembly or the Security Council, or on the basis of delegated authority by the Secretary-General, so as to make it directly responsible to one of the main organs of the United Nations, while integrated with the Secretariat in an appropriate form.
173. Were soundings with Member Governments, based on the aforementioned legal and political principles and rules and on the regulations regarding financial responsibilities set out below, to show that a number of Governments in their planning would be willing to take into account the possibility of having to provide promptly — on an emergency basis, on specific appeal from the United Nations — men and matériel to a United Nations operation of the kind envisaged in this report, a question arises regarding the conditions under which such a desirable stand-by arrangement could be utilized.
174. Under the Charter, and under the "Uniting for Peace" resolution, a formal decision on a United Nations operation must be taken by the General Assembly or by the Security Council. It must be regarded as excluded that the right to take such a decision, in any general terms, could properly be considered as delegated to the Secretary-General. Short of an explicit decision by the General Assembly or the Security Council with a specific authorization, the Secretary-General, thus, cannot be considered as entitled to appeal to a Member nation for military personnel to be dispatched to another Member country in a United Nations operation.
175. The terms of the delegation in each operation thus far have set the limit of the Secretary-General's authority. Thus, for example, as apparent from the description of the new body, the decision relating to UNEF, which was to be implemented by the Secretary-General, qualified the operation as being one of a paramilitary nature, while the absence of an explicit authorization for the Force to take offensive action excluded the

organization by the Secretary-General of units for such action, and consequently, the units generally were equipped only with weapons necessary for self-defence. Had there been any remaining doubts in this respect, the legal basis on which the General Assembly took its decision would have made this limitation clear.

176. Similarly, the Security Council decision on the United Nations Observation Group in Lebanon qualified the kind of operation that the Secretary-General was authorized to organize by the very name given to the unit to be established. That name excluded the creation of a paramilitary force and imposed, in fact, such limitations on the operation as to call for great restraint regarding the arming of the unit and its right of self-defence.

177. The General Assembly decision concerning the arrangements in relation to Jordan was in such broad terms as to provide possibilities for the organization of any kind of operation, short of one possible only under Chapter VII. In this case, however, as in the case of UNEF, a certain incompleteness in the terminology of the decision was covered by the conclusions following from the legal basis on which the decision was taken.

178. Confirmation by the Assembly of the interpretation of the question of authority given above would be useful. This interpretation would signify that a Member country, in deciding upon a contribution of men or matériel to a United Nations operation on the basis of such stand-by understandings as may have been reached, could rely upon the explicit terms of the executive authority delegated to the Secretary-General in determining the use which could be made of the units provided; it being understood, naturally, that in the types of operation with which this report is concerned this could never include combat activity. There will always remain, of course, a certain margin of freedom for judgement, as, for example, on the extent and nature of the arming of the units and of their right to self-defence. In the case of UNEF, such questions of interpretation have been solved in consultation with the contributing Governments and with the host Government. The Advisory Committee on UNEF set up by the General Assembly has in this context proved to be of especially great assistance.

179. In the preceding paragraph I have touched upon the extent to which a right of self-defence may be exercised by United Nations units of the type envisaged. It should be generally recognized that such a right exists. However, in certain cases this right should be exercised only under strictly defined conditions. A problem arises in this context because of the fact that a wide interpretation of the right of self-defence might well blur the distinction between operations of the character discussed in this report and combat operations, which would require a decision under Chapter VII of the Charter and an explicit, more far-reaching delegation of authority to the Secretary-General than would be required for any of the operations

discussed here. A reasonable definition seems to have been established in the case of UNEF, where the rule is applied that men engaged in the operation may never take the initiative in the use of armed force, but are entitled to respond with force to an attack with arms, including attempts to use force to make them withdraw from positions which they occupy under orders from the Commander, acting under the authority of the Assembly and within the scope of its resolutions. The basic element involved is clearly the prohibition against any initiative in the use of armed force. This definition of the limit between self-defence, as permissible for United Nations elements of the kind discussed, and offensive action, which is beyond the competence of such elements, should be approved for future guidance.

180. The clear delimitation of the right to use force which has been set out above as a basic rule for the type of operations discussed in this report should dissipate any objections against the suggested stand-by arrangements which would be based on the view that they go beyond the measures which the Charter permits the General Assembly to take and infringe upon prerogatives of the Security Council. The principles outlined above put UNEF on the same level, constitutionally, as UNOGIL, for example, qualifying it so as to make it an instrument of efforts at mediation and conciliation. It may be noted in this context that UNOGIL has not given rise to any constitutional objections; the fact that the Group was created by the Security Council is in this case irrelevant, as the Council acted entirely within the limits of Chapter VI of the Charter, and as a similar action obviously could have been taken by the General Assembly under Article 22.

181. In the case of UNEF, the General Assembly decided to organize an Advisory Committee under the chairmanship of the Secretary-General, to assist the operation. In practice, this arrangement has proved highly useful. In principle, it should be accepted as a precedent for the future. Extensive operations with serious political implications, regarding which, for practical reasons, executive authority would need to be delegated to the Secretary-General, require close collaboration with authorized representatives of the General Assembly. However, it would be undesirable for this collaboration to be given such a form as to lead to divided responsibilities or to diminished efficiency in the operation. The method chosen by the General Assembly in the case of UNEF seems the most appropriate one if such risks are to be avoided. The Committee is fully informed by the Secretary-General and his associates. There is a free exchange of views in closed meetings where advice can be sought and given. But ultimate decisions rest with the Secretary-General, as the executive in charge of carrying out the operation. Dissenting views are not registered by vote, but are put on record in the proceedings of the Committee. It is useful for contributing countries to be represented on such an advisory committee, but if the contributing States are numerous the size of the committee

might become so large as to make it ineffective. On the other hand, it is obviously excluded that any party to the conflict should be a member. Normally, I believe that the same basic rule regarding permanent members of the Security Council which has been applied to units and men in the recent operations should be applied also in the selection of members for a relevant advisory committee.

182. In the administration of UNEF at Headquarters, certain special arrangements were made on an ad hoc basis to provide expert military guidance. Thus, a senior Military Adviser and three officer assistants were attached to the Executive Office as consultants. The Military Adviser, and the Under-Secretary representing the Secretary-General on current matters relating to the Force, were assisted by a group of military representatives from the countries providing contingents, sitting as an informal military advisory committee. Once the operation was firmly established, these arrangements could be and were reduced and simplified, but in the initial stage they proved to be of great value organizationally and also as an added means of maintaining close contacts with contributing Governments.

183. A parallel arrangement was that by which, for a period, a personal representative of the Secretary-General was stationed in the capital of the host country as a liaison officer directly in contact with the Government.

184. In view of the very great diversity likely to characterize the experience in practice of using United Nations units within the scope of this report, it is impossible to enunciate any principles for organizational arrangements at Headquarters or in the host country that should be made in anticipation of each case. There will always be developed, as a matter of course, the forms of liaison for which there will be a clear need.

185. The question, however, is of interest in this context, as it has a bearing on the problem whether or not such stand-by arrangements as those for which the principles and rules set out here would provide, would call for any kind of nucleus of military experts at United Nations Headquarters. At some stage, a standing group of a few military experts might be useful in order to keep under review such arrangements as may be made by Member Governments in preparation for meeting possible appeals for an operation. I would consider it premature, however, to take any decision of this kind at the present time, since the foreseeable tasks that might evolve for the Secretariat do not go beyond what it is now able to cope with unassisted by such special measures. Were a more far-reaching understanding than I have indicated to prove possible, the matter obviously would have to be reconsidered and submitted again in appropriate form to the General Assembly, which then might consider the organizational problem. Pending such a development later, the present working rule, in my view, should be that the Secretariat, while undertaking the soundings mentioned above and the necessary continuing contacts with the Governments, should not take any measures beyond keeping the situation under

constant review, so as to be able to act expeditiously, if a decision by the General Assembly or the Security Council should call for prompt action.

186. It may be reiterated in passing that the United Nations Secretariat has by now had extensive experience in establishing and maintaining United Nations operations involving military personnel and, without improvising or augmenting unduly, can quickly provide any operation of that nature with efficient communications service in the field and with Headquarters, with transportation and vehicles for local transport, with well-tested administrative and accounting systems and expert personnel to man them, and with effective procurement and security arrangements.

187. The financial obligations of Member countries to the United Nations are of two kinds. On the one hand, there are such obligations as are covered by the scale of contributions established by the General Assembly; on the other, there are certain voluntary commitments outside that scale, such as United Nations technical assistance or the United Nations Children's Fund. While, of course, contributions from individual Member nations to United Nations units for field operations may always be made on a voluntary basis, thus being lifted outside the scale of contributions, the principle must be that, as flowing from decisions of one of the main organs of the United Nations, such contributions should be subordinated to the normal financial rules. Any other principle would seriously limit the possibility of recruiting the necessary personnel from the most appropriate countries and achieving the best geographical distribution, since most countries are not likely to be in a position to assume the additional financial burdens involved and since, unless otherwise agreed, all contributing countries should be treated on the same basis.

188. In the initial stages of UNEF, Member nations assumed certain additional burdens beyond those which would follow from the application of normal rules governing contributions to the United Nations. Later, financial relations were adjusted so as to be based on full compensation for extra and extraordinary costs, financed under the normal scale of contributions. The underlying rule is that a contributing country, by such action, should not be subjected to financial sacrifices beyond those obligations which would be incurred if it were not contributing directly to the operation. On the other hand, naturally, contributing countries should not shift to the United Nations any costs which, in any case they would have had to meet under their normal domestic policy.

189. I believe that, as part of the stand-by arrangements, it should be established that the costs for United Nations operations of the type in question, based on decisions of the General Assembly or the Security Council, should be allocated in accordance with the normal scale of contributions. The United Nations in this way should assume responsibility for all additional costs incurred by a contributing country because of its participation in the operation, on the basis of a cost assessment which, on

the other hand, would not transfer to the United Nations any costs which would otherwise have been incurred by a contributing Government under its regular national policy.

190. With relation to the men engaged in one of its operations, the United Nations should naturally assume all responsibilities necessary to safeguard the normal interest of those so employed. Thus, they should be fully compensated by the United Nations for any losses of earning power or social benefits which may be suffered because of their service with the United Nations. In view of the great variety of regulations applied by various countries, it is impossible to go beyond this general statement of principle; the details would have to be worked out with each contributing Government, as appropriate.

191. With relation to a host Government, it should be the rule that as the United Nations units are dispatched to the country in the interest and with the consent and co-operation of the host Government, that Government should provide all necessary facilities for the operation. This, in principle, should be done without any compensation, in case such facilities are in the possession of the host Government itself. Thus, for example, contributions of government services or government-owned property placed at the disposal of the United Nations for its operation should not be subject to compensation.

192. Concerning the claims of private citizens in the host country, the applicable rule is that the United Nations should pay compensation for the use of their property or services, whenever the host Government would have been obligated to pay for similar services or uses. The question whether the United Nations, in its turn, should be reimbursed by the host Government for such outlays would properly be settled through negotiation, in the light of the circumstances in each separate case.

193. The approach indicated in this chapter suggests a way in which the United Nations, within the limits of the Charter, may seek the most practical method of mustering and using, as necessary, the resources — both of nations and its own — required for operations involving military personnel which may be conceived in response to the needs of specific conflict situations. The national resources likely to be available for such purposes, if our limited experience is a gauge, are no doubt substantial, but they cannot now be calculated or even estimated, and even their availability at any particular time would probably be subject to considerable fluctuation, for political and other reasons. Formalizing the principles and rules outlined above, however, would afford a strengthened basis on which to expedite the mobilization of voluntary aid towards meeting urgent need. Their approval by the Assembly, thus clarifying and regularizing important legal and practical issues, would also ensure a more efficient use of any aid extended to the Organization, were it again to have to appeal to Member nations for such assistance.

Hammarskjöld's report is a much studied and highly valued document. Since the time of its composition, however, the United Nations not only became involved in the Congo, but has engaged in peace-keeping operations in Yemen and Cyprus. (The role of the United Nations in the transfer of West Irian from the Netherlands to the temporary sovereignty of Indonesia, subject to an apparent requirement to hold a plebiscite within five to ten years after the transfer, could conceivably also be identified as a peace-keeping operation. The character of the participation by the United Nations in the peaceful resolution of tensions between the Indonesian and Dutch governments was, however, primarily a matter of providing an intermediary; it stretches undesirably the already vague notions of peace-keeping and policing to consider the nominal United Nations role in the West Irian dispute as an instance.)

These recent peace-keeping experiences have led professional commentators to question the validity of some of the principles laid down by Hammarskjöld in his report. Marion McVitty, an observer of the United Nations activities during the past two decades, has concluded that it is necessary to revise these principles if the UN forces are to be able to carry out their peace-keeping functions.

In the following article, "The Need for Agreed Rules to Guide Future United Nations Peace-Keeping Operations" (United World Federalists, Washington, D.C., 1965) pp. 8–20, Mrs. McVitty proposes the future peace-keeping operations of the United Nations be given limited authority to impose martial law. Mrs. McVitty enumerates six powers that go beyond what Hammarskjöld's report calls for. Each of them represents only a slight revision, but when taken together they amount to an important proposal that might enhance considerably the potential effectiveness of the United Nations forces.

The most important suggestion is to grant the United Nations the power to impose martial law for a designated time period, specified in advance by the invoking authority and, wherever possible, agreed upon by the responsible officials in the host territories. A second important suggestion is to qualify somewhat Hammarskjöld's principle that the United Nations should only be authorized to use force in self-defense. Mrs. McVitty thinks that United Nations forces will be able to carry out their peace-keeping activities successfully only if they are given the right to use force as a *last resort* for such purposes as maintaining their essential positions, their lines of communication and supply, and to gain access to the whole area covered by their mandate. It seems probable, for instance, that if Mrs.

McVitty's principles had been operating in the Congo, UN forces would have acted differently in a number of situations.

Mrs. McVitty argues for "a general instrument" that would combine flexibility with some fixed guidelines. She also favors bringing it into being gradually through a series of transition steps that Member States would take in leading up to the adoption of the complete scheme. Whether this set of transition steps can be generalized for the solution of other world order problems is a consideration to bear in mind.

MARION H. McVITTY

Wanted: Rules to Guide UN Peace-Keeping Operations of the Future

Temporary UN Powers in an Emergency

In a local community when a disaster, or other emergency, has made unusual protective measures necessary, martial law is instituted. In such local crises, although military forces are used, their function is primarily a large-scale police action. The "military" rule is known to be temporary and without prejudice to the rights and claims of those involved, or to the restoration of full local civilian authority.

It is not possible, of course, to draw a perfect analogy between martial law in the event of local emergencies and UN peace-keeping capabilities in an international crisis. There is, however, enough similarity in the two situations to illuminate a potential application of the general principle to United Nations collective security actions.

When a crisis arises in which the United Nations is requested to take emergency policing action, the UN could be given emergency powers, defined to meet the particular situation, applicable to the geographical area and to the parties concerned, for an agreed period of time specified at the outset and renewable if necessary.

The heart of this suggestion is the possibility that in an emergency there may be some "willing suspension" of national sovereignty to the extent immediately required for the limited time specified.

United Nations experience to date, particularly with UNEF, ONUC, and UNFICYP, indicates the nature of the powers which the UN might need to expedite emergency policing actions in future. These powers in turn suggest certain safeguards which might be required to ensure against abuses. However, it must be understood that the powers and safeguards outlined hereafter cannot be considered definitive, but should be taken as illustrative of what should, and could, be done.

Temporary Powers Indicated

The United Nations should have control of the forces placed at its disposal. During the agreed emergency period, contingents should not be permitted to be withdrawn by contributing States or to be expelled by the host territory without United Nations permission. The United Nations should be permitted to institute common disciplinary standards for all national contingents in an emergency force, and the UN should be responsible for the consistency of their application.

The United Nations should have the right to internationalize, disarm, or otherwise neutralize local armed forces in the host territory. UN contingents are usually insufficient to give the UN preponderant force in the area of a peace-keeping operation. Under certain circumstances, local forces as a whole, or in part, may oppose, or obstruct, a UN mandate. By "internationalizing," or incorporating, local forces to augment its own, or by "neutralizing" or disarming local forces, particularly "irregulars" (uniformed or unidentified armed bands not under the full control of local authorities), the United Nations might accomplish its objectives without unduly enlarging the number of contributed contingents, and maintain control with a minimum use of force.

The United Nations should be able to control unauthorized assistance from outside the area of UN operations. When it is advisable for the UN to decide that outside assistance shall not be given to any of the parties involved in an emergency situation except through the United Nations, itself, the United Nations should be able to enforce that stipulation. It should, therefore, have the right to halt the importation of unauthorized materials and personnel, or to take them into custody. Effective measures to this end would presumably include the right of search, the control of roads, railways, airports, etc. to the extent necessary. The power suggested in the next paragraph would also be an adjunct to this end.

The United Nations should have competence over individuals opposing, or impeding, a UN mandate. Recalcitrant individuals involved in a particular emergency situation should be liable to UN apprehension, detention and disposition. A UN legal unit would, no doubt, need to be available to undertake the proper disposal of such cases. Individuals likely to come under UN competence in this sense would know in advance what actions would make them liable to UN apprehension and within what geographical area this could occur.

UN forces should be authorized to use the minimum degree of force necessary to fulfil their mandate. UN forces should have the right of self-defense when physically attacked. They should have the right to use force *as a last resort* in maintaining their essential positions, their lines of communication and supply, to gain access to the whole area covered by their mandate, and to exercise the powers suggested in these rules. By the judicious application of one or another of these legitimate uses of minimum force after negotiation and persuasion have failed, the UN police should be able to fulfil the functions of UN peace-keeping mandates.

The UN must have dependable sources of revenue to cover the cost of emergency operations undertaken. Although financial responsibility for UN peace-keeping operations may be dealt with as a separate problem, an agreed special formula for emergency assessments is a proper adjunct to other legal rules governing UN peace-keeping operations. Should such a formula and other financing methods be adopted in isolation from the other temporary powers suggested here, the formula and methods might thereafter be added to them.

Indicated Safeguards

Strict adherence to the voluntary nature of UN peace-keeping actions undertaken without reference to Chapter VII of the Charter should be maintained. The host territory should not be subjected to temporary UN powers without its consent. A nation requesting UN assistance, or permitting a UN operation in its territory, would know in advance that this entailed assent to the possible temporary suspension of certain internal prerogatives identified with domestic jurisdiction as enumerated above. Similarly, UN members would offer to contribute contingents only if they were willing to leave them at the disposal of the United Nations for an agreed and specified period in a particular crisis situation.

United Nations peace-keeping forces should not be deployed to decide an issue by force of combat. It should be understood that UN peace-keeping operations are undertaken to pacify a threat to, or breach of the peace, rather than to determine the outcome of the cause. Settlement of the issues in dispute should be sought by other agencies. UN police should, therefore, be deployed in the interest of law and order, and not on the side of any of the parties, no matter how just the case of any one of them may seem.

None of the temporary powers of the UN should be permitted to prejudice the internal political and constitutional situation within host territories, or the status quo ante of the parties. UN police action should to the greatest extent possible be undertaken without prejudice to the rights, claims or positions of the parties. This safeguarding principle has been recognized as valid in the past and has been pursued in practice. However, it may be well to formalize it in relation to the exercise of temporary UN authority. "Internationalization" or "neutralization" of local forces, for instance, should not be undertaken in such a way as to restrain the troops of one faction while leaving the troops of another faction free to gain advantage. Nor should one faction be free to import arms while the other is not.

Limiting factors should restrain undue use of force by UN police. Two of the proposed UN temporary powers should by their nature tend to limit the need to use force in carrying out a UN mandate. No military force and little police coercion should be required to exercise competence over recalcitrant individuals, and this competence should reduce the likelihood of concerted opposition by depriving it of leadership. The power to "internationalize" or "neutralize" local forces in whole or in part should give the UN preponderant power in the area, and recognition of the fact of that preponderance should deter armed opposition to the fulfilment of a UN mandate. A further safeguard against undue recourse to force might be appended in the form of peaceful procedures to be followed prior to the use of force by UN police in exercising their authority, or in maintaining their positions, contact with each other, or access to their facilities and to all of the area covered by the mandate.

Extension of the emergency period should require the consent of governments actively involved. Host territories would in fact have a veto power over the extension of an emergency period which they were unwilling to continue. Nations contributing contingents would not be bound to leave them at the disposition of the UN for an extension of the emergency period without their further consent. However, other nations might be willing to replace the contingents which might be withdrawn at the end of the initial period. Such newly volunteered forces would then become bound to UN disposition for the duration of the extended period.

Recourse to legal appeal should be provided for individuals who might come under temporary UN competence. While such individuals might be able in due course to obtain redress of grievances through their own national governments, statelessness or other impediments, might prevent them from doing so. An appropriate imternational tribunal might be set up *ad hoc* in a place removed from the emergency area in order to ensure that all individuals affected by UN jurisdiction would have access to prompt and equitable appeal.

Executive responsibility for the exercise of temporary powers may require a broader UN base. The Secretary General should be the chief executive and administrative official responsible for carrying out a UN peace-keeping operation. In the execution of temporary emergency powers, the personal responsibility of the Secretary General might be expected to be increased by the extension of actual UN authority, and to be reduced by the greater precision and clarity of his mandate. It is possible, therefore, that the area in which he, himself, would render decisions might be considerably narrowed, but within that narrowed area his personal decisions might be more momentous. To ensure the maximum degree of confidence in the UN executive, it might be wise to formalize the device of "advisory committees" with which the Secretary General consulted in carrying out the UNEF and ONUC operations. An appropriate committee, similarly composed for each future emergency action might have certain limited powers *pro tem* as an executive arm of the Assembly or Security Council. These powers should probably be no more than the right to determine the final directive if a decision of real moment had to be made which was not clearly covered by Assembly or Security Council resolutions, and over which the UN membership might be too evenly divided, or be otherwise incapable of prompt clarifying action.

In addition to the powers and safeguards of the type suggested, the agreed instrument of rules should at the outset define the new concept of collective security as separate and distinct from coercive enforcement action under Chapter VII of the UN Charter. Chapter VII would remain valid for the purposes for which it was intended, should the need arise to implement its provisions.

Acceptability

It is important to note that the "willing suspension" of national sovereignty required to implement this proposal is limited in degree, occasional in time, not fully applicable to all members in every event, and susceptible of review by governments in the light of known circumstances. The voluntary commitment of UN member governments would pass through several stages, and a number of conditioning factors would intervene, before that commitment had any binding legal force.

At first, governments would be asked to agree to legal guidelines for *possible* use in future international emergencies. Thereafter when a crisis arose the Security Council, or the General Assembly, would determine if the instrument of general rules should be invoked to meet the event. Should it be invoked, a further determination would have to be made as to the duration of its application. This might be for a short period of a few months or even weeks, or longer according to the apparent need. An extension of the initial period would require still another formal decision after some experience had been gained.

Although these decisions would be taken by the usual method of the appropriate UN body acting on the issue, individual member governments would not thereby be bound against their will, except in respect of their financial obligation to contribute to the costs. Otherwise the emergency powers would be applicable primarily to the host territory and to the nations contributing contingents. The powers could not be applied by any UN body to these two categories of nations without their own freely determined action—either in *requesting* UN assistance, or in *volunteering* to contribute forces. Unauthorized intervention in an emergency area would be prevented by national governments unless they had lost control of nongovernmental agencies or individuals, in which case the UN would exercise a competence which those governments did not in fact possess. Deliberate unauthorized intervention by a government must naturally be taken to make that nation a party to the threat to peace, in which case UN restraints upon it of the limited character described would be a minimum form of control knowingly incurred by the government in question

The general application of collective financial responsibility has already been accepted in principle by a very substantial number of UN members. Explicit definition of that principle in a special scale of assessments, and clarification of the implications and implementations of the new concept of collective security might serve to remove some of the political and constitutional reservations which have impeded unanimous agreement on the financial obligation thus far.

Flexibility

A further examination of the procedures involved in implementing an agreed general instrument of rules will show that there would be a pervading and continuous interplay between the available norms of the legal guidelines and *ad hoc* decisions as to their application.

The instrument of rules would make the practical powers available, but an *ad hoc* decision would determine when they were to be applied. The instrument might specify permissible outside limits for the duration of emergency powers, while an *ad hoc* decision would be made as to the actual length of the period in a given case. The instrument might specify that a committee should be established with limited executive authority to augment that of the Secretary General, but the composition of such a committee would be chosen *ad hoc* to ensure that its membership was appropriate to the operation being undertaken. The instrument would give the UN control over forces contributed, but the Secretary General would decide *ad hoc* which contingents volunteered could be suitably used.

Implementation

The necessary legal guidelines for future UN peace-keeping operations could be set out in a general instrument to be adopted by any 7 members of the Security Council and by a two-thirds majority of the General Assembly. Such an instrument should define the new concept of collective security, the emergency powers which could be invoked by the UN, and the essential safeguards to avoid abuses.

The degree of legal planning proposed is likely to improve the orderly and effective exercise of collective security by the international organization without unduly curtailing the sovereign independence of member States.

Nothing suggested violates the present UN Charter. The proposal is based on accepted principles contained therein, and on precedents already set. At most it interjects where the Charter is silent some clarifying definition of proper and effective means for preserving international security without recourse to armed combat.

The instrument required and its implementation conduce to the conviction that it is less formal, and less formidable, than a supplementary treaty. It is more nearly a formulation of model rules to guide rather tentative new experiments in the more efficient exercise of executive operations undertaken to preserve world peace. Hence, the present Committee of Twenty-one, or a similar *ad hoc* body, might be charged with preparing the instrument.

If a general instrument of rules of the kind proposed could be considered *in the absence of a crisis in being,* it is believed that it would be acceptable to a substantial majority of UN members, and there is no apparent need for its unanimous adoption, although that would be desirable. Clearly unless it were universally approved, it could not be universally applied. However, it might be applicable in a given case to an extent sufficient to warrant its use, even if some few States declined to be bound by its provisions. As the UN had more opportunity to demonstrate both its impartiality and its efficacy under these rules, the instrument might acquire universal acceptance in due course.

It may be argued that the instrument of rules might make the parties involved in a crisis situation unwilling to request a UN Peace Force when the interposition of such a Force seemed essential to the Security Council or General Assembly. Application of the rules might seem to the parties too big a price to pay for pacification of an emergency situation out of which each side hoped for some change in the *status quo,* or some advantage. Experience to date, however, suggests that a UN Peace Force is not now requested unless those concerned cannot gain their ends or control the situation by any means available to them. Should such rules as are suggested here actually inhibit recourse to UN peace-keeping operations, it may be pertinent to question whether without such rules the UN should in future become involved in peace-keeping operations in which it may be overwhelmed or discredited. Perhaps, it would now be wiser to set the minimum terms likely to ensure successful UN action before the UN is thrust into precarious efforts to save well-nigh hopeless situations. In the anxiety attendant upon serious crises, it is likely that proper rules will be acceptable as reasonable terms by both the parties and the world community as a whole.

NOTES AND QUESTIONS

1. Do you suppose that Mrs. McVitty's proposals would be acceptable to the United Nations? Does the United Nations have the capacity to accept and reject? When referring to "The United Nations" here, does one primarily refer to the views of the Secretary-General and the Secretariat, or to the views of the political organs? That is, are these executive-administrative, or political issues?
2. Which governments would favor the adoption of Mrs. McVitty's proposal? Which would oppose it?——for what reasons?
3. Compare the advantages and disadvantages of *a structured approach* to peace-keeping based upon principles of authority agreed upon in advance, with an *ad hoc approach* based upon the exigencies of the situation and upon the will of the relevant majority in the political organs of the United Nations. This comparison goes to the root of many world order issues—for instance, the debate on whether it is desirable or not to establish authoritative and detailed definitions of aggression and self-defense for purposes of interpreting Articles 2(4) and 51 of the Charter. To what extent are these two approaches complementary?

The last selection in this section is an essay by Louis B. Sohn, "The Role of the United Nations in Civil Wars," *Proceedings of the American Society of International Law* (1963) pp. 208–216. As previously noted, civil wars are likely to be frequent and intense in the years ahead, and as well, to involve the participation of the Great Powers in support of each rival faction. A way to express the point is to say that civil wars have emerged in the nuclear age as a very significant form of international violence. Sohn's essay summarizes past practice of the United Nations, depicts the legal issues, and argues for a limited United Nations role.

THE RÔLE OF THE UNITED NATIONS IN CIVIL WARS

By Louis B. Sohn

The relationship between international law and civil wars has always been a difficult one. While some civil wars have been treated as if they were for all practical purposes equivalent to international wars, in others, divergent rules of international law have been applied. This is due in large part to the fact that there is an infinite variety of civil wars, each of which has different international repercussions.

It has been said that

> a civil war exists when two opposing parties within a State have recourse to arms for the purpose of obtaining power in the State, or when a large portion of a State rises in arms against the legitimate Government.

Unfortunately, "even in the most highly developed societies, underlying inequalities and resulting strains produce riots, revolutions, and civil wars." In many countries "military rebellion is a recognized mode of carrying on political conflict." In some countries in the last 150 years on the average more than one revolution occurred per year, and in one region over seventy revolutions took place during a recent ten-year period. It is not likely that the situation will improve in the near future; in fact, in consequence of the establishment of some fifty new states in recent years, the number of revolutionary changes in the world may increase rather than diminish in the remaining decades of this century.

What should be the attitude of the United Nations toward this constant local upheaval in several areas of the world? Two types of fringe situations may be separated from the core of the problem. In the first place, the United Nations has in the past shown constant interest in revolts of non-self-governing peoples against the colonial Powers, and regardless of objections raised against interference in matters of domestic jurisdiction, it can be said that a "colonial revolution is now legally as well as practically a matter of concern to the whole community." In any case, the era of emancipation of colonial territories is quickly approaching an end, and it can be expected that in a few years all nations will comply with the General Assembly's declaration on the granting of independence to colonial countries and peoples. In the second place, it is necessary to treat differently wars waged by two parts of a country which in fact constitute two separate states. The hostilities which took place between North Korea and South Korea belong clearly to this category, and the intermittent fighting between the two Chinese Governments, on the mainland and on Taiwan, might also be so classified. In such case, there is not a civil war but a regular international war, even though one side to the conflict is not recognized by most states as the legitimate government of the territory under its control. In neither conflict was there any doubt about the belligerency status of both sides.

Once those extraneous problems are put aside, it might be necessary to distinguish between two basic types of revolutions: a "palace" revolution where the former government is replaced by a new group with a minimum of bloodshed; and a real civil war, where a prolonged military struggle for the control of the government takes place.

In current international relations we are becoming blasé in respect to the repeated ritual of new governments being installed in various countries in accordance with the whims of a group of military leaders. After a decent interval of a few days, as soon as it is clear that the putsch has not encountered any real opposition in the country, we recognize the new government and acknowledge its authority to rule the country. This is a far cry from the tendency in the past to insist that "unconstitutional" governments are not entitled to recognition. It may be recalled that at the Central American Peace Conference held in Washington in 1907, the Central American Republics agreed not to recognize

> any other Government which may come into power in any of the five Republics as a consequence of a *coup d'état,* or of a revolution against the recognized Government, so long as the freely elected representatives of the people thereof have not constitutionally reorganized the country.

This provision was further elaborated in the General Treaty of Peace and Amity of the Central American States, signed in Washington in 1923, by which various leaders of a revolution were disqualified from being elected to high governmental offices. The United States, though not a party to these treaties, agreed to follow a similar non-recognition policy with respect to this group of states, but in other areas different policies were often pursued. The requirement of constitutionality was seldom followed by other states, and in the United Nations "despite the fairly large number of revolutionary changes of government . . . there was not one single instance of a challenge of credentials" in the early years, and in later years difficulties arose only in the cases of China in 1950 and Hungary in 1956, and these were due to the special circumstances which accompanied the changes of government in those countries and not merely to the revolutionary character of the new governments. Apart from such special cases, the United Nations does not pay any attention to the legitimacy of any government, and a revolutionary government's right to represent its country is undisputed.

Even in case of a prolonged civil war, the winning faction has usually no difficulty in obtaining acceptance by the United Nations. For instance, when, after several years of struggle, Fidel Castro removed the Batista Government, no questions were raised over the legitimacy of the Castro Government. Difficult questions arise only when a government has come into power with the assistance of another state. This was alleged in the Czechoslovak Question in 1950, but the Security Council was prevented by a veto from investigating the facts. The General Assembly condemned, however, "the use of Soviet military forces to suppress the efforts of the Hungarian people to reassert their rights," and affirmed "the right of the Hungarian people to a government responsive to its national aspirations and dedicated to its independence and well-being." While the General Assembly repeatedly called upon the Soviet Government to "desist forthwith from any form of intervention in the internal affairs of Hungary" and to withdraw its armed forces from Hungary, no attempt was made to enforce these resolutions. However, as a gesture of censure the General Assembly approved a report of its Credentials Committee to "take no decision regarding the credentials submitted on behalf of the representatives of Hungary," as they "had been issued by authorities established as a result of military intervention by a foreign power." Despite this decision, the Hungarian delegates were allowed to participate in the debates of the General Assembly on the basis of Rule 29 of the Rules of Procedure of the General Assembly, which allows the provisional seating of representatives until "the General Assembly has given its decision."

The power of the United Nations to intervene in civil wars is circumscribed by two provisions of the Charter: the domestic jurisdiction clause in Article 2, paragraph 7, and the restriction of the authority of the Security Council to "the maintenance of international peace and security" (Article 24). Thus the Security Council is concerned only with "international" peace and not with "internal" or "domestic" peace. A civil war normally disturbs only domestic peace, and the United Nations should not intervene. If, however, a civil war constitutes a threat to international peace, the United Nations can "take effective collective measures for the prevention and removal" of such a threat (Article 1, paragraph 1, of the Charter); and "enforcement measures under Chapter VII" to maintain or restore international peace in such a situation are expressly exempted from the prohibition relating to intervention "in matters which are essentially within the domestic jurisdiction of any state" (Article 2, paragraph 7, of the Charter, *in fine*).

Thus the question of the power of the United Nations to intervene in a civil war depends on the factual situation: Does a particular civil war in fact create a threat to international peace? Such threat might arise, if other countries assist either the government in power or the insurgents, or if two groups of countries give assistance to both sides in the civil war. In Central America the traditional rule has been that "In a case of civil war no Government of Central America shall intervene in favor of or against the Government of the country where the conflict takes place.'' This rule was combined with agreements ''not to intervene, under any circumstances, directly or indirectly, in the international political affairs of any other Central American Republic,'' and not to permit any person ''to organize or foment revolutionary activities within its territory against a recognized Government'' of any such republic or ''to organize armed expeditions or to take part in any hostilities which may arise in a neighboring country or to furnish money or war supplies to the contending parties.'' Elaborate provisions concerning ''the duties and rights of States in the event of civil strife'' are also contained in inter-American agreements of 1928 and 1953. These provisions are directed mainly against the rebels, and against starting or promoting civil strife. Export of arms and war material to the government is therefore permitted, except in case of a recognition of the belligerency of the rebels, after which the ordinary rules of neutrality are to be applied to both sides. The two agreements are intended to implement the generally accepted inter-American principle of non-intervention which was formulated in a sweeping manner in Article 15 of the Charter of the Organization of American States, which reads as follows:

> No State or group of States has the right to intervene, directly or indirectly, for any reason whatever, in the internal or external affairs of any other State. The foregoing principle prohibits not only armed force but also any other form of interference or attempted threat against the personality of the State or against its political, economic and cultural elements.

The United Nations Charter imposes on the Members of the United Nations the obligation to ''refrain in their international relations from the threat or use of force against the territorial integrity or political independence of any state, or in any other manner inconsistent with the purposes of the United Nations'' (Article 2, paragraph 4). In its ''Essentials of Peace'' Resolution, the General Assembly interpreted this provision broadly, and called upon every nation to

> refrain from any threats or acts, direct or indirect, aimed at impairing the freedom, independence or integrity of any State, or at fomenting civil strife and subverting the will of the people in any State.

In the ''Peace through Deeds'' Resolution a year later, the General Assembly condemned ''the intervention of a State in the internal affairs of another State for the purpose of changing its legally established government by the threat or use of force,'' and solemnly reaffirmed that

> whatever the weapons used, any aggression, whether committed openly, or by fomenting civil strife in the interest of a foreign Power, or otherwise, is the gravest of all crimes against peace.

The General Assembly and the Security Council actually applied these rules in several situations. Already in the Greek Question, which arose prior to the adoption of these resolutions, the General Assembly considered that "the continuous aid given by Albania, Bulgaria and Yugoslavia to the Greek guerillas endangers peace in the Balkans, and is inconsistent with the purposes and principles of the Charter of the United Nations," and called on these countries "to cease forthwith any assistance or support in any form to the guerillas in fighting against the Greek Government." In the Chinese case in 1950, the General Assembly called upon all states to "respect the right of the people of China, now and in the future, to choose freely their political institutions and to maintain a government independent of foreign control," and to refrain from seeking "to create foreign-controlled regimes within the territory of China." The Security Council in 1958 rejected the contention that the situation in Lebanon was purely internal and dispatched an Observation Group to Lebanon to ensure that there was no illegal infiltration of personnel or supply of arms or other matériel across the Lebanese borders. In 1959 the Security Council sent a subcommittee to Laos to investigate reports of foreign assistance to guerrillas there, and that subcommittee concluded that, while some equipment and supplies from the territory of the Democratic Republic of Viet Nam had reached the guerrillas, it was not clear whether any regular troops of that Republic had crossed the frontier. Among the many issues involved in the Congo Question, there was also the problem of foreign assistance. The General Assembly, for instance, called upon

> all States to refrain from the direct and indirect provision of arms or other materials of war and military personnel and other assistance for military purposes in the Congo during the period of military assistance through the United Nations, except upon the request of the United Nations through the Secretary-General.

The Security Council also urged the "immediate withdrawal and evacuation from the Congo of all Belgian and other foreign military and paramilitary personnel and political advisers not under the United Nations Command, and mercenaries," and called upon all states to take measures "to prevent the departure of such personnel for the Congo from their territories, and for the denial of transit and other facilities to them."

This survey shows quite clearly that the United Nations has developed a constant practice of condemning and, when possible, preventing, the rendering of support to rebel forces against an established government. In the Congo Question the additional precedent was established that assistance to the government itself should be provided only through United Nations channels. This is quite contrary to prior precedents. During the early years of the United Nations the Security Council refused to condemn assistance rendered by the United Kingdom in Greece and Indonesia. When the United States proclaimed the Truman Doctrine and agreed to send military assistance to Greece and Turkey, these agreements were made subject to the condition that such assistance will be withdrawn if "the Security Council of the United Nations finds (with respect to which finding the United States waives the exercise of any veto) or the General Assembly of the United Nations finds that action taken or assistance furnished by the United Nations makes the continuance of assistance by the Government of the United States pursuant to [these agreements] unnecessary or undesirable"; but no such finding was ever made by the United Nations. Similarly in later years, while complaints were sometimes made to the United Nations with respect to military assistance rendered by one government to another, no resolutions condemning such assistance were ever adopted, except in the Hungarian Case, where the government supported by the Soviet Union was not considered by the United Nations as a real government of Hungary but merely as a puppet.

The final question is whether the United Nations itself should assist any Member government which is in trouble because of a dangerous rebellion and whether it should, whenever it deems it desirable, try to encourage a change in government either by itself taking action against that government or assisting an insurrection against it. In the Spanish Case, the General Assembly adopted a far-reaching resolution, in which it expressed its conviction that "the Franco Fascist Government of Spain, which was imposed by force upon the Spanish people with the aid of the Axis Powers . . . does not represent the Spanish people," and recommended that

> if, within a reasonable time, there is not established a government which derives its authority from the consent of the governed, committed to respect freedom of speech, religion and assembly and to the prompt holding of an election in which the Spanish people, free from force and intimidation and regardless of party, may express their will, the Security Council consider the adequate measures to be taken in order to remedy the situation.

At the same time, the General Assembly debarred Spain from membership in the specialized agencies of the United Nations and recommended that all Members of the United Nations recall their ambassadors from Madrid. Though the regime in Spain did not change, the General Assembly revoked its recommendations in 1950, and in 1955 Spain was admitted to the United Nations as part of an arrangement involving simultaneous admission of sixteen states. As already mentioned, the General Assembly has repeatedly called for the holding of free elections in Hungary under United Nations auspices, but here also no effect was given to these resolutions.

But if there is a civil war raging in a country, should not the United Nations take vigorous steps to support one side or another, depending on the "justness" of their cause, even if no threat to the peace is directly involved? Is not the establishment by force of a totalitarian government contrary to the basic principles of the United Nations Charter, and should not the United Nations do something about it? Should the United Nations, to paraphrase the Constitution of the United States, try to maintain a "democratic form of government" in each Member state, or at least in those Member states in which an attempt is made, through civil war, to establish democracy or to destroy it? If a civil war should be waged in a country on the scale of the Spanish Civil War, should the United Nations try at least to stop it, even if there is no foreign intervention? What is the paramount interest of the world community in a civil strife?

There is clearly a conflict here between the interest of the United Nations in the maintenance of international peace and the right of a people to self-determination and enjoyment of fundamental freedoms. In the interest of peace, the United Nations should either support the legitimate government or the stronger party in order to bring the conflict quickly to an end, before other nations become involved. The right of self-determination seems to imply that the matter should be left to the people itself, even if a prolonged conflict would result therefrom. But the right of self-determination could also form the basis of United Nations intervention on the side which is more likely to grant a greater measure of freedom to the people.

Judge Jessup once answered firmly "yes" to the question: "Shall the preservation of the world's peace be exalted over the attainment of a 'republican form of government' in every country of the world?" He added that

> if we allow a civil strife to broaden and degenerate into a general international war between the advocates of two opposing factions, representing two opposing theories of government, we settle nothing.

On another occasion, Judge Jessup said that

> the interest of the world community in peace is greater than the assertion of an individual or group of individuals that his or their rights are being disregarded. If the state has relinquished its right to resort to war, so the individual must relinquish any right to overthrow his own government by force.

The international community would have to be prepared "to render assistance to any of its members whose local forces are inadequate to preserve domestic peace and tranquillity." In some cases an international police force might be dispatched to restore peace, in others there might be "resort to collective blockade or quarantine of the state in which the civil war has broken out." While this might result in sustaining sometimes the "right" and sometimes the "wrong" side, this is preferable—according to Judge Jessup—to the situation in the past when "each outside state or each group of individuals in such outside states" was "free to reach its own conclusion and to intervene on one side or the other."

Judge Jessup's injunction was not followed in the Congo Question. While some United Nations activities in that case were directed against foreign intervention and the prevention of shipment of foreign arms into the Congo, other actions went much further. Thus, the Security Council, taking into account that a threat to international peace and security was involved, urged that

> the United Nations take immediately all appropriate measures to prevent the occurrence of civil war in the Congo, including arrangements for the cease-fire, the halting of all military operations, the prevention of clashes, and the use of force, if necessary, in the last resort.

Later, the Council, deploring "all armed action in opposition to the authority of the Government of the Republic of the Congo," declared that "all secessionist activities against the Republic of the Congo are contrary to the *loi fondamentale* and Security Council decisions," and demanded that "such activities which are now taking place in Katanga shall cease forthwith." The Council also declared "full and firm support for the Central Government of the Congo, and the determination to assist that Government in accordance with the decisions of the United Nations to maintain law and order and national integrity."

The answer thus to our original question seems to be that every civil war, if not ended quickly, is likely to become a threat to the peace, and the United Nations would be entitled to step in to remove such a threat. As a minimum, the United Nations would have the authority to establish a blockade on land and sea of the territory in which the civil war is waged in order to ensure that no foreign assistance would be given to either side. If invited by the government concerned, and perhaps even if invited by the rebels, it might send a peace force to assist in a cease-fire and to police the truce line. But should the United Nations force also be entitled to disarm the rebels, if so requested by the government? Or, even more drastically, should it arrest the government and disarm its forces, if its investigation should show that the rebels and not the government have the confidence of the population? Or, if it is not clear who should rule the country in accordance with the wishes of the people, should the United Nations establish a temporary government drawn from groups not involved on either side of the civil war, and arrange for an internationally supervised election? At present, the answer seems to be "no" to these three questions, except when a secessionist movement threatens the integrity of the country which, because of particular circumstances, is entitled to special protection by the United Nations, as in the Congo Question. It might even be doubtful that a different answer would be desirable in the near future. If the United Nations could effectively maintain international peace and, in addition, prevent civil wars from becoming threats to the peace, it would have done enough to improve our present situation; we should not burden it with more until better means are devised to cope with the problem of peaceful change on the international and domestic level.

NOTES AND QUESTIONS

1. Sohn suggests that many of the vexing political and legal problems arise from the difficulty of construing the relationship between the UN and a civil war in the light of the domestic jurisdiction principle in Article 2(7). See the note at the end of Chapter 7 for some discussion on this matter. When does a civil war threaten international peace? It is difficult to generalize an answer. Political considerations weigh heavily: one might be tempted to conclude that a civil war threatens international peace whenever a requisite majority says so. The United Nations has been called upon to act in relation to civil strife only when the United States and the Soviet Union can agree on the broad objectives of the peace-keeping mission, as in the cases of Cyprus and Yemen.
2. For an analysis of the relationship between civil war and international order different from that of Sohn, see Millis, **I-1C**. How does Millis conceive of the role of international organization?
3. McVitty is much more involved than is Hammarskjöld with the problems that arise in civil strife. Could this reflect the fact that cold war issues are too deeply embedded in much of the phenomena of civil strife?
4. Assuming that the Clark-Sohn world was in being, to what extent do you think that the answers to the three questions posed by Sohn in the last paragraph of his article should be changed from no to yes? Is the Clark-Sohn world compatible with rival national interventions in civil wars? What would a United Nations organized along Clark-Sohn lines do about the civil war in South Vietnam? Could a civil war on such a scale arise in a disarmed world? Where would the weapons come from? On what principles would the mission of the United Nations be based? Should the consent of the incumbent guide the mission at the outset, or should the mission be defined in light of removing the dangers to world peace? Should the United Nations prevent intervention by states interested in the outcome of the civil strife, or should the Organization seek to reestablish domestic peace? Who should decide which mission on the basis of what criteria? If the mission is one of internal pacification, should the United Nations seek a negotiated peace between the insurgents and the incumbent, or should it take sides on the basis of the will of the international community, or on the basis of a set of rules agreed upon in advance? What sort of rules would be appropriate? Would it be appropriate to help the insurgents win an anticolonial war in view of the condemnation by the Organization of the colonial system? Would it be appropriate to regard a commitment to uphold the human rights of the inhabitants as relevant to the response by the United Nations to the existence of civil strife?

C. Proposals for a World Police Force

The question of whether or not it is necessary or feasible to establish an effective international police force is generally thought to depend upon first resolving the major political and ideological conflict and tensions that exist in interstate relations. According to this view, a discussion of a police force that centers on such matters as the basis and methods of recruitment, size, available weapons, structure of field command, and such other problems is premature. Agreement on the details of a police system is a derivative from, rather than a precondition for, agreement on these more underlying political problems.

This skepticism is by no means capricious; nevertheless, it seems worthwhile to study the composition, structure, and operation of various proposals for police forces for at least three reasons. First, a depiction of the obstacles to acceptance of these proposals illuminates the character of international political processes. Second, the very act of investigation may enhance the prospects of political acceptability by removing the subject from the realm of fantasy and nightmare. For serious study may show that it is feasible to establish a police force and that if established, the dangers of its attempting to rule the world are insubstantial. And third, the process of study may serve educational purposes by pointing out that the acceptance of a police force as a realistic political objective is a preferable alternative to the risks of maintaining order in international society without one. It may be that statesmen and public opinion from societies with even the most conflicting ideologies and hostile belief systems will come to recognize that it is possible to establish a system in which recourse to violence is effectively outlawed, thereby allowing each society to concentrate on the pursuit of its own most cherished goals. It seems likely that such a recognition, if it comes, will be the product of three factors; some common interests, i.e., survival; the belief that other methods are as effective as international violence to pursue competitive goals; and the firm knowledge that recourse to violence is effectively eliminated as an instrument for achieving goals of other actors.

We have already noted that both U Thant and Hammarskjöld recommend that the next step in the development of an international police force should consist of the various Member States designating and training special troops to be available for whatever occasion the United Nations may call upon them. The initial reading is from Derek Bowett's important work, *United Nations Forces* (Praeger, New York, 1964) pp. 313–330, in which an appropriate frame of reference is developed for the evaluation of the full range of various proposals which have been suggested in this field. Categorizing these proposals into three classes, Bowett proceeds to analyze each of the three kinds of police forces in terms of two major kinds of activities: peace-keeping and enforcement. In the following paragraphs, he gives his interpretation of this distinction.

I. ENFORCEMENT FUNCTIONS

It is anticipated in Chapter VII of the Charter that the United Nations may, in the last resort, have to take armed action against a State which has been deemed an aggressor and has refused to heed the directives of the Security Council. It is also possible under Chapter VII that United Nations Forces may have to enforce the decisions of the Security Council for ending a breach of the peace, or even a serious threat to the peace in circumstances in which, though no State has been determined to be an "aggressor," one or both parties refuse to comply with an order for provisional measures under Article 40. In such circumstances, a United Nations Force is likely to be acting *against* certain elements or governments, will be engaged in hostilities, and will need to be a fully fighting, military Force. Loosely speaking, it may be said to be engaged in "belligerent functions" though the term "enforcement measures" is to be preferred. It is also possible that a United Nations Force could be used to enforce a judicial decision, although this has never yet been done. This could be done by the Security Council characterising a State's refusal to comply with the decision as a "threat to the peace, breach of the peace, or act of aggression" under Article 39, and hence using its power under Chapter VII to secure this end: or it may be that, in relation to judgments of the International Court of Justice, Article 94 of the Charter gives an entirely separate legal foundation for such action. In any event, the action would be directed against the recalcitrant State and would partake of the character of enforcement action whether technically taken under Chapter VII or not.

So far, the only unequivocal United Nations enforcement action has been in the case of the Korean conflict, though doubts have been expressed as to the correctness of designating the military effort a "United Nations Force." On 27 June 1950 the Security Council recommended that members "furnish such assistance to the Republic of Korea as may be necessary to repel the armed attack and to restore international peace and security in the area." The view has been expressed in Chapter 3 that, whilst the Korean action was not that which the Charter specifically envisaged in Article 42, it was nevertheless enforcement action under Chapter VII of the Charter.

II. "PEACE-KEEPING OPERATIONS" FOR THE MAINTENANCE OF INTERNATIONAL PEACE AND SECURITY

A United Nations Force may also be established for the purpose of maintaining international peace and security rather than enforcing its restoration. Such a Force is different in nature from the one described above, for although it may be armed and become involved in fighting, its main purpose and intention is not military. There are many different situations in which such a Force might be used, and indeed has been used, for the circumstances in which international peace might be jeopardised vary considerably. To some extent, therefore, it is possible to indicate various sub-categories within this rather broad category, though these are not mutually exclusive. The first five are in fact functions already assumed by United Nations Forces: the remaining categories, 6–9, are functions which may be anticipated in the future.

Bowett's enumeration of the five peace-keeping operations already undertaken by the Organization include: (1) *ceasefire, truce and armistice functions entrusted to "observer" groups,* (2) *frontier control,* (3) *interpositionary functions,* (4) *defence and security of United Nations zones or areas placed under United Nations control,* and (5) *the maintenance of law and order in a State;* in addition, he lists four functions which might be undertaken in the future: (1) *plebiscite supervision,* (2) *assistance and relief for national disasters,* (3) *prevention of international crimes*, and (4) *disarmament functions*. For a full exposition of these matters, see pp. 266–274. See also Morgenthau's and Waskow's distinctions between police and army in this section.

D. W. BOWETT

Structure and Control of United Nations Forces

I. TYPES OF FORCE

THERE is no scarcity of plans for "international police Forces" or "United Nations Peace Forces" or however a Force for the United Nations may be called. In 1930 Lord Davies identified three main schemes for the organisation of an "international police Force":

(1) A Force might be made up of quotas drawn from members of the League of Nations under the supervision of a general staff at the headquarters of the international authority, remaining under national control in peacetime, and falling automatically under command of the international authority on being mobilised;

(2) A Force comprising, after abolition of all national forces, a complete self-contained international army, navy and air force under the sole direction and control of the international authority;

(3) A composite Force made up of national quotas formed around a specialised contingent enlisted, equipped and controlled by the international authority.[1]

He said with great penetration that, "It may be possible to produce a host of proposals, but these will probably be variations of one of the three schemes . . . ," and in weighing the advantages and disadvantages of each of his three schemes, displayed an uncanny acumen.[2]

Hence, Clark and Sohn's 1958 "Gestalt" scheme[3] is an elaboration of Lord Davies' second scheme. Annex II of "World Peace through World Law" sets out a plan for the organisation, command and maintenance of a world peace Force whose growth would accompany a stage-by-stage disarmament of the world.

In a monograph entitled "International Policing," published by the New Commonwealth Institute in March 1935, Professor Hans Wehberg concluded that League members should try "to create at least the nucleus of an international police." This, he thought, would be "a new and great experiment" which mankind must have the

[1] Davies, *The Problem of the Twentieth Century* (1930), at p. 368.

[2] After each of his three schemes, Lord Davies set out its advantages and disadvantages, anticipating the American International Law Society's *Report of Committee on Study of Legal Problems of the United Nations*, Proceedings, American Society of International Law (1957) at pp. 227–228.

[3] *World Peace through World Law* (1960) 2nd ed. (revised), Annex II.

courage to try. Wehberg's is a modest variation of Lord Davies' third scheme.

In a work under the title "International Sanctions,"[4] published under the auspices of the Royal Institute of International Affairs in 1938 the group of members responsible for the report identified the following types of "international police Forces":

(1) An overwhelmingly powerful Force, consisting of all arms, under the complete control of an international body;
(2) A Force made up of ear-marked national contingents; or
(3) A combination of (1) and (2), *i.e.*, a centrally controlled Force around which ear-marked national contingents would form.

The resemblance between these and those proposed by Lord Davies is obvious.

In 1962 a monograph entitled "Keeping the Peace"[5] was published by the Wyndham Place Trust. The group responsible for the work saw the ultimate International Peace Force developing in stages:

(1) The present stage of *ad hoc* Forces, constituted for particular emergencies;
(2) Forces made up of ear-marked national units;
(3) Light standing Forces operating in a fully armed world;
(4) A stronger standing force in a fully armed world;
(5) A Force becoming supra-national, in a disarming world; and
(6) A world peace Force in a disarmed world.

If we eliminate, at this stage, those proposals which deal with a type of Force appropriate to some stage of disarmament and concentrate on types appropriate to the immediate future it becomes clear that there are three basic types of Force:

(1) A Force made up of national contingents provided by United Nations Member States but under the control of the United Nations;
(2) A permanent Force, established as a permanent organ of the United Nations and under its control;
(3) A composite Force combining a permanent nucleus with supporting national contingents, *i.e.*, a combination of (1) and (2).

Which type is appropriate, or even feasible, depends upon what functions one envisages for the Force, and the functions will determine not only the type appropriate but also questions of command structure, operational role, desirable methods of raising, of financing, the application of the laws of war, the necessity for bases, logistic support and permanent legal arrangements. Hence it will be necessary to consider each basic type, and any variations within that

[4] Royal Institute of International Affairs, *International Sanctions* (1938) at pp. 122, 123.
[5] Wyndham Place Trust, *Keeping the Peace* (1962).

basic type, in terms of the different functions which may be envisaged for the Force.

1. *A Force made up of national contingents provided by United Nations Member States but under the control of the United Nations*

This type of Force is, essentially, the type provided for in Chapter VII of the Charter, and also the type of Force which, although not the same as the Force contemplated in Articles 42 and 43 of the Charter, has been used by the United Nations in Korea, UNEF, ONUC, UNTEA and various observer groups.

The kind of national contingents required will, of course, depend upon the functions envisaged for the Force, hence the following broad generalisations are possible.

(a) *Enforcement functions*—military units equipped for armed hostilities on a scale (and of a size) dependent on the degree of resistance likely to be encountered;

(b) *Peace-keeping operations*—either military units lightly armed, *or* military observers recruited from governments as individuals rather than as units; *or* a combination of both when the observers may need armed protection.

The provision of these units, or individual personnel, can be either by way of a prior undertaking by States to contribute—the Article 43 Agreements with the Security Council or other "stand-by agreements" with either the Council or the General Assembly—or else on a voluntary, *ad hoc* basis as has so far been the case. There is the important variant of these which lies in between these two methods of providing forces in that it envisages that contributions will be voluntary but nevertheless planned for in advance, as when a State complies with the Assembly's invitation in the Resolution on Uniting for Peace to maintain within its armed forces units capable of being used at short notice upon call by the Assembly or the Council. This was essentially the "Pearson Plan" for peace-keeping operations: Mr. Pearson, the Canadian Secretary of State for External Affairs, suggested that:

"Even if governments are unable to give the United Nations a 'fighting' force ready and organised to serve it on the decision of the Security Council, they should be willing to earmark smaller forces for the more limited duty of securing a cease fire already agreed upon by the belligerents. We might in this way be able to construct a halfway house at the crossroads of war, and utilise an intermediate technique between merely passing Resolutions and actually fighting." [6]

As a first step he proposed the establishment of a "permanent mechanism by which units of the armed forces of member countries could be endowed with the authority of the United Nations and made available at short notice for supervisory police duties."

[6] Pearson, "Force for the UN" (1957) 35 *Foreign Affairs* at p. 401. For a similar proposal see the U.K. Foreign Secretary, Mr. Selwyn Lloyd at the 14th Session: *Off.Rec.G.A.*, 14th Sess., 798th Plen. Mtg., 17 September 1959.

Admitting that he was not proposing "anything very new," Mr. Pearson:

(1) Urged that non-permanent Members of the Security Council "should be invited to signify a willingness in principle to contribute contingents to the United Nations for purposes that are essentially noncombatant, such as, for example, the supervision of agreed cease fires and comparable peace supervisory functions";

(2) Suggested as a concomitant of effective organisation "some type of central United Nations machinery" made up of the Secretary-General, a permanent Military Adviser and a small staff;

(3) Recommended the use of an advisory committee similar to that constituted when UNEF was established;

(4) Recommended the revitalisation of the Peace Observation Commission of which the Peace Supervision Force would be an "extension in space"; and

(5) Suggested that model agreements be prepared in advance governing financial, administrative and legal procedures under which national contingents would be made available to the United Nations.

The "Pearson Plan" was really a proposal for certain steps to improve the UNEF prototype. It remains, therefore, a plan for this first type of Force, and not a plan for a permanent Force. The second of the suggestions enumerated above is the only one that comes anything near to a proposal for a permanent nucleus, but even this is really directed to increasing the strength of the personnel within the Secretariat on whom the Secretary-General may rely for advice: it is not the kind of permanent United Nations Military Staff which is referred to below in connection with the composite type of Force.

2. *A permanent Force, established as a permanent organ of the United Nations and under its control*

The initial attractions of this idea are apt to be lessened when one distinguishes between the different functions to be envisaged for a United Nations Force.

(a) ENFORCEMENT FUNCTIONS

These will require military units as outlined in 1 (a) above.

However, once the Force is envisaged as a permanent Force rather than composed of national contingents, there arise a number of problems of which perhaps the greatest is finance.[7] To be within the

[7] See Frye, *A United Nations Peace Force* (1957), pp. 72–73: he estimates that a Force of 500,000 would cost a minimum of $1,500 million per year, approximately 30 times the normal UN budget. One possibility of reducing the size of a UN permanent Force, capable of undertaking major enforcement actions, would be to give to the UN Force an overwhelming weapons

scope of the sort of finance which States may be expected to provide for a United Nations Force (and prior to any real reduction of the costs of maintaining national forces consequent upon disarmament) the Force would have to be of so minimal a size as to be useless against any but the smallest States. The inherent injustice in financing a Force capable of use against only the small, under-developed States is likely to make any proposal for such a force totally unacceptable. Clark and Sohn, neither of whom can be said to be lacking in optimism, reach this same conclusion that at the present time, or in the immediate future and pending complete disarmament, a permanent Force for enforcement functions is impractical.[8]

However, the fact is that such proposals are being made, and at the eleventh session of the Assembly the Foreign Minister of Pakistan expressed the hope that:

> ". . . without undue delay the international Force envisaged in Chapter VII of the Charter will be established on a permanent basis for enforcing the rule of law in all international disputes. Even though this permanent international Force may not be stronger than the national armed forces, its moral force, with the backing of the whole civilised world, would be an effective deterrent to any potential aggressor. This international Force, comprising for the present the units made available to the United Nations by the armed forces of Member States under General Assembly Resolution 337 (V), should eventually be recruited and paid for by this Organisation and located, under its own commanders, in various strategic areas of the world." [9]

The Pakistani proposal thus looks beyond the stage of what may be called the " Pearson Plan " to a stage at which a truly international and permanent Force should be created. No details were given of the size and cost of the Force envisaged.

(b) PEACE-KEEPING OPERATIONS

For this function the proposal for a permanent Force begins to be feasible, for it could generally be expected to be on a smaller scale than the Force required under (a) above. However, ONUC developed to a size of 20,000, so that the financial implications must not be under-estimated. A more realistic size might be in the region of 5–10,000.

The scheme put forth by Cannon and Jordan [10] in 1957 envisaged a lightly armed infantry brigade of 7,000 men, formed of national contingents from nations other than the Permanent Members of the Security Council and controlled by the General Assembly, not the Security Council. The financing of the Force was to be borne (by

superiority. But this is only feasible as a long-term plan in conjunction with general disarmament, and was so conceived by Lord Davies, *op. cit.*, p. 377. For suggestions that, under disarmament, the UN Force might retain a monopoly of the atomic weapon, see *post*, pp. 544–545.

[8] *World Peace through World Law*, p. 315.

[9] *Off.Rec.G.A.*, 11th Sess., Plen. Mtgs., Vol. 1, 601st Mtg.

[10] " Military aspects of a Permanent UN Force," in Frye, *A United Nations Peace Force* (1957) pp. 161–171.

apportionment by the Assembly) by all United Nations Members with the exception of those contributing troops: States would be entitled to an allowance for the facilities, services or equipment donated by them.

There would not seem to be any real need to confine the power to control the Force to the Assembly: indeed, it may be surmised that any proposal to do so would meet with the bitterest opposition by the Soviet Union.[11] The most that could be expected, and even this is highly problematical, is an acceptance of the principle which the International Court of Justice accepted in the *Expenses Case*, and which in a sense [12] lies behind the Resolution on Uniting for Peace, that, if the Security Council by reason of the veto fails to discharge its responsibilities and instruct the use of the Force in situations clearly calling for its use, the Assembly has the power to do so.

The International Law Association has recently devoted a good deal of attention to the problem of establishing a permanent United Nations Force for peace-keeping operations only (and to this extent its inquiry was more limited than the very wide terms of the Pakistani proposal). Professor Schwarzenberger, the Rapporteur of the Committee on the Charter of the United Nations, argued strongly for a study of a proposal to establish a permanent Peace Force of between 2,000 and 10,000 men,[13] and a definite proposal was submitted by which the Conference would have resolved:

> " 1. To recommend that the General Assembly of the United Nations consider at its next session, as a matter of urgency, the establishment of a permanent United Nations Peace Force and Observer Corps to assist the Organisation in the fulfilment of its obligations regarding the maintenance of world peace and international security;
>
> 2. To request the Committee on the Charter of the United Nations to examine . . . any of the problems raised in the Rapporteur's Report, as well as those involved in the establishment of a permanent United Nations Peace Force and Observer Corps, with a view to submitting a Report to the next Conference." [14]

This resolution was not, however, adopted: instead the Conference requested the Committee:

> " To examine, if necessary with the assistance of outside experts, any of the problems raised in the Rapporteur's Report, as well as those involved in the establishment of a permanent United Nations Peace Force and Observer Corps, with a view to submitting a Report to the next Conference." [15]

[11] See Schwarzenberger's *Report on Legal Problems of a UN Force, Report of the 49th Conference of the I.L.A.*, p. 151: " . . . proposals for a permanent United Nations Force might appear less extravagant than while it had to be taken for granted that such a Force would have to operate under the direction of the General Assembly." He lists five situations in which the Security Council might find it possible to operate an " interposition " Force.

[12] " In a sense " because the literal wording of the Resolution on Uniting for Peace is apt to include enforcement action as well as " peace-keeping operations," and it is only the latter which concern us here.

[13] *Report of the 48th Conference of the I.L.A.* (New York, 1958) at p. 510.

[14] *Ibid.*, p. 519.

[15] *Ibid.*, p. xiv.

Notwithstanding his excellent Report to the 49th Conference at Hamburg in 1960,[16] which he supported by the most persuasive arguments, Dr. Schwarzenberger failed to gain even the Committee's approval of that part of a draft resolution which *considered*:

> "in the light of the experiences gained in the practice of the United Nations, *that* the establishment and maintenance of United Nations Forces on the pattern of the United Nations Emergency Force is entirely in accordance with the letter and spirit of the Charter of the United Nations, and that further developments on these lines, especially in the direction of creating some more permanent framework and cadres of military and technical personnel, are in the best interest of the United Nations." [17]

Rather the Conference requested the Committee to carry out a further study with a view to reporting at an early date on the following specific questions:

(1) Whether it would be useful to prepare draft standing orders for the guidance of United Nations Commands in case of need;
(2) What are the respective legal implications, advantages and disadvantages, on the one hand, of *ad hoc* United Nations Forces and, on the other, permanent United Nations Forces;
(3) What are the respective legal implications, advantages and disadvantages, on the one hand, of United Nations Forces, consisting of contingents contributed by Member States and, on the other hand, a United Nations Force, based on the method of individual enlistment; and
(4) What are the rules governing civil and criminal liability resulting from the activities of a United Nations Force and the proper jurisdiction to which such matters should be referred.[18]

The reactions of the International Law Association to these proposals are instructive in that they indicate very clearly that reserve (or even hostility) to the idea of a permanent Force is not confined to politicians.

3. *A composite Force combining a permanent nucleus with supporting national contingents*

It was this kind of compromise, composite type of Force which, in 1930, Lord Davies felt to offer the best solution.[19] Again, however, one has to distinguish the two different types of function to be envisaged for the Force before the type of composite Force becomes clear.

[16] *Report of the 49th Conference of the I.L.A.* (Hamburg, 1960), at pp. 96, 130; and see for reference to this report, *ante*, pp. 279, 287.
[17] *Ibid.* (49th) at p. 112.
[18] *Ibid.* (49th) at p. 124.
[19] *Op. cit.*, p. 380. But note that the functions of the "international police force" were, for him, essentially those of repelling aggression and enforcing decisions of judicial and arbitral tribunals: these are the functions in practice least exercised so far by UN Forces. The permanent element would, in his plan, have had a marked weapons superiority over the national contingents.

(a) ENFORCEMENT FUNCTIONS

In all likelihood the permanent nucleus would have to be on a reasonably substantial scale. The permanent Force of 7,000 planned by Cannon and Jordan was, in the event of a situation developing which called for enforcement action or even serious military combat falling short of that (as in the Congo) to be either withdrawn or reinforced by national contingents.[20] Thus, in the event of reinforcement, the United Nations Force of one brigade would be no more than a permanent nucleus for a larger Force of this composite type.

There is, however, no axiomatic size for such a nucleus; the reasons for a smaller, or larger, nucleus of a permanent character would be reasons of finance, political acceptability, military convenience and the like. It is possible that the permanent nucleus could be no more than a standing Headquarters Military Staff from which could be drawn a United Nations Command, and this is a proposal which we shall develop under the next head.

(b) PEACE-KEEPING OPERATIONS

Prima facie, a permanent nucleus for this kind of function would be smaller than that required for enforcement functions. The proposals of Trygve Lie, as Secretary-General, in 1948,[21] for a United Nations Guard of 800 (500 of which would be reservists) was one kind of nucleus, although envisaged for somewhat more limited functions than the entire "peace-keeping" bracket includes. His later proposals for a United Nations "Legion" in 1951 [22] envisaged a quasi-permanent nucleus in the form of a United Nations Volunteer Reserve, although these would have been designed for enforcement action.

It may well be that a modest beginning could be made by establishing as a permanent nucleus only a United Nations Headquarters Military Staff which could be entrusted with advance planning of different kinds of operations, both enforcement and peace-keeping, and with the training of officers from States which were in principle, or even by commitment in a stand-by agreement, prepared to contribute national contingents to serve under this nucleus. In the event of an actual operation the United Nations Military Staff would then use the national contingents, and assume command over them, in a somewhat less *ad hoc*, or improvised, way than has been the United Nations' practice hitherto. Such a beginning, combined with the co-operation of Member States in the form of a definite ear-marking of units of their national forces or, even better, the conclusion of stand-by agreements whereby States undertook an obligation to make such units available to the United Nations, would signify a real advance in methods of maintaining international peace.

[20] *Loc. cit.*, p. 162.
[21] *Ante*, pp. 18–20.
[22] *Ante*, pp. 25–26.

Lord Robertson (formerly General Robertson), in the House of Lords debate on 20 February 1963, advocated "the immediate creation . . . of a headquarters, containing a strong political and military planning staff and a logistic nucleus. . . . This staff should owe allegiance to the Secretary-General through its own Chief of Staff . . . they should be the servants of the United Nations." He continued:

"Such a headquarters would, in my view, have functions roughly as follows. In the first place, it would make a study of the various kinds of intervention that the United Nations might be called upon to make, whether by force or by showing a presence, and a study of those ancillary activities which might be associated with intervention, such as the temporary assumption of responsibility for civil affairs, to which the Motion most properly draws attention. Second, as part of this study, the staff should devise and recommend a sensible system of control to ensure proper, prompt and constant direction and a reasonable chain of military command. Thirdly, it should collect information and collate it on the various parts of the world where information might be needed. Fourth, and most important, it should be authorised to consult with the governments of those States who agree, and who should be pressed to agree, to earmark forces . . . to consult them about their composition, their state of readiness, their training and so forth, and to make inspections. Fifth, this staff should plan the logistics of intervention, and the infrastructures needed for it—by which I mean the telecommunications, the chain of airfields and so on." [23]

There is increasing evidence of a recognition that the creation of a permanent Headquarters Military Staff is a logical and necessary next step in the improvement of the United Nations peace-keeping machinery. A study by the World Veterans Federation concluded that "all members of the Study Group agreed that a permanent planning organisation within the United Nations should be set up as soon as possible." [24] Significantly, this study was based upon the comments of senior military officers who had had actual experience with United Nations military operations.[25] Similar conclusions have recently been made in specialist papers prepared for the International Conference on United Nations Security Forces as a Means to Promoting Peace, to convene in Oslo in February 1964.[26]

[23] Parl.Debates (Hansard) H.L., Vol. 246, No. 43, cols. 1392–1393. See also Lord McNair (*ibid.*, col. 1402), speaking in like vein, Lord Tweedsmuir (col. 1405) and the Earl of Lucan (col. 1409).

[24] *The Functioning of Ad hoc United Nations Forces* (1963), p. 13. The functions to be assumed by the planning organisation included 1. A periodic review of national availabilities of Member States in supplying units for an *ad hoc* emergency Force; 2. The operational, logistical and administrative problems to be encountered, including the question of standardisation of equipment, particularly vehicles and light arms, and the establishment of standard operational procedures; 3. Preliminary arrangements for the establishment of a UN Force headquarters, once authorised.

[25] *Ibid.*, Annex A. The officers were General Burns, Air Marshal Miller, Lieut.-General Sean MacEvin and Maj.-General von Horn.

[26] "Earmarking of Forces for the Use of the UN," p. 8; "Establishment of a Permanent Planning Staff within the UN Secretariat"—Introduction to Second Lecture; Bowitz, "The Central and Military Administration of UN Forces," p. 13.

It will be one of the major aims of the present study to argue for the creation of such a United Nations Headquarters Military Staff, and the functions which such a Staff could perform will be outlined in the succeeding sections of this study.

4. *The pros and cons of permanent and ad hoc Forces*

It would be inappropriate to reach the above conclusions without a brief examination of the kind of points which are made for and against a permanent Force, an examination all the more interesting since it shows that the objections to a permanent Force relate either to a Force of a kind totally different to that which we now propose, or else are largely misconceived.

(a) THE ARGUMENTS FOR A PERMANENT FORCE

These have been put by various people, in various forms, at different times.[27] Essentially they are the following:

(1) The improvisation inherent in an *ad hoc* Force leads to inefficient use of resources, uncertainty as to whether a suitable Force can be collected together, and delay in the use of the Force, which could have serious consequences for international peace.[28]

(2) With the dissipation of an *ad hoc* Force, and with no permanent Force remaining in being, much of the experience gained is lost. It is not enough to commit experience to paper for future reference: experience means also the experience of people in handling a given set of problems, so that permanent personnel become more important than permanent records.[29]

(3) The decision to use the Force must always remain a political decision, but the additional decision of how to constitute a Force—which is necessary when reliance is placed on *ad hoc* Forces—adds further complicating factors which could be avoided if a permanent Force were established.[30]

(4) Personnel of a permanent Force recruited as individuals would not remain members of national forces and would therefore be able to assume the international loyalty and *esprit de corps* which

[27] See Lord Davies, *op. cit.*, pp. 377–9; Schwarzenberger's *Report on Legal Problems of a United Nations Force, loc. cit.*, pp. 96–98 and the discussion following this Report at pp. 99–123; *Report of Committee on Study of Legal Problems of the United Nations, Proceedings of A.S.I.L.* (1957) pp. 227–8; Frye, *op. cit.*, Chap. VII.

[28] For a frank confession of these weaknesses see the address by U Thant to the Harvard Alumni Association at Cambridge, Massachusetts, on 13 June 1963 (Press Release SG/1520).

[29] The post-UNEF assurance of the Secretary-General that the experience of the UN was satisfactorily embodied in such records as his *Summary Study of Experience, etc.* (A/3943) and in the experience of the UN Secretariat (para. 186) must be regarded as having been shaken by the Congo operations.

[30] See Green in *Report of the 49th Conference of the I.L.A.*, pp. 114–116; and see *ante*, pp. 109–111, 206–207, on problems of composition of UN Forces.

Secretariat members assume, and would become subject to rights and obligations under Article 100 of the Charter.[31]

(5) The possibility of recruitment of individuals in a permanent Force secures, in addition to the advantages in (4) above, a Force which cannot be dissipated by the withdrawal of national contingents.[32]

(6) In operations of an indefinite nature States are unwilling to see contingents of their national forces committed indefinitely.[33]

(7) Member States might be more prepared to finance a permanent international Force, than a Force comprised of relatively few national contingents.

(8) Service with a United Nations Force requires special skills [34] which cannot be readily imparted to an *ad hoc* Force, and which should be retained.

(9) Consent to the presence of the Force would be more readily forthcoming.[35]

(10) Unity of command and better control over the Force could be achieved.[36]

(11) The permanent Force could become a nucleus around which a larger Force could be constituted, by the contribution of national contingents, for the larger peace-keeping operations (like the Congo) or even enforcement action.

(12) The permanent Force would constitute a "pilot scheme" so as to build up the experience and confidence necessary for the progression to general disarmament, in which a larger United Nations Force would be necessary.

(b) THE ARGUMENTS AGAINST A PERMANENT FORCE

(1) The type of Force required for a particular operation will vary according to the situation, and *ad hoc* Forces give the necessary flexibility to meet different situations.

This was very much the argument used by Hammarskjoeld in his *Summary Study of the Experience derived from the establishment and operation of the Force* (UNEF).[37] Interestingly enough,

[31] On the status of members of UNEF see A/3943, para. 128.
[32] See *ante*, pp. 113, 208–209, on withdrawal of national contingents.
[33] For the reservations of States in contributing national contingents see *post*, p. 381.
[34] For example, skills in dealing with communications problems on a bilingual basis or in "policing" a situation with all the limitations on the use of arms inherent in that function as opposed to normal combat operations.
[35] *Proceedings of the A.S.I.L.* (1957) p. 228. This "advantage" was stated to exist on the assumption that *ad hoc* Forces required the consent of the territorial State for their operation: on the reasons for not entirely sharing this assumption see *post*, pp. 413–417.
[36] For the impact of this on matters of discipline and the application of the laws of war see *post*, pp. 511–513.
[37] A/3943, paras. 153–154. For his acceptance of the idea of an expanded military staff within the Secretariat see para. 185. He visualised a "standing group of military experts" to keep under review any stand-by arrangements which States might be prepared to conclude with the UN.

U Thant, speaking on 13 June 1963,[38] continued the Secretary-General's traditional opposition. He stated that:

"In my opinion, a permanent United Nations Force is not a practical proposition at the present time . . . Many difficulties still stand in the way of its evolution. Personally, I have no doubt that the world should eventually have an international police Force which will be accepted as an integral and essential part of life in the same way as national police forces are accepted."

However, the reasons against a permanent Force given by U Thant are not the variety of situations to be encountered, and the flexibility of the *ad hoc* system, but rather doubts "whether many governments in the world would yet be prepared to accept the political implications of such an institution and, in the light of our current experience with financial problems, I am sure that they would have very serious difficulties in accepting the financial implications." Hence, the Secretary-General advanced no more reasons of an intrinsically persuasive character against a permanent Force, but rather the simple political fact that governments are not prepared to accept the idea.

(2) The selection of personnel for a permanent Force would be difficult.[39]

This argument has never seemed particularly persuasive to the present writer. Whether secondment from national forces or individual recruitment is chosen, the problems are much the same as in recruiting the United Nations Secretariat—and this has never seemed insurmountable! Clearly some kind of quota system could be devised to prevent over-reliance on a few nationalities,[40] and, even though exclusion of nationals from the Permanent Members might be desirable, there would still be plenty of available and sufficiently expert personnel of the right calibre and qualifications.

(3) The financial implications.

This is, in a relative sense, an extremely strong objection and it is, as we have seen, still the objection which U Thant is raising. No one with any knowledge of the financial difficulties which the United Nations has experienced over UNEF and ONUC would deny the seriousness of this objection. However, it has to be placed in perspective, and it must first be said that, as one conceives of a peace-keeping Force or even a permanent Military Staff, and not a Force capable of enforcement action, so does one's conception of the cost involved alter, and the validity of the objection diminish. It may be recalled that the Secretary-General's estimate for his 800-man Guard Force in 1949 was $4m. per annum.[41] Frye's estimate for a force of

[38] SG/1520.

[39] See Saario in *Report of the 49th Conference of the I.L.A.*, p. 103. A similar argument was used by the U.K. in opposing the Secretary-General's proposals for a UN Guard in 1949: see *ante*, p. 20.

[40] The formula suggested by Clark and Sohn for a disarmament Force (*op. cit.*, p. 324) limiting the number of any one nationality to 3 per cent. of the total strength is one kind of solution: in relation to the UN Secretariat there has long been a fixing of the desirable number of posts for any one nationality.

[41] *Ante*, p. 19.

7,000 men was $25m. per annum when not in action.[42] UNEF, of 6,000 strong in 1958, was costing approximately $20m., and ONUC, of 16,000, approximately $120m.; in both cases, however, large parts of the upkeep was the burden of the participating States and not the United Nations.[43] Astronomic though these sums might be, viewed relatively they are reduced to their proper perspective, and they make a rather favourable comparison to the sums States are prepared to spend on their defence budgets or even single items in those budgets.[44] Moreover, as the recent examples of UNTEA and the Yemen Group show,[45] on some occasions the States directly concerned may be prepared to assume the entire cost of the operations.

Basically, the objection of finance is an objection to the assessment of a permanent Force as an institution of high priority in the maintenance of peace and security. The moment that one accepts that such a Force could make a contribution to the maintenance of international peace and security of the same order as the vast standing armies of the Member States, the objection of finance loses a great deal of its force.

Finally, it may be said that what is proposed above is not even, as a first step, a standing, permanent Force but rather a permanent Headquarters Military Staff. If one visualises a Staff of, say, fifty experienced officers,[46] the cost may well be in the order of $500,000 per annum: by any standards a not oppressive sum for more than a hundred Member States.

(4) Political unacceptance of the idea.

There is little doubt that the majority of Member States, as represented by their governments, show relatively little enthusiasm for the idea.[47] Quite apart from the question of cost, there are

[42] *Op. cit.*, pp. 78, 167. This cost is likely to be doubled when the Force is deployed in a State's territory on a peace-keeping operation. The cost of ONUC at a strength of 6,000 for six months only has recently been estimated by the Secretary-General to be $25m: *UN Review*, Vol. 10, No. 9, October 1963, p. 45.

[43] *Post*, pp. 468–471.

[44] Frye, *op. cit.*, p. 78 cites the cost of a Forrestal aircraft-carrier as $200m. In *NATO, Facts about the North Atlantic Treaty Organisation* (1962) at p. 105 the total defence expenditures for the NATO countries are given, and the following figures are taken from the table there produced:

	Currency Unit	*1958*	*1959*	*1960*	*1961 (Forecast)*
Canada	Million Can. $	1,740	1,642	1,654	1,703
France	Million New Frs.	16,569	17,926	18,940	19,800
U.K.	Million £s Strlg.	1,591	1,589	1,652	1,701
U.S.A.	Million U.S. $	45,503	46,614	46,545	51,093

It is believed that the Soviet Union's defence expenditure in 1961 was £4,960 million.

[45] *Ante*, pp. 85, 260.

[46] For details see *post*, p. 350.

[47] For observations on the sectional interests of States, real or imaginary, which militate against a permanent Force, see Frye, *op. cit.*, p. 34.

many[48] who distrust the idea because of a fear that the Force may be used to interfere with State sovereignty, or may be used to augment the Secretary-General's power in an improper way,[49] or used by a group or *bloc* of States in a way designed to further their regional interests rather than the purposes and principles of the Charter and the interests of the Members as a whole.[50] There is a certain validity in these objections, but they go to the desirability of establishing a proper system of political control[51] rather than to the establishment of a permanent Force as such. Moreover, since we are for the present talking in terms of a permanent United Nations Military Staff, and in the more remote future perhaps a permanent Force of 5–10,000 men, the very limited size of the Force is such that it can scarcely be regarded as a potential aggressor against States.

It may be that governments also instinctively dislike proposals which imply some restraint on their freedom of action—and certainly a permanent United Nations Force will be utilised to curb certain forms of action—but this is scarcely an objection which ought to carry much weight once the Force is conceived as an instrument designed to ensure that governments abide by the obligations they have already assumed under the Charter with regard to the limitation of the use of force. The other comment which must be made on the objection of "political unacceptance" is that governments may be becoming divorced from the opinions of their people. Ill-informed as the general public may be, gallup polls in the United States have revealed a majority view in favour of a permanent Force for the United Nations,[52] and one suspects that a good many States would find a similar view amongst their people.[53]

[48] See *Report of the 49th Conference of the I.L.A.* for observations by Tunkin (U.S.S.R.), p. 104, Perera (Ceylon), p. 109.

[49] *Ibid.*, statement by Sztucki (Poland), p. 121.

[50] See *ante*, p. 215, for comments on the role of the African States in the Congo operations.

[51] As to this see *post*, p. 353 *et seq.*

[52] For details see Frye, *op. cit.*, pp. 66–67. See also the celebrated Resolution 109 of the U.S. Congress in July 1958 that:

"(a) A Force of a similar character (to UNEF) should be made a permanent arm of the United Nations;

(b) Such a Force should be composed of units made available by members of the United Nations: provided, that no such units should be accepted from the Permanent Members of the Security Council;

(c) Consideration should be given to arrangements whereby individuals would be allowed to volunteer for service with such a Force: provided, that individuals who are nationals of permanent Members of the Security Council such not be acceptable;

(d) Equipment and expenses of such a force should be provided by the United Nations out of its regular budget."

Hearings before the Sub-committee on International Organisation and Movements of the Committee on Foreign Affairs, House of Representatives, 85th Congress, 2d Session (July 24, 1958).

[53] For a very instructive debate on a United Nations Force in the House of Lords on 20 February 1963 see Parl.Debates (Hansard) H.L., Vol. 246, No. 43, cols. 1371-1436. Lord Ogmore called for a small permanent Force, recruited

A final, and perhaps the most important, comment is that unless a beginning is made in this modest way it is difficult to see how the long-term plans for general disarmament which (at least from the standpoint of the proposals of the United States) envisage a United Nations Force of a permanent kind can ever be found acceptable. An experiment to build up confidence must be begun soon.

(5) The unconstitutionality of the proposal in terms of the United Nations Charter.

The objection has been made[54] that, since the Charter envisages a Force constituted by means of national contingents provided by States pursuant to agreements under Article 43, to establish a permanent Force would be to act *ultra vires.* This is an objection which has, in one sense, already been rejected by Member States generally and by the International Court of Justice in the *Expenses Case,* for it rests on the premise that the only type of Force permissible for the United Nations is the Article 43 type of Force: not one of the Forces so far established has been of this type and the different constitutional bases for United Nations Forces have already been examined to demonstrate the invalidity of this premise.[55]

However, to show the invalidity of this premise is not to answer the whole objection, for no permanent Force has yet been established. The full answer to the objection lies in the doctrine of implied powers[56]: as Seyersted has said:

> "Indeed, it appears that while intergovernmental organisations, unlike States, are restricted by specific provisions in their constitutions as to the aims for which they shall work, such organisations are, like States, in principle free to perform any sovereign act, or any act under international law, which they are in a factual position to perform to attain these aims, provided that their constitutions do not preclude such acts."[57]

Nothing in the Charter specifically precludes the establishment of a permanent Force, and, as we have seen,[58] both the Assembly and the Security Council have powers wide enough to enable them to establish a permanent Force as a subsidiary organ for purposes necessary to the maintenance of international peace and security.[59]

as individuals on a long-term basis, with a UN Command and having combined "military, naval and air units and a military-civil affairs component" (col. 1375). He also argued for a permanent Command structure immediately, and a gradual build-up of the individually-recruited element of the Force, gradually displacing the national contingents. He was supported by Earl Attlee, the Lord Bishop of Chichester, Lord Robertson, Lord McNair, Lord Tweedsmuir, and the Earl of Lucan.

[54] *Report of the 49th Conference of the I.L.A.*, observations by Tunkin (U.S.S.R.), p. 104; Litwin (Poland), p. 106; Krishna Rao (India), p. 116.

[55] *Ante*, pp. 274–312.

[56] See generally Seyersted, "United Nations Forces" (1961), B.Y.I.L. pp. 447–470.

[57] *Ibid.*, p. 456.

[58] *Ante*, pp. 274–312.

[59] But see *ante*, pp. 288, 291–293, on the question whether the functions of a Force established by the Assembly can include "enforcement action."

5. *Military, paramilitary or police Force?*

In the Second and final (UNEF) Report [60] to the General Assembly the Secretary-General described UNEF as a "paramilitary" body. This troubled General Burns, who made the following comment in his book:

"I objected to the use of the term 'paramilitary' to describe UNEF or its functions. The Oxford English Dictionary defines 'paramilitary' as 'having a status or function ancillary to that of military forces.' Examples are constabularies or gendarmeries organised more or less on military lines and having functions of maintaining order in turbulent areas, with a regular military force behind them. But UNEF was and is unquestionably formed of military units, from the regular forces of the nations contributing. It is not ancillary to any 'other' military force.

This inappropriate (in my view) use of the term 'paramilitary' perhaps arises from a misapprehension that a military force in all situations invariably and necessarily uses all the arms and means at its disposal to achieve its object. This, of course, is not so, as an army can give 'aid to the civil power' under great restrictions as to its use of arms. In my view, *UNEF is certainly a military force*, but with a strictly limited and defined task and mode of action prescribed for it.

"Possibly 'paramilitary' in the text was used to allay the doubts of some supporters of the Resolution." [61]

When Trygve Lie made his proposal for a United Nations Guard he took pains to emphasise that it would be "entirely non-military." Soviet spokesmen objected even to the light arming of the Guard suggested by the Secretary-General, arguing that so armed the Guard would be a "real armed force" and, for that reason alone, unacceptable.

During the interval between the World Wars it became fashionable to speak of an "International Police Force." The abbreviation "IPF" was used as if it were as generally known as "UN" is today. Others referred to an "international army" or simply an "international force." Frye entitled his book *The United Nations Peace Force*. Mr. L. B. Pearson, Canadian Minister for External Affairs in 1957, now the Prime Minister of Canada, coined the expression "Peace Supervision Force" in his article in the April 1957 quarterly issue of *Foreign Affairs*. For West New Guinea (West Irian) the Secretary-General created a "United Nations Security Force." The United Nations Force in the Congo has not yet been given a distinctive name but is referred to indifferently as the "United Nations Force in the Congo," or the "ONUC (UNOC) Force" or, simply, but inaccurately, "ONUC" or "UNOC." The expressions a "United Nations Military Force" or a "United Nations Armed Force" are consciously, almost self-consciously, avoided.

This preference for euphemisms can be explained, in part, by the feeling that the United Nations ought to be engaged in keeping the peace and not in fighting wars: it overlooks the fact that the United Nations may have to engage in hostilities indistinguishable from

[60] A/3302, para. 10.

[61] *Op. cit.*, p. 313.

warfare in their practical effect in order to keep the peace. The larger explanation is due to a desire to distinguish between the different functions which have in the past been, and may in the future be, entrusted to a United Nations Force.[62]

According to function, UNEF, ONUC and the UNSF are more "police" than "military." The fact remains that a United Nations Force made up of national military contingents will, and is expected to, behave like a military force. The distinguishing mark of a military force is its disciplined response to command, not the fact that its members bear arms and are uniformed.

Many purely civilian organisations wear uniforms and lawfully bear arms. In his article in the *British Year Book* (1961), Dr. Seyersted treats the United Nations Guard and the United Nations Field Service as examples of United Nations "semi-military" bodies. Dr. Seyersted also treats as "semi-military" United Nations military observer groups, UNTSO, UNOGIL and UNMOGIP. The observers are "military" but are not organised as a military body under formal military command. In dealing with his role as "Chief of Staff" of UNTSO General Burns said:

"The title 'Chief of Staff' in military usage denotes a senior officer controlling a more or less extensive staff, and responsible either to a military commander or to a Minister of Defence, or to a Government.

"The Chief of Staff UNTSO is not at the head of a staff, but is the administrator of the corps of United Nations Military Observers and the director of their operations. He is responsible to and receives instructions from the Security Council, usually in the form of its Resolutions. He communicates with the Security Council through the Secretary-General, to whom in the first instance he addresses his routine and day-by-day reports.

"The title, though not terminologically accurate, has established itself through usage."[63]

Kelsen had this to say about the accuracy of designating an armed Force as a police Force:

"Another terminology, the correctness of which is doubtful is to designate as an international 'police' Force only a permanent and separate armed Force at the direct disposal of the central organ of an international security community. A police force is an armed force used in the performance of a police action. A police action is any enforcement action performed by an organ of a community for the welfare of its members, their health, morals, prosperity and, especially, their security. However, it is not a sanitary police force or a police force for the purpose of morals or economics, but a *security police force* with which an international security organisation is concerned . . .The difference between a 'police force' for the maintenance of internal order and an 'armed force' for defence against external aggression is irrelevant within an international security organisation."[64]

[62] Thus Poirier, *La Force Internationale d'Urgence* (1962) Part Two, Chaps. I and II, devotes two chapters to the role and nature of UNEF to arrive at the conclusion that UNEF is an international police force and not a military force in the sense of the Charter. Burns was convinced that UNEF was a military force.

[63] *Op. cit.*, p. 295.

[64] U.S. Naval War College, *International Law Studies—Collective Security under International Law, 1954* (1956) at pp. 114–5.

Kelsen's views of the functions of a "security police force" are essentially pre-UNEF; that is to say, they are stated far too narrowly and do not include the variety of functions which have been listed above.[65] This whole controversy over nomenclature seems a somewhat sterile one. The analysis of functions attempted above discloses that United Nations Forces may be entrusted with tasks which involve a greater or lesser risk of combat activity, or even no risk at all: they will accordingly be armed to a greater or lesser extent, or not at all (as with many of the observer groups). The present study has adopted the all-embracing title of "United Nations Forces" to allow for the discussion of United Nations bodies *composed of military personnel,* as opposed to the civilian Secretariat, for whatever purpose or function.

The problem of nomenclature does, of course, assume importance when one discusses proposals for a permanent Force since it will raise the problem of the size, type and equipment of the Force and, indeed, one of the arguments against a permanent Force has been that it would commit the United Nations to a particular type of Force when other types may well be needed. It is believed that this argument has little merit. The permanent nucleus which should be aimed at in the immediate future, namely, a Headquarters Military Staff and soon afterwards a small unit of 5–10,000 men, would be a *military* Force: but it would have to be a versatile Force so that it would be trained, and in the event either armed or not armed, to tackle any of the various functions we have listed. The outstanding merit of the Ghanaian and Nigerian riot police (220 and 120 strong respectively) in the Congo stemmed from their training, not the fact that they were called "police" rather than "military," and there is no reason why a military unit should not be trained to deal with riots as well as armed hostilities. Equally there is no reason why its officers should not be trained in the duties of observers, although a reserve panel of observers might be necessary for situations in which greater numbers of observers would be required,[66] and part of the Force, if necessary, detailed to act as guards for the observers.

[65] *Ante,* pp. 267–274.
[66] *Post,* p. 548.

The next reading is also from Bowett's book and consists of his proposal for the establishment of a permanent United Nations Military Force, as well as a summary statement of the arguments for and against the establishment of such a permanent force. The proposal itself is the concluding chapter in his book, and is very carefully worked out: "Conclusions," *United Nations Forces* (Praeger, New York, 1964) pp. 561–569. The plan calls for four stages in which the political and military measures are coordinated in a manner as to permit sufficient trust in the forces to arise so that the entire process of transition can take place. The proposal is based upon a comprehensive and detailed analysis of all the peace-keeping activities of the United Nations and exhibits a rare mixture of political acumen and legal craftsmanship. The excerpt containing the pros and cons of the arguments on the establishment of a permanent international police force is not only valuable for its enumeration, but as a forthright response to the conclusion reached by both U Thant and Hammarskjöld that it is not presently possible to do more than create stand-by forces.

D. W. BOWETT

Conclusions

NEARLY twenty years have elapsed since the signing of the United Nations Charter. Yet, despite the prominence given to Chapter VII in the Charter, and despite a general agreement that the system of collective security established by the Charter can only operate upon the assumption that the United Nations is given the armed forces necessary to maintain international peace and security, the Charter scheme has not yet been implemented. The history of the attempts to implement this scheme and the alternative scheme which many envisaged could be established under the Resolution on Uniting for Peace of 3 November 1950 has been briefly described in Chapter 2. At the time of writing, however, there is no real "scheme" in existence, and the Cyprus situation [1] has revealed only too clearly the weakness of the United Nations Organisation in dealing with a situation which requires a military force but in which the United Nations is entirely dependent on the voluntary provision of national contingents by those very few States which accept a concept of obligation—albeit at this stage a moral rather than a legal obligation —towards the United Nations and the Purposes and Principles for which it stands.

The extraordinary thing is that the United Nations has been able to establish military forces at all. And yet, since 1948, there has never been a time in which, in one or several parts of the world, a group or Force comprising military personnel was not operating in the name of the United Nations. Whether in the form of observer groups,[2] or of a military Force such as that in Korea,[3] engaged in hostilities indistinguishable from war, or of a "peace-keeping" Force like UNEF in the Middle East [4] or ONUC in the Congo [5]—and whether 200 or 20,000 strong—United Nations Military Forces have in fact played a not insignificant part in maintaining the peace and security of the world. All these military operations have been described in Part One of the present study, and the postscript gives a brief account of the latest military operation, that in Cyprus.

Each and every one of these military operations represented an exercise in improvisation, and, however critical this study may have been at times, the determination and skill of those responsible calls for a special and sincere tribute. Yet the question which must be asked is why the United Nations Organisation, comprising 114 States,

[1] See *ante*, pp. 552–560.
[2] *Ante*, Chap. 4.
[3] *Ante*, Chap. 3.
[4] *Ante*, Chap. 5.
[5] *Ante*, Chap. 6.

is content to entrust its responsibilities for the maintenance of international peace and security to a system based on improvisation and chance? Not one of these States would contemplate looking after its own security in so haphazard a manner and yet for nearly twenty years it has remained the basis upon which United Nations military operations have been established. It has not been the intention of this study to answer that question in terms of the reasons behind the policies of Member States, but rather to examine the problems which have been encountered and the principles and practices which have emerged as solutions, complete or partial, to these problems.

However, the conclusion to which the present writer has been forced is that none of these problems can be properly solved except by establishing a permanent United Nations Military Force. The functions which are capable of attribution to a United Nations Force have been outlined in Chapter 8. These, it may be recalled, fell broadly into the two main categories of "enforcement" functions directed against a State or States and "peace-keeping" functions which, whilst possibly including the use of armed force, do not envisage that such force will be used directly against a State. The former, except for the action in Korea, have never been undertaken by the United Nations and Article 42 of the Charter has never been used. The latter have become very much the kind of military operations which the United Nations has been prepared to undertake and it may thus be argued that in initiating a scheme for a permanent Force it is a "peace-keeping" Force which ought first to be aimed at. There are other reasons why it is advisable to concentrate on a Force with peace-keeping functions. These are, first, that such a Force will not need to be of the same order of size as a Force designed for enforcement action [6]; secondly, the doubt over whether the General Assembly could legally authorise enforcement action [7]; thirdly, the likelihood that situations calling for a "peace-keeping" role will be more frequent than situations calling for enforcement action; and, lastly, the likelihood that Member States will find a proposal for a peace-keeping Force both politically and economically more acceptable.

Therefore, on the basis of the experience of the past and in the light of the principles which have emerged, there is every justification for proposing a scheme which would give to the United Nations a permanent military Force for peace-keeping purposes. This will not necessarily mean that the Force could not be used for enforcement action; as we shall see, it could also form the nucleus of a larger Force designed for enforcement action and created by strengthening the permanent nucleus with national contingents from Member States. However, its primary role will be a "peace-keeping" role. Such a scheme or plan can only be introduced gradually, for this is

[6] *Ante*, pp. 316–317, 320.
[7] *Ante*, pp. 288–293.

not a moment in time at which great changes can be effected: rather is it a time for the slow evolution of a machinery which can command the trust and confidence of States. The scheme which follows is, in effect, a ten-year scheme to be completed in four stages. The scheme may therefore be set out in the following stages and footnotes will refer the reader to those parts of the study in which the details of the scheme are enlarged upon.

I. STAGE ONE (TO BE COMPLETED WITHIN THREE YEARS)

1. *The United Nations Headquarters Military Staff* [8]

The Security Council or, failing agreement in that organ, the General Assembly, should appoint a United Nations Chief-of-Staff and authorise the Secretary-General to begin the recruitment of a permanent United Nations Headquarters Military Staff of approximately fifty experienced military officers in consultation with the Chief-of-Staff. These would be recruited as individuals for terms of service of, say, five to seven years and would range from a Commander down to experts in communications, transportation, ordnance, intelligence, civil affairs and medical services.[9]

The Military Staff, when constituted, would undertake the following tasks:

(1) A study of the different kinds of peace-keeping operations likely to be undertaken by a United Nations Force composed of national contingents and of the ideal composition and command structure for such a Force in any given type of operation.

(2) A survey of the operational, logistical and administrative problems (including standardisation of equipment and of operational procedures, joint civilian-military operations) encountered in the past and likely to be encountered in the future.[10]

(3) Liaison with the Member States which have declared their willingness in principle to provide contingents for a United Nations Force,[11] such liaison to include a periodic inspection of any such contingents by the United Nations Headquarters Military Staff.

(4) The organisation of joint exercises in which contingents assigned for United Nations duty by several Member States could participate under United Nations Command.

(5) The formulation of plans for a United Nations Staff College and of training schemes to be undertaken by such a College for the instruction of senior officers drawn from the armed forces of States declaring their willingness to provide contingents for the United Nations.

(6) The formulation of model Regulations for the Force,[12] Status

[8] *Ante*, pp. 349–352.
[9] See the diagram on p. 350.
[10] *Ante*, Chap. 11.
[11] *Ante*, pp. 330–337.
[12] *Ante*, pp. 334, 336, 372, 376.

of Forces Agreements [13] and Stand-by Agreements [14] for submission to the political organs of the United Nations for discussion and adoption.

(7) The negotiation of contracts and charterparties with public and private associations designed to ensure that the Staff could call on supplies and transport as and when needed.[15]

2. *The political control organs* [16]

Whilst the initiative in carrying out this scheme ought to come from the Security Council (or rather ought to begin there), should this be rejected the General Assembly should assert its secondary responsibility [17] and pass the Resolutions referred to above in connection with the establishment of the Headquarters Military Staff: the budgetary responsibility would in any event be upon the Assembly.

Moreover, whether or not the Security Council assumes the initiative, there would be every advantage in the General Assembly establishing a committee of limited composition, adequately representing the East, the West and the non-aligned States (and with due regard to equitable geographical distribution) which could assume the continuing political control of a United Nations Force in any particular operation which became hamstrung by a veto in the Security Council.[18] Thus the principal burden of political responsibility would be assumed by the Member States and not, as has so often been the case in the past, by the Secretary-General. The practice of vesting continuing political control in the Secretary-General,[19] which has been symptomatic of a shirking of responsibility by Member States, would therefore cease and Member States would be able to devise forms and procedures for exercising this responsibility, whether within the Security Council or the General Assembly (and the committee now proposed).

The political control organ, the Security Council or the General Assembly (according to where the initiative stemmed from)—or even, ideally, a joint committee of both organs [20] in view of the financial implications of the scheme—would also undertake the following:

(1) The consideration and approval of the contracts of service of the members of the United Nations Headquarters Military Staff and of the general plan for the composition of such a Staff submitted by the Secretary-General and the Chief-of-Staff.

(2) The consideration and approval of the plans for a United Nations Staff College.

[13] *Ante*, pp. 432–455.
[14] *Ante*, pp. 371–377.
[15] *Ante*, pp. 405–406.
[16] *Ante*, pp. 353–359.
[17] For the constitutional basis for the Assembly's authority to establish a Force, see *ante*, pp. 285–298.
[18] *Ante*, pp. 355–357.
[19] *Ante*, p. 357.
[20] *Ante*, pp. 354–356, 376.

(3) The consideration and approval of the drafts for Standing Regulations for the United Nations Force,[21] a basic Status of Forces Agreement,[22] and the basic Stand-by Agreements.[23]

(4) A study of the problems involved in establishing and operating a United Nations Force, in particular of such problems as the relevance of consent and of the principle of non-intervention,[24] the application of the laws of war,[25] means of financing the cost of the Force.[26]

(5) The establishment of a system of Claims Commissions to deal with claims arising out of the operations of the Force.[27]

(6) The establishment of the nucleus of an Observer Corps, either by creating an Observer section within the United Nations Headquarters Military Staff (to be supplemented by a revitalised Panel of Observers, held in reserve) or by extending the basic Stand-by Agreements to include the provision of observers by Member States.[28]

II. STAGE TWO (TO BE COMPLETED WITHIN TWO YEARS)

1. *The United Nations Headquarters Military Staff*

The Military Staff would enter into negotiations with Member States, at the purely military level, in an attempt to reach a provisional understanding on the size and kind of forces a Member State would contribute under a Stand-by Agreement.[29]

It would also draw up plans for the individual recruitment of certain specialised branches of the United Nations Force, for example, a bilingual communications section, vehicle and aircraft maintenance and repair staff, engineers, an observer section,[30] etc.

2. *The political control organs*

These would undertake the following tasks:

(1) The negotiation of Stand-by Agreements with particular States.[31]

(2) The negotiation of Agreements for transit, operational bases, training areas and other facilities to be furnished by States.[32]

(3) Approval of the principle of direct individual recruitment of certain specialised arms of the Force.

[21] *Ante*, pp. 334, 336, 372, 376.
[22] *Ante*, pp. 432–455.
[23] *Ante*, pp. 371–377.
[24] *Ante*, pp. 196–200 and Chap. 12.
[25] *Ante*, Chap. 15.
[26] *Ante*, Chap. 14.
[27] *Ante*, pp. 149–151, 242–248, 375, 383, 447–448.
[28] *Ante*, pp. 315, 330, 548.
[29] *Ante*, pp. 376–377.
[30] For a discussion of the advantages of individual recruitment see *ante*, pp. 334–335.
[31] *Ante*, pp. 376–377.
[32] *Ante*, 405, 455–467.

(4) Consideration of the establishment of an Arms Purchasing Agency, of a United Nations Code of Military Law and of a system of United Nations Courts-Martial.[33]

III. STAGE THREE (TO BE COMPLETED WITHIN TWO YEARS)

1. *The United Nations Headquarters Military Staff*

This would be developed and expanded and a clearer separation made between the Headquarters Staff of the Chief-of-Staff and the Staff of the Commander so as to permit the latter to assume the structure of a true military Command.

An infrastructure appropriate to a multi-purpose Force of 10,000 men would be studied and proposed to the political control organs.

2. *The political control organs*

These would turn to the following tasks:

(1) The devising of a scheme whereby Member States would allocate national contingents to the exclusive control of the United Nations for a fixed period of, say, two years during which they would be placed under exclusive United Nations Command and stationed in bases or training areas made available to the United Nations. Such a scheme would ensure that the size of the Force did not at any one time exceed 10,000 men and would include contingents from States drawn from different areas of the world.[34]

(2) The negotiation and conclusion of a base or bases agreements to provide bases large enough to accommodate the permanent Force of up to 10,000 men.[35]

(3) The consideration of a scheme for individual recruitment of the entire Force, such individuals to be phased in gradually so as to decrease reliance on national contingents.

(4) The establishment of an Arms Purchasing Agency, of a United Nations Code of Military Law and of a system of United Nations Courts-Martial.

IV. STAGE FOUR (TO BE COMPLETED WITHIN THREE YEARS)

1. *The United Nations Headquarters Military Staff*

The Staff would undertake the study of the problems involved in the assumption by the Force of the functions envisaged for the Force in the Disarmament Treaty,[36] and in the light of the results of the study of this problem by the political organs. In particular, it would study the problems involved in augmenting the permanent Force by

[33] For argument as to the necessity for these see *ante*, pp. 353, 378, 512–513.
[34] *Ante*, pp. 334, 377–378.
[35] *Ante*, pp. 458–467.
[36] *Ante*, Chap. 16.

contingents of national States in order to constitute a Force of far greater size for enforcement of a Disarmament Treaty.

2. *The political control organs*

These would undertake:

(1) The implementation of the scheme for individual recruitment of the entire Force.

(2) The revision of the Stand-by Agreements with Member States so as to adapt these to the necessity for providing a composite Force for disarmament enforcement, comprising the permanent, individually-recruited nucleus and the supporting national contingents drawn from the Member States.

(3) The consideration, in close co-operation with the Disarmament Conference, of the means whereby the United Nations Force could be assigned to functions envisaged for such a Force in the Disarmament Treaty.

(4) The study of the relationship between the Inspectorate, and any police attached to the Inspectorate,[37] to be established under the Disarmament Treaty and the United Nations Force.

This elaboration of the tasks to be undertaken by the Headquarters Military Staff and the political control organs has not included an assignment of tasks to the Secretary-General. This does not mean, however, that at all stages the political control organs may not delegate to the Secretary-General the general task of co-ordinating the work of the Military Staff with their own work, or of assisting either the political organs or the Military Staff by way of preparing studies and reports, or even of negotiating on behalf of one or the other the various agreements which have to be concluded. These powers of delegation already exist in the Charter and require no special emphasis.

The scheme, in concentrating upon the establishment of a United Nations Force, has also omitted the variety of problems which might ideally be considered in any development of the powers and effectiveness of the United Nations. Thus it may be said that proposals for the alteration of the composition of the Security Council, for the abandonment of the veto on certain questions, and, even more relevantly, for the development of an adequate machinery for peaceful change may all have to be considered at some juncture. This last proposal, for a machinery for peaceful change,[38] is directly relevant in the sense that, without such machinery, a United Nations Force may be tied down to the task of keeping the peace almost indefinitely in a situation in which there is no power in the United Nations to compel, in the last resort, the acceptance of a political solution which will remove the necessity for the presence of a Force. Yet all these proposals are not strictly necessary for the

[37] *Ante*, pp. 531–538.
[38] *Ante*, pp. 525–526.

creation of a United Nations Force. They have been omitted because it is believed that, even without any radical revision of the Charter, there is every point in establishing a United Nations Force and little to be gained by refraining from doing so pending an acceptance of other, allied proposals.

Finally, it may be noted that, whilst the scheme has obvious implications for disarmament [39]—and, indeed, in the Fourth Stage both the Military Staff and the political organs would undertake studies of the problems involved in utilising the Force for disarmament functions—the essential thesis which this study has developed is that the creation of a United Nations Force ought not to be made dependent upon disarmament but should be undertaken *now*. There will thus be created a United Nations Force which can be utilised for present purposes and, when that time comes, adapted and strengthened for any disarmament functions which a Disarmament Treaty may entrust to it. States in entering into a Disarmament Treaty will not be called upon to perform an act of faith by committing themselves to disarmament without any real guarantee that the United Nations Force essential to the whole scheme for disarmament will be created—as is now the case with both the Soviet and the Western proposals on disarmament. The Force will be in existence, there will be several years of experience by the United Nations in the techniques of recruiting, supplying, commanding and, above all, of controlling the Force, and thus the problems of creating a Force for disarmament purposes will be reduced to problems of a totally different order from those which now perplex the disarmament negotiations. All that will be required will be the adaptation and strengthening of an existing institution.

In the immediate future, however, the United Nations will have a Force which will be capable of making a significant contribution to the maintenance of international peace and security. The permanent nucleus will at no stage exceed 10,000 men—or such other limit as the Member States feel disposed to set to it bearing in mind the financial implications of the Force and possible distrust of it. It could, itself, be utilised for no more than a " peace-keeping " operation of limited size. For larger peace-keeping operations or for enforcement action ordered by the Security Council it would have to be enlarged by the national contingents provided by Member States. It is, therefore, a permanent nucleus of which the most important part would be the experienced planning staff, the Headquarters Military Staff, and the network of agreements and arrangements by which the United Nations would be prepared *in advance* to meet a host of different situations. It would put at an end the uneconomical, piecemeal and highly hazardous system which at present operates and would replace it by a system which will afford some guarantee that the United Nations will be able to discharge its responsibility

[39] *Ante*, Chap. 16.

for the maintenance of international peace and security. This is the immediate need, and the scheme set out in these conclusions is no more than an attempt to state how this need can be met. It needs for its implementation some little money,[40] some considerable effort by States and, above all, a modicum of goodwill and sincerity on the part of States to achieve the Purposes and Principles for which they established the United Nations Organisation.

[40] *Ante*, pp. 324–325, 479–481.

It is obvious that any attempt to study the necessity and feasibility of establishing an international police force requires the examination of a large number of variables specifying the kind of international political system in which the police force will be expected to operate. The character of the military environment is, of course, a particularly important variable. Bowett's proposal, for example, was concerned with the establishment of an international police force in the contemporary military environment. On the other hand, our next author, Arthur Waskow is, like Clark and Sohn, concerned with a disarming and disarmed world.

There are two broad sets of considerations. The first has to do with the extent that the assumptions or realities about armaments influence the kinds of proposals about police forces that can or should be implemented at a given time. It will, of course, make a difference whether total force levels are relatively high or low, whether there is or is not a wide dispersion of thermonuclear weapons, and whether there is or is not the possibility of technological breakthrough in weapons systems. In order to facilitate thinking about these issues, however, it would be useful as an initial matter to keep in mind four different environments of national security: (1) an arms race, (2) an armed world in which the arms race has ceased, (3) a disarming world, and (4) a disarmed world.

Because Waskow is concerned with the disarming and disarmed world, his report, *Quis Custodiet? Controlling the Police in a Disarmed World* (Peace Research Institute, Washington, D.C., April, 1963) pp. 1–42, is necessarily more speculative than the proposals of Bowett. It should also be acknowledged that in some ways the article may seem wildly imaginative, due, in part, to the fact that the author is dealing with a disarmed world. The article is a synoptic piece based on essays written by six distinguished scholars—Lincoln P. Bloomfield, Roger Fisher, Hans J. Morgenthau, J. David Singer, Richard C. Synder and Walter Millis—and built around the topic of how to achieve and maintain an effective, but controlled, police system in a disarmed world. See *Quis Custodiet?*, vol. II, Appendices, A-F (Peace Research Institute, Washington, D.C., April, 1963). The invitation to think seriously about a disarmed, and perhaps, warless world—to free oneself, as it were, from the strictures of the contemporary world—might be expected to produce an innovative perspective. This process of imagining life in a different international system is not only productive of ideas but constitutes a necessary preparation for the kinds of politically acceptable rules, procedural devices, and institutional structures that might be capable of bring about the change contemplated.

The article by Waskow performs several useful functions in this chapter sequence. To begin with, it makes clear all the major issues that have arisen in connection with the establishment of a police force and brings into sharper focus the materials that have been previously read. Secondly, it is a bridge between the more modest proposal of Bowett for strengthening the coercive power of the existing world community and the more radical proposals of Clark and Sohn. Although Waskow writes about policing a disarmed world, he does not envisage so drastic a revision of the existing one as do Clark and Sohn. Finally, despite the speculative nature of the subject, Waskow places a good deal of emphasis upon developing "scenarios" or hypothetical situations of conflict and crisis in a disarmed world. This adds concreteness to the subject and encourages us to think of the functions of a police force in more behavioral terms.

Arthur I. Waskow

QUIS CUSTODIET?

CONTROLLING THE POLICE IN A DISARMED WORLD

The term "international police force" has become remarkably diverse in its meanings. It conjures up to different persons visions ranging anywhere from a large-size military force possessing all modern weapons to an observation corps of men wearing blue armbands. Particularly troublesome in discussions of an international police force has been the question whether it should be oriented to military activity--should be capable of acting like one of the present national armies of the world.

Indeed, in some discussions of a future disarmed world it has sometimes been assumed (rather than suggested or argued) that only a "world army" would be adequate to keep the peace, symbolize and support the agreed-upon international order, and punish nations that attempted to violate the agreements establishing that order. This assumption is frequently embodied in the phrase that in a disarmed world an international police force would need to have at its disposal such preponderant physical force "that no state could challenge it," in the words used by the United States Treaty Outline on General and Complete Disarmament in a Peaceful World.

This assumption requires careful examination. At least two major problems present themselves in regard to such a "world army." First of all, there is serious doubt that agreements to create such a force would be forthcoming from present governments of present nation-states. This doubt of the world-wide political acceptability of a "world army" would not, however, seem so important in itself, if it were not for the underlying reason for the existence of such uneasiness on the part of some governments. After all, governments have changed their minds before on what was acceptable to them, and might do so on this point too.

But the reason that many governments fear the results of creating a "world army" is that they fear such an army might prove to be uncontrollable. They suggest that if naked and unanswerable physical power were to be made available to any institution it might soon become ungovernable and might begin to interfere in matters that it was not intended to affect--such as the domestic affairs of the various States.

In more exact terms, this fear of a "world army" is based on the assumption that such a sizeable force could only be controlled, financed, and supported by a true government or that alternatively, in order to finance and protect itself, the force would itself take on governmental attributes.

---

*See appended papers by Millis and Morgenthau.

Presumably one or the other of these developments would result from the need of a world army to make myriad political decisions concerning the recruitment, training, and disposition of large numbers of men and from the temptation (indeed necessity) to decide how and when to use the only powerful military force in the world on which side of what disputes. Such decisions--either to act or to refrain--would seem to be "governmental" decisions, simply because of the size of the power to be used or withheld.

* * *

The Problem of Political Consensus

What is likely to disturb many governments is the unlikelihood of achieving among the present conflicting interests in the world a sufficient political consensus on which to construct either a government or a series of "peace-keeping" institutions with quasi-governmental authority to settle political disputes. Many scholars as well are dubious of the possibility of constructing enough political consensus to provide institutions capable of controlling a large-scale "world army."

What is meant by such a consensus is agreement either on a future image of the way the world should look and run, or agreement on the kinds of political institutions and rules within which a disagreement on the future could be worked out in practice. Either sort of consensus (on political substance or political procedures) would require a partial surrender of the right and power to make independent national definitions of the national interest or of the means to be used in advancing the national interest.

The present outlook does not seem good for such a consensus among States whose participation would be crucial to a disarmament agreement. Between the Soviet Union and the Federal Republic of Germany, between the authorities in mainland China and the United States, between Nigeria and the Republic of South Africa, there does not seem to be any likely useful consensus on an image of the future world. Nor does any consensus seem at present to exist on the sorts of political institutions that each major State would think to be worthy of its trust as procedural bases for pursuing its national interest.

It is sometimes argued that achievement of a world-wide disarmament agreement would itself create a broader consensus on each level--procedural and substantive. It is possible, but not at all certain, that this would occur. It is also conceivable, for example, that States which are now willing to allow to some international institutions some limited authority to decide some limited political questions are willing to do so precisely because they feel that their own possession of armed power and the international authority's lack of it gives them an automatic protection against enforcement of such international decisions, whenever they choose to consider that such decisions threaten their own vital interests. If this situation were to be transformed so that the State had too little armed force to prevent an international institution from enforcing its decisions, the State might be less ready to concede even the present authority to make political decisions to international bodies. In this fashion, the expectation and consideration of a disarmament agreement might bring about in some States a reduction, not an increase, in the willingness to permit certain decisions to be made by international institutions, and therefore a reduction, rather than an increase, in the amount of political consensus on which could be built institutions capable of controlling a "world army."

It is also sometimes argued that no disarmament agreement will be reached unless and until the political climate in conflicting States has changed so much that not only agreement on disarmament *per se* but adequate *political* agreements could be achieved sufficient to establish political institutions capable of controlling a "world army." This argument raises two questions: first, whether the achievement of disarmament *per se* is separable from settlement of political conflicts; and secondly, whether, if it is so separable, the United States should or should not be prepared to accept the one--disarmament--without the other.

The second question involves among others the problem of timing: that is, whether it is better to wait for disarmament until it can be achieved together with political agreements, or to accept disarmament *per se* if it is possible to get it. In any case, the question is outside the scope of this report.

The first question, however--may the achievement of disarmament be separable from political settlements?--lies near the heart of the problem being examined by this report. It is at least conceivable, taking into account the way in which various governments have during the last fifteen years distinguished the problem of arms control and disarmament from the pursuit of their national interests, that agreement on disarmament and political agreements are separable. It may well be that many governments now regard disarmament not as a way of establishing a world order acceptable to all nations, but as a way of changing the means of independently pursuing the national interest. This view of disarmament would assume that States had taken into account both the increasing danger involved in using military means of advancing the national interest, because of the scale of modern weaponry, and the increasing difficulty of actually using military means, because of the increasing deterrent effect of the large-scale weaponry. In other words, the interest in disarmament may have arisen from a growing acceptance of "the hypertrophy of war" as a means, rather than from a growing acceptance of world order as an end. In the event that this view has directed the attention of some governments to the possibility of achieving disarmament, such governments may not regard it as necessary or desirable to change their political goals as a concomitant of changing from military to other means of pursuing those goals.

If this view of disarmament as a means be taken by several or possibly even one of the major States, it is possible to see that agreement on disarmament could be made an issue separable from agreement on political settlements. And it is thus possible to imagine a situation in which neither as a prerequisite to nor as a result of a disarmament agreement is there any enlargement of the area of political consensus between States. In that case, to recapitulate the previous argument, the absence of sufficient political consensus may prevent the establishment of international political institutions capable of effectively controlling an armed force so large as to be a "world army."

If these doubts are correct, there may be one of a variety of outcomes of an attempt to press for a disarmament agreement grounded upon creation of a "world army." These might be:

1. Rejection of the proposed disarmament agreement by one or more of the States whose acceptance is crucial.

2. Acceptance of the agreement and attempts by each State to protect its national interests against the feared "world army" by means of penetrating and taking over the decision-making apparatus of the army, with one of two results:

a. Successful subversion of the world army so that its decisions favor one major interest in the world against others;

b. Failure of any one of the competing "subverters" to succeed, but the paralysis of the official decision-making apparatus, so that an unofficial political apparatus arises within the "army" itself and it becomes an independent political force along the lines of the Praetorian Guard or certain elements of the French Army in recent years.

In the context of this third possibility, it should be noted that present concern for preserving "civilian command and control" over the military use of nuclear weapons has at its base a similar concern about the possibility of independent and unauthorized "quasi-political" decisions to use such weapons. If the problem is thought to exist concerning the armed forces of a well-integrated, heavily traditionalized, and well-consensused national government, it may be seen to be a fortiori a problem in the discussion of new, ill-consensused, and barely integrated political structures controlling a large world army equipped with the sorts of weapons national armies now possess.

* * *

The New-Model Police

Because it is likely that none of these outcomes would be acceptable to the United States and that each would be seen as a threat to American national interests, it is necessary to examine a version of an international police force that would be unlikely to result in such outcomes. For that reason, the remainder of this report will examine a possible version of an international police force that would not be equivalent to a "world army" and that would not possess the amount of concrete physical power "that no State could challenge." The questions to be examined are whether such non-"military" police forces could

(1) effectively enforce a world-wide disarmament agreement;
(2) prevent rearmament or a recourse to international war; and
(3) be susceptible of political control that would not require deep and broad political consensus among States.

In contradistinction to the kind of military force generally imagined, this report will proceed to discuss a force that might be constructed on the model of true police functions. Six basic assumptions concerning such a police force will be stated here in summary form, to be justified and discussed below in detail.

(1) If a Great Power should make a whole-hearted political decision and commitment to break the disarmament agreement, no presently imaginable international force could suppress such a whole-hearted violation.

(2) The task therefore is to create a kind of international police force that can deter such a whole-hearted decision from being made.

(3) The way to do this would be to create a series of graded deterrent responses to more and more serious violations, so that early in the process of violation the violator would be confronted with very small police-style detachments; as his violations grew the size of the force opposed to them would grow; etc. At each response step, the violator would have to reexamine the depth of his commitment to the violation and the repercussions of resisting the amount of force brought to bear by the international police force.

At most levels, despite the increase in power brought to bear by the international police force, the violator would probably have the sheer physical force capable of resisting.

(4) The use of physical force to resist the international police force would be likely to increase the determination of other nations to present the violator with still higher levels of force. This increased determination would permit the international police force to bring larger levels of force into play. Thus police responses would be governed by the principle that the more international consensus there came into being, the more force could be used.

(5) The most effective way to present such a series of graded deterrent responses to a would-be violator and at the same time make it unlikely that he would commit his own full prestige to the violation (and thus make it an issue of national honor from which he could not retreat) would be to treat each violation as if it were an act of private persons.

(6) In addition to presenting "graduated deterrents" of the sort described to violators of a disarmament agreement, opportunity would be afforded them of pursuing their national interest by an extremely wide range of non-military techniques. In this fashion the "stick" of graduated deterrents would deflect nations away from risking violations of the disarmament agreement, while the "carrot" of wide opportunities to be achieved by other means would attract their energies to non-armed means of intense competition and conflict.

The basic enforcement task confronting any institution created to uphold a disarmament agreement may be seen as one of nullifying efforts at "secession" from the agreement. We shall first examine this problem of secession in more detail; next examine the kinds of activities a police force might undertake in order to deter secession; and then examine the kinds of activities a police force would deliberately eschew, in order to allow each nation such scope for pursuing its interests that secession would not come to seem attractive.

* * *

The Problem of Secession

Even in societies that are well-integrated, that are built on a relatively broad political consensus, and that have several generations of effective governments behind them, it has been true that an ideological or political "secession" by a large fraction of the society is difficult for the central government to handle. It would be even more likely that in a world that had rather recently committed itself to a disarmament agreement, a world still deeply riven by ideological and economic conflict, a "secession" from the agreement by one of the great States or great interests in conflict would be extremely difficult or impossible for any central institution to handle.

That this difficulty would probably exist even if a sizeable army were at the disposal of the central institution can be made clear from an examination of the American Civil War. In 1861 there had existed for more than two generations a government with broad powers to make crucial decisions concerning the economy, foreign policy, and defense. The central military establishment had a unified tradition, its officers had attended the same academy and had fought on the same side in a succession of wars against the Indians and Mexico, and it had on many, many occasions taken both a symbolic and an effective role as the _ultima ratio_ of the existing order--that is, the Constitution. The United States Army had in fact at its disposal "sufficient armed forces and armaments so that no state could challenge it."

And yet, in 1861, when a major component interest withdrew its ideological and its political commitment from the central government, the Army

---

*See appended paper by Fisher.

was unable to stop that withdrawal. If there had been any doubt as to the situation before the secession of Virginia, the withdrawal of that "Great Power" made it clear that the Army could not control the situation. Indeed, the Army itself split: those officers and men with prior commitments to the seceding states reconstituted themselves in what might be called a "United States Army in miniature." The remaining institution that called itself "the United States Army" had in fact not much more of the force-in-being than the segment which had withdrawn.

What happened in 1861 seems inherent in the nature of federal government, or even in the nature of any government not built on an absolutely monolithic, undifferentiated society. The "great powers" living under such a government, whether they be semi-sovereign states and provinces, or powerful social and economic interest groups, are bound to have a major influence upon the armed forces of the central institution. It is hard to imagine how the withdrawal of one or more of them could have any effect other than the collapse of the central institution as a central and unifying force.

It is of course possible in such instances for the central institution to reestablish its authority. But it seems probable that this can only be done through full-scale war or through renegotiation of the original agreement. Renegotiation assumes the effective independence of the parties negotiating; and the experience of the American Civil War indicates how difficult and bloody the imposition of central authority by military means can be.

In other words, once the secessions of 1861 had taken place, it would have been extremely difficult or impossible for the Union to be reconstituted except through either renegotiation of the Constitution between the North and South or a war every bit as destructive as any war that could be imagined between a North and South that had never agreed to the Constitution in the first place. If it be assumed that the intention of a world disarmament agreement would be to deter the coming of war in a more effective fashion than it is being deterred without disarmament, then it seems clear that the prospect of a full-scale war intended to enforce the disarmament agreement would be a contradiction in terms.

Three means are available to deal with the problem typified by the history of 1861: first, making extremely unlikely a decision by any major interest or Great Power to "secede" from the disarmament agreement; second, so arranging affairs that if such a "secession" came about nevertheless, there would be in fact if not in appearance means of renegotiating the original agreement; and third, preparing for the ultimate eventuality that the agreement might be abandoned and rearmament undertaken by the Great Powers rather than attempting to use full-scale war to reimpose the agreement. (In this last case, the agreement would in a sense have been a way of putting all States on "non-alert status." Each State, or at least each Great Power, would know that if it felt rearmament absolute necessary, it could rearm; but the disarmament agreement would have been used as a way of requiring it and its opponents to spend considerable time in rearming.)

This review of the difficulty of controlling a major "secession" would suggest

(1) that the ultimate constitutional arrangements for an international police force should take into account the effective physical power of veto possessed by great interests and States in the world; and

(2) that the structure of the police force should be so shaped as to deter, rather than suppress, a secession.

* * *

The Stick: Graduated Deterrents

Both these ends could be accomplished by providing the police force with a series of graded responses to more and more serious violations of the agreement; by making it possible for the police force to cross each successive level of response only upon achievement of a broader consensus among States that it should be crossed; and by making it impossible for the police force to cross an ultimate threshold of response that would be threatening to the vital interests of a Great Power, without its consent. Let us examine each of these aspects of a policy of "graduated deterrents."

Orienting a police force to the deterrence rather than suppression of secession would require that every effort be made to enforce the agreement without engaging the prestige of the nation in which a violation has occurred. Selective responses, using small amounts of force carefully directed to the precise end intended, would be most likely to avoid engaging national prestige. For such selective and "fractionated" responses are least likely to be seen as a head-on challenge to national authority, the national purpose and character, or national policy. In addition, using the least possible amount of violence against persons is likely to help prevent outbursts of public anger against the international police force.

It would therefore seem wise to have the international police force act wherever possible as if particular persons and property, rather than the State as such, were the entities to be controlled. The general principle would be to direct all enforcement to the particular site of the violation, rather than to the seat of government; to the individual human beings actually carrying out the violation, rather than to those who had ordered them to do so; and to precisely those acts of the violating persons which constituted a violation, rather than to all of their lives or behavior. In this fashion, the police force would be able to halt violations by exerting a minimum of physical force. The national government would have to decide whether it wished to risk the results of protecting the violator with all the majesty of the state from the limited acts of the police force. If the national government avoided direct commitment of its full prestige, the decision whether to resist or obey the commands of the police force would be met by individual persons, and a decision to resist would be a heavy, lonely burden. This technique would avoid as long as possible the engagement of national prestige, and would place upon the national government the onus of deciding to engage its prestige and to accept the consequences of doing so.

In addition, to avoid making martyrs of the individuals controlled and thus prevent a surge of national anger against the international police force, the force would be wise to avoid the use of violence against persons wherever possible and to restrict its acts against property to the minimum necessary. Thus weapons that temporarily disorient or incapacitate the victim without killing (like tear gas or vomiting gas, or perhaps newer substances like tranquilizers, hallucinogens, etc.) would be preferable at the first response level of enforcement. Thus also, arrest and imprisonment of violators might be avoided as long as it was possible to end the violation without removing or punishing the violator. And where possible, the destruction or removal of machinery crucial to continuation of the violation (such as critical missile components, rifle bolts, the electric power lines to a tank factory, etc.) would be preferable to deliberately harming the violating persons.

The aim of the police force should thus be to demand that the fewest possible people change their behavior in the least possible way, so that a violation should cease but no other "events" take place. Confronting individuals with such demands is the means most likely to achieve their acquiescence.

Since such police-style responses to violation of an agreement are minimally threatening to national governments' belief that if necessary they can interpose their own power, the authority to order such minimal responses is most likely to be granted to the international institution with minimal power of national veto. In other words, States are less likely to demand a veto over the use of small than of large amounts of force. And so the principle of the more consensus, the more force would mean that very little consensus among States, as expressed constitutionally through their votes, would be required to order the police force to send a few men, very lightly armed with non-lethal weapons, to nip a small violation in the bud.

Above this initial response level, however, the use of growing amounts of force would require the agreement of more nations or effective interest groups. Thus if three policemen armed only with tear gas and a set of pliers to rip out some electrical connections were resisted in the State where they were seeking to stop a violation, sending a more powerful force would require a larger vote of the "court" or "council" in command. It would seem that in such a case the violator would be more likely to find other States most hostile to claims of "State's rights" and most willing to permit a higher level of force to be employed. In other words, a greater consensus would be most likely to emerge if the first and minimal steps of the international police force had been resisted.

It is possible that expectation of just such a response would be most likely to deter a violator from resisting the international police force, and that confrontation with just such a response would be most likely to deter him from going still further. If the police force acted both early enough and with enough precision, the political process within the violating nation would be more likely to bring about a careful and disguised retreat. The likely results may be compared to the Soviet refusal to escalate the Cuban encounter of 1962 when it was clear that an escalation by them would bring further escalation by the United States.

An international police force would be similarly bringing to bear the fear of escalation, though the "escalator" would be a chiefly police and partly political one, rather than military. The value of the use of larger and larger detachments of police to symbolize the political escalation would be the dramatic, international-consensus-creating impact of resistance to a flesh-and-blood force of high legitimacy.

It might be objected that this model of withdrawal from a higher level of violation is applicable only where a superior force is clearly in the background and might be used if escalation went far enough, not where a cut-off point in capability is apparent as in the suggested international police force. Yet there is a possible analogy to the suggested course of events in the early Federal history of the United States--an analogy that indicates it may be reasonable to expect withdrawal even where superior force is not available. Although the Federal government in 1794 did not have sufficient armed force at its disposal to overawe a state like Pennsylvania, and although no state would previously have been likely to grant it such force willingly, it was able to build a consensus that more force should be put at its disposal when its police officers in western Pennsylvania were roughly handled by tax-refusing distillers of whisky. The result was that four states sent their militia at President Washington's call, and the Whisky Rebels promptly backed down. A carefully restricted initial use of a tiny police force (one marshal) had been a sufficiently effective symbol that resistance to him produced a wider consensus for providing a larger force. If the Federal Government had tried to coerce the State of Pennsylvania, it could hardly have succeeded no matter how much force the other states provided.

Precisely because some States could not be physically coerced, the constitutional arrangements of a police force should make it legally clear as well as physically ineluctable that any Great Power could, in case of what it considered dire necessity, force renegotiation of the original disarmament agreement. In short, the Great Powers should be granted a legal as well as physical veto over the use of any international force sizeable enough to interfere with their vital interests. This veto would come into effect only at the highest threshold of international response to violations, and it would constitute the ultimate institutionalization of the principle of "more consensus, more force." The Great Power veto should, however, apply _only_ to the disposition of large forces and certain safeguards should be granted to possible victims of its use.

Treating the grant of the veto power as an institutionalization of the requirement for renegotiation of the disarmament agreement suggests some of the safeguards that would probably be needed. The veto should necessarily be publicly cast (unlike the one-of-twelve veto that turns the Anglo-Saxon jury into a quasi-confederal local government). And when the veto is cast in order to prevent a majority of the voting entities from stepping up the level of enforcement to the strength they consider necessary to be effective, the majority should then have the authority to cancel or relax or redefine the particular provision of the disarmament agreement whose enforcement had been in question. Thus a veto would really be the opening signal for a renegotiation of the agreement, so that the agreement as a whole need not dissolve because part of it is violated. What might be called "controlled partial rearmament" could then be one possibility. Another might be a reshaping of the agreement to meet changes in the world environment that had taken place since the original negotiations. A third might be an agreement to strengthen the international police force permanently, and a strengthening of the institutions controlling the police in the direction of making them more nearly a world government. That is what happened as a result of each American crisis in federal-state relations, from the Whisky Rebellion to the Civil War.

In all these fashions, then, the principles of _minimal use of force against minimal targets_, _graduated responses as a deterrent_, and _the more consensus, the more force_ should enable an international force to function as police, not as an army; to uphold the agreed-upon international order against almost all eventualities without expropriating the ultimate power of States to withdraw in part or wholly from that order if they so determined; and to provide each State signatory to a disarmament agreement with the assurance that enforcement of the agreement was highly likely but that any failure of enforcement would be highly visible and in such a case the State's own safety would be protected.

* * *

The Carrot: Non-Lethal Equivalents of War

To this point we have been concerned with what might be called the "stick" in a disarmament agreement: the institutions most likely to warn nations against and keep them from breaking the agreement and resorting to rearmament. It is necessary to examine also the "carrot": that is, the arrangements most likely to draw nations away from the possibility of rearmament by making other choices more attractive.

These arrangements may not at first blush seem to involve questions of political control over an international police force, but in fact they do concern the question of what the force would not try to do. For as a complement to the "true police" model of international force set out here, it would be necessary to restrain the force from interfering in a whole range of national behavior that is frequently thought to be necessary to control in a disarmed world. In short, there is an integral relation between the effectiveness of an international force as here sketched out in keeping the world disarmed, and the effectiveness of the force in _not_ preventing nations from carrying on their conflicts by unarmed means. _Adequate political control means both that the force accomplish what it is intended to accomplish, and that the force refrain from acts that it is intended to refrain from_.

In the kind of world sketched here, there would be many occasions on which intense conflict between the still-independent nations would lead to confrontations somewhat similar to traditional "wars." Having given up traditional war, however, the States would have to settle such disputes by other means. It is usually assumed that these means would be the "peacekeeping arrangements" suggested by the United States Treaty Outline for General and Complete Disarmament. Undoubtedly many such confrontations could indeed in the disarmed world be settled by reference to the International Court of Justice, to various mediation services, to various organs of the United Nations, etc. But if the possibilities set out in Part I above concerning absence of political consensus do indeed arise, then on many occasions one or both sides in such "war-like" confrontations are likely to refuse to accept the procedures or the substance of settlement via international institutions. In short, there may be occasions on which two independent States insist on their independence, save for the avoidance of rearmament and war.

In such a situation, the results may be remarkably similar to those obtained in the 1950's and 1960's when certain kinds of war were "abolished" not by agreement but by deterrence and fear. In other words, the sub-war or quasi-war exercise of national power by means of propaganda, subversion, economic aid, economic embargo or boycott, espionage, bribery, etc., may occur in the disarmed as well as in the hyper-armed world.

If the sort of international police force outlined here is to be created, careful consideration must be given to the question whether it should or should not be permitted to intervene if particular States attempt to use such "non-lethal equivalents of war."

It should be clear that the power to intervene in the use of political and economic pressures by particular States is almost inevitably equivalent to a world-governmental power to interfere in domestic political affairs; for such non-lethal equivalents of war would probably involve the very stuff of political and economic life. On the other hand, some of these techniques would, if used, skirt the very edges of "violence." If one State finds itself too effectively coerced by such techniques there may arise in that State a demand for rearmament to defeat the "non-lethal" coercive tactics of "the enemy."

These contradictory considerations suggest that although some sort of authority to define the line between "armed" and "unarmed" coercion may have to be granted to some international institution, many activities of States that are now considered illegitimate may have to be made legitimate or at least deliberately ignored. In other words, if most of the "violent" and "lethal" side of the line is spelled out as illegitimate in great detail (as it would be in a disarmament agreement), much of the "non-lethal" side of the line might have to be spelled out as legitimate, perhaps newly so. Then it could be hoped that the gray areas that remained after such careful spelling-out would be of lesser consequence, and that States might permit the final distinctions in this gray area to be made by an international body as particular cases arose.

Some analogies to the process here suggested may be seen in the way national governments over the last one hundred years have gone about eliminating violence from labor-management disputes. Just as certain forms of propaganda and economic pressure are of doubtful legitimacy under international law today, so the strike was of doubtful legitimacy under national law a century ago. The result was that when strikes did occur, they frequently involved considerable violence. The process of law-making during the past century tended to make a careful and rigid distinction between the strike as economic pressure and the use of private violence by labor or management. It was made clearer and clearer that sheer economic pressure was legal, and also clearer and clearer that sheer violence was illegal and would be punished. The clear permission to engage in economic struggle had a great deal to do with acceptance of the clear prohibition on violence. The government was essentially saying that it would allow labor and management to swing their own weight without let or hindrance, so long as they did not use violence. An international agreement along the same pattern would mean the legalization of many forms of pressure now considered only semi-legitimate, along with the precise outlawry and punishment of violence.

It should be pointed out that in recent years in many Western countries there has been movement in the direction of governmental or "neutral" settlement of strikes, rather than allowing them to be settled by sheer exercise of relative power. But this development came after that described above. It is not impossible to imagine that in a disarmed world, a succession of economic and political quasi-wars would stir some future generation to turn the police-only international institution into a true government, with power to intervene in political and economic struggles between governments. But it should be remembered that such a development could arise only from a far higher level of world consensus than now exists.

We may now review the model of one kind of international police force that has been set forth. It would be small; oriented to the use of police rather than military methods; prepared to meet violations early and to aim carefully at the specific violations rather than at the violating nation; ready to increase its use of force if authorized to do so by a wider international consensus; and unwilling to control conflict carried on between nations by political and economic means.

III. Three Police Missions

The sort of international force sketched out above would undertake to enforce compliance with an agreement on general and complete disarmament. Most of the description of its mission has so far been in terms of sheer disarmament--that is, of preventing the possession or manufacture of prohibited weapons. It might be argued that the force should concern itself with nothing else whatever. But many important questions arise about ways in which a disarmed world might be peculiarly vulnerable to threats other than rearmament. Should any of these threats be controlled by the international police force?

Let us imagine several possible situations. A small country that is far from its allies and is surrounded by larger hostile states is, simultaneously with its enemies, disarmed. It and its enemies are permitted to keep *x* men under arms per 1,000 population, in order to keep internal order. But before the disarmament agreement went into effect the small nation had been armed to the teeth with its own and its allies' men, whereas its enemies had kept a far smaller proportion of its men in the armed forces. Now its enemies can divert their legal "internal" police to the conquest of the small country, since its internal police are smaller than theirs. Or the larger states can simply have thousands of women and children "walk in" on their neighbor's territory and set up housekeeping. Should the international police force remain quiet, simply because the agreement on arms production has not been violated?

Or again: a major civil war begins in an under-developed country with rich but untapped resources. Two separate "governments" claim the right to form from their own adherents the "internal police" provided under the disarmament agreement, and to manufacture the legal quota of arms. Some major States that have been struggling for the allegiance and alliance of the under-developed country begin to sell arms to the warring "governments," each claiming that it is selling only in amounts legal under the disarmament agreement and only to the true government.* Should the international police force remain aloof?

Each of these examples, added to the world history of the last fifteen

---

*The legality or illegality of delivery of arms from one nation to another, even within the limits allowable to the recipient nation, would not be a simple matter to resolve. Further study is required as to the problems that would be raised on the one hand by requiring every nation, however small, to produce its own weapons for internal security, or on the other hand by permitting some nations to act as suppliers with the implied dangers of allowing such nations more easily to gain unauthorized possession of large supplies of arms.

years, suggests that two missions in addition to arms-elimination are likely to concern an international police force: the restoration of internal order in situations where domestic disorder is involving other nations and threatening the peace; and the protection of international boundaries from incursions by lightly armed or unarmed forces.

Neither of these missions is self-evidently essential for an international police force that is concerned with enforcing disarmament. "Walk-ins" by unarmed men into the territory of a weaker neighbor could conceivably be tolerated on the ground that weaker neighbors would have to think up their own unarmed means of defense, or suffer the classic fate of weaker neighbors: to lose "wars" to their stronger enemies. Domestic civil wars could conceivably be tolerated on the ground that to intervene would be a worse remedy than the disease, and nations in turmoil could be allowed to suffer their classic fate: bitterness, division, atrocities, misery, and brotherly hatred. Yet both these situations seem more likely to breed rearmament than do propaganda wars, economic embargoes, or even espionage. Somehow threats to the national territory and struggles for control over the symbols of governmental legitimacy seem to release the dammed-up springs of violence more easily than most other forms of conflict. For that reason, it seems likely there will be a considerable amount of pressure in the disarmed world to cope with a Congo crisis, a Kashmir crisis, a Sinai crisis before such crises could revive the arms race--just as there has been such pressure in the hyper-armed world to cope with these crises before they could escalate into war.

Political arrangements for an international police force might therefore include arrangements to carry out the missions of coping with internal disorder that becomes a threat to the peace and of coping with boundary incursions. These preparations might be made even if other sorts of conflict--such as propaganda "wars," competitive economic aid and boycotts, and even espionage--are specifically exempted from the jurisdiction of the international police force (as suggested above). But preparing to cope with internal disorder and border incursions that might breed rearmament need not be of as high an order of priority as preparation by the international police force to enforce the disarmament agreement itself.

For that reason, it may be suggested that the principle of "more consensus, more force" should be applied at a gentler gradient to the domestic-order and national-boundary missions than to the arms-eliminating one. In other words, a given level of force could be dispatched to cope with an arms violation upon agreement of fewer nations than would be required if the same level of force were being dispatched to deal with a boundary or domestic-order problem. Such an arrangement would recognize the centrality of the disarmament agreement itself and the secondary nature of the other missions.

In a sense, such a graded system of missions would place disarmament per se in the center of a circle, with high-level guarantees of enforcement; boundary maintaining and domestic order (where it concerns the peace of the world) in the next outermost circles; and totally outside the enforcement area, economic pressure and propaganda, etc.

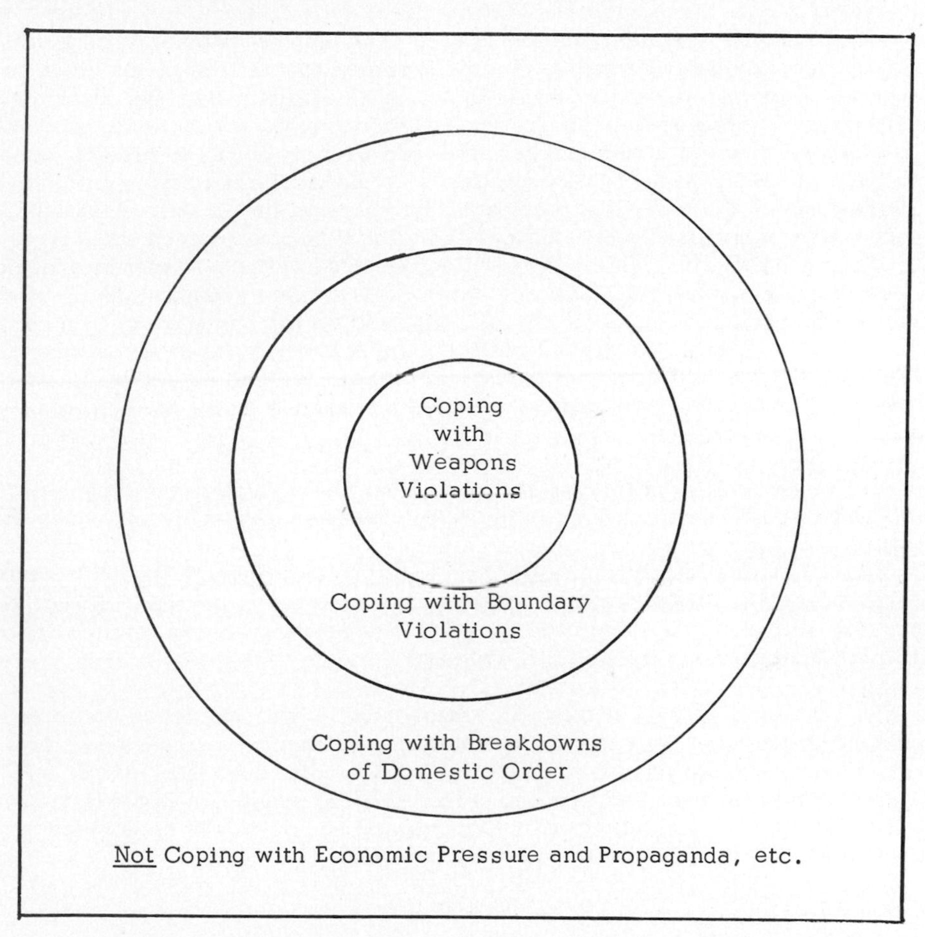

In the innermost circle, enforcement is most highly valued, and therefore a given level of force can be ordered into action earlier and with a lower degree of international consensus than in the proximate and mediate circles. In the outermost area, enforcement is not desired and so no force can be ordered into action.

To "constitutionalize" such an arrangment would probably require a separation of the forces required to deal with each of the three major missions. For one thing, the three missions themselves require considerably different sorts of training and equipment. Making a tank factory inoperative is a quite different sort of operation from defending a border against lightly armed or unarmed invaders or infiltrators, and both are quite different from managing a city in turmoil. In some instances the types of work involved might overlap, but the basic training required for forces intended to carry out each mission would be distinct. Secondly, the very existence of the total force levels in "international" hands that would be required to be prepared for all three missions might well arouse some fear in national governments of a coup by the international force itself, if it were able to take concerted action. Separation of the police force into three quite distinct services with three separate chains of command would minimize the likelihood of concerted action and make such a coup less likely. Finally, the gradation of the three forces as to consensus levels necessary to order action undertaken might make it wise to have three separate "councils" or "courts," voting under different procedures, for the control of each.

Some precedent for this sort of arrangement exists in the proposals of the United States and U.S.S.R. in their draft treaties on general and complete disarmament for separate organization and control of the proposed International Disarmament Organization (an inspection and verification system) and the proposed "peace" or "police" forces. A separation of the police force itself into three separate institutions to cope with three separate problems would simply build upon this already-recognized approach.

It may be useful at this point to sketch the ways in which the three different forces might be expected to operate. It should be made clear, however, that the description is intended to be only indicative; the kinds of weighted votes that are proposed, for instance, are suggested in order to make concrete the principles outlined above and should not be considered specific suggestions for constitutional provisions.

* * *

Enforcing Disarmament*

It seems clear that this mission would be the one that most nations

---

*See appended paper by Fisher.

would want carried out most effectively. At the upper level of consensus, therefore, it would seem that only the very Greatest Powers should be able to force a renegotiation of the agreement by interposing their veto and then only against an operation of such size that their own vital interests might be endangered by it. This might mean, for example, that 5,000 or more men using tanks, machine guns, and mortars could only be ordered into action against a disarmament violation if the four Greatest Powers (the United States, the Soviet Union, United Europa, and China, to take a conceivable future configuration) were in unanimous agreement and had support from one or a few other states.

Let us imagine that each of these four had a seat on a nine-nation "court" that could issue "warrants" for police action.* Then at the very lowest level of police response, one could imagine any two of the nations represented on such a "court" ordering a force of up to ten men, armed only with incapacitating gas and billy-clubs, to enforce a cease-and-desist order aimed at some violators of disarmament. The two votes might be enough to order this done even against the wishes of a majority, so long as a majority on the court or council had previously determined the existence of violation. In between these two extremes, one or more other levels of response could be built in-- a simple majority of the nine could perhaps order 200 men armed with rifles to enforce an order, a majority vote of the nine including at least two of the Greatest Powers could order the use of 1,000 men armed with submachine guns, etc.

It should be noted that this sort of voting system builds upon and enriches the sort of arrangement already existing in the Security Council, where "procedural" votes are not subject to veto but "substantive" votes are, or in the United States Senate, where one-fifth of the members can require a roll-call vote, a majority can pass a bill, two-thirds are necessary to ratify a treaty, and unanimous consent is required to circumvent the standing rules.

One might therefore construct the following scenario for a disarmament violation:

In Country Zee, a third-rank power with an elective seat on the Disarmament Police Court, a disagreement arises as to the intentions of hostile

---

*If there were a nine-nation "council" like the Security Council that issued "directives" to take police measures, it might make little difference. On the other hand, it might be wise to distinguish a "court" that examined "legal" questions such as the breadth and meaning of a particular clause of the disarmament agreement from a "council" that ordered various kinds of police measures in order to enforce abandonment of practices the "court" had decided were violations. Further study of these various roles would be useful.

Country Queue which has been running a propaganda campaign against Zee and which has just had two of its spies caught in Zee's border guards. A strong faction in Zee's cabinet argues that Queue is preparing its own people for recovery of an irredenta, and is infiltrating the border guard in order to prevent their resisting when the lightning attack comes. The faction argues that the world is unlikely to resist or reverse a fait accompli if Queue conquers the disputed territory, and therefore a stronger defense system is essential. The ten light tanks allowed Zee under the disarmament agreement are not enough, and--since Zee has no aggressive intentions whatever--the faction argues there is nothing wrong with making twenty more tanks.

A "peace party" in the cabinet disagrees, and urges that instead Zee step up its own propaganda services and perhaps offer Queue a technical assistance mission that can keep its eyes open for trouble. But Zee's president finally compromises on construction not of more tanks but of bullet-proof cars without windows and with a specially tough transmission and tire system, capable if necessary of being used with machine guns inserted as defensive armored cars. No specific prohibition of this vehicle is found in the disarmament agreement, and so the "peace party" acquiesces.

The inspectors of the International Disarmament Organization discover this activity and report it to the Disarmament Police Court. Queue charges that these "automobiles" are really forbidden tanks. Zee indignantly denies this. The Court decides, 6-3, that they are indeed tanks, and issues a cease-and-desist order to the manager of the plant that is making the tanks and all his subordinates. Two of the dissenters are Greatest Powers who approve of Zee's government and dislike Queue's, and the third is of course Zee itself.

Under the court finding, two of the States represented on the court order a single policeman, unarmed, to serve the cease-and-desist order on the plant manager. He tries to do so, but five local Zeean policemen bar his way and when he refuses to leave the premises charge him with trespassing and cart him off to jail. This causes an uproar in the world press, and Zee releases the policeman with apologies but refuses him access to the tank factory.

At this point the same two States that had ordered the policeman to serve the order are joined by two others of the Court's majority, providing enough votes to command the Police Force to send six men, armed with tear gas and pistols, to serve the cease-and-desist order and to resist any force used against them. A warning is first broadcast from International Disarmament Police helicopter to the tank factory, and then the six men are landed. They find the front gate locked, shoot off the lock, proceed across the open grounds toward the main factory office, but are ordered to halt by fifteen of Zee's police. They read the "no-resistance" order from Police Court in a loud voice, are ordered to halt again, and fire tear gas at the fifteen Zeean policemen in their path. But the policemen are wearing gas masks and announce they will use their guns on any Disarmament Policemen who advance. All do advance, the local police fire, three Disarmament Police are killed, one is wounded, and the rest withdraw.

At this point the world press explodes. Three of the famed and honored Disarmament Police have been killed, Zee is resisting the world's finest Court, the whole disarmament agreement is in jeopardy, the nightmare of nuclear war is recalled. Some groups and individuals within the two Greatest Powers that supported Zee start calling for repudiation of its acts, and other groups for still stronger support of Zee's just quarrel. One of these Greatest Powers privately warns Zee that it had better not pursue its undoubtedly just cause, for fear of world repercussions. It offers to issue formal warnings against any incursions by Queue if Zee will abandon the armored-car project. The Disarmament Police Court is called into session and several speeches are made urging dire action against Zee, but the Court votes (five members in favor, three opposed, one abstaining) to try once more to send a minimal force. The five promise that as a majority they will send a larger force if this one is resisted.

So five Police again appear at the gates of the tank factory. This time the manager invites them in and before they can formally serve the cease-and-desist order tells them it was all a mistake, he wasn't making bullet-proof cars anyhow, and offers to show them the plant. They serve the order upon him anyway, but inspectors learn that production of the cars has stopped.

Of course this scenario deals with a relatively easy case. But the principles can be seen from it. If one of the Greatest Powers had begun the same kind of semi-violation, the force needed to arouse sufficient anger from the rest of the world to cause a Greatest Power to think twice might have been greater. It is conceivable that a Greatest Power might have carried through its violation regardless of world responses or the probable doubts and divisions that would arise in its own population as it killed more and more Disarmament Police who were obeying Court orders. It is even conceivable that a Greatest Power might ultimately use the veto when some other State proposed sending a force of more than 5,000 men to carry out the Court's decrees. But then the Court majority (which had found the Greatest Power in violation in the first place) would revise or cancel that part of the disarmament agreement which was being violated, thus allowing other States to take appropriate action in their own defense. Thus the Greatest Power would probably have gained little from its violation, although there might be the problem of a possible time advantage gained over its neighbors, especially if the renegotiation process took the majority a long time to complete.

A special question arises in connection with violations by a Greatest Power, however. That is the question of a violation involving nuclear weapons or other mass-destruction weapons of relatively easy deliverability. It is sometimes argued that in order to cope with the possibility of such a violation, the Disarmament Police would have to have nuclear weapons at their disposal.

Several considerations make this argument rather questionable. First of all, it might not be easy to threaten to use nuclear weapons against the Disarmament Police themselves--a prospect that might otherwise argue in favor of the possession by the Police of some nuclear weapons as a self-protective deterrent. It might not be easy to threaten the Police in this way because it is possible that the relatively high mobility, small size, and ease of dispersing the home bases of such a force might keep it from presenting a suitable target for mass annihilation weapons. The degree of vulnerability the Police might have to nuclear attack requires further study; but the principle should be kept in mind that if the Police are not themselves vulnerable, there may be less reason for them to possess nuclear deterrents.

The second consideration is more troublesome. What if a State threatens to use nuclear weapons against another State, and neither the other State nor the Disarmament Police possess "deterrent" nuclear weapons? First of all, it should be said that one must assume an inspection and verification system through the International Disarmament Organization that should be able to discover in the early stages any program for the production of new nuclear weapons. The discovery of a new production program would lead either to enforcement of the ban, or, if enforcement were resisted, to renegotiation or abandonment of the agreement on general and complete disarmament.

Only the clandestine salting-away of nuclear weapons in the possession of States before the disarmament agreement went into effect need therefore be of any concern. Such an act would itself probably not be easy to accomplish under inspection arrangements at Stage III of General and Complete Disarmament that are contemplated by the American and Soviet draft treaties, and if various proposals for "knowledge inspection" of high officials were adopted, might be almost impossible. It is also important to note that only States already possessing such weapons could carry out a "salting-away" program. (Since the number of States possessing nuclear weapons will increase over time, the questions of timing in achievement of a disarmament agreement that were mentioned on p. 6 above may affect the nature of the Disarmament Police.) Thus relatively few States could turn up with "surprise" nuclear weapons, and even these States would have the relatively few weapons that could have been hidden despite the inspection process.

For these reasons it may be argued (as Walter Millis does in his appended paper, pp.A-29-A-30), that it would be extremely difficult for any nation to use a few nuclear weapons as blackmail in a world in which practically all other arms had been eliminated. The usefulness of nuclear weapons in the present world are either (1) as deterrents to the use of nuclear weapons by the other side; or (2) as a final back-up to the use of a whole range of military forces, intended either to compel acquiescence in a defeat achieved on a lower level of force or to turn a military defeat on a lower level of force into a victory at the nuclear level. The first purpose would not apply in the postulated world, and the second would be unworkable. For the violating nation would be in the position of having to jump an extremely wide firebreak between political and nuclear warfare, not having available any sizeable conventional military forces.

If Nation Arr, as a result of the humiliation of impending political defeat, decided to force its opponent Ess to withdraw its political advantage by suddenly revealing a small nuclear stockpile and threatening Ess's largest city with destruction, it is likely that Arr would be ignored. Political ends are extremely difficult to achieve with threats of mass destruction, and generally require more subtle and precise pressures. For example, it is difficult to imagine the United States enforcing racial integration upon South Africa not by using conventional political pressures and police and military force, but by threatening the destruction of all Johannesburg unless the government abolished apartheid. Or imagine a similar situation as it might occur in the disarmed world: a threat to annihilate New York unless the United States stopped giving economic aid to Brazil. Would such threats be believed or obeyed, even if there were no opposing nuclear capability to deter them (as there would not be, at this moment, if South Africa were threatened as described)?

For these reasons, it is hard to imagine the effective use of small hidden stocks of nuclear weapons by a violator nation. This does not mean, however, that such behavior is impossible. If the bare possibility is to be guarded against, some such arrangement might be examined as that described in the appended paper by Singer, p. D-5. He proposes that nuclear weapons be kept in the <u>possession</u> of a special division of an international police force, but that the international police force be unable to <u>use</u> them; and that they be so disposed as to be reachable and <u>usable</u> by but not in the <u>possession</u> of nations that had possessed nuclear weapons at the time of the disarmament agreement. This might be done, for example, by having a small stock of deterrent missiles stored outside but near the territory of former nuclear powers, guarded by a detachment of the international police force that was incapable of firing them, and physically reachable by the former nuclear power in case of such dire necessity as the threat of the use of such weapons against them.

Such an arrangement would have the drawback of failing to eliminate the weapons feared by all--and feared precisely because controls are so hard to create that can prevent unauthorized use of them between extremely hostile States. The Singer approach, however, might be useful as an interim arrangement during the last stages of the disarming process and the first period in the disarmed world. How useful it would be then, and whether it would continue to be as useful thereafter, would be problems to be examined carefully in the light of estimates of the risk of attempted use in the disarmed world of clandestine stocks of nuclear weapons as against the risk of the unauthorized or illegitimate use of the public stocks.

It should be clear, however, that even this approach does not contemplate the possible use of weapons of mass destruction by the Disarmament Police. The possibility of such use would make the Disarmament Police into a world army, with all the problems attendant upon such a body as pointed out above. Indeed, a Disarmament Police able to use nuclear weapons might be even less controllable than present national nuclear forces if its home base were so small or so widely dispersed as to be relatively invulnerable to nuclear attack, since in such a case the force itself could only with great difficulty be effectively deterred by threatening nuclear retaliation against it.

* * *

Policing Borders

The protection of national boundaries would probably rank as a second desideratum of nations that were surrendering the possession of enough armed force to become uncertain of protecting their own borders. Most States, it should be pointed out, could probably accomplish this end with their own legally retainable forces, since an attack might normally be expected from a neighbor of approximately equal strength that would therefore be deterred from attacking. Thus the United States could adequately protect Alaska from Soviet raids, the Soviets could protect Siberia from China, Kenya its territory from Somalia, etc. But some small nations ill-placed near overwhelmingly stronger enemies may demand additional protections from the international police force. Thus Thailand might fear Chinese incursions, Cuba the United States, Israel the Arabs, Turkey the Soviet Union.

Such fears are of course in the nature of an inter-nation system and are precisely what we mean when we call some States more powerful than others. Eliminating the weapons of war cannot possibly eliminate the various imbalances of relative power. The border-protecting function, however, is one that has been peculiarly associated with the armed forces, is a peculiarly sacred function of the State, and is probably difficult to carry out by other means than armed force. (The complete exertion of political and economic pressures by each of two States upon the political loyalties and alliance of a third is, on the other hand, a relatively easy function to carry out without armed force.)

It seems likely, therefore, that border protection would occupy a high place on the agenda of an international police force, but not so high a place as the enforcement of disarmament. Thus the amount of consensus required to bring to bear a given amount of force in protecting borders should probably be greater than the amount of consensus necessary to dispatch the same size force to eliminate a disarmament violation. This might at first blush seem easy to do, simply by moving the scale of votes and forces set out above for the Disarmament Police. For example, on a nine-nation court perhaps it would require four votes to send up to ten men to act as a border patrol, seven votes to send up to 500 men, and unanimity among the Greatest Powers plus two other votes to send 2,000 men. But this treats the problem a little too simplistically.

For those States that are most likely to be feared as possible invaders of their neighbors are precisely the Greatest Powers. It is they who are most likely to have the overwhelming imbalance of population and resources vis-a-vis small neighbors that it would make it easy for them to take territory even without breaking the provisions of the agreement on the sheer numbers and kinds of weapons and soldiers that they could have. So the demand for safeguards along these lines are more likely to come from weak neighbors of the Greatest Powers, and these neighbors are the more likely to object to a veto arrangement that cuts deep into the effective defense of their borders. How reconcile a demand that the Border Police be used most easily against the Greatest Powers, with a demand that the Greatest Powers have the loudest voice in determining when the strongest units of the Border Police could or could not come into play?

Several safeguards could be mobilized for the small neighbors of one of the Greatest Powers. First of all, it might be reasonable that as an added responsibility concomitant with their possession of the ultimate veto power, the Greatest Powers accept from the very beginning the establishment of a small but permanent force of Border Observation Guards just outside their own boundaries. In order for this to be done they would have to accept as well a special responsibility for defining their own borders more precisely and publicly than other States would do.

In other words, a special degree of "non-alert status" in the border-incursion field would be imposed upon those States that would least need to fear incursions upon themselves and would be most able to invade the territory of their neighbors. Whereas the Border Police would intervene in most cases only when a dispute arose, on the boundaries of the Greatest Powers they would be on constant guard. The guards on their borders would not possess heavy weapons of the sort that could only be brought into play by unanimous consent of the Greatest Powers, but would be alert to the earliest signs of infiltration or attack.

Secondly, provision could be made that if one of the Greatest Powers did veto a majority vote to use large-scale defensive forces, then not only the boundary agreements but also the disarmament agreement would be open to renegotiation by the majority of the States voting. If the weaker State had through disarmament surrendered the comparative weapons advantage that was offsetting the Greatest Power's population advantage, then renegotiation of the disarmament agreement could permit the endangered State to redress the balance.

With these special provisions regarding the Greatest Powers in effect, the rest of the operations of the Border Police could be carried out according to the same principles as those under which the Disarmament Police would operate. The minimal possible use of force, the treatment of violators so far as possible as private individuals rather than as agents of the State, the successive thresholds of response to violations made dependent upon successive levels of international consensus--all these would apply, so that the Border Police could begin by patrolling boundaries with binoculars and end by defending them with machine guns.

* * *

Coping with Domestic Disorder*

Only on some occasions (as Millis points out in his appended paper, pp.A-39 - A-40) has the world worried too much over bloody and disastrous

*See appended paper by Bloomfield.

struggles that take place within the borders of a single State. One of the bloodiest wars of human history, the Taiping Rebellion in China from 1851 to 1864, hardly made a ripple on the consciousness of most Westerners, although some Western forces did intervene on one side in the struggle. In many instances, no doubt, breakdowns of domestic order in a disarmed world will arouse neither great fears of international involvement nor intense demands for a restoration of peace on humanitarian grounds.

And yet certain kinds of domestic disorder are certain to arouse a number of different and conflicting hopes and fears in the world outside the struggling nation. In a world in which the ideological and political struggle between various forms of libertarian, authoritarian, and totalitarian societies continues, in which conflicting nations seek clients, allies, and friends among third parties, and in which gulfs still separate the rich and the hungry, some domestic revolutions and civil wars are certain to involve outside powers. Whether it is a revolution against some local communist government that upsets the Soviet Union, or a bloodbath of English colonials that outrages the United Kingdom, or a civil war in Latin America that threatens to destroy some crucial American property and thus disturbs the United States, some instances of internal disorder that in the armed world might once have been dealt with by national armed forces from outside will have to be dealt with differently in a disarmed world.

On the other hand, no major power is likely to enjoy the prospect of an international intervention in case of domestic disorder in its own country. The prospect of an international force "restoring order" in a Mississippi racial conflict or supporting a movement for Ukrainian independence would not please the United States or the Soviet Union, respectively. It is probably lucky that it is precisely in the Greatest Powers that social organization and the legitimacy of the State are best developed, so that internal convulsions are least likely there.

Since it is in the weaker and less effectively organized States that internal upheaval is both more likely and more easily coped with, the principle of "more consensus, more force" can probably be applied fairly easily, by way of graduated votes and ultimate veto, to what might be called the Special Situations Police. The gradient of increased force would probably be very gentle indeed, so that only after considerable delay and with wide agreement would powerful contingents be sent to intervene within a State.

Because the impact of domestic disorder on the central problem of preserving the disarmament agreement is likely to be considerably delayed, a time lag might well be built into the political control of a Special Situations Police. For example, to use again the nine-nation court suggested above, any four votes on such a board might be made enough to send a small unarmed force to the borders of a nation in turmoil with the sole job of sealing it off from outside interference by individual nations, and to send such a force as soon as a breakdown in order is clear. After four months of continued breakdown and no effective government, however, the same four votes might become sufficient to send up to 500 men, armed as municipal police would be armed, to eliminate sheer violence in major cities without taking sides in any political conflicts. After more time or with a larger vote, the Special Situations Police might be ordered to recognize one or another group as the legitimate government and to aid it in reimposing order.

The aim of the Special Situations Police would be to act as much as possible as a true police force would, especially since the keeping of order in daily life is precisely the job that present police forces in all nations undertake. It would become a quasi-military force (in support of one or another "government," for example) only on unanimous agreement of the Greatest Powers, so that they would scarcely need to fear its use in their own internal troubles. This would also guarantee the support of the Greatest Powers for any action by the Special Situations Police in support of a secessionist movement, in support of a central government as against a secessionist movement, or in support of one group claiming to be the central government as against another. Where such unanimous agreement could not be obtained, the Special Situations Police would be limited to police-style action intended merely to end street violence and put the internal struggle on a political plane.

IV. Control through Organization*

In the three preceding sections, a general explanation has been made of the principles by which a non-military international police force would function, of the ways in which its various missions might be undertaken, and of the means by which political control over each of these missions could be asserted at top command levels. But a crucial element of political control is the internal make-up of the institution being controlled: its financing, the way in which it is divided into units, the recruitment, training, and promotion of personnel, etc. It is necessary to examine ways in which such organizational arrangements could be made to undergird the kind of true police force here discussed.

The question of independent or nationally-donated financing for an international police force and of transnational or national-unit recruitment of its personnel are in principle closely related. The question at stake is whether the international police force should be able to take independent action (with its own money and "its own" units composed of men of mixed nationalities who have been carefully trained for international loyalties) or should be compelled to rely on nationally contributed funds that could be withheld if the nation wished and on nationally trained and earmarked units that might refuse to obey international orders as against orders from their own nation.

At bottom, this debate is the same as that over the veto as against freedom of action for the international police force, and it can be resolved the same way. For some purposes the veto is unavoidable; for others it cannot be permitted. For some sorts of action earmarked national detachments and national financial contributions may be unavoidable; for others, independent funds and transnational units should be used.

For example, if the use of a contingent of 5,000 men with mortars and tanks is made subject to veto by any one of the four Greatest Powers, then a special unit could be created of 5,000 men, 1250 of whom come from, are trained by, and are dominantly loyal to each of the Big Four. The use of the veto by any one of them would also mean in effect the withdrawal of its one-fourth of the special unit, thus crippling the unit and rendering it unusable. The financing of such a special unit would be by equal contributions from the Big Four, so that through finances as well the Big Four could exert a partial or qualified veto over the actions of this particular kind of special unit.

---

*See appended papers by Singer (in toto) and Fisher (pp.C-32 - C-44).

Yet at the same time, the units that would respond to a vote of any two of the Court members should be transnational units, trained by the international police force itself, made up of men loyal to the international police force, and financed from its own funds.

For these purposes, the international police force would need to have facilities for recruiting limited numbers of men, training them in very specific tasks, inculcating in them loyalty to the international police force, and paying them out of its own funds. Small police training centers scattered around the world, some of them perhaps aboard ship on the high seas or on isolated islands, would be suitable for such purposes.

In addition, some independent income would under such a scheme be made available to the international police force, but its amounts and sources carefully restricted. License fees for fishing on the high seas or recovering minerals from Antarctica, if limited in total amount, might be example of appropriate sources of income.

Even within the three separate Police Forces here proposed, there would be many careful subdivisions of function. Units trained as experts in making missiles unfunctional could scarcely be used to close down officers' training schools, and so legal safeguards against unauthorized use of the Force would be made still more effective.

As one form of these specialized units, the large quasi-military force from the Big Four (described above), would be trained, equipped, and financed differently; but whenever it was in legitimate use (that is, when the Greatest Powers had unanimously agreed to use it) it would come under the general command of the top commanders of the regular transnational sections of the Force. Its men, although they might have received most of their training from their own countries, would have to have some special training in how to work with each other as an international unit and in following orders from the general command of the Police Force. Such a special quadri-national unit would be kept "in being" as a Police Force unit, rather than left split up in the home countries, in order to make it impossible to use them as national armed forces of the Big Four.

Promotion lines within the Force would probably have to bypass such a large special "veto-able" unit, since high command within the Force should go to officers trained and practiced in transnational units and with international loyalties.

Finally, the problem of total size of the various Police Forces in combination would be a question of concern to the various States. Only with careful operations analysis could reasonable estimates be made of how many men would be necessary on active duty and in reserve to be prepared to cope with the fairly likely occurrence of several different kinds of violations subject to different levels of police response at the same moment in history. What can be said is that on first examination the forces involved might conceivably be somewhere near the force levels possessed by the United States in time of peace: that is, 137,472 men on active duty and 289,928 men on reserve, in 1930. To some extent, the international police force levels will depend on the levels of force retained by the various states to preserve their own internal security. The internal security levels are a matter that would also require intensive operations analysis.

V. Possible Objections to this Approach

The entire approach of police rather than military actions, minimal responses gradually increased, dependence on increased consensus for the use of more force, and the avoidance of political questions and quasi-"governmental" decisions wherever possible is open to several objections.

One, put forcefully by Morgenthau in his appended paper, is that police action necessarily contemplates not only the punishment or elimination of discrete violations, but also the general defense of the established order. Since he believes that in crises this second function is likely to depend on "military" force and that the "established order" being defended will take on governmental qualities, Morgenthau argues that distinctions of police from military responses and of "government" from a police-management institution are likely to dissolve.

The argument being set forth in this report is that in any particular crisis the nations that have constructed the disarmament agreement can determine whether--with enough agreement among them--they will allow the "police-management institution" to turn itself into a temporary government, or will insist upon reasserting their national sovereignty and renegotiating or even abandoning the agreement. This report further suggests that the possibility that in a crisis either of these choices might be made will in almost every case deter States from pressing their plans for violation to the point at which such a decision will confront the world. In other words, the possibility that the police-management institution might become even a temporary world government and the possibility that the disarmament agreement might break down will both be so frightening to most States that they will retreat before either choice is made. Thus on most occasions, violations will be dealt with in police-only fashion, and neither ultimate sanction will be invoked.

Since the Greatest Powers would both legally and physically be able to prevent the police-management institution from turning itself into a government, for them the ultimate deterrent would be the fear of rearmament.

A second major objection, closely connected with the first, is that action by an international police force to enforce the disarmament agreement upon private individuals rather than upon the State as such would be an utter negation of national sovereignty and itself would be a "governmental act." As Morgenthau pointed out in the work-conference discussions, however, treatment of the slave trade as an international crime in which quasi-international forces could enforce the law upon private individuals rather than upon their States is an example of the possibility of using such techniques in some cases without destroying or even damaging national sovereignty.

In response to his own point, however, Morgenthau suggested that the slave trade was not truly comparable to the weapon trade--that whereas the slave trade was on the periphery of national interest, armaments and military force were at the very heart of sovereignty and could not be divorced from it, and hence treating individual possessors of arms as private persons to be acted upon by international institutions would indeed work a revolution in national sovereignty.

This contention is at the center of any objection to the model of an international police force that has been sketched out above. If arms are indeed the heart of the State, then the approach suggested here cannot begin to be followed in the first place, since the basic assumption of this report is that disarmament will have been entered upon by States seeking to preserve and revivify, not to give up, their independence. In support of this argument, it should be reiterated that at the moment at which war hypertrophies--that is, becomes too dangerous, large, and unwieldy for the political unit that is trying to wield it--it may cease to be the heart of that political unit and instead become an unwelcome cancer to be cut away, without abandonment of the independent life of that political unit.

This disagreement cannot be easily resolved by argument since it hangs upon basic differences in assessment of such concepts as sovereignty, order, and the distinctions between force and violence. The disagreement might, however, be resolved by research of various kinds into concrete cases of the transfer of military power with or without political sovereignty.

VI. Possible Directions of Research*

It is often as difficult for scholars to imagine futures quite different from the present or the past as for politicians to construct such futures. The tool most often used in so "imagining" the future is disciplined conversation, wisdom, and analogy; and these are the techniques that have been chiefly used in preparing this report. No modern scholar or scientist, however, can be satisfied by such armchair thinking alone. He knows that such methods can generate hypotheses, but only an attempt to examine such hypotheses through research in the "real" world can confirm or confute them.

"What real world?" is the problem that confronts anyone attempting to think about a disarmed world. Is there any real disarmed world available on which we can try out our hypotheses? If not, we may be condemned to rest, discontent, with competing "wisdoms": you choose your "wise" man, I'll choose mine.

But there are some researchable worlds that are real and somewhat like disarmed worlds, and other researchable worlds that are disarmed and somewhat like real worlds. There are even some worlds available that are both real and at least disarmable, if not disarmed. Let us examine the possibilities of researching each of these three kinds of world.

* * *

Historical Research

The worlds that are real and "somewhat like disarmed" are in human history. Disarmament of every size of political unit has not occurred as yet in that history, but disarmament of some sizes of political units has occurred. The duchies of France have been disarmed, and the city-states of Greece and Italy, and the tribes of Indian America, and many other such units. The examination of these disarmaments has been neglected, and yet would be of crucial importance to answering some of the questions raised by this report.

Specifically requiring an answer is the problem set forth in Parts II and V: is military force always and inextricably connected with sovereignty

---

*See appended paper by Snyder.

and government?

Out of human history the first obvious answer seems to be "Yes." When the duchies of France disarmed, they transferred not only their military power but their political decision-making authority, their sovereignty, to the King of France. And this principle would seem at first blush to apply to all the other disarmament processes that have been mentioned.

Yet the answer is not so easy. For the answer is built upon our long-after knowledge of two situations long separated in time. We know that in year X the barons were effectively independent and had their own armies; in year X-plus-200 they were no longer independent and no longer had their own armies; and we can see that the two changes were closely related to each other. But what about the transition periods? Was there a span of years in which the barons no longer had military force at their command but were able to order their own bailiwicks as they liked--regardless of the King and other barons? To answer that question would require an extremely close examination of the process by which a whole series of disarmaments took place.

Another aspect of the question of the relation between military force and political independence and conflict is the history of the means by which States that for one reason or another have not been able to or did not wish to resort to war have carried on bitter political and economic struggles, acting as independent States but acting as if they had no weapons. Examination of this point would require careful research into the long periods of time in which the race for colonies in the New World was carried on by European powers with minimal recourse to war but maximal competitive use of money and intelligence; into the extreme propaganda "wars" carried on in recent years between Egypt, Jordan, and Saudi Arabia; into the competition between England and the United States for dominance over Canada, after the 1817 Great Lakes disarmament agreement; and into other such struggles.*

Within what have been recognized as States, as well as between them, "wars" have not been unknown; and "disarmament" agreements have sometimes been reached to end these wars in fashions that throw some light on the policing of disarmament. Thus Morgenthau in his appended paper discusses the creation of Robert Peel's Metropolitan Police in England as an attempt to enforce disarmament of the London footpads. In these

---

*See Arthur I. Waskow, "Non-Lethal Equivalents of War," paper prepared for the 1962 Summer Institute on "Alternative Ways of Handling Conflict" of the American Academy of Arts and Sciences.

intra-State disarmaments too we require more research on the period of transition. For example, what of the Bow Street Runners created several years before Peel's police as a voluntary police force deliberately not connected with the State and deliberately intended only to deal with discrete violations of law, not to uphold the established order? What were the problems and failures of the Bow Street Runners, what were their successes, what can they teach us of the transition period? Similar research also needs to be done into such problems as the period of vigilante organizations in Western America during transition between the mob and the sheriff; the transitional period in which strikes grew both less violent and more legal; and the transition from large-scale race riots to other means of carrying on racial conflict.

The emphasis on transitional periods in this proposed research is based on the belief that an agreement on disarmament *per se*, with no surrender of political independence, may represent a transitional period--possibly a long one--between national and world sovereignty. Or it may, if the police institutions are carefully constructed, represent the establishment on a permanent basis (so far as any political institutions are permanent) of what might have been merely a transitional state, national sovereignty without military forces. In either case, the study of historical transitions of like nature would be extremely useful.

Other sorts of research in the real world would provide important information on particular aspects of the sort of police force discussed here. An historical examination of the problems of recruitment and training of men into new loyalties in such transnational institutions as monastic orders, the French Foreign Legion, and the World Health Organization would be useful in assessing similar problems of an international police force. Comparisons of historical examples of attempts to coerce a State's behavior by confronting it with a challenge to its whole value and power system, as against examples of confronting its citizens as particular private persons, would cast some light upon the effectiveness of precision in enforcement as a police technique.

* * *

Simulation and Operations Analysis

The second category of research that might be fruitful is the study of worlds "that are disarmed and somewhat like real worlds." These worlds can be made to exist through the recently developed disciplines of simulation and operations analysis.

Through these disciplines, alternative models of future disarmed worlds can be created, each with its own form of policing institutions, and each model can be fed to operations analysts, to computers, and to simulated national governments made up of experimental teams of human beings.

The requirements of different sorts of international police forces for information channels, levels of armed force, organizational structures, financing, etc., could be mapped out by operations analysts. In particular, they could examine a number of variables bearing on an international police force that have been mentioned in the discussion above with such gross estimates as "probable" and "possible" attached to them. For example, in this report it has been suggested that an international police force of the kind discussed here might have a minimal "home base," hardly attackable by nuclear weapons. This view requires careful operations analysis, with attention to the transport, communication, information storage, housing, etc., that an international police force would require. Again, operations analysis of the political and technological requirements of various forms of rearmament could assess the time lag likely to be imposed on different nations in responding to partial breakdowns of the disarmament agreement, and thus operations analysis could assess the concept of the disarmament agreement as a means of putting States on a "non-alert status." Research into the possibilities of incapacitating weapons in police enforcement of disarmament, of the integrity of national borders, and of domestic order might also be carried on by means of operations analysis. In all these ways, particular facts about particular aspects of the real world that are now known or are easily discovered by experiment could be put together into a system different from the present world, and the new "system"--that is, the disarmed world--could be examined.

A second form of "invented world" research would be the exploration, through "gaming," of possible and probable reactions of various sorts of governments and of various kinds of international police forces to various sorts of world crises. For example, such "gaming" could present teams of experimental subjects who were "playing" the governments of various states with such scenarios as that described on pp. 23-25 above. Then a study of the interacting responses of the various "game governments" might throw considerable light on the role of the international police force. Such exercises might be especially useful if identical crisis scenarios were presented to game worlds in which various versions of international police forces existed, in order to compare the various responses when only that variable had been altered.

* * *

Action Research

Finally, there is the possibility of doing research on worlds "that are both real and at least disarmable, if not disarmed." This third category of research contemplates the construction of experiments in disarmament in the real world, by means of using small regional agreements on disarmament. This type of "action research" is obviously the most difficult of all to try, but it might offer the most reliable results.

One can imagine, for example, different sorts of international police forces set up to enforce disarmament in several different sections of Latin America, the Middle East, Africa, and a small section of Central Europe. The differences in effectiveness and workability of the different arrangements, including the approach set forth in this report, would be studied before any attempt would be made to decide on the way in which a world-wide disarmament should be enforced.

The historical research and the approaches of operations analysis and simulation are obviously much simpler to undertake. They do not require international agreement, and they do not require policy commitments from the United States that might later be difficult to undo, even if proved unwise.

NOTES AND QUESTIONS

1. Since Waskow raises many of the crucial issues that have arisen in connection with the establishment of an international police force, it would be useful to go through his essay evaluating both his way of stating the questions and the solutions he offers. The most important general categories are: the distinction between police and army, the use by the police of graduated deterrents and non-lethal equivalents of war, an evaluation of the three police missions, and voting procedures for invoking various kinds of responses to particular violations.
2. Which of his suggested research areas do you think is most valuable?——why?
3. The distinction between police and army is being increasingly employed by scholars working on world order problems. The following excerpt from an essay by Professor Hans J. Morgenthau, "Political Conditions for a Force," *International Military Forces*, edited by Lincoln P. Bloomfield (Little, Brown, 1964) pp. 175–186, clarifies this distinction:

HANS J. MORGENTHAU

Political Conditions for a Force

I

A police force, domestic or international, must meet two requirements: it must be reliable, and it must be effective. While obviously it cannot be effective if it is not reliable, it can be reliable without being effective, and it is for this reason that the two prerequisites must be distinguished. A police force, in order to be reliable, must be loyal to the political authorities and share their conceptions of law and justice. A police force, in order to be effective, must stand in a certain relation of power to that fraction of the population which is likely to call forth police action by breaking the law.

The police within the state are the instrument of a central authority which is supposed to be endowed with a will culminating in decisions, and it is these decisions that the police are called upon to put into practice. In legal terms the police have the function of enforcing the laws; in political terms they have the function of upholding the authority of the government; in social terms they have the function of protecting a status quo as defined by the laws and expressed in the government's policies. In a well-ordered society the police are but rarely called upon to enforce a change in the status quo; the enforcement of new race relations against groups committed to an outlawed status quo is a case in point in our society. In revolutionary societies, on the other hand, the police force is the main weapon with which a revolutionary minority imposes its will upon a recalcitrant population.

It follows that the police force will be reliable in the performance of its functions only if it has either been forged into so disciplined an instrument of the government's will that it will execute whatever orders it is given regardless of content, or else if its convictions and interests are at the very least not openly at odds with those of the government. Thus the police force, knowingly or without knowing it, is bound to be deeply involved in the political controversies of the society in which it operates.

Lenin maintained correctly against his opponents within the Marxist camp that the dictatorship of the proletariat could not afford to take over the enforcement agencies of its bourgeois predecessor and use them for its own purposes; forged for the purpose of maintaining the rule of an exploiting minority over the exploited majority, they could not be so used. Instead the proletariat had to create its own police, open and secret, appropriate to the special tasks of a new society. During certain periods of violent labor struggles in our society, the police force, regardless of the legal merits of the case, tended to transform itself into a protective guard for the employers, reinforced at times by the latter's private police. The police have at times refused to enforce the law for the protection of members of racial minorities. In certain regions of the United States they have habitually used their power to deprive such members of their rights through positive action. During the crisis at the University of Mississippi in 1962, state and federal police tried to enforce incompatible legal rules and conceptions of justice. Wherever a society is rent by deeply felt controversies, even though they do not lead to open violence, the political preferences of the police are likely to color the performance of its function.

On a lower level of motivation the police, frequently individually and sometimes collectively, have yielded to the temptation of private gain and neglected to enforce the law against certain types of violations, of which traffic, gambling, vice, and housing code violations are outstanding. If this corruption occurs on a massive scale, the police may transfer their loyalty altogether from the legal government to another, private one in the form of a crime syndicate. The police in our society remain a reliable instrument of law enforcement because normally no more than an insignificant number of them will be opposed to the legal order they are called upon to enforce.

The reliable performance of its functions by the police force within the state is thus not a simple technical matter to be expected with mechanical precision. Quite the contrary, it depends upon political, social, and moral conditions which may or may not be present in individual members of the police or the police force as a whole. These conditions must be created and maintained through a continuous effort of the political authorities. In other words, the functioning of a police force depends not only upon its internal technical qualities, but also upon the political, social, and moral climate within which it operates. If the latter is not favorable, the former will avail little.

The effectiveness of a police force is determined, aside from its reliability, by the power relation that exists between itself and the recalcitrant fraction of the population. For the police to be effective, that power relation must meet three prerequisites.

Of all the citizens of a particular society only a very small fraction must be engaged at any one time in breaking the law. If large numbers of citizens simultaneously break the law, as they did with regard to prohibition and rationing and as they are still doing with regard to gambling, the police force, although it meets the standards of reliability, ceases to be an effective agency of law enforcement. Second, however great the differences in power are within a given society, the combined power of law-abiding citizens must be distinctly superior to any combination of even the most powerful lawbreakers. If it is otherwise, as in the case of the medieval feudal lord and his modern counterpart in the form of private concentrations of economic power, the police are bound to be almost as impotent as the citizenry at large. Finally, the police force must be manifestly capable of coping effectively with all foreseeable threats to the legal order. This obvious capability serves to deter attacks upon the legal order that go beyond the piecemeal violations of individual legal rules. In other words, its visible readiness for effective action makes its actual employment in good measure unnecessary.

This quality of unchallengeable superiority, aside from being the result of the reputation for reliability, is a function of the two other prerequisites. In consequence the government is able to rely upon a numerically small and lightly armed police force to maintain law and order. In the absence of these prerequisites the state would need a numerous and heavily armed police force in order to meet frontal attacks upon the legal order itself. That is to say, the state would need an army rather than a police force, and the relations between government and people would be tantamount either to civil war or a military dictatorship.

II

It follows from what has been said thus far that the problems with which an international police force must come to terms are posed by the peculiar character of the international society since that character affects both the reliability and effectiveness of the force.

First of all, an international police force by definition cannot be at the service of a single government to which it gives allegiance and whose orders it executes unquestionably because of that allegiance. An international police force can only be the instrument of an international organization, such as the United Nations. It is this relationship that makes its reliability a continuous problem. In a society of nation-states it is possible for some outstanding individuals to transfer their loyalty from their respective nation-state to an international organization either on a particular issue or even in general. But it is too much to expect that large masses of individual members of different nations could so transfer their loyalties that they would execute reliably and without question whatever orders the international organization might give them. The reliability of an international police force cannot be taken for granted by virtue of the morale and discipline which we have come to expect from the domestic police.

The reliability of an international police force is a function of the legal order and the political status quo it is called upon to uphold. Yet the enforcement of an international legal order and the protection of an international status quo present a police force with problems quite different from those the national police has to solve. Great international conflicts which lead to the violation of international law and conjure up the danger of war and therefore call for the intervention of an international police force are typically the ones in which the survival of the existing legal order and of the political status quo is at stake. The task which the international police force must here perform is not the defense of the legal order and of the political status quo against piecemeal violations, but against an all-out attack. What is at stake here is not the enforcement of a particular legal rule, but the survival of the legal order itself.

One nation or group of nations will be committed to the legal order as it is and to the existing political status quo; another nation or group of nations will be opposed to them; a third will be indifferent. The members of the international police force belong to all of these three types of nations, and their sympathies concerning the issues at stake are bound to vary with the preferences of their respective nations. The members of an international police force will be a reliable instrument of an international organization only in the measure that their legal preferences and political sympathies happen to coincide with the policies of the international organization they are called upon to support.

In consequence the international organization commanding a police force will have to cope with three different contingencies with which national political authorities do not have to deal under normal circumstances. If the challenge to the legal order and the political status quo emanates from or is supported by a great power, the police action reverts to the traditional pattern of a coalition war. That is to say, an army composed of contingents of the nations supporting the legal order and the political status quo will be opposed by contingents of the nation or nations opposed to the legal and political status quo, with the contingents of neutral nations tending to one or the other side. This was the pattern of the Korean War. That this war was called a police action by the supporters of the status quo did not affect the nature of the operation. At best it made it easier for certain nations, which otherwise might have been inclined toward neutrality or a half-hearted effort, to join the defense of the status quo or to commit themselves more fully to it.

If the status quo is challenged by a nation of the second or third rank which has a vital stake in changing it, the sympathies and interests of many other nations are likely to be actively engaged on one or the other side. This contingency will confront an international police force with choices that are bound to be detrimental to its reliability or efficiency or both. If the international police force is composed of national contingents assembled in advance of and without regard to this particular conflict, those of its national contingents which are out of sympathy with the status quo may not be relied upon to defend it. If the international police force is being assembled *ad hoc* in view of this particular conflict and hence is being composed only of reliable national contingents, it faces the risk of being too small to provide an effective defense of the status quo against the forces opposing it.

Even if an international police force appears at the beginning of a conflict to be a reliable and effective instrument of an international organization, it is still faced with an ever present threat to its reliability and effectiveness. An international police force may be politically cohesive at the beginning of a conflict on the basis of a community of sympathy and interests on the part of the nations to which its individual members belong. Yet it is a moot question whether and to what extent such a community of sympathy and interests can survive the initial stages of the conflict. New interests may replace or modify the initial ones; new opportunities may present themselves for the pursuit of old ones. As the interests of the nations concerned change, so will the reliability of the respective contingents of the international police force to defend a status quo which may run counter to those interests. A multinational military force, be it called an international police force or an army, is thus always threatened with partial or total disintegration. Its survival as a reliable and effective force depends upon the persistence of the national interests on which it rests.

What distinguishes an international police force from a national one is, then, the lack of an automatic commitment to a particular legal order and political status quo. Such a commitment can be taken for granted, at least normally and except for piecemeal or marginal deviations, in a national police force. It cannot be taken for granted in an international one, but must there be created and re-created and maintained for each issue. The task an international organization faces in fashioning a police force for a particular issue parallels that of a group of nations seeking political and military support for a particular status quo. The international police forces which have been organized by the United Nations have reflected both the composition and the political and military character of the two-thirds majorities of the General Assembly to which they owed their existence. That is to say, no nation which did not support the police action by its vote in the Security Council or General Assembly supplied contingents for the police force, and of those who so supported it only a small minority supplied contingents. The contributions of these nations were a manifestation of their political interests and military capabilities.

Thus, of the then sixty members of the United Nations only sixteen provided in 1950 armed forces of any kind against North Korea, and of these only the United States, Canada, Great Britain, and Turkey can be said to have contributed more than token forces. South Korea and the United States provided about 90 percent of the armed forces that fought in Korea on the side of the United Nations. For the United Nations Emergency Force stationed along the Egypt-Israel armistice demarcation line, the international frontier south of the Gaza Strip, and at the Gulf of Aqaba the following nations provided troops: Brazil, Canada, Colombia, Denmark, Finland, India, Indonesia, Norway, Sweden, and Yugoslavia. The United Nations force in the Congo was originally composed of contingents from Ethiopia, Ghana, Guinea, Morocco, Tunisia, Sweden, and Ireland. The composition of that force subsequently changed according to changes in the policies of some of the participating nations. However, what remained as the distinctive feature of the United Nations force in the Congo was the numerical predominance of contingents from African nations, which had a special interest in the pacification of the Congo without the intervention of non-African nations. What this United Nations force had in common with that of the Middle East was the absence of great-power contingents, pointing to the policy of the United Nations to use its armed forces for the purpose of isolating the territorial issues from great-power intervention.

The tenuous character of an international police force reflects the tenuous character of the commitment of a number of sovereign nations to a particular legal order and political status quo. The deficiencies of an international police force are the deficiencies of the international order revealed in the perspective of a particular task. In a world of sovereign nations the idea of a reliable and effective international police force, after the model of the national police, is a contradiction in terms. An international police force, by dint of being international rather than national or supranational, cannot be more reliable and efficient than the political interests and military capabilities of the nations supporting it allow it to be.

This situation would not be materially affected by arms control or limited disarmament. As best the control and limitation of national armaments might increase the effectiveness of an international police force in conflicts among major powers, provided that the stabilization and decrease of national armed forces were to go hand in hand with a corresponding increase in the strength of the international police force. Without the latter proviso, arms control and disarmament might well have an adverse effect upon the effectiveness of an international police force; for they might adversely affect the ability and willingness of national governments to put armed forces at the disposal of an international organization. The best that can be expected from arms control and limited disarmament is a change in the distribution of armed strength between national forces and the international police force in favor of the latter. But the basic political issue bearing upon the reliability of an international police force will continue to make itself felt even in a partially disarmed world; for such a world would still be a world of sovereign nations.

The situation would be radically different in a totally disarmed world. Total disarmament can no more be envisaged in isolation from the over-all structure of international relations that can an international police force. Total disarmament requires as its corollary the existence of a supranational authority capable of committing organized force to the defense of the legal order and the political status quo. In other words, total disarmament and world government go hand in hand; they complement each other. In a totally disarmed world the problem of an international police force ceases to exist and reappears in the form — new in its dimensions and old in its substance — of the police of a world government.

We turn our attention now to the proposals of Clark and Sohn for the establishment of a United Nations Peace Force as set forth in Annex II of their book. In conjunction with this Annex it seems useful to read the following article by Thomas C. Schelling, "Strategy: A World Force in Operation," *International Military Forces,* edited by Lincoln P. Bloomfield (Little, Brown, 1964) pp. 212–235, that raises a series of troublesome and vexing questions about the possibility of relying upon the kind of World Peace Force that Clark and Sohn recommend. Schelling is quite pessimistic about the Clark-Sohn approach, but he elucidates some of the hard questions that must be answered if the Clark-Sohn plan, or some comparably drastic revision of world order, is ever to become a politically acceptable possibility for the governments of leading states.

THOMAS C. SCHELLING

Strategy: A World Force in Operation

The relation of an international military authority to the industrial (once nuclear) powers in a disarmed world is an intriguing one. We should not expect much success in finding an ideal strategy for it. It is hard enough to find one for the United States, Britain, or the Soviet Union in the familiar world of competitive military force.

And unless we expect a nationally disarmed world to be a stagnant one — hardly likely in the first few decades, if only because of the novelty of the environment — it might not be wise even to look for an enduring strategy for the international force. If national disarmament and an internationalization of military force are ever accomplished, it will probably not be as a revealed religion but as a political-military experiment. We had better not burden the organization with the need to know in advance the solution to all its strategic problems, or even what all those problems will be.

The "strategy" of an international armed agency is not just its military techniques. It is also its "foreign policy." The problem is not only one of equipping and training an efficient force that can conquer a country or halt some hastily mobilized army. It includes whom to invade, when, on what provocation, with what "war aim," or whom to defend against what. It involves who the "enemy" would be in a world in which it may be politically awkward to talk about enemies and in which "enemies" may not always be nations but governments or civil-war factions within nations, or movements not identified with territories and nations. The distinction between civil war and international war, not too clear at present, may become less clear. Those who argue today whether it is better to be red or dead may have to decide whether disarmament is worth a war in arriving at a policy for the international force.

If we think of an international authority as a "police force — to use a term that is often applied — the correct analogy is not overtime parking and burglary, but school integration, general strikes, looting in the wake of a disaster, election frauds, labor racketeering, collusive price fixing, and the problems of jury rigging, police kickbacks, and the third degree. The "policing" function is not just a matter of blue-suited men on motorcycles, but the entire issue of law and order and individual rights. For our international military authority, we do not even know yet what "laws" it will be asked to enforce. And in making its plans to restrain an aggressor or to dampen hostility the international authority may not be allowed the conceptual advantage of a clearly identified "criminal."

We have at least three areas to explore. One is the *organization* of the force — how it is staffed and financed, where it is housed, where it buys its supplies, and what "security" functions it performs other than tactical military functions. The second is its *foreign policy* — what it is supposed to deter, to compel, or to obstruct, and what its military relations are to be with nations and with other international agencies. Third are the *techniques* by which the threat or application of military (or non-military) violence is to be used to support that policy.

"Strategy" may suggest that we should confine ourselves to the third area. And so we should, if we could, leaving organization and foreign policy to other studies. But the strategy of our international authority, like that of a nation, is constrained by its economic base and internal organization. The strategy of an island nation differs from that of a continental power; the strategy of a rich nation differs from that of a poor one; and the strategy of a unified nation differs from that of one plagued by civil war or dissidents. A nation's strategy depends on whether it can keep secrets, whether its enemies can, and whether it can bluff its enemies, surprise them, keep them guessing, or promote discord among them. The strategy of a nation depends on its vulnerability to sabotage, to paralysis of decision, to inter-service rivalry, and to the desertion or revolt of its troops. The same applies to an international force. We do not know whether an international military organization whould have independent financial means of support, secure access to supplies, and its own intelligence service. We do not know because it has not been decided. And some of these decisions should depend on their implications for the organization's strategy.[1]

THE ORGANIZATION OF THE FORCE

A good place to begin is with money. We need some idea of how much money the force would require. This depends on which "force" we are talking about — a single international force, a strategic force separate from a tactical or limited-war force, a deterrent force separate from intervention force, or a force that can confront major powers as distinct from the force used to monitor small countries. If it is to be a force that can deter, repel, or conquer one major power or all of them at the same time, it is likely to be expensive enough to dominate the budget.

It will presumably need an "invulnerable nuclear deterrent," probably a more flexible and diversified deterrent than the major powers require now, with some redundancy as a safeguard against defection and sabotage. It will need good armed reconnaissance and worldwide surveillance and some military capability in space. It may also have to consider more selective, discriminating action than national forces have considered necessary. If it is to have a capacity to invade and conquer large and small countries without (or with little) use of nuclear weapons, it will need well trained, well equipped airborne and amphibious troops. And it would probably have to maintain standards of quality and comfort that would meet the highest existing national standards. Such a force would probably cost something closer to $25

[1] Something else not decided — and the language of this chapter must, for that reason too, be ambiguous — is how the international armed forces will fit into some larger organization. There will be some parliamentary or formalized diplomatic body at the top, and there has to be some executive authority, military or civilian, over the armed forces or over each separate service or command. Whether there will be some executive-administrative body above the armed forces (as with the United Nations Secretariat) or parallel to them (or even subordinate to them for purposes of procurement, research, etc.), whether the international armed forces will be purely military or jointly military and civilian, how much autonomy they will have — even whether, like the Roman senate during Hannibal's invasion, a distrustful political authority will appoint a partnership of generals who rule on alternate days — must go unstipulated.

billion than to $10 billion (nearer to half the American than to twice the British present defense budget).

During the first decade or so of the arrangement there will be a number of countries that can mobilize more than a million men under 35 who have had military training. Some countries, like the United States, China, Britain, or Japan, would require amphibious invasion (unless Canada or Russia accorded unmolested access) or airborne attack. If prolonged war with selective strategic bombing is not to be inevitable, if victim countries are not to be invaded by their main rivals as allies or recruits of the international force, if the force is not to be exhausted in its first campaign and lose control, and if it is to deter adventurism or panic rearmament in other countries while attending to its victim, the force will have to have sizable, professional, peacetime ground-air-naval capability. (In fact, a military organization that can *really* threaten to keep the peace and to prevent rearmament may look so large and so expensive that it is politically unacceptable.)

This cost — $10 to $25 billion — is not just financially significant. It is strategically significant. The money will come mostly from a very few countries — the large industrial countries. In fact, it will come from precisely those countries that are the main potential "enemies" of the strategic force. It will come either through national contributions, through taxes levied by an international agency, or through business enterprises owned by the international agency and operating in those countries. The financial vulnerability of the force to a few major countries is therefore important.

Parliaments have traditionally been reluctant to give military establishments financial autonomy, sometimes on grounds that a self-sufficient military force can be a threat to political institutions while a short financial tether can ensure civilian control. A parliament can starve a military establishment into submission to its wishes (or can provoke, by its attempt, a coup or civil war). So can an international military establishment be starved by a major contributor nation or by several major contributors. It can be starved selectively if some of its contributors can hold up appropriations for particular functions or capabilities.

Not only is this a threat to the military force — a vulnerability to non-violent financial blockade — but it raises questions about the force's authority. Has the military force (or the agency that controls it) the right to collect the taxes to support itself? Can it use military violence to extract the money it needs to maintain itself? Is financial delinquency a *casus belli*? And may the military organization negotiate in the event of a few financial defections, for higher contributions from more willing countries, possibly by the implicit promise of favors to come?

A possibility is to make the armed organization financially independent. It might manage some strategic industries — international airlines and canals, for instance. It might acquire patent rights arising out of its military assets and its research and development, licensing them for commercial use. It might be granted real estate, so that it, too, can become a territorial entity. But it seems unlikely that the armed organization could live off its own assets, though a good many commercial benefits may come out of the multiple technical activities and properties that accrue to the force. But if it depends in part on its own earnings, may it use violence to protect its properties located within nations and to assure their profitable operation? Like the salt tax of earlier times, a few critical monopolies, perhaps especially related to foreign trade, might give a good deal of non-violent leverage to the force. Whether it would want to use it, of course, is another matter.

Next consider how the military authority will spend its money. Most powerful nations have possessed within their territories the industrial base of their war potential. Even countries as dependent on foreign trade as Britain and Japan manufacture most of their own weapons. Control of the industrial base and critical supplies is strategically important to a military force. Without its own industrial base, an international force designed to cope mainly with the big industrial powers would be dependent on its likely enemies not only for money but also for war materials and for research and development of new military capabilities.

Embargo is thus a weapon that can be used against the international force — not just deliberate hostile embargo, but malingering slowdowns and induced difficulties of delivery. Subtle sabotage could be a problem. In a crisis, if a strike occurs at a German or American plant producing re-entry vehicles for the international Polaris force, or if a high incidence of defectives shows up in the delivery of some critical weapons, the organization may have a sticky problem on its hand. And if there is a straightforward denial of access, the international force (or its controlling authority) has to decide not only whether a *casus belli* exists but how long it can afford to negotiate before it feels the pinch of supplies.

Some deliberate dispersal and redundancy of supply would look attractive to the force. It may want to be dependent on no single country for any important military item. It may want to be assured of excess capacity around the world so that, in a crisis, it can forego the output of particular countries. But this raises two problems. One is the high cost of duplicate facilities for complicated items. The second is that a latent "Nth country problem" would be aggravated.

Much that has been said about production and procurement applies to research and development, for which the force would also be dependent on its most likely enemies. If it is to finance all its own research and development outside the major industrial countries, this will probably be at a high cost both in outlay and in reliability. Probably the best that can be hoped for is that some kind of "oligopolistic competition" among three to six major industrial powers would keep the force from being too dependent on any single country or alliance.

In any case, the international force would have to think about the reliability and security of alternative contractors. The letting of a long-term weapon contract will almost surely lead to conjecture as to the political and security motives for choosing one country rather than another. (A country that is interested in the weakening or discrediting of the international force may be tempted to consider bad technological advice to achieve its purpose.) This consideration in turn raises the question whether the force will contract through governments or with private firms, and since the force may want some immunity from strikes and other disruptions in the privately organized economies, the answer is likely to be that it contracts through governments unless it invests in its own 'internationalized" arsenals and laboratories on neutral soil.

The loss of industrial secrecy under a worldwide disarmament arrangement might substantially spread military technology around the world. This spread would be relevant to a possible resumption of the arms race as well as to violation of the rules of disarmament. To pose the question in extreme form: how many countries have the right to share in providing nuclear weapons to the international force? Do the present nuclear powers retain, under the heading of "industrial security," the nuclear secrets they possess? Must they share them with each other? Is the technology to be disseminated throughout an "open world" that at some stage, by breakdown or re-negotiation, may begin to rearm itself?

We should keep in mind that it is difficult in any country to divorce military considerations from domestic economics. Any organization that has ten or twenty billion dollars of procurement to undertake will be obliged to think about depressed areas, balance of payments problems, equity in the distribution of contracts, and the industrial growth of more than a hundred countries. What we now call "lobbies" and "military-industrial complexes" may not be purified out of existence by the internationalization of military procurement. And if the United States and the Soviet Union are still in the race to see who will be first on Mars, it is unlikely that an international military procurement organization could stay aloof, and be universally considered aloof, from the impact of its procurement on the relative space technologies of the two countries.

In addition to financial, logistical, and industrial questions, there are some questions of political and administrative organization that would affect the strategy of the force. One is whether it should have its own military intelligence service or should rely on some open "inspection" system to which all nations have equal access. Can it have "spies," and not just "inspectors"?

A second is whether it can keep its military plans and deployments secret from the countries that it works for. Political as well as military secrecy and surprise are involved, because the countries that might be the subjects of military action by the international force would also be represented in the organization. If they know exactly what kind of attack to expect and when, which actions will trigger a response and which will be allowed, or when a military deployment is a bluff and when it means business, the international force will be unlike a national force in its relation to the enemy.

Particularly if the force engages in any kind of "bargaining" — in deterrent threats or ultimatums — it might be embarrassed to have its internal decisions and plans known to its adversary. And if, say, it were about to launch a preemptive invasion intended to be as efficient and bloodless as possible, surprise might be crucial.

Within nations, military organizations usually have secrets that are not available to the voters, political representatives, nor even the entire cabinet. Presumably the chief executive of a country has the right to any information he wants, but he may not know what he wants or whether it exists. The occurrence of military coups and revolts demonstrates that secrets can be held within a military organization. And there can be a legitimate recognition, particularly in times of crisis or war, that since any sharing of secret information with civilian authorities may compromise security, those who have a right to know certain things may prefer not to exercise it.

So we can properly imagine the military organization's having its own intelligence system separate from the intelligence arrangements of the "political authority," or the "inspection force," or whatever else there is. We may also suppose that it can have the legal right to make secret war plans. Whether it could keep secrets in fact, given its non-national personnel system and its political relations with other international agencies, is not easy to say. The answer probably depends on how far one is willing to compromise certain political principles in the interest of military effectiveness. If the organization is confined to a very few nationalities in its top ranks — the nationalities that reflect the former nuclear powers — it may be possible to keep information from the representatives of a hundred other countries. But there is still a problem in keeping secrets from potential adversaries among the major powers.

As Germany, Russia, or the United States becomes a possible target for military action, its representatives may have to be eased out of positions of confidence, their "security clearance" withdrawn, perhaps in a way that did not tip them off to what was happening. This would be difficult, even if one relied on very specially indoctrinated senior personnel who were allowed a good deal of autonomy. If their plans were reviewed by higher civilian authority, the same problem would arise there.

The nature of the problem is suggested by our own government: only the Congress can declare war. If the international force is to be responsive to some representative arrangement, the countries that are most likely to be enemies of the force are precisely the ones most likely to be strongly represented in the legislative branch. The problem is a little like that of a Congressional declaration of civil war against, say, New England. Bargaining between the federal government and a secessionist bloc of states under the threat of war, the development of operational military plans, and particularly any action based on surprise, would be affected by the presence in the Congress of legislators from New England who could not be constitutionally excluded from debate.

While the most tangible problems here may be those of operational secrecy, the more important ones relate to bargaining. Imagine that during the Cuban crisis the Russians by right had had a man sitting beside the President in the White House who not only knew what information was available to the President but also could overhear all the policy discussions. Just what risks to take, how far to let things go, with what limited objectives to take action if action were taken, what minimum Soviet responses would meet our demands, and all that — these are things that one usually wants to keep the potential enemy from knowing.

Of course, it can sometimes help to let the enemy know certain things. If in the Cuban crisis the Russians really miscalculated, and if it was in both our interests that they not miscalculate, it might have been better if they had had better knowledge of how the United States was going to react. When one is not bluffing, it helps if the adversary can authentically learn the fact. (But unless it had secret intelligence in addition, it could not be sure it wasn't being left out of something.)

At some stage, some formality like "declaration of adversary relation" might be required in order to put a country on notice and to exclude it from the inner councils of the organization. The question arises whether at that point the country could cancel its obligations to put up money, sell goods, permit access, provide information, and participate in political-military planning. This not only has to be considered a procedural question, but also as a factor inhibiting the determination of an adversary relationship. How does a legislature deal with illegal secession or civil war by some of those represented in it? (The filibuster comes to mind.)

These questions of security, surprise, and command are affected by another organizational question: whether there is to be a single international military force or several for different purposes. If the latter, what are to be the control and coordination arrangements between the several military organizations?

American forces are now represented in NATO, but there are United States commands, including the Strategic Air Command, to which the North Atlantic Treaty Organization (NATO) countries have had no access by virtue of the NATO treaty. Similarly, an international "strategic force" that is mainly oriented toward deterring the major industrial nations might be quite separate from other international forces whose functions are lower in the scale of violence, oriented toward different areas of trouble, and possibly less concentrated among a few main governments.

From the point of view of military organization, one would probably set up a strategic command separate from the force that is to cope with smaller-scale violence, denying the latter force access to the former. But such a separation of functions does not solve the political problem of who controls the strategic force: whether it tends to be considered the agent of, or the enemy of, the major industrial nations that formerly were (and potentially are) major nuclear powers. If, for the reasons of finance, technology, industrial power, security, and military experience already mentioned, the strategic command is the captive of the United States and the Soviet Union, it may be regarded as a monopoly of force by the great powers. But if control over the strategic command is widely spread, "democratically" or "popularly" diffused among many lesser countries, it may become essentially a device by which a few big nations are policed militarily for the benefit of the small ones. Control over the strategic command will be determined by the arrangements made for its financing, staffing, procurement, and so forth.

THE FOREIGN POLICY OF THE FORCE

These considerations bring into focus the novel position of the force in a disarmed world. We usually think of the Western alliance and the Soviet bloc, or the United States and the Soviet Union, as the principal potential enemies that may need to be deterred, detained, or kept disengaged *from each other* by an international force. But in a disarmed world the United States and the Soviet Union are likely to have a common interest in mantaining their superior mobilization base for the event of war or rearmament. Whether or not they collaborate, they may be of a mind on a number of issues in opposition to lesser countries (including their former allies). Certain preparatory actions that might be considered grounds for military threat and intervention might be available only to the major nations, perhaps the largest two. Threats of intervention might be directed not at one of these countries at the urging of the other, but at both of them at the urging of many other countries, or at the autonomous discretion of an international authority itself. Their maintenance of a technical mobilization base for rearmament, either deliberately or as a natural consequence of industrial and scientific activity, might be an example of such an issue.

Whether the force will be primarily the agent of great or small nations will affect its military strategy, because a main ingredient of that strategy will be threats of intervention. Beliefs about which threats are real and which bluffs, what kind of violence is threatened, and what the likelihood is that the violence will be contained or will get out of hand — these will depend on who controls it. War with a major country or bloc will always be dangerous business no matter what uniform the attackers wear.

An example of such a crisis of credibility is NATO at the present time. There has been much discussion of which deterrent threat will be more credible to the Russians — a United States deterrent "umbrella," independent national deterrents, or a fifteen-nation NATO deterrent. There are also disagreements over the nature of the Soviet threat to be deterred — a large-scale Soviet attack, small Soviet mischief, or Soviet response to an unpremeditated outbreak of violence (like Hungary) — for which appropriate NATO deterrents can be designed. Strategy depends not only on what is credible, but also on what contingencies and actions it is politically possible to contemplate and to plan.[2] And these in turn depend on where political control over strategy lies. Deterrence strategy is at least as much political as military,

[2] NATO is seriously precluded from acknowledging certain contingencies and making plans for them by the political sensitivity of the issues. Similarly it is often reported that the Russian and Chinese communists feel constrained — or used to feel constrained — to argue by "proxy," using Yugoslavia or Albania as euphemistic code words for Russia and China.

at least as much concerned with command structure as with the destructive potential of a military force.

There is another important question about the separation of commands. It seems unlikely that an international strategic force would intervene often against major powers. It would be too serious an event. A force may frequently intervene in smaller-scale affairs, of which the Congo, Laos, the Arab-Israeli dispute, Goa, or a Castro revolution might be examples. If there is a single force, its experience is likely to be dominated by small wars, brush fire engagements, police actions, and so forth. Its budgetary orientation may reflect the crises that it is called on to manage during its first several years, unless a "strategic" force is separately emphasized.

At the same time, if we reflect on how an international force might deal with, say, Vietnam, we do not know whether the job would fall under the strategic command or the limited-war or counter-insurgency command. An international force might be no more willing, perhaps less willing, than the United States to support a local force against externally supplied and externally indoctrinated insurgents. An international force might identify the target as Hanoi, Peiping, or Moscow, not the Laotian-Vietnamese border. And if it wanted credibly to threaten that it would not forever tolerate an externally supported revolt but would sooner or later use its military coercive power on North Vietnam or China, it would surely have to coordinate its local actions with its strategic plans. In other words, if most local problems are part of a strategic contest between East and West (or some such blocs) and if a significant element in local wars is some elusive participation of major powers, the relation between local and strategic responsibilities becomes an important matter of policy. It is not a foregone conclusion that in the interest of peace and quiescence the international force should pretend that local violence is a local problem when it is not.

THE TECHNIQUES OF THE FORCE

The techniques by which violence or the threat of violence would be used by the international strategic command should depend on the policy it is supposed to carry out. Even with a fairly explicit idea of what the force is supposed to do, such questions as whether continued disarmament will be worth a war cannot be answered in advance.

The least ambitious purpose that might be served by an international strategic command would be ceremonial. The major nuclear powers might like to support a façade, a pretense that an international force is aimed at them as well as at smaller countries. They might commit themselves to the notion of an international force capable of policing the entire world against everything, adhere nominally to their verbal commitments, and be quite slow about setting up any actual capability. (Some proposals for NATO nuclear forces may serve as illustrations of such an "international" force.) A force might, for example, consist of "national contributions" and solemn declarations by all parties that the progressive integration of the world would bring the force closer and closer to true unification and some eventual autonomy.

At the other extreme the most ambitious goal is probably a force whose primary function is to maintain its military supremacy against all possible adversaries. The critical thing here is the irreversibility of the arrangement. The armed authority would be charged with the mission of making sure that only by sufferance could any nation withdraw from the arrangement and rearm itself. The primary objective of such an organization would not be the deterrence or prevention of war among "disarmed" nations, but the deterrence or prevention of rearmament. As long as significant rearmament was forestalled, the international force would still be in business. It might not win all its wars; it might not prevent wars; but at least it would have the ultimate capability to do so. And as a last resort it could launch preventive war and military occupation against its potential enemies.

A less ambitious objective is to police disarmed nations against the temptations toward violence and aggression, protecting disarmed nations either by active defense or deterrence of attack. This is an easier role to fill because it implies weaponry and tactics effective against disarmed nations and applied in support of an international status quo. The difference between deterring war and deterring rearmament might be compared with the difference between deterring Soviet attack on Europe and deterring Soviet resistance to an armed "rollback" of the Iron Curtain. One is external and passive; the other is internal and active. Rearmament for major industrial countries would be largely an "internal" affair. Except for countries quite vulnerable to blockade, rearmament could be stopped only by force or coercion inside a country, not by containment at its borders.

An important role to consider for an international strategic command is that of a *buffer force*. Instead of being responsible for preventive war against a country that initiated rearmament, it might maintain a protective deterrent shelter within which other countries could catch up. Such a buffer force might not even be obliged to enter an arms race if it could exercise a sufficient deterrent influence — hold a "balance of power" and keep the situation stabilized until the rearmament of other countries had superseded their dependence on the force. Part of its purpose would be to induce or to permit countries to rearm with a view to stabilized deterrence and self-defense rather than with a view to pre-emptive action. The role of such a buffer force in the event of war itself might not be to win against all countries or against those that start it, but just to make winning a war costly and uncertain for the side that starts it. The international authority might, in other words, pursue a "minimum deterrence" strategy against war itself while providing shelter in the early stages of a rearmament race.

Its role might then be comparable to that of the American armed forces since the end of World War II. The United States has tried to deter, to contain, to guarantee, and otherwise to preserve peace and the status quo. It did not undertake and apparently did not seriously consider preventive war against a nuclear-arming Soviet force. An international force might be equally reluctant or unable to consider preventive war in the face of a large nation's persistent armament program.

If the military organization is intended to guarantee its own supremacy and the irreversibility of the disarmament arrangement by deterring rearmament if it can, and forcibly stopping it if deterrence fails, we get a very different strategy. We get a strategic force absolutely committed to preventive war in the interest of peace and disarmament. (It is even committed to it in the interest of the subjects of the country that it might preventively attack.) And it would confront a dilemma.

The dilemma is that war is war; and to act prematurely, impatiently, and without negotiating not only might create needless violence and damage but also would be a major political act. If instead the force procrastinates, negotiates, provides "one more chance," and waits for internal political decisions or a change of government, it may be confronted with an increasingly difficult military situation. As it waits it will be confronted with an enemy of increasing strength and an increasingly unattractive war, while its threat to initiate a forestalling war becomes less persuasive, and other countries become anxious and hedge against rearmament themselves.

The three main kinds of military action that the force could take against a united country would be pain, conquest, and obstruction. By "pain" I mean sheer coercive damage. Nuclear or other weapons might be used to inflict civil damage at a rate sufficient to induce the government to change its mind and bend to the will of the international authority. By "conquest" I mean invasion or occupation sufficient to put the international authority into the role of occupying power. By "obstruction" I mean military action designed to retard a country's rearmament, to make it more costly than the country could manage, to spoil it altogether or to impede it sufficiently to prevent a major threat to the security of other countries. This might be done either by selective bombing or by selective invasion and occupation of key facilities.

Activities aimed at causing confusion, revolt of the population, civil war, or *coup d'état* could come under any of these three headings but would, of course, involve different tactics.

It is not obvious that we should want a force, even were it charged with the most ambitious responsibilities, to have excellent capabilities to carry out those missions. We might prefer the international force itself (or the nations controlling its decisions) to be deterred by at least some prospect of difficulty or even failure. We might, in other words, want the force itself to be under strong incentive to consider military intervention only as a last resort.

Militarily we can distinguish at least three different kinds of deployment for the international strategic force. In one, strategic weapons and personnel would be kept in neutral territories — on the high seas, in special areas reserved to the international force (perhaps island bases), or perhaps distributed in enclaves in some politically acceptable proportions. Except for contingents that happen to be within the victim country, the international armed force would then be in the same position that national armed forces usually are with respect to war: to conquer they have to penetrate enemy territory.

In a second mode of deployment, forces could be kept deliberately within the countries that are most likely to be "enemies." This would mean keeping strategic forces within the larger industrial countries. It might include the option of moving more forces into a country toward which threats were being made or with which war was imminent. Moving extra forces into the United States or the Soviet Union would of course be a major political move and might be subject to restriction of access. The purpose of being within the country, other than ceremonial, would be to minimize the cost and delay of invasion, occupation, or selective destruction — i.e., of war. Particularly for non-nuclear invasion — a quick capture of strategic points in the country — mobile forces already within the country, properly distributed, might enhance the likelihood of quick success. The force could occupy Moscow more reliably with ground forces located thirty miles away than by relying on airborne troops in bad weather. An amphibious landing on the coast of Japan, France, or the United States would be harder than just moving troops already located within these countries.

The third mode of deployment — and it might look a little unmilitary — would be to put critically vulnerable parts of a country's economy and essential services directly into the hands of an international force. If the force can control the supply of water, electricity, fuel, transport, and communication to American, German, or Soviet cities, it might minimize strategic bombing, selective occupation, and other violence. To coerce a country, like the landlord who shuts off the utilities when a tenant refuses to move, the force could put on the squeeze by shutting down services. Rather than bomb electric power installations the force might press a key that sets off a charge of dynamite already installed.

If one really believed in the reliability and permanence of an international arrangement, such schemes for providing the authority with "hostages" might be more efficient, even more humane, than providing it with bombers and shock troops. One could even go further and let the force have a monopoly of critical medicines to use for bacterial warfare on a transgressor country. As soon as it starts an epidemic, it sends its medical units in to make sure that no one suffers who co-operates. Those who oppose it — military forces, government leaders, or anyone else — are without essential vaccines and must decide for themselves whether to stay at large and suffer or to surrender to be cured.

These gimmicks undoubtedly suffer from novelty, even from meanness, and would not be acceptable. They probably also go too far in assuming that the scheme is really for keeps. They give the international force too great an assurance of easy victory. The cards should be stacked in favor of the international force, but not with complete reliability. The decision to intervene by force in a sovereign country should always be a hard one. Furthermore it is worth some extra cost to keep the forces of organized violence out of sight, in reserve, and confined by tradition. No matter how strongly the entire arrangement is opposed to military traditions, uniformed troops are likely to seem more civilized than schemes patterned on the "protection" rackets or a paternalistic big brother.

Nevertheless there may be something in the notion of "prior occupation," i.e., of having strategic forces already located where they can accomplish "strategic" missions by simple tactical means — throwing switches and using only the conventional weapons of armored infantry.

The "enemy" of the force may also look for unconventional techniques of deterrence. One, which works especially well in a totalitarian country, would be a government's using its own population as hostages. If a Chinese government could threaten to hold out in such a way that an international force would have to kill large numbers of Chinese, either directly or in the economic consequences of strategic bombing, the force and its political leadership might be substantially deterred.

A threat of this sort might be implicit in any country's determination to rearm unless stopped by military action. Such a determination presents the international authority with the dilemma mentioned earlier. Shall it inflict war damage on a violator, or should it abandon the disarmament agreement in the interest of peace? It hardly seems possible to answer this question in advance. The United States government did use Union forces to prevent secession by the Southern states from an agreement they had entered voluntarily, but the basic arrangement had been in effect for over four score years and was a good deal more than a disarmament agreement.

If the victim has nuclear weapons or can acquire them, it can threaten reprisal of its own. Against whom? If the international force has no homeland — no women, children, or industrial assets toward which it feels a strong attachment — there may be no way to hurt it except to engage it militarily. But the force will be acting at least with the acquiescence, and almost surely at the urging, of other major powers. If the victim has nuclear weapons that it can deliver on countries, it need not threaten to seek out the Quonset huts of an international island-based force; it can threaten to detonate weapons in Russia, China, Britain, Ghana, America, or wherever the military move against it originates politically.

Where might the United States, Japan, or the Soviet Union acquire nuclear weapons for reprisal? One possibility is that it retained them, contrary to agreement, in secret and secure locations. If other countries are believed to have hedged in this way, even the "honorable" countries may feel obliged to do likewise. (It is not out of the question that an agreement would even provide for some "minimum deterrent" buffer stock of weaponry, at least in the early stages.)

But if we assume — unreasonable though it may be to assume — that no country has its own nuclear weapons, there are still ways to get them. *Somebody* has them and knows how to use them. If they cannot be stolen from the force by burglary, they may be stolen or access provided by an insider. In a crisis nuclear weapons belonging to the international agency but located within particular countries might be captured or production and assembly facilities taken. Finally, for the most honorable of reasons, part or all of the international strategic nuclear force might secede in favor of the intended victim.

There are those who believe that military officers could be recruited and indoctrinated with exclusive loyalty to the international authority and that their reliability would be unquestioned. It is worthwhile to question whether this is desirable; even so, one must wonder whether it could be accomplished, particularly within the first few decades of the arrangement. Flag officers of the organization are likely to have been loyal and outstanding military officers who had served national governments. It would take the organization some twenty or thirty years to recruit youngsters under twenty, put them through the equivalent of Annapolis, and raise them in an international military tradition to flag rank.

Furthermore, it should not be a foregone conclusion that this kind of abstract loyalty can be bred into military officers, especially if they are born and raised in important countries that command their affection as well as their early allegiance. And even if it can, it remains to be proved that the best personnel of an international force are men who, after reaching maturity, can turn their backs on their homelands and "emigrate" into a government that has no population, no territory, no cultural tradition, and no family ties. The capacity to incur allegiance to an abstract organization, or even to "mankind" generally, may not be a capacity highly correlated with the other qualities we want in our senior military officers or even our junior ones.

But supposing that this abstract loyalty is desirable and that the international authority should appear to have promoted it successfully, we still could not be sure of it. It will be hard to cultivate officers finer than Robert E. Lee, whose devotion to his country has, to my knowledge, not really been questioned. He confronted a dilemma at the peak of his career — one that he could surely never have anticipated by a prior decision — and had to decide where his highest allegiance lay.

We still refer today to the Civil War as a conflict between North and South, rather than between America and the South; a military showdown between an international force and a major country may not appear as a showdown between the United States and mankind, or Russia and mankind, or a United Western Europe and mankind. It may appear as an East-West conflict or a European-Asian conflict, with an international force controlled by one bloc against another.

Similarly, military coups and civil wars throughout history — even in some of the most civilized and idealistic nations — have often found national military establishments not unified on one side or the other. One has to consider therefore the possibility that, in a major showdown between an international force and an important country or a bloc of countries, some of the international military forces or personnel would side with the victim country. They might refuse to take military action against it; they might split off and join it; or they might attempt to take over the international organization itself. So there *are* ways that countries in defiance of the international force could acquire weapons, including some of the best.

If we assume, then, that major countries may get nuclear weapons, "counter-deterrence" against the international authority or its supporters through threat of nuclear reprisal is meaningful. Furthermore, the delivery of these weapons might not be difficult if the nations are themselves substantially disarmed.

It is not likely that the international force would provide every country with an air defense or ballistic missile defense network against the possibility of nuclear attack. (Besides adding tens of billions to the possible cost, an effective system of active defense would look so militarized that countries might prefer to maintain small, national, nuclear deterrent offensive forces instead.) Thus a Soviet Union that got control of some nuclear-missile submarines or bomber aircraft with nuclear weapons and wanted to threaten western Europe or the North American hemisphere might pose a threat against which the international force could provide no direct shelter. The force might hope to *deter* such an attack; but if the result is just mutual deterrence, it has failed in the mission of capturing or disarming the delinquent country.

For a major industrial country a technique of defense against the international force might be sabotage. For two reasons the force might be susceptible. The first, already adverted to, is its likely inability to maintain tight internal security of the kind that national military forces hope to maintain. The problems of security clearance and personnel selection, together with the multi-national political access to information, would pose acute problems. And in an acute crisis of national loyalties the same possibilities of military defection mentioned earlier might provide opportunities for sabotage. In fact "honorable" sabotage of strategic forces might be easier, safer, and more conservative than revolt or defection by military forces.

A second vulnerability to sabotage is in the production process. A military force that buys complex equipment in the major industrial countries might risk certain vulnerabilities that had been embedded in the equipment it purchased. One may suppose that acceptance of complex equipment would be conditional on inspection by officers of a nationality other than the producers'. Nevertheless an "encrypted" vulnerability might be built into certain equipment — that is, secret vulnerabilities that did not affect the reliability of the equipment but could be triggered by those who knew about them. (This might be more likely in unique pieces of equipment — the central command-control headquarters of the international authority or the electronics of a missile force.)

Except for retaliation and sabotage, disarmed countries should be vulnerable to attack by a professional, well equipped, international force. In fact, preventive conquest might be militarily simpler for the force than defense of one country against another. If large numbers of ill-equipped American reservists invade Canada, the force can probably stop them most effectively by occupying critical parts of the United States, taking over or immobilizing government facilities, communications, and other essential services.

Non-violent resistance may be a problem for the force. What can be accomplished by non-violent resistance to the force depends on what the international force is after. That in turn raises the question of the "war aim" of the force when it does take action against a major adversary.

If the most feasible and most humane military action available to the force is pure conquest (military occupation of a country's government) the force will be good at achieving total victory — unconditional surrender — but not lesser objectives. Is the country then to be occupied indefinitely? Is a regime put in that is favorable to the nations that backed the international force? Or are the illegal facilities dismantled, the miscreants punished, and the country turned loose again? The extent of popular resistance may depend on what is expected to happen after the country has suffered a humane blitzkrieg.

It is worth noting that the temptation for the force to launch preventive occupation may be as strongly motivated, perhaps more strongly motivated, when two competing power blocs are both violating the agreement. In fact a force that can painlessly convert a bipolar cold war into victory for one side by invading and conquering either power bloc may ignite the same apprehensions that the possibility of pre-emptive attack does now. If somebody is eventually going to be conquered by the international force, pre-emptive control of that force by one side or the other may begin to appear imperative.

CONCLUSION

To speak of these contingencies may seem contrary to the spirit of a disarmament agreement and a peace-keeping world military organization. The whole arrangement only makes sense if there are decent prospects for the cooperation of the major powers. To suppose that something like the present East-West struggle continues, or that other competing power blocs emerge to continue a cold war, and that some major country or bloc provokes the international force into action, may seem like imagining the worst. In fact, not just imagining the worst but contradicting the premise on which it is all established.

But we are discussing the "strategic problems" of the force. One may hope that the eventual actions of any such military force are purely ceremonial, that its strategic problems never become real. But to the extent that it is meant to be a real force, capable of handling actual problems, we have to ask what those problems might be.

Two tentative conclusions can be put forward. First, it is unlikely that an international strategic command would have a completely reliable, credible capability to intervene and to stop any rearmament of a major industrial power. Its "deterrent" against rearmament will certainly be subject to some doubt. It will suffer from some of the same disabilities as a national deterrence force. As a coercive military organization it will be quite imperfect.

Second, it would probably be unwise and unsafe to have it any less imperfect. The international force can itself be a threat to peace, even to disarmament, and surely to the freedom and independence of nations. The more nearly omnipotent it is, the less reassurance it would provide. The greater its military superiority over individual nations, the more it can be viewed as a potential "enemy" by the nations that it is set up to guard. The more decisive its potential role, the more crucial becomes the capture of its political control or its disablement by those who cannot hope to control it.

If we are to have someday an international military force, we probably want one that is itself deterred. To create an instrument of painless world conquest, one that can overcome both passive and active resistance of national governments and national populations, might be to create extraordinary political instability. Indivisible, centralized, coherent power may be a good deal less conducive to peace and reasurrance than a more diffuse, less decisive, less tempting instrument of control.

A world disarmament arrangement is unlikely to be viable if it requires a "perfect" strategic military force to deter violation and secession. Unless a quite imperfect deterrent can be believed adequate to forestall competitive violation, the arrangement should be abandoned or postponed.

Suppose an international strategic force were as likely to split apart as to stay together under crisis. Suppose it were believed appreciably vulnerable to various forms of sabotage. Suppose that individual nations could get hold of nuclear weapons and a capacity to deliver them on population centers. Suppose there were doubts whether the political arrangements were conducive to the force's timely action in a crisis — at least as many doubts as have ever been raised about American intervention on behalf of Europe. What is the consequence?

The consequence may be a significant deterrent, a deterrent based not on the certainty of decisive intervention but on a likelihood of intervention too great to ignore. A deterrent force does not have to *guarantee* that it can win the engagement.

This brings us back to the concept of "buffer." Instead of threatening to intervene against the rearming nation the force might be charged only with maintaining enough deterrence against war itself to permit other nations to take steps for their own protection. In the event of a rearmament race the international buffer force would try to ensure that no nation or group of nations could get a decisive headstart over its rivals.

Particularly since deterrence may depend on the absolute reprisal damage with which a nation can threaten an aggressor, not on just relative strengths, an international buffer might deter a rearming country's aggression long enough to permit other countries to develop at least "minimum deterrent forces" by themselves.

Under this concept the international force might even be authorized to assist in the laggards' rearmament. By simply threatening to facilitate the defensive, deterrent rearmament of the laggards (turning over its own production facilities to them, providing technical assistance, or giving some of its own weapons to them) the force might reduce the attractiveness to any nation of rushing back into an arms race. If this were the expected outcome of a rearmament race, there might appear little advantage in initiating such a race and no desperate haste to join a race that may or may not have begun.

How definitely and exactly can we hope to specify what the force is supposed to do? Can we rule out certain functions, such as its assisting laggards in their own rearmament? Can we make sure in advance that it will intervene (or that it will not intervene) in certain kinds of rearmament? Can we decide that it should engage in nuclear reprisal against a country that starts war, but not against a country that starts rearmament; or, choosing the opposite, can we guarantee that it will use nuclear weapons to deter or obstruct rearmament but not against a country that initiates conventional war?

I suspect we cannot. We can talk about the alternatives and can perhaps arrange weaponry, deployment, doctrine, political controls, and national military capabilities in a way that enhances the likelihood of certain decisions and reduces the likelihood of others. But no one can say in advance whether those who enjoy political control of the force will have the resolve, temerity, prudence, audacity, restraint, brutality, responsibility, or whatever else it takes, to launch war when they ought to, to threaten it credibly, to limit war properly if it occurs, or to abstain in the face of temptation. It is unlikely that we can deny the nations that politically control the force any ability to disband it, to redistribute its assets, or to charge it with grand new responsibilities that were never dreamed of before.

What could be decided in advance, and ought to be decided, is whether the force is to be viewed as an experiment in power politics or as a religious institution. If every war is a holy war, if the force cannot admit compromise or even occasional defeat, if every flaw in its strategy is to be construed as a doctrinal contradiction, if its leadership is to be considered the embodiment of disinterestedness and saintliness, and if any affront to the force is to be considered heresy, the demands on strategy will be exorbitant. The one thing we cannot do is to design a military force and strategy to support a doctrine of absolute self-righteousness.

NOTES AND QUESTIONS

1. Clark and Sohn state their approach to the role of the police force in the General Comment introducing Annex II, pp. 314–320. Note that Clark and Sohn say that "while a world police force can and should be moderate in numbers, it must be strong enough to provide reliable protection against any foreseeable violation of world peace." (p. 315.) Is such an expectation compatible with Schelling's assertion that "A world disarmament arrangement is unlikely to be viable if it requires a 'perfect' strategic military force to deter violation and secession"? Compare Schelling's view of the "strategy" of the World Peace Force with that of Clark and Sohn. Which do you find more realistic?——for what reasons?
2. Note that Schelling estimates the cost of the police force to be in the neighborhood of $25 billion, whereas Clark and Sohn estimate $9 billion (p. 320). How do you account for this discrepancy? It may be a consequence of Schelling's assumption that the police force would need a nuclear deterrent that was "more flexible and diversified" than that possessed by the major nuclear powers today. Clark and Sohn seem to imagine a more moderate military potential, especially with respect to nuclear weapons. Both in their General Comment (p. 319) and in Article 4(6) of Annex II (p. 330) Clark and Sohn envisage only very exceptional recourse to nuclear weaponry by their police force, and then only after formal authorization by the General Assembly and release and transfer by the United Nations Nuclear Energy Authority. Is this a practicable scheme? Can nuclear weapons be kept operational under such a system of separated authority and control? Is the time sequence realistic? What would be the purpose of using nuclear weapons after a delay of several days? Could a credible deterrent be maintained by the United Nations Police Force on this basis? Of course, Clark and Sohn rely upon the transforming impact of total disarmament to a much greater extent than does Schelling. It is rather interesting that although Schelling seems to assume higher requirements of military effectiveness for the police force, he entrusts a far less ambitious role to such a force than do Clark and Sohn. One way to highlight the difference in approach is to say that Schelling thinks of the force as an "army," whereas Clark and Sohn conceive of it as a "police establishment." A police department doesn't need a strategy or a foreign policy in Schelling's sense to carry on its business, whereas an army does. Which image of a peace force seems most realistic?
3. Schelling raises many problems connected with defining the mission of the police force in a world of continuing conflict. Schelling, projecting the existing world of tensions and hostility into a disarmed world, is of the opinion that the police force will either have to remain aloof from dangerous situations of violence, or take sides in the world power struggle and thereby alienate an important segment of the world community. Evaluate Schelling's idea of "buffer." Is it realistic to suppose that one mission of an international force might be to help "innocent" states to rearm in time to take on the "aggressor"?

The Financing and the So-Called Financing Problem

10

A. The So-Called Financing Problem

The Nineteenth Session of the General Assembly was virtually paralyzed by what is commonly referred to as the financing crisis. This crisis is a product of many factors, but the most salient is the persistent refusal of the Soviet Union and France to pay their assessed share of the major peace-keeping operations carried on in Suez and the Congo. The refusal of these countries to pay goes back to an objection to the use of the General Assembly to circumvent the veto in the event that the permanent members of the Security Council cannot agree among themselves. These efforts have been reviewed in detail in the course of the discussion of the Uniting for Peace Resolution in Chapter 5B.

There we noted the case for removing the obstructive veto if international peace was in danger, but we also noted the case for honoring the veto as expressive of a divided world. The financing crisis suggests the extent to which political consensus is a precondition to the continuing effectiveness of an international organization in the peace-keeping area. The Uniting for Peace Resolution, and the competence to authorize the use of military force and to assess Member States for peace-keeping activities that has been assumed by the General Assembly, disclose the pressures upon the Organization to act when peace has been breached. Given the veto in the Security Council, the choice is between a certain measure of constitutional opportunism through resort to devices that evade the veto, and organizational paralysis. The United Nations was perhaps more mindful of its peace-keeping functions in Suez and the Congo than in upholding the original expectations of the Big Five with regard to the scope of the veto. Has this been a wise choice?

It is difficult to compare the impact of some hypothetical past with the actual course of events. How can we say what would have happened in Suez or the Congo if the United Nations had not been able to act? Great Power interventions might have taken place and the states of Asia and Africa might have completely lost interest, even to the extent of mass withdrawal, had the United Nations not been able to protect the victims of Anglo-French and Belgian aggression in the two situations. Of course, we cannot say, but it is evident that there is no easy choice between action and non-action by the United Nations when peace is breached and political consensus among the principal powers is absent.

The financial crisis that besets the Organization we call "the so-called financing problem." The crisis is not really about money. The amounts involved are very minor, given the level of expenditures of the governments involved. Although some of the small states in default have been contending financial hardship, the crisis that has paralyzed the Organization is a consequence of political default by France and the Soviet Union without either contention of financial hardship by the defaulting states, or actual inability.

Although the crisis is not about money, the effect of nonpayment was to place the United Nations on the edge of bankruptcy. The Organization is unable to pay its bills unless its principal members meet their financial obligations. Recall Brierly's conclusion at the end of his selection in the last chapter, to the effect that an international organization in the security field had to proceed on the assumption that not all states would be equally willing to participate in collective security operations, but that such equal participation was not *necessary*. In fact, that given the decentralized and conflicted character of international society it was undesirable, if not *impossible*, to insist upon equal participation. On this basis, Brierly imposes "a minimum obligation, negative in character," that asks of *all* states only that they deny neutral rights to any state designated by an international organization as an "aggressor" and refrain from interfering with the security operation undertaken. Those states most interested because they belong to the region, "or by reason of their wider interests," are expected to bear a disproportionate burden as they "should be prepared to undertake whatever action is necessary" to uphold the peace. Does Brierly point to a way toward overcoming the financing crisis? Some concept of unequal burdens already exists. States have never been asked to participate in the staffing and manning of peace-keeping forces except on a voluntary basis. This has created few problems even though the burdens have been unequally shared.

Why must the financial burdens of the Organization be equally shared? Why not allow the Big Five to retain a financial veto over peace-keeping operations, at least insofar as their own participation is concerned? This would give the Organization the capacity it needs to act when two-thirds or more of the Assembly favors action, and yet it would exhibit a measure of deference to the original expectations created by placing a right of veto in the Charter and would acknowledge the relevance of a political consensus to the formation of legal obligations in international society. Such a middle course also allows and member of the Big Five that opposes the action being taken by the United Nations to avoid the need to justify meeting the financial obligation to its own domestic society. It might be difficult to persuade the United States to pay its share of peace-keeping bills if the United Nations had acted against its perceived vital interests by intervening in Guatemala, say, in 1954 to protect the leftist leader, Jacobo Arbenz Guzmán, against being overthrown by a coup organized and administered quite avowedly by the United States. So long as power remains decentralized, efforts to coerce principal states to subordinate their national prerogatives in the interests of building an effective international organization in the peace-keeping field seem unrealistic.

Of course, no solution would be simple. The Soviet Union has used its refusal to pay as a basis for renegotiating the premises of any action in the peace-keeping field, and not just the premises of financial obligation. It wants more than to be released from the obligation to pay—it wants a return to preeminence of the Security Council.

On the other hand, the United States might not be able "to accept" a solution that required it to pay most of the bills in the peace-keeping area. It would not be desirable for the Organization to become too dependent upon the backing of any particular Member. And although the burden of financing has remained trivial in the context of American governmental spending, there are limits beyond which a domestic willingness to pay disappears. The United States Congress has not been happy about approving the payment of such a large share of the financial obligations by the United States. This feeling in Congress undoubtedly influenced the way in which the United States went about its unsuccessful campaign to put pressure upon the Soviet Union to pay the amounts assessed by the General Assembly. Confidence in the Organization was alleged by United States officials to depend upon the willingness of principal members, at least, to pay for all peace-keeping operations whether in favor or against the formation and execution of any particular one. This suggests the fundamental issue of whether the United Nations is an international or a supranational organization, whether it is an autonomous actor carrying out its own policies with a measure of independence, or merely a passive instrumentality for the realization of the convergent interests of dominant nation-states. The United States has treated the so-called financing issue as if it was promoting an autonomous role for the United Nations. After the crisis developed, expressing an unexpectedly stubborn Soviet refusal to relinquish the prerogatives of national sovereignty, the United States has apparently had some second thoughts, and has shown a willingness to negotiate toward a compromise on the present debt and to work out a mutually satisfactory basis with the Soviet Union for financing peace-keeping in the future. The prospect of hostile majorities in the General Assembly has sharpened with the increasing stridency of the Afro-Asian bloc, as evidenced, for instance, during the debates of December, 1964 in the Security Council on the Stanleyville operation. The Secretary of State, Dean Rusk, has pointed out that states paying less than 5 per cent of the annual budget and representing less than 10 per cent of the world's population can potentially mobilize a two-thirds majority in the General Assembly. From this perspective the United States seems no more ready than the Soviet Union to build up the autonomous role of the United Nations at this point. It is true, for what it is worth, that the official United States model of a disarmed world calls for a much more autonomous role for the United Nations than does the Soviet model. See discussion of general and complete disarmament, **IV-4**.

With this setting as a background it is appropriate to move to our first selection, a long extract from an Advisory Opinion of the International Court of Justice that deals with the authority of the General Assembly to make the special assessments under Article 17(2) to pay for UNEF and ONUC and a summary of Separate and Dissenting Opinions. This Advisory Opinion, "Certain Expenses of the United Nations," *Reports of Judgments, Advisory Opinions and Orders* (1962) pp. 151–181, was rendered as part of the United States campaign to put pressure on the Soviet Union with regard to the financing issue. It was also an attempt to involve the Soviet Union, however indirectly, in the activities of the ICJ, an organ of the United Nations for which the Russians have never had much use. In addition, recourse to the World Court was conceived as a way to depoliticize the financing issue and to strengthen the relevance of law to the operations of the political organs of the United Nations. See Chapter 2. An Advisory Opinion is rendered by the World Court, if requested, and provided it accepts jurisdiction, to answer legal questions by either the General Assembly or the Security Council (and, with Assembly authorization, by other organs, and by specialized agencies of the UN). See UN Charter, Article 96.

The opinion in the *Certain Expenses Case* has aroused great interest. First, it represents an attempt to give the ICJ a hot political issue that the political organs were unable to settle. To what extent can a political question be "settled" by treating it as a legal question? This raises the issues relevant to the discussion of pacific settlement procedures. See Chapter 8. Second, it discloses the application of legal techniques to a difficult problem of statutory construction in the context of Charter interpretation, thereby recalling the selections of Kelsen, Chapter 9A, and Alexandrowicz, Chapter 6. Third, it suggests the extent to which political disagreements are translatable into legal disagreements. This phenomenon is expressed by the range of opinions filed by the World Court and by the correlation between the national affiliation of a judge and his analysis of the legal questions put to him by the Assembly. The opinion of the Court was delivered on July 20, 1962. By a vote of 9 to 5 the Court agreed that the financing of UNEF and ONUC "constituted 'expenses of the Organization' within the meaning of Article 17(2)," thereby confirming the authority of the General Assembly to make the controversial assessment. There was a majority opinion and three separate concurring opinions filed by judges who supported the conclusions of the majority opinion but preferred to give a separate legal rationale. In addition, five dissenting judges, including the Soviet and the French members of the Court, each wrote a separate opinion. In sum, the Court produced nine opinions: a lot of advice, much of it conflicting, and a jurisprudential goldmine.

Resolution 1731 (XVI) of General Assembly requesting advisory opinion—objections to giving opinion based on proceedings in General Assembly—interpretation of meaning of "expenses of the Organization"—Article 17, paragraphs 1 and 2 of Charter—lack of justification for limiting terms "budget" and "expenses"—Article 17 in context of Charter—respective functions of Security Council and General Assembly—Article 11, paragraph 2, in relation to budgetary powers of General Assembly—role of General Assembly in maintenance of international peace and security—agreements under Article 43—expenses incurred for purposes of United Nations—obligations incurred by Secretary-General acting under authority of Security Council or General Assembly—nature of operations of UNEF and ONUC—financing of UNEF and ONUC based on Article 17, paragraph 2—implementation by Secretary-General of Security Council resolutions—expenditures for UNEF and ONUC and Article 17, paragraph 2, of Charter [1]

CERTAIN EXPENSES OF THE UNITED NATIONS (ARTICLE 17, PARAGRAPH 2, OF THE CHARTER).[2] I.C.J. Reports, 1962, p. 151.

International Court of Justice,[3] Advisory Opinion of July 20, 1962.

[Resolution 1731 (XVI), adopted December 20, 1961, by the General Assembly, read:

The General Assembly,

Recognizing its need for authoritative legal guidance as to obligations of Member States under the Charter of the United Nations in the matter of financing the United Nations operations in the Congo and in the Middle East,

1. *Decides* to submit the following question to the International Court of Justice for an advisory opinion:

"Do the expenditures authorized in General Assembly resolutions 1583 (XV) and 1590 (XV) of 20 December 1960, 1595(XV) of 3 April 1961, 1619(XV) of 21 April 1961 and 1633 (XVI) of 30 October 1961 relating to the United Nations operations in the Congo undertaken in pursuance of the Security Council resolutions of 14 July, 22 July and 9 August 1960, and 21 February and 24 November 1961, and General Assembly resolutions 1474 (ES-IV) of 20 September 1960 and 1599 (XV), 1600(XV), and 1601(XV) of 15

1 Caption by the Court.

2 Full text of majority opinion, except for introductory matter, and digests of remainder, by Wm. W. Bishop, Jr.

3 Composed for this case of President Winiarski, Vice President Alfaro, and Judges Basdevant, Badawi, Moreno Quintana, Wellington Koo, Spiropoulos, Sir Percy Spender, Sir Gerald Fitzmaurice, Koretsky, Tanaka, Bustamante y Rivero, Jessup, and Morelli.

April 1961, and the expenditures authorized in General Assembly resolutions 1122(XI) of 26 November 1956, 1089(XI) of 21 December 1956, 1090(XI) of 27 February 1957, 1151(XII) of 22 November 1957, 1204(XII) of 13 December 1957, 1337(XIII) of 13 December 1958, 1441(XIV) of 5 December 1959 and 1575(XV) of 20 December 1960 relating to the operations of the United Nations Emergency Force undertaken in pursuance of General Assembly resolutions 997(ES-I) of 2 November 1956, 998(ES-I) and 999 (ES-I) of 4 November 1956, 1000(ES-I) of 5 November 1956, 1001(ES-I) of 7 November 1956, 1121(XI) of 24 November 1956 and 1263(XIII) of 14 November 1958, constitute 'expenses of the Organization' within the meaning of Article 17, paragraph 2, of the Charter of the United Nations?"

The second paragraph of the resolution asked the Secretary General to transmit the resolution, and "all documents likely to throw light on the question," to the Court.]

Before proceeding to give its opinion on the question put to it, the Court considers it necessary to make the following preliminary remarks: [4]

The power of the Court to give an advisory opinion is derived from Article 65 of the Statute. The power granted is of a discretionary character. In exercising its discretion, the International Court of Justice, like the Permanent Court of International Justice, has always been guided by the principle which the Permanent Court stated in the case concerning the *Status of Eastern Carelia* on 23 July 1923: "The Court, being a Court of Justice, cannot, even in giving advisory opinions, depart from the essential rules guiding their activity as a Court" (P.C.I.J., Series B, No. 5, p. 29). Therefore, and in accordance with Article 65 of its Statute, the Court can give an advisory opinion only on a legal question. If a question is not a legal one, the Court has no discretion in the matter; it must decline to give the opinion requested. But even if the question is a legal one, which the Court is undoubtedly competent to answer, it may nonetheless decline to do so. As this Court said in its Opinion of 30 March 1950, the permissive character of Article 65 "gives the Court the power to examine whether the circumstances of the case are of such a character as should lead it to decline to answer the Request" (*Interpretation of Peace Treaties with Bulgaria, Hungary and Romania* (*First Phase*), *I.C.J. Reports 1950,* p. 72). But, as the Court also said in the same Opinion, "the reply of the Court, itself an 'organ of the United Nations', represents its participation in the activities of the Organization, and, in principle, should not be refused" (*Ibid.,* p. 71). Still more emphatically, in its Opinion of 23 October 1956, the Court said that only "compelling reasons" should lead it to refuse to give a requested advisory opinion (*Judgments of the Administrative Tribunal of the I.L.O. upon complaints made against the Unesco, I.C.J. Reports 1956,* p. 86).

[4] The English text of the majority opinion is authoritative.

The Court finds no "compelling reason" why it should not give the advisory opinion which the General Assembly requested by its resolution 1731 (XVI). It has been argued that the question put to the Court is intertwined with political questions, and that for this reason the Court should refuse to give an opinion. . It is true that most interpretations of the Charter of the United Nations will have political significance, great or small. In the nature of things it could not be otherwise. The Court, however, cannot attribute a political character to a request which invites it to undertake an essentially judicial task, namely, the interpretation of a treaty provision.

In the preamble to the resolution requesting this opinion, the General Assembly expressed its recognition of "its need for authoritative legal guidance." In its search for such guidance it has put to the Court a legal question—a question of the interpretation of Article 17, paragraph 2, of the Charter of the United Nations. In its Opinion of 28 May 1948, the Court made it clear that as "the principal judicial organ of the United Nations", it was entitled to exercise in regard to an article of the Charter, "a multilateral treaty, an interpretative function which falls within the normal exercise of its judicial powers" (*Conditions of Admission of a State to Membership in the United Nations* (*Article 4 of the Charter*), *I.C.J. Reports 1947–1948,* p. 61).

The Court, therefore, having been asked to give an advisory opinion upon a concrete legal question, will proceed to give its opinion.

The question on which the Court is asked to give its opinion is whether certain expenditures which were authorized by the General Assembly to cover the costs of the United Nations operations in the Congo (hereinafter referred to as ONUC) and of the operations of the United Nations Emergency Force in the Middle East (hereinafter referred to as UNEF), "constitute 'expenses of the Organization' within the meaning of Article 17, paragraph 2, of the Charter of the United Nations".

Before entering upon the detailed aspects of this question, the Court will examine the view that it should take into consideration the circumstance that at the 1086th Plenary Meeting of the General Assembly on 20 December 1961, an amendment was proposed, by the representative of France, to the draft resolution requesting the advisory opinion, and that this amendment was rejected. The amendment would have asked the Court to give an opinion on the question whether the expenditures relating to the indicated operations were "decided on in conformity with the provisions of the Charter"; if that question were answered in the affirmative, the Court would have been asked to proceed to answer the question which the resolution as adopted actually poses.

If the amendment had been adopted, the Court would have been asked to consider whether the resolutions *authorizing the expenditures* were decided on in conformity with the Charter; the French amendment did not propose to ask the Court whether the resolutions *in pursuance of which the operations in the Middle East and in the Congo were undertaken,* were adopted in conformity with the Charter.

The Court does not find it necessary to expound the extent to which the proceedings of the General Assembly, antecedent to the adoption of a resolution, should be taken into account in interpreting that resolution, but it makes the following comments on the argument based upon the rejection of the French amendment.

The rejection of the French amendment does not constitute a directive to the Court to exclude from its consideration the question whether certain expenditures were "decided on in conformity with the Charter", if the Court finds such consideration appropriate. It is not to be assumed that the General Assembly would thus seek to fetter or hamper the Court in the discharge of its judicial functions; the Court must have full liberty to consider all relevant data available to it in forming an opinion on a question posed to it for an advisory opinion. Nor can the Court agree that the rejection of the French amendment has any bearing upon the question whether the General Assembly sought to preclude the Court from interpreting Article 17 in the light of other articles of the Charter, that is, in the whole context of the treaty. If any deduction is to be made from the debates on this point, the opposite conclusion would be drawn from the clear statements of sponsoring delegations that they took it for granted the Court would consider the Charter as a whole.

Turning to the question which has been posed, the Court observes that it involves an interpretation of Article 17, paragraph 2, of the Charter. On the previous occasions when the Court has had to interpret the Charter of the United Nations, it has followed the principles and rules applicable in general to the interpretation of treaties, since it has recognized that the Charter is a multilateral treaty, albeit a treaty having certain special characteristics. In interpreting Article 4 of the Charter, the Court was led to consider "the structure of the Charter" and "the relations established by it between the General Assembly and the Security Council"; a comparable problem confronts the Court in the instant matter. The Court sustained its interpretation of Article 4 by considering the manner in which the organs concerned "have consistently interpreted the text" in their practice (*Competence of the General Assembly for the Admission of a State to the United Nations, I.C.J. Reports 1950,* pp. 8–9).

The text of Article 17 is in part as follows:

> "1. The General Assembly shall consider and approve the budget of the Organization.
> 2. The expenses of the Organization shall be borne by the Members as apportioned by the General Assembly."

Although the Court will examine Article 17 in itself and in its relation to the rest of the Charter, it should be noted that at least three separate questions might arise in the interpretation of paragraph 2 of this Article. One question is that of identifying what are "the expenses of the Organization"; a second question might concern apportionment by the General Assembly; while a third question might involve the interpretation of the phrase "shall be borne by the Members". It is the second and third questions which directly involve "the financial obligations of the Members", but it is only the first question which is posed by the request for the advisory opinion. The question put to the Court has to do with a moment logically anterior to apportionment, just as a question of apportionment would be anterior to a question of Members' obligation to pay.

It is true that, as already noted, the preamble of the resolution containing the request refers to the General Assembly's "need for authoritative legal guidance as to obligations of Member States", but it is to be assumed that in the understanding of the General Assembly, it would find such guidance in the advisory opinion which the Court would give on the question whether certain identified expenditures "constitute 'expenses of the Organization' within the meaning of Article 17, paragraph 2, of the Charter". If the Court finds that the indicated expenditures are such "expenses", it is not called upon to consider the manner in which, or the scale by which, they may be apportioned. The amount of what are unquestionably "expenses of the Organization within the meaning of Article 17, paragraph 2" is not in its entirety apportioned by the General Assembly and paid for by the contributions of Member States, since the Organization has other sources of income. A Member State, accordingly, is under no obligation to pay more than the amount apportioned to it; the expenses of the Organization and the total amount in money of the obligations of the Member States may not, in practice, necessarily be identical.

The text of Article 17, paragraph 2, refers to "the expenses of the Organization" without any further explicit definition of such expenses. It would be possible to begin with a general proposition to the effect that the "expenses" of any organization are the amounts paid out to defray the costs of carrying out its purposes, in this case, the political, economic, social, humanitarian and other purposes of the United Nations. The next step would be to examine, as the Court will, whether the resolutions authorizing the operations here in question were intended to carry out the purposes of the United Nations and whether the expenditures were incurred in furthering these operations. Or, it might simply be said that the "expenses" of an organization are those which are provided for in its budget. But the Court has not been asked to give an abstract definition of the words "expenses of the Organization". It has been asked to answer a specific question related to certain identified expenditures which have actually been made, but the Court would not adequately discharge the obligation incumbent on it unless it examined in some detail various problems raised by the question which the General Assembly has asked.

It is perhaps the simple identification of "expenses" with the items included in a budget, which has led certain arguments to link the interpretation of the word "expenses" in paragraph 2 of Article 17, with the word "budget" in paragraph 1 of that Article; in both cases, it is contended, the qualifying adjective "regular" or "administrative" should be understood to be implied. Since no such qualification is expressed in the text of the Charter, it could be read in, only if such qualification must necessarily be implied from the provisions of the Charter considered as a whole, or from some particular provision thereof which makes it unavoidable to do so in order to give effect to the Charter.

In the first place, concerning the word "budget" in paragraph 1 of Article 17, it is clear that the existence of the distinction between "administrative budgets" and "operational budgets" was not absent from the minds of the drafters of the Charter, nor from the consciousness of the Organization even in the early days of its history. In drafting Article 17, the drafters found it suitable to provide in paragraph 1 that "The General Assembly shall consider and approve *the budget* of the Organization". But in dealing with the function of the General Assembly in relation to the specialized agencies, they provided in paragraph 3 that the General Assembly "shall examine the *administrative budgets* of such specialized agencies". If it had been intended that paragraph 1 should be limited to the administrative budget of the United Nations organization itself, the word "administrative" would have been inserted in paragraph 1 as it was in paragraph 3. Moreover, had it been contemplated that the Organization would also have had another budget, different from the one which was to be approved by the General Assembly, the Charter would have included some reference to such other budget and to the organ which was to approve it.

Similarly, at its first session, the General Assembly in drawing up and approving the Constitution of the International Refugee Organization, provided that the budget of that Organization was to be divided under the headings "administrative", "operational" and "large-scale resettlement"; but no such distinctions were introduced into the Financial Regulations of the United Nations which were adopted by unanimous vote in 1950, and which, in this respect, remain unchanged. These regulations speak only of "the budget" and do not provide any distinction between "administrative" and "operational".

In subsequent sessions of the General Assembly, including the sixteenth, there have been numerous references to the idea of distinguishing an "operational" budget; some speakers have advocated such a distinction as a useful book-keeping device; some considered it in connection with the possibility of differing scales of assessment or apportionment; others believed it should mark a differentiation of activities to be financed by voluntary contributions. But these discussions have not resulted in the adoption of two separate budgets based upon such a distinction.

Actually, the practice of the Organization is entirely consistent with the plain meaning of the text. The budget of the Organization has from the outset included items which would not fall within any of the definitions of "administrative budget" which have been advanced in this connection. Thus, for example, prior to the establishment of, and now in addition to, the "Expanded Programme of Technical Assistance" and the "Special Fund", both of which are nourished by voluntary contributions, the annual budget of the Organization contains provision for funds for technical assistance; in the budget for the financial year 1962, the sum of $6,400,000 is included for the technical programmes of economic development, social activities, human rights activities, public administration and narcotic drugs control. Although during the Fifth Committee discussions there was a suggestion that all technical assistance costs should be excluded from the regular budget, the items under these heads were all adopted on second reading in the Fifth Committee without a dissenting vote. The "operational" nature of such activities so budgeted is indicated by the explanations in the budget estimates, e.g. the requests "for the continuation of the operational programme in the field of economic development contemplated in General Assembly resolutions 200 (III) of 4 December 1948 and 304 (IV) of 16 November 1949"; and "for the continuation of the operational programme in the field of advisory social welfare services as contemplated in General Assembly resolution 418 (V) of 1 December 1950".

It is a consistent practice of the General Assembly to include in the annual budget resolutions, provision for expenses relating to the maintenance of international peace and security. Annually, since 1947, the General Assembly has made anticipatory provision for "unforeseen and extraordinary expenses" arising in relation to the "maintenance of peace and security". In a Note submitted to the Court by the Controller on the budgetary and financial practices of the United Nations, "extraordinary expenses" are defined as "obligations and expenditures arising as a result of the approval by a council, commission or other competent United Nations body of new programmes and activities not contemplated when the budget appropriations were approved".

The annual resolution designed to provide for extraordinary expenses authorizes the Secretary-General to enter into commitments to meet such expenses with the prior concurrence of the Advisory Committee on Administrative and Budgetary Questions, except that such concurrence is not necessary if the Secretary-General certifies that such commitments relate to the subjects mentioned and the amount does not exceed $2 million. At its fifteenth and sixteenth sessions, the General Assembly resolved "that if, as a result of a decision of the Security Council, commitments relating to the maintenance of peace and security should arise in an estimated total exceeding $10 million" before the General Assembly was due to meet again, a special session should be convened by the Secretary-General to consider the matter. The Secretary-General is regularly authorized to draw on the Working Capital Fund for such expenses but is required to submit supplementary budget estimates to cover amounts so advanced. These annual resolutions on unforeseen and extraordinary expenses were adopted without a dissenting vote in every year from 1947 through 1959, except for 1952, 1953 and 1954, when the adverse votes are attributable to the fact that the resolution included the specification of a controversial item—United Nations Korean war decorations.

It is notable that the 1961 Report of the Working Group of Fifteen on the Examination of the Administrative and Budgetary Procedures of the United Nations, while revealing wide differences of opinion on a variety of propositions, records that the following statement was adopted without opposition:

> *"22. Investigations and observation operations undertaken by the Organization to prevent possible aggression should be financed as part of the regular budget of the United Nations."*

In the light of what has been stated, the Court concludes that there is no justification for reading into the text of Article 17, paragraph 1, any limiting or qualifying word before the word "budget".

Turning to paragraph 2 of Article 17, the Court observes that, on its face, the term "expenses of the Organization" means all the expenses and not just certain types of expenses which might be referred to as "regular expenses". An examination of other parts of the Charter shows the variety of expenses which must inevitably be included within the "expenses of the Organization" just as much as the salaries of staff or the maintenance of buildings.

For example, the text of Chapters IX and X of the Charter with reference to international economic and social cooperation, especially the wording of those articles which specify the functions and powers of the Economic and Social Council, anticipated the numerous and varied circumstances under which expenses of the Organization could be incurred and which have indeed eventuated in practice.

Furthermore, by Article 98 of the Charter, the Secretary-General is obligated to perform such functions as are entrusted to him by the General Assembly, the Security Council, the Economic and Social Council, and the Trusteeship Council. Whether or not expenses incurred in his discharge of this obligation become "expenses of the Organization" cannot depend on whether they be administrative or some other kind of expenses.

The Court does not perceive any basis for challenging the legality of the settled practice of including such expenses as these in the budgetary amounts which the General Assembly apportions among the Members in accordance with the authority which is given to it by Article 17, paragraph 2.

Passing from the text of Article 17 to its place in the general structure and scheme of the Charter, the Court will consider whether in that broad context one finds any basis for implying a limitation upon the budgetary authority of the General Assembly which in turn might limit the meaning of "expenses" in paragraph 2 of that Article.

The general purposes of Article 17 are the vesting of control over the finances of the Organization, and the levying of apportioned amounts of the expenses of the Organization in order to enable it to carry out the functions of the Organization as a whole acting through its principal organs and such subsidiary organs as may be established under the authority of Article 22 or Article 29.

Article 17 is the only article in the Charter which refers to budgetary authority or to the power to apportion expenses, or otherwise to raise revenue, except for Articles 33 and 35, paragraph 3, of the Statute of the Court which have no bearing on the point here under discussion. Nevertheless, it has been argued before the Court that one type of expenses, namely those resulting from operations for the maintenance of international peace and security, are not "expenses of the Organization" within the meaning of Article 17, paragraph 2, of the Charter, inasmuch as they fall to be dealt with exclusively by the Security Council, and more especially through agreements negotiated in accordance with Article 43 of the Charter.

The argument rests in part upon the view that when the maintenance of international peace and security is involved, it is only the Security Council which is authorized to decide on any action relative thereto. It is argued further that since the General Assembly's power is limited to discussing, considering, studying and recommending, it cannot impose an obligation to pay the expenses which result from the implementation of its recommendations. This argument leads to an examination of the respective functions of the General Assembly and of the Security Council under the Charter, particularly with respect to the maintenance of international peace and security.

Article 24 of the Charter provides:

> "In order to ensure prompt and effective action by the United Nations, its Members confer on the Security Council primary responsibility for the maintenance of international peace and security . . ."

The responsibility conferred is "primary", not exclusive. This primary responsibility is conferred upon the Security Council, as stated in Article 24, "in order to ensure prompt and effective action". To this end, it is the Security Council which is given a power to impose an explicit obligation of compliance if for example it issues an order or command to an aggressor under Chapter VII. It is only the Security Council which can require enforcement by coercive action against an aggressor.

The Charter makes it abundantly clear, however, that the General Assembly is also to be concerned with international peace and security. Article 14 authorizes the General Assembly to "recommend measures for the peaceful adjustment of any situation, regardless of origin, which it deems likely to impair the general welfare or friendly relations among nations, including situations resulting from a violation of the provisions of the present Charter setting forth the purposes and principles of the United Nations". The word "measures" implies some kind of action, and the only limitation which Article 14 imposes on the General Assembly is the restriction found in Article 12, namely, that the Assembly should not recommend measures while the Security Council is dealing with the same matter unless the Council requests it to do so. Thus while it is the Security Council which, exclusively, may order coercive action, the functions and powers conferred by the Charter on the General Assembly are not confined to discussion, consideration, the initiation of studies and the making of recommendations; they are not merely hortatory. Article 18 deals with "*decisions*" of the General Assembly "on important questions". These "decisions" do indeed include certain recommendations, but others have dispositive force and effect. Among these latter decisions, Article 18 includes suspension of rights and privileges of membership, expulsion of Members, "and budgetary questions". In connection with the suspension of rights and privileges of membership and expulsion from membership under Articles 5 and 6, it is the Security Council which has only the power to recommend and it is the General Assembly which decides and whose decision determines status; but there is a close collaboration between the two organs. Moreover, these powers of decision of the General Assembly under Articles 5 and 6 are specifically related to preventive or enforcement measures.

By Article 17, paragraph 1, the General Assembly is given the power not only to "consider" the budget of the Organization, but also to "approve" it. The decision to "approve" the budget has a close connection with paragraph 2 of Article 17, since thereunder the General Assembly is also given the power to apportion the expenses among the Members and the exercise of the power of apportionment creates the obligation, specifically stated in Article 17, paragraph 2, of each Member to bear that part of the expenses which is apportioned to it by the General Assembly. When those expenses include expenditures for the maintenance of peace and security, which are not otherwise provided for, it is the General Assembly which has the authority to apportion the latter amounts among the Members. The provisions of the Charter which distribute functions and powers to the Security Council and to the General Assembly give no support to the view that such distribution excludes from the powers of the General Assembly the power to provide for the financing of measures designed to maintain peace and security.

The argument supporting a limitation on the budgetary authority of the General Assembly with respect to the maintenance of international peace and security relies especially on the reference to "action" in the last sentence of Article 11, paragraph 2. This paragraph reads as follows:

> "The General Assembly may discuss any questions relating to the maintenance of international peace and security brought before it by any Member of the United Nations, or by the Security Council, or by a State which is not a Member of the United Nations in accordance with Article 35, paragraph 2, and, except as provided in Article 12, may make recommendations with regard to any such question to the State or States concerned or to the Security Council, or to both. Any such question on which action is necessary shall be referred to the Security Council by the General Assembly either before or after discussion."

The Court considers that the kind of action referred to in Article 11, paragraph 2, is coercive or enforcement action. This paragraph, which applies not merely to general questions relating to peace and security, but also to specific cases brought before the General Assembly by a State under Article 35, in its first sentence empowers the General Assembly, by means of recommendations to States or to the Security Council, or to both, to organize peace-keeping operations, at the request, or with the consent, of the States concerned. This power of the General Assembly is a special power which in no way derogates from its general powers under Article 10 or Article 14, except as limited by the last sentence of Article 11, paragraph 2. This last sentence says that when "action" is necessary the General Assembly shall refer the question to the Security Council. The word "action" must mean such action as is solely within the province of the Security Council. It cannot refer to recommendations which the Security Council might make, as for instance under Article 38, because the General Assembly under Article 11 has a comparable power. The "action" which is solely within the province of the Security Council is that which is indicated by the title of Chapter VII of the Charter, namely "Action with respect to threats to the peace, breaches of the peace, and acts of aggression". If the word "action" in Article 11, paragraph 2, were interpreted to mean that the General Assembly could make recommendations only of a general character affecting peace and security in the abstract, and not in relation to specific cases, the paragraph would not have provided that the General Assembly may make recommendations on questions brought before it by States or by the Security Council. Accordingly, the last sentence of Article 11, paragraph 2, has no application where the necessary action is not enforcement action.

The practice of the Organization throughout its history bears out the foregoing elucidation of the term "action" in the last sentence of Article 11, paragraph 2. Whether the General Assembly proceeds under Article 11 or under Article 14, the implementation of its recommendations for setting up commissions or other bodies involves organizational activity—action—in connection with the maintenance of international peace and security. Such implementation is a normal feature of the functioning of the United Nations. Such committees, commissions or other bodies or individuals, constitute, in some cases, subsidiary organs established under the authority of Article 22 of the Charter. The functions of the General Assembly for which it may establish such subsidiary organs include, for example, investigation, observation and supervision, but the way in which such subsidiary organs are utilized depends on the consent of the State or States concerned.

The Court accordingly finds that the argument which seeks, by reference to Article 11, paragraph 2, to limit the budgetary authority of the General Assembly in respect of the maintenance of international peace and security, is unfounded.

It has further been argued before the Court that Article 43 of the Charter constitutes a particular rule, a *lex specialis,* which derogates from the general rule in Article 17, whenever an expenditure for the maintenance of international peace and security is involved. Article 43 provides that Members shall negotiate agreements with the Security Council on its initiative, stipulating what "armed forces, assistance and facilities, including rights of passage, necessary for the purpose of maintaining international peace and security", the Member State will make available to the Security Council on its call. According to paragraph 2 of the Article:

> "Such agreement or agreements shall govern the numbers and types of forces, their degree of readiness and general location, and the nature of the facilities and assistance to be provided."

The argument is that such agreements were intended to include specifications concerning the allocation of costs of such enforcement actions as might be taken by direction of the Security Council, and that it is only the Security Council which has the authority to arrange for meeting such costs.

With reference to this argument, the Court will state at the outset that, for reasons fully expounded later in this Opinion, the operations known as UNEF and ONUC were not *enforcement* actions within the compass of Chapter VII of the Charter and that therefore Article 43 could not have any applicability to the cases with which the Court is here concerned. However, even if Article 43 were applicable, the Court could not accept this interpretation of its text for the following reasons.

There is nothing in the text of Article 43 which would limit the discretion of the Security Council in negotiating such agreements. It cannot be assumed that in every such agreement the Security Council would insist, or that any Member State would be bound to agree, that such State would bear the entire cost of the "assistance" which it would make available including, for example, transport of forces to the point of operation, complete logistical maintenance in the field, supplies, arms and ammunition, etc. If, during negotiations under the terms of Article 43, a Member State would be entitled (as it would be) to insist, and the Security Council would be entitled (as it would be) to agree, that some part of the expense should be borne by the Organization, then such expense would form part of the expenses of the Organization and would fall to be apportioned by the General Assembly under Article 17. It is difficult to see how it could have been contemplated that all potential expenses could be envisaged in such agreements concluded perhaps long in advance. Indeed, the difficulty or impossibility of anticipating the entire financial impact of enforcement measures on Member States is brought out by the terms of Article 50 which provides that a State, whether a Member of the United Nations or not, "which finds itself confronted with special economic problems arising from the carrying out of these [preventive or enforcement] measures, shall have the right to consult the Security Council with regard to a solution of those problems". Presumably in such a case the Security Council might determine that the overburdened State was entitled to some financial assistance; such financial assistance, if afforded by the Organization, as it might be, would clearly constitute part of the "expenses of the Organization". The economic problems could not have been covered in advance by a negotiated agreement since they would be unknown until after the event and in the case of non-Member States, which are also included in Article 50, no agreement at all would have been negotiated under Article 43.

Moreover, an argument which insists that all measures taken for the maintenance of international peace and security must be financed through agreements concluded under Article 43, would seem to exclude the possibility that the Security Council might act under some other Article of the Charter. The Court cannot accept so limited a view of the powers of the Security Council under the Charter. It cannot be said that the Charter has left the Security Council impotent in the face of an emergency situation when agreements under Article 43 have not been concluded.

Articles of Chapter VII of the Charter speak of "situations" as well as disputes, and it must lie within the power of the Security Council to police a situation even though it does not resort to enforcement action against a State. The costs of actions which the Security Council is authorized to take constitute "expenses of the Organization within the meaning of Article 17, paragraph 2".

The Court has considered the general problem of the interpretation of Article 17, paragraph 2, in the light of the general structure of the Charter and of the respective functions assigned by the Charter to the General Assembly and to the Security Council, with a view to determining the meaning of the phrase "the expenses of the Organization". The Court does not find it necessary to go further in giving a more detailed definition of such expenses. The Court will, therefore, proceed to examine the expenditures enumerated in the request for the advisory opinion. In determining whether the actual expenditures authorized constitute "expenses of the Organization within the meaning of Article 17, paragraph 2, of the Charter", the Court agrees that such expenditures must be tested by their relationship to the purposes of the United Nations in the sense that if an expenditure were made for a purpose which is not one of the purposes of the United Nations, it could not be considered an "expense of the Organization".

The purposes of the United Nations are set forth in Article 1 of the Charter. The first two purposes as stated in paragraphs 1 and 2, may be summarily described as pointing to the goal of international peace and security and friendly relations. The third purpose is the achievement of economic, social, cultural and humanitarian goals and respect for human rights. The fourth and last purpose is: "To be a center for harmonizing the actions of nations in the attainment of these common ends."

The primary place ascribed to international peace and security is natural, since the fulfilment of the other purposes will be dependent upon the attainment of that basic condition. These purposes are broad indeed, but neither they nor the powers conferred to effectuate them are unlimited. Save as they have entrusted the Organization with the attainment of these common ends, the Member States retain their freedom of action. But when the Organization takes action which warrants the assertion that it was appropriate for the fulfilment of one of the stated purposes of the United Nations, the presumption is that such action is not *ultra vires* the Organization.

If it is agreed that the action in question is within the scope of the functions of the Organization but it is alleged that it has been initiated or carried out in a manner not in conformity with the division of functions among the several organs which the Charter prescribes, one moves to the internal plane, to the internal structure of the Organization. If the action was taken by the wrong organ, it was irregular as a matter of that internal structure, but this would not necessarily mean that the expense incurred was not an expense of the Organization. Both national and international law contemplate cases in which the body corporate or politic may be bound, as to third parties, by an *ultra vires* act of an agent.

In the legal systems of States, there is often some procedure for determining the validity of even a legislative or governmental act, but no analogous procedure is to be found in the structure of the United Nations. Proposals made during the drafting of the Charter to place the ultimate authority to interpret the Charter in the International Court of Justice were not accepted; the opinion which the Court is in course of rendering is an *advisory* opinion. As anticipated in 1945, therefore, each organ must, in the first place at least, determine its own jurisdiction. If the Security Council, for example, adopts a resolution purportedly for the maintenance of international peace and security and if, in accordance with a mandate or authorization in such resolution, the Secretary-General incurs financial obligations, these amounts must be presumed to constitute "expenses of the Organization".

The Financial Regulations and Rules of the United Nations, adopted by the General Assembly, provide:

> "Regulation 4.1: The appropriations voted by the General Assembly shall constitute an authorization to the Secrtary-General to incur obligations and make payments for the purposes for which the appropriations were voted and up to the amounts so voted."

Thus, for example, when the General Assembly in resolution 1619 (XV) included a paragraph reading:

> "3. *Decides* to appropriate an amount of $100 million for the operations of the United Nations in the Congo from 1 January to 31 October 1961",

this constituted an authorization to the Secretary-General to incur certain obligations of the United Nations just as clearly as when in resolution 1590 (XV) the General Assembly used this language:

> "3. *Authorizes* the Secretary-General . . . to incur commitments in 1961 for the United Nations operations in the Congo up to the total of $24 million . . ."

On the previous occasion when the Court was called upon to consider Article 17 of the Charter, the Court found that an award of the Administrative Tribunal of the United Nations created an obligation of the Organization and with relation thereto the Court said that:

> "the function of approving the budget does not mean that the General Assembly has an absolute power to approve or disapprove the expenditure proposed to it; for some part of that expenditure arises out of obligations already incurred by the Organization, and to this extent the General Assembly has no alternative but to honour these engagements". (*Effects of awards of compensation made by the United Nations Administrative Tribunal, I.C.J. Reports 1954,* p. 59.)

Similarly, obligations of the Organization may be incurred by the Secretary-General, acting on the authority of the Security Council or of the General Assembly, and the General Assembly "has no alternative but to honour these engagements".

The obligation is one thing: the way in which the obligation is met—that is from what source the funds are secured—is another. The General Assembly may follow any one of several alternatives: it may apportion the cost of the item according to the ordinary scale of assessment; it may apportion the cost according to some special scale of assessment; it may utilize funds which are voluntarily contributed to the Organization; or it may find some other method or combination of methods for providing the necessary funds. In this context, it is of no legal significance whether, as a matter of book-keeping or accounting, the General Assembly chooses to have the item in question included under one of the standard established sections of the "regular" budget or whether it is separately listed in some special account or fund. The significant fact is that the item is an expense of the Organization and under Article 17, paragraph 2, the General Assembly therefore has authority to apportion it.

The reasoning which has just been developed, applied to the resolutions mentioned in the request for the advisory opinion, might suffice as a basis for the opinion of the Court. The Court finds it appropriate, however, to take into consideration other arguments which have been advanced.

The expenditures enumerated in the request for an advisory opinion may conveniently be examined first with reference to UNEF and then to ONUC. In each case, attention will be paid first to the operations and then to the financing of the operations.

In considering the operations in the Middle East, the Court must analyze the functions of UNEF as set forth in resolutions of the General Assembly. Resolution 998 (ES-I) of 4 November 1956 requested the Secretary-General to submit a plan "for the setting up, with the consent of the nations concerned, of an emergency international United Nations Force to secure and supervise the cessation of hostilities in accordance with all the terms of" the General Assembly's previous resolution 997 (ES-I) of 2 November 1956. The verb "secure" as applied to such matters as halting the movement of military forces and arms into the area and the conclusion of a cease-fire, might suggest measures of enforcement, were it not that the Force was to be set up "with the consent of the nations concerned".

In his first report on the plan for an emergency international Force the Secretary-General used the language of resolution 998 (ES-I) in submitting his proposals. The same terms are used in General Assembly resolution 1000 (ES-I) of 5 November in which operative paragraph 1 reads:

> "*Establishes* a United Nations Command for an emergency international Force to secure and supervise the cessation of hostilities in accordance with all the terms of General Assembly resolution 997 (ES-I) of 2 November 1956."

This resolution was adopted without a dissenting vote. In his second and final report on the plan for an emergency international Force of 6 November, the Secretary-General, in paragraphs 9 and 10, stated:

> "While the General Assembly is enabled to *establish* the Force with the consent of those parties which contribute units to the Force, it could not request the Force to be *stationed* or *operate* on the territory of a given country without the consent of the Government of that country. This does not exclude the possibility that the Security Council could use such a Force within the wider margins provided under

> Chapter VII of the United Nations Charter. I would not for the present consider it necessary to elaborate this point further, since no use of the Force under Chapter VII, with the rights in relation to Member States that this would entail, has been envisaged.
>
> 10. The point just made permits the conclusion that the setting up of the Force should not be guided by the needs which would have existed had the measure been considered as part of an enforcement action directed against a Member country. There is an obvious difference between establishing the Force in order to secure the cessation of hostilities, with a withdrawal of forces, and establishing such a Force with a view to enforcing a withdrawal of forces."

Paragraph 12 of the Report is particularly important because in resolution 1001 (ES-I) the General Assembly, again without a dissenting vote, "*Concurs* in the definition of the functions of the Force as stated in paragraph 12 of the Secretary-General's report". Paragraph 12 reads in part as follows:

> "the functions of the United Nations Force would be, when a cease-fire is being established, to enter Egyptian territory with the consent of the Egyptian Government, in order to help maintain quiet during and after the withdrawal of non-Egyptian troops, and to secure compliance with the other terms established in the resolution of 2 November 1956. The Force obviously should have no rights other than those necessary for the execution of its functions, in co-operation with local authorities. It would be more than an observers' corps, but in no way a military force temporarily controlling the territory in which it is stationed; nor, moreover, should the Force have military functions exceeding those necessary to secure peaceful conditions on the assumption that the parties to the conflict take all necessary steps for compliance with the recommendations of the General Assembly."

It is not possible to find in this description of the functions of UNEF, as outlined by the Secretary-General and concurred in by the General Assembly without a dissenting vote, any evidence that the Force was to be used for purposes of enforcement. Nor can such evidence be found in the subsequent operations of the Force, operations which did not exceed the scope of the functions ascribed to it.

It could not therefore have been patent on the face of the resolution that the establishment of UNEF was in effect "enforcement action" under Chapter VII which, in accordance with the Charter, could be authorized only by the Security Council.

On the other hand, it is apparent that the operations were undertaken to fulfil a prime purpose of the United Nations, that is, to promote and to maintain a peaceful settlement of the situation. This being true, the Secretary-General properly exercised the authority given him to incur financial obligations of the Organization and expenses resulting from such obligations must be considered "expenses of the Organization within the meaning of Article 17, paragraph 2".

Apropos what has already been said about the meaning of the word "action" in Article 11 of the Charter, attention may be called to the fact that resolution 997 (ES-I), which is chronologically the first of the resolutions concerning the operations in the Middle East mentioned in the request for the advisory opinion, provides in paragraph 5:

> "*Requests* the Secretary-General to observe and report promptly on the compliance with the present resolution to the Security Council *and* to the General Assembly, for such further *action as they may deem appropriate in accordance with the Charter.*"

The italicized words reveal an understanding that either of the two organs might take "action" in the premises. Actually, as one knows, the "action" was taken by the General Assembly in adopting two days later without a dissenting vote, resolution 998 (ES-I) and, also without a dissenting vote, within another three days, resolutions 1000 (ES-I) and 1001 (ES-I), all providing for UNEF.

The Court notes that these "actions" may be considered "measures" recommended under Article 14, rather than "action" recommended under Article 11. The powers of the General Assembly stated in Article 14 are not made subject to the provisions of Article 11, but only of Article 12. Furthermore, as the Court has already noted, the word "measures" implies some kind of action. So far as concerns the nature of the situations in the Middle East in 1956, they could be described as "likely to impair . . . friendly relations among nations", just as well as they could be considered to involve "the maintenance of international peace and security". Since the resolutions of the General Assembly in question do not mention upon which article they are based, and since the language used in most of them might imply reference to either Article 14 or Article 11, it cannot be excluded that they were based upon the former rather than the latter article.

The financing of UNEF presented perplexing problems and the debates on these problems have even led to the view that the General Assembly never, either directly or indirectly, regarded the expenses of UNEF as "expenses of the Organization within the meaning of Article 17, paragraph 2, of the Charter". With this interpretation the Court cannot agree. In paragraph 15 of his second and final report on the plan for an emergency international Force of 6 November 1956, the Secretary-General said that this problem required further study. Provisionally, certain costs might be absorbed by a nation providing a unit, "while all other costs should be financed outside the normal budget of the United Nations". Since it was "obviously impossible to make any estimate of the costs without a knowledge of the size of the corps and the length of its assignment", the "only practical course . . . would be for the General Assembly to vote a general authorization for the cost of the Force on the basis of general principles such as those here suggested".

Paragraph 5 of resolution 1001 (ES-I) of 7 November 1956 states that the General Assembly "*Approves provisionally* the basic rule concerning the financing of the Force laid down in paragraph 15 of the Secretary-General's report".

In an oral statement to the plenary meeting of the General Assembly on 26 November 1956, the Secretary-General said:

> ". . . I wish to make it equally clear that while funds received and payments made with respect to the Force are to be considered as coming outside the regular budget of the Organization, the operation is essentially a United Nations responsibility, and the Special Account to be established must, therefore, be construed as coming within the meaning of Article 17 of the Charter".

At this same meeting, after hearing this statement, the General Assembly in resolution 1122 (XI) noted that it had "*provisionally approved* the recommendations made by the Secretary-General concerning the financing of the Force". It then authorized the Secretary-General "to establish a United Nations Emergency Force Special Account to which funds received by the United Nations, outside the regular budget, for the purpose of meeting the expenses of the Force shall be credited and from which payments for this purpose shall be made". The resolution then provided that the initial amount in the Special Account should be $10 million and authorized the Secretary-General "pending the receipt of funds for the Special Account, to advance from the Working Capital Fund such sums as the Special Account may require to meet any expenses chargeable to it". The establishment of a Special Account does not necessarily mean that the funds in it are not to be derived from contributions of Members as apportioned by the General Assembly.

The next of the resolutions of the General Assembly to be considered is 1089 (XI) of 21 December 1956, which reflects the uncertainties and the conflicting views about financing UNEF. The divergencies are duly noted and there is ample reservation concerning possible future action, but operative paragraph 1 follows the recommendation of the Secretary-General "that the expenses relating to the Force should be apportioned in the same manner as the expenses of the Organization". The language of this paragraph is clearly drawn from Article 17:

> "1. *Decides* that the expenses of the United Nations Emergency Force, other than for such pay, equipment, supplies and services as may be furnished without charge by Governments of Member States, shall be borne by the United Nations and shall be apportioned among the Member States, to the extent of $10 million, in accordance with the scale of assessments adopted by the General Assembly for contributions to the annual budget of the Organization for the financial year 1957;"

This resolution, which was adopted by the requisite two-thirds majority, must have rested upon the conclusion that the expenses of UNEF were "expenses of the Organization" since otherwise the General Assembly would have had no authority to decide that they "shall be borne by the United Nations" or to apportion them among the Members. It is further significant that paragraph 3 of this resolution, which established a study committee, charges this committee with the task of examining "the question of the *apportionment* of the expenses of the Force in excess of $10 million . . . and the principle or the formulation of *scales of contributions different from the scale of contributions* by Member States to the ordinary budget for 1957". The italicized words show that it was not contemplated that the committee would consider any method of meeting these expenses except through some form of apportionment although it was understood that a different *scale* might be suggested.

The report of this study committee again records differences of opinion but the draft resolution which it recommended authorized further expenditures and authorized the Secretary-General to advance funds from the Working Capital Fund and to borrow from other funds if necessary; it was adopted as resolution 1090 (XI) by the requisite two-thirds majority on 27 February 1957. In paragraph 4 of that resolution, the General Assembly decided that it would at its twelfth session "consider the basis for financing any costs of the Force in excess of $10 million not covered by voluntary contributions".

Resolution 1151 (XII) of 22 November 1957, while contemplating the receipt of more voluntary contributions, decided in paragraph 4 that the expenses authorized "shall be borne by the Members of the United Nations in accordance with the scales of assessments adopted by the General Assembly for the financial years 1957 and 1958 respectively".

Almost a year later, on 14 November 1958, in resolution 1263 (XIII) the General Assembly, while "*Noting with satisfaction* the effective way in which the Force continues to carry out its function", requested the Fifth Committee "to recommend such action as may be necessary to finance this continuing operation of the United Nations Emergency Force".

After further study, the provision contained in paragraph 4 of the resolution of 22 November 1957 was adopted in paragraph 4 of resolution 1337 (XIII) of 13 December 1958. Paragraph 5 of that resolution requested "the Secretary-General to consult with the Governments of Member States with respect to their views concerning the manner of financing the Force in the future, and to submit a report together with the replies to the General Assembly at its fourteenth session". Thereafter a new plan was worked out for the utilization of any voluntary contributions, but resolution 1441 (XIV) of 5 December 1959, in paragraph 2: "*Decides* to assess the amount of $20 million against all Members of the United Nations on the basis of the regular scale of assessments" subject to the use of credits drawn from voluntary contributions. Resolution 1575 (XV) of 20 December 1960 is practically identical.

The Court concludes that, from year to year, the expenses of UNEF have been treated by the General Assembly as expenses of the Organization within the meaning of Article 17, paragraph 2, of the Charter.

The operations in the Congo were initially authorized by the Security Council in the resolution of 14 July 1960 which was adopted without a dissenting vote. The resolution, in the light of the appeal from the Government of the Congo, the report of the Secretary-General and the debate in the Security Council, was clearly adopted with a view to maintaining international peace and security. However, it is argued that that resolution has been implemented in violation of provisions of the Charter inasmuch as under the Charter it is the Security Council that determines which States are to participate in carrying out decisions involving the maintenance of international peace and security, whereas in the case of the Congo the Secretary-General himself determined which States were to participate with their armed forces or otherwise.

By paragraph 2 of the resolution of 14 July 1960 the Security Council "*Decides* to authorize the Secretary-General to take the necessary steps, in consultation with the Government of the Republic of the Congo, to provide the Government with such military assistance as may be necessary". Paragraph 3 requested the Secretary-General "to report to the Security Council as appropriate". The Secretary-General made his first report on 18 July and in it informed the Security Council which States he had asked to contribute forces or matériel, which ones had complied, the size of the units which had already arrived in the Congo (a total of some 3,500 troops), and some detail about further units expected.

On 22 July the Security Council by unanimous vote adopted a further resolution in which the preamble states that it had considered this report of the Secretary-General and appreciated "the work of the Secretary-General and the support so readily and so speedily given to him by all Member States invited by him to give assistance". In operative paragraph 3, the Security Council "*Commends* the Secretary-General for the prompt action he has taken to carry out resolution S/4387 of the Security Council, and for his first report".

On 9 August the Security Council adopted a further resolution without a dissenting vote in which it took note of the second report and of an oral statement of the Secretary-General and in operative paragraph 1: "*Confirms* the authority given to the Secretary-General by the Security Council resolutions of 14 July and 22 July 1960 and requests him to continue to carry out the responsibility placed on him thereby". This emphatic ratification is further supported by operative paragraphs 5 and 6 by which all Member States were called upon "to afford mutual assistance" and the Secretary-General was requested "to implement this resolution and to report further to the Council as appropriate".

The Security Council resolutions of 14 July, 22 July and 9 August 1960 were noted by the General Assembly in its resolution 1474 (ES-IV) of

20 September, adopted without a dissenting vote, in which it "fully supports" these resolutions. Again without a dissenting vote, on 21 February 1961 the Security Council reaffirmed its three previous resolutions "and the General Assembly resolution 1474 (ES-IV) of 20 September 1960" and reminded "all States of their obligations under these resolutions".

Again without a dissenting vote on 24 November 1961 the Security Council, once more recalling the previous resolutions, reaffirmed "the policies and purposes of the United Nations with respect to the Congo (Leopoldville) as set out" in those resolutions. Operative paragraphs 4 and 5 of this resolution renew the authority to the Secretary-General to continue the activities in the Congo.

In the light of such a record of reiterated consideration, confirmation, approval and ratification by the Security Council and by the General Assembly of the actions of the Secretary-General in implementing the resolution of 14 July 1960, it is impossible to reach the conclusion that the operations in question usurped or impinged upon the prerogatives conferred by the Charter on the Security Council. The Charter does not forbid the Security Council to act through instruments of its own choice: under Article 29 it "may establish such subsidiary organs as it deems necessary for the performance of its functions"; under Article 98 it may entrust "other functions" to the Secretary-General.

It is not necessary for the Court to express an opinion as to which article or articles of the Charter were the basis for the resolutions of the Security Council, but it can be said that the operations of ONUC did not include a use of armed force against a State which the Security Council, under Article 39, determined to have committed an act of aggression or to have breached the peace. The armed forces which were utilized in the Congo were not authorized to take military action against any State. The operation did not involve "preventive or enforcement measures" against any State under Chapter VII and therefore did not constitute "action" as that term is used in Article 11.

For the reasons stated, financial obligations which, in accordance with the clear and reiterated authority of both the Security Council and the General Assembly, the Secretary-General incurred on behalf of the United Nations, constitute obligations of the Organization for which the General Assembly was entitled to make provision under the authority of Article 17.

In relation to ONUC, the first action concerning the financing of the operation was taken by the General Assembly on 20 December 1960, after the Security Council had adopted its resolutions of 14 July, 22 July and 9 August, and the General Assembly had adopted its supporting resolution of 20 September. This resolution 1583 (XV) of 20 December referred to the report of the Secretary-General on the estimated cost of the Congo operations from 14 July to 31 December 1960, and to the recommendations of the Advisory Committee on Administrative and Budgetary Questions.

It decided to establish an *ad hoc* account for the expenses of the United Nations in the Congo. It also took note of certain waivers of cost claims and then decided to apportion the sum of $48.5 million among the Member States "on the basis of the regular scale of assessment" subject to certain exceptions. It made this decision because in the preamble it had already recognized:

> "that the expenses involved in the United Nations operations in the Congo for 1960 constitute 'expenses of the Organization' within the meaning of Article 17, paragraph 2, of the Charter of the United Nations and that the assessment thereof against Member States creates binding legal obligations on such States to pay their assessed shares".

By its further resolution 1590 (XV) of the same day, the General Assembly authorized the Secretary-General "to incur commitments in 1961 for the United Nations operations in the Congo up to the total of $24 million for the period from 1 January to 31 March 1961". On 3 April 1961, the General Assembly authorized the Secretary-General to continue until 21 April "to incur commitments for the United Nations operations in the Congo at a level not to exceed $8 million per month".

Importance has been attached to the statement included in the preamble of General Assembly resolution 1619 (XV) of 21 April 1961 which reads:

> "*Bearing in mind* that the extraordinary expenses for the United Nations operations in the Congo are essentially different in nature from the expenses of the Organization under the regular budget and that therefore a procedure different from that applied in the case of the regular budget is required for meeting these extraordinary expenses."

However, the same resolution in operative paragraph 4:

> "*Decides further* to apportion as expenses of the Organization the amount of $100 million among the Member States in accordance with the scale of assessment for the regular budget subject to the provisions of paragraph 8 below [paragraph 8 makes certain adjustments for Member States assessed at the lowest rates or who receive certain designated technical assistance], pending the establishment of a different scale of assessment to defray the extraordinary expenses of the Organization resulting from these operations."

Although it is not mentioned in the resolution requesting the advisory opinion, because it was adopted at the same meeting of the General Assembly, it may be noted that the further resolution 1732 (XVI) of 20 December 1961 contains an identical paragraph in the preamble and a comparable operative paragraph 4 on apportioning $80 million.

The conclusion to be drawn from these paragraphs is that the General Assembly has twice decided that even though certain expenses are "extraordinary" and "essentially different" from those under the "regular budget", they are none the less "expenses of the Organization" to be apportioned in accordance with the power granted to the General Assembly by Article 17, paragraph 2. This conclusion is strengthened by the concluding clause of paragraph 4 of the two resolutions just cited which states that the decision therein to use the scale of assessment already adopted for the regular budget is made "pending the establishment of a *different scale of assessment* to defray the extraordinary expenses". The only alternative—and that means the "different procedure"—contemplated was another *scale* of assessment and not some method other than assessment. "Apportionment" and "assessment" are terms which relate only to the General Assembly's authority under Article 17.

At the outset of this opinion, the Court pointed out that the text of Article 17, paragraph 2, of the Charter could lead to the simple conclusion that "the expenses of the Organization" are the amounts paid out to defray the costs of carrying out the purposes of the Organization. It was further indicated that the Court would examine the resolutions authorizing the expenditures referred to in the request for the advisory opinion in order to ascertain whether they were incurred with that end in view. The Court has made such an examination and finds that they were so incurred. The Court has also analyzed the principal arguments which have been advanced against the conclusion that the expenditures in question should be considered as "expenses of the Organization within the meaning of Article 17, paragraph 2, of the Charter of the United Nations", and has found that these arguments are unfounded. Consequently, the Court arrives at the conclusion that the question submitted to it in General Assembly resolution 1731 (XVI) must be answered in the affirmative.

For these reasons,

THE COURT IS OF OPINION,

by nine votes to five,

that the expenditures authorized in General Assembly resolutions 1583 (XV) and 1590 (XV) of 20 December 1960, 1595 (XV) of 3 April 1961, 1619 (XV) of 21 April 1961 and 1633 (XVI) of 30 October 1961 relating to the United Nations operations in the Congo undertaken in pursuance of the Security Council resolutions of 14 July, 22 July and 9 August 1960 and 21 February and 24 November 1961, and General Assembly resolutions 1474 (ES-IV) of 20 September 1960 and 1599 (XV), 1600 (XV) and 1601 (XV) of 15 April 1961, and the expenditures authorized in General Assembly resolutions 1122 (XI) of 26 November 1956, 1089 (XI) of 21 December 1956, 1090 (XI) of 27 February 1957, 1151 (XII) of 22 November 1957, 1204 (XII) of 13 December 1957, 1337 (XIII) of 13 December 1958, 1441 (XIV) of 5 December 1959 and 1575 (XV) of 20 December 1960 relating to the operations of the United Nations Emergency Force undertaken in pursuance of General Assembly resolutions 997 (ES-I) of 2 November 1956, 998 (ES-I) and 999 (ES-I) of 4 November 1956, 1000(ES-I) of 5 November 1956, 1001 (ES-I) of 7 November 1956, 1121(XI) of 24 November 1956 and 1263(XIII) of 14 November 1958, constitute "expenses of the Organization" within the meaning of Article 17, paragraph 2, of the Charter of the United Nations.

Judge Spiropoulos accompanied his concurrence in the majority opinion by a brief declaration.[5] Judges Sir Percy Spender, Sir Gerald Fitzmaurice and Morelli appended statements of their separate opinions. President Winiarski and Judges Basdevant, Moreno Quintana, Koretsky and Bustamante y Rivero each gave a dissenting opinion.

In his concurring opinion, Sir Percy Spender urged that the Court "ought not . . . go beyond the limits of what is reasonably necessary to permit it to answer the question," and concluded that it was not "necessary to express any opinion upon the validity or regularity of the resolutions pursuant to which the operations in the Congo and the Middle East were undertaken." Looking at Article 17 of the Charter, he stated:

> The word "budget" in Article 17 (1) covers all finance requirements of the Organization and the word "expenses" in Article 17(2) covers all expenditure which may be incurred on behalf of the Organization, which gives effect to the purposes of the United Nations. There is, upon the proper interpretation of Article 17, no legal basis for confining these words to what has been described as "normal", "ordinary", "administrative" or "essential" costs and expenditure, whatever precisely these terms may denote. The expenditures referred to in the question put to the Court were of a character which could qualify them as incurred in order to give effect to the purposes of the Organization. It was in these circumstances for the General Assembly, and for it alone, to determine, as it did, whether these expenditures did qualify as those of the Organization and to deal with them pursuant to its powers under Article 17(2).
>
> Once the General Assembly has passed upon what are the expenses of the Organization, and it is apparent that the expenditure incurred and to be incurred on behalf of the Organization is in furtherance of its purposes, their character as such and any apportionment thereof made by the General Assembly under Article 17(2) of the Charter cannot legally be challenged by any Member State. . . .
>
> It is, moreover, evident that once the Secretary-General, who, under Article 98 of the Charter, is bound to perform such functions as the General Assembly or the Security Council may entrust him with, is called upon by either organ to discharge certain functions, as he was in respect to the operations in both the Congo and the Middle East, and in discharging them he engages the credit of the Organization and on its behalf incurs financial obligations, then, unless the resolution

[5] Judge Spiropoulos declared that the General Assembly resolutions authorizing the financing of the operations in the Middle East and the Congo created obligations on the Members, but declined to express an opinion on the conformity with the Charter of the several resolutions relating to the United Nations operations in the Middle East and the Congo, because the General Assembly rejection of the French amendment offered to the resolution asking the advisory opinion showed "the desire of the Assembly that the conformity or non-conformity of the decisions of the Assembly and of the Security Council concerning the United Nations operations in the Congo and the Middle East should not be examined by the Court."

> under which he acts, or what he does, is unconnected with the furtherance of the purposes of the Organization, the moneys involved may properly be dealt with by the General Assembly as "expenses of the Organization". Once they have been, the action of the General Assembly would not be open to challenge by a Member State even if the resolutions under which he was called upon to act were not in conformity with the Charter and even if he should exceed the authority conferred upon him. . . .[6]

In his careful concurring opinion, Sir Gerald Fitzmaurice expressed some of his "reservations on certain points of principle having wider implications, though they do not affect the final conclusion reached in the present case." In the majority opinion, he "would have preferred to see less reliance on practice and more on ordinary reasoning." He would examine carefully what expenditures fall within the category of "expenses" and are also "validly incurred, for a purpose which was itself valid and legitimate." He could not accept the position that merely because an expense had been apportioned by the General Assembly, it was automatically validated. But as a "*de facto* solution" he accepted the proposition that

> when, on the basis of an item which has been regularly placed on the agenda, and has gone through the normal procedural stages, the Assembly, after due discussion, adopts by the necessary two-thirds majority, a resolution authorizing or apportioning certain expenditures incurred, or to be incurred, in the apparent furtherance of the purposes of the Organization, there must arise at the least a strong *prima facie* presumption that these expenditures are valid and proper ones.

"Expenses of the Organization" would include:

> A. All those expenditures, or categories of expenditures, which have

[6] Explaining his ideas of interpretation, Sir Percy Spender said: "The cardinal rule of interpretation that this Court and its predecessor has stated should be applied is that words are to be read, if they may so be read, in their ordinary and natural sense. If so read they make sense, that is the end of the matter. If, however, so read they are ambiguous or lead to an unreasonable result, then and then only must the Court, by resort to other methods of interpretation, seek to ascertain what the parties really meant when they used the words under consideration. . . ."

He pointed to the difficulties in looking to the intention of the parties, particularly when a multilateral treaty, and especially one to which later parties might adhere, is in question. Of such a treaty as the Charter, he said: "It may with confidence be asserted that its particular provisions should receive a broad and liberal interpretation unless the context of any particular provision requires, or there is to be found elsewhere in the Charter, something to compel a narrower and restricted interpretation." He added: "Despite current tendencies to the contrary the first task of the Court is to look, not at the *travaux préparatoires* or the practice which hitherto has been followed within the Organization, but at the terms of the Charter itself. . . . The purpose pervading the whole of the Charter and dominating it is that of maintaining international peace and security and to that end the taking of effective collective measures for the prevention and removal of threats to the peace. Interpretation of the Charter should be directed to giving effect to that purpose, not to frustrate it. . . ."

normally formed part of the *regular* budget of the Organization, so that a settled practice (*pratique constante*) of treating them as expenses of the Organization has become established, and is tacitly acquiesced in by all Member States.

B. *In so far as not already covered by head A:*

I. administrative expenditures;

II. expenditures arising in the course, or out of the performance by the Organization of its functions under the Charter;

III. any payments which the Organization is legally responsible for making in relation to third parties; or which it is otherwise, as an entity, under a legal obligation to make; or is bound to make in order to meet its extraneous legal obligations.

Turning to heading "B.II," he said:

There are broadly two main classes of functions which the Organization performs under the Charter—those which it has a duty to carry out, and those which are more or less permissive in character. Peace-keeping, dispute-settling and, indeed, most of the political activities of the Organization would come under the former head; many of what might be called its social and economic activities might come under the latter. Expenses incurred in relation to the first set of activities are therefore true expenses, which the Organization has no choice but to incur in order to carry out a duty, and an essential

---

He added: "The nature of the authority granted by the Charter to each of its organs does not change with time. The ambit or scope of the authority conferred may nonetheless comprehend ever changing circumstances and conditions and embrace, as history unfolds itself, new problems and situations which were not and could not have been envisaged when the Charter came into being. The Charter must accordingly be interpreted, whilst in no way deforming or dislocating its language, so that the authority conferred upon the Organization and its various organs may attach itself to new and unanticipated situations and events."

Although admitting that it is "a general principle of international law that the subsequent conduct of the parties to a bilateral—or a multilateral—instrument may throw light on the intention of the parties at the time the instrument was entered into and thus may provide a legitimate criterion in interpretation," he found difficulty "in accepting the proposition that a practice pursued by an *organ* of the United Nations may be equated with the subsequent conduct of *parties* to a bilateral agreement and thus afford evidence of intention of the parties to the Charter (who have constantly been added to since it came into force) and in that way or otherwise provide a criterion of interpretation. Nor can I agree with a view sometimes advanced that a common practice pursued by an organ of the United Nations, though *ultra vires* and in point of fact having the result of amending the Charter, may nonetheless be effective as a criterion of interpretation." This was particularly true when a minority of members of the organ opposed the decision reached by a majority. He concluded:

"The question of constitutionality of action taken by the General Assembly or the Security Council will rarely call for consideration except within the United Nations itself, where a majority rule prevails. In practice this may enable action to be taken which is beyond power. When, however, the Court is called upon to pronounce upon a question whether certain authority exercised by an organ of the Organization is within the power of that organ, only legal considerations may be invoked and *de facto* extension of the Charter must be disregarded."

function which it is bound to perform. . . . Even without Article 17, paragraph 2, the Organization could require Member States to contribute to these expenses.

. . . Even if it should be the case (and on this I do not express any final view) that there is no positive obligation to contribute to the expenses of carrying out social and economic activities of a permissive character (except for Member States supporting or not opposing the activity concerned), I consider that where such an activity is closely connected with, arises out of, and, in short, is basically part of a peace-keeping endeavour, and necessary for, or directly contributory to the success of that endeavour, the activity in question takes on the nature of an essential activity, the expenses of which are expenses of the Organization to which all Member States are bound to contribute, irrespective of their votes.

Consequently, my concurrence in the Opinion of the Court extends no less to the civil than to the military expenditures incurred under the Resolutions specified in the Request.

Judge Morelli summarized his concurring opinion as follows:

(1) "Expenses of the Organization", within the meaning of Article 17, paragraph 2, of the Charter are expenses which have been *validly* authorized by the General Assembly under paragraph 1 of that Article;

(2) The resolutions in which the General Assembly authorized the expenditures relating to the Emergency Force and the operations in the Congo are *valid* resolutions, irrespective of the validity of the General Assembly and Security Council resolutions by which the Emergency Force was established and the operations in the Congo decided upon;

(3) Consequently, the expenditures relating to the Emergency Force and the operations in the Congo constitute "expenses of the Organization" within the meaning of Article 17, paragraph 2, of the Charter.

In his dissenting opinion, President Winiarski thought it necessary to examine the conformity with the Charter of the resolutions authorizing the expenditures. He stated:

The Charter has set forth the purposes of the United Nations in very wide, and for that reason too indefinite, terms. But—apart from the resources, including the financial resources, of the Organization—it does not follow, far from it, that the Organization is entitled to seek to achieve those purposes by no matter what means. The fact that an organ of the United Nations is seeking to achieve one of those purposes does not suffice to render its action lawful. The Charter, a multilateral treaty which was the result of prolonged and laborious negotiations, carefully created organs and determined their competence and means of action.

The intention of those who drafted it was clearly to abandon the possibility of useful action rather than to sacrifice the balance of carefully established fields of competence, as can be seen, for example, in the case of the voting in the Security Council. It is only by such procedures, which were clearly defined, that the United Nations can seek to achieve its purposes. It may be that the United Nations is sometimes not in a position to undertake action which would be useful for the maintenance of international peace and security or for one or another of the purposes indicated in Article 1 of the Charter, but that is the way in which the Organization was conceived and brought into being. . . .

Reliance has been placed upon practice as providing justification for an affirmative answer to the question submitted to the Court. The technical budgetary practice of the Organization has no bearing upon the question, which is a question of law. . . . if a practice is introduced without opposition in the relations between the contracting parties, this may bring about, at the end of a certain period, a modification of a treaty rule, but in that event the very process of the formation of the new rule provides the guarantee of the consent of the parties. In the present case the controversy arose practically from the beginning in 1956. . . .

In respect of the financing of the United Nations operations in the Congo, the General Assembly resolutions decided that the expenses should be apportioned among the Member States according to the ordinary scale of assessments, but these resolutions . . . were not followed and the number of Member States which refuse to pay is too large for it to be possible to disregard the legal significance of this fact. I would recall that the military operations in Korea were paid for by voluntary contributions as were a number of "civilian" operations in which there is also to be discerned a certain connection with international peace and security. It is therefore difficult to assert, in the case before the Court, either that practice can furnish a canon of construction warranting an affirmative answer to the question addressed to the Court, or that it may have contributed to the establishment of a legal rule particular to the Organization, created *praeter legem,* and, still less, that it can have done so *contra legem.*

. . .

. . . in the case referred to the Court, it is established that some at least of the Member States refuse to comply with the decisions of the General Assembly because they dispute the conformity of those decisions with the Charter. Apparently they are of opinion that the resolutions cannot be relied upon as against them although they may be valid and binding in respect of other States. What is therefore involved is the validity of the Assembly's resolutions in respect of those States, or the right to rely upon them as against those States.

. . .

A refusal to pay, as in the case before the Court, may be regarded by a Member State, loyal and indeed devoted to the Organization, as the only means of protesting against a resolution of the majority which, in its opinion, disregards the true meaning of the Charter and adopts in connection with it a decision which is legally invalid; in such a case it constitutes a grave symptom indicative of serious disagreement as to the interpretation of the Charter. . . .

A serious legal objection to the validity of the General Assembly resolutions authorizing and apportioning the expenses may be briefly formulated as follows: these resolutions ignore the fact that the resolutions authorizing the operations have the character of recommendations. By levying contributions to meet the cost of the operations from all States in accordance with Article 17, paragraph 2, the resolutions of the General Assembly appear to disregard the fundamental difference between the decisions of the Security Council which are binding on all Member States (Chapter VII of the Charter) and recommendations which are not binding except on States which have accepted them.

. . .

The difference between binding decisions and recommendations constitutes one of the bases of the whole structure of the Charter. Decisions are the exception in the system of the means provided for the maintenance of international peace and security; they are taken in grave cases and it is only in those cases that Member States have consented to accept the necessary limitation of the exercise of their sovereignty. Recommendations are never binding and the United Nations must in all its activities ever have in view that its means of action are thus limited.

. . . it is apparent that the resolutions approving and apportioning these expenses are valid and binding only in respect of the Member States which have accepted the recommendations.

It is difficult to see by what process of reasoning recommendations could be held to be binding on States which have not accepted them. It is difficult to see how it can be conceived that a recommendation is partially binding, and that on what is perhaps the most vital point, the financial contribution levied by the General Assembly under the conditions of paragraph 2 of Article 17. It is no less difficult to see at what point in time the transformation of a non-binding recommendation into a partially binding recommendation is supposed to take place, at what point in time a legal obligation is supposed to come into being for a Member State which has not accepted it.

In an elaborate dissenting opinion Judge Koretsky explained his dissent, believing that the Court should not have given any advisory opinion, that it reached the wrong conclusions, and that the validity or compatibility with the Charter of the several actions was crucial.[7] He criticized the majority opinion because it "limits the powers of the Security Council and enlarges the sphere of the General Assembly. The Opinion achieves this by (a) converting the recommendations that the General Assembly may make into some kind of 'action', and (b) reducing this action, for which the Security Council has the authority, to 'enforcement or coercive action', particularly against aggression." After long discussion of the practice of the United Nations, he stated:

Even the fact that those expenses have never been included in the regular budget proves that it is impossible to argue that these expenses might be apportioned under Article 17, paragraph 2, of the

[7] Judge Koretsky criticized in detail the U.N. actions with respect to the Middle East and the Congo, beginning with the Nov. 4, 1956, General Assembly resolution, which he found at fault in that it directed the Secretary General to secure the cessation of hostilities, and that the General Assembly "has assumed a task of setting up the United Nations Force. One should state that the Charter does not include such a

> Charter. It has been said more than once that peace-keeping operations should be financed in another way.
>
> At the San Francisco Conference the necessity was at any rate realized of establishing a special procedure for assessment of eventual expenditures for operations of this kind. It is the Security Council which has, first of all, to decide about the financial implications of concrete peace-keeping operations. Article 43 gave directives as to how to arrange financial questions which might arise from these operations. Article 17 has nothing to do with these questions unless the Security Council should ask that necessary measures be taken by the General Assembly.
>
> One cannot consider that decisions of the Security Council regarding the participation of any Member State in concrete peace-keeping operations are not obligatory for a given Member. Its obligation to participate in a decided operation was based on Articles 25 and 48 of the Charter. Agreements envisaged in Article 43 proceed from this general obligation. Article 43 says that all Members undertake to make available to the Security Council *on its call* armed forces, etc. Agreements must (not may) specify the terms of participation, the size of armed forces to be made available, the character of assistance, etc., envisaging all the ensuing financial consequences as well. The General Assembly may only *recommend* measures. Expenses which might arise from such recommendations should not lead to an obligatory apportionment of them among all Members of the United Nations. That would mean to convert a non-mandatory recommendation of the General Assembly into a mandatory decision; this would be to proceed against the Charter, against logic and even against common sense.
>
> This applies even more to resolutions adopted not in conformity with the Charter. It is not within the power of the General Assembly "to cure" the invalidity of its resolutions enumerated in the Request by approving the financial provisions of these resolutions.

Judge Basdevant dissented because of his "conviction that the request for opinion has not been presented in a proper fashion." He pointed out that, under Article 65 of the Court's Statute, requests asking an advisory opinion must contain "an exact statement of the question upon

---

notion as a United Nations Armed Force. Even the Security Council itself is not authorized to set it up."

He pointed out further that "The whole history of financing the United Nations operations in the Middle East, mentioned above, shows that in no case could it have been carried out according to the regular scale of assessments, as those operations had an anti-Charter but at the same time a peace-keeping character." He added that "if, in regard to the operations in the Middle East, one could state that they were implemented *ultra vires*, beyond the powers permitted to the General Assembly by the Charter, then, regarding the operations in the Congo, we may say that they were carried out *ultra vires* as well as *ultra terms* of the mandates given to the Secretary-General."

Explaining his views on interpretation, he said: "I am prepared to stress the necessity of the strict observation and proper interpretation of the provisions of the Charter, its rules, without limiting itself by reference to the purposes of the Organization; otherwise one would have to come to the long ago condemned formula: 'The ends justify the means'."

which an opinion is required." The request did not specifically ask whether the expenditures had been properly authorized; no criteria were laid down by which the Court might determine whether "expenditures authorized" were "expenses of the Organization." Furthermore, the request related only to expenditures authorized prior to December 31, 1961, and did not ask the Court for "guidance to the other principal organs of the United Nations on what should be done in respect of their undertakings in the Congo and in the matter of the Emergency Force. Where it would have been possible to obtain from an opinion requested of the Court collaboration in the present work of the United Nations, it has been sought to obtain from the Court only a retrospective evaluation of what was done up to the end of 1961."

Judge Moreno Quintana emphasized in his dissenting opinion that:

> The exercise of the right to administer world affairs goes together with the duty of furnishing the necessary means for the accomplishment of that duty. It is therefore the obligation of the Members of the Security Council to pay the expenses incurred by such operations as those in the Middle East and the Congo.
>
> Hence, a legal interpretation of the provision in question leads to the view that the expenses referred to in Article 17, paragraph 2, of the Charter are the current administrative expenses of the Organization, and not other expenditure such as that resulting from the undertaking of operations by military forces.

He concluded also that "The circumstances in which the question put to the Court in the request for an advisory opinion is worded do not, in view of the resulting limitation of its competence, permit the Court conscientiously to accomplish its task in the present case."

Judge Bustamante's dissenting opinion starts with the view that it is essential to determine whether the resolutions with respect to action in the Middle East and the Congo conform to the Charter, and in general he appears to believe that they do. However, he would require that appropriate organs of the United Nations determine the legality of these actions before the Court could answer the question properly. He said, in part:

> . . . in principle, I am of opinion that expenditures validly authorized by the competent organ for the carrying out of an armed action with the purpose of maintaining international peace and security constitute "expenses of the Organization". But in the case of the expenditures authorized for the operations in the Middle East and the Congo, it is for the competent organ of the United Nations to pronounce on the legal objections put forward by certain States against the relevant resolutions. Only after this pronouncement on the legality or the non-legality of these resolutions would, in my opinion, a reply to the request be possible.
>
> In consequence, I conclude that the expenditures referred to in the request for an advisory opinion would constitute expenses of the Organization if, after consideration of the legal objections raised by certain Member States, the competent organ of the United Nations succeeds in determining as *legal* and *valid* the resolutions by virtue of which the expenses in question were incurred.

Since this definition has not been given and having regard to the limitations of the request, the Court—in my view—cannot declare whether the expenditures in question are or are not expenses of the Organization within the meaning of Article 17, paragraph 2, of the Charter. But if the Court must in voting reply categorically "yes" or "no" to the question put in the request, my reply can only be negative for, according to the foregoing, I am not in a position to assume the responsibility for an affirmative characterization of the legality of the expenditures.

NOTES AND QUESTIONS

1. For an analysis of the Advisory Opinion, see Leo Gross, "Expense of the United Nations for Peace-Keeping Operations: The Advisory Opinion of the International Court of Justice," *International Organization*, vol. XVII (Winter, 1963) pp. 1–35; see also, James F. Hogg, "Peace-Keeping Costs and Charter Obligations—Implications of the International Court of Justice Decision on Certain Expenses of the United Nations," *Columbia Law Review*, vol. LXII (November, 1962) pp. 1230–1263.
2. The General Assembly did adopt, by a vote of 76-17-8, a resolution "accepting" the majority opinion. The debates indicated that it was not clear exactly what was being adopted. What does it mean to "adopt" advice?
3. What does it mean to call the opinion of the Court "advisory"? How does this question relate to the discussion of the authority of the General Assembly "recommendations" to create obligations? See Chapter 5. What is the relation between community consensus and legal obligations?
4. What does the opinion in the case of *Certain Expenses* disclose about the limits of the adjudicative process? Can political controversies be fractionated into legal issues? Was the question put to the World Court a polycentric question in the sense meant by Lon Fuller? See Chapter 8. Was it desirable or undesirable to request an Advisory Opinion? Do you think that it has enhanced the prestige or relevance of the Court as a principal organ of the United Nations? How would Clark and Sohn handle this sort of question in their judicial and conciliation system? See Article 96(3) in the Clark-Sohn Charter. Does this authoritative power to interpret the Charter—that is, authority vested in the Court—betray an excessive confidence in the adjudicative process, given the system of order that is projected? Recall the famous response of President Andrew Jackson to the United States Supreme Court: "John Marshall has made his decision, now let him enforce it." Might not the same situation exist, but in accentuated form in the Clark-Sohn world?
5. For a study of the financing of peace-keeping operations, past and future, see Derek Bowett, *United Nations Forces* (Praeger, New York, 1964) pp. 468–483. Bowett's final sentence in the relevant chapter confirms the characterization of the existing financial crisis of the Organization as a so-called financing problem: "the argument that the finance is not available is, as such, nonsensical; it means no more than that the *will* to finance the operations is not present." (p. 483.)

B. The Financing Problem

If we conceive of life in a drastically altered international system with a large UN Police Force and a World Development Authority having a budget of up to 50 billion dollars per year, then the need to have assured sources of revenue is indeed significant, and not only for political reasons, but for fiscal reasons as well. Clark and Sohn envisage a very large budget for the United Nations and propose a quite elaborate revenue system to finance it. See Annex V, pp. 349–358, and **IV-6**.

The Clark-Sohn plan combines a number of considerations. The result is a very complicated scheme for fixing the budget and creating a scale of assessments. First, there is a complete acceptance of the role of the United Nations as an autonomous actor; it must be able to obtain payment from all Members, whether or not they approve of the particular policies undertaken by the Organization. Second, there are various checks upon the danger that the Organization might aggrandize and take for itself too great a functional role in world affairs. There are also limits upon what any one Member may be asked to contribute. The budget ceiling for the Organization, except for emergency financing, is fixed at 2 per cent of the value of the world gross product. Furthermore, states are given some discretion in deciding how to raise the revenue to meet their assessed obligations. Third, the revenue is to be raised by direct assessment of individuals, thereby involving both the nation-state in the revenue-raising process and individuals in a direct fiscal relationship to the Organization. Fourth, Clark and Sohn present a complicated formula for assessments on the basis of an ability to pay scale. Fifth, various devices are introduced into the procedures for the allocation of funds by the World Development Authority and elsewhere in the structure to give the states contributing most of the revenue to the Organization a proportionately larger influence in forming policy to govern the use of funds than the smaller contributors.

Is this "an acceptable package" for financing in the Clark-Sohn world? Is it workable once established? Is it fair in its distribution of functions and powers? Is it more objectionable to some nations than to others? Would some nations be reluctant to assume such heavy burdens? Which ones would need most convincing? How could the Clark-Sohn plan be changed to make it appear more acceptable to the main groupings of states in the world today? How can they be convinced that this aspect of transition is in their interests?

The next selection is a very careful article by Norman J. Padelford on the financial crisis, "Financial Crisis and the Future of the United Nations," *World Politics*, vol. XV, no. 4 (July, 1963) pp. 531–568. Padelford offers a series of suggestions for mitigating, if not overcoming it. The value of the article is to disclose in a highly competent fashion the characteristics of the real financing problem. This gives a basis for an intelligent analysis of both the "so-called financing problem" that presently faces the United Nations, and the real financing problems that must be solved in the Clark-Sohn world. As such, it clarifies the character of a strategy for the transition period.

FINANCIAL CRISIS AND THE FUTURE OF THE UNITED NATIONS*

By NORMAN J. PADELFORD

THE financial difficulties of the United Nations have become one of the pressing issues of contemporary international affairs. They have roots that extend to the heart of the politics of the Organization and its procedure. Beyond this they raise serious questions about the ability of the institution to function effectively in the future. To grasp the complex problems associated with the UN financial situation it is necessary to view the matter in some perspective.

I. Overall Expenses of the United Nations

The United Nations is no exception to the general rule that it costs money to run deliberative bodies and operating programs. As in the national scene, the UN has also found itself confronted with appeals and demands that have resulted in rising expenditures and the need for appealing for ever larger contributions. From an initial operating budget of $25 million, the expenditures of the United Nations and the affiliated Specialized Agencies have risen to $480 million in 1962.[1]

These comprise the assessments for the Regular Budget, the Specialized Agencies, and the peace-keeping operations in the Middle East and the Congo, together with voluntary contributions for the special voluntary programs such as the Expanded Program of Technical Assistance and the Special Fund. The relationship of these component expenses is shown in Figure 1. This of course does not represent the entire

* The author is indebted to the Brookings Institution for permission to draw upon data developed for its recent project on the United Nations Financing System. He is also appreciative of assistance by Richard H. Solomon, Catherine McArdle, and Margaret Windus on the research and computations.

[1] The most generally useful sources on UN finances are the Annual Reports of the Advisory Committee on Administrative and Budgetary Questions to the General Assembly, the Financial Reports and Accounts for each calendar year combined with the Report of the Board of Auditors, and the Official Records of the Fifth Committee of the General Assembly on Administrative and Budgetary Questions. Much useful information will also be found in the Hearings before the Committee on Foreign Affairs, House of Representatives, 87th Congress, 2nd Session, on S. 2768, a Bill to Promote the Foreign Policy of the United States by authorizing the Purchase of United Nations Bonds and the Appropriation of Funds therefor, June 27 to July 26, 1962 (cited hereinafter as *Purchase of United Nations Bonds*). See also Norman J. Padelford, *The Rising Cost of United Nations Membership* (Cambridge, M.I.T. Center for International Studies, C/63-2, 1963), one of a series of papers prepared for the Brookings project.

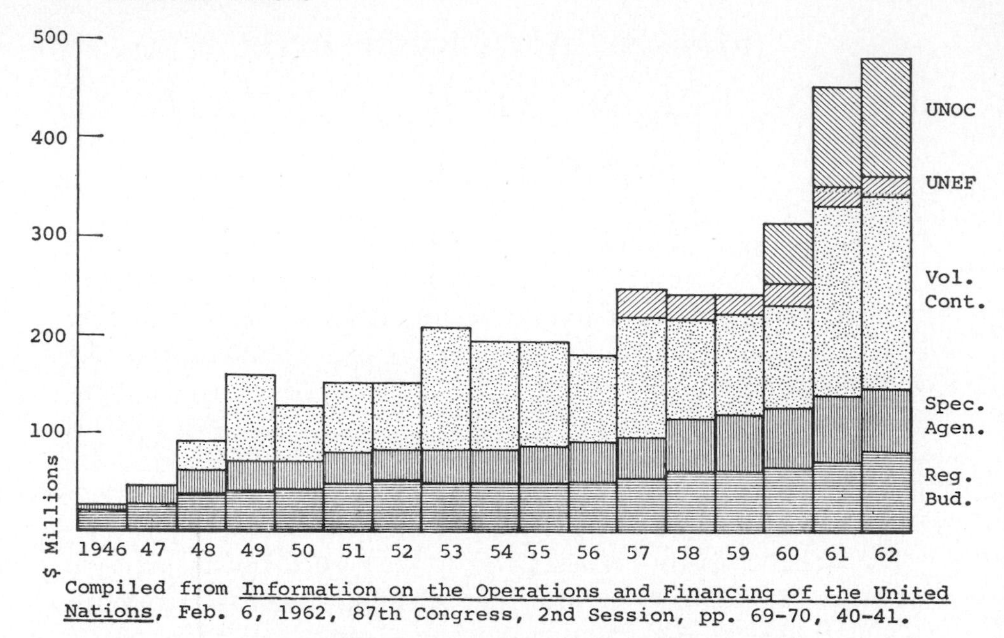

FIG. 1. RISING COST OF THE UNITED NATIONS

"cost" to member states of participating in the United Nations, for there are also expenses for maintaining permanent missions in New York and Geneva, communications, travel, attendance at meetings, and the time and salaries of the numerous personnel involved in planning and executing national policies with respect to the United Nations.

Taken in comparison with the amounts spent on the League of Nations—$6,128,000 at its height in 1935—the annual expenses of the United Nations seem very large. But compared with government expenditures in many states, they are really very small.

In noting the rise in UN expenses since 1946, it should be borne in mind that the purchasing power of the dollar has declined about 20 per cent in this period of time. Thus, if the direct outlay for the UN in assessments and contributions were to be expressed in terms of a constant-value dollar, the current level would more nearly approximate $390 million.

In considering what has happened to UN expenses over seventeen years it must also be borne in mind that in 1945-1946 the United States and others countries were supporting the United Nations Relief and Rehabilitation Administration to the extent of over $1 billion. This was administered separately from the United Nations as such, but the expenditures for it must not be overlooked. Furthermore, between 1947 and 1950 over $412 million was laid out for the International

Refugee Organization. Taking these expenditures into account, the United Nations and its affiliated programs are in fact costing a good deal less today than international activities did in the immediate post-war period.

In the area of routine annual operating expenses the rise from $19 to $82 million over sixteen years has been fairly moderate, considering the many demands that have been thrust upon the Organization, the continual series of meetings held under UN auspices, the doubling of the membership, and the gravity of the world situation. These expenses would of course have become much higher had some of the more expensive special voluntary programs such as technical assistance or the emergency peace-keeping operations in the Middle East and the Congo been put on the Regular Budget instead of being covered by voluntary contributions or placed on special assessment accounts. Figure 1 shows what the cumulative total has amounted to.

By decision of the General Assembly, the operating expenses of the Organization are apportioned among the member states according to a scale of assessment that is based on relative national income and revised periodically. Apportionments currently range from a minimum of .04 per cent to a high of 32.02 per cent. Not counting the states admitted at the XVIth and XVIIth sessions, at the present time 32 states pay the minimum rate of .04 per cent. An additional 48 are assessed less than 1 per cent, 14 are assessed at rates ranging from 1 to 5 per cent. Only 4 countries pay over 5 per cent—France, the United Kingdom, the Soviet Union, and the United States.[2] All of the states admitted since mid-1961 will pay less than 1 per cent. The four major powers contribute 60 per cent of the UN's operating expense revenue.

The cost pattern of the programs financed by government voluntary contributions shows a much steeper rise and now accounts for 43 per cent of the overall UN expenditures. The income for these programs—refugee work, relief, UNICEF, technical assistance, and the like—has indeed provided, on an average, twice as much income and outlay as the Regular Budget since 1956. This is, therefore, a substantial element in the UN financing picture. Without this form of support many undertakings could not have been carried forward as they have been. At the same time it must be noted that the number of states contributing to these programs has varied greatly, from as few as 18 for the Economic Fund for the Congo to 92 for the Children's Fund. EPTA and the Special Fund have enlisted pledges from 97 member states for

[2] General Assembly Resolution 1691 (XVI), December 18, 1961, set the apportionment rates for 1962, 1963, and 1964.

1963. This is the high-water mark for the number of states contributing. Contributions have also varied enormously, as might be expected. One thing that stands out in this area is the large giving record of the United States. The percentages of U.S. contributions to the totals of these programs are summarized in Table I. In every instance the United States has given more than its apportionment share under the assessment system. No other state has as consistent a record of liberal giving.

TABLE I. PER CENT OF UNITED STATES CONTRIBUTIONS TO TOTALS OF VOLUNTARY PROGRAMS, 1946-1961

Program	Per Cent	Program	Per Cent
Children's Fund	62.1	UNHCR Current Programs	38.3
UNRWA	68.4	Special Fund for Hungarian Refugees	51.3
UNKRA	65.1	United Nations Special Fund	41.0
EPTA	49.4	Economic Fund for the Congo	65.7
UN Refugee Fund	35.5	Fund for Algerian Refugees	49.6

Since 1946 the United States has contributed voluntarily over $1 billion to UN activities. The nation can take pride in the leadership it has shown in supporting the worthwhile causes represented by these programs. Much good has been done through them in alleviating want and despair and enabling some activities to go on that otherwise could not have gotten off the ground.

The expenditure curve for the nine Specialized Agencies most closely associated with the United Nations shows a close parallel to that of the UN Regular Budget, as seen in Figure 1, and requires little comment. Suffice it to say that the $70 million figure is a relatively modest one, considering the number of agencies involved and the global nature of the services they render.

The factor that has done more than anything else in recent years to catapult United Nations expenditures has been the maintenance of the United Nations Emergency Force in the Middle East since 1957 and the military operations in the Congo since the summer of 1960. Table II shows what this has done to UN costs and assessments since 1956. Putting aside for the moment considerations of attitude on how the costs of these operations should be shared—and this has been at the heart of much of the dispute over what to do about UN finances—it is this jump in assessments from $48 million to approximately $221 million in six years that has alarmed Members of the UN and led to rising opposition to paying assessments. Many have alleged that payments were becoming "unbearable." Far from lightening the burden of the

TABLE II. UN ASSESSMENTS, 1956-1962

			Members
1956—Regular Budget		$ 48,330,000	76
1957—Regular Budget		49,088,050	
UNEF		15,028,988	
	Total	64,117,038	76
1958—Regular Budget		51,502,289	
UNEF		25,000,000	
	Total	76,502,289	83
1959—Regular Budget		61,500,000	
UNEF		15,205,000	
	Total	76,705,000	82
1960—Regular Budget		58,347,514	
UNEF		20,000,000	
UNOC		48,500,000	
	Total	126,847,514	82
1961—Regular Budget		69,399,839	
UNEF		19,000,000	
UNOC		120,000,000	
	Total	208,399,839	99
1962—Regular Budget		82,144,740	
UNEF		19,500,000	
UNOC		120,000,000	
	Total	221,644,740	99*

* Not including states admitted at XVIth Session.

assessments seriously, the increase in membership that has taken place during this same period has principally brought into the Organization a large number of low-income countries upon whom any assessment, however small, might seem onerous. Thus, the effect of the increase in membership has been rather to heighten the chorus of those calling for reductions and for the Great Powers to pay more of the bill. How real the burden is has concerned not a few observers as the costs have crept up and defaults in payments have multiplied. Obviously the burden varies greatly from country to country, depending upon such variables as the capital structure, national income, the stage of development, and the competitions that exist for the allocation of scarce resources.

II. Current Cost of United Nations Membership

The amounts assessed each state for participation in the United Nations and the Specialized Agencies, *plus* the voluntary contributions made by it to the various voluntary programs, express in one way what the United Nations is costing member states. Table III gives these figures for each state in 1961. These include the assessments for UNEF and the Congo operation, with allowance for the rebates that were authorized that year for states receiving technical assistance from the UN. For comparative purposes, the states have been listed in a rank order regression from the country with the largest total payments to that with the smallest.

The figures show that the cost of participating in the United Nations at this time ranges from $201,541,993 on the part of the United States to $45,193 for Dahomey. The median in the cost curve falls at $325,972. This is the amount paid by Uruguay, a state which was assessed to pay .12 per cent on the normal scale of apportionment of UN expenses. The figures given in Table III do not indicate what each state actually paid, for many defaulted on one or more of their assessments in 1961 and 1962. The "cost" represented in this table is therefore what membership would have cost *if* each state paid in full what was assigned to it in addition to the voluntary contributions which it actually made.

Expressing the national assessments and contributions as a percentage of the total received by and due to the UN, the high and low percentages will be seen in Column 4 to extend from 46.91 per cent for the United States—all of which was paid—to .011 per cent for the smallest contributor, with the median located at .076 per cent. The large voluntary contributions made by the United States explain the 14 per cent excess over the 32.51 per cent the country was assessed, as shown in Column 5. Aside from the United States, the United Kingdom, Canada, Sweden, the Netherlands, Denmark, Norway, New Zealand, and the UAR, the record reveals that most UN members have been providing a smaller percentage of the total support than their assessment ratios, owing to the weighting introduced by the voluntary contributions. The Soviet Union and most of its satellites stand far below their apportionment levels in this respect.

The contributions made to the UN through assessments and voluntary payments express the external monetary cost of membership to the various states. They do not tell, however, what the cost amounts to in terms of the resources and productivity of each country. If the payments made *and* due to the United Nations are taken as a percentage of each state's gross national product, a fairly objective measure of the relative cost of UN membership can be obtained. GNP statistics do not tell the entire story about each country's means or its ability to pay, but GNP is a reasonably straightforward, stable index of national capacity that is almost universally accepted. It is a politically neutral concept. It does not bring into question controversial issues, such as a nation's economic effectiveness, the form of its government, or the extent of governmental control over the economy. It affords a fairly objective basis on which to compare relative means at any given time. Estimates of the gross national product of each Member of the United Nations, made with the assistance of the 7090 Computer at the M.I.T. Computation Center, are given in Column 2 of Table III. These show a spread from an estimated $525 billion for the United States in 1961 to $33 million for Congo Brazzaville.

By figuring each nation's payments to the United Nations as a percentage of its GNP, the percentages shown in Column 3 of Table III are reached. The principal fact which emerges from this calculation is the very small percentage of GNP which payments to the UN represent. No state contributes as much as one-half of 1 per cent of its GNP to the United Nations. Few even approach this figure. The contributions of 63 of the 97 states compared in 1961 fall between .015 and .035 per cent. Aside from the special situation of China, whose assessments are based on the resources of mainland China, and of Liberia, which has made large voluntary contributions for the Congo operation, there is a relatively small difference in the percentages of GNP being tapped. In a few instances—particularly in the cases of Congo Brazzaville, Libya, Gabon, Togo, Laos, and Somalia, which are among the states with the lowest incomes—UN payments do represent a somewhat higher burden, but only to a fractional degree.

What does stand out prominently in the comparison of UN payments as a percentage of GNP is that United Nations membership is costing the Soviet Union, Byelorussia, and the Ukrainian SSR, which have an estimated combined GNP of $169 billion, only a hair more than it is costing Peru, which has an estimated GNP of $1.8 billion, and less than it is costing India with an estimated GNP of $31 billion. In terms of individual means the discrepancy is no less striking. For with its large population the estimated per capita GNP of India in 1961 was only $73, and that of Peru $164, while that of the Soviet Union was figured at $746. The percentage of GNP being devoted to the United Nations

TABLE III. THE COST OF UNITED NATIONS MEMBERSHIP

UN Members by Rank Order of Payments to UN	*Assm'ts. & Contrbn's. 1961, US $**	*GNP, 1961 U.S. $ (millions)*	*Payments to UN as % of GNP, 1961*	*% Total UN Contrbn's. 1961*	*Normal Assm't. Scale*
United States	201,541,993	525,437	.038	46.910	32.51
United Kingdom	37,713,116	73,491	.051	8.778	7.78
USSR	35,438,809	169,621	.021	8.249	13.62
France	21,238,174	60,628	.035	4.943	6.40
Canada	16,515,883	37,293	.044	3.844	3.11
Sweden	8,642,794	12,706	.068	2.012	1.39
China	8,331,831	1,705	.489	1.939	5.01
Netherlands	8,232,175	11,701	.070	1.916	1.01
India	8,198,340	31,435	.026	1.908	2.46
Italy	7,999,045	33,412	.024	1.862	2.25
Australia	6,816,300	7,262	.039	1.587	1.79
Japan	6,333,369	41,179	.015	1.474	2.19
Ukraine SSR	4,669,773	incl. in USSR	—	1.087	1.80
Denmark	4,165,898	6,190	.067	.970	.60
Belgium	4,161,554	12,646	.033	.969	1.30
Brazil	3,231,989	18,082	.018	.752	1.02
Norway	3,220,606	4,642	.069	.750	.49
Poland	3,049,760	17,480	.017	.710	1.37
Czechoslovakia	2,293,115	8,902	.026	.534	.87
Argentina	2,226,681	9,852	.023	.518	1.11
New Zealand	2,049,603	3,812	.054	.477	.42
Mexico	1,962,302	11,236	.017	.457	.71
Turkey	1,826,324	6,326	.029	.425	.59
Spain	1,786,262	8,638	.021	.416	.93
UAR	1,580,791	4,149	.035	.368	.32
Austria	1,566,614	5,985	.026	.365	.43
Venezuela	1,500,050	7,437	.020	.349	.50
South Africa	1,489,326	7,752	.019	.347	.56
Byelorussia SSR	1,322,067	incl. in USSR	—	.308	.47
Pakistan	1,179,831	6,707	.018	.275	.40
Yugoslavia	1,149,535	5,274	.022	.268	.35
Finland	1,127,336	4,688	.024	.262	.36
Indonesia	974,464	9,165	.011	.227	.47
Philippines	966,524	6,209	.016	.225	.43
Rumania	887,327	8,021	.011	.207	.34
Iran	867,220	2,428	.036	.202	.21
Chile	863,113	4,555	.019	.201	.27
Colombia	834,277	5,082	.016	.194	.31
Hungary	773,204	6,598	.012	.180	.42
Cuba	620,432	2,633	.024	.144	.25
Thailand	607,978	2,461	.025	.142	.16
Greece	505,424	3,320	.015	.118	.23
Nigeria	451,744	2,921	.015	.105	.21
Israel	419,071	2,597	.016	.098	.14
Liberia	406,822	164	.248	.095	.04
Peru	386,081	1,853	.021	.090	.11
Portugal	379,561	2,402	.016	.088	.21
Ireland	373,025	1,896	.020	.087	.16
Morocco	353,109	2,070	.017	.082	.14
Uruguay	325,972	1,275	.026	.076	.12
Bulgaria	301,898	4,101	.007	.070	.16

TABLE III (continued)

UN Members by Rank Order of Payments to UN	*Assm'ts. & Contrbn's. 1961, US $**	*GNP, 1961 U.S. $ (millions)*	*Payments to UN as % of GNP, 1961*	*% Total UN Contrbn's. 1961*	*Normal Assm't. Scale*
Iraq	284,650	1,435	.020	.066	.09
Burma	276,701	1,304	.021	.064	.08
Sudan	265,136	1,124	.024	.062	.06
Ghana	243,853	1,541	.016	.057	.07
Ceylon	227,254	1,363	.017	.053	.10
Jordan	223,175	265	.084	.052	.04
Ecuador	187,169	941	.020	.044	.06
Ethiopia	182,758	1,288	.014	.043	.06
Lebanon	181,439	575	.032	.042	.05
Malaya	167,358	2,927	.006	.039	.17
Tunisia	155,760	764	.020	.036	.05
Saudi Arabia	149,383	1,155	.013	.035	.06
Afghanistan	146,960	721	.020	.034	.06
El Salvador	141,232	549	.026	.033	.05
Guatemala	140,468	699	.020	.033	.05
Luxembourg	138,103	504	.027	.032	.06
Libya	135,739	89	.153	.032	.04
Costa Rica	131,726	488	.027	.031	.04
Honduras	123,722	396	.031	.029	.04
Dominican Rep.	118,595	721	.016	.028	.05
Haiti	118,484	403	.029	.028	.04
Bolivia	117,793	344	.034	.027	.04
Senegal	109,791	247	.044	.026	.06
Panama	107,301	436	.025	.025	.04
Laos	106,648	137	.078	.025	.04
Guinea	101,500	167	.020	.024	.04
Iceland	101,421	192	.053	.024	.04
Nicaragua	99,783	319	.031	.023	.04
Paraguay	94,484	205	.046	.022	.04
Cambodia	90,237	505	.017	.021	.04
Albania	80,573	370	.021	.019	.04
Cameroun	77,696	343	.023	.018	.04
Madagascar	74,661	559	.013	.017	.04
Ivory Coast	73,571	333	.022	.017	.04
Togo	65,182	63	.103	.015	.04
Nepal	65,026	491	.013	.015	.04
Congo (L)	60,382	1,257	.005	.014	.04
Yemen	60,226	367	.016	.014	.04
Central Afr. Rep.	59,783	131	.046	.014	.04
Mali	57,735	392	.015	.013	.04
Cyprus	57,653	227	.025	.013	.04
Congo (B)	56,515	33	.171	.013	.04
Upper Volta	55,796	397	.014	.013	.04
Somalia	55,286	78	.071	.013	.04
Chad	53,258	293	.018	.012	.04
Gabon	53,075	46	.115	.012	.04
Niger	48,973	271	.018	.011	.04
Dahomey	45,193	182	.025	.011	.04

* Figures given include total amounts assessed, after rebates where granted under Resolutions A/1732-1733 (XVI), whether paid in full or not, plus voluntary contributions.

by the people of the United Kingdom is approximately twice that of the Soviet Union. In the case of the Netherlands, it is three times that of the USSR.

The bearing of these percentages must be viewed of course in the light of each state's unique circumstances. In countries where large sectors of the national economy are controlled by the government, payment may be somewhat easier to make than where most of the wealth is in private hands. Among most of the newer countries there are naturally great needs and pressures to devote the maximum possible resources to economic and social development. As UN costs and assessments rise, increased payments will tend to seem most onerous to those whose economic growth rate does not keep pace with the rising costs, for the "marginal value" of each extra dollar they are called upon to pay will seem greater to them than to those with a cushion of larger resources and income. Countries having difficulties in obtaining hard currencies find payments more difficult to make than those with ample foreign exchange. Thus, although the percentages of GNP represented in UN payments are in no wise large, there are variables that differentiate the load which any given percentage, however small, may constitute. And in all countries appropriations for the United Nations are to some extent in competition with demands for local interests and needs and with such basic concerns as national defense. The GNP computations throw much doubt, however, on assertions that UN costs are an unduly heavy burden on the economies of member states, especially where states are receiving substantial foreign aid from the United States or elsewhere.

Senator Hubert Humphrey in a recent Hearing inserted in the public record an estimate that the "total cost of the operations of the United Nations to the United States" since 1946, including the cost of all refugee programs, has been $1,864,218,000 for 17 years. This is slightly over $100 million a year, or, as he figured it, "approximately 75 cents per man, woman and child per year for the entire operations" of the United Nations for 17 years. To carry his estimate one point further, the $100 million a year "is one-fourth the cost of the *Enterprise* carrier; that is less than the cost of the maintenance of one division of troops in West Germany, troops without equipment or not having been delivered, just arrived."[3]

Dollar outlay figures for participation in the United Nations give

[3] Hearing before a Subcommittee of the Committee on Foreign Relations, U.S. Senate, *Review of United States Participation in the United Nations*, 88th Congress, 1st Session, March 13, 1963, 35-36.

only one side of the picture. There are intangible elements, not readily reducible to dollar figures, which lie on the *asset* side of the ledger. These must not be overlooked when contemplating what the United Nations is costing member states. For instance, if the United Nations were not in existence, many states would have to spend something more than they now are for national security, for additional representation costs, for information-gathering, and the like. There are, furthermore, numerous benefits which states receive from the presence of the institution and its various programs.

Many of the developing countries receive tangible amounts of economic or technical assistance. There are the advantages of the ease of negotiating simultaneously with many governments at the UN headquarters. Dollar symbols cannot be attached to the political support that can be marshaled behind national positions at UN meetings, or against policies that run counter to vital interests. World-wide publicity can be gained for leading statements or positions taken at the United Nations. Information gathered by UN agencies on such matters as economic, demographic, political, and other conditions in various parts of the world is invaluable. UN instrumentalities have also made contributions to maintaining peace and security that cannot be reduced to dollar terms. These have often benefited the large powers as well as the smaller states. For the United States in particular, there is a prestige value in having the headquarters of the world organization in New York, attracting as it does leaders and visitors from all over the world. These things all offset, to varying degrees, outlays made to support the United Nations and its various operations and programs. To consider the dollar costs of membership in the United Nations without at the same time considering the advantages and benefits derived from the presence of the Organization gives an unbalanced and unreal picture of the cost of the United Nations.

III. Financing Peace and Security Operations

The special assessments needed to support the peace-keeping operations in the Middle East and the Congo have been the principal factor behind the sharp rise in UN costs since 1956 and the source of its financial woes. Because of the magnitude of the added payments and dispute over who should pay for these operations, many states have opposed proration of these expenditures at the normal scale of apportionment and withheld some or all of their assessments.

A statement supplied to the Congress by the Department of State in 1962 contained the nub of the opposition which these assessments raised:

"This opposition was based primarily on three propositions. First, it was contended that the Charter contemplated that peace and security actions should be carried out primarily by the five permanent members of the Security Council who would furnish their troops without cost to other U.N. members. Accordingly it was argued that the five permanent members of the Security Council should pay considerably more than their ordinary assessment percentages for peace and security operations such as UNEF and ONUC, particularly since in neither case were they furnishing manpower. Second, it was maintained that in accordance with principles of equity the 'aggressors' who made U.N. peace and security actions a necessity, plus 'parties in interest' should pay all or most of the expenses. Finally, it was argued that regardless of other considerations, some member states had such limited financial resources that they simply could not contribute on the basis of the regular scale of assessments to the expenses of such costly operations as UNEF and ONUC."[4]

Mindful of the first and last of these arguments where they were sincerely advanced, and desirous of seeing the UN peace-keeping efforts succeed, Washington made a series of voluntary contributions to the UN expressly for these operations from 1957 to 1962. The amounts of these contributions are shown in Table IV. In the first years of UNEF, the contributions were used to reduce the total budget costs and the

TABLE IV. UNITED STATES VOLUNTARY CONTRIBUTIONS TO UNITED NATIONS PEACE-KEEPING OPERATIONS, 1957-1962

Year	*UNEF*		*UNOC*	
1957	3,170,850			
1958	9,750,000			
	1,191,581	(waivered airlift)		
1959	3,500,000			
1960	3,200,00		3,900,000	
			10,317,622	(waivered airlift)
1961	1,800,000		15,305,596	
1962	1,320,000		11,400,800	
Total	23,932,431		40,924,018	

SOURCE: Compiled from Appendices 14 and 15, *Purchase of United Nations Bonds*, 374-75.

[4] *Purchase of United Nations Bonds*, 340. The United Nations military operation in the Congo is referred to in this statement as ONUC; the Anglicized initials UNOC will be employed elsewhere

balance was then assessed against all members. Later the procedure was modified so that the contributions were applied only to the assessments of states least able to pay. As a result of negotiations at the United Nations, the criterion chosen for determining who should be included in the list of those having reduced assessments was qualification for assistance under the UN Expanded Program of Technical Assistance. With increasing numbers of states registering demands for relief from the assessments after the magnitude of the Congo operation became fully evident, the General Assembly declared that these were "extraordinary expenses," "essentially different in nature" from the normal operating expenses, and that a "procedure different from that applied in the case of the regular budget" should be employed. Accordingly, after further declaring that the Members of the Security Council have a special responsibility for maintaining international peace and security, the General Assembly decided in December 1961 to grant rebates extending from 50 to 80 per cent for states receiving or eligible to receive technical assistance from the UN. At the same time it appealed to all member states who were in a position to do so to make voluntary contributions to offset the deficit created by the rebates and to assist the general financing.[5]

This "mixed" arrangement, embodying both voluntary and assessment elements and exceptions from the normal scale of apportionment, was at most an expedient hammered out after laborious negotiation. Apportionment of some part of the cost to all member states by assessment emphasized the responsibility of each state, no matter how small or poor, for assuming some part of the costs of Organization peacekeeping functions. The singling out of the Permanent Members of the Security Council as having a "special responsibility for the maintenance of international peace and security and, therefore, for contributing to the financing of peace and security operations" laid it on the line that those Members who refused to pay their assessments for these activities—namely, France and the Soviet Union—were shirking on the job in the sight of the majority in the General Assembly. The rebate feature acknowledged that there are differences in the capacities of states to bear the added amounts needed to defray peace-keeping costs. The pro-

[5] See Resolutions 1732 (XVI) and 1733 (XVI), adopted December 20, 1961. The final vote on the first resolution, to provide for the Congo financing, was 66-13-15; on the resolution for UNEF, 61-11-24. The XVIIth General Assembly was unable to decide how to finance the UNOC costs after July 1, 1962, and passed the problem on to a Special Working Group that was asked to report not later than April 1, 1963. Meanwhile, standing obligations were to be met out of voluntary contributions and proceeds from the bond sale. See Resolutions 1854 (XVII), December 19, 1962, and 1864 (XVII) and 1865 (XVII), December 20, 1962.

vision for voluntary contributions helped to make it feasible to lighten the burden on the developing countries. And the arrangement permitted United States assessments to remain at no more than one-third of the total, in keeping with United States law.[6]

Although this compromise package succeeded in obtaining a two-thirds vote in the XVIth General Assembly, it was essentially a stop-gap measure and had some serious limitations. Other than appeals for voluntary contributions, it contained no provision for making up the deficits resulting from the rebates granted to states eligible to receive them. No penalty or sanction was built into the system to induce those inclined to be wayward in payment to fulfill their assessments. Nor was any provision made for support of the Organization in the event there were non-payments. To be sure, Article 19 of the Charter does stand in the background as a mild sanction. It has not yet been tested. It provides that a state "shall have no vote in the General Assembly if the amount of its arrears equals or exceeds the amount of the contributions due from it for the preceding two full years." But it then permits exceptions to be made if the Assembly finds that non-payment is due to "conditions beyond the control" of a state. What are the "conditions beyond the control" of a Member that would excuse failure to pay in the eyes of the Assembly? The Charter gives no guidance on this point. Hence, the General Assembly must decide the point when it may be raised. Without explicit guidance or precedents, it remains to be seen how the Assembly will interpret the Article and whether it will take firm action when the time of testing is reached, whoever the parties may be that are in arrears. Diplomacy may be able to find some carrot-and-stick formula that will induce sufficient payments to keep the Organization going. But it is by no means sure that the United Nations will not undergo a major constitutional crisis if large numbers of Members continue to hold back their payments and efforts are made to apply Article 19.

[6] The limitation placed by the United States Congress upon American contributions will be found in Public Law 495, July 10, 1952, 82nd Congress, 2nd Session, as follows:

"No representative of the United States Government in any international organization after fiscal year 1953 shall make any commitment requiring the appropriation of funds for a contribution by the United States in excess of 33 1/3 per centum of the budget of any international organization for which the appropriation for the United States contribution is contained in this Act: *Provided*, however, that this section shall not apply to the United States representatives to the inter-American organizations.

"No representative of the United States Government to any international organization of which the United States is now a member shall, unless specifically authorized in an appropriation Act or other law, make any commitment requiring the appropriation of funds for a contribution by the United States in excess of 33 1/3 per centum of the budget of such international organization." (66 Stat. 549, 550-51.)

IV. Financial Crisis

The crux of the financial crisis that has confronted the United Nations since 1961 lies in the failure of an increasing number of states to pay their assessments on time or in full, and the refusal of some—led by France and the Soviet Union—to pay one or another of their peace-keeping obligations. Table V summarizes the situation. The difficulty

Table V. Summary of Assessments Due and Received as at December 31, 1962

	Total Amount Assessed US $	*Amount Received (incl. credits)*	*Per Cent Received*	*Balance Due US $*
1959 Reg. Budget	61,500,000.00	61,497,944.00	99.99	2,056.00
1960 Reg. Budget	58,347,514.00	58,302,054.00	99.92	45,460.00
1961 Reg. Budget	69,347,807.00	64,924,123.10	93.55	4,475,715.90
1960 for New Member States	52,032.00			
1962 Reg. Budget	74,124,117.00	60,899,485.62	82.16	13,224,631.38
UNEF 1957	15,028,988.00	11,040,057.00	73.46	3,988,931.00
UNEF 1958	25,000,000.00	17,740,741.00	70.96	7,259,259.00
UNEF 1959	15,205,000.00	10,850,117.00	71.36	4,354,883.00
UNEF 1960	20,000,000.00	15,269,623.91	76.35	4,730,376.09
UNEF 1961	18,989,898.00	14,106,255.32	74.24	4,893,744.68
1960 for New Member States	10,102.00			
UNEF 1962	9,750,000.00	7,330,554.50	75.19	2,419,445.50
Congo 1960	48,500,000.00	31,185,891.38	64.30	17,314,108.62
Congo 1961	100,000,000.00	69,829,562.93	69.83	30,170,437.07
Congo 1962	80,000,000.00	51,274,933.54	64.09	28,725,066.46

Source: United Nations Secretariat, *Statement on the Collection of Contributions as at 31 December 1962*, ST/ADM/SER.B/168, January 2, 1963, Table ix.

Note: The assessments for both the UNEF and the Congo accounts for 1962 covered expenses only through June 30. The Congo account extended back to November 1, 1961. The XVIIth Session of the General Assembly did not decide upon the assessments for the remainder of the calendar year or for 1963 before adjourning in December 1962.

is clearly seen in the failure of the UNEF account to receive more than 76 per cent of the amount needed in any year, and of the Congo assessments to net more than 69 per cent of the amounts required from the membership. Furthermore, it will be seen that in 1962 the percentage received for the Regular Budget took a sharp drop. What this adds up to is that, as of the end of 1962, Members of the United Nations owed the Organization $122 million for expenses dating from 1957 through 1962. To this amount must be added the expenditures that have been accumulating since July 1, 1962, at the rate of $1 million a month for

UNEF and $10 million a month for UNOC. The UN bonds, to which 58 countries had either subscribed or pledged a total of $139,003,937 up to March 1963,[7] will take care of a part of the current running expenses. But this will not enable the Organization to become fully solvent unless large numbers of member states resume paying their assessments.

TABLE VI. NUMBERS OF STATES HAVING BALANCES DUE ON ASSESSMENTS
(Figures as of December 31, 1962)

	1957		*1958*		*1959*	
	*R.B.**	*UNEF*	*R.B.*	*UNEF*	*R.B.*	*UNEF*
African[1]	0	1	0	1	0	1
Arab[2]	0	7	0	8	0	8
Asian[3]	0	2	0	2	0	2
Latin American	0	7	0	7	2	10
Soviet Bloc	0	9	0	9	0	9
Western European	0	2	0	2	0	2
Other[4]	0	1	0	1	0	1
	0	29	0	30	2	33

	1960			*1961*			*1962*		
	R.B.	*UNEF*	*UNOC*	*R.B.*	*UNEF*	*UNOC*	*R.B.*	*UNEF#*	*UNOC#*
African	0	1	6	3	7	10	8	12	14
Arab	0	9	6	2	9	7	4	9	7
Asian	0	2	5	1	4	5	6	6	6
Latin American	4	13	18	8	16	18	15	18	20
Soviet Bloc	0	9	10	1	9	10	9	9	10
Western European	0	2	6	1	3	6	3	3	8
Other	0	1	2	1	1	2	2	1	2
	4	37	53	17	49	58	47	58	67

* Regular Budget # Through June 30, 1962, only
[1] Except Arab League members and South Africa
[2] Arab League members
[3] Except for China (Taiwan)
[4] China (Taiwan), Israel, South Africa
SOURCE: Compiled from *Statement on the Collection of Contributions as at 31 December 1962, op.cit.*

The mounting wave of defaulting is depicted in Table VI. As of the beginning of 1963, 25 states had paid nothing at all on their UNEF assessments, and 48 had paid nothing on their Congo levies. The procession of non-payers has been led by a nucleus of Arab, Latin American, and Soviet bloc states who withheld payments first on UNEF, then

[7] *United Nations Review*, x (March 1963), 2.

on the Congo. Since 1960 some of these states have withheld or delayed their payments for the Regular Budget assessments. None of the principal groupings of states has stood by the Organization en masse. Not a few of those who have been most vocal on the matter of the UN's playing a major role in maintaining international peace and security, and who voted for its engaging in these activities, have been among the major defectors. Included among these also are some who have received the principal benefits from the UN in the form of economic and technical assistance. It is such a record that raises the question of how seriously some Members mean to take their obligations under the Charter. Practice appears to deny what has been accepted in principle—namely, that maintaining international peace and security and supporting the Organization are responsibilities of all.

Speakers at the XVIIth session of the General Assembly, as on other occasions, hailed the "concept of universality of the United Nations," declaimed on its ability to meet the outstanding problems of international relations with firmness and wisdom, and underscored a worldwide "determination for its survival and development." The actions of some Members indicate that there is a considerable gulf between professions and actions. So long as large numbers of states continue to withhold payments for activities voted in a bona fide manner by large majorities in the General Assembly, the situation cannot fail to raise serious doubts about the future of the Organization. Unless it can pay its bills, it cannot for long fulfill the functions assigned to it by the Charter and confidence in it is likely to wane. The comparison is not to be pressed too far, but it cannot escape note that the fall-off in UN support today bears a resemblance to what happened to the League of Nations in the 1930's after the Manchurian episode.

The records show that by the end of 1962 less than one-quarter of the Members had paid all of their assessments for the period from 1957 to 1962, or from the date of their admission to the United Nations. Indeed less than one-half of the Members had paid all of their dues for the normal running expenses. As Table VII shows, only 41 states paid their assessments for supporting UNEF in full, and only 32 for the Congo operation. In the small company of 25 states fulfilling all assessments, 7 were Western European countries, 7 Asian states, 7 African members, and 4 classed as "others," including the United States.

It is not possible to document precisely what relationship may exist between United States foreign aid programs and payments to the United Nations. Examination of the records shows that there is relatively little correlation between the amounts received and constancy in

TABLE VII. STATES HAVING PAID THEIR OBLIGATIONS IN FULL AS OF DECEMBER 1962

	Reg. Bud.	*UNEF*	*UNOC*
Afghanistan	*		
Australia	*	*	*
Austria	*	*	
Burma	*	*	*
Cambodia		*	
Cameroon	*	*	*
Canada	*	*	*
Cent. Afr. Rep.	*	*	*
Ceylon	*	*	*
Chad	*		
Cyprus	*	*	*
Denmark	*	*	*
Dominican Rep.	*		
Ecuador		*	
El Salvador	*		
Ethiopia	*		
Fed. Malaya	*	*	*
Finland	*	*	*
France	*	*	
Gabon	*	*	*
Iceland	*	*	*
India		*	*
Indonesia	*	*	*
Iraq	*		
Ireland	*	*	*
Israel		*	*
Italy		*	*
Ivory Coast	*	*	*
Japan	*	*	*
Jordan	*		
Lebanon	*		
Liberia	*	*	*
Libya	*		*
Luxembourg	*	*	
Madagascar	*	*	
Mali	*		
Mexico	*		
Morocco	*		
Netherlands	*	*	*
New Zealand	*	*	*
Nigeria	*	*	*
Norway	*	*	*
Pakistan		*	*
Peru	*		
Philippines	*		*
Portugal	*	*	
Somalia	*	*	
South Africa	*	*	
Spain	*		
Sudan			*
Sweden	*	*	*
Thailand	*		
Togo	*		
Tunisia	*	*	*
Turkey	*	*	*
United Kingdom	*	*	
United States	*	*	*
Venezuela	*	*	
Yugoslavia	*	*	
59	52	41	32

SOURCE: Compiled from *Statement on the Collection of Contributions as at 31 December 1962, op.cit.*

meeting UN obligations. Some of the largest recipients of American aid have been among the chief withholders. A few of the larger beneficiaries of U.S. aid, such as Japan, the Netherlands, Norway, and Turkey, have met all of their payments. On the other hand, some countries that have received no U.S. aid, such as Australia, Canada, Finland, and New Zealand, have fulfilled all of their contributions. It is noted that no Latin American country has paid all of its obligations, and that one of America's principal allies, France, has been a leading standout against paying for the Congo operation.

The United States is the only Permanent Member of the Security Council that has met all of its financial obligations to the Organization when due. The United Kingdom has done so, with the exception of a short fall over this last year when it held up its Congo payment pending settlement with the UN of certain sums due to it. It is now fully current. China has been behind for some time, but it made a payment in April 1963. The Soviet Union paid its Regular Budget assessment in January 1963, but continued to withhold on the peace-keeping accounts the $60 million due from it. Likewise France continued to withhold the $14 million assessed to it for the Congo. Such policies are hardly in keeping with the responsibility given the Permanent Members of the Security Council when the Charter was drafted.

There is no simple explanation for the failure of so many states to meet their responsibilities to the United Nations. A few have found it difficult to locate ready funds to meet certain payments when due. A plotting of the overall assessment curve alongside the record of payments does show, as seen in Figure 2, that as the assessment gradient

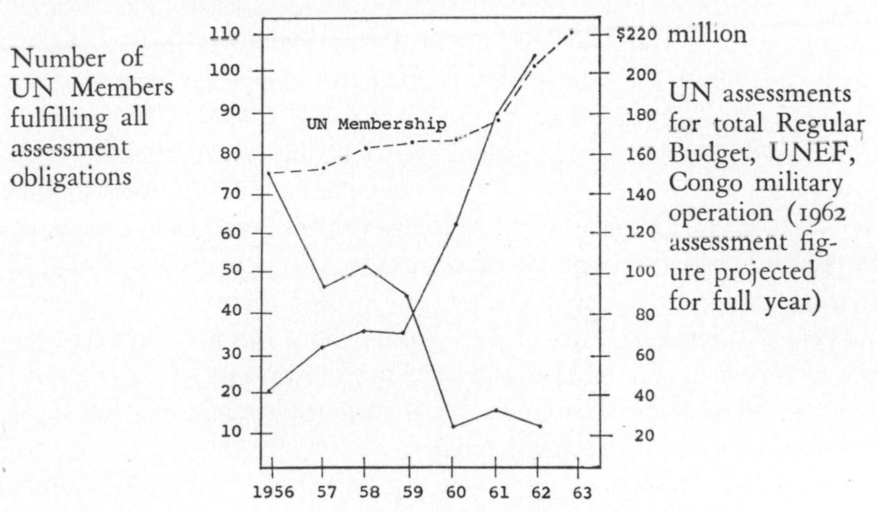

FIG. 2. FULFILLMENT OF UN ASSESSMENTS COMPARED WITH RISING CHARGES

has risen since 1959, the percentage of states fulfilling their obligations has dropped, notwithstanding the increase in membership. The plot lines show that after the assessment level passed the $100 million mark, fulfillments fell off precipitously. The fact that this coincides with the admission of the large number of new countries with low incomes suggests that the rising cost of UN membership is responsible, in part at least, for the financial crisis. But there is obviously more to it than this. For the numbers of Members fulfilling their obligations were already falling sharply before the assessment curve reached $80 million, and the defaulting parties are by no means limited to the low-income states.

Twelve of the 18 states having the highest apportionment rate—that is, above 1 per cent—failed to make their full payments in 1961 or 1962. Each of these 12 states had a GNP in excess of $8 billion in 1961. Moreover, among these 12 are 5 of the states with the highest national incomes in the UN membership. At the other end of the spectrum, 19 of the 25 states paying all of their assessments as of December 30, 1962, are in the minus 1 per cent apportionment category and 11 of their number had a GNP of less than $2 billion in 1961. If states with as small a national income as this can pay their assessments, those with a much larger GNP should be able to pay theirs.

In the majority of cases, payments to the United Nations appear to have been withheld for political rather than economic or financial reasons. Soviet and French refusals have been based upon outright opposition to measures taken by the Organization. Others have followed suit out of similar reasons or sheer opportunism. Delegates from African, Arab, and Soviet bloc states have argued that the peace-keeping costs should be borne by the states whose actions called forth UN intervention or who were in some way accessories to the causal circumstances. Lower-income countries have argued that the bulk of the costs should be borne by the Members of the Security Council, who have a primary responsibility for maintaining peace and security. Others have insisted that the situations in the Near East and in the Congo are of no direct concern to themselves and on this ground have rationalized non-payment. A few appear to have withheld payments as a part of a movement to bring about a testing of the question whether there is a legal liability to pay for this type of activity.

The Soviet Union has argued that expenses for peace-keeping cannot be imposed as binding upon member states save by a decision of the Security Council; that the latter must define all conditions relating to such financing and that the General Assembly has no right to assume such a function. In the case of UNEF it is argued that, since this force was called into being by an emergency session of the Assembly, there was a violation of the Charter and assessments for it are of no validity. In the case of the Congo force, although this was in response to a Congolese request and authorized by the Security Council, it is argued that the operations in the Congo were carried out in circumvention of the Council; hence the financing is said to impose no obligation.[8] This

[8] This argument is summarized in the report of the Working Group of 21, *Financing of United Nations Peace-keeping Operations*, UN Document A/5407, March 29, 1963, 4-5.

ex parte argument running in two different directions disregards the language of the Charter.

Article 17, paragraph 2, of the Charter clearly lays down the proposition that "the expenses of the Organization shall be borne by the Members as apportioned by the General Assembly." It makes no qualifications with respect to any kind of expenses. The withholdings of so many states served to bring into question, nevertheless, the scope of the Assembly's power and of the Members' commitments. It was to obtain "legal guidance" on these points that the XVIth Assembly, acting under proddings from the United States and others who have paid their assessments, decided to ask the International Court of Justice for an advisory opinion on whether the expenditures authorized by a series of Assembly resolutions, and pro-rated among the Members by separate assessments, constituted "expenses of the Organization" within the meaning of Article 17, paragraph 2, of the Charter.[9] It was the hope of those who supported this move, taken on the recommendation of a special subcommittee known as the Working Group of 15,[10] that a favorable opinion would not only clarify the power of the General Assembly with respect to UN finances but also settle the question of obligation by the member states to pay levies.

The advisory opinion of the Court, handed down on July 20, 1962, by a highly divided bench, has not settled the issue.[11] Space does not permit a full review here of the ten opinions that emerged from the deliberations of the fourteen judges who considered the questions. These have been carefully reviewed elsewhere.[12] It must suffice to say that the majority opinion, rendered by nine judges, held that the expenditures authorized by the various General Assembly resolutions for UNEF and the Congo operation constituted "expenses of the Organization" within the meaning of Article 17, paragraph 2, of the Charter, and as such were to be "borne by the Members as apportioned by the

[9] Resolution 1731 (XVI) on Administrative and Budgetary Procedures of the United Nations on the report of the Fifth Committee (A/5062), passed on December 20, 1961, by a vote of 52-11-32. The text will be found in *Purchase of United Nations Bonds*, 390; and the list of countries voting on the resolution in *ibid.*, 458-59.

[10] The text of the Report of the Working Group of 15 is contained in UN Document A/4971 (XVI), November 15, 1961.

[11] The opinion, entitled "Certain Expenses of the United Nations (Article 17, par. 2 of the Charter), Advisory Opinion of 20 July 1962," will be found in *International Court of Justice, Reports* (The Hague 1962), 151-308. The opinion will also be found in *Purchase of United Nations Bonds*, 469-598. Summaries of the opinion will be found in *United Nations Review*, IX (August 1962), 11-13, and *International Organization* XVI (Autumn 1962), 865-71.

[12] See Leo Gross, "Expenses of the United Nations for Peace-keeping Operations: The Advisory Opinion of the International Court of Justice," *International Organization*, XVII (Winter 1963), 1-35.

General Assembly." Reflecting the position taken by the United States, the majority affirmed that the General Assembly, and only the General Assembly, has the authority to apportion the expenses of the Organization and that these might be apportioned either according to the regular scale or to a special one adopted for a specific purpose. Furthermore the Court reasoned that the Assembly might utilize funds voluntarily contributed or it might "find some other method or combination of methods for providing the necessary funds." Refusing to take a narrow interpretation of the powers of the General Assembly, the majority enunciated the view that "While it is the Security Council which, exclusively, may order coercive action, the functions and powers conferred by the Charter on the General Assembly are not confined to discussion, consideration, the initiation of studies and the making of recommendations; they are not merely hortatory. Article 18 deals with 'decisions' of the General Assembly on 'important questions.' These 'decisions' do indeed include certain recommendations, but others have dispositive force and effect. Among these latter decisions, Article 18 includes suspension of rights and privileges of membership, expulsion of Members, 'and budgetary questions.' "[13]

In the final analysis, the Court held that expenditures must always be tested "by their relationship to the purposes of the United Nations." If they are within the purposes of the United Nations and are incurred as a result of resolutions passed by the Security Council and the General Assembly, and of measures taken at the direction of the Secretary-General acting thereunder, they are legitimate "expenses of the Organization."

Without denigrating the reasoning set forth in the various opinions written by the minority judges, we must pass on to the sequel to the Court's opinion. The immediate result of the Court's deliberation was to return the issue to the General Assembly with almost as many differing interpretations as before it was sent to the Hague. A majority opinion was mustered for the thesis that the peace-keeping expenditures voted by the General Assembly were legitimate "expenses of the Organization" and that Members were under obligation to pay their assessments for these. But strong judicial support was also lent to the contentions that apportionments voted by the Assembly in these instances were only recommendations and not binding upon Members who failed to consent to the majority votes in the Assembly. In debating matters at the XVIIth General Assembly session, it was not lost

[13] *Purchase of United Nations Bonds*, 479.

to sight that the Court's reply was only an advisory opinion, not a judgment. The Assembly did adopt, by a roll call vote of 76-17-8, a resolution "accepting" the opinion. But delegates of some countries did not omit to point out that this was only a legal opinion, that each Organ is its own interpreter of the Charter in last analysis. It was also emphasized that an advisory opinion, unlike a decision of the Court, does not require compliance by a Member under Article 94 of the Charter. And it was maintained that countries are under no more legal constraint than before to pay assessments which they believe to be illegal or otherwise non-obligatory.

In the majority voting to "accept" the Court's opinion were numbers of states that had been delinquent in their payments to one or both peace-keeping accounts—43, to be exact.[14] From this fact, and from the votes on four related steps—namely, (1) requesting the Secretary-General to explore all possible avenues to wipe out the arrears on the Regular Budget (voted 96-11-1);[15] (2) establishing a Working Group of 21 to report on methods for financing peace-keeping operations and paying arrears thereon (78-14-4);[16] (3) authorizing the Secretary-General to continue expending substantially the same sums for UNEF and the Congo operations up to June 30, 1963 (two votes: 76-11-8 and 75-12-13);[17] and (4) calling a special session of the Assembly to convene before June 30, 1963, in order to consider the financial situation of the Organization, including a report from the Working Group of 21 (77-0-21)[18]—there may be room for hope that numbers of Members will sooner or later resume paying. The Soviet and French delegates, however, declared that their countries would not pay where they felt no obligation.

Conceivably, a combination of these steps, together with the Court's opinion, possible reduction in the Congo expenses, and persistent diplomacy, may turn the tide. If further strife in the Congo can be averted and the UN force reduced to something on the order of 8,000 men, with expenses held to an estimated $30 million for the second half of

[14] The vote is recorded in UN Document P/V.1199. The text of the resolution, 1854 (XVII), adopted at the 1199th plenary meeting, December 19, 1962, will be found in *United Nations Review*, x (January 1963), 103.

[15] Resolution 1863 (XVII), Working Capital Fund for the Financial Year 1963, section B, par. 1, 1201st plenary meeting, December 20, 1962; text in *ibid.*, 107.

[16] Resolution 1854 (XVII), cited above, section B, paragraphs 1-6.

[17] Resolution 1864 (XVII), United Nations Emergency Force, adopted at 1201st plenary meeting, December 20, 1962. Text in *ibid.*, 107. Resolution 1865 (XVII), United Nations Operations in the Congo, adopted at 1201st plenary meeting, December 20, 1962, *ibid.*

[18] Resolution 1866 (XVII), Convening a Special Session of the General Assembly, adopted at the 1201st plenary meeting, December 20, 1962; text in *ibid.*, 107-8.

1963 and further reductions reasonably likely in 1964, this would contribute substantively to an alleviation of the UN's difficulties. Solid evidence that the Congolese are making progress in relieving the UN of tasks it has had to assume in their country would undoubtedly encourage some hesitant Members to resume their payments, for hope could then be seen that the endless spiral of expenditures and assessments would come to a halt. It is this, quite as much as the differences over the handling of the Congo business, that has alarmed many Members. On a different front, the rumblings heard in the 87th Congress about continuing large U.S. foreign aid grants and liberal subventions to the UN if other states continue to hold back on their obligations could not fail to convey a warning that the large voluntary contributions heretofore made by the United States to keep the UN going might dry up unless others reformed their practices. The proof of a change will be attested only when payments resume their normal patterns of completion.

V. Looking to the Future

If the actions taken in the closing days of the 1962 General Assembly session marked a turning in the UN crisis, as many delegates asserted, there is still much to be done to place the Organization on a solid financial basis.

Aside from accepting the opinion of the International Court of Justice on the validity of the expenses in the Middle Eastern and Congo peace-keeping operations and the binding obligation of the assessments therefor, the General Assembly in its December 1962 resolution explicitly affirmed "the collective financial responsibility of Members of the United Nations" and indicated that arrangements must be made, "within the letter and spirit of the Charter," to clear up the arrears owing to the institution. At the same time it acknowledged that "peace-keeping operations, such as those in the Congo and in the Middle East, impose a heavy financial burden upon Member states, in particular on those having a limited capacity to contribute financially." It accepted that a "different procedure is required" to meet these expenditures than to meet those applied for the Regular Budget, and called for consideration of a "possible special scale of assessments." In establishing a special Working Group of 21 to examine administrative and budgetary procedures, it instructed this group to study anew "the criteria for the sharing of the costs" of peace-keeping operations, including "special factors" relating to particular operations that might suggest variations in the methods of sharing, and the "degree of economic development" of member states. And it also directed its subcommittee to give "particular attention" to "a special financial responsibility of members of the Security Council" for meeting peace-keeping costs.

This omnibus resolution was obviously a compromise package. Conceivably a proposal with somewhat stiffer terms on the payment of arrearages or with fewer concessions to those who want a special scale could have gotten a majority. It is difficult to tell without access to the full diplomatic record. The chances are it would have been a less impressive vote. However this may be, a solid consensus was evidenced that something should be done about matters. The Working Group was given a definite mandate. A time was set for a special session of the Assembly. And the Soviet bloc and France were isolated in their opposition to efforts to put the UN on more solid ground.

We have spoken at length about the action of December 20, 1962, for it seems likely that whatever is done from this point on will rest in part upon elements agreed upon then.

Although the Working Group of 21 was not able to reach agreement upon any specific course of action to recommend to the General Assembly for solving the UN's financial problems, its deliberations did help to clarify positions further while at the same time affording an opportunity for exploring suggestions with respect to a special scale.[19] One of the most important things that emerged with the Committee's report was a formal appeal that member states "who are in arrears and object to making payments to meet the expenses of these peace-keeping operations on political or juridical grounds are invited nevertheless to make a special effort toward solving the financial difficulties of the Organization by making this payment." This clearly revealed that the great majority of the group were in favor of the payment of arrears and of reestablishing the financial stability of the UN.

Looking ahead, numerous ways can be seen in which efforts might be made to collect what is due to the United Nations and to resolve its needs for future funds. For purposes of convenience, we will group those that can be touched upon here under six general headings.[20]

[19] For the report of the Working Group, see Document A/5407, March 29, 1963, *Financing of United Nations Peace-keeping Operations.*

[20] Numerous proposals were discussed in the former Working Group of 15; for its Report, see Document A/4971 (XVI), November 15, 1961. These, and other suggestions advanced outside of the UN, are analyzed at some length in a research memorandum prepared by the author for the Brookings Institution, entitled *Financing Future United Nations Peace and Security Operations* (Cambridge, M.I.T. Center for International Studies, C/62-22, October 15, 1962). Reference may also be made to three other research memoranda prepared for the Brookings project, containing discussions of pro-

A. COLLECTION OF ARREARS AND CURRENT ASSESSMENTS

Aside from possible further appeals for payment of contributions and the invocation of Article 19 if need be, there are other measures that may be taken to strengthen the financial situation. One of these is the suggestion that the General Assembly create an office of United Nations Minister of Finance at the Under-Secretary level. Such an officer, if he was of national cabinet standing and world repute, and was authorized to deal directly with the highest fiscal officers of member states instead of with diplomats in New York, might be helpful in procuring earlier and fuller payment of assessments and in stimulating increased voluntary contributions. Such an officer could also be a valuable aide and counselor to the Secretary-General in planning UN operations and in ensuring utmost efficiency in the use of available resources. This appointment would carry no reflection upon the work of the Comptroller and his aides, who presumably would be under the supervision of the Minister or Under-Secretary. These officials have rendered able service in the sphere allotted to them. Experience with the voluntary programs has demonstrated, however, that leaders who have been in a position to make direct personal and official contact with the chief fiscal authorities of member states who control budgets and payments—i.e., the ministers of finance—have been most effective in eliciting large and prompt payments to their funds. Ambassadors in New York are several stages removed from those who determine the fiscal affairs of their countries and are seldom in direct line of communication with them. A person of the experience and stature of a Eugene Black or a Paul Hoffman, able to contact at once the highest authorities, might serve as a model for a UN Minister of Finance. Senator Leverett Saltonstall of Massachusetts has already suggested that the United States take the lead in securing approval of such a step.[21] The recent appointment of Eugene Black, former President of the World Bank, as Financial Adviser to the Secretary-General is indeed a move in the right direction. Mr. Black will not only aid the Secretary-General in approaching governments to pay their arrearages but advise him generally on dealing with financial matters. His long experience and wis-

---

posals relating to the main sources of UN funds: John G. Stoessinger, *The Financing of United Nations Peace and Security Operations* (Washington, Brookings Institution, October 1962, mimeograph); Walter R. Sharp, *The Voluntary Programs* (same); Norman J. Padelford, *Some Thoughts on the Financing of the Special Voluntary Programs* (same). Various proposals are also discussed in J. David Singer, *Financing International Organization: The United Nations Budget Process* (The Hague 1961), 138-46.

[21] *Congressional Record*, 87th Congress, 2nd Session, April 5, 1962, 5611.

dom in handling problems of international finance should be most helpful to the Organization.

Evidence that appeals directly to governments are having some effect is afforded by the fact that 23 states made payments to the Regular Budget, UNEF, and UNOC between the first of January and early April 1963.

B. BUILDING UP A CONTINGENCY RESERVE

One of the most important steps to restoring the financial vitality of the United Nations and enabling it to cope with future emergencies would be to have a sizable reserve that could be drawn upon to get an operation started until such time as the General Assembly could decide how the activity was to be further financed. A small reserve has existed in the item for Unforeseen and Extraordinary Expenses voted each year by the General Assembly and backed by the Working Capital Fund. Responding to diplomatic initiative by the United States and others, the XVIIth General Assembly voted to raise the amount that might be expended under this heading in 1963 to $10 million [1862 (XVII)], and to increase the Working Capital Fund from $25 to $40 million [1863 (XVII)], to be covered by assessment at the normal scale. This will not go far in an emergency on the order of the Congo crisis, but it will provide at least a small backlog. If the Working Capital Fund can eventually be built to something on the order of $100 million through unexpended accumulations, a larger reserve could be maintained, both for peace-keeping and for other types of extraordinary expenses. This might not take care of all expenses of future operations involving international forces or other large operations of an emergency or extraordinary nature, but it would certainly be a help to have such a "bank account" in reserve.

It has been suggested alternatively that a separate standing Fund for Peace and Security be established that would be available expressly for such purposes and be larger in amount than what might be divertible from the Working Capital Fund or other sources.[22] Amounts ranging from $25 million to $500 million have been mentioned as a base figure for such a fund. Although the latter would more than have sufficed for the Congo from 1960 through 1962, it would hardly have footed the bill for an operation such as the defense of the Republic of Korea in the Korean War, had that been left to the United Nations.

[22] See Advisory Committee on Administrative and Budgetary Questions, *First Report to the General Assembly at Its Fifteenth Session*, GAOR, XVth Session, Supplement No. 7 (A/4408), 1960, 9.

Such a fund might be raised from regular or special assessments, voluntary contributions, loans, or some combination of these. One possibility might be to use proceeds from the bond sale as the nest egg. Another might be to have a consortium of interested states advance the capital stake through a long-term, interest-free loan to be repaid gradually out of amounts set aside in the Regular Budget or from special assessment. It has even been suggested that private individuals, groups, and philanthropic foundations might be allowed to contribute to such a fund as a means of expressing their interest in the maintenance of international peace and security. Complications could conceivably arise from the latter course under some conditions. If, for instance, private contributions were to compose the bulk of the fund, would such large contributors be entitled to claim a voice in determining when and how the fund should be spent? This could become awkward. It would seem better to have such a fund sought from member states through contributions or loans and be backed for long-term sustainment and pay-off of any loans involved by amounts set aside in the Regular Budget. Ultimate control of expenditures from this fund should rest in the hands of the General Assembly in common with other expenses of the Organization. The Security Council acting under the powers given to it by the Charter to maintain international peace and security, and the Secretary-General acting under instructions from either the Security Council or the Assembly, should be able to draw upon this for duly authorized operations. This might not care for all expenses in every type of situation involving a UN peace and security action. But it would provide a source that could be tapped until the General Assembly had time to reach agreement upon other procedures.

C. FURTHER USE OF DEFICIT FINANCING

Some suggestions have been made that the United Nations treat the 1962 bond issue as an opening gambit for covering other emergencies in a like manner. Although the response to the present bond issue might warrant grounds for believing that another issue could be successfully floated, it seems sounder on the whole to the present writer, both from a fiscal and from a political point of view, for an international institution such as the United Nations, dependent as it is upon external sources of money and having no large independent resources of its own upon which to base credit, to be kept on a straightforward contribution and pay-as-you-go basis. Unless employed with utmost care, deficit financing of controversial operations could easily land the Organization in quicksands of trouble. It would be better to cover the costs of future peace and security and other extraordinary expenses by resort to a special fund or by instituting a special scale of assessment, or both. This applies with equal validity in my opinion to any extensive soft-loan economic development program.

D. DEVELOPING A SPECIAL SCALE FOR FUNDING EXTRAORDINARY EXPENSES

Notwithstanding that the scale of assessment applicable to the Regular Budget makes extensive allowances for the position of the countries with low capacity to pay, it is obvious from the UN debates that many of the low-income states would like to see "extraordinary expenditures," such as those for peace-keeping in the Middle East and the Congo, covered by a separate scale of assessment—one that would place a larger share of the burden on the higher-income states.

In considering the issue of a special scale there are certain principles other Members feel must not be ignored. These are first that every member state should expect to pay something on UN expenses; there should be no exemptions. Second, any deficit occasioned by a reduction in apportionment ratios should be broadly divided and not left to be shouldered by a few Members, voluntarily or otherwise. Third, it would be reasonable to make some allowance for those who place forces at the disposal of the Organization, particularly where there is danger to life. Fourth, no state must be required to pay more than one-third of the total assessment. And fifth, as the economic growth of states proceeds, they should expect to have their apportionment ratios readjusted to correspond with their increased capacity to pay.

Four alternative possibilities may be suggested for a special scale. In the first place, the United Nations might keep the essentials of the 1962 financing arrangements—that is to say, separate accounts and assessments for each major peace-keeping operation, the 80-80-50 per cent rebate feature for countries on the EPTA list, and an appeal for voluntary contributions to make up the deficit due to the rebates. This formula has not proved altogether satisfactory. And it throws a heavy responsibility upon one or a few countries that are willing to make up the differential by voluntary contributions. These should not always be counted upon.

A second plan would be to keep the rebate feature but apportion the resulting deficit among all member states not eligible for reductions and add this to their assessments in accordance with the normal scale. This would reduce or eliminate dependence upon voluntary contributions. It would spread the load more widely. Voluntary contributions would still be possible, but if none were given, the budget would still be in balance, assuming that all Members paid their assessments. Reapportionment of the deficit would inevitably raise the ratios of states not granted rebates. In the case of all excepting the five largest payers, this would add less than one-half of 1 per cent to their assessments. For the United States this would add more than 5 per cent and bring the total demanded of it to something over 37 per cent.[23] Although the United States has in fact supplied over 47 per cent of the support for UNEF and UNOC, this has resulted from the combination of assessments and voluntary contributions. As we have seen, the Congress has made it unmistakably clear, by the permanent restriction clause enacted with the 1952 appropriation legislation, that the United States shall not be obligated to pay more than 33 1/3 per cent of any UN apportionment. This was deliberately established by the Congress. It rests as well, as Deputy Assistant Secretary of State Richard N. Gardner has pointed out, upon a fundamental principle long accepted by the General Assembly that in an association of sovereign states, where each nation has one vote, it is not in the interest of the organization to depend too much upon the financial contributions of any one state.[24] Unless there were to be a major change in circumstances, it is hardly likely that the United States Congress would take readily to a call for this country to pay a larger assessment than one-third of the whole.

United States Delegate Francis T. Plimpton told the Working Group of 21 that the United States would not pay assessments for the peacekeeping operations for the last six months of 1963 in excess of the established 32.02 per cent, and that for any succeeding periods would consider going above this only if the UN financial situation were markedly improved and others had shown a comparable willingness to pay.[25] In my opinion the United States should hold to this position. It would seem that 110 member states should be able to find among them ways and means of providing the balance. Moreover, the United States should not be asked to pick up the tab that others refuse on political grounds to pay. The other Members of the United Nations should not expect the United States alone to assume what is a joint responsibility and obligation. Even in the sphere of voluntary contribu-

[23] See John G. Stoessinger, "The Price of Peace: Who Should Pay?" *Saturday Review*, November 3, 1962, 21-22. An estimate of the rates that would be payable by various states will be found in Padelford, *Financing Future United Nations Peace and Security Operations*, Table III, 63. The pages that follow this table suggest some possible modifications in this plan.

[24] Richard N. Gardner, "Financing the UN," *Department of State Newsletter* (April 1963), 23.

[25] *Christian Science Monitor*, March 7, 1963.

tions, there is a question whether the United States has not been too ready to advance large sums while others hold back. The Charter creates responsibilities that encompass the entire membership. This should be honored.

A third type of approach was suggested, in differing ways, by numbers of states during the meetings of the Working Group of 21. This would apportion expenses below a basic amount, such as $5 to $10 million, among all Members according to the normal scale; then apportion up to half of a next stage—say, $20 to $25 million—among all states on the same scale, with the balance being paid by the Permanent Members of the Security Council and the "developed" states; followed by other similar divisions on the same principles until a $100 million maximum was reached, above which all amounts would be apportioned by an *ad hoc* scale of assessment.

A fourth plan would be to develop a separate scale that would provide a simple, straightforward ratio of assessment for each state without resort to reductions, deficits, and the need for voluntary contributions or reapportionments. Such a scale could be constructed around the same basic data as the regular scale. It could start the percentage of payment at a low point for the lowest-income states and gradually raise the percentages as GNP and economic growth rates rise. Small increases in percentages above the normal scale could perhaps be introduced for the middle and higher income levels. By careful construction such a scale could stay within the 33 1/3 per cent limit for the United States and still do no injustice to any member state. Such a scale could have as its minimum starting point .008 per cent instead of the present .04 per cent. This would correspond almost exactly with the 80 per cent reduction authorized for the developing countries under the 1961 Congo and UNEF resolutions. The reduction percentages might then decrease by slowly graduated steps, closely corresponding to rising GNP and the rising points on the normal scale, until something approximating the plus $9 billion GNP rate and the normal apportionment point of 1.00 per cent were reached, at which reductions from the normal level might stop. Above this point there might be slowly graduated increases in the apportionment rate, corresponding again to rising GNP and the rising points on the normal scale, extending possibly to a maximum addition of 1.30 per cent in the case of the United States. The United States assessment rate might then rest at 33.32 per cent, within the legislatively established limits. Table VIII illustrates a scale constructed on this principle.

Variations could of course be made in the reductions or increases

TABLE VIII. ILLUSTRATIVE SPECIAL SCALE OF ASSESSMENTS FOR EXTRAORDINARY EXPENSES

	Normal Assessment		*Per cent of total*		
35 states at	.04	to be assessed .008 =	.28%	80% reduction.	GNP $30-559 million
10	.05	.008	.08		
1	.06	.01	.01		
4	.07	.02	.08		
3	.09	.03	.09		
1	.10	.04	.04		
1	.11	.04	.04		
3	.13—.14	.05	.15		
3	.15—.16	.07	.21		
3	.20	.08	.24		
3	.21—.23	.10	.30		
2	.24—.26	.12	.24	50% reduction.	GNP+$4.5 billion
1	.32	.20	.20		
2	.36—.38	.22	.44		
3	.40—.41	.24	.72		
4	.42—.45	.27	1.08		
3	.52—.53	.38	1.14		
2	.56—.58	.45	.90		
1	.74	.66	.66		
1	.86	.77	.77		
2	1.01	1.01	2.02	No reduction.	GNP+$9 billion
1	1.03	1.05	1.05	*Increase begins.*	GNP+$13 billion
1	1.17 Czechosl.	1.20	1.20		
1	1.20 Belgium	1.30	1.30		
1	1.28 Poland	1.38	1.38		
1	1.30 Sweden	1.50	1.50		
1	1.66 Australia	1.86	1.86	12% increase.	GNP+$17 billion
1	1.98 Ukraine	2.25	2.25		
1	2.03 India	2.35	2.35	15% increase.	GNP+$30 billion
1	2.24 Italy	2.55	2.55		
1	2.27 Japan	2.52	2.52		
1	3.12 Canada	3.60	3.60	15% increase.	GNP+$37 billion
1	4.57 China	4.57	4.57	(Special case)	GNP $1.70 billion
1	5.94 France	6.50	6.50	9% increase.	GNP+$60 billion
1	7.58 U.K.	8.18	8.18	7.8% increase.	GNP+$73 billion
1	14.97 USSR	16.17	16.17	8% increase.	GNP+$169 billion
1	32.02 USA	33.32	33.32	4% increase.	GNP+$525 billion
104	100.00%		100.00%		

from the Regular Budget norm as the Committee on Contributions and the Assembly might see fit. Thus, special allowance could be made in the assessments of states providing manpower for UN forces. Such a scale would be straightforward. It would avoid the rebate, deficit, and reapportionment problem. It would be adaptable. It would conform to the principles of the December 1962 resolution and remain within the acceptable ceiling for the highest apportionment. Furthermore, it would be adaptable for raising funds for other extraordinary expenses approved by the General Assembly in the future.

Special scales and dual standards are awkward to administer and can lead to further disputes. Notwithstanding their attractiveness under present circumstances, there is much that can be said against freezing matters into a formal mold at this time. Experience with financing extraordinary expenditures is still fairly limited. There would be advantages in keeping the method of handling these flexible, learning from additional experience what may be the most suitable ways of meeting different conditions. It is difficult to predict what the requirements of future peace-keeping operations may be. Furthermore, it is quite apparent that the differences presently separating the powers are not conducive to universal accord on any one formula. If the expenditures in the Congo can be sharply reduced in the near future, the need for a special scale of assessment may disappear. In my opinion it would be better to try other means of clearing up indebtedness and funding emergency operations until a wider diversity of experience has been gained or there is a larger measure of consensus among states.

E. RELYING UPON PARTIES AT INTEREST TO BEAR COSTS

United Nations costs for peace and security activities could be reduced or held to a minimum if the parties directly involved in situations calling for UN intervention were to assume the primary expenses, other than those of UN meetings, investigations, and good offices. The procedure in the Korean War is a case in point. There the parties responding to the UN appeal to aid in the defense of the Republic of Korea bore the costs of the armed forces that they themselves put at the disposal of the Supreme Commander, and the United States paid for the transportation, supplies, etc., which it provided. The principal expenditures of the UN were for the holding and servicing of meetings to consider the situation, communications among the parties involved, the time and travel expenses of the Secretary-General and other members of the Secretariat, the costs of the UN Commission which was already in Korea, and the refugee and reconstruction program undertaken by UNKRA, which was based upon special voluntary contributions.

Another case is the temporary United Nations administration in West Irian in 1962-1963 (UNTEA). While the United Nations provided the administrative personnel to administer this territory in the interim between Dutch and Indonesian rule, and while it arranged for the Pakistani troops that were sent to the island for police duty, the expenses of this operation were borne by the Netherlands and Indonesia in equal parts, according to the agreement of August 15, 1962.[26] The United Nations expenses were thus limited principally to those of the mediation team that was able to secure the agreement, and the time and costs involved in the UN meetings to discuss the situation and approve the various arrangements.

Not all situations requiring UN interposition are equally susceptible of handling in these manners. When observation or investigation commissions are needed in a region where hostilities are occurring or emotions are highly inflamed in regard to a contested area—as, for example, on the Greek borders in 1948-1949—the UN should be free of all ties and normally assume the costs of the teams it dispatches. Similarly, when it engages in a mediatorial effort—as in the Palestine fighting in 1948 or in the negotiations leading up to the Hague Agreement for the independence of Indonesia in 1949—it should be in a position to act quite independently of the parties and expect to foot the expenses of its mediator or good-offices committee. And when it is necessary for the United Nations to act rapidly to assemble and station an international force or commission to take over an area where fighting has been going on, in order to allow the parties to disengage or to keep them separated from one another, it should never have to wait for agreement to be reached among the contestants on such a detail as the financing of the peace force. The interests of world peace and security are paramount in such a situation. It is for such circumstances as these that the Organization needs to have stand-by funds for extraordinary and emergency expenses. The UN may always ask member states to volunteer assistance of different kinds. This may include not only money but also such things as an airlift—as the United States did at the beginning of the Congo crisis—supplies, use of strategic bases, communication facilities, personnel, and so forth. There are many ways in which UN expenses can be held down. It is to the interest of all Members that this be done wherever possible without sacrificing the mission the Organization is called upon to perform.

F. DEVELOPING INDEPENDENT MEANS OF INCOME

In looking to the future, one alternative that never ceases to intrigue some minds is the possibility of international organizations' having independent sources of revenue. The UN does have some direct income —e.g., from its sale of publications and stamps, the operations of its postal administration, the gift and souvenir shop, catering service, in-

[26] *United Nations Review*, IX (September 1962), 4-5, 39-42.

vestment income, staff assessment-tax equalization fund, and so on.[27] These bring in modest sums that are useful, but they do not involve the kinds of money needed to fund large and expensive operations or to reduce assessments or voluntary contributions. Furthermore, there are limits to their possibilities for expansion.

Private donations have played a part in the overall financial support of the United Nations. Some of these have been very substantial and contributed significantly to the UN's activities, as in the instance of the $8 million gift of John D. Rockefeller, Jr., for the land and headquarters of the UN in New York and the Ford Foundation grant of $6 million for the construction of the UN Library building. A host of small contributions have continually flowed into many of the refugee, relief, Children's Fund, and other humanitarian programs. Some movements have been started by groups, such as the Quakers, to develop regular support for UN projects. Others have volunteered to buy UN bonds and to promote a UN endowment fund.[28] But all of these add up to only a small proportion of the UN's needs. They beg questions of how far private support for an intergovernmental agency should be encouraged, whether this will undermine government responsibility or raise issues of non-governmental participation in decision-making on the use of such funds. They are doubtful as steady, dependable sources of income.[29]

Of a different nature qualitatively are such proposals as giving the United Nations the benefits of a surcharge upon such things as international mails, cables, air and sea transportation, passports, use of weather satellite data, and the like, to be levied and collected by states but turned over to the UN. Suggestions have also been made that it be permitted to levy service charges for technical assistance activities rendered to governments. And, going a step farther, it has been proposed that the Organization be given jurisdiction over the polar regions, over activities in outer space, and the right to collect a percentage of the revenues derivable from the exploitation of petroleum and other riches found beneath or in the sea beyond the limits of national jurisdiction.[30] Pro-

[27] These are discussed in a research paper for the Brookings project by Marcia Rosenfeld, entitled *Existing Sources of Independent Revenue for the United Nations* (Washington, Brookings Institution, October 1962, mimeograph).

[28] An extensive examination of these and other private support efforts will be found in another research memorandum for the Brookings project by Norman J. Padelford, *Private Support of the United Nations* (Cambridge, M.I.T. Center for International Studies, C/62-11, October 1962).

[29] J. David Singer, *Financing International Organization,* 145. See also Arthur N. Holcombe, *Strengthening the United Nations* (New York 1957), 259-61.

[30] A number of these proposals are set forth in an offset memorandum by Eugene Staley, "Direct Revenue for the United Nations" (Stanford, Stanford Research Institute,

ceeding even farther, to the point of requiring a sweeping change in the basic premises upon which the United Nations rests, are proposals that would give the Organization outright powers of taxation upon individuals, groups, and associations.[31]

Revenues of a fairly substantial nature, even possibly equaling or surpassing those derived from assessments, might conceivably be obtained from a system of levies, surcharges, and royalties if the member states were ready to allow the United Nations to impose and collect such charges. Many of the claims that have been made in this direction lack adequate supporting analysis, however.[32] Some of the proposals, such as taking over the polar areas or getting into outer-space activities, could easily result in far-reaching expenditures with little definite assurance of substantive income in the near future. As Howard Taubenfeld has wisely remarked: "It would be more humane for the U.N. to raise funds and develop the needy areas on earth, charging interest and living off it, than to raise the huge sums necessary for realizing gains from the remote areas, thus draining the resources represented by the investment capital from needy human beings."[33]

There is little evidence that states are ready to concede jurisdiction to the United Nations either over important potential mineral deposits beneath the high seas or over the business of international transactions, communications, and circulation. The surcharge levied upon shipping in the Suez Canal after 1956 was agreed upon only as an exceptional measure to pay for the work of reopening, deepening, and improving the facilities of the Canal. States may be willing on other specific occasions to authorize similar limited surcharges for reimbursement of a particular activity. It has yet to be demonstrated, all things considered, that it would be desirable to confer unrestricted powers upon the UN or any other world body to raise independent revenues. The power of an independent purse could become the prelude to the seizing and exercising of independent power. This could be detrimental to national independence and even ultimately to personal freedom. A number of questions

November 13, 1961). Some are further developed by John H. E. Fried in a research memorandum for the Brookings Institution, entitled *United Nations Revenue Through Levies on International Activities* (Washington, Brookings Institution, November 1962, mimeograph). The field as a whole is critically appraised by Howard J. Taubenfeld in a paper entitled *Long-Range Possibilities of Independent Revenue for the United Nations* (Washington, Brookings Institution, October 1962, mimeograph).

[31] For example, Grenville Clark and Louis Sohn, *World Peace Through World Law* (2d edn., New York 1961), xxxvii-xxxix, 349-58.

[32] U.S. Senate Subcommittee on the United Nations Charter, *Budgetary and Financial Problems of the United Nations*, Staff Study No. 6 (Washington 1954), 19.

[33] Taubenfeld, 48-49.

raised in the Congress some time ago still hold with respect to taxation proposals:

> (1) Would not a direct tax on individuals cause resentment among the people and lose public support for the U.N.? (2) Would the American people, already objecting to extensive foreign aid programs, agree to substantial increases in U.N. expenditures? (3) Could agreement be reached on the kind of taxes that would be fair and equitable in view of the various conditions that exist in different states? (4) Who would be responsible for the collection of such taxes? (5) What machinery would be set up for the enforcement of tax laws against individual citizens?
>
> These may not be insuperable problems. But given the present state of world affairs they are tough enough to make unlikely the adoption of any U.N. tax system in the near future.[34]

There is one area in which the United Nations can deal with its financial situation within its own bounds. This is in maintaining a strict control upon unnecessary expenditures. The problem is not a lack of monitoring of the expenses of authorized activities. A careful watch is kept upon these. The real problem is the tendency of UN debates and agendas to become longer and longer; to require more meetings in which to get business done. This is in part a by-product of the admission of large numbers of new members. But it is also a result of an inclination on the part of many delegates to speak on nearly every question, to exercise freely their right of reply, and to feel that they must restate positions they have set forth in committee meetings when subjects come to plenary gatherings for final action. This is a sphere that calls for restraint and selectivity—where silence will not impair vital interests. Restraint can also be practiced in requests for unnecessary documentation. The conduct of the XVIIth session of the General Assembly under the presidency of Sir Zafrullah Khan of Pakistan afforded a model of business-like procedure that deserves to be emulated by future meetings and other organs. In the area of economic and technical assistance, temptations can easily arise to ask for UN assistance in order to be on the list with other countries and for the prestige this may gain in internal politics. But such temptations must be kept in hand if UN finances are to remain viable. Members need to remind themselves that the Organization does have built-in limitations; that it must be kept solvent if it is to accomplish its purposes.

The "problem" of UN finances cannot be resolved unless all Members are prepared to work at it together and along all fronts simultaneously. The pinching off of sustenance, whether it be in the nature of po-

[34] Senate Subcommittee on UN Charter, Staff Study, 21.

litical or of financial support, is bound to impair the health of an international organization no less than an embolism in the blood stream of an individual. If the United Nations is to remain at all effective in the settlement of international disputes and maintenance of peace, if it is to assist economic and social advancement in a meaningful way during the Decade of Development, there must be a freeing of the flow of its lifeblood, a reknitting of the vessels of its support. The small and emergent countries have a vital stake, perhaps even greater than the more developed countries, in the continuance and effectiveness of these activities.

The purposes for which the United Nations was founded, and which have come to be seen in a larger light in the expanded world community of the 1960's, cannot be served without assuring the institution adequate financial means. They cannot long be maintained if there are to be self-appointed evaders of the common responsibility for paying for what the Organization legitimately and concertedly decides to undertake. Nor can blind cutting or curbing of expenditures on the familiar "meat-axe" principle known in the Congress in Washington serve the interests of the Members. At the same time there is need for preserving an enlightened sense of balance with respect to the number and cost of activities the Organization should be asked to assume. For its future can be put in jeopardy by undue haste and zeal as well. This is no doubt a part of what Secretary of State Dean Rusk had in mind when he recently remarked that an "increased sense of responsibility among all" is needed in approaching the problems and the future of the United Nations.[35]

[35] Press conference, March 8, 1963.

NOTES AND QUESTIONS

1. For the most complete study of the evolution of the financing problem and the prospects for its solution, see John C. Stoessinger and Associates, *Financing the United Nations System* (The Brookings Institution, Washington, 1964). Various transition proposals are made in the book to augment the independent sources of United Nations revenue without involving any real act of commitment on the part of nations. Is the solution to UN financing to find an independent source of revenue? Does this line of search overlook the fact that the financing issue has been used to argue about the extent to which a political consensus of the Big Two is a precondition for peace-keeping?
2. How does Padelford propose handling peace-keeping operations that require special assessments? How do Clark and Sohn handle the issue of special assessments to meet unforeseen contingencies?

C. Beyond Financing and So-Called Financing

Many of the political and constitutional issues underlying the so-called financing problem of the United Nations became clearly visible as the 19th Session of the General Assembly prepared to meet in the fall of 1964. With the United States assuming vigorous leadership, a sizeable group of the members declared their intention to invoke Article 19 of the Charter against those states which, not having met Assembly assessments for UNEF and ONUC operations, were now more than two years in arrears in meeting their overall financial obligations to the Organization. In pressing this position, these states relied heavily upon the Advisory Opinion of the ICJ (see Section A of this chapter) as an authoritative basis for the invocation of Article 19, especially in view of the fact that the General Assembly had "accepted" the Opinion. See Memorandum on Article 19 prepared by the United States State Department Legal Advisor's Office, *Department of State Bulletin,* vol. 51 (November 9, 1964), pp. 681–690. France, the Soviet Union, and those states commonly aligned with the latter, indicated that such action would not induce them to pay the assessments; rather they continued to maintain the position that the assessments were unconstitutional and that the Advisory Opinion was not legally binding upon the Assembly or any of its Members. Some observers felt that if Article 19 were invoked, these delinquent states might have become quite obstructive to the work of the Organization and perhaps might even have withdrawn altogether from Membership.

Since the United States refused to alter its position, the stage was now set for a "confrontation"; that is, should one of the alleged defaulting states attempt to cast a vote in the General Assembly, it would be challenged by one of those members who held the United States' position. See Article 19. Because many individuals, including the representatives of the states most concerned, felt that such a confrontation might involve serious political consequences for the working of the Organization, procedures were worked out to avoid this. Thus it was that the General Assembly during its entire 19th Session held no recorded votes, and a series of informal meetings were held to carry on with the work of the Assembly. This situation hampered the Assembly and in February of 1965 the Assembly directed Quaison-Sackey, then President of that body, to form a Special Committee on Peace-Keeping Operations. The Committee, consisting of 33 members, was expected to work out an agreement under which the immediate financial problems of the United Nations could be met and normal voting procedures could be established in the Assembly. At the same time, the Committee was requested to engage in a comprehensive review of the peace-keeping operations of the Organization.

The Committee met during the spring and summer of 1965. Their discussions and debates were quite spirited and in the main characterized by obviously sincere and conscientious efforts on the parts of the delegates to come to grips with the problems of future peace-keeping operations. See A/AC/PV, pp. 1–17. At the same time, it became clear that the states held such divergent views on the issues raised by these problems that it would be impossible to reconcile them before the 20th Session of the Assembly was to be convened. Attention then shifted to the immediate crises.

From the very outset, the political problem raised by the possibility of the invocation of Article 19, certain members had suggested that a special fund be set up inside the United Nations for use in non-peace-keeping operations, that the states be asked to make voluntary contributions to this fund and that these contributions would be considered as a portion of the overall expenses paid by the various members. This formula, it was thought, would save the legal positions of the contending parties and at the same time permit the Organization to return to normal operation. Both the United States and the U.S.S.R. showed some willingness to agree to this formula but each set conditions concerning its operation that were unsuitable to the other. In August of 1965, however, the United States recognized that it was not politically feasible to invoke Article 19 against the Soviet Union and Ambassador Arthur Goldberg announced at a meeting of the Special Committee that the United States therefore would no longer insist upon it. With this statement the Committee was able to achieve a consensus and President Quaison-Sackey announced at the opening of the 20th Session of the General Assembly the following:

The General Assembly is now resuming the work of its nineteenth session and I call the 1331st plenary meeting to order.

I wish first of all to welcome all representatives who are present here today.

The members of the General Assembly will recall that when we met last at the 1330th meeting on 18 February 1965, the Assembly adopted resolution 2006 (XIX) establishing a Special Committee on Peace-Keeping Operations to undertake, as soon as possible, a comprehensive review of the whole question of peace-keeping operations in all their aspects, including ways of overcoming the present financial difficulties of the Organization. The Special Committee has been very active during the last few months and Members will have seen the reports of the Special Committee. These are contained in documents A/5915 and Add. 1 and A/5916. In particular, I should like to draw the attention of the Members of the General Assembly to the statement which I, as Chairman of the Special Committee, made at the conclusion of the eighteenth meeting of the Committee which represented the consensus in the Committee. I should now like to read out this statement:

In the light of the statements made in the Committee, without prejudice to the positions taken therein and on the basis of paragraph 11 of the Committee's report of 15 June, I take it that the consensus is:

(a) That the General Assembly will carry on its work normally in accordance with its rules of procedure;

(b) That the question of the applicability of Article 19 of the Charter will not be raised with regard to the United Nations Emergency Force and the United Nations Operation in the Congo;

(c) That the financial difficulties of the Organization should be solved through voluntary contributions by Member States, with the highly developed countries making substantial contributions.

I take it that the General Assembly adopts the reports of the Special Committee.

If I hear no objection, it is so decided.

As Members are aware, the work entrusted to the Special Committee in terms of General Assembly resolution 2006 (XIX) has only been dealt with in part by the Committee. It is my understanding that there is general agreement that it is necessary to complete the work covered by the Assembly resolution I just mentioned. If it is acceptable to the Members of the General Assembly, I would propose that the modalities for the continuance of the work should be decided upon at the twentieth session.

If I hear no objection, it is so decided.

During the course of the debate and the discussion of the Special Committee, the Secretary-General and the President of the Assembly assumed the responsibility of preparing a report. This Report (A/AC. 121/4) summarized the issues which had been raised, recorded the views concerning these issues and offered some guidelines for future discussion and action. The Report was regarded by all the participants as remarkably accurate, exceptionally thorough, and a very helpful contribution to the thinking about these problems. In addition, the Report represents the state of current thinking by various states on the problems of establishing an international police force, and for these reasons it is reproduced below. Like the memorandum of Dag Hammarskjöld in Chapter 9, it is a document that must be read carefully. It raises many issues in a succinct, analytical style. The various definitions of peace-keeping, the range of constitutional and political positions which have been taken on the allocation of functions on peace-keeping between the Security Council and the General Assembly, and the review of various methods prepared for financing peace-keeping operations.

Special Committee on Peace-Keeping Operations: Report of the Secretary-General and the President of the General Assembly

INTRODUCTION

1. On 18 Feburary 1965, the General Assembly, during the course of its nineteenth session, adopted resolution 2006 (XIX) on the subject of a comprehensive review of the whole question of peace-keeping operations in all their aspects. The resolution reads as follows:

> "*The General Assembly,*
>
> "*Concerned* at the situation at its nineteenth session,
>
> "*Deeply anxious* to resolve urgently the problems which have arisen at that session, so as to enable the Organization to continue to fulfil its objectives,
>
> "*Considering* it necessary to ensure as soon as possible the normalization of its work,
>
> "1. *Invites* the Secretary-General and the President of the General Assembly, as a matter of urgency, to make arrangements for and to undertake appropriate consultations on the whole question of peace-keeping operations in all their aspects, including ways of overcoming the present financial difficulties of the Organization;
>
> "2. *Authorizes* the President of the General Assembly to establish a Special Committee on Peace-keeping Operations, under the chairmanship of the President of the Assembly and with the collaboration of the Secretary-General, the composition of which will be announced by the President after appropriate consultations;
>
> "3. *Instructs* the Special Committee, taking into account the consultations envisaged in paragraph 1 above, to undertake as soon as possible a comprehensive review of the whole question of peace-keeping operations in all their aspects, including ways of overcoming the present financial difficulties of the Organization;
>
> "4. *Requests* the Special Committee to submit a report to the General Assembly as soon as possible and not later than 15 June 1965."

In accordance with operative paragraph 1 of the above resolution, the Secretary-General and the President of the General Assembly undertook extensive consultations with a large number of Member States. The Secretary-General and the President of the Assembly wish to place on record their deep appreciation of the unfailing courtesy and the unstinted co-operation extended by Member States, without which the consultations would not have been so helpful and constructive as they have turned out to be.

2. In the preparation of the present report which, it is hoped, will assist the Special Committee in carrying out the important task entrusted to it by the General Assembly, the Secretary-General and the President of the Assembly have, apart from the valuable

consultations referred to in paragraph 1 above, also benefited considerably from the formal meetings of the Special Committee which were conducted in a constructive and co-operative manner and during which many helpful ideas and positive suggestions were submitted by the members.

3. The Secretary-General and the President of the General Assembly have attempted in sections I to IV of the report to place before the members of the Special Committee an account of the views and suggestions made both during the informal consultations and the formal meetings of the Special Committee on the different aspects of the matter covered by General Assembly resolution 2006 (XIX). In section I, there is also a short account of the experience of the United Nations in the field of peace-keeping operations. It is hoped that this will help to ensure a proper perspective in dealing with the problem.

4. In section V, the Secretary-General and the President have indicated some broad conclusions that can be drawn from the views expressed by the members and made certain observations which, it is hoped, will contribute in some measure towards the normalization of the work of the General Assembly and in solving the problems that confront the Organization.

I. GENERAL

5. The term "peace-keeping operations" which, according to the decision taken by the General Assembly on 18 February 1965, is to be reviewed in all its aspects by the Special Committee, is not defined as such in the Charter, nor has any effort been made in any United Nations body at any time in the past to attempt a clear and precise definition of this term. It is therefore not surprising that there does not appear to exist among the States Members of the United Nations even a general consensus as to what constitutes a "peace-keeping operation" as that term is referred to in General Assembly resolution 2006 (XIX). Some include under this term all measures taken by the Organization in the maintenance of international peace and security, either for the peaceful adjustment of a situation likely to impair the general welfare or friendly relations among States, or for the pacific settlement of disputes or for initiating action with respect to threats to the peace, breaches of peace and acts of aggression. Others give the term a more restricted interpretation.

6. Some of the views bearing on this question and which were expressed during the informal consultations and the formal meetings of the Committee are indicated below:

(a) Peace-keeping operations are operations of a military, para-military or non-military character which are to be conducted by the United Nations for the maintenance of international peace and security, with the exception of those which fall under the category of enforcement action under Chapter VII of the Charter. According to this view, such operations are of a non-mandatory and non-coercive nature and require an invitation from or at least the consent of the country on whose territory an operation is to take place and do not place any obligations on Member States as to contributions in the form of personnel and logistical support. Such operations should not be allowed to constitute or be a pretext for any type of foreign intervention or to infringe on the national sovereignty of any country. If armed personnel is involved, the use of force should be limited strictly to the requirements of self-defence. These operations could take different forms, such as:

(i) Observation of conditions on one side or on both sides of a frontier;

(ii) Fact-finding and observation in regard to alleged interference from outside in the domestic affairs of a Member State;

(iii) Observation or supervision of a cease-fire line;

(iv) Missions of mediation and conciliation;

(v) Missions connected with investigation or observation to clarify the factual situation;

(vi) Assistance to a country to maintain law and order where requested by that country and in conditions in which international peace and security might otherwise be disturbed.

(b) Another view is that the term "peace-keeping operation" connotes an operation of an executive nature which interposes a United Nations presence in a situation likely to lead to a breach of the peace, but the activity involved may constitute nothing more than either the employment of peaceful means which is of the parties' own choice, within the meaning of Article 33, or a measure for the peaceful adjustment of a situation which the General Assembly can recommend under Article 14. These operations are qualitatively different from the expedition of a military force with a clearly coercive mission.

(c) Yet another view is that the concept of peace-keeping operations is a new one that should be incorporated into the Charter as soon as possible by the inclusion of a new chapter which could be placed between the present Chapters VI and VII. Peace-keeping operations are conducted on the territory of one or more States, Members of the United Nations or not, at their request or with their consent, and undertaken by military contingents supplied chiefly by medium and small Powers. The only objective of these operations would be to preserve peaceful conditions but it does not exclude, during the operations, recourse to coercive action in given circumstances and for a limited period of time.

(d) It has been observed that it is unnecessary to decide each and every one of the characteristic features of these operations, that it may suffice to spell out that these operations can be carried out only with the consent of the State or States which are parties to the dispute and that it is a question of military operations in which the Member States participate in a manner which is fundamentally different from that provided under Chapter VII of the Charter.

(e) Some members feel that any operations which involve the use of armed force, whatever the reasons for initiating such operations might be, are "actions" within the meaning of Chapter VII and fall entirely within the exclusive prerogatives of the Security Council.

(f) Another view is that the exclusive competence of the Security Council covers all operations that involve the establishment of a force, military or otherwise, except for the mere purpose of observation and investigation, whether or not the action is initiated under the provisions of Chapter VII of the Charter.

7. It will be obvious from the preceding paragraphs that the concept of "peace-keeping" is capable of widely differing interpretations and, as such, incapable of being

accurately and clearly defined to the satisfaction of all Member States. It might be useful in this connexion if an attempt were to be made to outline the experience of the United Nations in this undefined and broad field—an experience which indicates very clearly the varied nature of such activities.

8. What are called the peace-keeping operations of the United Nations have varied greatly in size, nature and objective. There have also been wide variations in methods of financing. United Nations peace-keeping operations of various types and sizes have been organized in response to critical situations in Greece, Palestine, Kashmir, Suez and Gaza, Lebanon, Jordan, the Congo, West Irian, Yemen and Cyprus. It may be noted that only in the cases of the United Nations Emergency Force (UNEF) and the United Nations Temporary Executive Authority (UNTEA) did the initiative for setting up these peace-keeping missions come from the General Assembly.

9. There is great diversity both as regards the situations dealt with by United Nations peace-keeping efforts and the type of operation set up to deal with those situations. In some of the situations, for example in Kashmir, Palestine, Lebanon and Cyprus, fighting was actually going on when the United Nations action was taken. In most of them, outbreaks of violence have been a continuous possibility, and actual incidents involving the use of armed force have been regular occurrences throughout the existence of the United Nations Truce Supervision Organization in Palestine (UNTSO) and the United Nations Military Observers Group in India and Pakistan (UNMOGIP). Some situations, notably the Congo, Lebanon and Cyprus, have been made more difficult by threats of external interference and the fears and suspicions which such threats inevitably arouse.

10. Broadly speaking, United Nations peace-keeping operations may be divided into two main categories, namely, observer operations (UNTSO, UNMOGIP, United Nations Observation Group in Lebanon (UNOGIL) and United Nations Yemen Observation Mission (UNYOM)) and operations involving the deployment of armed forces (UNEF, United Nations Operation in the Congo (ONUC), UNTEA and United Nations Force in Cyprus (UNFICYP)). In three cases (Palestine, India-Pakistan and Cyprus) a mediator has also been appointed, at one stage or another, while in the cases of Palestine and the Congo, conciliation commissions were also set up.

11. The mandates of the various observer operations have varied widely, ranging from the observation and maintenance of a truce agreement (UNTSO and UNMOGIP) to a much more limited task of reporting, as in the cases of UNOGIL and UNYOM, and most lately in the Dominican Republic. The mandates of the various forces have also varied greatly. UNEF operates on the Armistice Demarcation Line in Gaza and on the International Frontier, covering a distance of about 450 kilometres. ONUC, with its more complex mandate, including assistance to the Government of the Congo, was far more involved with events of all kinds within the boundaries of the Congo. UNTEA had a very limited and transitional task, while UNFICYP is of necessity involved by its mandate in the intricacies of the Cyprus problem and the relations between the Greek Cypriot and Turkish Cypriot communities.

12. The national make-up of the armed forces involved in peace-keeping operations has also varied widely according to their role and location. The troops of UNTEA came from a single country, while thirty-six countries provided military personnel for

ONUC. The different characteristics and demands of each operation have meant that troops of a nationality which was entirely acceptable in a previous peace-keeping mission did not prove to be acceptable in another mission. The organization and type of military personnel required also vary according to the task to be performed.

13. The conduct of these operations, whatever their size or nature, involves constant thought, direction and frequent decisions both in the field and at United Nations Headquarters. The decisions required of both the Secretary-General and the senior military and civilian officials in the field are often urgent ones which involve lives and the possibility of quick and serious deterioration of a situation. Both speed and wisdom are essential in such decisions and a great responsibility therefore rests upon the Secretary-General and his representatives in the field, for the urgency of the situation sometimes makes full consultation with the representative organs of the United Nations or with national representatives impossible. These decisions relate, for example, to such complex matters as the interposing of United Nations forces, to directives which may put United Nations troops in a position where they have to use minimum force in exercising their legitimate right of self-defence, and where emergency measures have to be taken to prevent a breakdown of law and order. In observer operations, urgent decisions are also required in emergencies where a rapid and firm intervention by the peace-keeping mission is required.

14. Involving as they do by their very nature the most delicate political considerations as well as, more often that not, a very sensitive military situation, both main types of peace-keeping operations have to be conducted with the utmost care and with constant supervision at all levels. The difference in the relative importance of various aspects of the problems concerned as seen at United Nations Headquarters and in the areas of operation themselves also requires a constant interchange of information and directives between United Nations Headquarters and the field.

15. The Secretary-General and the Secretariat at Headquarters require from the chief military and civilian officials in the field regular and immediate information as to developments on the spot, for the information of the Security Council and of Member States, as well as for their own needs. Advice on the position of the peace-keeping operation and on its potential capacity to deal with probable future situations is also essential. The military and civilian heads of operations in the field also normally require constant advice and direction from Headquarters so that their activities may conform to wider political considerations, to the mandate laid down by the Security Council or General Assembly, and to the Secretary-General's concept of that mandate.

16. The logistic support of these operations, especially those involving sizable bodies of troops, is also a large and continuing responsibility both at Headquarters and in the field, a responsibility which is often complicated by the diverse make-up of the peace-keeping operations and by the uncertain and short-term nature of financing arrangements, as in UNFICYP.

17. Although the General Assembly has usually been responsible for the financial arrangements for peace-keeping operations, the methods of financing have varied widely. Some are charged to the regular budget (UNTSO and UNMOGIP, UNOGIL and the Mediator on Cyprus). Others, such as UNEF and ONUC, function on a more

complicated basis—on a special account outside the regular budget, on *ad hoc* financing and a combination of assessed and voluntary contributions. A third category, notably UNTEA and UNYOM, have been financed on the basis of a sharing of costs by the Governments principally concerned, while UNFICYP is financed by voluntary contributions. In the case of the small United Nations operation in the Dominican Republic, in the absence of any specific provision for the financing of the operation, the Secretary-General is acting under the provisions of paragraph 1 (a) of General Assembly resolution 1985 (XVIII) of 17 December 1963 and paragraph 3 of resolution 2004 (XIX) of 18 February 1965.

II. CONSTITUTIONAL

18. The conflicting views enumerated in the preceding section regarding the concept of peace-keeping operations are based largely on conflicting interpretations of the relevant provisions of the Charter and, in particular, on the provisions relating to the respective functions and powers of the Security Council and the General Assembly. The consultations which the Secretary-General and the President of the General Assembly held with Member States and the debates in the formal meetings of the Special Committee have helped to some extent to crystallize the views concerning this aspect of the problem. An attempt has been made in the following paragraphs to deal with the main points that were brought up.

19. There appears to be general agreement that the functions and powers of the Security Council and the General Assembly should be understood as complementary and not as contradictory. Article 24, paragraph 1, of the Charter states:

> "In order to ensure prompt and effective action by the United Nations, its Members confer on the Security Council primary responsibility for the maintenance of international peace and security, and agree that in carrying out its duties under this responsibility the Security Council acts on their behalf."

Further, Article 25 of the Charter states:

> "The Members of the United Nations agree to accept and carry out the decisions of the Security Council in accordance with the present Charter."

The specific powers granted to the Security Council for the discharge of the duties referred to in Article 24, paragraph 1, are laid down in Chapters VI, VII, VIII and XII of the Charter. The General Assembly also bears its responsibility in maintaining international peace and security. The general functions and powers of the General Assembly relating to the maintenance of international peace and security are defined in Articles 10, 11, 12, 14, 15 and 35 of the Charter.

20. It is frequently stated that all enforcement actions are the exclusive prerogatives of the Security Council under the provisions of the Charter. However, a serious difference of view exists as to what constitutes enforcement action. Many Members hold that enforcement action is action covered by Articles 41 and 42 of Chapter VII of the Charter which is exclusively within the competence of the Security Council. According to this view, action taken at the request or at least with the concurrence of a party or parties and which is of a non-mandatory and non-coercive nature is not enforcement action and as such does not fall within the exclusive competence of the Security Council.

21. The opposite view is that, according to the Charter, it is only the Security Council that can take decisions on any questions connected with the adoption of measures for the maintenance of international peace and security, which include operations involving armed forces of the United Nations. The utilization of United Nations armed forces in any instance, without any exception whatsoever, is an enforcement action and must therefore be governed by the corresponding provisions of Chapter VII of the Charter. In other words, the establishment of United Nations armed forces aimed at maintaining or restoring international peace and security is by agreement of the permanent members of the Security Council on all fundamental matters relating to their authorization, utilization and financing. According to this view, the broader participations in decisions on matters relating to the practical implementation of the operations of the United Nations aimed at the maintenance of international peace and security must be ensured by expediting the enlargement of the composition of the Security Council. The responsibility of the General Assembly consists of the consideration of any questions related to the maintenance of international peace and security and the adoption of suitable recommendations on such questions, taking into account the terms of reference of the General Assembly as laid down in the Charter. Furthermore, any question on which action becomes necessary is transferred by the General Assembly to the Security Council, but if the Council is unable to adopt a decision on any given concrete question related to the maintenance of international peace, nothing can prevent the General Assembly from considering the whole question anew in order to adopt new recommendations based on the terms of reference of the Assembly.

22. Another view is that enforcement action includes not only measures provided for in Articles 41 and 42 but all measures the purpose of which is the establishment of a force, military or otherwise, charged with the task of intervening against a State or inside a State, even when the latter consents and where the effective use of arms is theoretically limited to restricted or exceptional circumstances. This would exclude operations the purpose of which is to conduct observations, surveillance or enquiry, even when military personnel are used and even when such personnel are numerous, provided that such military personnel do not constitute units under a military commander and provided that they are not charged with their own security, since the latter is a task for the local forces. In other words, whenever an operation involves the use of armed personnel other than for the mere purpose of observation and investigation, such operation is enforcement action within the sole competence of the Security Council.

23. In connexion with the functions and powers of the Security Council, considerable importance is attached to General Assembly resolution 1991 A (XVIII) of 17 December 1963 on the question of equitable representation on the Security Council. In that resolution, the General Assembly recognized that it was necessary to enlarge the membership of the Security Council to provide for a more adequate geographical representation of non-permanent members and to make it a more effective organ for carrying out its functions under the Charter. The Charter amendment to this effect, decided upon by the General Assembly in the aforementioned resolution, will come into force when it has been ratified by two-thirds of the Members of the United

Nations, including all the permanent members of the Security Council. As at 31 May 1965, seventy-two Member States, including one permanent member of the Security Council, have ratified this Charter amendment and there is every reason to hope that the amendment will come into force before long.

24. Although it is not explicitly stipulated in the Charter, it seems to be the general opinion that in view of the primary responsibility for the maintenance of international peace and security conferred upon the Security Council by Members of the United Nations for the purpose of ensuring prompt and effective action by the Organization, any question which involves or may involve peace-keeping operations should be examined in the first instance by the Security Council in order that an appropriate decision could be adopted as promptly as possible by that organ.

25. It seems equally acceptable that if the Security Council is unable for any reason whatever to adopt decisions in exercise of its primary responsibility for the maintenance of international peace and security, there is nothing to prevent the General Assembly from considering the matter immediately and making appropriate recommendations in conformity with its responsibilities and the relevant provisions of the Charter. The General Assembly, if not in regular session, may be called into emergency session of the purpose referred to in the preceding paragraph upon the request of the Security Council or by a majority of the States Members of the United Nations. If the General Assembly is called upon to deal with a situation in these circumstances, it may under the relevant provisions of the Charter make recommendations to the Members of the United Nations or to the Security Council or to both, but there appears to be considerable support for the view that the Assembly should, in the first instance, address its recommendations back to the Council.

26. It was evident during the consultations that Members agree that if the General Assembly resolved by the required two-thirds majority to make recommendations to the Security Council, the weight of such recommendations, supported by a substantial majority of the membership of the United Nations, would have a very significant effect upon the subsequent action by the Security Council. It is likewise to be expected that the General Assembly will duly take into account and give the most serious weight to the views expressed and positions taken in the Council, including those by the permanent members, when the Council was previously seized of the matter at issue.

27. During the consultations, it was apparent that there was a difference of opinion concerning the scope and nature of the recommendations the General Assembly is authorized to make under the provisions of the Charter relating to the maintenance of international peace and security. This has understandably given rise to conflicting positions and has even led some to conclude that the position can be rectified only by an early revision of the Charter through the inclusion of provisions to deal with situations not adequately covered in the present Charter.

28. Article 11, paragraph 2, concerning the competence of the General Assembly to deal with questions relating to the maintenance of international peace and security, reads as follows:

> "The General Assembly may discuss any questions relating to the maintenance of international peace and security brought before it by any Member of the United Nations, or by the Security Council, or by a State which is not a

Member of the United Nations in accordance with Article 35, paragraph 2, and, except as provided in Article 12, may make recommendations with regard to any such question to the State or States concerned or to the Security Council or to both. Any such question on which action is necessary shall be referred to the Security Council by the General Assembly either before or after discussion."

The difference in interpretation has arisen largely on the exact meaning of the word "action" in the second sentence of the above quoted provision of the Charter. Some Members relate this word to the enforcement action covered by Chapter VII of the Charter which, in their view, is action directed against a State. They admit that such action is beyond the competence of the General Assembly. They do, however, make a distinction between such action and action taken with the consent or concurrence of the party concerned and not against that party. In regard to action of the latter type, they hold that the General Assembly is not obligated under Article 11, paragraph 2, to refer the question to the Council for decision. Another view is that, when implicitly or explicitly describing as coercive actions only those operations directed against a State, to the exclusion of those which have as their object action against disturbers of the peace, communities or provinces, a distinction is established which is not justified either by the Charter or by experience, and that enforcement action occurs whenever the use of force is provided for in an operation authorized with or without the consent or concurrence of the parties. According to this view, the action covered by Article 11, paragraph 2, includes not only the measures provided for in Chapter VII of the Charter, in Articles 41 and 42, but also measures the purpose of which is the establishment of a force, military or otherwise, charged with the task of intervening against a State or inside a State even when the latter consents and where the effective use of arms is theoretically limited to restricted or exceptional circumstances. This would leave aside the operations the purpose of which is to conduct observation, surveillance or enquiry, even when military personnel are used and even when such personnel are numerous, provided that such military personnel do not constitute units under a military commander and provided that they are not charged with their own security since the latter is a task for the local forces. Yet another view is that "action" covers any decision on matters relating to the practical implementation of the operations of the United Nations aimed at the maintenance of international peace and security.

29. Mention was also made by many Members in this connexion of Article 14 which, in their view, gives the General Assembly the competence to "recommend measures for the peaceful adjustment of any situation, regardless of origin, which it deems likely to impair the general welfare or friendly relations among nations." However, there does not appear to be any clear consensus regarding the scope of the term "measures."

30. Although, in terms of the provisions of the Charter, the General Assembly, if called upon to consider a question relating to the maintenance of international peace and security, is empowered to make recommendations to the Members of the United Nations or to the Security Council or to both, it appears to be widely accepted that if the Assembly is considering a question that involves or might involve a peace-keeping operation, it should make appropriate recommendations to the Council in the first instance in view of the latter's primary responsibility in such matters.

31. Apart from the difficulty in defining the precise scope of the General Assembly's recommendations, there is a very wide difference of views regarding the steps to be followed in the event of the Security Council being unable to act promptly in conformity with the recommendations of the Assembly.

32. Some Members hold the view that if the Security Council is unable to act even on the second attempt and in spite of the strong recommendations of the General Assembly, it would be realistic to accept the inability of the Organization to intervene in the given situation and to seek help outside the United Nations framework. This view does not, however, appear to be supported by the majority of Member States. In fact, there are some who would like to see the General Assembly empowered, in such a situation, to authorize the peace-keeping operation. Others suggest a more flexible approach and would have the General Assembly, at that stage, make appropriate recommendations for measures possibly not involving the establishment of a peace-keeping operation to deal with the situation.

III. FINANCIAL

33. Operative paragraphs 1 and 3 of resolution 2006 (XIX) make reference to the need for "overcoming the present financial difficulties of the Organization." It does not seem necessary to dwell at any great length on the history of this aspect of the problem with which the Members of the United Nations are very familiar.

34. The Special Committee is, needless to say, concerned with the whole question of the financing of peace-keeping operations. However, it is widely accepted that the immediate task is the restoration of the solvency of the Organization and that this should be achieved through voluntary contributions by Member States. It has been suggested, in this connexion, that the highly developed countries should make substantial contributions.

35. The question of the financing of future peace-keeping operations has received considerable attention. Views on this important question often differ widely, as shows in the paragraphs which follow:

(a) The view that appears to be shared by a substantial number of Member States is that, in case the financing of a peace-keeping operation is not covered by special arrangements, it should fall under the competence of the General Assembly to make assessments according to Article 17 of the Charter. These special arrangements include those envisaged in Article 43 of the Charter, as well as other arrangements such as sharing the total costs between parties who desire the particular peace-keeping operation or financing wholly or in part through voluntary contributions. If the General Assembly is required to distribute the costs of a particular peace-keeping operation, the principle of the collective responsibility of all Member States shall apply, although the assessment may be made according to a special scale which would duly take into account the special responsibility of the permanent members of the Security Council, the degree to which a State is involved in the situation giving rise to a peace-keeping operation, and the economic capacity of Member States, particularly of the developing countries.

(b) Another view is that the question of the reimbursement of expenditure required for the execution of emergency measures adopted by the Security Council to deter or repel aggression through the United Nations armed forces should be decided in conformity with the principle that aggressor States bear political and material responsibility for the aggression they commit and for the material damage caused by that aggression. This does not, however, preclude the possibility that situations may arise where, in order to execute the above-mentioned emergency measures of the Security Council, it will be necessary for Member States to take part in defraying the expenditure involved in the maintenance and use of United Nations armed forces established in order to maintain international peace and security. According to this view, any question relating to the creation and use of armed forces, including the financing of such forces, is within the exclusive prerogative of the Security Council.

(c) A third view is that it is incumbent upon the Security Council to lay down the mode of financing of the operation which it has decided upon or recommended, either in accordance with a scale to be determined when the expenses are divided among the Members, or in accordance with the system of voluntary contributions.

(d) Another view is that the method of financing a peace-keeping operation through voluntary contributions is most unsatisfactory inasmuch as there is a large degree of uncertainty about what amounts will be actually available, and therefore the planning and advance arrangements essential to an efficient and economical operation are sorely hampered.

36. It is obvious from the preceding paragraphs that the question of financing future peace-keeping operations will need more detailed examination. In this connexion several suggestions of an organizational nature have been made:

(a) One proposal is for the establishment by the General Assembly of a standing finance committee made up of the permanent members of the Security Council and a relatively high percentage of those Member States in each geographical area that are large financial contributors to the United Nations. This committee would make suitable recommendations by a two-thirds majority to the General Assembly, on the basis of which the Assembly would apportion the expenses of the peace-keeping operation. In making its recommendations, the Committee would consider various alternative methods of financing, including direct financing by countries involved in a dispute, voluntary contributions and assessed contributions.

(b) Another proposal is for the establishment by the Security Council, under Article 29 of the Charter, of a committee which would assist it in exercising its financial powers. The composition of the committee could be laid down on a broader footing than that of the Council itself, which would make it possible to initiate in practice a dialogue between the Council and the most representative and most interested elements within the General Assembly.

(c) A third proposal is for the establishment of a committee consisting partly of Security Council members and partly of States nominated by the General Assembly from among non-members of the Council, with terms of reference agreed by both the Council and the General Assembly.

(d) Another proposal aimed at giving an institutional form to voluntary contributions is for the creation of a fund, made up of voluntary contributions, from which appropriations would be made by the General Assembly to meet the costs of a given peace-keeping operation.

(e) A proposal that appears to have very considerable support is for a strict compliance with regulation 13.1 of the Financial Regulations of the United Nations which requires that "no council, commission or other competent body shall take a decision involving expenditure unless it has before it a report from the Secretary-General on the administrative and financial implications of the proposal." The provisional rules of procedure of the Security Council contain no provision giving effect to this regulation and in practice it has seldom been observed. It has been suggested further that any resolution involving expenditure on a peace-keeping operation should as far as possible include in it an indication as to how the required financing is to be provided or secured.

37. During the consultations, several Members stressed the necessity of giving special attention to the problem of the continued financing of UNEF and the amortization of the bond issue.

44. A related question is the role of the Military Staff Committee. Several members expressed the view that the Military Staff Committee should be activated and given a positive role in future peace-keeping operations. It was suggested in this connexion that the participation in the work of the Military Staff Committee should be broadened so as to associate with it those Member States that would participate in peace-keeping operations. Another suggestion was aimed at the implementation of Article 47, paragraph 4, which provides for consultation between the Military Staff Committee and appropriate regional agencies.

45. Reference was also made to the composition of peace-keeping forces. The following views were expressed in this connexion.

(a) In order to ensure that the utilization of force by the United Nations should be in keeping only and exclusively with the interest of peace and should not in any manner be related to unilateral aims or purposes of individual States or groups of States, it is necessary that in the contingents of armed forces and the command over those forces participation be ensured on behalf of "all three groups of Member States, namely, the Western Powers, the neutralist Powers and the socialist Powers."

(b) It would be inadvisable to include contingents from any States that are permanent members of the Security Council. A view was expressed that it might not however be wise to proscribe the use of such contingents altogether and for all time.

(c) Another suggestion was that the peace-keeping operations should consist of troops from States that are not members of the Security Council.

(d) The principle of fair geographical distribution should be adhered to.

(e) When the operation is being undertaken at the request of a Member State, the concurrence of that State regarding the composition of the forces should be obtained.

V. OBSERVATIONS AND CONCLUSIONS

46. The necessity for the development and strengthening of the United Nations as a really effective instrument for the preservation and maintenance of international peace and security is an accepted fact. Needless to say, in order to achieve this objective, it is necessary to observe strict compliance with the provisions of the Charter, which has

been described as the starting point and the common denominator among all the Members of the Organization. It has been suggested that a complete solution, acceptable to all, of all the problems confronting the Organization in its main purpose of maintaining international peace and security might necessitate a revision of various provisions of the Charter. But it is evident that the vast majority of the Members of the Organization are confident that with goodwill and co-operation it should be possible to find some acceptable formula, within the terms of the Charter, to overcome the difficulties that face the Organization.

47. It would be correct to say that the problems that confront the United Nations have largely been due to the fact that the Organization has been, over the last decade or so, called upon to deal with situations in a manner not explicitly spelled out in the Charter. It is a fact that the concept of collective security, which is embedded in the Charter, has undergone significant changes over the last twenty years. This is not to deny the primary responsibility of the Security Council for maintaining international peace and security, nor is any attempt being made or contemplated to minimize the responsibilities of the permanent members of the Security Council.

48. What would appear to be necessary is for the Members of the United Nations, and particularly the permanent members of the Security Council which have a major responsibility in this regard, to face up to the realities of the situation and, in keeping with their obligations under the Charter and their common desire to enable the Organization to fulfil its objectives, take practical measures for overcoming the difficulties that confront the Organization.

49. The Charter of the United Nations contains numerous provisions aimed at dealing with situations involving the maintenance of international peace and security. It is contended by some that these provisions are incomplete and inadequate. At the same time it is a fact that the situations involving the restoration or maintenance of international peace and security vary so considerably that it would be very difficult to attempt to rewrite the Charter to include absolutely clear and precise provisions to deal with every given situation to the satisfaction of all Members. Much of the controversy seems to be at times somewhat academic in nature and one is led to wonder if there are in fact such serious differences in interpreting the Charter. In fact, there is a great deal of merit in the view that wider use of peaceful means of settling disputes, as provided for in the Charter, should be encouraged.

50. The circumstances that led to the establishment of the Special Committee and the general concern of the Members of the Organization to avoid a repetition of the unfortunate experience of the first part of the nineteenth session have understandably highlighted the need for ensuring the normal functioning of the General Assembly when it resumes in September. During the consultations undertaken by the Secretary-General and the President of the General Assembly, the view was repeatedly expressed that there should not be recurrence of the situation that prevented the General Assembly from functioning normally when it met last. This undoubtedly is one of the immediate tasks before the Committee and must necessarily deserve special attention.

51. Another equally important and pressing question relates to the present financial difficulties facing the Organization. There appears to be substantial support for the view that it is of prime importance to restore the solvency of the Organization by voluntary contributions by the entire membership of the Organization, it being under-

stood that this arrangement shall not be construed as any change in the basic positions of any individual Members and should be accepted as a co-operative effort by all Member States, aimed at the strengthening of the United Nations with a view to creating a climate in which the future may be harmoniously planned. If this view is generally acceptable, it is expected that the members of the Special Committee may wish to authorize the Secretary-General to take appropriate steps, in consultation with Member States, towards this end.

52. There remains the wider question of the comprehensive review that the Special Committee has been asked to undertake of the whole question of peace-keeping operations in all their aspects, including the authorization of operations, the composition of forces and their control, and the financing of such operations. It is accepted that such a review, the scope and importance of which are considerable, cannot be completed by 15 June, by which date the Special Committee is required to submit a report to the General Assembly. The comprehensive review must necessarily begin with a clear definition of the term "peace-keeping operations", at present interpreted in several different ways which cannot be reconciled to the satisfaction of everyone without further study. Undoubtedly, there has already been some noticeable progress in this matter, inasmuch as the views have become clearer and do not appear to be so far apart. It would, however, seem appropriate and advisable for the Special Committee to agree at this stage upon certain guidelines, within the terms of the Charter, which could apply to future peace-keeping operations. It must be borne in mind, in this connexion, that peace-keeping operations vary so much in so many ways that a considerable degree of flexibility will be required in dealing with each individual situation. However, the following broad guidelines may be found useful and practical:

(a) The Members of the United Nations have conferred on the Security Council primary responsibility for the maintenance of international peace and security.

(b) The General Assembly also bears its share of responsibility in maintaining international peace and security. The general functions and powers ot the Assembly relating to the maintenance of international peace and security are contained in Articles 10, 11, 12, 14, 15 and 35 of the Charter.

(c) The functions and powers of the Security Council and of the General Assembly should be understood as complementary and not as contradictory.

(d) In view of the primary responsibility for the maintenance of international peace and security conferred upon the Security Council by the Members of the United Nations for the purpose of ensuring prompt and effective action by the Organization, any question which involves or may involve peace-keeping operations should be examined, in the first instance, by the Security Council in order that appropriate action may be taken as promptly as possible by that organ.

(e) If the Security Council is unable for any reason whatever to adopt decisions in the exercise of its primary responsibility for the maintenance of international peace and security, there is nothing to prevent the General Assembly from considering the matter immediately and making appropriate recommendations in conformity with its responsibilities and the relevant provisions of the Charter.

(f) According to Article 11, paragraph 2, of the Charter, the General Assembly may choose to refer the question back to the Security Council with appropriate recommendations. If the General Assembly resolves by the required two-thirds majority to make such recommendations, it is to be expected that the weight of such recommendations, supported by a substantial majority of the membership of the United Nations, will have a very significant effect upon the subsequent action by the Security Council. It is likewise to be expected that the General Assembly will duly take into account and give the most serious weight to the views expressed and positions taken in the Security Council when the Council was previously seized of the matter at issue.

(g) The financing of peace-keeping operations should be done in conformity with the provisions of the Charter, and the General Assembly and the Security Council should co-operate in this respect.

(h) In each case involving a peace-keeping operation by the United Nations, various methods of financing may be considered, such as special arrangements among the parties directly involved, voluntary contributions, apportionment to the entire membership of the Organization and any combination of these various methods.

(i) If the costs of a particular peace-keeping operation, involving heavy expenditure, are to be apportioned among all the Members of the Organization, this should be done according to a special scale, due account being taken of: (1) the special responsibility of the permanent members of the Security Council; (2) the degree to which particular States are involved in the events or actions leading to a peace-keeping operation; and (3) the economic capacity of Member States, particularly of the developing countries.

(j) No decision involving heavy expenditure on a peace-keeping operation shall be taken without advice of the financial implications involved in the operation. The Secretary-General shall, in conformity with regulation 13.1 of the Financial Regulations of the United Nations, submit a report on the administrative and financial implications of the proposal.

53. It is obvious that the guidelines indicated above are neither comprehensive nor fully adequate to meet the varying needs that may arise. There is no doubt that these questions need more detailed study.

54. The Secretary-General and the President of the General Assembly sincerely hope that this report may help the members of the Special Committee in carrying out successfully the mandate given to them by the General Assembly.

NOTES AND QUESTIONS

1. One way of looking at the resolution to the so-called financing problem is that the principle of voluntary contribution has now emerged as one of the major methods of financing peace-keeping operations in the United Nations. Recall on this matter Brierley's position stated in Chapter 9.

   Ambassador Goldberg's statement to the Special Political Committee raised some new problems in this connection. After making clear that the United States had not abandoned its view on Article 19, he went on to say the following:

   > At the same time, we must make it crystal clear that if any Member can insist on making an exception to the principle of collective financial responsibility with respect to certain activities of the Organization, the United States reserves the same option to make exceptions if, in our view, strong and compelling reasons exist for doing so. There can be no double standard among the Members of the Organization.

It is not clear from this statement whether Ambassador Goldberg intended to include matters other than peace-keeping within the purview of this statement. If so, the problem of financial viability of the Organization has become even more uncertain. Even if it should only apply to the peace-keeping area, this announcement of reservation by a major power with regard to the vital function of the Organization, is serious indeed.

2. Not clearly spelled out in the Report is the intricate relationship that might exist between invoking armed forces, command in the field, and financing. Furthermore, these matters are likely to be related to the particular type of armed force; as Waskow suggested in Chapter 9, there might be different procedures for different kinds of armed force.
3. The Mexican Delegation was responsible for the suggestion in paragraph 26 of the Report. For a fuller exposition of that position, see A/AC. 121 PV.2, pp. 33–37.
4. The Brazilian delegation believed that these peace-keeping operations, not having been foreseen in the Charter, should be dealt with by constitutional amendment. Do you believe that it would be sensible to push for constitutional amendment in this area, or would you prefer to see this develop in a slow evolutionary fashion? Consider the fact that the amendment to the Charter enlarging membership in the Security Council and the Economic and Social Council did finally take place after a period of vigorous action by various states. In terms of system transformation, which seems to you most appropriate?
5. The Report called upon the members to study the contents contained therein and to write back a formal reply on their reactions to it. Thus far (August 1, 1965), some 18 replies have come in and it is accurate to say that only a few of them show serious attention to the problems which were raised in the Report. However, the Secretary-General and other interested parties are pursuing the matter and the replies possibly may be a productive source of ideas for future discussion and action by the Organization. See A/AC. 121/5.

11

Evaluating the United Nations

Prior chapters in this volume have examined the main structural and functional characteristics of the United Nations, both as it operates within the existing international system and as it might be expected to operate in the Clark-Sohn world. In this chapter the readings offer an overall assessment of the impact of the United Nations upon the course of world politics. Perhaps a useful way to approach the subject-matter of this chapter is to try and conceive of the character of world politics if, on the one hand, the United Nations did not exist and if, on the other hand, it existed in whatever ideal form seems most responsive to the problems of legal and political order that remain unsolved. Thus one has, in effect, four models to compare: first, a world without any global international organization; second, a world with the United Nations as we know it; third, a world with a United Nations revised along the lines proposed by Clark and Sohn; and fourth, a world with your own conception of the ideal form of a global international organization.

In order to emphasize the structural nature of the comparisons proposed, we suspend any concern with the transition problem, that is, concern for transforming one structural model into another. At the same time, as is very clear in the essay by Stanley Hoffmann, "An Evaluation of the United Nations," *Ohio State Law Journal,* vol. 22 (Summer, 1961) pp. 427–449, the materials in this chapter deal with the political adequacy of the United Nations, and therefore assess the achievements and failures of the Organization in the existing international political system. Given the major political trends and conflicts of our times, what can we expect from the United Nations? In addition to this question, it is important to consider how to adapt the organizational character of the United Nations to political realities so as to maximize its contribution to world public order. The short excerpt from Alvin Z. Rubinstein's article, "More Responsibility for Russia?," *Current* (September, 1964) pp. 37–41, is an example of such an approach, offering, in particular, a suggestion for how it might be possible to involve the Soviet Union more constructively in the activities of the United Nations, and thereby make the Organization less of an arena for cold war politics and more of an arena for the maintenance of minimum world order.

Of course, the most difficult reconciliation to achieve is that of national sovereignty and world order. Members of the United Nations continue to give primary attention to the pursuit of their national interests, even if this pursuit endangers the stability of international relations. To create a more stable basis for world order it is necessary to persuade states to redefine their national interests in light of the common cause of war prevention and to translate that common cause into operative policies, making its recognition into something more than mere rhetoric. Even antagonistic states, given this perceived fear of unmanageable conflict, possess strongly convergent interests in an improved system of world order. We need to use ingenuity of the sort exhibited by each of the authors in this chapter to capitalize upon these convergent interests, while recognizing the limit of and inhibitions upon international cooperation that arise from the continuing reality of antagonistic interests. A first step is to acknowledge that international political harmony is not a precondition for meaningful international collaboration in the cause of world order. In this regard, it seems useful to assess the degree to which it is rational to subordinate cold war issues in various contexts of United Nations action. Dag Hammarskjöld advanced the thesis in the celebrated introduction to his last Annual Report as Secretary-General that it is both possible and necessary to exclude cold war politics from the operations of the Secretariat: "Two Differing Views of the United Nations Assayed," *International Organization*, vol. 15 (World Peace Foundation, Boston, 1961) pp. 549–563. Hammarskjöld's views also bear upon the overall role of the United Nations as a source of order in world affairs.

Hoffmann's article, in particular, highlights the ambiguity of the United Nations in relation to world order, for the Organization is a center of conflict as well as of common enterprise. All the disagreements that go on outside the Organization are introduced into it whenever a controversial subject is under consideration. In this respect, the United Nations is a reflection of, rather than an alternative to, international anarchy.

AN EVALUATION OF THE UNITED NATIONS

STANLEY HOFFMANN

Sixteen years have passed since the Charter of the United Nations was drafted at the San Francisco Conference. Sixteen years after the Versailles treaty, the League of Nations was on the verge of facing, and failing to meet, its biggest challenge: an evaluation written in the summer of 1935 would have been, on the whole, a positive one. Thus, any assessment of the United Nations' contribution to contemporary world order has to be cautious and provisional.

At any given time, the kind of order which exists in the world depends on the nature of the international system; the methods and the rules by which a minimum of security, assent and flexibility is insured depend on the structure of the world, on the domestic political systems, on the trans-national forces and on the scope and means which characterize the relations between the actors on the international scene.[1] Before 1919, world order consisted of two main elements: on the one hand, the legal norms which tried to delimit the rights and duties of the states and to regulate their competition or their cooperation in various areas; on the other hand, the empirical rules of behavior which resulted from the distribution of forces, from the calculations and strategies of the states, for instance, the "laws" of the balance of power system of the eighteenth and nineteenth centuries. The creation of an international organization was supposed to bring a drastic change into world politics and world order. It was intended to close the gap which had so often appeared between the legal order and the empirical one. At the same time, the legal order was becoming far more ambitious: international law would stop being the reflection of power relations which left sovereignty intact or submitted the sovereignty of a given state merely to those restrictions which were imposed by the greater force of its combined enemies. International law would become instead a body of rules determining the conduct of states independently from power relations and curbing the essential attribute of sovereignty, the right to resort freely to violence. International organization would be the motor of this new law. The world was assumed to be capable, so to speak, of leaping from Hume to Kant.

The drama of both the League and the United Nations has resided in one basic ambiguity and in one deep abyss. The ambiguity is that of the very concept of international organization.[2] It is a

[1] For further elaboration, see the author's "International Systems and International Law," to be published in World Politics (October 1961).

[2] See Walter Schiffer, The Legal Community of Mankind (New York, 1954).

fictitious community; it represents no revolution in the structure of the world. The basic unit remains the state, but in order to be able to play an effective role in discharging such functions as the maintenance of peace, the settlement of disputes, the emancipation of non-self-governing territories, the protection of human rights or the promotion of economic cooperation, the organization should dispose of some real political power *over* the states, *i.e.*, enjoy a modicum of autonomy and supremacy. In reality, however, decisions within the organization are made *by* the states. Hence a contradiction: the basis of action and obligation is supposed to be an emergent community spirit, *as if* the states were no more than agents of this international community, *as if* the organization expressed a general will no longer divided into separate and antagonistic wills, no longer confiscated by governments. But the reality of action is precisely one of governmental interests, which remain most frequently divergent and which, even when they converge on the organization, tend to use it as an instrument, and to exploit the community fiction for their own purposes. Consequently, the efficiency and authority of the organization depend ultimately, not on its Charter, but on the state of the world outside. But it is here that we find an abyss opening under the organization. After 1919 and after 1945 there has been a tremendous difference between the kind of world which was supposed to be the starting point, the condition and the milieu of the organization's functioning, and the world which had emerged from a global war. Versailles did not create a world of satisfied nation-states and of safe democracies, in which public opinion operating freely across borders, and statesmen who recognize as a new international legitimacy the dogmas of open diplomacy and world parliamentarism would serve as trans-national forces. Now, the organization is unable to create through its own power the reality which the founders of the Organization had failed to deliver.

In the case of the League, it proved to be impossible to overcome the ambiguity and to bridge the abyss. Obviously, the deeper the latter, the stronger the former. But the paradox of the United Nations until now is that despite that abyss, the organization has been able to survive. Although totally different from the world envisaged at San Francisco, the post-war international system has, so to speak, found various uses for the United Nations; consequently, the role the United Nations plays has little in common with the role an international organization was supposed to play, in the grandiose Wilsonian design for a new world order: it is a more modest but far less utopian task and therefore the basic ambiguity, which, as we will see, is of course still there, is less destructive. I would like to examine first how and to what extent the United Nations has been able to adapt to the post-war world despite the abyss I mentioned, and secondly, what are the uses of the organization in the present international system.

II

1. In the case of the League of Nations, it became clear only gradually that the main authors of the Covenant did not agree on what they expected from the organization, and that the post-war world fitted the expectations of none of them. It took just a few months to make it clear that the world in which the United Nations was operating had no resemblance with the world envisaged by the men who made the Charter.

The world envisaged by them was full of complexities and contradictions. It was assumed, in the first place, that the Big Five would remain responsible for the maintenance of peace and act as a new Concert (but no longer restricted to Europe) in charge of security; hence, the well-known provisions of Chapter VII and the theory of the chain of events, the extension of the principle of unanimity to admissions and amendments. In the second place, the Charter embodied also another inheritance from the nineteenth century, but this one was a product of that very liberal utopia of international relations which had *opposed* the practices of the European Concert, and whose victory over those practices Wilson had tried to insure in the Covenant of the League. It was the expectation that major disputes between states would, on the whole, be few and limited. The solemn assertion of a very broad "domestic jurisdiction" principle showed that one still believed that domestic affairs and international ones could be kept separate. Another distinction was made between breaches of peace or threats to peace, and less explosive disputes. It was assumed that a hierarchy could be maintained, and that the lesser disputes could ordinarily be solved by traditional diplomatic techniques. In the third place, the Charter provisions on economic and social matters and the statutes of the World Bank and International Monetary Fund postulated a world which, after a brief period of reconstruction, would no longer be plagued by permanent financial difficulties (balance of payment troubles being primarily solved by domestic efforts), in which economic development would be assured mainly by private investors at ordinary conditions of security and profit, and in which quantitative restrictions and discriminatory measures would be gradually removed from world trade.

One can defend those postulates by saying that they were not at all utopian, but realistic in the sense of defining the only conditions in which an international organization can properly function.[3] Whereas the egalitarianism of the League had a utopian flavor, the Charter at least recognized that the success of an organization which is not a super-state depends on the existence of a concert of great powers which will be the driving force within and the mechanism thanks to which the world outside will be made such that an international organization has some chance of playing a useful role. As for the liberal conception of international relations which coexisted with the new Concert, did it not simply express the idea that an organization which is not a super-state can be effective only as long as not every dispute which it handles is a matter of life and death for some of its members? When such a matter arises, it is the Concert of the Big Five which must deal with it (and the Security Council was indeed made capable of overcoming the domestic jurisdiction clause in the case of Chapter VII). But one must assume that the organization will not have to live in the climate of tragedy all the time, for, indeed, the more often such a climate takes over, the smaller are the chances of great power solidarity. However, if this was realism, it belonged to the category which Raymond Aron has called "wrong realism"—the mistake which results from a misinterpretation of reality rather than from idealistic illusions.[4] The United Nations was launched in a world torn by the conflict between East and West, by the storm of decolonization, and by the quest for development.

2. The history of the Organization, and especially the history of what happened to its Charter, is that of a race, the race of the United Nations to escape from the consequences of the contrast between the world postulated by the Charter and the real world. Because of this contrast, the Organization was faced with the risk of a triple paralysis. First, the conflict between East and West was threatening not only to destroy the collective security function and apparatus, but also to cripple the procedure for the peaceful settlement of disputes by the Security Council. The race away from deadlock took the well-known form of a transfer of power to the General Assembly: on the one hand, more and more ordinary disputes and situations were brought before it, under art. 11, par. 2; on the other hand, the Uniting-for-Peace revolution of 1950, voted during the Korean crisis, constituted a daring attempt at shifting responsibility for collective security from the Security Council to the General Assembly, unburdened by the veto. Secondly, the violence of most of the disputes which broke out in the

---

[3] See I.L. Claude, Swords into Plowshares (2d ed., New York, 1959), Chapters 4 and 8.

[4] Raymond Aron, "En quête d'une philosophie de la politique étrangère," III Revue Française de Science Politique, 69-91.

post-war world, particularly between colonial powers and their colonies and protectorates or between the new states, was such that too faithful an observance of the careful tags with which the Charter tried to define a hierarchy of conflicts, and too persistent a respect of the prohibition against intervention in domestic affairs, would have condemned the organization to permanent frustration. The race, here, led on the one hand to an implicit or explicit rejection of the exception of domestic jurisdiction whenever a state invoked it in a case where its domestic troubles had serious international repercussions, and on the other hand to a discarding of the labels of the Charter by the Security Council and by the General Assembly. Ad hoc procedures were substituted for explicit references to such and such an article. Consequently, instead of the cautious and gradual diplomatic methods of Chapter VI, the Organization has resorted to a far more energetic "policy of presence" and to collective intervention. Thirdly, the kind of massive irrelevance to post-war economic problems other than the reconstruction of western Europe, which seemed to be the fate of the United Nations and of its agencies, was avoided by a determined switch of attention to problems of technical assistance and economic development.

This triple race away from paralysis presents two aspects which are worth noting. First, in order to justify practices which were so thoroughly at variance with its original Charter, the Organization had to accentuate, rather than overcome, the fundamental ambiguity I have described: it has interpreted its Charter as if this document were the equivalent of a national constitution, whose provisions frequently lose their old meaning or receive a new interpretation, without any formal amendment, but through the practices of governmental organs and thanks to the underlying political consensus. The trouble is, of course, that the international milieu is not a community yet, but the trend toward behaving as if it had, in Mr. Hammerskjöld's vocabulary, passed from the stage of an "institutional pattern of coexistence" to that of a "constitutional system of international cooperation,"[5] is nowhere more clear than in the role played by the Secretary General. Both Mr. Lie and Mr. Hammerskjöld—the former with excessive gusto, and the latter despite his initial reluctance—have acted not merely as administrators in charge of a secretariat, nor even as trustees discharging the functions which heavy and clumsy political organs cannot perform efficiently, but as leaders speaking for that international interest or community whose "existence" justifies the twisting of the Charter. It is precisely when the normal interplay of states' clashing

[5] Address by Mr. Hammerskjöld at the University of Chicago Law School, 6 United Nations Review No. 12 (June 1960), 26-30.

policies threatens to reduce the Organization to impotence, that the Secretary General becomes the organ of continuity and "fills the vacuum" by taking an initiative.[6]

Secondly, the postulates on which the re-interpretation of the Charter is based describe a world which is the exact opposite of the world assumed by the original postulates, but whose "realism" is just as questionable. On the one hand, it is now assumed that the conflict between the big powers should not prevent the exercise of collective security even against one of them, and indeed, in the practice of the United Nations, collective security has been set in motion only in the Korean case, and the only nations condemned as aggressors have been Red China and the Soviet Union! Breaches of peace which do not pit East against West have been handled with methods stronger than those envisaged by Chapter VI, but far less drastic than those of Chapter VII. On the other hand, it is also assumed that the very scope of the disputes between old and new states, or between the new ones—disputes in which the old barrier between domestic and international affairs collapses, and in which force is almost always used—makes collective intervention by the Organization not only desirable but likely to succeed.

3. Precisely because those new assumptions are of dubious validity, the outcome of the race has been most ambiguous. It is easy to point out that the Organization has been unable to eliminate all those factors of present-day world politics which resisted its attempts at asserting its role; but it is also easy to show that the Organization has nevertheless survived and played a remarkable part.

In many ways, the race looks like a circular circuit rather than a straight run away from the pitfalls of the Charter. The postulate of the need for big-power unity seems largely vindicated; whenever there has been a direct clash between East and West, the role of the Organization has been limited. The fact of "bipolarity" has been stronger than the machinery of "Uniting for Peace," collective security has been tacitly abandoned as a function of the United Nations,[7] and the procedure of resorting to an emergency session of the General Assembly when the Security Council is paralyzed has been used, not in order to organize collective security against a large or even a small power (ex-

6 See for instance the Secretary General's statement at the opening meeting of the General Assembly's third emergency special session on August 8, 1958, his initiatives in the Congo crisis in July 1960 and again in February 1961. Throughout the summer of 1960, the resolutions submitted by Tunisia and Ceylon to the Security Council on the Congo followed the suggestions spelled out by the Secretary General in his statements or reports.

7 See I.L. Claude, "The United Nations and the Use of Force," 532 International Conciliation (March 1961).

cept during the Korean war), but as a way of restoring peace or solving disputes without resort to coercion, after a failure of the Security Council. Even when the issue at stake was not a direct clash between East and West, one major condition of United Nations' success in restoring peace or in reaching a settlement has been at least a tacit concert of the Big Two. The postulate according to which the Organization would be most effective if the majority of disputes were not too violent or too deep has also been largely vindicated: the United Nations has dealt with countless conflicts in which the international status or the domestic regime of nations was involved, but it has repeatedly failed to reach a substantive settlement. The expansion of the technical assistance program, the switch in the lending policies of the World Bank—from Europe to the rest of the world—the creation of the International Finance Corporation and the International Development Association do not amount to a massive transfer of aid from bilateral to United Nations channels. The "haves" remain reluctant to abandon control of their funds. Various short-circuits such as the fiasco of the International Trade Organization or the failure to stabilize the price of primary products or the resistance to SUNFED have marked the limits of United Nations action in this area.

The lesson is clear: *legal* impotence has been overcome, *political* limitations have not been removed. The failure to influence the Soviet Union or China in cases such as Hungary and Tibet, not to mention disarmament; the inability to solve the issues of Kashmir or the Arab-Israeli conflict, as well as the difficulties of the United Nations operation in the Congo; the slowness of the process of erosion by which the underdeveloped countries try to squeeze more money for capital development from the richer nations: all those facts show how deep an abyss there remains between the world as it is and the world as it ought to be in order to allow the United Nations to play the major role which both its founders and their successors wanted. Consequently, the basic ambiguity of international organization cannot fail to appear as a persistent obstacle; the world community has rarely looked more fictitious. In an area such as Laos, in which East and West clash directly, the "United Nations presence" established by the Secretary General was bound to evaporate; in the Congo crisis, there have been moments when the deadlock between conflicting camps—East and West, moderates and radicals among the new nations—was such that any attempt at pursuing a "United Nations policy" became both an exercise in fiction and a peril for the Secretary General. Indeed, in so far as this ambiguity is both summed up in, and revealed by, the Secretary General's role and fate, nothing is more discouraging for the believers in an international community than the destruction of one Secretary by the brutal attacks from the Soviet Union (which followed degrading pressures of United States witchhunters) and the threats to the position of the other Secretary which come both from the Eastern bloc and from certain new nations whose policies conflict with the "international interest" as defined by Mr. Hammerskjöld.

However, despite such unfavorable circumstances, the Organization has done far more than survive. The contrast with the League in this respect is most remarkable. The Covenant was gradually emasculated, and when the "time of troubles" came, the nations' reactions were centrifugal. On the contrary, the United Nations has emerged as one of the most interesting aspects of contemporary international relations. The Organization has become indispensable as a result of a double process. On the one hand, each camp needs the United Nations as a field of manoeuvre; in this respect, the United Nations is neither a substitute for traditional diplomacy nor the beginning of a world community, but the form of multilateral diplomacy which corresponds to the extension of the international system to the whole world. The cold war involves not only an attempt by each bloc to preserve its own forces and, if possible, to weaken the adversary. One of its main stakes is the allegiance of the new and underdeveloped nations; consequently, it becomes necessary for both East and West to be present in the United Nations, which provides them with unprecedented possibilities of influence and mobilization. Even if the Organization cannot directly affect the "core area" held by each superpower, it can exert a more subtle action on the balance of power in the area of the "third world." The revolution against colonialism operates with a similar dialectic; here, the very divisions among the major powers (and not only between East and West) give an advantage to the smaller nations and incite them to exploit to the hilt an organization which those divisions put under their numerical control. Similarly, in the battle for economic development, the needy nations use the Organization as a lever against the richer ones and the latter dare not protest too much because it is precisely for the support of those poorer nations that they compete. Thus, there is a convergence of conflicting interests on the Organization as an arena of major importance. On the other hand, there are areas in which the Organization is useful not merely as an instrument to be used *by each group* in the international competition but as an institution necessary *to all members* because of identical or convergent interests in joint action. In such cases the United Nations is more than an arena, it is a force. Thus, the United Nations contributes to the establishment of a new world order in two distinct ways. First, it is the framework in which the nations hammer out many (although, as we have noticed and shall see again, by no means *all*) of the empirical rules of behavior and of the legal norms which are supposed to prevent the present international system from resembling the war of all against all. Secondly, it is one (and only one) of the elements of stability and order in the present world.

III

Thus, the role of the United Nations in the present international system is double. The Organization reflects the system; but it also affects it—both negatively and positively.

1. Precisely because the United Nations, since 1955, has opened its doors to almost all states, the Organization is a very faithful mirror of post-war world politics. It shows both the disastrous and the hopeful sides. Let us examine the disastrous aspects first. The present international system is a revolutionary one. As such, it presents two characteristics which account for many of the United Nations' own features. In the first place, it is a heterogeneous system. The diplomatic field embraces the whole world for the first time, but there are huge differences: (1) between states, both from the viewpoint of power (contrast between the states that dispose of a capacity of general destruction, and the others) and from the viewpoint of authority (difference between well-established states, and new nations, sometimes in search of their proper borders); (2) between political regimes, both from the viewpoint of the domestic formula of legitimacy and from that of economic policy; (3) between levels of economic development; (4) between ideological camps. Those factors of heterogeneity are felt in United Nations debates on practically any subject, whether the Organization discusses the future of colonialism or tries to draft covenants on human rights or attempts to intervene in the endlessly complicated disarmament dialogue which has been going on among the superpowers. The United Nations mirrors both the universal but superficial adherence of all states to the principles of conduct expressed in the Charter, and the reality of negative solidarities which link members of blocs or groups and divide the world into contending factions.

In the second place, a revolutionary system is one in which the relations between states are no longer marked by any moderation in scope or means. The end of moderation in scope entails the following developments. On the one hand, the violence of the competition between states brings about the collapse of the zone of domestic affairs and of the principle of non-intervention; the choice of a regime determines the international conduct of a state and each major contender tries to influence the choices of lesser ones. United Nations' discussions on the French Cameroons in 1959, and even more the debates on the Congo, have reflected this aspect: not only is the United Nations' operation in the Congo caught in the contests between Congolese leaders, but various groups of states fight for the recognition of antagonistic leaders. On the other hand, in a revolutionary period, "functional" sectors previously removed from the political struggle and left to the free activities of private citizens become once again stakes in the struggles of the states: consequently, not only has the sphere of international economic affairs become one of the main battlefields, but even more technical subjects have been affected with a political interest. United Nations' discussions on economic development or on the right to nationalize natural resources have reflected this extension of world politics, while many of the specialized agencies were faced with the dilemma of eliminating from their agenda controversial issues in order to stay out of politics—but at the cost of irrelevance—or else facing the storm, but at the risk of possible deadlock. As for the end of moderation in means, it entails in particular the unlimited resort to techniques of propaganda and subversion against the enemy camp or in order to obtain the allegiance of third parties; it also entails the willingness to use force in order to wrest local gains and the determination to exploit fully the temporary advantages one may enjoy in the technological race. A list of the problems discussed by the United Nations shows that this is indeed what has kept the organization so busy, despite all the restraints which the principles of the Charter were supposed to impose on the behavior of the members. But this is also what makes agreement on the international control of atomic energy, or on reserving outer space for peaceful uses, impossible to obtain.

By definition, a revolutionary system is one in which world order is almost non-existent; and to the extent to which the United Nations has been a mirror of the system, it has been permanently threatened with paralysis. The United Nations translates into parliamentary terms the fundamental divisions of the world. The danger of paralysis has even augmented over time. Thus, the more membership has increased, the more difficult it has become to obtain a two-thirds majority in the General Assembly; the outcome of debate is often either no resolution at all, or a compromise version which verges on the meaningless.[8] Similarly, the United Nations has suffered not only from the fact of the cold war between East and West, but also from its evolution. Soviet tactics have switched, after Stalin's death, from an essentially defensive attitude, reflected in Russian behavior and arguments in

[8] See for instance, during the 14th session of the General Assembly, the failure to adopt a resolution on Algeria; during the 15th session, the failure of the resolution proposing sanctions against the Union of South Africa because of apartheid, and the compromise resolution on Algeria.

the United Nations, to a much more daring strategy which adds to the continued defense of the integrity of the Soviet bloc a determined effort to win over uncommitted nations, or at least to exasperate their antagonism toward the West. The fifteenth session of the General Assembly has been particularly spectacular in this respect. The effect of this change on the United Nations has been a faithful reflection of the effect in the world. It has meant not so much a net addition to the strength of the Soviet bloc, as a loss of influence for the United States (which finds it far more difficult to get its own viewpoint adopted by two thirds of the members, must more and more frequently leave the initiative to the uncommitted nations, and merely tries to soften or weaken their suggestions) and an increasingly deep split between moderates and radicals among the uncommitted nations.

This shift in Soviet tactics poses a very serious problem for the United Nations. Until recently, the organization's efficiency in political matters was limited by two main obstacles: the "impenetrability" of the Soviet bloc, which became sufficiently recognized so that issues like Tibet or Berlin were either barely discussed or avoided altogether, and the rockbottom obstacle which stops any international organization, *i.e.*, the unwillingness of any state to accept a substantive settlement of a dispute which goes against its interests. Here, the United Nations merely reflected the contradiction between the extension of the diplomatic field and the maintenance (and mushrooming) of separate sovereignties. Those obstacles were serious enough, for they contributed to the reluctance of UN members to allow the establishment of a permanent non-fighting force. Many states feared that it might be used either in an East-West dispute, thus endangering world peace, or against their own interests, should a conflict involving them arise. However, in between those limits there remained the area described by the Secretary General in his report to the fifteenth Assembly: "Keeping newly arising conflicts outside the sphere of bloc differences,"[9] filling the power vacuum between those blocs whenever a conflict breaks out there, so as to prevent them from rushing in. This was feasible as long as both superpowers tacitly agreed on the need for "decolonization" or on the way of handling the crises which this process provoked. But if each superpower tries to affect the process in such a way that the outcome will be a "friendly" new state, the dream of the UN filling the gap becomes the nightmare of the UN turned into a battlefield. The contrast between the Suez and Congo crises indicates the extent of the deterioration. In the Suez crisis, the UN was able to act without too many difficulties because of a joint pressure

---

[9] 7 United Nations Review No. 4 (Oct. 1960) 24.

from the U.S. and the U.S.S.R. toward a restoration of the status quo, and because of the support of most "uncommitted" nations for such a policy. Consequently, the Secretary-General was able to act as the "executive" of the Assembly, which gave him massive political backing. In the case of the Congo, the superpowers agreed only on one thing, the need for Belgian withdrawal,[10] but each one chose his own favorite among the contending leaders, and the Afro-Asian nations split and chose sides as well; consequently, from October 1960 to February 1961, the Secretary General, far from filling any vacuum, was left on his tightrope walking above a political vacuum, as was shown in most spectacular fashion by the failure of both the Security Council and the General Assembly to adopt any resolution at all in December. The long race from the Security Council to the General Assembly, from the Assembly to the Secretary, seemed to have ended in fiasco. The lesson is clear—the UN can escape from total paralysis only to the extent to which, in the sphere considered to be *the* proper UN sphere of action by the Secretary General, the states that belong to neither bloc are able to reconcile their differences and to resist the pulls and pushes of both blocs.

Is this possible? The answer is yes. Here we must turn to a far more positive side of the picture. The present revolutionary system contains one fundamental element of stability—the fear of total war. The very uncertainty which marks the danger of "escalation" has acted as a dampener on limited wars as well. Consequently the contest between the two blocs, including the competition for allegiance of the other nations, is primarily a non-military one and each superpower tries to seduce or subvert, but not to conquer or coerce. Two chances open therefore for the United Nations. First, the amount of arm-twisting which each superpower can do at the expense of the smaller nations is limited, and the United Nations reflects the desire of the latter to preserve their independence from outside encroachments, wherever they may come from, just as much as it reflects the blocs' efforts to penetrate this independence. Whatever their ambiguity, the resolutions adopted by the Security Council in February 1961 and by the General Assembly two months later, concerning the Congo, as well as the resolution adopted by the Assembly's emergency session on August 21, 1958, concerning the Middle Eastern crisis, show the restraints which the need to gain consent imposes on the superpowers. The failure of the Soviet plan to "reorganize" the Secretariat indicates the same thing. Secondly, the fear of general war re-enforces the desire of all states, and particularly of those which have the weapons of gen-

[10] Even on this point the two states have disagreed about the speed with which it should take place and the scope it should have.

eral destruction, to "keep talking." Negotiations may be fruitless, but the dialogue must be maintained and the UN provides an ideal forum for such a dialogue. But we are here at the limit between the United Nations' role as a mirror and its role as an actor.

2. Every contemporary development toward world order has two faces; one which threatens chaos, one which promises order. There is a negative contribution by the United Nations which tends too often to be submerged behind pious expressions of faith or gallant efforts at presenting what may well be inevitable as being actually beneficial. It results from the fundamental ambiguity which was mentioned in the beginning. It expresses itself in three ways.

There is, first, a contradiction between the realities of international politics and the fictions which the UN seeks to preserve in order to be able to operate. Now, any resort to fictions conceals a weakness and multiplies difficulties. One such fiction is the principle of equality, according to which each member has one vote. Equality symbolizes the idea of homogeneity, but as we know, the members represented in the UN are neither equal in power nor homogeneous from any point of view. The idea of homogeneity and the dream of community combine in producing "majoritarianism"—the belief that the resolutions adopted by two thirds of the members really represent the opinion of mankind. Another fiction, which has gotten the Organization into all kinds of trouble, is that of non-intervention. We have seen that the UN has actually reversed the hierarchy established by the Charter, and rejected the exception of domestic jurisdiction invoked by a member whenever there was an international interest attached to the matter. But the principle of non-intervention is one to which each member clings for himself, and which the UN must proclaim in its own operations; it was supposed to be the guideline of its action in the Congo. Unfortunately, the revolutionary character of world politics has played havoc with the principle. In a situation of quasi-civil war, non-intervention can only mean staying out completely; once one goes in, it becomes almost meaningless. Indeed, in the Congo crisis, the myth of non-intervention has had three effects: it has managed to infuriate in turn each of the Congolese factions, which interpreted the "neutrality" of UNOC as an act of hostility. It has obliged the Secretary General and the members to resort to highly debatable devices in order to justify intervention while preserving the dogma of non-interference in domestic affairs: thus, the idea that what makes UN intervention necessary, and what explains the crisis, is the persistence of Belgian intervention, or—at the time when Mr. Hammerskjöld's antagonism with Mr. Lumumba was at its most heated—the distinction between internal political conflicts, which were "off-limits," and "flagrant violations of elementary human rights," which had to be stopped.[11] Finally, the myth of non-intervention itself collapsed, when the Security Council adopted a resolution asking for reorganization of the Congolese army. The main trouble with the resort to fictions is that they increase the resistance of minorities; a state or a faction which objects to a UN resolution finds in the lack of realism of the organization a good reason to stick to its guns. In a world where states are not equal, where they have no obligation to obey, and no way of being obliged to obey resolutions adopted by UN majorities, and where domestic and international problems are intertwined, the UN exposes itself to failure either when it tries to bully a reluctant state (be it a Communist state like Russia, a colonial power like Portugal, a racist country like South Africa, or the industrial nations which have been resisting SUNFED) or when it pretends to respect a principle which will merely give to the pygmies some rope with which they can bind Gulliver.

Secondly, there is a contradiction between the nature of the problems submitted to the Organization and the way in which they are handled by it. On the one hand, there is an excessive fixation on procedure: the emphasis is put less on the methods by which the issue could be solved, even less on the substance of a solution, than on the measurement of "international public opinion" as represented by the delegates. In other words, the UN tends to indulge in "barometrics" rather than in diplomacy. This is a by-product of the transfer of power to the General Assembly, but the practice of inviting "interested" states which are not members of the Security Council to come and present their views generalizes this development. Hence huge amounts of time are spent on finding the right words or the right sponsors. It is a search for the degree of indignation, concern or exhortation which will make the machine tilt—I mean, obtain the necessary two-thirds majority. Much of the criticism of parliamentary diplomacy is unfair; the length and heaviness of debate and its inevitable propaganda aspects should not make one forget that there is as much negotiation going on behind the scenes as there is posturing on the rostrum. What is seriously disturbing, however, is that so many of the secret discussions and deals in the lobbies are concerned not with action, but with wording—with symbols rather than substance. On the other hand, when the Organization in emergencies resolves to act, there is another kind of fixation. The extinction of fires, I mean the end of the use of force, seems to be the ideal and the goal; it is, of course, a fine and noble task, especially in a world in which "escalation" and general embroilment are permanent threats. But there is a formalism in this

[11] Statement by the Secretary General to the Security Council, 7 United Nations Review No. 4, 47 (Oct. 1960).

approach, which is not without its own peril.[12] Groups or nations often resort to force because it is the last avenue which remains open to them for the redress of a grievance or because underlying problems have received no solution. The United Nations, by putting so much more energy into the admittedly more spectacular act of rushing to smother the flames than into the difficult task of rebuilding the charred house, tends to leave too many cinders smoldering in the ashes. This was the weakness of UN action during the Suez crisis. The handling of the Congo emergency has shown a tendency to concentrate once more on the avoidance of "military solutions"; it was made inevitable both by the danger of foreign military intervention at the request of the various contending factions, and by the difficulty of recognizing openly that the cause of the drama was the lack of preparation of the Congolese for independence and the absence of any Congo-wide nationalism. However, as long as the source of the trouble remains hidden, the Organization has no choice but to see the domestic political struggles continue, the peril or the reality of outside military help resume, the lack of competent Congolese administrators and technicians persist, and its own forces treated as a party to the conflicts without disposing of all the means a party ordinarily can use. A policy of presence with limited authority may bring about the worst of all worlds. This contradiction between the nature of the problems and the UN approach tends to aggravate matters, to the extent to which attention is diverted from what is fundamental to what is merely an effect, and often from what is relevant to what is not. In particular, the concentration on the evil of force incites nations either to shift their strategy from outright violence to subtler forms of intervention (which may go unnoticed or be handled far less energetically by the UN) or else to provoke new explosions after the problems which led to previous ones have remained unsolved long enough.

There is a third contradiction, this time between the stakes of political conflicts in the world and the means at the disposal of the Organization. Those means are extremely limited: small sums of money, either for the regular budget, or for economic programs, or for special operations such as UNEF and UNOC, sums which are obtained only after painful debates, and at the cost of heavy arrears or defections; then, there are mechanisms such as emergency forces, observers, committees of conciliation or investigation, mediators and special representatives; finally, there are resolutions, pure and simple. As we have seen, there is no collective security machinery, the organs which the Uniting-for-Peace resolution was supposed to establish have faded

[12] See Père R. Bosc, "Ideologies et Institutions de l'O.N.U. depuis 1945," Revue de l'Action Populaire No. 147 (April 1961), 403-14.

away, and the emergency forces themselves are doubly limited by the principle of consent of the host and by the freedom of withdrawal of the participants. The result is that the UN impact on world affairs remains necessarily limited. The UN does not reach domestic opinion, does not affect the choice of a regime, the selection of alliances, the military policies of the main powers. Attempts to handle vital problems with insufficient means may aggravate international troubles in two ways. On the one hand, whenever the UN hits (deliberately or accidentally) a vital interest of a state, and in particular whenever the UN seems to threaten what a nation considers to be its very fabric or its essential values—in other words, the image the citizens have of their nation—the reaction is bound to be violent and bitter: French attitudes toward the UN because of Algeria, South African refusals to cooperate with UN Committees, Portugal's walk-out over Angola are only the more extreme examples. The total fiasco of UN action in the field of human rights, *i.e.*, the most sensitive area of governments' relations with their citizens, points to the same moral. On the other hand, the contrast between stakes and means tends to weaken the UN as an instrument for the solution of disputes and thus to reduce the effectiveness of one of the few elements of order available in the present international system. Thus, the presence of 20,000 men in the Congo looks at times like the attempt of a few shipwrecked passengers on a raft trying to stop a storm. Coping with interventions from abroad, and with civil war and political turmoil within, is simply too much for an expeditionary force which far from being able to seal off hermetically the Congo from the outside world, must suffer the consequences of decisions taken elsewhere—for instance in Casablanca—or in the Congo itself—for instance in Matadi. The force which was supposed to act as a buffer is too weak to be effective; and the other two contradictions—the myth of non-intervention, the fixation on force—added to the present one tend to perpetuate the crisis, even if only in softened form. One may well ask if an endless, if muted, terror, is better than a terrible end—or will prevent it ultimately.

3. The more positive effects of the UN on the international system are, however, far from negligible. The organization contributes to a transformation of three aspects of the system.

In the first place, the Organization has a double impact on the structure of the world. On the one hand, there is a subtle action on the international hierarchy, one might almost call it a gradual subversion. The effect of "bipolarity" on the hierarchy is in many ways neutralized, i.e., the super-powers, far from possessing an influence proportional to their potential (specially their military potential) are obliged to let smaller powers enjoy greater freedom of action than in many periods of history. Two qualifying remarks must be made. First, the UN does not "destroy" the international hierarchy, not only because it does not have the means to do so, but also because it has shown, in its treatment of states on which the Organization wanted to put pressure, a healthy respect for differences in power, i.e., small states have been dealt with far less cautiously than either the Soviet Union (even in the Hungarian case), or the United States (see the resolution of April 22, 1961 on Cuba), or even the United Kingdom and France. Secondly, what prevents the superpowers from playing toward the small nations a role corresponding to their overwhelming might is primarily the double factor I have singled out before, the desire to avoid general war, and the resulting reliance on persuasion or subversion rather than violence for the recruitment of clients and friends. This is the fundamental cause which explains why, in the international hierarchy of today, sheer military strength is less decisive than it has been in the past. The very destructiveness of the nuclear arsenal, which gives to the superpowers a superiority great powers never had before, also tends to neutralize this advantage as long as a war has not started.

However, the UN has not only benefited from this singularity, it has exploited and enlarged it. The transfer of power to the General Assembly has given to the weaker states a splendid opportunity to push their advantage to the hilt, and they have used it. In the UN, because of their number, they can even thwart the designs of the superpowers. The debate on the Congo has shown for instance that the very violence of Soviet attacks on the UN operation has brought the African and Asian nations close enough together to allow them to compromise for the preservation of UNOC, and both the Soviet Union and the United States, despite their objections to various provisions, had to follow. As Mr. Hammerskjöld put it recently, "the United Nations has increasingly become the main platform—and the main protector of the interests—of those many nations who feel themselves strong as members of the international family but who are weak in isolation. Thus, an increasing number of nations have come to look to the UN for leadership and support in ways somewhat different from those natural in the light of traditional diplomacy. They look to the Organization as a spokesman and as an agent for principles which give them strength in an international concert in which other voices can mobilize all the weight of armed force, wealth, an historical role and that influence which is the other side of a special responsibility for peace and security."[13] It is precisely this role of the UN as a counter-

[13] 7 United Nations Review No. 4, 27 (Oct. 1960).

vailing force that corrects the effects of the traditional hierarchy, to which a statesman like General de Gaulle objects so strongly, for he is attached to the classical formula of a directory of the great powers. Paradoxically, such a directory was more powerful in the League, despite a very egalitarian Covenant, than in the UN, despite a hierarchical Charter. Thus, each small state sees in the UN the one forum in which it not only "is somebody," but in which it is able to make its presence felt. Furthermore, in so far as the processes of parliamentary diplomacy resemble those of any parliamentary system marked by a multiplicity of factions and consequently by great difficulty at reaching compromises, certain small states gain considerable prestige and influence by playing a key role as brokers and conciliators, due not to their own strength but to their political position. They are the "friends of all parties," the truly non-aligned states, which play the role which isolated but centrally located and skillful personalities played in the Parliament of France's Third Republic, for instance, Ireland, Sweden, Tunisia, and often Canada and Yugoslavia.[14]

On the other hand, the UN influences the structure of the world by accelerating the increase in the number of states. The very prestige conferred by membership in the UN, and the opportunities for influence which are thus opened, are factors which confirm many nationalist leaders in their desire to press not only for full-fledged independence rather than mere internal autonomy within a crumbling empire, but also against mergers between newly independent nations. Furthermore, the Organization's own interpretation of its powers under Chapter XI, its very strict supervision of political developments in trusteeship territories, its attacks on colonialism both in separate instances of trouble and as a matter of principle, have made of the UN a matrix of new states.

Both aspects of this action on the structure of the world tend to strengthen the basic ambiguity of international organization, for there is a sharp contrast between the "community" symbolized by the UN (with its predominance of the smaller nations and its collective drive for independence from colonial rule) and the outside world, in which the superpowers remain the leaders and in which the increase in the number of states only multiplies the prospects for disputes and crises, consequently undermining whatever community there may be. What matters here, however, is that the UN does more than reflect this ambiguity, which may well condemn it to impotence at frequent intervals, it is one of its chief architects.

In the second place, the Organization affects the means at the disposal of the states in their relations. The role of the UN in this

[14] See Sidney D. Bailey, The General Assembly, Ch. 2 (London, 1960).

respect consists of fostering at least a partial return to moderation. It has been felt in three areas. First, there is the area of the one identical aim of all states, the avoidance of general war and the desire to see even limited conflicts purged of violence because of the danger of extension. There, the UN has not been able to affect the superpowers directly, despite pleas for the suspension of nuclear tests and for disarmament, but it has skillfully handled the "limited war" in Korea—except for the blunder of crossing the 38th parallel in Oct. 1950 without sufficient awareness of the consequences—and it has developed numerous techniques, put up various kinds of alarm bells to prevent clashes between smaller nations or within a smaller nation from becoming trial grounds for a direct East-West clash. The tacit consent of both superpowers in this respect—a negative concert which does not prevent either from trying to affect the outcome of the dispute as long as resort to force is avoided or maintained at a low level—has been continuous. French and British evacuation of Egypt in 1956, U.S. withdrawal from Lebanon in 1958, and the Soviet retreat from the Congo after the fall of Lumumba have been possible not only because of the fear of war but also because the UN provided both a guarantee against excessive loss of face and a fairly impartial mechanism for removing the element of violence—without prejudging the result of the contest. This is the area in which the Secretary General has played a vital role, and acted as the representative of the one identical purpose of all segments of mankind.

A second aspect of this action of the UN corresponds to convergent interests of the various members, *i.e.*, the setting up of instruments for technical and administrative assistance as well as the expansion of channels for multilateral economic aid. The logic of the competition has forced not only the West to retreat from its hostility and to concede that a sizable portion of its aid should be granted through the UN (although the risk of giving too much control to the recipients is an unpleasant one) but also the East to abandon its initial refusal to participate at all. The desire of the underdeveloped countries for aid devoid of the political strings or implications of bilateral agreements has conversely forced them to accept, in the case of loans from the World Bank, more of a check on their own plans than they often might have wished. The results remain limited, but the partial convergence of competing interests on common channels is definitely an element of stability, whereas the separate channels of bilateral and regional agreements perpetuate the centrifugal elements of the present international system. In this area, it is the Secretariat whose role must be underlined.

A third aspect of the stabilizing role of the UN is more controversial: in the parts of the world which are not under the control of the Soviet Union, the United Nations has made it almost impossible for the stronger states to employ toward the lesser ones the more brutal means of coercion traditionally used; this is a result of, both, the fear of general war and the increased role of small powers within the United Nations. The best example was the Suez affair. It is a doubly controversial "improvement" of world politics. The Soviet bloc feels under no compulsion to observe similar restraints, and the outcry against a "double standard" of UN action arises quite legitimately. This abandonment of gunboat diplomacy also has its hypocritical aspects, since it does not prevent bigger powers from trying to impose their will on lesser ones by methods of subversion. Nevertheless there is here a partial contribution to a partial world order, and it must be taken into account as one of the consequences of the existence of the Organization.

In the third place, the UN has an impact on the trans-national forces that cut across borders. The action of the UN in this respect is twofold. On the one hand, the Organization reenforces those "separatist" solidarities which bind various nations into groups or blocs. Those entities are usually created outside the UN, but once again the world organization is more than just a mirror, it is a catalyst and an accelerator. It is easier to meet in the lobbies of the UN than in Accra or Bandung. The blocs or groups are, with the exception of the Soviet one, anything but united. Recent votes on Algeria or on the Congo reveal for instance a three-way split among the Afro-Asians.[15] But the fact is that the basic negotiating unit tends to become the bloc, that drafts are discussed first by each caucus, and that deals between groups take place only at a later stage, after a common stand has been thrashed out within each of the principal groups, or after attempts at achieving unity within them have failed.[16] The very fact that most of the major issues of international politics are brought before the UN and to a vote obliges groups which would otherwise remain vague associations of states with ideological affinities, to react in a way which either consolidates their solidarity, or decisively shows that it was fictitious.

---

[15] The Pakistani resolution on the Congo, adopted by the General Assembly on April 15, 1961, received the support of 12 African and 12 Asian states (in addition to Turkey); 7 African states voted against it; 6 African and 8 Asian states abstained. The paragraph of the resolution on Algeria which decided the organization of a referendum by the United Nations was supported by 27 African and Asian states, rejected by 11 African ones, while 5 Asian ones abstained. The resolution as a whole was supported by 31 African and Asian states and opposed by 6 African states, while 7 abstained. The resolution asking for sanctions against South Africa was supported by 23 African and 7 Asian nations and opposed by one Asian state; 13 Asian and 1 African state abstained.

[16] See Thomas Hovet, Bloc Politics in the United Nations (Cambridge, 1958).

It will be interesting to see, in this respect, to what extent a sub-group of the Afro-Asian group such as the French-speaking African one is just a transition from the former Community to totally different alignments, or to what extent on the contrary it is a genuine bloc. The UN, in which such groups rub against one another, puts them to a kind of test of truth which would probably operate much more slowly if the Organization did not exist.

Partial and often divisive solidarities are however not the only ones which the UN consolidates. The Organization also strengthens the germs of universalist tendencies which can be detected in the present world. Thus, the UN crystallizes elements of a new international legitimacy which are still weak and questionable but which might otherwise get lost altogether in the turmoil of separate interpretations and calculations. The origin of those elements is double. There is first of all the internationalization of European principles—those of the old Liberal ethos of international relations—as was shown, for instance, by the Bandung provisions on coexistence. They simply reflect the fact that the vision of a world of harmonious nation-states uncoerced by superior power is a kind of common denominator in a universe where nationalism still spreads. Secondly, there is this fear of war and the resulting restraint on the competition for allegiance which I have mentioned. What results is a kind of consensus on principles such as the avoidance of force, the need for an international presence in emergencies, the right to self-determination and the right to economic development. Needless to say, the balance sheet is mixed; not only does the Soviet bloc have its peculiar interpretation of each of those principles, but, as we have seen, there is not any of them which does not have its own limitations, drawbacks or dangers. However, there has never been any international legitimacy without inequities or flaws, and the role of the UN consists precisely of trying to put some flesh on those bones—for there can be no international legitimacy without a minimum of performance.

The United Nations tries to strengthen these principles not only by promoting common actions, but also by fostering a process of what I have elsewhere called "political mobilization," or a gradual leveling of concern.[17] The UN accelerates the effects of the extension of the diplomatic field to the whole world, by obliging all its members to take stands on all questions, thus bringing home to an unprecedented degree the idea that what concerns one part of the planet may affect all the others. The UN is unable to achieve "one world" in the sense of an orderly and unified system for collective security, the settlement

[17] "National Attitudes and International Order: the National Studies on International Organization," XIII International Organization 202.

of disputes, etc.; such a system requires a unity, or an overwhelming convergence, of national attitudes and responses. But at least the UN tries to bring about the prerequisite, "one world," in the sense of universality of concerns. This is precisely the area in which the League of Nations, with its de facto predominance of the Council, its essentially European aspect, and even more its link with the status quo of the peace treaties, had failed most dismally.

IV

Ambiguity has been the key of our assessment of UN history and of UN action. It remains at the center of any projection one may try to make into the future.

If we look at the general trend of UN action in the world, it becomes almost too easy to denounce the Organization as the second most powerful force of disruption of the status quo, next to Communism. The break-up of Empires, approval of measures of economic nationalism which hit mainly Western interests, a majority of anti-status quo nations which obliges the West to choose between ineffective and unpopular opposition, and giving its blessing to resolutions which weaken its positions further—all those aspects of the role of the UN may give serious worry to statesmen who fear that the only beneficiaries of disruption will ultimately be the Communists. On the other hand, we must not forget that the assault on the status quo which is thus being waged is in many ways a conservative revolution, inspired by slogans and principles which belong to the Western, and particularly to the Liberal heritage. If the cry for political and economic self-determination and the desire for welfare and development provide Communism with admirable opportunities and turn more often than not against the West in the present phase, they may at a future date provide in reverse the West with opportunities and serve as barriers against Communist imperialism. The UN merely accelerates a liquidation of the status quo which would proceed anyhow; the degree to which this should mean a liquidation of the West depends on the West's reactions far more than on UN actions.[18]

If we look at potential UN contributions to a new world order, we must realize first that such an order will still be based on the state as the main unit, and consequently that order will be possible only if conditions of stability are resolved in the international system. Now, for such a restoration we cannot count on material developments (for they may tend to accentuate the competition), on general common

---

[18] On this point see Lincoln P. Bloomfield, The United Nations and U.S. Foreign Policy (Boston, 1960) and the author's "Sisyphus and the avalanche: the United Nations, Egypt and Hungary," XI International Organization, 464-9.

principles (for they may be interpreted in conflicting ways), or even on what Raymond Aron calls the dawn of universal history (for there are violently divergent manners of living the same history).[19] We cannot count on legal prescriptions, for international law loses much of its authority in revolutionary systems. We cannot count on the UN to maintain or establish such conditions of stability as an equilibrium of power between the major states (for the Organization has no responsibility in preserving the balance of terror and no way of checking nuclear diffusion) or a return to the limited state in domestic regimes, or an end of the ideological clash between East and West. But a restoration of stability presupposes also a return to moderation in the scope and means of international relations and it is here that the UN becomes important. Moderation in scope would necessitate both the end of the cold war, and improved political and economic relations between the western powers and the newly independent states. Moderation in means would require a strengthening of the measures taken to prevent the outbreak of general war or of wars which could degenerate into global conflicts. The end of the cold war is beyond the possibilities of anyone at this time; but on the other two issues, despite the persistence of the cold war which interferes with a reconciliation of "North" and "South" and makes agreements on disarmament or even arms control unlikely, the United Nations has a major role to play. It is not an exclusive role, but it is a crucial one precisely because the Organization is the only agency which includes almost all states and symbolizes, in its weaknesses as well as in its strengths, the idea of a universal world order. Nothing is more important therefore than to avoid wasting United Nations' efforts on areas where failure is guaranteed; nothing is more important than to exert leadership so that in the two areas where constructive action is possible, the United Nations do indeed contribute to world order, rather than fail to act altogether, or even act to increase tensions further.[20]

---

19 Dimensions de la Conscience historique, Ch. VIII (Paris, 1961).

20 For recent evaluations of the UN, see Erich Hula, "The UN in crisis 27 Social Research, 387-420, and Hamilton Fish Armstrong, "UN on trial," 39 Foreign Affairs, 388-415.

NOTES AND QUESTIONS

1. What is, according to Hoffmann, the conflict between the world postulated by the Charter and the real world? How can this conflict be eliminated? Should the Charter be adapted to the real world? How would such an adaptation compare with that proposed by Clark and Sohn?
2. In what areas does Hoffmann find the impact of the United Nations to have been most constructive?——for what reasons? How might the United Nations be strengthened, given Hoffmann's line of analysis? What next steps might be appropriately taken?

3. What does Hoffmann mean by the negative role of the United Nations in the existing international system? To what extent is this negative role a consequence of Hoffmann's characterization of the system as a revolutionary one? Hoffmann seems to suggest that the ideas of domestic jurisdiction and collective intervention have been altered by political developments in ways that were not anticipated in 1945. Is Hoffmann's view consistent with that presented in Chapter 7. How does the financing crisis reflect the double role of the United Nations in international politics?
4. Do Clark and Sohn take adequate account of the persistence of international conflict in their plan for a reconstructed United Nations? Is there an assumption in their proposals that states will be reasonable under all circumstances in settling their disputes? How does one deal with a powerful and unreasonable state in a disarmed world?

TWO DIFFERING CONCEPTS OF UNITED NATIONS ASSAYED: INTRODUCTION TO THE ANNUAL REPORT OF THE SECRETARY-GENERAL ON THE WORK OF THE ORGANIZATION, 16 JUNE 1960—15 JUNE 1961[2]

DAG HAMMARSKJÖLD

I.

Debates and events during the year since the publication of the last report to the General Assembly have brought to the fore different concepts of the United Nations, the character of the Organization, its authority and its structure.

On the one side, it has in various ways become clear that certain Members conceive of the Organization as a static conference machinery for resolving conflicts of interests and ideologies with a view to peaceful coexistence, within the Charter, to be served by a Secretariat which is to be regarded not as fully internationalized but as representing within its ranks those very interests and ideologies.

Other Members have made it clear that they conceive of the Organization primarily as a dynamic instrument of governments through which they, jointly and for the same purpose, should seek such reconciliation but through which they should also try to develop forms of executive action, undertaken on behalf of all Members, and aiming at forestalling conflicts and resolving them, once they have arisen, by appropriate diplomatic or political means, in a spirit of objectivity and in implementation of the principles and purposes of the Charter.

Naturally, the latter concept takes as its starting point the conference concept, but it regards it only as a starting point, envisaging the possibility of continued growth to increasingly effective forms of active international cooperation, adapted to experience, and served by a Secretariat of which it is required that, whatever the background and the views of its individual members, their actions be guided solely by the principles of the Charter, the decisions of the main organs, and the interests of the Organization itself.

The first concept can refer to history and to the traditions of national policies of the past. The second can point to the needs of the present and of the future in a world of ever-closer international interdependence where nations have at their disposal armaments of hitherto unknown destructive strength. The first one is firmly anchored in the time-honored philosophy of sovereign national states in armed competition of which the most that may be expected in the international field is that they achieve a peaceful coexistence. The second one envisages possibilities of intergovernmental action overriding such a philosophy, and opens the road toward more developed and increasingly effective forms of constructive international cooperation.

It is clearly for the governments, Members of the Organization, and for these

[2] General Assembly *Official Records* (16th session), Supplement 1A. Title cited from *United Nations Review*, September 1961 (Vol. 8, No. 9), p. 12.

governments only, to make their choice and decide on the direction in which they wish the Organization to develop. However, it may be appropriate to study these two concepts in terms of the purposes of the Organization as laid down in the Charter and, in this context, also to consider the character and the significance of the decisions of the Organization as well as its structure.

II.

The purposes and principles of the Charter are set out in its Preamble and further developed in a series of articles, including some which may seem to be primarily of a procedural or administrative nature. Together, these parts of the Charter lay down some basic rules of international ethics by which all Member States have committed themselves to be guided. To a large extent, the rules reflect standards accepted as binding for life within states. Thus, they appear, in the main, as a projection into the international arena and the international community of purposes and principles already accepted as being of national validity. In this sense, the Charter takes a first step in the direction of an organized international community, and this independently of the organs set up for international cooperation. Due to different traditions, the state of social development and the character of national institutions, wide variations naturally exist as to the application in national life of the principles reflected in the Charter, but it is not too difficult to recognize the common elements behind those differences. It is therefore not surprising that such principles of national application could be transposed into an agreed basis also for international behavior and cooperation.

In the Preamble to the Charter, Member nations have reaffirmed their faith "in the equal rights of men and women and of nations large and small," a principle which also has found many other expressions in the Charter.

Thus, it restates the basic democratic principle of equal political rights, independently of the position of the individual or of the Member country in respect of its strength, as determined by territory, population, or wealth. The words just quoted must, however, be considered as going further and imply an endorsement as well of a right to equal economic opportunities.

It is in the light of the first principle that the Charter has established a system of equal votes, expressing "the sovereign equality of all its Members," and has committed the Organization to the furtherance of self-determination, self-government, and independence. On the same basis, the Charter requires universal respect for and observance of human rights and fundamental freedoms for all "without distinction as to race, sex, language or religion."

It is in the light of the latter principle—or, perhaps, the latter aspect of the same basic principle—that the Charter, in Article 55, has committed the Members to the promotion of higher standards of living, full employment, and conditions of economic and social progress and development, as well as to solutions of international economic and related problems. The pledge of all Members to take joint and separate action, in cooperation with the Organization, for the achievement of these purposes has been the basis for the far-reaching economic and technical assistance channelled through or administered by the Organization, and may rightly be considered as the basic obligation reflected also in such economic and technical assistance as Member governments have been giving, on a bilateral basis, outside the framework of the Organization.

It would seem that those who regard the Organization as a conference machinery, "neutral" in relation to the direction of policies on a national or international basis and serving solely as an instrument for the solution of conflicts by reconciliation, do not pay adequate attention to those essential principles of the Charter to which reference has just been made. The terms of the Charter are explicit as regards the equal political rights of nations as well as of individuals and, although this second principle may be considered only as implicit in the terms of the Charter, they are clear also as regards the demand for equal economic opportunities for all individuals and nations. So as to avoid any misunderstanding, the Charter directly states that the basic democratic principles are applicable to nations "large and small" and to individuals without distinction "as to race, sex, language and religion," qualifications that obviously could be extended to cover also other criteria such as, for example, those of an ideological character which have been used or may be used as a basis for political or economic discrimination.

In the practical work of the Organization these basic principles have been of special significance in relation to countries under colonial rule or in other ways under foreign domination. The General Assembly has translated the principles into action intended to establish through self-determination a free and independent life as sovereign states for peoples who have expressed in democratic forms their wish for such a status. Decisive action has in many cases been taken by Member governments, and then the United Nations has had only to lend its support to their efforts. In other cases, the main responsibility has fallen on the Organization itself. The resolution on colonialism, adopted by the General Assembly at its fifteenth session, may be regarded as a comprehensive restatement in elaborated form of the principle laid down in the Charter. Results of developments so far have been reflected in the birth of a great number of new national states and a revolutionary widening of the membership of the Organization.

The demand for equal economic opportunities has, likewise, been—and remains—of special significance in relation to those very countries which have more recently entered the international arena as new states. This is natural in view of the fact that, mostly, they have been in an unfavorable economic position, which is reflected in a much lower per capita income, rate of capital supply, and degree of technical development, while their political independence and sovereignty require a fair measure of economic stability and economic possibilities in order to gain substance and full viability.

In working for the translation into practical realities in international life of the democratic principles which are basic to the Charter, the Organization has thus assumed a most active role and it has done so with success, demonstrating both the need and the possibilities for such action.

Further, in the Preamble to the Charter it is stated to be a principle and purpose of the Organization "to establish conditions under which justice and respect for the obligations arising from treaties and other sources of international law can be maintained." In these words—to which, naturally, counterparts may be found in other parts of the Charter—it gives expression to another basic democratic principle, that of the rule of law. In order to promote this principle, the Charter established the International Court of Justice, but the principle permeates the approach of the Charter to international problems far beyond the sphere of competence of the

Court. As in national life, the principle of justice—which obviously implies also the principle of objectivity and equity in the consideration of all matters before the General Assembly or the Security Council—must be considered as applicable without distinction or discrimination, with one measure and one standard valid for the strong as well as for the weak. Thus, the demand of the Charter for a rule of law aims at the substitution of right for might and makes of the Organization the natural protector of rights which countries, without it, might find it more difficult to assert and to get respected.

The principle of justice can be regarded as flowing naturally from the principles of equal political rights and equal economic opportunities, but it has an independent life and carries, of itself, the world community as far in the direction of an organized international system as the two first-mentioned principles. It has deep roots in the history of the efforts of man to eliminate from international life the anarchy which he had already much earlier overcome on the national level, deeper indeed than the political and economic principles which, as is well known, were much later to get full acceptance also in national life. Long before the United Nations and long before even the League of Nations, governments were working toward a rule of justice in international life through which they hoped to establish an international community based on law, without parliamentary or executive organs, but with a judicial procedure through which law and justice could be made to apply.

The Charter states and develops the three principles mentioned here as a means to an end: "to save succeeding generations from the scourge of war." This adds emphasis to the concept, clearly implied in the Charter, of an international community for which the Organization is an instrument and an expression and in which anarchic tendencies in international life are to be curbed by the introduction of a system of equal political rights, equal economic opportunities, and the rule of law. However, the Charter goes one step further, drawing a logical conclusion both from the ultimate aim of the Organization and from the three principles. Thus, it outlaws the use of armed force "save in the common interest." Obviously, the Charter cannot, on the one side, establish a rule of law and the principle of equal rights for "nations large and small," and, on the other hand, permit the use of armed force for national ends, contrary to those principles and, therefore, not "in the common interest." Were nations, under the Charter, to be allowed, by the use of their military strength, to achieve ends contrary to the principle of the equality of Members and the principle of justice, it would obviously deprive those very principles of all substance and significance. One practical expression of this approach, which may be mentioned here, is that the organs of the United Nations have consistently maintained that the use of force, contrary to the Charter as interpreted by those organs, cannot be permitted to yield results which can be accepted as valid by the Organization and as establishing new rights.

In the Charter, the right to the use of force is somewhat more extensive than may seem to be the case from a superficial reading of the phrase "save in the common interest." Thus, apart from military action undertaken pursuant to a decision of the Security Council for repression of aggression—that is, for upholding the basic Charter principles—the Charter opens the door to the use of armed force by a nation in exercise of its inherent right to resist armed attack. This is a point on which, both in theory and in practice, the development of international law is still at a very early stage. As is well known, no agreement has been reached on a definition of aggression, beyond that found in Article 2, paragraph 4, of the Charter, and the Organization has several times had to face situations in which, therefore, the rights and wrongs in a specific case of conflict have not been clarified. It would be a vitally important step forward if wider agreement could be reached regarding the criteria to be applied in order to distinguish between legitimate and illegitimate use of force. History is only too rich in examples of armed aggression claimed as action in self-defense. How could it be otherwise, when most cases of armed conflict are so deeply rooted in a history of clashes of interests and rights, even if, up to the fatal moment of the first shot, those clashes have not involved recourse to the use of armed force?

In recognition of this situation and in the light of historical experience, the Charter makes yet another projection into international life of solutions to conflicts tested in national life, and establishes the final principle that the Organization shall "bring about by peaceful means and in conformity with the principles of justice and international law, adjustment or settlement of international disputes or situations which might lead to a breach of the peace." This principle, as quoted here from Article 1 of the Charter, is further developed specifically in Article 33, which requires parties to any dispute, the consequence of which is likely to endanger the maintenance of international peace and security, to "seek a solution by negotiation, enquiry, mediation, conciliation, arbitration, judicial settlement, resort to regional agencies or arrangements, or other peaceful means of their own choice." It is in this sphere that the Security Council has had, and is likely to continue to have, its main significance, both directly as a forum before which any dispute threatening peace and security can be brought up for debate and as an organ which directly, or through appropriate agents, may assist the parties in finding a way out and, by preventive diplomacy, may forestall the outbreak of an armed conflict. It seems appropriate here to draw attention especially to the right of the Security Council under Article 40 to "call upon the parties concerned to comply with such provisional measures as it deems necessary or desirable" for the prevention of any aggravation of a situation threatening peace and security, and to the obligation of Members to comply with a decision on such measures.

It is in the light of the approach to international coexistence in our world today, which is thus to be found in the Charter, that judgment has to be passed on the validity of the different conceptions of the Organization which in recent times have become increasingly apparent. As already pointed out, the basic principles regarding the political equality of nations and their right to equal economic opportunities are difficult to reconcile with the view that the Organization is to be regarded only as a conference machinery for the solution, by debate and joint decisions, of conflicts of interest or ideology. It seems even more difficult to reconcile these principles with a view according to which equality among Members should be reflected in the establishment of a balance between power blocs or other groupings of nations. The same difficulty is apparent as regards the principle of justice and the principle prohibiting the use of armed force. It is easier to apply the conference concept to the principle of prevention of conflict through negotiation, but also on this point the difficulties become considerable if it is recognized that such solutions as may be sought by the Organization should be solutions based on the rules of equality and justice.

III.

The General Assembly, the Security Council, and other collective organs of the United Nations have features in common with a standing international diplomatic conference, but their procedures go beyond the forms of such a conference and show aspects of a parliamentary or quasi-parliamentary character.

While decisions of a conference, in order to commit its participants, must be based on their subsequent acceptance of the decisions, the organs of the United Nations act on the basis of voting, with the decisions being adopted if supported by a majority. However, the decisions of the Assembly have, as regards Member States, only the character of recommendations (except for financial assessments and certain other types of organizational action) so that obligations like those arising out of an agreement, coming into force after a conference, do not normally flow from them. But although the decisions, legally, are only recommendations, they introduce an important element by expressing a majority consensus on the issue under consideration.

Naturally, such a formula leaves scope for a gradual development in practice of the weight of the decisions. To the extent that more respect, in fact, is shown to General Assembly recommendations by the Member States, they may come more and more close to being recognized as decisions having a binding effect on those concerned, particularly when they involve the application of the binding principles of the Charter and of international law.

Both those who regard a gradual increase in the weight of decisions of the General Assembly as necessary, if progress is to be registered in the direction of organized peaceful coexistence within the Charter, and those who oppose such a development, have to recognize that, with certain variations in individual cases, the practice still is very close to the restrictive Charter formula. Experience shows that even countries which have voted for a certain decision may, later on, basing themselves on its character of merely being a recommendation, refuse to follow it or fail to support its implementation, financially or in other respects.

What has been said applies generally to the collective organs of the Organization, but, as is well known, the Charter has gone one step further beyond the conference concept, in the direction of the parliamentary concept, in the case of the Security Council. In Article 25, Member States of the United Nations have agreed to "accept and carry out the decisions of the Security Council in accordance with the present Charter," thus, by agreement, making the decisions of the Council mandatory, except, of course, when such decisions take the form of "recommendations" within the terms of Chapter VI or certain other articles of the Charter. They have further, in Article 49, undertaken to "join in affording mutual assistance in carrying out the measures decided upon by the Security Council."

This agreed mandatory nature of certain Security Council decisions might have led to a demand for unanimity in the Council, a unanimity which was the rule for the Council of the League of Nations. Even so, however, the arrangement would have gone beyond the conference principle with its requirement that no decision reached in an international organ should be binding on an individual Member short of his agreement. With the present arrangements, requiring a majority of seven and the concurring votes of the permanent members, a bridge between the traditional conference approach and a parliamentary approach is provided by the commitment in Article 25 to agree to the carrying out of the decisions in the Council which should be considered as giving the Council its authority by general delegation as indeed stated in Article 24, paragraph 1.

What clearly remains within the Council of the traditional conference and agreement pattern is the condition that its decisions of a nonprocedural character must be supported by the unanimous vote of the five permanent members, thus avoiding for those members the risk of being bound by a decision of the Council which has not met with their agreement. It may be observed that this special position for the permanent members, apart from other reasons, has the justification that, without such a rule, the other Members of the Organization, in complying with a Security Council decision, might find themselves unwillingly drawn into a big power conflict.

In spite of the delegated authority which the Council may be considered as exercising, and the condition that decisions must be agreed to by the permanent members, the experience of the Organization, as regards the implementation of Council decisions, is uneven and does not indicate full acceptance in practice of Article 25. In this case also, examples can be given of a tendency to regard decisions, even when taken under Chapter VII, as recommendations binding only to the extent that the party concerned has freely committed itself to carry them out; there is here a clear dichotomy between the aims of the Charter and the general political practice at its present stage of development. Such cases refer not only to Members outside the Council, or, perhaps, Members inside the Council, who have not supported a specific decision, but also to Members within the Council who have cast their votes in favor of a decision but who later on are found to reserve for themselves at least a right to interpret the decision in ways which seem to be at variance with the intentions of the Council. The ambiguity of this situation emerges with special force in cases where such attitudes have been taken by permanent members of the Council, who are considered to shoulder the responsibility for the maintenance of peace and security which is reflected in the special position they hold within the Council. Obviously, the problem whether the intended legal weight is given to decisions of the Security Council arises in practice not only in cases of noncompliance but also in cases of a refusal to shoulder the financial consequences of a decision of the Council.

These observations—which have been limited to a reminder of the Charter rules and a factual reminder also of the experiences in practice—point to a situation which in any evaluation of the United Nations must be given the most serious consideration by Members. For the judgment on the various concepts of the United Nations which are put forward, it is one thing to note what the Charter stipulates; it is an entirely different but ultimately more important question as to what the situation is in practice and what, in fact, is the weight given to decisions of the Organization when they go beyond the conference pattern of agreement.

For those who maintain the conference concept of the Organization, it is natural to side-step the mandatory nature of decisions by the Security Council. For those who take a different view, it is equally natural and essential to work for a full and general acceptance of the Charter rules. Were those to be right who hold that the Charter on the points discussed here, and, maybe, also as regards the five basic principles discussed in the first part of this Introduction, is ahead of our time and the political possibilities which it offers, such a view still would not seem to justify the conclusion that the clear approach of the Charter should be abandoned. Rather, it would indicate that Member nations jointly should increase their efforts to make political realities gradually come closer to the pattern established by the Charter.

In the light of such considerations, the significance of the outcome of every single conflict on which the Organization has to take a stand, and the weight given to its decisions in such a conflict stand out very clearly. A failure to gain respect for decisions or actions of the Organization within the terms of the Charter is often called a failure for the Organization. It would seem more correct to regard it as a failure of the world community, through its Member nations and in particular those most directly concerned, to cooperate in order, step by step, to make the Charter a living reality in practical political action as it is already in law.

Were such cooperation, for which the responsibility naturally rests with each single Member as well as with all Members collectively, not to come about, and were the respect for the obligations flowing from Article 25 of the Charter to be allowed to diminish, this would spell the end of the possibilities of the Organization to grow into what the Charter indicates as the clear intention of the founders, as also of all hopes to see the Organization grow into an increasingly effective instrument, with increasing respect for recommendations of the General Assembly as well.

What this would mean for the value of the Organization as protector of the aims, principles and rights it was set up to further and safeguard, is obvious. The effort through the Organization to find a way by which the world community might, step by step, grow into organized international cooperation within the Charter, must either progress or recede. Those whose reactions to the work of the Organization hamper its development or reduce its possibilities of effective action may have to shoulder the responsibility for a return to a state of affairs which governments had already found too dangerous after the First World War.

IV.

The growth of the United Nations out of the historic conference pattern—which, as observed earlier in this Introduction, at all events naturally remains the starting point in all efforts of the Organization—is clearly reflected in what, in the light of experience, may seem to be a lack of balance in the Charter. While great attention is given to the principles and purposes, and considerable space is devoted to an elaboration of what may be called the parliamentary aspects of the Organization, little is said about executive arrangements. This does not mean that the Charter in any way closes the door to such arrangements or to executive action, but only that, at the stage of international thinking crystallized in the Charter, the conference approach still was predominant, and that the needs for executive action, if the new Organization was to live up to expectations and to its obligations under the Charter, had not yet attracted the attention they were to receive in response to later developments.

The key clause on the executive side may be considered to be Article 24 in which it is said that "in order to assure prompt and effective action by the United Nations, its Members confer on the Security Council primary responsibility for the maintenance of international peace and security." On that basis the Security Council is given the right, under Article 29, to establish such subsidiary organs as it deems necessary for the performance of its functions, the right under Article 40 to decide on so-called provisional measures, the right to use, for the purposes of the Charter, under certain conditions, armed forces made available to the Council, the right under Article 48 to request from governments action on the Council's behalf, as well as the right to request of the Secretary-General to "perform such . . . functions as are entrusted to him" by the Council.

The various clauses here briefly enumerated open a wide range of possibilities for executive action undertaken by, and under the aegis of, the Security Council. However, no specific machinery is set up for such action by the Council, apart from the Military Staff Committee, with planning responsibilities in the field of the possible use of armed force by the Security Council under Chapter VII of the Charter. In fact, therefore, the executive functions and their form have been left largely to practice, and it is in the field of the practices of the Organization that cases may be found in the light of which it is now possible to evaluate the ways in which the Organization may develop its possibilities for diplomatic, political, or military intervention of an executive nature in the field.

The forms used for executive action by the Security Council—or when the Council has not been able to reach decisions, in some cases, by the General Assembly—are varied and are to be explained by an effort to adjust the measures to the needs of each single situation. However, some main types are recurrent. Subcommittees have been set up for fact-finding or negotiation on the spot. Missions have been placed in areas of conflict for the purpose of observation and local negotiation. Observer groups of a temporary nature have been sent out. And, finally, police forces under the aegis of the United Nations have been organized for the assistance of the governments concerned with a view to upholding the principles of the Charter. As these, or many of these, arrangements require centralized administrative measures, which cannot be performed by the Council or the General Assembly, Members have to a large extent used the possibility to request the Secretary-General to perform special functions by instructing him to take the necessary executive steps for implementation of the action decided upon. This has been done under Article 98, as quoted above, and has represented a development in practice of the duties of the Secretary-General under Article 97. The character of the mandates has, in many cases, been such that in carrying out his functions the Secretary-General has found himself forced also to interpret the decisions in the light of the Charter, United Nations precedents, and the aims and intentions expressed by the Members. When that has been the case, the Secretary-General has been under the obligation to seek guidance, to all possible extent, from the main organs; but when such guidance has not been forthcoming, developments have sometimes led to situations in which he has had to shoulder responsibility for certain limited political functions, which may be considered to be in line with the spirit of Article 99 but which legally have been based on decisions of the main organs themselves, under Article 98, and thus the exclusive responsibility of Member States acting through these organs. Naturally, in carrying out such functions the Secretariat has remained fully subject to the decisions of the political bodies.

This whole development has lately become a matter of controversy, natural and, indeed, unavoidable in the light of differences of approach to the role of the Organization to which attention has been drawn earlier in this Introduction. While the development is welcomed by Member nations which feel a need of growth as regards the possibilities of the Organization to engage in executive action in protection of the Charter principles, it is rejected by those who maintain the conference concept of the Organization. The different opinions expressed on the development are only superficially related to this or that specific action and the way in which it is considered to have been carried through. They are also only superficially related to the choice of means used for translating decisions into action. The discussion regarding the development of executive functions is basically one confronting the same fundamentally different concepts of the Organization and its place in international politics, which could be seen also in the different attitudes toward the legal weight of decisions of the Organization.

It is in this context that the principle embodied in Article 100 of the Charter is of decisive significance. This principle, which has a long history, establishes the international and independent character of the Secretariat. Thus, it is said that the Secretary-General and the staff of the Secretariat "shall not seek or receive instructions from any Government or from any other authority external to the Organization," and that they "shall refrain from any action which might reflect on their position as international officials responsible only to the Organization." In the same Article, the Members of the United Nations undertake to respect "the exclusively international character of the responsibilities of the Secretary-General and the staff and not to seek to influence them in the discharge of their responsibilities."

The significance of the principle stated in Article 100 is a dual one. It envisages a Secretariat so organized and developed as to be able to serve as a neutral instrument for the Organization, were its main organs to wish to use the Secretariat in the way which has been mentioned above and for which Article 98 has opened possibilities. But in doing so, the principle also indicates an intention to use the Secretariat for such functions as would require that it have an exclusively international character.

In the traditional conference pattern, participants in a meeting are mostly serviced by a secretariat drawn from the same countries as the participants themselves, and constituting a mixed group regarding which there is no need to demand or maintain an exclusively international character. It is therefore natural that those who favor the conference approach to the United Nations tend to give to Article 100 another interpretation than the one which the text calls for, especially in the light of its historical background and its background also in other clauses of the Charter.

There is no reason to go more deeply into this special problem here. Suffice it to say that, while the Organization, if regarded as a standing diplomatic conference, might well be serviced by a fully international Secretariat but does not need it, the other approach to the Organization and its role cannot be satisfied with anything less than a secretariat of an exclusively international character, and thus cannot be reconciled with a secretariat composed on party-lines and on the assumption that the interests represented in the main organs in this manner should be represented and advocated also within the Secretariat. Thus, again, the choice between conflicting views on the United Nations Secretariat is basically a choice between conflicting views on the Organization, its functions, and its future.

In order to avoid possible misunderstandings, it should be pointed out here that there is no contradiction at all between a demand for a truly international Secretariat and a demand, found in the Charter itself, for as wide a "geographical" distribution of posts within the Secretariat as possible. It is, indeed, necessary precisely in order to maintain the exclusively international character of the Secretariat, that it be so composed as to achieve a balanced distribution of posts on all levels among all regions. This, however, is clearly something entirely different from a balanced representation of trends or ideologies. In fact if a realistic representation of such trends is considered desirable, it can and should be achieved without any assumption of political representation within the ranks of the Secretariat, by a satisfactory distribution of posts based on geographical criteria.

The exclusively international character of the Secretariat is not tied to its composition, but to the spirit in which it works and to its insulation from outside influences as stated in Article 100. While it may be said that no man is neutral in the sense that he is without opinions or ideals, it is just as true that, in spite of this, a neutral Secretariat is possible. Anyone of integrity, not subjected to undue pressures, can, regardless of his own views, readily act in an "exclusively international" spirit and can be guided in his actions on behalf of the Organization solely by its interests and principles, and by the instructions of its organs.

V.

After this brief review of the principles of the Organization, of the character of its decisions, and of its structure, especially as regards arrangements for executive action, presented only as a background for the consideration of what basic concepts and approaches should guide the development of the Organization, it may be appropriate, in conclusion, to give attention to the activities of the Organization and their relevance to the current international situation.

For years the Organization has been a focal point for efforts to achieve disarmament. This may still be considered as the main standing item on the agenda of the General Assembly. However, in recent years these efforts of the Organization have been running parallel to other efforts which are either outside of it or only loosely tied to the work of the United Nations. This may be justified on the basis that a very limited number of countries hold key positions in the field of armaments, so that any effort on a universal basis and by voting, to reach a decision having practical force, would be ineffective, unless founded on a basic agreement between those few parties mostly concerned. Therefore, direct negotiations between those countries are an essential first step to the solution, through the United Nations, of the disarmament problem, and do not in any way derogate from the responsibilities or rights of the Organization.

The situation may serve as an example of a problem which has become increasingly important in the life of the Organization: the right way in which to balance the weight of the big powers and their security interests against the rights of the majority of Member nations. Such a majority naturally cannot expect the big powers, in questions of vital concern to them, with their superior military and economic strength, automatically to accept a majority verdict. On the other hand, the big powers cannot, as Members of the world community, and with their dependence on all other nations, set themselves above, or disregard the views of, the majority of nations. An effort to balance the big power element and the majority element is found in the Charter rules regarding the respective competence of the

General Assembly and the Security Council and regarding the special position of the big powers within the Council. Other efforts to solve the same problem are reflected in the way in which the disarmament problem has been attacked in recent years. No fully satisfactory or definitive formula has been found, but it must be sought, and it is to be hoped that when the time comes for a Charter revision, agreement may be reached on a satisfactory solution.

What is true of the disarmament problem is, of course, true also of those more specific questions in which security interests of big powers are or may be directly involved, as for example the Berlin problem. The community of nations, represented in the United Nations, has a vital interest in a peaceful solution, based on justice, of any question which—like this one—unless brought to a satisfactory solution, might come to represent a threat to peace and security. However, the problem of the balance to be struck between the rights and obligations of the big powers and the rights and obligations of all other nations applies, in a very direct way, also to this problem which is now so seriously preoccupying the minds of all peoples and their leaders. The United Nations, with its wide membership, is not, and can, perhaps, not aspire to be a focal point in the debate on an issue such as the Berlin question, or in the efforts to solve it, but the Organization cannot, for that reason, be considered as an outside party which has no right to make its voice heard should a situation develop which would threaten those very interests which the United Nations is to safeguard and for the defense of which it was intended to provide all Member nations with an instrument and a forum.

Reference has already been made in this Introduction to the work of the Organization devoted to furthering self-determination, self-government, and independence for all peoples. In that context it was recalled that the General Assembly, at its last session, adopted a resolution regarding the colonial problem which elaborates the basic principles of the Charter in their application to this problem.

This is, likewise, a question which for years has been before the General Assembly and it is likely to remain a major item until a final result is achieved which reflects full implementation of the basic principles in the direction indicated by last year's resolution. Experience has shown that peaceful progress in that direction cannot be guaranteed solely by decisions of the General Assembly or the Security Council, within the framework of a conference pattern. Executive action is necessary, and neither the General Assembly nor the Security Council—which has had to deal with situations in which the liquidation of the colonial system has led to acute conflict—has abstained from such action in support of the lines upheld. As in the past, executive action by the Organization in the future will undoubtedly also be found necessary if it is to render the service expected from it under the terms of the Charter.

It is in conflicts relating to the development toward full self-government and independence that the Organization has faced its most complicated tasks in the executive field. It is also in the case of executive action in this context that different concepts of the Organization and of its decisions and structure have their most pointed expressions. As regards this specific aspect of the work of the United Nations, the front line has not been the usual one between different bloc interests, but more one between a great number of nations with aims natural especially for those which recently have been under colonial rule or under other forms of foreign domination, and a limited number of powers with other aims and predominant interests. This seems understandable if one takes into account that a majority of nations wishes to stand aside from the big power conflicts, while power blocs or big powers tend to safeguard their positions and security by efforts to maintain or extend an influence over newly emerging areas. The United Nations easily becomes a focal point for such conflicting interests as the majority looks to the Organization for support in its policy of independence also in relation to such efforts, while power blocs or countries with other aims may see in the United Nations an obstacle in the way of their policies to the extent that the Organization provides the desired support. How this is reflected in the attitude toward the development of the executive functions of the United Nations can be illustrated by numerous examples. It may be appropriate in this context to say in passing a word about the problem of the Congo and the activities of the United Nations in that country.

Different interests and powers outside Africa have seen in the Congo situation a possibility of developments with strong impact on their international position. They have therefore, naturally, held strong views on the direction in which they would like to see developments in the Congo turn and—with the lack of political traditions in the country and without the stability which political institutions can get only by being tested through experience—the doors have been opened for efforts to influence developments by supporting this or that faction or this or that personality. True to its principles, the United Nations has had to be guided in its operation solely by the interest of the Congolese people and by their right to decide freely for themselves, without any outside influences and with full knowledge of facts. Therefore, the Organization, throughout the first year of its work in the Congo, up to the point when parliament reassembled and invested a new national government, has refused—what many may have wished—to permit the weight of its resources to be used in support of any faction so as thereby to prejudge in any way the outcome of a choice which belonged solely to the Congolese people. It has also had to pursue a line which, by safeguarding the free choice of the people, implied resistance against all efforts from outside to influence the outcome. In doing so, the Organization has been put in a position in which those within the country who felt disappointed in not getting the support of the Organization were led to suspect that others were in a more favored position and, therefore, accused the Organization of partiality, and in which, further, such outside elements as tried to get or protect a foothold within the country, when meeting an obstacle in the United Nations, made similar accusations. If, as it is sincerely to be hoped, the recent national reconciliation, achieved by parliament and its elected representatives of the people, provides a stable basis for a peaceful future in a fully independent and unified Congo, this would definitely confirm the correctness of the line pursued by the United Nations in the Congo. In fact, what was achieved by parliament early in August may be said to have done so with sufficient clarity. It is a thankless and easily misunderstood role for the Organization to remain neutral in relation to a situation of domestic conflict and to provide active assistance only by protecting the rights and possibilities of the people to find their own way, but it remains the only manner in which the Organization can serve its proclaimed purpose of furthering the full independence of the people in the true and unqualified sense of the word.

The United Nations may be called upon again to assist in similar ways. Whatever mistakes in detail and on specific points critics may ascribe to the Organization in the highly complicated situation in the Congo, it is to be hoped that they do not lead Members to revise the basic rules which guide the United Nations activities in such situations, as laid down in the first report of the Secretary-General to the Security Council on the Congo question,[3] which the Council, a year ago, found reason, unanimously, to commend.

Closely related to a policy aiming at self-government and independence for all is the question of economic and technical assistance, especially during the first years of independence of a new Member State. The United Nations and its agencies and affiliated organs have at their disposal only very modest means for the purpose, but a rich experience has been gathered and the personnel resources are not inconsiderable.

Last year the Economic and Social Council and the General Assembly had to consider proposals designed to open up new possibilities for the Organization to respond to the demands of Member governments facing all the problems of newly achieved independence. Naturally, the problems which are of special importance for such countries are basically the same as those which face all countries which have been left behind in economic development. Therefore, the urgent attention required by newly independent countries in this respect can in no way justify a discrimination in their favor against other countries with similar difficulties.

This year the General Assembly will have before it proposals initiated by the Scientific Advisory Committee and endorsed by the Economic and Social Council for a conference under United Nations aegis, intended to provide possibilities for a break-through in the application of the technical achievements of present times to the problems of the economically less developed countries. It is sincerely to be hoped that, in the interest of international cooperation and the acceleration of the economic progress of those countries, this proposal will meet with the approval of the General Assembly.

So far, the economic and technical activities of the United Nations have been less influenced by the conflict between different concepts of the role of the Organization than its activities in other fields. However, it is impossible to isolate the economic and technical problems from the general question discussed in this Introduction. While receiving countries should have full freedom to take assistance from whatever source they find appropriate, they should not be barred, if they so wish, from getting all the assistance they need through United Nations channels or under United Nations aegis. The Organization is far from being able to meet all such demands, as donor nations continue to show a strong preference for bilateral approaches on a national or a group basis. Again, the problem arises of the basic concept of the United Nations. With the conference approach to the work of the Organization a choice is made also in favor of bilateral assistance, while the alternative approach opens the door to a development under which international assistance, in implementation of the principle of equal economic opportunities for all, would be channelled through the Organization or its related agencies to the extent that this is desired by the recipient countries and is within the capacity of the Organization.

Basic to the United Nations approach to economic and technical assistance is the principle, under all circumstances, that, although the Organization has to follow its

[3] Document S/4389 and Adds.1–6.

own rules and maintain its own independence, its services are exclusively designed to meet the wishes of the recipient government, without the possibility of any ulterior motives and free from the risk of any possible influence on the national or international policies of that government. Whatever development the executive activities of the Organization may show in the field, there should never be any suspicion that the world community would wish or, indeed, could ever wish to maintain for itself, through the United Nations, a position of power or control in a Member country. Were political groups in a country really to believe in such a risk, the explanation would seem to be that, as has indeed happened in the case of governments of Member countries with long established independence, they may find it difficult to accept the judgment of the majority of the nations of the world as to what in a specific situation is necessary in order to safeguard international peace and security, when such a judgment appears to be in conflict with the immediate aims of the group. With growing respect for the decisions of the Organization and growing understanding of its principles, the risks for such misinterpretations should be eliminated.

. . . the Organization has now reached a stage in its development where Member nations may find it timely to clarify their views on the direction in which they would like to see the future work of the Organization develop.

NOTES AND QUESTIONS

1. Hammarskjöld writes of two different concepts of the United Nations in his opening paragraph. What are they? Do some nations hold one concept and some another? Which concept is held in the West?——in the Communist world?——in the third world? Do all Western states adhere to the same concept? Are some Western states closer to Communist states than they are to each other?
2. Hammarskjöld writes that there is no agreement on what constitutes aggression within the meaning of the Charter. He writes that "it would be a vitally important step forward if wider agreement could be reached regarding the criteria to be applied to distinguish between legitimate and illegitimate use of force." Do you agree? What sorts of criteria might serve as the basis for agreement? Why is it difficult to reach an agreement? It is a matter of record that the Soviet Union has consistently, since the League, favored the adoption of an authoritative definition of aggression and that the United States has opposed all efforts at definition. How do you account for these opposing postures? For a detailed defense of the United States' outlook, see Julius Stone, *Aggression and World Order: A Critique of United Nations Theories of Aggression* (University of California Press, 1958).
3. In Section V of Hammarskjöld's Introduction consideration is given to balancing off the interests of the big powers against those of the majority of states. This is a problem that has been fundamental to the operations of the Organization in all aspects of its work. Do the big powers have more or less relative influence as a consequence of the existence of the United Nations? How does one answer such a question? Is the same answer appropriate for each of the big powers? Which of the big powers would lose most or gain most from the adoption of the Clark-Sohn plan? Why? Would any of the smaller powers lose?

   Should the financing problem be solved by translating differences in financial contribution into differences in political authority in the Organization? How does one reconcile the idea of "sovereign equality" in Article 2(1) of the Charter with differentiations in the status of members? Note that Clark and Sohn abandon the phrase "sovereign equality" in their revision of Article 2(1). Why? But also note that Clark and Sohn reserve "to all nations or their peoples all powers inherent in their sovereignty, except such as are delegated to the United Nations." What are these powers inherent in sovereignty? To what extent do they survive the Clark-Sohn revision? To what extent is a stable world order compatible with the prerogatives of national sovereignty? Does the sovereignty of weak states endanger world peace? If not, is it not the fact of power rather than the freedom to use it that constitutes the danger?——or is it the combination of power and sovereignty that must be broken up? Is sovereignty connected with the idea of domestic jurisdiction? Is the suppression of human rights a matter of sovereign prerogative under existing international law? Is such suppression a danger to world peace? How? How do Clark and Sohn, in light of their statement of Article 2(1) and their adoption of a Bill of Rights in Annex VII, pp. 365–370, envisage the connection between world peace and the promotion of fundamental human rights?

ALVIN Z. RUBINSTEIN

More Responsibility for Russia?

How the Soviet Union might be more deeply involved in the United Nations is considered by an associate professor of political science at the University of Pennsylvania. His study, The Soviets in International Organizations *(Princeton University Press), is based on research conducted under the auspices of the Center of International Studies at Princeton.*

"Given the present state of affairs, Western attempts to convince the Soviet Union that strengthened international organizations are to its interest are politically and ideologically foredoomed to failure. *Only Moscow's conviction that increased participation would facilitate closer relationships with the neutralists, indeed that it was necessary for such a development, might bring about a modification of Soviet attitude and behavior;* for whatever the current position of Moscow might be on international organizations, conditioned as it is by Soviet perspectives on the West and Western policies, a growing commitment by the politically important underdeveloped countries could prove a trend too strong for the Soviet Union long to withstand. And in this reconstitution of the institutions and environment of the world beyond the Soviet orbit lie the most promising hopes for the consequent erosion of Soviet ideology.

"It is with this long-run objective in mind that a number of moves should be tried; they will at least clear the atmosphere and show the neutralists that the West does not seek to manipulate these organizations to advance its own interests, but desires to work with underdeveloped countries in a genuine partnership for economic progress and international stability.

"The problem can be approached in two ways, each of which would, it is hoped, reinforce the other: first, associate the U.S.S.R. more intimately and intensively in the planning . . . of activities; and second, improve the cooperation between the Western and neutralist countries.

"For more than a decade and a half, the Soviet Union has been kept on the periphery of policy-making and administration in international organizations—initially through its own choice, and later as a consequence of Western control which barred the Soviets from positions of authority. In its criticisms of Western high-handedness and anti-Soviet attitudes, Moscow has ground for grievance. That it has contributed to the present state of affairs by its own actions and attitudes goes without saying. But this is not the place to review or assess responsibility for the genesis and generation of cold war politics; it is our purpose here to suggest ways of diminishing negativism in international organizations. The Soviet Union has not been accorded responsibility or status commensurate with its position as a great power and should be brought more directly into the decision-making levels of international organizations. There is no guarantee, and perhaps little likelihood, that greater responsibility for policy would lead to extensive Soviet commitments, any more than the long Western pre-eminence resulted in full-fledged Western support." But increased responsibility for the Soviet Union might moderate some of its unjustified criticisms of international organizations.

"First, a Soviet citizen should be made the head of one of the specialized agencies. At present, all the Directors-General are Westerners, with the exception of Dr. Sen (of the FAO) who is an Indian. The time is overdue for an 'internationalization' of the top executive posts. The changing composition of these organizations should be reflected in the decision-making levels. Though no rigid, troika-type arrangement should be adopted, a redressing of national representation is needed. The danger that an organization headed by a Soviet citizen might become subservient to Soviet interests, or be turned into a Soviet-front organization, is remote, because the membership of each organization is the ultimate judge of the Director-General's competence and impartiality, and has the authority and means to remove unfit officials. We cannot *a priori* assume that a Soviet Director-General would not function in a way satisfactory to the great majority of the member nations. For its part, Moscow would stand to lose considerable prestige among the neutralists if it sought to use a Soviet Director-General to promote Soviet interests.

"Second, Moscow should be made the headquarters of one of the specialized agencies. Though most of them are now engaged principally in activities pertaining to underdeveloped countries, their headquarters are all located in Western European countries. Whereas, at the time the agencies were originally established, the overwhelming majority of members came from the Western world and the activities were Western-oriented, there is no longer any justification for the geographic concentration of the agencies. It would be thoroughly appropriate for some of those agencies which are most active in underdeveloped countries, e.g., FAO, WHO, ILO, UNESCO, to relocate in other parts of the world. In the decentralizing process, one of the new centers could be Moscow or Leningrad. The Soviets currently use the forums of international organizations to reach the opinion-molding elite, as well as the mass audiences, of other countries. Establishment of the site of a specialized agency in Moscow would provide non-Communist officials with an opportunity to reach more of the Soviet public. Working in the Soviet Union, either as governmental representatives or as members of the Agency Secretariat, would give neutralist officials new insights into the nature of Soviet society and the operation of Soviet 'socialism.' The West should make the proposal in conjunction with several of the leading neutralist countries, or encourage the neutralists to make it alone. The Soviet Government might well reject a proposal to establish the headquarters of an international organization in the U.S.S.R., but the responsibility and the onus should be theirs.

"Third, consideration could be given to holding alternate sessions of the General Assembly in New York and Moscow. This might entail impossible administrative problems for the Secretariat, but not until they have been carefully explored should the idea be rejected. The Soviet Government has occasionally suggested that UN headquarters be transferred from New York to West Berlin, Vienna, Geneva, or some other city, in order to lessen Western control over the UN. Dissatisfaction with New York as the site of General Assembly sessions also exists among some neutralists. . . .

"Fourth, the West is wasting a unique opportunity by failing to challenge the Soviet Union to enter into a joint program of helping underdeveloped countries within the framework of international organizations. Secretary-General U Thant called on member nations to make this 'the decade of development.' The Soviets have indicated their support for SUNFED but have never stated how much they would be prepared to contribute; also, they persistently hold that an agreement on disarmament must be reached before more money can be diverted to the needs of underdeveloped countries, a view generally shared by the Western countries. The West should reverse its position and offer to match any contribution made by the Soviet bloc. By stating its willingness to contribute to SUNFED, or to any other program for aiding underdeveloped countries, an amount equal to that which the Soviet bloc is prepared to give, the West would do much to wrest the initiative on this issue from Moscow. The more money that the U.S.S.R. can be induced to direct into economic development through international channels, the better will be the prospects for political stability in underdeveloped countries. So far, the Soviets have reaped impressive political harvests from meager contributions to UN programs. It is to the advantage of the West and the neutralists that Moscow increase its contribution. . . .

"Disarmament is one pressing problem; economic development is another. We cannot do much about the first, but we can significantly attack the second. Aid channeled through international organizations offers potential political and economic returns that are far greater than those currently received from the massive bilateral programs. It could place developmental activities on a more economically rational basis and do much to take the cold war out of programs for helping needy nations. Suitably presented, such a program of development would be one challenge that the Soviets could not afford to ignore.

"Fifth, the West has been remiss in squandering prospects for strengthening international organizations in the interest of temporary political triumphs of dubious merit. Its preoccupation with winning minor parliamentary skirmishes with the Soviet Union is endangering its opportunities for cooperation with the neutralist nations. For example, whether the Communist-controlled World Federation of Trade Unions is accredited to the International Atomic Energy Agency is a matter of no importance. Yet, by debating this issue with the Soviets, the West serves the Soviet objective of publicizing the organization and intensifies the politicization of IAEA. To involve organizations in circular political debate prevents useful work from being accomplished and engenders among neutralists a bitterness that is directed primarily against the West as the bloc responsible for setting the tone of the proceedings. Accreditation can be granted all non-governmental organizations which desire it, without in the least adversely affecting the operations of the specialized agencies. It would merely provide an opportunity for officials of, let us say, the WFTU to make a few speeches, reiterating views that have already been stated by Soviet delegates. The agencies' work is far too important to be impeded by endless, parliamentary wrangling. Since the West still dominates the proceedings of the specialized agencies, it must be held largely responsible for the lamentable waste of time and effort afflicting the agencies.

"These suggestions, even collectively, would seem inadequate to the task of stimulating an expanding Soviet interest in international organizations, particularly when they are juxtaposed to the general Soviet repugnance toward engaging in meaningful cooperation with capitalist countries, and the marginal role assigned to international organizations in the Soviet approach to international affairs. However, in the context of the growing importance of underdeveloped countries to Soviet policy, it is possible that Soviet leaders would increase their commitment to the so-called 'non-political' activities if they thought it necessary for the advancement of their influence among the neutralists. Certainly, the Soviets now support in principle any economic and social program which is strongly favored by neutralist countries. But it is also true that they have shown a continued illiberality toward new programs, even when the money was intended for underdeveloped countries. This, however, is not damaging to them for several reasons.

"First, as long as bilateral aid remains the major source of foreign assistance for neutralist countries, the 'token' contributions of the U.S.S.R. to international organizations is not critical in view of their considerable bilateral aid programs. Second, the neutralists do not regard Western contributions as significantly greater than those of the Soviet bloc, since the bulk of Western aid to underdeveloped countries is given to those who are allied with the West and is also channeled bilaterally. Accordingly, the difference between the amounts of Western and Soviet support for the economic and social programs of international organizations is not significant, in view of the difference between the amounts of foreign aid rendered through international and bilateral channels. Third, the neutralists share the Soviet view that Western concepts dominate the allocation of resources available to international organizations and that this acts as a legitimate deterrent to larger Soviet commitments. Finally, seeing that international organizations show no promise of developing as major sources of capital, the neutralists have no stake in making a political issue of strengthening them.

"One clear fact emerges from an examination of international organizations: namely, that the combination of Western and neutralist cooperation is sufficient to make any economic and social proposal a reality; further, the Soviet Union, for political reasons, will not oppose a proposal enjoying neutralist approval and will participate and contribute, though often only minimally. Cooperation between the neutralist and Western nations is essential for the future of international organizations; when the two conflict, the Soviets are afforded the opportunity for political mischief. If they work in concert, each can advance its own interests: the West can improve its relations with underdeveloped countries, retain an important measure of influence in international organizations in which it no longer commands a voting majority, and strengthen institutions through which economic progress and orderly international change might be channeled; the neutralists will find international organizations indispensable for obtaining serious consideration for their views, for developing closer ties with other underdeveloped countries through cooperation rather than competition, and for encouraging the wealthy nations to devote more of their resources to the well-being of the poor nations. The neutralist nations have within their reach an opportunity to convince the Western nations that they are not out to get whatever they can for themselves by playing on the cold war rivalry. By evidencing a readiness to cooperate within an international framework, the neutralists may encourage greater support from the Western countries; by attributing political value to international organizations, they may also induce Moscow to increase its commitment.

"Such developments will not end the cold war. Nor, in the short run, should they be expected to decrease international tension. But they could conceivably result in greater Soviet cooperation in the task of helping the poor countries, and then, inadvertently but inevitably, in strengthening international organizations as a consequence of greater Western-neutralist cooperation and growing Soviet participation. . . .

"In the past, the United States supported international organizations because they supported the United States. The introduction of numerous neutralist nations has complicated the operation of these organizations and the possibilities of obtaining a consensus which would permit the continuation and expansion of their established purposes. The West's preoccupation with the efforts of the Soviet Union to exploit these organizations for the furtherance of Soviet objectives, coupled with its excessive concern that the newly independent countries, inexperienced and impatient, will be used as pawns against the West, has given rise to suspicions on both sides that forestall the mutual benefits that the West and the neutralists stand to gain from an effectively functioning system of international organizations. . . .

"The time has come for the United States, as the leading Western power, to act in a manner that leaves no doubt of its wholehearted commitment to international organizations, to the task of promoting economic and social development in concert with underdeveloped countries. International organizations can serve as valuable bridges between the West and the new nations, over which can pass not merely goods, but knowledge and understanding. By transforming them into cold war arenas, the West demeans the very institutions that it created and that are capable of playing an important role in promoting international stability. Let Western delegates, led by the United States, devote themselves to the problems in which the underdeveloped countries have a vital interest; let them seek to resolve differences, to negotiate genuinely, and to concentrate on the goals that are mutually shared. For the West, the dialogue with the underdeveloped countries is the only one worth pursuing in international organizations. Efforts to dominate, to dictate policy, to bend these organizations to narrowly conceived political objectives, will result only in widening the gulf between Western and neutralist nations, and in emasculating international organizations, an end which Moscow devoutly desires and from which it alone stands to gain." *(The Soviets in International Organizations)*

NOTES AND QUESTIONS

1. How does Rubinstein propose persuading the Soviet Union to participate more constructively in the affairs of the United Nations? Do you think it is in the interests of the United States and of the United Nations to increase the role of the Soviet Union as Rubinstein proposes? What political assumptions relative to Soviet intentions is it necessary to make?——on the basis of what evidence?
2. Do the arguments advanced by Rubinstein with respect to the U.S.S.R. also bear upon the issue of whether it is advisable to admit Peking China to the Organization?
3. What might be done to persuade other states or groups of states to participate more fully and responsibly in the Organization—for example, France, Japan, the Latin American and the Afro-Asian states?
4. Some have suggested that the United States makes insufficient use of the United Nations. For a general analysis from the perspective of foreign policy rather than international order, see L. P. Bloomfield, *The United Nations and United States Foreign Policy* (Little, Brown, Boston, 1960); compare the internationalist orientation in the final chapter of Inis L. Claude's *Swords into Ploughshares* (3rd rev. ed., Random House, New York, 1964). Recently, the United States has been criticized for not making greater use of the United Nations in connection with the settlement of the civil war in South Vietnam. See Don R. Larson & Arthur Larson, *Vietnam and Beyond: A New American Foreign Policy and Program* (Duke University Press, 1965) pp. 30–42.

   The consideration of such a proposal, the arguments for and against it, suggest both the opportunities for and the limitations of United Nations' action in the present world, especially in the context of civil war. How can the United Nations pacify civil strife without taking sides? As the opposing factions in most civil wars since the end of World War II correspond to cold war factions, how is it possible to define a mission and recruit a staff for a United Nations undertaking? The Congo operation, the initial consensus among principal powers, and the intense conflict once it disappeared, disclose both the positive and negative aspects of making use of the United Nations in the event that a civil war is alleged to be a threat to international peace and security.

   How do Clark and Sohn reconcile the unity of mission and staff needed for effective peace-keeping with the persistence of international conflict? Can you offer any methods of approach? Some of these problems were considered in Chapter 9.

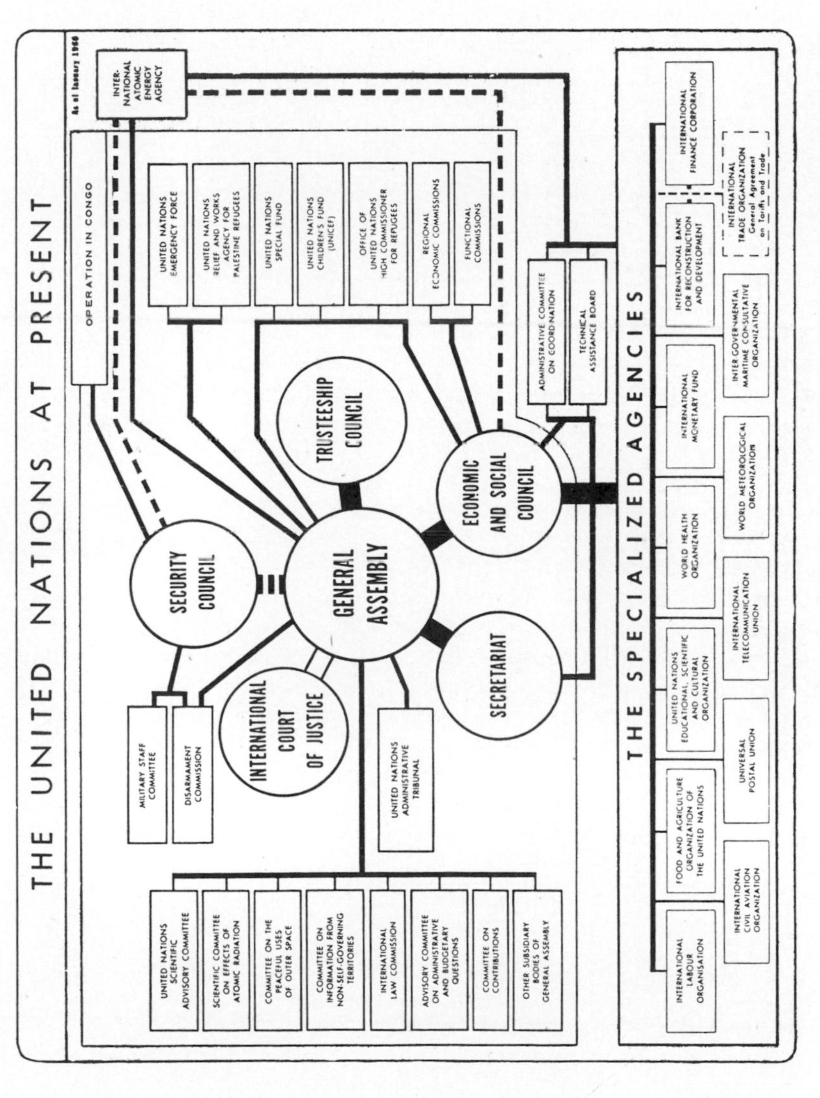

Adapted from *Yearbook of the United Nations 1959*, with permission of the UN

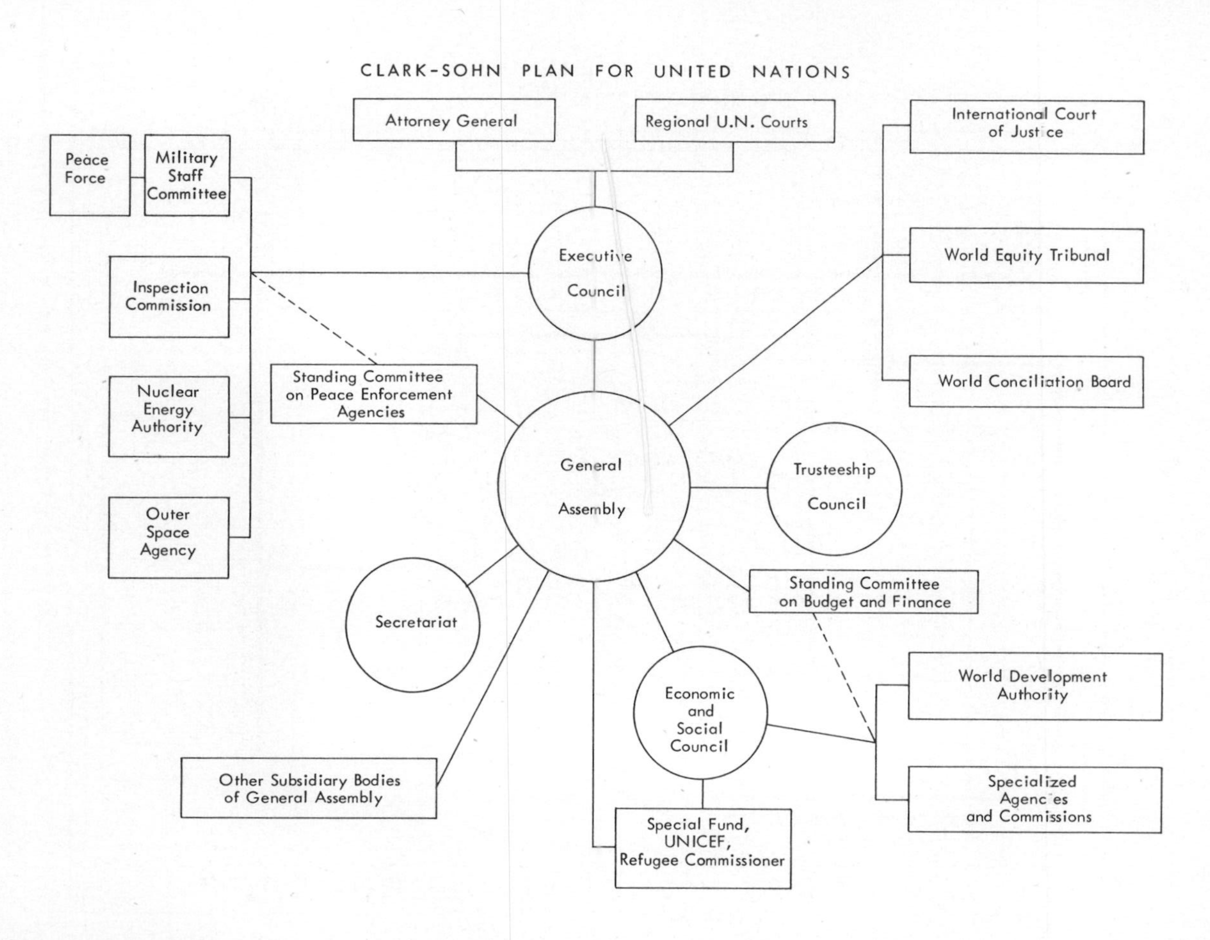
CLARK-SOHN PLAN FOR UNITED NATIONS
Attorney General
Regional U.N. Courts
Peace Force
Military Staff Committee
International Court of Justice
Executive Council
World Equity Tribunal
Inspection Commission
Standing Committee on Peace Enforcement Agencies
World Conciliation Board
Nuclear Energy Authority
General Assembly
Trusteeship Council
Outer Space Agency
Secretariat
Standing Committee on Budget and Finance
World Development Authority
Economic and Social Council
Other Subsidiary Bodies of General Assembly
Specialized Agencies and Commissions
Special Fund, UNICEF, Refugee Commissioner

The Editors

RICHARD A. FALK. Albert G. Milbank Professor of International Law and Practice at Princeton University. Co-editor of *World Politics*. Author of *Law, Morality and War in the Contemporary World*, and *The Role of Domestic Courts in the International Legal Order*.

SAUL H. MENDLOVITZ. Professor of International Law at Rutgers University School of Law. Consultant to the World Law Fund, New York. Editor of *Legal and Political Problems of World Order*.

Notes on Authors

CHARLES HENRY ALEXANDROWICZ. Holder of the Associate Chair of International Legal Organization at the University of Sydney. Author of *International Economic Organizations*, and *Constitutional Developments in India*.

SYDNEY D. BAILEY. Author and editor of many works on parliamentary government and international affairs. He served as Director of the Quaker United Nations Program. His books include *The United Nations: A Short Political Guide*, and *The Secretariat of the United Nations*.

D. W. BOWETT. Lecturer in Law, University of Cambridge. Fellow, Queens College and former UN Legal Officer. Author of *The United Nations* and *Self-Defence in International Law*.

JAMES L. BRIERLY. Deceased. He was Chichele Professor of International Law and Diplomacy at the University of Oxford, editor of the *British Year Book of International Law* and an original member of the International Law Commission. His *Law of Nations* is considered a classic. His other works include *The Basis of Obligation in International Law*, and *The Outlook for International Law*.

NICHOLAS DEB. KATZENBACH. Attorney-General of the United States. Formerly Professor of Law at the University of Chicago. Co-author with Morton A. Kaplan of *The Political Foundations of International Law*.

CLYDE EAGLETON. Deceased. Formerly Professor of International Law at New York University and Director of the Institute of International Law. Author of *Forces that Shape our Future, United Nations and the United States*, and *Analysis of the Problem of War.*

WOLFGANG FRIEDMANN. Professor of International Law at Columbia University School of Law. Author of several books, including *Law in a Changing Society, Introduction to World Politics*, and *The Changing Structure of International Law.*

LON L. FULLER. Carter Professor of General Jurisprudence, Harvard University Law School. Author of *The Law in Quest of Itself*, and editor of *Basic Contract Law*, and *The Problems of Jurisprudence.*

LELAND M. GOODRICH. Professor of International Organization and Administration at Columbia University. Professor Goodrich was a member of the International Secretariat, United Nations Conference on International Organization in 1945. Author of several books including *The United Nations*, and *The United Nations and the Maintenance of International Peace and Security.*

DAG HAMMARSKJÖLD. Secretary-General of the United Nations until his death in 1961. Posthumously awarded the Nobel Peace Prize in 1961.

ROSALYN HIGGINS. Research scholar attached to the Royal Institute of International Affairs. Author of *The Development of International Law through the Political Organs of the United Nations* and *Conflict of Interest.*

STANLEY HOFFMANN. Professor of Government, Harvard University. Editor of *Contemporary Theory in International Relations* and author of *The Politics of Defeat: The Road to Vichy and the Vichy Regime.*

THOMAS HOVET, JR. Professor of International Relations at New York University. Author of *Bloc Politics in the United Nations.*

MORTON A. KAPLAN. Professor of Political Science and Chairman of the Committee on International Relations at the University of Chicago. Author of *System and Process in International Politics*, co-author with Nicholas deB. Katzenbach of *The Political Foundations of International Law*, and editor of *The Revolution in World Politics.*

HANS KELSEN. Formerly Dean of the Faculty of Law at the University of Vienna and associated with the Graduate Institute of International Studies in Geneva. Author of numerous books, including *The General Theory of Law and State, The Principles of International Law*, and *Law and Peace.*

GABRIELLA R. LANDE. Presently research associate at the Center of International Studies, Princeton University. Author of *The United Nations Emergency Force.*

MARION H. MCVITTY. United World Federalist representative to the UN. Past Chairman of the Conference Group of the US Organizations for the UN. Editor of the *Independent Observer,* and author of *Current Disarmament Proposals.*

HANS J. MORGENTHAU. Albert A. Michelson Distinguished Service Professor of Political Science and Modern History and Director of the Center for the Study of American Foreign and Military Policy, University of Chicago. Among his books are *Politics Among Nations, The Purpose of American Politics,* and *Politics in the 20th Century.*

HERBERT NICHOLAS. Fellow, New College, Oxford University. Author of *The United Nations as a Political Institution,* and *Britain and the United States.*

NORMAN J. PADELFORD. Professor of Political Science and a member of the senior staff of the Center for International Studies at M.I.T. Chairman of the Board of Editors of *International Organization.*

KEITH S. PETERSEN. Associate Professor of Government at the University of Arkansas. Recipient in 1958 of the Rockefeller Fellowship for the Study of International Organization at the World Affairs Center for the United States in New York City.

ALVIN Z. RUBINSTEIN. Associate Professor of Political Science at the University of Pennsylvania. Author of *The Soviets in International Organizations.*

OSCAR SCHACHTER. Director of the General Legal Division of the UN Secretariat. Visiting Lecturer of International Law and Organization at Yale University Law School. Member of the Board of Editors of the *American Journal of International Law* and member of the Commission for the Study of the Organization of Peace.

THOMAS C. SCHELLING. Professor of Economics, Harvard University, and Associate at the Center for International Affairs, Harvard University. Author of *The Strategy of Conflict* and *International Economicx,* and coauthor with Morton H. Halpern of *Strategy and Arms Control.*

KRZYSZTOF SKUBISZEWSKI. Docent, University of Poznan, Poland, and visiting scholar, Columbia University, in 1964.

LOUIS B. SOHN. Bemis Professor of International Law, Harvard Law School. Served as Consultant, Legal Department, UN, and to the US Arms Control and Disarmament Agency. His books include *Cases and Other Materials on World Law*, *Cases on United Nations Law*, and *World Peace through World Law* (with Grenville Clark).

A. J. P. TAMMES. Professor of Public International Law and International Relations at the University of Amsterdam. Member of the Netherlands Delegation to several sessions of the General Assembly of the United Nations. He has served as Rapporteur of the Sixth (Legal) Committee of the General Assembly of the United Nations.

U THANT. Secretary-General of the United Nations since 1961. Former delegate from Burma to the UN.

ARTHUR I. WASKOW. Resident Fellow of the Institute for Policy Studies, Washington, D.C. Author of *The Limits of Defense*, and *The Worried Man's Guide to World Peace*.

FRANCIS O. WILCOX. Dean, Graduate School for International Studies, Johns Hopkins University. Co-editor with Carl M. Marcy of *Proposals for Changes in the United Nations*.

Permissions*

Clyde Eagleton. "Covenant of the League of Nations and the Charter of the United Nations. Points of Difference." Reprinted by permission from the *Department of State Bulletin* (August 19, 1945) pp. 263–269.

Leland M. Goodrich. "From League of Nations to United Nations." Reprinted by permission of the World Peace Foundation from *International Organization*, Vol. I, No. 1 (1947) pp. 3–21.

Rosalyn Higgins. "Law, Politics and the United Nations." Reprinted by permission from *The Development of International Law Through the Political Organs of the United Nations* (Oxford University Press, London, 1963) pp. 1–10.

* Permissions are listed to correspond to the sequence of the materials included in this volume.

A. J. P. Tammes. "The Introduction of a New Legislative Technique." Reprinted with permission from *Decisions of International Organs as a Source of International Law, Recueil des Cours*, Vol. II, Academie de Droit International (Leyden: A. W. Sijthoff, 1958) pp. 265–284.

Report of Committee on Study of Legal Problems of the United Nations. "Should the Laws of War Apply to United Nations Enforcement Action?" Reprinted by permission of the American Society of International Law from the *Proceedings* of the Society for 1952, pp. 216–220.

Oscar Schachter. "The Relation of Law, Politics and Action in the United Nations." Reprinted by permission of the Academy of International Law from *Recueil de Cours*, Vol. I (Leyden: A. W. Sijthoff, 1963) pp. 191–200.

The Advisory Opinion of the International Court of Justice in "Conditions of Admission of a State to Membership in the United Nations" (28 May 1948). Reprinted by permission of the publisher from *Cases on United Nations Law* by Louis B. Sohn (New York: Foundation Press, 1956) pp. 9–20.

United Nations. All materials reproduced in this volume from United Nations documents were graciously given to us by Miss Alice Smith, The Office of Public Inquiries, the United Nations.

Leland M. Goodrich. "The United Nations Security Council." Reprinted by permission of *International Organization*, Vol. XII, No. 3 (1954) pp. 273–287.

D. W. Bowett. "The Security Council: Functions and Powers." Reprinted with permission from *The Law of International Institutions* (New York: Praeger, 1963) pp. 30–37).

Gabriella R. Lande. "The Changing Effectiveness of General Assembly Resolutions." Reprinted by permission of the American Society of International Law from the *Proceedings* of the Society for 1964, pp. 162–173.

Krzysztof Skubiszewski. "The General Assembly of the United Nations and its Power to Influence National Action." Reprinted by permission of the American Society of International Law from the *Proceedings* of the Society for 1964, pp. 153–162.

Keith S. Petersen. "The Uses of the Uniting for Peace Resolution Since 1950." Reprinted by permission of the World Peace Foundation from *International Organization*, Vol. XIII, (1959) pp. 219–232.

Francis O. Wilcox. "Representation and Voting in the United Nations General Assembly." Staff Study No. 4 (United States Government Printing Office, 1954) pp. 1–23.

Thomas Hovet, Jr. "How the African Bloc Uses its Votes." Reprinted by permission from *Current* (March, 1964) pp. 26–27.

United States Department of State. "Would Weighted Voting Help the U.S.?" Reprinted by permission from *Current* (September, 1963) pp. 28–29.

Charles Henry Alexandrowicz. "The Secretary-General of the United Nations." Reprinted by permission of the British Institute of International and Comparative Law from *International and Comparative Law Quarterly*, Vol. XI (1962) pp. 1109–1130.

Sydney D. Bailey. "The Troika and the Future of the United Nations: The Secretary-General." Reprinted by permission of the publisher from *The Secretariat of the United Nations* (rev. ed., New York: Praeger, 1962) pp. 33–59.

Morton A. Kaplan and Nicholas deB. Katzenbach. "The Institutions of International Decision-Making." Reprinted by permission from *The Political Foundations of International Order* (New York: John Wiley & Sons, 1961) pp. 265–283.

Louis B. Sohn. "Step-by-Step Acceptance of the Jurisdiction of the International Court of Justice." Reprinted by permission of the American Society of International Law from the *Proceedings* of the Society for 1964, pp. 131–136.

Lon L. Fuller. "Adjudication and the Rule of Law." Reprinted by permission of the American Society of International Law from the *Proceedings* of the Society for 1960, pp. 1–8.

James L. Brierly. "The Prohibition of War by International Law." Reprinted by permission from *The Basis of Obligation in International Law* (Oxford: Clarendon Press, 1958) pp. 280–296.

Hans Kelsen. "Sanctions in International Law under the Charter of the United Nations." Reprinted with permission from the *Iowa Law Review*, Vol. 31 (1946) pp. 499–503, 513–543.

Wolfgang Friedmann. "National Sovereignty, International Cooperation and the Reality of International Law." Reprinted by permission from the *UCLA Law Review*, Vol. 10 (May, 1963) pp. 739–753.

U Thant. "United Nations Peace Force." An Address to the Harvard Alumni Association delivered in Cambridge, Massachusetts (June 13, 1963). Permission to reproduce this document as it appears in *International Military Forces: The Question of Peacekeeping in an Armed and Disarming World* by Lincoln P. Bloomfield has been given by the publisher, Little, Brown & Company.

Herbert Nicholas. "An Appraisal." From *International Military Forces: The Question of Peacekeeping in an Armed and Disarming World* by Lincoln P. Bloomfield. Copyright © 1964, by the Massachusetts Institute of Technology. Reprinted by permission of the publisher, Little, Brown & Company (Boston: 1964) pp. 105–125.

Dag Hammarskjöld. "United Nations Emergency Force." UN Document A/3943 (October 9, 1958). Permission to reproduce this document as it appears in *International Military Forces: The Question of Peacekeeping in an Armed and Disarming World* by Lincoln P. Bloomfield has been given by the publisher, Little, Brown & Company.

Marion H. McVitty. "Wanted: Rules to Guide UN Peace-Keeping Operations of the Future." Reprinted by permission of the United World Federalists from *New Federalist Papers,* No. 1 (1965) pp. 1–50.

Louis B. Sohn. "The Role of the United Nations of Civil Wars." Reprinted by permission of the American Society of International Law from the *Proceedings* of the Society for 1963, pp. 208–216.

D. W. Bowett. "Structure and Control of United Nations Forces" and "Conclusions." Reprinted by permission of the publisher from *United Nations Forces* (New York: Praeger, 1964) pp. 313–330, 561–569.

Arthur I. Waskow. "Quis Custodiet? Controlling the Police in a Disarmed World." Reprinted by permission of the author from Peace Research Institute Report (Washington, D.C., April, 1963) pp. 4–42.

Hans J. Morgenthau. "Political Conditions for a Force." From *International Military Forces: The Question of Peacekeeping in an Armed and Disarming World* by Lincoln P. Bloomfield. Copyright © 1964, by the Massachusetts Institute of Technology. Reprinted by permission of the publisher, Little, Brown & Company (Boston: 1964) pp. 175–186.

Thomas C. Schelling. "Strategy: A World Force in Operation." From *International Military Forces: The Question of Peacekeeping in an Armed and Disarming World* by Lincoln P. Bloomfield. Copyright © 1964, by the Massachusetts Institute of Technology. Reprinted by permission of the publisher, Little, Brown & Company (Boston: 1964) pp. 212–235.

International Court of Justice. Advisory Opinion, "Certain Expenses of the United Nations." Reprinted from *Reports of Judgments, Advisory Opinions and Orders* (1962) pp. 151–181.

Norman J. Padelford. "Financial Crisis and the Future of the United Nations." Reprinted with permission from *World Politics*, Vol. XV, No. 4 (July, 1963) pp. 531–568.

Stanley Hoffmann. "An Evaluation of the United Nations." Reprinted by permission of the publisher from the *Ohio State Law Journal*, Vol. 22 (Summer, 1961) pp. 427–449.

Dag Hammarskjöld. "Two Differing Views of the United Nations Assayed: Introduction to the Annual Report of the Secretary-General on the Work of the Organization, 16 June 1960—15 June 1961." Reprinted by permission of the World Peace Foundation from *International Organization*, Vol. 15 (1961) pp. 549–563.

Alvin Z. Rubinstein. "More Responsibility for Russia?" Reprinted by permission from *Current* (September, 1964) pp. 37–41. Also appeared in A. Z. Rubinstein's *The Soviets in International Organizations*. Copyright © Princeton University Press, 1964.